International Directory of
COMPANY HISTORIES

International Directory of COMPANY HISTORIES

VOLUME 121

Editors

Derek Jacques and Paula Kepos

ST. JAMES PRESS

A part of Gale, Cengage Learning

Detroit • New York • San Francisco • New Haven, Conn • Waterville, Maine • London

International Directory of Company Histories, Volume 121

Derek Jacques and Paula Kepos, Editors

Project Editor: Miranda H. Ferrara

Editorial: Virgil Burton, Donna Craft, Peggy Geeseman, Julie Gough, Hillary Hentschel, Sonya Hill, Keith Jones, Matthew Miskelly, Lynn Pearce, Laura Peterson, Paul Schummer, Holly Selden

Production Technology Specialist: Mike Weaver

Imaging and Multimedia: John Watkins

Composition and Electronic Prepress: Gary Leach, Evi Seoud

Manufacturing: Rhonda Dover

Product Manager: Jenai Drouillard

Gale
27500 Drake Rd.
Farmington Hills, MI, 48331-3535

LIBRARY OF CONGRESS CATALOG NUMBER 89-190943
ISBN-13: 978-1-55862-788-8
ISBN-10: 1-55862-788-X

This title is also available as an e-book
ISBN-13: 978-1-55862-803-8 ISBN-10: 1-55862-803-7
Contact your Gale, a part of Cengage Learning sales representative for ordering information.

BRITISH LIBRARY CATALOGUING IN PUBLICATION DATA
International directory of company histories, Vol. 121
Derek Jacques and Paula Kepos
33.87409

Printed in Mexico
1 2 3 4 5 6 7 15 14 13 12 11

Contents

Preface

The St. James Press series *The International Directory of Company Histories* (*IDCH*) is intended for reference use by students, business people, librarians, historians, economists, investors, job candidates, and others who seek to learn more about the historical development of the world's most important companies. To date, *IDCH* has profiled more than 11,370 companies in 121 volumes.

INCLUSION CRITERIA

Most companies chosen for inclusion in *IDCH* have achieved a minimum of US$25 million in annual sales and are leading influences in their industries or geographical locations. Companies may be publicly held, private, or nonprofit. State-owned companies that are important in their industries and that may operate much like public or private companies also are included. Wholly owned subsidiaries and divisions are profiled if they meet the requirements for inclusion. Entries on companies that have had major changes since they were last profiled may be selected for updating.

The *IDCH* series highlights 25% private and nonprofit companies, and features updated entries on approximately 35 companies per volume.

ENTRY FORMAT

Each entry begins with the company's legal name; the address of its headquarters; its telephone, toll-free, and fax numbers; and its web site. A statement of public, private, state, or parent ownership follows. A company with a legal name in both English and the language of its headquarters country is listed by the English name, with the native-language name in parentheses.

The company's founding or earliest incorporation date, the number of employees, and the most recent available sales figures follow. Sales figures are given in local currencies with equivalents in U.S. dollars. For some private companies, sales figures are estimates and indicated by the abbreviation *est.* The entry lists the exchanges on which the company's stock is traded and its ticker symbol, as well as the company's NAICS codes.

Entries generally contain a *Company Perspectives* box which provides a short summary of the company's mission, goals, and ideals; a *Key Dates* box highlighting milestones in the company's history; lists of *Principal Subsidiaries*, *Principal Divisions*, *Principal Operating Units*, *Principal Competitors*; and articles for *Further Reading*.

American spelling is used throughout *IDCH*, and the word "billion" is used in its U.S. sense of one thousand million.

SOURCES

Entries have been compiled from publicly accessible sources both in print and on the Internet such as general and academic periodicals, books, and annual reports, as well as material supplied by the companies themselves.

CUMULATIVE INDEXES

IDCH contains three indexes: the **Cumulative Index to Companies**, which provides an alphabetical index to companies profiled in the *IDCH* series, the **Index to Industries**, which allows researchers to locate companies by their principal industry, and the **Geographic Index**, which lists companies alphabetically by the country of their headquarters. The indexes are cumulative and specific instructions for using them are found immediately preceding each index.

SPECIAL TO THIS VOLUME

This volume of *IDCH* contains entries on Liechtensteinische Landesbank AG, Liechtenstein's oldest financial institution, and Planned Parenthood, the oldest and largest family planning organization in the United States.

SUGGESTIONS WELCOME

Comments and suggestions from users of *IDCH* on any aspect of the product as well as suggestions for companies to be included or updated are cordially invited. Please write:

The Editor
International Directory of Company Histories
St. James Press
Gale, Cengage Learning
27500 Drake Rd.
Farmington Hills, Michigan 48331-3535

St. James Press does not endorse any of the companies or products mentioned in this series. Companies appearing in the *International Directory of Company Histories* were selected without reference to their wishes and have in no way endorsed their entries.

Notes on Contributors

Stephen V. Beitel
Writer and copyeditor based in East Amherst, New York.

Joyce Helena Brusin
Writer and essayist; contributor to the *Encyclopedia of World Governments.*

Ed Dinger
Writer and editor based in Bronx, New York.

Evelyn Hauser
Researcher, writer, and marketing specialist based in Germany.

Louise B. Ketz
Author, editor, book producer, and literary agent based in New York City; contributor to *Scribner Encyclopedia of American Lives.*

Eric Laursen
Writer and editor based in Buckland, Massachusetts.

Mary C. Lewis
Chicago–based editorial services professional specializing in reference books, educational publishing, copyediting, and developmental editing.

Judson MacLaury
Retired historian of the U.S. Department of Labor; author of *To Advance Their Opportunities* (2008) and of numerous articles, reviews, and encyclopedia entries.

Grace Murphy
Writer based in upstate New York with specialties in health care, business, and reference.

Marie O'Sullivan
Researcher, writer, and editor based in Ireland; expertise includes international education, student mobility, and globalization; editor and writer for the IIEPassport Study Abroad Directories.

Roger Rouland
Writer and scholar specializing in company histories, literary criticism, literary essays, and poetry; freelance photographer specializing in nature photography.

Helga Schier
Writer, editor, and translator (German/English) based in Los Angeles.

Roger K. Smith
Writer and writing instructor in Ithaca, New York; contributor to the *Gale Encyclopedia of World History: Governments,* CQ Press's *Political Handbook of the World,* and other reference titles.

List of Abbreviations

€ European euro
¥ Japanese yen
£ United Kingdom pound
$ United States dollar

A

AB Aktiebolag (Finland, Sweden)
AB Oy Aktiebolag Osakeyhtiot (Finland)
A.E. Anonimos Eteria (Greece)
AED Emirati dirham
AG Aktiengesellschaft (Austria, Germany, Switzerland, Liechtenstein)
aG auf Gegenseitigkeit (Austria, Germany)
A.m.b.a. Andelsselskab med begraenset ansvar (Denmark)
A.O. Anonim Ortaklari/Ortakligi (Turkey)
ApS Amparteselskab (Denmark)
ARS Argentine peso
A.S. Anonim Sirketi (Turkey)
A/S Aksjeselskap (Norway)
A/S Aktieselskab (Denmark, Sweden)
Ay Avoinyhtio (Finland)
ATS Austrian shilling
AUD Australian dollar
Ay Avoinyhtio (Finland)

B

B.A. Buttengewone Aansprakeiijkheid (Netherlands)
BEF Belgian franc
BHD Bahraini dinar
Bhd. Berhad (Malaysia, Brunei)
BND Brunei dollar
BRL Brazilian real
B.V. Besloten Vennootschap (Belgium, Netherlands)
BWP Botswana pula

C

C. de R.L. Compania de Responsabilidad Limitada (Spain)
C. por A. Compania por Acciones (Dominican Republic)
C.A. Compania Anonima (Ecuador, Venezuela)
C.V. Commanditaire Vennootschap (Netherlands, Belgium)
CAD Canadian dollar
CEO Chief Executive Officer
CFO Chief Financial Officer
CHF Swiss franc
Cia. Compagnia (Italy)
Cia. Companhia (Brazil, Portugal)
Cia. Compania (Latin America [except Brazil], Spain)
Cie. Compagnie (Belgium, France, Luxembourg, Netherlands)
CIO Chief Information Officer
CLP Chilean peso
CNY Chinese yuan
Co. Company
COO Chief Operating Officer
Coop. Cooperative
COP Colombian peso
Corp. Corporation
CPT Cuideachta Phoibi Theoranta (Republic of Ireland)
CRL Companhia a Responsabilidao Limitida (Portugal, Spain)
CZK Czech koruna

D

D&B Dunn & Bradstreet
DEM German deutsche mark (W. Germany to 1990; unified Germany to 2002)
Div. Division (United States)
DKK Danish krone
DZD Algerian dinar

E

E.P.E. Etema Pemorismenis Evthynis (Greece)
EBIDTA Earnings before interest, taxes, depreciation, and amortization
EC Exempt Company (Arab countries)
Edms. Bpk. Eiendoms Beperk (South Africa)
EEK Estonian Kroon
eG eingetragene Genossenschaft (Germany)
EGMBH Eingetragene Genossenschaft mit beschraenkter Haftung (Austria, Germany)
EGP Egyptian pound

Ek For Ekonomisk Forening (Sweden)
EP Empresa Portuguesa (Portugal)
ESOP Employee Stock Options and Ownership
ESP Spanish peseta
Et(s). Etablissement(s) (Belgium, France, Luxembourg)
eV eingetragener Verein (Germany)
EUR European euro

F
FIM Finnish markka
FRF French franc

G
G.I.E. Groupement d'Interet Economique (France)
gGmbH gemeinnutzige Gesellschaft mit beschraenkter Haftung (Austria, Germany, Switzerland)
GmbH Gesellschaft mit beschraenkter Haftung (Austria, Germany, Switzerland)
GRD Greek drachma
GWA Gewerbte Amt (Austria, Germany)

H
HB Handelsbolag (Sweden)
HF Hlutafelag (Iceland)
HKD Hong Kong dollar
HUF Hungarian forint

I
IDR Indonesian rupiah
IEP Irish pound
ILS Israeli shekel (new)
Inc. Incorporated (United States, Canada)
INR Indian rupee
IPO Initial Public Offering
I/S Interesentselskap (Norway)
I/S Interessentselskab (Denmark)
ISK Icelandic krona
ITL Italian lira

J
JMD Jamaican dollar
JOD Jordanian dinar

K
KB Kommanditbolag (Sweden)
KES Kenyan schilling
Kft Korlatolt Felelossegu Tarsasag (Hungary)
KG Kommanditgesellschaft (Austria, Germany, Switzerland)
KGaA Kommanditgesellschaft auf Aktien (Austria, Germany, Switzerland)
KK Kabushiki Kaisha (Japan)
KPW North Korean won
KRW South Korean won
K/S Kommanditselskab (Denmark)
K/S Kommandittselskap (Norway)
KWD Kuwaiti dinar
Ky Kommandiitiyhtio (Finland)

L
L.L.C. Limited Liability Company (Arab countries, Egypt, Greece, United States)
L.L.P. Limited Liability Partnership (United States)
L.P. Limited Partnership (Canada, South Africa, United Kingdom, United States)
LBO Leveraged Buyout
Lda. Limitada (Spain)
Ltd. Limited
Ltda. Limitada (Brazil, Portugal)
Ltee. Limitee (Canada, France)
LUF Luxembourg franc
LYD Libyan dinar

M
mbH mit beschraenkter Haftung (Austria, Germany)
Mij. Maatschappij (Netherlands)
MUR Mauritian rupee
MXN Mexican peso
MYR Malaysian ringgit

N
N.A. National Association (United States)
N.V. Naamloze Vennootschap (Belgium, Netherlands)
NGN Nigerian naira
NLG Netherlands guilder
NOK Norwegian krone
NZD New Zealand dollar

O
OAO Otkrytoe Aktsionernoe Obshchestve (Russia)
OHG Offene Handelsgesellschaft (Austria, Germany, Switzerland)
OMR Omani rial
OOO Obschestvo s Ogranichennoi Otvetstvennostiu (Russia)
OOUR Osnova Organizacija Udruzenog Rada (Yugoslavia)
Oy Osakeyhtiö (Finland)

P
P.C. Private Corp. (United States)
P.L.L.C. Professional Limited Liability Corporation (United States)
P.T. Perusahaan/Perseroan Terbatas (Indonesia)
PEN Peruvian Nuevo Sol
PHP Philippine peso
PKR Pakistani rupee
P/L Part Lag (Norway)
PLC Public Limited Co. (United Kingdom, Ireland)
PLN Polish zloty
PTE Portuguese escudo
Pte. Private (Singapore)
Pty. Proprietary (Australia, South Africa, United Kingdom)
Pvt. Private (India, Zimbabwe)
PVBA Personen Vennootschap met Beperkte Aansprakelijkheid (Belgium)
PYG Paraguay guarani

Q
QAR Qatar riyal

R
REIT Real Estate Investment Trust
RMB Chinese renminbi
Rt Reszvenytarsasag (Hungary)
RUB Russian ruble

S
S.A. Sociedad Anónima (Latin America [except Brazil], Spain, Mexico)
S.A. Sociedades Anônimas (Brazil, Portugal)
S.A. Société Anonyme (Arab countries, Belgium, France, Jordan, Luxembourg, Switzerland)
S.A. de C.V. Sociedad Anonima de Capital Variable (Mexico)
S.A.B. de C.V. Sociedad Anónima Bursátil de Capital Variable (Mexico)

S.A.C. Sociedad Anonima Comercial (Latin America [except Brazil])
S.A.C.I. Sociedad Anonima Comercial e Industrial (Latin America [except Brazil])
S.A.C.I.y.F. Sociedad Anonima Comercial e Industrial y Financiera (Latin America [except Brazil])
S.A.R.L. Sociedade Anonima de Responsabilidade Limitada (Brazil, Portugal)
S.A.R.L. Société à Responsabilité Limitée (France, Belgium, Luxembourg)
S.A.S. Societe Anonyme Syrienne (Arab countries)
S.A.S. Societá in Accomandita Semplice (Italy)
S.C. Societe en Commandite (Belgium, France, Luxembourg)
S.C.A. Societe Cooperativa Agricole (France, Italy, Luxembourg)
S.C.I. Sociedad Cooperativa Ilimitada (Spain)
S.C.L. Sociedad Cooperativa Limitada (Spain)
S.C.R.L. Societe Cooperative a Responsabilite Limitee (Belgium)
S.E. Societas Europaea (European Union Member states)
S.L. Sociedad Limitada (Latin America [except Brazil], Portugal, Spain)
S.N.C. Société en Nom Collectif (France)
S.p.A. Società per Azioni (Italy)
S.R.L. Sociedad de Responsabilidad Limitada (Spain, Mexico, Latin America [except Brazil])
S.R.L. Società a Responsabilità Limitata (Italy)
S.R.O. Spolecnost s Rucenim Omezenym (Czechoslovakia)
S.S.K. Sherkate Sahami Khass (Iran)
S.V. Samemwerkende Vennootschap (Belgium)
S.Z.R.L. Societe Zairoise a Responsabilite Limitee (Zaire)
SAA Societe Anonyme Arabienne (Arab countries)
SAK Societe Anonyme Kuweitienne (Arab countries)
SAL Societe Anonyme Libanaise (Arab countries)
SAO Societe Anonyme Omanienne (Arab countries)
SAQ Societe Anonyme Qatarienne (Arab countries)
SAR Saudi riyal
Sdn. Bhd. Sendirian Berhad (Malaysia)
SEK Swedish krona
SGD Singapore dollar
S/L Salgslag (Norway)
Soc. Sociedad (Latin America [except Brazil], Spain)
Soc. Sociedade (Brazil, Portugal)
Soc. Societa (Italy)
Sp. z.o.o. Spólka z ograniczona odpowiedzialnoscia (Poland)
Ste. Societe (France, Belgium, Luxembourg, Switzerland)
Ste. Cve. Societe Cooperative (Belgium)

T

THB Thai baht
TND Tunisian dinar
TRL Turkish lira
TTD Trinidad and Tobago dollar
TWD Taiwan dollar (new)

U

U.A. Uitgesloten Aansporakeiijkheid (Netherlands)
u.p.a. utan personligt ansvar (Sweden)

V

V.O.f. Vennootschap onder firma (Netherlands)
VAG Verein der Arbeitgeber (Austria, Germany)
VEB Venezuelan bolivar
VERTR Vertriebs (Austria, Germany)
VND Vietnamese dong
VVAG Versicherungsverein auf Gegenseitigkeit (Austria, Germany)

W–Z

WA Wettelika Aansprakalikhaed (Netherlands)
WLL With Limited Liability (Bahrain, Kuwait, Qatar, Saudi Arabia)
YK Yugen Kaisha (Japan)
ZAO Zakrytoe Aktsionernoe Obshchestve (Russia)
ZAR South African rand
ZMK Zambian kwacha
ZWD Zimbabwean dollar

40 Acres and a Mule Filmworks, Inc.

75 South Elliott Place
Brooklyn, New York 11217-1207
U.S.A.
Telephone: (718) 624-3703
Fax: (718) 624-2008
Web site: http://www.40acres.com

Private Company
Incorporated: 1986
Employees: 15
NAICS: 512110 Motion Picture and Video Production

■ ■ ■

The Brooklyn, New York–based 40 Acres and a Mule Filmworks, Inc., is the privately held production company of director Spike Lee. The innovative and often controversial African-American filmmaker's company has produced about 40 feature films and documentaries, as well as numerous music videos, since its launch in the mid-1980s. Notable works include *Do the Right Thing*, *Malcolm X*, *Clockers*, *Summer of Sam*, *Inside Man*, and *Miracle at St. Anna*. Not content to limit itself to filmmaking, 40 Acres sold merchandise related to Lee and his films through its now-defunct Spike's Joint stores, and creates commercials through its successful Spike DDB unit. The company's best-known advertising endeavor is a series of commercials for Nike featuring Lee with basketball star Michael Jordan. Spike DDB has also worked with numerous prominent clients and produced several ads which made their debuts during the Super Bowl.

SPIKE LEE: ATLANTA BORN, BROOKLYN RAISED

Born in Atlanta in 1957 as Shelton Jackson Lee, Spike Lee was raised in a middle-class neighborhood in Brooklyn, New York, by his jazz musician father, who introduced him to music, and his schoolteacher mother, who made him familiar with African-American literature. He did not grow up with a particular interest in film, however. The seeds for a film career were planted following his mother's unexpected death in 1977. A student at Morehouse College at the time, Lee often went to the movies with friends wanting to buoy his spirits during this period. There he developed a taste for the work of directors such as Bernardo Bertolucci, Akira Kurosawa, and Martin Scorsese, but it was not until after he saw Michael Cimino's *Deer Hunter* that he told friends he wanted to become a filmmaker. His goal was to make films that captured the black experience.

Following his years at Morehouse, Lee returned to New York to enroll in the graduate film program at New York University's Tisch School of the Arts. There he produced a 45-minute film, *Joe's Bed-Stuy Barbershop: We Cut Heads*, which earned him a 1983 Student Academy Award from the Academy of Motion Picture Arts and Sciences. After earning his degree, he worked for a movie distribution house while raising funds to produce his first film, *The Messenger*, a semiautobiographical film about a bicycle messenger. The money never came through, however, and in the summer of 1984 Lee was forced to abandon the project.

KEY DATES

1986: Company is established by film director Spike Lee.
1989: *Do the Right Thing* is released.
1990: Spike's Joint opens in Brooklyn.
1991: Record label is launched.
2004: Los Angeles story development office closes.

FIRST FEATURE FILM: 1986

Rather than become discouraged, Lee turned his attention to a low-budget idea. With a budget of just $175,000, Lee filmed *She's Gotta Have It* in black and white over a span of 12 days and then edited the picture in his apartment on a rented machine. He was able to secure distribution through Island Pictures, which released the film in 1986. Not only did the film find a receptive black audience, it proved popular on the art-house circuit, grossing nearly $8 million.

She's Gotta Have It provided Lee with critical acclaim as a producer, director, and writer, as well as for his acting ability. The success of the film also allowed Lee to form his own production company in 1986, which he called 40 Acres and a Mule Filmworks. The name was drawn from the post–Civil War effort by Union General William Tecumseh Sherman to provide a livelihood for newly freed slaves by allocating to each of them 40 acres of land and to many a surplus army mule. (The order was later rescinded by President Andrew Johnson, and the land was returned to the former owners.) The company set up shop in a renovated three-story firehouse in the Fort Greene section of Brooklyn.

Although his first film was a light comedy, Lee's next effort, *School Daze*, ostensibly a musical comedy, ruffled some feathers by examining color discrimination within the black community. Drawn from Lee's years at Morehouse, the film pits light-skinned blacks with "good" hair against darker-skinned blacks with kinky hair. In 1988 *School Daze* was released by Columbia Pictures. Despite a lack of support from the distributor, the film grossed $15 million.

Lee used the success of his first two films to begin doing commercials. In 1988 40 Acres began producing a popular series of Nike Air Jordan spots that featured basketball superstar Michael Jordan and Lee as Mars Blackmon, the comic relief role he played in *She's Gotta Have It*. The Blackmon character was so popular that Lee had felt the need to announce that the character would not appear in any further films. However, Lee decided to revive the basketball fanatic character for the Air Jordan commercials. Appearing on-screen with the biggest star in sports for a high-profile ad campaign raised Lee's public profile, as well as that of 40 Acres.

DO THE RIGHT THING RELEASED: 1989

Having demonstrated a willingness to court controversy, Lee turned his attention to black-white tensions with his 1989 film *Do the Right Thing*, which examines relationships between blacks and Italian Americans in the Bedford-Stuyvesant section of Brooklyn. Because of the riot that the story culminates in, some observers feared that *Do the Right Thing* would lead to real-world violence. It did not materialize, however, and for the most part the film received critical approval. In 2007 the American Film Institute recognized *Do the Right Thing* as one of the top 100 American films of all time.

From the very start of 40 Acres, Lee demonstrated a shrewd business sense. He kept a journal with each film and published it along with the script. The company also sold T-shirts out of the Fort Greene office and added other apparel, eventually launching a mail-order business that by the summer of 1990 was generating $75,000 each month. Taking advantage of the popularity of the apparel, Lee opened a retail shop a block from the production offices in July 1990 under the name Spike's Joint. Lee's films also created hit singles in the music industry, such as "Da Butt" from the *School Daze* soundtrack and "Fight the Power" from the *Do the Right Thing* soundtrack. As a result, Lee formed a record label at Columbia Records in 1991, 40 Acres and a Mule Musicworks.

Lee's first film of the 1990s, *Mo' Better Blues*, a story about a jazz trumpeter inspired by his father, was more romance than social commentary and received lukewarm reviews. It was, however, the start of a relationship between Lee and actor Denzel Washington. After Lee made the 1991 film *Jungle Fever*, which examined interracial romance, Lee and Washington worked together again on the biographical picture *Malcolm X*. It was the project of a lifetime for Lee, who had long admired the legendary black Muslim leader, but the film proved a struggle on multiple fronts. Lee had to rework a script that had been started by novelist James Baldwin, who died before completing it, and then finished by another writer. Moreover, Lee fought over the budget with the studio producing the picture, Warner Brothers, and made up the shortfall in the funds by giving back part of his $3 million salary and raising additional money by selling foreign rights to the film and turning to prominent blacks for support. The end result was a sprawling film nearly three and a half hours long. Although it received two Academy Award nominations (for Best Actor and Best Costume Design), the film did not win any Oscars.

Malcolm X generated box-office sales of less than $50 million but was a phenomenal success for Lee in merchandising. The iconic "X" logo of the film came to adorn shirts, baseball caps, and any number of other products. To sell these and other products associated with Lee, 40 Acres opened a second shop in Los Angeles, Spike's Joint West, in October 1992.

NEW YORK DEVELOPMENT OFFICE OPENS: 1992

Lee opened 40 Acres' first story development office in New York in 1992. Although Lee refused to live in Los Angeles, he did open a second story development office there in 1998 and maintained it until 2004. Along the way, Lee also formed the 40 Acres Institute to help educate aspiring filmmakers. Saturday morning seminars were held at the Long Island University campus in Fort Greene and featured such notables speakers as Scorsese, Robert De Niro, and John Singleton.

Lee and 40 Acres continued its prolific pace of film production during the balance of the 1990s. *Crooklyn*, an homage to growing up in Brooklyn in the 1970s, was released in 1994, followed a year later by an adaptation of the Richard Price novel *Clockers*, and 1996 brought *Girl 6*, written by African American and future Pulitzer Prize–winning playwright Suzan-Lori Parks. Other notable works during the 1990s included *Get on the Bus*, *He Got Game*, and *Summer of Sam*. In the meantime, Lee directed several documentaries, including *4 Little Girls*, which deals with the death of four Sunday school students in the 1963 bombing of a Birmingham, Alabama, church. The film was nominated in the Best Documentary Feature category by the Academy of Motion Picture Art and Sciences. In this same period, Lee directed music videos for a wide range of artists, including Michael Jackson, Bruce Hornsby, and Tracy Chapman; continued to direct commercials for the likes of Converse, Taco Bell, and Ben & Jerry's; and 40 Acres produced feature films such as *Drop Squad* and *Tales from the Hood*, which were not directed by Lee.

EMPHASIS ON TELEVISION IN THE NEW CENTURY

In the first decade of the 21st century, the Los Angeles story development office closed, as did some ancillary operations, including the record division and the Spike's Joint shops. The commercial unit, Spike DDB, remained viable. With or without Lee directing, 40 Acres also maintained a full slate of projects, including feature films and documentaries. In 2001 Lee directed an adaptation of Roger Guenveur Smith's one-man show, *A Huey P. Newton Story*, for the cable television channel Starz, opening a new avenue for 40 Acres's output. Two non-Lee-directed 40 Acres films, *3 A.M.* and *Good Fences*, both starring Danny Glover, were produced for Showtime Entertainment, and Lee availed himself of television distribution of his work throughout the decade.

In 2002 Showtime and Lee began negotiating on what was to be 40 Acres' first television series, *Sucker Free City*. The series, created by writer Alex Tse, was supposed to deal with the conflicts among San Francisco's African American, Latino, and Asian street gangs; unfortunately, scheduling conflicts and management changes at Showtime doomed the production in its infancy. However, the Lee-directed two-hour pilot for the series, released by Showtime as a television movie, showed the project's potential. "It takes only a few minutes of 'Sucker Free City' to come to this conclusion: Showtime blew it," critic Tim Goodman wrote in the *San Francisco Chronicle*. The series "would have been, without question, the best thing on Showtime and reason enough to pay extra for the channel."

Lee also found that cable television offered a viable outlet for documentaries. In 2002 Lee directed *Jim Brown: All American*, about the life of the football Hall of Famer and civil rights activist, for HBO Films. *When the Levees Broke* (2005) and *If God Is Willing and da Creek Don't Rise* (2010), also for HBO Films, examined New Orleans in the aftermath of Hurricane Katrina, and 2009's *Kobe Doin' Work*, produced for ESPN Films, documented a day in the life of basketball star Kobe Bryant. Lee's adaptation of the hit Broadway musical *Passing Strange* was also released for the small screen that year, on the Sundance Select on-demand video service.

BOX OFFICE SUCCESS WITH *INSIDE MAN*: 2006

The company's new emphasis on television and documentaries was not an abandonment of theaters or feature films. However, Lee's first three films of the new millenium, *Bamboozled*, *The 25th Hour*, and *She Hate Me* were all huge disappointments at the box office. Of the three, only *The 25th Hour* was critically well received, making several prominent critics' best-of-decade lists. Lee's fortunes would turn, however, in his fourth collaboration with Denzel Washington, *Inside Man*. The film, a relatively conventional bank heist thriller, was the biggest hit in 40 Acres' history, topping the box office on its opening weekend and pulling in almost $90 million domestically. Any thought that 40 Acres would abandon challenging, socially engaged material in favor of more commercial fare was immediately undercut by Lee's next feature, 2008's *Miracle at St. Anna*, a World War II drama which told the story of black GIs serving in Italy.

Ed Dinger

PRINCIPAL DIVISIONS

Spike DDB.

PRINCIPAL COMPETITORS

Gotham Pictures Inc.; New Deal Entertainment; Tribeca Enterprises LLC.

FURTHER READING

Chappell, Kevin. "20 Years Later: Spike Lee: Still Gotta Have It." *Ebony*, September 2006, 98.

Fitzgerald, Sharon. "Spike Lee: Fast Forward." *American Visions*, October–November 1995, 20.

Goodman, Tim. "Review: *Sucker Free City*." *San Francisco Chronicle*, February 11, 2005, E1.

Grimm, Matthew. "The Rebel as Hero, as Auteur, as Crossover Marketer." *Adweek's Marketing Week*, July 16, 1990, 4.

Lally, Kevin. "40 Acres ... 20 Years." *Film Journal International*, March 2006, 10.

McDowell, Jeanne. "He's Got to Have It His Way." *Time*, July 17, 1989, 92.

Norment, Lynn. "A Revealing Look at Spike Lee's Changing Life." *Ebony*, May 1994, 28–30, 32.

Whitaker, Charles. "Doing the Spike Thing." *Ebony*, November 1991, 82.

A123 Systems, Inc.

321 Arsenal Street
Watertown, Massachusetts 02472
U.S.A.
Telephone: (617) 778-5700
Fax: (617) 778-5749
Web site: http://www.a123systems.com

Public Company
Founded: 2001
Employees: 1,627
Sales: $91.05 million (2009)
Stock Exchanges: NASDAQ
Ticker Symbol: AONE
NAICS: 335911 Storage Battery Manufacturing; 335912 Primary Battery Manufacturing

■ ■ ■

A123 Systems, Inc., is one of the world's leading producers of high-powered lithium-ion batteries. The company designs, develops, and manufactures its rechargeable lithium-ion batteries and battery systems for the consumer products, transportation, and power-grid markets in the United States and abroad. A123 Systems also provides research and development services for commercial clients and governmental entities. Based on the company's proprietary nanophosphate technology, its batteries are designed to be safer and to have more energy, a longer life, and a faster rechargeable capacity than traditional lithium-ion batteries.

ORIGINS OF A123 SYSTEMS: 2001–02

A123 Systems traces its roots to technology that was developed at the Massachusetts Institute of Technology by Yet-Ming Chiang, a professor of materials science and engineering. During the summer of 2001 Chiang met with the Venezuelan start-up entrepreneur Ric Fulop and the electrical-power technologies engineer Bart Riley to discuss forming a battery firm that was based on Chiang's research. By fall A123 Systems, Inc., was established.

The primary business objective of A123 Systems was to develop a commercially viable battery that was based on one of Chiang's theories: particular materials when mixed together would spontaneously develop into a working battery and would have greater storage capacity than traditional batteries. Chiang's idea was received favorably by investors, and an initial round of venture financing in late 2001 generated $8.3 million. Before the year was over, Chiang was also awarded a $100,000 Small Business Innovative Research grant for his work on lithium iron phosphate.

In early 2002 Motorola, Inc., and QUALCOMM, Inc., each seeking a high-performance battery for their products, also became A123 Systems investors. That same year the founding trio hired the company's first 15 employees, beginning with David Vieau, a nine-year veteran executive from American Power Conversion who was tapped to be the chief executive officer and president. The company also licensed Chiang's key ideas: a self-assembling battery and another that

COMPANY PERSPECTIVES

Founded in 2001, A123 Systems' proprietary Nanophosphate technology is built on a new nanoscale materials initially developed at the Massachusetts Institute of Technology. A123 Systems is now one of the world's leading suppliers of high-power lithium ion batteries designed to deliver a new combination of power, safety and life.

Our breakthrough technology, innovative multinational manufacturing model and experienced executives are providing the power to change the game for today's Transportation, Electric Grid and Commercial manufacturers.

involved lithium-ion batteries, which initially seemed to have little to do with A123 Systems's immediate future.

NEW BATTERY MODEL: 2002–06

Before Chiang's self-assembling battery idea was licensed, he made a discovery that would ultimately fuel the production of the company's first commercial product. As part of his grant research work Chiang was experimenting with lithium iron phosphate, which was nontoxic as well as safer and less expensive than materials used in traditional lithium-ion batteries. Because lithium iron phosphate stored less energy than traditional batteries and charged and discharged slowly, Chiang made alternations to it by mixing in trace quantities of metals. He discovered that this modified material, which was called nanophosphate, could deliver surges of electricity that were greater than that generated by traditional lithium-ion batteries. Even though this discovery seemed impressive, it was not related to the company's self-organizing battery and it did not appear to be commercially viable.

Regardless, the company decided to license both Chiang's self-assembling battery concept and the lithium-ion battery. By late 2002 the test results for the self-assembling battery were turning out less positive than expected, so the founding trio decided to shift their focus on the modified lithium-ion battery.

In 2003 Vieau and Fulop met with Stanley Black & Decker, Inc., representatives, who sought a power source for a new line of power tools. Vieau and Fulop believed that Chiang's lithium-ion battery was well suited for cordless power tools because it delivered more power than a home circuit, it recharged fast, and it was not susceptible to catching on fire, unlike traditional lithium-ion batteries. It also had a lifespan 10 times that of a conventional battery and five times the power and could be produced using mostly traditional manufacturing methods.

Stanley Black & Decker was impressed with A123 Systems's sales pitch. In early 2005 A123 Systems signed an exclusive agreement with the tool maker to develop a commercially viable lithium-ion battery that was based on Chiang's proprietary technology. By November A123 Systems had established manufacturing facilities in Asia and was producing its lithium-ion battery for Stanley Black & Decker, which began selling the battery to consumers in 2006.

ENTRANCE INTO THE AUTOMOTIVE MARKET: 2006–07

The battery that was designed for Stanley Black & Decker illustrated that A123 Systems could successfully develop commercial applications from its technology. It also generated an important revenue stream and interest in the company. The A123 Systems battery was noticed by the U.S. Department of Energy, which commissioned the company to begin working on battery applications for hybrid electric vehicles.

In 2006 A123 Systems landed a General Motors (GM) commission to develop battery packs for GM's plug-in hybrid electric vehicle (PHEV), the Volt, which made its debut in late 2010. That same year the company also entered into a General Electric (GE) research partnership to develop a no-emissions hybrid bus that was reliant on battery power.

A123 Systems received additional venture capital in 2006, with new investors including OnPoint Technologies, a private equity firm that was funded by the U.S. Army; GE Energy Financial Services; and the company's chairman, Gururaj Deshpande. By 2007 A123 Systems's lithium-ion batteries had become the industry standard within select markets.

NEW CONTRACTS AND BATTERY APPLICATIONS: 2007–09

In May 2007 A123 Systems acquired a leading fabricator of aftermarket plug-in hybrid modules, Hymotion, Inc., whose Battery Range Extender Module (BREM) allowed a standard vehicle to be converted to a PHEV. Hymotion provided A123 Systems with hybrid plug-in technology and BREM engineering expertise. Later that year A123 Systems garnered another $30 million in venture capital, which it used to improve manufacturing

KEY DATES

2001: A123 Systems is founded.
2006: A123 Systems's batteries debut in a line of power tools sold by Stanley Black & Decker, Inc.
2006: A123 Systems signs a deal to develop a car battery for General Motors.
2009: A123 Systems goes public.
2010: A123 Systems opens the largest lithium-ion automotive battery factory in North America.

capacity for cordless tools and to ramp up research on the Volt battery cell. The company also secured contracts with BAE Systems for its buses, Saturn to power its hybrid Vue, and the U.S. Army to develop battery packs for soldiers.

In 2008 A123 Systems developed a new battery pack for the Toyota Prius that converted the vehicle into a PHEV. The company also joined a three-way partnership with Th!nk Global, a Norwegian electric vehicle company, and GE Energy Financial Services, an A123 Systems investor. GE contributed $4 million to Th!nk and increased its investment in A123 Systems to $20 million, while A123 Systems was commissioned to develop a rechargeable lithium-ion battery for the City, Th!nk's new car model. That same year the U.S. Advanced Battery Consortium awarded A123 Systems a $12.5 million grant to develop PHEV battery-cell technology.

The following year the company signed a contract with Chrysler to provide lithium-ion batteries for its new line of ENVI cars. As part of the Chrysler deal, A123 Systems agreed to build a Michigan factory to produce battery cells that could be combined in different sized automotive battery packs to fit different vehicles. In April 2009 A123 Systems completed a new round of private financing that provided the company with $69 million to develop its battery manufacturing operations in Michigan. The financing also furthered the company's research and development of smart-grid energy storage systems.

NEW CONTRACTS AND JOINT VENTURES: 2009

In September 2009 A123 Systems staged an initial public offering (IPO) of 25.6 million common shares on the NASDAQ. The company initially planned to open its IPO with shares priced at $8 to $9.50, but interest was great enough to boost the price to $13.50 at the opening bell. The stock closed its opening day at $20.29.

That same month Edison Material Company signed a pilot-program pact with A123 Systems to acquire two Smart Grid Stabilization Systems to provide standby reserve capacity. In October the company signed an agreement with the Tianjin Battery Joint-Stock Company. The three-year deal licensed A123 Systems's proprietary manufacturing and battery-cell design to Tianjin, which agreed to purchase from the company all the necessary materials that were required for battery-cell production.

In December A123 Systems formed the joint venture Shanghai Advanced Traction Battery Systems (ATBS) with the Chinese auto manufacturer SAIC. ATBS was formed to develop, produce, and sell batteries for a vehicle traction system that was used in Chinese electric and hybrid vehicles. By targeting the world's largest auto market, ATBS became the preferred provider of energy storage systems for all electric and hybrid SAIC vehicles. SAIC controlled a 51 percent stake in ATBS and A123 Systems claimed the minority share.

DEVELOPMENT OF MICHIGAN MANUFACTURING: 2009–10

Before the close of 2009 A123 Systems received a $250 million grant through the U.S. Department of Energy's Battery Initiative, which the company used to build a lithium-ion battery manufacturing facility in Livonia, Michigan. The company also received from the state of Michigan a $10 million incentive grant to establish a battery-production facility, a forgivable $4 million loan for the creation of jobs, a $2 million grant to develop and enhance energy-efficient technologies, and $125 million in Michigan state tax credits covering a 15-year span.

In early 2010 the company was commissioned by Fisker Automotive to provide lithium-ion batteries for the Karma, a new PHEV. A123 Systems additionally agreed to provide batteries for another Fisker vehicle, the Nina, and to invest $23 million in Fisker as part of a strategic partnership. A123 Systems also signed a deal with Navistar International to manufacture batteries for the heavy-duty truck maker's joint-venture all-electric vehicle Navistar-Modec EV Alliance.

In September 2010 A123 Systems opened the largest lithium-ion manufacturing facility in North America in Livonia. The facility closely duplicated one of the company's South Korean plants.

CHANGING REVENUE STREAMS AND THE FUTURE

In August 2010 Chrysler and A123 Systems ended their collaboration. That same month A123 Systems spun off 24M Technologies, which was formed to develop a hybrid-energy storage system that merged both lithium-ion and flow-battery technologies. A123 Systems supported the new venture with financing and took a seat on the company board.

During the latter half of the first decade of the 21st century the company's dominant source of revenue shifted from the consumer products market to the transportation market, and it also began serving the power-grid industry. The company's annual revenues rose from $41.3 million in 2007 to $91.1 million in 2010. However, the company, which was still in the infrastructure-building stage, reported net losses of $34.2 million for the second quarter of 2010, prompting concerns from some investors that A123 Systems was too dependent on government funding. In response to these concerns, company officials announced that A123 Systems would eventually wean itself off of government funding.

Despite its net losses, A123 Systems entered 2010 as one of the top-five battery suppliers for electric and hybrid vehicles. This fact and industry projections for the markets A123 Systems served boded well for future profitability. The power-grid battery market was expected to be worth more than $3 billion by 2015, while the transportation battery market was expected to generate $50 billion to $100 billion by 2020. The company was counting on such growth to power its own future development and profitability.

Roger Rouland

PRINCIPAL SUBSIDIARIES

A123 Securities Corporation; A123 Systems Co., Ltd. (China); A123 Systems Materials Co., Ltd. (China); A123 Systems GmbH (Germany); A123 Systems (Zhenjiang) Co., Ltd. (China); Enerland Co., Ltd. (Korea); Changchun Farad Electric Co., Ltd. (China); Changchun Guoji Electronic Technology Co., Ltd. (China; 45%); A123 Systems Hong Kong, Ltd.

PRINCIPAL DIVISIONS

Automotive and Transportation; Consumer Products; Power Grid.

PRINCIPAL COMPETITORS

Ener1, Inc.; Johnson Controls, Inc.; Valence Technology, Inc.

FURTHER READING

Aragon, Lawrence. "A123 Revs up IPO Market, Not Backers." *Private Equity Week*, September 28, 2009, 7.

Beene, Ryan. "A123: 2010 Marks 'Michigan Ramp-Up.'" *Crain's Detroit Business*, May 3, 2010, E013.

Buderi, Robert. "The A123 Story: How a Battery Company Jumpstarted Its Business." Xconomy.com, January 24, 2008. Accessed November 4, 2010. http://www.xconomy.com/2008/01/24/the-a123-story-how-a-battery-company-jumpstarted-its-business/.

Bullis, Kevin. "An Electrifying Startup: With a New Battery from A123 Systems, Electric Cars Could Come to Dominate the Roads." *Technology Review*, May–June, 2008, 68.

———. "Ric Fulop, 33: A123 Systems: Energizing Rechargeable Batteries." *Technology Review*, September–October, 2008, 74.

Henderson, Tom. "A123 a Success Story in Clean Technology." *Crain's Detroit Business*, November 16, 2009, E8.

Huang, Gregory T. "A123 Opens Lithium Ion Battery Plant in Michigan, Wants to Create Global Hub for Electric Vehicles." Xconomy.com, September 13, 2010. Accessed November 4, 2010. http://www.xconomy.com/detroit/2010/09/13/a123-opens-lithium-ion-battery-plant-in-michigan-wants-to-create-global-hub-for-electric-vehicles.

———. "A123 Systems Spins off New Battery Firm, Drops Out of Chrysler Deal, Posts Quarterly Loss." Xconomy.com, August 11, 2010. Accessed November 4, 2010. http://www.xconomy.com/boston/2010/08/11/a123systems-spins-off-new-battery-firm-drops-out-of-chrysler-deal-posts-quarterly-loss.

Stoffer, Harry. "Lithium Ion Batteries Power Converted Priuses." *Automotive News*, June 16, 2008, 8.

Academy of Motion Picture Arts and Sciences

8949 Wilshire Boulevard
Beverly Hills, California 90211
U.S.A.
Telephone: (310) 247-3000
Fax: (310) 859-9351
Web site: http://www.oscars.org

Nonprofit Company
Founded: 1927
Incorporated: 1927
Employees: 174
Sales: $80.51 million (2009)
NAICS: 813920 Professional Organizations

■ ■ ■

The Academy of Motion Picture Arts and Sciences is a professional organization devoted to the advancement of the arts and sciences of motion pictures. It is best known for the annual Academy Awards, known worldwide as the "Oscars." Based in Beverly Hills, California, the nonprofit organization has a membership of 6,000 motion picture professionals, most of whom work in the United States, but in recent years the organization has become more international in scope. The Academy maintains the Science and Technology Council that not only provides a forum to foster advances in technology but also preserves the history of motion picture science and technology. The Academy Film Archive preserves the history of film by collecting and restoring motion pictures. Educational outreach and the maintenance of the Margaret Herrick Library, a research library, are other important Academy activities. The Academy offers Student Academy Awards and each year bestows as many as five Nicholl Fellowships in Screenwriting. In addition, the Academy serves the general public by operating the Academy Museum of Motion Pictures and sponsoring lecture series, exhibitions, and film retrospectives.

ACADEMY FOUNDED: 1927

The seeds for the Academy were planted during a Sunday dinner in early 1927 at the Santa Monica beach home of Louis B. Mayer, a well-known movie mogul. The film industry was at a crossroads. Not only did it have to contend with public pressure over what many considered indecent content in Hollywood films but also organized labor was making its presence felt. A few weeks earlier the Studio Basic Agreement was signed between nine film studios and unions representing carpenters, electricians, musicians, painters, and stagehands. Moreover, the silent era of films was coming to an end and there was no clear consensus on a standard for sound-on-film. It was against this backdrop that Mayer and three of his guests, the producer Fred Beetson, the director Fred Niblo, and the actor Conrad Nagel, discussed the possibility of creating a single organization that could police screen content, resolve technological issues, and settle labor disputes. A dinner was planned for the following week with a larger group to discuss the idea further.

In January 1927, 36 film industry people met at the Ambassador Hotel in Los Angeles and became the founders of the International Academy of Motion

COMPANY PERSPECTIVES

Founded in 1927 by 36 of the most influential men and women in the motion picture industry at the time, the Academy is an honorary membership organization whose ranks now include more than 6,000 artists and professionals.

Picture Arts and Sciences. When it came time to incorporate, the word *International* was omitted. Among the original 36 were notables such as Douglas Fairbanks, George Cohen, Cecil B. De Mille, Jesse Lasky, Harold Lloyd, Edwin Loeb, Mary Pickford, Irving G. Thalberg, and Jack Leonard Warner. In May the Academy received a charter as a nonprofit corporation from the state of California. Fairbanks was named the first president.

A week after incorporation an organizational banquet was held at the Biltmore Hotel in Los Angeles. Of the 300 guests that night, 231 wrote $100 checks to become the Academy's pioneer members. They were divided among five branches: Actors, Directors, Producers, Technicians, and Writers. As the industry became more specialized, further branches were added. From the outset, membership was by invitation only.

AVERTED STRIKE AND CONDUCTED SEMINARS

The Academy wasted little time in making its influence felt. The East Coast financial backers of the studios were pressing for 10 percent salary cuts on all studio personnel, who objected and were on the verge of a strike. The Producers branch was able to work with the Academy's other branches to find ways to reduce production costs without affecting salaries and thus averted the strike. While working on preventing the strike, the Academy was looking for a suitable home. Temporary offices were taken before suitable accommodations were found on the mezzanine floor of the Roosevelt Hotel. It was large enough to house a library, and soon a screening room was added with all the industry's new competing sound systems. Here, unreleased pictures could be shown to church officials, educational leaders, and other key opinion-makers of the day.

In keeping with its mandate, the Academy conducted a series of seminars on lighting, which served as the foundation for the organization's first book, *Report on Incandescent Illumination*, published in 1928. Sound seminars were also conducted and led to the 1931 publishing of *Recording Sound for Motion Pictures*. The Academy also published *Introduction to the Photoplay*, which was based on lectures given at the University of Southern California. Another publishing effort during the early years of the Academy was the 1933 launch of the *Screen Achievements Records Bulletin*, which kept track of production titles and director and writer credits. This was followed four years later by the *Academy Players Directory*, a casting publication that included pictures of actors and the names of their agents or industry contacts.

FIRST OSCARS PRESENTED: 1929

Initially, the Awards of Merit were of secondary importance to the Academy, so much so that a year passed before the subject was seriously addressed. The awards committee created a five-member board of judges, drawn from the five branches of the Academy, to recognize special achievement in 12 categories. The movie art director Cedric Gibbons created the trophy that would take the name of Oscar during the 1930s. The first winners were named in February 1929, but it was not until May of that year that the awards were presented at a black-tie dinner held at the Roosevelt Hotel. The Oscars were distributed in a matter of five minutes. Their importance was so minor that three of the Best Actor nominees were no-shows.

Indifference to the Academy Awards was short lived, however. The awards program took shape during the 1930s. The calendar year for eligible films was first adopted in 1933, so that the 1934 awards recognized 17 months of films to complete the transition to the new system. Early on, the studio bosses were able to control nominations and essentially select the winners, but by the third year of the awards program the full Academy membership became involved in both the nomination procedure and the final voting. Not everyone received statuettes during this period. Supporting actors and actresses received plaques until 1944, while film editors initially received certificates of merit, then plaques, before being issued statuettes in 1944. The categories also came and went during this period, and between 1931 and 1943 the number of Best Picture nominees ranged from 8 to 12, before being set at 5. The Academy began using sealed envelopes to announce the winners in 1941.

The Academy Awards eventually became more than mere industry recognition. The general public took an interest as well, and the Academy Awards as an entertainment program began to develop during the late 1930s, when the first radio broadcast of the ceremony was aired. After World War II television gained popularity, so much so that the motion picture industry saw

KEY DATES

1927: The Academy of Motion Picture Arts and Sciences is established.
1929: The first Academy Awards ceremony is held.
1937: The Academy's bylaws are rewritten.
1975: The Academy moves into new headquarters.
2004: The Academy adopts a new admissions policy.

ticket sales plummet. Even though television was viewed as a mortal enemy in many quarters, there was no denying that the medium was not a mere fad. In 1953 the Academy gave in and the first Academy Awards ceremony was telecast.

BYLAWS REWRITTEN: 1937

After 10 years of being in existence, the Academy recognized that its mission had evolved significantly. The idea that it would arbitrate labor-management disputes was quickly abandoned. In 1937 the bylaws were rewritten to take the organization out of this arena. In the public eye, the Academy was simply the presenter of the annual Oscars, but the organization continued to fulfill much of its original mandates. The Academy's Research Council evolved into the Science and Technology Council, and the Academy library became a major repository for motion picture–related collections. The National Film Information Service was established in 1972 to make library materials available to historians and students outside of the Los Angeles area.

The Academy also played an important role in elevating the academic study of the motion picture arts. During the 1960s the Academy established a scholarship program for film students and began issuing grants to support internships at colleges and film-related organizations. In 1986 the Academy awarded its first Nicholl Fellowships in Screenwriting. It quickly grew into a major international screenwriting competition. A Film Festival Grants Program was added in 1999. To encourage film scholarship, the Academy established in 2000 the Academy of Film Scholars Program to make grants available to established historians, scholars, writers, and researchers.

Public outreach was another area of emphasis. The Visiting Artists Program was launched in 1970 to send Academy members throughout the United States to give filmmaking presentations. Several lecture series were created, starting in 1974 with the Marvin Borowsky Lecture, named in honor of the late screenwriter and professor. In 1975 the Academy moved into its new enlarged headquarters, which included a state-of-the-art theater, where postscreening discussions could be held with members of a film's cast and crew.

As the century came to a close, the Academy acquired a former Beverly Hills water treatment plant to create a facility to house the organization's library holdings and its growing film archive. The building was dedicated in 1991 and in 2002 was renamed the Fairbanks Center for Motion Picture Study, in honor of Fairbanks, the Academy's first president. The film archive moved again in 2002 to a new facility, the Pickford Center for Motion Picture Study, named for Mary Pickford, who was the wife of Fairbanks and a cofounder of the United Artists film studio.

REVISED ADMISSIONS POLICY: 2004

To keep pace with the times, the Academy implemented a new admissions policy in 2004. The immediate goal was to curb the growth of the Academy, which officials believed had become too unwieldy as it approached 6,000 members. Moreover, the ranks had become heavily tilted toward U.S. members. The new policy brought in more people from the independent and international film communities. As a result, the focus of the Academy Awards began to drift away from mainstream films, and more independent and foreign films received recognition, often at the expense of blockbuster films on which the industry depended.

In 2009 the matter came to a head when the Indian film *Slumdog Millionaire* was selected as the Best Motion Picture of the Year, while the more widely seen *Dark Knight* and *Wall-E* failed to even receive nominations. A short time later, the Academy doubled the number of Best Picture nominees to 10. Even though that was the same number of films recognized a half-century earlier, there were substantially more films released during the 1940s. Nevertheless, it was a change that made sense for an organization that instead of being a group of company-town insiders interested in dealing with matters of mutual concern was fast becoming an advocate of world film.

Ed Dinger

PRINCIPAL DIVISIONS

Academy Museum of Motion Pictures; Fairbanks Center for Motion Picture Study; Margaret Herrick Library; Pickford Center for Motion Picture Study.

FURTHER READING

Cieply, Michael. "Academy Expands Best-Picture Pool to 10." *New York Times*, June 25, 2009, C1.

———. "Film Executive to Lead Academy That Bestows Oscars." *New York Times*, August 20, 2009, C2.

———. "Honor Just to Be Asked in, as Film Academy Tightens Its Ranks." *New York Times*, December 1, 2008, C1.

———. "With Oscar Show Salvaged, a Planned Film Museum Is Back in Play." *New York Times*, February 23, 2008, B12.

"Happy 60th Oscar!" *People Weekly*, April 11, 1988, 85.

"Hollywood Launches Academy of Movie Art." *New York Times*, May 5, 1927.

Osborne, Robert. *50 Golden Years of Oscar*. La Habra, CA: ESE California, 1979.

Advanced Drainage Systems, Inc.

4640 Trueman Boulevard
Hilliard, Ohio 43026
U.S.A.
Telephone: (614) 658-0050
Toll Free: (800) 821-6710
Fax: (614) 658-0204
Web site: http://www.ads-pipe.com

Private Company
Founded: 1966
Employees: 4,000
Sales: $1.20 billion (2009)
NAICS: 32612 Plastics Pipe, Pipe Fitting, and Unlaminated Profile Shape Manufacturing; 326122 Plastics Pipe and Pipe Fitting Manufacturing; 424610 Plastics Materials and Basic Forms and Shapes Merchant Wholesalers

■ ■ ■

Advanced Drainage Systems, Inc. (ADS), is a global leader in the manufacture of high-density polyethylene pipe. Its products are used for drainage systems in residential, commercial, and public construction and include culverts, drains, fittings, gaskets, grates, screens, leaching chambers, grease interceptors, and storm sewers. Its systems have also been used in noted sports centers, including Dodger Stadium in Los Angeles, California, and Turner Field in Atlanta, Georgia. In 2010 ADS broadened its product line to include the manufacture of concrete pipes.

FIRST YEARS: EARLY FIFTIES TO EARLY SEVENTIES

In 1951 the creation of high-density polyethylene (HDPE) was developed by the research chemists Paul Hogan and Robert Banks of Phillips Petroleum. In 1954 Phillips introduced HDPE commercially under the brand name Marlex, but the product was not the success Phillips initially expected. The first widespread use of HDPE was in the wildly popular hula hoop. Sales from the toy allowed Phillips to improve the HDPE production process and expand the quality levels. This resulted in new and more varied uses for the material, including piping.

In 1966, when Marty Sixt and Ron Martin founded Advanced Drainage Systems, Inc., in Hilliard, Ohio, they developed a corrugated HDPE pipe that had the potential for being used industrially. The structural strength and durability of the ADS pipe, which was tested at Ohio State University, was found suitable for use in industrial applications and provided some significant advantages over the then prevalent clay piping. Even though ADS began as a small regional manufacturer for agricultural applications, the versatility of its initial product allowed ADS to consider marketing its pipe more extensively.

In 1973 ADS recruited Frank Eck as its vice president of sales and marketing. Eck had earned a degree in chemical engineering, served in World War II, and then attended Harvard Business School. He initially worked in the petrochemical industry and held marketing and managerial positions with leading companies in the emerging plastics industry, such as American Cyana-

COMPANY PERSPECTIVES

At ADS, we continually enhance the products and services we offer to our customers, helping them to solve water management issues, which ultimately improves the quality of life.

Our culture is results oriented and promotes competitiveness and a desire to win, hard work, integrity and mental toughness.

mid Company and Celanese Plastics Company. Eck's skills and leadership were recognized by ADS, and soon he was named president of the company.

MARKETING AND DEVELOPMENT: 1982–96

Under Eck's direction, ADS became known for its marketing proficiency and product development. ADS promoted its pipes for uses in mining, forestry, recreation, and agriculture. It added a distinctive green stripe to all its pipes, identifying its manufacturer and attesting to its quality. It 1982 the company introduced pipes with larger diameters than its original four-inch pipe. The 18- and 24-inch pipes significantly increased the applications for the company's products. That same year ADS also produced the SB2 pipe with geothermal and hazardous waste functions, which further diversified its market.

In 1987 ADS created the N-12 dual-wall corrugated pipe, which had a smooth interior. With its improved flow characteristics this large-diameter pipe was suitable for storm sewers, highways, and heavy-duty commercial applications, opening even more markets for the company's HDPE products. The following year the company developed the AdvanEDGE drainage pipe. This pipe was designed as a slim vertical panel that could be easily and quickly installed in a narrow trench. AdvanEDGE pipes became popular for being installed along highways, in building foundations, and under golf courses, athletic fields, and airport runways.

During the early 1990s ADS continued to expand its products and product applications with larger pipes and new coupling systems. It introduced the ADS 3000, a triple-wall pipe that was created to compete with polyvinyl chloride (PVC) pipe, without the health and environmental dangers that were associated with PVC. ADS 3000 pipes were used in agriculture for field irrigation and grain aeration, in residential and commercial properties for basement drainage and driveway culverts, and in recreational applications for park, golf course, and athletic field drainage and storm water management.

Since its founding, ADS had been working with industry regulators and government agencies to increase the acceptance of its products. In 1993 ADS began installing and testing HDPE pipe in 30 residential subdivisions in Columbus, Ohio. By 1996 the city had approved the pipe for under pavement sewer and drainage.

GLOBAL GROWTH AND ACQUISITIONS: 2000–05

In 2000 ADS opened a pipe manufacturing plant in El Salvador. The company chose that location not just because El Salvador itself was an expanding market but also because it offered a central distribution point for many developing Central American countries and for southern Mexico. The facility was created through a strategic alliance between ADS and Industrial De Tuberias, a Salvadoran pipe company. That same year ADS participated in the Golf, Irrigation, Landscape, Turf Sporting Grounds International Conference and Expo in Guangzhou, China, where the company introduced its products to the Asian market. In 2002 the company opened a plant in Chile.

Meanwhile, as ADS was moving into the global marketplace, the company was expanding its products and facilities through a series of acquisitions. In 2001 ADS acquired the Inline Drain & Drain Basin Division of Nyoplast, USA, a manufacturer of PVC surface drain pipes and fittings. This move signaled ADS's intention to penetrate the storm sewer market and challenge the concrete pipe manufacturers. Two years later, in a joint venture with Infiltrator Systems, Inc., of Old Saybrook, Connecticut, ADS created StormTech for the development and manufacture of underground storm water retention chambers. These chambers provided a less expensive and safer storm water management alternative to runoff ponds.

By 2005 ADS had five international plants, including facilities in Mexico and Puerto Rico. That same year ADS acquired Hancor, Inc., of Findlay, Ohio. Hancor was ADS's greatest competitor. Combining the two companies created the largest HDPE pipe manufacturer in North America, with nearly 40 plants and estimated sales of over $700 million. When the deal was announced in April, the terms of the agreement were not made public. However, in May ADS raised $110 million through a private placement deal in a transaction with National City Corporation, an Ohio-based bank.

KEY DATES

1966: Advanced Drainage Systems, Inc. (ADS), is founded.
1987: N-12 dual-wall corrugated pipe is introduced.
2000: El Salvador plant is opened.
2005: ADS acquires Hancor, Inc.
2010: ADS acquires Foltz Concrete Pipe Company.

Combined, ADS and Hancor cornered about 70 percent of the North American market for corrugated HDPE pipe, which made them the largest players in an industry that reported revenues of $2.3 billion annually. Both companies challenged the supremacy of concrete pipes in drainage applications and had similar successes. For example, Hancor supplied Lowe's and ADS supplied Home Depot. Furthermore, their strengths were complementary, in that Hancor was focused on material development and ADS had the marketing savvy.

STRATEGIES AND PLANS: 2005–10

ADS had continued to lobby for HDPE pipe to be accepted for a variety of applications and, by 2005, ASTM International (originally the American Society for Testing and Materials), a global standards organization, had included corrugated plastic pipe in the permitted materials for storm sewers. This change supported further expansion for HDPE pipe in a market where it still had a relatively small penetration.

By 2007 ADS had formed a dedicated team to work with regulators on construction standards. The U.S. Federal Highway Administration, which was motivated at least in part by increases in the price of steel and concrete, issued a resolution that called for a variety of materials to be considered in setting storm water drainage specifications. The following year the Florida Department of Transportation certified ADS's flagship N-12 pipe for a 100-year service life. The expanding recognition of the value of HDPE pipe in heavy-duty construction applications validated ADS's efforts.

In 2008 ADS became the sole sales and marketing provider for all BaySaver Technologies, Inc., products. BaySaver systems separated and filtered pollution from storm water. As a component of any storm water drainage system, its systems assisted in the compliance with all federally mandated regulations set by the Clean Water Act, and this alliance increased ADS's storm water market appeal. That same year the Freedonia Group conducted a market research study on the future of large-diameter pipe. The study indicated that the market for large-diameter pipe in the United States would grow annually by 2.2 percent and that the country would need more than 200 million feet of pipe by 2012. It also predicted that even though concrete pipe would still predominate, the use of plastic pipe would grow more rapidly, increasing annually by 4 percent.

In 2009 ADS announced a joint venture with Tigre S.A., a PVC pipe manufacturer that was based in Brazil. The new venture established the company Tuberias Tigre ADS Limitada to produce ADS corrugated pipe and Tigre solid-wall pipe and sell both products in South America. ADS also opened two manufacturing facilities in Canada. That same year ADS acquired another corrugated HDPE pipe manufacturer, Century Plastics, Inc., of Hayfield, Minnesota.

In April 2010, in a move that shocked some who saw the company as singularly committed to plastic pipes, ADS acquired Foltz Concrete Pipe Company. Joe Chlapaty, the chief executive officer of ADS, explained to Angie DeRosa of *Plastics News* that the move was an expansion of ADS offerings rather an abandonment of plastic piping: "There is no change of philosophy, just a broadening."

With the 2010 purchase of Foltz Concrete, ADS was in a position to provide for the varied needs of an aging pipe infrastructure. It was already a major plastic pipe manufacturer, but the Foltz Concrete acquisition clearly indicated that ADS wanted to become a major manufacturer of both plastic and concrete pipes.

Grace Murphy

PRINCIPAL COMPETITORS

CONTECH Construction Products Inc.; Diamond Plastics Corporation; J-M Manufacturing Company, Inc.; Charlotte Pipe & Foundry Company.

FURTHER READING

"ADS." *Underground Construction*, February, 2010, 49.

"Advanced Drainage Systems (ADS) and Infiltrator Systems Inc. of Old Saybrook, Connecticut Created the Joint Venture StormTech, a Company That Engineers and Manufactures Chambers for Use in Underground Storm Water Detention and Retention Systems." *Water and Waste Water International*, September 2003, 5.

DeRosa, Angie. "Advanced Drainage Buys Hancor." *Plastics News*, April 11, 2005, 1.

———. "ADS Buys into Concrete Pipe." *Plastics News*, April 5, 2010, 1.

"Education's Paying Off for Plastic Pipe." *Chemical Business Newsbase*, February 20, 2007.

"Feed/Drain System Keeps Athletic Turf Healthy." *Public Works*, February 1999, 26.

Griswold, Matt. "Advanced Drainage Expands Pipe Empire." *Plastics News*, June 15, 2009, 1.

Newpoff, Laura, "Advanced Drainage Opens Pipe Plant in El Salvador." *Business First-Columbus*, May 12, 2000, 7.

"US Large Diameter Pipe Market." Freedonia Group. January 2008. Accessed November 10, 2010. http://www.reportlinker.com/p096500/US-Large-Diameter-Pipe-Market.html.

Wilson, Paul. "Frank E. Eck, 1923–2007: Chief Took Drainage Company to New Level." *Columbus Dispatch* (Ohio), December 15, 2007.

Aecon Group Inc.

20 Carlson Court, Suite 800
Toronto, Ontario M9W 7K6
Canada
Telephone: (416) 293-7004
Toll Free: (877) 232-2677
Fax: (416) 293-0271
Web site: http://www.aecon.com

Public Company
Founded: 1877 as Adam Clark Plumbing & Gas Fitting
Incorporated: 1957 as Prefac Concrete Co. Ltd.
Employees: 4,557
Sales: CAD 2.26 billion ($2.15 billion)
Stock Exchanges: Toronto
Ticker Symbol: ARE
NAICS: 212321 Construction Sand and Gravel Mining; 236116 New Multifamily Housing Construction (except Operative Builders); 236210 Industrial Building Construction; 236220 Commercial and Institutional Building Construction; 237110 Water and Sewer Line and Related Structures Construction; 237120 Oil and Gas Pipeline and Related Structures Construction; 237130 Power and Communication Line and Related Structures Construction; 237310 Highway, Street, and Bridge Construction; 237990 Other Heavy and Civil Engineering Construction; 238210 Electrical Contractors; 238290 Other Building Equipment Contractors; 332312 Fabricated Structural Metal Manufacturing; 332313 Plate Work Manufacturing; 541690 Other Scientific and Technical Consulting Services

■ ■ ■

Aecon Group Inc. is the largest publicly traded construction and infrastructure development firm in Canada. Serving both the private and public sectors throughout Canada and selectively in international locales, the company operates in three business segments: concessions, industrial, and infrastructure.

EARLY PREDECESSOR COMPANIES: 1877–57

Aecon Group is a result of more than a century of growth through acquisitions, organic development, and geographic expansion. The company claims its roots in at least 18 forerunner companies but accepts Armbro Construction, founded in 1929, as its principal predecessor while Prefac Concrete Co. Ltd., incorporated in 1957, is the legal forerunner to Aecon Group, having acquired Armbro during the 1980s.

Aecon Group traces its roots to many independent Canadian companies whose foundings spanned more than 100 years. The first such company was established by the Scottish immigrant Adam Clark, who in 1877 launched Adam Clark Plumbing & Gas Fitting in Hamilton, Ontario, that developed into a multitrade contracting operation. Two decades later, during the peak of the Klondike Gold Rush, the entrepreneur Jack Lockerbie founded the plumbing company Lockerbie & Hole in Edmonton, Alberta, that grew into a leading mechanical construction and industrial fabrication firm.

In 1910 the Foundation Company was established in Montreal, Quebec, and eventually developed into a major civil contractor. Two years later the Jackson-Lewis Company was founded in Toronto, Ontario, and

COMPANY PERSPECTIVES

Aecon is Canada's largest publicly traded construction and infrastructure development company. For over a century, we've been delivering superior projects of every size and shape for our clients.

Over the years, we've become one of the most diverse companies in our industry. Our expertise spans all elements of design, build, operate, procure and finance in the areas of buildings, civil, industrial, mechanical, nuclear and utility construction. Whether it's a small building renovation, a project-financed infrastructure development, or a complex industrial fabrication and module assembly project, Aecon prides itself in being able to handle virtually any challenge for our clients.

became one of Canada's first general contracting firms. Armbro Construction was established in 1929 in Brampton, Ontario. Armbro soon developed into a leading Canadian road builder and aggregate supplier.

During the Great Depression years Leo Alarie performed contract work for farmers in the area surrounding Timmins, Ontario, before later incorporating his company as Leo Alarie & Sons Construction Ltd. Alarie's company eventually developed into an infrastructure construction business in northern Ontario. During World War II the heavy civil contractor C.A. Pitts General Contractor Ltd. was established in Ontario and later became part of Aecon Group's infrastructure division. In 1957 Prefac Construction was formed.

LANDMARK WORK AND FORMATION OF MORE FORERUNNERS: 1960–88

During the 1960s Aecon Group's forerunners were involved in major Canadian infrastructure projects, such as the construction of Highway 401 and the Gardner Expressway in Ontario and new airports in Toronto and Montreal. In 1972 the Foundation Company was involved in construction work on the Canadian landmark CN Towers.

In 1973 South Rock Limited was formed in Medicine Hat, Alberta, and developed into an infrastructure construction firm in Alberta. That same year the construction firm Karson Kartage Inc. was established in Carp, Ontario. In 1975 Nicholls-Radtke was established in Cambridge, Ontario, and still another, the Ontario-based Miwel Construction Limited, was formed in 1980.

In 1987 Prefac Enterprises Inc. (formerly Prefac Concrete Co. Ltd. until 1986) acquired complete control of Armbro Investments Ltd. (formerly Armbro Construction), making Armbro a wholly owned Prefac subsidiary. At the time of the acquisition Prefac was a small metal-fabricating operation while Armbro was a sizable private construction and real estate company. Armbro's interests had grown to include retirement homes, steel fabrication, construction, and aggregate supply. Through the purchase alone, Prefac's annual revenues grew from less than CAD 7.5 million to more than CAD 100 million. After acquiring Armbro, Prefac went public and was listed on the Toronto Stock Exchange that same year. In 1988 Prefac changed its name to Armbro Enterprises Inc.

DIVESTITURES, BOARD CONFLICT, AND RESTRUCTURING: 1990–95

Armbro divested its retirement home business and steel fabricating subsidiary in 1990. That same year the company was rocked by a recession. Within 18 months the firm's stock fell from CAD 8.87 to CAD 1.70, and it lost money as real estate values plummeted. After the real estate market and Armbro's stock began bottoming out, the Toronto-Dominion Bank seized company stock that had been used to secure loans for Prefac to make its 1987 acquisition.

In March 1992 John Beck, the president and a director of Armbro with an 11 percent stake in the company, asked the board of directors for a special meeting to propose a new slate of directors, several of which were with Armbro before the Prefac acquisition. Two days later Beck was fired and replaced by Alan Chapple, who came to the company with Prefac's purchase. However, Beck was not done making moves. As a major shareholder, he called for another special meeting and by April 1992 Beck had regained his former post as president and helped refashion the board of directors. Chapple was soon gone, and Beck assumed the roles of chairman and chief executive officer (CEO).

In 1995 the company finalized an agreement to repay all bank debt. Armbro offered the bank an option to acquire about 66 percent of the company on a diluted basis with the expectation that most of the shares would be returned to the firm. In September the firm finally reemerged from a long restructuring, repaid its debt through a new bank loan and equipment

KEY DATES

1877: Aecon Group Inc.'s first forerunner is established in Ontario.
1929: Armbro Construction is established.
1987: Prefac Enterprises Inc. acquires Armbro.
2000: The company acquires BFC Construction Corporation.
2001: The company adopts the name Aecon Group Inc.

financing, received its stock shares back from the bank, and watched its stock rebound. The company's revenues that year grew 20 percent, and Armbro's balance sheet moved out of the red.

PARTNERSHIPS, JOINT VENTURES, AND MAJOR CONTRACTS: 1995–99

Between 1995 and 1996 Armbro was awarded a CAD 11.4 million contract for grading a new runway at Pearson International Airport in Toronto and a CAD 30 million contract to widen and reconstruct a stretch of Queen Elizabeth Way (QEW) highway in Ontario. During the mid-1990s Armbro formed a partnership with Amec Inc. to create Canadian Highways International Corporation (CHIC). CHIC won a CAD 1 billion contract for the development, design, and construction of Highway ETR 407, the new 69-kilometer all-electronic toll highway in Toronto, and was awarded a 35-year contract to manage and maintain the tollway. CHIC also landed a CAD 120 million contract to construct a 45-kilometer tolled portion of Highway 104 in Nova Scotia.

In 1996 Banister Pipelines purchased Nicholls-Radtke. In late 1997 Armbro formed the 50-50 joint venture Capital Projects Group Inc. (CPGI) with Strait Crossing Inc. Among CPGI's larger successes was the CAD 1 billion contract to build Confederation Bridge between New Brunswick and Prince Edward Island. In 1998 Armbro purchased Miwel Construction Limited, which specialized in concrete paving, concrete curbs, and barrier walls. The following year Armbro acquired Innovative Steam Technologies (IST), a developer of steam generators.

By the late 1990s a majority of Armbro's revenue growth stemmed from joint ventures and public-private partnerships, including a Czech Republic airport redevelopment contract and toll project work on Highways 104 and 407. In 1999 CHIC gained a 33 percent interest in Derech Eretz Highways Ltd., a consortium of Israeli and Canadian companies that was chosen to finance, design, construct, and operate the new Cross Israel Highway, the first electronic tollway in Israel.

DEVELOPMENT OF A GROUP MENTALITY: 2000–03

In 2000 Armbro acquired the pipeline-construction contractor BFC Construction Corporation (previously Banister Pipelines) after joining with the German construction corporation Hochtief AG, which provided loans that were converted into nearly 50 percent of Armbro stock. Beck became chairman and CEO of the newly merged firm, which became the largest public construction company in Canada. In 2001 Armbro adopted the name Aecon Group Inc. The following year Hochtief increased its ownership in Aecon to one share less than 50 percent.

After acquiring BFC, Aecon continued to consistently win government contracts for bridge and road work in Ontario. Aecon also increasingly landed contracts for public and private buildings in the commercial, educational, and residential sectors. Between 2000 and 2003 Aecon was hired to construct high-rise condominiums in Toronto and Ottawa, a student residence hall for the University of Toronto, a science complex for the University of Guelph, and a casino in Washington state.

In addition, in 2002 an Aecon-forged consortium assumed management of the Mariscal Sucre International Airport in Quito, Ecuador, with Aecon holding a majority interest, in a lead-up to construction of a new international airport. That same year the firm also won contracts from energy companies, including a CAD 61 million award to build a hydroelectric dam on the Toulnustouc River and a CAD 108 million award to build a northern Quebec power plant. In 2003 it received a CAD 30 million contract to build a gas-fired power plant in New Brunswick. IST also began generating revenues by licensing its Once through Steam Generator (OTSG) technology to a German company for sale throughout Europe and Russia.

RAPID DEVELOPMENT OF BUSINESS: 2004–07

Aecon bought in 2004 Cegerco CCI, which specialized in the construction of industrial, institutional, and residential buildings. That same year Hochtief offered to acquire the 51 percent of Aecon that it did not own.

The offer was rejected by the Aecon board, which deemed it too low, and Hochtief withdrew its proposal and later sold its stake in Aecon to a consortium of financial service companies.

In 2004 IST began actively marketing its OTSGs in Europe and in the United States. IST also formed two partnerships between 2006 and 2007. The subsidiary joined with TEi-Struthers to manufacture Enhanced Oil Recovery steam generators for the extraction of oil from tar sands. It also partnered with the Italian-based Macchi to develop and sell industrial and heat-recovery boilers in North America, the Middle East, and Europe.

In 2005 Aecon's industrial division landed three contracts with energy firms in western Canada: to rebuild a Suncor Energy facility, to help construct a Petro Canada refinery, and to perform pipe fabrication and assembly work for a Nexen Inc. oil sands project. The following year Aecon won contracts for work at the Bruce Power nuclear generating station to devise and install a system that transferred spent fuel to dry storage containers; fabrication and assembly work for Canadian Natural Resources Limited's cogeneration facility; and fabrication and assembly work at Petro Canada's RCP 1.1 Sulphur Plant. In 2007 the industrial division earned a CAD 116 million contract to build the East Windsor Cogeneration Centre.

During the middle of the decade Aecon's building division earned contracts for a Seattle luxury hotel, a Halifax health center, a Montreal senior home, a science building at Saint Mary's University in Halifax, the Orleans Arts Centre Facility in Ottawa, and a health system facility in Ajax, Ontario. Its infrastructure division landed an airport parking lot expansion contract in Montreal, a joint venture contract for CAD 77 million tunnel in the York municipality, a design and construction contract for a rail–transit line tunnel for Go Transit, and a CAD 87 million QEW lane-construction and bridge-refurbishing contract.

ACQUISITIONS, ALLIANCES, AND FURTHER GROWTH: 2007–09

In 2007 Aecon acquired the Karson Group and Leo Alarie & Sons Construction Ltd. The following year Alarie & Sons partnered with Peter Kiewit Sons Co., a major western Canadian contractor, to begin a three-year CAD 230 million refurbishing of two hydroelectric dams near Timmins, Ontario.

During the latter half of the decade Aecon's infrastructure division was awarded alliance contracts with energy firms. For example, in 2008 Union Gas awarded an alliance contract to Aecon to install gas mains, service gas lines and pipelines, perform engineering pipeline construction, and maintain infrastructure. That same year Aecon signed a four-year CAD 180 million alliance contract with Enbridge Gas Distribution to perform distribution construction work in Enbridge's territory in Ontario.

Aecon reached financial close in 2008 on a build-finance project, a CAD 112 million renovation and expansion of the Toronto Rehabilitation Institute's University Centre. Under terms of the contract, the company received final payment when construction was completed. The infrastructure division also landed a CAD 105 million contract to widen and reconstruct a 15-kilometer stretch of Highway 401.

In 2009 Aecon purchased South Rock Ltd., an Alberta-based road building construction firm, and Lockerbie & Hole (in 2001 Lockerbie & Hole had acquired Adam Clark Company Limited, the earliest of Aecon Group's predecessor companies). That same year Lockerbie & Hole won a CAD 125 million award from Consumers' Co-operative Refineries Ltd. to enhance processing units at the Regina Oil Refinery.

REVENUE INCREASES AND A NEW DECADE

By 2009 the company had more than doubled its revenues in a decade, reporting sales of CAD 2.3 billion and earnings of CAD 44 million. During the decade Aecon progressed from being primarily an Ontario road builder to a national contractor providing a variety services. It also preserved its status as a public company after rebuffing a takeover offer from Hochtief, which through its financing had actually placed Aecon in a position to expand.

In 2010 Aecon acquired GCCL Contracting Ltd., a paving, asphalt, and construction firm; Cow Harbour Construction Ltd., an environmental reclamation services firm; and a minority stake in the Churchill Corporation, a diversified construction company based in Alberta. In June 2010 Aecon's infrastructure division was part of a joint venture that earned a CAD 1.7 billion contract to design and build the Lower Mattagami Hydroelectric Complex for Ontario Power Generation. Aecon also landed a contract for Suncor Energy, representing one of the largest industrial projects in the company's history. The contract involved field construction of Suncor's Firebag 3 plant facilities and was expected to require as many as 600 Aecon workers.

In late 2010 the company realigned its division structure by integrating the buildings division into the infrastructure division. The company's two other divisions were concessions and industrial. Aecon also sold its interest in the Cross Israel Highway for CAD 77.8 million but retained its interest in Derech Eretz Highways Ltd. that operated the highway.

Roger Rouland

PRINCIPAL SUBSIDIARIES

Aecon Construction Group Inc.; Aecon Construction and Materials Limited; Corporacion Quiport S.A. (Ecuador; 42.3%); Derech Eretz Highways Ltd. (Israel; 25%); Found Energy Inc.; Groupe Aecon Québec Ltée; Leo Alarie & Sons Construction Ltd.; Lockerbie & Hole Inc.; South Rock Ltd.; West Carleton Sand & Gravel Inc.

PRINCIPAL DIVISIONS

Concessions; Industrial; Infrastructure.

PRINCIPAL COMPETITORS

AMEC PLC; Bovis Lend Lease; PCL Employees Holdings Ltd.

FURTHER READING

"Aecon Restructures Its Buildings Division." *CNW Group*, September 27, 2010.

"Armbro Principals Agree to Peace Plan." *Globe and Mail* (Toronto), April 1, 1992, B17.

"Bank Would Get Real Estate in Armbro Restructuring Plan." *Globe and Mail* (Toronto), May 5, 1993, B12.

"Israel: Aecon to Sell Interest in Cross Israel Highway Concession for CAD 77.8 Million While Retaining Interest in Operating Company." *TendersInfo News*, July 16, 2010.

"Using 'Absolute Precision': Aecon Construction and Materials Specializes in Highway Construction and Builds throughout Canada." *Construction Today*, February 2007, 48.

Affinion Group, Inc.

6 High Ridge Park
Stamford, Connecticut 06905
U.S.A.
Telephone: (203) 956-1000
Toll Free: (800) 251-2148
Fax: (203) 956-1005
Web site: http://www.affiniongroup.com

Private Company
Incorporated: 1974 as Compu-U-Card of America, Inc.
Employees: 3,000
Sales: $1.38 billion (2009)
NAICS: 541990 All Other Professional, Scientific, and Technical Services

■ ■ ■

Based in Stamford, Connecticut, Affinion Group, Inc., is a major affinity direct marketer, providing membership, insurance, and loyalty programs. The company primarily serves the financial services industry, including 18 of the 20 largest financial institutions in the United States. Affinion designs and administers programs for its partners; develops customized products and services; creates marketing campaigns that make use of direct mail, online marketing, point-of-sale marketing, and telemarketing; and provides the necessary fulfillment and customer service to support the programs. Membership products include credit monitoring, identity-theft resolution services, and discount shopping; loyalty products include points-based programs for credit and debit cards. Affinion also markets accidental death and dismemberment as well as other insurance programs and checking account enhancement programs.

COMP-U-CARD OF AMERICA

Affinion was founded by Robert Perlman in Stamford, Connecticut, in 1973 as Comp-U-Card of America, Inc.. His idea was to serve as a broker of consumer products by developing a computer database of prices for such big-ticket items as televisions, stereos, washers and dryers, and refrigerators. The company distributed free membership cards that allowed consumers to use the phone to find the best deal and place an order. Comp-U-Card added a small mark-up to the price of the products for its service. Because it held no inventory, the company had little overhead.

To grow his business, Perlman accepted venture capital from Walter A. Forbes, a 1968 graduate of Harvard Business School, who was in charge of the venture capital arm of a Cambridge, Massachusetts, consulting firm. Forbes also became a member of Comp-U-Card's board of directors. It was soon clear that Perlman's and Forbes's visions for the company differed greatly, and in 1976 Forbes used his position on the board to oust Perlman and become chief executive officer himself. Under Forbes, Comp-U-Card began charging shoppers an annual fee and launched a telephone and catalog shopping club.

Forbes's enthusiasm for electronic shopping persuaded private investors to invest $14 million to fund his vision, which included personal computers connected to his database through telephone modems. Comp-U-Card continued to lose money, but Forbes

COMPANY PERSPECTIVES

Your business, and your customers, deserve more. Affinion Group provides a diverse range of proven products and services to help you attract new customers, strengthen relationships with existing customers, and produce significant new revenues that go straight to your bottom line.

soon found a profitable business line to pursue. In 1982 he forged an alliance with Banc One of Columbus, Ohio. The agreement allowed him to offer free Visa credit cards with Comp-U-Card memberships to the bank's 22 million customers.

GOING PUBLIC AND A MAJOR MERGER

Also in 1982 Forbes changed the company's name to CUC International (CUC) and then convinced Morgan Stanley to take CUC public in 1983, despite a decade without profits and a loss of $2.5 million on just $4 million in sales in 1982. In its initial public stock offering CUC earned $18 million. Forbes then began to form alliances with other major credit card companies to sell shopping memberships to their card customers. In 1985 and 1986 he acquired the insurance and package enhancement products of Financial Institutions Services, Inc., and Madison Financial Corporation, both of which were well established, having been in business since 1971. Forbes expanded CUC further in 1988 with the acquisition of National Card Control, Inc., a loyalty solutions and package enhancement program provider.

In 1995 Forbes formed a partnership with Hospitality Franchise Systems (HFS), the owner of the Avis car rental company, Century 21, Days Inn, and Ramada Inn. The agreement with HFS allowed CUC to sell its travel- and shopping-club services to HFS customers. It appeared to be a good fit, joining the affluent customers of HFS with a smart marketing operation to create an enviable profit center, and two years later, in 1997, Forbes approached HFS about an acquisition. Discussions ensued and eventually the two companies merged, creating Cendant Corporation. The plan was for Henry Silverman from HFS to serve as CEO and Forbes to be chairman for two years, and then they would reverse roles in 2000.

What seemed like a good combination on the surface soon proved a catastrophe. The company cultures were incompatible. HFS was known for its tight controls, and CUC had an improvisation style that included less than stringent accounting practices. The situation grew worse in April 1998 when HFS executives discovered that CUC had falsified earnings.

In light of CUC's financial improprieties, Forbes was soon forced out, the blow cushioned somewhat by a $47.5-million severance package. CUC executives were also fired. Forensic accountants then discovered the true extent of the deceit: $511 million in fabricated profits over the course of three years that allowed CUC to meet Wall Street expectations and maintain its stock price. There were also numerous personal expenses that Forbes charged to CUC.

CUC CHARGED WITH FRAUD

Authorities soon determined that CUC had committed the largest accounting fraud in U.S. history to that time, costing investors an estimated $19 billion. Forbes and his chief lieutenant, E. Kirk Shelton, were charged with securities fraud and other violations by the government. In 2005 Shelton was found guilty and sentenced to 10 years in prison. He was also ordered to pay $3.3 million in restitution to Cendant.

After two months of deliberations, a jury was unable to agree on the charges against Forbes, who maintained that he had been unaware of what Shelton had been doing. A second jury also deadlocked. Finally in October 2006 a third jury found Forbes guilty. In January 2007 he was sentenced to 12 years and 7 months in prison and ordered to pay $3.3 billion in restitution.

AFFINION GROUP FORMED: 2005

Although Cendant survived CUC's financial scandal, its stock price dropped much lower than the underlying value of the company. In 2004 Cendant split into four companies, and in October 2005 the marketing services unit was sold to private-equity firm Apollo Management L.P. for $1.8 billion. It assumed the name of the corporate entity created to complete the deal: Affinion Group, Inc. After Affinion recorded revenues of $1.14 billion and a net loss of $431.6 million in 2006, Apollo filed for an initial public offering of stock in June 2007 that it hoped would raise $600 million.

By November 2007, however, Apollo had decided to postpone the offering. North American membership was declining, due in part to consolidation in the banking industry. Because so many customers were busy integrating their operations, Affinion postponed launching new programs. Affinion's international division, on

KEY DATES

1973: Robert Perlman founds Compu-U-Card of America, Inc.
1982: Walter A. Forbes renames the company CUC International.
1983: CUC International goes public.
1997: CUC International merges with Hospitality Franchise Systems, creating Cendant Corporation.
2005: Cendant sells its marketing services unit, which becomes Affinion Group, Inc.

the other hand, was doing well, having added 500,000 new members during 2007. Affinion also generated revenues of $1.32 billion in 2007, while narrowing its net loss to $190.8 million.

Nearing the end of the first decade of the twenty-first century, Affinion looked to boost revenues by focusing on new areas of growth, such as credit card protection services, the management of which banks were increasingly outsourcing to third parties. In early 2008 Affinion acquired about 500,000 customers for its cardholder protection service from an unnamed bank. With a single call, customers could cancel and replace stolen credit cards, arrange for emergency cash, and monitor their credit, among other services. Later in 2008 Affinion unveiled a new identity theft protection service called Card Patrol, which was quickly adopted by more than 100 financial institutions.

Revenue for 2008 was $1.4 billion, but in 2009 fell to $1.38 billion, due mostly to the high cost of insurance in North America and the impact of a strong U.S. dollar on the company's international business. Later in the year, the company also spent $135 million to acquire Minnesota-based Connexions Loyalty Travel Solutions, a premium travel loyalty rewards program administrator. At the same time, Apollo once again filed for an initial public offering of stock that it hoped would raise $400 million. Whether Affinion would follow through with the offering remained to be seen.

Ed Dinger

PRINCIPAL OPERATING UNITS

Affinion North America; Affinion International.

PRINCIPAL COMPETITORS

AEGON Direct Marketing Services, Inc.; Vertrue Incorporated; Webloyalty.com, Inc.

FURTHER READING

"Affinion Group to Acquire Travel & Loyalty Solutions Provider." *Hartford Commercial Record*, May 21, 2010.

Elkind, Peter. "A Merger Made in Hell." *Fortune*, November 9, 1998, 134.

Farrell, Greg. "Trial Digs Up Two Views of Walter Forbes." *USA Today*, July 7, 2004.

Farzad, Roben, and Amy Barrett. "Cendant's Credibility Problem." *Business Week*, March 13, 2006, 56.

Hartman, Curtis, and Joseph P. Kahn. "Comp-U-Card International Inc.." *Inc.*, May 1984, 180.

Lee, Richard. "Affinion to Acquire Connexions for $135M." *Stamford-Norwalk Advocate*, May 27, 2010, B010.

Ozanian, Michael K. "Card Game." *Financial World*, October 29, 1991, 23.

Petre, Peter. "The Man Who Computerized Bargain Hunting." *Fortune*, July 9, 1984, 137.

Airsprung Group PLC

Canal Road
Trowbridge, Wiltshire BA14 8RQ
United Kingdom
Telephone: (+44 1225) 754 411
Fax: (+44 1225) 777 423
Web site: http://www.airsprung-furniture.co.uk

Public Company
Founded: 1871
Employees: 578
Sales: £42.81 million ($69.12 million) (2009)
Stock Exchanges: London
Ticker Symbol: APG
NAICS: 337121 Upholstered Wood Household Furniture Manufacturing; 337910 Mattress Manufacturing

■ ■ ■

With its main production units located in Trowbridge, Wiltshire, and Chorley, Lancashire, Airsprung Group PLC is one of the UK's leading manufacturers and distributors of divan beds, mattresses, sofa beads, and bedsteads. The group produces over 600,000 beds and mattresses annually, making it the second-largest bed producer in the United Kingdom. Bed, mattress, and upholstered furniture brands include Airsprung Beds, Cavendish upholstered furniture, Gainsborough Beds, Hush divans and mattresses, and Hush-a-Bye beds. The group's "One Stop Shop" contract furniture division offered customized services to a host of markets, including hotels and other hospitality venues, universities and schools, healthcare and residential care facilities, and contract furnishers. The group also produces Airofreem, a range of polyurethane foams and fiber products used in the manufacture of furniture, packaging, bedding, and insulation. Airsprung's Arena Design is an integrated design agency offering multimedia graphic design solutions, including brand imaging, print design, web design, interior displays, signage, and exhibition stands.

FROM PALLIASSES TO PROFITS

In 1871 Hedley Chapman established Chapman's, a factory in Trowbridge, England, that manufactured straw-filled bedding mats, otherwise known as palliasses. In 1891 John Yates bought Chapman's for £11,000. In the early 1900s he modernized the factory by introducing mass production techniques. In 1934 his son Fred took charge of the company. Chapman's soon opened a new plant and machinery in place to manufacture the recently developed interior spring mattress.

John Yates's grandson, also called John Yates, first went to work in the family business in 1936 at age 21, and had urged his father to invest in the new spring mattress machinery. In 1946, soon after his return from serving in World War II, he took the helm of the business. He hoped to use new technologies to increase production of mattresses (still using coconut fiber for fill) from 30 a day to 100. It was during the 1940s that the name "Airsprung" first came to be used, after a competition among employees for a new slogan. After Fred Yates died in 1957, John became chairman of the company. The business continued to grow, producing

COMPANY PERSPECTIVES

The Airsprung Group is committed to meeting the ever-changing needs of our consumer and trade partners through product innovation and versatility, building on our tradition of quality and value for money.

both beds and upholstered furniture. In 1965 the company formally changed its name to Airsprung, and in 1968 it moved to a new 28-acre site in Trowbridge.

In 1991, 100 years after his grandfather bought Chapman's, Yates took the company public. Yates retained a 40 percent stake in Airsprung Furniture Group PLC. In 1995 Yates stepped down as chairman, and by 1999 he retired as president at age 84. By that time, the company was worth £80 million, with manufacturing facilities in 10 locations throughout Britain producing 14,000 mattresses a week.

A NEW CENTURY AND NEW CHALLENGES

In 1998, as conditions in the furniture market weakened, Airsprung had decided to focus its business on bed manufacture, a move that analysts forecasted could result in a £5 million profit. Airsprung closed its factory in Casterbridge, which produced plastic toilet seats and veneer tables, having cost the group £8.1 million. Unable to compete with the low-cost imports from China, the factory's losses ate into Airsprung's profits, and by May 1999 the group found itself £1.7 million in debt.

The furniture market continued to soften, and in February 2002 Airsprung announced that it expected its pretax profits for the year ending on March 31, 2002 to be about £300,000, significantly less than the £1.3 million forecast by analysts. In an effort to cut costs and boost sales, the group embarked on a series of restructuring, recruitment, and training programs, which included a reduction of middle and upper management, the acquisition of new machinery, the implementation of new procedures and controls, and a repositioning of some of its upholstery and bed companies. Airsprung also closed its sites in Dursley, Gloucestershire, and Queenslie, Glasgow, in Scotland, resulting in the loss of more than 100 jobs.

In May 2002 Tony Lisanti was appointed chief executive officer of Airsprung. By October 2002 Airsprung had formed a joint venture with W.E. Rawson Ltd., marking its entrance into polyester filling production. The following month, the group launched a trade loyalty plan, whereby retailers accrued air travel points with the purchase of any Airsprung product. At that point, the group's £1.8 million restructuring program was about 80 percent complete, but Airsprung found itself facing a takeover bid as it tried to overcome a final stumbling block, staff shortages in Trowbridge. Lisanti planned to offset these shortages by increasing the number of female employees and instituting a voluntary night shift.

2003: GROUP'S VALUE PLUNGES

When it failed to find backers for the £23.9 million deal, the potential buyers of Airsprung pulled out of the takeover bid in March 2003, and the group's value plunged to £16.6 million. Despite efforts to transform Bymacks, its upholstery firm, into an upmarket manufacturer, the subsidiary still suffered a significant drop in sales due to competition from inexpensive imports. The restructuring costs associated with its Peter Guild subsidiary, a manufacturer of luxury furniture, also had a negative impact on profits. The fall-off in demand resulted in a pretax loss of £471,000 for the year ending March 31, 2003, and a £7.5 million drop in sales.

Airsprung sold Okehampton-based Sprung Slumber in October 2003 to Steinhoff UK for £5.4 million to concentrate on its Trowbridge plant. In January 2004 Airsprung closed the loss-making Bymacks plant in Gloucestershire, temporarily shifting production to the Cavendish firm before moving it overseas.

In June 2004 Lisanti announced that the two-year restructuring program had been completed. To retain a competitive edge, Airsprung planned to focus on product design and marketing. Airsprung also planned to close its four-year-old wood mill at a cost of £1.9 million and outsource all cabinet production in a further effort to cut costs.

Airsprung was unprepared for the steep rise in steel prices in July 2004. As steel prices rose by 35 to 40 percent, the group estimated that cost rises would increase its raw material costs by £800,000 for the year. Airsprung issued a second profits warning in November 2004. To offset costs, Airsprung planned to double the outsourcing of its products from 20 percent to 40 percent, beginning with a plan to manufacture its wooden bed products in Central Europe. This was followed in March 2005 with the shedding of 11 jobs in the back offices of its Trowbridge plant when improvements in trading failed to materialize.

KEY DATES

1871: Hedley Chapman founds Chapman's, a straw mattress factory.
1891: John Yates buys Chapman's.
2003: Airsprung sells Sprung Slumber to Steinhoff UK.
2009: Airsprung acquires Hush-a-Bye Limited.
2010: The company changes its name from Airsprung Furniture Group PLC to Airsprung Group PLC.

For the year ending March 31, 2005, the group reported pre-tax losses of £3.0 million from £4.1 million the previous year on sales of £39.7 million, reflecting an annual drop in sales revenue of about £10 million.

In July 2005 the last members of the Yates family on the executive board were removed. Airsprung reduced the number of board members from five to two, and John Yates's two sons, Jeremy and Stephen, and a third member all stepped down. Stephen Yates remained in his position as the group's marketing director, while Jeremy continued on as head of the Gainsborough and Peter Guild furniture divisions. The remaining executive directors were Tony Lisanti and finance director Tean Dallaway.

RETURN TO PROFITABILITY

In September 2005 Airsprung reported that trading had improved in the previous four months and credited the growth to productivity gains following the restructuring. The following month Lisanti and five fellow directors bought five million Airsprung shares from Cynthia Yates, widow of John Yates, for £500,000, giving the board members a 21.57 percent stake in the group. The other large shareholders were Cynthia Yates's sons Jeremy and Stephen Yates and Redbird Holdings, a Panama-based investment firm that held 29.12 percent. In that same month, Airsprung sold the Peter Guild subsidiary to Sistra, a move that saw the group's shares rise by more than 10 percent.

After announcing in June 2006 plans to create two new subbrands for the midmarket trade and sell off part of its Trowbridge manufacturing site, by September 2006 Airsprung had returned to profitability. In January 2007 the group launched a rebranding campaign for its Airsprung beds. The new "bed of roses" theme was communicated through point of sale materials, window and in-store displays, web design, and press advertising. Airsprung also embarked on a redevelopment plan of its Trowbridge site after it found itself with nine acres of empty buildings as wood and bed springs were imported.

In February 2009 Airsprung acquired Hush-a-Bye Limited for £300,000, with plans to manufacture it alongside the group's Hush brand as part of its Sleep Collection. By September of that year, revenue for the first half of the fiscal year had risen by £23.1 million, and the group was able to resume dividend payments to its shareholders. In June 2010 the company changed its name from Airsprung Furniture Group PLC to Airsprung Group PLC.

Marie O'Sullivan

PRINCIPAL SUBSIDIARIES

Airsprung Beds; Airofreem; Arena Design; Cavendish; Gainsborough Beds & Sofa Beds; Hush Sleep Collection; Hush-a-Bye Beds.

PRINCIPAL COMPETITORS

Dorlux Beds Ltd.; Silentnight Group Limited; Slumberland Limited.

FURTHER READING

"Airsprung Is Warning of Soaring Loss." *Western Daily Press,* February 7, 2004.

"Airsprung Looks to Comfier Future." *Western Daily Press,* November 30, 2002.

"Airsprung See Increase in Profits." *Western Daily Press,* December 11, 2009.

"Airsprung Shake-Up: Brothers Step Down." *Western Daily Press,* July 9, 2005.

"Airsprung's Solution to Sweet Sorrow." *Western Daily Press,* October 19, 2005.

Bolitho, Nigel. "Airsprung Furniture Bouncing Back," *Investors Chronicle,* June 18, 2007.

"Firm Bounces to the Aid of City's Homelessness Charity." *Bath Chronicle,* March 12, 2009.

Herbstein, Denis. "Airsprung Hit by Raw Material Costs," *Financial Times,* June 18, 2005.

"No Time to Relax at Beds Group." *Western Daily Press,* December 6, 2006.

Smy, Lucy. "Airsprung Sells Sprung Slumber," *Financial Times,* October 4, 2003.

American Museum of Natural History

Central Park West at 79th Street
New York City, New York 10024-5192
U.S.A.
Telephone: (212) 769-5000
Toll Free: (800) 462-8687
Fax: (212) 769-5006
Web site: http://www.amnh.org

Nonprofit Company
Founded: 1869
Employees: 1,262
Sales: $174.67 million (2009)
Total Assets: $1.05 billion (2009)
NAICS: 561520 Tour Operators; 611310 Universities; 712110 Museums

■ ■ ■

The American Museum of Natural History (AMNH) is a nonprofit organization that provides cultural, educational, and scientific services. With more than 30 million specimens and artifacts, the museum is one of the world's leading scientific institutions. Located in a landmark structure in New York City's Central Park, the museum is part of the University of the State of New York.

MUSEUM FOUNDING AND DEVELOPMENTAL YEARS

The AMNH traces its conception to Albert S. Bickmore, a scientist from the Harvard Museum of Comparative Zoology. While other major cities had fostered an interest in scientific exploration through museums by the mid-19th century, New York City had failed to follow suit. The point was not lost on Bickmore, who in 1866 presented his idea for a natural history museum to the New York congressman William E. Dodge. During the next two years the idea crystallized in the minds of members of New York City's elite. Then in December 1868, 20 men, many of whom were city powerbrokers, sent a letter to Andrew H. Green, the comptroller of Central Park, urging the city to develop a museum. The signatories included Dodge's son, the banker John Pierpont Morgan, and the philanthropist Theodore Roosevelt Sr.

In April 1869 the American Museum of Natural History was established by an act of the New York Legislature. John David Wolfe, one of the museum's early proponents, was named the museum's first president and Bickmore became the museum's only scientist.

The Arsenal on Central Park's east side became the first home to the museum, which in 1871 opened with a series of exhibits. The museum struggled to find space for the new collections that Bickmore had acquired, and after Robert L. Stuart became president in 1872, the city purchased a four-block parcel on Manhattan Square between West 77th and 81st Streets and Columbus Avenue and Central Park West, across from Central Park. The museum had funds to build only a relatively small structure, but its two architects, J. Wrey Mould and Calvert Vaux, who where known for previous Central Park architecture, created an enormous design. President Ulysses S. Grant laid the cornerstone for the

COMPANY PERSPECTIVES

The Mission of the American Museum of Natural History is to discover, interpret, and disseminate—through scientific research and education—knowledge about human cultures, the natural world, and the universe.

museum's first dedicated structure in 1874, and President Rutherford B. Hayes officiated the opening of a one-sided modest red brick museum with Victorian Gothic structure in 1877.

EDUCATION, EXPEDITION, AND ROOSEVELT HALL: 1880–1924

With public interest and funding waning by the end of the 1870s, Bickmore devised another idea. In 1880 he began offering free lectures to school teachers to improve science education. Initially, the audience was small, but as Bickmore brought in visual aids and guest speakers, attendance grew and the lectures became a museum staple.

The industrialist Morris K. Jesup became museum president in 1881, and he initiated a 50-year period of museum-commissioned exploration. In 1888, with only one side of Mould and Vaux's plan constructed, the museum hired Josiah Cleveland Cady to design the south side along 77th Street. Cady's design reflected changes in architectural taste. He envisioned a massive Romanesque structure in pink granite in the style of a castle with jutting bays and a double stairway. Cady completed the first section of his grandiose plan in 1892, when construction was again put on hold.

Bickmore's lectures continued to grow in popularity, and by 1894 more than 18,000 teachers attended his weekly lectures. In 1895 Jesup hired Franz Boas as assistant curator of the Department of Ethnology. The following year the museum opened its Hall of Northwest Coast Indians. Boas also organized a five-year comparative-cultures expedition for Jesup that covered Siberia, China, Alaska, and Canada's northwest coast.

In 1891 Henry Fairfield Osborn was hired as the first curator of the museum's Department of Vertebrate Paleontology to develop a dinosaur fossil collection. Nine years later the museum opened the Hall of Prehistoric Life. Jesup died in 1908 and was succeeded by Osborn. Carl Akeley, a creator of lifelike mammal dioramas, joined the museum in 1913 to develop the African Mammals Hall. The Hall of Ocean Life also began its long developmental history after Osborn proposed its construction in the museum's southeast courtyard.

City financial woes, coupled with the onset of World War I, put construction on hold until 1921, when New York City renewed its funding and approved a memorial hall that commemorated the late Theodore Roosevelt. Planning for and construction of a southeast wing commenced along the empty Central Park West block in 1922. With Romanesque architecture out of vogue, the new wing followed a Roman-type design. Construction on the Hall of Ocean Life was completed two years later. However, hall preparation work, which included completion of marine dioramas, the updating of specimen collections, and the hanging of whale models and skeletons from the ceiling, took another six years.

NEW HALL DEVELOPMENT: 1926–36

In 1926 the museum received a donation of Indian subcontinent mammals from an expedition by Arthur S. Vernay and Colonel J. C. Faunthorpe and preparation for a new hall began. In 1930 the museum opened its South Asiatic Hall, which displayed the Vernay and Faunthorpe specimens and mammal habitat exhibits. That same year the museum unveiled its Hall of Ocean Life. Five years later, in 1935, the Art Deco–fashioned Hayden Planetarium opened.

In 1936, after six years of construction, the museum opened Roosevelt Memorial Hall, which featured Roosevelt dioramas and busts of Bickmore and Osborn. At the same time the museum opened the Roosevelt Rotunda, directly above Roosevelt Memorial Hall, and the Akeley Hall of African Mammals, named for Carl Akeley, who conceptualized, designed, and provided expedition specimens, sketches, and photographs for the hall.

NEW HALL OPENINGS: 1942–87

Albert E. Parr became the director of the museum in 1942. Determined to guarantee the museum's future success, he decided to stake out a philosophical direction for the next two decades that stressed an interpretative approach to the museum. During the 1950s the museum began developing new exhibits and opened the Whitney Hall of Oceanic Birds, the Hall of Man and Nature, the Hall of North American Forests, and the Hall of North American Mammals. During the 1960s the museum opened several new halls, including the

KEY DATES

1869: The American Museum of Natural History is established.
1877: Construction of the first part of the museum is completed.
1993: Ellen V. Futter becomes the first female president of the museum.
2000: The museum's newly remodeled Hayden Planetarium opens.
2009: A renovation of the museum's original castle facade is completed.

Hall of North American Small Mammals, the Chapman Memorial Hall of North American Birds, the Hall of Primates, the Hall of Eskimos, the Hall of Eastern Woodlands Indians, the Hall of Plains Indians, and the Hall of African Peoples.

In October 1964, 23 gemstones were stolen from the museum, including the priceless 100-carat De Long Star Ruby and the Star of India sapphire. Jack R. Murphy and two other men were responsible for the heist, which was the largest jewelry theft in U.S. history. Murphy and his accomplices entered the museum after hours through an open bathroom window and stole the jewels after discovering that a protective alarm was not working. Murphy and an underworld boss behind the heist were arrested within two days, and most of the jewels were recovered. However, the De Long Star Ruby remained missing for nearly a year when museum officials received word that the holders of the ruby would return it for a $25,000 ransom. The billionaire John D. MacArthur agreed to pay the ransom, and after making the money drop as instructed, a museum official recovered the ruby without incident.

Exhibit halls that opened during the 1970s included the Hall of Mexico and Central America, the Hall of Pacific Peoples, the Morgan Memorial Hall of Gems, the Guggenheim Hall of Minerals, and the Hall of Reptiles and Amphibians. During the 1980s the museum opened the Stout Hall of Asian Peoples, the Hall of South American Peoples, the Ross Hall of Meteorites, and the Dana Education Wing. The wing featured two theaters, a lecture room, the Calder Laboratory, and the White Natural Center.

In 1985 the museum received an anonymous gift of the world's largest cut gemstone, the nine-and-a-half pound light-blue topaz stone, dubbed the Brazilian Princess. Attendance grew to a peak of 3.1 million annual visitors by 1987. That same year the museum hired its first paid president, George D. Langdon Jr., in an effort to better compete with New York's other cultural institutions.

RENOVATED FOSSIL HALLS AND NEW PRESIDENT: 1990–96

In 1990 the museum closed its dinosaur exhibit to make way for construction of six new halls. The following year the AMNH debuted inside the Roosevelt Rotunda a five-story-tall Barosaurus cast, which was the tallest self-supporting dinosaur display in the world and only one of two specimens displayed in the world. In 1992 the museum opened its new $11 million Research Library featuring 1 million scientific texts. The following year the AMNH established its Center for Biodiversity and Conservation to bring attention to threats to species diversity and the natural habitat. The museum also opened an upgraded Hall of Biology and Human Evolution.

In 1993 Ellen V. Futter became the first female president of the museum and only the second paid one. Futter was hired with the expectation of modernizing the museum, improving fund-raising, making the institution more competitive with other tech-laden cultural institutions, and enhancing the museum's educational programs. Futter's changes dovetailed with the museum's renovation and construction projects throughout the decade.

Between 1994 and 1996 significant renovations of the fossil floor occurred that restored original architecture. In the process the exhibit layout was redesigned so fossils were arranged according to evolutionary relationship rather than to chronological order. Openings on the fossil floor during this period included the Hall of Primitive Mammals, the Hall of Advanced Mammals, the Hall of Saurischian Dinosaurs, the Hall of Ornithischian Dinosaurs, and the Hall of Vertebrate Origins. All told, the floor included more than 1 million specimens, the largest collection of vertebrate fossils in the world.

RENOVATIONS AND OPENINGS: 1997–2002

During the late 1990s the museum embarked on a second major reconstruction and expansion program that was centered around a new planetarium with a new wing, the Rose Center for Earth and Space. In 1997 the original Hayden Planetarium was demolished and construction on a new planetarium began. The following year the AMNH opened its new $17.8 million Hall of Biodiversity, which displayed the interdependency of life forms and the threats to biodiversity.

In 1999 the AMNH opened the Starr Natural Science Building to store scientific research and museum collections. The museum also established the Institute for Comparative Genomics to support genetic diversity research. Before the decade closed, the museum opened the first of three parts to the Rose Center: the Gottesman Hall of Planet Earth, which featured a geological collection of rock specimens and classic-outcropping models.

The $210 million Rose Center for Earth and Space and the Hayden Planetarium opened to the public in 2000. The planetarium was a glass cube-like structure that rose 87 feet inside and appeared suspended within a glass cube from the outside. It featured the world's most advanced star projector, which was capable of projecting 9,100 stars onto the planetarium's dome and displaying the surface of any object within the earth's solar system. That same year the AMNH also opened the third prong of the Rose Center, the Cullman Hall of the Universe, which displayed the discoveries and theories of modern astrophysics.

In 2001 the museum added a Columbus Avenue entrance and opened its Discovery Room. The family-focused Discovery Room provided an interactive entrance to the museum's contents for children aged five to 12. In 2002 the museum reopened its newly renamed main auditorium, the Samuel J. and Ethel LeFrak Theater, which had been restored to Cady's original 19th-century design.

FINANCIAL WOES AND HALL REOPENINGS: 2001–04

During the 1990s the AMNH doubled its budget and workforce as it expanded exhibits, underwent renovation and addition projects, and accommodated attendance increases that rose to 5 million visitors annually by 2000. Following the terrorist attacks on the World Trade Center in New York on September 11, 2001, the museum suffered a drop in attendance of more than 50 percent. By 2002 attendance had rebounded to about 4 million visitors per year, but the city decreased the museum's annual funding by $1.5 million. Forced to cut its budget by more than $10 million, the museum decided to close several museum entrances, reduce hours, and institute a hiring and wage freeze. By 2003 the AMNH had also slashed 300 staff.

Other cuts were made as well, and some scientific staff became disgruntled. The museum shifted to displaying more visitor-appealing exhibits on things such as chocolate and baseball, but elected to sell its house journal *Natural History* and put an axe to the Micropaleontology Press, a publisher of original research. Some longtime officials feared the museum was sacrificing real science for so-called popular science.

In 2003 the museum reopened the renovated and recently renamed Milstein Family Hall of Ocean Life. The $25 million renovation included the addition of a video wall, interactive computers, refurbished dioramas, and new models of sea life and ocean ecosystem displays. The main feature of the hall was the well-known 21,000-pound replica of a blue whale, which had been in the original 1933 hall but was newly repainted and made more realistic.

That same year the museum opened the renovated Ross Hall of Meteorites, which featured new exhibits of rocks from the moon and Mars and the reinstalled 34-ton Ahnighito. The museum also began digitizing its entire collection, with a goal of making images of its 30 million artifacts available online. In 2004 an earthquake monitoring station was installed in the Hall of Planet Earth.

EDUCATIONAL PROGRAMS, FINANCIAL STRUGGLES, AND FUTURE CHALLENGES: 2006–10

In the weeks following the 2006 debut of the box-office hit *Night at the Museum*, the museum's attendance rose 20 percent. The AMNH was the fictional setting for the movie, in which museum exhibits came to life at night. The museum created a brochure that responded to frequently asked questions about the museum and things seen in the movie. The AMNH also began offering sleepovers for groups with children eight to 12 years old.

In 2006 the New York State Board of Regents gave the museum authority to offer comparative biology master's and doctoral degrees. The AMNH, which became the first U.S. museum with doctoral-degree-granting capacity, began recruiting students in 2007. That same year the museum opened the renovated Audubon Gallery, which explored the relationship of humans to the natural world, and the Spitzer Hall of Human Origins, which used artifact specimens to trace human evolution.

In 2009 the museum's endowment shrank by $170 million. The institution lost an additional $3.1 million due to a decease in three of its main revenue streams: city public funding, regular charitable contributions, and bookings for gala events. In an effort to slash 10 percent of its operating budget, the museum reduced its payroll through buyouts, layoffs, and attrition. Its net assets fell from $810.2 million in 2008 to $663.8 million in 2009. However, the AMNH concluded an $850 million fund-raising campaign and closed the year with a balanced budget.

That same year the AMNH completed the largest restoration in its history, a two-year $37 million renovation of the 117-year-old Romanesque castle facade on West 77th Street. The facade opened to the original 1877 hall, which was the first of 25 connected structures within the museum.

As the museum moved into a new decade, Futter faced a few significant challenges. The biggest challenge was to balance a reduced budget while maintaining AMNH programs. A second related challenge involved balancing the hard-core science with popular science to keep both the scientific community and museum visitors happy and returning.

Roger Rouland

PRINCIPAL COMPETITORS

Brooklyn Children's Museum; Children's Museum of Manhattan; Guggenheim Museum; Metropolitan Museum of Art; Museum of the City of New York; Museum of Modern Art; New York Hall of Science; Sony Wonder Technology Lab; Sports Museum of America; Whitney Museum of American Art.

FURTHER READING

Boxer, Sarah. "What 'Astronomical' Means." *New York Times*, January 29, 2000.

Donadio, Rachel. "Museum Staff Says Cutbacks Begat Ice Age." *New York Observer*, December 7, 2003.

Dunlap, David W. "Everything but Ahab." *New York Times*, December 7, 2000.

Goldberger, Paul. "Natural History Museum Plans Big Overhaul." *New York Times*, January 27, 1995.

Gonzalez, George. "Museum Official Arrives for Delong Ruby." *Palm Beach Post*, September 4, 1965, 1.

Gray, Christopher. "The Face Will Still Be Forbidding, but Much Tighter and Cleaner." *New York Times*, July 29, 2007.

Honan, William H. "Barnard's President to Head Museum of Natural History." *New York Times*, June 29, 1993.

"Picture Darkens for City's Museums." *Crain's New York Business*, February 2, 2009, 1.

Preston, Douglas J. *Dinosaurs in the Attic: An Excursion into the American Museum of Natural History*. New York: St. Martin's Press, 1986.

Aquatic Company

8101 East Kaiser Boulevard, Suite 200
Anaheim, California 92808
U.S.A.
Telephone: (714) 993-1220
Toll Free: (800) 877-2005
Fax: (714) 998-3062
Web site: http://www.aquaticbath.com

Wholly Owned Subsidiary of Tomkins plc
Founded: 1947 as Lasco Products Group
Incorporated: 1965 as Lasco Industries Inc.
Employees: 1,038
Sales: $140.3 million (2009)
NAICS: 332913 Plumbing Fixture Fitting and Trim Manufacturing; 326191 Plastics Plumbing Fixtures Manufacturing; 332998 Enameled Iron and Metal Sanitary Ware Manufacturing

■ ■ ■

Created in 2010 through the merger of Lasco Bathware and Aquatic Whirlpools, Aquatic Company designs and manufactures bathware, showers, and hydrotherapy products, including soaking tubs and whirlpools. With manufacturing facilities in Pennsylvania, Michigan, Nevada, Texas, Virginia, and Washington, the company produces more than 330 products and accessories. Aquatic Company's customers include architects, designers, builders, hotels, hospitals, universities, and the general public. The company is headquartered in Anaheim, California, and employs 950 people. With annual sales of $140 million, Aquatic Company sells more than 25 percent of all bath fixtures sold in the United States.

LASCO PRODUCTS GROUP AND AQUATIC WHIRLPOOLS

Lasco Products Group was founded in 1947, and in 1965 the company was renamed Lasco Industries Inc. Headquartered in Montebello, California, the company manufactured plastic pipes and other products for a growing construction industry. In 1970 Philips Industries Inc., an Ohio-based manufacturer of automotive products, acquired Lasco Industries. Philips was experiencing growth itself, with more than 20 subsidiaries and facilities in over 10 states. For several years, plastics had been used in the production of tires, auto bodies, seats and other car parts. The acquisition gave Philips greater control over quality and volume. In turn Philips's economic health fueled the direction and capacity of Lasco's operations. By 1972 Lasco Industries had plants in Fountain Valley, California; Florence, Kentucky; and Three Rivers, Michigan.

By 1980, Lasco's 33rd year in business, the company was producing whirlpool tubs for indoor use as well as plastic pipes, fixtures, and fiberglass reinforced panels for tubs and showers. By the late 1980s the company had returned to the name Lasco Products Group and moved its corporate headquarters to Anaheim, California. In 1989 sales reached $160 million, and Lasco Products had more than 1,300 employees in plants in California, Georgia, Kentucky, Tennessee, and Texas.

COMPANY PERSPECTIVES

Aquatic is the world leader in innovative bathware and showers, offering the broadest and most inspiring selection of luxury hydrotherapy, everyday and accessible products. With every detail, every design, every feature, Aquatic builds showers and baths with that mantra in mind. Spanning luxury hydrotherapy, everyday bathing and accessible products, our customers will feel inspired from the moment they set eyes on the right shower or bath to the moment they step into it and for years to come.

The 1990s featured more noteworthy events for Lasco Products. In 1990, Lasco Products' 43rd year, the company became a subsidiary of London-based Tomkins Group plc as part of its $550 million acquisition of Philips Industries. The decade's other highlights included a name change to Lasco Bathware Inc. and a growing product line of plastic pipes and fittings and tub and shower products. By 1999 the company had factories in nine states and more than 1,400 employees.

Also in 1999 Tomkins acquired Aquatic Whirlpools for £9.2 million. Brad Roten and Dean Morgan had founded Aquatic Whirlpools in Leander, Texas, in 1989 and built a customer base of elite Texans and hotels in the region. Aquatic performed well and achieved $14 million in revenue in its first four years. During its first decade, the Texas firm refined its designs of jetted tubs, adding, for instance, therapeutic jets targeted at elbows and other joints, and established a national network of distributors for various markets, adding hospitals, fitness clubs, contractors, and interior designers to its growing list of clients.

TOMKINS GROUP

At the start of the 21st century, Lasco Bathware took advantage of new technologies, using three-dimensional, computer-aided drafting (CAD) software to lessen expenses in product testing and clients' presentations. Lasco also sought to streamline its budget in the face of new air pollution control regulations for the manufacturing of polystyrene. From the mid- to the late 1990s, as the U.S. Environmental Protection Agency instituted changes in air quality standards, Lasco and Aquatic began compliance efforts, upgrading equipment and procedures. In 2005 Aquatic Whirlpools' air bathtubs became popular. Although air bathtubs, owing to their bubbling and foaming water, resembled whirlpool products, it was the gentler flow of water that distinguished air bathtubs from jetted tubs, with their more aggressive flow. Other available features included underwater lights, Shiatsu-style massaging jets, and remote controls. Lasco's variations included underwater sound systems, a design that drew from a German luxury car's sleek form, and a breakthrough that enabled users to add bath oils and fragrances without clogging the jets. Meanwhile Lasco Bathware targeted the aging population with products such as threshold-flexible showers.

In 2007 Tomkins sold two of its Lasco businesses. Dutch manufacturer Aalberts Industries N.V. acquired Lasco Fittings, the division responsible for manufacturing plastic plumbing parts, for $104 million. In another deal, Lasco Composites LP, a Kentucky-based maker of fiberglass reinforced panels, was sold to the Connecticut industrial manufacturer Crane Company for $43.5 million. Tomkins stated that the divestments were part of its strategy of streamlining its portfolio by disposing of noncore businesses.

Aquatic Whirlpools and Lasco Bathware remained a part of Tomkins's strategic plans. In 2009, despite the economic slowdown, Lasco Bathware began a $1.7 million expansion of its manufacturing operations in Halifax County, Virginia, to accommodate growth. The expansion, which included a planned increase in the Virginia plant's workforce of more than 20 percent, also involved a factory in Austin, Texas, where Aquatic's whirlpool tubs were made. Equipment was shipped from the plant in Texas to the plant in Virginia. The factory in Virginia was partially rebuilt to house the incoming machinery. Job training in specialized skills such as robotics were among Lasco's plans for the expanded operation, which included production of Aquatic's whirlpools. On another front, in 2009 Aquatic hired researchers to report on future potential markets. They predicted that the aging baby boomer population would produce a greater demand for accessible bathroom products and fixtures, presenting Aquatic with an opportunity to expand its customer base.

AQUATIC COMPANY

In 2010 Tomkins merged Lasco Bathware and Aquatic Whirlpools into one company named Aquatic Company. Gary Anderson, previously president of Lasco Bathware since 2008, became president of the new company. Aquatic company consisted of three product groups: Hydrotherapy, Everyday, and Accessible. Hydrotherapy and Everyday products comprised the majority of Aquatic's tubs, showers, and bath accessories, close to 300 of more than 330 total products as

KEY DATES

1970: Philips Industries Inc. acquires Lasco Industries.
1989: Aquatic Whirlpools is established.
1990: Lasco becomes a subsidiary of Tomkins Group plc.
1999: Tomkins acquires Aquatic Whirlpools.
2010: Tomkins merges Lasco and Aquatic Whirlpools; the new company is named Aquatic.

of 2010. Each product group featured distinct elements. The Everyday product group offered cost effectiveness and a product line known as sectionals, for remodeling jobs and new construction in which tub or shower installation were made problematic by walls, ceilings, and doorways already in place. Hydrotherapy, another product group, featured tubs with whirlpool jets, soakers with consistently heated water temperature, air baths, and combination whirlpool and air baths. The third product group, Accessible, incorporated the practice of universal design along with aspects in common with other product groups, such as various color choices and acrylic coating on the tubs and showers.

During 2010 Aquatic drew attention for its product innovations. The Accessible products group debuted a line of tubs with unique, patent-pending features. Consumers wanting sustained independence for daily routines such as bathing were actually a fairly broad and diverse population. They ranged from those in wheelchairs or walkers to seniors with restricted mobility to those approaching retirement age whose homes required adjustments in anticipation of waning mobility. Because this customer base had a range of needs and mobility, product developers needed to respond accordingly. Aquatic's innovations for this product category included an automated tub door that lowered and rose for ease of access, a fast-acting drain for ease of exit, and a variety of colors that reduced the impression of being in hospital or long-term care settings.

Aquatic launched other products at bathroom builders' expositions in 2010. These included whirlpool and soaker tubs with a flat-rimmed design known as a skirted tub, targeted at upscale new construction or renovation. The company also introduced a sheet-molded sectional shower system featuring a low threshold, an improvement in safety for users with somewhat limited mobility. In addition, Aquatic announced it had become a vendor to Choice Hotels International, making the manufacturer's tubs and other items eligible for purchase by more than 6,000 franchise hotels, inns, and other lodging establishments in more than 30 countries. By combining two strong subsidiaries and their respective expertise and products, Tomkins was clearly determined to stay in the world's bathrooms.

Mary C. Lewis

PRINCIPAL COMPETITORS

Jacuzzi UK Group plc; Kohler Company; MAAX Bath Inc.; Masco Bath Corporation; Toto USA Inc.

FURTHER READING

Arkin, Sarah. "Halifax County Company Adding 50 New Jobs." *Danville (VA) Register & Bee*, January 24, 2009.

Hawkins, Lori, and Tim Green. "Central Texas Companies Make Fastest-Growing List." *Austin American-Statesman*, October 13, 1995.

"Lasco Bathware." *Professional Builder*, December 1999, 95.

"Lasco Enters the High-End Designer Bath Market." *Kitchen & Bath Business*, June 2005, 18.

Miazga, Mike. "For All Walks of Life." *Plumbing & Mechanical*, June 2010, 40–43.

Peters, Rick. *Remodeling for Easy Access*. New York: Hearst Books, 2006, 4, 10–11, 64–65.

Petty, Gary. "Good Clean Fun." *Fleet Owner*, September 1, 2007.

Stone, Jim. "Coming into Compliance." *Pollution Engineering*, February 2008, 35–36.

Vida, Herbert J. "Spa Users Turn to Great Indoors." *Los Angeles Times*, September 25, 1983.

Washington State Department of Ecology. *Lean & Environment Case Study: Lasco Bathware, Executive Summary*, Seattle: Pollution Prevention Resource Center, April 2007.

Associated British Foods plc

Associated British Foods plc

Weston Centre
10 Grosvenor Street
London, W1K 4QY
United Kingdom
Telephone: (+44 207) 399-6500
Fax: (+44 207) 399-6580
Web site: http://www.abf.co.uk

Public Company
Founded: 1882
Incorporated: 1935 as Food Investments Ltd.
Employees: 96,000
Sales: £9.3 billion ($14.7 billion) (2009)
Stock Exchanges: London
Ticker Symbol: ABF
NAICS: 311412 Frozen Specialty Food Manufacturing; 311212 Rice Milling; 311230 Breakfast Cereal Manufacturing; 311312 Cane Sugar Refining; 311313 Beet Sugar Manufacturing; 311423 Dried and Dehydrated Food Manufacturing; 311811 Retail Bakeries; 311812 Commercial Bakeries; 311821 Cookie and Cracker Manufacturing; 445110 Supermarkets and Other Grocery (Except Convenience) Stores; 551112 Offices of Other Holding Companies

■ ■ ■

Associated British Foods plc (ABF), operating as a multibillion-dollar international conglomerate, characterizes itself as a "family of businesses." ABF subsidiaries, whether self-developed or acquired through merger or acquisition, retain their individuality in name, operations, and clientele, yet maintain strong connections with the parent's central management. From its roots as a Canadian bakery, the company evolved to become Britain's top manufacturer of bread, controlling more than one-third of the U.K. market. By the early 1990s, the company expanded the food business to include tea, coffee, biscuits (cookies), crispbread, frozen foods, and edible oils. With sales and manufacturing operations in Europe, the Americas, Africa, and Asia, ABF employs about 96,000 people in 44 countries.

ABF's five major business segments are Sugar, Agriculture, Retail, Grocery, and Ingredients. The Sugar segment, which is based in nine countries throughout Europe, Africa, and China, is the world's second-largest producer, while the British Sugar business is the sole processor of the United Kingdom's sugar-beet crop. The Agriculture segment provides the food, drink, and animal-feed sectors with products, services, and technology. The Primark value fashion and clothing chain leads ABF's Retail segment, with more than 200 stores in Belgium, Germany, Ireland, the Netherlands, Portugal, Spain, and the United Kingdom. The Grocery segment encompasses a number of international manufacturers of grocery products, including the well-known brands Ryvita, Kingsmill, Mazola, and Twinings. The Ingredients segment, which is the world's second-largest producer of baker's yeast, focuses on providing high-value food and nonfood ingredients to hotel and food service outlets, as well as to the global bakery market.

COMPANY PERSPECTIVES

We aim to achieve strong, sustainable leadership positions in markets that offer potential for profitable growth, and deliver quality products and services that are central to people's lives.

EARLY HISTORY

The seeds of the company were planted in Toronto, Canada, in 1882, when George Weston, then 18, bought a bread-delivery route. During the following 36 years, he built a number of successful bakeries in that area. George Weston Ltd., the Toronto-based chain of bakeries and supermarkets that resulted from that growth, consistently ranked among North America's top businesses throughout the 20th century.

When George Weston's son Garfield took over the bakery business upon his father's death in 1924, he had much more in mind than simply maintaining or building up the chain of local bakeries his father had founded: he was determined that it grow into an international business. Eleven years later, in November 1935, he took a giant step toward that goal by purchasing seven bakeries in England, Scotland, and Wales and adding them to his newly formed Food Investments Ltd., which was promptly renamed Allied Bakeries Limited. All seven bakeries remained in operation throughout the 20th century, three under their original names.

Within four years, Garfield Weston had 18 bakeries and 4 biscuit factories throughout the British Isles, beginning decades of expansion into Europe, Africa, Australia, Asia, and North America. The expansion went beyond food products to encompass seed production, milling, canning, retail grocery and clothing outlets, restaurants, vehicle parts, fuel, and basic research.

The expansion was not always steady, however. At the onset of World War II, wartime restrictions and shortages of supplies began to slow production, while high taxes and voluntary defense contributions reduced profits. Nevertheless, expansion picked up again in the postwar period. A postwar excess-profits tax refund was wholly invested in expansion and equipment. In 1948 Garfield's son Garry Weston joined the board of directors. The following year, the company purchased two Australian firms: Gold Crust Bakeries in Adelaide and Gartrell White in Sydney. By the end of the decade, profits had surpassed £2 million a year.

A growth spurt in the 1950s added dozens of new bakeries, tea shops, restaurants, and catering businesses. Many of these were in newly constructed shopping centers, which provided one-stop convenience for consumers. Food stores purchased by the company were refashioned into supermarkets to suit new shopping habits. This diversification led to a name change in 1960, to Associated British Foods. By 1964 the company claimed to be the largest baker in the world and one of the largest millers, in addition to being one of the largest grocers in the United Kingdom. Rapid growth continued during the 1960s, with the acquisition of A.B. Hemmings, Ltd., a chain of 230 bakery shops in the London area; the entire chain of Fine Fare food shops; and a 51 percent interest in the South African Premier Milling Company.

NEW MARKETS IN THE SEVENTIES AND EIGHTIES

In 1970 ABF also opened the largest bakery in Western Europe, in Glasgow, Scotland. A year later, ABF's Fine Fare opened its first two superstores. As the 1970s progressed, the Stewart Cash Stores in Ireland, which ABF had acquired some 20 years before, followed suit, opening their first hypermarket (a store that carries department-store merchandise as well as groceries). In 1978 ABF expanded into a new market, frozen foods, buying an ice cream factory and a pizza bakery. Garfield died in October 1978 and Garry advanced to the chairmanship of ABF. The family no longer sought the public eye, keeping a low profile since 1983, when an attempt by six Irish Republican gunmen to kidnap a family member was foiled.

Despite difficulties such as fluctuation of the pound and climatic conditions affecting crops, ABF continued to expand and prosper. In 1980 a subsidiary, Twinings Tea, opened its first North American factory, in Greensboro, North Carolina, and also opened the Grosvenor Marketing Company in Paramus, New Jersey. Additional bakeries and other businesses were acquired. ABF's continual program of monitoring and modernizing kept products and services up to date and operations efficient.

GROWTH OF MAJOR SUBSIDIARIES IN THE 20TH CENTURY

Some of ABF's subsidiaries are much older than their parent. The Twining Crosfield Group, for example, dates back to a coffee shop purchased by Thomas Twining in 1706, when coffee was the fashionable drink for men. Tea, introduced early in the 17th century, had been popularized as a drink for ladies by Queen Catherine,

KEY DATES

1882: George Weston begins his career in the bakery industry.
1935: Seven bakeries are acquired and operate under the name Allied Bakeries Limited.
1949: The firm enters the Australian market with the purchase of two companies.
1960: The firm changes its name to Associated British Foods (ABF).
1978: The company expands into the frozen food industry.
1980: Subsidiary Twinings Tea opens a factory in North Carolina.
1997: ABF sells its retail food businesses to Tesco.
2005: The company acquires Littlewoods Stores Holdings Limited and St. James Street Properties Limited.
2009: ABF acquires Azucarera Ebro, Spain's leading sugar producer.

the wife of Charles II of England, at midcentury. The consumption of tea by men, however, was usually for medicinal purposes only (it was widely regarded as a remedy for headaches). When Twining introduced tea as a sideline, he found it was so popular that in 1717 he converted Tom's Coffee House into the Golden Lyon, London's first tea shop.

Twinings Tea, exported to nearly 100 countries at the start of the 21st century, was arguably ABF's most widely known brand name. A winner of the Queen's Award for export achievement, it consistently dominated its market. In 2000 Twinings acquired a Sweden-based food distributor, introduced four new organic teas, and introduced new packaging to the Australian market.

The Ryvita Company, purchased by ABF in 1949, also won the Queen's Award for export with the crispbread that has long been its principal product and probably ABF's second best-known brand name. Increasing interest in health foods made Ryvita and the company's other main product, Crackerbread, popular in many countries in the 1980s. By the early 1990s, Ryvita eclipsed its competition with an 80 percent share of the market. ABF hoped to parlay the brand's strength into increased sales with the late 1988 introduction of a crossover product. Ryvita High Fibre Corn Flakes coupled the original product's reputation as a health food with a marketing emphasis on environmentalism. The product came in recycled packaging. Demand for high-fiber foods and the availability of new extrusion technology resulted in the development of Allinson branded products, as well as other extruded breakfast cereals and cereal products. In 1998 Ryvita entered the Russian market and also introduced Ryvita Currant Crunch. Rising popularity of organic products also led to new product launches, including the Organic Allinson crackerbread.

RESTRUCTURING OF ALLIED BAKERIES

Allied Bakeries, the group of bakeries Weston purchased at the time of its incorporation, continued to function as part of ABF's largest subsidiary. Over the course of the company's history, this segment grew to include some 40 wholesale bakeries and close to 1,200 retail bakery shops and restaurants throughout the British Isles. When the addition of in-house bakeries in many supermarkets put a slight crimp in the wholesale baked-goods business, Allied Bakeries countered this trend with a line of partially baked goods and a line of frozen bakery products, both of which could be completed at an in-house bakery or by the retail consumer at home. By mid-1994, however, a string of losses in the Bakers Oven retail chain led to that operation's divestment. The sale, which encompassed two bakeries and more than 400 retail locations, generated £8.95 million. Allied Bakeries restructured itself into four operating units in 1998. Its Kingsmill brand continued to be a leader in the late 1990s.

Other subsidiaries included Cereal Industries and Fishers Agricultural Holdings, which supplied animal feeds and livestock marketing services, and Fishers Seed and Grain, which produced agricultural seeds. The Allied Grain Group marketed seeds and fertilizers and was the United Kingdom's largest grain trader at the start of the new millennium. ABR Foods supplied wheat by-products to several types of industry: baking and brewing, food and pharmaceutical manufacturers, animal feed, and packaging products. Poor market conditions, however, led to its sale in September 2000 to Roquette Frères. Allied Mills produced more than one million tons of flour each year, making it one of the leading flour mills in the United Kingdom. British Sugar processed 1.55 million tons of sugar in 2000, the second-largest crop in its history.

ABF's Burton's Gold Medal Biscuits long ranked as one of the largest biscuit manufacturers in the United Kingdom. As consolidation swept through the biscuit market in the late 1990s, Burton's stood as the second largest in the industry. The business unit, however, faltered in the late 1990s as competition increased and as the Russian economy experienced a severe decline.

Famous for its Jammie Dodgers and Wagon Wheel products, the subsidiary was sold to Hicks, Muse, Tate & Fürst in October 2000, as a result of continued poor performance.

The firm's Irish retail group operated as the largest supermarket chain in Ireland (as Quinnsworth stores in the Irish Republic and Stewarts and Crazy Prices in Northern Ireland) throughout much of its history. This group also included retail clothing stores (Penneys in Ireland and Primark in the United Kingdom) focusing on fashions for young people. Many of these stores opened in the 1960s. Although they continued to do a thriving business through the 1980s, they were battered by cutthroat price wars in the early 1990s. ABF sold its retail food business to Tesco in 1997, which included Quinnsworth, Crazy Prices, and Stewarts, in order to focus on its other retail ventures.

AB Ingredients, formed in 1982, and AB Technology, formed in 1987, constituted new directions for ABF. AB Ingredients developed and manufactured new ingredients and additives for Allied Bakeries and for other independent companies. It also developed improved bakery processes. AB Technology specialized in high-tech improvements for several types of industry, including food production. The company continued to focus on research and development through its Ingredients and Oils business segment.

LAGGING PROFITS AND EXPANSION: EARLY TO MID-NINETIES

It took a strong central management, an efficient reporting system, and vigilant personnel and investment programs to hold together so many relatively independent companies of disparate size and design, in widely separated geographic locations. ABF's continual expansion testified to its strength, but its structure, marked by an intricate system of holding companies and representation, was difficult to penetrate and analyze.

An early 1990s recession put ABF in what an anonymous analyst with Charles Stanley & Co., Ltd., called "an unenviable situation." Cautious consumers and ready-to-please retailers squeezed profit margins on virtually all of the company's products. Sales declined from £4.81 billion in 1991 to £3.95 billion in 1992, and pretax profits dropped from £332.3 million to £267 million during the same period. The company responded with a major reorganization encompassing the core bakery division as well as the British Sugar plc operations acquired in 1991, closing factories and eliminating a net of nearly 1,500 jobs from 1992 to 1994. Net results rebounded in 1993, when the company recorded £4.39 billion in revenues and £338 million in pretax profits. Financial performance continued to improve in 1994, as sales increased to £4.48 billion and pretax profits increased to £360 million.

With finances back on track, ABF made two key acquisitions in 1995. U.S.-based Abitec Corporation and AC Humko Corporation, specialty oils and cheese analogs (imitation cheese) businesses, were purchased as part of the company's efforts to penetrate that market. The next year, the firm began a joint venture with the Lianhua Gourmet Powder Company of Henan Province, China, and with Henan Lianhua BSO Pharmaceutical Company Ltd. Both ventures were related to its glucose and dextrose operations. Profits increased nearly 15 percent in 1996, due to U.K. flour milling and baking operations as well as the company's expansion into the United States. Marked growth in ABF's animal-feed subsidiaries, the Twining companies, Burton's Biscuit operations, and the retail grocery and textile units also had a positive effect on the year's earnings. ABF's stock ended the year at an all-time high, the only U.K. food manufacturer to do so.

DECLINING MARKET CONDITIONS: LATE NINETIES

In 1997 ABF purchased the One-Up chain of stores as part of its effort to focus on its retail clothing operations. With the sale of its retail food interests in Ireland, the firm's Penneys and Primark units continued to grow. The company's milling and baking operations, however, suffered in 1997, because of a poor harvest caused by bad weather and a surplus in the plant baking market. A drop in sugar prices also began to affect British Sugar's operations despite record production levels.

The following year was a tough one for the firm. Profits declined and market conditions continued to deteriorate because of the adverse effect the strengthening of the pound sterling had on sales. British Sugar also came under fire by the European Commission when it was fined for price-fixing in the late 1980s. ABF appealed the fine. George Weston Foods also recorded a decline in profits.

In 1999 profits continued to fall while sales rose a modest 3 percent. Sugar prices plummeted and the subsidiary ABR was negatively affected by a surplus in Europe in the wheat starch and glucose industry. Flour prices also fell, prompting Allied Mills to introduce new products such as organic flours. The firm's U.K.-based grocery units, as well as George Weston Foods, faced increased competition. The glass-packaging unit also experienced hardship as the U.K. market declined.

Some of ABF's subsidiaries did see growth, however. ABN and Fishers, animal-feed subsidiaries, acquired six mills from Dalgety Feed Ltd. and continued forging relationships in Asia. Allied Grain, as well as Germain's seed-coating operations, maintained profits. ABF's retail unit recorded a 23 percent increase in sales due in part to its expansion. The firm's U.S. interests, Abitec and AC Humko, also saw positive results in 1999. With the acquisition of German-based Rohm Enzymes, a leading enzyme producer catering to the food, industrial, and animal-feed markets, ABF strengthened its food ingredients businesses. That division also acquired SPI, a U.S.-based ingredients company.

RESTRUCTURING IN THE 21ST CENTURY

In May 2000 Garry Weston retired as chairman of the company because of poor health. As the U.K. agriculture industry continued to decline into the new millennium, ABF also had to deal with flat and declining prices and margins in the food retailing and manufacturing industries. Despite these setbacks, the firm recorded a 4 percent increase in profits in 2000. To remain competitive in adverse market conditions, the company underwent a series of restructuring events in 2000, including the sale of its Allied Frozen Food and ABR Foods units. Increasing competition in the biscuit market led to the sale of Burton's. The firm's industrial fats business was also divested.

Management also focused on strengthening its core operations by implementing an aggressive acquisition strategy. In an April 2000 *Grocer* article, CEO Peter Jackson stated, "There is no bigger priority than looking for the right acquisition." In keeping with the new strategy, ABF acquired four sugar-beet plants in Poland, securing its position as the largest foreign investor in the Polish sugar industry. The firm also purchased the polyols business of Lonza Inc., a U.S. subsidiary of the Swiss Lonza Group. With management uncertain about future economic conditions in many of its core markets, it continued to restructure traditional business units. The company also sought international growth through acquisitions and focused on the development of new technologies.

In 2001 the Westons owned slightly more than half of ABF's equity through Wittington Investments Ltd., the firm chaired by Garry's oldest son, Guy, and profits before taxes had increased by 12 percent to £191 million ($275.3 million). ABF's ongoing restructuring program included further divestments, and the acquisition of two sugar factories in China and Kerry SPP, the bakery-ingredients business of Ireland's Kerry Group. The acquisitions spree continued in 2002 beginning in April with the purchase of Unilever's Mazola corn oil business in the United States, Canada, and Puerto Rico. This was followed in October with the acquisition of Novartis AG's food and drinks division, which included the popular Ovaltine brand, for £171 million ($257 million). In September 2003 the ABF's U.S. subsidiary, ACH Food Companies, Inc., acquired the bottled oils business of Bunge Limited. The year closed with ABF's purchase of the ethnic food company, G Costa, which included the Blue Dragon line of products.

Operating profits had increased to £478 million ($876 million) in 2004 with sales up 5 percent to £5.17 billion ($9.5 billion). In March, ABF entered into an agreement with Unilever to buy its Mexico-based food oils and fats brands for $110 million. This was followed by the acquisition of the Billington Food Group in August, and the U.S. herbs and spices business and Sydney-based yeast and bakery ingredients business from Australia's Burns, Philp & Company Limited for £730 million ($1.35 billion). In keeping with the family tradition, when Jackson announced in September 2004 that he would be retiring the following April, it was another George Weston, Garry's middle son, who was appointed to succeed him.

EXPANSION AND CONSOLIDATION

ABF's U.K. Retail segment expanded substantially in July 2005 with the acquisition of 120 stores from Littlewoods Stores Holdings Limited and St. James Street Properties Limited from LW Finance Limited for £409 million ($717 million). ABF planned to turn 30 to 40 of the units into Primark stores and sell the remaining stores to other high-profile retailers, such as Next, New Look, TK Maxx, and Debenhams. In 2006 the Sugar business expanded with the April acquisition of 51 percent of Africa's largest sugar producer, Illovo Sugar Limited. This was followed in July with the closure of two U.K. sugar plants in York and Allscott and the consolidation of the remaining four factories. The move mirrored the consolidation of ABF's Polish sugar production the previous year. This restructuring, combined with the purchase of 11,000 tons of sugar quota in Poland and 83,000 tons of sugar quota in the United Kingdom, put ABF in a strong position as Europe's least-expensive sugar producer.

The expansion of Primark paid off, with ABF reporting in April 2007 a 28 percent increase in profits after opening 23 new stores. By 2008 Primark and the Retail segment would overtake the Sugar business as ABF's most profitable segment. In May 2007 ABF announced that it was acquiring the Indian food brand Patak's from the founding Pathak family. The Patak's and Blue Dragon brands were integrated the following year to create a new world foods business within the Grocery segment. In September ABF bought 20 percent of Jordans, a breakfast cereal and cereal-bar manufacturer, for an estimated £15 million ($30.3 million). The following June, ABF took control of Jordans when it increased its stake in the company to 62 percent, and merged it with its Ryvita operation to strengthen ABF's position in the healthful eating market. Although economic conditions were worsening, and the costs of raw materials and energy rising, ABF reported operating profits of £664 million ($1.2 billion), and a 21 percent increase in revenue of £8.2 billion ($15.2 billion) for 2008.

ABF's European sugar business was further strengthened in 2009 with the acquisition of the leading sugar producer on the Iberian Peninsula, Azucarera Ebro in Spain. Nevertheless, with many countries in recession, ABF decided to sell its Polish sugar business, British Sugar (Overseas) Polska SP. Z.o.o. to Pfeifer & Langen Polska S.A. The Retail segment continued to expand in 2009 with new Primark stores opening in Belgium, Germany, the Netherlands, and Spain. In January 2010 ABF issued a first-quarter statement that showed company revenues up 17 percent over the previous year. Primark continued to be a major earner for ABF, reporting a 20 percent increase in half-year profits in April 2010. Although summer sales slowed at the retail chain during the global downturn, analysts were still predicting a 6 percent increase in full-year sales. With the Sugar segment also performing well, ABF shares had risen a staggering 28 percent in 2010, a considerable achievement during difficult economic times.

Updated, April Dougal Gasbarre; Christina M. Stansell; Marie O'Sullivan

PRINCIPAL SUBSIDIARIES

AB Agri Limited; AB Brasil Industria e comercio de Alimentos LTDA (Brazil); AB Enzymes GmbH (Germany); AB Enzymes Oy (Finland); AB Food & Beverages (Thailand) Limited; AB Food & Beverages Australia Pty Ltd; AB Food & Beverages Philippines, Inc.; AB Mauri Food, S.A. (Spain); AB Mauri India (Private) Limited; AB World Foods Limited; ABF European Holdings & Co SNC (Luxembourg); ABF Grain Products Limited; ABF Investments plc; Abitec Corporation (USA); ABNA (Shanghai) Feed Co., Ltd (China); ACH Food Companies, Inc. (USA); Alimentos Capullo S.de R.L.de C.V. (Mexico); Anzchem Pty Limited (Australia); Azucarera Ebro, S.L.U. (Spain); Bo Tian Sugar Industry Company Limited (China; 65%); British Sugar (Overseas) Limited; British Sugar plc; Calsa de Colombia S.A.S.; Cereform Limited; Compania Argentina de Levaduras S.A.I.C; Food Investments Limited; Foods International S.A.S. (France); G. Costa and Company Limited; George Weston Foods (NZ) Limited (New Zealand); George Weston Foods Limited (Australia); Germain's (Ireland) Limited; Germain's Technology Group NA Inc. (USA); Germain's Technology Group Polska Sp. z.o.o. (Poland); Guangxi Bo Hua Food Co., Ltd (China; 71%); Guangxi Boqing Food Co., Ltd (China; 60%); Guangxi Boxuan Food Co., Ltd (China; 70%); Harbin Mauri Yeast Co., Ltd (China; 85%); Hebei Mauri Food Co., Ltd (China); Illovo Sugar (Malawi) Limited (39%); Illovo Sugar Limited (South Africa; 51%); Innovative Cereal Systems LLC. (USA); Jacksons of Piccadilly Limited; Kilombero Sugar Company Limited (Tanzania; 28%); Liaoning Liaohe Aimin Feed Co., Ltd (China); Liaoning Liaohe Yingpeng Feed Co., Ltd (China); Lojas Primark Portugal-Exploracao, Gastao e Administracao de Espacos Comerciais S.A. (Portugal); Maragra Acucar SARL (Mozambique; 38%); Mauri Fermentos II, SA (Portugal; 96%); Mauri La-Nga Fermentation Co., Ltd (Vietnam; 66%); Mauri Lanka (Private) Limited (Sri Lanka); Mauri Maya Sanayi A.S. (Turkey); Mauri Products Limited; Patak's Breads Limited; Patak's Foods Limited; Premier Nutrition Products Limited; Primark Deutschland GmbH (Germany); Primark Netherlands NV; Primark NV Belgium; Primark Republic of Ireland; Primark Stores Limited; Primark Tiendas S.L.U. (Spain); R. Twining & Co., Ltd (USA); R. Twining and Company Limited; Serrol Ingredients Pty Limited (Australia); Shanghai AB Food & Beverages Co., Ltd (China); SPI Pharma Inc. (USA); SPI Pharma S.A.S. (France); Talisman Guernsey Limited (Guernsey); The Billington Food Group Limited; The Jordans & Ryvita Company Limited (62%); Twinings North America Inc. (USA); Ubombo Sugar Limited (Swaziland; 31%); Wander AG (Switzerland); Yeast Products Company (Ireland); Zambia Sugar plc (46%).

PRINCIPAL DIVISIONS

Sugar; Agriculture; Retail; Grocery; Ingredients.

PRINCIPAL COMPETITORS

Nestlé S.A.; Südzucker AG; Tesco PLC.

FURTHER READING

"ABF Hit by Tough Market." *Grocer*, April 22, 2000, 8.

Crosland, Jonas. "Associated British Foods Weathers the Storm." *Investors Chronicle*, April 21, 2009.

Davies, Charles. *Bread Men: How the Westons Built an International Empire*. Toronto: Key Porter Books, 1987.

Fletcher, Nick. "Associated British Foods Bucks Trend as FTSE Falls on Economic Fears." *Guardian*, August 24, 2010. Accessed October 19, 2010. http://www.guardian.co.uk/business/marketforceslive/2010/aug/24/associatedbritishfoods-vedantaresources.

———. "Primark Slowdown Hits Associated British Foods Shares." *Guardian*, September 13, 2010. Accessed October 19, 2010. http://www.guardian.co.uk/business/marketforceslive/2010/sep/13/primark-slowdown-associated-british-foods.

Hawkes, Steve. "Associated British Foods Looks Tasty in Tough Times." *Times* (London), February 26, 2008, 55.

———. "Associated British Foods Takes Control of Jordans as It Aims for a Perfect Mix." *Times* (London), June 3, 2008, p. 39.

Puliyenthuruthel, Josey. "U.K. Food Group Rises with Yeast." *Daily Deal*, July 23, 2004.

Tigert, D. *George Weston Limited: A Corporate Background Report.* Toronto: Royal Commission on Corporate Concentration, 1977.

Urry, Maggie. "George Weston to Take Chief Executive's Role at Associated British Foods." *Financial Times*, September 24, 2004, 23.

AstraZeneca PLC

15 Stanhope Gate
London, W1K 1LN
United Kingdom
Telephone: (+44 20) 7304-5000
Fax: (+44 20) 7304-5151
Web site: http://www.astrazeneca.com

Public Company
Founded: 1999
Employees: 62,700
Sales: $32.8 billion (2009)
Stock Exchanges: New York London Stockholm
Ticker Symbol: AZN
NAICS: 325412 Pharmaceutical Preparation Manufacturing

■ ■ ■

AstraZeneca PLC is one of the world's leading pharmaceutical companies. Its corporate headquarters are in London, and its research and development headquarters are in Sodertalje, Sweden, south of Stockholm. Of its more than 62,000 total employees, the company employs 11,000 people in drug research and development at 17 research and development facilities in the United Kingdom, United States, Sweden, France, Canada, India, China, and Japan. AstraZeneca has sales in more than 100 countries worldwide, including the emerging markets of Russia, Brazil, India, and China. AstraZeneca focuses its drug research, development, and manufacturing on six key medical areas: cardiovascular, central nervous system, gastrointestinal, infection, oncology, and respiratory and inflammation. AstraZeneca resulted from the 1999 merger of two European pharmaceutical companies: Astra AB of Sweden, which made pharmaceutical products and medical devices, and Zeneca PLC of the United Kingdom, a bioscience company that focused on pharmaceuticals, agricultural and specialty chemicals, and disease-specific health care services.

ASTRA: EARLY DEVELOPMENT

Astra AB was formed in Sweden in 1913 by the initiative of more than 400 doctors and apothecaries, who became the company's first shareholders. Two products (Digitotal, a heart medication, and Glukofos, a nutritional supplement) emerged from Astra's facilities in 1914, and the company began to prosper. When the apothecary Hjalmar Andersson Tesch joined Astra in 1915 as the company's new president, he brought with him a number of his own pharmaceuticals. Astra's product line then comprised a variety of medicines and chemical compounds. Government restrictions on imports during World War I created a demand for Astra's products, and the company bought new factory buildings to meet that demand. By the end of the war, Astra was reporting handsome profits.

ASTRA: INTERWAR DIFFICULTIES

The years following the war proved less successful. In an attempt to create a company of international stature, the Swedish chemical company AB Svensk Fargamnesindustri acquired Astra's entire capital stock. The directors of

COMPANY PERSPECTIVES

AstraZeneca is a global, innovation-driven, integrated biopharmaceutical company. Our mission is to make the most meaningful difference to health through great medicines that bring benefit for patients and add value for our stakeholders and society.

Svensk assumed that the shortage of raw materials during the war would persist in the postwar years, but prices for raw materials dropped as war shortages disappeared. The company faced imminent bankruptcy, as its manufacturing costs grew larger than the prices its products could command in the marketplace.

A solution seemed possible when Sweden's first socialist government announced plans to create a nationalized pharmaceutical monopoly and authorized the state liquor monopoly to purchase Svensk Fargamnesindustri. Within months, however, the socialist government fell, and its successor was staunchly opposed to the new monopoly. From 1921 until 1925, the government sought a private buyer who would release the state from its responsibilities. A purchaser was finally found in the form of a private consortium, and Astra became an independent company once again.

The company's new hierarchy, which included board members Erik Kistner and Richard Julin and company president Börje Gabrielsson, reorganized many of Astra's operations. The most important of these changes allowed for the formation of the company's own distribution network. In just a few years, the company was again profitable. With the establishment of research and development facilities in the 1930s, Astra began to create more innovative products, such as Hepaforte, a treatment for pernicious anemia, and Nitropent, a medication for angina pectoris.

Astra's growth during the years prior to World War II resulted from not only its development of new products but also its aggressive expansion and acquisition strategy. By 1940 Astra subsidiaries were operating in Finland, Latvia, and Stockholm and Hässleholm, Sweden.

Restricted imports and shortages of raw materials during World War II placed Astra's products at a premium, and once again profits increased. Astra constructed a new central laboratory and established a subsidiary to supervise management of and distribution to Astra's numerous branch offices. The company established new subsidiaries in Denmark, Argentina, and the United States.

ASTRA: DEVELOPMENT OF XYLOCAINE AND POSTWAR GROWTH

In the postwar years, a number of successful pharmaceuticals emerged from Astra's laboratories. These included Ferrigen, an iron preparation, and Sulfadital, a sulfa medication. The most important of all the products Astra developed during this period was Xylocaine, a local anesthetic synthesized in 1943. For years Xylocaine remained one of Astra's most popular products. By 1984 local anesthetics constituted 24 percent of Astra's total group sales, and Xylocaine alone contributed SEK696 million.

The worldwide production of Xylocaine began in earnest during the 1950s, along with a significant increase in research and development spending. Throughout the 1950s the company produced a number of successful new products, including Secergan (an antiulcer medication), Ascoxal (a treatment for oral infections), Jectofer (an injectable iron preparation), and Citanest (another local anesthetic). In the 1960s Astra continued to expand both at home and abroad. The company acquired a manufacturer of nutritional products and a distributor of medical supplies. It created and built new operations in Western Europe, South and Central America, and Australia. It joined with England's Beecham Research Laboratories in an attempt to develop synthetic penicillin.

By the 1970s Astra had formed separate divisions for its diverse activities: a pharmaceutical division dedicated to its array of drugs; a chemical products division encompassing agricultural products, nutritional products, cleansers, and recreational items; and a division responsible for medical equipment and rust-prevention products. By the end of the decade, however, Astra announced that it would concentrate solely on producing pharmaceuticals, and the company sold all its other holdings.

ASTRA: REEMPHASIS ON PHARMACEUTICALS

With a renewed commitment to the manufacture of pharmaceuticals, Astra's unique and highly efficient research units emerged as the company's strongest assets. By 1984 Astra's three most important products (Xylocaine, the heart disease medication Seloken, and the bronchodilator Bricanyl) were generating more than half the company's revenues. The development of several

KEY DATES

1913: Astra AB is formed in Sweden.
1926: Imperial Chemical Industries (ICI), parent company of Zeneca PLC, is founded in the United Kingdom.
1943: Astra develops Xylocaine, which becomes the world's largest-selling local anesthetic.
1993: Zeneca PLC is demerged from ICI.
1996: Astra's Losec becomes the world's best-selling prescription drug.
1999: Astra AB and Zeneca PLC merge to form AstraZeneca PLC.
2001: AstraZeneca introduces Iressa, a drug to treat lung cancer.
2003: AstraZeneca introduces the cholesterol-lowering statin Crestor.
2006: AstraZeneca completes its acquisition of the British biotechnology pioneer Cambridge Antibody Technology (CAT).

new drugs helped push Astra's pretax earnings over the one billion kroner mark in 1985. Sales of the asthma drug Pulmicort propelled total revenues to over SEK6.2 billion in 1988, by which time the company's pretax earnings had risen to SEK1.5 billion.

Although Astra's financial performance was beginning to attract the attention of investors worldwide, a core group of stockholders remained dissatisfied. Sweden's well-to-do Wallenberg family, which owned a 10 percent stake in Astra, launched a search for a replacement for CEO and president Ulf Widengren. In 1988 they hired an unlikely candidate: 44-year-old chocolatier Hakan Mogren. Mogren turned the company's former marketing program on its head, rescinding licenses and instead beefing up Astra's own distribution and sales organization. He established subsidiaries where there had previously been licensees and added nearly 1,000 sales representatives worldwide by the end of 1990. Mogren chose a tough market for his first outing, launching the antiulcer drug Losec in competition with Glaxo Pharmaceuticals' best-selling Zantac. Fortunately, Astra enjoyed a close relationship with longtime U.S. distributor Merck, which became an important ally in the competition, playing an especially vital role in convincing the U.S. Food and Drug Administration to approve Losec as a first-tier ulcer treatment. Astra formed a 50-50 joint venture with Merck called Astra Merck, Inc., which marketed the drug under the name Prilosec in the United States. In his first two years at the helm, Mogren boosted sales by nearly 50 percent, from SEK6.3 billion to SEK9.4 billion, and increased pretax earnings by SEK1 billion.

ASTRA: TRANSFORMATION UNDER MOGREN

The new leader intensified his transformation of Astra in the early 1990s, propelling the company into the ranks of the pharmaceutical industry's fastest growth vehicles. Mogren more than doubled the sales force, from about 3,000 in 1990 to nearly 7,000 by mid-decade, and boosted the company's roster of subsidiaries to 40 nations worldwide. These assertive moves succeeded in increasing the company's sales and income at a truly astonishing rate. Total sales quadrupled, from SEK9.4 billion in 1990 to nearly SEK39 billion in 1996, while pretax net mushroomed fivefold, from SEK2.5 billion to over SEK13 billion. Losec became the world's top-selling drug in 1996, with an estimated 200 million prescriptions and $3.5 billion revenues.

Mogren's reign was not without problems, however. In 1995 the company suffered an embarrassing scandal when Lars Bildman, head of Astra's North American operations, was fired and faced criminal charges for defrauding the company of more than $1 million. Additionally, Bildman's alleged sexual harassment of female employees resulted in several lawsuits. The company settled the suits, but its reputation suffered. Analysts also worried about what would happen to Astra when Losec's patents began expiring in 1999, and they expressed concern over the vagueness of the company's strategy to handle the losses. Some criticized Astra's venture with Merck, saying that Astra Merck missed important sales opportunities because of an inexperienced sales staff. Most troubling to analysts was the paucity of Astra's drug "pipeline." Because drugs can take years to test and find approval, their development must begin years before their launch. Astra's critics felt that the company had far too few promising new drugs in development.

In 1997 the company's shares began to underperform compared with the rest of the industry. Rumors of a merger or acquisition in Astra's future started to circulate, and in fact the company had held extensive merger talks with British pharmaceuticals company Zeneca PLC in 1996. Those talks foundered because Zeneca felt that Astra's relationship with Merck was a barrier. In 1998, however, Astra and Merck dissolved their venture, and in December of that year Astra and Zeneca announced their merger into a new company called AstraZeneca PLC. In freeing itself from its obligations to Merck, Astra made a deal wherein it would pay Merck between $675 million and $1 billion upon completion of the merger, $950 million the following year, and continue to pay royalties to Merck for products sold in the United States at least through 2008.

ZENECA: ROOTS IN ICI

Zeneca Group PLC was the result of a demerger from Imperial Chemical Industries (ICI). Formed in 1926, ICI was one of the United Kingdom's oldest and most renowned chemical corporations. By the end of the 1980s, ICI's pharmaceutical division was the company's most profitable business. Yet it held many different product lines and operations in widely diverse geographical regions, and while pharmaceuticals and agrochemicals grew rapidly, ICI was ill prepared to manage the complexities of its own businesses.

The prospects of a fully mature chemicals market, which meant intense competition, lower growth, and overcapacity in many regions throughout the world, convinced management at ICI that a comprehensive restructuring of the company was necessary. This realization was brought to a head when Hanson PLC acquired a small amount of stock in ICI, thus fueling speculation that executives at Hanson were preparing for a hostile takeover. The result was a series of meetings and consultations with Warburgs, ICI's merchant bank advisors, who established a strategy to separate the company into two new groupings, ICI and ICI Bioscience, which was named Zeneca.

During its 65-year history, ICI had developed into an extremely complex and fully integrated organization with more than 120,000 employees working in 130 countries around the globe. Management decided to continue operating ICI as a chemical company in traditional markets, while the demerger gave Zeneca all ICI's former pharmaceutical, agrochemical, and specialty products. When Zeneca was formed, it took approximately 30,000 employees from ICI with it.

ZENECA: INDEPENDENCE

Zeneca Ltd. was established as a 100 percent wholly owned subsidiary of ICI on January 1, 1993. By June of the same year, however, Zeneca existed as a totally separate company from ICI. Zeneca's market capitalization was actually more than that of ICI and placed the newly established company in the top 25 firms with the highest capitalization in the United Kingdom. By the end of fiscal year 1993, the first full year of Zeneca's operation, sales had increased approximately 12 percent to an impressive total amount of £4.44 billion, and the company's profit margin increased by an astounding 42 percent, to £647 million. Zeneca's pharmaceutical operation immediately catapulted it into the ranks of the top 20 pharmaceutical companies worldwide.

By 1995 Zeneca was operating at full capacity. The company's group sales, composed of pharmaceutical, agrochemical, and specialty products, amounted to £4.8 billion, and operating profit increased to £894 million. Zeneca was ranked number two in worldwide sales of anticancer drugs, and it ranked as one of the top six agrochemical firms around the globe. The company had expanded to include facilities in more than 25 countries, and it sold its products in more than 100 nations.

ZENECA PHARMACEUTICALS, ZENECA AGROCHEMICALS, AND ZENECA SPECIALTIES

Zeneca Pharmaceuticals provided the largest portion of the company's sales, with more than £2 billion in 1995. Its research and development efforts focused on treating a wide variety of cancers and disorders of the respiratory, cardiovascular, and central nervous systems, including Casodex, an oral prostate cancer drug; Arimidex, for use by breast cancer patients; Tomudex, a cell-killing agent for advanced stages of colorectal cancer; and Accolate, a tablet developed to prevent asthma attacks. To expand its presence overseas, Zeneca also purchased a 50 percent share in Salick Health Care, Inc., one of the leading providers of comprehensive cancer and chronic disease care in the United States.

Herbicide products made up approximately two-thirds of Zeneca Agrochemicals' £1.6 billion in sales for 1995. Innovative herbicides such as Touchdown, Falcon, and Surpass, the latter specifically developed for use in maize, were extremely successful in the marketplace. The company's leading herbicide, Gramoxone, was adopted by farmers the world over. Zeneca Plant Sciences (ZPS), part of the company's agrochemical operation, concentrated on developing vegetables, fruits, and fiber crops with enhanced characteristics. In 1995 ZPS began working closely with Nippon Paper, a Japanese firm, and Shell Forestry, a U.S. subsidiary of Shell Oil, to develop trees with modified lignin, which resulted in the tree pulp needing less chemical treatment and thereby producing a higher quality of paper.

Zeneca Specialties made and sold high-performance pigments that put the color in plastics and paints for cars; developed smudge-resistant inkjet dyes used in the printing of magazines and in color photocopying equipment; supplied products to control contamination caused by unwanted bacteria such as the fungi and algae in swimming pools; manufactured a host of leather finishes; designed water-based resins for use in adhesives, paints, and inks; and even developed a low-fat alternative to meat that had no cholesterol and was high in fiber.

Beginning in 1995, Zeneca focused on a unique approach to the treatment of cancer. The company was one of the first pharmaceutical firms in the world that approached cancer not as a disease ultimately to be cured but as a chronic disease with which patients could learn to live. Zeneca was so successful in its approach and in developing breast cancer and prostate cancer drugs that the direction of cancer research changed within the pharmaceutical industry as a whole, and many companies began to follow Zeneca's lead in cancer research.

ZENECA: RUMORS OF A TAKEOVER

Almost from the moment Zeneca demerged from ICI, rumors began to circulate that it was ripe for acquisition. The company was certainly an attractive prospect for interested buyers. Between its spinoff and 1996, the company doubled its pretax profits, and its stock value more than tripled. In 1997 the company was the second-largest seller of cancer drugs. Additionally, the overall trend in the pharmaceuticals industry at that time was for small- to medium-sized companies such as Zeneca to be taken over by industry giants. Furthermore, 1997 saw the beginnings of a downturn for the company, as patents on its most successful drugs, Zestril (a heart medication) and Nolvadex (a cancer drug), were due to expire at the beginning of the 21st century. Some analysts were concerned that Zeneca did not have enough drugs in late-stage trials to compensate for the loss. Other analysts thought that Zeneca had not made alliances with biotechnology companies fast enough.

Nonetheless, the company was determined to maintain its independence. David Barnes, Zeneca's CEO, held a hard line, saying that any competitor had to be willing to pay a substantial premium for control of Zeneca. Nevertheless, the company was ruling out no possibilities, and it conducted talks with several suitors. Zeneca rejected merger talks with Astra AB in 1996 because of that company's close relationship with Merck, and 1998 negotiations with GlaxoWellcome and SmithKline Beecham were scuttled when the two larger companies balked at Zeneca's premium. Finally, in December 1998 Zeneca announced its impending merger with Astra, which had recently disentangled itself from its obligations to Merck.

ASTRAZENECA: A MARRIAGE OF EQUALS

Investors greeted the news of the merger warmly: the day after the deal was announced, Astra's share price increased 13 percent, and Zeneca's rose 7.5 percent. The new company, AstraZeneca PLC, would be the number-three pharmaceuticals firm in the industry. The $37 billion merger was completed on April 6, 1999, 80 days after its announcement, and the new company's stock was listed on the London, Stockholm, and New York stock exchanges. AstraZeneca was headed by Tom McKillop (formerly the CEO of Zeneca) as chief executive and Percy Barnevik (of Astra) as chairman.

In many ways, the two companies seemed a perfect match. They were of comparable size (valued at over $30 billion each), so they entered the merger on equal footing. One of the first steps AstraZeneca took after the merger was to streamline its operations and focus solely on its pharmaceuticals business by spinning off the agricultural and chemical holdings Zeneca had brought to the merger. The company merged its agrochemical business with that of Novartis (another drug company) in 2000. A year after its merger, the company had achieved sales of $15.8 billion, with an operating profit of $4 billion.

Nonetheless, the new company faced challenges. Although the combined drug portfolios created a stronger pipeline than the companies had held independently, AstraZeneca still faced patent loss on some of its major drugs. Losec in particular accounted for nearly 40 percent of the company's total sales. When Losec's patent expired in 2001, other companies were able to produce it and sell it generically at a lower price. AstraZeneca immediately put in place a strategy to offset the losses by defending secondary patents on the drug while simultaneously bringing replacement products to the market, namely Nexium, which was launched on March 19, 2001. Within 17 weeks of its release, Nexium, dubbed "the purple pill" in the United States, was ranked third in the market for new prescriptions in its class.

THE PROMISE OF IRESSA

In December 2001 AstraZeneca submitted a new drug to the U.S. Food and Drug Administration (FDA) for approval. The drug, Iressa, was a promising new treatment for advanced cases of the most common type of lung cancer. It was also being studied for the treatment of breast, colorectal, and gastric cancer. In July 2002 Japanese drug regulators approved Iressa for the treatment of lung cancer. This decision made Iressa the first drug in a new class of cancer medications known as molecular-targeting drugs to reach the market anywhere in the world.

Cancer specialists were especially hopeful about Iressa and the other drugs in its class because they promised to attack cancer cells exclusively and leave healthy cells unharmed. A drug's ability to draw such a distinction promised far fewer side effects for patients. Iressa's benefits, however, proved elusive for the majority of patients. Although highly effective in a small number of people, only about 1 in 10 patients dramatically improved.

Iressa became controversial just months after Japan approved it. Cases of interstitial pneumonia, a potentially fatal condition, were noted among increasing numbers of Japanese patients taking the drug, and a number of deaths were reported. Concerned physicians called for a temporary ban, while the Japanese media accused AstraZeneca of falsifying or suppressing information about the drug's detrimental side effects. AstraZeneca issued an emergency warning regarding the possibility of fatal side effects but maintained that interstitial pneumonia was associated with many cancer treatments and also appeared in cases of untreated cancer. The company maintained that the potential benefits of the drug to patients with advanced cases of lung cancer outweighed any risks associated with its use. Ironically, Iressa also proved more effective among Japanese patients, 30 percent of whom showed improvement.

In May 2003 the FDA approved Iressa for treatment of lung cancer cases in the United States. The low survival rate among individuals suffering from non–small cell lung cancer (the most common type of lung cancer) and the drug's remarkable effectiveness for some of them were said to convince FDA regulators of the need to approve the drug.

CRESTOR TAKES THE STAGE

In August 2003 the FDA approved AstraZeneca's new cholesterol-lowering drug, Crestor. Intended to compete with pharmaceutical rival Pfizer's drug Lipitor, Crestor was expected to generate eventual sales of $2.5 to $3 billion annually, helping to offset the loss of revenue as AstraZeneca's top-selling gastrointestinal drug Prilosec (Losec in Europe) lost its patent protection.

Concerns regarding the safety of Crestor surfaced over the following year. Questions centered around the drug's effects on the kidneys and on reports of patients who developed a potentially fatal muscle-damaging condition called rhabdomyolysis. The consumer protection group Public Citizen called for Crestor's removal from the U.S. market. AstraZeneca maintained that the level of side effects seen with Crestor was consistent with other statins on the market. The company nonetheless issued a letter to physicians, reminding them of the pronounced effectiveness of Crestor and urging them to follow label indications closely when prescribing it. The letter advised physicians to start new patients on the lower recommended doses of the drug and increase doses gradually and only when necessary.

In June 2005 the FDA limited use of the once-promising lung cancer treatment Iressa to existing or previous users and participants in clinical trials. Clinical trial results had been released that indicated Iressa did not prolong life among trial participants. The FDA's restriction was one step short of withdrawing the drug from the market and preserved its use among the particular patients for whom Iressa proved especially effective.

BIOTECHNOLOGY ACQUISITIONS STRENGTHEN AND ADD VARIETY

In June 2006 AstraZeneca completed acquisition of the British biotechnology pioneer Cambridge Antibody Technology (CAT). The deal capped a two-year alliance between the companies in the key AstraZeneca medical areas of respiratory medicine and inflammatory disease. Observers noted the potential difficulty of integrating a biotechnology firm into a well-established pharmaceutical company. "Integration is a sensitive and delicate issue across most industries," wrote Salamander Davoudi in the *Financial Times* on January 29, 2007, "but it is especially so in biotechnology, which is somewhat dependent on an informal network, key talent, agility, and a lack of bureaucracy." Hamish Cameron, the new CEO of CAT, stressed that the transition had to be managed properly or key CAT scientists would leave and the company's unique culture would be destroyed. To stave off a defection of CAT staff, AstraZeneca offered a first-year retention bonus to former CAT employees.

In April 2007 AstraZeneca acquired the U.S.–based biotechnology company MedImmune Inc. for $15.6 billion. The move allowed AstraZeneca to expand its pipeline of experimental drugs and biological medicines and also to acquire an interest in vaccines for the first time. David Brennan, CEO of AstraZeneca, told the *Financial Times* on April 24 that MedImmune's "compelling fit" justified the high purchase price. (Brennan had become CEO in 2006.)

In December 2008 AstraZeneca announced it would investigate opportunities to develop lower-cost versions of the biological medicines manufactured by its rivals as soon as their patent protections expired. The move mirrored efforts by two other pharmaceutical giants, Eli Lilly and Merck, to shift some focus to the development of generic drugs originally developed by rivals. The biological medicines of interest to AstraZeneca were known as "biosimilars" because they underwent a complex manufacturing process that made them impossible to copy exactly. Some analysts attributed AstraZeneca's interest in developing generics to possible shortages of new drugs in the company's own pipeline.

PARTNERING WITH ACADEMIA AND OTHERS

In June 2009 AstraZeneca announced plans to permit the U.S. eye care company Alcon access to its "library" of experimental drug compounds. Like most other giant drug companies, AstraZeneca maintained a library of a million or more drug compounds but struggled to find ways to use them in safe and effective new medicines. The five-year deal with Alcon limited research to the development of promising treatments in ophthalmology, or eye care.

That same month, AstraZeneca said it would share its library of drug compounds with Medicines for Malaria Venture, a nonprofit group, in order to find new drugs to fight the disease, which remained widespread in many parts of the world. A month later, AstraZeneca announced plans to share its compounds library with academic researchers from the commercial arm of the UK organization the Medical Research Council (MRC). The new arrangement allowed both AstraZeneca and the council to screen their combined libraries of compounds against specific biological targets. According to the terms of the deal, both companies would retain ownership of their compounds and negotiate licensing agreements with each other for any compounds chosen for further development.

APPROVALS AND CHALLENGES END THE DECADE

In March 2010 the cholesterol-lowering drug Crestor, developed in the early part of the decade, won FDA approval to fight heart disease in patients whose cholesterol was normal but who exhibited at least two serious risk factors for heart disease. The approval cleared the way for a vast new market of potential Crestor users.

In April 2010 AstraZeneca reached an agreement to pay $520 million to settle claims it had illegally marketed the psychiatric medication Seroquel. The U.S. Department of Justice had accused the company of marketing the schizophrenia and psychosis drug for "off-label" uses, including treating aggression, Alzheimer's disease, attention-deficit/hyperactivity disorder, depression, and insomnia. Other charges against AstraZeneca had included marketing the drug to physicians who were not specialists in schizophrenia and psychosis, the only conditions for which it was approved.

UNCHANGING DIRECTION, 2010

In 2010 AstraZeneca assured potential investors that it was not changing direction and that it would retain its core strategies of strengthening its pipeline and focusing on research and development. The company expected, however, to accelerate efforts to acquire innovation from outside AstraZeneca in the form of partnerships and to continue aggressively investing in emerging markets.

Thomas Derdak
Updated, April D. Gasbarre;
Lisa Whipple; Joyce Helena Brusin

PRINCIPAL SUBSIDIARIES

AstraZeneca UK Ltd (England); AstraZeneca Reinsurance Ltd (England); AstraZeneca Treasury Ltd (England); NV AstraZeneca SA (Belgium); AstraZeneca Dunkerque Production SCS (France); AstraZeneca GmbH (Germany); AstraZeneca Holding GmbH (Germany); AstraZeneca SpA (Italy); AstraZeneca Farmaceutica Spain SA (Spain); AstraZeneca AB (Sweden); AstraZeneca BV (Netherlands); AstraZeneca Canada Inc. (Canada); AZ Reinsurance Ltd (Cayman Islands); IPR Pharmaceuticals Inc. (Puerto Rico); AstraZeneca LP (USA); AstraZeneca Pharmaceuticals LP (USA); Zeneca Holdings Inc. (USA); Medimmune, LLC (USA); AstraZeneca Pty Ltd (Australia); AstraZeneca Pharmaceuticals Co., Ltd (China); AstraZeneca KK (Japan).

PRINCIPAL COMPETITORS

GlaxoSmithKline PLC; Merck & Co., Inc.; Novartis AG; Eli Lilly and Company; Pfizer, Inc.

FURTHER READING

Barrett, Amy, and Kerry Capell. "Prilosec Time Is Just about Up." *BusinessWeek*, January 8, 2001, 47.

"Corporate Profile: The Arranged Marriage." *Independent* (London), February 24, 1999.

"Crestor Wins Approval as a Drug to Prevent Heart Disease." *New York Times*, February 9, 2010.

Davoudi, Salamander. "Pioneer in Need of Protection." *Financial Times*, January 29, 2007, 11.

Jack, Andrew. "AstraZeneca Targets 'Biosimilars.'" *Financial Times*, December 23, 2008.

Jack, Andrew, and Richard Milne. "View from the Top: David Brennan, Chief Executive of AstraZeneca." *Financial Times*, April 17, 2009.

Moore, Stephen D. "Astra's Successful Ulcer Drug May Become Bellyache." *Wall Street Journal*, November 26, 1996.

Owen, Geoffrey, and Trevor Harrison. "Why ICI Chose to Demerge." *Harvard Business Review*, March–April 1995, 133–40.

Pilling, David. "Hard Lessons from Japan's Drugs Market." *Financial Times*, June 24, 2003.

Pollack, Andrew. "F.D.A. Restricts Access of Cancer Drug, Citing Ineffectiveness." *New York Times*, June 8, 2005.

Stevenson, Richard W. "A Certain Glow on Sweden's Astra." *New York Times*, November 22, 1992.

Atrium Companies, Inc.

3890 West Northwest Highway, Suite 500
Dallas, Texas 75220-8108
U.S.A.
Telephone: (214) 630-5757
Fax: (214) 630-5001
Web site: http://www.atriumcompanies.com

Private Company
Founded: 1948 as Lumberman Sash & Door Co.
Employees: 7,000
Sales: $755 million (2007 est.)
NAICS: 332321 Metal Window and Door Manufacturing

■ ■ ■

Dallas, Texas–based Atrium Companies, Inc., is North America's largest manufacturer of vinyl and aluminum windows and swing and sliding patio doors. The company also offers entry doors, shutters, and specialty products, including impact-resistant doors and windows, sound-suppression windows, decks and railing systems, and patio enclosures. In addition to the Atrium Windows and Doors flagship brand, other brands include Champion Window, Darby Doors, HR Windows, North Star, Safe Harbor, Silent Guard, Superior Windows & Doors, and Thermal Industries. Atrium maintains about 80 manufacturing and distribution centers spread across 23 states, mostly in the southwestern United States as well as in Mexico. The company became majority owned by a pair of investment firms, Kenner & Company and Golden Gate Capital, following a financial restructuring in 2010.

POST–WORLD WAR II ROOTS

In 1948 what later became Atrium Companies was founded by Joe Fojtasek in Dallas, Texas, as Lumberman Sash & Door Company. The company was originally a building materials distributor, but in response to the housing boom that developed after World War II, it began manufacturing wood windows and doors in 1953. Aluminum products were added through the acquisition of Irving-based Skotty Aluminum Products, which was founded in 1960. Extruders Inc., founded in Wylie, Texas, in 1975, would later supply aluminum for sister companies. Wood products continued to be manufactured by Atrium Door & Window Company, based in Dallas, and along the way, vinyl windows and doors were added as well. On the distribution side, Atrium Door and Window Distributors of Arizona opened in 1979, and Atrium Windows & Doors—Colorado followed in 1986.

All manufacturing and distribution assets became part of Fojtasek Companies, Inc., in 1988. In that same year, the company supplemented its holdings with the acquisition of another Irving company, H-R Windows. The following year, North Texas Die & Tool was formed. In 1990 the company launched Dow-Tech Plastics in Carrollton, Texas, to produce rigid and flexible vinyl extrusions that sister companies used to make vinyl and aluminum windows and doors.

The Fojtasek operations in the Dallas area were faced with unionization efforts in the early 1990s. For

COMPANY PERSPECTIVES

Our values begin and end with honesty and integrity. We approach our business with passion, enthusiasm and a commitment to continuous improvement and a dedication to excellence in products and service. We strive to provide a safe and rewarding work environment focused on continuous improvement that will empower our employees to reach their individual and collective potential. Our vision is to be the preferred brand of fenestration products throughout North America, based on quality, reliability, and value. And we will conduct our business as responsible corporate citizens in our communities and provide appropriate returns for our shareholders.

many years Fojtasek relied heavily on its Hispanic work force, a large number of them recent immigrants. The Amalgamated Clothing and Textile Workers Union sought to organize the production workers at Atrium Door & Window, H-R Windows, Extruders, and Skotty Aluminum. Most of the workers started at minimum wage and did not earn enough to acquire company-sponsored health insurance. Moreover, workers charged that management made little effort to accommodate their language limitations. Many supervisors did not speak Spanish, and written instructions were only available in English. Hence, the union found fertile ground with Fojtasek Companies' 750 workers, which in 1993 voted by a three-to-one margin to organize.

LABOR COMPLAINTS

Fojtasek Companies hardly embraced its new union, which in late 1993 filed a complaint with the National Labor Relations Board, charging that the company persisted in an anti-union campaign despite losing the election. Union officials claimed that work rules had been changed in violation of labor law and active union members had been illegally demoted, fired, laid off, suspended, or transferred. The company defended the job cuts as seasonal, said the firings were for just cause, and insisted that it was no longer fighting the union but actually negotiating its first contract.

Amalgamated Clothing filed more charges of unfair labor practices in early 1994. The company responded by filing a petition to have the union decertified. The union also alleged workplace safety violations at H-R Window and Skotty Aluminum. When the U.S. Occupational Health and Safety Administration (OSHA) attempted to inspect the plants, however, they were denied entry by management, which also refused to present paperwork on safety procedures. The company claimed that the union was simply using OSHA as a way to harass management. OSHA was not deterred, and eventually federal inspectors were allowed in the plant. The result was $243,000 in assessed fines for safety problems. In August 1994 the company reached a settlement with OSHA that cut the amount to $142,500.

The Union and Fojtasek Companies continued to battle in court over other charges while contract negotiations dragged out. Finally in May 1995 a labor contract was agreed upon. It called for an 11 percent increase in base pay over three years and improved health insurance benefits. Two fired workers who complained of civil rights violations were also reinstated, and the company agreed to pay approximately $240,000 in back wages and compensation to settle sexual discrimination charges. All the pending lawsuits and unfair labor practice charges were withdrawn.

FOUNDER'S RETIREMENT

While Fojtasek Companies was fighting with the union, there was a change at the helm. Joe Fojtasek retired as president and chief executive officer in early 1994, turning over the post to his son, Randall S. Fojtasek, who had been with the company since 1989. The elder Fojtasek remained chairman, while his son began to grow the business. At the time of the change in upper management the company was generating annual sales of nearly $100 million.

Under Randall Fojtasek, Fojtasek Companies launched Atrium Door and Window Distributors of Texas and Atrium Door and Window Distributors of Nevada in 1994. In July 1995, he engineered a private equity recapitalization of the company in which Heritage Partners Inc. became the majority owner. Another recapitalization took placed in November 1996 with the Dallas investment firm of Hicks, Muse, Tate & Furst Inc. This transaction was set up earlier in the month when Fojtasek Companies was merged into a new Delaware corporation, FCI Holding Corp. The surviving entity assumed the named Atrium Companies, Inc. Hicks, Muse then paid $135 million for an 80 percent stake in the company, with Heritage and Atrium officers holding the rest of the stock.

Despite the change in ownership, Randall Fojtasek remained CEO and continued to grow Atrium. In 1996 it acquired Kel-Star Building Products and Woodville

KEY DATES

1948: Joe Fojtasek founds Lumberman Sash & Door Company.
1960: Skotty Aluminum Products is formed.
1988: The newly renamed Fojtasek Companies begins to manufacture windows and doors.
1996: Fojtasek Companies becomes Atrium Companies, Inc.
2010: Atrium Companies emerges from bankruptcy.

Distributors. It also formed Atrium Door and Window Company of the Northeast, Atrium Door and Window Company of New England, and Atrium Door and Window Company of New York. For the year, Atrium Companies recorded revenues of $156 million. In 1997 Atrium Door and Window Company–West Coast was created out of an H-R Window Supply unit that acquired Anaheim, California–based Gentek Building Products. Masterview Window Company, LLC, of Phoenix, Arizona, was purchased in 1998 for about $27 million.

WING INDUSTRIES GAINING CONTROL

A third recapitalization under the watch of Randall Fojtasek was completed in October 1998. Wing Industries, a Greenville, Texas–based manufacturer that focused on wood interior doors, acquired the Hicks Muse 80 percent stake for $225 million. Wing was controlled by New York investment firm Ardshiel Inc., and GE Investment Private Placement Partners II, an arm of General Electric Company. Another buildings-product company owned by Ardshiel and GE Investment, the R.G. Darby Company, was then folded into Atrium, creating a combined company that generated annual revenues of nearly $400 million.

Randall Fojtasek remained Atrium's CEO and oversaw further acquisitions in 1999. In January, Delta Millwork, Inc., a door manufacturer based in Orlando, Florida, was combined with the R.G. Darby operations. Heat, Inc., a vinyl and door company, was acquired in May, bringing a pair of subsidiaries: Yakima, Washington–based Best Build, Inc., and Pittsburgh, Pennsylvania–based Thermal Industries. Also in May, Atrium purchase another vinyl and door company, Denver, Colorado–based Champagne Industries, Inc.

Randall Fojtasek left Atrium in the fall of 1999 to join a new Dallas-based investment firm, Brazos Private Equity Partners, LLC. It was founded by a pair of Hicks Muse veterans, Jeff Fronterhouse and Patrick McGee, who came to know Fojtasek when Hicks Muse had acquired Atrium. They recruited Fojtasek to join Brazos to help with the acquisition of family-owned businesses. Fojtasek was well-suited to the task because of his experience guiding Atrium through three private equity transactions.

ACQUISITIONS IN THE NEW CENTURY

With ties to the Fojtasek family severed, Atrium entered the new century. In 2000 the company acquired North Carolina–based Ellison Window and Door and Ellison Extrusion Systems, Inc., for about $127 million, while also shedding most of the Wing assets. The company also sold its Atrium Wood Patio Door division in the summer of 2000. In this way, Atrium exited the marginally profitable wood door category to focus on its core aluminum and vinyl business, which was enjoying much faster growth, especially vinyl windows, in the southeastern United States. As a result of the Ellison acquisition, Atrium became the largest non-wood window and door manufacturer in the United States, with $501 million in revenues in 2000.

Atrium experienced another growth spurt in 2003 when it completed several acquisitions. Early in the year most of the assets of Miniature Die Casting of Texas, L.P., a Fort Worth–based zinc die cast hardware manufacturer, was purchased for $3.3 million. Next, in April 2003, Atrium added Danvid Window Company, a Dallas-based aluminum and vinyl window manufacturer. In October 2003, Atrium paid about $17 million for Aluminum Screen Manufacturing Ltd., L.L.P., Aluminum Screen Products, Inc., and Aztec Screen Products, adding screen manufacturing capabilities and distribution operations in Dallas, Houston, Phoenix, Las Vegas, and Ciudad Juarez, Mexico. Finally, at the close of 2003 Atrium spent $53 million in cash and stock to acquire Superior Engineered Products Corporation, an Ontario, California–based manufacturer of windows and other building materials.

NEW OWNERS

In December 2003 the ownership of Atrium again changed hands. Kenner & Company, Inc., a private investment group based in New York, created an investment group with Atrium's CEO, Jeff L. Hull, members of his management team, and other investors, including the likes of UBS Capital Americas and Merrill Lynch Ventures. KAT Holdings, Inc., was formed to accomplish the transaction, and it was merged with Atrium, with Atrium the surviving corporation.

Atrium continued to pursue external growth in 2004. It acquired a pair of Fort Lauderdale, Florida, companies for $12 million in cash and stock: Robico Shutters Inc. and Expert Installation Service Inc. The deal helped Atrium increase its presence in the fast-growing Florida housing market. Atrium also looked to the West Coast in 2004, spending nearly $6 million on Palm Springs, California–based West Coast Custom Finish, a distributor and installer of aluminum and vinyl windows for home construction in southern California. These acquisitions brought additional debt, leading Atrium to refinance its existing credit line to cut interest expense while extending debt maturities.

Atrium Companies increased sales to $800 million in 2005, according to the *Dallas Morning News*. A year later that amount grew to $835 million. Atrium continued to pursue acquisitions in 2007. In March of that year it added North Star Vinyl Windows & Doors, a Canadian vinyl profile extruder that brought new sales opportunities in Canada as well as northern United States.

New business would take on greater importance as the housing market began to collapse in 2006 and 2007. Very much dependent on new housing, Atrium saw revenues drop to $755 million. The company had taken on considerable debt in recent years and soon found it was unable to meet its obligations to creditors. As a result, in early 2010 Atrium filed for Chapter 11 bankruptcy protection as part of a plan worked out with creditors to recapitalize the company. When Atrium emerged from bankruptcy protection in April 2010, Golden Gate Capital and Kenner & Company controlled 92.5 percent of the reorganized company. Having shed a good deal of debt, Atrium was well positioned to resume its growth as the economy and housing market eventually improved.

Ed Dinger

PRINCIPAL SUBSIDIARIES

Atrium Windows & Doors; Champion Window, Inc.; R.G. Darby Co., Inc.; Thermal Industries, Inc.

PRINCIPAL COMPETITORS

JELD-WEN, Inc.; Pella Corporation; Silver Line Building Products Corporation.

FURTHER READING

Bowen, Bill. "Plants Hit with Union Charges." *Dallas Business Journal*, January 14, 1994.

Craver, Richard. "Welcome, N.C., Window-Door Factory Quietly Becomes Major Employer." *High Point Enterprise*, June 17, 2002.

Kunde, Diana. "Firm, Union Go Head to Head." *Dallas Morning News*, November 21, 1993.

———. "Fojtasek Employees OK First-Ever Labor Contract." *Dallas Morning News*, May 20, 1995.

Perez, Christine. "Window Maker Takes Shine to Pinnacle Park." *Dallas Business Journal*, May 11, 2001.

Wallach, Dan. "Dallas-Based Builder to Close Woodville, Texas, Plant." *Beaumont Enterprise*, January 3, 2002.

Austria Technologie & Systemtechnik AG

Am Euro Platz 1
Vienna, A-1120
Austria
Telephone: (+43 1) 68 300 0
Fax: (+43 1) 68 300 9290
Web site: http://www.ats.net

Public Company
Founded: 1987
Employees: 5,500
Sales: €372.2 million ($495.32 million) (2009)
Stock Exchanges: Vienna
Ticker Symbol: ATS
NAICS: 334412 Bare Printed Circuit Board Manufacturing; 423690 Printed Circuit Boards Merchant Wholesalers

■ ■ ■

Austria Technologie & Systemtechnik AG (AT&S) is a leading manufacturer of printed circuit boards (PCB) in Europe, Asia, and India. AT&S products are used as electromechanical linking elements, mainly in the telecommunications, automobile, medical equipment, defense, and aerospace industries. The company also offers services such as electronics design and component assembly. AT&S boasts an international list of clients that includes General Electric Company, Honeywell International Inc., Motorola Inc., Nokia Corporation, and Siemens AG. Headquartered in Vienna, Austria, the company operates major production plants in China, Korea, and India and has a service and design center in Germany.

COMPANY FOUNDING: 1987

The history of AT&S was based on three separate companies: a Körting Elektronik factory in Fehring, Austria, that produced circuit boards for television sets; an Eumig plant in Fohnsdorf, Austria, that was known for its production of radios, movie cameras, and film projectors; and a Voestalpine AG production facility in Leoben, Austria, that manufactured steel.

Körting was founded in Leipzig in 1889 to produce eloctromechanical devices, transformers, lighting technology, and eventually technical supplies for radio. In 1948, after World War II, the company moved to West Germany. Growing demand in the radio and television sector made expansion necessary, so in 1970 Körting agreed to a joint venture with the company Gorenje in Velenje, Slovakia. Four years later, in 1974, Körting opened Körting Elektronik in Fehring to cover the parent company's need for PCBs. However, a year later demand in the radio and television sector plummeted, so Gorenje took over the main production plant in West Germany. In 1978 Gorenje closed the main site, making way for a grouping of the Fehring plant with a Eumig plant nine years later.

Founded in 1919, Eumig began manufacturing radios and cameras, particularly instant cameras. In 1977 Eumig opened a plant in Fohnsdorf to relieve unemployment rates in an economically disadvantaged area. Eumig, like most other Austrian companies after World War II, was a state-owned company, so it had to

COMPANY PERSPECTIVES

AT&S Group strategy is geared towards innovation as well as organic, profitable and sustainable growth. We aim to achieve undisputed leadership in our target markets. The Group also aims to open up additional market potential by consistently continuing and proactively designing technological trends.

follow political decisions over economic prudence. When Eumig lost its contract with Polaroid for the production of instant cameras in 1978, its revenues began to decline steadily. By 1981 Eumig had to declare bankruptcy. The Fohnsdorf plant remained in operation until it was grouped with the Körting plant in Fehring and the Voestalpine plant in Leoben.

The steel manufacturer Voestalpine was founded in 1938 in Linz, which was then part of the German Reich, and refounded in 1948 in Vienna as part of the state-owned conglomerate of industrial companies that would eventually become the Österreichische Industrie Holding AG (ÖIAG). ÖIAG carried out a dual role as the Austrian Republic's investment and privatization agency by focusing on increasing the value of the investments entrusted to it and by monitoring its investments for exit scenarios and privatizing the companies that it oversaw. The Voestalpine PCB plant in Leoben was established in 1982 as an investment in association with IBM. When IBM announced its withdrawal from Austria in 1987, AT&S was founded to take over the plant.

PRIVATIZATION AND AUTOMATION: 1989–99

About to loose IBM as its main customer, AT&S set about establishing a broader customer base. However, by 1989 the company was reporting massive losses, in part because of the economic slump during the mid- to late 1980s and because Austria hosted two other PCB manufacturers, Körting in Fehring and Eumig in Fohnsdorf, that were competing against one another. Willi Dörflinger, the managing director of AT&S, approached ÖIAG and suggested that three production facilities should consolidate. Realizing the benefits of combining the facilities, ÖIAG agreed with the consolidation. In 1991 E+E Leiterplattenholding was founded under the leadership of Dörflinger and Helmut Zoidl, the managing director of Eumig Fohnsdorf. The three plants began operating under the names of AT&S Fehring, AT&S Fohnsdorf, and AT&S Leoben.

During the early 1990s AT&S began investing heavily in upgrading its capacity and technology. By focusing on full automation and multilayer PCBs, the company hoped to increase its share of the mobile telephone market.

Meanwhile, privatization efforts in Austria accelerated, and in 1993 the Austrian parliament issued its final privatization act, which indicated that the state was going to sell all state-owned industrial activities, including AT&S. To avoid a hostile takeover by a competitor, Dörflinger and Zoidl approached ÖIAG to suggest a management buyout. In 1994 AT&S was awarded to Zoidl, Dörflinger, and Hannes Androsch and was renamed AT&S GmbH. In 1995 the company was transformed into a stock company, AT&S AG, and offered up to 25 percent of its stock to employees.

Now a private company, AT&S was ready to reap the fruits of its investments. Around 1994 the cell phone market began to boom, and the company was able to attract international cell phone manufacturers such as Nokia. Contracts with Siemens and Sony Ericsson soon followed.

To maintain its lead, the company pursued an aggressive strategy of technological renewal and advancement. In 1998 the new Fehring production facility was opened. The second production factory in Leoben, the most modern of its kind in Europe, was nearly finished and plans for a logistics and design center in Nörvenich, Germany, were well under way. In early 1999 AT&S acquired Indal Electronics, India's largest PCB manufacturer, and a former Siemens plant in Augsburg, Germany. Production capacity was at an all-time high. Riding on these successes, AT&S went public and was listed on the Frankfurt Stock Exchange in July 1999.

MARKET CONSOLIDATION AND EXPANSION IN ASIA: 2000–05

AT&S began the new century well positioned in the European market. The company pursued a strategy of expansion and international acquisitions to ensure further growth. Beginning in 2000 AT&S built a new production facility in Shanghai, China, to supply its partners Nokia and Siemens, which had facilities located in China. The factory began production in 2002. One year later AT&S was one of the top three producers of high-density interconnection–microvia boards and was supplying about 40 percent of all mobile phones sold in Europe and about 15 percent of the global handset market.

KEY DATES

1987: Austria Technologie & Systemtechnik AG (AT&S) is founded.
1999: AT&S is listed on the Frankfurt Stock Exchange.
2008: AT&S is delisted from the Frankfurt Stock Exchange to trade exclusively on the Vienna Stock Exchange.
2010: AT&S shareholders approve capital gain program.

Having outgrown its local headquarters, the company moved from Leoben to Vienna in 2003. From there AT&S oversaw the acquisition of AIK Electronics in Klagenfurt, the extension of the Indian plant by 50 percent, and the establishment of a purchasing center in Hong Kong. That same year the company consolidated its infrastructure to focus on three major applications of its PCBs: automotive, industrial, and telecommunications.

In 2005 Dörflinger moved from the management board to the supervisory board. Harald Sommerer became the new chief executive officer and continued the strategy of expansion by buying the Indian circuit board designer ECAD, making AT&S one of the major global players not only in the production but also in the design of PCBs. AT&S was well on its way to becoming a total solutions supplier, designer, and producer of PCBs.

NEW STRUCTURE AND FOCUS: 2005–10

In 2005 Sommerer also began a long-term restructuring process of the company, aiming to lower production costs while remaining competitive in the global marketplace. AT&S shifted its Austrian plants to focus on the European market, while its Asian plants kept a broader outlook on the world market. With this in mind, AT&S reduced its European production by relocating operations from the Fohnsdorf plant to the second plant in Leoben. At the same time, the company acquired the Korean PCB manufacturer Tofic Co. Ltd. In 2006 AT&S ramped up a second plant in Shanghai, China, and then a third one the following year. A second plant was built in Nanjangud, India, in 2008. That same year AT&S also expanded to the United States by opening AT&S Americas LLC near San Jose, California.

In 2008 AT&S was delisted from the Frankfurt Stock Exchange and thereafter was traded exclusively on the Vienna Stock Exchange. Meanwhile, the company began another round of restructuring. The company shifted its mass production of PCBs to Asia and India to take advantage of lower production costs and offset a decline in demand. By 2009 all high-volume orders were filled in Asia and India, while the two Austrian plants in Leoben only supplied European customers in the industrial and medical markets.

In fiscal year 2009 AT&S reported a loss of €37.6 million. The company indicated three main reasons for the loss: the initial cost of its restructuring, a longer than expected recuperation process following the Tofic acquisition, and the ongoing global recession, which began in late 2007. The company announced in July 2010 plans to issue €100 million in stock in a capital gains program.

AT&S indicated that the positive effects of the restructuring program would be felt after 2010. The focus on the high-end mobile device sector, which accounted for 60 percent of the company's business, strongly connected AT&S to several international customers. The industrial sector, which encompassed 28 percent of the company's business, provided service to European and U.S. customers with specialized needs for measurement and control technology, computing, and aerospace. The automotive sector made up 12 percent of the company's business and promised further growth considering that the electronics used in automobiles were expected to increase in complexity. With its commitment to proactive technological development, AT&S was well equipped to meet the future demands of the market.

Helga Schier

PRINCIPAL DIVISIONS

Automotive; Industrial; Mobile Device.

PRINCIPAL OPERATING UNITS

AT&S Austria; AT&S China; Vertriebs, Service & Design Center Nörvenich (Germany); AT&S India; AT&S Korea.

PRINCIPAL COMPETITORS

Elcoteq SE; Flextronics International Ltd.; Simclar Group Limited.

FURTHER READING

"AT&S: Grünes Licht für Wandelanleihe." DerStandard.at, July 7, 2010. Accessed November 1, 2010. http://derstandard.at/

1277337602023/ATS-Gruenes-Licht-fuer-Wandelanleihe.

Fürstler, Gerhard. "AT&S: Vorwurfsvoller Betriebsratsbrief an Helmut Zoidl." Boerse-express.com, July 7, 2002. Accessed November 1, 2010. http://www.boerse-express.com/pages/183100.

Gold, Steve, and Roy Sakelson. "Conducting a Successful Strategy: How AT&S Captured Europe's Cell Phone Market." Circuitree.com, January 1, 2001. Accessed November 1, 2010. http://www.circuitree.com/Articles/Cover_Story/a2c109e9ca7d7010VgnVCM100000f932a8c0.

Sakelson, Roy. "AT&S and China: Waking the Giant." Circuitree.com, May 1, 2004. Accessed November 1, 2010. http://www.circuitree.com/Articles/Feature_Article/8a28dce9230f7010VgnVCM100000f932a8c0____.

Von Fellhuber, Martin. "AT&S leidet unter der schwachen Konkurrenz." Wirtschaftsblatt.at, February 4, 2008. Accessed November 1, 2010. http://www.wirtschaftsblatt.at/home/boerse/analysen/ats-leidet-unter-der-schwachen-konkurrenz-277528/index.do.

Bavaria N.V.

Postbus 1, De Stater 1
Lieshout, NL-5737 ZG
Netherlands
Telephone: (+31 0499) 42-81-11
Fax: (+31 0499) 42-82-69
Web site: http://www.bavaria.com

Private Company
Founded: 1719
Employees: 949
Sales: $477 million (2004)
NAICS: 312120 Breweries

■ ■ ■

Bavaria N.V. is a Netherlands-based brewery whose name reflects its brewing method rather than its Netherlands locale. Nonetheless, the name was the subject of trademark litigation in Europe for years. Bavaria sells standard and low-alcohol pale lagers under the Bavaria and Hollandia labels. It also offers a non-alcohol beer; Claro, a beer brewed from rice; a variety of malts, including apple, caramel, karkade, and lemon flavors; sweet beers Bavaria 8.6 and Bavaria 8.6 Red; Bavaria Crown, a premium lager; and private label beers for the supermarket trade in Europe. Each year the company produces more than 600 million liters of beer, making it the second-largest brewery in the Netherlands. All told, the company's products are sold in more than 100 countries across the globe. Beer is brewed locally in Russia and South Africa as well as in the Netherlands. Bavaria is owned and managed by the seventh generation of the founding Swinkels family.

SEVENTEENTH-CENTURY ROOTS

Bavaria N.V. traces its brewing heritage to 1680, when forebears of the Swinkels family began brewing beer in an old farmhouse near Lieshout in the Dutch province of Brabant. Their product could then be traded for foodstuffs and other products. The brewery as a truly commercial enterprise did not begin until 1719, when Laurentius Moorees turned the farmhouse into a profitable brewery that produced about 88 kegs of beer a year, which he sold in surrounding communities. Moorees also made wine and brandy. The Swinkels family became involved when Moorees's daughter Brigitta married Ambrosius Swinkels.

A grandson of Moorees, Jan Swinkels, born in 1851, eventually took charge of the brewing business and was responsible for expanding production as well as distribution of the beer. His three sons, Franciscus, Petrus, and Johannes, inherited the brewery and grew the business further. In 1910 a malting plant was opened and began making malt for the family operation as well as for sale to other breweries. The plant's kiln was put to a different use when conditions in World War I forced it into service to dry vegetables for food for the local population. Although the Netherlands was not directly involved in the war, the country's brewers were adversely affected. They joined together to purchase barley from the United States, but the first cargo ship was sunk by a German U-boat. Fortunately, the breweries were well insured, and the Swinkels family

COMPANY PERSPECTIVES

The traditional brewing of Bavaria beer has been handed down from generation to generation. With each generation adding a little something of its own, craftsmanship has now been married to modern management.

was able to use some of the insurance money they received to make improvements to its operations.

THE NEW CENTURY

To keep pace with demand for their "Brebntse *biertje*," or "beer from Brabant," following the war, the Swinkels brothers increased production by building a new brewery in 1924. Seeking to improve quality, the brothers began paying visits to Belgium, Germany, and other countries to learn how other brewers operated and to incorporate some of their practices at home. They learned of a variety of yeast, for example, that had been developed in Czechoslovakia and was well suited for brewing beer in cold temperatures. They began using the yeast, stored in ice-filled cellars, to create a bold-tasting beer. The filtering process was also improved, resulting in a clear, golden color.

The most important trips the Swinkelses took, however, were to the region of Bavaria in Germany, where they learned how to produce the low-fermentation lagers that were becoming increasingly popular in the 1920s. The brothers decided to switch production from traditional Dutch ales to the new Bavarian beer. Taking the suggestion of a German master brewer, Georg Kraus, the brewery adopted the Bavaria trade name in 1925 to emphasize this change in direction. While Bavaria N.V. always emphasized that it was a Dutch brewery, the use of the Bavaria trademark would become a contentious issue several decades later.

Another development that prompted a change in the business was the growing popularity of bottled beer. Thus, in 1933, the company broke ground on a new bottling plant. Capable of filling and capping 2,000 bottles per hour, the new facility opened early the following year. The demand for higher quality malt necessitated a new malting plant as well. Construction on the facility began in 1938, and it was operational by the time Europe was once again plunged into a world war. This time, however, the Netherlands felt the war's direct effects.

During World War II the country was invaded by Nazi Germany and occupied for four years. Again the malting plant kiln was used to dry vegetables. After the country was liberated, the Swinkels family lost little time in adding more germination boxes to produce malt well beyond the needs of the family brewery. This excess was then sold to other Dutch brewers and was also exported.

GROWTH AND EXPANSION

Bavaria expanded into soft drinks in 1955, selling the product under the name 3-ES, a reference to the three Swinkelses who were in charge of the family business at the time. Nevertheless, beer remained at the heart of the company. The postwar years also saw a significant increase in beer consumption in the Netherlands. As a result, the malting plant was expanded again in 1964, when production was doubled to 12,000 tons a year. Later in the decade the malting industry underwent a significant change because of new European Union rules that opened up closed markets. To protect its position and to take advantage of this opportunity, Bavaria constructed one of the first European tower malting systems, in which steeping was conducted on the top floor and germination and kilning took place on lower flowers. This fully automated, compact semicontinuous system became operational in the early 1970s. A second tower was added in 1981. The 1987 acquisition of a facility in Wageningen increased malting capacity. With that facility's modernization a year later, malting capacity reached 120,000 tons per year.

It was not until 1970 that Bavaria began selling its beer outside of the Netherlands, entering markets in southern Europe. The company even pursued business in Africa and the Middle East, where Islamic countries prohibited alcoholic beverages. In 1978 Bavaria developed and introduced a non-alcohol beer, which proved so popular that in the 1980s it would be introduced in the Netherlands. A switch in advertising taglines in 1985 signaled Bavaria's emergence from provincial status. In place of the phrase "brewed in our own Brabant," the company opted for "Right. Time for a Bavaria first."

Bavaria continued to grow in the 1990s, adding a second germination tower was added to the maltings operation in 1991 and a second kilning tower four years later. Not only was capacity added but quality was also improved. In addition, beer production increased from 3 million to 4 million hectoliters of beer in the first half of the 1990s. Some of that increased production would

KEY DATES

1719: Laurentius Moorees establishes the commercial brewery that will evolve into Bavaria N.V.
1910: The brewery opens a malting plant for its own use and for sale to other breweries.
1925: The Bavaria N.V. name is adopted.
1996: Bavaria enters the U.S. market.
2009: The company wins an international legal dispute over the use of the Bavaria name.

be put to use in 1996, when Bavaria entered the United States, the world's most important beer market.

"HOLLAND" ADDED TO LABEL

In 1995 the Bavaria company added the word "Holland" to its beer label. Nevertheless, the company's use of the word "Bavaria," which the Swinkels family had trademarked in 1947, irked breweries located in the German region of Bavaria. As long as Bavaria N.V. had been content to serve merely the Dutch market, they and German brewers had coexisted without a problem. Now that Bavaria was competing in multiple markets, however, the Germans charged the Dutch with marketing malfeasance. Complicating the matter were European Union rules that went into effect in 1992 to protect region-specific food products, such as Italy's Parma ham and Greece's Feta cheese. Bavaria N.V. maintained that such rules did not apply to the use of "Bavaria," because, in addition to a locale, the word designated the brewing technology the Dutch company employed. Moreover, Bavaria N.V. had always promoted its Dutch origins, as evidenced by the addition of "Holland" to its label.

The new geographic protection laws included a registration process, which a coalition of 650 German brewers from Bavaria initiated in 1992. Bavaria N.V. did not learn of the process until five years later. In 2001 German brewers were successful in winning protection, leading to legal battles in German, Spanish, and Italian courts as well as the European Union's highest court, the European Court of Justice in Luxembourg. In July 2009, after eight years of litigation, the Luxembourg court finally issued a ruling that denied the German brewers from using geographic trademark laws against Bavaria N.V. At the same time, the court upheld the Germans' right to the name "Bayerisches bier," the German phrase for "Bavarian beer." In essence, the Dutch and German brewers were told to return to peaceful coexistence.

GROWTH AND CONTROVERSY IN THE NEW CENTURY

Despite legal wrangling, Bavaria N.V. continued to expand in the new century. It improved control over its supply of barley in 2003 by forging an alliance with the Agrifirm agriculture cooperative, resulting in the Holland Malt joint venture. To increase malting capacity for the new joint venture, Bavaria N.V. opened a new state-of-the-art plant in Eemshaven, Netherlands, in 2005. The company also looked to grow its business in the United States. In 2008 it entered into a partnership with California-based World Brews, which repositioned the brand, improved distribution, and developed a new marketing plan.

Bavaria N.V. was the subject of controversy on other fronts in the 2000s. In 2007 it was one of three breweries that were determined by the European Commission to have acted as a price-fixing cartel to control 95 percent of the Dutch beer market from 1996 to 1999. The three were found to have colluded to carve up among themselves beer sales to restaurants, bars, supermarkets, and hotels. The other brewers named were Heineken and InBev. A fourth company, Grolsch, was also involved in the cartel but escaped penalty because it informed on its partners and provided information on the practices of other European brewers. For its part, Bavaria was fined €22.9 million.

WORLD CUP CONTROVERSIES

Bavaria was also involved in a pair of controversies related to soccer's World Cup in both 2006 and 2010. The company did not pay FIFA, the organizer of the World Cup, to be a sponsor of the event (Budweiser acquired the rights to be the official World Cup beer), but it hoped to take advantage of the tournament's popularity to promote its own beer. In 2006 the World Cup was held in Germany, prompting Bavaria N.V. to give away what they dubbed *leeuwenhosen* (*leeuwen*, Dutch "lions"; *hosen*, German "pants") with the purchase of its products. The overalls were orange, the team color of the Dutch, and included a lion's tail in honor of the team mascot. They were also adorned with the Bavaria N.V. logo. FIFA decided that the brewer was guilty of engaging in "ambush" marketing, and when Dutch supporters showed up for a game between the Netherlands and Ivory Coast, stadium security denied entry to fans wearing the *leeuwenhosen*. About 1,000 of them simply removed the garment and watched the game in their underwear, creating the kind of international publicity for Bavaria N.V. that it could never have hoped to buy.

FIFA again involuntarily helped promote the Dutch brewer in the 2010 World Cup in South Africa. This time Bavaria had about three dozen women wear orange minidresses under their outer clothing and seated them all in the same section of the stands during a game between the Netherlands and Denmark. Although the company took care this time to not place a logo on the dresses, the group was evicted from the stadium during the first half after they removed their outer garments and tossed them to the crowd to reveal the orange minidresses. The two women responsible for recruiting the women in South Africa were detained and questioned, and British soccer commentator Robbie Earle, who had supplied many of the tickets to the game, was sent home. Again, Bavaria N.V. received incalculable publicity, bringing further awareness to an old brewery that was just beginning to scratch the surface of its market potential.

Ed Dinger

PRINCIPAL COMPETITORS

Heineken NV; Heisterkamp-Grolsch Vastgoed B.V.; In-Bev Deutschland Vertriebs GmbH & Co. KG.

FURTHER READING

"EU Decides That Dutch Brewer Bavaria NV Can Use Word 'Bavaria' in Its Beer." *Guardian* (London), July 2, 2009.

"EU to Rule Against InBev, Heineken, Grolsch, Bavaria Over Dutch Cartel—Source." *Europe Intelligence Wire*, April 17, 2007.

Glickman, Elyse. "The Real Dutch Treat: Bavaria Beer." *BIN*, January 2008.

Smith, Heather. "'Lederhosen Incident' Shows Soccer Group's Tough Marketing Rules." *Fulton County Daily Report*, August 22, 2006.

BEAULIEU®
of AMERICA

Beaulieu of America, L.L.C.

1502 Coronet Drive
Dalton, Georgia 30720
U.S.A.
Telephone: (706) 876-2900
Toll Free: (800) 227-7211
Fax: (706) 695-6237
Web site: http://www.beaulieu-usa.com

Private Company
Founded: 1978
Employees: 7,500 (est.)
Sales: $1.18 billion (2008 est.)
NAICS: 314110 Carpet and Rug Mills; 313210 Broadwoven Fabric Mills

■ ■ ■

The Beaulieu Group, L.L.C., a privately held company that does business as Beaulieu of America, Inc., is the third-largest producer of carpet in the world. Since divesting itself of area rug and hard-surface flooring manufacturing facilities in 2002, the company has concentrated on broadloom, including residential, commercial, and indoor/outdoor carpeting. The company's growth has been characterized by vertical development, initiated in 1981 when it began manufacturing the yarn used in its carpets, as well as global expansion, including the formation of Beaulieu Canada and Beaulieu Australia.

BEGINNINGS: FROM BELGIUM TO GEORGIA

Beaulieu, meaning "beautiful place" in French, has its roots in the carpet company that Roger de Clerck and his wife, Anne-Marie, founded in Belgium in 1959. After his firm became a leading European carpet manufacturer, De Clerck divided his operations among several of his children and entrusted his daughter Mieke and her young husband, Carl Bouckaert, with exporting the business to the United States. In 1978, one day after their marriage, the Bouckaerts moved to Georgia.

The Bouckaerts began their independent U.S. venture in the Dalton, Georgia, facilities of the bankrupt Barwick Industries, once the largest tufted carpet fabricator in the country. Dalton was considered the capital of tufted carpets (made by inserting tufts of yarn through a backing fabric) and was headquarters for several of its leading manufacturers. With Carl serving as the CEO of Beaulieu of America, the Bouckaerts decided to provide a different product and used their new facility to make woven polypropylene Oriental rugs.

At the time, the market for woven polypropylene rugs was small (less than $1 million in annual retail sales through Sears, Roebuck and Company), but the Bouckaerts trusted in the Beaulieu vision that DeClerck expected them to fulfill. By 1981 the company was strong enough to begin producing its own polypropylene yarn. Beaulieu's Belgian forebear also manufactured its own yarn, but producing fabric was still a novelty for U.S. carpet manufacturers. It took Beaulieu of America several years to perfect the process and adapt it to the hot Georgia climate.

EXPANSION AND ACQUISITIONS

Once Beaulieu had successfully extruded its own yarns, it began producing enough to sell to other carpet

COMPANY PERSPECTIVES

Where Innovation Meets Inspiration.

makers. By 1984 Beaulieu opened a second facility (in Chatsworth, Georgia), and in 1987 it increased its yarn production capacity by adding a plant in Bridgeport, Alabama, that produced nylon polymers and yarn.

One of Beaulieu's customers, Ed Ralston, owner of D & W Carpets, went into partnership with the Bouckaerts. In 1988 the Bouckaerts and Ralston purchased Conquest Carpet Mills, which began to use Beaulieu yarns in its carpets. The partners then acquired three additional competitors in Dalton and another in Chatsworth. Beaulieu's 1990 attempt at a hostile takeover of Horizon Industries was thwarted by Horizon stockholders, but shortly thereafter the company acquired Coronet Carpets, the seventh-ranked organization in the industry, and Coronet Canada, the second-largest carpet manufacturer in Canada.

As part of a joint venture formed in 1988, Beaulieu created Epsilon Products to produce polypropylene resin. The resin, used in the production of carpet yarn as well as in the automotive and packaging industries, provided another element in the Beaulieu vertical integration strategy. By 1993 Beaulieu of America had annual sales of $752 million, second in the industry, from its manufacture of resin, yarns, and backing for its own products as well as for other carpet makers, as well as from its manufacture of finished residential and commercial broadloom and rugs.

In 1993 Ralston sold out his interest in Beaulieu while remaining its chief operating officer for four more years. The company continued to expand throughout the world, acquiring an Australian carpet maker, Sterling Carpet Mills, and creating Beaulieu Australia in 1995. In 1998 Beaulieu purchased Peerless Carpet Corporation, further increasing its Beaulieu Canada holdings and making it the largest carpet manufacturer in Canada. Beaulieu had $1.5 billion in revenue that year.

In the beginning of 1999, Beaulieu acquired Columbus Mills and Marglen Industries and created a new residential sales and service structure based on the company's distribution networks: independent retailers, mass marketers, and home centers. This strategy supported teams that could sell the full range of Beaulieu products to a specific distribution channel rather than focusing on a small group of products sold to a variety of distributors. Beaulieu expected this effort to enhance its ability to introduce new products successfully and increase customer feedback for product development.

HARD SURFACES AND HARD TIMES

In late 1999 Beaulieu decided to add hard surface floor coverings to its soft surface products, making it the most comprehensive and integrated flooring organization in the United States. It purchased Pro Group Holdings, with its subsidiaries L. D. Brinkman, the largest hard surface distributor in the United States, and Hollytex, Inc., a top-end carpet manufacturer. After these acquisitions, the Beaulieu offerings included wood, laminate, vinyl, and ceramic tile. The company had a nationwide distribution network for all its products, from resins to finished flooring.

Beaulieu's vigorous expansion moves in the late 1990s left the company with extensive debts. According to Carl Bouckaert, in *U.S. Business Review* in January 2006, "a bad acquisition in 1999 plagued the company for almost four years." The company also agreed to pay $8.7 million in settling a class-action suit that alleged carpet price fixing with other industry leaders. Rretail demand slowed in early 2000, and the cost of the raw materials for fiber production, including petroleum, increased. The company defaulted on its loan payments.

Beaulieu was estimated to have lost close to 20 percent of its sales volume in 2001, and the company's dramatic downturn required dramatic measures. Beaulieu implemented a drastic reorganization plan, cutting both the product line and sales force in half, reducing inventory by $129 million, and making significant reductions in its marketing budget. At first it attempted some consolidation, limiting its hard surface distribution to the West and Southwest and closing 30 hard flooring warehouses. However, Beaulieu finally divested L. D. Brinkman entirely and returned the hard surface flooring business to its former shareholders.

In addition to eliminating hard surface flooring from its product line, Beaulieu decided to concentrate its core business on broadloom carpets. In January 2002 the company sold its area rug business to Springs Industries and part of its fiber production to Shaw Industries, one of its chief competitors. By February 2002 the company had reduced its debt and begun making a profit. Beaulieu divested itself of ambitions to be the largest floor covering supplier as it shed its acquisitions. Chief operating officer and president of Beaulieu's residential division, Ralph Boe, who was hired in 2001 in the midst of Beaulieu's financial crisis, told *National Floor Trends* in January 2003, "It's not

KEY DATES

1978: Beaulieu of America is founded in Dalton, Georgia.
1981: Yarn extrusion production begins.
1999: Beaulieu acquires Pro Group Holdings.
2002: Beaulieu consolidates and focuses on broadloom carpets.
2007: Beaulieu launches Bliss product line.

important to be the biggest, but it is important to be the best."

INNOVATION, GROWTH, AND TAX TROUBLES

Even while distressed by the failure of its foray into hard surface flooring, Beaulieu continued developing processes and products that supported its reputation for innovation, begun when it initially decided to produce its own yarn. In 2000 Beaulieu, which already used recycled polyethylene terephthalate (PET) in manufacturing its yarns, had joined with the Turner Foundation to support an effort at doubling the bottling recycling rate. The company then introduced Nexterra carpet tiles, consisting of 85 percent recycled materials. In 2003 it introduced Magic Fresh, a carpet treatment aimed at reducing smells from pets, common household odors, and tobacco. It then launched training programs for carpet installers, updated its Internet access for customers, introduced a rewards incentive program for retailers, and developed a consumer financing program.

By 2005 the company's profits were increasing again, its bottom line had improved by 10 percent, and the Beaulieu Group had become the third-largest carpet manufacturer in the world. Beaulieu's annual sales were greater than $1 billion by 2007, but its troubles were not over. After an investigation that had lasted more than 10 years, Beaulieu pleaded guilty to filing a false tax return and agreed to pay taxes and fines totaling over $32 million. Part of the plea agreement required Mieke and Carl Bouckaert to relinquish their roles in the daily operations of the company, although they retained their positions on the board of directors. No individuals were charged with any crimes, but Beaulieu was placed on probation for five years.

NEW DIRECTIONS

Despite management shifts, Beaulieu maintained its focus on carpeting as its core business and continuing its environmentally friendly policies. These included powering plants with wind power, practicing strong pollution prevention measures, and using recycled materials in manufacturing its products.

In 2007 the company decided to target a new customer base. Based on extensive consumer focus groups, the company launched the Bliss carpet line, created to appeal specifically to women as well as respond to the health concerns that had boosted the sales of wood flooring. The new carpet line added fashionable styles to its classic look by using new dyes, new fibers, and new patterns. It included antimicrobial technology to reduce the growth of stain-causing bacteria, mold, and mildew and was certified with Green Label Plus for low volatile organic compound (VOC) emissions. It also combined stain-resistant and odor-reducing treatments. The Bliss line also was marketed with new user-friendly sales tools. Bliss was designed to be the new Beaulieu flagship product.

Although 2009 was challenging for the flooring industry as new home sales and consumer spending were seriously affected by the difficult economy, Beaulieu maintained its optimistic view. The company instituted economies, including employee furloughs, that kept plants open while reducing costs. Sherwin-Williams, preeminent in the property-management field, named Beaulieu its supplier of the year. With its new female-focused marketing strategy, Beaulieu gained 0.6 percent market share during that time and ended the year with 11.5 percent of carpet industry sales.

Beaulieu chose to expand its business through collaboration rather than acquisition. In an alliance with Armstrong World Industries, a highly recognized name in flooring, Beaulieu carpets began manufacturing and marketing carpets using the Armstrong brand. This partnership, which combined Armstrong's hard surface products with Beaulieu's carpets, provided streamlined purchasing for builders and buyers and created, in a new way, a single source for all flooring needs.

By 2010 Beaulieu was expanding its extrusion operations and added 50 new jobs. According to President and CEO Boe in *National Floor Trends* in January 2010, "We will continue to uncover new opportunities, show our customers we value their business, and continue to give them product, merchandising, and promotional reasons to do business with Beaulieu."

Grace Murphy

PRINCIPAL SUBSIDIARIES

Beaulieu Canada; Beaulieu Australia.

PRINCIPAL DIVISIONS

Residential Carpet; Commercial Carpet; Fibers and Fabrics: International.

PRINCIPAL COMPETITORS

Interface, Inc.; Mohawk Industries; Shaw Industries; Dixie Group; Milliken.

FURTHER READING

Boe, Ralph. "2010 Industry Outlook: Beaulieu of America—Ralph Boe Speaks about His Company's Services." *National Floor Trends*, January 2010.

Bond, Patti. "Dalton's Beaulieu Buys Two Texas Companies." *Atlanta Journal-Constitution*, December 14, 1999.

Broadhurst, Mike. "Its Operations Retooled, Beaulieu Readies Debut of New High-Performance Carpet Line." *National Floor Trends*, January 2003.

"Carpeting Success: Beaulieu Group Has Become the Third-Largest Carpet Manufacturer in the World—The Company Has a History of Innovation and Acquisitions." *U.S. Business Review*, January 2006.

Deaton, Thomas M. *Bedspreads to Broadloom*. Acton, MA: Tapestry Press, 1993.

Dunham, Stacey. "Beaulieu of America." *HFN: The Weekly Newspaper for the Home Furnishing Network*, June 14, 1999.

Hucal, Michelle. "Negative Waste, Clean Energy, Green Carpet: Beaulieu Commercial's Carpet Manufacturing and Recycling Plants Are Powered by Wind, Inspired by Sustainable Initiatives." *Environmental Design & Construction*, July 2008.

Jackson, Kelly. "Tax Breaks Sought for Beaulieu Expansion." *Chattanooga Times/Free Press*, January 4, 2010.

Smith, Ellis. "Beaulieu Rolls Out Bliss." *Chattanooga Times/Free Press*, June 13, 2010.

White, Jennifer. "Beaulieu Residential to Quit Hard Surface Business." *HFN: The Weekly Newspaper for the Home Furnishing Network*, March 18, 2002.

BELKIN®

Belkin International, Inc.

12045 East Waterfront Drive
Playa Vista, California 90094-2536
U.S.A.
Telephone: (310) 751-5100
Toll Free: (800) 223-5546
Fax: (310) 898-1111
Web site: http://www.belkin.com

Private Company
Founded: 1983
Incorporated: 1985 as Belkin Components
Employees: 1,000
Sales: $1.35 billion (2009 est.)
NAICS: 334290 Other Communications Equipment Manufacturing; 334419 Other Electronic Component Manufacturing; 335311 Power, Distribution, and Specialty Transformer Manufacturing; 335911 Storage Battery Manufacturing; 335931 Current-Carrying Wiring Device Manufacturing

■ ■ ■

Belkin International, Inc., designs, manufacturers, and supplies consumer electronics–related wares, specializing in electronic connectivity and power products. The company operates both in the commercial business-to-business and consumer markets, selling its products worldwide through an online store, commercial resellers, retailers, and distributors. Belkin's product lines include universal serial bus (USB) and computer-networking hubs; cables; surge protectors; switches; routers; upgrade cards; server room and rack mounts; liquid-crystal-display rack-mount consoles; cabled and desktop keyboard, video display unit, and mouse (KVM) solutions; iPod and iPhone accessories; laptop and notebook accessories; MP3-device accessories; home-theater networking products; and media-player accessories. The company has offices in Europe, Latin America, the Asia-Pacific region, and Africa, including locations in the United Kingdom, Australia, China, Germany, the Netherlands, and the United Arab Emirates.

COMPANY ORIGINS

Belkin was founded by Chet Pipkin in Hawthorne, California, in 1983. Pipkin enjoyed fiddling with engines, televisions, and radios, and while attending the University of California, Los Angeles (UCLA), he worked part time for a firm that supplied connector components for military electronics. During this time, Pipkin recognized the value in identifying niche markets and filling a need in those markets. While still a student, he visited computer dealers and found out that some were so dissatisfied with products they had purchased that they turned to building computer cables themselves. Others complained of steep prices and long wait times for merchandise. In 1981 Pipkin dropped out of UCLA to start his own business; his first product was computer cables.

Initially, Pipkin's work space was the kitchen table in his parents' home in Hawthorne. Then he moved out into the garage and driveway. Erroneously thinking there was not much money to be made in cables, his

COMPANY PERSPECTIVES

Belkin is a leader-driven technology innovator in its various product lines, consistently expanding into new and groundbreaking global markets. We strive for leadership in technology, market share, production, and fill rate. We do this while maintaining a solid financial foundation and the highest standards of quality, integrity, and customer service. Our culture exemplifies the diversity of the world in which we operate. It consists of talented professionals who are eager to excel, who are rewarded for individual effort, and who comprise our successful specialized teams.

initial goal was simply to build enough profit to fund a business that would sell high-end computer products. Pipkin later admitted that he did not choose the electronics industry because of any affinity with computers. As he told the *Los Angeles Business Journal* in 1998, computers "don't do anything for me. I could just as easily be selling any other product on the face of the earth."

Pipkin began putting together computer cables with a makeshift staff that included his machinist father, brother, girlfriend-later-turned-wife, and friend Steve Bellow. The company was named for Bellow and Pipkin, being a combination of the first three letters of Bellow's name and the last three letters of Pipkin's name. Pipkin's father, Chester, designed and then built some of the firm's early cable-making machines to avoid what would have otherwise been a considerable outlay of cash to purchase them. In 1982 Pipkin rented office space, and the next year he established Belkin. The company's early customers were local, mostly independent, computer shops. For its first year in business, Belkin logged an admirable $178,000. For a while, Belkin focused on copper cable assemblies.

As one of hundreds of cable-making companies in a crowded and fragmented U.S. market, the business struggled during its early years. The company occasionally had a tight balance sheet and had to negotiate with suppliers to make ends meet. Belkin's earliest customers were largely value-added resellers (VARs), which in turn serviced information technology departments of other firms, usually businesses and corporate offices, often outfitting their operations with computers for the first time.

INTERNATIONAL DISTRIBUTION AND EARLY GROWTH

In 1985 the company was incorporated as Belkin Components. It was that year that Ingram Micro Inc. of Santa Ana, California, an international distributor, added Belkin products to its catalog. Inclusion in Ingram's catalog established Belkin as a quality supplier of cables.

In 1988 Belkin was listed as number 112 on the *Inc.* 500 list, a ranking exclusively for U.S.-headquartered private, independent companies based on percentage of revenue growth over a three-year period. As the computer industry grew, however, so did the competition among computer accessory companies. Belkin found itself in a tightening market, and Pipkin believed he needed to develop a business strategy beyond computer cables in order to survive and expand.

From the company's beginning, Pipkin worked to identify emerging niche markets and fill needs with quality products. Belkin showed an interest in Apple products as early as 1989 as the market for connectivity products just began to grow. That year, Belkin debuted a media filter that allowed Apple's TokenTalk card to be connected through IBM-type cabling. The TokenTalk card enabled Macintosh II computers to interact with personal computers (PCs) connected in an IBM token-ring network, and the filter helped facilitate this connection.

THE NINETIES: NEW PRODUCT LINES AND INITIAL PRODUCTION FACILITIES

As Belkin's business began to expand, Pipkin tried his hand at myriad other cables that connected computers to peripheral devices. In the early 1990s, Belkin added additional product lines, including surge protectors, keyboard pads, and peripheral-sharing devices. In 1992 Belkin introduced its first printer-sharing device, which allowed multiple computers to use one printer. This product was part of the company's line of "intelligent printer sharing devices" called Sprinter II.

During the mid-1990s, Belkin launched a line of ergonomic accessories, including a mouse pad and wrist support products. In 1995 Belkin debuted a component that could connect up to seven small-computer-system-interface devices to the parallel port of a desktop or laptop computer. The following year, the company launched its Air Metro wireless printer-sharing system.

Belkin set up its first production facility, outside of Hawthorne, in Compton, in the southern Los Angeles County area, which was known for gang violence.

KEY DATES

1983: Belkin is founded by Chet Pipkin.
2002: The company changes its name to Belkin International, Inc.
2006: Belkin surpasses $1 billion in annual sales.
2007: Mark Reynoso is appointed company president.
2010: Reynoso becomes CEO.

Initially, Pipkin was concerned about the city's stigma and his ability to recruit workers. The rent was inexpensive and Compton sat between a Los Angeles airport and two harbors, making it well placed for a company shipping nationally and expanding internationally. Belkin did suffer $100,000 in damage during the riots that followed the Rodney King trial in 1992. The company, though, used this to its advantage. It was offered a sizable tax incentive to stay in Compton when it was ready to expand to larger facilities in 1996. Belkin's subsequent plant was a new 240,000-square-foot facility that employed 350 workers.

INTERNATIONAL EXPANSION AND RAPID SALES GROWTH

Fueling Belkin's expansion was the rapid development and popularity of computers, and the need resulting for cables. Because most computers at the time needed to be plugged into a wall outlet and were probably connected to other machines, cables were essential. Belkin also started to expand internationally, beginning in the mid-1990s with an office in the United Kingdom as a foothold in Europe and with plans to broaden the company's operations into Latin America and then East Asia.

Belkin added cell-phone cables and accessories to its product line in 1997. By the end of the year, Belkin's revenues were nearly $90 million, 70 percent higher than the year before, with cables representing nearly 70 percent of sales. Belkin was supplying major retailers such as Fry's Electronics and Computer City with cables and plugs and also marketing its wares to major international distributors in California, including Ingram Micro and Merisel. To take sales to the next level, Pipkin planned to begin selling directly to original equipment manufacturers (OEMs). Belkin controlled half of the retail PC cable market and hoped to find similar success in the OEM market.

By 1998 Belkin was one of Los Angeles's 100 fastest-growing companies, according to the *Los Angeles Business Journal*, with revenues having grown from $43 million in 1995 to more than $100 million in 1997 and nearly $180 million in 1998. Cable sales continued to dominate the company's business, but Belkin continued to launch new products. For example, in 1998 the company launched a line of products to make old printers compatible with new iMac computers.

In 1999 Belkin acquired the engineering and development company eTEK Labs Inc. of Rochester, New York, which specialized in connectivity. This acquisition dovetailed with Belkin's interest in expanding its research, development, and engineering department, which played an ever-expanding role in company growth.

A NEW CENTURY: NEW MARKETS AND NEW PRODUCTS

Belkin Components opened the new century ranked number 30 on *Inc.*'s Inner City 100, a list of the 100 fastest-growing businesses in the urban centers of the United States. In 2001 Belkin opened an 800,000-square-foot distribution facility in Indiana. That same year, the company acquired Micra Digital Pty Ltd., a leading manufacturer of computer cables, networking merchandise, and phone cables and accessories in Australia. This acquisition in the Asia-Pacific region represented the next step for Belkin's global expansion following its move into Europe.

Pipkin prided himself on observing industry trends and being the first to market with a new product. For example, when the iPod debuted in 2001, Belkin soon followed with a line of iPod accessories that garnered several industry awards and within five years accounted for as much as 20 percent of the company's revenues. During the first years of the 21st century, Belkin also introduced a new line of network interface cards, a hands-free in-car cell-phone kit, a notebook computer security lock, and a USB Ethernet adapter. The company also expanded its line of products for the European game market, debuting a game mouse and an advanced game pad. Belkin in 2002 entered the fledgling Bluetooth market with a line of products that included a mouse, PC cards, USB adapters, PC- and Palm-compatible keyboards, and printer adapters. Just two months after entering the market, Belkin became the leading Bluetooth accessory maker.

Reflecting its increasing global presence, the company changed its name to Belkin International, Inc., in 2002. Between 1998 and 2003, the firm grew at a yearly rate of 285 percent, and by 2003 Belkin had more than 1,000 workers and about $465 million in annual sales. Meanwhile, Belkin had penetrated 80 percent of the small-office and home market for computer cables, was a leading player in the switch-box market, was strong in surge-protector sales, and had entered the market for local-area network mobile-device products and accessories.

In 2004 Belkin added to its market-leading Bluetooth line with the launch of a Bluetooth hands-free headset, a Bluetooth GPS navigation system, and a Bluetooth wireless keyboard and mouse set. The following year, Belkin debuted its Pre-N wireless networking product line, which was designed to support wireless N, a wireless standard in development at the time. Products included a wireless router, a wireless desktop network card, and a wireless notebook card. Belkin in 2005 joined with power-tools manufacturer Stanley Works to produce a line of Stanley-branded extension cords, surge protectors, and power accessories for the outdoors and workshops.

AWARDS AND MANAGEMENT CHANGE

Belkin surpassed the $1 billion mark in annual sales in 2006. By that time, the company had garnered numerous awards in nearly every category for which it created a product. Among the innovative products for which the company had been recognized were Nostromo n52, an all-in-one keyboard and game pad; various TuneBase products, which played MP3s and often included other functions; the MediaPilot, a wireless keyboard with built-in mouse that acted as a universal remote for entertainment and computing electronic devices; various Belkin Pure AV Home Theater Power products; iPod accessories; and a KVM switch, which controlled numerous computers at once.

By 2007 Belkin was a world leader in its field of connectivity and power products with 1,300 employees, and the company had achieved 25 consecutive years of record-breaking revenue growth. Belkin had European offices in the United Kingdom, Germany, and the Netherlands, as well as Asia-Pacific offices in Australia and China and a regional headquarters in Hong Kong. After nearly 25 years with complete control of his company, Pipkin in 2007 turned over the company presidency to Mark Reynoso while remaining CEO and chairman. Reynoso, a former vice president of marketing and sales, had been with Belkin since 1996.

MARKET EXPANSION

In 2007 Jumpnode, a leader in appliance-enabled software (AeS), signed an OEM agreement with Belkin. Initially, the corporate alliance was designed to produce Pulse, a network monitoring and remote access device for small and medium-sized businesses that used Jumpnode's AeS platform. The platform integrated an appliance on site at a business with hosted software to allow for network monitoring.

Belkin hoped that products such as Pulse would carve out a new market for network monitoring and remote access products for small to medium-sized businesses, and in 2007 the company began sharpening its focus on the commercial market and targeting smaller VARs. The VAR market represented only 30 percent of company sales, a figure that the company wanted to see rise to 50 percent because of the commercial market's growth potential. To that end, the company expanded its field sales representative force to sell high-end products such as Pulse.

Belkin in 2007 also signed a deal with Bell Microproducts Inc., one of the world's largest distributors of computing technology and storage products. Bell agreed to distribute Belkin's entire line of 40,000 products in the United States and Canada. Bell also began using Belkin products at its integration centers and offered them to its network of resellers, expecting Belkin's wares to help Bell become a one-stop store for consumers' storage needs.

PARTNERSHIPS AND NEW PRODUCTS

Belkin used several partnerships to launch new products during this period. For the gaming market, the company in 2007 rolled out its n52te, an improved gaming keyboard powered by Razer software. Belkin also joined with Eastman Kodak Company to release a Bluetooth USB adapter that wirelessly saved, printed, and transmitted photos from camera phone to PC using Kodak technology. Belkin partnered with Amimon, Inc., a supplier of technology for the wireless transmission of high-definition (HD) video, to jointly build a device able to wirelessly deliver HD content from an HD video source device to HD televisions. Belkin also joined with Ingram Micro to improve the Belkin-produced V-7 cables, originally released in 2007. The new V-7 was designed to provide a greater variety of cable capabilities. In addition, the company released a desktop phone for Skype that made free Skype Internet calls without the need for turning on a computer, as well as an Ethernet desktop and wall-plug adapter, based on Intellon Corporation's plug technology, which could be used in North America and abroad.

Among other product introductions around this time, Belkin's power products, particularly its line of

Conserve products, proved very popular with industry critics and consumers. This line included the eight-outlet Conserve surge protector, a clamp-on surge protector, and a compact surge protector. Belkin in 2009 announced it would establish 45 service centers in India, including ones in Thiruvananthapuram and Kochi. The center openings were part of Belkin's ongoing global expansion and its concerted push into Asian territories.

NEW CEO, NEW HEADQUARTERS

Reynoso was promoted to the additional position of CEO in January 2010, succeeding Pipkin who remained chairman. Reynoso was charged with continuing to guide product development creation and take Belkin to the ranks of a multibillion-dollar firm. Also in 2010, Belkin left Compton and moved into a newly built 150,000-square-foot headquarters in the Playa Vista area of Los Angeles. The new facility housed all of Belkin's administrative, research and design, product development, marketing, and sales operations.

In early 2010 Belkin (which had been the first consumer electronics maker to capitalize on iPod accessories) unveiled an initial line of products designed to take advantage of the release of Apple's iPad tablet computer. The products included three sleeves to protect the computer from getting scratched.

Belkin beefed up its energy-conservation portfolio in 2010, acquiring Zensi, a leader in energy sensing and monitoring technology. The acquisition was part of the company's strategy to expand its Conserve energy-management product line. Previously focusing primarily on the office, Belkin planned a late 2010 rollout of additional economical Conserve products for the home. The Zensi purchase included patent-pending licenses for technology developed at the University of Washington and Georgia Institute of Technology. Kevin Ashton, a cofounder of Zensi who had served as the firm's CEO, was named general manager of a newly formed Conserve business unit. Belkin also made a substantial investment in Juice Technologies, a supplier of energy-optimization products, battery-charging technology, and plug-in hybrid-electric vehicle technology. The investment provided further evidence that Belkin was committed to an increased focus on energy-management products.

Midway through 2010, Belkin appeared well positioned to maintain market dominance in its well-carved-out niches. At the same time, the company was expanding into the energy-conservation market. Belkin was also actively expanding its global footprint, with plans in place for the Middle East, North Africa, and South Africa in the near term, as well as continued expansion of operations in Europe and the Asia-Pacific region.

What initially made Belkin successful was its ability to identify, before other companies, emerging niche markets, be out in front of product development and product release for those markets, and then dominate sales within those niches. With Pipkin gradually turning over product development activities and executive oversight of day-to-day operations to Reynoso, it appeared that much of Belkin's future success in niche markets was left for Reynoso to chart.

Roger Rouland

PRINCIPAL SUBSIDIARIES

Belkin Business Systems Inc.; Belkin Consulting Inc.; Belkin Corporation; Belkin Inc.; Belkin Limited (Australia); Belkin Components B.V. (Belgium); Belkin Trading (Shanghai) Company Ltd. (China); Belkin s.r.o. (Czech Republic); Belkin SAS (France); Belkin GmbH (Germany); Belkin Asia Pacific Limited (Hong Kong); Belkin India Pvt. Ltd.; Belkin K.K. (Japan); Belkin B.V. (Netherlands); Belkin Coöperatief UA (Netherlands); Belkin New Zealand Ltd.; Belkin Pte. Limited (Singapore); Belkin EMEA S.L. (Spain); Belkin Sàrl (Switzerland); Belkin Ltd. (United Arab Emirates); Belkin Limited (UK).

PRINCIPAL COMPETITORS

Cisco Systems, Inc.; D-Link Corporation; NETGEAR, Inc.

FURTHER READING

"Belkin Components Acquires Australia's Micra Digital." *AsiaPulse News*, January 29, 2001, 339.

Cassano, Erik. "CEO Chet Pipkin Shares the Secrets behind Belkin Corp.'s Success." *Smart Business Los Angeles*, August 2006.

Cole, Benjamin Mark. "A Real Cable Guy: Chet Pipkin Has Used His Love of Tinkering to Build a $90 Million-and-Growing Computer Accessories Empire." *Los Angeles Business Journal*, March 17, 1997, 12.

Fenn, Donna. "A Business Grows Straight Outta Compton." *Inc. Online*, May 1, 2003. Accessed November 8, 2010. http://www.inc.com/magazine/20030501/25437.html.

Rosenfeld, Jill. "Belkin Components Chief Constantly Looks to Future." *Los Angeles Business Journal*, November 16, 1998, 36.

Black Diamond Equipment, Ltd.

2084 East 3900 South
Salt Lake City, Utah 84124
U.S.A.
Telephone: (801) 278-5552
Fax: (801) 278-5544
Web site: http://www.blackdiamondequipment.com

Public Company
Founded: 1989
Incorporated: 1991
Employees: 475
Sales: $92 million (2009)
Stock Exchanges: NASDAQ
Ticker Symbol: BDE
NAICS: 339920 Sporting and Athletic Goods Manufacturing; 423910 Sporting and Recreational Goods and Supplies Merchant Wholesalers

■ ■ ■

Headquartered in Salt Lake City, Utah, Black Diamond Equipment, Ltd., specializes in designing and manufacturing mountaineering and backcountry skiing gear. Its products include crampons, ice picks, ice screws, pitons, carabiners, backpacks, gloves, helmets, headlamps, telemark skis and bindings, and the AvaLung II, an avalanche safety device. Black Diamond has 475 employees worldwide, and most are exceptionally skilled and enthusiastic users of Black Diamond products. The company operates manufacturing plants in Salt Lake City and China, a distribution center in Germany, and a sales and marketing office in Switzerland. In 2010 the investing group Clarus Corporation acquired Black Diamond and took the company public.

ORIGINS

Black Diamond Equipment, Ltd., was formed on December 1, 1989, by 40 former employees of Chouinard Equipment, a bankrupt manufacturer of rock-climbing equipment in California. The employees acquired the assets of their one-time employer in a leveraged buyout structured as an employee ownership plan. Financial support also came from rope supplier Michael Beal and Japanese distributor Naoe Sakashita. One of the cofounders was Peter Metcalf, formerly the general manager of Chouinard Equipment. Metcalf became president and chief executive officer (CEO) of the newly formed company.

In 1991 Black Diamond Equipment established its headquarters in Salt Lake City, Utah. The company paid a little over $1 million for a seven-acre property where it located its offices, manufacturing, warehousing, and an outlet store. The new location offered a convenient testing ground for climbing and skiing gear, as well as access to knowledgeable experts in relevant sports. Black Diamond had 48 employees and revenues of $7 million in its first year. About one-third of sales came from backcountry skiing products.

Most of Black Diamond's climbing equipment was produced at its Salt Lake City headquarters, while facilities in Italy supplied shoes, boots, and ropes, and a

COMPANY PERSPECTIVES

We're a company of users—it's who we are. We're the greatest dreamers about what could be, and the harshest of critics about what exists and because of this—the creation of Black Diamond is a process which will never end. The company today is more committed than ever, thanks to the many people here in the U.S., at Black Diamond Europe and at Black Diamond Asia whose limitless energy and hands-on involvement have created a promising future for all climbers and skiers worldwide.

Texas subcontractor, Flatland Mountaineering, produced climbing harnesses. The company hired another Utah firm, Chums Ltd., to install custom automation equipment to speed up its carabiner production in 1992. Also in 1992 Black Diamond developed a line of plastic telemark ski boots, called Terminator, in conjunction with SCARPA of Italy. Sales grew quickly in the early 1990s, exceeding $20 million in 1995.

CONTINUED GROWTH

Black Diamond also grew quickly in the 1990s, expanding its range of products, particularly those related to backcountry skiing gear, through acquisitions. In 1996 it acquired Bibler Tents, a high-altitude tent-making company, and moved manufacturing of the tents from Boulder, Colorado, to the Salt Lake City headquarters. In 1998 the company acquired Franklin Climbing Equipment, a small, eight-person maker of holds for climbing walls based in Seattle.. In 1998 it acquired Ascension, a maker of climbing skins (a product that is attached to skis to provide traction when scaling slopes), moving production to Salt Lake City as well. By the end of the decade, Black Diamond had 250 employees and annual revenues of $30 million.

In 2000 Black Diamond began leasing a new warehouse in Salt Lake City's Ninigret Park. It also updated its electronic distribution systems. The following year the company began selling LED headlamps designed for backpackers as well as climbers and skiers. These soon became one of Black Diamond's best-selling items. In 2002 the company made another acquisition: Skye Alpine Inc., a manufacturer of ski bindings and climbing skins.

THE AVALUNG AND PRODUCT SAFETY

In October 1999 Alex Lowe, a Black Diamond employee, died in an avalanche. Lowe, dubbed the world's best climber by *Outside Magazine* shortly before his death, and other Black Diamond employees had been known to rise in the wee hours of the morning to hit the backcountry slopes before work. Several other Black Diamond employees had been lost to avalanches over the years, so it was natural for the company to focus on developing an avalanche safety device. The AvaLung debuted in 1999.

The AvaLung, invented by psychiatry professor and backcountry skiing enthusiast Tom Crowley, was a vest with a network of porous tubes that deployed in the event of an avalanche, allowing the user to breathe air from the snowpack. Black Diamond spent $500,000 making the design practical. The first version, retailing between $200 and $300, was not a big seller. The lighter, smaller, and, at $100, less expensive AvaLung II was introduced in 2001. It was credited with saving a skier trapped for half an hour under five feet of snow in February 2002.

The seriousness of Black Diamond's approach to product design and quality control stemmed from its clear awareness that climbers and other athletes depended on its equipment for survival and that product failure could easily lead to fatalities. The company voluntarily recalled several products, such as the lithium ion batteries for its headlamps in 2004 and a speed buckle harness in 2006, although no incidents had been reported. Meanwhile, the company continued to roll out new products, such as an extensive line of Freeride skis in 2007. In 2008 Black Diamond earned the safety certification of the International Mountaineering and Climbing Federation, the industry's highest standard.

THE CLARUS DEAL AND GOING PUBLIC

In the 2000s Black Diamond continued to experience consistent revenue growth primarily through word-of-mouth marketing and a business model emphasizing vertical integration, controlling rather than outsourcing every element of product design, development, manufacture, testing, and distribution. In 2004 the company took a major step toward expansion by launching an Asian subsidiary, which was fully operational two years later. Black Diamond Asia is a wholly owned factory and global distribution center in Zhuhai, China, staffed by company employees and operated according to the same procedures and quality

KEY DATES

1989: Peter Metcalf and 39 cofounders establish Black Diamond Equipment, Ltd., from bankrupt Chouinard Equipment.
1991: Black Diamond opens its headquarters in Salt Lake City, Utah.
1992: The company develops the Terminator ski boot with SCARPA of Italy.
1996: Black Diamond acquires Bibler Tents.
1998: Black Diamond acquires Franklin Climbing Equipment.
2000: The company introduces LED headlamps.
2001: The company introduces AvaLung II.
2004: Black Diamond opens a factory in Zhuhai, China.
2010: Clarus Corporation acquires Black Diamond and Gregory Mountain Products; the new corporate entity goes public.

control standards as the home facility in Utah. The company also employed more than 150 people in Europe, with a sales and marketing office in Reinach, Switzerland, which opened in 1996.

By 2009 Black Diamond's annual revenue reached $92 million, an average growth rate of around 15 percent per year since 1989. CEO Peter Metcalf wanted to continue to grow the company, but Black Diamond's core market was relatively limited, consisting of the most serious practitioners of some of the world's most rugged athletic pursuits. Expanding to appeal to a broader customer base would require more money. As reported by the Associated Press on May 11, 2010, Metcalf commented, "We haven't put capital into this business since I started it in 1989." He quickly found a solution to this dilemma, however.

Black Diamond found a buyer in the Clarus Corporation, a Connecticut-based investing group. Clarus had no business operations of its own but held cash reserves from the sale of a software company it formerly owned. In a $135-million deal, Clarus acquired both Black Diamond and a smaller outfit, Gregory Mountain Products of Sacramento, California. Gregory's speciality, sophisticated mountaineering backpacks, was not part of Black Diamond's catalog of products.

Peter Metcalf became president and CEO of the new publicly traded company, while Warren B. Kanders of Clarus served as chairman of the board. Clarus moved its offices to Black Diamond's headquarters in Salt Lake City and intended to change its name to Black Diamond Equipment. Clarus (BDE) began trading on the NASDAQ on June 11, 2010. Metcalf expressed optimism that the acquisition would unleash Black Diamond as a force on the global market without compromising the company's ethical integrity and unique way of doing business. "Corporate social responsibility is linked with our mandate as a public company to create value for our stockholders," Metcalf said when the deal was completed on June 1, as reported on that same date by *Business Wire*. "We will expand selectively and deliberately in relevant markets and appropriate tiers of distribution. For Black Diamond, growth is not an end in itself, but is a means to accomplishing greater goals."

Frederick C. Ingram
Updated, Roger K. Smith

PRINCIPAL SUBSIDIARIES

Black Diamond Equipment AG (Switzerland); Black Diamond Equipment Asia.

PRINCIPAL DIVISIONS

Ascension Enterprises; Beal Ropes; Bibler Tents; Franklin Climbing Equipment; Scarpa Mountain Boots.

PRINCIPAL COMPETITORS

Backcountry Access, Inc.; K2 Inc.; Metolius Climbing, Inc.; Mountain Hardwear Inc.; Petzl; Skis Rossignol S.A.; Voilé Mountain Equipment.

FURTHER READING

Blum, Jonathan. "Black Diamond's Death-Defying Revenue Climb." *Fortune Small Business*, November 21, 2008.

Boulton, Guy. "AvaLung Might Be a Lifesaver in Avalanche." *Denver Post*, October 13, 2002.

Foy, Paul. "Utah Gear Maker Black Diamond to Go Public, Join with Another Company." Associated Press, May 11, 2010.

Gorrell, Mike. "Black Diamond's New Line Built for Backcountry and Resorts." *Salt Lake Tribune*, January 21, 2007.

McHugh, Paul. "The Retooling of Chouinard Equipment." *San Francisco Chronicle*, March 19, 1990.

Metcalf, Peter. "Lessons Learned (How a Mountain Climbing Experience Helped Build a Business)." *Inc.*, April 1, 1995, 35.

Osborne, Steve, and Kristina Kunzi. "Adventure Capitalists," *Utah Business*, May 2001, 30.

Thalman, James. "Recent Mergers Will Lead to Salt Lake Growth for Black Diamond." *Deseret News*, August 17, 2010.

Van De Mark, Donald, and Susan Lisovicz. "Mt. Climbing Mogul." *CNNfn: Business Unusual*, February 10, 1998.

Venn, Tamsin. "Employees to Buy Chouinard." *STN*, August 1, 1989, 4.

Blue Nile, Inc.

705 Fifth Avenue South, Suite 900
Seattle, Washington 98104
U.S.A.
Telephone: (206) 336-6700
Toll Free: (800) 242-2728
Fax: (206) 336-7950
Web site: http://www.bluenile.com

Public Company
*Founded:*1999
Employees: 190
Sales: $302.1 million (2009)
Stock Exchanges: NASDAQ
Ticker Symbol: NILE
NAICS: 448310 Jewelry Stores; 423940 Jewelry, Watch, Precious Stone, and Precious Metal Merchant Wholesalers

■ ■ ■

Mark Vadon, founder of Blue Nile, Inc., considered himself intelligent, discerning, and in complete control of his life. When he began to shop for an engagement ring, however, he was in over his head. To the well-educated Vadon, the choices were endless and confusing, due in large part to the commission-based sales of local jewelry retailers. With thousands of dollars at stake, a consumer needed to know if salespersons were truly being honest about the diamonds they were selling. Unwilling and unable to put his trust in traditional jewelry stores, Vadon turned to the Internet for help. What he found was the aptly named Internet Diamonds Web site. The rest, as they say, is history. Internet Diamonds was reborn as Blue Nile, Inc., in 1999 and quickly established itself as the Internet's largest online source for diamonds and fine jewelry.

FOUNDING: 1999

Mark Vadon attended Harvard University, where he received undergraduate degrees in American history and European social theory, then went on to Stanford University for his MBA. He then became a "Bainie" working in the San Francisco office of Bain & Company, the well known management consulting firm, in 1992. Vadon worked as a consumer products strategist, which proved invaluable in his later endeavors. He was still employed as at Bain when he began looking for an engagement ring in 1998.

After giving up on traditional retail jewelers and disingenuous salespersons, Vadon started surfing the web. He found an informative site called Internet Diamonds, which featured detailed descriptions of various diamonds and a toll-free number to call for assistance. Vadon found what he considered an outstanding engagement ring at an excellent price. He was so impressed by the online experience, and its business potential, that he contacted the site's owner, Doug Williams, a diamond wholesaler based in Seattle, Washington. Vadon flew to Seattle, met with Williams, and expressed an interest in buying the diamond website.

Vadon returned to San Francisco and met with a number of venture capitalists. By late spring 1999 the 29-year-old Vadon had raised an initial $6 million in

COMPANY PERSPECTIVES

We started our business in 1999 with a mission of creating a better way for consumers to purchase diamonds and fine jewelry. Since that time, we have only become more convinced of the value of the core tenets of our customer proposition—vast selection, high quality products at a tremendous value, customization, convenience, and, of great importance to our customers, education and guidance. Blue Nile empowers consumers with transparency and in-depth product information that put them in control of the purchase experience.

funds, selling his idea with relative ease in the dot-com boom. Vadon then lined up suppliers and distributors and turned Internet Diamonds into a full-service, user-friendly online store to sell baubles to bachelors.

After sealing the deal in May 1999, Vadon renamed the fledgling company "Blue Nile," which he considered more in tune with his goals for the online jeweler. Within a few months Vadon had raised a $32 million infusion of capital for Blue Nile, $10 million of which went into a major marketing effort launched in November. The massive print and television campaign was created by the San Francisco office of Leagas Delaney, which had made a name for itself promoting a host of clients including adidas, Goodyear, Harrods, Hyundai, and watchmaker Patek Phillipe. Most of the campaign went into television advertising and targeted sports-related events, including ABC's *Monday Night Football* and ESPN programming., Sales for Blue Nile's maiden year reached $14 million, while online shopping as a whole racked up total retail sales of almost $26 billion for the same period.

INTERNET SUCCESS DURING THE DOT-COM CRASH

By 2000 the Internet's overcrowding began to thin as dot-coms large and small failed. Blue Nile, however, did not stumble or fall, but rather it flourished. Early in the year Vadon was again raising funds, and one investor of note was Microsoft cofounder Paul Allen's Vulcan Ventures, Inc., which joined a host of well-known firms willing to bank on Blue Nile's future. Part of the funding went into adding new products to Blue Nile's online store while remaining true to its status as a luxury jeweler. Sterling silver trinkets and classy watches (such as Swiss Army, Tag Heuer, Seiko, and Kenneth Cole) joined the Web site's diamonds. Blue Nile was careful, however, not to expand into noncore items and stayed within the bounds of fine jewelry. The addition of the lower-priced sterling silver pieces helped attract customers who could not spend thousands for jewelry. Vadon and his marketing staff also believed silver would attract more women to the Blue Nile site, which still catered primarily to men.

Much of the e-tailer's appeal was its no-nonsense approach to selling. The company's website was divided into simple categories for prospective buyers, with headings for engagement rings, jewelry, watches and accessories, or shopping by specific product (earrings, men's or women's items) or material (such as diamond, pearl, gold, platinum). Yet most impressive about the Blue Nile web shop was its emphasis on information. An educated consumer was Blue Nile's best customer, and a plethora of information was just a mouse click away.

Presented in a straightforward manner under the link "Education," Blue Nile provided online shoppers with subheadings about diamonds, pearls, gemstones, platinum, gold, silver, and even pewter, while its "Buying Guide" was broken down into categories such as engagement rings, necklaces, bracelets, watches, and other fine gifts. Because diamonds were Blue Nile's claim to fame, the diamonds link offered almost everything shoppers would want or need to know about purchasing the ultimate rock, especially under the "Build Your Own Engagement Ring" link and subsequent pages.

ACCOLADES

Blue Nile not only thoroughly covered the famed four Cs of diamond buying (color, clarity, cut, and carat weight) but it also threw in two additional all-important Cs as well: certification and care. Even the labyrinthine grading system of the Gemological Institute of America (GIA) and American Gem Society Laboratories (AGSL) were broken down into simple terms, as every Blue Nile diamond was certified by either the GIA or the AGSL (certificates were available for viewing online).

By the end of 2000 Blue Nile had gained a reputation for excellence and was lauded by business and lifestyle publications, receiving accolades from *Forbes* magazine as a "*Forbes* Favorite" among Internet retailers. It was also voted *Fortune* magazine's "Best of the Web" jewelry site. Blue Nile finished fiscal year 2000 with sales of $44.4 million.

EXPLORING NEW OPTIONS

In 2001 Blue Nile began researching a leap of faith: actual retail stores bearing its name. Despite its begin-

KEY DATES

1999: Blue Nile, Inc., is established in Seattle, Washington, as an online jewelry site.
2002: *Time* magazine names Blue Nile as a "Best Indulgence" in its "Best Website for Business" rankings.
2003: Blue Nile receives Bizrate.com's "Circle of Excellence" Platinum Award.
2004: Blue Nile goes public on the NASDAQ.
2008: Diane Irvine succeeds founder Mark Vadon as CEO.

nings as the antithesis of traditional jewelry retailing, Vadon believed that Blue Nile's three largest markets (New York, San Francisco, and Seattle) might benefit from physical locations. The stores, however, would remain true to Blue Nile's basic business tenets; that is, no commissioned sales staff, no hard sell, and plenty of information and assistance. The pluses to the proposed storefronts included off-the-street impulse buyers, the opportunity for customers to try on jewelry, and the further branding of the Blue Nile name.

Blue Nile's sales and products continued to grow in the spring and summer of 2001. Then came the terrorist attacks against the United States on September 11, 2001, and businesses throughout the United States and abroad suffered. Blue Nile was no exception, yet before the end of the year sales rebounded. Not only were sentimental favorites like engagement rings and engraved lockets in high demand, but also Blue Nile's patriotic sterling silver bracelet, adorned with a flag, sold out several times over. Sales for the online retailer reached $48.7 million for fiscal year 2001.

LARGEST ONLINE JEWELER

More praise came in 2002 from *Time* magazine, when Blue Nile was called "Best Indulgence" from the periodical's "Best Websites for Business" roundup. Blue Nile had not only more than quintupled its sales in a mere three years (from $14 million in 1999 to a phenomenal $72 million for 2002), but also the firm had become the Internet's largest online jeweler, with more than 30,000 independently certified diamonds to choose from and dozens of settings in gold, platinum, and sterling silver to dazzle even the most selective buyer. More significant, at least to many, was the pricing: as much as 20 to 40 percent lower than traditional jewelers, along with free shipping and a 30-day money-back guarantee.

According to a *Time* magazine article in February 2003, online jewelry sales topped $1 billion for 2002 and Blue Nile had become the major player in the virtual jewelry trade. Many Internet shoppers came directly to Blue Nile through its "anchor tenant" agreements with AOL, MSN, and Yahoo!. Shoppers simply had to click a jewelry tab on any of the three browsers to arrive at Blue Nile's home page. The simplicity and effectiveness of Blue Nile's browser links mirrored its matured approach to advertising, favoring less expensive online ads and direct mail over much more expensive ads for television, print, and radio.

In 2003 Blue Nile received a rare commendation from Bizrate.com, the Internet retailing rating service, by earning its "Circle of Excellence" Platinum Award. The Platinum Award denoted the best of the best, in this case the top e-tailers who met a stringent set of criteria. Only 20 Internet retailers were so honored.

Another online rating service, Internet Retailer, declared Blue Nile as its "Best of the Web" recipient in 2003, while Blue Nile also received mentions in a number of national publications, including *Time*, *InStyle*, *Newsweek*, *Fortune*, and *Forbes*. Sales for fiscal year 2003 more than measured up to all the praise at $129 million, making it Blue Nile's best year to that time.

EQUAL-OPPORTUNITY RETAILER

Mark Vadon believed Blue Nile's outstanding success was due in large part to its bucking of the usual retail methods. As he commented to *USA Today* on October 23, 2003, "Everything we do is heresy. Instead of marketing to women, we market to men. Instead of trying to push our gross margins as high as possible, we sell as cheap as we possibly can. Instead of hiding information, we're all about educating our consumer and making him feel comfortable."

Clearly, many men did feel comfortable buying from Blue Nile's well-stocked virtual shelves and turned the relatively young e-tailer into a winner. Women, too, had begun shopping at Blue Nile, and its client base continued to grow, as did the company's headquarters. Blue Nile's 115 employees moved to new office space of more than 20,000 square feet in Seattle.

PUBLIC OFFERING

Blue Nile's rosy picture continued into 2004, the year Vadon led the company to public ownership. Sales were up 79 percent in 2003 and another 49 percent, year-to-year, in early 2004. When the company issued its initial public offering on the NASDAQ in May, investors eagerly snapped up the shares. The share price jumped almost 40 percent on the first day.

In the following years, Blue Nile found increasing success in selling the formerly hard-to-market large diamonds as consumers became more willing to make large jewelry expenditures online. In November 2005 a Blue Nile five-carat diamond solitaire sold for $170,000, followed by a three-carat diamond engagement ring for $114,000. By 2006 the company showed an increase of 72 percent in purchases of $20,000 or more. Blue Nile also started selling expensive pinks, reds, and other colored diamonds, taking advantage of their growing popularity and bringing to a wider public a category hitherto available primarily to a privileged few.

CHANGING OF THE GUARD

A decade after Vadon went online to buy his fiancée's engagement ring, he was ready to step back from running the company that grew out of that experience. In February 2008 he moved to the new position of executive chairman and named longtime associate Diane Irvine to succeed him as CEO and join the small but growing cadre of women who had made it into corporate executive suites. In the fall Blue Nile launched international shipping to 12 new countries in Europe and Asia. Foreign sales had doubled in 2007, more customers worldwide were shopping on the web, and the company had received numerous requests to add more countries to its shipping roster. International commerce had become a permanent part of the Blue Nile business plan.

Cementing Blue Nile's premier status as it entered the post-Vadon leadership period in 2008 was its elevation to *Chain Store Age*'s list of "High Performance Retailers." Blue Nile was number two on the list and was the first Internet company to reach the prestigious list. Inclusion was based partly on growth in revenues from $14 million in the company's first year to $319 million in 2007, a year that saw Blue Nile's net income grow by 34 percent to $17.5 million. Blue Nile had become the nation's second-largest diamond ring merchant after Tiffany's.

NEW MARKETING APPROACHES

Blue Nile continued adding new marketing wrinkles to keep ahead of rivals like Amazon.com and a number of former brick-and-mortar jewelers who were venturing into the online marketing waters. Paradoxically one of its first moves was a step backward, technologically, from the world of pure cybermarketing. In November 2008 Blue Nile launched a personal shopping service whereby customers could consult about their purchases with expert advisers via telephone. The company also introduced an improved online shopping system that allowed customers to choose from more than 150 settings for the stones that they wanted.

In 2009 the entire website and search process were redesigned to give customers a more vivid experience and more detailed information on stones and settings and to allow them for the first time to compare different stones side by side. Later that year Blue Nile enhanced the Web site further with a feature that displayed more than 1,300 rings that other customers had recently designed and purchased.

In September 2010 Blue Nile developed an iPhone application, bringing the capabilities of its powerful Web site search and design tools to the cell phone. The "app" even included a button that activated a telephone contact with one of its personal shopping advisers. To better satisfy the new customers that Blue Nile expected to draw in with these marketing initiatives, in 2010 it increased its selection of available diamonds to more than 73,000 stones.

As evidence that its marketing program was having an impact, Blue Nile reported record-breaking second quarter sales of $76.6 million in 2010, an increase of 9.7 percent year to year. International sales growth was even stronger that quarter, at 28.2 percent (Blue Nile was then available in 40 countries), and the revenues of $9.1 million were also a record. Although consumer demand slowed significantly in June 2010, Blue Nile expected annual sales to reach $325 to $335 million by the end of the year.

Blue Nile's future looked as bright as one of its flawless cut diamonds. Although the recession of 2008–09 had seriously disrupted the retail jewelry sector, it had forced numerous store closures and thereby reduced the company's competition. The expectation was that Blue Nile would continue to flourish, both domestically and internationally. In the company's second quarter 2010 report, CEO Irvine maintained in August that even though consumers overall were pulling back on major purchases, "our competitive position remains stronger than ever .... This positions us well to continue to gain market share in the industry, regardless of overall consumer trends."

Nelson Rhodes
Updated, Judson MacLaury

PRINCIPAL COMPETITORS

Tiffany & Co.; Zale Corporation; Signet; QVC, Inc.; Walmart; DeBeers.

FURTHER READING

Acohido, Byron. "He Turned Web Site in the Rough into Online Jewel." *USA Today*, October 20, 2003.

Beres, Glen A. "Online Jewelers Make Major Strides in Sales, Profit Growth." *Diamond Intelligence Briefs*, January 24, 2003.

"Blue Nile Announces Second Quarter 2010 Financial Results." Blue Nile Press Release, August 5, 2010. Accessed October 7, 2010. http://investor.bluenile.com/releasedetail.cfm?ReleaseID=497000.

Foley, Michael F., and Thomas Melville. "What Men Want." *Success*, April 2001, 20.

Hamilton, Anita. "Click and Clink." *Time*, February 10, 2003.

Kim, Nancy J. "Diamond E-Tailer Aims $10M Ad Blitz at Men." *Puget Sound Business Journal*, November 12, 1999, 10.

Mamer, Karl. "Red Hot Blue Nile." *Luxury Magazine*, Spring 2002.

Markels, Alex. "Baubles and Browsers." *U.S. News & World Report*, September 23, 2002.

Shin, Laura. "These Jewelry Sites Are True Gems." *USA Weekend*, June 15, 2003.

Tice, Carol. "Blue Nile Building Up Steady Current of Sales." *Puget Sound Business Journal*, August 25, 2000, 8.

Burkhart Dental, Inc.

2502 South 78th Street
Tacoma, Washington 98409
U.S.A.
Telephone: (253) 474-7761
Toll Free: (800) 562-8176
Fax: (866) 401-6648
Web site: http://www.burkhartdental.com

Private Company
Founded: 1888 as Tacoma Dental Deport
Incorporated: 1893 as Burkhart Dental Supply
Employees: 360
Sales: $142.8 million (2009)
NAICS: 423450 Dental Equipment and Supplies Merchant Wholesalers; 522220 Leasing in Combination with Sales Financing; 541410 Interior Design Consulting Services; 54161 Management Consulting Services; 611710 Educational Support Services

■ ■ ■

Burkhart Dental, Inc., is one of the top five dental supply companies in the United States, providing dental equipment and supplies to more than 5,000 dental practices. It also offers equipment maintenance and repair, dental office design, dental practice support, consulting, and educational services, as well as finance and leasing services. Burkhart Dental sells its supplies and equipment through sales representatives and online. Based in Tacoma, Washington, and serving 16 states west of the Mississippi River, the company has 18 branch offices and 3 distribution centers. Burkhart Dental, a company that is family owned and operated, has been controlled by the Burkhart family since its founding.

COMPANY ORIGINS: 1888–1910

Burkhart Dental was established by Dr. William E. Burkhart in 1888. Burkhart, who had just launched his dental practice in Tacoma a year earlier, identified a need for providing dentists with necessary supplies in what was becoming a developing region of the Pacific Northwest. Burkhart joined with Dr. Cyrus Van Winter, a friend and fellow dentist, to found the Tacoma Dental Depot in the Mason Block Building.

Burkhart was also an experienced printer and editorial member of the *Archives of Dentistry*, and he decided in 1890 to start his own dental periodical targeting dentists in the Pacific Northwest. Designed to share information on treatments, create a community of dentists, and advertise his company's dental products, the first issue of *Pacific Dental Journal* appeared in 1891. The publication was discontinued in 1897.

In November 1891 Burkhart dissolved his partnership with Van Winter and the company's name was changed to Burkhart Dental Supply. The company was incorporated in 1893. Ever the dental entrepreneur, Burkhart launched the Tacoma College of Dental Surgery that same year. Burkhart served as president of the school and taught operative dentistry until 1895. Three years later, in 1898, the college was relocated to Portland, Oregon, and subsequently became the University of Oregon School of Dentistry.

COMPANY PERSPECTIVES

It is the purpose of Burkhart Dental Supply to provide the dental products, services and information which will enhance the success of the dental profession, and to provide those services with the highest degree of quality, reliability and integrity, to enable all employees of Burkhart Dental Supply to work together to meet this challenge in a secure and rewarding environment for the mutual benefit of the clients of, and the people who are, Burkhart Dental Supply.

During the 1890s Burkhart Dental Supply grew rapidly. Around 1905 Burkhart retired from active practice as a dentist and focused on his supply business. His youngest son, Archie Needham, joined the company in 1910.

WAR YEARS AND NEW GENERATIONS OF BURKHARTS: 1913–54

In 1913 Burkhart Dental Supply moved its headquarters to the 18-story National Realty Building, which was the tallest building west of the Mississippi River. After being elected board secretary in 1916, Archie eventually replaced his father as company president and kept the company in stable condition through the Great Depression. William Burkhart died in 1937.

Burkhart Dental Supply's revenues plummeted during World War II, so the company responded by consolidating its executive offices. In September 1945, just as the war was drawing to a close with the surrender of Japan, Archie died at the age of 53. Archie's death meant that his two sons, Everett and Perry, who were both naval officers serving in the Pacific Theater, were called home.

The two Burkhart brothers immediately entered the family business, with Everett becoming president and Perry becoming vice president and treasurer. The company had only two other employees in 1945. Despite their titles, Perry excelled at managing the company and helped direct Burkhart Dental Supply into a renewed position of business viability and Everett helped expand the company's geographical sales reach. By the 1950s the company was growing, and in 1954, after calling the W. R. Rust Building home for 30 years, Burkhart Dental Supply moved into a new headquarters.

RAPID GROWTH AND BUSINESS EXPANSION: 1960–80

During the 1960s many companies began adding dental insurance to their benefits packages, which increased the demand for dentists. In response, dentistry schools expanded the scope of their activities and evolved with advances in equipment, technology, and treatment procedures. All these factors resulted in greater sales for Burkhart Dental Supply. In addition, the company decided to add equipment repairs and equipment building to its business activities.

Everett and Perry determined that the company's growth justified a new corporate headquarters, so in 1968 Burkhart Dental Supply moved to its custom-built Center Street Building. The building doubled the size of space for dental merchandise and repair operations. It also included eight "operatories," or dental work space stations, that served study clubs in the area and provided functional work space for dentists to increase their education.

When Burkhart Dental Supply moved to the Center Street location, the company had 32 employees at its home office. By that time, it had established a branch office in Yakima, Washington, and had expanded its sales territory to include all of Washington and Alaska and parts of Idaho, Montana, and Oregon. During the 1960s Burkhart Dental Supply also began a practice of making its employees minor shareholders in the company, which essentially gave them a stake in the success of the growing business, a strategy that later helped retain personnel when other dental supply companies went public.

During the early 1970s the company opened a third branch office in Spokane, Washington. Each of its three branch offices had its own local sales representatives and merchandise warehouse. To make order processing more efficient, Burkhart Dental Supply eventually consolidated all of its distribution to a warehouse in Tacoma. The company also added a new computer system in 1978 to further streamline purchasing and inventory control activities and trim overhead expenses.

GEOGRAPHICAL EXPANSION UNDER NEW LEADERSHIP: 1981–99

In 1981 Perry and Everett both made plans to retire, which set the stage for a non-Burkhart to run the company for the first time in its 93-year history. In July 1981 Perry retired and was succeeded as chief executive officer and board vice president by Gary Halsan, who started working for the company as a delivery boy. Halsan took one more step up the corporate ladder when he

KEY DATES

1888: The company is founded by Dr. William E. Burkhart, the only dentist to ever run the company.

1893: The firm is incorporated as Burkhart Dental Supply.

1984: Perry Burkhart Jr. becomes company president.

1987: Three new branch offices open, making Burkhart Dental Supply the leading dental supply firm in the Northwest.

2006: Lori Burkhart Isbell takes over as president, representing the fifth generation of Burkharts to run the company.

became president and chairman of the board following Everett's retirement in December 1981. However, Halsan died unexpectedly a year later at the age of 42. Perry reassumed the position of president until 1984, when his son Perry Burkhart Jr. became president. Perry Jr. had joined the company 10 years earlier as a territory account manager and equipment specialist after working as a chemical engineer for another company.

Perry Jr. assumed control of the company at a time when both inflation and interest rates were rising throughout the country. Despite the economic situation, Perry Jr. embarked on a plan to greatly expand the reach of the company into the West and Midwest. By drawing on new technology, he employed a computerized management system to better consolidate inventory from all branches and improve the company's purchase system. In 1987 Burkhart Dental Supply added to three more branches in Portland and Eugene, Oregon, and Anchorage, Alaska. This expansion made the company the leading dental supply firm in the Northwest.

In 1991 Burkhart Dental Supply moved into a larger office and warehouse corporate complex that provided additional space for merchandise. The 36,000-square-foot facility included corporate offices and the company's distribution center. The following year Perry Jr. delivered laptop computers to all company account managers to ensure the precise entry of orders and the documentation of each account's purchase history.

The new order-filling system would be needed because the 1990s proved to be a period of unparalleled business expansion for Burkhart Dental Supply. In 1990 an office was established in Denver, Colorado, and three years later more branches were opened in Phoenix, Arizona; Sacramento, California; and Union City, California. Having successfully entered the West and Southwest, Burkhart Dental Supply set its sights on Texas and Oklahoma. In 1997 Burkhart Dental Supply acquired a dental supply business with offices in Fort Worth, Texas, and in Tulsa and Oklahoma City, Oklahoma. It also opened a new branch office in Houston, Texas, in 1998. To ensure adequate distribution for these new locations, a Dallas Distribution Center was established. While the company successfully expanded, it continued to dominate its home territory. As it closed the decade, the company reported that at least 25 percent of the dentists in its home region were customers.

FURTHER EXPANSION IN THE NEW CENTURY

In 2000 the company debuted on the *Puget Sound Business Journal*'s list of the Largest 100 Private Companies in Washington. That same year Burkhart Dental Supply logged $80 million in revenues, making it the 95th fastest growing company in Washington. Merchandise, such as day-to-day dental supplies and instruments, accounted for about two-thirds of the company's sales while larger equipment, such as dental chairs, generated the other one-third. The company, which boasted of a full-service dental supply business, was also providing office design, continuing education, consulting, and office management services, in addition to its sales and repair operations.

Burkhart Dental Supply opened its 15th branch office in Salt Lake City, Utah, in 2001 and its third distribution center in Reno, Nevada, in 2004. The success of Perry Jr.'s expansion plans were evident by 2004, when Burkhart Dental Supply moved into the ranks of the top-five dental suppliers in the country. In addition, since he took the reins of the company in 1984, the company's annual revenues had risen from $13 million to $117 million. Meanwhile, the strategic alignment of its network of branches and distribution centers helped drive branch sales growth approximately 8 percent annually. By yearend 2005 Burkhart Dental Supply reported $124.4 million in sales.

NEW LEADERSHIP AND STEADY GROWTH

Perry Jr. retired in 2006. He was succeeded as president by a member of a fifth generation of Burkharts, his daughter Lori Burkhart Isbell, who had been an elementary school teacher for four years before joining the dental supply business. By the time Burkhart Isbell took over, the company was the 66th largest private business in Washington. The company shortened its name to Burkhart Dental, Inc., and by 2008 it was providing dental supplies to more than 5,000 customers from branch offices in states running from Texas and to the West Coast.

In the latter half of the first decade of the 21st century, Burkhart Dental took steps to remain on the cutting edge of the dental supplies it offered. In 2008 the company began distributing Milestone Scientific products, specifically its STA System, a state-of-the-art computer-controlled local anesthesia delivery system that provided for painless administration of local anesthesia. Burkhart Dental also became a provider for Cadent, a supplier of iTero, a digital image impression system for tooth preparation.

Before the decade closed Burkhart Dental added branch offices in Boise, Idaho, and Las Vegas, Nevada. In January 2010 the company opened its 18th branch office in Austin, Texas. With offices in 16 midwestern and western states, the company reported revenues that surpassed $140 million in 2010. Burkhart Dental anticipated continued growth of 6 percent to 8 percent per year. Perry Jr.'s expansion strategy had largely defined the company's territory up until his retirement. If the expansion under Burkhart Isbell was a harbinger of things to come, the company could expect a gradual increase in the number of branch offices within its defined sales area, from the Mississippi River to the West Coast.

Roger Rouland

PRINCIPAL SUBSIDIARIES

ADC Group Financial Services; Practice Leadership Center; Reeve Burkhart Dental Supply Co.; Summit Dental Study Group.

PRINCIPAL COMPETITORS

Benco Dental Supply Company; Henry Schein, Inc.; Patterson Companies, Inc.

FURTHER READING

Broberg, Brad. "Dental-Equipment Supplier Has Deep Roots." *Puget Sound Business Journal,* June 14, 2002.

"Cadent Signs iTero Distribution Agreements with Henry Schein, Benco, Burkhart, and Goetze." *Business Wire,* February 2, 2009.

Genna, Chris. "Burkhart Dental Supply Enters Fifth Generation." *Puget Sound Business Journal,* June 23, 2006.

Keith, Jack. "Tacoma, Wash., Companies Honored with Family Business of Year Awards." *News Tribune* (Tacoma, WA), November 8, 2004.

"Milestone Scientific Expands Domestic Sales Network with Addition of Three New Dental Distributors." *PR Newswire,* July 16, 2008.

Monk, Becky. "How It's Done." *Puget Sound Business Journal,* June 23 2006.

Smith, Rob. "Dental Supply Firm's Roots Date Back to 1889." *Puget Sound Business Journal,* June 21, 2000.

———. "Top 100 List Features New Firms." *Puget Sound Business Journal,* June 23, 2000.

Wilson, Chris. "Burkhart to Pass Dental Business to Sixth Generation." *Puget Sound Business Journal,* June 25, 2004.

Cardiac Science Corporation

3303 Monte Villa Parkway
Bothell, Washington 98021
U.S.A.
Telephone: (425) 402-2000
Toll Free: (800) 426-0337
Fax: (425) 402-2001
Web site: http://www.cardiacscience.com

Public Company
Founded: 1913
Incorporated: 2005
Employees: 617
Sales: $156.85 million (2009)
Stock Exchanges: NASDAQ
Ticker Symbol: CSCX
NAICS: 339112 Surgical and Medical Instrument Manufacturing; 541910 Marketing Research and Public Opinion Polling

■ ■ ■

Cardiac Science Corporation develops, manufactures, and markets devices that are used in the diagnosis and treatment of cardiovascular conditions and diseases. These include devices to monitor the cardiovascular system, blood pressure monitors, pulse oximeters to measure blood oxygen content, spirometers to measure the volume of air entering and leaving the lungs, and electrocardiogram (ECG) systems for use during cardiac stress tests. Cardiac Science also manufactures automated external defibrillators (AEDs) for emergency use in public spaces, such as hotels, airports, and schools, as well as automated and traditional defibrillators for use in hospitals and other medical settings. An AED detects abnormal heart rhythm, determines whether the abnormal rhythm is life threatening, and delivers an electrical shock to correct the rhythm if necessary. Cardiac Science also provides its customers with related supplies and accessories, such as wall cabinets to store devices, carrying cases, replacement batteries, and training devices. Besides devices and products, the company offers related maintenance, training, and support services. Headquartered in Bothell, Washington, Cardiac Science sells its products through its own sales force, independent distributors, direct sales representatives, and third-party distributors.

A TRIO OF BEGINNINGS: 1913–91

The Cardiac Science Corporation of 2010 combined the expertise and brand-name recognition of three prominent medical device companies: Burdick Company, Cardiac Science, Inc., and Quinton Cardiology Systems, Inc. Cardiac Science Corporation dates its history back to the founding of the Burdick Company in 1913 by F. F. Burdick and F. A. Anderson. The Burdick Company developed and manufactured the first infrared lamp for medical use. It went on to become a pioneer in the development and manufacture of electrographic technology to measure and record heart rates and cardiac activity during stress tests.

In 1953 Wayne Quinton of Quinton Cardiology Systems, a related medical technology company, collaborated with Dr. Robert Bruce to develop the first mechanical treadmills that were expressly designed to

> **COMPANY PERSPECTIVES**
>
> Cardiac Science is a global leader in the development, manufacture, and marketing of diagnostic and therapeutic cardiology products and services. We provide a full spectrum of cardiology products and services that help protect hearts and save lives.

conduct cardiac testing at an elevated heart rate. These pioneering products formed the foundation of modern cardiac stress testing.

Cardiac Science was formed in 1991 for the purpose of developing heart rhythm analysis software called RHYTHMx. When installed in AEDs, the RHYTHMx technology could detect and treat heart arrhythmias without the need for human intervention. The RHYTHMx software eventually received approval from the U.S. Food and Drug Administration (FDA) and became the foundation for the first fully automatic bedside defibrillator used in hospitals. It was marketed under the Powerheart brand.

ACQUISITIONS CREATE CARDIAC SCIENCE CORPORATION: 2002–05

In 2002 Quinton Cardiology Systems became a publicly traded company on the NASDAQ. The following year it acquired the Burdick Company, which had become a market leader in the distribution of noninvasive products used in cardiology diagnosis and treatment. The $24 million Burdick acquisition allowed Quinton Cardiology Systems to broaden its portfolio of products that were intended for use in physicians' offices.

Three years later, in 2005, Quinton Cardiology Systems acquired Cardiac Science. The new company became known as Cardiac Science Corporation. Like Quinton Cardiology Systems, the new company was traded on the NASDAQ. The merger united the four most prominent brands in cardiac technology: Burdick, HeartCentrix, Powerheart, and Quinton. It also produced revenues of $100 million during the company's first year.

INNOVATIONS AND GROWTH: 2006–07

In September 2006 Cardiac Science announced the launch of new HeartCentrix software that would allow electrographic devices, heart monitors, and other cardiology devices to communicate directly with the electronic medical record systems kept in physicians' offices and hospitals. The HeartCentrix software could be used by a patient's physician to order a number of tests directly from the patient's electronic medical chart and have the results returned to the chart. Physicians could examine the results from within their offices or from a remote location using Internet access.

Cardiac Science announced in January 2007 plans to partner with Benco Dental, a dental equipment and supply distributor, to sell and distribute Powerheart AEDs to dentists and dental practices across the country. The partnership was prompted in part by the state of Florida's requirement that all dental offices in the state keep an AED on hand and by the American Dental Association's recommendation that dental practices throughout the United States do the same. "More and more, dentists are attentive to the risk of a patient or employee suffering from cardiac arrest in their offices," said Charles Cohen, the president of Benco Dental, in a *PR Newswire* January 10, 2007, press release that announced the venture. "This risk is very real, caused by the stress and fear many people have before a dental exam, the sedation required for some procedures, and demographic changes that are bringing more elderly patients into the practice for, in many cases, surgical procedures."

Public interest in readily available AEDs increased as the American Heart Association and other organizations stressed the importance of immediate treatment for sudden heart attacks and cardiac arrest. Cardiac Science went on to partner with public and private institutions throughout the United States and abroad, including school districts, sports clubs, and transportation authorities, to increase the availability of AEDs in heavily trafficked public areas.

In May 2007 Cardiac Science announced a settlement in its long-standing patent litigation with Philips Healthcare, a rival technology company. The litigation had centered on defibrillation-technology patents that were held by both companies. Under the settlement, all claims by each side were dismissed and each company was granted rights to the contested technology patents that were part of the suit. In exchange for a one-time payment of $1 million, Cardiac Science was also granted perpetual rights to certain defibrillation-technology patents held by Philips that were not named in the suit.

GROWTH AND REALIGNMENT

In March 2008 Cardiac Science completed the largest single order of ECG systems in its history when it supplied Mexico's Instituto de Seguridad y Servicios So-

KEY DATES

1913: The Burdick Company is founded.
1953: Wayne Quinton and Dr. Robert Bruce collaborate to develop treadmills expressly designed to conduct cardiac testing at an elevated heart rate.
1991: Cardiac Science, Inc., is founded.
2003: Quinton Cardiology Systems, Inc., acquires the Burdick Company.
2005: Cardiac Science merges with Quinton Cardiology Systems to create Cardiac Science Corporation.

ciales de los Trabajadores del Estado with 282 ECG systems. The systems included communication features that granted health care practitioners in remote areas access to cardiologists in more populated parts of the country. Kurt Lemvigh, the international vice president of Cardiac Science, told the industry publication *Health and Medicine Week* on March 24, 2008, that "the scale of this delivery illustrates the international demand for new generations of ECG technology and Cardiac Science's ability to meet that demand with advanced informatics solutions."

That same month Cardiac Science realigned its leading product brands, which included Burdick, HeartCentrix, Powerheart, and Quinton behind a single Cardiac Science brand. "We believe our solitary focus on noninvasive cardiology elevates our product and service offerings and differentiates us in the medical devices field," said company president and chief executive officer John Hinson in a *PR Newswire* March 6, 2008, press release. "Going forward, our 95-year heritage and track record, comprehensive product and service offerings, and the strengths of our predecessor companies will be concentrated into a single, overarching story of dependability."

LOOKING FORWARD

In August 2009 Cardiac Science initiated a voluntary field correction after determining that approximately 75,000 AEDs manufactured between 2003 and 2009 might fail during a cardiac resuscitation attempt. The voluntary action followed the company's receipt of approximately 180 related consumer complaints. Cardiac Science instituted more stringent testing of the individual components used in its AEDs and announced that all forthcoming units would be free of the components identified as problematic. The company also announced plans to issue a software update to address issues in existing units.

The following December Cardiac Science announced a voluntary recall of approximately 12,200 AEDs that were determined to be potentially unreliable during a cardiac resuscitation attempt. In April 2010 the FDA responded by suggesting that upwards of 280,000 AEDs may be defective. In March Cardiac Science updated its response plans and announced that it would replace approximately 24,000 AEDs in use by U.S. hospitals and emergency medical responders. Frequently in heavy use, AEDs in hospitals and first-response vehicles were considered to be more likely to exhibit or develop problems. "We have worked constructively with the FDA to address their concerns and are pleased to bring this matter to a close," said company president and chief executive officer Dave Marver, according to the *Puget Sound Business Journal* on July 19, 2010. "We are now focused on executing the updated recall quickly and effectively."

In 2010 Cardiac Science remained a global leader in the development, manufacture, and marketing of AEDs, ECG systems, and other medical devices used in diagnostic and therapeutic cardiology. While marketing its products in over 160 countries around the world, the company maintained facilities in the United States, including Washington, California, and Wisconsin; in Europe, including Denmark, France, and the United Kingdom; and in Asia, including China.

Joyce Helena Brusin

PRINCIPAL SUBSIDIARIES

Cardiac Science, Inc.; Quinton Cardiology, Inc.

PRINCIPAL COMPETITORS

GE Healthcare; Medtronic, Inc.; Midmark Corp.; Philips Healthcare; Royal Philips Electronics N.V.; Scott Care Corp.; Spacelabs Healthcare; Welch Allyn, Inc.; ZOLL Medical Corporation.

FURTHER READING FURTHER READING:

"Cardiac Science Announces Settlement of Patent Litigation with Philips." *Health and Medicine Week*, May 14, 2007.

"Cardiac Science and Benco Dental Partner to Distribute Powerheart AEDs." PR Newswire, January 10, 2007.

"Cardiac Science Delivers Largest Order of Electrocardiograph Systems in Company History." *Health and Medicine Week*, March 24, 2008.

"Cardiac Science Notifies AED Customers of Nationwide Voluntary Medical Device Correction." *PR Newswire*, November 13, 2009.

"Cardiac Science Replacing 24,000 AEDs." *Puget Sound Business Journal*, July 19, 2010.

"Cardiac Science Unveils Major Brand Change; Strategy to Lift Brand Awareness." *PR Newswire*, March 6, 2008.

"Instrumentarium Sells US Cardiology Business Spacelabs Burdick Inc to Quinton Cardiology Systems Inc." *Nordic Business Report*, December 24, 2002.

Mills, James Edward. "Defibrillator Maker to Expand in Deerfield," *Wisconsin State Journal*, March 2, 2005.

"Officials at Cardiac Science Corporation Discuss Recent Developments." *Health and Medicine Week*, July 30, 2007.

Club de hockey Canadien, Inc.

1260 rue de la Gauchetiere O.
Montreal, Quebec H3C 5L2
Canada
Telephone: (514) 932-2582
Fax: (514) 932-8736
Web site: http://canadiens.nhl.com

Private Company
Founded: 1909
Employees: 110
Sales: $130 million (2008)
NAICS: 711211 Sports Teams and Clubs

■ ■ ■

Club de hockey Canadien, Inc., is the parent company of the storied Montreal Canadiens franchise of the National Hockey League. The Canadiens are one of the most successful teams in all of professional sports, having won the Stanley Cup, the NHL's championship trophy, a record 24 times. The team plays in the 21,273-seat Bell Centre, one of the busiest arenas in the world. Both the Canadiens and the Bell Centre are owned by a partnership group controlled by three of the Molson brothers, whose family is best known for its brewery.

EARLY 20TH-CENTURY ROOTS

While ice hockey is regarded as Canada's game, it was originally more the passion of those of English descent rather than of French descent. The English formed athletics clubs, while the French preferred clubs where they could socialize and enjoy the pleasures of dining and dancing.

Hockey had become popular with university students in Ontario, Canada, in the late 1800s, leading to the rise of amateur leagues, the winner of which received the Stanley Cup, a silver bowl donated by the English governor general of Canada, Lord Stanley of Preston. It was first awarded in 1893. One of those leagues was the four-team Eastern Canada Hockey Association (ECHA), but it was amateur in name only. In 1909 three of the four teams decided to disband the ECHA and form a new league, leaving the Montreal Wanderers team and its uncooperative owner to fend for itself. The Wanderers joined with other amateur clubs to form the National Hockey Association (NHA).

In need of a larger fan base, the NHA looked to Montreal's French-speaking community, which comprised two-thirds of the city's population of 465,000. In early December 1909 the NHA announced that it would include a French-Canadian team to be called le Canadien, which the newspapers quickly turned plural. The new owner of the Canadiens was 24-year-old J. Ambrose O'Brien, who was neither a French Canadian nor from Montreal but from the small town of Renfrew. He had been snubbed by the ECHA in his attempts to secure a place in its new league for his Renfrew Creamery Kings, but of greater importance, he came from a wealthy mine-owning family. For the good of the fledgling NHA, O'Brien agreed to back the Canadiens until French-speaking ownership could be secured. A team was quickly organized, and the Montreal Canadiens played their first game on January 5, 1910, at the Jubilee Arena, defeating the Cobalt Silver Kings 7-6.

COMPANY PERSPECTIVES

On December 4, 1909, two days after the founding of the National Hockey Association, the hockey world sees the birth of the Montreal Canadiens at Montreal's Windsor Hotel thanks to businessman J. Ambrose O'Brien.

The Silver Kings were one of three teams that folded after the NHA's inaugural season. While the league was preparing for its annual winter meeting to sort out its problems, a wrestling promoter, a French-speaking young man named George Kendall (who did business as "George Kennedy" to placate his respectable stove-manufacturing father), laid claim to the rights to the "Canadiens" name as the owner of a sporting association known as Le Club athlétique Canadien. Interested in owning a hockey team, Kendall demanded an NHA franchise or at least the chance to purchase the Canadiens. Although Kendall was prepared to go to court, the NHA owners were more than happy to award him a franchise for $7,500 and transfer ownership of the Canadiens to him.

FIRST STANLEY CUP: 1916

Kendall proved to be an excellent owner, turning a $4,000 profit in his first year with the Canadiens, a feat unmatched by the other clubs in the league. More importantly, he was successful in building a following for the team among French Montrealers; however, he made the mistake of signing an Irish Catholic defenseman, offending those who demanded an all-French-Canadian team. Kendall tried to accommodate that demand and persuaded the league to allow the Canadiens to sign only French-Canadian players, but it soon grew obvious that there were not yet enough talented French-Canadian players available. The desire to assemble a winning team soon took precedence over cultural purity, and no one protested when Kendall petitioned the league for the right to sign English-speaking players. In 1916 the team won its first Stanley Cup, which at the time was contested, unsuccessfully, by the NHA and Pacific Coast Hockey Association champions.

To rid themselves of the Toronto team's bellicose owner, Eddie Livingstone, the other NHA owners abandoned the league en masse to form the National Hockey League in November 1917. The Canadiens were a founding member and officially changed the team name to *club de hockey Canadien*. The letters *CH* now adorned their red-white-and-blue jerseys, creating what became an iconic look.

By this time the world was at war and would soon be visited by an influenza epidemic that swept the globe in 1918, killing some 50 million people. Kendall was one of its victims. He died in October 1921 at the age of 39. The Canadiens' new owner was an American of French-Canadian descent, Leo Dandurand, whose family had immigrated from Montreal to Illinois.

Dandurand had been sent to Montreal to complete his education and in 1913 went into business with a major Montreal sports figure, Joseph Cattarinich, a lacrosse star. They became involved in horse racing and over the years would own or manage some of the best racing facilities in North America. Dandurand would also own a string of winning thoroughbreds and head the Montreal Jockey Club. When the Canadiens became available following Kendall's death, Dandurand eagerly bought the club in November 1921 for $11,000.

THE MONTREAL FORUM: 1924

Dandurand not only assembled a Stanley Cup–winning team in 1924 but also played a key role in promoting the league, using his contacts to launch NHL franchises in the United States in Boston, Chicago, Detroit, and New York. The NHL also awarded a second franchise to Montreal to appeal to the city's English-speaking population. Known as the Maroons, the new team joined the NHL for the 1924–25 season, becoming the Canadiens' chief rival. The Maroons played in a new state-of-the-art arena, the Montreal Forum. In the Forum's third year, the Canadiens also became a tenant.

During the Great Depression of the 1930s, both the Canadiens and the Maroons struggled. The Maroons were unable to participate in the 1938–39 season and in May 1939 informed the NHL that the team was relinquishing its franchise, leaving only the Canadiens to represent Montreal in the league. In 1940 the Canadiens also came close to folding, but the owner of the Forum and former manager of the Maroons, the Canadian Arena Company, acquired the team. Serving as the Canadiens president was Donat Raymond, who had made his fortune in hotels before cofounding and serving as president of the Canadian Arena Company.

After winning the Stanley Cup in 1931, the Canadiens struggled on the ice through much of the next decade, winning no additional Cups and twice failing to make the playoffs. Due to Raymond's deep pockets, the Canadiens were able to hang on until the economy picked up with the increase in defense spending during World War II. He was able to assemble another championship-caliber club, and the Canadiens again

KEY DATES

1909: The Canadiens hockey team is established.
1917: The National Hockey League is formed.
1924: The Montreal Forum opens.
1940: The Canadian Arena Company buys the team.
1957: The Molson family acquires the team.
2009: The Molson family reacquires the team.

won the Stanley Cup in 1944, repeating the feat two years later. During Raymond's presidency, the team would win further Cups in 1953, 1956, and 1957.

In 1957 the Canadian Arena Company sold the Canadiens and the Forum to Hartland Molson, owner of Molson Breweries of Canada Ltd. Molson took control of a team that was in the midst of a golden era, as the Canadiens won three more consecutive Stanley Cups: five in a row altogether. The Canadiens then won back-to-back Cups in 1965 and 1966, and lost in the finals the following year before closing out the 1960s with two more Stanley Cups.

ANOTHER OWNERSHIP CHANGE: 1971

The Forum underwent a major renovation in 1968, but soon more significant changes were in store for the Canadiens. In 1971, because of changes in Canada's tax laws, the Molson family sold the Canadian Arena Company to Placements Rondelle Ltée, owned by brothers Peter and Edward Bronfman. They took over the reigning NHL championship team, and during the Bronfmans' seven years of ownership, the Canadiens would win another three Cups. A fourth championship in a row followed in 1979, but by this time the team was under different ownership as the Bronfman family had sold the Canadiens to Molson Breweries of Canada in 1978.

During the Canadiens' second association with the Molson family, the team experienced a mild drought, failing to win another Stanley Cup until 1986. The Canadiens won their 24th Cup in 1993. By this time the Montreal Forum was an outdated facility, despite periodic renovations, so construction began on a new, larger arena, the $230 million Molson Centre, which opened in March 1996. Seating for hockey increased by 5,000 to more than 21,000 seats. Moreover, a large number of those new seats, about 1,400, were found in 135 luxury suites, which generated $12 million in annual revenues, a significant increase over the $3 million produced by the VIP suites the Forum had offered. The new arena also provided Molson and the Canadiens with other revenue streams. Not only were the number of concession outlets increased, but the Molson Centre also boasted three restaurants with a combined seating capacity of 1,000.

The Molson Companies had always considered the Canadiens to be a "heritage asset," but by the end of the 1990s management began to question whether owning a hockey team and arena helped it in the pursuit of its core mission: selling beer. Making matters worse, Molson had to pay C$10 million in annual taxes on its arena, more than the amount the five other Canadian franchises combined paid, and a far cry from the $4.1 million paid by the 20 NHL teams in the United States. Each year, Molson lost C$5 million to C$7 million on its hockey operation, a fact that did not sit well with shareholders. The team was also suffering through its worst stretch since the 1930s, missing the playoffs in both 1995 and 1999.

NEW U.S. OWNER: 2001

In June 2000 Molson announced that it wished to sell a controlling interest in the Canadiens by the end of the year. A deal with a new owner was not struck, however, until May 2001 when Colorado businessman George N. Gillett Jr. agreed to pay $275 million for an 80.1 percent stake in the Canadiens and 100 percent of the Molson Centre. Molson retained a 19.9 percent interest in the team. In March 2002 Gillett sold the naming rights on the arena to Bell Canada. Thus, the Molson Centre became the Bell Centre in September 2002.

Gillett began to rebuild a franchise that had fallen on difficult times. In 2009 the Canadiens franchise celebrated its 100th anniversary, and a new generation of the Molson family grew interested in reestablishing a relationship with the team after learning that Gillett was interested in finding a coinvestor. In June 2009 brothers Geoff, Andrew, and Justin Molson agreed to buy the Canadiens and the Bell Centre for $500 million to $550 million. They received a team that according to *Forbes* magazine was worth $339 million, the third highest valuation in the NHL. The team also appeared to be on the rise, making a deep run into the playoffs in 2010.

Ed Dinger

PRINCIPAL SUBSIDIARIES

Arena des Canadiens Incorporated; Hamilton Bulldogs Hockey Club.

PRINCIPAL COMPETITORS

Boston Professional Hockey Association, Inc.; Hockey Western New York, LLC; Ottawa Senators Hockey Club Limited Partnership.

FURTHER READING

Branswell, Brenda. "Les Canadiens—in Name Only?" *Maclean's*, January 29, 2001, 55.

Davies, Tanya. "A Hockey-Beer Marriage Is Saved." *Maclean's*, April 26, 1999, 12.

Diamond, Dan, et al. *Total Hockey*. Kingston, NY: Total Sports, 1998.

Jenish, D'Arcy. *The Montreal Canadiens: 100 Years of Glory*. Scarborough, Ont.: Doubleday Canada Limited, 2008.

Marino, Jonathan. "NHL's Canadiens to Molson Family." *Mergers & Acquisitions Report*, June 29, 2009, 31.

Mouton, Claude. *The Montreal Canadiens: A Hockey Dynasty*. New York: Van Nostrand Reinhold, 1980.

"New Majority Owner for the Montreal Canadiens and Sale of the Molson Centre." *Market News Publishing*, May 1, 2001.

O'Brien, Andy. *Fire-Wagon Hockey: The Story of the Montreal Canadiens*. Toronto: Ryerson Press, 1967.

CNN Worldwide

One CNN Center
Atlanta, Georgia 30303
U.S.A.
Telephone: (404) 827-1700
Fax: (404) 827-1099
Web site: http://www.turner.com

Wholly Owned Subsidiary of Time Warner Inc.
Founded: 1980 as Cable News Network, Inc.
Incorporated: 1980
Employees: 4,000
Stock Exchange: New York
Ticker Symbol: TWX
NAICS: 515210 Cable and Other Subscription Programming, Cable Television Networks; 515120 Television Broadcasting; 515111 Radio and Satellite Radio Networks; 519130 Internet Broadcasting

■ ■ ■

Since its founding, CNN Worldwide has broadcast the news nonstop. As originators of a 24-hour all-news cable television network, Ted Turner and a team of producers, journalists, and others developed the programming, policies, and strategies that propelled the network into the top ranks of global newscasting. Over a 30-year span, CNN progressed from a single Atlanta-based news network in 1980 to 24 networks and related media accessed by more than 2 billion people in 2010. The network's coverage of unfolding events (particularly the catastrophic) and its system of news bureaus located around the world strengthened CNN's reputation among its peers and its users. As of 2010, CNN's primary business segments were: CNN/U.S., HLN, CNN.com, CNN International, and CNN Networks/ Services.

TED TURNER

For more than a decade before founding the Cable News Network, Ted Turner built several lucrative businesses. These included Turner Outdoor Advertising, which he inherited in 1963; the Atlanta Braves baseball team and the Atlanta Hawks basketball team, which he acquired in 1976 and 1977, respectively; and the initially failing Atlanta-based television station WJRJ, which he bought in 1970. Turner renamed the station WTCG and then WTBS, revived its programming and popularity, and instituted other changes from 1976 to 1979, most notably satellite broadcasting to cable systems throughout the United States.

In this broadcasting venture, Turner's pioneering approach was apparent. He termed his innovation a TV "superstation" whose scope via technology and subscribers was extensive. Then, around 1978, although his experience with programming consisted largely of sports telecasts, broadcasts of movies, and reruns of TV shows he had acquired, Turner's interest turned to newscasting. After exploratory discussions with his own management and with other networks' executives, Turner became convinced of the potential profitability of an all-news network. Eschewing a partnership or joint venture, he hired Reese Schonfeld, an independent journalist and producer, as head of his fledgling operation.

COMPANY PERSPECTIVES

CNN, the original 24-hour news network on cable, continues to invest in newsgathering to deliver the most comprehensive, nonpartisan news and analysis to global audiences across all platforms.

FIRST CNN BROADCAST

CNN's first broadcast occurred June 1, 1980. By the end of the network's first month, other members of the press had weighed in on CNN's on- and off-camera performance. One of them, Tony Schwartz, noted in his June 29, 1980, article in the *New York Times*, "In a brief time, CNN has set a tone that is serious, professional and credible, whether one tunes in during its prime-time newscast from 8 to 10 P.M., or during the late-evening and midday hours." While Schwartz acknowledged challenges such as developing a distinct brand of reportage and managing coverage of large-scale events, he joined peers in giving CNN a general thumbs up.

Unlike the major networks' approach, which tended toward sophisticated visual effects, impressive studio sets, and well-known journalists such as Walter Cronkite of CBS and David Brinkley of NBC, CNN initially relied on simple, straightforward delivery of the news. In 1982 the network launched CNN2, a second 24-hour news channel that had continuous headlines. Later called Headline News and then HLN, the channel aired in locations such as airports, a choice that indicated awareness of viewers whose fast-paced lifestyles still included commitment to keeping pace with world events. In 1982 CNN began airing in Asia and added CNN Radio.

In its first decade there were other signs of optimism for CNN. While the network derived some revenue from carrying advertisements, it also had subscribers, another source of income. By contrast, the Federal Communications Commission (FCC) forbade the major networks from charging subscription fees. Between 1982 and 1985 CNN's staff grew from 800 to over 1,050; during that period, revenues increased from about $40 million to about $130 million. In 1987 CNN relocated to a new headquarters in downtown Atlanta. The 1980s ended with CNN officially on the list of the White House Press Corps, a reflection of the network's well-earned credibility.

IN THE FIELD

By the end of CNN's first decade, two strengths had emerged: a straightforward approach to journalism and a preemptive commitment to newsgathering that left competitors, even correspondents at better known networks such as NBC and CBS, second on the scene of newsworthy events. With millions in revenue and hundreds on staff, the potential for scoops had soared. To realize their potential, CNN needed not only dedicated professionals but field offices (known as bureaus) and equipment. Events were needed too: big ones that captured the public's attention and gave viewing the news an urgency that extended beyond a prime-time slot.

During the 1990s numerous important events created a near traffic jam in broadcasting schedules. In addition to building a reputation for besting the competition, CNN's provided TV coverage that took full advantage of the medium's visual element. In surveying CNN's first two decades in a June 1, 2000, article for suburban Chicago's *Daily Herald*, Ted Cox concluded, "Looking back at the past 20 years, it's amazing to consider how many of those images belong exclusively to CNN, such as the *Challenger* explosion in 1986 or the beginning of the Persian Gulf war with the bombing of Baghdad in 1991 or O.J. Simpson's slow-speed chase in his Ford Bronco in 1994." The role the network played in etching such events on the public consciousness firmly associated CNN with up-to-the-minute global reporting, validating its brand and its motto as "the most trusted source of news in the world."

STRATEGIES FOR MAINTAINING QUALITY

Even as CNN defined for itself, its viewers, and its peers the terms and examples of uncompromising, hard-nosed, real-time broadcast journalism, management remained sharply aware of the revenue demanded to maintain this quality. Examining the prospects for the years ahead, Turner and his executives considered strategies that included acquisitions, mergers, and partnerships with CBS, Viacom, Microsoft, and other media enterprises. By 1995 a major deal was under way with Time Warner Inc. The FCC studied details of such a merger, finding the package in compliance with antitrust laws, and in 1996 Turner Broadcasting merged with Time Warner at a cost of $7.57 billion.

The multibillion-dollar Time Warner merger signaled the extent to which Ted Turner's operations had mushroomed over the years. His acquisitions of MGM Entertainment Company and New Line Cinema Corporation, while expensive, resulted in critically ac-

KEY DATES

1980: Cable News Network airs its first day of programming.
1982: CNN2 (later Headline News and HLN) debuts as CNN's second 24-hour news channel; CNN begins airing in Asia.
1996: Turner Broadcasting System, Inc., and Time Warner Inc. merge.
2001: CNN is the first TV channel to broadcast news of the terrorist attacks on New York City's World Trade Center.
2010: CNN observes its 30th year in operation.

claimed box office successes such as *The Shawshank Redemption* and *The Lord of the Rings* trilogy. Initially, it seemed that these entities bore little relevance to CNN. A shift was under way, however. The network had proved it could handle global news on an ongoing basis, and the merger with Time Warner offered new territory and opportunities for CNN.

EVOLUTION OF PROGRAMMING IN THE NEW CENTURY

By 2001 CNN had fully matured as a news operation. When the World Trade Center was destroyed in a terrorist attack that year, CNN brought to the devastating crisis the New York bureau's expertise and ready equipment, guided by management's efficient supervision of crews on site and at headquarters in Atlanta. The network's overarching professionalism focused the world's attention on a traumatic situation, all the while maintaining a calm yet substantive treatment of evolving circumstances. CNN's performance heralded the onset of a decade of dominance for the network in this type of programming.

At the same time, however, other programming styles began to emerge at CNN. In a format similar to those of traditional talk shows, CNN introduced programs featuring hosts who conducted in-depth interviews, often with one guest per show. Sometimes the hosts were not journalists, as with radio personality and author Glenn Beck. Sometimes the topics stretched the definition of "news" to include issues of popular culture, celebrities in entertainment and sports, and subjects guaranteed to stir debate. With programs such as *Larry King Live* and *The Situation Room*, the network extended its lineup to incorporate shows akin in scope and tone to broad-based print magazines, such as *Time* and *People*. The hope was that, disaster or not, viewers' choice would remain CNN.

NEW LEADERSHIP AND NEW MEDIA

Twenty-first-century lives demanded mobility and innovation. Computers, cell phones, and other devices became ubiquitous, especially among the highly desirable 25- to 54-year-old audience segment. As Jim Walton assumed leadership of CNN on Ted Turner's departure in 2003, the company began enthusiastically to combine state-of-the-art technology with the breadth of multimedia offerings from parent companies Time Warner and Turner Broadcasting augmenting CNN's own established newsgathering know-how in order to serve their target audiences' lifestyles.

Outcomes for the period 2005–2010 entailed expansion of website development in several foreign languages that aligned with existing international bureaus, seizing a leading role in providing digital news content, and pursuing joint ventures and partnerships with, for example, *Money* magazine and online video giant YouTube. In 2007 CNN and YouTube cosponsored a presidential debate for which audience-participants created and posted their own video recordings on YouTube for a question-and-answer segment.

Even in these new-media configurations, however, CNN remained true to its beginnings in its commitment to connections between evolving news and an audience in a democracy requiring informed citizens. In 2010, CNN's 30th year, the network announced the debut of CNNNewsource, which replaced CNN's subscription to the Associated Press news syndication service. The new CNN service was designed for in-house ownership of editorial content to be shared across all of the company's news delivery platforms. As 2011 approached, CNN's multimedia perspective viewed a landscape of links activated on all company fronts.

Mary C. Lewis

PRINCIPAL SUBSIDIARIES

CNN Airport Network; CNN Arabic.com (U.A.E.); CNN.co.jp (Japan); CNN.com; CNN.com International Edition (UK); CNN.com Korean (Republic of South Korea); CNN en Español–Mexico; CNN International Asia Pacific; CNN International South Asia; CNN International Europe/Middle East/ Africa; CNN International in Latin America; CNN International North America; CNN/Money Online; CNNPolitics.com; iReport.com; Turner Private Networks Inc.

PRINCIPAL DIVISIONS

CNN en Español; CNN en Español Radio; CNN International; CNN Mobile; CNN News Services; CNN Radio; HLN.

PRINCIPAL COMPETITORS

Bloomberg L.P.; FOX News Network LLC; MSNBC Cable, LLC; Yahoo! Inc.

FURTHER READING

Auletta, Ken. *Media Man.* New York: W.W. Norton & Company, 2004, 40–48.

Broderick, James F., and Darren W. Miller. *Consider the Source: A Critical Guide to 100 Prominent News and Information Sites on the Web.* Medford, NJ: Information Today, 2007, 53–56.

Cox, Ted. "Impact of Images Is Hard to Miss." *Arlington Heights (IL) Daily Herald,* June 1, 2000.

Joyner, Tammy. "'We'll Continue to Be What We Are': The Global News Conglomerate Closes in on Its Third Decade." *Atlanta Journal-Constitution,* May 30, 2010.

Li, Kenneth. "CNN Cancels AP Subscription." *Financial Times,* June 22, 2010.

Project for Excellence in Journalism and the Pew Internet & American Life Project. "Cable TV—Economics." *The State of the News Media 2010.* Accessed November 4, 2010. http://www.stateofthemedia.org/2010/cable_tv_economics.php.

Rice, Marc. "Turner Seals Deal with Time Warner." *Albany (NY) Times Union,* October 11, 1996.

Schwartz, Tony. "TV View: Cable News Network—In Search of an Identity." *New York Times,* June 29, 1980.

Seelye, Katharine Q. "Debates to Connect Candidates and Voters Online." *New York Times,* July 23, 2007.

Turner, Ted, with Bill Burke. *Call Me Ted.* New York: Grand Central Publishing, 2008, 249–52, 337–41.

Whittemore, Hank. *CNN: The Inside Story, How a Band of Mavericks Changed the Face of Television News.* Boston: Little, Brown, 1990, 5–9, 298–300.

Coinstar, Inc.

1800 114th Avenue S.E.
Bellevue, Washington 98004
U.S.A.
Telephone: (425) 943-8000
Toll Free: (800) 928-2274
Fax: (425) 637-0253
Web site: http://www.coinstar.com

Public Company
Founded: 1991
Incorporated: 1993
Employees: 2,600
Sales: $1.15 billion (2009)
Stock Exchanges: NASDAQ
Ticker Symbol: CSTR
NAICS: 812990 All Other Personal Services; 333313 Office Machinery Manufacturing

■ ■ ■

Coinstar, Inc., operates a network of automated, self-service coin counting and processing machines that provide customers with a means of converting loose change into cash. It also owns Redbox, which rents DVDs from its own network of kiosks. The Coinstar units, located in supermarkets, financial institutions, and mass merchants, count loose coins and issue vouchers listing the total number, denominations, and dollar value of the coins processed, minus an 8.9 percent processing charge. Coinstar also receives handling fees from consumer giants such as Pepsi, Kraft, General Foods, and Kroger, whose coupons Coinstar passes along to consumers on printouts.

JAR OF COINS

Jens Molbak came up with the idea for Coinstar in 1988, when he was a graduate student in business at Stanford University. One night, the story goes, while sitting in his dorm room, thinking about the jar of coins on his dresser, he hit upon the idea of finding a way to turn a service into a business. The penny held special significance for Molbak, who, as a 10-year-old, washed 28,011 flowerpots for a penny apiece at his Danish immigrant parents' plant nursery in Washington. As noted by Fred Vogelstein and David Brindley in *U.S. News & World Report* on April 21, 1997, the $280.11 he collected taught Molbak "that there was real money in coins."

Molbak's idea was to provide a service to coin hoarders in which for a small fee they would be able to trade their coins for more usable cash. In 1989 Molbak turned his idea into part of a graduate school project and stood outside San Francisco Bay-area grocery stores with a clipboard interviewing people about what they did with their change at the end of the day. "We talked to 1,500 people, and it turned out that three out of four had coins at home, with an average of about $30 [sitting unused] at any one time," Molbak said in a February 10, 1997, *Forbes* article, as reported by William G. Flanagan and Alexandra Alger. As a result of his research, Molbak estimated that there was about $8 billion worth of change sitting in jars in the United States. He arrived at this number by subtracting the estimated value of the coins in circulation from the value of all U.S. coins produced during the previous 25 years. The remainder, $8 billion, equaled a bit more than $30 per adult.

COMPANY PERSPECTIVES

Our vision for Coinstar is to be the world's leading supplier of valuable services that make life easier for consumers. Coinstar was founded on a truly innovative idea of turning consumer change into cash, conveniently, at a self-service kiosk. Over time, the company has expanded its footprint and product lines, leveraging our expertise in automated retail, bringing incremental value to consumers and retail customers at the front of the store. Just as we did in the early days, we will continue to innovate, focusing on consumer needs—and we will look both inside and outside the company to add even greater value to our automated retail offering.

FOUNDING OF COINSTAR

It took Molbak a few years to raise the capital for his private company and perfect the green-and-yellow Coinstar machine, which combined ATM-style computer software and Las Vegas slot machine technology. Adapted from an electronic coin counter made by a Swedish company named Scan Coin, the machine cost about $12,000 and contained a computer, modem, video screen, and printer. Its sorting equipment was sensitive enough to kick out keychains, foreign coins, and lint while counting 600 coins per minute. An online network allowed all sorts of information to be transmitted, including how many slugs had been inserted, how much each machine took in by the minute and in what denominations, whether it needed servicing, and when the machine's coffers were full. By the time the machine design was complete, the company held five patents on it.

In 1991, degree in hand, Molbak founded Coinstar. By 1992 Coinstar's machines were installed in four San Francisco supermarkets, each of which received a small portion of Coinstar's fees for promoting the service. In addition, stores benefited from the fact that Coinstar users had to go to a cash register with their machine voucher to collect their money; company surveys showed that three out of four spent part of their voucher in the store. Three years later, in 1995, Coinstar had placed 263 machines in stores. In 1996 the company had about 900 units in use in 18 states, with its largest concentration in Los Angeles. There, 347 machines took in about $5,000 per week and dispensed $4,625 in vouchers, more volume than all the rest combined.

PUBLIC OFFERING

The company began a national rollout of its machines in the late 1990s. Flush with $63 million in loans, which it had secured in the fall of 1996, Coinstar had a total of 2,000 machines in 23 states by spring 1997. By year's end, it had increased its presence by about 3,000 machines in supermarkets and in two new markets (financial institutions and Target stores) nationwide. The company also began its "Coins That Count" campaign, offering customers the chance to donate their change to local nonprofits through Coinstar machines.

By 1996, however, Coinstar had yet to turn a profit, and its annual financial losses had grown since 1991. This was due to the expense of expanding its business, attributable in turn to the cost of its machines. Between 1995 and 1998, the company lost about $52 million in the United States. In the summer of 1997, Coinstar went public with an initial public offering on the NASDAQ, hoping to net more than $60 million in the deal. However, it had to settle for $29.3 million, selling one-third fewer shares for $10.50 instead of the original target of $15. A secondary offering of four million shares took place in July 1999.

Despite dramatic increases in revenue, the company remained unprofitable, mainly because of the high depreciation costs on new machines. In 1998 Coinstar recycled more coins than the U.S. Mint produced (15.84 billion versus 15.81 billion) and revenues doubled to $47.7 million. Nonetheless, the company lost $24 million that year. Although Coinstar's price per share almost doubled its initial price by late 1999, analysts expressed concern about the company's long-term viability when weak third-quarter results, caused by a nationwide shortage of coins, led to a drop in the company's stock price by half, back to about $11.

OVERSEAS EXPANSION

In 1998, with about 4,900 machines in 37 states, Coinstar began to look overseas toward the potential market in euros. By midyear, the company had formed a new wholly owned subsidiary called Coinstar International, Inc., in an effort to expand its overseas operations. The company anticipated that approximately $23 billion worth of various European currencies needed to be converted into the common currency during the following years. It also raised the transaction fee for its money-changing service to 8.9 percent, turning over 1 percent to supermarkets. In early 1999 the company placed three machines in Toronto stores and signed two separate agreements with supermarket chains in the

KEY DATES

1991: Jens Molbak founds Coinstar.
1992: Coinstar machines are installed in four supermarkets in San Francisco.
1997: The company makes an initial public offering.
1998: The company forms Coinstar International, Inc.
1999: Coinstar forms Meals.com, Inc.; the company's secondary offering of four million shares takes place in July.
2001: David Cole replaces Molbak as CEO and initiates diversification effort.
2008: Coinstar acquires control of Redbox.
2010: Coinstar sells its prepaid card and international transfer businesses.

United Kingdom. In 2001 the company continued its push into Britain, signing up two more chains.

Coinstar also attempted to add to its revenue streams with a turn-of-the-millennium upgrade of its website and in-store kiosks. This allowed customers to log onto www.my-meals.com and gain access to a recipe center and their personal grocery lists. They could then print out their list at their supermarket kiosk and receive grocery coupons. Supermarkets, for their part, could then track consumers' shopping patterns.

GROWTH THROUGH HARD TIMES AND INTO THE NEW MILLENNIUM

Finally, in early 2000, Coinstar felt confident it had hit upon a recipe for success. Sales had jumped from $77.7 million in 1999 to $103 million in 2000, while losses stayed fairly constant between $21 million and $23 million. Coinstar converted Meals.com into a wholly owned subsidiary and sold 11 percent of Meals.com's shares to a consortium of investors, a virtual who's who of Seattle's tech scene, for $5.5 million. Daniel Gerrity took over as Coinstar's chief executive, while Molbak assumed the positions of chair and chief executive of Meals.com. In late 2000, however, Gerrity resigned, after only nine months in the top job.

Coinstar's "Coins That Count" program continued to thrive and became a permanent consumer service that provided nonprofit organizations with the opportunity to use Coinstar machines to raise money. This service offered consumers the choice of making a tax-deductible donation with their coins instead of receiving a voucher for the money they deposited in a Coinstar machine. The nonprofit organization received 92.5 percent of the funds collected.

In May 2001 Coinstar announced its first profit of $11,000 for its first quarter from its more than 8,500 machines. The company's net loss had been $24 million in 1998, $21.4 million in 1999, and $22.7 million in 2000. It continued to lose money overall because of the losses of its Meals.com subsidiary. Around that time, Molbak announced his resignation as chair of Coinstar, planning to continue working at Meals.com. The company's ailing Web site had lost $21 million since its inception. As a result, in June, the subsidiary laid off 31 employees, one-third of its workforce, and attempted to buy back outstanding shares of Meals.com. Later in the year Coinstar sold the entire Meals.com operation to Nestle USA.

MOVING BEYOND THE COIN-CHANGING BUSINESS

The sale of Meals.com was not the only big change of 2001. Founder Jens Molbak withdrew entirely from Coinstar and was replaced as CEO by David Cole. With experience in retailing and consumer products, Cole was a good fit for Coinstar. Although the company had finally turned its first profit, there was a sense that it was approaching maximization of the coin-changing business. Coinstar's machines were installed in most of the major grocery chains, and the growth in installations of new machines was slowing down. In addition, many potential customers were put off by the 8.9 percent coin-changing service charge.

Cole's strategy for avoiding stagnation was to move beyond coin-counting and develop new services and revenue streams using the existing base of installed coin machines. The idea was to offer various prepaid options on to which users could load the value of their coins rather than simply taking a voucher for the cash value. To add to the revenue stream, Coinstar added bill acceptors to its kiosks. In addition, to place its machines into more stores, the company focused on the "fourth wall," the neglected space between the check-out lanes and the store entrance. Coinstar shared the revenue generated, and thus both parties profited. Another new goal was to capture "unbanked" consumers who had no convenient way to move cash and paychecks to debit cards or other prepaid instruments.

ACQUISITION, EXPANSION, AND DIVERSIFICATION

To realize these goals and move the company forward again, Coinstar embarked on an aggressive multiyear acquisition and expansion campaign. Through partnering with merchants and service providers, Coinstar began to realize expanded revenues from the coin-heavy and the unbanked. As early as 2001 it started to pilot a MasterCard–branded "Truth Card" in 52 stores. In a pilot program in Las Vegas and Houston in 2003, Coinstar distributed prepaid debit cards and payroll debit cards through MasterCard and others. The payroll card was marketed to employers who were willing to drop paper checks and issue cards to employees without bank accounts. That same year Coinstar partnered with Financial Stored Value Systems to create a wide network of kiosks for participating employees. The decision by Safeway stores, which had 1,000 Coinstar coin-changing kiosks, to not renew its contract in 2003 no doubt reinforced its decision to diversify.

Coinstar introduced several other prepaid weapons into its kiosk arsenal. It made gift cards available for a wide range of dining, clothing, and entertainment providers. In 2005 Amazon.com agreed to allow customers at 12,000 Coinstar locations to purchase Amazon gift cards with no Coinstar service charges. As early as 2001 Coinstar was piloting a topping-off service for holders of prepaid mobile phone cards and adding a pilot in the United Kingdom in 2003. In 2006 Coinstar kiosks offered gift cards for iTunes and Virgin Digital.

In 2004 Coinstar acquired major prepaid product distributor CellCards of Illinois, extending its reach to a new realm: point-of-sale locations in drug stores. The following year it acquired Mundo Communications Network. Serving 2,300 western U.S. retail locations, Mundo featured prepaid MasterCards, cell phone airtime, gift cards, and prepaid long-distance calls. To handle bill payments, prepaids, online computer games, and other new product and service needs, Coinstar developed the smaller, more powerful TOP-UP kiosk.

The international market had long beckoned Coinstar. In 2006 it purchased Travelex Money Transfer, the world's third-largest international money transfer company, operating at 17,000 locations in 138 countries. The following year it acquired GroupEx Financial Corp., a large transfer company serving Latin America.

Entering the entertainment realm, in 2004 Coinstar acquired American Coin Merchandising, an operator of over 167,000 coin-operated kiddy rides, skill-cranes, and other entertainment machines. In what would turn out to be a key move for its future, in 2005 Coinstar paid $20 million for a substantial minority interest in Redbox, a McDonald's unit that rented DVDs for one dollar from 800 self-service kiosks mostly in McDonald's restaurants. A few years later, Coinstar exercised an option to acquire a majority interest in Redbox. It was perhaps the best move Coinstar ever made.

NEW LEADERSHIP RETURNING TO THE COMPANY'S ROOTS

At this juncture CEO David Cole retired. He was replaced by chief operating officer Paul Davis. Soon afterward Gregg Kaplan, former CEO of Redbox, became president and also replaced Davis as COO. Most of the diversification of the Cole era was soon thrown out. In 2009 Coinstar sold its entertainment business to National Entertainment Network, Inc., after taking a $65.2 million loss. In 2010 it sold its electronic payment services to InComm, Inc., for $40 million. This included the entire portfolio of prepaid cards for a wide range of services. That same year Coinstar sold its international money transfer services to Sigue Corporation for $41.5 million.

Coinstar sold its prepaid card and money transfer operations because they were not producing significant revenues. Entertainment was sold because it was no longer needed after serving a very special purpose for Coinstar: reeling in the retailing giant Wal-Mart. According to *BusinessWeek Online* on February 11, 2008, "Coinstar bought its entertainment division … as a way to get its coin-counting machines into Wal-Mart's superstores." Replacing the old coin-operated stationary kiddy rides were thousands of new coin machines and Redbox kiosks.

The dismantling of the diversification effort of the 2000s pared Coinstar down to its original coin-changing core, plus the up-and-coming Redbox. The sold-off businesses constituted a relatively small fraction of total revenues and profits, and Redbox, with 67 percent of revenues before the spinoffs and its revenues growing astronomically every year, was poised to become the tail wagging the dog. This tail, incidentally, was helping Coinstar weather the recession of 2008–09 and the ensuing slow recovery.

BACK ON TRACK WITH REDBOX

Only one cloud remained on Coinstar's horizon. Redbox had become embroiled in a legal battle with Hollywood studios over the timing of the availability of movies for rental. At stake was the public's chance to rent movies when they were at their "hottest," right after release. The studios saw immediate rental as a threat to DVD prices and various other revenue streams and wanted to force Redbox to wait 28 days or more before renting new titles.

Happily for Coinstar, Redbox was able to strike deals with a number of the studios. By agreeing to pay

Sony Pictures up to $460 million, Redbox was granted the right for five years to rent all new Sony titles on their release date. Redbox reached similar agreements with Lions Gate Entertainment and Paramount. Redbox won a less advantageous result, however, when it reached a two-year agreement with Warner Home Video for $124 million that made Warner DVDs available 28 days after release.

The future looked bright for Coinstar and Redbox. Kroger had agreed to allow new Redbox kiosks into 2,600 of its supermarkets. Redbox began adding titles in the new medium of Blu-ray to its network of 22,000 kiosks. Coinstar was confident enough in its future to invest in ecoATM, a company that was developing a kiosk where consumers could turn in their old cell phones and receive a payment. Coinstar wanted to be in a position to profit from the estimated $7 billion worth of phones retired annually. Was this an opening to a new era of diversification? Only time would tell.

Carrie Rothburd
Updated, Judson MacLaury

PRINCIPAL SUBSIDIARIES

Coinstar Money Transfer Ltd.; Coinstar International, Inc.; Redbox.

PRINCIPAL COMPETITORS

Global Payment Technologies, Inc.; Continental Coin Processors; Netflix.

FURTHER READING

Flanagan, William G., and Alexandra Alger. "'It's Found Money': Finally, There's an Easy Way to Cash in All That Extra Change." *Forbes*, February 10, 1997, 214.

Grover, Ronald, and Olga Kharif. "Hollywood vs. Redbox." *BusinessWeek*, August 24, 2009, 38.

Levisohn, Ben. "Coinstar: Counting More Than Coins; Shares Get a Jolt after the Company Announces a Deal to Boost the Number of DVD Rental and Coin Machines at Wal-Mart." *BusinessWeek Online*, February 11, 2008.

Stepankowsky, Paula L. "Coinstar Leveraging Coin Machine Network with More Services." *Dow Jones News Service*, July 7, 2001.

Tarnowski, Joseph. "Eyes Front: Coinstar Is Thinking about Ways to Help Retailers Turn the Front of the Store from a No Man's Land into a Gold Mine." *Progressive Grocer*, May 1, 2005, 26.

Tice, Carol. "Coinstar Adds Services, Plans to Shed Meals.com." *Puget Sound Business Journal*, June 29, 2001, 59.

Vogelstein, Fred, and David Brindley. "No More Wrapping and Rolling." *U.S. News & World Report*, April 21, 1997, 85.

Colefax Group PLC

19–23 Grosvenor Hill
London, W1K 3QD
England
Telephone: (+44 20) 7493-2231
Fax: (+44 20) 7495-3123
Web site: http://www.colefaxgroupplc.com

Public Company
Founded: 1934
Incorporated: 1939 as Sibyl Colefax and John Fowler Limited; 1984 as Colefax Group PLC
Employees: 360
Sales: $102.8 million (2010)
Stock Exchanges: AIM (London)
Ticker Symbol: CFX
NAICS: 442110 Furniture Stores; 442291 Window Treatment Stores; 442299 All Other Home Furnishings Stores

■ ■ ■

Colefax Group PLC designs, distributes, and sells luxury furnishings for the high-end residential market in the United Kingdom, United States, and continental Europe. The company sells fabrics, wallpapers, upholstered furniture, window trimmings, and other related furnishings. The company's fabrics brands include Colefax and Fowler, Cowtan & Tout, Jane Churchill, Larsen, and Manuel Canovas. Colefax is also a major international decorating firm with offices in the United Kingdom, United States, France, Germany, and Italy. About 20 percent of the firm's business comes from the decorating division. The London-based company garners more than half its annual sales from the United States.

COMPANY ORIGINS

Colefax Group has its roots in a small decorating company for the wealthy and well known, formed through the perhaps unlikely partnership between John Fowler and Sibyl Colefax. Sibyl Colefax was part of the upper-crust English establishment who had been forced to make a living after she lost £50,000 in the Wall Street crash of 1929 and her husband, a well-known London attorney, died in 1936. She moved to a smaller house, and soon pictures of her home appeared in *Vogue House & Garden Book*. Colefax had begun to offer her services as a decorator to the very wealthy and prominent socialites who were part of her social set by 1934.

John Fowler, half as old as Colefax, in a few short years had become one of Britain's leading decorators, highlighted by his inclusion in a 1938 *House & Garden* feature of prominent designers. That year he accepted Colefax's invitation to work at her firm. Although their personalities appeared worlds apart, as decorators, they worked well together, and both initially utilized the Regency Revival style that was immensely popular in the 1930s. By 1939 the company was formally renamed Sibyl Colefax and John Fowler Limited, with Fowler taking a smaller share of the business and Colefax maintaining a majority stake.

The coming of World War II stalled the fledgling business as both Colefax and Fowler spent much time on the war effort. Nonetheless, Colefax found time to

COMPANY PERSPECTIVES

Colefax Group PLC is an international designer and distributor of luxury furnishing fabrics and wallpapers and a leading international decorating company. Sales are made under the brand names Colefax and Fowler, Cowtan & Tout, Jane Churchill, Larsen, and Manuel Canovas. The Group strategy is to build and expand its portfolio of luxury international fabric brands. Each fabric brand in the Group has a separate design studio and a separate marketing strategy promoting a distinctive look.

write missives to friends gently reminding them of her business, mentioning, per Martin Wood in his 2007 book *John Fowler: Prince of Decorators*, that she and Fowler had "lovely old furniture ... and, as ever, can do any jobs ... allowed by [wartime] Regulations." Colefax fell ill and in 1944 was forced to sell her stake, which was purchased by Nancy Tree (later Nancy Lancaster) for £15,000.

Colefax died in 1950, but her name would live on with the company. Lancaster, a transplant from Virginia who had been a client of Fowler's, loved English country houses and their traditional style. Fowler had a keen sense of the historical and was an expert in creating a unity of colors, patterns, and textures. Ultimately, their two strengths were wed as the business took off in the 1950s.

THE RISE OF THE ENGLISH COUNTRY STYLE

During the 1950s Fowler helped to popularize a particular image of the country house as one filled with expensive antiques, beautiful fabrics, and symmetrical designs reminiscent of the 18th century. In 1956 Fowler became an advisor for the National Trust of Britain, contributing significantly to the redecoration of its properties.

Fowler and Lancaster engaged in the design and decoration of numerous famous and luxurious houses in Britain, including Chequers, Uppark, and Buckingham Palace, as well as many more modest projects. Fowler's style, even after World War II when restrictions on materials were lifted and the company came to decorate many architecturally significant interiors, was humble while still elegant. However, it was through his exposure to Lancaster's love of the English country home and his often contentious collaboration with her that Fowler fine-tuned his style.

REDESIGN OF COLEFAX AND FOWLER

By 1960 Lancaster's son Michael Tree was handling her finances, and it had become clear that the company needed to be restructured to stabilize financially. Fowler invited Tom Parr, then in business with a well-known decorator, to join the firm as a financial assistant. Tree agreed with Fowler's decision to appoint Parr, who was later credited with saving the company. Parr added business acumen and a concern for retailing and distribution that had been missing from the firm. He quickly set about transforming the company into a modern commercial enterprise. In 1969 Fowler retired from the company.

The company in the 1970s opened a retail outlet in Belgravia, a wealthy neighborhood in London. By the mid-1970s Colefax and Fowler still was a somewhat sleepy decorating firm, with about 70 employees working from a London design office. After Fowler's death in 1977, however, the company underwent a major redesign.

Following Colefax and Fowler's initial retailing successes in the 1960s and 1970s, the company began distributing its collections to trade markets in the United Kingdom and abroad in the early 1980s. The year 1985, a particularly strong one for Colefax, highlighted a burgeoning trend: throngs of Americans flocking to Colefax's showroom on Bond Street in London to furnish their U.S. homes with English antiques, art objects, chintzes, and paintings. A renaissance in the English Country style, which seemed to offer an immediate pedigree for the residential home and credibility for the businessperson, and the strength of the dollar versus the pound also contributed to the popularity of this trend. By 1987 Colefax had unveiled a new suite of occasional furniture to blend with an interior of antiques within a traditional setting.

GOING PUBLIC

David Green, of Carlton Communications, Inc., became chief executive of Colefax and Fowler in 1986. By 1988 the company had three retail outlets and 1,500 product distributors. Within three years Green had helped the company double its revenues as the firm expanded to 120 employees. Also in 1988 the company held an initial public offering (IPO). By that time the company's board had moved the company toward a retail business. That year Colefax set up shop in the

KEY DATES

1934: Sibyl Colefax opens a decorating business in London.
1939: A year after John Fowler joins Colefax's firm, the company becomes Sibyl Colefax and John Fowler Limited.
1944: Colefax sells her majority interest in the company to Nancy Tree (later Lancaster).
1969: Fowler retires from the company.
1986: David Green becomes chief executive of the company and begins a rapid diversification.
1988: The company goes public.

United States with the £9.9 million purchase of the New York–based Cowtan & Tout, a fabrics and wallpaper designer and distributor. The acquisition was funded in part by the public float of 7.5 million shares of stock. Colefax was already distributing Cowtan & Tout products outside the United States, and the purchase allowed the company greater control over distribution and production.

Colefax made two more acquisitions before the end of the decade. In 1989 the company acquired the international furnishing designer and distributor Jane Churchill for £1 million as part of Green's strategy to develop a field of well-known quality brands. The London-based business included the consultancy services run by the company's owner Jane Churchill. Colefax soon expanded the Churchill operations. Colefax also acquired in 1989 the Devon, England–based manufacturer LM Kingcome for £1 million. Financed by a secondary public offering, the Kingcome acquisition brought along a high-end handmade upholstered furniture business specializing in quality sofas.

Colefax nearly doubled its revenues in the first year of the new decade, and earnings in 1990 grew by nearly 50 percent. The company had also led the Jane Churchill operation out of the red and into profitability. By 1990 Colefax's conversion from a design and decorating firm to a distributor of high-end furnishings was evident in sales figures. A full 80 percent of revenues came from the company's product division, driven by what the company called a "faded elegance" style, as European sales rose 22 percent in a year and U.S. sales rose 15 percent. Colefax had modified its product line for European distributors to appeal to the desire for brighter and brasher colors. In the German market the company created items that were more functional and neutral in color.

During the early 1990s a housing slump in the United States coupled with a relatively slow economy contributed to a slide in Colefax's profits. Although sales were more limited than in previous years, the company's brands remained strong, and European annual revenues rose. By 1993, however, profits took a major hit. Pretax earnings for Colefax fell in the 1992–93 year from £704,000 to a loss of £395,000.

RISING PROFITS AND ADDITIONAL ACQUISITIONS

It was not long before the economy was on the road to recovery. Colefax began to return to profitability by 1994. Jane Churchill and Cowtan & Tout performed particularly well. The company in 1996 experienced additional improvement, propelled by a housing market on an upswing, but was far still from reaching its late 1980s heights. With its stock in 1996 worth only about half its IPO value, Colefax saw profits that were far from returning to their 1989 high of £4 million.

In 1997 Colefax announced it would roll out a "more informal" furnishings line to compete with the Swedish furnishings group IKEA, which had begun to make its mark on UK tastes, a departure from the floral chintz of the past. With its bottom line improving, Colefax in 1997 acquired the U.S. fabrics firm Jack Lenor Larsen for £4 million and placed it under the control of subsidiary Cowtan & Tout. The Larsen brand, known for its interwoven textiles, was soon introduced to UK and European markets. In 1998 Colefax acquired the Paris-based fabric manufacturer Manuel Canovas SA for $8.8 million (Colefax paid some $6.7 million, issuing new shares to cover the balance). Colefax expected the acquisition to provide the company with both a solid clientele base in Europe as well as woven-fabric products to complement the company's printed fabrics portfolio.

Overall sales for Colefax continued to rise in the late 1990s, led by activities in the United States, while UK revenues fell due to tough market conditions. By the late 1990s, Colefax had become what Leslie Geddes-Brown in the August 1998 issue of *Town & Country* called "a 460-person conglomerate, one of the most aggressively expansionist in the design world." The firm's five distinct brands of Colefax and Fowler, Cowtan & Tout, Jane Churchill, Larsen, and Manuel Canovas offered American, European, and modern styles, allowing it to service a broader range of wealthy homeowners.

A NEW CENTURY, DIFFICULT MARKET CONDITIONS

By 2000 the company's revenues of £63.9 million generated pretax profits of £5.1 million. Meanwhile,

U.S. sales had grown to more than 55 percent of all company revenues, and UK revenues had slipped to about 20 percent. Writing in the *Financial Times* (July 22, 2000), David Harold Blackwell acknowledged the company's illustrious past but observed that "Colefax & Fowler, which virtually invented the English country-house look in the 1930s, remains a brand associated with wealthy home owners. But it has changed dramatically over the past decade or so, and it would now be fair to describe it as a US company listed in London."

By 2001 housing markets in the United Kingdom and United States were weakening. In January 2003 the value of Colefax stock slid to 65 1/2 pence, its lowest point in three years. Dependency on the U.S. market brought a downside as losses in the value of the dollar meant losses for the company. In August 2004 Colefax pulled out of the London Stock Exchange's main market after 16 years. The company listed on the junior market AIM, designed for smaller and high-growth companies. AIM involved less regulatory control and also offered listees certain tax advantages.

FLUCTUATIONS IN THE ECONOMY

The company's U.S. sales increased in 2005 despite the declining luxury housing market. After a better-than-expected year, Colefax stock climbed in August 2006 to an all-time high of 190 pence. Housing booms in the United Kingdom and United States helped drive the improvements in profits and share value.

The year 2007 began with strong growth in the industry for high-end furnishings, as the market for luxury homes boomed. The *Evening Standard* of London reported on July 23, 2007, that "the influx of wealthy foreigners to London seeking classic English furnishings has driven Colefax Group's profits to a record" for the 2006–07 year. Sales of £71 generated pretax earnings of £5.93 million. Operations in the United Kingdom and continental Europe did particularly well. The company's stock performed very well, although a Colefax share buyback that began the previous year had cut into available stock.

By 2008 Colefax was following the market trends and targeting luxury clientele. By late 2008, however, the economic downturn had impacted company sales. Most of the company's major markets were embedded in recession by 2009. Earnings for 2008–09 were sliced nearly in half, and Colefax responded by reducing its dividend.

THE LUXURY HOUSING MARKET AND THE FUTURE FOR COLEFAX

Colefax's future and finances were clearly tied to the UK and U.S. housing markets, and as those markets suffered late in the decade, so did the company. To cut its business losses, Colefax during the 2009–10 year sold its noncore Manuel Canovas Beachwear Division but would have to later assume an after-tax disposal cost of £757,000.

By mid-2010 Colefax reported much-improved annual results for the previous year. Green conceded that uncertainties such as the recovery of the housing market and the strength of the dollar, as well as rising raw material costs from Colefax suppliers, made the future unclear. In Colfax's 2010 annual report, he stated that the company's performance "will be about striking the right balance between controlling our costs and investing in the future to make sure that we are in a strong position to take full advantage of any recovery."

Roger Rouland

PRINCIPAL SUBSIDIARIES

Colefax and Fowler Limited; Sibyl Colefax and John Fowler Limited; Kingcome Sofas Limited; Colefax and Fowler Holdings Limited; Cowtan & Tout Incorporated (USA); Manuel Canovas SAS (France); Colefax and Fowler GmbH (Germany); Colefax and Fowler Srl (Italy).

PRINCIPAL COMPETITORS

Galiform PLC; House of Fraser Limited; Inter IKEA Systems B.V.; Harvey Nichols Group Limited; Liberty PLC; NEXT PLC; ScS Upholstery; Steinhoff UK Retail Limited.

FURTHER READING

Apple, R. W. "Buying British." *New York Times Magazine*, April 14, 1985.

Blackwell, David Harold. "In Search of a Golden Thread." *Financial Times*, July 22, 2000.

"CEO Interview: David Green—Colefax Group PLC." *Wall Street Transcript Digest*, April 23, 2001.

Fallon, James. "French Connection for Colefax." *HFN The Weekly Newspaper for the Home Furnishing Network*, March 30, 1998, 21.

"Impressive Upgrade from Colefax's Broker." *Investors Chronicle*, January 27, 2010.

Mesure, Susie. "Colefax Struggles to Paper over Cracks." *Independent* (London), July 23, 2003.

"Recession Pulls Cushion from under Colefax." *Financial Times*, July 21, 2009.

"Smart Recovery at Colefax." *Investors Chronicle*, July 27, 2010.

Wood, Martin. *John Fowler: Prince of Decorators*. London: Frances Lincoln, 2007.

Columbian Home Products, LLC

550 North Rand Road
Lake Zurich, Illinois 60047
U.S.A.
Telephone: (847) 307-8621
Fax: (847) 726-4706
Web site: http://www.columbianhp.com

Private Company
Founded: 1871 as Bellaire Stamping Company
Employees: 145
NAICS: 339999 All Other Miscellaneous Manufacturing

■ ■ ■

Headquartered in Lake Zurich, Illinois, Columbian Home Products, LLC, is a privately held manufacturer of cookware, bakeware, cooking accessories, canning supplies, and tea kettles. Its flagship brand, Granite Ware, is made from a combination of porcelain and steel to produce a wide variety of roasters, pots and pans, seafood pots, canning pots, bakeware, Mexican cookware, and casual cookware. Manufacturing is done in Terre Haute, Indiana. The Joyce Chen unit, which is based in Walnut, California, produces woks and stir fry skillets, cutting and food preparation tools, bamboo steamers, cutting boards, and ornate tea kettles. The products are also sold under the China Village label. Snow River Products, which operates out of Crandon, Wisconsin, offers crafted wooden bowls, cutting boards, carts, and specialty items such as cedar grill planks, pastry boards, and sink boards. Other Columbian brands include Italian Villa cookware and accessories; Mexican Fiesta calderos, fajita pans, and accessories; and Country Cabin cast iron cookware. Columbian products are carried by a wide variety of retailers in the United States and Canada, including Ace Hardware, Bed Bath & Beyond, Target, and Wal-Mart. Columbian is owned by its chief executive officer, Dick Ryan.

ORIGINS: 1871–99

Columbian traces its history to Bellaire, Ohio, where in 1871 the Bellaire Stamping Company was formed to produce mason jars and kerosene lamps. Bellaire Stamping then turned its attention to cookware. At the time, easy-to-clean, lightweight enamel cookware was gaining in popularity over traditional cast iron cookware, which was more expensive. To enter this new market, Bellaire Stamping acquired the Belmont Glass works and began developing a porcelain enameling process. The work was interrupted by a devastating fire, however, so Bellaire Stamping moved to Harvey, Illinois. A new plant opened in 1890 that was designed solely to produce porcelain enameled utensils.

Bellaire Stamping was well aware of the Columbian Exposition of 1893 that was held in Chicago to commemorate the 400th anniversary of Christopher Columbus's first voyage to the New World. The exposition was a seminal moment in U.S. history that not only affected architecture for years to come but also spurred U.S. industrial might well into the 20th century. Bellaire Stamping won design awards at the exposition. Thus, it was not surprising that the company latched onto the Columbian name when it decided to change its image at the turn of the century, following

COMPANY PERSPECTIVES

The name has changed several times over the last 125 years, but the business remains the same—producing porcelain on steel cookware.

another devastating fire that totally destroyed the Harvey plant in 1899.

TERRE HAUTE PLANT: 1902–35

The principals of Bellaire Stamping, Wilbur Tallman, Wilbur Topping, Henry Dalzell, and Charles Gorby, elected to rebuild the plant using the insurance money from the fire and new capital. Financial incentives from the city of Terre Haute, Indiana, persuaded the owners to relocate, and in April 1902 a new enamelware plant opened on the north side of the city. The company reemerged as Columbian Enameling and Stamping Company and offered products under the Columbian brand as well as under the Dresden, Amethyst, and Atlas labels.

The new Terre Haute plant was massive, consisting of 14 brick and steel buildings with a combined floor space of 172,500 square feet. Powered by steam, the state-of-the-art facility had only one drawback: it lacked sufficient lighting, which limited work hours and prevented Columbian from taking advantage of the demand for enameled cookware. This problem was corrected in 1913, when generators were installed to light the facility, and the plant became operational 24 hours a day.

Europe was soon at war and the United States was eventually involved as well. Like many U.S. companies, Columbian began producing war materials. Because of its expertise, the company produced metal helmets and other goods. Following the war, Columbian gained national notice because it was involved in one of the country's most publicized labor disputes.

During the early 1930s the company negotiated a one-year agreement with the United Garment Workers Union that called for voluntary union membership, but the two parties quickly fell out over a number of issues. The union responded by seeking mandatory union membership for all nonmanagement positions. Columbian and the union returned to the negotiating table in November 1934, and after five months of fruitless talks, union members voted to strike. In March 1935 union members walked off the job.

VIOLENT STRIKE: 1935

Columbian responded to the strike by closing the plant. In June 1935 the management announced that if the plant reopened, it would be with nonunion employees. When eight armed uniform guards occupied the plant a few days later, an angry mob attacked the plant and the police had to rescue the guards. Tensions escalated further when in mid-July a 50-man security force armed with shotguns and submachine guns entered the plant. Another mob formed and in the altercation that followed many people were hurt and 150 arrests were made.

The Indiana national guard was ordered into Terre Haute to maintain martial law, a situation that lasted for six months. In the meantime the plant reopened with new workers. The National Labor Relations Board (NLRB) ruled that the company had to rehire as many of the former workers as possible, but the matter was not finally settled until it reached the U.S. Supreme Court. In 1939 the Court ruled in *Labor Board v. Columbian Enameling and Stamping Co.* that the NLRB order was void because the Wagner Act, which established the NLRB and the right to collective bargaining, was not effective until a few weeks after the strike began. During this interim period the Court asserted that there was no evidence that Columbian executives knew that the union wished to initiate collective bargaining or that Columbian executives refused to begin collective negotiations.

GENERAL HOUSEWARES: 1939–95

Columbian resumed production under the protection of martial law, but the fight with the union left wounds in the community that only time would heal. Columbian continued to manufacture enamel cookware under the Granite Ware name as an independent company until 1968. In that year it was acquired by General Housewares Corporation, which had been founded a year earlier by John H. Muller Jr., a former marketing executive with General Foods. With $50,000 of his own money, $1.5 million raised through a public stock offering, and $5 million in borrowed funds, Muller had launched the company by acquiring a Minnesota manufacturer of outdoor furniture, ladders, and ironing boards. Other acquisitions followed and Muller eventually focused on two primary groups: tabletop giftware and cookware. The latter was based at the Columbian operation in Terre Haute.

During its time under General Housewares ownership, Columbian replaced its longtime enamel pots with ones that relied on heavier and smoother metals offering a porcelain-like finish. By 1980 General Housewares was

KEY DATES

1871: Bellaire Stamping Company is founded in Bellaire, Ohio.
1902: The company relocates to Terre Haute, Indiana, as Columbian Enameling and Stamping Company.
1935: A strike leads to martial law in Terre Haute.
1968: The company is sold to General Housewares Corporation.
1998: Columbian Home Products, LLC, is formed.

the only manufacturer of enamelware in the United States due to stiff competition from manufacturers in countries that enjoyed duty preference. Staying the course proved wise for General Housewares because in 1980 the U.S. International Trade Commission provided temporary trade protection to manufacturers of enamelware. As the only remaining U.S. producer, General Housewares was rewarded for its patience.

General Housewares looked to make inroads in the upper end of the cookware market. In keeping with this change in direction, General Housewares added to its Cookware Group in 1983 by acquiring Leyse Aluminum Co. for $7.8 million in cash and notes. Based in Kewaunee, Wisconsin, Leyse Aluminum was an industrial customer fabricator and decorative metals finisher that also produced professional cookware. At the time, the Cookware Group accounted for $45 million of General Housewares' total sales of $74 million.

Overseas competition led to changes in the Cookware Group during the early 1990s. The stainless steel segment was no longer profitable, so it was sold. In the meantime, a new line of nonstick cast aluminum cookware was introduced, and the enamelware business was strengthened by the acquisition of the Normandy line from the National Housewares Corporation. During the mid-1990s the cast iron lines of cookware were divested, leaving Granite Ware as the main focus of the Cookware Group.

DICK RYAN: 1998

General Housewares decided to make the switch from a manufacturing company to a distribution and marketing operation. In keeping with this strategy, the Granite Ware line was sold in March 1998 to Dick Ryan, the former president of the Cookware Group. To accomplish the acquisition, he formed Columbian Home Products, LLC, drawing on the name of Granite Ware's parent. Besides the brand and inventory, Columbian acquired the Terre Haute plant, where the company was headquartered.

As the new incarnation of Columbian plotted its course, it continued to face overseas challenges, in particular from producers in China, Mexico, and Taiwan, who sought to dump porcelain-on-steel cookware in the U.S. market. In 2000 the International Trade Commission voted to continue the antidumping order, much to the satisfaction of Columbian.

With some measure of security from unfair foreign competition, Columbian expanded through acquisitions. In 2001 it acquired Snow River Products, a Vermont manufacturer of cutting boards, bowls, and wooden kitchen accessories. A year later Snow River acquired the Woodworking Division of Bemis Manufacturing Company, a producer of hardwood, acrylic, and poly cutting boards. Its Crandon, Wisconsin, plant then became the home for Snow River. Also of note in 2002, Columbian became the exclusive distributor of Cinsa S.A. de C.V.'s Mexican-produced cookware.

As the decade unfolded, Columbian continued to grow both organically and through acquisitions. In 2003 the company acquired Joyce Chen, Inc., a company founded by the Chinese immigrant Joyce Chen, who popularized Mandarin cuisine in the United States. She opened a restaurant in Cambridge, Massachusetts, in 1958 and then authored a cookbook in 1964 that led to the cooking series *Joyce Chen Cooks* on the Public Broadcasting Service. During the 1970s she developed her own line of Chinese cookware. She passed away in 1994. The family sold Joyce Chen along with the subsidiary Keilen Ltd. to Columbian.

In 2006 Columbian forged an alliance with the Television Food Network, G.P. The company was selected to develop a cookware line for the network's popular cooking series *Iron Chef America*. The line featured a new type of cast iron cookware that was lightweight and had nonstick surfaces. Even though cast iron was one of the oldest materials in cookware, it was making a comeback and Columbian was well positioned to take advantage of the trend. Over the course of its history, the company had overcome fires, labor strife, and foreign competition, and there was every reason to believe that it would remain viable for many years to come.

Ed Dinger

PRINCIPAL SUBSIDIARIES

Joyce Chen, Inc.; Snow River Products.

PRINCIPAL COMPETITORS

Meyer Manufacturing Co. Ltd.; Newell Rubbermaid Inc.; Swiss Diamond International Sàrl.

FURTHER READING

Barmash, Isadore. "Houseware Maker Thrives as Families Stay at Home." *New York Times*, May 6, 1982.

"Columbian Home Products Acquires Joyce Chen, Inc." *Gourmet Retailer*, March 2003, 10.

"High Court Voids NLRB Hiring Order." *New York Times*, February 28, 1939.

Porter, Thyra. "General Housewares Sells off Cookware." March 23, 1998, 1.

Roznowski, Tom. *An American Hometown: Terre Haute, Indiana, 1927*. Bloomington: Indiana University Press, 2009.

Sarkar, Dipa. "Historical Treasure: Don't Take It for Granite." *Tribune Star* (Terre Haute, IN), July 7, 2007.

"Terre Haute Tense under Martial Law." *New York Times*, July 25, 1935.

Cooper Tire & Rubber Company

701 Lima Avenue
Findlay, Ohio 45840
U.S.A.
Telephone: (419) 423-1321
Toll Free: (800) 854-6288
Fax: (419) 424-4212
Web site: http://www.coopertire.com

Public Company
Founded: 1914 as M&M Manufacturing
Incorporated: 1960
Employees: 13,000
Sales: $2.78 billion (2009)
Stock Exchanges: NYSE
Ticker Symbol: CTB
NAICS: 326211 Tire Manufacturing (except Retreading); 423130 Tire and Tube Merchant Wholesalers

■ ■ ■

Cooper Tire & Rubber Company designs, manufactures, and markets replacement tires for passenger cars, light trucks, sport utility vehicles, motorcycles, racing vehicles, and commercial trucks. The company is the fourth-largest tire manufacturer in North America and the ninth-largest worldwide, and it operates 67 manufacturing, design, technical, sales, and distribution facilities in 10 countries. Besides the Cooper tire lines, the company's other proprietary brands include Avon, Mickey Thompson, Mastercraft, Dean, and Dick Cepak. These brands are sold through tire dealers, wholesale distributors, and regional and national tire chains.

EARLY 20TH-CENTURY ORIGINS

In 1914 brothers-in-law John F. Schaefer and Claude E. Hart bought the M&M Manufacturing Company in Akron, Ohio. Schaefer and Hart entered the industry in the midst of a period of vigorous growth, for between 1910 and 1916 tire production doubled every two years. As real incomes increased over the decade and the Ford Motor Company introduced its more affordable Model T, the demand for tires increased. Tire manufacturers increased capacity, designed new machinery, and promoted their new products.

During the second decade of the 20th century Ohio was a hub of tire manufacturing: one-third of the 134 tire companies in the United States were located in the state, and Akron alone supplied one-third of the country's rubber goods. Located in the "rubber capital of the world," M&M Manufacturing produced tire patches, cement, and repair kits. These products were in high demand during the early years of the automotive tire industry because the first pneumatic tires were easily punctured. Poor tire quality also prompted consumers to seek rebuilt tires, so in 1915 Schaefer and Hart purchased the Giant Tire & Rubber Company, a tire rebuilding business, in Akron.

In 1917 the Giant Tire & Rubber operations were moved to Findlay, Ohio, into buildings that had been abandoned by the failed Toledo Findlay Tire Company. That same year Ira J. Cooper, whose name would later come to represent the company, joined Giant's board of directors. Fire destroyed the main building of the Giant plant in 1919, but reconstruction of a new, single-story plant began immediately. As Giant rebuilt and

COMPANY PERSPECTIVES

One company, one team, one goal: creating superior value, for our customers, employees, partners and shareholders.

continued to grow, Cooper became involved in forming his own company to manufacture new tires, the Cooper Corporation, which began operations in 1920. As founder, Cooper emphasized dedication to three principles: good merchandise, fair play, and a square deal. This "Cooper Creed" would serve as a corporate doctrine for many years to come.

INDUSTRY CONSOLIDATION: 1920–46

The tire industry underwent several changes during the 1920s. New tire and rim designs made it easier for consumers to replace worn or punctured tires, and improved durability meant they would have to do so less often. Lower pressure tires that were developed during the decade improved comfort and road handling. Furthermore, technological advances in the manufacturing process helped larger companies gain economies of scale that made them more competitive and promoted a consolidation of the industry during the 1920s and 1930s.

In 1930 the Giant Tire & Rubber Company and Cooper Corporation merged with the Falls Rubber Company of Cuyahoga Falls, Ohio, to form the Master Tire & Rubber Company. Within one year, production at the three plants totaled 2,850 tires per day. At that time the company marketed tires under several brand names, including Falls, Giant, Sterchi, Hoover, Savage, Linco, Williams, Swinehart, Tigerfoot, and Englert. When the company began downsizing during the 1930s, all the tire operations were brought to Findlay by 1936.

Ira J. Cooper died in 1941, the first year the Cooper oval trademark was registered and used. In those early years of the brand's identification, the logo also included a banner proclaiming the tires' "armored-cord" construction. The company's red, white, and blue logo would become one of the most easily recognized emblems in the tire industry.

During World War II the company manufactured pontoons, landing boats, waterproof bags, inflatable barges, life jackets, and tires to benefit the Allied war effort. In 1946 the company's name was officially changed to Cooper Tire & Rubber Company, in recognition of Cooper's contribution to the Master Tire & Rubber Company.

POST–WORLD WAR II EXPANSION: 1947–65

The postwar era heralded expansion at both Cooper and in the industry as a whole. Three major factors contributed to the growth of the business: increasing disposable incomes, development of the interstate highway system, and suburbanization. As Americans' disposable income increased, they had more money available to purchase cars, so much so that car sales skyrocketed. Likewise, the expansion of the interstate highway system and suburbanization meant that Americans spent more time driving, which in turn meant more wear and tear on tires and increased demand for replacement tires. Furthermore, rail transportation was supplanted by buses, taxis, and trucks for local and long-distance needs. In 1956 Cooper purchased a plant from the Dismuke Tire & Rubber Company in Clarksdale, Mississippi. The refurbished factory helped Cooper meet demand for tubes and tread rubber.

Between 1947 and 1964 Cooper developed its own national wholesaling system. The company strengthened its ability to supply private brand customers and earned retailer loyalty by pledging not to open its own sales outlets. This marketing scheme simultaneously enabled Cooper to avoid the vagaries of the retail market.

Cooper went public in 1960. The distribution of shares facilitated another decade of growth for the company. That same year it acquired a plant in Auburn, Indiana, where all automotive and custom engineered rubber parts were produced. In 1964 an industrial rubber products division was established as a separate corporation known as Cooper Industrial Products Inc. A second industrial products plant near El Dorado, Arkansas, was acquired to expand those operations.

Capital improvements at the corporate headquarters during the 1960s included a new warehouse, which made operations at the Findlay plant more efficient. A research and engineering building was added to the location in 1964 to accommodate testing, laboratories, tire design, engineering, and sales training operations. That same year the company completed the first phase of construction on its new tire plant in Texarkana, Arkansas. The following year the production facilities in Texarkana, El Dorado, Auburn, and Clarksdale were expanded. Original outlets in Los Angeles, California, and Atlanta, Georgia, were replaced with new and

KEY DATES

1914: M&M Manufacturing is purchased by John F. Schaefer and Claude E. Hart.
1941: The Cooper trademark is registered.
1946: Company name is changed to Cooper Tire & Rubber Company.
1960: Cooper goes public.
1964: Cooper's industrial rubber products division is established.
1974: Cooper begins production of steel-belted radial tires.
1985: Cooper makes first global acquisition, Rio Grande Servaas, S.A. de C.V.
1997: Cooper acquires Avon Rubber PLC.
2004: Cooper sells automotive unit.
2005: Cooper acquires China's Cooper Chengshan (Shandong) Passenger Tire Company Ltd. and Cooper Chengshan (Shandong) Tire Company Ltd.

enlarged Cooper factory branches. Before the decade came to a close, the Texarkana plant was expanded and a modernization plan was completed.

CONVERSION TO RADIAL TIRES: 1970–80

During the 1970s Cooper worked to convert from bias-ply to radial tire manufacture. Bias tires had been produced by placing cords in rubberized fabric at an angle of 25 to 40 degrees to the direction traveled. Radial tires were originally conceived in 1913, but the first practical application of the idea was not achieved until 1948. Radial tires had cords or belts that were arranged at a 90-degree angle to the direction traveled. Advantages of radial construction included improved wear, improved handling, and lower fuel consumption. The disadvantages, however, prohibited many companies from making the conversion until the 1970s. Radial tires included more complex and time-consuming production requirements, incompatibility with bias tires on the same vehicle, and diminished cushioning. For a brief period, many manufacturers in the industry compromised by introducing a bias-belted tire, but steel-belted radials became the norm by the late 1970s.

Cooper completed research and development of its own radial tire manufacturing equipment and in-house product testing in 1973 and began full-scale production of steel-belted radial passenger tires at the Findlay and Texarkana plants the following year. During this time Cooper purchased a plant in Bowling Green, Ohio, for the manufacture of reinforced hose and extruded rubber products. Within three years, the plant was upgraded to produce rubber trunk, car door, window, and sunroof seals.

Near the end of the decade the U.S. government imposed the Uniform Tire Quality Grading System to regulate the manufacture and labeling of bias and belted tires. A voluntary system of tire grading had been proposed by the National Highway Traffic Safety Administration and accepted by the Rubber Manufacturers Association in 1966, but the guidelines were expensive and hard to enforce. The federal government advanced regulations several times during the 1970s, but grading did not begin until 1979 for bias-belted tires and 1980 for radial tires.

COUNTERCYCLICAL STRATEGIES: EARLY TO MID-EIGHTIES

The 1980s were years of significant change for Cooper and the tire industry overall. Many U.S. manufacturers scrambled to lower production capacity as the domestic market became saturated. From 1979 to 1987 a total of 23 U.S. plants were closed in the rush to downsize. However, while many U.S. tire manufacturers consolidated in the face of steadily falling automobile sales, Cooper executives calmly delineated strategies for continued growth and expansion of production. Cooper based its plans on several consistent factors. Its executives observed that there was as yet no other form of personal transportation that could provide the speed and convenience of the automobile and, therefore, no alternatives for the pneumatic tire. Cooper executives also noticed that as auto manufacturing in the United States improved, consumers kept their cars longer. Furthermore, as the average age of cars increased, so did the demand for replacement tires. As a result, when its competitors deserted plants, Cooper bought and upgraded them. By overhauling older facilities, Cooper added capacity for one-third the cost of building new ones.

In 1981 the Texarkana plant reached a production record of more than 5 million tires. The following year a three-phase expansion project at Texarkana was undertaken and three building additions at the Findlay plant were completed. Production capacity continued to increase with the purchase of a radial tire plant at Tupelo, Mississippi, and even more expansion at the Findlay plant.

By 1983 Cooper was ranked on the *Fortune* 500 register of the United States' largest industrial companies, and a year later its net sales exceeded $500 million. Two years later, in 1985, Cooper made its first foreign acquisition, that of Rio Grande Servaas, S.A. de C.V., in Piedras Negras, Mexico, a manufacturer of inner tubes. That same year Cooper was listed among the 101 Best Performing Companies in the United States.

CAPITAL IMPROVEMENTS: MID- TO LATE EIGHTIES

Research and development at Cooper were enhanced by several capital investments during the decade. A technical center for design, research, development, and testing was completed in 1984 at the Auburn engineered products plant. The following year saw the completion of an addition to Findlay's research and engineering complex. A third addition enhanced the Findlay facility in 1988.

Distribution was also improved during the 1980s, with centers opening or expanding in Atlanta; Moraine, Ohio; and Tacoma, Washington. Cooper warehousing capacity totaled 3.2 million tires by mid-decade. By the end of the 1980s the distribution centers at Findlay and Moraine were granted foreign trade subzone status from the U.S. Department of Commerce. This designation suspended Cooper's payment of duty on imported raw materials.

As the company celebrated its 75th anniversary, Cooper's emphasis on the replacement tire market was vindicated. Statistics showed that the replacement tire market was three times larger than the original equipment market and had grown much faster over the decade. Investors appreciated the company's performance as well. Cooper's stock rose 6,800 percent during the 1980s, and its per share price amounted to 14 times its earnings, which insulated Cooper from takeover threats.

INTERNAL IMPROVEMENTS AND EXPANSION OVERSEAS: 1990–99

Cooper's capital investments and focus on the replacement tire market continued to pay off during the 1990s. The company's efficient means of production propelled it to the highest gross profit margins in the industry at 33 percent. When larger competitors turned to the replacement tire market and tried to undercut Cooper's prices, its high margins gave the company leeway to join in the price wars.

Despite a lingering U.S. recession, Cooper's net sales topped the $1 billion mark in 1991. Cooper responded to this increase in sales by concentrating on expanding its capital investments. In 1990 the company purchased a 1.8-million-square-foot tire manufacturing plant in Albany, Georgia, then in 1993 it expanded its Findlay and Bowling Green locations. A $10.5 million upgrade of the Clarksdale facility began in 1994 and construction of a new plant in Mt. Sterling, Kentucky, got under way in 1995. Ongoing cost-cutting efforts almost doubled Cooper's operating margin from the late 1980s to the early 1990s.

Meanwhile, Cooper's net sales increased from $1.2 billion in 1992 to $1.4 billion in 1994, and its net revenues climbed to $128.5 million. Over the next two years sales continued to grow, totaling $1.6 billion in 1996. However, high raw material costs that could not be passed on to customers in the form of price increases began to cut into Cooper's net revenues in the intervening years. Profits declined and Cooper's usually high-flying stock suffered as well, dropping from a high of $39.50 per share in 1993 to less than $18 per share in 1996.

International sales totaled less than 10 percent of the company's total revenues in 1996. The Ohio firm then boosted its foreign operations in 1997 with the acquisition of Great Britain's Avon Rubber PLC for $110.4 million. The purchase gave Cooper a plant in England, distribution throughout France, Germany, and Switzerland, and a foothold in several emerging markets in Asia. It also added $169 million to Cooper's sales column and $6.5 million to the bottom line. In 1999 Cooper allied with Italy's Pirelli S.p.A., the world's sixth-largest tire manufacturer. This strategic deal gave Cooper access to Pirelli's high-performance tire technology, and while Cooper sold Pirelli tires in North America, Pirelli distributed Cooper tires in its South American market.

ADVERSITY AND OPTIMISM: 2001–05

Despite these efforts, Cooper was still struggling. In 2001 the company settled 32 class action lawsuits alleging that it made faulty tires whose tread separated while on the road. Even though the settlement acknowledged no liability, Cooper agreed to pay a $55 million fine and institute a five-year warranty enhancement program. That same year, after announcing a plunge in profits in the fourth quarter of 2000, Cooper initiated a reorganization that closed or reduced production at 22 plants and cut 1,000 jobs.

During the next two years the tire industry experienced slow growth and the market demand declined significantly. By June 2003 Cooper had instituted U.S. plant shut downs for brief periods to reduce inventories. Its Findlay plant was shut down for a week and other plants were shut for four days. That same year Cooper announced that it had signed a contract with Hangzhou Zhongce Rubber Company in China to distribute 250,000 to 350,000 radial truck tires each year in the U.S. market.

In September 2004 Cooper sold its automotive unit to the Cypress Group and Goldman Sachs Capital Partners for $1.2 billion. Cooper announced plans to use the capital to reduce its debt, repurchase shares, and invest in its tire operations. The sale enabled Cooper to focus entirely on its tire business, which helped reposition the company in the industry.

When Kumho Tire, a South Korean tire manufacturer and the world's eleventh-largest producer, made its initial public offering in January 2005, Cooper purchased a 10.4 percent strategic stake in the company. The following October Cooper also purchased a majority ownership in China's Cooper Chengshan (Shandong) Passenger Tire Company Ltd. and Cooper Chengshan (Shandong) Tire Company Ltd. Besides increasing its manufacturing capacities, this purchase augmented Cooper's strong Chinese distribution networks.

EXPANSION AND RECESSION: 2005–10

After a recall of 49,000 Hangzhou Zhongce tires in August 2005, Cooper ended its contract with that company. Two years later, in 2007, Cooper entered a joint venture with Kendra Rubber Industrial Company of Taiwan and Cooper Kendra began production. That same year Cooper also formed a partnership with Corporacion de Occidente S.A. de C.V., a Mexican tire manufacturer. The new company, Cooper Tire and Rubber de Mexico, was created to market, sell, and distribute all the joint venture's brands.

At the same time, Cooper focused on improving the performance of it U.S. operations. A significant operational change involved switching the company's supply chain from a regional, history-based structure to an integrated, pull-based system that improved planning and productivity. Cooper also reduced production in the United States and, in late 2008, announced it was closing the Albany plant.

Despite a global economic recession that began in late 2007 and a resultant decline in North American sales, by late 2009 Cooper was preparing for a more positive future. Anticipating an acceleration in the growth of the tire market, the company invested $22.3 million in research and development in 2009. Cooper then spent $10 million in automation and retooling at the Findlay plant and announced plans to hire up to 100 new employees. In May 2010 it increased its stake in Cooper Chengshan (Shandong) Tire Company to 65 percent.

Responding to increasing costs of raw materials, the company announced price increases in early 2010 and again midyear. By the second quarter of 2010 Cooper's North American Tire Operations reported an increase of $148 million in sales over 2009 and its International Tire Operations reported a similar increase of $55 million. Colin Whitbread noted in AutomotiveWorld.com on August 5, 2010, that the company described its expectations for the future as "cautiously optimistic." Clearly, Cooper was still driving steady.

April D. Gasbarre
Updated, Grace Murphy

PRINCIPAL OPERATING UNITS

North American Tire Operations; International Tire Operations.

PRINCIPAL COMPETITORS

Bridgestone Corporation; Compagnie Générale des Établissements Michelin; Goodyear Tire & Rubber Company.

FURTHER READING

Abelson, Reed. "Companies to Watch: Cooper Tire and Rubber." *Fortune*, October 9, 1989, 82.

Bremner, Brian, and Zachary Schiller. "Three Who Bucked the Urge to Merge—and Prospered." *BusinessWeek*, October 14, 1991, 94.

Byrne, Harlan S. "Cooper Tire and Rubber: Ohio Company Sets the Pace in the Replacement Market." *Barron's*, November 26, 1990, 39.

Clothier, Mark. "Cooper Tire Raising Prices up to 6.5% in November." *BusinessWeek*, September 17, 2010.

Dubashi, Jagannath. "Cooper Tire: Retreading Growth." *Financial World*, August 3, 1993, 17.

Gorr, Ivan. "Cooper Tire: Successful Adaptation in a Changing Industry." *Journal of Business Strategy*, Winter 1987, 83–86.

Holzinger, Albert G. "A Successful Competitor." *Nation's Business*, April 1993, 59–60.

Roberts, Ricardo. "Cooper Wants to Drive Away from Its Auto Parts Business." *Mergers and Acquisitions Report*, April 5, 2004.

Schiller, Zachary. "Why Tiremakers Are Still Spinning Their Wheels." *BusinessWeek*, February 26, 1990, 62–63.

Whitbread, Colin. "US: Cooper Tire's Outlook 'Cautiously Optimistic.'" AutomotiveWorld.com, August 5, 2010. Accessed October 22, 2010. http://www.automotiveworld.com/news/components/83221-us-cooper-tire-s-outlook-cautiously-optimistic.

Decide with Confidence

D&B

103 JFK Parkway
Short Hills, New Jersey 07078
U.S.A.
Telephone: (973) 921-5500
Toll Free: (800) 234-3867
Fax: (973) 921-6056
Web site: http://www.dnb.com

Public Company
Founded: 1841 as the Mercantile Agency
Incorporated: 1933 as R. G. Dun-Bradstreet Corporation
Employees: 5,000 (est.)
Sales: $1.69 billion (2009)
Stock Exchanges: New York London Tokyo Geneva Zurich Basel
Ticker Symbol: DNB
NAICS: 511140 Database and Directory Publishers; 523999 Miscellaneous Financial Investment Activities

■ ■ ■

The Dun & Bradstreet Corporation, now known as D&B, is the leading provider of business information worldwide, priding itself on its indispensability as a facilitator of business-to-business commerce for nearly 170 years. Derived from a global database of more than 140 million companies, D&B's integrated array of products and services includes D&B Risk Management Solutions for minimizing credit exposure, D&B Sales & Marketing Solutions for identifying profitable customers, D&B Supply Management Solutions for efficient management of suppliers, and D&B Internet Solutions for fast, web-based access to reliable business information. In 2001 the company launched a new branding initiative, officially changing its name to D&B, its familiar acronym, and creating a new logo along with the tagline "Decide with Confidence."

COMPANY ORIGINS

Dun & Bradstreet traces its origins to Lewis Tappan, who in 1841 left Arthur Tappan & Company (a New York silk trading firm that he ran with his elder brother) to found a credit information bureau called the Mercantile Agency. Tappan had long been aware of the need for better credit reporting. As the borders of the United States expanded westward, traders were moving beyond the easy view of the East Coast merchants and bankers who kept them supplied and capitalized. Information on the creditworthiness of these far-flung businesses was collected by individual trading houses and banks in a scattershot fashion, and Tappan saw that centralizing the process of collecting information would result in greater efficiency. Accordingly, he took out an advertisement in the *New York Commercial Advertiser* on July 20, 1841, and opened shop 11 days later on the corner of Hanover and Exchange streets in Manhattan.

The Mercantile Agency operated by gathering information through a network of correspondents and selling it to subscribers. The agents were attorneys, cashiers of banks, merchants, and other competent persons, anyone who might have an impartial familiarity with local merchants through business or civic affairs. Over the years people as famous as U.S. presidents

COMPANY PERSPECTIVES

At D&B we are building a culture focused on winning in the marketplace and creating shareholder value. We believe that superb leadership will enable our transformation by driving the results that will lead to the achievement of our aspiration— *to be the most trusted source of commercial insight so our customers can decide with confidence.*

Abraham Lincoln, Ulysses S. Grant, Grover Cleveland, and William McKinley, as well as presidential candidate Wendell Willkie, would serve as agents for the company that Tappan founded.

The Mercantile Agency opened branch offices in Boston in 1843 and Philadelphia in 1845. In 1846 Benjamin Douglass, a young New York businessman with connections in the southern cotton trade, joined the firm. When Lewis Tappan retired in 1849, Douglass and Tappan's brother, Arthur, ran it as partners until 1854, when the elder Tappan sold out to Douglass. Then in 1859 Douglass sold out to Robert Graham Dun, who immediately changed the firm's name to R. G. Dun & Company. That year the company published its first reference book of credit information, the *Dun Book*.

EXPANSION

As the nation grew and commerce boomed in the decades following the Civil War, Dun kept up with it by establishing new branch offices. The firm expanded into the South, west to California, and north into Canada. An office in San Francisco opened in 1869. In 1891 there were 126 Dun branch offices.

Robert Dun Douglass, who was Benjamin Douglass's son and Robert Graham Dun's nephew, became general manager of the firm in 1896. After his uncle died in 1900, the company operated as a common-law trust with Douglass in charge as executive trustee. He retired as general manager in 1909 and was succeeded by Archibald Ferguson.

R. G. Dun also began to expand overseas at about this time. The firm opened its first office in London in 1857 and, by the end of the century, added five more foreign offices, in Glasgow, Paris, Melbourne, Mexico City, and Hamburg. From 1901 to 1928 R. G. Dun opened 41 overseas branches, scattered across Europe, South Africa, and Latin America.

REORGANIZING

In 1931 R. G. Dun acquired National Credit Office (NCO), a credit-reporting service. The firm then reorganized into a holding company called R. G. Dun Corporation, which assumed control of the assets of both NCO and the original R. G. Dun & Company. NCO president and former owner Arthur Dare Whiteside became president of the new entity.

In 1933, at the nadir of the Great Depression, R. G. Dun merged with one of its main competitors, the Bradstreet Company. Because the two companies overlapped each other in many activities and resources, an amalgamation at that time made sense. Bradstreet had been founded in Cincinnati, Ohio, in 1849 by John Bradstreet, a lawyer and merchant whose ancestors included Simon Bradstreet, a colonial governor of Massachusetts, and the prominent colonial American poet Anne Bradstreet. A large file of credit information had come into John Bradstreet's possession as he was overseeing the liquidation of an estate, and he decided to enter the same business in which Lewis Tappan had pioneered eight years earlier. In 1855 Bradstreet packed up and moved to New York, where he challenged the Mercantile Agency directly. Two years later the firm started publishing a semiannual reference book that offered more extensive coverage than the early *Dun Book*.

John Bradstreet died in 1863 and was succeeded by his son, Henry, who ran the firm until it incorporated in 1876 under the name the Bradstreet Company. A group headed by Charles F. Clark then ran the company until 1904, when Clark died and was succeeded by Henry Dunn. Dunn retired in 1927 and gave way to Clark's son, Charles M. Clark. The younger Clark was still chief executive when Bradstreet merged with Dun in 1933. The new company changed its name to R. G. Dun-Bradstreet Corporation and then to Dun & Bradstreet, Inc., in 1939.

ACQUISITIONS

Business remained slow for Dun & Bradstreet through the 1930s and during World War II and then picked up again after the war ended. In 1942 the company acquired Credit Clearing House, a credit-reporting agency that specialized in the clothing industry. In 1958 the company began operating its own private wire network, which linked 79 of its major offices. This allowed credit information to be handled more expeditiously.

In 1961 Dun & Bradstreet acquired R.H. Donnelley Corporation. Donnelley, best known for publishing the Yellow Pages telephone directories, was founded in Chicago in 1874 and also published trade magazines. The next year Dun & Bradstreet acquired Official

KEY DATES

1841: Lewis Tappan founds a credit information bureau called the Mercantile Agency, which over the years evolves to become Dun & Bradstreet, or D&B.
1849: Another credit information bureau, the Bradstreet Company, is founded in Cincinnati, Ohio, by John Bradstreet, a lawyer and merchant.
1859: The Mercantile Agency is sold to Robert Graham Dun, who changes the company's name to R. G. Dun & Company; the company publishes its first reference book of credit information, the *Dun Book*.
1933: R. G. Dun & Company merges with the Bradstreet Company, becoming R. G. Dun-Bradstreet Corporation.
1939: R. G. Dun-Bradstreet Corporation is renamed Dun & Bradstreet, Inc.
1958: The company begins operating its own private wire network, linking 79 of its major offices and allowing credit information to be handled more expeditiously.
1961: Dun & Bradstreet acquires R.H. Donnelley Corporation, a company founded in Chicago in 1874 and best known for publishing the Yellow Pages telephone directories.
1962: The company acquires Moody's Investors Service, a provider of financial data for investors on publicly owned corporations through its series of Moody's manuals.
1996: Dun & Bradstreet divides itself into three new publicly traded corporations: Cognizant Corporation, the Dun & Bradstreet Corporation, and A.C. Nielsen.
2000: The Dun & Bradstreet Corporation splits into two companies, spinning off Moody's Investors Service.
2003: D&B acquires Hoover's, Inc.

Airline Guides and added it to the Donnelley division. The company also acquired Moody's Investors Service, which provided financial data for investors on publicly owned corporations through its series of Moody's manuals.

In 1962 Arthur Dare Whiteside retired and was succeeded by J. Wilson Newman, who headed Dun & Bradstreet until 1968. Under Newman, Dun & Bradstreet embarked on a course of expansion and technological improvement. In 1966 Dun & Bradstreet acquired Fantus Company, which specialized in area development surveys, and in 1968 it bought book publisher Thomas Y. Crowell. When Newman retired that year, he was succeeded by former University of Delaware president John Perkins, who served as chairman for one year.

In 1971 Dun & Bradstreet acquired Corinthian Broadcasting, which owned five CBS television affiliates and publisher Funk & Wagnalls. In 1973 the company changed its name to the Dun & Bradstreet Companies Inc. It had acquired some 40 businesses since J. Wilson Newman inaugurated this expansion in 1960 and had seen its annual sales rise from $81 million in 1960 to $450 million in 1973. In 1973 the Dun & Bradstreet Corporation was formed to become the parent company.

In 1978 Dun & Bradstreet acquired Technical Publishing, a trade and professional magazine publisher. The next year it acquired National CSS, an information-processing technology company. In 1983 it diversified into computer software when it acquired McCormack & Dodge, which published systems software for mainframe computers. The following year it cut back a bit on diversification when it spun off Funk & Wagnalls and sold most of its Corinthian Broadcasting television assets to A.H. Belo. The company, however, acquired Datastream, a British business information company.

It also acquired the market research firm A.C. Nielsen. Nielsen, famous for its television ratings service, was founded in Chicago in 1923 by Arthur C. Nielsen Sr. Chief executive officer of Dun & Bradstreet Harrington Drake was a longtime friend of the Nielsen family, and the two companies had been discussing a merger on and off since 1969.

RESTRUCTURING

Dun & Bradstreet continued restructuring itself through divestiture and acquisitions from the late 1980s into the 1990s. It sold Official Airline Guides to Propwix, an affiliate of British Maxwell Communications, in 1988 and Zytron, Petroleum Information, and Neodata in 1990. Also in 1990 the company announced its intention to sell two divisions of Dun & Bradstreet Software: Datastream International, Ltd., and Information Associates, Inc. The company sold Donnelley Marketing, the IMS communications unit, and Carol Wright Sales in 1991.

By 1993, however, Dun & Bradstreet began shifting gears and entering a phase of acquisitions. Through the various divisions of Dun & Bradstreet, the company focused on acquiring smaller, primarily information-based companies. For example, it acquired a majority interest in Gartner Group Inc., an international market research firm, on April 8, 1993. Also in 1993 the company formed HealthCare Information Inc. to conduct research in the health-care industry, and on February 17, 1994, HealthCare Information acquired Lexecon Health Service Inc.

That same year, A. C. Nielsen, IMS America, and Dun and Bradstreet Information Services each made multiple acquisitions. The Dun & Bradstreet Corporation acquired Pilot software, an online software company. Also in 1994 Dun & Bradstreet announced that it would be getting out of the magazine publishing business, in the process ceasing publication of *D & B Reports*.

On January 9, 1996, Dun & Bradstreet announced plans to divide itself into three new publicly traded corporations. The first was Cognizant Corporation, which consisted of IMS International, the Gartner Group, Nielsen Media Research, Pilot Software, and Erisco. Next was the Dun & Bradstreet Corporation, made up of Dun & Bradstreet Information Services, Moody's Investors Service, and R.H. Donnelley. A.C. Nielsen was the third. The Dun & Bradstreet Corporation was to continue its historically successful financial information services.

In 1997 Dun & Bradstreet announced the release of two coding systems designed to simplify the process of making purchases on the Internet. The first was the Data Universal Numbering System (DUNS), which employed nine-digit company identification tags. The DUNS, developed in the 1960s, had previously been used only internally by Dun & Bradstreet. The second release was an Internet database of the Standard Products and Service Code (SPSC). This database provided 11-digit codes that identified product types so Internet users could more easily find companies that provided particular products or services.

CORPORATE REALIGNMENT AND STRATEGIC ALLIANCES

Dun & Bradstreet realigned its corporate structure again in 1998 by spinning off R.H. Donnelley. According to the new structure, the Dun & Bradstreet Corporation would retain its two main financial information businesses, Moody's Investors Service and the Dun & Bradstreet (D&B) operating company. Donnelley, the top independent seller of Yellow Pages advertising in the United States, would become a fully independent, publicly traded company. The spinoff brought improved financial flexibility to Dun & Bradstreet, as about $450 million of the corporation's existing debt was assumed by Donnelley. With a net income of $280.1 million in 1998, the Dun & Bradstreet Corporation achieved its second consecutive year of double-digit earnings growth.

In 1999 the D&B operating company established strategic alliances with such enterprise software companies as SAP AG of Germany, SAS Institute, Siebel Systems, and Oracle Corporation, aiming to embed its data into customers' system software and position itself amid the rising current of e-commerce. Also in 1999 D&B launched a new Internet business, eccelerate.com, designed to leverage D&B's worldwide database for online business-to-business transactions.

Despite these strides, however, 1999 was a year of reckoning for the company. While Moody's continued to produce phenomenal results, boasting a fourth consecutive year of double-digit revenue growth, the core business was underperforming and the stock was lagging. Market watchers said the company had been too slow to adjust to the Internet revolution and its assets were poorly leveraged. After management announced midyear that Dun & Bradstreet would fall short of its revenue and earnings goals, leading shareholders urged the board of directors to sell the company. The internal turmoil led the board to ask for the resignation of CEO Volney Taylor. By year's end, the company planned to lay off nearly 5 percent of its workforce in data collection.

BLUEPRINT FOR GROWTH

In early 2000 Dun & Bradstreet split again, spinning off Moody's Investors Service as an independent, publicly traded company. Incoming CEO Allan Loren, former executive vice president of the American Express Company, faced a daunting turnaround challenge at a corporation that had divested a hefty proportion of its largest and most profitable assets. To transform Dun & Bradstreet and address both its immediate and long-term goals, Loren crafted a strategy the company called its "Blueprint for Growth." The central short-term goal was to improve the company's earnings, particularly through the aggressive expansion of its Internet presence. The plan aimed to make Dun and Bradstreet a leading player in business-to-business (B2B) e-commerce; its target was for the company to derive 80 percent of its total revenue from Internet-related businesses by 2004.

The Blueprint for Growth focused on three interrelated strategies for "reengineering" the company over the long term. The first aim was to give the Dun & Bradstreet brand a makeover. The company was still known as one of the most trusted sources of credit information but faced the danger of being perceived as a "legacy" brand and losing its relevance to the contemporary market. Secondly, Loren's blueprint brought flexibility to the company's financial model, creating efficiencies at all levels of operation in order to free up capital to reinvest in new ventures. To achieve this aim required implementing the third plank: renovating the culture inside the company through intense focus on leadership cultivation and raising the motivation to win in the marketplace. As Loren put it in a 2005 interview with Brian Hanessian and Carlos Sierra of the *McKinsey Quarterly*: "I said, 'If you're telling me we have such high fixed costs that we can't invest in the company then we should sell it.' ... Nobody liked hearing that, but it got the dialogue on reengineering started. ... We faced up to the consequences of not investing."

CONVERTING INFORMATION INTO BUSINESS INSIGHT

To leverage and reposition the brand, the company officially changed its name in 2001 to D&B, the already familiar acronym, and launched a new logo along with the tagline "Decide with Confidence." Taking advantage of its company's core asset, its database of business information, D&B expanded the range of its value-added products, investing in signature tools and services including Global DecisionMaker, Portfolio Management Solutions, and Data Integration Toolkit. Most importantly, in 2002 the company introduced the DUNSRight Quality Process, a proprietary information service building on the nearly universal DUNS numeration system. These innovations brought immediate financial rewards. In 2002 D&B delivered earnings per share (EPS) growth of 26 percent, while the company's revenue from Internet business soared to 65 percent, up from 17 percent two years earlier.

In February 2003 the company further strengthened its complement of products with the $119 million acquisition of Hoover's, a prominent provider of information on private and publicly traded companies through its website, Hoovers.com. This key acquisition meshed tightly with D&B's newly clarified mission of driving value and profitability for its customers by converting information into "business insight."

Having completed D&B's successful turnaround, Loren retired in 2005, and another former American Express executive, Steve Alesio, took his place. That year the firm celebrated a milestone in its accumulation of information when its global business database reached 100 million records. By 2009 that number had surpassed 140 million, a clear sign that the company had more than adequate resources to devote to the backbone of its enterprise, data collection.

D&B consolidated its position in the world of electronic commerce and information by acquiring AllBusiness.com for $55 million in 2007. That year, for the second consecutive year, the company earned the number-one ranking in the financial data services category of *Fortune* magazine's list of most admired companies.

In another planned executive succession, Sara Mathew, who had risen to become company president in 2007, took over as board chair and CEO in 2010. Mathew was not only the first woman to lead the storied finance outfit but the first from a foreign background. Born and raised in India, Mathew had worked her way up in the business world, starting out as a clerk at Proctor & Gamble. She inherited an institution in sound financial health, prepared to add to its illustrious record.

Claire Badaracco; Douglas Sun
Updated, Terry Bain; Erin Brown; Roger K. Smith

PRINCIPAL SUBSIDIARIES

Hoover's, Inc.; All Business.com, Inc.

PRINCIPAL COMPETITORS

Equifax Inc.; infoUSA Inc.; Dow Jones (News Corporation); Experian PLC; Yahoo! Finance.

FURTHER READING

Bharadwaj-Chand, Swati. "Dun and Bradstreet Identifies Web as Major Focus Area." *Times of India*, February 17, 2001.

"D&B Acquires D&B Australia for $205 Million." Associated Press, August 31, 2010.

Dun & Bradstreet: The Story of an Idea. New York: Dun and Bradstreet, 1966.

Gilpin, Kenneth N. "New Dun and Bradstreet Split Planned If the I.R.S. Agrees." *New York Times*, December 19, 1997, D2.

Greenberg, Ilan. "Dun & Bradstreet Finds Its Strength in Data Management." *San Jose (CA) Mercury News*, August 18, 1999.

Hanessian, Brian, and Carlos Sierra. "Leading a Turnaround." *McKinsey Quarterly*, no. 2, 2005, 83–93.

King, Julia. "D&B Software Users Cheer Sell-Off Plan." *Computerworld*, January 15, 1996, 4.

Krell, Eric. "Running Down the Numbers." *Business Finance*, December 2008, 32–34.

Oppel, Richard A., Jr. "Credit Giant Feels Heat of Agitators." *New York Times*, October 31, 1999.

Pine, Michael. "Dun's Do-Over: Two of Dun & Bradstreet's Three Parts Are Worth More Than the Whole." *Financial World*, July 8, 1996, 44–45.

DALSA Corporation

605 McMurray Road
Waterloo, Ontario N2V 2E9
Canada
Telephone: (519) 886-6000
Fax: (519) 886-8023
Web site: http://www.dalsa.com

Public Company
Incorporated: 1980 as DALSA Inc.
Employees: 1,000
Sales: CAD 162.5 million
Stock Exchanges: Toronto Stock Exchange
Ticker Symbol: DSA
NAICS: 333314 Optical Instrument and Lens Manufacturing

■ ■ ■

DALSA Corporation is a Waterloo, Ontario, Canada-based designer and manufacturer of high-performance digital-imaging equipment and a provider of semiconductor wafer manufacturing. The company serves the "machine vision" market with digital-imaging components that are used in automated inspection systems for manufacturing and such industries as electronics, flat-panel displays, and semiconductors. In addition to cameras, DALSA offers frame grabbers and ancillary software. DALSA's Sensor Solutions business provides products used in digital still photography, broadcast videography, medical applications such as X-ray imaging and medical and dental radiography, and remote sensing for military and aerospace applications. DALSA's Semiconductor Fabrication division consists of a silicon wafer foundry that produces microelectromechanical systems and complementary metal-oxide-semiconductor chips used in products including cameras, cell phones, optical-networking equipment, smoke detectors, ink-jet printing, and industrial and automotive controls. DALSA is a public company listed on the Toronto Stock Exchange.

FOUNDER, CYPRUS BORN: 1941

DALSA was founded by Savvas Georgiou Chamberlain, who was born in Nicosia on the island of Cyprus in 1941. A child of Greek parents, Chamberlain came from an upper-middle-class family whose life was disrupted by political unrest in the island nation, twice losing all of their property. Despite the turmoil, he grew up fascinated by radio, which led to an interest in physics and mathematics. In 1960 he immigrated to England to study electrical engineering at the University of Southampton, where he earned an undergraduate degree and a master's degree before receiving his doctorate in 1968. After a stint as a researcher for the United Kingdom's Plessey Company Limited, a major electronics manufacturer, Chamberlain immigrated with his family to Canada in 1969 to become an assistant professor of electrical engineering at the University of Waterloo.

In the same year that Chamberlain came to Canada, Willard S. Boyle, a Canadian, and American George E. Smith invented the charge-coupled device (CCD) at the Bell Labs in New Jersey. Instead of chemical film, the CCD relied on a photoelectric effect to

COMPANY PERSPECTIVES

DALSA has led the evolution of digital imaging for over a quarter century and has earned its reputation as a global leader in high performance imaging and semiconductors. DALSA, its employees and partners are committed to enabling industry, art and exploration through innovative technology.

capture image information, essentially converting light into electrical signals. Chamberlain was one of many to pursue the concept of digital imaging because of this breakthrough work, which would eventually earn Boyle and Smith a Nobel Prize. Starting in 1970 Chamberlain began working with his graduate students in the development of CCD image sensors that would one day become the heart of digital cameras. Later in the 1970s he took a leave of absence to work with International Business Machines Corporation (IBM) and Bell-Northern Research to pursue applications for CCDs and other new image-sensor technologies.

DALSA FOUNDED: 1980

In 1980 Chamberlain formed DALSA Inc. to serve as a two-person consultancy, while hoping to one day manufacture CCD devices. He worked with IBM and Northern Telecom in the integration of CCD into manufacturing processes but was unable to persuade them to commercialize his CCD technology. The young company worked out of office space in a strip mall. At one point the employees constructed their own "clean room" where they could build sensor chips. In November 1984 Chamberlain, aided by some graduate students, raised enough funds through venture capital to create chip-producing equipment. Because most potential investors thought DALSA's revenue potential was too limited, he had to turn to the University of Waterloo's technology transfer office to secure $350,000 in seed money.

DALSA began producing chips in 1985 and from the start the venture was profitable. Despite a lack of business experience, Chamberlain served as chief executive, bringing a unique perspective to the job. "I didn't know much about business," he told *Canadian Business* in a 2008 profile, "but I knew conservation of money. … I kept track of the money coming in, and the money going out. Later on, I was told that paper was cash flow." His math background also led him to limit growth of the company to less than 30 percent a year, "otherwise I would very quickly go bankrupt, or borrow so much money that somebody else would own the company."

An important development in DALSA's history came in 1988 when the company introduced the first thermographic diagnostic imaging sensors, which greatly increased light sensitivity. Because of the increasing demands of running DALSA, Chamberlain finally resigned his post at the University of Waterloo a year later, although he continued to teach a course at the school for several more years. In 1990 DALSA introduced its first standard products, cameras used for postal inspection. Cameras were now very much at the heart of DALSA's business. In 1991 the company opened a new manufacturing facility that tripled its capacity and allowed it to produce complete cameras for specific high-end applications, including the sorting of mail and the search for manufacturing flaws in integrated circuit boards. In 1993 the company introduced an industry-leading 25-megapixel sensor. Sales rose steadily to CAD 7.83 million in 1994 and nearly CAD 11 million in 1995. To keep pace with demand, DALSA expanded further doubling its capacity.

TAKEN PUBLIC: 1996

Over the years, Chamberlain had rewarded employees with shares of stock in lieu of large salaries in order to grow the company. By the mid-1990s, when DALSA began posting healthy profits, many of these shareholders were looking for liquidity. As a result, Chamberlain, despite his belief that the company should wait until revenues were greater, agreed to take DALSA public on the Toronto Stock Exchange and provide a way for shareholders to sell stock. The initial public offering raised CAD 22.9 million in 1996. Revenues for the year improved to CAD 14.6 million. Of that amount, only CAD 923,000 came from sales in Canada, almost as much as Asia generated. The United States accounted for CAD 7.64 million in sales and Europe for CAD 5 million.

For much of DALSA's history, its technology ranged far ahead of the market and the company was forced to wait for the cost of computer processing to decrease before digital imaging became economically viable. In 1975, for example, the cost of one million instructions per second (MIP) was $1 million. A quarter century later that cost was reduced to just $1 per MIP. "As the price comes down, it helps our business," Chamberlain told *Canadian Business* in a 2002 article, "because our customers can take these big frames, which have a lot of information and are able to process them cheaply enough."

KEY DATES

1980: DALSA Inc. is founded by Savvas Chamberlain.
1985: Chip production begins.
1996: Company is taken public.
1999: Silicon Mountain Design is acquired.
2007: Chamberlain retires as CEO.

DALSA unveiled the world's fastest line scan camera, dubbed the Piranha, in 1998. In addition to organic growth, DALSA expanded through an acquisition in the summer of 1999, paying $11.5 million for Colorado Springs, Colorado-based Silicon Mountain Design, a CCD high-speed camera specialist that focused on military and high-end applications. In early 2000 DALSA spent another $3 million to acquire Tucson, Arizona-based MedOptics Corp., a small medical-imaging company. Both moves were part of a strategy to act as a consolidator in what was still very much a fragmented industry filled with small, niche players. The moves also led to a new growth strategy announced in late 2000 that resulted in four strategic business units focused on high-growth opportunity markets: Vision for Machines, Life Sciences, Vision Systems, and Digital Camera.

The acquisitions also helped to drive revenues to CAD 38 million in 1999 and a further 40 percent to CAD 53.3 million in 2000, while earnings improved from CAD 5.2 million in 1999 to CAD 6.2 million in 2000. More importantly, diversification helped to insulate DALSA from the collapse of the semiconductor market in 2001. Unlike many competitors, the company was able to continue its sales growth, albeit at a modest level, to CAD 56.4 million while recording net income of CAD 4 million. DALSA also completed the year with $9 million in cash and was in a position to pursue further acquisitions in anticipation of market improvements.

FOUNDRY ACQUIRED: 2002

In January 2002 DALSA acquired a major stake in the Bromont, Quebec, semiconductor foundry of Ottawa, Canada-based Zarlink Semiconductor Inc., the former chip division of Mitel Corp., for CAD 21.6 million. DALSA had been outsourcing the manufacture of silicon wafers to the Bromont foundry as well as two foundries in Europe and the United States. Not only could the company now consolidate its operations, it could design wafers and manufacturing processes without relying on a third party, thus gaining greater control over its business. Only days after the Zarlink transaction, DALSA acquired the CCD image-sensors business of Royal Philips Electronics of the Netherlands to create the foundation for the company's Professional Imaging group. These acquisitions helped to increase revenues to CAD 112.6 million in 2002.

In 2000 DALSA established a digital-cinema division to develop the world's sharpest-resolution digital movie camera that it hoped would revolutionize the motion-picture industry. The roots of this effort had actually begun a few years earlier when NHK, a Japanese pioneer in high definition, enlisted DALSA to develop a high-resolution camera sensor. Once DALSA had a state-of-the-art sensor in hand, however, NHK abandoned the project, prompting DALSA to use its research to build a cinema camera. That work came to fruition in 2004 when the company introduced the Origin camera. In that same year DALSA established a presence in Los Angeles, the heart of the movie industry, through the acquisition of Broadcast Plus, a camera rental business that was to serve as a distribution point for the Origin and a second-generation digital camera called the Evolution. Although the cameras were well received for their technology, they were not embraced by film studios, and were used only to make some short films, a few commercials, and a skydiving sequence in a James Bond film.

Shooting films in a digital format was supposed to lower production costs because the purchase of film stock, developing, and printing, all major expenses, could be postponed, providing producers with greater financial flexibility. Unfortunately, the use of digital cameras led to the creation of massive amounts of data that postproduction companies were not equipped to handle. The film industry was likely to one day embrace digital photography, but DALSA did not have the luxury of waiting. In 2008 it decided to cut its losses by closing the digital-cinema division and licensing its camera technology to Arnold & Richter Cine Technik GmbH, a German camera maker. In 2009, however, this deal fell through and DALSA elected to turn over the technology to employees who formed a start-up company called Cine Flow.

CHAMBERLAIN RETIRES AS CEO: 2007

In 2007 Chamberlain retired as CEO and turned over day-to-day control to longtime lieutenant Brian Doody. Chamberlain stayed on as chief technology officer and chairman, then relinquished the chief technology officer post in October 2009. He remained chairman in a nonmanagement capacity. After DALSA generated record revenues of CAD 206 million and record earnings of CAD 21.9 million in 2008, Doody had to contend with the impact of a recession in 2009. The company cut costs and as a result was able to remain profitable, netting CAD 500,000 on diminished revenues of CAD 162.5 million. In 2010 the Ontario government awarded DALSA with a CAD 23.4 million grant to help support the company's ongoing research and development efforts. Although the company had hoped to have reached CAD 500 million in annual sales by this point, and while that level appeared well in the future, there was every reason to believe that DALSA would continue to enjoy steady growth in the years to come.

Ed Dinger

PRINCIPAL SUBSIDIARIES

DALSA Semiconductor; Rad-icon Imaging.

PRINCIPAL COMPETITORS

Agfa-Gevaert N.V.; MEMC Electronic Materials, Inc.; Panavision Inc.

FURTHER READING

Beebe, Paul. "Digital Camera Firm Expands Colorado Springs, Colo., Operations." *Colorado Springs (CO) Gazette*, October 14, 2004.

"Dalsa Blames Recession for Drop." *Kitchener (Ontario) Record*, May 1, 2009, p. C8.

"Dalsa Celebrates 30 Years." *Northumberland News* (Cobourg, Ontario), June 30, 2010, E4.

"Dalsa to Continue Cost-Cutting." *Kitchener (Ontario) Record*, January 30, 2009, E8.

"Dalsa's Dream Fades to Black; the Company's Digital-Cinema Division Never Caught on as Hoped and Will Be Discontinued." *Kitchener (Ontario) Record*, October 31, 2008, E1.

Flavelle, Dana. "Dalsa Corp.'s Chips Defy Economic Dip." *Toronto Star*, August 19, 2002.

"How Dalsa's Big Screen Dreams Ended on the Cutting Room Floor; Digital Camera Considered Top Quality, but Lacking 'Name Recognition.'" *Kitchener (Ontario) Record*, November 29, 2008, C1.

Marx, Bridget R. "Dalsa to Purchase Philips' CCD Business." *Optoelectronics Report*, February 15, 2002, 4.

Powell, Doug. "Company Sees Future in Image Sensor Technology." *Computing Canada*, July 6, 1994, 16.

Wahl, Andrew. " The Founder, Chair and Former CEO of Dalsa Corp. on Growth, the Undervaluing of R&D and Why He's Not Ethnic." *Canadian Business*, February 28, 2008.

———. "Meet the Professor." *Canadian Business*, March 4, 2002, 118.

Dana-Farber Cancer Institute

44 Binney Street
Boston, Massachusetts 02115
U.S.A.
Telephone: (617) 632-3000
Toll Free: (866) 408-3324
Fax: (617) 632-4421
Web site: http://www.dana-farber.org

Nonprofit Company
Founded: 1947 as Children's Cancer Research Foundation
Incorporated: 1951 as Children's Cancer Research Foundation
Employees: 4,000
NAICS: 622310 Specialty Hospitals

■ ■ ■

Founded by Sidney Farber, the Dana-Farber Cancer Institute (DFCI) is a nonprofit organization dedicated to cancer treatment and research located in Boston, Massachusetts. In addition to developing diagnostics, treatments, and ways to prevent cancer, DFCI researches AIDS treatments and cures for other diseases. Each year about 300,000 patients visit the institute, which is the primary teaching affiliate of Harvard Medical School. The DFCI is also involved in community-based programs throughout New England related to the prevention, detection, and control of cancer. The DFCI's researchers are involved in about 700 clinical trials each year.

FOUNDER SIDNEY FARBER

Sidney Farber was born in Buffalo, New York, in 1903. He earned his medical degree at Harvard Medical School in 1927. After postdoctoral work at Boston's Peter Bent Brigham Hospital, he joined the staffs at Harvard Medical School and at Children's Hospital, as an assistant in pathology and a resident pathologist, respectively. Farber eventually became a professor of pathology at Harvard. He also developed an interest in cancer in children, in particular leukemia, which became the focus of his career.

In 1947 Farber took the unprecedented step of trying to treat children with cancer by starting a clinic, the Children's Cancer Research Foundation, at Children's Hospital. In November Farber began a clinical trial on a new experimental drug created to treat leukemia. Out of the 16 children in the trial, 10 achieved temporary remission. Farber published his results in the June 3, 1948, issue of the *New England Journal of Medicine.*

THE JIMMY FUND

Farber's clinical trial caught the attention of the Variety Club of New England, a charitable organization formed by the entertainment community that was looking for a local cause to support. The Variety Club chose the small outpatient clinic Farber had opened at Children's Hospital and began supporting Farber's treatment and research efforts. In 1948 the Variety Club arranged for time on the popular *Truth or Consequences* radio program on May 22 to raise money for the foundation. One of Farber's 12-year-old patients, who Farber insisted be called Jimmy in order to protect the boy's

COMPANY PERSPECTIVES

The mission of Dana-Farber Cancer Institute is to provide expert, compassionate care to children and adults with cancer while advancing the understanding, diagnosis, treatment, cure, and prevention of cancer and related diseases.

privacy, was interviewed at his bedside at the clinic by the show's host, Ralph Edwards. As they talked about baseball, members of the Boston Braves Major League Baseball team and their manager arrived in a surprise visit.

The Braves gave Jimmy souvenirs and announced that the next day's doubleheader at Braves Field would be called Jimmy's Day. Edwards then told listeners that if the foundation received $20,000 in donations, Jimmy would receive a television and be able to watch Braves games while in the clinic. The response was overwhelming. The show raised 10 times more than the amount asked. The Variety Club quickly realized the potential for an ongoing fund-raising effort.

In 1949 the Variety Club launched the Jimmy Fund/Variety Club Theater Collections Program. The Jimmy Fund also became the favorite charity of the Braves, and after the franchise was relocated to Milwaukee, the Boston Red Sox stepped in and adopted the fund as its official charity. As a result of fund-raising efforts by the Jimmy Fund and other sources, a $1.47-million, four-story building, named the Jimmy Fund Building, was constructed on Binney Street to house Farber's clinic. In 1958 four more floors were added to accommodate research laboratories.

FARBER'S RESEARCH AND LEGACY

Farber's research led to discoveries of chemical agents that inhibit the development of leukemia as well as other malignant diseases. Farber was also a pioneer in what would become known as total care, making clinical care and nutrition, social work, and counseling services all available in a single location. In the mid-1950s he converted an entire inpatient floor to pursue this approach and created a standard for pediatric cancer care that would be emulated around the world. Farber also proved to be a highly effective advocate for federal spending on cancer research, often appearing before the U.S. Congress to appeal for greater appropriations for the National Cancer Institute. Due in large measure to his efforts, the annual budget of the institute increased from $48 million in 1957 to $176 million in 1967.

While children remained his focus, Farber sought to extend the advances made in treating pediatric cancer to older patients. In 1969 he oversaw the Children's Cancer Research Foundation's transition to providing services to patients of all ages. In March 1973 Farber died of a heart attack at the age of 69. A year later the foundation was renamed the Sidney Farber Cancer Center in his honor. The name was changed again in 1976 to the Sidney Farber Cancer Institute.

MORE ADVANCES AND A MAJOR BENEFACTOR

During the 1960s Sidney Farber Cancer Institute researchers developed a way to control bleeding, a common side effect of chemotherapy treatment. The researchers were also responsible for a number of advances in the 1970s. They pioneered the strategy of combination chemotherapy, which made use of multiple drugs to combat different forms of cancer. As a result, cure rates improved significantly for some forms of adult non-Hodgkin's lymphoma, osteogenic sarcoma, soft-tissue sarcomas, acute lymphoblastic leukemia, breast cancer, advanced testicular cancer, acute myelogenous leukemia, and large cell leukemia.

One of Farber's major benefactors over the years was the Charles A. Dana Foundation, established by industrialist Charles A. Dana. His son, Charles A. Dana Jr., learned about Farber's work and arranged for a $300,000 grant in 1962, the first of several major grants to be awarded to the Children's Cancer Research Foundation. In 1976 the foundation, now called the Sidney Farber Cancer Institute, opened a new building and named it the Charles A. Dana Building. In 1983 the institute received a $10-million challenge grant from the Dana Foundation, kicking off a five-year, $38 million fund-raising campaign. That same year the Sidney Farber Cancer Institute's name changed again to the Dana-Farber Cancer Institute (DFCI).

During the 1980s the DFCI continued to make progress in the treatment of cancer. It pioneered the bone marrow transplant procedure that allowed the use of greater amounts of chemotherapy and radiation to effectively treat childhood leukemia. DFCI researchers also helped develop immunotoxins, a new generation of anticancer drugs. Moreover, the DFCI established the Dana-Farber's Breast Evaluation Center to advance breast cancer detection and treatment and in 1989

KEY DATES

1947: Dr. Sidney Farber founds the Children's Cancer Research Foundation.
1973: Sidney Farber dies.
1974: The Children's Cancer Research Foundation is renamed the Sidney Farber Cancer Center.
1976: The Sidney Farber Cancer Center is renamed the Sidney Farber Cancer Institute.
1983: The Sidney Farber Cancer Institute is renamed the Dana-Farber Cancer Institute.

opened the Brain Tumor Clinic to further the effort to combat brain cancers in children and adults.

NEW PROGRAMS AND MORE NEW CLINICS

The DFCI's multifaceted work continued in the 1990s. Researchers demonstrated that susceptibility to developing cancer could be passed from one generation to the next, found a relationship between a section of DNA and the aggressiveness of prostate cancer, enjoyed some success in causing tumor cells to grow more slowly, and developed a way to disarm immune system cells that offered hope for a way to avoid tissue and organ transplant rejection. In other developments, the DFCI forged an alliance to develop a new generation of antitumor drugs. In 1992 it established the Cancer Risk and Prevention Clinic, devoted to the early detection and prevention of women's breast cancer.

In 1993 the DFCI launched the Women's Cancers Program. It also established the High Risk Research Clinic to provide genetic testing, identify individuals at risk, and provide genetic and psychological counseling. Another new program, formed in conjunction with Massachusetts General Hospital and Brigham and Women's Hospital, was Dana-Farber/Partners Cancer Care, which brought together the resources of the participating institutions for the benefit of cancer patients. The DFCI also formed the Dana-Farber/Harvard Cancer Center in 1999 to consolidate the research efforts of Boston-area institutions.

FINDING JIMMY

For many years the identity of the child known as Jimmy of the Jimmy Fund was unknown. While it was generally assumed that Jimmy had died young of leukemia, Farber had mentioned over the years that the boy had reached adulthood. In 1990 the newly hired director of special events at the Jimmy Fund, Christina Zwart, was asked to learn the fate of the child made famous by the radio broadcast of 1948. She followed a multitude of leads but was unsuccessful in finding "Jimmy." The task became so time-consuming that eventually she had to abandon the effort.

As the Jimmy Fund approached its 50th anniversary, the fund's executive director, Mike Andrew, received a letter in February 1997 from a woman in Maine named Phyllis Clauson, who claimed her brother was Jimmy and that he was alive. Because there had been numerous people over the years making similar claims, Andrews set aside the letter, which was then misplaced for 10 months before the DFCI assistant director of communications, Karen Cummings, wrote back to Clauson. A short time later Cummings received a call from a man who said, "Hello this is Jimmy. I heard you were looking for me." The man on the line was Einar Gustafson, who soon produced proof that he was indeed Jimmy. Gustafson's proof included the Braves uniform presented to him in the hospital and correspondence with Farber.

Gustafson had married, become a father and a grandfather, and made his living as a truck driver, all the while uninterested in calling attention to himself. "In my day, we were taught to keep things quiet," he explained, according to Dan Shaughnessy of the *Boston Globe* (January 23, 2001). After speaking with Cummings, Gustafson spent the next two and half years promoting the Jimmy Fund at functions and by recording public service announcements. He died in January 2001 after suffering a stroke at the age of 65.

EXPANSION IN THE 21ST CENTURY

The DFCI continued to expand in the twenty-first century, making progress in research as well as in treatment. The Cancer Vaccine Center opened in 2005, and the Patient Navigator Program was established a year later to help underserved populations. In 2008 an adult cancer care clinic was established in Londonderry, New Hampshire, to spare cancer patients in the area a trip to Boston for their treatment. The DFCI also enjoyed success in fund-raising.

In 2005 a longtime patron, businessman Jack Blais, acquired the naming rights to the New England Patriots football team's indoor practice facility for $15 million and donated it to the DFCI, which renamed it the Dana-Farber Field House. In addition to the visibility it received, the DFCI was also allowed to use the Patriots' Gillette Stadium for events, and it received hundreds of game tickets donated by the team that were given to patients and used for fund-raising activities. Later in the year the Blais family donated $16.5 million to establish a protein research facility, the Blais Proteomics Center. In 2007 the DFCI launched a $1 billion fund-raising campaign, the largest of its kind in New England history, to build a 13-floor tower and create a medical center that was more patient friendly. As a result, the DFCI was well equipped to meet future needs in both care and research.

Ed Dinger

PRINCIPAL OPERATING UNITS

Dana-Farber/Brigham and Women's Cancer Center at Faulkner Hospital; Dana-Farber/Brigham and Women's Cancer Center at Milford Regional Medical Center; Dana-Farber/New Hampshire Oncology-Hematology; Dana-Farber/Brigham and Women's Cancer Center in Clinical Affiliation with South Shore Hospital.

PRINCIPAL COMPETITORS

University of Texas M.D. Anderson Cancer Center; Memorial Sloan-Kettering Cancer Center; Roswell Park Cancer Institute.

FURTHER READING

Allen, Scott. "Dana-Farber Aiming for $1b to Boost Care." *Boston Globe*, January 31, 2007.

"Dr. Sidney Farber, a Pioneer in Children's Cancer Research." *New York Times*, March 31, 1973.

Mrowca, Maryann. "Dana-Farber Cancer Institute Marks 40 Years in Battle against Illnesses." *Boston Globe*, October 13, 1996.

Negri, Gloria. "The Jimmy Fund: 40 Years Helping Kids with Cancer." *Boston Globe*, August 22, 1988.

Shaughnessy, Dan. "A Mystery Story with Happy Ending: Even Dana-Farber Was Left Clueless." *Boston Globe*, May 17, 1998.

———. "The Original 'Jimmy' of Cancer Fund Dies." *Boston Globe*, January 23, 2001.

Talcott, Sasha. "Man Buys, Donates Rights to Patriots' Practice Facility to Cancer Institute." *Boston Globe*, August 16, 2005.

DeNA Co., Ltd.

30-3, Yoyogi 4-chome, Shibuya-ku
Tokyo, 151-0053
Japan
Telephone: (+81 3) 5304 1701
Fax: (+81 3) 5304 1770
Web site: http://www.dena.jp/en

Public Company
Founded: 1999
Employees: 1,323
Sales: ¥48.11 billion ($514 million) (2009)
Stock Exchanges: Tokyo
Ticker Symbol: 2432
NAICS: 511210 Software Publishers

■ ■ ■

Based in Tokyo, Japan, DeNA Co., Ltd., offers e-commerce and mobile e-commerce services. The company originally offered bidding services in Japan, creating an online space where buyers and sellers could complete transactions reliably and safely. The concept has since been extended to mobile devices with the development of the Pocket Bidders service, providing users with a comprehensive shopping site as well as the ability to use their personal computer bidder's ID. In turn, DeNA operates the official shopping mall for these bidding services. DeNA also has several e-commerce subsidiaries, including Mobaoku Co., Ltd., a mobile phone auction site; Mobakore Co., Ltd., a joint-venture shopping site geared toward young women; PAYGENT Co., Ltd., an online payment services site; and Air Link Co., Ltd., a travel services site. In addition, DeNA offers Mobage-town, a free online mobile gaming portal for mobile devices that provides content from social networking sites. Even though the games are free, many users purchase game accessories or enhancements for their cartoon avatars. DeNA is also involved in Internet advertising through Pocket Affiliate, which connects mobile and personal computer website owners with prospective advertisers, and Pocket Match, a pay-for-performance advertising placement service. Outside of Japan, DeNA operates Jia Jia Cheng, a free mobile phone networking site in China. The 2010 acquisition of ngmoco Inc., a California iPhone game developer, enabled DeNA to enter the U.S. market. DeNA is led by its founder, Tomoko Namba, who owns 15 percent of the company.

HARVARD-EDUCATED FOUNDER

Born in 1962, Namba earned an English degree from Tsuda College. After graduation she was hired by the consulting firm McKinsey & Co. in Tokyo. She interrupted her career to earn a master of business administration at Harvard University. She returned to McKinsey, where she became the third Japanese woman to make partner. During the late 1990s she made her mark by helping Japanese companies, such as Sony, to begin doing business online. When she suggested launching an auction site, Sony executives urged her to consider starting her own site. Thus, Namba quit McKinsey in 1999 to become an Internet entrepreneur.

Namba did not lack financial backers. Besides Sony, she received seed money from a job-hunting firm and

COMPANY PERSPECTIVES

We have been working to develop e-commerce since the market first emerged. Today we have grown to be a company providing services that make our users happy and give added value to the mobile e-commerce market.

Since the company's launch our motto has been to always try something new. This pursuit of new ideas is part of our DNA. It's what drives us forward.

We have built this company from the ground up with our ideas, know-how and user input as the basic building blocks that have given us a technological edge up. Now we are steadily moving ahead with an eye toward expanding the horizon of our operations as we bring new ideas to life.

the Sumitomo trading house. For a company name Namba combined "DNA," the acronym for deoxyribonucleic acid, and "e" for e-commerce to coin DeNA. She formed the company in March 1999 in the trendy Shibuya district of Tokyo and assembled a team of engineers and developers.

An ambitious launch date for the Bidders auction site was set for November of that year. The company came close to missing its deadline when in October Namba learned that an outside firm she hired to write the software for the online bidding system was unable to complete the project. She contacted one of her investors, Kazutaka Muraguchi, a general partner of Nippon Technology Venture Partners. He borrowed engineers from some of his portfolio companies to write the necessary code and helped Bidders launch on schedule.

NICHE PURSUITS: 2001–05

Although making the launch date was a notable achievement for DeNA, the Bidders service did not fare well against the deep pockets of Yahoo! Inc., Japan's auction service. As a result, DeNA was forced to look for niche opportunities. For example, in February 2001 it launched the Oikura site, which auctioned off used electronics, furniture, and other items from a network of registered secondhand stores. Namba claimed the idea had first come to her during her days at Harvard, when she saw how prevalent used furniture was among students, even the wealthiest ones. Oikura proved popular with both buyers and sellers, helping DeNA to raise $4.1 million in a fourth round of funding in 2001.

Despite DeNA's financial backing, the company came close to bankruptcy. However, DeNA's willingness to adapt and pursue other e-tailing opportunities allowed it to survive and even become profitable by 2003. DeNA also proved to be more nimble than Yahoo by branching into mobile auctions in 2004 with the launch of Mobaoku and worked aggressively to gain market share in this sector. Mobaoku's success provided the necessary foundation for taking DeNA public. An initial public offering of stock was completed in 2005 and shares of DeNA began trading on the Tokyo Stock Exchange.

EXPANSION INTO NEW MARKETS: 2006–07

The next important development for DeNA was the February 2006 launch of the mobile game community Mobage-town. Even though the site could only be accessed through certain carriers, it quickly gained a following with young people in Japan because of the superior graphics, virtual worlds, and choice of multiplayer games. Many of the site's early users were Mobaoku members, which provided Mobage with some immediate momentum. Within hours of launching the site traffic was soaring. By the end of the first month Mobage was receiving 4 million page hits per day. Initially, the site's popularity centered on mah-jongg and Japanese chess games, but new games were added regularly, so that within two years the site offered more than 120 games. An important factor in the popularity of Mobage was the limited number of ads. Only a quarter of the site's revenues were drawn from advertising. The rest came from the sale of enhanced avatar characters and accessories such as clothing and virtual weapons.

To appeal to older users, Mobage added news, weather, sports, and commuting information services. These additions gained increasing importance in December 2007, when teen stalker fears in Japan led the government to ban wireless carriers from permitting people under the age of 20 to use interactive mobile websites such as Mobage. The ban created a major challenge for DeNA, given that among teenagers 60 percent of boys and 40 percent of girls were regular Mobage users and that the chat element was a large part of many games. However, not all retailers enforced the ban. Independent mobile phone retailers were less diligent about turning on the filtering feature than were the shops owned by Japan's three major wireless carriers. Also, many teens were able to persuade their parents to sign a release form that increased their age. The ban was hardly a fatal blow, but it did curtail Mobage's growth.

KEY DATES

1999: DeNA Co., Ltd., is founded.
2006: The Mobage mobile game site is launched.
2007: DeNA founds the Chinese subsidiary Jia Jia Cheng.
2008: DeNA founds the U.S. subsidiary DeNA Global.
2010: DeNA acquires ngmoco Inc.

As Mobage was being launched in 2006, DeNA was also looking into expanding in China, which was a vast market with significant potential for mobile phone services. In February 2007 DeNA established the subsidiary Jia Jia Cheng, a free social networking site. Many of the popular Mobage features were modified to appeal to Chinese users, such as a short messaging feature instead of e-mail, which was not supported by Chinese phones. Other features included chat rooms, diaries, and message boards.

ACQUISITIONS AND PARTNERSHIPS: 2008–10

The prospects of China were enticing, but DeNA recognized that the United States, whose mobile gaming industry lagged well behind Japan, held a great deal of potential as well. In January 2008 DeNA formed the U.S. subsidiary DeNA Global in San Mateo, California. That same year the company launched MobaMingle, which was essentially an English-language version of Mobage. Even though MobaMingle offered much of the same social networking and avatar features as Mobage, it provided only a handful of games in the United States, where most handsets lacked the necessary flash memory to run the applications.

A strong yen, which was enjoying a 15-year high against the dollar, also allowed DeNA to spur further growth through acquisitions. In 2009 DeNA bought a 50 percent stake in Waptx Ltd., a British operator of tx.com.cn, a Chinese cell phone social networking site. Established five years earlier, the site recorded daily page views of around 1 million and had attracted more than 30 million users. DeNA reported sales of over $500 million in 2009 and was poised to reach the $1 billion mark the following year.

The company was clearly a prominent player in its field, as demonstrated by an alliance it forged with the much larger Yahoo Japan Corp. In April 2010 DeNA agreed to make its social games available to personal computer users in Japan under the name Yahoo! Mobage. By combining their games and customer bases the partners hoped to dominate Japan's personal computer social game market.

ACQUISITION OF NGMOCO: 2010

In October 2010 DeNA reached an agreement to acquire ngmoco Inc. for $300 million in cash, stock, and stock options, plus $100 million in performance milestones. The firm had been founded two years earlier as an iPhone game developer by the longtime game executive Neil Young and the industry veterans Bob Stevenson, Alan Yu, and Joe Keene. The start-up enjoyed quick success with the launch of its flagship game, Rolando, in which users guided a character through an animated landscape. Young was able to attract ample venture capital to acquire three other game developers: Miraphonic in 2009 and Freeverse and Stumptown Game Machine in 2010.

The combination of DeNA and ngmoco offered advantages for both parties. For a game developer such as ngmoco, being part of a major social game platform company such as DeNA offered greater opportunity for growth. DeNA added a strong lineup of new games and a development platform that worked on not only iPhones but also smartphones. More important, ngmoco was expected to greatly aid DeNA in gaining traction in the Western market. The company's long-term strategy was to enable developers to create games that could be used across devices as well as across borders. Namba made it clear that she believed such universal capability would become a reality. "The big tide in social gaming is coming, right now," she told Hiroko Tabuchi in the *New York Times* on October 13, 2010. "We'd like to capture it and quickly become the world's No. 1 mobile gaming platform." She also told Chris Morrison of *Inside Social Games* on October 15, 2010, that she hoped to grow DeNA's revenues to $4 billion by 2014, half of which would come from Japan, and the remainder from the rest of the world. "This is not a formal announcement of a plan," she explained, "but what I aspire to."

Ed Dinger

PRINCIPAL SUBSIDIARIES

Air Link Co., Ltd.; DeNA Global, Inc.; EVERYSTAR Co., Ltd.; IceBreaker U.S., Inc.; MiniNation, Inc.; Mobakore Co., Ltd.; Mobaoku Co., Ltd.; PAYGENT Co., Ltd.

PRINCIPAL COMPETITORS

Konami Corporation; Square Enix Holdings Co. Ltd.

FURTHER READING

Morrison, Chris. "Interview: DeNA Global CEO Tomoko Namba on Ngmoco and Growing to $40 Billion." *Inside Social Games*, October 15, 2010.

Nagata, Kazuaki. "Mobage-town a Rising-Star Site of Mobile Users, but Filters Loom." *Japan Times*, January 23, 2008.

Schoenberger, Chana R. "Queen of Mobile." *Forbes Global*, May 19, 2008, 32.

Tabuchi, Hiroko, "Japanese Game Maker on a Buying Spree." *New York Times*, October 13, 2010, p. B8.

Terada, Shinichi. "Internet Business Try Luck in Overseas Markets." *Japan Times*, May 15, 2008.

"Tomoko Namba." *BusinessWeek*, July 2, 2001, p. 32.

Wayabayashi, Daisuke. "DeNA's Namba Takes Deal Plunge." *Wall Street Journal*, October 17, 2010.

Eby-Brown Company, LLC

280 West Shuman Boulevard, Suite 280
Naperville, Illinois 60566
U.S.A.
Telephone: (630) 778-2800
Toll Free: (800) 553-8249
Fax: (630) 778-2830
Web site: http://www.eby-brown.com

Private Company
Founded: 1887
Incorporated: 1887
Employees: 2,200
Sales: $4.5 billion (2009 est.)
NAICS: 424410 General Line Grocery Merchant Wholesalers; 424450 Confectionery Merchant Wholesalers; 424940 Tobacco and Tobacco Product Merchant Wholesalers

■ ■ ■

Eby-Brown Company, LLC, based in Naperville, Illinois, is one of the largest product distributors to convenience stores in the United States. By 2010 Eby-Brown was servicing 13,500 clients in 28 U.S. states with candy, tobacco products, assorted merchandise, beverages, and refrigerated and frozen foods. Its Wakefield Sandwich Company division offers clients a range of sandwiches and other prepared foods and drinks. Eby-Brown also provides marketing support for its retail partners. In operation since 1887, the privately owned firm has been managed by members of the Wake family from the 1950s. Eby-Brown has distribution centers in Eau Claire, Wisconsin; Montgomery, Illinois; Plainfield, Indiana; Ypsilanti, Michigan; Springfield, Ohio; Rockmart, Georgia; and Baltimore, Maryland.

JACOB EBY FOUNDS A COMPANY

In 1887 Jacob Eby established a firm to produce candy and tobacco products in Aurora, Illinois, not far from Chicago. The company ceased candy manufacturing in 1912. Eby continued operating the business, with various partners and name changes, until 1930, when he sold his interest to R. H. Youngen and A. E. Hallman. The new owners renamed the company Eby-Youngen. In turn, Youngen and Hallman sold the firm in 1946 to Lyle Brown Sr., who changed the name to Eby-Brown Co.

Eby-Brown already had a unit in nearby Joliet, and by the mid-1950s it had set up a third unit, in Elgin, Illinois, which in 1956 was purchased by two of its salesmen, W. H. "Mike" Michael and W. S. "Bill" Wake. These partners soon bought the unit of Eby-Brown that was based in Aurora, and they began to expand the company, starting with the purchase of J. C. Theis Company in 1960.

Eby-Brown concentrated on distributing tobacco and candy to the burgeoning convenience store industry. Convenience stores were small retailers, typically located in urban or suburban neighborhoods, in small towns, or along busy roads, that sold candy and snacks, tobacco products, and grocery items (often at high markups), as well as alcoholic beverages.

In the mid-1960s Eby-Brown began holding an annual trade show that brought together company officials,

> **COMPANY PERSPECTIVES**
>
> We are an organization of people dedicated to providing superior service at competitive prices. All of us have an individual responsibility to fulfill our customers' needs to the best of our ability. When we are a good supplier to our customers, their successes become our successes.

product vendors, and retailers to socialize and make deals. The company also pioneered in automated product tracking in the 1970s, and its systems grew in sophistication as computer technology advanced.

THE WAKE FAMILY TAKES CONTROL

Mike Michael and Bill Wake headed Eby-Brown until 1983, when Bill Wake bought out his partner's share. In 1985 Bill Wake's sons Thomas G. "Tom" and Richard W. "Dick" Wake became joint presidents and CEOs, while Bill Wake remained as chairman and his wife Barbara served as chief financial officer. The Wakes avoided publicity and Chicago society, and vital decisions were made by the tight-knit group at the top. They gave division managers autonomy to make decisions, however, and they welcomed suggestions from employees. Even as Eby-Brown's workforce grew to more than 1,000, the company fostered a family-like atmosphere, which encouraged many employees to remain for decades.

Eby-Brown and convenience stores sought to respond to the declining popularity of tobacco products. Many operators responded by diversifying their product categories, stocking more grocery items, frozen foods, and prepared foods ranging from sandwiches to fried chicken, frozen yogurt, and popcorn. In 1986 Eby-Brown began distributing a full range of food preparation equipment to its retail partners and also providing training and promotional materials. Eby-Brown executives admitted that they expected little profit from equipment; rather, they anticipated that expanded food service would lure more customers into stores and stimulate greater overall sales.

By 1983 Eby-Brown's annual sales had reached $380 million. Five years later this amount had swelled to $581 million, ranking the company third among U.S. tobacco, candy, and convenience distributors, although its distribution was limited to Illinois and regions in adjoining states. In 1989 Eby-Brown bought the assets of financially distressed Schiller Inc., with five distribution centers in Michigan. Later the same year, Eby-Brown's purchase of Smith-Harris Distributors of Indianapolis, Indiana, further widened its territory. Indicative of its extended distribution network, Eby-Brown by 1991 held annual trade shows in three states; they included more than 200 exhibition booths and were attended by more than 2,700 retail buyers.

ACQUISITIONS AND STEADY EXPANSION

By 1991 Eby-Brown's total sales jumped to $961 million as it worked with more than 22,000 outlets in nine U.S. states. Chain stores accounted for about 52 percent and independents 48 percent of the company's sales that year. During the 1990s convenience distribution concentrated in larger firms, and Eby-Brown was one of the first distributors to cross into several states in what had been a mostly localized industry.

National chain discounters, supermarkets, and drugstores opened more outlets, draining business from independent convenience stores and the smaller wholesalers that supplied them, forcing many out of business. To maintain its profitability and competitive position, Eby-Brown in 1993 made a $200 million purchase of Bosart Company, whose territory covered West Virginia and western Pennsylvania.

In the 1990s Eby-Brown and many competing distributors turned to value-added services to stand out from rivals and boost profits, adopting category management and Efficient Consumer Response approaches that were already standard in supermarkets. By tracking orders and sales of individual products more closely, distributors could save money by devising more efficient shipping schedules. Eby-Brown's proprietary IRIS (Intelligent Reporting Information System) allowed retailers to access comprehensive information over the Internet about shipments of specific products to single stores or whole regions, as well as examine inventory in Eby-Brown's warehouses. The company used its computerized sales reports to assist stores in setting up products on their shelves for optimal turnover and also supported retailers' installation of electronic scanners at points of sale.

COOPERATIVE VENTURES AND CONTINUED EXPANSION

Eby-Brown joined three other leading regional warehouses to form the National Distribution Alliance (NDA) in 1994. The alliance offered an integrated

KEY DATES

1887: Jacob Eby founds tobacco- and candy-producing firm in Aurora, Illinois.
1956: Mike Michael and Bill Wake begin to take control of Eby-Brown.
1983: Bill Wake buys out Mike Michael and prepares to transfer leadership to his sons Tom and Dick Wake.
1994: Eby-Brown cofounds National Distribution Alliance.
2007: Eby-Brown introduces the Wakefield Sandwich Company line of prepared food.

national distribution service targeting major chain convenience retailers. Eby-Brown and its partners each promised to service NDA's clients within its core distribution area. The member companies set general policies together, but each client was assigned a particular NDA partner to work with. The addition of a fifth member in 1996 extended NDA's network to the entire United States.

On its own, Eby-Brown's most important client was Speedway SuperAmerica LLC, a subsidiary of Marathon Ashland Petroleum LLC. Their relationship was strengthened when Speedway chose Eby-Brown as the exclusive distributor for its chain convenience stores by spring 1999, adding 1,150 stores for a total of more than 2,400. In 1998 Eby-Brown resumed acquisitions, buying the J. L. Lester Company of Georgia, which gave the company a presence in the Southeast. F. A. Davis and Sons in Baltimore fell into Eby-Brown's hands in 2000.

Convenience store distributors such as Eby-Brown were adept at handling small amounts of slow-selling products. Thus wholesalers or retailers used Eby-Brown to purchase smaller quantities of items, which their regular suppliers often would not provide. Eby-Brown leveraged its expertise in candy and tobacco to bring in retail clients and expand its overall sales even as the cigarette market contracted.

As early as the mid-1980s, the company stocked orders for grocery wholesalers to ship to supermarkets and offered supermarkets its promotional skills to help move these products faster. To meet requests from clients, Eby-Brown arranged with a supermarket wholesaler to provide private-label products to be sold under the Top Care, Home Best, and Flavorite brands. As of 2004, however, company executives stated that sales of these brands remained meager.

CONTRACTION OF TOBACCO MARKET

After 2000 Eby-Brown made no significant acquisitions for the next decade. The company had attained its goal of becoming a leading convenience distributor in the eastern half of the United States. Eby-Brown's network spread over 28 states from Minnesota to Florida. Overall sales grew modestly, reaching $3.8 billion in 2003 and staying between $3 billion and $4.5 billion each year through 2010. The company usually ranked second or third nationally in tobacco and confectionery distribution throughout the decade.

In 2003 cigarettes still made up about 83 percent of Eby-Brown's revenues; candy and snacks about 5 percent. Candy and snacks were vital for the company's growth, especially as cigarette revenues declined at a rate that company vice president John Scardina estimated in 2010 at 3 to 4 percent annually. Eby-Brown distributed more than 4,600 SKUs (stock-keeping units) in candy and snacks (i.e., the company distributed more than 4,600 different candy and snack items), although most convenience stores had little display space for these products, and a few brands dominated sales. Recognizing that impulse purchases accounted for a large share of candy sales, Eby-Brown and other candy distributors persuaded manufacturers to support multivendor display racks designed to catch shoppers' attention.

DIVERSIFICATION IN FOOD OFFERINGS

Food service provided convenience distributors another strong field for growth as convenience stores continued to expand their offerings of prepared foods and foods with health claims. Eby-Brown collaborated with Sara Lee to introduce, in 2006, the Pronto Café concept, which featured hot coffee. In 1994 Eby-Brown had purchased a distribution center in Springfield, Illinois, where it set up a commissary that produced about 11 million sandwiches annually. Springfield became the home of Wakefield Sandwich Company, which launched in 2007 and offered convenience stores a line of hot and cold sandwiches, burgers, packaged salads, juices, and cut fruit in branded display units, coupled with category management and marketing support.

Eby-Brown continued to support tobacco retailing through its ORCHID (Optimized Replenishment of Cigarettes using Historical & Inventory Data) program, by which stores could automate cigarette orders to minimize quantity of both in-stock and out-of-stock items. Selected clients of Eby-Brown benefited from its Speed to Market program, in which the company offered detailed information by e-mail about newly ordered products before they were ready to ship, so that the stores could set up and promote the new items weeks ahead of time. Another means for the company to share information and marketing suggestions with its clients was through periodicals such as *Category Insights*, introduced in 2009 and published quarterly.

Eby-Brown adopted other high-tech innovations, including a voice pick system named Jennifer. Using this technology, a picker in a distribution center wears a headset and receives (and can respond to) audio instructions regarding an order to be picked. The picker does not have to carry around an actual pick list or a handheld device, allowing for a more rapid and precise selection of shipments. Another innovation was the installation of XATA tracking devices on the company's delivery trucks, which enabled the company to chart trucks' positions and map out more efficient delivery schedules.

After the death of Bill Wake in 2004, Tom and Dick Wake continued their family's leadership of Eby-Brown. By 2010 the company remained reliant on tobacco distribution even as further legal constraints were imposed on cigarette advertising and retailing. Company managers hoped that growth in candy and snacks, prepared food, and other merchandise would partly compensate for the shrinking tobacco market.

Stephen V. Beitel

PRINCIPAL SUBSIDIARIES

Eby-Brown Leasing, LLC; Eby-Brown Mid-Atlantic; Eby-Brown Plainfield; Eby-Brown Transportation, LLC; Elgin Eby-Brown Company; Indiana Eby-Brown Company; NewFreshCo Foods, LLC; Spnl Eby-Brown Company; Wakefield Sandwich Company.

PRINCIPAL COMPETITORS

Core-Mark Holding Company Inc.; GSC Enterprises, Inc.; Harold Levinson Associates Inc.; H. T. Hackney Company; McLane Company Inc.; S. Abraham & Sons Inc.

FURTHER READING

Balu, Rekha. "Trucking beyond Candy, Cigarettes." *Crain's Chicago Business*, June 23, 1997, 3.

Bennett, Stephen. "Private Label Pros and Cons: When Is the Time Ripe to Launch a Private-Label Program?" *National Petroleum News*, November 2005, 42.

Crecca, Donna Hood. "Staking a Claim." *Convenience Store News*, February 9, 1998, 40.

Donahue, Bill. "The Fresh Edge: Eby-Brown Angles for Fresh-Foods Lead with Wakefield Sandwich Division." *CSP Magazine*, October 2007, 181–91.

"Eby-Brown Makes Move into Michigan; Acquires Assets from Schiller Inc." *U.S. Distribution Journal*, May 1989, 1.

Echeandia, Lisbeth. "Nine Questions for Eby-Brown's." *Professional Candy Buyer*, January-February 2010, 26.

Francella, Barbara Grondin. "Technology Boosts Wholesalers' Services." *Convenience Store News*, May 3, 1999, 38.

Kaplan, Andrew. "Strength in Numbers." *U.S. Distribution Journal*, February 15, 1995, 28.

Kuhn, Mary Ellen. "Thinking Big at Eby-Brown: John Scardina Takes Both a Macro and a Micro View of the Candy Category as Merchandising Vice President for This Large Wholesale Distribution Company." *Confectioner*, March 2004, 12.

Quackenbush, Kate. "Brown Has Green in the Black: Buoyed by Eby-Brown's 'Speed to Market' Program, Green Oil Is Quickly Capitalizing on Emerging Sales Trends." *Convenience Store Decisions*, December 2006, 28.

Eskom Holdings Limited

P.O. Box 1091
Johannesburg, Gauteng 2001
South Africa
Telephone: (+27 011) 800-8111
Fax: (+27 011) 507-6358
Web site: http://www.eskom.co.za

Government Owned Company
Founded: 1923 as Electricity Supply Commission
Incorporated: 1923 as Electricity Supply Commission
Employees: 39,222 (2010 est.)
Sales: $6.99 billion (2009)
NAICS: 221122 Electric Power Distribution

■ ■ ■

Eskom Holdings Limited is a Johannesburg, South Africa–based utility company that generates 95 percent of the country's electricity and 45 percent of the electricity used in Africa. The company also operates electricity concessions in Mali and Uganda. Other Eskom ventures include Eskom Enterprises (Pty) Limited group, which provides support and maintenance services for other Eskom units, and Eskom Finance Company (Pty) Limited and Gallium Insurance Company Limited, providers of employee home loans and business risk insurance and management services. An affiliated nonprofit company, Eskom Development Foundation, serves as a corporate social investment vehicle. Although Eskom is a public company, the government of South Africa is the sole shareholder.

19TH-CENTURY ROOTS

The electrical utility industry began to take shape in South Africa in 1882 when Diamond City became the first African city to employ electric streetlights. South Africa made increasing use of electricity for mine lighting, trams, electric motors, and private lighting. By 1891 the first central power station in the country opened. Other power stations followed, and in 1906 a central electricity company was established to take advantage of the generating potential of the Victoria Falls, resulting in the creation of the Victoria Falls Power Company Limited (VFP). The hydropower concept proved impractical, however, and VFP changed its name in 1909 to Victoria Falls and Transvaal Power Company Limited, the emphasis now on building generating plants powered by the coal deposits in the Transvaal Colony.

In 1923 the South African government formed the Electricity Supply Commission (Escom) to develop and maintain affordable supplies of regional electricity for industry, railways and harbors, and government agencies. (Escom was also known by its Afrikaans name Elektrisiteitsvoorsieningskommissie, or Evkom.) The new commission established its headquarters in Johannesburg to manage the building of new power stations in Cape Town, Durban, Sabie, and Witbank. Although the Witbank station was financed and owned by Escom, it was designed, built, and operated by VFP.

NEW PLANT COMMISSIONED

Escom also took charge of a power station in Colenso as well as substations that had been under the control of

COMPANY PERSPECTIVES

Together building the powerbase for sustainable growth and development.

the Railway Administration as part of an effort to electrify a rail link between Glencoe and Pietermaritzburg. The coal-fired Glencoe power station and a similar unit in Witbank were commissioned in 1926. Two years later, coal-fired plants in Congella and Salt River were commissioned. Escom also made use of hydroelectricity. In 1927 it commissioned a new hydroelectric plant on the Sabie River to meet the needs of the gold mines in the Eastern Transvaal. This station was of further significance because it was the first project designed by the commission's own engineers.

Escom was not immune to the effects of the economic depression that dominated the 1930s. Nevertheless, demand for electricity continued to grow. The commission held off on the construction of new power plants, but the discovery of gold fields near Witwatersrand, coupled with the increase of gold prices that accompanied lean times, prompted Escom to begin construction of the Klip power station near Vereeniging. As with the unit at Witbank, it was operated as part of the VFP network. The station began operations in 1940.

Although the Klip station was commissioned, the construction of the Vaal power station was postponed owing to the impact of World War II. These complications were demonstrated by the loss of a new turbo generator set for the Congella power station that was lost when the ship carrying it was sunk by a German U-boat. The Vaal plant was not commissioned until 1952, and in the meantime, Escom contended with the problem of maintaining aging equipment. To make matters worse, Escom had to make do without its Rosherville workshop, which had been commandeered by the South African government to manufacture parts and instruments for sophisticated weapons. Demand for power fell off, then rebounded as the war progressed, but given its constraints Escom struggled to add new capacity.

VFP NETWORK ADDED

In 1944 Escom acquired the Port Shepstone power station. Further external growth followed through the 1940s after the war ended. The West Bank power plant and the central power station for the De Beers mines in Kimberley were added in 1947. A year later Escom acquired the Alice and King William's Town municipal power stations. In that same year, Escom absorbed the VFP power network to fulfill a mandate first laid out in South Africa's Power Act of 1910 and reiterated in the Electricity Act of 1922.

Extra capacity would be greatly needed during the economic expansion of the postwar years, as South Africa's major cities grew and industry expanded in the Northern Transvaal, the Witwatersrand region, and the Vaal Triangle urban complex that included Vereeninging, Vanderbijlpark, and Sasolburg. Although Escom doubled its capacity from 1945 to 1955, it fell far short of demand, and the company was forced to ration power. Because the supply of electricity was expected to double again over the next 10 years, Escom began building larger power stations. The coal-fired Komati power station commissioned in 1962, for example, had a capacity of 1,000 megawatts, but it paled in comparison to the plants that began construction later in the 1960s, including the 2,000-megawatt plant in Hendrina, the 2,100-megawatt plant in Arnot, and the 3,000-megawatt station in Kriel.

Also of great importance to the growth of Escom and the economic development of South Africa was the establishment of a national power network in the 1960s. This network linked Cape Province operations to the Transvaal power stations.

A new hydroelectric power station, Hendrik Verwoerd, became operational in 1971. It was followed by the Vanderkloof hydroelectric power station commissioned in 1977. During this decade Escom also added new coal-fired and gas-turbine power stations. Moreover, Escom pursued a nuclear power project, the Koeberg power station, to help meet the growing demand for power in the Western Cape. It was the first nuclear power plant on the continent.

ESKOM NAME ADOPTED

An even more ambitious expansion program was launched in the 1980s. The construction of coal-fired power stations in the Transvaal and what was then called the Orange Free State began in Tutuka, Lethabo, Kendal, Matimba, and Majuba. In addition, the distribution and transmission network was expanded. In the wake of a change in leadership in 1985, Escom was restructured, and it was replaced by a government-appointed electricity council, which in turn formed a management board. In 1987 the utility changed its name, combining Escom with the Afrikaans name Evkom to create Eskom.

The 1990s not only brought increased electrical power capacity to South Africa but also political changes

KEY DATES

1923: Electricity Supply Commission (Escom) is formed.
1948: Escom absorbs Victoria Falls Power Company operations.
1987: Escom changes its name to Eskom.
1999: Eskom Enterprises is formed.
2002: Eskom becomes a public company.

that impacted every aspect of the country. Since 1948 the South African government had enforced a policy of racial segregation known as apartheid that maintained minority rule of white inhabitants over a black majority, Asians, and other designated racial groups. Opposition to apartheid grew over the years, internally as well as internationally, leading to a trade embargo, and by 1990 the South African government launched negotiations to bring an end to apartheid. During these drawn-out talks, Eskom attempted to raise $200 million for expansion through a pair of bond issues on the Eurobond market, but in 1992 it was forced to shelve the offering as the negotiations hit a snag and were suspended. It was clear that until apartheid was eliminated and a new democratically elected multiracial government was in place, South African industry would be hamstrung.

Democratic elections were finally held in South Africa in 1994. Eskom then faced a power struggle of its own between its mostly white management and the Ministry of Public Enterprises, which at the behest of the new coalition government was pushing Eskom to name more blacks and Asians to senior positions. Eskom agreed to a target of 50 percent black managers and 20 percent women by the end of the 1990s. Eskom was eager to maintain its independence and avoid government-proposed five-year performance contracts that would give the government more control over Eskom's operations. Eskom's management was keen on expanding outside of South Africa to neighboring countries.

In the late 1990s the South African government's attempt to privatize Eskom led to dire consequences a decade later. Eskom's budgetary requests to build new power stations were denied by the government in the belief that private investment would soon follow. Although funds to build new power plants did not materialize, Eskom was able to forge technology and management agreements with Electricité de France and East Midlands Electricity of the United Kingdom.

ESKOM ENTERPRISES FORMED

In 1999 Eskom formed Eskom Enterprises to focus on nonregulated endeavors in South Africa and pursue energy and related services opportunities internationally. The subsidiary was involved in energy-related projects throughout Africa as well as in China and India. Also in 1999 Eskom formed the Eskom Development Foundation to support small business and community development as well as a school and clinic electrification program.

In 2002 the South African government enacted the Eskom Conversion Act, which converted Eskom into a public company. The utility became Eskom Holdings Limited, and South Africa's Minister of Public Enterprises appointed a board of directors, replacing the Electricity Council and Management Board. Despite its new structure, Eskom could not avoid the mistakes of the late 1990s when the country failed to begin the construction of new power plants.

The Cape region began experiencing power disruptions in 2006 caused by unexpected outages and increased demand that overwhelmed Eskom's reserve capacity. Matters only grew worse, so that in January 2008 the country declared a national electricity emergency. Eskom responded with a program of "load shedding," which meant turning off the power in different parts of the country on a rotating basis whenever the integrity of the power grid was threatened. It also stopped exporting power to neighboring countries. These rolling blackouts prevented more devastating nationwide blackouts. The blackouts also had a ripple effect on the global economy, as mine closures sent the price of platinum and palladium soaring to record heights.

To add much-needed capacity, Eskom reinstated three shuttered power stations in 2008. An expansion program was also launched, and in keeping with this effort an office was opened in London, to oversee the manufacture of new power-generating equipment. Several coal-fired stations began construction, including the Kusile Power Station in 2008. Eskom hoped to add 20,000 megawatts of power, electricity that would be needed if South Africa was to grow its gross national product by an anticipated 6 percent per annum, by 2025.

Ed Dinger

PRINCIPAL SUBSIDIARIES

Eskom Enterprises (Pty) Limited; Eskom Finance Company (Pty) Limited; Gallium Insurance Company Limited.

FURTHER READING

Bearman, Jonathan. "Battle of the Energy Giants." *African Business*, June 1995, 32.

Coupe, Stuart. "Manufacturing Apartheid: State Corporations in South Africa." *Business History*, October 1995, 133.

"Eskom Completes Project Financing of $260 Million for Wind and Solar Power Plants, South Africa." *OfficialSpin*, June 17, 2010.

"Eskom Secures $500m Capital Expansion Loan." *Modern Power Systems*, December 2008, 5.

Guzzo, Maria. "South African Energy Crisis Impacting Markets Globally." *American Metal Market*, February 6, 2008, 1.

Laurance, Ben. "Financial Notebook: Differing Priorities." *Guardian*, August 12, 1992, 9.

Nevin, Tom. "Eskom—Between a Rock and a Hard Place." *African Business*, April 2010, 80.

Etsy Inc.

55 Washington Street, Suite 512
Brooklyn, New York 11201
U.S.A.
Telephone: (718) 855-7955
Fax: (718) 732-2613
Web site: http://www.etsy.com

Private Company
Founded: 2005
Incorporated: 2006
Employees: 125
Sales: $180.6 million (2009)
NAICS: 454111 Electronic Shopping

■ ■ ■

Etsy Inc. is a privately owned online marketplace for handmade products, such as art, jewelry, housewares, and a variety of other items. Individuals sell their products on the site, paying Etsy a small fee for each item sold and a percentage of the total sale amount. Etsy serves 5 million buyers and sellers in more than 150 countries. Etsy maintains its headquarters in Brooklyn, New York, and operates branch offices in San Francisco and Berlin. In addition to corporate offices, the New York location also houses Etsy Labs, which serves as a community workspace where craft workshops and special events are held.

FOUNDER ROBERT KALIN

Etsy was founded by Robert Kalin, the son of a carpenter who early on learned the joys of working with his hands. He was an indifferent student in high school, more interested in photography than his studies. After high school, he attended art classes at the Museum of Fine Arts in Boston. He used his photography skills to make a fake graduate student ID that allowed him to take additional classes at the nearby Massachusetts Institute of Technology.

Kalin later moved to New York City and enrolled in New York University to study the classics, supporting himself with carpentry work and eventually earning a degree in the classics in 2004. In addition to carpentry jobs, he earned a living working as a bookstore clerk and a department-store cashier. Along the way he also became involved in website development. His Brooklyn landlord, who owned a restaurant, asked him to create a website for the restaurant. Kalin taught himself hypertext markup language (HTML) and within a month presented his landlord with a website.

Kalin then used his programming skills to work for a crafts website that offered advice to artisans. About this time, Kalin had difficulty selling an item he had made, a computer encased in wood. Disenchanted with eBay, an online auction site that he felt had become too large and corporate, Kalin decided to start his own online marketplace for artisans.

RAISING SEED MONEY

Kalin's grandfather, who had worked at major corporations including IBM and General Electric, urged him to develop a detailed business plan, but Kalin elected to just launch a site and make adjustments as necessary. To help start the company, Kalin enlisted the help of New

COMPANY PERSPECTIVES

Our mission is to enable people to make a living making things, and to reconnect makers with buyers.

York University friends Chris Maguire and Haim Schoppik, who were skilled programmers. They formed a company called Iospace. For seed money Kalin turned to people for whom he had worked: his former landlord and a pair of real estate developers who had hired him for carpentry jobs. He received $50,000 before launching the company and another $100,000 within six months.

Kalin and his partners were eager to launch their website. To speed up development, Maguire and Schoppik essentially moved into Kalin's Brooklyn apartment so that they could work night and day. Six weeks later the site was ready to launch. For a name Kalin chose Etsy. The origin of the name and Kalin's reason for choosing it are unknown.

LAUNCHING THE SITE

On June 18, 2005, Kalin and his partners launched the Etsy site. They were soon joined by Jared Tarbell, who served as vice president of visualizations. In its first year of operation, Etsy sold $166,000 in merchandise. Relying almost entirely on word of mouth, sales grew to $3.8 million in 2006.

It was also in 2006 that Kalin raised additional funds in an unusual manner. Kalin wrote a letter to the cofounders of the popular Flickr photo-sharing website, Stewart Butterfield and Caterina Fake, who the year before had sold their business to Yahoo! Butterfield and Fake were so taken by Kalin's letter that they invited him and his partners to visit them in San Francisco. Not only did Butterfield and Fake become Etsy investors, but they also helped the start-up company raise $615,000 in venture capital. Etsy would also raise money through Union Square Ventures, a venture capital fund established in 2003 to invest in Internet start-ups.

To keep pace with the growing business, Kalin and his partners looked to move into a larger space. Late in 2006 they moved into a 6,000-square-foot space in a former bank building in downtown Brooklyn. With the extra space they created Etsy Labs, where various pieces of equipment, such as sewing machines, were available for use free of charge. It also offered a book club, afternoon teas, and movie nights.

GRASSROOTS MARKETING DRIVES SALES

Sales soared to $26 million in 2007, as Etsy enjoyed excellent growth. A good deal of that success was the result of the Etsy Street Team, a concept that combined guerilla marketing and community building. Teams of Etsy advocates, primarily sellers on the site, formed in major cities, where they organized craft shows, passed out posters and buttons, and created a local arts community that simultaneously built the Etsy brand. Etsy also exchanged ad space with magazines that shared similar audiences, including *Good Magazine* and artist Mary Engelbreit's *Home Companion.*

Despite the success, problems soon arose that the partners had not foreseen. The site's interface was slow, and customer service struggled to keep up with the surge in site traffic. Moreover, the payment system was rudimentary. A new system was developed in 2007 that allowed buyers to make purchases from different sellers in a single transaction. Because Etsy was dealing with buyers and sellers from around the world, it added currency conversion capabilities and foreign-language support.

Also in 2007 Etsy opened an office in San Francisco to attract talent, and the company began scouting for office space in Europe, considering London and Berlin before deciding to open an office in the latter city. Etsy also sought further capital to support its expansion plans. In early 2008 it raised $27 million from Union Square Ventures, the German media company Hubert Burda Media, and technology investor Jim Breyer of Accel Partners. Other changes followed in 2008. Kalin stepped down as chief executive officer (CEO) in July, turning over day-to-day control to Maria Thomas while staying on as chief creative officer and chairman.

Thomas was a former executive of Amazon.com and National Public Radio. She had joined Etsy several months earlier as chief operating officer. A month after Thomas took charge as CEO, Schoppik and Maguire left the company. A short time later former Yahoo! employee Chad Dickerson joined Etsy as chief technology officer, a post he had held at Salon.com and InfoWorld Media Group/IDG.

Although gross sales increased to $87.5 million in 2008, Etsy continued to experience growing pains. The company promoted the idea that sellers could earn a living by selling their wares on the site, as exemplified by Etsy's "Quit Your Day Job" section, which profiled seller success stories. The company boasted that its top sellers earned six-figure incomes, when in truth only a few were self-sustaining entrepreneurs. The vast majority of sellers relied on Etsy as a secondary source of income,

KEY DATES

2005: Etsy is founded.
2006: Etsy moves into a 6,000-square-foot space in a former bank building to accommodate its growing business.
2007: Etsy opens an office in San Francisco.
2008: Etsy raises $27 million in venture capital.
2009: Etsy acquires Adtuitive.

and some objected to Etsy promoting itself as a kind of small business platform.

Etsy was also criticized for censoring its forums and banning outspoken members from posting comments. Several disgruntled members formed their own website, where Etsy was roundly criticized. The company also had to contend with accusations that some sellers were selling the work of others as their own.

ETSY BECOMES PROFITABLE

In 2009 Etsy faced direct competition for the first time as new craft marketplace sites began appearing. Thousands of Etsy sellers abandoned the site, but their loss was mitigated by the thousands of new sellers who joined the site as a result of the growing global awareness of the Etsy brand. Gross merchandise sales more than doubled to $180.6 million in 2009, and the company claimed that it had reached profitability.

Also in 2009 Etsy moved to a new 15,000-square-foot space near the Manhattan Bridge in New York and acquired a New York–based advertising company, Adtuitive, a start-up that brought five employees with skills Etsy hoped to exploit. In January 2010 Thomas left the company, and Kalin returned as CEO. The company continued to grow under his leadership. During the first half of 2010, sales increased to more than $130 million. After five years in business, Etsy had just begun to realize its potential and planned for an initial public offering in 2011.

Ed Dinger

PRINCIPAL SUBSIDIARIES

Etsy Labs.

PRINCIPAL COMPETITORS

ArtFire LCC; DaWanda GmbH; eBay Inc.

FURTHER READING

Bruder, Jessica. "The Etsy Wars." *Fortune Small Business*, July 2009, 94.

Evans, Teri. "Creating Etsy's Handmade Marketplace." *Wall Street Journal*, March 30, 2010.

Fenn, Donna. "Meet Rob Kalin, the Man behind Etsy.com." *Reader's Digest*, December 2009.

Macmillan, Kate. "Etsy Lets Art Sales Take Wing." *San Francisco Chronicle*, May 26, 2008.

Miller, Kerry. "An eBay for the Arts and Crafts Set." *BusinessWeek*, July 23, 2007, p. 70.

Pack, Thomas. "Web Users Are Getting Crafty." *Information Today*, March 2008, 36.

Evenflo Company, Inc.

1801 Commerce Drive
Piqua, Ohio 45356
U.S.A.
Telephone: (937) 415-3300
Toll Free: (800) 233-5921
Fax: (937) 415-3112
Web site: http://www.evenflo.com

Private Company
Founded: 1920
Employees: 105 (est.)
Sales: $300 million (2004 est.)
*NAICS:*339932 Game, Toy, and Children's Vehicle Manufacturing; 326299 All Other Rubber Product Manufacturing

■ ■ ■

Evenflo Company, Inc., is a worldwide leader in the development of innovative infant care products and equipment, and one of the leading manufacturers of baby and juvenile care products in the United States. Evenflo supplies a wide variety of products, ranging from infant and child car seats, strollers, high chairs, portable cribs, mattresses, and play yards to bath accessories, baby monitors, baby bottles, disposable and reusable baby bottle feeding systems, breastfeeding aids, and pacifiers. The company markets its products through the brand names Evenflo, Snugli, and ExerSaucer, among others. Evenflo has established marketing and sales operations throughout the United States, Canada, Mexico, and the Philippines. In the United States Evenflo sells its products through children's specialty stores and big-box stores. Safety and convenience are primary concerns for parents and caregivers shopping for infant and child care products. Evenflo has reached and maintained its place among the market's top three manufacturers by keeping these directives in mind when designing and promoting its products.

PYRAMID RUBBER COMPANY OF RAVENNA, OHIO

Evenflo was founded in 1920 in Ravenna, Ohio, a small manufacturing town located along a branch of the Ohio River and Erie Canal. Originally part of the Pyramid Rubber Company, Evenflo began as a manufacturer and distributor of infant care products, specializing in the manufacture of latex nipples for baby bottles. The company took its name from a nursing device invented by Erhart Kirkjan for which it obtained a patent in 1935. At that time, according to a 1989 oral history provided by former Pyramid Rubber Company president Cyril Porthouse, molded nipples for baby bottles were a brand new invention. Porthouse arrived at Pyramid in 1937 as an engineer and helped to rapidly increase production of the new patented design. Pyramid Rubber continued to specialize in Evenflo nipples and designed additional nipples to accommodate infants with cleft palates and other special needs.

Following World War II, production at Pyramid rapidly increased, and in 1947 Cyril Porthouse raised approximately $1 million to buy the Pyramid Rubber Company. He raised an additional $1.25 million to fund additional future growth. Pyramid marketed the

COMPANY PERSPECTIVES

At Evenflo Company, Inc., we devote ourselves to five important values at the heart of our company—passion, ownership, partnership, leadership, and social responsibility. These values originate from our steadfast mission to maintain and build on the trust between ourselves and the children, parents, and caregivers who use our products. We hire people whose passion for their work translates into products of the highest quality and safety possible. We allow our employees to take ownership of their work, encouraging them to innovate and develop products that meet the needs of growing families. We build and maintain mutually beneficial partnerships with retailers, departments, and product brands within our corporate family. We view market leadership in many of our product categories as much more than market share. We do not settle for less when it comes to bringing consumers the best baby and children's products available. We give back to our local communities by sharing our knowledge, expertise, and passion with parents and caregivers.

Evenflo nipple under both Evenflo and Vita-Flo brand names. Evenflo was sold in specialty retail drugstores and department stores, while the same product was sold in discount stores as Vita-Flo. When discount stores began selling the same goods as specialty stores, the Vita-Flo brand name was dropped.

POSTWAR GROWTH

In 1955 Pyramid Rubber acquired a 22.5 percent share in the A.G. Spalding & Brothers, Inc., sporting goods company, which was experiencing a downturn because of slow growth and inadequate management. Porthouse and other Pyramid executives approached the Spalding family and convinced them of their ability and willingness to turn the company around. Pyramid Rubber subsequently acquired control of the struggling company. Founded in 1876, Spalding was one of the most respected and recognized sporting goods companies in the world. It marketed a wide range of athletic and recreational goods, including products used in football, soccer, tennis, racquetball, basketball, and baseball.

In the 1950s the Evenflo division of Pyramid Rubber built the Harcourt plastics company, which enabled Evenflo to manufacture better quality plastic baby bottles. During the same era, Pyramid Rubber acquired the Oil City Glass Company, which had previously manufactured glass baby bottles for Evenflo. Pyramid also acquired another plastics company, Crater Manufacturing, of Pennsylvania.

Throughout the next 20 years, Evenflo's parent company, Pyramid Rubber, continued to acquire smaller companies, including Alfred Dunhill of London; AP Parts Company of Toledo, Ohio, also known as Questor Corporation; and the children's publisher Platt and Monk. By the time Cyril Porthouse retired in 1973, Pyramid Rubber was known as Questor Corporation and had become highly diversified. According to the oral history provided by Porthouse in 1989, mounting debt forced Questor Corporation to sell many of the smaller companies it had acquired. By 1976 all that remained were Evenflo and Spalding, which became known as Spalding & Evenflo Companies.

BEGINNING OF A NEW ERA

In 1977 Evenflo introduced an innovative and important new product to its market when it produced the first rear-facing infant car seat.

In 1984 the privately held Cisneros Group of Caracas, Venezuela, purchased Spalding & Evenflo Companies. Owned by Gustavo and Ricardo Cisneros, the Cisneros Group was best known for its ownership interests in international media and telecommunications businesses such as DIRECTV International and Univision.

In 1994 Evenflo introduced the ExerSaucer, a proposed safer alternative to baby walkers. Competing companies quickly turned out their own versions of the stationary infant entertainer. In 1995 Evenflo reached $954 million in sales, including about $634 million from direct sales. Licensed sales accounted for the remaining $320 million.

Despite these sales successes and continued profitability, in May 1996 the Cisneros Group announced plans to sell Spalding & Evenflo Companies in order to pursue opportunities offered by the worldwide telecommunications industry. In August 1996 the New York–based buyout firm Kohlberg Kravis Roberts & Company (KKR) agreed to purchase a majority stake in Spalding & Evenflo Companies. Cisneros Group and its management would continue to hold minority interests in the companies. Terms of the purchase were not announced, but financial publications later estimated the cost to have been around $1 billion.

KEY DATES

1920: Pyramid Rubber Company is founded.
1935: Evenflo nurser is patented.
1955: Pyramid Rubber acquires Spalding sporting goods company.
1997: Evenflo acquires Gerry Baby Products Company.
2007: Evenflo acquires the Swedish company Ameda.

In 1997 Evenflo acquired the Gerry Baby Products Company for a purchase price of $73 million in cash. Gerry's parent company, the Huffy Corporation, did not wish to make the investment necessary to build the third-place Gerry Baby Products into one of the top two industry leaders in baby and juvenile care products. Evenflo predicted the acquisition would help bolster its position as a market leader in baby products.

DEPARTURE OF SPALDING

In August 1998 KKR announced that it would split Spalding & Evenflo Companies into two separate freestanding companies. KKR retained an 80 percent share in both companies. Company spokesman Michael Kipphut told the *Tampa Tribune* (August 1, 1998) that "Spalding and Evenflo are two strategically unrelated businesses, and with their size and complexity, we believe that it is to their advantage to operate as separate corporate entities."

In 2001 Evenflo reached total sales of $350 million, of which $150 to $200 million was accounted for by sales of infant gear such as car seats, strollers, carriers, and high chairs. In 2003 Evenflo sold between $125 million and $175 million worth of the same types of infant gear, placing it in third place behind its chief competitors, first-place Dorel Juvenile Group, Inc., and second-place Graco Children's Products, Inc.

TURNED AROUND BY HARVEST PARTNERS

Harvest Partners, a private investment equity firm, acquired Evenflo in August 2004 for an undisclosed sum that was estimated in published reports to have been no more than $200 million. Harvest's existing diverse interests included gas turbine equipment, energy production components, building materials, communication supply equipment, bus manufacturing, vehicle accessories, and home health-care supplies. Harvest welcomed the acquisition of Evenflo as one that would increase its exposure in consumer products. "We've been looking at consumer-related businesses for the past couple of years now," said Harvest senior managing director Thomas Arenz in an interview with *Buyouts* (August 23, 2004). "We really like that Evenflo has a terrific brand and a great reputation among consumers," he added.

The sale marked the end of eight years of ownership by KKR, during which time competition with other baby and juvenile care product manufacturers increased. In addition, Evenflo sales tracked downward for the last three years prior to its acquisition by Harvest. Total sales in 2004 were estimated at approximately $300 million, down $50 million from three years earlier. Despite these figures, Harvest director Arenz remained optimistic. He mentioned existing Evenflo company management as an important draw in moving ahead with the acquisition. Arenz also cited potentially beneficial demographic trends. In the same *Buyouts* interview, he said, "There's been continued growth in the number of births, and the market itself has been very steady over time, growing in the low single digits. This is not a volatile or cyclical type of business."

Harvest Partners retained ownership of Evenflo until 2007, when it sold the company to an affiliate of the private equity firm Weston Presidio. Arenz described the strength of Evenflo's performance during the previous three years to *Business Wire* (February 8, 2007). "Evenflo has performed very strongly due to an outstanding management team … and ongoing positive industry trends." During its years with Harvest Partners, reported *Business Wire*, Evenflo continued to strengthen its executive management team, improve its sourcing strategy, and introduce new products into the marketplace.

BEST FOR BOTH MOTHER AND CHILD

In 2007 Evenflo acquired Ameda, a Swedish manufacturer of breast pumps and breast-feeding accessories. According to published reports, the acquisition of Ameda represented a defining moment in Evenflo's ongoing policy of providing products and services that were considered best for both mother and child. An account of the Ameda acquisition published in *Business Wire* (October 18, 2007) noted that research worldwide showed breast-feeding to be the preferred method of feeding for both newborns and infants. Evenflo CEO Robert Matteucci stated that "the addition of Ameda to our family of products further expands our ability to provide moms the widest range of options to enhance their breastfeeding experience."

In 2008 Evenflo announced plans to become the first U.S. baby bottle manufacturer compliant with the World Health Organization's (WHO's) International Code of Marketing of Breast Milk Substitutes. The code serves as a guide to manufacturers who market breast milk substitutes, baby bottles, and nipples to ensure that marketing practices do not undermine the practice of breast-feeding. To become compliant with the code Evenflo discontinued all baby bottle and nipple advertisements directed at consumers, altered its feeding packaging to adhere to WHO guidelines, and stopped offering or advertising baby bottles and nipples for sale on its website.

THE BUSINESS OF PRODUCT RECALLS

The nature of Evenflo products, along with the importance parents, caregivers, and Evenflo itself placed on product safety and effectiveness, meant that over the decades of its history Evenflo had recalled numerous products from store shelves. Evenflo was not alone in recalling products. For example, beginning in 1998 and ending in 2001, a total of four manufacturers, including Evenflo, recalled baby transportation products, such as infant car seat-and-carrier combinations. The individual items recalled by the four companies totaled ten million.

In April 2009 Evenflo released a statement addressing a series of three product recalls that had taken place over the previous four months. Recalled items included 831,000 high chairs and 213,000 stationary activity centers. In a statement following the last of the recalls, Evenflo reassured consumers of its strict standards and said it would never hesitate to recall any infant or juvenile care product that it perceived to have any potential hazard. "At Evenflo, our primary goal is always to put safety first," the company said.

Joyce Helena Brusin

PRINCIPAL SUBSIDIARIES

Ameda; Gerry Baby Products.

PRINCIPAL COMPETITORS

Gerber Products Company; Dorel Juvenile Group, Inc.; Graco Children's Products, Inc.; Kids II, Inc.; Sassy, Inc.

FURTHER READING

"A Bumpy Ride at Evenflo." *BusinessWeek*, May 14, 2001.

"Companies to Split; Close Tampa Office." *Tampa (Fla.) Tribune*, August 1, 1998.

"800 Infant Carriers Are Recalled by Evenflo." *New York Times*, March 5, 2008.

"Evenflo Adopts WHO Code." *Mothering*, January–February 2008.

"Evenflo Says It May Put Itself Up for Sale." *New York Times*, January 13, 2004, C4.

French, Dana. "Dorel Takes Over Top Spot in Gear Revenues: Top Three Manufacturers Stay Ahead of the Pack." *Home Accents Today*, February 2005.

"Gerry Baby Products Sold to Evenflo for $73 Million." *New York Times*, April 23, 1997.

MacFadyen, Kenneth. "Harvest Bottles Evenflo." *Buyouts*, August 23, 2004.

Romero, Simon. "Coup? Not His Style. But Power? Oh, Yes." *New York Times*, April 28, 2002.

"Top Three Gear Producers Dominate Field." *Home Textiles Today*, February 10, 2003.

Expedia Inc.

333 108th Avenue NE
Bellevue, Washington 98004
U.S.A.
Telephone: (425) 679-7200
Toll Free: (800) 397-3342
Fax: (425) 679-7240
Web site: http://www.expediainc.com

Public Company
Founded: 1996
Employees: 7,960
Sales: $2.95 billion (2009)
Stock Exchanges: NASDAQ
Ticker Symbol: EXPE
NAICS: 561510 Travel Agencies; 561520 Tour Operators; 561599 All Other Travel Arrangement and Reservation Services; 519130 Internet Search Portals

■ ■ ■

Expedia Inc. has reconfigured the world of travel. Formerly a start-up online travel division of Microsoft Network, Expedia has devised a broad scope of products and services such as discounted hotel rooms, rental cars, and packaged travel plans. The corporate travel market is part of its menu and has international operations in 31 countries. Expedia's cutting-edge technology simplifies customers' travel-related planning and online purchasing and keeps customers satisfied and the company profitable.

ONLINE TRAVEL SERVICES: 1996–98

When Microsoft Corporation launched Expedia on the Microsoft Network in October 1996, it was the first online travel service to be offered by a major technology company. Expedia allowed consumers to make air, car, and hotel reservations online and to browse a library of multimedia travel guides. Richard Barton, who worked in Microsoft's CD-ROM division and guided the team that created CD-ROM travel guides, was the initial developer of Expedia. When the CD-ROM market began to collapse, he was transferred to the company's multimedia group. He presented the concept to the Microsoft cofounder and chief executive officer (CEO) Bill Gates at the company's annual product review, and shortly thereafter Barton became Expedia's first president and CEO.

At first, Expedia accepted bookings only from consumers, not from offline travel agencies. At the time most consumers used the Internet for browsing rather than buying, so it was not clear whether they would use an online service to make travel reservations. In the November 21, 1996, issue of *Travel Weekly*, Joseph Kornik noted that Microsoft ran its first mainstream ad for Expedia in November. A full-page ad in the *Wall Street Journal* urged consumers to access "the same reservations system" that travel agents used and indicated that going online gave them a simple method of obtaining airline tickets, at no charge. However, the ad also gave travel agents the impression that e-commerce for travel services spelled unfortunate prospects for them. Evidently, more communication between websites such as Expedia and

COMPANY PERSPECTIVES

Our mission is to build the world's largest and most intelligent travel marketplace, connecting more travelers with the best travel booking services and destination information, and delivering value to travel suppliers and other companies that want to reach this unmatched audience.

traditional travel agents was needed for future coexistence.

Over the next several months a series of improvements followed. In May 1997 Expedia upgraded its website and added airline seat selection, real-time flight information, and an expanded directory of hotels and bed-and-breakfast inns. These improvements and other features likened consumers' choice of Expedia to that of contact with actual travel agents. The travel service also included new destinations in its Expedia World Guide, an element of its website that benefited from Microsoft's library of knowledge and therefore provided consumers with virtual travel publications about destinations.

Other improvements kept Expedia on track for progress. The company consolidated its Flight Wizard, Hotel Wizard, and Car Wizard onto a single screen. This simplified the website's practicality and reduced download time, which increased customer satisfaction. In early 1998 Expedia launched the Expedia Associates Program. Companies such as American Express Vacations, National Car Rental, National Leisure Group, and Hotel Reservations Network signed up for the program and agreed to cobrand their websites in return for use of Expedia's booking engine. The strategy of partnering with others in the industry whose offerings and products aligned with Expedia's interests and technology became a formula for success.

EXPANSION AND INITIAL PUBLIC OFFERING: 1998–99

In late 1998 Microsoft expanded Expedia's reach by launching travel service in the United Kingdom. The site gave information on fares for air travel and prices for hotel rooms and car rentals. According to Linda Fox in the November 11, 1998, issue of *Travel Trade Gazette*, the website also included a section known in the United Kingdom as a "holiday shop" that offered discounted, last-minute packaged vacations from 20 tour operators. A toll-free telephone number and an e-mail address were given as booking options for consumers. In addition, details about destinations were provided as a promotional tie-in with *Business Traveller* magazine.

By mid-1999 consumers had access to Expedia via websites in the United States, the United Kingdom, Germany, Canada, and Australia. In its third year of operation, Expedia ranked 25th among travel agencies in the United States. Industry projections had the company joining the top 10 by the end of the year. Expedia reported over $250 million in travel bookings in 1998 and projected an increase to over $750 million in 1999. Expedia's U.S. website had 3.9 million daily visitors in 1999 and gross bookings of $16 million per week. From an initial workforce of 40 employees mainly involved in technology development, the company underwent a 10-fold increase to more than 400 full-time employees, with 250 customer service representatives.

In November 1999 Microsoft offered an initial public offering (IPO) of Expedia, in which it sold 13.6 percent of Expedia's outstanding shares and retained the remaining 86.4 percent. The decision to sell a minority interest in Expedia was the first time that Microsoft had spun off one of its businesses. In its 1999 annual report Microsoft pointed out that Expedia was part of its MSN Portal business that in turn was part of the Consumer and Commerce group. By being part of the MSN Portal business, Expedia had access to Microsoft's interactive ability for helping consumers in making decisions on purchases ranging from cars to housing to news. For fiscal year 1999 Expedia reported revenues of $38.7 million.

ACQUISITIONS AND COMPETITION: 2000–01

In early 2000 Expedia and Travelocity were locked in competition for the top ranking among online travel services. Expedia had undertaken its IPO and reported revenues of $17.8 million for the fourth quarter of 1999. Meanwhile, Travelocity's upcoming activities included a planned takeover of Preview Travel and an alliance with Priceline.com. Karen Anderson observed in the February 7, 2000, issue of *Travel Agent*, "Now, analysts say, it's going to be an even closer fight. Expedia's sales of $1 billion last year were just behind the combined $1.2 billion sales of Preview and Travelocity." Expedia launched a multimedia advertising campaign that year and pushed further into expansion-related strategies.

In 2000 Expedia made two significant acquisitions that enabled it to offer a wider range of accommodations. It paid $82 million in stock for VacationSpot.com Inc. of Seattle, a reservation network

KEY DATES

1996: Microsoft Corporation launches Expedia, an online travel service, as part of the Microsoft Network (MSN).

1999: Expedia is spun off from Microsoft as a publicly traded company, with Microsoft retaining a majority interest.

2002: USA Networks Inc. acquires controlling interest in Expedia from Microsoft; USA Networks is renamed USA Interactive Inc.

2003: USA Interactive is renamed InterActiveCorp; InterActiveCorp acquires the remaining shares of Expedia.

2005: Expedia is spun off from InterActiveCorp.

for vacation homes, condo rentals, and bed and breakfasts. The company also acquired Travelscape.com Inc., a Las Vegas–based company that specialized in discounted hotel rooms, for $95 million in stock. These enterprises gave Expedia listings for 65,000 properties worldwide, low hotel rates in 240 cities, approximately 2 million room nights per year, and the expertise of Travelscape's customer service representatives at its call center. The acquisitions also indicated that Expedia was shifting its business model from primarily selling airline tickets to offering more lodging and package tour transactions and thus greater profitability.

Anticipating the upcoming debut of another rival, the online travel site Orbitz, Expedia began adding features and services in 2001. Early in the year Expedia introduced Expert Searching and Pricing (ESP), a flight search platform. With ESP, existing website features became one platform and gave consumers more choices and more control over their travel planning. The launch of ESP was a win-win event. Jessica Davis observed in the February 19, 2001, issue of *InfoWorld* that "a competitive environment keeps these companies on the road to improving the customer experience and value." In July 2001 USA Networks Inc. announced that it planned to purchase 75 percent of Expedia's shares from Microsoft for about $1.5 billion.

CHALLENGES AND PROGRESS

In September 2001 events beyond the control of anyone in the travel world captured everyone's attention. All online travel services were negatively affected by the tragedy of September 11, 2001, when terrorists flew hijacked airliners into New York's World Trade Center and the Pentagon. Before the disaster occurred Expedia had been growing, with gross bookings up 78 percent over the previous year. Even though air travel bookings dropped dramatically in mid-September for companies that included Travelocity, Priceline.com, and Expedia, by mid-October the company was reporting projected third-quarter sales of about $90 million.

Moreover, Expedia's plans were geared toward maintaining the progress forged in previous years. Impulse-driven travel was expected to decline as was travel for leisure. However, other means of sustaining growth at Expedia were under way. These included a discount program, in conjunction with Amazon.com, offered to consumers using Expedia exclusively. Another bolster involved continuing the pursuit of corporate travelers. They accounted for around 30 percent of Expedia's clients, but because trips were on that market's regular agenda corporate travel was worth Expedia's attention. Also, the growing use of e-mail as a marketing and promotions tool aligned with the company's customizing and information capabilities.

Fiscal year 2001 was a good year financially for Expedia. Compared to 2000 its revenue more than doubled to $222.2 million. Expedia's revenue was strengthened in part by increased wholesale sales of inventory from lodging and travel package suppliers, which gave the company merchant income in addition to its traditional commission income from airline ticket sales.

USA INTERACTIVE INC. AND EXPEDIA: 2002–04

In early 2002 Expedia completed its acquisition of Classic Custom Vacations for about $52 million. Classic Custom Vacations was a wholesaler whose focus was vacation packages to Mexico, cities in North America and Europe, and islands in Hawaii and the Caribbean. The purchase of Classic Custom Vacations involved about $5 million in cash and $47 million worth of Expedia's stock. After the acquisition Classic Custom Vacations remained a wholesaler and became a subsidiary of Expedia, with offices in San Jose, California.

In February 2002 USA Networks acquired controlling interest in Expedia. The following May USA Networks sold its entertainment assets to Vivendi Universal and then changed its name to USA Interactive Inc.

That fall Expedia launched Expedia Corporate Travel, which gave clients access to call-center reservation agents and online booking tools. Expedia's revenue climbed dramatically in 2002, reaching $590.6 million. The company's financial results were attributed to a significant and early investment in technology and diversification into wholesale accommodations, a strategy that enabled strong influence over prices and greater control of margins. Approximately 60 percent of Expedia's 2002 revenue came from the sale of wholesale accommodations, which the company called its merchant business.

The following year brought upper-level management and ownership changes for Expedia. Barton resigned as CEO of Expedia, becoming a board member of USA Interactive and a consultant to Expedia's new CEO, Erik Blachford. In March 2003 Expedia's board of directors accepted a $3.3 billion buyout offer from USA Interactive of Expedia's remaining shares. In June USA Interactive was renamed InterActiveCorp (IAC).

As Expedia sought to strengthen its position in the online travel industry, acquisitions became prominent. In 2004 three such purchases included controlling interest in the China-based online travel firm eLong Inc. When eLong held its IPO in 2004, Expedia bought 52 percent of the stock and became eLong's controlling company. That same year Expedia acquired Activity World, a tour booking company based in Hawaii, and Egencia, a French online travel agency. In 2004 Expedia reported revenues of $1.8 billion, and its international bookings neared $1.8 billion.

INDEPENDENCE: 2005–10

In 2005 an $8 billion spin-off from IAC was completed and Expedia Inc. became a stand-alone firm. Dara Khosrowshahi, formerly the chief financial officer of IAC, became Expedia's president and CEO. Joining the spin-off of Expedia and its websites were Expedia Corporate Travel, Hotels.com, Classic Custom Vacations, Hotwire.com, eLong, and TripAdvisor. For 2005 Expedia reported revenues of $2.1 billion, and its gross bookings had increased 22 percent from 2004.

Expedia continued its pursuit of excellence and leadership. For example, Hotwire, one of Expedia's subsidiaries, kept garnering great deals for consumers and high praise. From 2006 to 2008 Hotwire won the top slot in customer satisfaction for travel services from the survey and rating firm J. D. Powers. In 2008 Expedia acquired Venere, an online firm based in Rome that specialized in accommodations for vacation rentals, inns, and hotels in Italy, Spain, France, and the United Kingdom. That same year Expedia relocated its corporate headquarters to a newly built, 20-story office building in Bellevue, Washington.

The global economic crisis that began in late 2007 required Expedia to reassess its plans and strategies for its future. For example, Expedia engaged in several partnerships and affiliations with large hotel chains and tourism and convention groups. These partnerships involving ads, multimedia maps, and other visuals about destinations and related methods for increasing consumers' bookings. The combination of partnerships and other campaigns were centralized by Expedia in 2009, when it introduced Expedia Media Solutions, its advertising sales division.

That same year Expedia streamlined its structure. With more than 10 brands under its corporate umbrella, Expedia reorganized itself into three segments: Leisure, the TripAdvisor Media Network, and Egencia. Expedia.com, Hotels.com, the Expedia Affiliate Network, Hotwire.com, Classic Vacations, eLong, and Venere made up the Leisure segment. The TripAdvisor Media Network consisted of TripAdvisor, TripAdvisor.com, and over 10 search engines and directories, including Kuxun.cn (a China-based search engine), Cruise Critic, and SeatGuru. The third segment, Egencia, focused on business travel. Within these segments, Expedia tailored options for destinations and budgets. As Kevin Harlin remarked in the September 7, 2010, issue of *Investor's Business Daily*, "A slow economy means high inventory of rooms and flights, and budget-conscious shoppers on the prowl for them." By embracing technology, networks, and expertise, and attuning its activities to the existing climate, Expedia's go-to approaches gratified consumers, affiliates, and stockholders.

David P. Bianco
Updated, Mary C. Lewis

PRINCIPAL SUBSIDIARIES

Expedia has nearly 100 subsidiaries worldwide in the areas of travel planning and reservations.

PRINCIPAL DIVISIONS

Egencia; Expedia Media Solutions; Leisure; TripAdvisor Media Network.

PRINCIPAL COMPETITORS

Navigant International, Inc.; Orbitz Worldwide, Inc.; Priceline.com Inc.; Travelocity.com L.P.; Travelweb LLC.

FURTHER READING

Anderson, Karen. "Expedia's Two Web Site Buys Spur Race for Top Online Spot." *Travel Agent*, February 7, 2000, 8.

Davis, Jessica. "Net Prophet: Expedia and Travelocity Improve Search Features and Customer Experience." *InfoWorld*,

February 19, 2001, 84.

Fox, Linda. "Microsoft's Expedia to Be 'Top On-line Travel Service.'" *Travel Trade Gazette*, November 11, 1998, 96.

Harlin, Kevin. "Have Broadband, Will Travel." *Investor's Business Daily*, September 7, 2010, A9.

Kornik, Joseph. "Microsoft Touts On-line Agency in Mainstream Consumer Press." *Travel Weekly*, November 21, 1996, 1.

Limone, Jerry. "Expedia Buys Agency, Tour Unit." *Travel Weekly*, April 5, 2004, 1.

Mullaney, Timothy J., and Jay Greene. "Expedia: Changing Pilots in Mid-Climb." *Business Week*, February 24, 2003, 120.

Oser, Kris. "Survivor Tale." *Direct*, November 1, 2001, 107.

Quinlan, Michael. "Expedia's Challenge." *Travel Agent*, August 16, 1999, 20.

Standaert, Jeff. "Online Travel Firm Expedia Acquires California-Based Vacation-Package Company." *News Tribune* (Tacoma, WA), January 24, 2002.

Fabri-Kal Corporation

600 Plastics Place
Kalamazoo, Michigan 49001
U.S.A.
Telephone: (269) 385-5050
Toll Free: (800) 888-5054
Fax: (269) 385-0197
Web site: http://www.f-k.com

Private Company
Founded: 1950
Incorporated: 1950
Employees: 800
Sales: $260 million (2009 est.)
NAICS: 326199 All Other Plastics Product Manufacturing

■ ■ ■

Fabri-Kal Corporation is one of the largest U.S. manufacturers of thermoformed plastic containers, mainly for food and beverages. Since its founding in 1950, Fabri-Kal has supplied its containers to restaurants, food-service establishments, and consumer-goods manufacturers and retailers. The company embraces ecological sensitivity through its Greenware line of compostable plastic cups and plates, manufactured from a corn-based resin. Fabri-Kal is headquartered in Kalamazoo, Michigan, and has offices or production facilities in Hazleton and Mountain Top, Pennsylvania; Piedmont, South Carolina; and Los Angeles, California.

FOUNDING OF FABRI-KAL

In 1950 a group of seven investors, including Robert P. Kittredge (who eventually became sole owner and chairman of the board), created Fabri-Kal Corporation in Kalamazoo, Michigan. The new company started its business by acquiring the plastics unit of Kalamazoo Paper Box. In its early years, Fabri-Kal manufactured custom plastic packaging for prominent retailers, such as Sears Roebuck. About 1960 the company moved into larger quarters in Kalamazoo and began producing stock plastic components, such as lids and cups.

As the company's distribution expanded geographically, Fabri-Kal set up production in Hazleton, a small city in northeastern Pennsylvania, in 1967. The following decade saw the company start manufacturing plastic bottles with blowing plants in California and New Jersey. Another new venture for Fabri-Kal was supplying plastic containers for bedding plants for commercial plant growers. In 1981 the company established a third manufacturing center, in Piedmont, near Greenville, South Carolina. At about the same time, Fabri-Kal also erected a headquarters building in Kalamazoo.

In the 1980s Fabri-Kal stopped manufacturing plastic bottles and plant containers and focused instead on packaging foods and drinks offered by retailers and food-service establishments. The company specialized in thermoforming, a process in which powerful extruders heat and roll bulk plastic into wide, very thin sheets. The sheets are then moved onto molds and cooled until they have firmed and taken the desired shape. Fabri-Kal was innovative in developing packaging materials, introducing high-density polyethylene (HDPE) in the

COMPANY PERSPECTIVES

The mission of Fabri-Kal is to be a customer driven, world class manufacturer of quality packaging; be recognized as a leader in customer satisfaction; be a growing and financially sound company, providing a fair return to shareholders; assist employees in achieving an attractive lifestyle; and manage operations and create products in a safe and environmentally responsible manner.

1970s and polypropylene in the 1980s. The company also worked with polystyrene and polyethylene phthalate. Company officials believed thermoformed containers had the competitive advantage of being considerably lighter and less costly than ones made by injection molding and other competing technologies.

FABRI-KAL FLOURISHING

In the 1990s Fabri-Kal teamed up with Jackson Dairy of Jackson, Michigan, to create containers for the dairy's new line of premium ice cream. Introduced in 1994, the new line was packaged in rectangular containers made of HDPE, which protected the ice cream from air and moisture better than traditional paper containers did. Fabri-Kal made the containers in three sizes, including an unusual three-pint size, and the lids were identical for all sizes. In addition, Fabri-Kal designed and manufactured custom packaging for leading consumer-goods firms, including General Mills, Heinz, and Procter & Gamble.

In 1998 sales reached $123 million. By 1999 stock plastic products, mostly used by institutional food-service providers and convenience stores, constituted 55 percent of Fabri-Kal's revenues. Custom products, such as cereal bowls, dose cups for administering medicine to children, and yogurt and pudding cups, accounted for an estimated 45 percent of sales. The thriving custom work required the company to expand manufacturing capacity by installing three new thermoforming machines at the Hazleton plant in 1999. Most of the company's custom products were manufactured at Piedmont, while the Hazleton plant turned out most of the stock cups.

By the 1990s Chairman Kittredge's sons, Rob and John, had become company executives, serving as executive vice president and vice president of marketing, respectively. While the Kittredge family retained significant family control of Fabri-Kal well into the 21st century, the company drew upon other talented leaders, appointing John Kelly as president and chief executive offer (CEO) in 2001. In 2006 experienced packaging executive Mike Roeder became president and CEO, posts he still held as of 2010.

GOING GREEN

Also by the 1990s many environmentalists and a segment of the general public were blaming the consumer packaging and disposable containers that Fabri-Kal and its competitors manufactured for creating unnecessary waste and fostering dependence on petroleum. In response to the growing outcry, many packaging manufacturers sought ways of developing more ecologically sustainable products. Eventually Rob Kittredge prompted Fabri-Kal to join this trend by using polylactic acid (PLA), a compostable polymer based on fermented cornstarch, created by Cargill's NatureWorks unit. In 2002 NatureWorks started large-scale production of PLA, which made its price much more competitive with standard plastics derived from petroleum. In contrast to other plastics, PLA used only annually renewable and homegrown material. Another advantage was that corn prices were less volatile than those of oil, so Fabri-Kal could rely on stable supply costs.

Fabri-Kal researchers struggled to fabricate this novel plastic, which is brittle, crystallizes at low temperatures, and must be kept free of contamination with other plastics. One of the company's equipment designers, Universal Dynamics, helped reconfigure its thermoforming machinery to suit PLA's distinctive properties. By 2003 Fabri-Kal announced that it had created its first commercial application of PLA: clamshell cases that wrapped around and sealed retail items, such as CDs and DVDs, to help prevent theft. Fabri-Kal collaborated with Partner-Pak Inc., which marketed a sealing device for these clamshells, and by the start of 2005 the company rolled out its Greenware line of cups and lids. The following year it introduced Greenware round deli containers.

GREENWARE LINE

Because marketing surveys suggested that many food-service customers preferred to patronize establishments that used ecofriendly materials, Fabri-Kal promoted its Greenware line to potential clients by appealing to their desire to demonstrate their environmental responsibility to the public and to reduce their waste streams. Nonetheless, the Greenware line was not a roaring success when it was introduced, due to its comparatively higher prices and the clients' unfamiliarity with the PLA material. Furthermore, Greenware containers could be

KEY DATES

1950: Fabri-Kal Corporation is founded in Kalamazoo, Michigan.
1967: Fabri-Kal's second factory begins production in Hazleton, Pennsylvania.
1981: A new production plant opens in Piedmont, South Carolina.
2005: Fabri-Kal launches its ecofriendly Greenware line.
2009: *Plastics News* newspaper ranks Fabri-Kal the sixth-largest thermoformer in the United States.

used only for chilled contents, because PLA softens and bends when it is exposed to heat. Within a few years the brand found steady clients among universities and government institutions as well as chain retailers, such as PJ's Coffee of New Orleans. After growing by 60 percent yearly since 2005, Greenware represented 10 percent of Fabri-Kal's volume by the end of 2007.

Other Fabri-Kal products incorporated postconsumer recycled PET (RPET). Late in 2008 the company launched an Alur series of deli containers with 20 percent RPET, and the following April it announced a line of RPET dessert containers under the name Indulge. Meanwhile, in 2004 Fabri-Kal became one of the first packagers to license a production technique named CompelAroma, by which the company incorporated materials within the packaging designed to give off pleasant aromas when the container was opened or heated. The CompelAroma process could also prevent the contents from absorbing odors from the container.

SURGING REVENUES

Fabri-Kal's revenues surged after 2000, to about $225 million in 2006 and $250 million in 2007. Throughout the decade it ranked among the 10 largest thermoformers in the United States, and Fabri-Kal's production was threatening to exceed the capacity of its plants. Because its factories in South Carolina and Pennsylvania were hemmed in by surrounding properties and unable to expand, the company scouted for production sites in the Midwest. In 2008 a generous tax incentive and loan package helped convince Fabri-Kal to purchase a nearly 400,000-square-foot vacant factory in Kalamazoo, which contained enough space to set up as many as 12 thermoforming lines.

Fabri-Kal established an Innovation Center in its new facility, so product concepts could be designed and prototypes could be created in the same space in one or two days. The new facility also embodied Fabri-Kal's environmental ethic. The company renovated the building so that it used less energy for lighting, heating, and cooling and required less water for sanitation and landscaping, while retaining more than 99 percent of the original structure. In July 2010 Fabri-Kal received LEED (Leadership in Energy and Environmental Design) Silver certification for its new Kalamazoo facility from the U.S. Green Building Council. The award recognizes environmentally sensitive building design and operation.

Fabri-Kal's revenue growth persisted during the post-2007 economic recession, rising to some $260 million in 2009, when *Plastics News* ranked it as the sixth-largest thermoformer in the United States. In 2010 business was concentrated in mass-market retail products, institutional food-service providers, and popular chain restaurants. The company was positioned well for the future, riding a swelling trend toward environmentally friendly containers and packaging.

Stephen V. Beitel

PRINCIPAL COMPETITORS

Berry Plastics Corporation; Dart Container Corporation; Pactiv Corporation.

FURTHER READING

"Fabri-Kal Awarded LEED Certification." *Plastics News*, July 26, 2010, 10.

"Fabri-Kal Slates New Facility, Upgrades." *Plastics News*, February 25, 2008, 20.

Miller, Joanna. "Fabri-Kal: Cradle to Cradle." *Venture Magazine*, December 21, 2007.

Naitove, Matthew H. "Green Business Is Good Business for Fabri-Kal." *Plastics Technology*, December 2009, 18.

Parikh, Jane C. "Fabri-Kal Packaging Company Gets New President." *Kalamazoo Gazette*, February 11, 2006.

"PJ's Coffee of New Orleans Introduces Environmentally Friendly Cups." *Business Wire*, April 17, 2007.

Schut, Jan H. "Extruding Biopolymers: Packaging Reaps Cost Benefit of Going 'Green': Plastics Made from Renewable Carbon Chains, Not Fossil Carbon from Oil or Gas, Are Suddenly a Solid Commercial Reality." *Plastics Technology*, February 2007, 60.

"Technology Brings New Aroma Dimension to Thermoformed Packages." *Food Manufacturing*, March 2004, 36.

"Thermoformer Fabri-Kal Sweetens Recycling with Dessert Line That Continues Reuse Trend." *Packaging Strategies*, April 30, 2009, 7.

Thorne, Blake. "Keeping the Kal in Fabri-Kal." *Kalamazoo Gazette*, February 1, 2009.

FalconStor Software, Inc.

2 Huntington Quadrangle, Suite 2S01
Melville, New York 11747-4503
U.S.A.
Telephone: (631) 777-5188
Toll Free: (866) 668-3252
Fax: (631) 501-7633
Web site: http://www.falconstor.com

Public Company
Founded: 2000
Employees: 542
Sales: $89.5 million (2009)
Stock Exchanges: NASDAQ
Ticker Symbol: FALC
NAICS: 511210 Software Publishers

■ ■ ■

FalconStor Software, Inc., based in Melville, New York, provides network storage management software and related services to secure, back up, store, and recover business-critical data for companies of all sizes. Products include Virtual Tape Library (a disk-based emulation data backup system), Continuous Data Protector (a system that makes mirror images of data for quick recovery), Network Storage Server (a storage provisioning, virtualization, and monitoring system that works across disk arrays and connection protocols while also offering data protection services), File-Interface Deduplication System (a data repository that keeps online storage capacity to a minimum by reducing redundant information), and HyperFS File System (a file system for data-intensive applications that creates a large number of massive files). FalconStor also offers technical support, training, and the design and management of storage systems. FalconStor is a public company listed on the NASDAQ Global Market.

COMPANY FOUNDED

FalconStor was founded in 2000 by ReiJane Huai and several of his former employees at Computer Associates. Born in Taiwan to parents who hailed from mainland China, he was the son of a chief financial officer of a state-owned company. After earning a degree in computer science from National Taiwan University, he came to the United States for graduate school under scholarship at SUNY Stony Brook on Long Island, New York. Eager to start his career, Huai completed his two-year program in just nine months. In 1985 he went to work writing code and serving as manager of research and development for Roslyn Heights, New York-based Cheyenne Software Inc. It was a two-year-old company that developed sophisticated software programs for specialized uses and would find its niche in data storage management software, creating a backup enterprise software product called ARCServe. After two years Huai left to work at the legendary Bell Laboratories, fulfilling a childhood dream.

Huai returned to Cheyenne in 1988 to serve as vice president and chief engineer. The company was struggling with its marketing at the time and Huai was responsible for Cheyenne taking more control from its sales partners to grow annual sales to the $50 million mark by the early 1990s. In the fall of 1993 he was

> **COMPANY PERSPECTIVES**
>
> Vision: Innovation that delivers competitive business advantages.

named Cheyenne's president and chief executive officer. Cheyenne's growth soon stalled, and in 1996 Huai arranged to sell the company to Computer Associates International Inc. for $1.2 billion. CA's leader, Charles Wang, was a friend of Huai. The relationship had been forged in 1992 when Cheyenne provided the backup software component for Computer Associate's Unicenter software product.

HUAI'S DEPARTURE FROM CA

Huai and other Cheyenne employees joined CA, where Huai now became executive vice president and general manager of Asia. After three years, however, he and several of his Cheyenne colleagues were eager to launch a new company. They began meeting to discuss a new product and develop a business plan. The split from CA was amiable, and Huai discussed his plans with Wang. In February 2000 the new company was incorporated and some of the former Cheyenne employees left CA to lay the groundwork for the startup venture. In November 2000 Huai completed his planned exit from CA to join them. His former Cheyenne employees included Wayne Lam (who headed marketing), Wai Lam (who was in charge of engineering), and Wendy Petty (who would oversee sales). Other former Cheyenne would soon follow, including CFO Jacob Ferng, president of business development Bernard Wu, and chairman Barry Rubenstein.

Huai and his cofounders had become independently wealthy through the Cheyenne sale and had no little difficulty raising $10 million in seed money. As a name for the startup, they looked back to Cheyenne, which had been named after the Cheyenne II propeller airplane, and settled on a newer, faster plane, the Falcon jet. The result was FalconStor Inc. The "Stor" referred to the focus of the company, file storage. Starting in August 2000, several months before Huai left CA, FalconStor employees quietly set up shop in Melville, New York, and began work on a storage-area network software product called IPStor.

IPStor was designed to work with both of the competing standards for data storage: NAS (network attached storage), which delivered files through a local area network, and SAN (storage-attached network), which relied on a dedicated storage network. Moreover, IPStor did not tax the resources of individual servers, instead creating a "virtualized" system that could perform such functions as disk-failure recovery on a network-wide basis rather than rely on the traditional and more expensive server-based model. IPStor was intended for sale to companies that marketed computer storage hardware, storage service providers, and parties simply interested in licensing the product.

FIRST PRODUCT LAUNCHED

IPStor was introduced to the market in April 2001. In that same month, Fremont, California-based Network Peripherals Inc. (NPI), a publicly traded Ethernet switch manufacturer, invested $25 million in the company and received the right to integrate IPStor with a new IP switch. As part of the deal, NPI also acquired a 14-day option to merge with FalconStor. Given a slowdown in the information technology field, joining forces held a good deal of attraction for both companies and the option was soon exercised. The reverse merger allowed FalconStor to become a public company and also brought some financial security during a difficult business environment because NPI brought with it $65 million in cash. Another major factor in the company's emerging success was the work ethic of Huai, who essentially worked night and day. Others followed his lead, and the company thrived on its close-knit relationships.

The merger was completed in August 2001, and the combined company took the name FalconStor Software, Inc. The Fremont office was also closed, and the hardware business was dropped. The company's NASDAQ ticker symbol was also changed from NPIX to FALC. On the first day of trading under the new name, the price of the stock increased from $9.60 to $10.20, resulting in a market capitalization of about $455 million.

Sales of IPStor were slow to materialize, due in large measure to the deliberate decision making of most corporate IT departments, which often spent months evaluating products. Sales in 2001 totaled less than $5.6 million and increased a year later to $10.6 million, while FalconStor recorded an accumulated loss of nearly $25 million since the company's launch. To drive further growth, FalconStor beefed up its engineering staff as well as its sales force and technical support team in 2003. As a result, the company moved to a larger facility in Melville in November. The company's Asia/Pacific headquarters was moved to a larger site in Taiwan to support growth in that region. During the year, the company added virus-scanning capabilities to the NAS portion of IPStor, helping to increase sales 59 percent to $16.9 million in 2003. FalconStor also

KEY DATES

2000: FalconStor is founded.
2001: Merger is completed with Network Peripherals Inc.
2003: Company moves to a larger facility, in Melville, New York.
2005: FalconStor posts its first profitable year.
2008: The company's European business is expanded.

trimmed its net loss from $11.5 million in 2002 to $7.4 million in 2003.

FIRST PROFITABLE QUARTER

Demand in the marketplace for network-based storage products continued to rise. In 2004 FalconStor recorded its first profitable quarter. For the year, the company increased sales 69 percent to $28.7 million and narrowed its net loss to $5.9 million in 2004. Driving the increase were enhancements to the flagship product, which included the release of the ISCSI Storage Server, allowing small and midsize companies to enjoy the benefits of a SAN solution through an integration with Microsoft Windows Storage Server 2003.

FalconStor posted its first profitable year in 2005, netting $2.3 million on revenues of nearly $41 million. The greatest increase in sales came from the company's VirtualTape Library (VTL) software. FalconStor also benefited from a significant number of reorders, a testament to customer satisfaction. Moreover, its VTL solution was being adopted by a host of major industry players, including EMC, COPAN, Pillar Data Systems, and Sun/StorageTek.

Following a slow start, the company continued to grow in 2006 as the need for data storage increased alongside a steady increase in customers' data. IT departments were taxed with the responsibility of protecting this data while frequently backing it up despite geographic complications. As a result, the network-centric solutions offered by FalconStor became ever more attractive. Another key to success was a commitment to open architecture, which made FalconStor solutions suitable for any storage infrastructure and compatible with all hardware, software, and protocol. In this way, customers could make the greatest use of the systems in which they had already made sizable investments.

The vast market of China offered promise to the company. In 2006 FalconStor opened a second research and development operations in China to position the company for further growth in this region. Sales topped $55 million in 2006. Although the company posted a net loss of about $3.4 million, it spent $8 million more on software development, $20 million, than the prior year.

RECOGNIZED BY FORBES

Those investments in product development would pay dividends in 2007. Sales improved 41 percent to $77.4 million while operating income increased more than 200 percent and net income totaled $12.7 million. This performance garnered FalconStor a No. 5 ranking on the Forbes annual list of the 25 Fastest Growing Technology Companies in the United States. Although the economy took a turn for the worse in 2008, FalconStor was able to grow sales 12 percent to more than $87 million while increasing software development to more than $25 million and remaining profitable, netting $1.2 million.

In many ways, tough times played to FalconStor's strengths, as IT departments were asked to do more with less, making FalconStor solutions more attractive than ever. To stimulate business, the company launched a program in 2008 that helped its provider partners to develop and market timely turnkey applications that ran on any major hardware platform. Another important step taken in 2008 was an expansion of FalconStor's European business. The company's operation in Toulouse, France, now carried the entire product line. In Asia, FalconStor added a new revenue source by teaming with the Internet service provider unit of Chunghwa Telecom, Taiwan's largest information and telecommunications service provider, to offer online data backup for businesses as well as individuals.

A troubled global economy led to steep cuts in IT spending. As a result, FalconStor's ability to increase sales 3 percent to $89.5 million in 2009 was very much a success story. Although the company recorded a net loss of $3.1 million, it continued to increase spending on software development to $26.8 million rather than cut the budget to realize a short-term profit. In an interview with *Long Island Business News* published March 19, 2010, Huai said, "When the economy is bad, you can slow the business or increase your bet. A confident entrepreneur should increase the bet." In this way, FalconStor planned to have the infrastructure in place to take advantage of opportunities when the economy rebounded. Late in 2009 FalconStor added several new officials, including a new chief strategy officer to oversee the company's international marketing.

There was every reason to believe that FalconStor was well positioned to enjoy long-term, sustained growth.

Ed Dinger

PRINCIPAL SUBSIDIARIES

FalconStor SAS; FalconStor Software GmbH; FalconStor Software (Shanghai) Co., Ltd.; FalconStor.

PRINCIPAL COMPETITORS

Hewlett-Packard Company; Symantec Corporation; Tivoli Software.

FURTHER READING

Bernstein, James. "L.I. Software Company Gets New Leader." *Newsday*, October 9, 1993, 19.

Falk, William B. "'Dear Friends' / Wang and Huai: Same Cloth, but Different Cuts." *Newsday*, October 8, 1996, A03.

Harlin, Kevin. "Melville, New York Company's Products Help Keep Corporations' Archives Organized." *Investor's Business Daily*, October 4, 2007, 7.

Harrington, Mark. "Explaining the Not-So Obvious / FalconStor's Software Is New, Innovative and Complicated," *Newsday*, February 19, 2001, C13.

"Huai Leads Cheyenne to Greater Communication." *Long Island Business News*, February 28, 1994, S16.

Phan, Monty. "FalconStor Agrees to Merger." *Newsday*, May 8, 2001, A47.

———. "Merger Results in FalconStor Software." *Newsday*, August 24, 2001, A61.

Russell, Joy D. "Looking Strong, FalconStor Takes Off—Storage Over IP Is Its Flight of Fancy." *VARbusiness*, March 5, 2001, 23.

Schachter, Ken. "Rei's Vision." *Long Island Business News*, April 5, 2002, 5A.

Solnik, Claude. "Q&A with Melville-Based FalconStor Chief ReiJane Huai." *Long Island Business News*, March 19, 2010.

Federal-Mogul Corporation

26555 Northwestern Highway
Southfield, Michigan 48033
U.S.A.
Telephone: (248) 354-7700
Fax: (248) 354-8983
Web site: http://www.federal-mogul.com

Public Company
Founded: 1899
Incorporated: 1924
Employees: 43,000
Sales: $5.3 billion (2009)
Stock Exchanges: NASDAQ
Ticker Symbol: FDML
NAICS: 336399 All Other Motor Vehicle Parts Manufacturing; 339991 Gasket, Packing, and Sealing Device Manufacturing

■ ■ ■

Federal-Mogul Corporation manufactures precision components for cars, trucks, and construction vehicles, marketing its products to original equipment manufacturers (OEMs) and aftermarket customers in the United States and around the world under brand names such as "Federal-Mogul," "Signal-Stat," and "TRW." It also packages products for third-party private label brands. The company has over 100 manufacturing facilities in 34 countries. Federal-Mogul sells its own products to major global automakers, including BMW, General Motors, and Nissan. It distributes auto parts to automotive aftermarket customers, primarily independent warehouse distributors, but also local parts suppliers and parts retailers.

MUZZY-LYON COMPANY

The history of Federal-Mogul can be traced to 1899, when J. Howard Muzzy and Edward F. Lyon, two mill supply vendors in Detroit, Michigan, began searching for ways to produce better babbitt metal. Babbitt metal, an alloy of tin, antimony, and copper, had been patented in 1839 by Isaac Babbitt as an antifriction agent surrounding moving metallic locomotive parts. The use of babbitt metal remained the principal means of preventing rotating metallic shafts from overheating and wearing out. However, the introduction of combustible engines early in the 20th century prompted a need for new, improved babbitt metal.

Having developed an alternative formula for babbitt metal, Muzzy and Lyon left secure jobs at J.T. Wing and Company, a vendor of mill and factory supplies and rubber goods, where their friendship and business acumen had gradually matured.

Determined to be their own bosses in the market they knew best, the two partners opened their first facility in 1900, on Woodward Avenue in Detroit. During this time the mill and factory supply business was highly competitive, and many producers offered shoddy merchandise at inexpensive prices. However, Muzzy and Lyon established a reputation for high-quality products and were able to reinvest most of their profits back into the business. They used aggressive and imaginative advertising, providing money-back guarantees and

COMPANY PERSPECTIVES

We are a premier supplier of products, services and solutions to original equipment manufacturers that use our quality components in their vehicles and automotive systems, and to aftermarket customers who sell our world renown brand-name replacement parts through repair shops and retail outlets. We partner with a global network of suppliers whose commitment to excellence and on-time delivery is crucial to our success.

For more than a century, we have developed the innovative products our customers need to produce the next generation of vehicles. Now, as we write the history of our next 100 years, we continue to build on our position status as a market leader in product and service solutions to set ever higher standards and continually exceed customer, shareholder and employee expectations.

coupons good for prizes ranging from pocket rulers to firearms.

MOGUL METAL COMPANY

Whatever time Muzzy could spare from his primary responsibility of managing the financial and manufacturing end of the business, he devoted to experimentation with babbitt metals. Lyon, when not on the road selling company products, joined his partner in blending new formulas of tin, antimony, and lead. Their company soon garnered major orders from Clark Motor Company and the Sheffield Motor Company. As a result of the increased business, the partners formed a subsidiary company called the Mogul Metal Company.

At that time the traditional method of making motor bearings was to pour molten babbitt metal directly onto the motor block and shape the metal to fit by hand. Mechanics replaced worn bearings by laboriously gouging out the old metal and then pouring in the new. When Sheffield's parent organization, the Fairbanks Morse Company, inquired as to whether die cast metals could be manufactured to form standard-size bearings, Muzzy and Lyon began working on a method. They purchased a typecasting machine, and, by modifying it they were able to make some of the new parts themselves, while commissioning various machine shops to produce the rest. The design and construction of Muzzy's and Lyon's new machine remained a secret, and while the partners had limited mechanical and engineering experience, the machine proved successful.

The potential of the die-casting machine so impressed the partners that they decided to drop the mill supply business completely. The company would devote its entire resources to manufacturing and mechanizing automotive bearings and babbitt metals. They sold their products under the brand names of Duro (made according to a purchased formula) and Mogul (the formula developed by Muzzy and Lyon). Orders for their die-cast bearings began to arrive, and in 1910 an important order was placed for 10,000 connecting rod bearings for the massive Buick 10, one of the first cars to use parts produced by Mogul Metal. That year the partners nearly lost a large order from the Hudson Motor Company after they refused to compromise their secret processes by allowing Hudson engineers to inspect the plant.

FEDERAL-MOGUL CORPORATION

In 1923 Muzzy learned that Douglas-Dahlin, a large Kansas City–based parts distributor, stood in danger of bankruptcy while owing Mogul a large sum of money. S. C. Reynolds, vice president of Federal Bearing and Bushing, which also stood to lose money, called Muzzy to discuss the situation, proposing a trip to Kansas City to protect their interests. When Muzzy and Reynolds began discussing their companies and assessing their relative strengths and weaknesses, they realized the advantages of a merger. The Federal Bearing employees were expert bronze foundry men but lacked the capacity to produce babbitt. Muzzy and Lyon, on the other hand, operated a complete babbitt foundry but purchased bronze on the market. The companies merged in 1924, taking the name Federal-Mogul Corporation. To protect its investments, Federal-Mogul took over the nearly bankrupt Douglas-Dahlin Company, thus entering the parts distribution business.

In 1927 Federal-Mogul purchased U.S. Bearings Company, an Indiana distributor that resold replacement bearings. The following year, Federal-Mogul's involvement in the service business increased substantially with the acquisition of the Watkins Manufacturing Company of Wichita, Kansas. Following this major expansion, Federal-Mogul also purchased the Pacific Metal Bearing Company in San Francisco, primarily to supply its West Coast branches. In 1936 the corporation acquired the Indianapolis-based Superior Bearings Company, and in 1937 the service division went international with the acquisition of the former Watkins Rebabbitting Limited, with locations in Toronto, Montreal, and Winnipeg, Canada. By 1939

KEY DATES

1899: J. Howard Muzzy and Edward F. Lyon join forces to find ways to produce better babbitt metal.
1924: Federal-Mogul Corporation is formed.
1937: The company goes international with the acquisition of Canadian firm Watkins Rebabbitting Limited.
1953: The company merges with Bearings Company of America.
1955: The company acquires the Bower Roller Bearing Company and forms the Federal-Mogul-Bower Bearing Corporation.
1965: The company is renamed Federal-Mogul Corporation.
1992: The company purchases TRW Inc.'s automotive aftermarket business.
1998: The company completes its acquisition campaign with the purchase of four major firms.
2001: The company files for bankruptcy protection.
2007: The company emerges from Chapter 11 bankruptcy with Carl Icahn as board chairman.

Federal-Mogul was operating 53 service branches across North America.

World War II led to further expansion. By 1941 Federal-Mogul had more than 50 facilities devoted to military production, turning out millions of bearings, bushings, and seals for military applications. The company's marine division won highly competitive U.S. Navy tests for PT boat propellers and secured orders for over 24,000 Super Equi-poise wheels for every PT boat propeller used by all the Allied navies, including that of the Soviet Union. The marine division grew from a workforce of 50 in 1942 to nearly 1,000 by the end of the war. Moreover, from September 1939 to July 1945, the total area of Federal-Mogul plants increased nearly threefold, and annual sales were more than double the best prewar amounts.

Although postwar employee layoffs were necessary, the company continued to grow through acquisition. In 1953 Federal-Mogul merged with Bearings Company of America, marking the single largest acquisition in its history. The merger of the Bearings Company brought 610 new employees and approximately 121,000 square feet of manufacturing space into the organization.

FEDERAL-MOGUL-BOWER BEARINGS

Even more significant growth occurred in 1955 when Federal-Mogul acquired the Bower Roller Bearing Company. Soon thereafter, the corporation announced its third major merger in as many years, when the National Motor Bearing Company (National Seal Division) joined the new Federal-Mogul-Bower Bearing Corporation in July 1956. At the time of the merger, National was one of the country's largest manufacturers of oil seals and a variety of other specialized parts, ranging from grommets and gaskets to fiberglass ducts and railroad journal boxes.

The acquisition earned the company its first listing among *Fortune* magazine's 500 largest U.S. companies, ranking 350, with sales that exceeded $100 million that year. By the end of the 1950s, Federal-Mogul-Bower's service division had expanded from 58 to 96 branches, and the number of customers had doubled to over 10,000. The mergers and increased efficiency of the 1950s had increased annual sales to four times their 1949 level.

During the 1960s the corporation's timely response to innovations in automobile production ultimately resulted in large dividends. One such development involved the steady expansion of foreign automobile manufacturers, facilitated by mass production technology and the development of the European Common Market. Observing a threat to U.S. export sales, Federal-Mogul management began investing in foreign manufacturing operations and purchasing interests in various major European bearing firms.

Domestic expansion also continued, and the firm began to focus on manufacturing parts for the highly sophisticated missile market. In 1964 Federal-Mogul-Bower opened a new oil seal facility that was publicized as the most highly mechanized plant of its kind in the world. The following year, the company purchased Steering Aluminum, a piston factory, and the Vellumoid Company, a manufacturer of gaskets and gasket materials.

FEDERAL-MOGUL CORPORATION ... AGAIN

The company's name was changed back to Federal-Mogul Corporation in April 1965. In July 1966 Federal-Mogul's world headquarters officially relocated from downtown Detroit to its present location in Southfield, Michigan.

The early 1970s marked a domestic expansion into the southern states. A highly automated new plant in

Princeton, Kentucky, opened in late 1970, with 50,000 square feet devoted to producing super alloy metal powders. In 1971 a new plant in Virginia began manufacturing aluminum sleeve bearings, while another Federal-Mogul plant was introduced for the manufacture of bimetal bushings and bearings. The following year, an additional powdered metal parts plant was opened in Ripley, Tennessee, and, soon thereafter, a new 360,000-square-foot plant in Hamilton, Alabama, began producing tapered roller bearings ranging up to eight inches in diameter.

DIVERSIFICATION AND ACQUISITIONS

Economic recession in 1975 prompted management at Federal-Mogul to begin reassessing its long-term strategy. Although the company quickly recovered from the recession, recording its fourth consecutive year of record sales and earnings in 1979, management found that the company's earnings were overly reliant on the fortunes of automotive OEMs. In the 1980s chairperson and CEO Tom Russell placed increasing emphasis on a strategy of diversification, making acquisitions and entering into joint ventures to strengthen its manufacturing position.

In July 1985 Federal-Mogul acquired the Mather Company, a manufacturer of high-performance sealing products for the automotive and industrial markets and a leader in PTFE (Teflon) technology. In January 1986 the purchase of the Carter Automotive Company, Inc., a manufacturer and distributor of automotive fuel pumps and systems, and in September of that year, the acquisition of Signal-Stat, a manufacturer, marketer, and distributor for lighting and safety components, further strengthened its position. In August 1989 Federal-Mogul completed a joint venture agreement with a German manufacturer of seals and specialty molded products, and the new entity is called Dichtungstechnik G. Bruss GmbH & Co KG.

Dennis J. Gorley, who assumed Federal-Mogul's chief executive office upon Russell's 1989 retirement, accelerated his predecessor's diversification scheme. Gorley spearheaded Federal-Mogul's expansion into the automotive aftermarket, which promised higher profit margins and more stability than the OEM market. From 1989 to 1993 the firm continued to strengthen its operations through additional acquisitions, acquiring some of the best-known brands in automotive replacement parts and divesting itself of some peripheral OEM businesses.

Principal acquisitions included the vehicular lighting assets of R.E. Dietz and Co. in March 1990; a German manufacturer of automotive and diesel engine bearings Glyco AG, in October 1990; Brown & Dureau (Australia), and Sealed Power Replacement. The company made its largest purchase ever in 1992, when it bought TRW Inc.'s automotive aftermarket business (AAB). The former TRW operations expanded Federal-Mogul's presence in the European and Japanese markets and constituted nearly 20 percent of annual revenues in 1993.

IMPROVING EFFICIENCY AND WINNING AWARDS

During this period Federal-Mogul worked to improve efficiency through automation, capital improvements, and staff reductions. The company adopted bar code technology for inventory control and invested in guided vehicles, hand-held scanners, and computers for its Jacksonville, Alabama, worldwide distribution center. These modernizations cut order fulfillment time from three days to one. Federal-Mogul also moved to transform its export operations into international enterprises. By 1993, 21 percent of the company's sales were generated by businesses outside the United States and Canada, while another 13 percent of annual revenues came from exports.

The transition was not entirely smooth. Federal-Mogul recorded net losses in 1991 and 1992 totaling \$87.4 million. After the company reported a \$40.1 million profit for 1993, however, *Financial World* (January 18, 1994) praised the company's "sound acquisition strategy, good cost controls, and participation in international markets." In March 1993 Federal-Mogul's lighting and electrical division was named one of the first General Motors Worldwide Suppliers of the Year for its excellence in quality, service, and price.

In September 1995 the company acquired Seal Technology Systems (STS), one of Europe's leading designers and manufacturers of a specialized range of seals and gaskets for the automotive sector and other industrial markets. Chrysler Corporation recognized the company for outstanding manufacturing plant performance in the areas of quality, delivery, and warranty in May 1996, when it gave its Gold Pentastar Award to Federal-Mogul's Blacksburg, Virginia, engine bearing manufacturing facility. In November of that year, Dick Snell took the helm as chairman, CEO, and president of Federal-Mogul. Another accolade came in January 1997, when Federal-Mogul's engine bearings facility in Orleans, France, was honored with the first Platinum Award for supplier excellence from the Rover Group for winning the Gold Supplier Excellence Award three consecutive years. Concurrently, Federal-Mogul's

STS division won the Rover Group's Silver Supplier Excellence Award for the second consecutive year.

ACQUISITION SPREE

Beginning in October 1997 the company went on an acquisition spree, acquiring T&N PLC, one of the world's leading suppliers of high-technology automotive components, engineered products, and industrial materials. In January 1998 Federal-Mogul acquired privately owned Fel-Pro Inc. (the premier automotive and industrial gasket manufacturer for the North American aftermarket and OEM heavy-duty market, headquartered in Skokie, Illinois) and its subsidiaries. The acquisition of the venerable company (founded in Chicago in 1918 as Felt Products Manufacturing Company to manufacture Ford Model T car felt gaskets and washers) brought the Michigan giant capabilities in a broad variety of products, including custom and standard potting, encapsulation, and embedment compounds, resins, adhesives, sealants, epoxy, and polyurethane compounds. The $720 million ($225 million common stock and $495 million cash) acquisition also brought 1,800 new employees to Federal-Mogul.

In March 1998 Federal-Mogul strengthened its market position in Asia by increasing the company's ownership in KFM Bearing Co., Ltd. (the leading manufacturer of engine bearings, bushings, and related parts for automotive and other applications in Korea, a joint venture formed that year with Kukje Special Metal Co., Ltd.), from 30 percent to 87 percent. Also in March the company expanded its engine bearing operations in Europe when it acquired Gdansk, Poland–based Bimet SA, a manufacturer of engine bearings, bushings, and related products, bringing 600 employees and sales of $12 million to the company.

In October 1998 Federal-Mogul acquired Tri-Way Machine Limited and its subsidiary, J.I.S. Machining Ltd. Headquartered in Windsor, Canada, Tri-Way was a privately owned manufacturer of machines and machining systems serving the world metal-cutting industry. J.I.S. Machining was a machiner of power train components. Another acquisition that month was Cooper Automotive, a business unit of Cooper Industries, Inc., whose principal products included brakes and friction, lighting, chassis parts, ignition, and wiper blades.

A CENTENNIAL AND A NEW CENTURY

Its market position fortified by the acquisitions campaign of the 1990s, Federal-Mogul appeared to be well positioned for growth and innovation for years to come. To help build public interest in its centennial year of 1999, the company expanded beyond its traditional business-to-business marketing approach and engaged Bozell Worldwide to mount a direct advertising campaign. Bozell targeted car buffs through media buys on *Monday Night Football* and other National Football League telecasts.

Just at its apogee, latent internal problems and the external economy combined to put Federal-Mogul on a downward track that would only be reversed slowly and with difficulty. Company president Richard Snell proved to have been both overaggressive and overoptimistic in his acquisition binge. Integration of the new companies did not go well, and when Federal-Mogul's earnings failed to meet Wall Street's expectations in 1999, the stock plummeted as much as 91 percent in value. Worse still, two major streams of revenue, the automobile aftermarket and the North American commercial truck market, were severely curtailed in the economic downturn after the turn of the millennium.

Disappointed in this turn of events, the company's board of directors forced Snell out and brought in Steve Miller to apply his experience turning companies around to Federal-Mogul. A long-term restructuring was instituted, reorganizing the piston, engine bearing, and sealing product areas across geographic lines, and shedding 1,500 jobs. Nothing seemed to help, at least in the short run. The company posted a net loss of $1 billion in 2001.

LEGAL BATTLES

There was worse news looming, courtesy of some 1990s acquisitions, principally T&N PLC. Numerous plaintiffs were filing lawsuits against the company alleging harm from asbestos used in some of its products. Snell had attempted to stem the losses by quickly settling the claims out of court. Unfortunately, the settlements were like blood in the water to sharks, and soon a second wave of claims by plaintiffs hopeful of winning similar settlements. As a result, Federal-Mogul made annual cash payments of as much as $150 million to settle the raft of suits.

The combination of ruinous asbestos lawsuits and tough economic times pushed Federal-Mogul into filing for federal bankruptcy protection in October 2001. The company filed a Chapter 11 reorganization plan with creditors in March 2003. It hoped to emerge from bankruptcy within a year, but it was not that simple. First a federal court ruling prevented it from negotiating a needed loan. Then in 2004 a dispute over the pension plan of T&N PLC, the very company whose asbestos problem had pushed Federal-Mogul over the brink, delayed a hearing on the reorganization plan.

As the bankruptcy process wore on, two more CEOs, Frank Macher and Chip McClure, both from other positions within the company, came and went. They were followed in 2005 by José Maria Alapont, the Spanish former head of European operations for Delphi Automotive LLC. The central player in the fate of Federal-Mogul, however, was corporate buyout expert Carl Icahn. He had been interested in the company's problems for years, having bought a 5.2 percent stake in 2000 when its stock was a bargain. When the company was finally preparing in 2006 to emerge from bankruptcy, Icahn made a series of financial moves. The key one was the acquisition of rights to purchase up to 50.1 percent of the company's total equity from asbestos claimants, who were about to receive Federal-Mogul shares in a settlement.

RECOVERY BY 2010

The company's long march to solvency was completed with its emergence from Chapter 11 protection in December 2007. Icahn became the largest shareholder after exercising his stock purchase rights. Although six years was long time for a company to be under bankruptcy protection, experts did not consider it surprising, considering the thousands of claims in the complex issue of asbestos-related illness. Federal-Mogul was listed on the NASDAQ in 2008. Icahn became the nonexecutive chairman of the board, and by 2010 he controlled 75 percent of the company.

The Icahn era was a bit of a rollercoaster ride at first, and much of the course was dictated by the hand of the past as policies developed during the bankruptcy period continued to guide the company. In 2003 Federal-Mogul began to emphasize sales and production in European and, especially, Asian markets. CEO Alapont in 2006 announced plans to close plants, reduce the workforce, and shift production to low-cost countries. These policies, combined with booming economic conditions, led to record quarterly sales of $1.86 billion by 2008. Production from a raft of new orders that had been booked beginning in 2005 began to come on stream, enhancing the revenue outlook further.

The intense recession of 2008–09 hit the global economy, and the company went sharply into the red, laying off 4,000 employees and posting a net loss of $530 million in 2009. These clouds passed surprisingly quickly, however, and by the second quarter of 2010 sales had rebounded to a 22.3 percent gain over a year earlier. As the company looked more confidently to the future, Alapont and Icahn began to think about acquisitions again. Federal-Mogul set its sights on the emerging market spurred by electric and hybrid vehicle manufacturing. With billionaire Carl Icahn's deep pockets backing it up, the company's prospects for a successful acquisitions campaign looked very good.

Daryl F. Mallett
Updated, Daryl F. Mallett; Judson MacLaury

PRINCIPAL SUBSIDIARIES

BHW GmbH; Bimet SA; Carter Automotive Company, Inc.; Conaba S.A. de C.V. (51%); F-M Motorentiele Holding GmbH; Federal-Mogul Boliviana, S.A.; Federal-Mogul Bruss Scaling Systems (74%); Federal-Mogul Canada Investment Co.; Federal-Mogul Canada Ltd.; Federal-Mogul Cayman Investment Company Ltd.; Federal-Mogul Comercio International, S.A.; Federal-Mogul de Costa Rica, S.A.; Federal-Mogul de Guatemala, S.A.; Federal-Mogul de Venezuela C.A.; Federal-Mogul del Ecuador, S.A.; Federal-Mogul Distribuidora SAC (66%); Federal-Mogul Dominicana, S.A.; Federal-Mogul Funding Corp.; Federal-Mogul GmbH; Federal-Mogul Handelsgesell-schaft MBH; Federal-Mogul Holding U.K., Ltd.; Federal-Mogul Japan KK; Federal-Mogul Ltd.; Federal-Mogul New Zealand Ltd.; Federal-Mogul Panama, S.A.; Federal-Mogul Pty. Ltd.; Federal-Mogul S.A. de C.V. (61%); Federal-Mogul S.A. (France); Federal-Mogul S.A. (Switzerland); Federal-Mogul SpA; Federal-Mogul Uruguay; Federal-Mogul Venture Corp.; Federal-Mogul World Trade Chile Ltda (99%); Federal-Mogul World Trade de España, S.A.; Federal-Mogul World Trade B.C.; Federal-Mogul World Trade Hong Kong, Ltd.; Federal-Mogul World Trade, Inc.; Federal-Mogul World Trade Ltd.; Federal-Mogul World Trade Pte. Ltd.; Federal-Mogul World Trade SDN BHD; Federal-Mogul World Wide, Inc.; Federal-Mogul Westwind Air Bearings Ltd. (89%); Fel-Pro Chemical Products L.P.; Fel-Pro Inc.; Fel-Pro Specialty Sealing Products L.P.; Femosa Mexico S.A. (90%); Glyco AG; Glyco Antriebstechnik GmbH; Glyco B.V.; Glyco do Brasil; Glyco KG; H. Minoli S.A.I.C. (59%); In-De-Co.; KFM Bearing Co. Ltd. (87%); Manufacturas Metálicas Linan S.A.; Mather Seal Co.; Metaltec, Inc.; Raimsa S.A. de C.V. (70%); Servicios Administrativos Industriales, S.A.; Servicios de Components Automotrices, S.A.; Subensambles Internacionales S.A. de C.V.; T&N PLC; Villa Fane Auto Supply, Inc.

PRINCIPAL COMPETITORS

Dana Holding Corporation; GKN PLC; Johnson Controls, Inc.; Lear Corporation; MAHLE International GmbH.

FURTHER READING

"APS/Big A Auto Parts Challenge New Gasket Supplier to Speed Vendor Changeover." *Automotive Marketing*, November 1995, 108.

"Elliot Lehman and Lewis Weinberg." *Industry Week*, October 27,1980, 53.

Elstrom, Peter J. W. "Chaos Shattering Trade with Mideast." *Crain's Chicago Business*, January 21, 1991, 4.

"Federal-Mogul Corp. Continues Its Buying Binge." *Ward's Auto World*, April 1998, 57.

"Federal-Mogul Finishes Purchase." *Wall Street Journal*, February 25,1998, B6.

"Federal-Mogul, Southfield, MI, Has Completed the Acquisition of Fel-Pro, a Privately-Owned Manufacturer Headquartered in Skokie, IL, for $720 Million." *Rubber World*, March 1998, 12.

Green, J. Howard. "Doing Well by Doing Good." *Time*, May 20,1996, 42.

Hershey, Robert D., Jr. "Paradise Lost?: A Takeover of Workers' Dream Factory." *International Herald Tribune*, May 16, 1998, 19.

"Icahn Is Federal-Mogul Chairman." *Automotive News*, January 21, 2008, 51.

Melcher, Richard. "Warm and Fuzzy, Meet Rough and Tumble; A Takeover Puts a Manufacturer's Generous Perks to the Test." *BusinessWeek*, January 26, 1998, 38.

Panchapakesan, Meenakshi. "Federal-Mogul: Shifting Gears." *Financial World*, January 18, 1994, 24.

Sherefkin, Robert. "How the Merger Game Nearly Killed Federal-Mogul," *Automotive News*, February 12, 2001, 42H.

Fédération Internationale de Football Association

FIFA-Strasse 20
Zürich, PO Box 8044
Switzerland
Telephone: (+41 43) 222 7777
Fax: (+41 43) 222 7878
Web site: http://www.fifa.com

Nonprofit Company
Founded: 1904 as Fédération Internationals de Football Association
Employees: 361
Sales: CHF 1.09 billion ($1.06 billion) (2009)
NAICS: 813990 Sports Governing Bodies

■ ■ ■

The Fédération Internationale de Football Association (FIFA), the world's governing body for football (soccer), is responsible for regulating the rules of play, superintending international transfers of players, establishing uniform standards of refereeing, and organizing international competitions. FIFA-sponsored competitions include the World Cup, the Olympic Football Tournament, the World Youth (Under-20) World Cup, the Under-17 World Cup, the FIFA Women's World Cup, the FIFA Futsal World Cup (indoor football), and the FIFA Confederations Cup. In 2010 FIFA had 208 member associations. The legislative body of FIFA, the Congress, convenes every two years to determine and implement FIFA statutes and every four years to elect a president. The majority of the profits that FIFA receives from ticket sales, television rights, corporate sponsorship, and merchandising are awarded to the finalist teams in each competition, and the remainder is retained by FIFA to finance its administrative costs and its efforts to promote and develop the sport of football.

ORIGINS: 1904–29

The impetus for FIFA's formation arose from the spontaneous act of a 19th-century football player in Rugby, England. In 1823 a player for the home team scored a goal by picking up the ball and running with it. The loosely organized, largely uncodified sport of football was changed forever. The player's inspired use of hands divided the sport of football into two groups: association football, which forbade the use of hands and was distinguished by the use of a round ball, and Union football, which used an oval-shaped ball and whose derivatives included rugby and U.S. football. FIFA was formed to distinguish association football from Union football and to serve as a governing organization that could provide international standards and unity to the many national association football organizations. The driving force behind FIFA's formation was Robert Guerin, the president of France's national association football organization, who reportedly began spearheading an effort to create a governing body for an international association football after a match between Belgium and France. In May 1904 Guerin achieved his goal when delegates from Belgium, Denmark, France, the Netherlands, Spain, and Sweden gathered in Paris to

COMPANY PERSPECTIVES

Played by millions around the world, football is the heart and soul of FIFA and as the guardian of this most cherished game, we have a great responsibility. This responsibility does not end with organising the FIFA World Cup and the various other world cup competitions; it extends to safeguarding the Laws of the Game, developing the game around the world and to bringing hope to those less privileged. This is what we believe is the very essence of fair play and solidarity.

We see it as our mission to contribute towards building a better future for the world by using the power and popularity of football. This mission gives meaning and direction to each and every activity that FIFA is involved in—football being an integrated part of our society.

found FIFA and formally adopt the term *association football* as their own.

At the organization's inaugural meeting, Guerin was elected president of FIFA, a post he held for two years. The possibility of a tournament among FIFA members (the World Cup) was first discussed at the meeting in Paris, but it would be years before the organization's signature event was staged. However, during FIFA's annual Congress in 1920 momentum began to build toward staging a tournament. The meeting resulted in the election of M. Jules Rimet as president and the unanimous agreement that a FIFA championship should be staged.

Under Rimet's direction, FIFA moved laboriously toward organizing the first World Cup, its progress slowed by the many political difficulties inherent in reaching accord among disparate nations. It was not until the annual Congress in 1928 that a declaration was passed stating that FIFA would "organize a competition open to representative teams of all affiliated national associations." The divisive issue as to where the tournament was to be held was not resolved until the annual Congress in 1929, when FIFA officials agreed to stage the event in Uruguay, the reigning football champion for the previous two Olympic Games. For FIFA, with its European roots, the decision to hold the first World Cup in South America nearly led to an embarrassing failure.

FIRST WORLD CUP: 1930

Following the 1929 annual Congress, construction began on a 100,000-seat stadium in Montevideo, where the tournament was scheduled to take place during the summer of 1930. However, as preparations continued and the date of the first match neared, organizers grew worried when it became apparent that no European teams were interested in participating. The European teams were expected to spend upwards of two months away from home, which was a serious deterrent to players with jobs and a sacrifice the teams were unwilling to make. As late as two months before the first FIFA championship was scheduled to begin organizers still had not received a formal entry from a European country, but then Rimet exerted his formidable influence.

Rimet managed to convince four European nations to make the southward voyage, bringing France, Belgium, Yugoslavia, and Romania to Montevideo to compete against Argentina, Mexico, the United States, Chile, Brazil, Bolivia, Peru, Paraguay, and the host country, Uruguay. By the time the FIFA World Cup trophy was awarded to victorious Uruguay, the 13 nations had played 18 matches witnessed by more than a half million spectators. FIFA, with 46 member associations at the time, had successfully staged its first international event, the popularity of which supported the organization's mission to promote and govern what would become known as the "beautiful game."

POLITICS AND DIPLOMACY: 1934–38

Preparations for the second World Cup began soon after the closing ceremonies in Montevideo. For the next World Cup, FIFA's Congress decided that Europe should be the stage, but it required eight long conferences to select Italy as the host nation. Interest in the tournament had grown measurably, which prompted FIFA officials to implement two changes for the 1934 World Cup that became hallmarks of the unique competition in the decades to come. Instead of playing all the matches in one city, the 17 matches scheduled to be played were spread throughout the country, divided among eight cities, with Rome as the site for the final match. In addition, greater interest in the tournament (29 nations entered the 1934 World Cup) required qualification games to be played throughout the world to reach the 16 finalists scheduled to compete in Italy.

Italy won the 1934 World Cup and repeated the feat at the 1938 World Cup, which was held in France. The selection of France as the host country aggravated the tensions between Europe and South America,

KEY DATES

1904: The Fédération Internationale de Football Association (FIFA) is founded in Paris by delegates from six European nations.
1930: The first World Cup is held in Montevideo, Uruguay.
1950: The World Cup resumes after a 12-year hiatus caused by World War II.
1953: FIFA membership begins reorganization under continent-wide football confederations.
1970: The World Cup, held in Mexico, reaches largest worldwide television audience of any program to that time.
1991: The first FIFA Women's World Cup is held.
2002: The first World Cup is held in Asia; top FIFA officials charged with financial mismanagement and accepting bribes.
2009: FIFA's annual revenues top $1 billion.
2010: The first World Cup is held in Africa.

exacerbating the jealousies that had been building since the 1930 World Cup. In 1934 the reigning champion Uruguay had refused to travel to Italy as retribution for the lack of interest by European teams in the 1930 World Cup. Argentina, believing that the location of the World Cup would alternate between Europe and South America, had lobbied vigorously for the rights to the 1938 World Cup, but its efforts were in vain. The selection of a European nation for a second consecutive tournament led Argentina to boycott the event entirely, a decision aped by Uruguay, which was still miffed by the lack of European support. Other South American teams bowed out as well, leaving Brazil as the lone South American representative to enter the 1938 World Cup.

The tensions between Europe and South America, and later between Europe and the rest of the world, would dominate FIFA's activities as the popularity of the FIFA world championships increased, making the president's job in large part a political exercise in diplomacy. After the conclusion of the 1938 World Cup, however, political events of a far more nefarious nature called a halt to the quadrennial celebration of football. The outbreak of World War II canceled the tournaments scheduled for 1942 and 1946, invoking a 12-year respite from the heated battle for football supremacy.

POST–WORLD WAR II MATURATION

During the war years FIFA's membership increased from 57 associations in 1938 to 70 associations by the time the 1950 World Cup was under way. Rimet ushered FIFA and the sport into the postwar era. Perhaps mindful of the gulf separating European and South American nations during the 1938 World Cup, Rimet issued a mission statement in 1948 stating that it was FIFA's goal to bring world unity to the game of football. It was a novel concept, befitting the expansive reach of FIFA during the second half of the 20th century, but at the time Rimet issued the statement FIFA and its member nations were struggling to recover from the devastation wrought by the war. Of the 31 countries that originally entered the 1950 World Cup to compete for the 16 final positions, only 13 made the trip to Brazil, to whom FIFA, in an effort to achieve Rimet's unity, had awarded the rights to the fourth FIFA championship.

Following the 1950 World Cup Rimet implemented an organizational change that created FIFA's structure for the remainder of the century. From its outset FIFA had worked with regional federations, but beginning in 1953 FIFA authorized the formation of continental confederations. South America had been represented by its confederation, Confederacion Sudamericana de Futbol, the oldest unit affiliated with FIFA, since 1916, and was joined by other continental confederations in the wake of the 1953 ruling. The Union of European Football Association (UEFA) and the Asian Football Confederation were formed in 1954, followed by the Confederation Africaine de Football in 1956. North American, Central American, and Caribbean nations joined together in 1961 to form the Confederación Norte-Centromericana y del Caribe de Fútbol, and five years later Australia, New Zealand, and the South Pacific island-nations organized the Oceania Football Confederation.

LEADERSHIP AND A STRUGGLING ASSOCIATION: 1954–70

By the 1954 World Cup, Rimet's last as president, FIFA's member nations had recovered from World War II and their level of participation reflected a rejuvenated passion for competing internationally. Held in Switzerland, where FIFA had moved its headquarters in 1932, the 1954 World Cup marked the 50th anniversary of FIFA and attracted formal applications from 38 countries who played 57 qualifying matches and 26 final matches. Rimet's 24-year term as president was followed by two comparatively brief terms by Rodolphe William Seeldrayers (1954–55) and Arthur Drewry (1955–61), who oversaw the first worldwide television transmission of a World Cup at the 1958 tournament held in Sweden. Drewry was succeeded by Sir Stanley Rous, whose 13-year term marked the last time a European would control FIFA for nearly a quarter of a century.

Rous's ouster marked a turning point in FIFA's existence, not only because of the historic shift away from the European power base but also because the organization was suffering from years of institutional neglect and needed a new, dynamic leader. At the last two World Cups during Rous's presidency (1966 in England and 1970 in Mexico), attendance had eclipsed 1.6 million, each a record high. Furthermore, the 1970 tournament reached worldwide television audiences greater than any other event in history, which, coupled with the legions of spectators flocking to the event, suggested the existence of a commensurately strong FIFA. FIFA, however, was nearly bankrupt, struggling lethargically to stay afloat financially while the sport it governed and the worldwide tournament it sponsored stood ready for commercial exploitation.

ELECTION OF HAVELANGE: 1974

The individual who tapped into the marketability of football was Rous's successor, João Havelange, who served as president from 1974 to 1998. Havelange was Brazilian, the first non-European to preside over FIFA, and was keenly aware that FIFA's survival depended on securing lucrative deals with the corporate sector. One year after his election, Havelange completed a sponsorship deal with the Coca-Cola Company. The money from the sponsorship agreement replenished FIFA's coffers, giving Havelange the resources to focus on fostering football in the developing world.

The general sponsorship agreement with Coca-Cola proved to be instrumental to FIFA's growth during the 1970s, leading to the creation of the FIFA World Youth Tournament for the FIFA/Coca-Cola Cup in 1977, an international competition for players younger than 20 years old. Renamed the World Youth (Under-20) World Cup in 1981, the tournament served as Havelange's "ambassador" in developing countries and was just one of several new FIFA-sponsored tournaments that were created during Havelange's tenure. For the 1982 World Cup, hosted by Spain, Havelange expanded the tournament from the traditional 16 finalists to 24 finalists, thereby creating more room for African and Asian teams. For the first time at a World Cup, attendance eclipsed 2 million in Spain and television viewership soared into the millions. Havelange's recipe of combining big business with multimillion-dollar television agreements and incorporating a greater geographic diversity into FIFA-sponsored events had revolutionized the world of football.

SUCCESS AND CRITICISM OF HAVELANGE

Along with the praise for Havelange's success in increasing the might and scope of FIFA came an equal amount of criticism, with the harshest critics claiming that Havelange's efforts had sullied the sport. His style of management was described as autocratic and his behavior more like a head of state than like a president of a nonprofit organization. Havelange created a vast bureaucracy of FIFA committees, over which he presided with resolute control. For nearly a quarter century Havelange held onto the reins of power like no other FIFA president before him and, criticism aside, the financial and political power of FIFA increased exponentially.

In 1985 the FIFA Under-16 World Cup (renamed the Under-17 World Cup in 1991) was added to FIFA's ever-growing calendar of events, and in 1989 Havelange directed the development of the Futsal World Cup, the first indoor football international competition. In 1991 the FIFA Women's World Cup debuted in China, further broadening the scope of FIFA's involvement in football. With the addition of these international tournaments and a flourishing World Cup that included the participation of 112 countries in preliminary rounds for the 1990 finals, FIFA boasted a global reach that was unrivaled by any other sports organization. Havelange, for better or worse, had built an organization whose lucrative sponsorship deals had transformed the sport of football into big business.

The 1994 World Cup, hosted by the United States, drew a record 3.5 million spectators and reached a cumulative television audience of nearly 19 million viewers. However, Havelange's tight control over FIFA was beginning to slip. Before the 1994 World Cup the Brazilian football player Pelé had alleged that Havelange's son-in-law was involved in corruption within Brazilian domestic football. Havelange responded to the accusation by banning Pelé from the 1994 World Cup ceremonies. Havelange's reaction was regarded as a political mistake, one from which he never fully recovered, but before he made his exit he completed one more FIFA deal of epic proportions. In 1996 FIFA sold the worldwide television and marketing rights for the 2002 and 2006 World Cups to a partnership between the Bavarian media mogul Leo Kirch and the Swiss company Sporis (later renamed International Sport and Leisure [ISL]) for $2.2 billion, which was exponentially more than the $92 million paid for the television rights to the 1990, 1994, and 1998 World Cups combined.

GLOBAL EXPANSION AND CONTROVERSY UNDER BLATTER

Havelange announced his retirement in early 1998, touching off a power struggle between Joseph S. Blatter, the general secretary of FIFA, and Lennart Johansson, the head of the UEFA. Havelange supported Blatter and accused Johansson of conspiring to create a new European football empire. Johansson countered by explaining that Europe was the historical power base of football, where the UEFA countries generated a majority of football's income. A bitter campaign for the FIFA presidency ensued, ending two days before the opening ceremonies of the 1998 World Cup in France. Blatter emerged as the winner, with his victory promising the continued development of football as a worldwide sport.

The selection of Japan and South Korea as cohosts of the 2002 World Cup underscored FIFA's commitment to expanding the geographic horizons of football. However, before the 2002 games got under way FIFA was faced with a series of management crises. One of these was related to the collapse of ISL, a sports marketing company and FIFA's exclusive marketing rights partner. After the company went bankrupt in May 2001 with debts over $200 million, the liquidator assigned to the firm found evidence of a massive system for funneling bribes to sports officials, including FIFA representatives. In May 2002 Michael Zen-Ruffinen, the general secretary of FIFA, accused Blatter of financial mismanagement and corruption. These allegations, which were supported by Johansson and 10 other members of the executive committee, came amid Blatter's campaign for reelection to the FIFA presidency. Blatter, who was handily reelected at the FIFA congress in Seoul, was further accused of using financial incentives to rig the vote. The executives subsequently withdrew their allegations and a prosecutor in Zürich found insufficient evidence to move forward on them.

Nevertheless, the attributions of foul play by the organization's leadership persisted. A Swiss magistrate continued investigating the links between FIFA and ISL, even executing a raid on FIFA's headquarters in Zürich in November 2005 and confiscating documents from the offices of the president and general secretary. A 2006 television exposé on the British Broadcasting Corporation's *Panorama* program brought renewed scrutiny to the charge that FIFA leaders had pocketed kickbacks in exchange for granting ISL the lucrative marketing rights to the World Cup. In 2008 several former ISL executives who were on trial in Zug, Switzerland, admitted to paying roughly $100 million in bribes to officials of FIFA and other sports governing bodies. The judges ruled that FIFA officials had not testified in good faith and ordered the association to pay £57,000 in court costs. Blatter himself steadfastly maintained his innocence of any wrongdoing. Swiss prosecutors cleared him of the bribery charges in 2010, but the case against several other members of FIFA's executive committee was ongoing.

OVERCOMING SCANDAL AND LOOKING FORWARD

Despite these blemishes, FIFA continued to succeed in its worldwide stewardship of the game and grew rapidly during the first decade of the 21st century. By 2009 FIFA boasted 208 member associations, a membership larger than that of the United Nations. The financial data revealed that FIFA had realized the game's full potential as an entertainment vehicle. The organization's revenue increased steadily from $575 million in 2003 to $1.1 billion in 2009. During the same period FIFA built up its equity development from a mere $75 million to over $1 billion.

Besides administering worldwide competitions in men's, women's, and youth football, beach soccer, and indoor futsal, FIFA progressively expanded its humanitarian and international development work, from sponsoring grassroots football programs for children to training doctors and health officials in the developing world. In its preparations for the 2010 World Cup in South Africa, the first time that an African nation would host the competition, FIFA initiated a program called "Win in Africa with Africa" to build up the continent's football infrastructure. Dozens of new football pitches were laid across the continent and training courses were provided for member associations and the media. Although some South Africans complained about high ticket prices for the events and restrictions on local vendors and journalists, the 2010 World Cup reached record audiences on television and the Internet. An estimated 700 million people watched Spain defeat the Netherlands in the final match amid the deafening roar of the vuvuzela horns in the crowd. According to Gerald Imray of the Associated Press on September 23, 2010, Jerome Valcke, the general secretary of FIFA, said the remarkable success of the 2010 tournament set "'a new benchmark' for future World Cups."

Jeffrey L. Covell
Updated, Roger K. Smith

FURTHER READING

Boehm, Eric. "Jocks Itchy over Costly Cup." *Variety*, June 8, 1998, 1.

Coman, Julian. "Fight to Control the Game That Turned to Gold." *The European*, June 8, 1998, 8.

Hogan, Kevin. "World Cup Wired." *Forbes*, April 11, 1994, SI124.

Imray, Gerald. "Valcke Gives SAfrica's World Cup Glowing Report." Associated Press, September 23, 2010.

Islam, Shada. "Playing by New Rules." *Far Eastern Economic Review*, September 19, 1996, 64.

Jennings, Andrew. *Foul! The Secret World of FIFA: Bribes, Vote Rigging, and Ticket Scandals.* London: HarperSport, 2006.

Mackay, Duncan. "Blatter Cleared in ISL Case as FIFA Names Remain a Mystery." Insidethegames.biz, June 24, 2010. Accessed October 25, 2010. http://insidethegames.biz/index.php?option=com.

"Old Man's Game: Soccer." *The Economist*, January 6, 1996, 35.

"Why Switzerland Won after All." *The Economist*, July 9, 1994, 66.

"The World Cup of Bribery: International Soccer Tarnished by Corruption Case." *Der Spiegel*, February 29, 2008.

Fender®

Fender Musical Instruments Company

8860 East Chaparral Road, Suite 100
Scottsdale, Arizona 85250
U.S.A.
Telephone: (480) 596-9690
Fax: (480) 596-1384
Web site: http://www.fender.com

Private Company
Founded: 1946
Incorporated: 1959
Employees: 250 (est.)
NAICS: 339992 Musical Instrument Manufacturing; 334310 Audio & Video Equipment Manufacturing

■ ■ ■

Fender Musical Instruments Company is the world's leading guitar manufacturer and a prominent name in the music business. Its classic Telecaster and Stratocaster solid-body guitars have been mainstays of popular music almost since their inception in the early 1950s. Fender's reputation for producing quality amplifiers and electric guitars was already established in country music when rock and roll began to sweep the nation in the late 1950s and early 1960s. When early rock stars, including Buddy Holly, Jimi Hendrix, Eric Clapton, and the Beatles, began playing Fender's brightly colored guitars and basses, the company's success was ensured. Beginning in the mid-1990s, Fender made several acquisitions that enhanced its market position across the musical equipment industry. The company manufactures and markets instruments, custom-made amplifiers, and audio equipment under the Fender name and numerous other brand names, including Guild, Squier, Ovation, Gretsch, Jackson, Charvel, Tacoma, SWR, and Latin Percussion.

THE EARLY YEARS

Although Clarence Leo Fender, born in 1909 near Anaheim, California, never learned to play the guitar, the guitars and amplifiers he designed changed the course of popular music. Fender began tinkering with radios in 1922, and by the time he graduated from high school in 1928, he was operating an amateur "ham" radio station. He was also building amplifiers and public-address systems, and from 1930 until 1938, he supplemented his income as a California civil-service accountant by renting his homemade equipment for dances, political rallies, and baseball games. In 1938, he opened a repair shop, Fender's Radio Service, in Fullerton, California. The shop also sold phonographs and repaired amplifiers.

In the early 1940s Fender teamed up with Clayton "Doc" Kauffman, then a professional violinist and lap-steel guitarist, to design a phonograph record changer. They sold their design for $5,000 and formed K&F Manufacturing. In 1943 K&F Manufacturing developed a new pickup for electric guitars in which the strings passed through the magnetic coil. K&F filed for a patent on the pickup in 1944, which was granted in 1948. Fender later said that K&F built its first guitar to test the new pickup.

By 1945 Fender and Kauffman, working out of a shack behind the radio-repair shop, were manufacturing

COMPANY PERSPECTIVES

With an illustrious history dating back to 1946, Fender has touched and transformed music worldwide and in nearly every genre: rock 'n' roll, country and western, jazz, rhythm and blues and many others. Everyone from beginners and hobbyists to the world's most acclaimed artists and performers have used Fender instruments and amps, in the process making the company not only a revered music industry name, but also a cultural icon. It is our vision to continue championing THE SPIRIT OF ROCK-N-ROLL® throughout the world, and our mission to exceed the expectations of music enthusiasts worldwide.

amplifiers and lap-model Hawaiian steel guitars, which were sold as sets. Fender wanted to expand the business, taking advantage of the fact that many musical instrument companies had gone out of business during World War II, but Kauffman was worried about going into debt. When Kauffman decided to leave the company, Fender agreed to trade him a small press punch for his share of K&F Manufacturing.

In 1946 Fender renamed the business the Fender Electric Instruments Company. That same year, he signed an agreement with Radio & Television Equipment Company (Radio-Tel) of Santa Ana, California, which had been supplying parts for his repair shop, to be sole distributor for Fender amplifiers and guitars. Fender also turned over operation of his repair shop so he could concentrate on making musical instruments. By 1949 Fender amplifiers and guitars were firmly entrenched in the country music industry.

THE TELECASTER

In the spring of 1950 the Fender Electric Instruments Company introduced a single-pickup, solid-body electric guitar, which it called the Esquire. The company started taking orders for the Esquire, but before Fender could start full production, the guitar had been redesigned as a dual-pickup solid-body called the Broadcaster. The Broadcaster was renamed the Telecaster in 1951 because of a conflict with Gretsch Broadkaster drums. Although it was sometimes derided as a "canoe paddle," because of its plain solid-ash body and screwed-on fretted maple neck, the Telecaster became the first commercially successful solid-body electric guitar.

Other guitar makers had created solid-body electric guitars as early as the mid-1930s. In his 1994 book *Fender: The Inside Story*, Forrest White, former vice president and production manager for the Fender Electric Instruments Company, traces the concept of the Telecaster to a guitar that a part-time guitar maker in southern California, Paul Bigsby, created in 1947 for Merle Travis.

Fender supplied amplifiers for the Saturday night "Cliffe Stone Show" in Placentia, California, and there seems little doubt that Fender would have seen Travis play his custom-designed electric guitar on the show. In 1979 Travis wrote in the *JEMF Quarterly* that he loaned his guitar to Fender for a week to make a copy, and he argued for years that he, not Fender, should be considered the father of the solid-body electric guitar.

Despite the dispute, in 1951 Fender received a patent for "a new, original, and ornamental design for a guitar," and it was Fender who popularized the electric, solid-body guitar; both the Gibson Les Paul, itself a classic, and Fender's own Stratocaster were inspired by the Telecaster design. In *American Guitars: An Illustrated History* (1992), Tom Wheeler, former consulting editor for *Guitar Player* magazine, calls Fender "the Henry Ford of electric guitars and the Telecaster … his Model T." With the success of the Telecaster, which sold for $189.50, Fender closed his repair shop to devote all his energy to designing and manufacturing musical instruments. By late 1951 Fender had scored another coup with his invention of the first electric bass guitar, the Precision Bass. By the late 1960s, the combination of the Telecaster (and its successor, the Stratocaster) and the Precision Bass would revolutionize the performance and recording of popular music.

ASSUMING CONTROL OF DISTRIBUTION

Before long, however, Leo Fender became unhappy with his distribution arrangement with Radio-Tel, which seemed content to focus its marketing efforts on Fender's amplifiers and lap-steel guitars. In his book White quotes his former employer: "During this time, they (Radio-Tel) didn't sell hardly any of our (solid-body) guitars. [The guitars] just sat there in this garage, and termites got into them and ate through the bodies. We never found out about the termites until dealers started calling us about holes in the guitars. We ended up taking back 500 guitars and had to burn them all."

In 1953 Leo Fender formed Fender Sales, Inc., to take over distribution from Radio-Tel. Surprisingly, his partners in the venture were, or had been affiliated, with Radio-Tel, including Donald Randall, former sales manager who became president of the distribution

KEY DATES

1943: Clarence Leo Fender, with business partner Clayton Kauffman, designs a new pickup for electric guitars.
1946: Fender, now the company's sole proprietor, renames the company Fender Electric Instruments Company.
1951: Fender introduces the Telecaster guitar, for which the company receives a patent, and the Precision Bass, the first electric bass guitar.
1954: Fender introduces the Stratocaster guitar, which becomes the most popular solid-body electric guitar ever made.
1959: Fender Electric Instruments incorporates.
1965: Fender is acquired by CBS for $13 million.
1985: CBS sells its Fender division to a management company headed by William Schultz; the company name is changed to Fender Musical Instruments.
1987: Fender acquires Sunn, an amplifier company; Fender Custom Shop opens in Corona, California.
1995: Fender acquires Guild Guitar Company.
2007: Fender acquires Kaman Music Company.

company, and Charles Hayes, a former salesman. The third partner was F.C. Hall, who owned Radio-Tel. Later that year Hall purchased the Electro String Instrument Corporation from founder Adolph Rickenbacker, placing himself in the position of being both Fender's competitor and partner. When Hayes died in an automobile accident in 1955, Fender and Randall bought his interest in Fender Sales from his widow and ousted Hall. Fender and Randall each then owned 50 percent of the distribution company, although Fender continued to own 100 percent of Fender Electric Instruments.

THE STRATOCASTER

In 1954 Fender Electric Instruments introduced the Stratocaster. While the Telecaster may have looked like a canoe paddle, Tony Bacon and Paul Day, authors of *The Fender Book*, describe the Stratocaster as "in some ways [owing] more to contemporary automobile design than traditional guitar forms, especially in the flowing, sensual curves of that beautifully proportioned, timeless body." The Stratocaster also included a built-in vibrato and came in a variety of DuPont car colors. Although the Stratocaster took a while to catch on (during the year of its introduction, it barely outsold the older Telecaster), it became the most popular and most copied solid-body electric guitar ever made. It was also the guitar that would make Fender Electric Instruments worth millions of dollars and make Leo Fender an icon among rock musicians.

Building on the phenomenal success of the Stratocaster, Fender Electric Instruments introduced a line of less expensive guitars and amplifiers in 1955. The "studio instruments" were branded with the name "White," a tribute to Fender's production manager, Forrest White. Fender also attempted to transcend the top of the line with his Jazzmaster guitar design; unfortunately, it never really caught on. The company also introduced a three-quarter-sized solid-body guitar in 1955, an electric mandolin in 1957, a short-lived electric violin in 1958, and its first acoustic guitars in 1964. Fender dabbled briefly with brass instruments, buying a horn company and introducing the Hayes brand in 1954. However, the horn business, like the White brand, was abandoned a year later. Fender Electric Instruments, which had fewer than 15 employees in 1947, had more than 100 employees by the time it incorporated in 1959.

THE CBS YEARS

In 1964 Leo Fender, then 55, became ill and offered to sell Fender Electric Instruments to Randall, still his partner in Fender Sales, for $1.5 million. At the time, the company was producing 1,500 amplifiers, electric guitars, acoustic guitars, and other instruments per week, and was the largest exporter of musical instruments in the United States. Fender Electric Instruments employed 600 people, 500 of them in manufacturing.

Randall lacked the resources to purchase the company himself but agreed to find another buyer. After talking with several companies, including the Baldwin Piano & Organ Co., Randall negotiated a deal with the Columbia Broadcasting System. On January 5, 1965, CBS announced that a subsidiary, Columbia Records Distribution Corp., had purchased Fender Electric Instruments and Fender Sales for $13 million. The new Columbia Records division was known initially as Fender CBS, but that was changed to CBS Musical Instruments in 1966, as it acquired other companies, including Steinway & Sons and flute maker Gemeinhardt Co.

CBS began making changes almost immediately. Fender Electric Instruments had expanded haphazardly over the previous 20 years until it occupied 29 buildings scattered throughout Fullerton. To consolidate operations, CBS announced plans to build a 120,000-square-foot, $1.3 million facility, complete with a dust-free air-filtering system. The building was completed in 1966. CBS also began sending efficiency experts to Fullerton to analyze how the former Fender Electric Instruments Company operated. White, who had been responsible for production since 1954, commented in his book *Fender: The Inside Story*, "We had been invaded by a horde of 'know-it-all CBS experts' at both Fender Sales and the factory."

CONCERNS ABOUT QUALITY

Demoted from vice president to plant manager with the takeover, White quit less than two years later in a dispute over the quality of an amplifier that CBS planned to introduce. He wrote, "I asked all of my key personnel to come to the conference room. I told them that I had too much respect for Leo to have any part in building something that was not worthy of having his name associated with it."

Many other longtime Fender employees also believed that quality was declining as CBS cut back on product lines and produced few new models. Randall, who had become vice president and general manager under CBS, left the company in 1969, apparently more because of corporate politics than a concern over quality. In *Fender: The Inside Story*, White quotes him as saying, "Everybody at CBS was climbing the corporate ladder, stepping on everyone else's fingers as they climbed up. There was a tremendous amount of infighting." However, despite the management upheaval and concerns over quality, sales at CBS Musical Instruments almost tripled, from $20 million in 1971 to nearly $60 million in 1981.

Meanwhile, Leo Fender had been retained by CBS as a consultant in research and development from 1965 until 1970, although according to White, CBS executives made fun of his ideas. In 1972 Fender's consulting business, CLF Research, began manufacturing stringed instruments for Tri-Sonics, Inc., a company formed by White and Tom Walker, a former district manager at Fender Sales. Tri-Sonics changed its name briefly to Musitek, short for Music Technology, before finally settling on Music Man, Inc., in 1974. Fender was named vice president in 1974 and became president in 1975. The company was sold in 1984.

In 1980 Leo Fender and George Fullerton, another longtime Fender Musical Instruments employee who quit CBS, formed G&L Inc. to market instruments made by CLF. G&L originally stood for George and Leo, but when Fullerton sold out in 1986, receptionists began answering the telephone, "Guitars by Leo." The company was sold after Fender's death in 1991.

FENDER'S TURNAROUND

By the early 1980s Japanese competition was beginning to affect the bottom line at CBS Musical Instruments. CBS tried shifting some of its manufacturing to Korea to reduce tooling costs, but that experiment was abandoned the same year because of poor quality. CBS also recruited three top executives from Yamaha Musical Instruments. John McLaren was hired to head up CBS Musical Instruments, William Schultz was hired as president of the Fender division, and Dan Smith was named director of marketing for electric guitars.

In *The Fender Book*, Tony Bacon and Paul Day quote Smith: "We were brought in to kind of turn the reputation of Fender around, and to get it so it was making money again. It was starting to lose money, and at that point in time everybody hated Fender. We thought we knew how bad it was. We took for granted that they could make Stratocasters and Telecasters the way they used to make them, but we were wrong. So many things had changed in the plant."

In 1982 Schultz virtually shut down U.S. production of Fender guitars, focusing instead on reissuing limited editions of top-of-the-line "classic" Fender guitars from pre-CBS days. Schultz also formed a joint venture, Fender Japan, with two Japanese distributors, Kanda Shokai and Yamano Music. Fuji Gen-Gakki, which made Ibanez brand instruments, was licensed to manufacture Fender guitars, which were sold only in Japan. Fuji Gen-Gakki also manufactured lower-priced vintage Fender guitars under the Squier Series brand name. The Squier Series originally was intended for the Japanese and European market, but export to the U.S. market began in 1983.

A year later, with CBS a potential takeover target, the company began soliciting offers for its Fender Musical Instruments division. Among the companies expressing interest were the International Music Co. and Kaman Music Corporation, which manufactured Ovation guitars. In the end, however, CBS offered to sell to a management group headed by Schultz for $12.5 million. The leveraged buyout was completed in March 1985, and the company name was changed to Fender Musical Instruments.

According to *Forbes*, the management group borrowed $9 million and CBS took back a note for $2.5 million, which gave Fender Musical Instruments about $11 in debt for every $1 in equity. Making matters worse, the sale did not include the production facilities in Fullerton, which CBS sold separately. As a result, Schultz, chairman of the company, was forced to halt all

U.S. production of Fender guitars, and only Japanese-made instruments were listed in the 1985 catalog. Schultz also slashed employment at Fender Musical Instruments from 800 to about 90 workers, mostly in research and design.

EXPANSION

As part of his effort to rebuild the company, Schultz created the Fender Custom Shop in Corona, California, which produced about five models for a Vintage reissue series and began offering free or discounted guitars to rock music stars. In return, the musicians agreed to appear in Fender Musical Instruments advertisements. In 1986 Fender Musical Instruments introduced the American Standards model Stratocaster and Telecaster guitars. By 1996 the Corona plant, which also produced the company's amplifiers and speakers, employed about 600. Schultz, who moved company headquarters to Scottsdale, Arizona, in 1991, also opened guitar-manufacturing facilities in Mexico, China, and Korea.

In addition, Fender opened its Amp Custom Shop in Scottsdale in 1992. This enabled Fender to provide custom amplifiers along with custom guitars to its higher-profile and professional customers. In 1998 Fender reintroduced the Sunn line of amplifiers to the marketplace. Fender had acquired this legendary company, whose products had been endorsed by the Who, the Rolling Stones, and Jimi Hendrix, in 1987. Schultz saw great potential for growth in the amplifier and speaker market. In 2001 Fender debuted its CyberTwin amplifier, which attempted to combine the classic and the modern by allowing musicians a wide range of sound options, including emulation of old-fashioned tube amplifiers, using actual tubes combined with digital processing in an entirely new configuration.

Fender also expanded its operations into the acoustic market, importing guitars from manufacturers in Southeast Asia. More significantly, the company became the North American distributor for Manuel Rodriguez guitars. These guitars, handmade in Spain by the Rodriguez family since 1905, were widely recognized as among the highest-quality acoustic guitars in the world, regularly retailing in the thousands of dollars.

ACQUISITIONS AND CONTINUED GROWTH

In 1995 Fender acquired the Guild Guitar Company, a Rhode Island–based manufacturer of handmade electric and acoustic guitars played by Keith Richards, Eric Clapton, Jerry Garcia, Brian May, and Richie Havens. Although Fender kept Guild's Westerly, Rhode Island, plant open, the company shifted the guitar manufacturing to its Corona plant. Fender spokesman Morgan Ringwalk cited the more ideal climatic conditions in southern California, telling the New London, Connecticut *Day* (June 28, 2001) that "wood is a touchy material to work with, and being close to the ocean in Westerly really messes with it. Getting a consistent product is very tough." Guild foreman Gilbert Diaz questioned that decision, pointing out that Guild had made top-of-the-line guitars in Rhode Island for years, ocean humidity and all. A Guild Custom Shop was also opened in Nashville, Tennessee. In 1998 DeArmond guitars were introduced under the Guild name. Manufactured in Korea, with the pickups installed at the Corona plant, the DeArmond line was designed with affordability in mind.

In 1995 the company sold 1.1 million guitars, with sales across the industry growing an average of 10 percent a year. To keep pace with Fender's growing sales volume, the company opened a new facility in Corona in 1998. Built on a new 19-acre site, the $20 million state-of-the-art plant covered 177,000 square feet and produced all of Fender's U.S.-made guitars, with a capacity of more than 350 a day. The facility was designed with California's rigorous air-quality standards in mind. The company claimed that the plant's air emissions were 95 percent clean. South Coast Air Quality Management District spokesman Larry Watkins thought highly of Fender's air-quality control. With the Fender Custom Shop on the same site and the Amp Custom Shop moved from Scottsdale to Corona, all of Fender's U.S. manufacturing was consolidated in one place.

THE NEW MILLENNIUM

In 2000 Fender's reported revenue reached $280 million. For nearly two decades, the company's sales had grown more than 10 percent per year. Despite a slowing economy that led to staff cuts at its Corona facility in 2001, the company's reputation and market position were both unsurpassed. That same year the company awarded a contract for construction of a new headquarters in Scottsdale, from which to direct its worldwide operation.

In 2002 Fender acquired the Charvel and Jackson guitar brands and agreed to produce and distribute the Gretsch line. The following year the company picked up SWR amps, and in 2004 it acquired Tacoma Guitar, which produced instruments for Bob Dylan and other famous customers. Fender continued to market all these instruments under their original names but with the backing of its own formidable distribution network. These moves signaled the beginning of a new phase for

Fender. An even clearer sign was the creation of Fender-branded apparel. DaVinci Clothing Company released several lines of denim jeans and jackets, T-shirts, and other casual Fender wear in 2002. DaVinci's Christopher Wicks aspired for Fender to become "the Harley-Davidson of music—an entire lifestyle brand," as reported by Adam Tschorn in the *Daily News Record* (January 10, 2005). Sales of the clothing line topped the million-dollar mark in its first year on the market, surpassing expectations.

William Schultz, who masterminded Fender's return to the top of the market and saw the company into the new millennium, retired in 2005. He left the company in the hands of his longtime deputy, William Mendello. That year Fender streamlined its operations by completing construction of a giant warehouse in Ontario, California, to serve as the company's single global distribution center.

TRANSFORMING INTO A CONGLOMERATE AND SURVIVING A RECESSION

Fender's transformation into a major music-industry conglomerate, begun with the acquisition of Guild, culminated with the October 2007 purchase of the Kaman Music Corporation, a subsidiary of Kaman Corporation, for $117 million cash. Kaman was an aerospace company founded by Charles Kaman, an engineer known for his innovations in aeronautics. Kaman was also a guitar player, and his experiments applying engineering principles to the craftsmanship of musical instruments resulted in the innovative Ovation guitar, made of composite materials with a rounded back. Kaman Music also produced Takamine and Hamer guitars, several brands of percussion instruments, and an array of music accessories. The transaction made Fender the second-largest producer of musical equipment in the market, behind Yamaha Corporation, and secured Fender's position as the leading guitar manufacturer.

The steep recession that began in late 2007 meant no sales growth for Fender in 2009, yet Fender management was content not to lose ground in revenue or market share in a year when overall guitar sales dropped 20 percent. In another setback the company's long-term effort to trademark the well-known shape of its solid-body guitars failed in a federal appeals process in 2009. Lawyers for Fender had argued that the trademark was necessary to reduce counterfeiting, but smaller firms contended that granting Fender a trademark would eventually put them out of business. A bright spot for the company was the licensing agreement that made the Stratocaster a highly visible element in the popular video game *Rock Band*, produced by Harmonix Music Systems. To further connect the virtual and real worlds of music, Fender sealed a cobranding and joint marketing agreement with the software startup eJamming.com in January 2010. This online software application allowed musicians to produce music with simultaneous streaming audio.

Fender's chairman and CEO Mendello stepped down in July 2010 after more than 30 years with the company. The company's leadership succession had been carefully planned. Two board members, Mark Fukunaga and Michael Lazarus, became the new cochairs, while Larry Thomas became the new chief executive. Thomas had previously run Guitar Center, which called itself "the largest musical instrument retailer in the world." The new team inherited a private company in a strong financial position at the top of its market, continually innovating, and ready to rock and roll into the 21st century.

Dean Boyer
Updated, Heidi Wrightsman; Roger K. Smith

PRINCIPAL SUBSIDIARIES

Guild; Sunn; Squier; Tacoma; Gretsch; Jackson; Charvel; EVH; SWR: Kaman Music Corporation.

PRINCIPAL COMPETITORS

Gibson Guitar Corp.; Yamaha Corporation; Harman International Industries.

FURTHER READING

Bacon, Tony. *50 Years of Fender: Half a Century of the Greatest Electric Guitars*. San Francisco: Miller Freeman, Inc., 2000.

"Fender Buys Kaman." *Music Trades*, December 2007, 18.

Graham, Jefferson. "From Virtual to Real Rocker." *USA Today*, January 20, 2010.

"Guild's New Home Signals Fresh Start." *Music Trades*, July 2010, 76.

Matzer, Maria. "Playing Solo." *Forbes*, March 25, 1996, 80–81.

Natale, Tony. "Fender Musical Instruments Corp. CEO Makes the Company's Books Sing." *Mesa Tribune*, November 12, 2005.

Padgett, Mike. "Money in Music." *Business Journal*, March 23, 2001, 24.

Smith, Richard. *Fender: The Sound Heard 'Round the World*. Fullerton, CA: Garfish, 1995.

Wheeler, Tom. *American Guitars: An Illustrated History*. New York: Harper Perennial, 1992.

White, Forrest. *Fender: The Inside Story*. San Francisco: Miller Freeman, Inc., 1994.

FirstService Corporation

FirstService Building
1140 Bay Street, Suite 4000
Toronto, Ontario M5S 2B4
Canada
Telephone: (416) 960-9500
Fax: (416) 960-5333
Web site: http://www.firstservice.com

Public Company
Founded: 1972 as Superior Pools
Incorporated: 1988
Employees: 18,000
Sales: $1.7 billion (2009)
Stock Exchanges: Toronto NASDAQ
Ticker Symbols: FSV (Toronto); FSRV (NASDAQ)
NAICS: 531210 Offices of Real Estate Agents and Brokers; 531312 Nonresidential Property Managers; 531311 Residential Property Managers; 531110 Lessors of Residential Buildings and Dwellings; 531320 Offices of Real Estate Appraisers; 531390 Other Activities Related to Real Estate; 531120 Lessors of Nonresidential Buildings (Except Miniwarehouses); 541191 Title Abstract and Settlement Offices; 561730 Landscaping Services; 236118 Residential Remodelers; 238330 Flooring Contractors; 238320 Painting and Wall Covering Contractors; 541350 Building Inspection Services

■ ■ ■

FirstService Corporation is a leading global provider of real estate services, operating in three business segments: commercial real estate, residential property management, and property services. As one of the three largest global providers of commercial real estate services, with offices in 40 countries, FirstService operates primarily under the Colliers International brand. Colliers provides brokerage, valuation, property management, maintenance, project management, and corporate advisory services to investors, owners, and tenants. FirstService is the largest apartment manager in North America, with more than one million units managed, and is also the continent's leading property services provider through its contractor and franchise networks of construction, painting, restoration, and inspection companies.

COMPANY ORIGINS AND EARLY YEARS

FirstService Corporation traces its roots to a pool maintenance and facility management business, Superior Pools, established in 1972 by Jay Hennick while he was still a teenager. The business provided Hennick with the money to finance his college education and launch his own law practice. Upon graduating from college, Hennick began his professional career as a corporate attorney in Toronto before deciding to start his own corporation.

After tapping friends and relatives to raise start-up capital, Hennick established FirstService Corporation in 1988, with Superior Pools as the company's first service operation. In 1989 Hennick's company acquired College Pro Painters, a franchisor of exterior residential

COMPANY PERSPECTIVES

FirstService has grown into a global leader in real estate services. Our refined management style is built on seven powerful pillars we call "The FirstService Way." It continues to guide our Company's growth and attract strong management teams with visions that are similar to ours, visions for the future success of their businesses.

FirstService believes that our strongest competitive advantage is being partners with operating managers. We provide the strategic leadership to guide and support growth initiatives and our partners remain focused and committed on building a strong global company.

painting businesses. Two years later, FirstService acquired another property services firm, Chemlawn Canada, a leading residential lawn-care business.

During the 1990s, FirstService used acquisitions to enter the fields of property security, business services, and property management. In 1993 FirstService purchased Intercon Security Limited, a leading Canadian security systems and staffing firm. That same year, FirstService went public in Canada and raised CAD 10 million through its initial public offering on the Toronto Stock Exchange. FirstService doubled annual revenues during its first year as a public company, logging CAD 88.4 million in sales. In 1995 the company's stock was listed in the United States on the NASDAQ.

FirstService entered the business services market in 1995 by acquiring Toronto-based B.D.P. Business Data Services Limited, a major business-process outsourcing firm. The following year, the company secured a revolving credit facility and expanded its business services platform with the purchase of DDS Dyment Distribution Services, an Ohio-based distributor of trade marketing and promotional materials.

FirstService entered the residential property management business in the mid-1990s with a series of purchases. The company acquired two Florida-based full-service property management operations, Prime Management in 1996 and The Continental Group, Inc., the following year. The company also bought The Wentworth Group, Inc., operating primarily on the East Coast, in 1997 and the Arizona-based Rossmar Management Company in 1998.

EXPANSION AND ACQUISITIONS

In 1997 FirstService raised about $27 million in the United States through an offering of 2.5 million subordinate voting shares. The company used its additional financial resources to expand its property services segment, acquiring Paul Davis Restoration in 1997 and California Closets in 1998. With 150 global locations, the franchisor California Closets was the world's largest supplier of custom closets and home-storage units. FirstService in 1999 purchased North America's largest commercial swimming pool and recreation-facility management business, Beltsville, Maryland–based American Pool Enterprises Inc., into which Superior Pools was integrated.

In 1999 DDS Distribution purchased a Dallas-based order-fulfillment operation. The acquisition included warehouse and distribution centers in Dallas; Oklahoma City, Oklahoma; and Albuquerque, New Mexico. The additions made DDS one of the largest U.S. storage and distribution firms handling advertising, promotional, and in-store display materials. By the close of the decade, FirstService's annual revenues had increased 600 percent in six years to total more than $260 million.

Early in the first decade of the 21st century, FirstService expanded its security, business services, and property services platforms. In 2000 the company entered the U.S. security market with the acquisition of Security Services and Technologies of Philadelphia. FirstService in 2001 acquired Herbert A. Watts Ltd., Canada's largest business-processing service for contact centers and promotion fulfillment, and then renamed its business services unit the Resolve Corporation. In 2003 FirstService purchased the property services business Pillar to Post, a North American professional home inspection service.

FirstService in 2003 became the leading North American property management company after acquiring Cooper Square Realty, a leading New York residential management service. Following this acquisition, FirstService managed more than 2,000 properties in a total of 14 states, providing construction management, mortgage brokering, and real estate leasing and sales, as well as property management services. In 2004 Cooper Square acquired RMI Management, the largest community-association management firm in southern Nevada.

DEVELOPMENT OF COMMERCIAL REAL ESTATE BUSINESS

FirstService entered the commercial real estate business in 2004 with the $88 million purchase of a 70 percent

KEY DATES

1988: FirstService Corporation is incorporated.
1996: The company enters the residential property management business.
2004: FirstService enters the commercial real estate business.
2009: FirstService assumes control of the Colliers International brand.
2010: FirstService Real Estate Advisors and Colliers International combine operations under the Colliers name.

stake in Vancouver-based Colliers Macaulay Nicolls Inc. (CMN). CMN was the largest affiliate of the well-known Colliers International, a network of worldwide offices licensed to use the Colliers brand. CMN had 80 offices serving 20 countries, providing appraisal, brokerage, consulting, and property management services in the Asia-Pacific region and Latin America and on the West Coast in the United States. CMN managers and select employees collectively kept a 30 percent share in the firm, which continued to operate independently. With its subsequent acquisitions, FirstService used this same decentralized model of ownership.

In 2005 FirstService used CMN as a foundation for the establishment of FirstService Real Estate Advisors (REA), a global commercial real estate business. REA quickly expanded that year through a series of acquisitions giving the firm offices in Dallas; Phoenix, Arizona; Portland, Oregon; Toronto; and Vancouver, as well as in Asia. The company in 2005 also acquired for $100 million an 82 percent stake in the Los Angeles-based Colliers Seeley International Inc.

STRATEGIC ACQUISITIONS AND DIVESTITURES: 2005–07

With its CMN acquisition, FirstService had five business platforms: commercial real estate services, residential property management, property services, commercial property security, and business services. Between 2005 and 2006, FirstService began divesting nonstrategic businesses, including Chemlawn and its entire business services unit, Resolve Corporation, to focus on growing its property-related businesses. In 2006 FirstService acquired Cincinnati-based Handyman Connection, the largest remodeling and home repair franchisor in the United States, which became part of its property services business.

FirstService REA in 2006 began acquiring over a three-year period a series of international Colliers firms (including ones in Brazil, southeastern Europe, Russia, and the Netherlands) and adding commercial real estate specialty businesses. That year FirstService REA acquired a majority stake in Chicago-based Cohen Financial, the fifth-largest provider of commercial real estate loans in the United States, and the appraisal business PGP Property Valuation. In 2007 FirstService purchased PKF Consulting and PKF Hospitality Research, an association of auditors, accountants, and consultants for the hospitality industry, and MHPM Project Managers, Inc., Canada's largest provider of project management services. FirstService REA in 2007 also acquired an 80 percent share in Boston-based commercial real estate brokerage Meredith & Grew, a major affiliate of the ONCOR international network of real estate advisers.

In 2007 the company expanded its West Coast property management operations with the majority-stake acquisition of Southern California-based Merit Companies, Inc., the largest residential property manager in California. FirstService also purchased Field Asset Services, Inc., a U.S. leader in property preservation and maintenance with a network of more than 15,000 independent contractors. By the fiscal year ending in March 2008, FirstService's annual revenues had ballooned to $1.57 billion.

In 2008 FirstService sold its security business to ADT Security Systems for $187.5 million, paring its focus to three divisions: commercial real estate, residential property management, and property services. That year, the company's commercial real estate platform added a New York headquarters via the acquisition of a 65 percent stake in the Manhattan-based firm GVA Williams. The acquisition made FirstService an immediate player in the New York metropolitan commercial property business and provided a hub from which to expand the group's global operations. With the acquisition, FirstService's commercial property business was operating in 36 countries and was vaulted into the upper echelon of the top four global commercial real estate operations, trailing only CB Richard Ellis Group, Inc.; Cushman & Wakefield, Inc.; and Jones Lang LaSalle Incorporated.

RECESSION AND REBRANDING: 2008–09

In 2008 FirstService began orchestrating major commercial real estate deals in the greater New York City area. By late 2008, however, a growing recession and credit crisis created a glut of Manhattan-area sublease space, pushing up vacancy rates and pulling down rental prices in the company's largest commercial market.

FirstService in 2009 recorded sales of $1.7 billion, nearly doubling its revenues of a few years previous, but the company logged a net loss of $7.9 million, which was its first year in the red in the 21st century. FirstService was not the only major commercial property broker suffering. Cushman & Wakefield posted a loss of $127 million, while the global leader CB Richard Ellis eked out a $33 million profit. For the first quarter of 2009, all the leading commercial real estate brokerage companies in the United States reported net losses for the first time in recent history. By September 2009, major U.S. commercial real estate markets, including Manhattan, were stabilizing.

In September 2009 the company launched plans for a full-service Washington, D.C., regional commercial real estate headquarters. Later that year, FirstService REA became a minority shareholder of the London-based Colliers CRE plc. CRE, rebranded Colliers International, gave the firm access to its first Western European territory, including offices in Ireland, Spain, and the United Kingdom. Continuing its rebranding campaign, the company in November 2009 changed the name of its commercial property appraisal unit to FirstService PGP Valuation.

In 2009 the company became the controlling stakeholder in Colliers International Property Consultants. In the process, FirstService gained control of the Colliers International brand and owned the third-largest commercial real estate group in the world. By January 2010, FirstService REA had increased its stake in Colliers International to 70 percent, and Colliers International and FirstService REA that month merged their global real estate operations. The merged firm adopted the Colliers International name and the FirstService REA model for partnering with local management. At the time of the deal, FirstService's ownership of 70 percent of Colliers International included controlling stakes of other Colliers firms held under the subsidiary FirstService REA. The new Colliers International began fully integrating REA operations through a process propelled by a $20 million outlay for information technology to create collaboration. With the restructuring, the commercial property subsidiary PKF Hotel and Hospitality Consulting adopted the Colliers brand, and FirstService Williams changed its name to Colliers International.

GROWTH AND NEW COMPETITION

Although designed to establish greater coherence among its partner-subsidiaries and improve oversight and delivery of services, the merger was primarily a change in name to improve brand recognition. FirstService retained its original partnership business model, which left day-to-day operations in the hands of local affiliates, although the corporate office established measures for greater accountability for consistent service quality. With the merger, though, Colliers International became the second-largest commercial real estate operation in the world, according to *National Real Estate Investor* magazine and the Lipsey Company.

The Colliers rebranding set in motion some turmoil in the real estate arena, spawning the creation of a new national firm, Cassidy Turley, formed from former affiliates of Colliers as well as those from the firms NAI Global and Grubb & Ellis Company. As a result, Colliers lost affiliate offices in Baltimore, New York City, Washington, D.C., and other cities. During mid-2010, though, Colliers licensed its brand in other U.S. markets, including Long Island, New York; Cincinnati and Columbus, Ohio; Nashville, Tennessee; and Grand Rapids, Michigan.

FirstService also expanded its property management platform in 2010. The company's subsidiary TenantAccess expanded to serve the entire United States and hired an additional 350 property managers after the passage of the Protecting Tenant Foreclosure Act of 2009, which put additional obligations on entities foreclosing on properties. FirstService also acquired the New York City-based property manager Goodstein Management, Inc., and made its first non-U.S. residential property management acquisition with the purchase of Condominium First Management Services Ltd., the largest residential property services provider in the Canadian province of Alberta.

Roger Rouland

PRINCIPAL SUBSIDIARIES

American Pool Enterprises, Inc. (USA; 96.4%); Field Asset Services, Inc. (USA; 78.3%); FirstService Residential Management, Inc. (USA; 97.6%); FirstService Commercial Real Estate Services Inc. (d/b/a Colliers International) (93.1%); FirstService (USA), Inc.; FirstService Delaware, LLC (USA); FirstService Delaware, LP (USA); The Continental Group, Inc. (USA; 92%); The Franchise Company Inc. (87%); The Wentworth Group, Inc. (USA; 88.2%).

PRINCIPAL DIVISIONS

Commercial Real Estate Services; Residential Property Management; Property Services.

PRINCIPAL COMPETITORS

CB Richard Ellis Group, Inc.; Cushman & Wakefield, Inc.; Great Atlantic Management Company; Jones Lang

LaSalle Incorporated; The ServiceMaster Company; Trammell Crow Company.

FURTHER READING

Bubny, Paul. "Colliers Plays the Offense." *Real Estate Forum*, April 2010, 30–32.

"Cooper Square Forms Partnership with FirstService Corporation." *Real Estate Weekly*, May 21, 2003, 16.

Fleming, Sibley. "Colliers International Restructures to Become More Nimble." *National Real Estate Investor* online, January 6, 2010. Accessed November 9, 2010. http://nreionline.com/finance/news/colliers_international_restructure_0106.

Johnson, Ben. "Brokerage Juggernaut in the Making?" *National Real Estate Investor*, January 1, 2009.

McLeod, Lori. "Big Fish, Small Pond, an Ocean of Opportunity." *Globe and Mail*, August 11, 2007.

O'Flanagan, Linda Barr. "GVA Williams Finds Partner." *Real Estate Weekly*, September 17, 2008, 1.

Satow, Julie. "Commercial Firms Fight Back in a Post-Boom World." *New York Times*, June 16, 2010.

Silverman, Suzann D. "Largest Colliers Company Merges to Expand Business." *Commercial Property News*, November 1, 2004, 6.

Thangavelu, Poonkulali. "Consolidation Extends to CRE Servicing." *Mortgage Servicing News*, July 2006, 10.

Turcotte, Jason. "Williams the New 'Big Fish.'" *Real Estate Weekly*, October 22, 2008, 1.

FJ Management

1104 Country Hills Drive
Ogden, Utah 84403
U.S.A.
Telephone: (801) 624-1000
Web site: http://www.flyingj.com

Private Company
Incorporated: 1958
NAICS: 324110 Petroleum Refineries; 522320 Financial Transactions Processing, Reserve, and Clearinghouse Activities

■ ■ ■

Until it filed for bankruptcy protection in 2008, Flying J Inc., renamed FJ Management in 2010, was one of the nation's largest chains of truck stops, which the company helped to reconceptualize as "travel plazas." Flying J pioneered a novel concept in the truck stop industry: truckers deserve clean, friendly, comfortable facilities with a range of amenities, such as hotel and motel accommodations, restaurants, computer access, well-stocked convenience stores, and even bars. In July 2010 the company sold its highway hospitality network to a principal rival, Pilot Travel Centers, and with the proceeds was able to exit from bankruptcy and survive as a corporate entity. Operating under the name FJ Management, it retained an 11.7 percent ownership stake in the combined truck stop company, which was subsequently called Pilot Flying J. Also remaining in FJ Management's ownership portfolio are an oil refinery in the vicinity of Salt Lake City, Utah; the Transportation Alliance Bank, a small industrial loan institution catering to the trucking industry; and a half ownership of Transportation Clearing House (TCH), a financial services firm that sells fuel transaction cards to truck drivers and fleets. FJ Management is a private company owned principally by the descendants of founder Jay Call. Call's daughter, Crystal Call Maggelet, is president, CEO, and chairwoman.

PIONEERING THE TRAVEL PLAZA

O. Jay Call, a native of Idaho, came to Willard, Utah, in the mid-1960s to run a gas station he had bought from his family. Call's father had owned a gas station in Idaho. His relatives also owned the successful Maverik chain of convenience stores and service stations, founded in 1930. Call set out to build a chain of his own. By 1968 Call owned four gas stations; in that year, he organized his company as "Flying J," named for his love of flying. By the late 1970s Call had recognized an opening in the market for a different kind of truck stop.

The typical truck stops of the day were somewhat squalid, rough-and-ready places offering few amenities. The truck stop industry itself was highly fragmented. Call took a tip from the booming fast-food industry and its growing chains of restaurants offering consistency, quality, and cleanliness, as well as low prices. In 1979 Call debuted the Flying J "travel plaza" in West Haven, Utah, adding amenities such as a restaurant, motel, shower stations, and fuel islands for both cars and trucks. An early hallmark of the Flying J concept was its emphasis on cleanliness. Another was its low fuel prices, with which it lured customers.

COMPANY PERSPECTIVES

Flying J is a major national firm engaged in all facets of hospitality and other highway-related products and services, in addition to the exploration, production, refining, distribution, and marketing of petroleum products. We are a "results oriented" and "people driven" company. We are committed to: Providing premium hospitality and quality products, at a fair and competitive price, while continuing to enhance what we have to offer our guests/customers in order to help improve their position; Providing professional and personal growth opportunities to our people, while enhancing the effectiveness, competitiveness, and value of our properties and maintaining a leadership role in those industries in which we participate; Building our resource base and economic strength through skillful and profitable application of our human, financial, and technological resources; Serving and improving those communities and the society of which we are a part.

ADDING REFINERY OPERATIONS

In 1980 Flying J took a step to ensure its ability to keep its fuel prices low. The company moved into integrated operations, buying refinery and gas processing assets from Inter-City Gas Ltd., based in Canada. The $31 million purchase gave Flying J refineries and gas processing plants in Cut Bank, Montana, and Williston, North Dakota, as well as a number of retail gasoline and propane outlets in Montana, North Dakota, Oregon, and Washington. The sale also gave Flying J its own exploration operation, based in Williston. The company's refinery operations concentrated on blending, upgrading, and distributing petroleum fuels, rather than refining crude oil. The following year, the company was awarded a $4.9 million contract from the Defense Logistics Agency for gasoline and other petroleum products. However, the company's emphasis remained on its own chain of service stations and its drive toward vertical integration.

By the mid-1980s Flying J had expanded its operations through much of the Northwest. With 35 Flying J gasoline and truck stops and convenience stores, the company was achieving annual sales of some $240 million and a spot on *Forbes*'s list of the largest private companies in the United States. In 1986, Flying J made its next major move, more than tripling its annual sales with the $70 million purchase of the U.S. refining and retail operations from Canada's Husky Oil Ltd. The purchase included a 35,000 barrel-per-day refinery in Cheyenne, Wyoming; a pipeline stretching from Wyoming to Nebraska; and a refinery in Salt Lake City, Utah, with a capacity of 14,000 barrels per day, as well as a closed refinery, capable of 15,000 barrels per day, in Cody, Wyoming. The purchase also gave Flying J some 550 retail outlets and 40 gasoline stations and truck stops under the Husky brand name.

The acquisition made Flying J the largest independent oil company in the Northwest, and with it, Call set out to build Flying J into a national chain, starting with 50 Flying Js, including 15 former Husky stations to be converted to the Flying J concept. Although the company continued to lease its Husky stores to existing dealers, the Husky name would be phased out through the rest of the decade, allowing Husky Oil Ltd. to retain exclusive control of its brand. Call envisioned a chain of at least 300 Flying Js; once again turning to the fast-food industry, Call's original plan was to build a franchise concept for the truck stop industry. The Flying J franchise network proved to be short-lived, however. By the early 1990s the company had moved to maintain full ownership of the Flying J chain.

EXPANDING ON THE TRAVEL PLAZA CONCEPT

The company's core concept of the travel plaza was itself undergoing an expansion with a "next generation" of expanded food, lodging, and convenience amenities. Aiding the company was a rising trend in the trucking industry itself, as more and more husband-and-wife driving teams began to take to the road. While some in the industry regretted the slow passing of the traditional image of the rough-hewn truck stop, Flying J's travel plaza concept, with amenities including restaurants, lodging, barber shops and hairdressers, laundry facilities and showers, television lounges, arcade game rooms, and other comforts for the truck driver, coupled with its insistence on cleanliness, quality, consistency, and low fuel prices, proved attractive not only to the trucking industry, but to the automobile and recreational vehicle traveler as well.

By 1993 Flying J was operating 63 travel plazas and, coupled with its refinery operations, was generating between $800 and $900 million per year. By then, Call had stepped down from the day-to-day running of the company. He remained chairman of the company, and his family continued to hold a majority of the private company's shares. Call, together with his son and

KEY DATES

1968: Jay Call, owner of four gasoline stations, incorporates the Flying J company.
1979: First Flying J "travel plaza" opens in West Haven, Utah.
1980: Company begins vertical integration by acquiring refinery, gas processing, and oil exploration assets.
1986: Company acquires refining and retail assets in a $70 million deal with Husky Oil Ltd., tripling its size.
1995: Company opens its first Country Market Restaurant; turns over motel management to Crystal Inn, owned by Jay Call's daughter Crystal.
2003: Flying J founder Jay Call dies in a plane crash.
2008: Flying J makes top 20 on *Forbes* magazine's list of largest private companies; Flying J files for Chapter 11 protection.
2009: Crystal Call Maggelet, already chairman of the board, becomes president and CEO of Flying J.
2010: Flying J emerges from Chapter 11; Pilot Travel Centers buys Flying J travel center network; company is renamed FJ Management.

daughter, was developing another side business, Call's Investment, to build a new chain of all-suites hotels.

THE CRYSTAL INN AND COUNTRY MARKET RESTAURANT AND BUFFET

Dubbed the Crystal Inn after Call's daughter, the hotels would feature indoor pools, Jacuzzi tubs, and workout areas, as well as a kitchen to serve breakfast. The first Crystal Inn opened in Salt Lake City. By 1995 Call had stepped aside from that project as well, allowing daughter Crystal Call Maggelet and her husband to operate and expand the new hotel chain, closely linked with the family's Flying J chain.

Meanwhile, Flying J, now under the leadership of J. Phillip Adams, stepped up its expansion. By 1995 the company was operating nearly 90 travel centers, each up to 20,000 square feet, while continuing to upgrade its amenities offerings. In that year, the company introduced a new restaurant concept to its travel centers, opening the family-style Country Market Restaurant and Buffet, offering 24-hour, buffet-style service with seating for up to 150 people. The company turned over management of its Flying J motels to Crystal Inn, while making plans to add the all-suites hotel concept to some of its sites as well. With the state-of-the-art Flying Js costing up to $10 million to build, Flying J, which had been serving the freeway and interstate market, began developing a smaller-scale concept for the secondary roadways. The company also expanded its oil well operations with the acquisition of Cenex Inc.'s oil and gas production operations. The acquisition more than doubled Flying J's production to 6,000 barrels per day.

ENTERING THE CREDIT BUSINESS

By 1996 the chain had grown to 96 Flying Js, with the company announcing plans to add 15 to 20 travel centers per year toward the end of the century. With sales topping $1.3 billion in 1995, Flying J had climbed to number 152 on *Forbes*'s list of the largest private companies in the United States. The company, which had begun marketing to national trucking fleets in the early 1990s, was also getting into the credit business through the Transportation Clearing House, promoting its own TCH fuel transaction card. This initiative led to a conflict with Comdata, one of the leading credit transaction processors for the trucking industry. When Comdata and Flying J began negotiating to renew their contract in 1996, Comdata pressured Flying J to stop promoting its own card. Flying J refused, filing an antitrust suit and announcing that its travel centers would no longer accept Comdata's Comcheck card.

The break was complete when Comdata announced it would refuse to process transactions made at Flying J travel centers. Despite the inconvenience and negative publicity, the spat did not appear to threaten either company's business position. The two firms settled out of court in 2001, and Comdata agreed to accept transactions made with the TCH card. (Flying J announced it would accept Comdata methods of payment at its travel centers in June 2010, one month before relinquishing the centers to Pilot.)

BANKRUPTCY

The company's fortunes began to change in March 2003, when a small plane being piloted by Jay Call crashed in Idaho, killing the company's founder along with Richard "Buzz" Germer, retired head of Flying J's subsidiary, Big West Oil. Call's two children, Crystal Call Maggelet and Thad Call, began to take a more active role in the company's affairs, with Maggelet later becoming board chairwoman.

The company's next moves set the stage for its troubles. In 2005 Flying J's Big West Oil bought a closed refinery in Bakersfield, California, from Shell Oil for a reported price of $130 million. The unit, capable of processing crude oil at a rate of 70,000 barrels per day, needed numerous repairs and upgrades to meet state regulations. In 2006 Flying J acquired Longhorn Pipeline Holdings, owners of a 700-mile Texas pipeline from the Gulf Coast to El Paso to serve the growing southwest region. The pipeline was also in need of modifications before it could play the role the company anticipated. In Bakersfield local officials held up approval of the company's environmental mitigation plans until October 2008.

In both cases, the delays and added expenses put a drain on Flying J's finances. The company was still raking in substantial income from its truck stops and other assets and would probably have been able to ride out these setbacks in ordinary times, but times were not ordinary in the fall of 2008. The onset of a major financial crisis brought the credit market to a near standstill. To make matters worse, oil prices were plummeting from the summer's record highs of nearly $150 per barrel, creating a serious downturn for the industry. This was a double whammy that put Flying J into an immediate cash-flow predicament. The board of directors had no time to try to change course. Right before Christmas, Flying J and its two subsidiaries, Big West of California and Longhorn Pipeline, filed for Chapter 11 bankruptcy protection in a Delaware court.

RESTRUCTURING

Company officials expressed optimism that Flying J could survive a bankruptcy reorganization given its strong market position, but the board had lost its confidence in longtime CEO Phil Adams. Adams, it seemed, had violated the cardinal rule of executive behavior: in pursuing greater revenue, he had paid insufficient attention to the bottom line. "Although Flying J did fine" for years, Maggelet told Paul Beebe of the *Salt Lake Tribune* (August 10, 2009), "I think that you could argue, given the revenue growth that we had, that our profitability really didn't match our revenue growth." Adams departed the company in January 2009 and Maggelet assumed the titles of president and CEO.

In the hole for $1.4 billion, Flying J set about selling off assets to pay off its creditors under the guidance of the bankruptcy court. The Longhorn pipeline went for $340 million in June 2009; six months later, El Paso Corp. paid $103.5 million for Longhorn's oil and gas assets. Alon USA Energy, Inc., acquired the Bakersfield refinery in June 2010 for the bargain price of $40 million. However, these pieces were insufficient to get Flying J out of hock; it needed to put up its prized possession, its truck stops. It found a willing buyer in its close competitor, Pilot Travel Centers.

PILOT FLYING J

The transaction (not a merger per se) was concluded on July 1, 2010. The Federal Trade Commission expressed reservations about the deal due to its antitrust implications but signed off after Pilot agreed to divest itself of 26 travel centers to Love's Travel Stops and Country Stores. Pilot, renamed Pilot Flying J, now became the clear leader in interstate travel centers, possessing more than 550 units in 43 states and six Canadian provinces. The new company said it would maintain existing operations at Flying J travel centers and not rename them. "We are now one great company, two great brands," said Pilot's president and CEO James A. "Jimmy" Haslam III, as reported by Brian Straight in *Fleet Owner* on July 1, 2010. The new company ranked among America's top 10 private companies, expecting annual revenues between $20 billion and $30 billion.

Flying J, renamed FJ Management, became a minority shareholder in Pilot Flying J. Six days after the Pilot deal was concluded, the new company announced the bankruptcy court's approval of its restructuring plan. All Flying J's creditors would be paid in full with interest. Roughly 2,500 jobs would be lost, but the company managed to retain an equity stake in its main business, 50 percent of the TCH fuel card system, and full control of two side businesses: the oil refinery at North Salt Lake, and the small Transportation Alliance Bank, "a financial institution that understands the trucking industry," as described in the company's news release dated July 7, 2010. Industry observers expressed pleasant surprise at the unusual outcome, for rarely does a large company emerge alive from a bankruptcy proceeding. Although the company's future was impossible to foretell, Maggelet expressed optimism, telling Paul Beebe of the *Salt Lake Tribune* on August 1, 2010, that FJ Management was "not going to be a small company."

M. L. Cohen
Updated, Roger K. Smith

PRINCIPAL SUBSIDIARIES

Big West Oil Co.; Transportation Alliance Bank; Transportation Clearing House; Flying J Communications; Flying J Transportation.

PRINCIPAL COMPETITORS

TravelCenters of America; Love's Travel Stops & Country Stores.

FURTHER READING

Beebe, Paul. "Flying J's Bankruptcy a Tale of Rapid Growth without Corresponding Profit." *Salt Lake Tribune*, August 10, 2009.

———. "Successful Flying J Bankruptcy a Throwback to Different Time." *Salt Lake Tribune*, August 1, 2010.

Carey, Bill. "Comdata Ends Relationship with Flying J Truck Stops." *Nashville Tennessean*, June 3, 1996, 1E.

"Husky Acquisition Makes Flying J Biggest Independent in Mountain West." *National Petroleum News*, February 1986, 35.

Keahey, John. "Inn Idea Is Crystal Clear." *Salt Lake Tribune*, December 24, 1995.

Mansfield, Duncan. "Pilot to Acquire Flying J's 250 Travel Centers." Associated Press, July 15, 2009.

Pomerleau, Charlie. "Merger Official Today for Two Companies." *Ogden (Utah) Standard-Examiner*, July 1, 2010.

Smith, Gordon. "Space-Age Truck Stop Is Roadside Oasis." *San Diego Union-Tribune*, July 21, 1994.

Straight, Brian. "Pilot, Flying J Complete Merger." *Fleet Owner*, July 1, 2010.

Timmons, Tony. "Truck Stops Convert to 'Travel Plazas.'" *Las Vegas Business Press*, February 10, 1997, 3.

Foxconn Technology Co., Ltd.

No. 3-2 Chung-Shan Road
Tucheng City, Taipei County 236
Republic of China (Taiwan)
Telephone: (+886 2) 2268-0970
Fax: (+886 2) 2268-7176
Web site: http://www.foxconn.com

Public Company
Founded: 1990 as Q Run Technology Corporation
Incorporated: 1990 as Q Run Technology Corporation
Employees: 51,525
Sales: TWD 155.09 billion ($4.82 billion) (2009)
Stock Exchanges: TSEC
Ticker Symbol: 2354 (Taiwan)
NAICS: 334113 Computer Terminal Manufacturing; 333313 Office Machinery Manufacturing; 334111 Electronic Computer Manufacturing; 334119 Other Computer Peripheral Equipment Manufacturing; 334412 Bare Printed Circuit Board Manufacturing

■ ■ ■

The Taiwan-based Foxconn Technology Co., Ltd., manufactures a variety of computer, consumer-electronics, and communication products. The company produces magnesium and aluminum alloy structures and casings, heat sinks, server and computer cooling modules, and computer monitors. Foxconn Technology's products are used in the manufacture of mobile phones, notebook and desktop computers, projectors, digital cameras, electronic books, personal game consoles, and other items. The company has facilities in both Taiwan and China, as well as North Vietnam, Mexico, Slovakia, and Russia, and distributes its products in the Americas, Asia, and Europe. Hon Hai Precision Industry Co. is the major shareholder of Foxconn Technology, which is part of the Hon Hai group of companies, the world's largest manufacturer of consumer electronics, operating under the trade name of Foxconn.

COMPANY ORIGINS AND EARLY PRODUCTS

Q Run Technology Corporation, a forerunner of Foxconn Technology, was established in Tucheng City, Taiwan (Republic of China), in 1990. The company was launched to build computer terminals and related products. In 1993 Q Run garnered its first major contract, a commission from the U.S. firm NCD to develop 15-inch black-and-white high-resolution computer terminals. The following year, the company acquired factory facilities in Tucheng City.

Q Run became a public Taiwan company in 1994. In 1995 the company developed its MONIPUTER, a multimedia computer with rotating mount that featured a fax, modem, telephone and answering machine, and video-decompression capability. The following year Q Run completed its initial public offering on the Taiwan Stock Exchange (TSEC).

A NEW OWNER AND NEW PRODUCTS

In 1999 Q Run established a research and development department for video-related products and desktop

COMPANY PERSPECTIVES

Foxconn Technology is positioned as a professional original design manufacturer whose products and expertise include system assembly of 3C (computing, communication, and consumer-electronics) products, mechanical design, processing, and sales. It provides global customers with complete design capacity, fast volume manufacturing capability, and efficient customer service.

computers. That same year the company signed a $300 million supply deal with Compaq Computer Corporation, which often outsourced its computer-manufacturing business to Taiwan, to build about a million desktop computers. About the same time that Q Run secured the Compaq contract, Hon Hai Precision Industry Co., the world's 11th-largest computer connector manufacturer, with $1 billion in annual revenues, acquired Q Run. Hon Hai was looking to diversify, and it viewed Q Run as a midsize personal computer (PC) maker with money-making potential.

Q Run's research and development (R&D) department opened the new century with the development of new products, including a video board, an analog board, and a down converter board. Q Run in 2000 also began manufacturing the printed circuit board assembly (PBSA) for iMac computers. In 2002 Q Run, which had focused its business on computer manufacturing, began losing PC-assembly business after Compaq and Hewlett-Packard (HP) merged and took assembly contracts elsewhere. Hon Hai helped Q Run turn to another business, however, by lining up sizable orders from Japan's Nintendo to build GameCube consoles. In 2003 Q Run also began production of 15-, 17-, and 19-inch LCD TVs and high-resolution 26- and 32-inch models. In addition the company initiated plans to produce mechanical notebook computer components.

In 2003 Q Run reached a deal to purchase magnesium alloy parts and production equipment from Foxconn Advanced Technology Inc., another Hon Hai subsidiary. Q Run's revenues for the year approached TWD 24 billion, producing earnings of about TWD 500 million. With Q Run on the rise, Hon Hai in 2004 merged Q Run and another of its subsidiaries, Foxconn Precision Components Co., a cooler-module maker for electronics. The merged firm adopted the name Foxconn Technology Co., Ltd., and became part of the Hon Hai Group of companies that had grown into the world's leading manufacturing services provider for computer, communication, and consumer-electronics industries.

Hon Hai adopted the trade name Foxconn, and as it increasingly diversified and added to the number of its electronics-producing subsidiaries, its companies likewise used the Foxconn name. The Foxconn firms did business with each other and invested in each other, and in 2005 Foxconn Technology made indirect investments in several companies, some of which were Foxconn businesses, and most of which were engaged in the manufacture of computer components, motherboards, plugs, sockets, and carrier-current system products made in China. Foxconn Technology, like its parent, also invested in Innolux Display Corporation, a producer of thin film transistor–liquid crystal display (TFT-LCD) panel modules and LCD monitors, mainly used for desktop monitors, laptops, and mobile phones.

COMPANY WORKING CONDITIONS COME UNDER SCRUTINY

Working conditions at several Hon Hai companies first came under scrutiny in 2006 when the *Daily Mail* of London published a report on working conditions at Foxconn factories in China. This report put a spotlight on long hours, low pay, and what some claimed were harsh working conditions endured by workers. *Mail* photographers took unauthorized pictures, and reporters talked to employees who spoke on the condition of anonymity. The *Mail* reported that some employees worked 15 hours a day, for a monthly salary of £27, and lived in cramped company dormitories, where it was difficult to sleep.

The *Mail* article prompted Foxconn customer Apple Inc. to scrutinize its supplier. Apple sent a team of investigators to China. After interviewing 100 Foxconn employees, the investigators concluded that the working hours for employees often exceeded Apple's Supplier Code of Conduct, which limited the work week to 60 hours and required that employees receive at least one day off a week. Apple also reported that, in general, the company was in compliance with its code, that Apple had initiated a training program for Foxconn, and that Foxconn officials were taking measures to address areas where the company was in violation. *China Business News* of Shanghai, however, followed the *Mail* story with one of its own on employees who had fainted from working long hours.

Hon Hai responded by claiming defamation and filing a lawsuit against two *China Business News* staffers and requesting that their assets be frozen. Reporters

KEY DATES

1990: The company is established as Q Run Technology Corporation.
1999: Hon Hai Precision Industry Co. acquires the company.
2004: Q Run Technology Corporation and Foxconn Precision Components Co., both Hon Hai subsidiaries, merge into the newly formed Foxconn Technology Co., Ltd.
2010: During a span of 5 months, 10 worker suicides occur; the company announces it will no longer operate dormitories for its workers.

without Borders (RWB), an international journalistic watchdog, sent an open letter to Apple CEO Steve Jobs, published on the RWB Web site, urging the Apple chief executive to convince Foxconn officials to drop the lawsuit, which the company eventually did.

INVESTMENTS IN ASIAN BUSINESSES

In 2006, in an effort to strengthen its asset holdings in China, Foxconn Technology invested in Hongfujin Precision Industry Co., a computer components producer based in Shanxi Province, People's Republic of China. The following year Foxconn Technology invested more than $168 million in precision components and aluminum businesses.

In 2007 Li Hanming succeeded Guo Taicheng as chairman, and the company acquired a 9 percent stake in Advanced Optoelectronic Technology Inc., a Taiwanese company specializing in light-emitting diodes (LEDs), laser diodes, and chip LEDs. That same year the company announced plans to develop a $1 billion industrial park in North Vietnam. For 2007 the company recorded revenues of nearly TWD 135 billion, an increase of more than 70 percent from the previous year, and generated earnings of TWD 9.35 billion.

GLOBAL DIVERSIFICATION, IPHONES, AND JOINT VENTURES

In 2008 Foxconn Technology acquired the PC-manufacturing assets of Sanmina-SCI, a California-based global electronics manufacturing services provider, for about $85 million. That same year the company began construction of a $50 million, 5,000-employee manufacturing facility in St. Petersburg, Russia. The factory was a joint development with Hewlett-Packard, whose laptops and desktop computers were to be produced there.

Foxconn companies in 2008 were selected to be major component and assembly providers of the new Apple 3G iPhone. Foxconn Precision Components, a subsidiary of Foxconn Technology, was selected to produce phone cases, while Foxconn Electronics, another Hon Hai subsidiary, was chosen to do assembly work. By the end of 2008, Foxconn Technology's revenues had risen to nearly TWD 160 billion, although net income slipped to TWD 6.2 billion that year.

In 2009 Foxconn Technology expanded through acquisitions. The company's subsidiary Q-Run Holdings bought a 24 percent minority stake in UER Holdings Corporation, a computer-monitor manufacturer and wholesaler. In a move that could pay financial dividends for years to come, Foxconn Technology signed a joint-venture agreement with METRO AG, one of the world's largest retailers, and METRO's sales division with the leading chain of consumer electronics stores in Europe, Media Markt. Foxconn acquired a 25 percent stake in the venture, which was designed to bring hundreds of large-format Media Markt stores to China beginning in late 2010.

In mid-2009 Foxconn Technology and Hewlett-Packard jointly invested $3 billion to develop laptop-manufacturing facilities in Chongqing, China. The venture was projected to produce 20 million laptops a year for export. The companies were attracted to Chongqing because of its free-trade zone and relatively inexpensive land and labor costs. For 2009, Foxconn Technology's earnings climbed to TWD 18.57 billion on revenues of TWD 155.09 billion.

SUICIDES IN 2009 AND 2010

In July 2009 a Foxconn worker leaped to his death from a high-rise window after he lost a secret prototype iPhone. The worker, who was responsible for shipping iPhone prototypes to Apple, feared repercussions from his superiors and the reaction from Apple after the phone went missing, according to sources quoted in the *Daily Mail.* The suicide once again placed the Foxconn name in the news and raised the issue of working conditions at Foxconn factories.

Beginning in 2010 the Foxconn name became synonymous with a spate of suicides, with a total of 10 employees killing themselves in less than 5 months by leaping from Foxconn dormitory and factory windows. The suicides all involved relatively new hires between the ages of 18 and 24 and occurred on two Foxconn campuses in Shenzhen, where about half of Hon Hai's 800,000 workers in China were employed making products for Apple, Dell, and Hewlett-Packard. The deaths raised continuing questions about working conditions not only at Foxconn plants but in China in general. While the suicide rate for Foxconn workers was not abnormally high compared to China's overall high rate for a country, the fact that the suicides all occurred within a limited locale was unusual. Moreover, suicides had never occurred in such numbers at any Foxconn facility.

In late May 2010, after the ninth Foxconn employee suicide that year, the normally reclusive Gou called a press conference. In an effort to minimize growing global criticism of his company, Gou led a media tour of the Longhua facility in Shenzhen where the suicides had occurred to prove to the press that his factory was not, as some reports had claimed, a sweatshop. Media reports, however, pointed out that the factory was without air conditioning and that summer temperatures in the area reached 35°C (95°F) and humidity could be as high as 90 percent. Workers also complained of cramped conditions in dormitories that were sometimes infested with ants and cockroaches. Nonetheless, the Longhua factory town had its own hospital, Olympic-sized swimming pool, company cafeteria, and bookstore, among other amenities. Unfortunately, just one day after Gou's press conference, a 10th worker committed suicide. This time the local police and government said they were joining with the company to consider how to improve the living environment of the employees.

RESPONSES TO SUICIDE CRISIS OF 2010

After the suicides sparked three major Foxconn customers, namely, Apple, Hewlett-Packard, and Dell, to announce that they intended to look into the company's working conditions, Hon Hai and Foxconn Technology acted quickly to defuse the crisis. In June 2010 Foxconn Technology replaced Li Hanming as chairman with Lin Donglian. To demonstrate to both its workers and the world that Hon Hai was serious about safeguarding its workers, the parent company took several steps to prevent future suicides. The company installed iron bars in front of dormitory and factory windows to prevent workers from jumping from these locations, constructed 10-foot-high wire fences on rooftops, and placed large nets at the base of facilities. (The Chinese words the company used for these nets, *ai xin wang*, literally meant "nets of a loving heart.") The company also hired 100 counselors to watch and talk with workers, established a suicide hotline, and hired monks to exorcise evil spirits from the facilities.

The world press in its coverage of the suicides made much of the cramped conditions of the Longhua factory town dormitories and the relatively low wages, by Western standards, that Foxconn factory workers received. Hon Hai addressed both, announcing in June 2010 that the longtime "factory town" model was going to be abandoned in order to better separate, for employees, their working and living environments. In June 2010 Hon Hai began outsourcing Longhua housing arrangements to two Chinese real estate firms that would handle dormitory management for its 420,000 employees, or half of its total workforce, located in Shenzhen. The hope was that the real estate management firms could better help integrate workers into the local community and thereby help relieve pressures of factory work. Employees who previously lived free in company dormitories were to be given a housing stipend.

PAY RAISES

Then in a move that changed the wage landscape for factory workers in China during a period of just a few weeks in June 2010, employees at the Longhua factory town were given two pay raises that essentially doubled income for most workers to about $300 month. Existing employees were required to pass a three-month evaluation to receive the raise, while new employees were required to pass a three-month probation period.

Some industry analysts calculated that, if all Foxconn facilities adopted the same salary schedule, Hon Hai's annual profits would drop by more than 30 percent. Still other analysts noted that the pay increases were not likely to affect consumer costs, since the company had been gradually spreading its workforce around the globe. During mid-2010 several initiatives were put in play to more quickly relocate workers and production facilities away from Shanghai and Hon Hai's factory town and into northern and central China, where the cost of living and doing business and the government-mandated minimum wage were lower.

After doubling the pay for much of the Longhua workforce at the factory in Shenzhen, Hon Hai, to offset the rising cost of labor, began moving about three-quarters of its workforce from Shenzhen to the Langfang/Tiajin area in northeast China near Beijing. The monthly minimum wage for workers in Tianjin was $135, substantially less than workers receiving two 2010 raises in Shenzhen were paid. The move of about 300,000 employees was expected to be completed by October 2010.

THE FUTURE FOR FOXCONN TECHNOLOGY

Following the series of suicides, Foxconn Technology further diversified its manufacturing locations and its business activities. In June 2010 the company purchased LCD TV production plants in Slovakia and Mexico from Sony Corporation. That same month, Foxconn Technology reached an agreement with Hewlett-Packard to invest $60 million in a joint venture in Turkey to develop a 200-employee facility to produce HP desktop computers beginning early the next decade. Foxconn Technology in July 2010 announced plans to develop a new central China production facility in Chengdu, which could triple the company's workforce with workers who were hired at a starting monthly salary of about $235.

In 2010 Foxconn Technology denied media rumors that Terry Gou planned to liquidate the business and operate it as a holding company. The rumors were based on the assumption that such liquidations preceded the retirement of a company chairman or owner and the fact that Gou had previously announced he planned to retire by 2008. In 2010, however, Gou said that he would continue to lead Hon Hai companies for another full decade.

CHINA'S CHANGING LABOR MARKET

China was increasingly the scene of labor unrest during the summer of 2010, fueled in part by a growing shortage of workers and wage concerns. Industry analysts and experts on the Chinese economy held varying views on the country's future as a manufacturing center. Most agreed, however, that forces had combined to bring to an end an era of an overabundant low-cost labor force. Tao Dong, Credit Suisse's chief Asian economist, wrote in the *People's Daily* (June 30, 2010) that the suicides at Foxconn "signaled the end of an era on the mainland. Its role as the world's factory and the export-driven model of economic growth are being challenged by rising wages and a labor shortage in coastal areas."

Dong claimed that the new generation of migrant workers had higher expectations than its parents about living and working conditions and was more inclined to object to poor conditions. Moreover, a growing labor shortage meant that companies would need to listen to their workers. Dong predicted migrant worker wages would rise by as much as 30 percent in the first half of the decade and that policy makers and company leaders would pay greater attention to protecting worker dignity and improving employee living conditions. While other analysts did not anticipate such a rapid change in employee salaries, most industry insiders agreed that foreign companies were unlikely to abandon China because of the varied benefits of its manufacturing operations, including production efficiency, business logistics, and tax policies.

Several industry analysts in 2010 suggested that while salary increases would raise Foxconn Technology's operating expenses and lower its earnings, in the long term, the company should be more concerned about its ongoing reputation among its customers. The company had taken steps to offset wage hikes by shipping some production inland. Hon Hai was also expected to pass along some of its wage-related expenses to its customers. How its customers viewed the Foxconn brand after the 2010 tragedies, and whether the changes Hon Hai made in mid-2010 would be taken as positive over the long-term, remained to be seen. Entering the decade of the 2010s, Hon Hai companies together produced more than half of desktop PCs worldwide, and, as a brand, Foxconn traditionally had been viewed as one of the better, more reliable manufacturing partners, with its high-volume production capacity and low manufacturing costs.

DIVERSIFICATION

How the changing labor market in China impacted Foxconn Technology and its parent, Hon Hai, remained uncertain, although a loss of the parent company's major clients seemed unlikely, at least in the short term. Foxconn Technology had already begun global diversification of its manufacturing, with operations in Asia, eastern Europe, and Mexico. It had also followed moves by the parent company to take manufacturing away from its traditional locale of Shanghai and move inland.

As one of the smaller Hon Hai firms, behind Foxconn Electronics and Foxconn International Holdings, Foxconn Technology had carved its own niche. While the company shared customers with its parent, Foxconn Technology also had developed its own partnerships that were geared toward long-term business relationships. Moreover, Foxconn Technology had done so at a time when publicity regarding suicides was still fresh in the news, suggesting that the company had perhaps already weathered one major storm. How rising wages and a shrinking workforce impacted the company at time when it was growing was still uncertain.

Roger Rouland

PRINCIPAL SUBSIDIARIES

Foxconn Precision Components Holding Co., Ltd.; Q-Run Holdings Ltd.; Q-Run Technology LLC; Hua-Zhun Investment Co., Ltd.

PRINCIPAL COMPETITORS

Motorola, Inc.; Nokia Corporation; Sony Ericsson Mobile Communications AB.

FURTHER READING

Barboza, David. "A Chinese Factory Outsources Worker Dorms." *New York Times*, June 26, 2010, B1.

Dean, Jason. "The Forbidden City of Terry Gou." *Wall Street Journal*, August 11, 2007.

"Foxconn Factories Headed Inland, Spokesman Confirms." *People's Daily*, July 2, 2010.

"Foxconn Raise May Lead to Profit Plunge." *People's Daily*, June 8, 2010.

Hille, Kathrin, and Robin Kwong. "Chief Acts as Death Toll Rises at Foxconn." *Financial Times*, May 25, 2010.

Hull, Liz, and Lee Sorrell. "The Image Microsoft Doesn't Want You to See: Too Tired to Stay Awake, the Chinese Workers Earning Just 34p an Hour." *Sunday Mail* (London), April 18, 2010.

Kwong, Robin. "Foxconn to Scrap 'Factory Town' Model." *Financial Times*, June 8, 2010.

LaPedus, Mark. "Foxconn Saga: What Analysts Are Saying." *Electronic Engineering Times*, June 15, 2010.

Whitney, Lance. "Foxconn Raising Factory Salaries Again." CNET, June 7, 2010. Accessed October 22, 2010. http://news.cnet.com/8301-13579_3-20006945-37.html.

Wong, Stephanie, John Liu, and Tim Culpan. "Why Apple and Others Are Nervous about Foxconn." *BusinessWeek*, June 7, 2010.

French Connection Group PLC

Centro 1, 39 Camden Street
London, NW1 0DX
United Kingdom
Telephone: (+44 20) 7036 7200
Fax: (+44 20) 7036 7201
Web site: http://www.frenchconnection.com

Public Company
Founded: 1969 as Stephen Marks (London) Limited
Incorporated: 1972 as French Connection Group PLC
Employees: 3,173
Sales: £249.20 million ($373.80 million) (2010)
Stock Exchanges: London
Ticker Symbol: FCCN
NAICS: 424330 Women's, Children's, and Infants' Clothing and Accessories Merchant Wholesalers; 424320 Men's and Boys' Clothing and Furnishings Merchant Wholesalers.

■ ■ ■

French Connection Group PLC is a leading designer, retailer, and wholesaler of its own in-house clothing and accessories. The company's unique and innovative line includes men's, women's, and children's fashions; men's and women's toiletries; sunglasses and eyewear; watches; and footwear. The company operates under three principal brands: "French Connection," which accounts for approximately 80 percent of the company's sales; "TOAST," a home shopping–based women's fashion and homeware range; and "Great Plains," a fashion basics range. Led by its founder, Stephen Marks, French Connection made waves, and profits, with its now-discontinued controversial advertising campaigns built on its French Connection U.K. acronym. The French Connection's design teams are located in London, England, while manufacturing facilities are based in Europe and Asia. The company operates via branded retail stores, department stores, and multibrand fashion stores in over 50 countries, with more than 1,000 outlets worldwide.

FROM HAIRDRESSER'S SON TO HOTPANTS KING

Growing up in the Harrow area of north London, Stephen Marks helped his father in his hairdresser's shop. He left school at age 16. Marks's initial interest was in playing tennis, and in 1964, at age 18, he won the junior's title at Wimbledon. Tennis then was still an amateur sport, however, and Marks looked for ways to earn a living. Having seen how hard his father worked, Marks sought a different career direction. As Marks told Beverley D'Silva of the *Independent* (August 8, 1998), "My father used to leave home at 6:30 a.m. and get back at 9 p.m., 11 p.m. on Saturdays, earning enough to give us a comfortable life, but not that comfortable."

Marks went to work for a clothing manufacturer run by a family friend. As Marks told Julia Finch of the *Guardian* (March 31, 2001), "They gave me the most wonderful training, although I didn't realize it at the time, learning about everything from cloth buying to designing." Toward the end of the 1960s, Marks left the coat manufacturer for clothing designer and manufacturer Louis Feraud. Marks was behind the suc-

> ## COMPANY PERSPECTIVES
>
> French Connection is a destination brand on the British High Street. Born of a desire to be original, distinctive, and accessible, French Connection has given personality to its brand through stand-out campaigns and original designs. Sexy, stylish, and oozing attitude, French Connection celebrates personal style and individuality.

cessful launch of the company's Miss Feraud label. That success led Feraud's management to offer Marks a position as a director of the company. In the same *Guardian* article, Marks described the appointment: "I asked if that meant I got a share of the company and they said, 'No, you just get called a director.' That made me very depressed, because I wanted to get on in life. I didn't care what I was called."

A friend came to the aid of Marks, suggesting that he go into business for himself and promising him financial backing. In 1969 Marks struck out on his own, establishing Stephen Marks London Limited with just £17,000. The clothing was designed by Marks, who was joined by a pattern cutter and an accountant. Marks described his own role in the new company to the *Independent* on April 4, 1999, as that of "a salesman who 'had a sense of what was right and what was wrong,' who used to 'botch a collection together and sell it.'" Marks quickly displayed a flair for fashion, or at least a commercially successful fashion trend. On a trip to Paris, he discovered the newest French fashion phenomenon, hotpants. "I came back to London, had some run up, and showed them to a buyer at Miss Selfridge," Marks told the *Guardian*. "She took 36 pairs and sold them all in a day. She came back for 2,000 pairs, and I became the Hotpants King." By the end of its first year, the company had posted sales of £180,000.

THE FRENCH CONNECTION LABEL

Marks launched his own label, designing a line of suits and coats, although he was to become especially known for his youth-oriented fashions. By 1972 Marks's designs were generating £700,000 in revenues. That year Marks traveled to Hong Kong. "Once I saw Hong Kong I realized the potential of the Far East," Marks told the *Guardian* (March 31, 2001). "It was like a shining light in terms of price and quality. And so French Connection was born."

Marks then entered the retail arena, opening a furniture and clothing shop called Cane, then a second store, also in London, called Friends. The French Connection brand name came in the 1970s as Marks contracted to sell his designs through the Top Shop retail chain. Joining Marks was a freelance designer, Nicole Farhi, who became his companion and mother of his first child, and later the company's chief designer. "She was always criticizing my designs and saying she could do better. So in the end I said 'bloody get on with it then,' and she did," explained Marks in the *Guardian.* Farhi not only created the youth-oriented designs for the French Connection label, she also began to produce designs under her own name for an older, wealthier women's market.

French Connection soon became the company's retail store brand, as Marks began to open new stores in London and then throughout the United Kingdom. The Nicole Farhi brand was also transformed into its own retail format, however, French Connection remained the company's flagship brand. In 1984 the company turned toward the United States, partnering with American Michael Axelrod in a 50-50 joint venture Best of All Clothes (BOAC). The joint venture's role leaned especially toward wholesale sales of the French Connection brand, rather than a retail expansion of the company's store format. Two years later, as French Connection prepared to boost its expansion in the United Kingdom, the company was listed on the London Stock Exchange.

CONTROVERSIAL SUCCESS FOR THE NEW CENTURY

At the end of the decade, however, French Connection appeared to be on the brink of disaster. The company had been caught up short by the beginning of a new recession that affected not only the United Kingdom, but also the company's growing activities in the United States. Despite holding two-thirds of the company's shares, Marks resigned as CEO in 1989, a position taken up by Michael Shen. By then too, Marks's personal relationship with Farhi had ended, although they remained business partners. Threatened with the loss of his majority share and in order to rescue the company he had founded from collapse, Marks lent French Connection more than £3.5 million.

Arguments with Shen led Marks to take back the CEO position in 1991. Marks set to work rebuilding the company, bringing it back into renewed profit growth by mid-decade. Marks's personal fortunes also received a boost when Hard Rock Café, in which he had been one of the original financial backers and retained the second-largest holding of shares, was sold to the

KEY DATES

1969: Stephen Marks launches Stephen Marks (London) Limited.
1972: Marks opens his first French Connection retail store.
1984: The company launches the French Connection label in the United States through a joint venture with Best of all Clothing (BOAC).
1986: The company is listed on the London Stock Exchange.
1997: The company launches the first FCUK (French Connection United Kingdom) campaign.
2001: The company acquires 100 percent of BOAC and opens the first store in Tokyo.
2008: French Connection acquires the remaining 50 percent stake in its Japanese business, French Connection Japan Inc.
2010: French Connection sells Nicole Farhi label.

Rank Organization, allowing Marks to pocket a hefty share of the £300 million purchase price. By 1996 his company's operations were also growing, with 30 retail stores in the United Kingdom (primarily under the French Connection name but also under the Nicole Farhi signage) and 11 stores in the United States. That year the company was also able to pay its first stock dividends since 1991. Yet the company's strongest expansion was still ahead.

ADVERTISING EFFORTS

Until the mid-1990s French Connection had operated more or less without an advertising budget. In 1997 the company turned to the then-independent Trevor Beattie (who was shortly to form his own TBWA advertising agency) for assistance. Beattie quickly spotted opportunity in the company's own name. French Connection's United Kingdom office had long been addressing its correspondence with its Hong Kong office using the acronyms from FCUK to FCHK. The FCUK acronym had also been used in the company's stores. Beattie took the acronym and turned it into a UK sensation.

After an initial series of deliberately provocative ads featuring models wearing "fcuk fashion," the company rolled out a new and more playful billboard and press campaign, playing on the garbled appeal of the FCUK logo with such taglines as "I you want" and "night all long." Complaints from among others the Church of England (for the company's "fcuk Christmas" campaign) brought the company under investigation from the United Kingdom's Advertising Standards Association (ASA).

The controversy surrounding French Connection's advertising campaign helped put the company into high gear. Backed by a string of strong clothing designs, French Connection's sales took off, reaching £83 million in 1997 and topping £117 million by 1999. The company quickly added new stores, boosting its total number of French Connection and Nicole Farhi stores to more than 100 by the end of the decade. The company's wholesale arm was also performing strongly, adding a number of foreign concessions in Australia, the Netherlands, the Scandinavian market, Singapore, Hong Kong, Saudi Arabia, and Dubai.

EXPANDING GLOBALLY

Until then French Connection had built a strong, albeit niche, position in the United States. The success of the FCUK campaign gave the company a new base from which to attack the U.S. market, traditionally resistant to foreign retailers. By the end of 2000, the company's expansion in the United States led it to forecast growing to as many as 300 retail stores in that country, with immediate plans to expand to nearly 60 stores there by 2004. To consolidate its growth in the United States, the company acquired the 50 percent of the BOAC joint venture it did not own in 2001. As reported in *Corporate Money* on February 21, 2001, Stephen Marks explained, "Acquiring 100 percent ownership of our U.S. business is an important milestone for our global brand strategy. We believe that complete ownership will enable us to maximize French Connection's potential as it enters the next stage of its development in the U.S."

Meanwhile, French Connection had for some time been eyeing the Japanese market. In 2001 the company opened its first store in Tokyo, teaming up with a local partner, D'Urban, Inc., for a three-year partnership. The company expected to use that country as a springboard for expansion throughout the Far East.

French Connection made no secret of its plans to develop into a globally operating retailer, raising its French Connection and Nicole Farhi brands to true international status. The company's advertisements continued to draw criticism and complaints, as well as customers. By the end of its 2001 fiscal year, the company's sales had topped £193 million. In early 2001 the company was delighted to discover that its latest campaign, dubbed "fcukinkybugger," had been banned from the British national television. The company immediately launched a Web site featuring the full-length advertisement. The hundreds of thousands of teenagers sporting the company's "FCUK ME" T-shirts gave Stephen Marks and French Connection a strong base on which to bet its future growth.

CONTROVERSIAL MARKETING STRATEGIES

Adding fuel to the ASA fire, in August 2001 the company launched a range of soft furnishings adorned with the "fcuk" and "no 1 fcuk" logos. Two months later, the company entered into a partnership with Matthew Clark Brands to launch FCUK-branded flavored alcoholic beverages (FAB). This raised the hackles of the advertising standards authorities, who were concerned that the product and its marketing strategy might promote underage drinking.

In time for the 2002 World Cup, the company emblazoned T-shirts with "fcuk football" which flew off the shelves. Although the North American business had declined 30 percent in the aftermath of the September 11, 2001, terrorist attacks in the United States, the United Kingdom and Europe reported a sales increase of 17 percent, helped in part by the new range of FAB drinks and improved customer outreach via the company's Web site and additional store openings.

Marks was forced to backpedal on the company's "kinkybugger" campaign in March 2002, admitting that it "was a mistake for the brand because it was not our core focus," according to Mark Kleinman of *Marketing* (March 21, 2002). The ASA deemed that the FCUK brand brought advertising into disrepute and ordered that French Connection submit all its non-broadcast ads for prescreening for the following two years. Undeterred, Marks maintained that the company's controversial advertising strategy would continue as the company embarked on a series of brand extensions, including women's toiletries, sports and health drinks, sportswear, books, and CDs.

SETBACKS

Despite the fact that sales in the North American division were almost half the previous year's, in March 2003 the company announced plans to double the number of units in this region from 25 to 50 over the following three years. In addition, French Connection suffered a blow in May 2003 when it was forced to withdraw FAB drinks from the market on the basis that the product's gimmicky packaging appealed to underage drinkers. Three months later, the company had its hand slapped again by the ASA for an e-mail condom ad it considered highly offensive that used the tagline "Practice safe sex go fcuk yourself."

To add to these setbacks, in September 2003, Cincinnati-based Federated Department Stores, Inc., withdrew all FCUK-branded items from its 400 stores across the United States. Citing that the line of FCUK clothes and fragrances were not in keeping with the image it wished to convey to its young adult market, the products were removed from several high-profile chains, including Macy's, Bloomingdale's, and Burdines. Following this, in response to more than 100,000 complaints received in reference to the FCUK fragrance advertising campaign, which carried the slogan "scent to bed," French Connection was forced to withdraw all its ads from several teen magazines.

In 2004 the company's focus was on international expansion, beginning with a 50-50 joint venture with Hong Kong fashion retailer IT for construction of a 3,000-square-foot store there, and plans for new units in China. The U.S. retail market was also showing some recovery that year, with the North American division reporting a 9.1 percent increase in sales. The company identified the United States as its key growth area in 2004 and planned a mobile marketing campaign to launch its new digital radio station. FCUK FM aired in shops, online, and through digital television and mobile phones, and had SMS and MMS messaging capabilities through its own branded shortcode, 8FCUK.

In July 2004, after an anonymous retailer was quoted in the trade magazine *Draper's Record* describing the FCUK campaign as "tired" and "tacky," the company's share price fell almost 9 percent in a single day. French Connection quickly launched a new campaign, replacing the logo with a series of suggestive phrases such as "Don't make us say it" and "Something beginning with F." In November 2004 the company also tested an unbranded store format called "191," beginning with an outlet in London's Notting Hill, with the French Connection and FCUK brands only visible on labels and products. Unfortunately, these measures were not enough to turn around the FCUK brand, and in March 2005 the French Connection reported its first loss in nine years.

MAKING CHANGES TO SURVIVE THE RECESSION

Sales continued to slip, and by July 2005 the company was looking at a 40 percent drop in profits. In October 2005 the FCUK logo was removed from all clothing and billboards, but the slump deepened, and French Connection was forced to run its end-of-year sale 10 days before Christmas. In February 2006 the company launched a £2 million advertising campaign with the theme of "fashion vs. style." The following month, the company revealed that it had experienced its most disastrous year, with profits more than halved. In an effort to regain its edgy image, the company produced an ad featuring two female kung fu fighters kissing, only to again fall foul of the ASA after it was inundated with complaints. In July 2006 French Connection parted company with both its marketing director Griffiths and Trevor Beattie, the advertising guru credited with devising the once-provocative FCUK ad campaign.

As the economic climate worsened, the company fell further into the red, and sales in menswear performed particularly poorly. By 2009 the company had started to make dramatic changes. It closed all French Connection businesses in Japan, shuttered many stores in Denmark and Sweden, reduced its advertising budget, and downsized, beginning with the elimination of 50 head office jobs.

In March 2010 French Connection made the startling announcement that it was selling the Nicole Farhi designer label to OpenGate Capital for £5 million ($7.5 million). In the United States 17 of its 23 stores were closed after reporting losses totaling £3.2 million ($5.2 million). In July 2010, in an effort to rebuild its image, French Connection unveiled a new brand, Pippa, a collection of contemporary workwear essentials, with the fall line launched exclusively by Bloomingdale's. According to the company Web site, French Connection had returned to a healthy net operating margin. The company planned to continue its steady growth organically and through retail joint ventures and development of licensees, particularly in Australia and Asia.

M. L. Cohen
Updated, Marie O'Sullivan

PRINCIPAL SUBSIDIARIES

French Connection Limited; French Connection Retail Limited; NF Restaurants Limited; French Connection (Hong Kong) Limited (British Virgin Islands, operates in Hong Kong); Stephen Marks (London) Limited; French Connection No. 2 Pour Hommes Sarl (France); PreTex Textilhandels GmbH (Germany); French Connection Holdings Inc. (USA); French Connection Group Inc (USA); NF Trading LLC (USA); Louisiana Connection Limited (USA); Roosevelt Connection Limited (USA); Soho Connection Limited (USA); Water Tower Connection Limited (USA); Westwood Connection Limited (USA); French Connection (Canada) Limited (75%); Toast (Mail Order) Limited (Wales, 75%); YMC Limited (75%); French Connection Japan Inc.; FCUK IT Company (Hong Kong, 50%); FCIT China Limited (Hong Kong, 50%).

PRINCIPAL COMPETITORS

H&M Hennés & Mauritz AB; Industria de Diseño Textil, SA; Marks and Spencer Group PLC.

FURTHER READING

Benady, David. "FCUK America." *Marketing*, March 22, 2001.

D'Silva, Beverley. "Stephen Marks: No Marks for Subtlety." *Independent*, August 8, 1998, 16.

Fernandez, Joe. "Chief Exec Stakes Reputation on French Connection Recovery." *Marketing Week*, September 18, 2008, 8.

Garrett, Jade. "Sold on Bare-Faced Chic." *Independent*, March 20, 2001, 8.

Hume, Neil, and Matthew Kennard. "Share Placing Lifts French Connection." *Financial Times*, July 10, 2010, 24.

Jardine, Alexandra. "Style Offensive." *Marketing*, April 5, 2001.

Kuchler, Hannah, and John O'Doherty. "French Connection Offloads Nicole Farhi in Revamp." *Financial Times*, March 16, 2010.

Mesure, Susie. "French Connection Hit by Fresh Profits Alert as Slump Deepens." *Independent* (London), December 10, 2005.

Rankine, Kate. "Cool, Calm and Connected." *Daily Telegraph*, October 31, 1998.

Tempus, Dominic Walsh. "French Connection." *Times* (London), March 19, 2009.

Futbol Club Barcelona

Avinguda Arístides Maillol
s/n 08028
Barcelona, Catalonia
Spain
Telephone: (+34 93) 496-36-00
Fax: (+34 93) 496-37-67
Web site: http://www.fcbarcelona.cat

Nonprofit Company
Founded: 1899
Employees: 788 (est.)
Sales: €415.4 million ($577.9 million) (2009)
NAICS: 711211 Sports Teams and Clubs; 711310 Promoters of Performing Arts, Sports, and Similar Events with Facilities

■ ■ ■

Futbol Club (FC) Barcelona is a nonprofit sporting club of some 170,000 members centered around one of the world's most storied and valuable professional football (soccer) teams. Commonly known as Barça, the club has become a symbol of cultural pride and political defiance for its home city of Barcelona, which is the capital of the autonomous region of Catalonia, Spain. Barça's millions of fans identify with the organization's motto, "More than a club," by taking pride in its history of political dissent as well as its strong athletic record. Barça has won dozens of titles in Spanish leagues and has also been extremely competitive in European championships. Home games are played at Camp Nou, a stadium with a seating capacity of more than 100,000. In addition, Barça fields teams in other professional sports, including futsal (indoor soccer), basketball, handball, and roller hockey, and owns a pair of indoor arenas.

INTERNATIONAL SUPPORT AND NATIONAL STRIFE

For a club so closely tied to a regional identity, it may seem ironic that many of FC Barcelona's original players were Englishmen and that its founder was an immigrant from Switzerland. On the other hand, by the late 1800s British football (soccer) enthusiasts had been spreading the game for some time to wherever their parent country had business interests. Soccer had already taken root elsewhere in Spain, but Catalonia was slow to embrace the game due in large measure to preoccupations with civil unrest, a growing number of strikes, and the rise of Catalan nationalism. The man most responsible for the birth of FC Barcelona was Swiss-born soccer player Hans Gamper, who later took the Catalan name Joan Gamper. In October 1899 he placed an ad declaring his interest in forming a team, and later that year he organized the Futbol Club Barcelona.

One of the players, Englishman Gualteri Wild, became the club's first president. In less than a decade, however, the team almost folded. Many of the members had deserted by 1908, prompting Gamper to take over the leadership. He effectively refounded the club while declaring that "Barcelona cannot and should not die" (quoted from the team's Web site) and that it should have a pro-Catalan and service-oriented vision. Soon the club had over 200 members, and within a year it

COMPANY PERSPECTIVES

FC Barcelona is "more than a club" in Catalonia because it is the sports club that most represents the country and is also one of its greatest ambassadors. Also, for different reasons, FC Barcelona is "more than a club" for many people living elsewhere in Spain, who see Barça as a staunch defender of democratic rights and freedom.

acquired its first playing field, with a capacity of 6,000. Barça became extremely popular in Catalonia as it won numerous Catalan and Spanish championships. By the 1922–23 season, when the 30,000-seat Les Corts ("Cathedral of Football") was opened, the club counted more than 10,000 members.

Gamper's tenure as Barça president came to an end following Miguel Primo de Rivera's military overthrow of Spain's parliamentary government in 1923. The dictatorship banned Barça from flying the Catalan flag at its grounds or making announcements in the Catalan language, and Barça's membership files were registered with the police. The Barça club and its fans did not take these affronts lightly, however. In 1925, when Barça played host to an English team, the spectators stood for the British anthem but sat and jeered for the Spanish anthem. The government responded to this massive symbolic protest by closing the grounds for an extended period and forcing Gamper to resign his leadership. Despite these challenges, Barça won numerous Catalan matches and strove for respect at the national level as well. Barça also organized a basketball team in 1926.

FOOTBALL DURING THE GREAT DEPRESSION AND THE SPANISH CIVIL WAR

The Wall Street crash of 1929 led to the global Great Depression and the downfall of the Primo de Rivera regime in Spain. Despite this turmoil, membership in the soccer club remained at 10,000 in 1930; however, far more destructive political, social, and economic events were soon to follow. The Second Spanish Republic came into power in 1931, but following democratic elections in 1936 in which a Popular Front government of Marxist, liberal republican, and other left-wing factions took power, right-wing elements rebelled and racked the country with violence. In the bloody Spanish Civil War that followed (1936–39) the fascist general Francisco Franco led "Nationalist" right-wing forces against the left-wing "Republicans" that held power in Barcelona and many other parts of the nation. The war eventually involved other European powers, including Nazi Germany and Italy, both of which supplied Franco's fascist army with modern weapons of war. Meanwhile, an influx of left-wing volunteers from the Soviet Union, Mexico, and several other countries formed International Brigades to oppose the fascists.

Soon after the outbreak of the Civil War, Barça's antifascist president at the time, Josep Suñol, was intercepted while on his way to Madrid and summarily executed. A Nationalist warplane dropped a bomb on Barça's social club in 1938, and a short time later Barcelona was "liberated" by Franco's fascist regiments. Fortunately, the Barcelona team had been touring Mexico and the United States raising funds for the club when the civil war began. The team extended the trip as long as possible, but at the end of September 1937, the players were given a choice: return home or become exiles. Of the 16 players, 12 opted for a life of exile. The funds raised during the tour were placed in a Paris bank account, out of the reach of Spain's warring factions.

As a symbol of Catalan nationalism, Barça was kept under close scrutiny by the Franco government, which labeled the club subversive and separatist. The dictator forced FC Barcelona to change its name to the Spanish Club de Futbol Barcelona, and it reduced the team's coat of arms from four red bars (symbolic of the Catalan flag) to two. Despite these and other setbacks, the team won the Spanish Cup in 1942. However, the following season brought an incident that would never be forgotten by Barça supporters nor forgiven.

INTENSIFIED GOVERNMENT PRESSURE

General Franco, who was often called the Generalísimo (Great General), ruled Spain with a totalitarian government that controlled national industries, media, and cultural centers. In one of the first measures of the regime the Spanish Cup was renamed the Generalísimo Cup in his honor. Although few remained who openly resisted the Franco regime, many resented it, including a large number of Catalans. In 1943 Barça defended its title against Real Madrid, the team that most Catalans associated with the fascist government and with Franco personally. At Les Cort stadium in the first of the two-game series, Barça dominated the field and won 3–0. Before the start of the second match in Madrid, however, Franco's director of state security paid a visit to the locker room and issued a lightly veiled threat to the players, reminding them, according to the 1999 book *Barça: A People's Passion* by Jimmy Burns, "Do not

KEY DATES

1899: Joan Gamper founds the club, and Gualteri Wild is elected its first president.
1908: Gamper effectively refounds the club.
1922: Les Corts stadium opens.
1925: After FC Barcelona fans protest the national government, the dictator Primo de Rivera temporarily closes the stadium and forces Gamper to resign.
1951: Barça members and fans support a tram strike against the Franco dictatorship.
1957: Camp Nou stadium opens.
1968: The socially conscious Barça president Narcís de Carreras coins the phrase "more than a club" in his acceptance speech.
1979: Barça takes the prestigious Cup Winners Cup (CWC) for the first time.
1992: Barça wins the European Cup.
2006: Barça wins the European Cup for the second time; Joan Gamper Sports Centre opens; an advertising agreement is signed with UNICEF, reinforcing the global reach of the Barça name.
2009: Barça wins a record six titles with La Liga (its domestic league), the Spanish Cup, the Champions League, the Spanish Super Cup, the European Super Cup, and the World Club Cup.

forget that some of you are only playing because of the generosity of the regime that has forgiven you for your lack of patriotism." His message was clearly understood. Meeting little resistance for the rest of the game, Real Madrid won 11–1 and took the cup.

During the 1940s, Barça expanded beyond soccer, forming a handball team in 1942. Barça's membership approached 25,000 by the time the club celebrated its 50th anniversary, and that same year Barça reconstituted a roller hockey team which it had initially attempted to form during the 1942–43 season. In 1949 FC Barcelona won its first international soccer title, the Latin Cup.

CAMP NOU AND NEW GROWTH

Soccer remained at the heart of the club, and the team was so popular that by the start of the 1950s it had outgrown Les Corts. A new club president, Francesc Miró-Sans, took control in 1953 and pledged to build a new stadium. Four years later the 93,000-seat Camp Nou was inaugurated and club membership grew to 49,000.

After enjoying a run of success in the late 1950s, Barça experienced some difficult times in the 1960s, winning only a pair of Spanish Cups during the decade while Real Madrid dominated La Liga. Some of the decline was due to a lack of money available for procuring talented players. Nevertheless, the club continued to grow in membership, and Barça's role in symbolizing Catalan autonomy and opposition to the Franco regime intensified. The soccer team's fortunes were greatly improved with the arrival of Dutch star Johan Cruyff, who quickly endeared himself to Barça supporters when he told the press that he chose to sign with Barcelona rather than Real Madrid because he refused to play for a club linked to Franco. He then led the team in the 1973–74 season to its first La Liga title since 1959–60. The season was highlighted by a 5–0 victory over Real Madrid in the city of Madrid, which was one of the latter team's worst home losses in history. The 1973–74 season was momentous for another reason as well: it marked the near-end of Franco's longstanding dictatorial regime. As his grip on the nation loosened, the club was able to reclaim its Futbol Club Barcelona name and restore its coat of arms.

Barça added an indoor soccer team (futsal) in 1978, the same year Josep Lluís Núñez became the club president. Cruyff returned to serve as club manager in 1988 and assembled a powerful squad that would win four consecutive La Liga titles from 1991 to 1994 and several prestigious cups. After an impressive eight-year run during which the team secured 11 trophies, however, Cruyff left the club owing to disagreements with Núñez. His replacement, Bobby Robson, took the helm for just one memorable season, 1996–97, during which Barça achieved its domestic league and cup championships as well the UEFA Cup Winners Cup.

NEW CENTURY INITIATIVES

After Núñez resigned suddenly in 2000, he was succeeded as president by Joan Gaspart before Joan Laporta took charge in 2003. The soccer team struggled for a few years but rebounded in 2004–05 by winning La Liga and the Spanish Cup. By then Barça had become one of a handful of soccer clubs that was known as an international brand. In 2006 it joined forces with Juventus FC, Manchester United, and Paris Saint-Germain and appointed Warner Brothers Consumer Products as their master licensee for North, Central, and South America. It also signed an advertising agreement with UNICEF which greatly reinforced the club's global and democratic image. Meanwhile, Barça aimed at becoming more directly involved in North America, which was a vast market holding a great deal of promise for soccer. The club considered acquiring a Major League Soccer franchise in the United States, but nothing came to pass. Nonetheless 2006 was a watershed for Barça on the sporting field, as the club won its second European Cup and opened the Joan Gamper Sports Centre in Sant Joan Despí.

Barça was never more popular at home, and in 2007 the club announced a major renovation of Camp Nou that would increase seating to 106,000. The work, budgeted at €250 million, was slated to be completed in 2011 or 2012. In 2008 Barça signed a five-year strategic agreement with Soccer United Marketing that included several international matches and advertising initiatives, and the team soon enjoyed significant successes. In 2009 it won the major Spanish cups as well as the FIFA World Club Cup title. It took the La Liga title the following year as well, and at the 2010 World Cup, eight Barça players represented the Spanish team, including six starters. When the month-long tournament came to an end, the Spanish national team emerged victorious, taking home the first World Cup in its history. For a short time at least, regional differences were put aside as Real Madrid and Barça players and supporters joined in common cause and celebration.

Ed Dinger

PRINCIPAL COMPETITORS

Associazione Calcio Milan s.p.a.; Manchester United Limited; Real Madrid C.F.

FURTHER READING

Blitz, Roger, and Naomi Mapstone. "FC Barcelona Looks to US for Its Next Big Goal." *Financial Times*, October 18, 2008.

Burns, Jimmy. *Barça: A People's Passion*. London: Bloomsbury Publishing Plc, 1999.

———. "FC Barcelona President Nunez Quits." *Financial Times*, May 15, 2000.

"Four Top European Soccer Clubs: FC Barcelona, Juventus FC, Manchester United and Paris Saint-Germain Appoint Warner Bros. Consumer Products Master Licensee for the Americas." *CNW Group*, August 2, 2006.

Mahmud, Shahnaz. "MLS to Market FC Barcelona in the U.S." *Adweek*, May 16, 2008.

"Soccer Spurring Catalonia Pride." *New York Times*, March 10, 1974.

Games Workshop Group plc

Willow Road
Lenton
Nottingham, NG7 2WS
United Kingdom
Telephone: (+44-115) 900-4001
Fax: (+44-115) 916-8111
Web site: http://www.games-workshop.com

Public Company
Founded: 1975 as Games Workshop
Incorporated: 1991
Employees: 2,066
Sales: £126.5 million ($201.1 million) (2010)
Stock Exchanges: London
Ticker Symbol: GAW
NAICS: 339931 Doll and Stuffed Toy Manufacturing; 339932 Game, Toy, and Children's Vehicle Manufacturing; 451120 Hobby, Toy, and Game Stores; 454111 Electronic Shopping; 454113 Mail-Order Houses

■ ■ ■

Games Workshop Group plc operates the world's leading tabletop fantasy war-games business. Games Workshop (GW) designs, manufactures, and markets games and miniature game figures for a global market, selling its product lines via a network of over 300 company-owned hobby shops, nearly 4,000 independent retailers, mail order, and the Internet. GW's premiere product lines are Warhammer and Warhammer 40,000; the company also is licensed to design games based on J. R. R. Tolkien's *Lord of the Rings* trilogy and the subsequent films based on that series. Additionally, the firm publishes a monthly hobby magazine, *White Dwarf*, printed in more than 50 languages, and also operates Black Library, a publishing division for periodicals and books related to the Warhammer environments and characters.

GW has sales operations in the United Kingdom, the United States, Australia, Belgium, Canada, Denmark, France, Germany, Holland, Italy, Japan, New Zealand, and Sweden, with about 70 percent of its revenues generated outside the United Kingdom. The Nottingham, England-based company has manufacturing operations and distribution facilities in Nottingham; Memphis, Tennessee; and Shanghai, China.

COMPANY ORIGINS

Steve Jackson and Ian Livingstone met each other while still in high school in the 1960s and often played board games together. Jackson liked board games, and Livingstone liked miniatures, or game figurines. After graduation, they parted ways for a time until they reconnected in the 1970s, becoming roommates with another friend, John Peake, in West London. The three friends enjoyed playing games, were bored with their jobs, and decided to form their own game-based business, which they called Games Workshop. To help market their company, which was initially run out of their apartment, they launched *Owl and Weasel*, the first interactive games magazine, in 1975 and used the limited-circulation fan-

COMPANY PERSPECTIVES

Games Workshop markets a Hobby. We make and sell the best model soldiers in the world. The Games Workshop Hobby involves collecting, modelling, painting, and tabletop gaming with whole armies of these soldiers. Our strategy is to establish and develop the Games Workshop Hobby in each of the world's major economies.

zine to sell wooden boards for such games as Backgammon and Go, built mostly by Peake.

The partners' landlady in 1976 banished the business from the apartment building, so, for a short time, Games Workshop was run out of a van. The growth of business, however, forced Jackson and Livingstone to open their first true office, at the rear of a South London real estate office. That, too, was soon too small, and GW in 1977 relocated to a shop in Hammersmith in West London. By that time, Peake had left the company.

INITIAL GW EXPANSION

GW's biggest break came when the pair received an early copy of the new game Dungeons and Dragons (D&D); contacted its creator, Gary Gygax; and soon secured an exclusive three-year European D&D distribution agreement with TSR, which held the intellectual property rights to the game. TSR granted GW an exclusive license to distribute D&D merchandise in the United Kingdom and a license to produce its own D&D products in the United Kingdom, including the printing of game materials tailored to a U.K. audience. GW was licensed to print U.K. variations of D&D and Advanced Dungeons and Dragons publications, including rule books and the "Dungeon Floor Plan." As a result, GW printed a completely original D&D rule book that used the original American text but featured a new design, including new and original artwork. Rapidly growing interest in D&D dramatically increased interest in the new U.K. game company and increased GW's sales, allowing it to create a new fanzine, establish a miniatures-manufacturing company, and open retail outlets.

In 1977, after two years of printing the photocopied *Owl and Weasel*, which reached a specialized audience of about 200, GW began publishing a new fanzine, *White Dwarf*. Intended for a much wider circulation, the new fanzine featured a much more professional appearance. It provided information on GW products as well as games from other companies and became the major U.K. source of gaming news. Eighteen months after its launch, *White Dwarf* was being sold by newsdealers, which represented a step up from the subscription-only *Owl and Weasel*.

The release of the new fanzine was timed to preannounce and complement the opening of the first Games Workshop Hobby shop. After operating largely as a mail-order operation, GW in April 1978 opened its first retail outlet in the Hammersmith area of London. From the outset, the new shop and others that followed were staffed with avid and knowledgeable gamers. With publicity from *White Dwarf*, the store was a success, and other outlets followed in Birmingham, Manchester, Nottingham, Sheffield, and other U.K. locations. GW's shops sold all the leading role-playing games (RPGs), including RuneQuest, Middle Earth Roleplay, and Traveller. As a matter of course, almost all new RPGs issuing a U.K. edition made their way through GW shops.

Livingstone and Jackson soon realized that there was a greater profit margin in miniatures, the character figurines used for games, which were particularly popular with gamers between 10 and 14. To target this market, GW partnered with Bryan Ansell, already known for his miniature manufacturing through his initial company, Asgard Miniatures. In 1979 GW funded the formation of Citadel Miniatures Limited, a satellite manufacturing firm based in Nottingham, with Ansell placed in charge of its operation. For GW, Ansell's Citadel created and produced miniatures that the games company sold through mail order and at retail shops.

SEPARATION OF GW AND TSR

For a time, GW and TSR management discussed a merger of the two small but growing games companies. However, the companies appeared to be going different directions, and internal forces were working against a merger. Brian and Melvin Bloome, who represented two-thirds of the TSR board in the early years of that company, apparently were against such a merger even though the third member, Gary Gygax, who orchestrated the D&D distribution deal with GW, was actively promoting it. (According to Gygax, a merger would have stripped the Bloome brothers of their majority control of the firm.) Additionally, GW was just starting to develop its own product lines. Thus, GW's short but profitable relationship with TSR came to an end

KEY DATES

1975: Games Workshop is established by Ian Livingstone, Steve Jackson, and John Peake.
1979: Games Workshop helps establish Citadel Miniatures, with Bryan Ansell as general manager.
1986: Jackson and Livingstone sell Games Workshop to Ansell.
1991: The company is incorporated as Games Workshop Group plc after a management buyout led by Tom Kirby.
1994: Games Workshop goes public and is listed on the London Stock Exchange.

early in the decade, as indicated by TSR's March 1980 launch of a new subsidiary, TSR UK, that opened its first U.K. sales branch that year.

Early in its history, GW began sponsoring "Games Day" conventions throughout England. At one of these conventions in the early 1980s, Jackson and Livingstone met a publisher from Penguin who pitched a book concept. One of the ideas for the book included a brief interactive adventure that allowed the reader to select where to go next in the text; this idea, however, ended up being the overriding concept for the entire book. *The Warlock of Firetop Mountain*, published in 1982, turned out to be a classic in the field. Its popularity sparked Penguin to ask Jackson and Livingstone to write more books geared toward the target 10-to-14-year-old audience, and the Fighting Fantasy book series was born. Penguin kept asking the two to churn out more books, which they did, and for which they gained both a popular following and individual fortunes, as the series grew to include 59 books and sold more than 16 million copies in 23 languages.

Livingstone and Jackson worked at GW during the day and wrote at night and on weekends. Eventually, to limit their workload, the partners promoted GW executives to give them authority to run particular operations, and they put Ansell in charge of the entire company. Ansell named Tom Kirby as his general manager.

PRODUCT LINE EXPANSION AND CHANGE

Early in the 1980s, GW expanded its product lines, beginning with its own board games. One such game was based on the comic book character Judge Dredd and another on the British television series *Doctor Who*. Later that decade, the company released its first role-playing game, Judge Dredd—The Roleplaying Game and followed that with a second RPG, Golden Heroes. The company further expanded through the manufacture of war-gaming systems, which required the separate purchase of miniatures, under the Games Workshop brand name. The first and one of the most popular and enduring war games was Warhammer, a Tolkien-type fantasy cowritten by Ansell himself, and for which Citadel launched its own set of miniatures in 1983. About the same time, Ansell moved the entire company to Citadel's home city of Nottingham.

During the 1980s, the company also expanded into the area of video-game publication. The video-game boom, in many ways, grew out of the interest in role-playing games, and GW was at the cusp of this change in game-type popularity. During the mid-1980s, GW created several video games for Spectrum, a small but popular computer released in various versions in the United Kingdom by Sinclair Research Ltd. during the 1980s. The earliest computer games released by GW included *Battlecars*, a two-player game featuring a battle of cars, *D-Day*, which was based on World War II landings at Normandy, and *Tower of Despair*, which was an adventure game like many of GW's titles.

While Livingstone and Jackson were heavily involved in writing for the Fighting Fantasy book series, the two partners made the ambitious, bottom-line-oriented Ansell an offer: If he met certain sales targets, he could purchase GW. During the mid-1980s, the market for war games and miniatures rose, which was a market trend that played into Ansell's strength and original business. Warhammer miniatures sold quickly, while RPGs sales became sluggish. Considering the high profit margins of miniatures when marketed through GW stores, as compared to RPGs, role-play books, and board games, the company began to shift its strategy to producing war games that required miniatures to play.

BUYOUT AND CHANGE IN BUSINESS STRATEGY

Ansell soon met the targets established by Jackson and Livingstone, and in 1986 he led a Citadel management buyout of Games Workshop from the founders. Relaunched under new management with a guiding strategy of selling lead miniatures along with other accessories for games, Games Workshop adopted a clear plan for profitability based on market conditions.

The buyout was not met with jubilation on all fronts. Some customers and GW fans felt the firm had swapped its 1960s-styled enthusiasm for overt corporate materialism and marketing. Such corporatism was reflected in *White Dwarf*, which became a slicker, more marketing-oriented publication devoted to GW products at the exclusion of reviews of other products.

Under its new ownership and management, GW focused on publishing character-laden games to serve as a foundation for selling miniatures and accessories. In 1986, for example, with Warhammer in its third edition, the company issued Warhammer Fantasy Roleplay, which was the best-selling RPG in 1987 and a top-selling U.K.-based RPG for several years after its release. By 1988 GW had stopped selling games from most other manufacturers to concentrate on its own creations. Along with Warhammer and its RPG game, the most popular titles included Warhammer 40,000, a dark space-war game, and Dark Future, an example of a product that pushed the sales of miniatures. Set in a cyberpunk world of decay, Dark Future was a tabletop war game played with numerous miniatures.

Having witnessed Jackson and Livingstone cash in on their fiction, and watched the entrance of other RPG manufacturers into the associated-fiction market, GW decided to follow suit and publish its own fiction, with stories based on the specific characters, environments, and rules of the company's games. After several false starts trying to recruit writers, and tension between GW and writers, the company formed a new subsidiary, GW Books, based in Brighton, with David Pringle acting as editor and Ian Miller as art director. Pringle decided to contract with writers appearing in the pages of *Interzone* (a popular British magazine devoted to science fiction and fantasy), and the first GW books in the form of short-story anthologies and novels began appearing in shops in 1989. The setting for the first of these was the fantasy world of Warhammer. Industry reviews of the first books were mixed, and GW executive support for the book subsidiary quickly faded, especially after a change in management early the following decade.

THE EARLY NINETIES: INCORPORATION AFTER ANOTHER BUYOUT

In 1991 Games Workshop was incorporated following a leveraged management buyout of the company led by Kirby, the company chief executive. The buyout drew on capital from Bank of Boston, Charterhouse Development Capital, County NatWest Ventures, and ECI Ventures. Although the buyout was orchestrated on the selling end by Ansell, who had a majority interest in GW, Livingstone and Jackson still owned a portion and benefited financially from the sale. Following the buyout, GW largely retreated to its seminal business: tabletop games, especially war games that used numerous miniatures. Meanwhile, video-game production was limited to just a few publications. One particularly popular title during this period was *Space Hulk*. Similarly, book publication, while continuing, went through numerous editorial changes and was limited (Kirby, unlike Ansell, was not a big fan of science fiction and fantasy).

Kirby quickly led a retail expansion, nearly doubling the number of Games Workshop Hobby shops, the company-owned stores, in three years. As a result, sales rose. In the United States, revenues grew from £2.8 million to £5.1 million between 1992 and 1994, during a time when overseas earnings exceeded those generated in the United Kingdom.

By 1994 there were 80 shops in the expanding GW retail chain. That year, the company went public, offering its shares on the London Stock Exchange. Industry analysts cited several strengths regarding the initial public offering (IPO) of GW. For one, the company had no advertising budget, per se. New business came from word-of-mouth, from shop passersby, and especially from the company's self-promotion via *White Dwarf*, which had a worldwide circulation of 70,000 by 1994. GW also lacked any viable competition. Moreover, GW had plenty of room for growth, especially internationally.

Kirby also oversaw a well-planned international expansion of GW at a fairly rapid pace for a small company. By the time of its IPO, the company was opening four shops a year in France (along with 10 annually in the United Kingdom), with a new outlet in Paris leading all stores in sales in 1994. In Germany and Australia, GW took a more measured approach, creating a solid foundation of interest and enthusiastic gamers for its new staff before opening shops. In advance of openings in Germany, for example, GW in 1994 launched a German version of *White Dwarf* to help build interest. The following year, more U.K. openings followed as well as new debuts in France and Spain, with shops providing customers a place where they could come and actually play GW games. As a result of this expansion, GW was forced to double its U.K. production of miniatures to keep up with demand. These figurines were sold not only in GW shops but also through independent retailers (primarily in the United States), such as Toys "R" Us and Argos, and through mail orders.

MID-NINETIES: MANAGEMENT MOVES AND INTERNATIONAL EXPANSION

In January 1996 Stephen Godber was appointed Games Workshop managing director, and by that time Brian North was serving as chairman. Under the new executive team, the company continued its European expansion, including its first store opening in Germany as well as the establishment of a German subsidiary, along with ongoing openings in Spain, France, and Australia. By the close of the year, GW had a 95-store chain as it worked toward a long-term goal of starting shops in all of the world's major economic areas. GW in 1996 also began selling directly to U.S. retailers and established a distinct business operation in Canada that opened outlets the following year. A new operation was also established in Hong Kong, where the first store was opened early the following year.

In 1997 GW was the benefactor of a strong demand for fantasy war games. In particular, miniatures related to its Blood Angels and Orks titles sold well. GW also relaunched editions of Warhammer Fantasy Battle in five languages. By 1997 sales outside United Kingdom were outpacing those in GW's home ground, while North American sales grew more than 75 percent in one year.

In 1997 all U.K. operations were consolidated into a new headquarters in the Lenton neighborhood in Nottingham, where additional space was allocated to create Warhammer World, the firm's premier war-gaming system. Increasingly, Games Workshop began to hold gaming tournaments and other events at its headquarters, thereby building a destination for gamers worldwide. GW in 1997 also launched its Black Library division, which was developed by staffers Marc Gascoigne, Rick Priestley, and Andy Jones to initially publish *INFERNO!* magazine, a bimonthly anthology of stories, features, and comics based on the Warhammer titles. The development of the *Warhammer Monthly* anthology comic book series followed. Two years after its creation, Black Library released its first art book, *Inquis Exterminatus*, and a series of science fiction and fantasy novels.

Sales continued to rise in 1998, but profits were negatively affected by the value of the pound and the growth of local currency in various markets. The company that year released at Easter its U.S. football-type fantasy game Blood Bowl, a title with very mixed results. Despite stagnant profits, European expansion continued with new shop openings in Denmark, Holland, Italy, and New Zealand, as well as in other established markets, and GW closed the decade with nearly 200 retail outlets worldwide. To build a presence in Asian markets, GW in 1999 released its first products in Japan, Warhammer Fantasy Battle and related products.

SALES GROWTH AND NEW BUSINESSES IN THE NEW CENTURY

In January 2002 GW acquired Sabertooth Games, Inc., a manufacturer and wholesaler of collectible card games. The following year, GW, seeking an expanded publishing platform to develop its U.S. presence and push into new media areas, announced a new publishing program. The company launched a new stand-alone subsidiary, BL Publishing, dedicated to the publication of books, including those with the company's five-year-old Black Library imprint and a new publishing unit, Black Flame. BL Publishing was headquartered in Nottingham and had its books distributed in the United States by Simon & Schuster Inc. GW planned for Black Library to publish six to eight graphic works annually and Black Flame to make its mark publishing reprint and original fantasy novels and science fiction.

Beginning in the middle years of the first decade of the 21st century, GW increasingly turned to creating video games from its popular tabletop games. In 2004 the company began trying to convert a Warhammer title, Age of Reckoning, to a video game. Initially GW attempted to be involved in the video-game development but soon found that doing so was beyond its area of expertise. Such transformations from table to video included Dawn of War: Relic, a popular real-time strategy game that imitated the ambiance and feel of Warhammer 40,000, on which Dawn of War was based.

At its incorporation in 1991, Games Workshop had logged sales of about £17.5 million. Revenues rose incrementally over the next 10 years, and by 2001 annual sales neared £100 million. By 2004, however, company revenues peaked for the decade as they approached £160 million.

By the beginning of 2005, 70 percent of all GW revenues were derived from non-U.K. operations, and the company's chain of shops had grown to more than 350 outlets as the company increasingly emphasized its own GW Hobby shops rather than deals with independent retailers. The company also had expanded manufacturing operations to include not only Nottingham but also Wisbech, Cambridge, in the United

Kingdom and Memphis and Baltimore in the United States.

MID-DECADE DOWNTURN

With the excitement surrounding the *Lord of the Rings* film trilogy beginning to wane, GW in 2005 experienced a sharp decline in sales. Since the release of the first *Lord of the Rings* film in 2001, the company had benefited; sales of its tabletop game based on the trilogy helped to propel profits and revenues to record heights. After four years, it appeared that what the company called the "bubble effect" had finally burst. By April 2005 GW's stock had lost about 25 percent of its market value, and the company's profits were substantially marred that year.

The 2006 fiscal year was likewise financially challenging, as the company logged a 73 percent drop in profits from a year prior. The firm continued to blame the loss of *Lord of the Rings* revenues as well as its heavy investment in that game. Compounding GW's problems was the migration of game-playing customers to large retailers such as Wal-Mart and away from small shops. In response to the economic turmoil, GW began to cut its overhead and trimmed the number of its GW Hobby shops. Profits for fiscal year 2006 amounted to just £3.7 million, a sharp decline from the previous year's total of £13.9 million.

Unfortunately for GW, there was more bad financial news in 2007. By May the game maker had issued two profit warnings, forecasting earnings below expected levels. To help offset the decline, GW cut 10 percent of its workforce, shuttered 35 unprofitable or underperforming GW Hobby shops, and merged back-office positions in efforts to slash £7 million in annual overhead. The company's stock, meanwhile, had fallen from its 2001 high of 195 pence to 132½ pence, the second-lowest mark since 2001. For the 2007 fiscal year, GW posted a pretax loss of £2.9 million on revenues that were essentially flat at £111.5 million. The company attributed its plight to a European economic slowdown and promised a still-leaner organization.

LICENSING AGREEMENTS, IMPROVED SALES, AND MORE COST CUTTING

In March 2007 GW inked a six-year global licensing deal for its Warhammer 40,000 with the video-game producer Vigil Games of THQ Inc. The agreement expanded an existing pact with THQ that included interactive rights for games produced for handheld, console, and personal computer (PC) systems and added wireless device rights and all online rights. The pact also included rights to a forthcoming massively multiplayer online (MMO) game being developed by THQ. Earlier in the decade, THQ produced *Warhammer 40,000: Dawn of War* to critical and popular acclaim. With the subsequent release of the related hybrid title *Warhammer 40,000: Dawn of War—Dark Crusade*, this Warhammer project had sold in excess of two million copies. The third in that series, the MMO title, represented a move into a new arena for Warhammer and GW. MMO games, as their name suggests, are multiplayer ones that allow the potential for hundreds if not thousands of participants playing online and can be run via PC-connected game consoles. The 2007 agreement with THQ also included rights granted for Warhammer 40,000 and licenses for GW's Gorkamorka and Necromunda games.

By late in the first decade of the 21st century, given some missteps and false starts involving video games, GW had adopted a policy of working only with well-recognized video-game developers known for high-quality productions. During this period, GW began selling intellectual property rights to video-game producers and gaining royalties from each game sold. In addition to THQ and its Relic Entertainment studio, other partners included Mythic Entertainment, Inc. After more than 20 years of off-and-on active production of video games, the company believed its new policy and partners finally fit its situation and products. GW had finally begun to take seriously the production and financial value of a well-produced video game.

Nonetheless, GW also wished to keep separate product lines for video games and tabletop games, for each were played differently and required different activities from the player. The company recognized that a video-game player, unlike the core GW customer, could not hold a miniature and literally paint it, actions that gave true GW table-game fanatics great pleasure and that had given GW, in great proportion, a large share of its consistent business for more than 30 years.

In September 2008 GW unveiled *Warhammer Online: Age of Reckoning* via the Electronic Arts website. Subscriptions to play this Warhammer title online began at $14.99 month. Also that year, GW's balance sheet improved, and the company's income moved back into the black while revenues inched up. Given global recessionary conditions setting in, the company viewed the results as positive. Much of GW's progress came not from the shops but on the cost-cutting end, as the company eliminated nearly two-dozen stores. In 2008 GW also sold its interest in the collectible card game operation Sabertooth Games.

2009–10 AND BEYOND

The company's profit margin continued improving in 2009, as GW reported pretax earnings of £7.5 million on rising revenues of £125.7 million. During the year, the game maker also slashed net debt by £8.5 million, reducing it to £1.6 million. The company also refused to pay a dividend, something it had paid out earlier in the decade while experiencing substantial sales declines. The widening cost-cutting moves in 2009 included relocating stores to lower-rent areas, improving the efficiency of manufacturing operations, and slashing staff even further. The company also improved its inventory management controls and purchasing operations.

For the 2010 fiscal year, GW's sales improved slightly. The company opened 27 new hobby centers, but more centers were closed than debuted. North America and northern Europe saw growth, whereas continental European and Australian sales declined. Other highlights involved the company's two specialty businesses, Forge World and Black Library, which continued to achieve positive results. Forge World (a GW unit that manufactured variant vehicle and infantry miniatures) relaunched its website with improved order processing, while Black Library prepared for an October 2010 launch of e-books and audiobook downloads from its website.

By 2010 GW had grown much as a company since its days as a fledgling firm distributing D&D in the 1970s. The difficult economic times of the early 21st century, however, had forced the company to come full circle and return to a renewed focus on the development of quality products for its loyal customers. GW also anticipated a return to profitability in all the territories in which it operated. Substantial territory expansion, though, was not likely. Rather, the company was looking at smaller targets for growth, as in one-person-operated shops in both small towns and large-city suburbs in the United Kingdom. GW viewed areas outside its home country as "greenfield" territory, offering additional opportunities for future growth.

Roger Rouland

PRINCIPAL SUBSIDIARIES

Games Workshop Limited; Games Workshop International Limited; Games Workshop America Inc. (USA); Games Workshop Retail Inc. (USA); Games Workshop US Manufacturing LLC; Games Workshop (Queen Street) Limited (Canada); EURL Games Workshop (France); Games Workshop SL (Spain); Games Workshop Oz Pty Limited (Australia); Games Workshop Deutschland GmbH (Germany); Games Workshop Limited (New Zealand); Games Workshop Italia SRL (Italy); Games Workshop (Shanghai) Co. Limited (China).

PRINCIPAL DIVISIONS

The Black Library; Forge World.

PRINCIPAL COMPETITORS

Blizzard Entertainment, Inc.; DC Entertainment Inc.; Hasbro, Inc.; King Features Syndicate, Inc.; Konami Corporation; Lucasfilm Entertainment Company Ltd.; Marvel Entertainment, Inc.; Mattel, Inc.; Mythic Entertainment, Inc.; Sony Online Entertainment LLC; Wizards of the Coast LLC.

FURTHER READING

Baxter, Stephen. "Freedom in an Owned World: Warhammer Fiction and the *Interzone* Generation." *Vector*, no. 229 (2003). Accessed November 1, 2010. http://www.vectormagazine.co.uk/article.asp?articleID=42.

Capper, Andy. "Steve Jackson and Ian Livingstone." *Vice Magazine*, December 2009. Accessed November 1, 2010. http://www.viceland.com/int/v16n12/htdocs/steve-jackson-ian-livingstone-283.php.

Evans, Rhodri. "*Lord of the Rings* Loses Magic Spell." *Western Mail* (Cardiff, Wales), January 26, 2005, 8.

"Games Workshop Has Regained Its Moneymaking Magic." *Birmingham Post* (England), July 30, 2008, 19.

Hughman, John. "Model Results from Games Workshop." *Investors Chronicle*, July 27, 2010.

Lumsden, Quentin. "A Chance to Play for Profit." *Independent* (London), January 22, 1995, 7.

Marsh, Peter. "Games Workshop Seeks Further Conquests." *Financial Times*, October 27, 2003, 24.

McCarthy, Dave. "The History of Games Workshop." *IGN Online*, September 22, 2008. Accessed November 1, 2010. http://pc.ign.com/articles/911/911959p1.html.

McGrath, Melanie. "A Visit to the Fantasy World of Ian Livingstone." *Independent on Sunday* (London), June 2, 1998. Accessed November 1, 2010. http://www.independent.co.uk/arts-entertainment/a-visit-to-the-fantasy-world-of-ian-livingstone-1162339.html.

Sacco, Ciro Alessandro. "The Ultimate Interview with Gary Gygax." *TheKyngdoms.com*, August 11, 2005. Accessed November 1, 2010. http://www.thekyngdoms.com/forums/viewtopic.php?t=37.

gettyimages®

Getty Images, Inc.

601 North 34th Street
Seattle, Washington 98103
U.S.A.
Telephone: (206) 925-5000
Toll Free: (800) 462-4379
Fax: (206) 925-5001
Web site: http://www.gettyimages.com

Private Company
Founded: 1995
Incorporated: 1995 as Getty Communications PLC
Employees: 1,900
NAICS: 541990 All Other Professional, Scientific, and Technical Services

■ ■ ■

Getty Images, Inc., has reinvented itself more than once. It began life in 1995 as a stock photography company, mailing negatives to ad agencies and editorial clients and shuttling them to other customers when they were returned. Placing itself at the forefront of the digital revolution, Getty became the first visual content company to license its images online. Meanwhile, through a long series of acquisitions, it morphed into a broad-ranging media company, with offerings including video footage, multimedia, photography, and even music.

In the process Getty relocated from its original home in London to Seattle, launched itself as a publicly traded company, then went private again in 2008 when it was acquired by private equity investor Hellman & Friedman. Today Getty is one of the world's largest providers of visual content and a growing player in the audio field, working through its website, gettyimages.com; subsidiaries including iStockphoto, WireImage, FilmMagic, Jupiterimages, and Photos.com; and 21 offices worldwide serving clients in 100 countries.

ORIGINS

The birth of Getty Images as a visual content provider occurred through an acquisition, one of many to follow. On March 14, 1995, cofounders Mark Getty (a descendant of multibillionaire business executive Jean Paul Getty) and Jonathan Klein completed their first acquisition for what was initially known as Getty Communications PLC, purchasing Tony Stone Images. Ranked as one of the world's leading providers of contemporary stock photography, with $42 million in sales for the year preceding its acquisition, Tony Stone inaugurated Getty Communications' bid to become the world's preeminent provider of visual content. Getty and Klein's plan was to be consolidators in the fragmented industry, a strategy built on assessing and carrying out a steady stream of acquisitions that included not just contemporary stock photography but a range of formats and subject matter stretching from contemporary and archival stills and footage to news, current affairs, features, and celebrity material.

A year after the Tony Stone acquisition, Getty purchased Hulton Deutsch, one of the world's largest privately owned collections of archival photography. Renamed Hulton Getty and divided into 300 separate collections comprising approximately 15 million images,

COMPANY PERSPECTIVES

We are a leading provider of digital media worldwide, creating and distributing a range of assets—from royalty-free stock photography and editorial images to footage, music and multimedia—that help communicators around the globe tell their stories.

Hulton Getty drew the majority of its customers from the United Kingdom, primarily professional customers such as magazine, news, and book publishers. Tony Stone attracted similar users, but the Hulton collection was also used by advertising and design agencies, travel companies, and poster and calendar manufacturers.

For those customers interested in either collection, Getty initially offered the material through a network of international sales offices in the traditional manner. Catalogs were sent to interested parties, who then selected the specific images they wanted to use, for which privilege they paid a fee to the provider. Getty and its competitors were also preparing for a new era in the visual content industry. Digitization of photographs, which could then be displayed on the web, promised to expedite the selection and buying process for traditional customers and, potentially, spark demand among the general public. Accordingly, Getty established in-house departments charged with digitizing the images in each of its major collections.

Getty was working, meanwhile, to widen its geographic reach and the breadth and depth of its collection of images and footage. Marketing was in the hands of a group of strategically placed sales offices: London (the company headquarters), Boston, Chicago, Los Angeles, New York, Seattle, Toronto, Paris, Munich, Hamburg, and Vienna. Agent licensees extended Getty's reach to 20 countries. The objective was for Getty to be a one-stop destination for anyone interested in any form of visual content, which meant its management was continually either acquiring or in search of fresh content.

FROM STOCK OFFERING TO FUTURE ACQUISITIONS

One month after the Hulton Deutsch purchase, Getty acquired Fabulous Footage, a leading North American provider of contemporary stock footage. With content in three major categories (contemporary stills, archival stills, and contemporary footage), Getty had carved out a large enough presence within its first year of operation to attract the attention of investors. It went public in July 1996, completing an initial public offering on NASDAQ. It next moved to bolster its profile in Europe by acquiring, in November 1996, Amsterdam-based World View, the exclusive licensee of Tony Stone images in The Netherlands, Belgium, Sweden, and Denmark. The deal was consistent with a corporate strategy to work through wholly owned offices in major markets rather than through agents.

By the end of 1996, its first full year in business, Getty's sales totaled $85 million and net income stood at $2.7 million. Financial results would improve significantly as Getty added new collections and penetrated new segments of the visual content market. In November 1997 it made its first foray into photojournalism, purchasing the Liaison Agency, a New York–based photography agency regarded as one of the world's leading suppliers of news material. Through its own connections as well as production and distribution agreements with Gamma Presse Images SA, Liaison had contracts with roughly 750 photojournalists throughout the world and ranked magazine, book, and multimedia publishers in more than 50 countries as its primary customers. The deal brought Getty news content it previously lacked and bolstered its selection in existing categories.

BUILDING BUSINESS RELATIONSHIPS

The series of acquisitions, and the content they helped it to amass, gave Getty the leverage to develop strategic relationships with providers who could help it to better manage and market its collection. In 1997 Getty formed a development partnership with IBM that included creation of a new digital image distribution system. Based on IBM's Digital Library watermarking system, the system would enable a digital image to be visually identified as belonging to a copyright holder without detracting from the image's visual appeal. Concurrently Getty launched Hulton Getty On-Line, a website containing selected images from the Hulton Getty collection. Initially several thousand of the collection's 15 million images were put on display, the first stage of a plan that called for 500,000 archival images to be online by the end of 1998.

This foray into electronic commerce marked a new era stage in the company's evolution. No longer restricted to requesting material through catalogs, customers could examine and select images via the Internet. They could then contact the nearest Getty sales office to license the rights to their selections,

KEY DATES

1995: Jonathan Klein and Mark Getty acquire Tony Stone Images, creating Getty Communications.
1996: Getty Communications debuts on the NASDAQ.
1997: The launch of Hulton Getty On-Line ushers the company into electronic commerce.
1998: Getty Communications and PhotoDisc, Inc., merge, creating Getty Images, Inc.
1999: Getty Images acquires the Image Bank for $183 million.
2000: Getty Images acquires Visual Communications Group, Inc., for $220 million.
2001: Getty Images launches gettyworks.com, allowing online access to Getty collections.
2002: Getty Images moves from NASDAQ to the New York Stock Exchange.
2007: Getty Images purchases Pump Audio, a music licenser.
2008: Getty Images is acquired by Hellman & Friedman for $2.4 billion.

reproduction-quality copies of which they would subsequently receive in a variety of digital and analog formats. The ease of online use quickly prompted Getty and other providers to marshal their efforts to develop digital catalogs tailored for website display. Aiming to be leading provider of visual content on the Internet, Getty returned aggressively to the acquisition trail.

In July 1997 it completed two important purchases. First it acquired the work of Slim Aarons, one of the world's leading photojournalists. One week later Getty purchased Energy Film Library. Energy, whose customers included advertising companies, feature film producers, and industrial clients, controlled a 3,500-hour library of footage, the majority of which had been mastered to digital imagery for online search and distribution. This represented a major step toward Getty's goal of amassing the world's largest collection of moving imagery.

MERGER WITH PHOTODISC

Getty's next move created a new company and eventually prompted the relocation of headquarters away from London. In September 1997 the company agreed to a union with PhotoDisc Inc., the leading royalty-free digital stock photography provider and the largest provider of imagery on the Internet. Traditionally in the stock photo business, customers paid royalty fees to use images for a limited time in a particular medium. Royalty-free providers sold images for a flat fee, however, allowing customers to use the image in any media without time constraints. PhotoDisc brought another large trove of content to Getty but also gave it a presence in this new market.

The deal forming the new company, Getty Images, Inc., was consummated in February 1998. Mark Torrance, founder of PhotoDisc, became cochairman, serving alongside Mark Getty, while Klein retained the chief executive officer's responsibilities.

As details of the merger were being finalized, another acquisition was announced. In February 1998 Getty acquired Allsport PLC, a global sports photography agency. Getty planned to distribute Allsport's existing photographs and the agency's archive of four million edited images through its global network of sales offices and distribute the images digitally on the Internet. With the absorption of Allsport and the completion of the Getty/PhotoDisc merger, the company ranked as the largest visual content provider in the world, registering $185 million in revenue at the end of 1998, capping a three-year climb to the top. Leadership by revenue was a position Getty intended to maintain, an objective that called for the continued enhancement of the company's content collection and a concerted exploration of marketing opportunities in the digital age.

In March 1999 Getty announced it was relocating its headquarters from the United Kingdom to the United States, which now generated the majority of its revenue. Seattle, its new headquarters, was also the home of its closest rival, Corbis Corporation. The move reflected Getty's commitment to the potential of electronic commerce, Klein told Carol Tice of the *Puget Sound Business Journal* (May 7, 1999). "Because of the importance of technology, which is completely transforming our industry," he said, "we wanted to be close to that expertise."

As the move was taking place, Getty announced its largest acquisition to that time. In September it purchased the Image Bank from Eastman Kodak Company for $183 million. With 70 sales offices in 40 countries, the Image Bank owned significant contemporary and archival photography and film footage, representing the work of more than 1,500 photographers and more than 200 cinematographers. As the decade closed, Getty controlled more than 60 million still images and more than 30,000 hours of footage.

FURTHER ACQUISITIONS AND NEW RELATIONSHIPS

While Getty continued to expand through acquisitions in the new century, much of its attention shifted to forming partnerships and alliances with content originators and further developing its delivery model, especially its online platform. At the same time, the company devoted more attention to tailoring its offerings to specific markets and audiences.

In February 2000 it acquired Visual Communications Group, its largest competitor, from United News & Media PLC, for $220 million. Getty's plans for VCG's collections underscored the role of e-commerce as its primary route to new growth. The VCG purchase was followed by four more major acquisitions during the first half of the decade. In January 2003 Getty bought ImageDirect, which supplied music, entertainment, and fashion photography to newspapers, magazines, and websites. The following year it acquired Bongarts Sportfotografie GmbH, Germany's leading sports photography agency, and its sister company, Sportimage Fotoagentur GmbH, an international sports imagery distributor. In April 2005 Getty purchased London-based Digital Vision for $165 million in cash, augmenting its leading position in royalty-free imagery.

RECIPROCITY

Less than a month later, Getty acquired Photonica West from the Tokyo-based Amana Group for $51 million in cash. Photonica brought two major collections of rights-managed imagery that included the work of leading photographers in Europe, the United States, and Japan. The Photonica acquisition was part of a broader global production and reciprocal distribution effort that Getty was developing with Amana. The new alliance provided better distribution for Getty's collections in Japan through Amana, while Getty expected to represent and distribute Amana's imagery to the international market through its global network.

Such partnerships, with a wide range of counterparties, were becoming more important to Getty. In 2000 it signed deals to exclusively represent the work of celebrated photographer Arnold Newman and offer the National Geographic Society's image collection to professionals through its website. It also formed a partnership with Berkeley, California–based Ofoto to provide high-quality photographic printing services for Getty's Art.com fine art service. The following year brought deals with America Online to provide real-time access to sports images across several AOL brands through Allsport and with NBA Entertainment to act as the official photo source for professional basketball. In 2002 the National Hockey League picked Getty as its official photographer and photographic partner. A similar deal followed later that year with the Ladies Professional Golf Association.

In May 2002 CNN announced that Getty would be the exclusive distributor for still images collected from CNN footage. This dramatically increased the number of news images that Getty could offer to editorial customers. Partnerships, distribution deals, and service and licensing agreements followed, in 2003 with counterparties including Agence France-Presse, Business Wire, the Manchester United football club, General Motors, and Boeing and in the following year with Major League Baseball, the International Olympic Committee (as official photographer for the 2004 Summer Games in Atlanta), and the National Football League. The company also signed top photographers, such as award-winning photojournalist Tom Stoddart, to shoot exclusively for Getty.

GEOGRAPHIC EXPANSION AND NEW E-COMMERCE OFFERINGS

The company was also expanding and deepening its services geographically. After opening its first office in Brazil in 1998, Getty greatly expanded its presence there three years later. The previous year it had opened four new offices in Southeast Asia (Singapore, Manila, Kuala Lumpur, and Bangkok), widening a regional presence that already included Hong Kong, Australia, and New Zealand. In 2002 Getty greatly expanded the content collections it offered in Japan and opened a new office in Tokyo. A Japanese-language website followed in 2004.

Getty was also targeting China as a valuable new market. In November 2004 it established the largest photo bureau operating in Beijing, a hub for staff and freelance photographers covering China, Hong Kong, and Taiwan. In July 2005 the company added Getty Images China, based in Beijing and offering web-based access for Chinese editorial and advertising clients to imagery from all Getty collections, including content developed specifically for the Chinese market.

By 2000 Getty was a leader in digitizing and transferring visual content to the web, and it continued to refine and expand its online presence. In the fourth quarter of 1999, more than 30 percent of the company's $79.9 million total revenue came from e-commerce. In February 2001 it launched gettyworks.com, a comprehensive do-it-yourself website allowing clients to access images to create business communication materials such as reports, their own websites, and presentations.

An online news and sport photo service, Getty Images News and Sport, went live in August 2002. Two years later Getty announced a deal to make fine art prints of its best photography available to Amazon.com customers through a print-on-demand service housed on Amazon's online Home & Garden store.

TARGETING SPECIFIC AUDIENCES

The company's gettyimages.com website also aided the company's efforts to appeal to specific audiences. In May 2003 it launched an online full-service assignments capability through which clients could hire commercial photographers for commissioned photo shoots. Next month came gettyimages.com's Professional Directory, where photographers, illustrators, and their representatives could post portfolios for viewing by prospective clients. In May 2004 Getty announced the formation of an editorial contributors' group to provide marketing and distribution opportunities to well-known feature photographers. The new online offering Exclusive by Getty Images, launched in October 2005, made it easier for magazine and newspaper clients to access and secure rights to premium celebrity portraits, celebrity portrait archives, reportage features, and editorial specials.

Getty's focus on expanding and refining its services during the first half of the decade was set against the backdrop of a rollercoaster economy. After posting a record profit of $484.8 million in 2000 (a 95.6 percent increase over the previous year), the company in July 2001 laid off 300 people, or 13 percent of its staff. The cuts were part of a larger effort to reduce costs. The company broke even in the third quarter of 2001 and then returned to profitability as the economy recovered. In October 2002 it switched its listing from NASDAQ to the New York Stock Exchange.

ECONOMIC PRESSURES

With profits growing again, Getty was back on the acquisition trail in the second half of the decade. In February 2006 it purchased iStockphoto, a stock photography community based in Calgary, Canada. The deal gave Getty entree to a new niche business of providing photographs at low prices to individuals and companies with minimal image needs. In April the company added two new collections, Stockbyte and Stockdisc, when it acquired their parent, Pixel Images Holdings Limited of Ireland, for $135 million in cash. A month later it purchased Laura Ronchi, SpA, the leading provider of visual content in Italy. Another collection, the Michael Ochs Archives of music and entertainment imagery, was added in February 2007.

Getty was rapidly adding to its collection of celebrity and entertainment-related content. In August 2006 it announced a distribution partnership with Associated Press's AP Archive, bringing more news, sports, entertainment, and historical photos and videos into the fold. In March 2007 Warner Brothers Entertainment signed a licensing agreement that made thousands of original stills and film clips available to editors, publishers, and filmmakers via gettyimages.com. The following month Getty acquired its largest competitor, MediaVest, owner of WireImage, FilmMagic, and Contour Photos, for $202 million.

"Celebrity, entertainment and sports photography is a fast-growing and vital part of the imagery industry," Klein said in a press statement on April 26, 2007, after the MediaVest purchase was completed, "and this acquisition positions us to meet and exceed the demand for nearly instantaneous content. Growing our entertainment imagery business has been a key strategic focus, resulting in revenue growth of approximately 60 percent in each of the last three quarters of 2006."

DIVERSIFICATION: USER-GENERATED CONTENT AND MUSIC-LICENSING OPTIONS

Earlier in 2007 Getty purchased Scoopt, an aggregator and distributor of photographs and video footage by eyewitnesses to news events. Getty moved deeper into user-generated content the following year, when it formed a partnership with Yahoo! Inc. under which Getty editors could search Yahoo!'s Flickr service for images. Photographers would then be invited to become paid contributors to Getty, with the company licensing their work and paying them the same rates as its contract photographers.

An acquisition in June 2007 marked Getty's entry into another new business. For $42 million, the company purchased Pump Audio, a music licenser with a 700,000-track online archive of precleared music from independent and unsigned artists. Shortly thereafter Getty announced the launch of Soundtrack, a new music-licensing service available through gettyimages.com. Soundtrack provided direct access to more than 20,000 original tracks by independent artists and bands for use in broadcast and film production, advertising, and other media projects. Getty's objective was to build a music-licensing business in somewhat the same way it had built its visual content presence, and with many of the same clients. As reported by Antony Bruno of *Billboard.biz* on June 20, 2007, Klein stated, "Our ambition moving into music is part of an overall thrust to be a digital media company." In February 2008 Getty followed by concluding a partnership with the independent film studio Lionsgate to make its film scores and soundtracks available for commercial licensing.

As an economic downturn started to affect the company, Getty announced layoffs of 5 percent of full-time staff in August 2006, and in October it kicked off a restructuring plan that would entail $9 million in charges. Meanwhile the Securities and Exchange Commission launched an investigation into allegations that top executives had backdated stock-option grants and then profited from their sale. Several shareholders filed lawsuits the following spring. Although it denied any wrongdoing, the company agreed to restate its earnings to fiscal year 1998.

ACQUISITION BY HELLMAN & FRIEDMAN

By 2007 the company had totaled up well in excess of half a billion dollars in acquisitions, and it claimed to service 4 million unique visitors to its website with 3.2 million images per month. Although nearly all its content was delivered digitally, the company maintained 21 offices worldwide and serviced clients in 100 countries.

The visual image business was becoming more competitive, however, putting downward pressure on pricing. In August 2007 management announced it was lowering its full-year profit projection. Getty's share price fell 47 percent in 2007, prompting talk that it was looking for a buyer. On February 25, 2008, Getty announced that it was being acquired by Hellman & Friedman LLC, a San Francisco–based private equity firm, for $2.4 billion in cash and assumed debt. The deal was completed in July.

PARTNERSHIPS

Getty continued to develop its services while extending old partnerships and adding new ones. In August 2009 it launched two new web and mobile image products that allowed clients to apply its images to digital communications with high resolution. The new product built on the success of the $49 web-resolution product Getty had introduced two years earlier. The following May the company launched Stockphotorights.com, an online service giving image providers information and advice on licensing their content.

Getty still sought new content. In September 2008 it inked a deal with Time Inc. to make images from *Life* magazine available online. Getty would publish 3,000 new images each day at Life.com and archive thousands of historic *Life* photos. New distribution agreements were signed with Disney/ABC Television group, Bloomberg Photos, the *Washington Post*, and the *New York Daily News*, among others.

The company's Contour by Getty Images collection formed a partnership with the *Los Angeles Times* to carry the newspaper's high-end contemporary celebrity portraiture. Getty also formed strategic alliances with digital music providers, including Gracenote and Hello Music, that would allow it to integrate images with their products and services. These alliances would allow Getty to profit from the rise of the digital album, spurred by the 2009 launch of iTunes LP.

"What people want to see is stills, video, historic images of bands rehearsing, award shows—and we have all that," Klein said at a music industry gathering, as reported by Ben Cardew in *Music Week* on February 6, 2010. "We can package for the fan a very compelling digital album."

Looking ahead, Getty sought new content and ways to make it available to new audiences. "Other industries encountered very similar threats," Klein told *Music Week*, comparing the experience of the visual content business with that of digital music providers. "You have to be open for new business models even if they cannibalize your core business. Consumers will keep demanding what technology gives them."

Jeffrey L. Covell
Updated, Eric Laursen

PRINCIPAL SUBSIDIARIES

iStockphoto; WireImage; FilmMagic; Jupiterimages; Photos.com.

PRINCIPAL COMPETITORS

Agence France-Presse; Corbis Corporation; Reuters Media.

FURTHER READING

Bruno, Antony. "Getty Images to Acquire Pump Audio." *Billboard.biz*, June 20, 2007. Accessed October 20, 2010. http://www.billboard.biz/bbbiz/content_display/industry/e3i1f767c9b7cecd7a2eb3f399f64aac78f.

Cardew, Ben. "Light Is Shone on Digital Dilemma." *Music Week*, February 06, 2010.

Corcoran, Jason. "Rich Kid Who Found Getty Name Negative: How I Made It." *Sunday Times* (London), February 2, 2003.

Dahle, Cheryl. "Image Isn't Everything." *Fast Company*, June 2000.

Fox, Katrina. "Why Image Is Everything." *B&T Weekly*, January 20, 2006.

"Getty Images Teams with RealNetworks to Bring World-Class Images and Footage to Streaming Media Users." PR Newswire, September 14, 1999.

"Getty Images to Buy Image Bank." United Press International, September 22, 1999.

Goldstein, Alan. "Seattle-Based Getty Images Buys Photo, Video Collection from Eastman Kodak." *Knight-Ridder/Tribune Business News*, September 22, 1999.

Lee, Jaimy. "Getty Focuses on Its Image Development." *PR Week*, September 29, 2008.

Sorkin, Andrew Ross, and Michael J. de la Merced. "Getty Images Up for Sale, Could Fetch $1.5 Billion." *New York Times*, January 21, 2008.

Tice, Carol. "Stock Central: Seattle Is Now a Photo Capital." *Puget Sound Business Journal*, May 7, 1999, 1.

Ghirardelli Chocolate Company

1111 139th Avenue
San Leandro, California 94578
U.S.A.
Telephone: (510) 483-6970
Toll Free: (800) 877-9338
Fax: (510) 297-2649
Web site: http://www.ghirardelli.com

Wholly Owned Subsidiary of Chocoladefabriken Lindt & Sprüngli AG
Founded: 1852
Employees: 650
NAICS: 311320 Confectionery Chocolate Made from Cacao Beans

■ ■ ■

The Ghirardelli Chocolate Company is the longest continuously operating chocolate manufacturer in the United States. Even though it moved its headquarters and production facilities to San Leandro, California, in 1967, Ghirardelli's historic factory in San Francisco is now a key landmark in that city, where it functions as an urban mall called Ghirardelli Square and a hub for the chocolatier's brand image. The company has a significant business selling chocolate wholesale. During the 1990s Ghirardelli increased its retail business by selling bagged candies in grocery stores and other outlets, as well as Ghirardelli brand baking chocolate and cocoa.

Since 1998, when the Swiss confectioner Chocoladefabriken Lindt & Sprüngli AG purchased the company, Ghirardelli has broken out of its regional concentration in the western United States to sell its products nationally through large grocery chains and other outlets, including its own chain of 14 ice cream and chocolate stores in five states. Helping to make this shift successful was Ghirardelli's decision to enlarge its position as a maker of premium chocolate products. Its efforts helped ignite a major surge in this market.

EARLY YEARS

The Ghirardelli Chocolate Company was founded by Domenico Ghirardelli, who was born in Rapello, Italy, in 1817. After serving as an apprentice to a confectioner and spice importer, Ghirardelli moved to South America. He worked for a time in Montevideo, Uruguay, then settled in Lima, Peru. Ghirardelli's shop in Lima was next door to James Lick, a cabinetmaker. Lick decided to leave Peru for California, arriving in San Francisco in January 1848, just days before gold was discovered at Sutter's Mill. Lick had brought with him 600 pounds of Ghirardelli's chocolate. He soon wrote to Ghirardelli that he had sold all the chocolate and advised the confectioner to come north.

At first Ghirardelli sold chocolate, coffee, liqueurs, and other items to gold miners, and by 1852 he had established a store in San Francisco. By 1885 the company was importing 450,000 pounds of cacao beans a year as well as importing and grinding spices and selling coffee, wine, and liquor. However, chocolate manufacturing was the mainstay of the business. Ghirardelli retired in 1892, leaving the company to his sons, who in 1893 purchased a square block in San Francisco to expand the company's operations. This

COMPANY PERSPECTIVES

As America's longest continuously operating chocolate manufacturer, Ghirardelli has established its position as America's premium chocolate company for more than 150 years.

We are one of very few American manufacturers that make chocolate starting from the cocoa bean through to finished products. Throughout the process, we take special steps to ensure that our premium chocolate delivers our signature intense, smooth-melting chocolate taste.

area survived the earthquake and fire of 1906 and Ghirardelli continued to expand its facilities, erecting new buildings in what became known as Ghirardelli Square. By 1916 the site included an apartment building and a clock tower that soon made it a local landmark.

Business boomed during World War I, when the factory operated around the clock to produce chocolate for the armed forces. During the 1920s Ghirardelli became the largest chocolate factory west of the Mississippi. Besides bulk chocolate and cocoa, it made retail goods such as instant-chocolate malted milk powder. Ghirardelli also did a sizable business in mustard, of which it was the only manufacturer west of the Mississippi under both its own name and the Schilling brand.

FAMILY SELLS BUSINESS: 1958–67

By the time the founder's son, Domingo Lyle Ghirardelli, stepped down as president of the company in 1958, Ghirardelli was a vertically integrated operation that not only processed chocolate but also made its own cans and boxes, manufacturing everything it needed except for paper goods. However, Ghirardelli was reaching a crossroads. Its manufacturing plant used large and antiquated equipment that was labor intensive to use and required a great deal of maintenance. Ghirardelli imported cacao beans from the Ivory Coast, Panama, Samoa, and Colombia, each with different characteristics, and blending them for the proper taste and color was a sophisticated art.

The mustard business had come to a halt in 1947, when A. Schilling & Company, Ghirardelli's major customer, was acquired by McCormick & Company. Ghirardelli's sales were weak and its management was reaching retirement age. As a result, during the early 1960s the company announced that it would consider selling the business.

Ghirardelli received an offer for its land and buildings in 1962 from Mrs. William P. Roth and her son William Matson Roth. The Ghirardelli family accepted, and the Roths formed the Ghirardelli Center Development Company to renovate the buildings and convert them into the block of shops and restaurants now known as Ghirardelli Square. Then in 1963 the Golden Grain Company offered to buy the chocolate company. Another family-run business founded by Italian immigrants, Golden Grain had gained nationwide appeal with its introduction of Rice-A-Roni. Ghirardelli's machinery was mostly sold to scrap dealers and Golden Grain started from scratch, constructing a new, modern manufacturing facility in nearby San Leandro in 1967.

CHANGES IN OWNERSHIP: 1986–94

Ghirardelli continued producing wholesale chocolate for the confectionary, baking, and dairy industries and premium branded items for retail stores. By the mid-1980s the company was doing well but its business was still concentrated in the western United States and only accounted for a little over 10 percent of Golden Grain's total sales. In 1986 Quaker Oats, a food conglomerate based in Chicago, Illinois, acquired Golden Grain, and with it Ghirardelli. Quaker hung on to the chocolate maker for three years, then put it up for sale. Ghirardelli was then bringing in an estimated $35 million in annual sales. During this period Ghirardelli redesigned its packaging to give it a more modern and upscale look, and this change sparked an upsurge in sales.

In March 1992 Thomas H. Lee Company, a Boston, Massachusetts, investment firm, bought Ghirardelli. Terms of the sale were not made available, but later disclosures put the price at around $40 million. Annual sales had grown to about the same amount by the early 1990s, although industry watchers also noted that Ghirardelli faced harsh competition from other large chocolate producers such as the Hershey Company and Nestlé S.A.

John J. Anton was appointed as the president and chief executive officer (CEO) of Ghirardelli, and during his tenure he oversaw a surge in growth. The company had three soda fountain and chocolate shops in San Francisco, and in 1994 Ghirardelli announced it would open more stores in other cities in California and Chicago. Retail sales accounted for only about 15 percent of the company's total sales, but the company saw this as an opportunity for growth. Ghirardelli also

KEY DATES

1852: Domingo Ghirardelli establishes the company in San Francisco, California.
1893: Ghirardelli purchases a square block in San Francisco as its headquarters and production facility.
1963: The Golden Grain Company buys the company from the Ghirardelli family following sale of land and buildings the previous year.
1967: A new production facility is established in San Leandro, California.
1986: Quaker Oats acquires Ghirardelli.
1992: Thomas H. Lee Company acquires Ghirardelli; John J. Anton is named president and chief executive officer.
1996: John J. Anton buys out Thomas H. Lee.
1998: John J. Anton sells Ghirardelli to Chocoladefabriken Lindt & Sprüngli AG.
2006: Ghirardelli introduces a successful line of dark gourmet chocolate bars.
2009: Ghirardelli introduces an application that lets customers order company products from iPhones.

worked on expanding its presence in grocery stores with branded baking products such as cocoa and chocolate chips. During this period the company's branded products surpassed industrial products in the percentage of total sales. By 1994 around 60 percent of its total sales were in the branded products division. Total annual sales rose from $37 million in 1992 to $75 million in 1994.

NATIONAL EXPANSION AND A NEW OWNER: 1994–2000

By the mid-1990s Ghirardelli shifted to selling its products nationally. It pushed to get its products into more grocery stores and other retail outlets in major markets, particularly in big cities in the Midwest and Northeast. In November 1994 Ghirardelli announced a distribution deal with the Sam's Club food chain that was owned by Wal-Mart Stores, Inc. By then almost half the company's sales were in markets east of the Rocky Mountains, up from just 20 percent when Thomas H. Lee first acquired Ghirardelli. The company also expanded its product line, which doubled to 125 different food items by 1994. It marketed its baking goods in supermarkets by setting up displays, established a recipe center, and maintained a toll-free customer support line. With increased marketing and distribution, grocery sales grew 50 percent annually during the first half of the decade. Ghirardelli was also searching for new ways to make its brand more attractive and widely known, such as by launching an annual chocolate festival at its flagship Soda Fountain & Chocolate Shop in Ghirardelli Square in 1995.

In 1996 Anton bought out Thomas H. Lee with the help of two private investment firms, Hicks, Muse, Tate, & Furst, Inc., and C. Dean Metropoulos & Company. Remaining as president and CEO of the company, Anton kept Ghirardelli on its growth course. However, the new ownership was short lived. After weighing the possibility of taking the company public to raise needed capital for expansion, Anton announced in January 1998 that Ghirardelli had been acquired by Chocoladefabriken Lindt & Sprüngli, a leading producer of premium chocolates in Europe. Anton remained as president. Even though the decision to sell was difficult, he told David Lazarus in the *San Francisco Chronicle* on May 27, 2000, that "with Lindt, here was a company whose total focus was chocolate. The more I thought about that, the more excited I got."

FOCUSING ON GROWTH WITH NEW PRODUCTS: 2000–04

Lindt & Sprüngli was on an expansion drive, and its acquisition of Ghirardelli helped increase its share of the North American market. Lindt brand chocolates had a larger presence on the East Coast than on the West Coast, so Ghirardelli gave it better coverage of the entire country. Lindt & Sprüngli announced that it was pleased with Ghirardelli's growth, which had averaged 20 percent annually between 1995 and 2000 and reported sales of over $100 million in 2000.

If anything, Lindt & Sprüngli sped up Ghirardelli's pace of expansion, which was underpinned by a push to streamline the company's internal processes. In 2000 Ghirardelli completed a $45 million expansion of its 265,000-square-foot San Leandro plant, which quadrupled production capacity. To better accommodate its growing business with large retailers such as Wal-Mart, Ghirardelli adopted in 2004 a production scheduling program from JRG Software to improve factory planning productivity and reduce labor costs.

Meanwhile, Ghirardelli's focus during its first years under Lindt & Sprüngli's ownership was also on expanding its product line and reinforcing its standing as a premium chocolatier. In 1999 it introduced the Frappe Classico line of drink mixes. The following year it began selling new versions of its popular Ghirardelli Squares chocolates with varieties of fillings. Upgrades in packaging followed in 2003 and 2004, along with another new product, Caffe Whole Bean Coffees.

Ghirardelli was bolstering Lindt & Sprüngli's effort to expand in the United States, where it had its own chain of high-end stores. In 2000 the United States became the single-largest market for Lindt & Sprüngli, with sales totaling $204 million, topping its sales in Germany for the first time "The United States 'has become the most significant market for the group in terms of sales in the year 2000,'" the group chairman and CEO Ernst Tanner told Alice Ratcliffe of Reuters News on March 27, 2001. "I firmly believe the U.S. holds untold potential for us."

In 2001 Anton left Ghirardelli and was replaced as CEO by Kamillo Kitzmantel. Ghirardelli's new focus was to increase its share of the $1 billion premium chocolate market and to encourage Americans to raise their chocolate consumption from about 12 pounds per year to the European level of 25 pounds per year. Ghirardelli started selling its chocolate squares in Target and Safeway stores while its bite-sized chocolates were being carried by CVS, Walgreen's, Vons, and ShopRite. Overall, 10 percent of full-service grocery stores were carrying Ghirardelli Squares chocolates, a figure the company wanted to raise to 20 percent.

Accordingly, the company launched a $3 million advertising campaign in 2003. It was also looking for other ways to promote its brand. In 2004 it launched a new national contest, the Ghirardelli Chocolate Championship, that was held at state fairs and other events across the country.

SPARKING A PREMIUM CHOCOLATE BOOM: 2004–05

In March 2004 *Cook's Illustrated* named Ghirardelli's bittersweet premium baking chocolate its "Favorite Dark Chocolate," beating eight other well-known brands including Lindt & Sprüngli's. Over the next several years Ghirardelli and Godiva Chocolatier, Inc., jump-started a national consumer trend in favor of premium dark chocolates with more intense flavors. Between 2003 and 2005 U.S. sales of premium chocolates jumped from $1.4 billion to $1.8 billion. This represented a 28 percent growth rate, compared to the overall chocolate market, which had a 2 percent to 3 percent growth rate during the same period.

Ghirardelli began noting the percentage of cacao on its product packaging and moved to capitalize on its recognition as a high-quality chocolate maker by introducing new dark-chocolate products. In 2005 it increased the cacao content of its bittersweet baking chocolate to 60 percent. At about the same time it premiered a new extra bittersweet baking chocolate, with 70 percent cacao, as well as dark chocolate squares.

That same year it converted from cardboard boxes to open gray tubs known as totes, a switch that helped reduce its landfill contribution by 350 tons of per year. The switch also reduced costs. Previously, Ghirardelli paid $520,000 per year to buy 580,000 cardboard boxes to deliver its premium chocolate squares to its packagers. Disposal costs added another $2,700 annually. Ghirardelli expected to save $2 million over five years with the new system.

Cost reduction was important because the price of raw materials for Ghirardelli's products was going up steadily. Cacao prices started rising as early as 1989, and jumped up significantly in 2004 due to unrest in the Ivory Coast, which produced 40 percent of the world's supply. Commodity costs rose massively again three years later, which meant that Ghirardelli had to raise prices across the board. However, it expected that because of its positioning as a high-end chocolate producer customers would most likely accept higher prices.

DEVELOPING MORE PRODUCT AND REBRANDING IMAGE: 2006–10

In 2006 Ghirardelli launched a new line of intense dark gourmet chocolate bars in four flavors and then added three more in 2007. Ghirardelli was now processing nearly 150,000 pounds of chocolate per day at its San Leandro plant.

The company was also looking for other ways to expand its brand. In 2006 it concluded a deal with Tully's Coffee of Seattle in that Tully's would offer drinks made with Ghirardelli white and dark chocolate and caramel gourmet sauces. It also completed a deal with Friendly Ice Cream Corporation to introduce a branded Ghirardelli chocolate ice cream that was available only in Friendly's restaurants. That was followed by a deal with Cold Stone Creamery, Inc., to offer ice cream products with Ghirardelli chocolate chips and caramel squares as mix-ins. In 2008 the company introduced a new line of gourmet baking products that included a 100 percent cacao unsweetened baking chocolate.

In late 2007 a recession began to take hold of the country. Whereas some companies saw their sales decrease in response to the recession, Ghirardelli found that its sales were relatively unscathed. "People reward themselves for all the hardship they're going through by giving themselves a nice glass of wine or a nice chocolate," Fabrizio Parini, the senior vice president of marketing, told *Market News International*'s Claudia Hirsch on April 29, 2009. "And premium chocolate works better as that compensatory consumption than mass chocolate does." Parini also explained that Ghirardelli was in a particularly strong position because of its brand recognition and the relative affordability of its pricing compared to other premium chocolates.

Meanwhile, Ghirardelli was refurbishing and updating its branded presence. By early 2009 the company had 14 retail stores in five states, including its original Soda Fountain & Chocolate Shop in Ghirardelli Square. The company was also pushing its retail sales operation into the digital age. It added a feature to its website that allowed a visitor to click on a product to launch a Facebook application, creating an image on the visitor's wall and sending a message to others in the visitor's network, who could then provide comments and suggestions.

In October 2009 a new iPhone application through the Digby Mobile Commerce Suite followed, allowing customers to browse and purchase Ghirardelli products. "The way our customers shop with us is changing, and we want to be as accessible and convenient as possible for them," said Yvo Smit, the vice president of restaurant and retail at Ghirardelli, to *Information Technology Newsweekly* on October 6, 2009. "With this app, sending a thank you gift to clients following a meeting can be done on your way out the door."

A. Woodward
Updated, Eric Laursen

PRINCIPAL DIVISIONS

Baking; Confections and Beverages; Food Service.

PRINCIPAL COMPETITORS

Godiva Chocolatier, Inc.; Mars, Inc.; Nestlé S.A.

FURTHER READING

Carlsen, Clifford. "Ghirardelli Chocolate Plans National Rollout." *San Francisco Business Times*, April 29, 1994, 1.

Foley, Brian. "Savings Are Sweet at Local Plant." *Oakland (CA) Tribune*, January 1, 2006.

"Ghirardelli Rolls out iPhone App, Mobile Web Storefronts on Digby Platform." *Wireless News*, October 1, 2009.

"Ghirardelli Thrives on Old World Heritage." *Candy Industry*, August 1994, 51.

Hirsch, Claudia. "Reality Check: Some US Businesses Thriving, Even Now." *Market News International*, April 29, 2009.

Lawrence, Polly Ghirardelli, et al. *The Ghirardelli Family and Chocolate Company of San Francisco*. Berkeley, CA: Regional Oral History Office, the Bancroft Library, University of California, 1985.

McDonough, Susan. "Going Gourmet: Ghirardelli Chocolate Sells Nationwide." Associated Press, August 10, 2002.

O'Brien, Tom. "Swiss Chocolate, Smooth Success." *Swiss News*, December 1, 2002, 22.

Raine, George. "Sweet Sesquicentennial," *San Francisco Chronicle*, June 9, 2002, G3.

"Sales Leap 300% after Upscale Redesign." *Packaging*, February 1992, 15.

Goodwin PLC

Ivy House Foundry, Hanley
Stoke-on-Trent, ST1 3NR
United Kingdom
Telephone: (+44 1782) 220 000
Fax: (+44 1782) 208 060
Web site: http://www.goodwingroup.com

Public Company
Founded: 1883 as R. Goodwin & Sons
Incorporated: 1935 as R. Goodwin & Sons (Engineers) Ltd.
Employees: 822
Sales: £93.9 million ($151.4 million) (2010)
Stock Exchanges: London
Ticker Symbol: GDWN
NAICS: 541330 Engineering Services; 327124 Clay Refractory Manufacturing; 327125 Nonclay Refractory Manufacturing

■ ■ ■

Headquartered in Stoke-on-Trent in the United Kingdom, Goodwin PLC is the parent company of several subsidiaries in the mechanical and refractory engineering fields. Goodwin also owns Internet Central Limited, an Internet service provider based in the United Kingdom. Goodwin Steel Castings Ltd. for castings, Goodwin International Ltd. for machining, general engineering, valves, and pumps, and Easat Antennas Ltd. for radar antennas lead the mechanical engineering business. Hoben International Ltd. for powders, refractory cements, and minerals and Hoben Industrial Minerals Ltd. for mineral processing are the group's leading subsidiaries for refractory engineering. The company's subsidiaries serve more than 70 countries throughout the world. The group attributes 80 percent of its sales growth to the developing world, particularly the Pacific Basin, for which it manufacturers check valves for oil, gas, and the liquefied natural gas industries and steam valves for the power-generation industries.

GOODWIN'S FOUNDRY

Ralph Goodwin and his sons established R. Goodwin & Sons, iron founders and engineers, in the ancient Ivy House Estate in Hanley, Stoke-on-Trent, Staffordshire, in 1883. By the 1920s R. Goodwin & Sons was an iron foundry and engineering company supplying castings and equipment to local industry. On October 11, 1935, the company was incorporated as R. Goodwin & Sons (Engineers) Ltd. Over the next 15 years, R. Goodwin & Sons expanded with the acquisition of 35 percent of J. A. Domenet Ltd. and construction of a factory for sheet-metal work and medium and precision engineering.

On June 7, 1953, J.A. Domenet Ltd. was renamed Akron Standard (Engineers) Ltd. The company name changed again in 1977 to R. Goodwin International Ltd. It changed again in April 1994 to Goodwin International Ltd., becoming a wholly owned subsidiary of Goodwin PLC.

In 1952 the International Nickel Company granted R. Goodwin & Sons the license to produce spheroidal graphite iron, also known as ductile iron, a malleable

COMPANY PERSPECTIVES

The Company has an engineering commitment. Its investment criteria aim at the efficient economic supply of technically advanced products to growth markets. The core competence is mechanical and refractory engineering combined with an emphasis on innovative design and cost reduction to competitively manufacture.

Investing in new ideas has been a key factor in the development of the Company's subsidiaries so that the group is sufficiently diversified to avoid excessive dependence on a single product or market but sufficiently focused to ensure management is able to maintain a deep understanding of each of the individual businesses and the markets in which they operate as shown on the subsidiary websites.

material for use in castings. In 1958 Goodwin & Sons shares began trading publicly on the London Stock Exchange. On August 12, 1963, the company acquired W. H. Kirkham & Sons, which was renamed Hoben Quarries Ltd. Hoben expanded with the purchase of land in Brassington, Derbyshire, in March 1972 and, in 1994, its name was changed again to Hoben Industrial Minerals Ltd. It was in 1965 that R. Goodwin & Sons purchased Hoben Davis Ltd., which was renamed Hoben International Ltd. in March 1997.

On January 15, 1973, the goodwill and trading assets of the foundry division were transferred to a new company named Goodwin Steel Castings Ltd., while the status of R. Goodwin & Sons (Engineers) Ltd. changed to that of a holding company. In that same year, the company expanded with the founding of Goodwin GMBH in Dusseldorf, Germany. In 1978 British Coal commissioned R. Goodwin & Sons to develop and manufacture an electrically driven submersible slurry pump. By 1981 the first submersible pump units were installed in British Coal at the Cwm Washery in South Wales, with thousands of installations following into British Steel and the Central Electricity Generating Board between 1983 and 1994.

GOODWIN'S POSTCENTENARY EXPANSION

On February 1, 1982, R. Goodwin & Sons (Engineers) Ltd. changed its name to Goodwin PLC. In celebration of its centenary in 1983, the company coat of arms was granted with the motto, *On fonde per le monde* (One founds for the world). Every detail of the coat of arms was carefully selected to symbolize the company's engineering contributions, its international interests, and the English roots of the Goodwin family. Designed in black for its industrial connotations, red for the steel melting furnaces, and gold for the wealth that the business generated, the coat of arms was proudly adopted as the company's logo.

The following year, Goodwin became the first steel foundry to be accredited with BS5750 (ISO9001) by the British Standards Institution for its quality management. The company was also accredited with ISO14001 in 1999 for its environmental management systems. In 1986 Langley Alloys Ltd. granted Goodwin a license to manufacture Super Duplex Stainless Steel, the same year that Cosmopark Ltd. was incorporated. Goodwin purchased 75 percent of Cosmopark the following year, which was renamed Easat Antennas Ltd. By 1990 Haynes International Inc. had granted Goodwin the sole UK license to cast Hastelloy, a range of metal alloys used by the chemical processing industries.

In 1992 Goodwin became the only steel foundry to be audited and awarded a best-practice certificate for computer-aided methoding by the UK government's Energy Efficiency Office. The company expanded its presence in Asia the following year with the formation of Goodwin Korea Co., with Goodwin holding 95 percent of the shares. With the privatization of British Coal in 1994, which resulted in the closures of several mines and steel works in the United Kingdom, Goodwin decided to develop its European presence, primarily the steel and power sectors in Poland, Germany, Hungary, and the Czech Republic. Goodwin also moved into Africa, providing submersible slurry pumps to the gold, copper, and platinum mining industries.

MORE INTERNATIONAL EXPANSION

In 1997 Goodwin entered the Internet business with an initial investment of 47.5 percent of Internet Central Ltd., which was later increased to 82.5 percent of the share capital. In 2000 Goodwin received the Structural Steel Design Award for its castings for London's Paddington Station Phase 1 Masterplan. In 2002 sales outside Europe and the United Kingdom increased to £14.6 million. Some of the projects contributing to this figure included cable bands for two major bridges in China, valves for oil and gas rigs, and molds for gold and silver jewelry.

In 2005 Goodwin International was incorporated in order to expand the global sales of its submersible slurry

KEY DATES

1883: Ralph Goodwin and his sons establish R. Goodwin & Sons.
1935: R. Goodwin & Sons (Engineers) Ltd. is incorporated.
1958: The company's shares are traded publicly on the London Stock Exchange.
1982: R. Goodwin & Sons (Engineers) Ltd. changes its name to Goodwin PLC.
2010: The family of founder Ralph Goodwin holds 53 percent of the company.

pumps, particularly in India, China, and Brazil, where the company set up sales, manufacturing, and servicing outlets. With oil prices continuing to rise, the sale of Goodwin's valves to the international energy and petrochemical industries remained buoyant. Steam valves for the power-generation industry and the Radar Antenna Division were also performing well in 2005. In March 2007 Goodwin expanded its presence in Germany when it acquired 75 percent of Noreva GmbH, a nonreturn nozzle check valve manufacturer, for £2.8 million. The following year, Easat Antennas Ltd. won a contract worth more than $10 million to supply transportable air surveillance antennas.

In June 2008 Goodwin announced that it had acquired SRS Holdings Limited, a holding company for Specialist Refractory Services Limited, and all of its associated subsidiaries for £6 million. In September 2008 Goodwin took a 51 percent share in a joint venture with Goldstar Brazil, an industrial minerals company, and established a manufacturing plant São Paulo. In 2009 Goodwin won a U.S. defense contract worth £8.6 million, and included General Electric, the Royal Navy, and China's power stations among its customers. By investing in emerging markets, such as China, India, Thailand, and Brazil, the company's bottom line remained positive with sales in excess of £100 million at the close of the 2009 fiscal year.

LOOKING AHEAD

In preparation for the increased demand for car parts and jewelry that analysts projected would occur in 2011, Goodwin reorganized its engineering business to better position itself for this demand. Also, many of the power stations that Goodwin supplied burned fossil fuels, a strong attraction to energy producers that were keen to reduce greenhouse gases.

Forward-thinking chairman John Goodwin said to the Stoke-on-Trent *Sentinel* (September 1, 2008), "By 2020, using the cast components produced by Goodwin could potentially contribute to delivering power generation efficiency resulting in a reduction of 800 million tons of carbon dioxide emissions a year in China and India, based on these countries' anticipated output." In 2010 the family of founder Ralph Goodwin still held 53 percent of the business.

Marie O'Sullivan

PRINCIPAL SUBSIDIARIES

Dupre Minerals Limited; Easat Antennas Limited (92.5%); Gold Star Brazil Limited (51%); Gold Star Powders Private Limited (India, 80%); Goodwin (Shanghai) Valve Co. Limited (China); Goodwin India Private Limited (80%); Goodwin International Limited; Goodwin Korea Co. Limited (South Korea, 95%); Goodwin Refractory Services Limited; Goodwin Steel Castings Limited; Hoben International Limited; Internet Central Limited (82.5%); Jewelry Plaster Company Limited (Thailand, Associate, 49%); Noreva GmbH (Germany, 75%); Siam Casting Powders Limited (Thailand, 51%); SRS Guangzhou Limited (China, 51%); Ultratec Jewelry Supplies Limited (China, 51%).

PRINCIPAL DIVISIONS

Refractories; Engineering.

PRINCIPAL COMPETITORS

Antenova Ltd.; Cookson Group plc; W. R. Grace & Co.

FURTHER READING

Brown, Graeme. "Engineering Firm Goodwin Turns Over £68m in Nine Months." *Birmingham Post*, March 9, 2010.

"Demand from Emerging Markets Boosts Profits at Hanley Engineer Goodwin." *Sentinel* (Stoke-on-Trent), September 1, 2008.

"Goodwin Buys 75 Pct of German Co Noreva for Initial 2.8 Mln Stg in Cash." *Europe Intelligence Wire*, March 23, 2007.

"Goodwin (GDWN)." *Investors Chronicle*, January 7, 2005.

"Goodwin (GDWN)." *Investors Chronicle*, September 9, 2005.

Hofmann, Julian. "Goodwin's Cast Iron Returns." *Investors Chronicle*, September 10, 2009.

Hughman, John, "The Winning Family-Owned Companies." *Investors Chronicle*, May 7, 2010.

"Profits Stable for Goodwin." thisisbusiness-staffordshire.co.uk, September 14, 2009. Accessed November 11, 2010. http://www.thisisbusiness-staffordshire.co.uk/localnews/Profits-stable-Goodwin/article-1335110-detail/article.html.

Grote Industries, Inc.

2600 Lanier Drive
Madison, Indiana 47250
U.S.A.
Telephone: (812) 273-1296
Toll Free: (800) 628-0809
Fax: (812) 265-8440
Web site: http://www.grote.com

Private Company
Founded: 1901 as Grotelite Company
Incorporated: 1943 as Grote Manufacturing Company
Employees: 1,000 (est.)
Sales: $67 million (2009)
NAICS: 334413 Light Emitting Diodes (LED) Manufacturing; 336321 Vehicular Lighting Equipment Manufacturing; 327215 Glass Products Manufacturing Made of Purchased Glass; 334290 Other Communications Equipment Manufacturing

■ ■ ■

Grote Industries, Inc., has been a leading light in entrepreneurship and highway safety throughout its 100-plus years in business. The brainchild of William D. Grote (pronounced "GRO-tee"), the company revealed its innovative outlook through an early focus on plastics production. Fittingly, more than a century after the firm's founding, Edward Sitarski, a product development engineer at Grote, won the 2007 Idea of the Year Award from the Employee Involvement Association for his robotics efforts with LED vehicle lights. As a maker and distributor of vehicle lighting and related products, Grote Industries has served customers including automotive original equipment manufacturers, automotive parts retailers, the heavy-duty vehicle aftermarket, and marine and RV distributorships. On boats, semitrailer trucks, recreational vans, buses, loaders, cars, and other vehicles, the need for interior and exterior lighting has kept Grote at the industry's forefront.

AN EXCLUSIVE LICENSE FOR PLASTICS

By the early 1900s, scientists, engineers, and manufacturers had accrued sufficient knowledge of plastics to confirm their future marketability. As a chemicals broker in Kentucky, William Grote had a keen curiosity about what lay ahead for plastics. In 1901 Grote took a business trip to Europe, his entrepreneurial mission ignited by his chemistry background and the prospects of the plastics industry. Once abroad, he encountered a product at the frontier of thermoplastics: an injection molding machine. He bought four of the so-called Buchholz machines, acquired an exclusive license for operating them in the United States, and brought the machines home. The Grotelite Company was born.

Grotelite made plastic products as well as supplying custom-made molds to other manufacturers. According to Jeffrey L. Meikle's 1995 book *American Plastic: A Cultural History*, combs, eyeglass frames, steering wheels, and tool handles were among the outcomes of injection molding. In 1922 Grote acquired National Colortype Company, a maker of road signs, thereby channeling his efforts toward the transportation industry. When Grote's

COMPANY PERSPECTIVES

Grote Industries is a leading manufacturer and marketer of vehicle lighting and safety systems. Our company was founded in the heartland over 100 years ago and has remained family owned from the day William Grote opened the doors for business. With manufacturing locations in Canada, Mexico, and the United States, we are the only heavy duty lighting supplier that can boast to be truly a NAFTA company. We are an industry leading manufacturer, the first to receive our TS16949 certification in the heavy duty lighting industry. Our company is steeped in tradition with a continued focus on innovation as well as a strong commitment to providing quality products and service. We still hold firm to the family values and work ethics set forth by our founder all those years ago.

workers developed the first automatic injection molding machine in 1929, manufacturing became more efficient and set the stage for wider production. Further growth followed when the company made its injection molding material available commercially in 1936, diversifying the company's client base and raising its industry profile.

During World War II the company added metal boxes for storing ammunition to its line. In 1943 the Grotelite Company became Grote Manufacturing Company, with Walter F. Grote, Sr., who had been company president since 1935, carrying on his father's forward-thinking approach. After the war's end, machines that had stamped metal for the ammunition boxes were turned to the production of medicine cabinets for a building products division aimed at the burgeoning postwar construction industry. Grote Manufacturing remained a supplier for the military well into the 21st century. However, building on research and development that began in the late 1920s with the company's pioneering retro-reflective devices for automobiles, Grote refocused his company's postwar efforts on the emerging field of vehicle lighting. Cars, trucks, and other motor vehicles needed innovative lighting products, as well as new ways of making them.

IMPROVEMENTS IN VEHICLE LIGHTING

The 1960s were ripe for improvements in vehicle lighting. In his July 1965 article for *Fleet Owner*, David Weber observed: "The problems of vehicle lighting and night vision, and more broadly, communication between vehicles, are undergoing one of the most widespread research and development periods ever to hit the industry." A growing urgency surrounded vehicle lighting issues, particularly for trucks. Interstate highway systems were growing, but minimum standards for lights varied on federal, state, and local levels, leaving decisions about product features and quality in the hands of truck owners and of lighting product manufacturers such as Grote. Even though the cost of new lights tended to be relatively high, safety was considered by all parties to be of paramount importance.

Grote moved its headquarters and flagship facility from Kentucky to Madison, Indiana, in 1960, and five years later the company achieved two breakthroughs. The Turtleback Marker Lamp was the first vehicle marker made of plastic and glass instead of metal. Marker lights define a vehicle's dimensions for other traffic, and the Grote product's distinctive convex shape (hence Turtleback) withstood impact, while its rustproof housing increased durability. The other development of 1965 was a truck wiring system that eliminated the need for splicing. As Weber pointed out in his 1965 article, electrical problems drove up maintenance costs and kept a truck off the road. Grote's new products, and the problems they solved for truckers and firms hiring them, for the efficient delivery of goods, and for highway safety in general, affirmed the company's product development choices.

INNOVATION AND EXPANSION

In 1971, one year after the company sold its building products division, Grote acquired the Monarch Manufacturing Company, a Chicago-based maker of vehicle mirrors. Five years later Grote opened a factory in Ontario, its first site outside the United States. With the Canadian plant and the Monarch site, the company extended its geographic and product-related markets. In 1977 another innovation came about when Grote offered a vehicle lamp with two somewhat risky features: the lamp was both repairable and long-lasting. Because the lamp drastically reduced the need for replacement, it virtually invited some revenue loss from diminished repeat business. With the product's greater dependability and longevity, however, Grote saw an equally valuable increase in customer loyalty and confidence.

When Grote introduced a wiring harness system known as Ultra-Blue-Seal (UBS) in 1983, the industry had its first modular wiring for trailers. System attributes such as plug-together assembly and anti-corrosion sealing eased installation and repair. Then, in 1985, a distinctly important opportunity opened up. At

KEY DATES

1923: William D. Grote, founder of the Grotelite Company, obtains an exclusive license for the first plastic injection molding machines in the United States.

1965: Grote Manufacturing Company launches the vehicular lighting industry's first plastic and glass headlamp.

1976: The company establishes its first facility outside the United States.

1989: Grote introduces the first LED marker light.

2009: Grote debuts the vehicle industry's first pliable LED lighting film for commercial sale.

the behest of the National Highway Safety Transportation Administration, the Ford Motor Company was working on the prototype of a car with air bags and signed on Grote to design, manufacture, and install lights for the car's rear window. The job was done so well that Grote was contracted concurrently to engineer the high-mount rear lights on Ford's 1986 models. The company consequently became one of Ford's main suppliers.

SAFETY LIGHTS AND LEDS

Because of their size, long lifespan, extreme brightness, diverse applications, and all-around uniqueness, LEDs (light-emitting diodes) became a mother lode of products for Grote beginning in the 1980s. Since they were compact, LED were simpler to install than incandescent bulbs. What is more, they held up better against the impact of highway and road surfaces, were budget savers, and provided an extreme brightness crucial in poor weather conditions and at night. Diversity in product application meant that, over time, LEDs might surpass incandescent bulbs in trucks, buses, cars and other vehicles. Grote's engineers worked on the possibilities of LEDs and in 1989 generated a new product, the industry's first LED marker light. Like Grote's original Turtleback Marker Lamp, the 1989 product indicated profile and clearance along a vehicle's edges, but with the further advantages offered by an LED.

With the cooperation of some well-known shipping and vehicle rental companies, including Roadway Express, ABF Freight System, and Ryder, the new LED marker light was road-tested, emerging with outstanding results. "In fact," remarked John J. Dwyer, Jr., in the August 1990 issue of *Fleet Owner*, "not a single failure has been reported in over a year of field testing, according to Lynn Roney, manager, advanced technology at Grote." Although the company's research and development teams remained at the drawing board working to create cost-effective amber lights (also commonly used for indicator lights), the red marker light had clearly earned its seal of approval from users. Roney emphasized that other applications would be rolled out in the near term.

In 1991, two years after adding LEDs to its product lineup, Grote celebrated its ninth decade in business. Ora Spaid profiled the company in the February 1990 issue of *Indiana Business Magazine*, surveying its history and accomplishments, noting its 400 product offerings, and interviewing Bill Grote, third-generation president of the family-owned enterprise. Spaid observed, "This Indiana firm's advance to becoming the nation's largest maker of lighting and safety products for the commercial vehicle market raises the question. What is different about Grote? Put those questions to Bill Grote, the president, and the term 'aggressive' keeps turning up in his answers." With growth that included a 1990 employee count of nearly 1,000 (10 times its 1960 level) and a Madison factory expansion costing $7 million, Grote's progress was certifiable.

LEDS AND THE FUTURE

During the 1990s Grote maintained an assertive stance. Another plant opened in Ontario in 1992, a facility in Mexico followed in 1993, and within 15 years Grote expanded to Spain and then Germany. Cost considerations and lean manufacturing trimmed the workforce to just below 875 by 1995, the year the company was renamed Grote Industries, Inc. The decade ended with additions to the company's SuperNova product line of four-inch LED vehicle lights with patented lens innovations that garnered attention in the January 1999 issue of *Fleet Equipment*: "By using transparent dyes and a design that focuses light over a 40-degree arc, [Dominic] Grote said the SuperNovas increase both the brightness and intensity of light far beyond that of existing LED technology." Dominic Grote, concentrating on marketing and sales of the company's LED lights, represented his family's fourth generation in the business.

In 2001 Grote reached its centennial milestone, and the company's second century saw its continued success and pioneering product development. A federally issued deadline of 2001, for example, required that trucks with trailers meet conspicuity requirements by achieving standardized visibility levels by using red and white reflectors or reflective tape. Grote was among the lighting distributors offering products to assist fleet owners with compliance. In 2002 the company reported revenues of about $66.7 million. In 2008, having overcome issues of technology and cost, Grote made amber LED lights available for the first time. In 2009 the company debuted LightForm, the first thin, flexible LED lighting film, produced as power strips and extension strips, whose commercial availability made possible myriad applications in previously unworkable spaces and contexts. That same year Dominic Grote took over as company president and chief operating officer, steadfastly pursuing the founder's vision.

Indicators at the end of the first decade of the 21st century augured well for the company's future. In 2009 a report by Marcy Lowe and others, *Manufacturing Climate Solutions, Carbon-Reducing Technologies and U.S. Jobs*, numbered Grote among the companies with the specialized capability to produce energy-saving LED lights compatible with environmentally friendly upgrades in public transit. In 2010 Grote introduced a dome light for refrigerated trucks that featured energy-efficient LED motion sensors for automatic on-off switching that used power only when a person was present and moving about. As it had for more than 100 years, the company continued to apply its expertise in a diverse marketplace, solving problems, meeting challenges, and looking ahead.

Mary C. Lewis

PRINCIPAL SUBSIDIARIES

Gale Die Mold Co.; Grote Canada Ltd.; Grote Electronics; Grote Europe; Grote Industries Co. (Canada); Grote Industries LLC; Grote Manufacturing Company; Grote North America.

PRINCIPAL DIVISIONS

Core Products Engineering; Electrical Connections and Accessories; Electronics; Grote Trailer; Heavy Duty; Safety Systems; Signal Lighting; U.S. Aftermarket Sales.

PRINCIPAL COMPETITORS

Decofimex S.A. de C.V.; Dorman Products, Inc.; Hella KGaA Hueck & Co.; Jordan Industries, Inc.; Lexalite International Corp.; Magna International Inc.; Robert Bosch GmbH.

FURTHER READING

DuBois, J. Harry. *Plastics History U.S.A.* Boston: Cahners Books, 1972, 216–20.

Dwyer, John J., Jr. "LED Lamps Are Alive and Well." *Fleet Owner*, August 1990, 36.

"Grote Industries; Grote Introduces LightForm, the World's First Flexible LED Lighting Film at 2009 SEMA Show." *Marketing Weekly News*, November 21, 2009, 188.

"Grote Launches New LEDs That Use Brightest and Most Efficient Technology." *Fleet Equipment*, January 1999, 54–55.

"LED Lines Expanding." *Fleet Owner*, May 1, 2008.

Lowe, Marcy, Bengu Aytekin, and Gary Gereffi. "Public Transit Buses: A Green Choice Gets Greener." In *Manufacturing Climate Solutions, Carbon-Reducing Technologies and U.S. Jobs*. Durham: Duke University, Center on Globalization, Governance and Competitiveness, 2009.

Meikle, Jeffrey L. *American Plastic: A Cultural History*. New Brunswick, NJ: Rutgers University Press, 1995, 78–82, 332.

Spaid, Ora. "Grote." *Indiana Business Magazine*, February 1990, 41–42.

Weber, David. "Vehicle Lighting: What You Can Do ... What's Being Done for Your Future." *Fleet Owner*, July 1965, 86–93.

Wilson, Marilyn. "Conspicuity." *Fleet Owner*, August 2000, 74.

Habasit AG

Römerstrasse 1
Reinach, CH-4153
Switzerland
Telephone: (+41 61) 715 15 15
Fax: (+41 61) 715 15 55
Web site: http://www.habasit.com

Private Company
Founded: 1946
Employees: 3,600 (est.)
Sales: $119.3 million (2009)
NAICS: 326220 Rubber and Plastics Hoses and Belting Manufacturing

■ ■ ■

Habasit AG is a global market leader in the lightweight belting industry. It manufactures a range of products from conveyor and processing belts for factories and warehouses to timing and power transmission belts for automobiles. With the increasing automation of packaging and food-processing businesses comes a greater demand for conveyor and processing belts. To meet this demand, Habasit, a family-owned joint stock company, has expanded its physical operations and sales beyond its home base of Reinach, Switzerland. In 2010 Habasit had 34 affiliated companies, 17 production facilities, and more than 3,600 employees worldwide.

ORIGINS AND EARLY EXPANSION

Habasit was founded in Reinach in 1946 by Fernand Habegger and Alice Habegger-Fluck. The company's cornerstone was a patent for a new driving belt for power transmission made out of synthetic materials. The Habeggers focused largely on European sales during the company's first two decades and then in 1968 established an affiliate near Atlanta. The new unit, Habasit Belting, Inc., imported belts from the parent company's European plants, completed fabrication, and then distributed the end product.

Habasit Belting developed new markets for the company products in the United States, Mexico, and Central and South America and soon became Habasit's largest and most profitable affiliate. In 1990 the company set up a regional distribution and service center in Singapore under the name Habasit Far East. This regional center covered the nations of Southeast Asia, as well as China, South Korea, Taiwan, and Hong Kong.

Fernand Habegger died in 1992. By that time Habasit was generating sales of more than $303 million and was the second-largest lightweight belt manufacturer in the world.

STRATEGIC REORIENTATION

In 1993 the company's management under Fernand's son, Thomas Habegger, put in place a strategic reorientation program calling for the company to increase market share by 50 percent in five years with sufficient profitability both to ensure its continued independence and to finance future growth out of profits. Key goals included keeping its focus on manufacturing and selling belts; maintaining a small number of selected suppliers; adopting a uniform,

> ## COMPANY PERSPECTIVES
>
> Habasit is the worldwide market leader in the belting industry. Our key objective is to offer superior solutions for our customers. Anywhere. Any time. Based on over 60 years of experience and continuous innovation, you always receive the best solution for your application. Exactly the right products, right on time.

volume-based pricing policy; and considering its customer base in any diversification. "We integrated every aspect of our business and organization around our customers," Giovanni Volpi, chief executive officer and chairman of the board, said in *Paperboard Packaging*, October 2003, marking the strategic plan's 10th anniversary.

The goal was to grow both organically and through partnerships and acquisitions. In 1995 Habasit established Habasit Iakoka Pvt Ltd, a joint venture with the Iakoka group of Coimbatore, India, to expand its manufacturing and marketing base for sandwich spindle tapes and transmission and conveyor belting systems. Habasit agreed to move all its production of spindle tapes, used in weaving belts, to the new enterprise, investing $100 million in it over the next four years. By 2002 Habasit Iakoka was the world's largest producer of spindle tapes, used in 65 to 70 percent of spinning machines, and was exporting 30 percent of its production.

ACQUISITIONS

Habasit acquired a second U.S. facility (and its first manufacturing site in that country) in 1996 when it purchased Advanced Belt Technology L.P., a maker of seamless conveyor and power transmission belting in Middletown, Connecticut, renaming it Habasit ABT. This deal was followed quickly by the purchase of another company, Globe International Inc., a conveyor belt maker in Buffalo, New York. It was Habasit's sixth acquisition in three years, punctuating an acquisitions boom in the lightweight belting industry that was sparked by overcapacity and cutthroat competition. Through it all Habasit was able to maintain a nearly continuous streak of year-on-year revenue increases.

By the end of the decade Habasit acquired Plastomeccanica, an Italian plastic injection molding specialist, which would provide an entrée for Habasit into the growing area of plastic modular belting. The company also merged its three U.S. operations and located its headquarters in Gwinnett County, Georgia. The change was largely for administrative purposes, eliminating duplicate functions, but it was accompanied by a move to a new location that was double the size of the one Habasit had occupied for the past three decades and that included a training facility three times as large. "The demand is up," said Steve Broadwell, vice president of marketing, as reported by Lauren B. Worley of *Rubber & Plastics News* on June 12, 2000, "but at the same time we are aggressively seeking our market share."

DIVERSIFICATION INTO FOOD PROCESSING AND OTHER INDUSTRIES

Habasit further expanded its manufacturing footprint in 2001, when it purchased Charles Walker Holdings, one of the United Kingdom's oldest and largest belt makers. Its clients included Nestle and United Biscuits, and the plan was to maintain Walker's distinctive brand. "The impact will be positive, it's a win-win situation," said Walker chairman David Belford (who retained his position), as reported by James Graham in the *Yorkshire Post* on May 10, 2001. "This brings us greater financial, technical, and marketing resources than we had as a small, independent UK firm."

Walker brought to the deal an expertise in the food-processing and automotive industries. Food processing and packaging were automating rapidly at the time, creating an important new growth area for belt manufacturers. One of Habasit's most successful new products was HyGUARD, a belt treated with an antimicrobial additive to protect even tiny tracks in the belt against contamination. The company's R&D area continued to drive new products onto the market. In 2004, for instance, it introduced the world's only 1.5-inch tight-radius belt, a space-saving innovation that it expected would be especially useful in food-processing facilities (for such items as baked goods, seafood, meat, poultry, fruit, and vegetables).

Expansion continued in Asia as Habasit selected Hong Kong in 2002 to be its regional headquarters and fabrication and distribution center, aimed at tapping the growing markets of China and Taiwan. "Hong Kong provides an ideal environment for our company to grow in Asia," said Henry Jong, general manager of Habasit East Asia Ltd., as reported by the Xinhua News Agency on October 29, 2002. "With its sound financial system, its pool of high-quality manpower and the efficient government machinery, Hong Kong is a superb location for our East Asia regional headquarters. These competitive edges can further guarantee investment security."

KEY DATES

1946: Habasit is founded by Fernand Habegger and Alice Habegger-Fluck in Reinach, Switzerland.

1968: Habasit's first U.S. affiliate is established, near Atlanta, Georgia.

1999: Habasit acquires Plastomeccanica, a plastic injection mold specialist, inaugurating the company's move into plastic modular belting.

2002: Habasit establishes Hong Kong as its regional headquarters for expansion into China and Taiwan.

2007: Habasit opens Modular Belt Innovation Center in Reinach.

Habasit made another strategic investment in 2004 when it purchased a minority stake in Rossi Motoriduttori, an Italian maker of gear reducers, gear motors, electrical engines, and motor variators. The deal established a close resource-sharing partnership that would jointly target industries including food and beverage, printing and paper, materials handling, wood, textile, stone, and plastics.

FURTHER INVESTMENT AND ACQUISITIONS

In the United States, meanwhile, the company announced that Habasit Belting Inc. had purchased 25 acres near its Georgia facility for a new 50,000-square-foot plant that would later expand to more than 300,000 square feet. The company's rubber and plastic modular belt lines were growing especially fast, spurred by such advantages over traditional fabric and metal belts as easier cleaning and maintenance, lack of corrosion, and fewer instances of slippage and disengagement. Habasit had invested some $50 million in plastic modular belting, included the introduction of HabaGUARD. The new product had "taken the market by storm," according to a company official, as reported by Mike McNulty of *Rubber & Plastics News* on December 13, 2004. The new Georgia facility opened in June 2005.

The emphasis on plastic modular belting carried over to the United Kingdom, where Habasit and Rossi launched Habasit Rossi in Silsden, West Yorkshire, in 2006. The new unit would enable them to combine resources on HabasitLINK, a new range of plastic modular belts with a special hinge design allowing steam cleaning and localized repairs, often without removing the whole belt. The partnership grew closer as Rossi Motoriduttori established a direct operation in Oakville, Ontario, in partnership with Habasit Canada Ltd., to support customers in Canada and develop a North American sales network.

Habasit added another arm to its U.S. operations in 2006 with the acquisition of publicly held Summa Industries of Torrance, California, for $58.2 million and the assumption of $21 million in debt. Summa made plastic components for industrial and commercial markets and had plants in California, Florida, Michigan, Mississippi, Pennsylvania, Tennessee, and Canada. The acquisition, in addition to an expansion of its Middletown facility, would help Habasit build its business in polyurethane, plastic, and rubber-coated belts.

"Even when the economy slowed down, we continued to invest heavily in new product development," said Flieger, executive vice president of sales and marketing at Habasit Belting, according to McNulty. The company's strategy, Flieger added, was to work closely with distributors "and provide them with strong sales, technology and customer support." Summa would remain a separate company under the name Habasit Holding USA Inc. The acquisition also brought KVP Inc., a belt manufacturer owned by Summa and with a presence in the UK food and packaging industries, into the Habasit fold. Shortly thereafter Habasit sold one of Summa's component companies, Aquarius Brands, a drip-irrigation firm, to an Indian company, Jain Irrigation Systems, for $21.5 million.

DEFENDING ITS POSITION IN A DIFFICULT ECONOMY

Now the world's second-largest maker of plastic modular belts and of conveyor, transmission, and processing belts overall, Habasit announced in August 2007 that it was opening a new Modular Belt Innovation Center at its Reinach headquarters. The following year it increased its stake in Rossi Motoriduttori to 51 percent and announced a joint venture with the Italian company to manage a new production facility near Habasit's existing one in Georgia. Further accentuating the importance of the plastic modular belting business, the company announced in 2008 that it was merging Habasit Belting and KVP and reorganizing their operations as Habasit America, with two divisions. One division, fabric belts and gears, would be located in Buffalo, Middletown, and Suwannee, Georgia. The other division, plastic, would be situated in Reading, Pennsylvania, and Suwannee.

Amid the global economic downturn that was beginning to take hold, Habasit was also concentrating more attention on finding out and responding to customer needs. In the United Kingdom, Habasit Rossi launched a campaign in which potential customers were mailed an information packet and offered a free belting audit. Companies accepting the audit would be given access to the company's 24-7 service support. The objective was in part to highlight the advantages of retrofitting conveyor belts.

By the following year, 2009, the downturn's impact was fully felt at Habasit. The company's consolidated revenues had declined 2.9 percent in 2008 after posting a record figure the previous year but then fell 41.8 percent in 2009, although its earnings before interest and taxes remained positive, and its cash position actually improved. Habasit was continuing to invest in new product development and new and improved infrastructure and equipment. It also acquired the portion of Rossi it did not already own.

Eric Laursen

PRINCIPAL SUBSIDIARIES

Habasit Argentina S.A. (Argentina, Uruguay); Habasit Australasia Ltd. (Australia, New Zealand); Habasit GmbH (Austria); Habasit Belgium N.V. (Belgium, Luxembourg); Habasit do Brasil Ind. E Com. de Correias Ltda. (Brazil); Habasit Bulgaria; Habasit (Shanghai) Co. Ltd. (China); Habasit predst. u Republici Hrvatskoj (Croatia); Habasit Bohemia spol.s r.o. (Czech Republic); Habasit AB (Denmark); Habasit France S.A.S.; Habasit GmbH (Germany); Habasit East Asia Ltd. (Hong Kong); Habasit Hungaria Kft.; IBH Ltd. (Iceland); Habasit-Iakoka Pvt. Ltd. (Bangladesh, India); Habasit Italiana S.p.A.; Habasit Nippon Co. Ltd.(Japan); Habasit Macedonia; Habasit Netherlands BV; Habasit Norge A/S (Norway); Habasit Polska Sp. z o.o. (Poland); Habasit Hispanica S.A. (Portugal, Spain); Habasit Import/ Export Romania SRL; OOO Habasit Ltd. (Russia); Habasit-Predstavnistvo v Sloveniji (Slovenia); Habasit AB (Sweden); Habasit Rossi (Taiwan) Limited (Taiwan); Habasit Kayis San. Ve Tic. Ltd. Sti. (Turkey); Habasit Ukrain (Ukraine); Habasit Rossi Ltd. (UK); Habasit America (USA).

PRINCIPAL COMPETITORS

Forbo Siegling (Germany); Nitta Corporation (Japan).

FURTHER READING

Cediel, Luis. "Swiss Approach Is an Absolute 'Belter.'" *European Food & Drink Review*, Autumn 2002, 63.

"Habasit Holding, AG Announced Plans." *Seed Today*, November 4, 1998.

"Habasit Reorganizes for Continued Success: Weathering a Difficult Economy." *Paperboard Packaging*, October 2003, 48.

McNulty, Mike. "Spreading Outward: Acquisitions, Expansions Boost Habasit's Global Operation." *Rubber & Plastics News*, October 16, 2006, 10.

"New Chapter for Habasit as Belt Sales Drive Investment." *Packaging Today*, August 2007, 5.

Wenger, Rachel. "Worldly Gain: Dynamics of Globalization Forcing U.S. Belt Makers to Rethink Strategies." *Rubber & Plastics News*, June 11, 2001, 15.

Whitford, Marty. "Market in Motion: Purchases, New Materials Reshape Conveyor Belting." *Rubber & Plastics*, June 30, 1997, 11.

Harlem Children's Zone, Inc.

35 East 125th Street
New York, New York 10035-1816
U.S.A.
Telephone: (212) 360-3255
Fax: (212) 289-0661
Web site: http://www.hcz.org

Nonprofit Organization
Incorporated: 1970 as Rheedlen Centers for Children and Families
Employees: 1,200
Operating Revenue $83.6 million (2009)
NAICS: 624110 Child and Youth Services

■ ■ ■

Harlem Children's Zone, Inc. (HCZ), is a nonprofit corporation dedicated to rebuilding the community of Harlem in New York City. Taking a holistic approach, the organization offers a comprehensive slate of programs. HCZ's Baby College is a nine-week parenting workshop that addresses the needs of children up to the age of three. HCZ operates two charter schools under the Promise Academy name, and for parents of attending children HCZ offers the "Three Year Old Journey" and "Get Ready for Pre-K" programs. HCZ also runs the Harlem Gems all-day prekindergarten program to prepare children for kindergarten.

The Fifth Grade Institute, a free after-school program, prepares students for middle school. They are offered further support through the Truce Fitness and Nutrition Center, which provides free classes in karate, fitness, and dance; the A Cut Above after-school academic help program; and Boys to Men and Girl Power social development programs. Academic case management services are offered to both middle school and high school students, and the latter are also supported by additional youth development programs, the Learn to Earn after-school program, an employment and technology center, and a college preparatory program.

HCZ's College Success Office not only helps students to gain admission to appropriate schools but also provides academic support. In addition, HCZ offers programs to improve the quality of life in Harlem. Quality Pride organizes block and tenant associations. The Single Stop program helps residents secure public benefits as well as legal and financial guidance and domestic crisis resolution. HCZ also offers initiatives related to asthma and obesity. Project Class provides referrals to drug and alcohol abuse programs. Finally, HCZ runs a truancy prevention program, the organization's original mandate.

ORGANIZATION FOUNDED: 1970

HCZ was founded in 1970 as the Rheedlen Centers for Children and Families by Richard L. Murphy, who had grown concerned by the large number of young children, ages 5 to 12, he saw on the streets of Manhattan when they should have been at school. Concluding that they lacked proper parental guidance, he began working with parents and chronically truant children in Harlem and the Upper West Side of Manhattan. The organization was originally funded by the city's Criminal Justice Coordinating Council and later received backing from the Bureau for Child Welfare and

COMPANY PERSPECTIVES

Called "one of the most ambitious social-service experiments of our time," by the *New York Times*, the Harlem Children's Zone Project is a unique, holistic approach to rebuilding a community so that its children can stay on track through college and go on to the job market.

the Office of Special Services for Children as well as private donations. Rheedlen received its first public contract in 1977 to prevent child abuse and neglect. In May 1990 Murphy left Rheedlen to become New York City's commissioner for youth services. Taking over as president and CEO of Rheedlen was Geoffrey Canada, a man who was well prepared for the job and who would be instrumental in transforming the truancy program into a comprehensive effort to rebuild an entire neighborhood.

Canada was more than familiar with the lives of the people he served. He was born in 1954 in the South Bronx, the son of a chronic alcoholic father. His mother chose to raise Canada and his three brothers on her own, and despite privations she was able to instill a love for education. In time she would earn a master's degree from Harvard University. Although Canada did well at school, he could not avoid the streets, and like many in the community he was forced to learn how to fight. Unlike the majority of his peers, however, he was able to attend college, awarded a scholarship in 1970 to Bowdoin College in Brunswick, Maine.

After receiving a degree in psychology and sociology from Bowdoin, he earned a master's degree in education at the Harvard Graduate School of Education. He stayed in the Boston area, joining the faculty of the Robert White School, devoted to Boston's troubled inner-city youth. Unlike the children in his native Bronx, however, these street-tough children were white. It was an eye-opening experience for Canada. "Those poor white kids and I had more in common than any one of us expected," Canada told *Newsweek* in 2009. "It was my first glimpse of the role that class plays when you're poor in this country. Often people think it's race, and it's not." Canada was soon named director of the school.

BEACON SCHOOL FORMED: 1991

Canada returned home to New York City in 1983 and went to work for Murphy, serving as program director for Rheedlen's Truancy Prevention Program. A third-degree black belt, he soon opened a martial arts school, using tai kwon do as a way to teach conflict resolution skills. After succeeding Murphy as the head of Rheedlen, Canada opened the organization's first Beacon School in 1991. It was a year-round after-school center that offered educational, recreational, and youth development programs for young people from 5 to 21 years of age, and it became so popular that he was forced to create a waiting list. Realizing that he was turning away many children who could benefit from what Rheedlen had to offer, and aware that all too often the impact of programs was just temporary, Canada began to reevaluate Rheedlen's approach. He realized that in order to help poor children to become healthy, productive Americans, he needed to have an impact on the entire community in which they lived.

Another seminal moment in the development of Canada's holistic approach to helping impoverished children came when he and his colleagues noticed that families living in a particular apartment building were abandoning their apartments to live in homeless shelters because the building had become a drug bazaar. Rheedlen decided to make the building an unsuitable place for drug dealers, but that only served to relocate the trade to another building down the street. Rheedlen responded by reclaiming an entire block, and when the drug dealers merely moved to a neighboring block, the idea took root that an entire neighborhood needed to be secured in order to create a safe environment in which to raise children. In 1991 HCZ initiated the Neighborhood Gold program to organize tenants; it was followed two years later by Community Pride, a program to restore buildings and blocks and prevent homelessness, and the Harlem Peacemakers' Success in School program, which made classrooms and areas surrounding schools safer.

HARLEM CHILDREN'S ZONE PROJECT BEGINS: 1997

In 1997 Rheedlen launched the Harlem Children's Zone Project to provide a comprehensive slate of programs for a 24-block area of central Harlem. It contained 3,000 children, about 60 percent of whom lived below the poverty line. In order to make the effort effective, a large percentage of the residents needed to participate. The programs were designed to be fun and engaging; in addition Canada offered such inducements as free meals, $50 Old Navy gift certificates, and drawings that awarded rent money for a month.

In 1999 one of Rheedlen's longtime sponsors, the Edna McConnell Clark Foundation, offered Canada a $250,000 grant and the services of the Bridgespan

KEY DATES

1970: Rheedlen Centers for Children and Families is founded by Richard L. Murphy.
1990: Geoffrey Canada is named Rheedlen's president.
1997: Harlem Children's Zone Project is launched.
2002: The Rheedlen name is changed to Harlem Children's Zone, Inc.
2004: Promise Academy opens.

Group, a nonprofit consultancy, to develop a business plan for Rheedlen. Canada took advantage of the opportunity to devise a plan to steadily increase the organization's budget to $46 million over the course the next nine years. At the same time, however, the organization decided it needed to be more focused and not just run programs because there was funding available for them. In some cases, careful analysis demonstrated, these programs actually drained resources from the organization.

Rheedlen determined that its mission was to serve children in central Harlem. After a review of all its programs in 2001, it concluded that three of its services, the Neighborhood Gold program, the Jackie Robinson Senior Center, and the El Camino dropout prevention program did not meet this mandate. Neighborhood Gold was discontinued; management of the Jackie Robinson Senior Center was transferred to the Harlem Meals on Wheels; and responsibility for the El Camino program, which was located outside of the Harlem area, was transferred to another organization.

NAME CHANGE: 2002

The first phase of the new strategy was to launch a set of 10 programs to help the children and families in the 24 blocks of Harlem that the organization had already targeted. In 2000 the Baby College parenting workshops were established, and a year later the Harlem Gems preschool program and the HCZ Asthma Initiative were established. To help reinforce the program, Rheedlen changed its name in 2002, becoming the Harlem Children's Zone, Inc.

An impediment to the success of the HCZ program was the poor performance of the local public schools. In 2002 a new mayor, Michael Bloomberg, installed a new chancellor, Joel I. Klein, for the city's school system. Canada met with Klein and shared a plan in which HCZ would administer some of Harlem's public schools. Klein suggested that a quicker and more effective approach was for HCZ to sponsor charter schools, publicly funded schools that were run by nonprofits and other organizations but not under the purview of the local school board. It was a relatively new, and often controversial, concept, whose critics claimed that it was merely a way to weaken unions and undermine the public school system.

A skeptic of charter schools himself, Canada realized, however, that if HCZ opened its own schools in Harlem, it would have children under its care for a major part of the day and have a better chance of being a positive influence. Thus, in 2003 HCZ submitted its application for a charter school to the New York City Department of Education. Upon gaining approval, HCZ held a lottery for admission in April 2004, and the new charter school, named Promise Academy I, opened its door in September of that year. In its first year, the new school offered kindergarten and sixth grade. The school came to include elementary (kindergarten to third grade); upper elementary/middle (fourth through seventh grades); and high school (tenth and eleventh grades). In 2005 Promise Academy II opened with two schools, eventually offering kindergarten to fourth grade. In the future, HCZ expected the schools to offer kindergarten through twelfth grades.

SECOND PHASE BEGINS: 2004

Also in 2004 HCZ began the second phase of its strategy, which called for an increase in the annual budget to $24 million and adding to the program another 36 blocks north of the original Harlem area. The organization also established what it called a Practitioners Institute to share its programming experience with others interested in adapting it to their communities. Although HCZ was well occupied with running its new charter school and administering a full slate of other initiatives, it continued to look for further ways to serve the community. In 2006 HCZ created an obesity program to encourage healthy lifestyles for the children of Harlem.

In January 2007 HCZ began the third phase of its program, which expanded the area it served to 97 blocks. The budget kept pace, so that by fiscal year 2010 it exceeded $48 million. Although the success of this holistic approach could not be adequately measured for many years (not until the children who spent their entire lives in the program grew into adulthood), every indication was that HCZ was playing a positive role in revitalizing its community. Indicative of what HCZ had already achieved were the efforts to imitate the program. President Barack Obama advocated the creation of

"Promise Neighborhoods" around the country. In the fall of 2009 representatives from more than 100 communities traveled to New York for a conference to learn more about the HCZ program as a prelude to seeking federal support for starting Promise Neighborhoods. Whether they received federal funding on not, many community organizations and municipalities had committed to following the lead of HCZ and programs were already in the development stage across the country.

Ed Dinger

PRINCIPAL DIVISIONS

Promise Academy Charter Schools.

FURTHER READING

"Harlem on His Mind." *People Weekly*, April 10, 1995.

"He's the Angel of Harlem." *Newsweek*, February 23, 2009, E10.

Karpman, Michael. "Harlem Children's Zone Shares Insight with More Than 100 Communities." *Nation's Cities Weekly*, November 23, 2009, 8.

Lee, Felicia R. "On Sunday; Being a Man and a Father Is Being There." *New York Times*, June 18, 1995.

Quittner, Jeremy. "Harlem Becomes Epicenter of Educational Change." *Crain's New York Business*, March 20, 2006, 19.

Tough, Paul. "The Harlem Project." *New York Times*, June 20, 2004.

———. *Whatever It Takes: Geoffrey Canada's Quest to Change Harlem and America.* New York: Houghton Mifflin, 2008, 296 p.

Harmonix Music Systems, Inc.

625 Massachusetts Avenue, 2nd Floor
Cambridge, Massachusetts 02139
U.S.A.
Telephone: (617) 491-6144
Fax: (617) 491-7411
Web site: http://www.harmonixmusic.com

Division of MTV Networks
Founded: 1995
Incorporated: 1995
Employees: 300
NAICS: 511210 Software Publishers

■ ■ ■

Based in Cambridge, Massachusetts, Harmonix Music Systems, Inc., is a video-game developer that focuses on music games. Best known as the developer of the *Guitar Hero* series, the company also produced *Rock Band, Rock Band 2,* and *The Beatles: Rock Band.* Many of the company's employees are musicians and members of well-known bands. Founded by graduates of the Massachusetts Institute of Technology (MIT), Harmonix holds several patents related to real-time music creation and group musical interaction over a network. The company is a division of MTV Networks, a subsidiary of media giant Viacom.

HARMONIX FOUNDED

Harmonix was founded in 1995 by Alex Rigopulos and Eran Egozy, who met at MIT as graduate students. At MIT Rigopulos, a drummer in a Led Zeppelin/Pink Floyd cover band, earned a bachelor's degree in music followed by a master's degree in media arts and sciences, and Egozy, a virtuosic clarinetist, earned his bachelor's and master's degrees in electrical engineering. The two men shared an interest in finding a way for nonmusicians to enjoy the pleasures of making music through electronic means. During their time together at the MIT Media Laboratory, Rigopulos and Egozy became familiar with a computer music generation system based on an algorithm that could create spontaneous music, and they developed a way to control the system using a joystick, thus allowing a nonmusician to improvise solos. They formed Harmonix to commercialize this technology.

Rigopulos and Egozy raised $100,000 from family and friends to launch Harmonix Music Systems and develop their music improvisation software, which they called *The Axe: Titans of Classic Rock.* They needed more money, however, and devoted several months to pursuing additional funding with no success. After failing to win an MIT business plan competition, Egozy realized that one of the judges was a fellow fraternity brother, Brad Feld, a venture capitalist. Feld was impressed by the young entrepreneurs and not only invested $25,000 in Harmonix but also helped them raise an additional $500,000.

FIRST TITLE PUBLISHED

Harmonix published *The Axe* in 1997. It used what the creators called "jamware" to allow nonmusicians to create music using either a joystick or mouse that controlled the melodic contours, rhythms, and phrasing

COMPANY PERSPECTIVES

We are artists, developers, engineers, and gamers with one thing in common: a love for music. We make games that let people experience music in a whole new way.

while the program took care of pitch selection, rhythmic precision, and other technical components of the music. While the impressive technology received rave reviews, *The Axe* only sold about 300 copies. In 1998 Harmonix repackaged *The Axe* as *CamJam*, so that body gestures replaced the joystick or mouse. The company secured a contract to install *CamJam* at Disneyworld's Epcot Center, but despite the technical success, Harmonix lost money on the job.

Still in search of commercial success, Harmonix continued to attract investments. Japan's Softbank invested $2 million in 1998, and a year later Taiwanese computer manufacturer Acer invested another $2 million. By now Rigopulos and Egozy had turned their attention to karaoke and Japan, where karaoke bars were popular. It became apparent to the partners that interactive video gaming had a mass-market appeal, and it was the ideal vehicle to further their dream of bringing the music-making experience to nonmusicians.

Harmonix established an office in Tokyo and began developing contacts in the karaoke industry. In 1999 Rigopulos and Egozy attended the annual Karaoke Festa trade show and set up a booth to demonstrate a joystick fixed to a real guitar that allowed users to improvise guitar solos. The product failed to garner any attention, and the partners returned home to lay off 10 of their 25 staff members in order to conserve what remained of their cash, having spent $7 million of the $10 million they had raised. They also rewrote their business plan. Instead of being a music company, Harmonix became a game company in 2000.

FREQUENCY PUBLISHED

Rigopulos and Egozy now took note of *Beatmania* and other rhythm-action games that only required users to tap out musical beats. Their underlying technology was extremely simple compared to the sophisticated algorithms used by Harmonix products, but the games were popular and after years of struggle and frustration, Rigopulos and Egozy turned their attention to developing similar fare. Their first attempt was *Frequency*. Although the game was funded by Sony Computer Entertainment, Harmonix retained ownership of its intellectual property, a key to the company's future development. Sony published *Frequency* for its PlayStation 2 gaming console in 2001.

Frequency was more sophisticated than its intended audience, and it experienced poor sales despite excellent industry reviews. Harmonix developed a sequel, *Amplitude*, for Sony, which debuted in 2000 and performed no better. Sony was not willing to finance another Harmonix music title, leaving Rigopulos and Egozy with few options. A Japanese company, Konami, then gave them an opportunity to develop a karaoke game for the U.S. market, and they created their simplest game, *Karaoke Revolution*.

Players of *Karaoke Revolution* sang pop songs into a headset or microphone to score points. It became the most popular game the company had produced. Harmonix also learned to streamline the development process to decrease its expenses. As a result, Harmonix posted its first profit in 2004.

DEVELOPING *EYETOY* AND *GUITAR HERO*

Sony now asked Harmonix to develop a game for its new interactive camera with the stipulation that it not include music. Harmonix accepted the job and developed *EyeToy: AntiGrav*, a virtual hover-board game. While the game received poor reviews, it did find an audience. By 2005 *EyeToy* emerged as the company's top-selling product. Its success, however, was not satisfying for Rigopulos and Egozy, who now viewed Harmonix as a quirky video-game company that happened to employ musicians.

It was during this period of disillusionment that Rigopulos and Egozy were approached by RedOctane, a Silicon Valley–based peripheral manufacturing company, to create a guitar game. RedOctane was owned by brothers Charles and Kai Huang. The Huangs wanted to increase sales in the United States and decided it needed a rock music–based game that included a guitar peripheral that it could produce. Already fans of Harmonix, the Huangs approached Rigopulos and Egozy, who agreed to develop the game that would become known as *Guitar Hero*.

Because it was important to have *Guitar Hero* ready for sale during the holiday season, only nine months were allotted for development. The budget was also tight at one million dollars, limiting the amount of money Harmonix had available to license familiar guitar songs from the likes of Boston, David Bowie, and Black Sabbath. To stretch its dollars, Harmonix acquired only

KEY DATES

1995: Harmonix is founded.
1997: Harmonix introduces its first game.
2005: Harmonix introduces *Guitar Hero.*
2006: Viacom purchases Harmonix.
2007: Harmonix introduces *Rock Band.*

composition rights and hired a studio to record the songs. The game itself allowed players to perform like rock stars by using fret buttons and a strum bar in coordination with onscreen instructions.

GUITAR HERO RELEASED

When *Guitar Hero* was released in November 2005, the only major retailer to carry it was Best Buy, which placed an order of about 8,000 copies, due in large part to the high price of the game. Once consumers tried the game at demo kiosks, however, they had to have their own version. Best Buy began increasing its orders as it quickly sold out its stock. Unlike most games, sales of *Guitar Hero* did not diminish after the holiday season. Instead, sales continued to climb in January and February 2006 as *Guitar Hero* became a national phenomenon.

Harmonix developed a sequel, *Guitar Hero 2,* which RedOctane released in 2006. Sales eventually reached $1 billion in North America, faster than any video game in history. The success of *Guitar Hero* also brought the dissolution of the partnership between RedOctane and Harmonix. The former was acquired in 2006 by game publisher Activision for $99.9 million, a deal that included the rights to *Guitar Hero.* Also in 2006 Rigopulos and Egozy sold Harmonix for $175 million to Viacom, which folded the company into its MTV Networks division, and the partners stayed on to run the autonomous company.

Guitar Hero was not only a triumph for Harmonix. It was also a boon to the music industry, which was struggling to find a way to negotiate a digital world that had destroyed its traditional business model. *Guitar Hero* and similar games that followed sold downloads of songs to game players at twice the usual price. Moreover, artists who allowed their songs to used in these games experienced a surge in sales of all their work.

ROCK BAND RELEASED

To fulfill a contract obligation, Harmonix developed a final game for RedOctane, *Hero Encore: Rocks the 80s,* released in the summer of 2007. The company then developed a game for MTV called *Rock Band,* released in November 2007, which expanded on the idea of *Guitar Hero* by including other peripherals, such as bass, drums, and a microphone. After a dozen years of effort, Rigopulos and Egozy realized their dream, allowing nonmusical people to join together to enjoy the experience of making music. Harmonix refined the product further, resulting in *Rock Band 2,* released in 2008.

Shortly after Viacom purchased Harmonix, Dhani Harrison, son of the late George Harrison of the Beatles, began discussing the possibility of a game based on the Beatles with Rigopulos. Harrison's interest led to a five-song demo in 2008 that earned the support of the shareholders of Apple Corps, the Beatles' music production company. The project went into development and in September 2009 *The Beatles: Rock Band* was released. Harmonix also had a game in development with the popular band Green Day, and other titles were sure to follow as Harmonix continued to carve out its unique niche in the video-gaming industry.

Ed Dinger

PRINCIPAL COMPETITORS

Walt Disney Company; RedOctane, Inc.

FURTHER READING

Atwood, Brett. "'Jamware' Lets the Consumer Play Along." *Billboard,* June 14, 1997, 66.

"40 Under 40 Business's Hottest Rising Stars." *Fortune,* November 9, 2009, 79.

Fritz, Ben. "'Band' Redux Hits the Right Notes." *Variety,* September 15, 2008, 22.

Lopiccolo, Greg. "Harmonix's Amplitude: The Sound and the Fury." *Game Developer,* August 2003, 40.

Moltenbrey, Karen. "Sound Effects: Harmonix Re-Creates the Sights and Sounds from the Beatles for Its Latest Rock Band Title." *Computer Graphics World,* February 2010, 30.

Parker, James. "School of Rock." *Atlantic,* March 2009, 36.

Sussman, Daniel, and Greg Lopiccolo. "The Buzz on Harmonix's Guitar Hero." *Game Developer,* February 2006, 24.

Hästens Sängar AB

Nya Hamnvägen 7
Köping, 731 23
Sweden
Telephone: (+46 221) 274-00
Fax: (+46 221) 274-19
Web site: http://www.hastens.com

Private Company
Founded: 1852
Employees: 178
Sales: $90.3 million (2006)
NAICS: 337910 Mattress Manufacturing; 442110 Furniture Stores

■ ■ ■

In Swedish, "häst" means "horse," and for more than 150 years, horses, and horsehair, have been the foundation of success for Hästens Sängar AB. Beginning in 1852 as a maker of saddles and carriage furniture, the company evolved into a bed manufacturer that produced pieces on demand using natural filling material, principally, horsehair. Its blue-and-white checked pattern became familiar throughout Sweden and other Scandinavian countries, and from 1952, the company was the bed supplier to the Swedish royal family. However, Hästens was little known outside its home market and a few other western European countries until the 2000s, when it began pushing into the United States, western Europe, and some emerging markets.

As it expanded its sales effort, Hästens rode a wave of consumer interest in luxury bedding, especially in the United States. Between 2000 and 2005, the market value of the wholesale mattress industry jumped nearly 40 percent, to $6.4 billion, according to the International Sleep Products Association. Premium-priced mattresses (those priced at more than $1,000) represented 21 percent of that market in 2005, up from 14 percent in 2000. Hästens situated itself firmly within the luxury sector; its top-end Vividus king-size mattress set, introduced in 2006, was priced at $59,750. Hästens enjoyed a 40,000 percent increase in sales from about 1990 to 2010. By the end of the decade, the company was introducing new models and looking for more opportunities for global expansion.

FROM THE STABLE TO THE BEDROOM

In 1852 Hästens Sängar, a saddlery that made saddles and equipage for carriages, opened for business. Horsehair was the main material used to pad saddles, and saddle makers often produced beds filled with horsehair as a sideline. It is thought that Hästens first produced a bed the first year it commenced operations, although bedding only became its principal business decades later.

The product that evolved in its workshops was built from a specific assortment of materials: horsehair, which is hollow and does not retain moisture, enabling the mattress to dry quickly and discourage pests like dust mites; cotton for the upholstery, because it ventilates and quickly rejects perspiration; wool, which warms as well as cools, helping to maintain a comfortable temperature; flax for padding; down for pillows; and

> **COMPANY PERSPECTIVES**
>
> In an industry where everyone else focuses on cost, Hästens keeps its focus on quality. The vision of giving the world the best bed allows for no shortcuts. Over more than 150 years, Hästens has hand-crafted beds using nothing but all natural filling materials.

Nordic pine for the bed frame. Hästens extended a 25-year guarantee covering spring or frame breakage. The beds were regarded as so durable that owners often bequeathed them to their heirs.

ACCELERATED EXPANSION, GLOBAL REACH

In 1988 Jan Ryde, a fifth-generation descendent of the original owner, took control of the company as chief executive. He quickly embarked on an aggressive effort to expand the company's sales and geographic reach. He did so while keeping the company privately held. Hästens went from an item whose distinctive blue-and-white checks were known at best regionally to a luxury item available in 16 global markets by 2004. In that year the company experienced a 21 percent year-on-year increase in sales, to $61.2 million. Export sales rose 35 percent over five years, from $10.8 million in 2001 to $56.3 million in 2005. An important segment of its export market was the United States, where Hästens beds first became available in 2002. Two years later the company sold them at 16 locations in that country. At the time, the highest-priced bed Hästens offered in the United States cost $17,000, and the average price paid at its highest-selling store, in New York City, was $8,000. In 2004 the company employed 42 workers, and a year later the number had jumped to 56.

As Hästens grew in the mid-2000s, exports came to dominate its balance sheet. To build on and solidify its success, the company developed an ambitious marketing campaign, added new products to augment its core offering, and improved its business infrastructure to better manage higher turnover. In 2006 the Swedish Trade Council named Hästens Swedish exporter of the year.

The United States remained the company's largest growth market. By 2007 U.S. sales had jumped 66 percent in four years. By 2009 there were 23 Hästens retail locations in the United States, and its line of products included accessories such as down pillows and duvets, linens, and blue-and-white checked sleepwear. Its biggest U.S. seller was the $15,500 Excelsior model. Outside the United States, a store in Budapest opened in February 2008, giving Hästens its first Hungarian location, where the company expected to sell 100 beds within the year. The Far East was another important focal point. By 2006 the bed maker had an Asian distributor, then opened stores in Hong Kong and Shanghai. Hästens next reached into India, opening a store in Hyderabad in July 2008, with aggressive expansion plans there and throughout Asia. "We want to cater to the Mercedes-Benz, Rolex consumers," Sanjay Verma, country manager for Hästens (India), told the *Hindu* (July 26, 2008).

SELLING THE LUXURY

In the United States Hästens ran an ad campaign in 2007 featuring a photograph of a Vividus model bed with the comforter pulled back and a pair of stiletto heels to the side. "Who would spend $59,750 on a bed?" the blurb read. The following year, the company committed $10 million to a global advertising campaign helmed by the branding and advertising agency Barker/DZP. It launched a print ad headlined "Transcendence," in which an unclothed model floating several feet over a Hästens bed was accompanied by the tagline "The bed of your dreams."

"The essence of this campaign is to take the best bed in the world and visually place it at the intersection of consumer lifestyle aspirations and best quality sleep," John Barker, president of Barker/DZP, said in a June 2, 2008, *Business Wire* press release. "The Transcendence ad captures the physical and spiritual renewal you feel in the world's most luxurious bed." The company also worked to enhance its luxury appeal by striking deals with high-end hotels to place Hästens beds in their top-priced suites. By the end of 2008 these included the Peninsula in Chicago, the Hotel Bel-Air in Los Angeles, Blakes Hotel in London, and the Marbella Club Hotel in Marbella, Spain. By early 2009 the effort was expanding to India as well.

EXPANDING ITS LUXURY LINE OF BEDS

In 2010 the company announced a new interior design program aimed at encouraging leading architects, interior designers, and stylists in the United States to integrate Hästens beds into their projects. Participants would be entitled to preferred pricing on Hästens beds at associated retailers. "We are reaching out to the entire country for potential business partnerships," Janet Stein, country manager for the United States, told David Perry of *Furniture Today* (January 21, 2010). "We are also

KEY DATES

1852: Hästens is founded as a maker of saddles and carriage furniture.
1988: Jan Ryde takes control of Hästens.
2002: Hästens beds become available in the United States.
2006: Hästens launches the Vividus luxury model, which sells for $59,750.
2010: Hästens names Nick Braden as global president of Hästens.

reaching out to the interior design community with our new ID program. We would like to gain a greater presence in the U.S."

The brand's upscale image was burnished later in 2010 when Hästens created a new bed to be presented as a gift to Sweden's Crown Princess Victoria on her June 19 wedding. The $18,000 model, the "Royal Bed," would be made in limited quantities and sold for only a few weeks through the end of June at 10 Hästens stores in the United States. The Royal Bed was hardly the company's most high-end product, however. In 2006 Hästens had introduced the Vividus, which took 160 hours to assemble and was said to be among the most expensive beds sold in the United States. Fewer than a dozen Vividus beds sold during its first nine months, but over its first four years, 250 were purchased.

In 2009 Hästens broadened its line further with the Continental Bed Collection, three new beds ranging in price from $8,450 to $23,250. The Luxuria was the least expensive of the three; followed by an update of the Excelsior model with two additional layers of cotton, wool, and horsehair replacing the usual layer of flax; and the 2000T II, one of H ästens' most exclusive beds. The 2000 IT was an update of the Hästens 2000T, and the three-part bed consisted of a bottom-section spring system, a thick spring mattress, and a top mattress with extra layers. Hästens continued to address environmental concerns in its design, as the three new releases, as had all the company's previous models, received Sweden's Nordic Swan label, meaning that their frames were built from certified sustainable wood and the upholstery from natural materials.

LOOKING TO THE FUTURE

Hästens added other sleep-related products. In September 2009 it introduced the MindSpa application for the iPhone and iPod Touch designed to enable deep relaxation and better sleep. "Everything we do at Hästens leads to one ultimate goal: the perfect night's sleep," Ryde said in a September 23, 2009, press statement. The MindSpa application, which sold initially through the iTunes Apps Store and then was to be offered as a free download for those with the device, "is another tool for achieving that goal."

By then Hästens was established in 28 markets and selling through 330 retail stores worldwide. Still a mid-sized company, it worked to improve inventory turnover and accuracy, keep better track of quality issues, and generally run its operations more efficiently as it continued to grow.

In January 2010, to enlarge the company's expansion efforts, Hästens hired Nick Braden, the former general manager of Mars Drinks, as global president of Hästens worldwide. Based in Washington, D.C., Braden's job would be to search for strategic opportunities as well as oversee the centralized functions supporting the company's worldwide operations. Ryde remained as CEO. "I have been doing this for more than 20 years, and I am looking forward to refocusing my energies towards strengthening Hästens strategic direction and moving away from the management role," he said in a *Business Wire* press release on June 10, 2010.

Eric Laursen

PRINCIPAL COMPETITORS

Dux Interiors; E.S. Kluft & Co.; Hollandia International; Hypnos Ltd.; Magniflex; Organic Mattresses Inc.; Select Comfort; Stearns & Foster; VI-Spring.

FURTHER READING

Athavaley, Anjali. "What Makes a Mattress Cost $33,000?" *Wall Street Journal*, June 16, 2010.

Evans, Sandra. "A $20,000 Mattress? It's Enough to Keep You Up Nights." *Washington Post*, May 20, 2004.

Green, Penelope. "The Money's in the Mattress." *New York Times*, July 12, 2007.

"Hästens Beds Anoints Nick Braden as New Global President." *Business Wire*, June 10, 2010.

"Luxury Bed Maker Hästens Introduces Mindspa iPhone™ Application." *Vocus*, September 23, 2009.

Perry, David. "Hästens Bedding Aims to Expand Presence in U.S." *Furniture Today*, January 21, 2010.

Perry, David. "New Hästens Bed Celebrates Sweden's Royal Wedding." *Furniture Today*, June 15, 2010.

Peters, Meghan. "Hästens' Beds Are Pricey but Worth It, Say

Satisfied Customers." *Seattle Post-Intelligencer*, August 9, 2007.

Prihoda, Kate. " Hästens Releases Newest Collection of Luxury Beds." *Just Luxe*, October 8, 2009.

Rubin, Josh. "Hästens Beds: Hands-On Review." *Design*, October 21, 2009.

Indianapolis Colts, Inc.

7001 West 56th Street
Indianapolis, Indiana 46254
U.S.A.
Telephone: (317) 297-2658
Toll Free: (800) 805-2658
Fax: (317) 297-8971
Web site: http://www.colts.com

Private Company
Founded: 1953
Employees: 134
Sales: $248 million (2009)
NAICS: 711211 Sports Teams and Clubs

■ ■ ■

Indianapolis Colts, Inc., is the parent company of the Indianapolis franchise of the National Football League. The one-time professional football team of Baltimore, Maryland, the Colts have played in Indianapolis since its controversial relocation in 1984 by owner Robert Irsay. As of 2010 the team was owned by Irsay's son, James Irsay, who also serves as chief executive officer. Since 2008 the Colts have played in the 63,000-seat Lucas Oil Stadium, a multiuse, retractable-roof facility.

POST–WORLD WAR II ROOTS

The Colts franchise originated in late December 1946 when a Baltimore group headed by Robert Rodenberg, a minority stockholder in the Washington Senators baseball team, bought the bankrupt Miami Seahawks franchise of the All America Football Conference (AAFC), launched earlier that year to challenge the National Football League (NFL). Serving as president, Rodenberg relocated the Seahawks to Baltimore and renamed the team the Colts. In its inaugural season the Colts lost 11 games and about $250,000 for its investors. In 1950 the NFL and the AAFC merged under the NFL name. The Colts was one of four AAFC teams selected to join the NFL, but the team fared no better in the new league and folded after just one season.

In the meantime the New York Yankees, another former AAFC team, had transferred to Dallas, where it played as the Texans. In 1953 Carroll Rosenbloom, a Baltimore native, and several partners became the new owners of the Texans, and the team moved to Baltimore. While the team continued to wear the Texans colors of blue and white, its name was changed to the Baltimore Colts. A year later the team posted a three-win, nine-loss record, but by this time Rosenbloom had installed a new coach, Weeb Eubank.

GREATEST GAME EVER PLAYED

Under Eubank, the Colts improved in 1955, and a year later the team signed Johnny Unitas, a backup quarterback who no other team wanted. Drafted by the Pittsburgh Steelers right out of college, Unitas was quickly cut, and he got a job in construction while continuing to play semiprofessional football on weekends. Given an opportunity to play for the Colts when the team's starting quarterback broke his leg, Unitas proved to be more than capable. A year later he was

COMPANY PERSPECTIVES

Professional football came to Indianapolis March 28, 1984, when Colts Owner Robert Irsay moved the historic NFL franchise from Baltimore to Indianapolis—the friendly heart of the Midwest.

named the NFL's Most Valuable Player, and in 1958 Unitas led the Colts to an NFL championship, defeating the New York Giants in overtime in a game generally considered to be the greatest ever played in NFL history.

Eubank and Unitas led the Colts to another NFL championship in 1959. When the team struggled in 1961, however, Rosenbloom fired Eubank and hired Don Shula. Under Shula, the Colts in 1969 reached the Super Bowl for the first time. The opponent was the New York Jets, with its brash quarterback, Joe Namath, and head coach, Weeb Eubank. In one of the greatest upsets in sports, the Jets defeated the Colts, 16–7.

In 1970 the National Football League and the American Football League merged, creating one league, under the NFL banner, consisting of two conferences: the National Football Conference (NFC) and the American Football Conference (AFC). To establish an equal number of teams in each conference, three former NFL teams, the Browns, Steelers, and Colts, were moved to the AFC. The Colts did well in the AFC and reached the Super Bowl again in 1971. The team prevailed over the Dallas Cowboys, 16–13.

OWNERS TRADE TEAMS

Rosenbloom, who had bought out his minority partners by 1965, became unhappy with the team, especially after it received poor attendance at its three home preseason games following the 1971 Super Bowl win. At this time the Los Angeles Rams franchise was available for purchase due to the death of its principal owner, and businessman Robert Irsay purchased the team. After paying $19 million for the Rams, a record amount at the time, Irsay, a great admirer of Johnny Unitas, then traded the franchise to Rosenbloom for the Colts in July 1972. It was an unprecedented sports transaction, given that no players or facilities changed hands, just owners.

Irsay proved to be an intrusive team owner, one who liked to pace the sidelines during games and give occasional locker room speeches. In his first season as owner, Irsay fired the head coach after just five games. Again, in midseason 1974, Irsay fired his head coach. When Ted Marchibroda became coach in 1975, the team achieved some success and returned to the playoffs.

The following year Irsay had a conflict with Marchibroda, who was forced to resign. The players objected to Marchibroda's departure, which led to his reinstatement. When the team struggled again, in 1979, Irsay fired Marchibroda, and the Colts lapsed into mediocrity.

By the early 1980s the Colts' home base, Memorial Stadium, was one of the smallest venues in the league. That combined with the team's poor record contributed to dwindling attendance, which was 30 percent below the league average. Phoenix, Arizona; Memphis, Tennessee; and Jacksonville, Florida, urged Irsay to move the Colts to their communities, prompting Baltimore officials to upgrade Memorial Stadium. The state legislature supported the plan by passing a $23 million bond issue in 1980 to fund it. In 1984 the city offered a $15 million loan at generous interest rates and a six-year guarantee of at least 43,000 per game attendance to keep the Colts.

In 1982 Oakland Raiders owner Al Davis successfully defied the NFL, winning a federal antitrust suit, and moved his team to Los Angeles. In the meantime, Indianapolis, with a new domed stadium in development, became a serious candidate for an NFL expansion franchise, and city officials began to court Irsay. Word leaked out and in March that the Maryland House of Representatives voted to give Baltimore the power to seize control of the Colts through eminent domain.

THE COLTS MOVE TO INDIANAPOLIS

Faced with the prospect of losing the Colts, Irsay acted quickly, agreeing to the deal offered by Indianapolis. The mayor then called the chief executive of Mayflower Corp., who had promised to move the Colts for free on just 12 hours' notice. A dozen contract drivers were gathered, and on the snowy evening of March 28, 1984, Mayflower vans pulled up to the Colts' facility in Owings Mill, Maryland. By the next morning, the last of the vans departed for Indianapolis.

While Irsay was portrayed as a villain in Baltimore, he was given a hero's welcome in Indianapolis. The NFL did not contest the move, and Maryland eventually dropped its futile opposition when Irsay and the Colts promised to support Baltimore's efforts to secure an expansion team. Baltimore would eventually receive a team, but it would come from Cleveland, whose Browns became the Baltimore Ravens, and another city experienced the disappointment of losing a beloved team.

KEY DATES

1953: The Dallas Texans move to Baltimore and adopt the Colts name.
1972: Robert Irsay trades the Los Angeles Rams for the Baltimore Colts.
1984: The Colts move to Indianapolis.
2008: The Colts play for the first time in Lucas Oil Stadium in Indianapolis.

Irsay became less meddlesome with the Colts after the move to Indianapolis. His son, James Irsay, took on increasing responsibility with the organization. After graduating from college in 1982, he joined the team's professional staff. In 1984 he became vice president and general manager. He was also expected to inherit the team one day.

In 1988 Robert Irsay divorced James's mother, Harriet. As part of the divorce agreement, Harriet received a promise that James would receive the Colts upon his father's death. In 1989 Robert remarried, and he and his new wife signed a prenuptial agreement that made James's claim on the Colts clear. In 1993, however, Robert created a supplemental trust and did not inform Harriet, James, or his second wife.

When Robert suffered a debilitating stroke in November 1995, the supplemental trust took effect, and all of the parties learned of a provision related to the Colts: Three years after the death of Robert, a five-person trustee group had to vote unanimously for James to receive the team. The trustees would vote every year until the transfer was made.

JAMES IRSAY ASSUMES OWNERSHIP

Harriet threatened to sue because of the conflict between the 1988 and 1993 agreements. A settlement was reached in July 1996 that allowed Harriet and James to buy a controlling interest in the team, with the purchase paid for by Robert's estate. In January 1997 Robert died and James became owner and chief executive officer of the Colts.

In 1998 the team drafted quarterback Peyton Manning, and Irsay and the city negotiated an agreement to keep the Colts in Indianapolis that called for additional game-day revenues for the team. By 2000 an effort was launched to build a new stadium, one that had luxury boxes and amenities that other stadiums around the United States offered. In 2004 a plan began to take shape to expand the Indiana Convention Center by adding a retractable-roof stadium. The Colts' success on the field helped to sell the proposal.

After experiencing disappointment in the playoffs, the Colts won Super Bowl XLI in January 2007. In 2008 the team began playing in their new home stadium, Lucas Oil Stadium. The Colts once again played in the Super Bowl, in February 2010, but lost to the New Orleans Saints. Nevertheless, the team's support by the community was assured for many years to come.

Ed Dinger

PRINCIPAL SUBSIDIARIES

Indiana Farm Bureau Football Center.

PRINCIPAL COMPETITORS

Houston NFL Holdings, L.P.; Jacksonville Jaguars, Ltd.; Tennessee Football, Inc.

FURTHER READING

Battista, Judy. "For Manning and Colts, Super Bowl Loss Lingers." *New York Times*, September 18, 2010.

Beck, Bill. "Kicking Off the Tenth Season." *Indiana Business Magazine*, September 1993, 8.

"Colts Owner Robert Irsay Dies." *San Francisco Chronicle*, January 15, 1997.

Davis, Andrea Muirragui. "Convention, Stadium Linked." *Indianapolis Business Journal*, December 27, 2004, 3.

Eskenazi, Gerald. "Robert Irsay, 73, Executive in Shift of N.F.L. Colts, Dies." *New York Times*, January 15, 1997.

Peltz, John. "Bob Irsay's Tangled Legacy." *Indianapolis Business Journal*, September 29, 1997.

Steadman, John. *From Colts to Ravens: A Behind-the-Scenes Look at Baltimore Professional Football.* Atglen, PA: Schiffer, 1997, 244.

Wallace, William N. "Colts Franchise Traded for Rams; Players Remain." *New York Times*, July 14, 1972.

Innovia Films Ltd.

Station Road
Wigton, Cumbria CA7 9BG
United Kingdom
Telephone: (+44 1697) 342-281
Fax: (+44 1697) 341-452
Web site: http://www.innoviafilms.com

Private Company
Founded: 2004
Employees: 1,400
Sales: €400 million ($480 million) (2010)
NAICS: 326113 Unsupported Plastics Film and Sheet (except Packaging) Manufacturing

■ ■ ■

Innovia Films Ltd. is a global leader in the development, manufacture, and marketing of cellulose and biaxially oriented polypropylene (BOPP) films for packaging and labeling. Innovia was formed in October 2004 following the acquisition of the UCB Group's films business by a consortium led by Dennis Matthewman, who became Innovia's chairman, and Candover Investments PLC, a European private equity house. Innovia employs approximately 1,400 people at its 4 production sites and 15 sales offices in Europe, the Americas, and the Asia-Pacific region, and the company produces more than 120,000 metric tons (132,300 tons) of film per year. Its products serve a wide range of markets, from small self-adhesive labels for food, health and beauty, beverage, and industrial and household chemical packaging to durable and UV-resistant flat application graphics, such as those found on buses, windows, and other large signage sites. Innovia's research and development (R&D) investment program included the 2002 opening in Wigton, Cumbria, England, of a £12 million ($8.8 million) state-of-the-art research and technical facility for packaging and specialty films. Innovia's business is fueled by R&D, and the company's core competencies lie in surface engineering, exclusive process technologies, and knowledge of polymer properties. Its main brands include films for labels, packaging, and graphic arts applications, such as Rayoface, Rayofoil, Rayoweb, Rayoart, and NatureFlex, a completely renewable and compostable cellulose film.

INNOVIA'S ROOTS

In 1892 three English chemists, Charles Cross, Edward Bevan, and Clayton Beadle, discovered the process for manufacturing cellulose viscose. Sixteen years later Dr. Jacques E. Brandenberger, a Swiss research scientist, inventor, and entrepreneur, successfully produced cellulose film from the viscose. In 1913 Brandenberger opened La Cellophane SA with a factory in Bezons, France, thereby inaugurating the commercial production of thin transparent cellulose film and making possible Innovia Films' global success nearly a century later.

The first factory of the Société Industrielle de la Cellophane (SIDAC) was founded in Ghent, Belgium, in 1926. By 1932 SIDAC had established a distribution company in the United Kingdom, and, after opening its first production plant in 1934, SIDAC was renamed British Sidac Ltd. One of British Sidac's main investors was Baron Emmanuel Janssen, founder of Union

> **COMPANY PERSPECTIVES**
>
> Innovia Films' mission is to be recognised by our customers as a leading value-added speciality film supplier and a supplier of choice through innovation, quality products, exceptional service in all aspects of business, and close relationships/strategic alignment.

Chimique Belge, the progenitor of UCB SA, which would play a major role in Innovia's development later in the century. About this same time, in a factory that was originally designed for the manufacture of rayon, British New Wrap Co Ltd. was founded in Wigton, Cumbria, England, to produce cellulose film. In 1936 British New Wrap was renamed British Rayophane.

In 1935 British Cellophane Ltd. (BCL) was formed through a joint venture between La Cellophane SA and Courtaulds for the manufacture and sale of cellophane in the United Kingdom. Production began in Bridgwater, Somerset, England, in 1937 and was expanded with the founding of La Cellophane Española in Burgos, Spain, in 1942. Production of cellulose film developed considerably over the next three decades. During this time BCL established additional operations in Mexico and Canada, as well as a new site at Dalton, Lancashire, England.

THE DEVELOPMENT OF BIAXIALLY ORIENTED POLYPROPYLENE (BOPP)

The ICI film production company developed biaxially oriented polypropylene (BOPP) in 1961. The properties of this new Propafilm not only resembled those of cellophane but could be offered at highly competitive prices. Its bubble production process yields especially strong, tight-sealing wrinkle-resistant film. Coating enhances film qualities while adding a moisture barrier.

ICI established its first bubble and coater units for the production of BOPP in 1962 in Dumfries, Scotland. In 1963 British Rayophane and British Sidac merged, retaining the latter company's name. In 1967 British Sidac entered into an agreement with ICI to produce BOPP at a new £3 million factory at the Wigton site under the company name Sidex Ltd.

In 1973 British Sidac became a wholly owned subsidiary of UCB SA, and for the next several years consolidation characterized the European cellulose film industry. In 1987 UCB severed its ties with ICI and assumed full ownership of Sidex Ltd., while ICI formed ICI Films (Merelbeke) to continue production at the Ghent plant. In that same year UCB implemented an investment program for organic growth, which included raising annual production volumes of oriented polypropylene (OPP) from 10,000 to 35,000 metric tons (11,000 to 38,600 tons) and commissioning an additional bubble line and a new £10 million coater.

In 1996 UCB acquired British Cellophane Ltd. and the Cellophane trade name. On acquiring U.S. cellulose film producer Flexel Inc., based in Tecumseh, Kansas, in 1997 and the ICI Propafilm business in 1998, UCB became the world's largest producer of both cellulose and BOPP films. In 1999 UCB entered Australia with the opening of a £25 million plant in Melbourne. Also in 1999 UCB announced plans to build a multimillion-pound advanced research and technical center next to its production site in Wigton. According to UCB the center would boast unrivaled laboratory and analytical facilities equipped to test new films from conception to commercial production.

Innovations at the turn of the millennium included Propafilm RK, an antimist BOPP film for packaging fresh salads and produce, and Star-Twist Cellophane, a twistable color laminate that provided a high barrier against moisture, gas, and aromas. By the end of 1999, UCB's packaging films could be found on a wide range of popular brands, such as Twinings teas and infusions, Senzora BV's Tricel laundry detergent tablets, and Cadbury's Miniature Heroes range.

THE FORMATION OF INNOVIA FILMS

In 2000 UCB closed La Cellophane Espanola in Burgos, Spain, and expanded its presence in the Americas with the acquisition of Cydsa in Mexico. In February of that year, following the success of its Propafilm RK, UCB launched a two-sided acrylic-coated film with a metallized surface that surpassed the performance of earlier versions of high-barrier BOPP. Named Propafilm RMC, the film was suitable for packaging products such as wafers and biscuits and for high-speed flow-wrapping of chocolate-coated confectionaries. Another breakthrough was the development of Propafilm OS25, a self-tightening BOPP film that gave packaging a glossy, lacquered appearance and would not wrinkle over time. Developments in 2001 included Rayofoil, a ready-to-use metallized label facestock, and a new easy-peel Propafilm. In that same year UCB commissioned a third coater and bubble line at its Wigton facility, increasing film capacity by an additional 15,000 metric tons (16,500 tons) per year.

KEY DATES

1933: British New Wrap Co Ltd., formed in Wigton, Cumbria, England, begins cellulose film production.
1963: British Sidac Ltd. acquires British New Wrap.
1973: British Sidac becomes a wholly owned subsidiary of the UCB Group.
1996: UCB Films acquires British Cellophane Ltd. and the trade name Cellophane.
2004: Innovia Films Ltd. is formed following the acquisition of UCB Films by a consortium led by Dennis Matthewman and Candover Partners Ltd.

In 2002 the curl-free Rayoart BOPP film was launched, and UCB Films' long-awaited £12 million ($8.8 million) R&D center at Wigton opened its doors. Spanning 5,500 square meters (59,200 square feet) and employing 100 people, the new facility would significantly increase UCB Films' product development capabilities and bring new developments to the global market more quickly. The next year UCB Films was merged with its sister division, UCB Chemicals, and Solutia, a resin, additives, and adhesives business, to form Surface Specialties UCB, Inc. (SSI). As a single integrated business, SSI was poised to offer total packaging solutions to a broad range of business sectors.

In October 2004, however, a consortium led by Dennis Matthewman, former managing director of Hays Chemical Distribution, and Candover Investments PLC bought UCB's film business. In December 2004, with Matthewman as chairman, the UCB films business was renamed Innovia Films Ltd. The company announced in early 2005 that it would be closing its original UK-based cellophane production plant in Bridgwater and concentrate on further development of its facility in Wigton. In that same year the Wigton site was awarded the British Retail Consortium/Institute of Packaging Technical Standard Certificate for Hygiene in recognition of the many products the company has contributed to the food industry.

THE DEVELOPMENT OF NATUREFLEX AND OTHER ACHIEVEMENTS

In 2006 Innovia announced that it had developed a biodegradable cellulose film that would suit both industrial and home composting. The next year saw the Wigton site attain ISO 1400 certification for its environmental management standards. Building on this accomplishment, NatureFlex in February 2008 achieved CarbonZero status following a comprehensive Life Cycle Assessment (LCA). Within months the NatureFlex range received numerous accolades, including the DuPont Award for Packaging Innovation and Canada's Sustainable Packaging Leadership Award.

In May 2009 Innovia announced that a new €10 million cellulose film manufacturing line had begun production at its Wigton site. The state-of-the-art equipment replaced two lines built in the 1940s and was capable of producing some grades of film faster and with better quality. In a company press release dated May 25, 2009, Alexander van 't Riet, global sales and marketing director, stated, "The successful completion of this major project is testimony to Innovia Films' ongoing commitment to cellulose film, a reflection of the dedication and skills of our highly experienced engineering team and a clear demonstration of our belief and desire to continue to bring further developments in cellulose technology to our customers."

Innovia Films entered the in-mold label (IML) injection molding field in September 2009 with the development of RayoForm. The solid white RayoForm IW and clear RayoForm IC films gave a gloss effect to containers and, with the product's high stiffness, could be used to label large containers, such as 5–20 liter paint buckets. By 2010 Innovia had production sites in the United Kingdom, the United States, Belgium, and Australia. Since its development the company had also expanded the NatureFlex line to include NatureFlex NKM, a gleaming metallic film; NatureFlex NKC, a range of brightly colored films; and NatureFlex NK White, a solid white film. The company's metallized NatureFlex had become the wrapping of choice for a variety of high-profile confectionary brands, such as Thornton's Melts and Cadbury's Flake. Innovia's investment program, combined with its exemplary R&D facility, highly specialized workforce, and dedicated global sales team, positioned the company well to continue to expand and turn its resources into world-class film products.

Marie O'Sullivan

PRINCIPAL OPERATING UNITS

Innovia Films (Asia Pacific) Pty Ltd. (Australia); Innovia Films BVBA (Belgium); Innovia Films (Commercial) Ltd. (Brazil); Innovia Films Inc. (Canada); Innovia Films (Asia Pacific) Pty Ltd. (China); Innovia Films (France); Innovia Films (Commercial) Ltd. (Germany);

Innovia Films (Commercial) Ltd. (Malaysia); Innovia Films (Italy); Innovia Films (Commercial) Ltd. (Japan); Innovia Films SA de CV (Mexico); Innovia Films (Commercial) Ltd. (Poland); Innovia Films (Commercial) Ltd. (Russia); Innovia Films (Commercial) Ltd. (Spain); Innovia Films Inc. (USA).

PRINCIPAL COMPETITORS

Fuwei Films (Holdings) Co., Ltd.; SABIC Innovative Plastics; Shiner International, Inc.

FURTHER READING

"Another Name Change: UCB Now Innovia." *Australasian Business Intelligence*, December 3, 2004.

"The Best of Both Worlds." *Packaging Magazine*, June 3, 1999, 10.

"Innovia Films' NatureFlex™ Goes CarbonZero." *packagePrinting*, February 2008.

"Innovia Films Responds to Rumors of US Pull-Out." *Label & Narrow Web*, September 2008.

"Innovia Launches New Wood-Based Biodegradeable Plastic Film." *Chemical Business Newsbase*, February 26, 2010.

"Metallized Cellophane Wraps Up New Product Launch." *Paper, Film & Foil Converter*, December 2000, 68.

"A New Beginning for a Film Star." *Brand Packaging*, September 2003, 27.

"UCB Combination Film Gets European Launch." *Packaging Magazine*, April 8, 1999, 28.

"UCB Films Expands Films Range." *Candy Industry*, February 2000, 60.

"UCB Sells Films Business." *Converting Today*, July–August 2004, 5.

J. Choo Limited

4 Lancer Square, Kensington Church Street
London, W8 4EH
United Kingdom
Telephone: (+44 20) 7368-5000
Toll Free: (800) 506-9991
Web site: http://www.jimmychoo.com

Private Company
Founded: 1996
Incorporated: 2004
Employees: 96 (est.)
Sales: $143.5 million (2008 est.)
NAICS: 316214 Women's Footwear (except Athletic) Manufacturing; 316992 Women's Handbag and Purse Manufacturing; 448210 Shoe Stores

■ ■ ■

Founded in London in 1996, J. Choo Limited (JCL) is a leading designer and manufacturer of shoes and accessories, known by the name Jimmy Choo. The company has more than 115 stores in 32 countries, and its products are also sold in department and specialty stores around the world. Jimmy Choo merchandise is synonymous with luxury and high fashion, and many well-known celebrities and actors are customers. The company's product line includes shoes, handbags, small leather goods, sunglasses, eyewear, and fragrances. In early 2007 the company was valued at £185 ($365) million.

TAMARA MELLON AND JIMMY CHOO

Tamara Mellon and Jimmy Choo founded J. Choo Limited, which would be known as Jimmy Choo, in London, England, in 1996. Mellon was born in London and educated in England, the United States, and Switzerland. She was accessories editor at *Vogue* magazine when she approached Choo about a partnership. Jimmy Choo was born in Pedang, Malaysia, and exhibited artistic talent from a young age, designing his first pair of shoes by age 11. Choo graduated with distinction from England's Cordwainers College for Footwear Designers, and in 1986 he opened his own shoe-design business in London.

In 1988 Choo shot to fame when *Vogue* published an eight-page spread featuring his creations, and soon he was attracting high-profile customers, such as Britain's Princess Diana. With a rapidly growing list of clients, Choo recruited his niece, Sandra Choi, to help with the workload that also included providing a complete line of custom footwear for two annual fashion shows. In May 1996, financed by Tamara Mellon's father, Tom Yeardye, who became chairman of JCL, Mellon and Choo launched the "Jimmy Choo" label for ready-to-wear shoes, with production based in Italy and a boutique on Motcomb Street in London. Choo, whose strength was in making custom shoes based on preexisting designs, soon found the pressure of designing a full collection daunting. Choi, who became JCL's creative director, came to the rescue, sketching dozens of shoe designs.

The ready-to-wear line successfully made its way into leading department stores by 1998, and JCL

> COMPANY PERSPECTIVES
>
> To fully accessorize and capture the hearts of women around the world by building a full luxury house with shoes at its core.

opened its first U.S. store in New York City that same year. Located between 51st and 52nd Streets on fashionable Fifth Avenue, the 1,800-square-foot Olympic Tower flagship store housed the entire Jimmy Choo collection on three floors. The following year JCL established a store in Los Angeles, and "Jimmy Choos" were soon adorning the feet of Oscar nominees.

CHOO'S SHARE SOLD

By 2001 JCL was valued at about $30 million, and sales for that year exceeded $18 million. In November 2001 under mutual agreement, Mellon and Choo parted ways when Equinox Luxury Holdings Ltd. purchased his share for $10.6 million. Robert Bensoussan, former managing director of Gianfranco Ferre and president of Christian Lacroix, became chairman and chief executive officer (CEO) of Equinox and CEO of JCL, while Mellon became president. Choi remained creative director.

In April 2003 JCL launched a line of handbags that retailed from about $690 to $1,500. Made from calfskin, crocodile, satin, and sandblasted metal, the handbags were designed and produced in Italy. In August 2003 the company opened a store on Madison Avenue in New York, and its sensual lilac-toned, 1940s-inspired, boudoir-style decor beautifully showcased the brand's range of shoes and handbags. Within the first few weeks of opening, sales at the Madison Avenue store had exceeded estimates, and the interior design was so popular that customers were asking if they could purchase the furnishings. For 2003 JCL's business was 55 percent wholesale and 45 percent retail, achieving sales of about $40 million.

CHANGING PARTNERS AGAIN

In January 2004 JCL opened a 1,500-square-foot store on London's Bond Street, featuring the new boudoir-style interior that was now part of the Jimmy Choo brand. By April 2004 JCL achieved an even split between its retail and wholesale businesses. In May 2004 Mellon's father, Yeardye, died suddenly at the age of 73. Six months later Lion Capital acquired Equinox's 51 percent stake in JCL, as well as Yeardye's 27 percent stake, while Mellon and Bensoussan held 22 percent. At the time of the acquisition, JCL was valued at £101 ($187) million.

Sales reached $100 million in 2005. In April 2006 JCL opened five new stores in the United States, bringing the number of stores in the country to eighteen. Also in 2006 the company, now with 60 stores and shops around the world, celebrated its 10th anniversary. In February 2007 Lion Capital sold its share of JCL to TowerBrook Capital Partners LP and Gala Capital in a deal worth £185 million ($364.5 million), with TowerBrook as the majority shareholder. Bensoussan, Mellon, and Choi remained onboard in their respective positions of CEO, president, and creative director.

MORE STORES

Two months after the buyout, Joshua Schulman, a former executive of Kenneth Cole, Gucci, and Yves Saint Laurent, became the new CEO of JCL. Bensoussan, who still held a small share in the company and served on the board of directors, continued to work with TowerBrook on expanding its luxury portfolio. In May 2007 JCL opened its first store in Chicago, Illinois, bringing the number of U.S. stores to 21. In June 2007 JCL announced that it had signed a 10-year worldwide distribution licensing agreement with Selective Beauty SAS, a French fragrance manufacturer and distributor.

Also in June 2007 the newly renovated Jimmy Choo store on Madison Avenue was unveiled. With 3,000 square feet, it was the company's largest store, and it was designed with the intention of displaying the full range of Jimmy Choo's rapidly expanding collection. On the international front, the first Jimmy Choo store opened in China in October 2007, and its sixth store in Japan opened in July 2008. European openings in 2008 included new stores in Cannes, Barcelona, and Rome.

NEW DIRECTIONS

In April 2009 JCL formed a joint venture with Bluebell Far East Limited to own and operate Jimmy Choo stores in Hong Kong. In June 2009 the company launched Project PEP in partnership with the Elton John AIDS Foundation. Twenty-five percent of the Project PEP collection, which included totes, sandals, flats, clutches, and flip-flops ranging in price from $95 to $995, would be donated to the Simelela Rape Centre in Cape Town, South Africa. Also in June JCL teamed with H&M, launching a discount pump, and within months the relationship was extended to include a range

KEY DATES

1996: Tamara Mellon partners with Jimmy Choo to launch J. Choo Limited.
2001: Equinox Luxury Holdings Ltd. purchases Choo's share of J. Choo Limited.
2004: Lion Capital acquires a majority share.
2007: TowerBrook Capital Partners purchases the company.
2010: Tamara Mellon becomes chief creative officer.

of women's and men's apparel. Shoes retailed between €40 and €100, while handbags cost up to €200.

In October 2009 JCL and the Royal Horticultural Society collaborated with Hunter Boots to produce a designer Wellington that retailed for about £250. In January 2010 the company partnered with Ugg Australia to design a range of women's sheepskin boots. JCL also agreed to a new 12-year fragrance venture with Inter Parfums SA in October 2009 after Selective Beauty failed to launch a new scent. Under the deal, Parfums SA would create, develop, and distribute the Jimmy Choo range of perfumes.

In September 2009 the company unveiled Choo 24/7, a shoe collection of timeless styles, priced between $395 and $1,295. In April 2010 Mellon changed her job from president to chief creative officer, with Choi continuing in her position as creative director reporting to both Mellon and Schulman. In that same year, Mellon was awarded the Office of the Order of the British Empire for her outstanding contributions to British culture, philanthropic initiatives, and artistic collaborations.

Marie O'Sullivan

PRINCIPAL OPERATING UNITS

Shoes; Handbags; Small Leather Goods; Sunglasses; Eyewear.

PRINCIPAL COMPETITORS

Manolo Blahnik USA, Ltd.; Nine West Group Inc.; Prada SpA; Salvatore Ferragamo Italia S.p.A.

FURTHER READING

Anniss, Elisa. "Full Speed Ahead: Jimmy Choo Eyes Global Expansion." *Footwear News*, July 12, 2004, 1.

———. "Kenneth Cole Exec Lands at Choo." *Footwear News*, April 23, 2007, 4.

Chabbott, Sophia. "Choo Takes to the Road for 24:7." *WWD*, February 12, 2010, 27.

———. "Jimmy Choo Looks to Lenses for Growth." *WWD*, June 22, 2007, 3.

Conti, Samantha. "Jimmy Choo Sold to Private Equity Firm." *WWD*, February 5, 2007, 4.

———. "Jimmy Choo Unveils Project PEP." *WWD*, October 29, 2009, 11.

Singletary, Michelle. "If the Shoe Fits." *Washington Post*, June 25, 2009.

Socha, Miles. "Full Steam Ahead at Jimmy Choo." *WWD*, September 5, 2007, 37.

Ward, Andrew. "Jimmy Choo's First Steps into H&M Set to Trigger Stampede." *Financial Times*, November 14, 2001, 11.

Whitworth, Melissa. "The World of Tamara Mellon, Co-Founder of Jimmy Choo." *Europe Intelligence Wire*, January 30, 2010.

The Joffrey Ballet of Chicago

Joffrey Tower
10 East Randolph Street
Chicago, Illinois 60601-3617
U.S.A.
Telephone: (312) 739-0120
Fax: (312) 739-0119
Web site: http://www.joffrey.com

Nonprofit Company
Incorporated: 1954 as Robert Joffrey Ballet
Employees: 72
Operating Revenue: $12.8 million (2009 est.)
NAICS: 711120 Dance Companies

■ ■ ■

The Joffrey Ballet of Chicago is one of the premiere dance companies in the United States. The Joffrey made a truly American art out of ballet, which had been an almost exclusively European province, by presenting classic 19th- and 20th-century dances along with new American works. The Joffrey is renowned both for its preservation of bygone masterpieces, such as Vaslav Nijinsky's version of *Le Sacre du printemps* and Kurt Jooss's *The Green Table*, and for its development of modern ballet choreography. Founder Robert Joffrey's well-known ballets include *Pas de Déesses* (Dance of the goddesses), *Astarte*, *Remembrances*, and *Postcards*. Cofounder Gerald Arpino was one of America's best-loved and most prolific choreographers, whose works include *Sea Shadow*, *Incubus*, *Ropes*, *Light Rain*, and *Billboards*.

The company's repertoire also includes works by George Balanchine, Frederick Ashton, Laura Dean, Mark Morris, and many more contemporary choreographers. The Joffrey Ballet began as a touring company based in New York, and later had a bicoastal presence with a long-standing residency in Los Angeles. The company moved to Chicago in 1995. The Joffrey tours nationally and internationally, and offers workshops at schools and universities across the United States.

FOUNDERS JOFFREY AND ARPINO

Robert Joffrey was born in Seattle in 1928, the son of immigrants from very different backgrounds. His father, Joseph Joffrey, had come to Seattle from Afghanistan in 1916 with a brother. Joseph's name before it was anglicized was Dollha Anver Bey Jaffa Khan. Joseph and his brother first worked in sawmills to support themselves. Later they sold chili from a stand, and Joseph then opened a restaurant, the Rainbow Chili Parlor. Joseph Joffrey was a devout Muslim, yet he married a Catholic woman, Marie Gallette, a violinist from Italy who ended up a cashier in his restaurant. The two did not have much in common, and they did not get on easily. Robert Joffrey was their only child.

Young Robert was both bowlegged and asthmatic, and his pediatrician may have advised his parents to enroll him in some sort of physical activity to bolster his health. At eight years old Robert began boxing lessons, but he loved the dancing he had seen in movies, and he soon persuaded his parents to allow him to switch to dance lessons. His teacher immediately noticed his flair.

COMPANY PERSPECTIVES

Classically trained to the highest standards, The Joffrey Ballet expresses a unique, inclusive perspective on dance, proudly reflecting the diversity of America with its company, audiences, and repertoire which includes major story ballets, reconstructions of masterpieces and contemporary works.

When he was only 12 Joffrey appeared as a supernumerary in Michel Fokine's ballet *Petrushka*. At 15, Joffrey began studying ballet with Mary Ann Wells, a respected local teacher who had a lasting influence on him. Wells put him in her most advanced classes, and had him teach beginning students. Although he was still bowlegged and, at five feet four, considered too short to be a professional dancer, he was extremely talented and completely devoted to ballet.

In 1945, when Joffrey was 16, he met Arpino. Arpino's mother had known Joffrey's mother in Italy. Arpino was six years older than Joffrey and in the Coast Guard. When his ship stopped in Seattle, he looked up his mother's friend. Marie Joffrey sent the young man to find Robert at the dance studio where he was rehearsing. Arpino knew nothing of ballet, but when he walked in the door, the instructor liked his lean physique and dragged him into class. Arpino, too, had a natural gift for dance, and after this he frequently went AWOL from his ship in order to take more classes. He also fell in love with Robert Joffrey. The two were romantically involved for several years and remained close friends and artistic collaborators until Joffrey's death in 1988. The pair pretended to be cousins, but apparently Joffrey's family understood and accepted the nature of their liaison. The couple lived together in the Joffrey family home, then moved to New York in 1948.

INJURY LEADS TO TEACHING

In New York Joffrey and Arpino had numerous dance opportunities. Joffrey danced with Roland Petit's Ballets de Paris, while Arpino danced in several Broadway shows. By 1950 Joffrey also was teaching at New York's High School for the Performing Arts. In 1953 Joffrey suffered a terrible injury onstage, tearing a calf ligament so badly that his doctor advised him to give up dancing. As a result, Joffrey began focusing on teaching, with the idea of forming his own ballet company. He founded the American Ballet Center (better known as the Joffrey Ballet School) in 1953 on Sixth Avenue in Greenwich Village. That summer he presented several of his works at the annual Jacob's Pillow Dance Festival in Massachusetts.

In 1954 the newly created Robert Joffrey Ballet debuted a program of Joffrey's original works at the 92nd Street YMCA. The 92nd Street Y was an acclaimed venue for modern dance in New York, where the most esteemed choreographers, including Martha Graham and Agnes de Mille, premiered their works. It was unusual for a ballet company to be granted the space, but Joffrey's from the beginning was an unusual company that bridged the gap between classical and modern styles. Joffrey wrote *Pas de Déesses* for the 92nd Street Y recital, which proved to be one of his most enduring works.

Joffrey premiered another set of ballets the next year and began making an impression on notable dance critics. In 1955 Joffrey was invited to teach several of his dances to the English company Ballet Rambert. He returned to the United States to choreograph for theater, including a televised production of the fairy-tale opera *Griffelkin*. Joffrey received plenty of attention for *Griffelkin* and his other works, and he caught the eye of an agent at Columbia Artists Management, Inc. Columbia Artists wanted a small ballet company that could tour the country, something portable, classical, but accessible to audiences who had not seen much dance. Joffrey and Columbia Artists worked out an arrangement to fill this niche, and thus created the Robert Joffrey Theatre Dancers, Joffrey's first real company.

ON TOUR IN THE FIFTIES

Arpino was the principal dancer in the small troupe. There were only five other dancers because Columbia Artists would pay for only six and because no more could fit in a station wagon, their mode of transportation. Joffrey's idea for the company was that it would have a teenage image, although most of the members were actually in their late 20s and Arpino was 33. European ballet companies had typically presented a frosty veneer of enviable sophistication. By contrast, the Joffrey dancers were to project a front of youthful enthusiasm, of kids next door who just happened to be fantastic dancers. They performed four ballets a night in college and high school auditoriums, almost entirely in small towns. Most of the audiences had never seen ballet or, presumably, a live dance performance of any kind, and the Joffrey made a big impression.

Columbia Artists renewed the Joffrey's contract the next year. In 1958 the company gave 69 performances, almost all were one-night stands, with hundreds of miles of driving in between. By then, however, the company

KEY DATES

1950s: Robert Joffrey Theatre Dancers tour for Columbia Artists.
1962: The Joffrey Ballet embarks on its first international tour.
1964: The Joffrey group breaks with patroness Rebekah Harkness.
1966: Residency begins at New York's City Center.
1979: The Joffrey Ballet is close to bankruptcy.
1983: The Joffrey Ballet begins its first season at Music Center of Los Angeles.
1988: Robert Joffrey dies.
1995: The Joffrey Ballet moves to Chicago.
2007: Gerald Arpino retires.
2008: The company moves into the Joffrey Tower in Chicago.

had exchanged the station wagon for a more comfortable bus. They played in larger cities this time as well, including San Francisco and Seattle. The company continued to tour through 1961, adding dances by other choreographers. The troupe was welcomed and admired, with some dancers, particularly Arpino and ballerina Lisa Bradley, garnering warm reputations of their own.

The company had expanded to 17 dancers by 1961. That year Arpino showed his choreography for the first time, presenting *Ropes* and *Partita for 4*. He blossomed into a prolific and beloved choreographer, whose engaging modern works became the cornerstone of the Joffrey repertoire.

UNDER THE INFLUENCE OF REBEKAH HARKNESS

The Robert Joffrey Theatre Dancers had begun life as a portable troupe, geared for traveling. By the early 1960s, however, the company had matured and grown. Joffrey afforded new dancers for the touring company by paying them lower wages than his established dancers, $65 to $75 a week. There were many other expenses, as well, such as sets and costumes and labor to haul and organize equipment and set up the stage. In addition, the touring company did not make money when it was not performing. Joffrey's school brought in a steady income but by 1962 it was clear that it could not support the company as well. Joffrey had been given at least one significant anonymous donation that allowed the company time to rehearse and learn new works. Nevertheless, in order to keep going, the company (which changed its name to the Robert Joffrey Ballet in 1961) needed to attract a new source of funding. At that time, there was little government support for the arts. (The National Endowment for the Arts was not established until 1965, and many artists and organizations depended on private patronage.)

Joffrey considered disbanding the company in 1962, but he managed to keep it going with help from friends and family. Then he met Rebekah Harkness at a New York party. Harkness was the widow of William Hale Harkness, heir to the Standard Oil fortune, and was reputed to have inherited $60 million when Harkness died. She used her wealth to support dancers and musicians through her Rebekah W. Harkness Foundation. She was a composer herself, and had written music for several professional dance pieces. Joffrey agreed to audition his company for her, giving her a private showing.

In the summer of 1962 Harkness invited Joffrey and his whole company to her estate, Watch Hill, to spend 12 weeks choreographing and rehearsing. Many strings, however, were attached. Through an intermediary, she gave a musical score to Arpino, asking him to use it for a new dance piece. Arpino, not realizing the work was Harkness's, turned it down. Joffrey managed to get another choreographer to use the music, for a dance called *Dreams of Glory*, which the Joffrey would perform.

A WORLD TOUR

Partially because the Joffrey now had Harkness's deep pockets (thus part of its costs were subsidized), the U.S. Department of State sponsored the company to go on a world tour. The dancers would show audiences around the globe a piece of exciting American culture. In the winter of 1962, the Joffrey Ballet set off for its first international tour, with stops in Europe, the Middle East, India, and Afghanistan, the ancestral homeland of Robert Joffrey's father. The tour was in most ways a rousing success, with a command performance for the shah of Iran. *Dreams of Glory*, however, the piece set to Harkness's music, gave the company trouble. The ballet, about children in a museum imagining growing up to be president, was by all accounts a failure, and Harkness was irritated and upset.

Nevertheless, the tour led to an invitation to travel to the Soviet Union the next year. When the company returned to New York, Joffrey began choreographing new works to take to Russia. He again worked at Watch Hill, and this time Arpino agreed to write a dance to some new Harkness music. Harkness began having thoughts of starting her own ballet company and hiring Arpino as artistic director. Harkness also made her authority felt at Watch Hill. She objected to a piece choreographer Anna Sokolow was working on for the Joffrey, and eventually Harkness told the dancers to stop rehearsing it. It was evident that she wanted to do much more than write checks to the Joffrey Ballet. Although she was instrumental in getting the company its first international tour and then its Manhattan debut in 1963, she hindered the group by meddling with artistic decisions. The Joffrey performed for President John F. Kennedy in October 1963, then left for its tour of the Soviet Union. Harkness underwrote the tour, along with the State Department and another private donor. Again, the tour was a fantastic success, as Russian audiences had never seen this kind of ballet before.

In January 1964 the Joffrey set off on its last domestic tour for Columbia Artists, playing in major cities as well as many smaller towns. Relations between Harkness and Joffrey had grown chilly, although Harkness was still pumping money into the group, to the tune of possibly $40,000 to $50,000 a week. While the group was traveling, Harkness announced that she was starting her own company, the Harkness Ballet. She had asked Arpino to direct the new group, but he refused. Next, she offered Joffrey the job, and he, too, turned her down. Then Harkness asserted her rights to works Joffrey and others had created under her patronage, and to sets and costumes for which she had paid. Robert Joffrey was unsure what to tell his dancers. Harkness was offering them steady pay in her new company, and he did not know if he would be able to continue. Eventually, some Joffrey dancers joined Harkness's company, and Joffrey was forced to regroup.

IN NEW YORK AND LOS ANGELES: SEVENTIES THROUGH EIGHTIES

After the bitter break with Harkness, Joffrey was forced to start almost from the beginning again. The school was still running and it gave him a pool of new young dancers from which to choose. The company, however, had grown so large and sophisticated with the injection of Harkness's money that it was difficult to go back to a leaner organization. The company applied to the Ford Foundation for grant money. Because the Joffrey did not have nonprofit status, however, it was not eligible.

Normally, applying for nonprofit status was arduous and expensive, and could take a year of filing legal papers. However, the company had a lucky strike in its choice of lawyer, Howard Squadron. Squadron had been working on filing for nonprofit status for a Boston arts group that had folded before the process was completed. The Joffrey was able to use this almost finished application, and it became the nonprofit Foundation for American Dance almost overnight. The company's business director, Alex Ewing, twisted the arms of many of his Yale University classmates, who became Joffrey board members and contributors. In November 1964 the Robert Joffrey Ballet received an initial grant of $35,000 from the Ford Foundation, with the promise of more for the next year. The newly reorganized company made its debut in August 1965 at the Jacob's Pillow Dance Festival.

In 1966 the Joffrey was appointed the resident dance company of New York's City Center. The company's official name then became the City Center Joffrey Ballet. The company would have an annual season at the center with all expenses paid and approximately $17,500 a week. This initiated a fruitful period for the Joffrey. Robert Joffrey choreographed one of his most famous and popular ballets, *Astarte*, in 1967. The multimedia show seemed to capture the mood of the era like no other ballet, and it was featured on the cover of *Time* magazine. Joffrey also began reviving classic ballets, something he had always longed to do. He began putting on the works of ballet greats Léonide Massine and Frederick Ashton in the late 1960s. The company also expanded with the addition of an apprentice corps of young dancers who were being groomed for the main Joffrey. This began in 1968 as the Joffrey Apprentice Company. In 1971 the name was changed to the Joffrey II Dancers. Arpino created some of his most popular works in the early 1970s, including most notably *Trinity*.

FINANCIAL ISSUES LEAD TO CANCELLATIONS

The Joffrey was in the highest echelons of American dance, yet it was far from financially stable. In 1973 City Center management announced that it was reducing its funding for the Joffrey. The dance company was running a deficit of $1.3 million, and apparently the center's management thought the group was fiscally irresponsible. The company was rescued by another large grant from the Ford Foundation. Nevertheless, funding for the arts in New York began to dry up. The dance audience had grown enormously in the years since the Joffrey began touring, but now it was reaching a plateau. City government was faced with budget problems, too. In 1976 the City Center stopped supporting the Joffrey, which then changed its name back to simply the Joffrey Ballet. The company struggled to keep going. By 1979 the company was forced to lay off many of its dancers and cancel both its New York season and a planned international tour. Costs had risen enormously, and even with a severe escalation in ticket prices, the company could not pay its own way.

It looked as if the Joffrey would have to fold, and the company's business director began planning the company's bankruptcy filing. Then at the close of 1979, the National Endowment for the Arts stepped in with a special grant of $250,000 to keep the Joffrey going. It was an unusual move by the arts organization, and the Joffrey was put on a strict schedule of financial audits. The company, however, was saved. In 1980 Robert Joffrey hired a crop of new young dancers, mainly from Joffrey II, as he had had to let many of his mature stars with their higher salaries go.

THE REAGAN FAMILY INFLUENCE

In the early 1980s the Music Center of Los Angeles asked the Joffrey if it would consider becoming its resident dance company. The Joffrey then, in 1983, became a bicoastal company, with homes in both New York and Los Angeles. Some of the machinations behind the move to Los Angeles were apparently due to Nancy Reagan, wife of then U.S. president Ronald Reagan. Their son Ron had been a scholarship student at the Joffrey school, and then was inducted into Joffrey II. Ron Reagan was evidently an accomplished dancer who succeeded on his own merits. His parents, however, had influential friends and it pleased Nancy Reagan to have her son closer to her in California. Ron Reagan was a full member of the Joffrey Ballet for only a short time before resigning. Nonetheless, his presence seemed to attract many new donors with ties to the Republican Party. The Joffrey also began attracting corporate donations, something that was new at the time. Tobacco giant Philip Morris Companies Inc. began sponsoring the Joffrey in its 1981–82 season.

Los Angeles underwriters raised $2 million for the company's first two seasons in Los Angeles, and the Joffrey was able to pay off its debts. The relationship with the Music Center provided much needed financial stability in the early 1980s, yet there were still problems. The Music Center wanted the Joffrey to move all of its operations to Los Angeles by late 1984. The center, however, had not provided adequate rehearsal space or offices, so this move did not take place. The company maintained separate marketing departments for its New York and California shows, and the Joffrey had something of a split identity.

Robert Joffrey began bold plans for putting on major classic ballets over the next five years, but by 1985 a few of his intimates knew that he was ill with AIDS. The Joffrey put on Nijinsky's *Le Sacre du printemps*, a groundbreaking 1913 ballet, in Los Angeles in October 1987. Shortly afterward, Joffrey had to be hospitalized. He was very ill over the next year, although he would not admit publicly that he had AIDS, and his plans for the future of the company were laid out only as wishes, not as legally binding contracts. Joffrey died on March 25, 1988, at the age of 59.

THE JOFFREY AFTER JOFFREY

Robert Joffrey had recommended that the company's board appoint Arpino as artistic director. Although Arpino was a very different character from Robert Joffrey and not everyone on the board believed Arpino was capable of the responsibility, Joffrey's wishes were followed. Arpino had tended to stay in the background while Joffrey was alive, and Arpino put most of his energy into choreography. Joffrey, however, had ended up with little time for choreography while trying to keep the company afloat.

In 1989 the Joffrey's annual budget was more than $12 million, yet it still had a deficit of approximately $3 million. A member of the board of directors accused Arpino of having gone over budget on a ballet he was presenting at a gala in Washington, D.C., to honor President George H. W. Bush. Arpino proved that he had actually come in under budget for the dance, but bookkeeping errors had made it seem like the opposite.

Arpino found other financial errors, too, including the company's failure to pay $868,000 in payroll taxes to the Internal Revenue Service. One of the company's chief backers in Los Angeles, businessman David H. Murdock, offered to cover the deficit but only if Arpino were removed. This set off a struggle between the Joffrey's patrons and its artistic director. The Joffrey dancers warmly supported Arpino. In May 1990 several Joffrey directors resigned from the board, effectively leaving the company to Arpino. "I have regained the company," Arpino said in an interview with *Dance Magazine* in July 1990. "I did what I had to do—not just for myself, but for the arts and artists. We have to stand up for ourselves." Arpino swiftly raised money from new sources. In 1991, however, the company ended its relationship with the Music Center of Los Angeles, where Murdock was a powerful patron.

The company went on a national tour in 1992 but abruptly canceled its annual season in New York, citing the expense and lack of support from the city. The Joffrey kept going with an anonymous donation of $1.25 million that year. It was operating in the black but had to be cautious about expenditures. Its future was not certain. The company had a major hit in 1993 with Arpino's *Billboards*, danced to the music of pop singer Prince. It was the kind of broadly appealing show that had sustained Arpino's popular reputation.

A MOVE TO CHICAGO

By early 1995, however, the Joffrey was in serious financial trouble, owing back pay to many dancers. The company laid off its 43 dancers in January while a dispute with the dancers' union was hashed out. Later that year the company announced that it was moving to Chicago. Plans had existed from at least 1991 to move the company to the Windy City, where it had many patrons and a long history of successful performances. The company considered merging with Ballet Chicago but instead moved wholesale on its own, occupying new quarters downtown at 185 North Wabash Avenue. The Joffrey had the ecstatic support of Maggie Daley, wife of Chicago Mayor Richard M. Daley, and of Lois Weisberg, the Chicago commissioner of cultural affairs. The move was seen as a coup for the city, while the Joffrey was released from supporting an ever-more-expensive presence in Manhattan.

The Joffrey played a fall and summer season in Chicago, plus a holiday season of *The Nutcracker*. Ticket sales increased year after year in Chicago. By 2000 the company was raising some 40 percent of its budget from ticket sales and other earned income. It had a number of corporate donors, including Philip Morris, AT&T, and American Airlines. The Joffrey's new chairman of the board was the president and CEO of Chicago-based Sara Lee Corporation. Corporate and other donations made up 60 percent of the Joffrey's income. Once firmly settled in Chicago, the company finally began building cash reserves to keep it from the ups and downs that had made its past so difficult.

The first decade of the new millennium presented the Joffrey Ballet with its toughest test in its new home city. The economic impact of the terrorist attacks against the United States on September 11, 2001, severely affected the company. Tickets sales were down and investment losses were inhibiting potential donors. The resourceful and experienced Jon Teeuwissen was appointed executive director that December, which proved a fortunate move for the Joffrey. Teeuwissen quickly found a way to generate $2.3 million in funds, a large part of it through the diversion of money originally intended as capital expenditures. He also instituted a new business model that reduced operating expenses and, through schedule revisions, maximized ticket sales.

During this difficult period, the Joffrey made appearances in two Hollywood films that gave it valuable cachet as it sought to establish itself in its new hometown. In *Save the Last Dance* (2001), the aspiring dancer protagonist is inspired by watching a Joffrey performance. Director Robert Altman's *The Company* (2003), a documentary-style drama about a fictitious ballet company, used Joffrey dancers' experiences for much of its story line and the entire company was paid talent. The company also received an undisclosed fee for the film rights to the story.

ESTABLISHMENT OF PERMANENT FACILITIES

A major goal of the Joffrey in the first decade of the 2000s was the establishment of adequate facilities in its new city. For performance space, the answer was at hand: the magnificent Auditorium Theatre of Roosevelt University where the Joffrey was already giving most of its performances. In 2003 the company agreed to become the permanent ballet in residence there.

A headquarters for rehearsals and operations was another matter. In 2000, after working for five years to gain a permanent toehold in Chicago, the company appeared to have come upon the solution. Commonwealth Edison donated a five-story building to the Joffrey. Conveniently located in the new North Loop theater district and worth $4.5 million, it was the largest gift in the history of the company. The Joffrey immediately began planning on a $24 million development of the property. Unfortunately, the projected costs soon skyrocketed to some $40 million, and it was discovered that, for structural reasons, there could not be a big enough column-free space for rehearsals. In 2002 the company put the plan on hold.

Luckily, Mayor Daley's administration had come to support the Joffrey and wanted to make sure it had a prominent location in the theater district. An opportunity developed in 2004 in conjunction with a proposed 32-story condominium project just one block from the former Commonwealth Edison building. The Joffrey negotiated with the developer of the new building to acquire a condominium interest in 45,000 square feet of space, over two floors, for its headquarters and rehearsal space. An agreement was reached in 2005. The new facility cost a fraction of the renovation costs for the Commonwealth Edison building. Perhaps the crowning touch was that the new home was called the Joffrey Tower. The company quickly sold the old building, thus retiring existing debts and financing its new home.

In August 2008 the Joffrey moved into its gleaming new building on East Randolph Street. Administrators and performers were united under one roof, and the performers had three beautiful studios with floor-to-ceiling windows affording public views of the dancers at work. Furthermore, there was enough space to allow two simultaneous rehearsals in the full space used by each production. The next year the new Joffrey Academy of Dance began operations there, reviving the teaching tradition of the company's early years.

DEATH OF ARPINO

Before it could move into its new facility, the Joffrey lost a powerful link with its creative roots when cofounder and artistic director Arpino retired in 2007. Arpino was one of the last of the generation of choreographers that included Balanchine, de Mille, and his business and life partner Robert Joffrey. Arpino died the next year, but he had taken steps to ensure that the company would have all rights to his and Robert's choreographic legacy in perpetuity. In 2009 the Gerald Arpino Foundation was established to lease the rights to 35 ballets by the duo.

Before retiring, Arpino had overseen the lavish, two-season-long celebration from 2005 to 2007 of its 50th anniversary. In an artistic highlight, legendary choreographer Twyla Tharp personally directed a restaging of her *Deuce Coupe*, backed by Beach Boys music, that had made history at the Joffrey in 1973. The lavish observance of the 50th anniversary affirmed the company's arrival at the midpoint of the decade as an accepted and valued member of Chicago's cultural life. This was ratified by the appointment by Mayor Daley's brother William to the cochairmanship of the company's board of directors.

In addition to the death of Arpino, the end of the celebratory seasons saw the retirement of Executive Director Teeuwissen, who had helped bail the company out of debt and secure its new home. That meant the company had to fill the top two posts in short order. Arpino's replacement as artistic director was Ashley Wheater, assistant artistic director of the San Francisco Ballet and a former Joffrey dancer. For executive director, the company turned to Christopher C. Conway, a sitting vice president with extensive experience in arts management.

As the first decade of the 21st century wrapped up, the Joffrey was in a transition stage. One hint of its new directions was the addition in 2009 of nine dancers from various ethnic backgrounds, as the company actively sought to create a more diverse corps of dancers. While still planning a new course for the Joffrey, Wheater and Conway had to wrestle with the economic downturn of that began in late 2007, which, as with the 2001 recession, was biting into revenues and donations. Unfazed, the troupe planned a 2010–11 season that would culminate in two world premieres by leading choreographers. It remained to be seen how the troupe would balance redefining the company and retaining its recognizable identity as the Joffrey.

A. Woodward
Updated, Judson MacLaury

PRINCIPAL COMPETITORS

Ballet Chicago; Ballet San Jose; New York City Ballet; Pennsylvania Ballet.

FURTHER READING

Anawalt, Sasha. "Arpino Returns." *Dance Magazine*, July 1990, 17.

———. *The Joffrey Ballet: Robert Joffrey and the Making of an American Dance Company.* New York: Scribner, 1996.

Barzel, Ann. "The Joffrey Comes Home: Joffrey Ballet of Chicago." *Dance Magazine*, May 1996, 66.

Bauman, Risa. "Bi-Coastal Dance Troupe Adopts Single Marketing Strategy." *Direct*, March 1991, 26.

"Joffrey Cancels New York Season." *Dance Magazine*, February 1992, 12.

Reiss, Alvin H. "Arts Groups Come Back from Financial Precipice to Reach New Heights." *Fund Raising Management*, June 2000, 40.

Smith, Sid. "How the Joffrey Fared in the 'Company' of Altman; Dancers Describe 3-Month Chicago Shoot as Exhilarating and Exhausting." *Chicago Tribune*, December 8, 2002, 1.

———. "A Leap of Faith; When the Joffrey Ballet Came Here from New York, It Was Gambling with Its Life. But the Wager Is Paying Off—And the Biggest Winner May Be Chicago." *Chicago Tribune*, October 23, 2005, 14.

Troester, Maura. "Joffrey Back in Action." *Dance Magazine*, December 1995, 28.

Wernick, Ilana. "Joffrey Ballet Announces It Will Move to Chicago." *Back Stage*, September 15, 1995, 1.

Key Plastics, L.L.C.

21700 Haggerty Road, Suite 150N
Northville, Michigan 48167-8996
U.S.A.
Telephone: (248) 449-6100
Fax: (248) 449-4107
Web site: http://www.keyplastics.com

Private Company
Incorporated: 1986 as Key Plastics, Inc.
Employees: 4,100
Sales: $1.25 billion (2009 est.)
NAICS: 326199 All Other Plastics Product Manufacturing; 336360 Motor Vehicle Seating and Interior Trim Manufacturing; 336399 All Other Motor Vehicle Parts Manufacturing

■ ■ ■

Key Plastics, L.L.C., engages in the development and manufacture of thermoplastic components and subassemblies for the automotive industry. The company provides assembly of injection-molded parts, interior and exterior component painting, part-surface decoration, and radio prototyping via the company's own computer-aided-design/computer-aided-engineering (CAD/CAE) department. Key Plastics' product lines include exterior, interior, trim, and under-the-hood components. Its customers include a majority of original equipment manufacturer (OEM) and Tier 1 suppliers in both North America and Europe. In North America, the company is a leading manufacturer of exterior door-handle assemblies and pressurized coolant and power-steering bottles. Key Plastics has about two-dozen facilities in North America, Europe, and Asia and four technical centers. Since the founding by Key Plastics' original ownership group, it has been through two bankruptcies and subsequently has been controlled by two investment companies, including, since 2009, Wayzata Investment Partners LLC.

ORIGINS

Between the mid-1970s and the late 1980s, plastic applications in automobiles increased more than 10 percent. It was in fact new technology in tool design and manufacturing in the 1980s that first allowed the production of the plastic door handle in 1984. In 1986, in the midst of this increase in plastic automotive parts, Key Plastics, Inc., was established to acquire the plastics division assets of Key International Manufacturing, Inc. (KIMI), which had been in business for about two decades. Key Plastics was formed by a trio of former KIMI managers, including Joel Tauber, its former president, who became Key Plastics' chairman. Tauber was joined by George Mars and David Benoit. Mars had been the general manager of the KIMI plastics division and became cochairman and president of Key Plastics. Benoit had served as KIMI's CFO and was named executive vice president at Key Plastics. All three executives also became directors of the company and its largest stockholders.

The KIMI plastics division was a combination of two companies, Superior Plastics and Aline Plastics, which together had two manufacturing facilities and $20 million in annual revenues. Tauber, Mars, and

COMPANY PERSPECTIVES

Each of our global associates is motivated by a single goal: being responsive to the customer. This attitude stems from refocusing Key Plastics' internal culture on total customer responsiveness, which already is paying benefits for our company and our customers—and will continue to do so.

Benoit initially were attracted to the automotive industry because of its stable production schedule and established market. Moreover, they formed Key Plastics at an opportune time, when the industry was transitioning to the use of plastics to replace many heretofore metal components. The company's first major product, exterior door handles, became an enduring staple of the Key Plastics portfolio of products.

EARLY NINETIES: PRODUCT LINE AND FACILITY EXPANSION

During the early 1990s, Key Plastics established a second staple product, power-steering reservoirs, after landing a contract with Ford Motor Company in 1992. Key Plastics joined with Kuss Filtration to produce the reservoirs for Ford's Tracer and Escort models, with Kuss producing the insert-molded filter and Key Plastics providing the power-steering reservoir itself.

Beginning in 1992, the company also began investing millions to upgrade and acquire production facilities. Key Plastics built a new paint plant in Indiana and opened molding facilities in Indiana, Michigan, and Pennsylvania. In addition, in 1995 the firm established a foothold in Mexico, developing a manufacturing molding facility in Chihuahua.

The company underwent a management shift in 1995. Mars relinquished his seat as president while remaining cochair of the board. Leonard Griffin, a former executive of two plastics firms in Troy, Michigan (near Key's base in Novi, Michigan), including Rockwell International, replaced Mars as president. Benoit became CEO. During the next five years, the team of Griffin and Benoit improved production at existing facilities and accelerated the growth of the company both domestically and abroad. Griffin implemented a program to substantially drive down the parts-per-million defect rate and improve product quality, delivery time, and customer ratings. Key Plastics expanded into Canada, Portugal, the United Kingdom, Italy, France, Switzerland, and the Czech Republic. Meanwhile, the company enlarged from nine North American plants with $170 million in annual revenues to operations in nine countries with 34 facilities generating $600 million in sales, half of which were derived outside the United States.

INTERNATIONAL EXPANSION IN THE LATE NINETIES

Helping to drive its international expansion, Key Plastics made 12 acquisitions in five years. In 1996 the company bought Clearplas Ltd. of Coventry, England, and a minority stake in Portugal-based Materias Plasticas, S.A. (MaP), both of which had operations focusing on assembly, injection molding, and painting. Two years later, Key Plastics acquired complete control of MaP. In 1997, to broaden its assembly, injection molding, and painting capacity, the company made three purchases: three Aeroquip interior automotive plastics plants from Trinova Corporation; the assets of T.D. Shea Manufacturing Inc., an OEM supplier of decorative appliqués with two Indiana factories; and the French firm Ascot Ltd.'s Clearplas division, a supplier of custom-made injection-molded interior trim and dashboard and under-the-hood parts to the European auto industry. Key Plastics in 1998 completed three more acquisitions: Ontario-based Acco Plastics, Inc., with an injection-molding and assembly plant, which became Key Plastics' first Canadian operation; a Michigan division of Libralter Plastics, with a molding plant that became one of Key Plastics' largest; and Concentric Plastics businesses in the United States, Mexico, and the United Kingdom.

Key Plastics continued to land Ford contracts, including a 1996 deal for an integrated control panel for the Taurus model. Then, as a step up, Ford contracted Key Plastics in 1997 as part of a multiple-company creation of insert-mold decoration for the new Mercury Tracer and Escort. Key Plastics provided the molding and assembly technology.

In a 1998 restructuring, all of the firm's assets and liabilities were transferred to a new parent company named Key Plastics, L.L.C. The former parent, Key Plastics, Inc., became a subsidiary and changed its name to Key Plastics Holdings, Inc. In the process, Key Plastics restructured its debt and took on a new third-party investor, which purchased a 25 percent stake in the company.

In its largest acquisition to that time, Key Plastics in 1999 acquired the Italian Foggini Group of companies, a European Tier 1 supplier of plastic injection-molded parts with annual sales of $130 million. Foggini added 175 injection presses and 1,000

KEY DATES

1986: The company is formed to acquire the plastics division assets of Key International Manufacturing, Inc.
1999: Key Plastics acquires the Italian Foggini Group of companies.
2000: Key Plastics declares bankruptcy and later emerges owned by Carlyle Management Group.
2008: Key Plastics again files for Chapter 11, emerging a few months later controlled by Wayzata Investment Partners LLC.
2010: Key Plastics acquires two sizable German companies.

employees to Key Plastics' operations. Key Plastics made an initial outlay of $45 million toward the $113 million Foggini price tag and also agreed to assume Foggini debt and the cost of a 35 percent stake in the newly formed Key-Foggini Europe subsidiary.

As it moved toward the end of the decade, Key Plastics was North America's 16th-largest injection-molding operation. To enhance this status, Key Plastics at the end of 1999 began construction on a Grand Rapids, Michigan, injection-molding plant to further expand into the under-the-hood components market. The 119,000-square-foot plant replaced a factory of half its size and increased the number of injection-molding presses by 37 percent.

NEW CENTURY: BIGGER COMPANY, BIG DEBT PROBLEMS

By the end of the decade, Key Plastics had 16 manufacturing plants and 3 paint facilities in North America and 13 European painting and manufacturing facilities. Ford Motor Company, General Motors Corporation, and Chrysler Corporation (the so-called Big Three) were the company's major customers, although Key Plastics was providing plastic assemblies and components to automotive OEMs and Tier 1 suppliers worldwide. Key Plastics was ranked 104th on *Automotive News*' list of North America's largest original-equipment suppliers and was North America's largest independent producer of plastic door handles, pressurized bottles, and decorative bezels. Moreover, the Foggini acquisition gave Key Plastics the capacity to produce all interior trim components within the 700-ton-press range.

With bigger operations, however, came bigger debt. Key Plastics also faced growing competition among plastic parts suppliers to the auto industry and increased pressure to trim profits in order to secure contracts. Because of capital expenditures related to its string of acquisitions, Key Plastics found itself in serious financial trouble as it neared the new century. Late in 1999 the company filed an amendment with the Securities and Exchange Commission, noting it needed more time to secure additional equity to back its loans.

In early 2000 Key Plastics filed a similar amendment despite recording about $550 million in annual sales. In February 2000 Standard & Poor's (S&P), one of the four major credit rating agencies, downgraded the credit rating of Key Plastics from a B to a CCC-plus, a two-step drop. S&P cited the company's total number of 1,000 creditors, its total debt of more than $350 million, and concerns that Key Plastics could default on its loans. In March, Key Plastics told creditors it was in "dire financial circumstances" and needed still more time to generate capital to pay bills, or it would face bankruptcy. Seeking to appease creditors, the firm hired an investment banker to sell the company and promised it would not substantially increase its debt for 90 days.

Key Plastics filed for Chapter 11 bankruptcy in late March 2000. The filing accorded with a lender commitment of up to $125 million to fund restructuring costs. The bankruptcy was also undertaken in such a way as to avoid interruption of production. Prior to filing for bankruptcy, the company solidified retention bonuses for senior management. Having experienced managers and employees on staff was deemed essential to marketing the company to buyers, hence the "pay-to-stay" agreements.

By July 2000, the company had narrowed its list of suitors to four: Becker Group LLC; NYX, Inc.; Carlyle Group Inc.; and Oak Hill Capital Partners. Key Plastics ultimately accepted the bid from Carlyle Management Group (CMG), a Washington-based fund affiliated with the high-profile Carlyle Group. In March 2001 a U.S. bankruptcy judge approved CMG's bid of around $175 million in cash and debt assumption for Key Plastics, which at the time of its Chapter 11 filing had $331 million in assets and about the same amount of debt. The following month the deal was completed, and B. Edward (Ed) Ewing, the CEO of CMG, became Key Plastics' new CEO.

GROWTH UNDER CMG CONTROL

CMG committed $40 million in equity to Key Plastics and also helped put in place a new line of credit. The new owner's stated objective for the plastics manufacturer was to increase its size, line of products, and in-house product development. To manage its automotive industry acquisitions, CMG in 2002 established the Key Automotive Group (KAG). As a sign of its reemergence, Key Plastics that same year expanded its under-the-hood product line when it acquired the bankrupt Soo Plastics Inc. of Michigan, a manufacturer of plastic battery trays, fan shrouds, and other products previously not made by Key Plastics.

CMG's management encouraged a focus on fiscal discipline and improved customer satisfaction. By 2003 positive signs of Key Plastics' renewal showed in reduced parts-per-million defects and improved on-time deliveries. The company also initiated a cost-control program, making each plant supervisor responsible for the plant's own budget. In another sign of a renewal, the company in January 2003 opened a new world headquarters in Farmington Hills, Michigan, housing senior management, advanced engineering operations, CAD/CAE activities, sales, marketing, human resources, finance, and central purchasing.

In 2003 the company developed injection-molded parts that, when applied to voltage, transmitted light. The components, designed in Farmington Hills, were part of Key Plastics' in-mold decorating product line. This electroluminescence feature was designed to brighten a broad area or an entire plastic component as opposed to only a line or point of a component.

Also in 2003, CMG added a company to the ranks of the Key Automotive Group by acquiring Breed, a plastics-intensive manufacturer of seat belts, air bags, steering wheels, and other automotive safety-system products. The acquired firm changed its name to Key Safety Systems, Inc. Following the acquisition, KAG was active in 15 countries in North America, Europe, and Asia.

ACQUISITIONS AND INTERNATIONAL EXPANSION UNDER EWING MANAGEMENT

In July 2004 CMG ended its affiliation with the Carlyle Group and became known as the Ewing Management Group (EMG). The original CMG was used as an investment fund but included only what became known as KAG, which included Key Plastics and Key Safety Systems. The Carlyle Group fund, which was limited to a two-year investment window, raised about $590 million during its one full year of running Key Plastics and Key Safety. Nevertheless, it reinvested only about $120 million. After the fund ran its two-year course, Ed Ewing, chairman and CEO of the new EMG, acquired Key Automotive Group and became chairman and CEO of Key Plastics.

In 2004 Key Plastics established its first Japanese office to enhance its servicing of Asian automakers. Key Plastics also invested $18 million to develop a plant in Slovakia to serve PSA Peugeot Citroën and South Korea's Kia Motors Corporation, both of which had recently established factories in Slovakia. The Slovakian facility was the company's second Eastern European molding plant and was developed to follow potential customers and generate components for OEMs in that region. Key Plastics already had established operations in France, Italy, Portugal, and the Czech Republic.

Ewing named Tim Nelson, former group president for under-the-hood and exterior products, as president and COO in 2004. At the same time, Ewing named Daniel Ajamian as president of Key Safety Systems. Ed Ewing continued to serve as chairman and CEO of both companies.

In a move to more than double its operations in Europe, Key Plastics in 2004 acquired Netherlands-based Kendrion N.V.'s auto plastics unit, which specialized in injection molding, painting, and laser etching and generated annual sales of about $250 million. Like Key Plastics, the acquired unit produced door handles and interior trim products. The deal also enlarged Key Plastics' production capacity with the addition of four assembly facilities at Volkswagen AG plants in Belgium and Germany and factories in the Czech Republic, Portugal, and Spain.

EXPANSION INTO CHINA AND TECHNOLOGICAL DEVELOPMENTS

In 2005 Key Plastics entered China through a joint venture with Shanghai-based Jiehua Automotive Trim Development Center. The venture, Shanghai Key Automotive Plastic Component Company, Ltd., manufactured door handles, air vents, bezels, and under-the-hood components for OEMs in the domestic Chinese market. With the addition of the Shanghai operation, Key Plastics had over 5,000 employees worldwide.

EMG sold Key Safety Systems in 2007, opting instead to invest in two Chinese firms involved in chemical manufacturing and horticulture. That same year, EMG closed its New York office. The closing was a sign of things to come and that EMG, which had not completed an acquisition for Key Plastics during the previous three years, might be tightening its purse strings.

In March 2007 a new state-of-the-art paint system went online at Key Plastics' facility in Mexico that increased both the capability and capacity for injection-molded plastics painting. In January 2008 the company began production using its new technology for vacuum-formed appliqué trimming at its Felton, Pennsylvania, plant. This technology, providing appliqués for decoration of injection-molded plastic components, eliminated the need for the company to use third parties for appliqués.

A SHRINKING AUTO MARKET, ANOTHER BANKRUPTCY, AND A NEW OWNER

With the global economy worsening, the auto industry subsequently shrank, and OEM suppliers felt the effects. In late 2008 the Big Three awaited word from Washington, D.C., about an industry bailout to keep them afloat. Meanwhile, Key Plastics and other suppliers suffered through the loss of contracts. With debt mounting and the market for contracts constricting, the company began restructuring in late 2008 to improve its balance sheet and facilitate future growth. In December 2008 Key Plastics filed for Chapter 11 bankruptcy as part of a reorganization to swap equity for debt. The company obtained financing to ensure routine payment of employees and suppliers and announced product deliveries would continue uninterrupted.

In January 2009 a Key Plastics reorganization plan was approved by a Delaware court and company creditors. The plan eliminated $115 million in debt, added a $20 million equity investment in the firm from Wayzata Investment Partners LLC, and provided for a new $25 million line of credit. As a result of the restructuring, the leading firm providing the equity, Wayzata Investment, became the company's controlling stakeholder. All North American creditors were expected to receive full payments under the plan.

Although operations in Europe and Asia were unaffected by and not included in the restructuring, Key Plastics' French and Slovakian operations were insolvent at the time of the North American restructuring and under French bankruptcy protection. As a result, the company reduced production capacity and slashed jobs at its Slovakian and French facilities because of reduced demand. In 2009 Key Products sold these operations to the French firm Groupe Plastivaloire.

The so-called soft-landing bankruptcy for which Key Plastics filed was feasible because of Wayzata's sizable infusion of capital. The plastics company emerged from bankruptcy in early 2009 with 25 facilities worldwide and wasted little time in establishing a new management team. Wayzata named Eugene Davis, the chairman and CEO of Pirinate Consulting Group, LLC., chairman of Key. Pirinate specialized in corporate strategic planning and ran other firms for Wayzata as well. In April 2009 Davis named Terrence Gohl, Visteon Corporation's former interiors and lighting president, as CEO of Key Plastics. Gohl had joined Visteon about four years earlier just as that firm landed a contract to design and provide door trim and the cockpit for a new Dodge Ram truck. Gohl was charged with overseeing Key Plastics' global activities, directing strategic growth, and integrating the firm's worldwide operations.

Although the restructuring improved Key Plastics' balance sheet, the auto industry remained in a recession, reducing demand for company products. By May 2009 Key Plastics had closed its fourth facility in less than a year, a former Soo Plastics injection-molding facility, to cut overhead. Although the plant was closed, company officials planned to move operations from the shuttered plant to another facility.

GERMAN EXPANSION IN 2010

In the spring of 2010, the company expanded in Germany. Key Plastics acquired the business and assets of the insolvent Paulmann & Crone Gmbh, a German-based manufacturer of automotive in-mold decorative products and thermoset products. The acquisition overnight made Key Plastics a leader in the European market for injection-molded decorative components and expanded the company's customer base in Germany, particularly with BMW and Volkswagen.

The company also purchased the German-based OLHO Group, which designed, engineered, and manufactured in-mold decorated products, air vents, and interior items for international OEMs and Tier 1 companies. OLHO gave Key Plastics a market-leading status in automotive air vents and interior mechanism products and strengthened its capacity and presence in Germany, Portugal, China, and the Czech Republic. The acquisition included equipment and inventory from OLHO's German facility as well as OLHO's business in the Czech Republic. The OLHO acquisition was expected to generate $75 million in annual revenues for Key Plastics.

The German acquisitions in 2010 signaled that Wayzata, unlike EMG, was willing to invest in Key Plastics' global expansion. Moreover, the purchases expanded the company's European presence and helped it move into new product areas. As it moved through 2010, the company was in the first year of a three-year strategic plan aimed at strengthening its market position in the area of decorative parts, achieving growth with nontraditional customers, and identifying potential acquisition targets to help Key Plastics best use its strengths. Key Plastics' actions in 2010 suggested it was starting to do just that.

Roger Rouland

PRINCIPAL SUBSIDIARIES

Key Plastics Company, Canada; Key Plastics de Mexico, S. de R.L. de C.V.; Key Plastics Bohemia, s.r.o. (Czech Republic); Key Plastics Czech, s.r.o. (Czech Republic); Key Plastics Germany GmbH; Key Plastics GmbH (Germany); Key Plastics Kierspe GmbH (Germany); Key Plastics Löhne GmbH (Germany); Key Plastics P&C Vermögensverwaltungs GmbH (Germany); Key Plastics Italy Srl; Key Plastics Radicar Srl (Italy); Key Plastics Europe S.a.r.l. (Luxembourg); Key Plastics Portugal, S.A.; Key Plastics (Dalian) Co., Ltd. (China); Taian Wing Key Plastics Co., Ltd. (China); Key Plastics Japan.

PRINCIPAL DIVISIONS

North America; Europe; Asia; Advanced Technology Products & Services.

PRINCIPAL COMPETITORS

ADAC Automotive Inc.; Cascade Engineering, Inc.; Clarion Technologies, Inc.

FURTHER READING

Barkholz, David, and Ryan Beene. "Key Plastics Goes Inside Visteon for New CEO." *Automotive News*, April 13, 2009, 6.

"Key Forms JV with Chinese Firm Jiehua." *Plastics News*, May 23, 2005, 1.

Miel, Rhoda. "Carlyle to Add to Size, Product Line of Key." *Plastics News*, April 23, 2001, 46.

———. "Key Buying Kendrion's Auto Plastics Unit." *Plastics News*, September 13, 2004, 1.

———. "Key Plastics Files Chapter 11." *Plastics News*, December 22, 2008, 5.

———. "Key Reveals Finance Woes." *Plastics News*, March 13, 2000, 1.

———. "New Plant a Sign that Key Plastics Is Moving Out of Financial Troubles." *Automotive News*, August 6, 2004, 4.

Murphy, Tom. "Back on Track." *Ward's Auto World*, March 1, 2003.

Pryweller, Joseph. "Key Plastics Buys Two Firms." *Crain's Detroit Business*, June 22, 1998, 16.

Kobold Watch Company, LLC

1801 Parkway View Drive
Pittsburgh, Pennsylvania 15205
U.S.A.
Telephone: (412) 722-1277
Toll Free: (877) 762-7929
Fax: (412) 722-1577
Web site: http://www.koboldwatch.com

Private Company
Founded: 1998
Employees: 10
Sales: $110 million (2009 est.)
NAICS: 448310 Jewelry Store

■ ■ ■

The Kobold Watch Company, LLC, is a manufacturer of professional-grade watches for explorers, police, and military personnel as well as for luxury watch collectors. The company boasts that its watches reflect the values of ruggedness, durability, luxury, and exclusivity. To maintain the latter, the company has vowed to never produce more than 2,500 watches per year. In 2008 Kobold released a watch whose components were 89 percent made in the United States, and the company plans to manufacture a fully U.S.-made watch by 2015. This plan represents a major goal of the company's founder and owner, Michael Kobold, who actively runs the business.

FOUNDATION FOR A FUTURE

Michael Kobold was born in Germany into a family of wealth and luxury. When he was just 12 years old, his father, Klaus, gave him a special Christmas present: a Cartier watch. "I loved that watch," Kobold told Josh Dean of *Inc.* magazine in May 2007. "It was mechanical. It was high end. I thought this was my one watch for the rest of my life. ... I thought it was the perfect product. You buy one for life." Kobold's obsession was born.

Kobold soon began taking watches apart and putting them back together again. When he was 16, he began writing to watch experts, asking each to take him on as an apprentice. Gerd Lang of Chronoswiss, a famous German manufacturer of timepieces and his most idolized watchmaker, responded positively to Kobold's query. During the next two years, Kobold shadowed Lang, who taught him watch design and business fundamentals.

Lang was the first important person in Kobold's future career. The second was the English explorer Sir Ranulph Fiennes. While going to high school at the Frankfort International School in Germany, Kobold became an assistant driving instructor for a driving school that taught antiterrorism tactical driving. Sometimes he was dispatched to chauffer VIPs who came to speak at Frankfort International. One day he was sent to pick up Fiennes. Because they were running late, Kobold put on a speed-driving show, Fiennes was impressed, and a lifelong friendship began.

After he graduated from Frankfurt International, Kobold moved to the United States to enroll in Car-

COMPANY PERSPECTIVES

Kobold is a pioneer in the watch industry, and like the explorers that wear its watches to the ends of the earth, the company is not looking to stop just yet. With ideas for industry-leading watches, new marketing strategies, and a lasting devotion to mechanical timepieces, it can be expected that the Kobold Watch Company will always adhere to its mantra—Embrace Adventure!

negie Mellon University in Pittsburgh, Pennsylvania, where his father's company, Kobold Instruments, had a U.S. office. At Carnegie Mellon, Kobold's relationships with Lang and Fiennes would start to pay dividends. Kobold was an average student and struggled early on to excel in his studies. Then Jack Roseman, Kobold's entrepreneurship professor, suggested that Kobold should start a business for a class project. With $5,000 in seed money and Lang's good name to use with suppliers, Kobold launched the Kobold Watch Company in 1998. He registered for an Internet domain name, placed an initial advertisement in a watch magazine, and was online and operating for less than $600.

THE EARLY YEARS: 1999–2001

Kobold's first business headquarters was his college apartment, where he kept a small safe for company valuables. When he received an online order, he fastened a strap to a watch, placed the watch in a box, and mailed it. In 1999, Kobold's first full year in business, Fiennes stopped endorsing Rolex and began endorsing his friend's new business. At year-end 1999 Kobold's fledgling company had generated $85,000 in sales, although Kobold only earned $50 per watch.

Kobold's initial business involved a limited line of military and aviator watches made in Germany and Switzerland. From the very beginning, Kobold's watches were driven by a mechanical movement that along with jewels and special amenities tended to set his luxury watches apart from less expensive timepieces. These movements consisted of materials such as aerospace-grade titanium, surgical stainless steel, and near-scratchproof sapphire crystal.

After Kobold graduated from Carnegie Mellon in 2001, he shifted to designing and making his own watches. For $750 a month, Kobold leased a small industrial park office next to his father's company, and when he needed storage space, he used a corner of the Kobold Instruments factory.

GROWTH AND NAME RECOGNITION: 2002–04

In 2002 Kobold Watch released its Soarway line of watches and debuted the firm's Polar Surveyor Chronograph. Designed with input from Fiennes and another explorer, Ben Saunders, the Polar Surveyor was the world's first mechanical wristwatch that indicated Greenwich Mean Time, date, and local time-zone day information. Fashioned with and for polar explorers, the model became the flagship watch of the Soarway Collection. A limited-edition Polar Surveyor also was developed, becoming the first Kobold made in solid gold.

Kobold expanded his company's operations in 2003, when he hired a chief operating officer, a bookkeeper, and a watchmaker. He also contracted with two master watchmakers when needed. Kobold himself assembled watches until he hired his first watchmaker. However, after 2003 the jeweler's monocle in his desk was more for show than for work.

By 2004 Kobold Watch had established a growing and prestigious collection of customers and had placed itself among a rather elite group of competitors within the watch industry. A niche market that the company exploited was geared toward explorers. By late 2004 Kobold watches had been to both the North and South Poles, to Antarctica, in the Brazilian rain forests, and in deep ocean waters.

BUILDING A REPUTATION: 2004–05

Kobold Watch's design and manufacturing process was one in which Michael Kobold took an active role in the creation of each new model. Watches were designed in house and then parts were imported from Switzerland and Germany. Watches were then assembled at Kobold's small office. Even though a watch's gold or platinum components increased its price tag, the next most expensive part of a timepiece was its movement (the spring and gears assembly that actually made a watch run). Developing a movement was both expensive and complicated, so initially Kobold imported Swiss movements.

In 2004 Kobold released its new Polar Surveyor Chronograph with a second time zone. The new model also included a gold version that was fashioned from more than 110 grams of gold. The watch was driven by a Kobold-developed antimagnetic self-winding movement.

KEY DATES

1998: Michael Kobold establishes the Kobold Watch Company, LLC.
1999: Sir Ranulph Fiennes begins promoting Kobold watches.
2002: Kobold Watch releases its popular Soarway line of watches.
2008: Kobold Watch releases its Spirit of America Automatic timepiece.
2010: Michael Kobold reaches the summit of Mount Everest without supplemental oxygen.

By 2005 Kobold watches were so popular that the company enhanced its online sales with select distribution through chosen retail stores. The company's most successful line of watches were those based on the Surveyor, the largest line and the first Kobold developed for professional explorers. In 2005 Kobold debuted its Soarway Diver SEAL, which was designed and crafted especially for divers. The size was actually larger than previous Kobold models. The watch price ranged between $2,450 and $4,750.

MARKETING THE U.S.-MADE MANTRA: 2006–07

In September 2006 Kobold Watch released its commemorative Spirit of America timepiece in recognition of the fifth anniversary of the September 11, 2001, terrorist attacks against the United States. The watch was designed by Burton Morris, a U.S. artist, and made of Swiss parts that were assembled in the United States. The release of the new line coincided with a charity auction of celebrity-worn watches, with funds received given to the United Service Organization of New York City. The limited edition watch sold out in a matter of days.

In 2007 Kobold released another limited-edition watch, the Rattrapante Stirling Moss, which was timed to debut with the Monaco Grand Prix that May. The watch's design was a collaboration between the British Formula One driver Stirling Moss and Michael Kobold and featured a split-seconds chronograph mechanism and a caseback with Moss's signature. Moss designed the watch's most unique element: an aerospace-grade titanium bracelet featuring two curved, parallel bars that attached to the watchcase on each side. Designed to keep excessive oil and dirt from getting caught within the armband's components, this bracelet was a reproduction of a watch that Moss himself had worn since early in his career. Just 250 Rattrapante watches were produced.

The company also released its Large Soarway Diver in 2007, a watch designed in collaboration with the deep-sea diver Philippe Cousteau, the grandson of Jacques Cousteau. The Large Soarway Diver was the largest timepiece Kobold ever released, and its large dial featured a minimalistic front that was reminiscent of divers' watches from the 1960s. It was also antimagnetic, shock resistant, and waterproof to depths of 1,650 feet. That same year the company launched a redesigned Polar Surveyor. The new Surveyor represented the company's inaugural reworking of the renown ETA 7750, believed to produce the world's most accurate and reliable chronograph movements.

GROWING THE KOBOLD NAME AND PRODUCT LINES

Kobold Watch was increasingly making a name for itself, and Michael Kobold was generally the one associated with the brand's name recognition and popularity. According to Dean, Kobold was "residing in the rarified air of mechanical timepieces, a niche of the market based almost exclusively in Europe." Despite his efforts, Kobold paid himself only a low six-figure salary, choosing instead to filter the remaining company profits back into the business. After manufacturing expenses, that money went to advertising and exposure. In 2007 the company spent nearly $500,000 on advertising.

However, some of the company's best advertising was free. Michael Kobold liked to brag that Bill Clinton owned three Kobold watches, Gary Sinise regularly wore a Kobold on the CBS crime show *CSI: New York*, and dozens of famous explorers and adventurers approved the company's use of their name on its website as Kobold wearers. Interestingly, Kobold decided to never give his watches as gifts, even to his so-called ambassadors. They bought their Kobold timepieces just like all the other Kobold customers. The only regular discount given was 10 percent that was offered to military and law enforcement personnel.

The notion that a Kobold was something someone bought to use and treasure helped make his watches valuable. Michael Kobold vowed to never produce more than 2,500 watches per year, and many lines had only 250 watches and were then retired, which developed demand and protected the investment of Kobold owners.

PROMOTING CARS, WATCHES, AND THE UNITED STATES: 2007–08

In late 2007 Kobold Watch was hired by Land Rover to create a watch for the British automaker's 20th anniversary high-end Range Rover. The clock was to become a dashboard feature. Kobold watches for male and female wearers were also designed to be included in the purchase of the Range Rover. With a price tag of $145,000, the vehicle became the most expensive ever to be serially produced and sold in the United States. Land Rover also commissioned Kobold to design Land Rover–brand timepieces for its senior executives and noteworthy retailers. Fiennes, an advertising emissary for both firms, brought the two parties together.

The company launched its Spirit of America Automatic in July 2008. The concept of the company's 2006 Spirit of America collection was so popular that, less than two years after its debut, Kobold released the watch's next generation, dubbed the Spirit of America Automatic 10th Anniversary Edition. Approximately 89 percent of the watch's components were made in the United States, save the movement, which was produced from parts made in Germany. The company claimed that the watch was the first serially produced U.S. watch of the 21st century and called the timepiece the company's new flagship model. Despite the printing of "Pittsburgh, Pennsylvania" on the dial, the product did not warrant the "Made in the U.S.A." label, which required that all components be produced in the United States. The watch sold for $6,250.

By mid-2008 a global recession that began in late 2007 was beginning to affect the luxury watch market, and Kobold Watch was no exception. In response to slow sales Kobold began using e-mail newsletters with marketing software that was designed to segment what information was sent to each customer. The newsletters, which were sent to the company's list of those who owned at least one Kobold, announced product releases and charitable events that Kobold supported.

MOUNT EVEREST AND OTHER CHALLENGES FOR KOBOLD: 2008–10

In May 2008 Michael Kobold made his first trek to Mount Everest, accompanying Fiennes but remaining at base camp while Fiennes journeyed upward. Shortly after the excursion Kobold decided to attempt to climb to the summit of Mount Everest the following year and help his favorite charity in the process. As a result, he organized the 2009 Everest Challenge Expedition with the goal to raise $250,000 in donations for the Navy SEAL Warrior Fund.

In 2009 Kobold Watch released its limited-edition USS Pittsburgh Chronograph. The timepiece represented a unique collaboration between Kobold Watch and Chronoswiss. Designed as an homage to the nuclear submarine USS *Pittsburgh* and its crew, the dial displayed the ship's hull number just above the watch's hour register.

That same year Kobold and Fiennes joined a team to climb Mount Everest. With the aid of supplemental oxygen, Kobold accompanied his friend to the summit, where he planted a U.S. Navy SEAL flag. In May 2010 Kobold was again part of an Everest excursion team, along with his wife, Anita, and Fiennes. Both husband and wife made it to the top without supplemental oxygen. Anita, whom Kobold met on a previous excursion, was a professional mountain climber.

THE FUTURE FOR KOBOLD WATCH

In 2010 Kobold Watch released a new variation on a proven theme: the Spirit of America Titanium, which sold for $3,350. As with the 2008 model, over 89 percent of the watch was produced in the United States. Following the release of this timepiece, Michael Kobold established a goal of creating a watch that earned the "Made in the U.S.A." label by using just U.S. suppliers. His target date was 2015.

Kobold Watch faired better during the global recession than its competitors, a majority of which had suffered a sales decline of approximately 30 percent. The company adjusted to the decrease in sales by attending fewer watch shows, making fewer business trips, and spending less on entertainment. The fact that Kobold Watch was Internet-based helped. As Michael Kobold told the website Off the Cuff on November 22, 2009, being an Internet company "has definitely helped in that we are able to focus on watchmaking and keep the business geared toward customer service. It's also easier for us to keep in direct contact with our customers." Kobold noted that the company needed to actively advertise and that he needed to help promote Kobold watches by making public appearances. He explained to Off the Cuff that "a big part of my job is to be seen, to meet people and to generate interest in and awareness of the brand."

Roger Rouland

PRINCIPAL COMPETITORS

Rolex S.A.; Omega SA; Officine Panerai; Breitling S.A.

FURTHER READING

"The American Way." *Robb Report*, December 1, 2008.

Dean, Josh. "The Greatly Improbable, Highly Enjoyable, Increasingly Profitable Life of Michael Kobold." *Inc.*, May 2007, 126.

———. "The Kobold Adventure Story." 2010 Everest Challenge, 2009. Accessed October 26, 2010. http://everest-challenge.com/the-kobold-adventure-story.

"The Interview: Michael Kobold (Part I)." Off the Cuff, November 22, 2009. Accessed October 26, 2010. http://offthecuffdc.com/the-interview-michael-kobold-part-i.

Khadka, Ayush. "Armchair Explorer Makes It to the Top." eKantipur.com, June 1, 2009.

"Kobold's American Dream." *International Watch*, June 2007, 58.

Milk, Leslie. "Read My Wrist." *Washingtonian*, November 2007.

Smith, Alex. "Rugged Re-Design." *International Watch*, May 2007, 154.

Smith, Nick. "The Hands-on Manager." *IET: Collective Inspiration*, February 17, 2009.

Tiku, Nitasha. "Update: Made in the U.S.A.—Almost." *Inc.*, November 1, 2008.

Kuoni Travel Holding Ltd.

Neue Hard 7
Zürich, CH-8010
Switzerland
Telephone: (+41 44) 277 44 44
Fax: (+41 44) 271 52 82
Web site: http://www.kuoni-group.com

Public Company
Incorporated: 1906 as Travel Bureau
Employees: 9,070
Sales: CHF 3.89 billion ($3.78 billion) (2009)
Stock Exchanges: Zürich
Ticker Symbol: KUNN
NAICS: 561510 Travel Agencies; 561520 Tour Operators

■ ■ ■

Kuoni Travel Holding Ltd. oversees one of the world's leading leisure travel companies. Based in Zürich, Switzerland, the company has branch offices in more than 40 countries in Europe, North America, Africa, Australia, India, and Asia and provides travel arrangements all over the world. As an internationally established brand, Kuoni offers classic travel, while regional sub-brands provide vacations of different types, scales, and prices. Services are available through various distribution channels, such as retail offices, agents, call centers, and the Internet. Kuoni Destination Management, its business-to-business division, offers an international network of sales and destination management operations. Destination Management organizes and arranges packages for groups, individual travelers, seminars, conventions, special interest and incentive tours, and sports events by providing tailor-made services that include hotel accommodation, transportation, restaurants, meeting venues, activities, and themed events.

FOUNDING AND DEVELOPMENT: 1906–86

In 1906 Alfred Kuoni, a native of Chur, Switzerland, moved to Zürich to open the Travel Bureau. One of the company's first organized tour packages took Swiss citizens on a guided tour of Egypt. In 1925 the Travel Bureau was reincorporated as a joint-stock company, with shares remaining within the Kuoni family. Through the years leading up to World War II the Travel Bureau expanded from its original location to include a number of sales offices located throughout Switzerland. Despite its success in its home market, the company recognized early on that Switzerland was too small for its growing ambitions. As a result, the company opened its first international office in Nice, France. Further international moves were thwarted by the buildup to and outbreak of World War II.

The Travel Bureau's international expansion began almost immediately after the war. In 1948 the company opened subsidiaries in Italy and France. It also continued to pioneer new and exotic travel destinations, such as chartered flights to Africa. In 1957 the Kuoni family established the Kuoni and Hugentobler Foundation to group the family's share of the company. Much later, when the company was publicly listed, the founda-

COMPANY PERSPECTIVES

Kuoni aims to be the most admired leisure travel company in the world, with a global market leadership position in the premium, specialist and destination segments, and selective local leadership positions in the standard packaged holiday segment. Kuoni serves consumers primarily through direct relationships, both offline and online, and takes full advantage of its broad knowledge base, top lifestyle brand and best people.

tion became the company's first primary shareholder, and up until 2003 it controlled 25 percent of the voting rights, while only holding 6.3 percent of the capital.

The Travel Bureau began looking farther afield during the 1960s. In 1963 the company made its first entry into Asia by opening a branch office in Japan. Two years later the Travel Bureau entered what eventually became one of its most important single markets when it acquired Challis and Benson Ltd. in the United Kingdom. The importance of the UK market to the Travel Bureau was recognized in 1970, when the company changed its name to Kuoni Travel Ltd.

The company's listing on the Zürich stock exchange in 1972 fueled further growth, while opening up the company's shares to new partners, including SwissAir, which built up a 30 percent share in Kuoni. The public listing enabled the company to step up its international growth. In 1973 Kuoni established subsidiaries in Germany, Greece, and Spain. The following year the company strengthened its position in the UK market when it acquired Houlders World Holidays.

In line with its international network, Kuoni also diversified its product line. In 1977 the company began marketing its first around-the-world tour. During the 1980s Kuoni started acquiring properties in many of its most popular destinations, adding a number of hotels, including the Hawksbill Beach Hotel in Antigua in 1981 and the Discovery Bay Beach Hotel in Barbados in 1984. In 1986 Kuoni became the first tour company to offer around-the-world charter flights on the Concorde supersonic jet. Aware that this latter product catered only to the company's high-end and high-margin clientele, Kuoni decided to launch a new brand name, Helvetica, to encompass its discount tour and travel operations.

EUROPEAN EXPANSION AND ATTEMPTED TAKEOVER: 1990–95

The worldwide travel industry remained highly fragmented during the 1990s, with many small-scale operators competing against a few quickly growing industry heavyweights. Kuoni, which had already captured the lead in the Swiss market, was determined to maintain a leadership position as the travel industry moved toward a consolidation drive during the late 1990s. The company acquired Reiseburo NUR Neckermann in 1987, boosting its position in the Austrian market. Three years later the company regrouped its Austrian activities to launch the NUR Neckermann Reisen AG joint venture with Germany's Neckermann Touristic. Kuoni controlled 49 percent of the joint venture.

The company continued to consolidate its dominance of the Swiss market by acquiring Privat Safaris, Switzerland's leading operator of tours to eastern Africa, and Reisebüro Popularis, which combined retail offices with direct sales operations to market discounted tour and travel packages. Given Kuoni's strong position in the Swiss market and its growing share internationally, it eventually became a target for a takeover attempt.

When SwissAir sold its 30 percent holding in 1992, the sale created an opportunity for Germany's Kaufhof AG to attempt to acquire a 50.1 percent majority of Kuoni. However, because of the Kuoni and Hugentobler Foundation, Kuoni retained majority control of the company's voting rights, which provided the leverage to prevent the takeover attempt. Three years later, in 1995, the Kuoni and Hugentobler Foundation bought out Kaufhof's stake in the company. The company then changed its name to Kuoni Travel Holding Ltd., a move that also reflected a new diversification drive. That same year the company acquired Danzas Reisen AG, a Switzerland-based specialist in business travel services. The Danzas acquisition led Kuoni to create a dedicated business travel unit. The company also acquired the retailer Kewi Reisen and integrated its majority share of Railtour Suisse SA, which it had acquired the year before.

EXPANSION INTO OTHER WORLD MARKETS: 1996–2000

With its independence secured, Kuoni launched its own acquisition drive during the mid- to late 1990s. In 1996 Kuoni added France's Voice SA and the Scandinavian-based Scanditours. The company moved into the Netherlands with the acquisition of Special Traffic. Kuoni also expanded into the potentially huge Indian market by acquiring SOTC Holiday Tours, which

KEY DATES

1906: Alfred Kuoni founds the Travel Bureau.
1925: The Travel Bureau is incorporated as a joint-stock company.
1970: The Travel Bureau is renamed Kuoni Travel Ltd.
1972: The company is traded on the Zürich stock exchange.
1995: Kuoni Travel Ltd. is renamed Kuoni Travel Holding Ltd.
2009: The company institutes a cost-reduction program that centers around procurement and production.
2010: The company acquires a 32 percent share in Et-china.com.

provided the basis for its Kuoni India Ltd. subsidiary. Two other acquisitions completed the company's busy year: Rotunda Tours, which extended Kuoni into South Africa, and CIS Intersport, a Swiss company that catered to the growing demand for sports-oriented vacation packages.

In 1997 Kuoni entered a joint venture with Peninsular and Oriental Steam Navigation Company, based in Hong Kong, to launch P&O Travel Ltd. with offices in Bangkok and Singapore. The joint venture strengthened Kuoni's position in the Asian market, which, despite the austere economic climate in the region at the end of the decade, was anticipated to become one of the world's stronger vacation markets. Closer to home, Kuoni continued lining up acquisitions, especially Voyages Jules Verne, a UK-based upscale tour operator, and Switzerland's Manta Reisen, which specialized in scuba and other deep-sea vacations. In 1998 the company acquired the German business travel specialist Euro Lloyd Reisebüro, which it combined with its other German operations into the new subsidiary BTI Euro Lloyd. That same year Kuoni launched a joint venture with Italy's Gastaldi Tours.

Kuoni faced a major setback in 1999. The company pursued a merger with First Choice Holidays, the number-three travel operator in the United Kingdom. The merger, which had been agreed on by both sides, was thwarted by the rival UK operator Airtours PLC, which offered a higher per-share price for First Choice. When the majority of First Choice's shareholders chose to back the Airtours offer, Kuoni pulled out of the merger talks.

After the collapse of the merger, Kuoni redirected its strategic focus to other markets, especially the one in the United States. In 1999 Kuoni acquired the upscale travel company Intrav, based in St. Louis, Missouri. The Intrav acquisition gave Kuoni a strong opening into the booming U.S. market for luxury vacations. The following year the company acquired T Pro, a New York–based destination management specialist and the number-three incoming services provider to the U.S. market.

CONTINUED EXPANSION: 2000–06

Kuoni strengthened its hold on the Swiss travel market in 2000, when it bought a 49 percent share in ITV, Switzerland's third-largest tour group. It also expanded its presence in Scandinavia and India. In Scandinavia the company purchased a 49 percent share in Apollo Resor in Stockholm, Sweden, and then acquired Denmark's Dane Tours. That same year Kuoni acquired Sita Travel, which made Kuoni the leading travel group in India.

In 2001 Kuoni restructured most of its Scandinavian holdings into a single subsidiary headquartered in Stockholm and sold its share in NUR Neckermann Reisen. That same year Kuoni established Reisen Netto, a direct sales discount brand. In 2002 Kuoni became the leading destination management provider in the United States by adding Allied Tours LLC to its U.S. subsidiaries Intrav and T Pro. The following year Kuoni acquired the French travel operator Vacances Fabuleuse, which specialized in high-end travel to and in the United States, thus consolidating its foothold in North America.

Between 2003 and 2005, amid an ongoing crisis in the travel industry due to the wars in Afghanistan and Iraq, an outbreak of the severe acute respiratory syndrome in 2003, and the Indonesian tsunami in December 2004, Kuoni was forced to refocus on its core businesses of leisure travel and destination management. Thus, Kuoni sold its U.S. subsidiary Intrav to First Choice Holidays and its business travel division BTI Central Europe to the UK-based business travel specialist Hogg Robinson. At home, Kuoni established cost saving measures by implementing shorter workweeks and unpaid vacation days.

To mark its 100-year anniversary, Kuoni commissioned a study of future travelers' wishes and needs. The study revealed that individualized vacation packages and niche traveling will likely increase. According to the study, future travelers will expect more care and comfort. Also, future travelers will expect travel to be an opportunity for socializing, meeting, and learning while experiencing the world. To meet the needs of future travelers, Kuoni launched a global rebranding effort in 2006. All of its subsidiaries began using the Kuoni name and logo and offered the same quality care and comfort. The purpose of this rebranding effort was to create a new culture of travel that incorporated lifestyle, fashion, art, architecture, music, and literature to provide a holistic travel experience.

GLOBAL RECESSION AND RECOVERY: 2007–10

By the end of 2007 the world economy was beginning to sag because of a global recession. To prevent or at least diminish the effects of the recession on its revenues, Kuoni restructured itself into three strategic business divisions: SBD Style, for brand- and service-driven products; SBD Smart, for vacations that offer outstanding value for money; and SBD Destinations, for local land arrangements.

Meanwhile, Kuoni continued its global rebranding efforts, which culminated in September 2008 with the Global Launch Event in London and the opening of several flagship stores throughout Europe. The rebranding efforts were enhanced by three acquisitions that fit the new approach to travel: UTE Megapolus in Russia, which specialized in high-end travel; Carrier Ltd. in the United Kingdom, which specialized in luxury travel; and Cotravel, a Swiss educational travel company. Kuoni also purchased a 60 percent share in the Swiss direct sales giant Direkt Reisen.

However, despite its aggressive efforts to rebrand and restructure itself, Kuoni was unable to fend off the effects of the global recession. In August 2009 the company announced a 12 percent decrease in its revenues for the year. Kuoni immediately reacted by implementing a three-year cost-reduction program that focused on consolidating its online distribution and synchronizing its booking and inventory for its worldwide network.

Despite a slowdown of acquisitions in 2009 and 2010, Kuoni planned to continue its strategy of expansion, particularly in China, where in 2010 the company purchased a 32 percent share in Et-china.com in anticipation of continued growth in the Asian market. Given its stature as a strong global player, Kuoni was anticipated to weather future economic crises, political events, and natural disasters that affect travel behaviors through acquisitions and further consolidation.

M. L. Cohen
Updated, Helga Schier

PRINCIPAL SUBSIDIARIES

Apollo Sweden; Apollo Norway; Apollo Denmark; UTE Megapolus (Russia); Kuoni United Kingdom; Kuoni Benelux; Kuoni Switzerland; Kuoni France; Kuoni Italy; Kuoni Spain; Kuoni India; Kuoni China; Kuoni Belgium; Hub Switzerland; Hub United Kingdom; Hub Scandinavia; Kuoni Connect.

PRINCIPAL DIVISIONS

SBD Style; SBD Smart; SBD Destinations.

PRINCIPAL COMPETITORS

Carlson Wagonlit Travel; First Choice Holidays PLC; Thomas Cook Holdings Ltd.; TUI Travel PLC.

FURTHER READING

"Anhaltende Verstimmung bei Kuoni." NZZ Online, August 20, 2006. Accessed October 21, 2010. http://www.nzz.ch/2006/08/20/wi/articleEEDRT.html.

Carey, Christopher. "Intrav Accepts $115 Million Buyout from Swiss Travel Firm." *St. Louis Post-Dispatch*, July 20, 1999, C12.

Court, Mark. "We'll Fight Them on the Beaches." *Sunday Telegraph* (London), May 2, 1999, 6.

Drees, Caroline. "Kuoni Slips on Capital Increase News." *Reuters*, March 28, 2000.

Gelnar, Martin. "Kuoni's First Choice Merger Seen Falling Through." *Reuters*, June 2, 1999.

Hager, Emil. "Die ganze Welt aus einem Guss." *Schweizertouristik*, July 16, 2010.

Hebeisen, Beat D. "Kuoni denkt vermehrt an die Aktionäre." *Finanz und Wirtschaft*, March 19, 2005.

Hofmann, Birthe. "Kuoji: Zwangsferien für Reiseprofis." *Beobachter*, October 2003. Accessed October 21, 2010. http://www.beobachter.ch/arbeit-bildung/artikel/kuoni-zwangsferien-fuer-reiseprofis/.

"Kuoni Maps out European Expansion Strategy." *Financial Times*, March 29, 1999.

"Kuoni on Hunt for Takeovers." *Financial Times*, March 29, 2000.

Langenscheidt KG

Mies-van-der-Rohe Straße 1
Munich, D-80807
Germany
Telephone: (+49 89) 36096-0
Fax: (+49 89) 36096-222
Web site: http://www.langenscheidt.de

Private Company
Founded: 1856
Employees: 1,400
Sales: EUR 242 million ($336.8 million) (2008 est.)
NAICS: 511130 Book Publishers

■ ■ ■

Langenscheidt KG, founded in 1856 by Gustav Langenscheidt in Berlin, Germany (and later based in Munich), is a family-owned publishing company specializing in dictionaries and other reference books, language-learning materials, and travel guides for leisure travelers, businesspeople, students, and children. Four generations of Langenscheidts have built a global enterprise from a single self-study program for French developed by Gustav Langenscheidt and Charles Toussaint. The publisher's content is available in print, audio, and electronic formats, and the company offers its products online and in bookstores, office supply stores, convenience stores, drugstores, and grocery stores. Combining under one roof subsidiaries and brands such as Langenscheidt, Berlitz, Polyglott, Hexaglot, APA, Mentor, and Axel Juncker, Langenscheidt KG operates over 30 companies in 11 countries, with 1,400 employees worldwide.

THE FIRST GENERATION: OVERCOMING LANGUAGE BARRIERS

In 1851, 18-year-old Gustav Langenscheidt began his *Wanderjahre*, traveling throughout Europe in the tradition of the journeyman. To overcome language barriers he studied French with Charles Toussaint. Together they developed the first self-study program based less on grammar and more on speaking and reading, henceforth known as the "Methode Toussaint-Langenscheidt." Their method was characterized by simple everyday sentences, an easily accessible phonetic transcription system, and the constant repetition of newly acquired knowledge. These remain the didactic staples of any self-study program. Langenscheidt offered his "Brieflichen Sprach- und Sprechunterricht für das Selbststudium der französischen Sprache" (Self-study letters for learning to speak the French language) to several publishers, but no one was interested. Convinced of the worthiness of his product, he founded his own publishing house in Berlin in 1856, and by 1868 he had set up his own printing press to accommodate his unique phonetic transcription system. The French program was so successful that it became the prototype for many more language program to come. English was the second language to be added, in 1861, and Hebrew, added in 1923, was the last.

Recognizing that vocabulary is among the most important ingredients to language learning, Langenscheidt in 1863 commissioned the authors Carl Sachs and Césaire Villatte to compile a French-German/German-French dictionary. Research and writing took years longer than expected, and the complete 4,000-page opus was not published until 1880. The Sachs-

COMPANY PERSPECTIVES

The Langenscheidt Publishing Group has been a leading publisher of travel, language, and reference products for 150 years. From our bestselling bilingual dictionaries and phrasebooks to maps and travel guides, the Langenscheidt name has come to represent quality in every corner of the globe. Established in 1856, our company is world famous for catering to the needs of language students, educators, travelers, business people, and native speakers around the world.

Villatte dictionary became the prototype for many future Langenscheidt dictionaries.

The development of the English edition, named after its original authors Eduard Muret and Daniel Sanders, took even longer. Editorial work began in 1869, however, the first complete edition of the Muret-Sanders dictionary did not hit the market until 1901, 30 years after its commission and six years after Gustav Langenscheidt's death in 1895.

THE SECOND GENERATION: PRODUCT DEVELOPMENT IN SERIES

Langenscheidt's son Carl began to recycle and reuse content by consistently developing books in series. The "Notwörterbücher" (essential dictionary), first published in 1883 as a less voluminous and more practical edition of the Sachs-Villatte and Muret-Sanders dictionaries, became the "Taschenwörterbücher" (pocket dictionary), which was eventually available in "big" and "small" editions; in editions focused on travel, business, and school; and in languages as diverse as Albanian, Russian, and Slovak. Carl Langenscheidt developed his line of products into a recognizable brand name, and quite literally so, as the first letter of his last name, the capital *L*, became the company's logo.

In 1905 Carl Langenscheidt teamed up with the Deutsche Grammophon Gesellschaft to create the first all-audio language program available on records. Offering English to those who had neither time nor leisure nor aptitude to learning a language through reading and writing, Langenscheidt became a trendsetter once more. Also realizing that increasing mobility in the new century had created the opportunity and need for more international travel, and realizing that the language needs of a traveler are vastly different from those of a serious language learner, Carl Langenscheidt expanded his company's product line in 1912 with the launch of the Metoula language guides, which offered language instruction organized according to themes relevant for travel. The line encompassed more than 30 languages up until the early 1960s, when they were reissued under the Langenscheidt name. This self-study series eventually became available in numerous languages and editions offering targeted materials for beginners and advanced students, business and leisure travelers, children, and adults.

POSTWAR EXPANSION

During World War II, production came to a halt because of the rationing of paper, key employees' participation at the front, and the virtual destruction of the company's publishing building. Content and machines went up in flames, and work could not resume until 1947. The 1948–49 blockade of Berlin forced the family to establish branch offices near Berchtesgaden in southern Germany. The relationships forged through this move proved helpful years later when the company was forced to relocate permanently because of the escalation of the Cold War.

Although Carl Langenscheidt had created an impressive publishing list, Karl-Ernst Tielebier-Langenscheidt, who was a grandson of Carl Langenscheidt and had joined the company in 1948, made Langenscheidt into an international publishing force. In 1951 Langenscheidt reissued its pocket dictionary, signaling a fresh start after World War II with a new and revised edition. In 1956, in time for the company's 100-year anniversary, Tielebier-Langenscheidt continued his father's marketing strategy and created the firm's long-standing logo, a blue *L* on a yellow background.

In 1955 Langenscheidt took over Polyglott, a competing publisher of language and travel guides. By the end of the 1950s, the Polyglott Reiseführer became the most successful travel guide series in German-speaking countries. Polyglott eventually offered guides to hundreds of countries and cities the world over.

Like his grandfather, who had developed the first all-audio language program, Tielebier-Langenscheidt recognized the opportunities of new media. In 1960 the company struck its first international cooperation deal with the BBC. The publishing house supplied printed language-learning materials for *Walter and Connie—English by Television*, a television show on language developed by the BBC. Within only two months, 150,000 copies of the books were sold.

In 1961 the Berlin Wall divided the city into East and West. Tielebier-Langenscheidt immediately realized

KEY DATES

1856: Gustav Langenscheidt founds his own publishing company with a French self-study program.
1956: Company marks its 100-year anniversary with a new logo, a blue *L* on a yellow background.
1983: Langenscheidt introduces the world's first electronic dictionary.
2002: Company acquires Berlitz Publishing.
2010: Langenscheidt begins offering a variety of applications for the iPad, iPhone, and other smartphones.

that a publisher would not survive in a divided city in the middle of East Germany, and moved his family and his editors to the West. The first two years in Munich were difficult, with the editorial offices situated in the family's apartment. Nevertheless, employee loyalty, a strong entrepreneurial spirit, and the relationships forged in southern Germany by the branch office near Berchtesgaden proved successful. In 1963 the first postwar Langenscheidt publishing building was completed.

The postwar economic boom brought foreign workers to West Germany. Realizing the need for a language program to foster integration in German society, Langenscheidt developed the "Deutsch als Fremdsprache" (German as a foreign language) program. Outside Germany the program was distributed by the Goethe-Institut, an organization seeking to improve West Germany's international image. By 1971 Langenscheidt had become an internationally recognizable name.

ACQUISITIONS AND INNOVATION IN THE LATE 20TH CENTURY

In 1981 Andreas Langenscheidt, the eldest son of Carl Langenscheidt, joined the company. Before becoming the publisher's managing partner in 1990, Andreas Langenscheidt helped his father build up the company's U.S. operations. The cartographic companies American Map and Hagstrom Map were acquired and then became subsidiaries of the firm's U.S. division, Langenscheidt Publishers Inc., established in 1983.

In 1983, in keeping with the company's tradition of technical innovation, Langenscheidt and the Japanese electronics giant Sharp Corporation developed the world's first electronic dictionary. Ten years later, Langenscheidt accelerated its venture into this field by acquiring Hexaglot, a specialist in electronic dictionaries.

In 1988 Langenscheidt acquired a majority holding of the Bibliographisches Institut & F.A. Brockhaus AG (BIFAB) to thwart a foreign takeover by publishing and media mogul Robert Maxwell. BIFAB, German royalty among dictionary publishers, carried the two most recognizable German dictionary lines, the *Brockhaus Konversations-Lexikon*, an encyclopedia written for the general public, and the *Duden*, the premier name in German spelling.

Despite taking over such traditional heavyweight works, Langenscheidt remained at the forefront of technical innovation, publishing CD-ROM editions of the *Brockhaus* and the *Duden* in the 1990s. The first complete LexiROM edition of the *Brockhaus*, developed in cooperation with Microsoft Corporation, was available in 1995, followed two years later by a CD-ROM edition of the *Duden*, which already incorporated the German spelling reform that took effect in 1998. Through its string of acquisitions and its innovations on the technical front, the company grew more than sevenfold by the end of the 20th century.

NEW PRODUCTS IN A NEW CENTURY

Further expansion, a rejuvenation of the publishing list, and a search for new distribution venues characterized Langenscheidt KG at the beginning of the 21st century. In 2002 Langenscheidt acquired Berlitz Publishing, strengthening the company's corporate foothold in the United States and establishing it as a premier global player in foreign language self-study and travel publications.

Langenscheidt also sought to broaden its customer base by pursuing a younger, less serious clientele. In 2004 comedian Mario Barth's *Deutsch-Frau/Frau-Deutsch*, a dictionary offering "German" translations of "woman speak," became an instant best seller. It also eventually led to the establishment in 2010 of the Langenscheidt Entertainment series, which included titles offering lighter takes on language, such as translating between lawyers and clients, doctors and patients, employees and superiors, and even dogs and their owners.

Equally committed to technological innovation, the company published a new generation of electronic Langenscheidt and Duden dictionaries in cooperation with Sharp in 2006. Although technology was a vital ingredient of Langenscheidt's success, it also created difficulties. In 2007 Langenscheidt KG reported a 3.9 percent decline in revenues, thanks to the poor performance of the cartography and knowledge divisions, which were hardest hit by competition from Internet content providers such as Wikipedia and online navigation services such as MapQuest.

The 2005 print edition of the *Brockhaus* had reported losses, and thus, in 2008, Langenscheidt began to offer *Brockhaus* content on the Internet. Later in 2008 the Brockhaus division of BIFAB was sold to Bertelsmann, and the remainder of BIFAB was sold to Cornelsen a year later. In 2010 Langenscheidt sold its U.S. cartographic subsidiaries American Map, Hagstrom Map Company Inc., Alexandria Drafting Company, and Hammond World Atlas Corporation.

The shedding of the encyclopedia and map division allowed the company to refocus on its core products in language and travel. The travel division entered a cooperation deal with Michelin in 2008, through which Langenscheidt became the exclusive distributor of the world-renowned Michelin travel guides. In 2009 the Langenscheidt travel division relaunched the popular Polyglott series, adopting a new look and adding a series of more exotic titles.

The language division focused on technological rejuvenation, entering a cooperation agreement with the Swiss company Mobileman GmbH in 2008. By 2010 Langenscheidt KG had plans to offer 1,000 applications for the iPad, iPhone, and other smartphones. Langenscheidt also began offering language courses on Facebook. At the same time, the company, which remained owned and managing by its founding family, continued its tradition of editorial renewal by launching a new division in 2010 called Langenscheidt Kinder- und Jugendbuch, which offered titles teaching language through storytelling.

Helga Schier

PRINCIPAL SUBSIDIARIES

APA Publications GmbH & Co.; Axel Juncker Verlag GmbH; GeoGraphic Publishers GmbH & Co. KG; Langenscheidt Verlag GmbH; Mentor Verlag GmbH; Polyglott Verlag GmbH; Blay-Foldex (France); Berlitz Publishing Company, Inc. (USA).

PRINCIPAL COMPETITORS

Ernst Klett Verlag GmbH; HarperCollins Publishers, Inc.; Rand McNally & Company; Random House, Inc.

FURTHER READING

Ebert, Maria. *150 Jahre Langenscheidt, 1856–2006: Eine Verlagsgeschichte.* Berlin: Langenscheidt, 2006.

Haupt, Christine. "Von einem, der auszog, das Geschäftemachen zu lernen." *Personal Finance,* August 2002. Accessed August 27, 2010. http://www.christinehaupt.com/Langenscheidt.pdf.

Heintze, Dorothea. "Babylons Erbe." *Zeit Online,* April 19, 2007. Accessed August 26, 2010. http://www.zeit.de/2007/17/Babylons_Erbe.

Langenscheidt, Florian, ed. *Lexikon der deutschen Familienunternehmen.* Cologne, Germany: Deutsche Standards Editionen, 2009.

Milliot, Jim. "Langenscheidt Agrees to Buy Berlitz Publishing." *Publishers Weekly,* February 18, 2002, 16.

Reid, Calvin. "Universal Map Acquires American Map and Affiliates." *Publishers Weekly,* August 20, 2010. Accessed August 26, 2010. http://www.publishersweekly.com/pw/by-topic/industry-news/publisher-news/article/44218-universal-map-acquires-american-map-and-affiliates.html.

LAZARD

Lazard LLC

Clarendon House
2 Church Street
Hamilton, HM 11
Bermuda
Telephone: (+441) 295-1422
Toll Free: (800) 823-6300
Fax: (+441) 292-4720
Web site: http://www.lazard.com

Public Company
Incorporated: 1848 as Lazard Frères
Employees: 2,292
Sales: $1.62 billion (2009)
Total Assets: $135 billion (2010)
Stock Exchanges: New York
Ticker Symbol: LAZ
NAICS: 523110 Investment Banking and Securities Dealing; 523120 Securities Brokerage

■ ■ ■

Lazard LLC is a leading financial services firm and one of the world's top 10 mergers-and-acquisitions specialists. The company originated in 1848 and for decades was among the world's leading private investment banking houses, not turning public until 2005. Some of Wall Street's most legendary deal makers (men such as André Meyer, Felix Rohatyn, Steven Rattner, and Bruce Wasserstein) have worked for Lazard. Throughout the 20th century the company operated as three separate and autonomous firms: Lazard Frères & Co. LLC; Lazard Brothers & Co., Limited; and Lazard Frères & Cie. All three carried the Lazard name but remained devoted to their respective New York, London, and Paris locations, and relations between the three were sometimes acrimonious. Michel David-Weill, the fourth generation of Lazard family members to head the firm, merged the three houses into a single corporate entity in 2000.

The company, whose official headquarters is now located in Bermuda, conducts business on every continent, with a stable base on each side of the Atlantic. Although the financial industry has been consolidating, resulting in the rise of a small number of gigantic banks, Lazard remains steadfast to its tradition as a modestly sized boutique specializing in full-service, client-oriented investment and financial advisory services.

FROM MERCHANTS TO MERCHANT BANKERS

The Lazard dynasty began modestly enough, as three brothers (Alexandre, Elie, and Simon), from France's Alsace region, left their native country to settle in New Orleans, Louisiana, in 1848. There, the Lazard brothers founded the Lazard Frères (*frères* means "brothers" in French) dry goods store. A year later, Lazard Frères & Co. followed the rest of the world's fortune seekers to the gold rush in California. In San Francisco the company quickly expanded its business from its range of dry goods to include banking and merchant banking

COMPANY PERSPECTIVES

The core of Lazard's success is its simple business model of Financial Advisory and Asset Management, with a focus on excellence, intellectual rigor, integrity and creativity. The firm provides value to its shareholders, premium service for its clients, and an environment that attracts and breeds top talent. Lazard is committed to investing in the success and growth of the global Lazard franchise.

services, as well as exchange services for the foreign currencies market.

This last activity encouraged the company to return to France, where the Lazards opened a second office in Paris in 1852. The Paris office, which initially counseled the French government on its gold purchases, quickly focused on its financial advisory business. Lazard Frères et Cie, as the Paris branch was named, began working closely with France's government and the Banque de Paris, establishing itself as the preeminent investment banker in the French capital.

In the late 1850s another member of the Lazard family, Alexandre Weill, left France to join to the three Lazard brothers, his cousins, in the United States. The family business continued to grow, adding new services to its financial portfolio (including arbitrage services), making the shift away from its dry goods business complete by the 1870s. By 1876 Lazard Frères had abandoned all of its other activities to focus solely on its financial services business. The following year, the partners opened a third office, in London, in order to be present in that financial center. The London office adopted the name Lazard Brothers & Co.

Originally a unified company, the Lazard financial empire developed into a multiheaded organization during the later years of the 19th century. Precipitating the change in the company was the rise to control of Alexandre Weill, who, as the only member of the four partners to have male children, supplied the heirs to the family's financial empire. Weill's decision to move the San Francisco office to New York, placing the company at the heart of that booming financial center, prompted discord among his cousins and set the scene for a segmentation of the three company branches. Lazard Frères & Co. opened its New York office in 1880 and quickly carved a place for itself among the top Wall Street investment banking firms.

THE HOUSES OF LAZARD

Each of the three Lazard offices concentrated on its local market, placing the company's name at the center of the three main financial centers of the day. The lack of a rapid means of communication among the offices meant that each conducted its own business independent of the others and, at the same time, developed its own corporate cultures and its own partnership organizations. Nevertheless, the Weill family, which initially took over operations of the Paris branch, maintained their ownership of the branch offices and continued to receive the largest share among any of the other partners. The latter were, in fact, partners in name only. Although each of the Lazard partners received a share of the company's profit pool (the amount was later determined from the Paris office), they did not receive any equity in the company.

The separation into distinct houses took place at the dawn of the 20th century. In 1908, the London office became a separate company, which was a prelude to the company leaving, in large part, the Lazard/Weill family's control. This move was forced upon the company by the British government in 1919, when the Bank of England enacted new rules prohibiting ownership of banks in the United Kingdom by foreign companies. Lazard Brothers came under the control of S.P. Pearson & Sons when the Weill family sold nearly half of its stake in the London office. Pearson eventually built up its ownership of Lazard Brothers, reaching some 80 percent of that company's shares, in the 1930s. Pearson maintained its position in Lazard Brothers until the end of the 20th century, when it agreed to sell its stake back to the Weill family.

The Weills continued to control the New York and Paris branches. During the initial decades of the 20th century, the Paris office was led by David David-Weill (who added the hyphen to the family name), Alexandre Weill's grandson. David-Weill then transferred leadership of the company to his son Pierre. The outbreak of World War II, however, forced Pierre David-Weill to flee Paris and Europe for the United States, where he took over control of the New York office. David-Weill was joined by André Meyer, as both were named resident partners of Lazard Frères & Co. in 1943. In Paris, Lazard Frères & Cie ceased operations under the Nazi occupation.

A SHIFT TO NEW YORK

The devastation of the European financial scene during the war caused the focus of Lazard's activity to shift to its New York office. The rebuilding of much of the European and world's economies helped promote Wall

KEY DATES

1848: Lazard Frères is founded in New Orleans, Louisiana.
1852: Lazard Frères et Cie is opened in Paris.
1876: Company is focused exclusively on banking activities.
1877: Lazard Brothers is opened in London.
1880: Lazard Frères moves to New York.
1908: Lazard Brothers separates from other branches.
1984: Lazard Partners is formed, in beginning of effort to unite the three Lazard firms.
1997: Lazard Asset Management takes over all Lazard asset-management operations.
2000: All Lazard operations are combined under Lazard LLC's direction.
2005: After 157 years as a private firm, Lazard goes public with an initial public offering.

Street as the world's financial capital, and Lazard established itself among the top financial services firms. Helping to solidify the company's reputation was the arrival of Felix Rohatyn in 1948. Rohatyn forged a reputation as one of the era's great deal makers, most notably when he led the management team that helped New York City stave off bankruptcy in the mid-1970s. With Meyer and Rohatyn at the head of the New York office, Lazard Frères & Co. became the strongest of the three Lazard houses and one of the market's top mergers-and-acquisitions specialists.

Meanwhile, a new generation of the David-Weill family was preparing to make its mark on the family-owned company. In the 1950s Pierre's son Michel David-Weill joined Lazard Frères & Cie, which had been devastated by the war years. Michel David-Weill succeeded in turning around that company by the end of the decade, reestablishing the Lazard name as the preeminent name in investment banking in Paris. In 1961 David-Weill, who inherited the family's controlling share of the Lazard empire, was named a general partner of New York-based Lazard Frères & Co.

The 1970s saw the balance of power shift within the global Lazard empire, which by then included offices worldwide. The failing health of Meyer gave David-Weill an opportunity to take over direction of the New York branch as well as the Paris branch, uniting the two formerly separate offices under the same chief for the first time since the beginning of the century. David-Weill was named senior partner of Lazard Frères & Co. in 1977.

Meanwhile, in London, the third member of the Lazard investment family was struggling against a new wave of competitors entering the British financial markets in the 1970s. Struggling to keep up in its market, Lazard Brothers finally sought help in the form of a merger with another company. This move, however, was blocked by the other two members of the Lazard group.

CREATING A GLOBAL NETWORK

The Lazard Brothers crisis served to open up an opportunity for David-Weill to buy back some of the shares in the London office from Pearson. In 1984 David-Weill set up Lazard Partners, a private limited U.S. partnership, joining his own and related Lazard shares into the new vehicle. Pearson in turn contributed its holdings in Lazard Brothers, taking a 50 percent share of Lazard Partners, which then gained 100 percent control of the London office. Although the deal did not give David-Weill outright control over the London Lazard branch, it did bring together the three branches into a more cooperative, globally operating network.

David-Weill's timing was right. Although the Paris branch was reaping the benefits of the French wave of nationalizations of its banking industry, which Lazard Frères et Cie helped coordinate, David-Weill had correctly recognized the growing globalization of the international marketplace, as mergers and acquisitions began to cross borders, a trend that especially picked up in the 1990s. Meanwhile, Lazard had shunned, in large part, the wave of leveraged buyouts that washed across the financial world during the 1980s, thereby avoiding the fallout as the world economy slumped in the late 1980s and early 1990s.

In 1989 David-Weill was named senior partner at the Lazard Brothers branch, marking the first time since the beginning of the century that one person held the leadership position in all three Lazard firms. The move toward formally uniting the three branches under a single management only came slowly, however.

UNITING THE EMPIRE

In the mid-1990s the three Lazard firms took a number of steps toward unification. Among these was the creation of Lazard Capital Markets, which was formed in 1995 as a single globally operating entity providing underwriting services to Lazard clients in all three branches. More significantly, the three offices began a common profits pool from which to pay its partners.

David-Weill himself decided the amount partners were to be paid. The move was not well received by the company's partners, given that the New York office generated twice the amount of profits of either the London or Paris offices. The company lost a number of its partners, particularly a number of its brightest stars, who were tempted away by the promise of better compensation at one of the newly emerging investment banking giants.

Lazard found itself caught up in a new trend. As mergers-and-acquisitions specialists became involved in a series of megamergers, which in turn were creating a new breed of huge, globally operating companies, the banking firms themselves began to take on scale to meet their new clients' needs. The emergence of giants such as Morgan Stanley Dean Witter and Goldman Sachs had come to dwarf the three individual Lazard houses. Lazard, which had long ranked among the top-tier mergers-and-acquisitions houses, found itself slipping in the ranks, and even dropped out of the top 10 entirely in 1997.

In that year, the three Lazard firms took a new step toward their own in-house merger, when the New York-based Lazard Asset Management absorbed the other Lazard companies' asset-management operations. Lazard, however, continued to find difficulty in recruiting (and even keeping) the industry's top banking stars. The retirement of Rohatyn, who was named the U.S. ambassador to France in 1997, shook up the company. Lazard was equally shaken by the defection of Édouard Stern, David-Weill's son-in-law and purported successor, who left the company that same year. Replacing Rohatyn and Stern as top rainmaker was Steven Rattner, a former journalist who had gained an international reputation as a top deal maker during the 1990s. Rattner, named CEO of Lazard Frères & Co., was credited with helping to clarify some of Lazard's operations, such as revealing the amount paid to each partner, while also persuading David-Weill to cut his own 15 percent share of the New York office's profits back to just 10 percent in an effort to appease disgruntled New York partners.

Rattner, however, did not remain with Lazard for long. His own political ambitions (he was popularly tipped for a role in the presidential cabinet in the event of a win by Al Gore) brought him to step back from active management of Lazard in 1999, before leaving the company altogether in 2000. By then, however, David-Weill had used his own funds to buy out Pearson's share of Lazard Partners, giving him majority control of the three pieces of the Lazard empire.

In 2000 David-Weill announced his decision to rejoin the pieces to create a single, globally operating entity, Lazard LLC. Based in the company's traditional Paris headquarters, the newly united Lazard hoped to regain some of its former luster in the world's international market. In these years, the global investment banking marketplace was changing rapidly, with the merger of several major players into a few so-called superbanks such as JPMorgan Chase and Morgan Stanley. Nevertheless, Lazard remained dedicated to its modest size and, especially, to its status as one of the few remaining private partnership companies in the industry, a position that enabled the company to provide a higher degree of discretion to its clients.

GOING PUBLIC

Although David-Weill had succeeded in uniting his family's empire under his control, the company was threatened by the depletion of top executives and the ongoing disharmony among the firm's branches and shareholders, not to mention the consolidation of its competitors. To engineer Lazard's turnaround, David-Weill hired one of Wall Street's heavy hitters, Bruce Wasserstein, in 2002. Wasserstein, elder brother of the celebrated playwright Wendy Wasserstein, had helped bring off major mergers such as AOL's marriage to Time Warner and Morgan Stanley's to Dean Witter.

With full executive authority as Lazard's new CEO, Wasserstein set about replenishing the company's management with rising and established talent. He siphoned off funds from the company's profit pool to pay the new managers top dollar, to the chagrin of the firm's directors. The strategy soon showed results; Lazard scored high fees in 2004 for its role in two high-profile deals, the $59 billion merger of Bank One and JPMorgan Chase and Sprint's $35 billion acquisition of Nextel.

Nonetheless, Wasserstein had a more ambitious plan to build the company: He wanted to take the house of Lazard public, shifting majority control from the board to the managing directors. Such a move was a major gamble. David-Weill bitterly opposed it but ultimately failed to block it. The two men publicly agreed that Wasserstein would resign if he failed to complete an initial public offering (IPO) by the end of 2005. The IPO took place on May 5 of that year, ending Lazard's reign as the last of the major private investment banks. The company sold 34.2 million shares at an initial share price of $25. The company's working partners assumed roughly two-thirds ownership, with Wasserstein himself taking the largest share, over 11 percent of the company. Most market analysts regard the move as highly successful for the company, dramatically increasing its market capitalization. Wasserstein is also credited with markedly improving and rationalizing the firm's organizational structure, which had been widely described by observers as Byzantine.

GROWTH THROUGH ACQUISITIONS

Following Lazard's transformation into a publicly held company, the firm shored up its global position in the world of high finance with several acquisitions. In 2007 the company acquired Carnegie, Wylie & Company. This financial advisory company was Australia's largest independent business in that sector, with an extensive presence in the Asia-Pacific region. Lazard also took a 50 percent stake in Grupo MBA, the parent company of the Latin American investment bank MBA Banco de Inversiones.

In addition to the company's strong geographic base, Lazard's business model also proved its mettle through changing economic times. Although mergers and acquisitions customarily fluctuate along with the boom and bust of the business cycle, Lazard built up a secondary specialty of advising companies going through financial restructuring, such as during a bankruptcy crisis. Revenues from this sector of the firm increased markedly as the U.S. economy headed into a severe recession in 2008. Rounding out the business, the asset-management division provided more steady earnings to balance the periodic swings in advisory fee intake.

Wasserstein, credited with restoring Lazard to administrative and financial health, died in October 2009 at the age of 61. His successor was hired from within the company: Kenneth M. Jacobs, formerly chief of North American operations. In early 2010 the company welcomed the return of Rohatyn as a special adviser to Jacobs.

M. L. Cohen
Updated, Roger K. Smith

PRINCIPAL SUBSIDIARIES

Lazard International Holdings, Inc. (USA); Lazard Frères & Co. LLC (USA); Lazard Asset Management LLC (USA); Lazard Funding Limited LLC (USA); Lazard & Co., Holdings Limited (UK); Lazard & Co., Limited (UK); Compagnie Financière Lazard Frères SAS (France); Lazard Frères Gestion SAS (France); Lazard Frères Banque SA (France); Maison Lazard SAS (France).

PRINCIPAL COMPETITORS

Bank of America Merrill Lynch; Citigroup Inc.; Daiwa Securities Group Inc.; Deutsche Bank AG; Fidelity Management and Research Corp.; The Goldman Sachs Group, Inc.; JPMorgan Chase & Co.; Morgan Stanley, Inc.; The Nomura Securities Co., Ltd.; UBS AG.

FURTHER READING

Bianco, Anthony. "The Taking of Lazard." *Business Week*, November 6, 2006, 54.

Cave, Andrew. "Lazard Men Quit and Go Private." *Daily Telegraph* (London), March 1, 2000.

Cohan, William D. *The Last Tycoons: The Secret History of Lazard Frères & Co.* New York: Doubleday, 2007.

de la Merced, Michael J. "New Leader at Lazard Is an Insider." *New York Times*, November 18, 2009, B1.

Gledhill, Dan. "Lazard Bows to Rival's Pressure." *Independent on Sunday* (London), October 1, 2000, 1.

Lenzner, Robert. "Assault on the House of Lazard." *Forbes*, September 4, 2000.

Owen, David. "Adapting to Change Not Easy for an Icon." *Financial Times*, November 10, 2000.

Reed, Stanley. "The Leadership Question at Lazard Frères." *Business Week*, June 21, 1999, 170.

Washington, Sharon Walsh. "Lazard to Combine Global Offices." *Washington Post*, June 8, 1999, E3.

Liechtensteinische Landesbank AG

Städtle 44
P.O. Box 384
Vaduz, 9490
Liechtenstein
Telephone: (+423) 236 88 11
Fax: (+423) 236 88 22
Web site: http://www.llb.li

Public Company
Founded: 1861 as Zins- und Credit-Landes-Anstalt
Employees: 1,054
Total Assets: CHF 49.4 billion ($45.4 billion) (2009)
Stock Exchanges: Swiss
Ticker Symbol: LLB
NAICS: 522110 Commercial Banking

■ ■ ■

Liechtensteinische Landesbank AG (LLB) is the Principality of Liechtenstein's oldest financial institution. According to the company's website, the majority of the company's share capital is held by the Principality Liechtenstein, amounting to 17.7 million, or 57.5 percent, of the bank's 30.8 million bearer shares, each with a par value of 5 Swiss francs. LLB is the parent company of the LLB Group, which provides comprehensive wealth management services for its clients through universal banking, private banking, fund and trust services, and asset management. LLB has a state guarantee on savings deposits and medium-term notes. In addition to its main headquarters in Vaduz, Liechtenstein's capital city, LLB has locations in Switzerland (Basel, Geneva, Lugano, Uznach, and Zurich), Austria (Vienna), the Cayman Islands, United Arab Emirates (Abu Dhabi), Hong Kong, and the Virgin Islands.

THE PRINCIPALITY OF LIECHTENSTEIN

Located between Switzerland and Austria, the Principality of Liechtenstein is a small nation of about 35,000 people governed by a hereditary constitutional monarchy. With German as its official language and the Swiss franc as its currency, Liechtenstein ranks as one of the world's most industrialized nations, also boasting one of the highest gross domestic product per person. The country, originating from the Austrian Liechtenstein family, began as an independent principality of the Holy Roman Empire in 1719. After the French occupied the nation for a number of years, it was a sovereign state beginning in 1806 and part of the German Confederation beginning in 1815. When the confederation dissolved in around 1866, Liechtenstein declared its neutrality, which it would maintain through both World War I and World War II. Until the First World War, the country maintained close relations with Austria but, finding itself financially distraught after the conflict, turned to Switzerland for a customs and monetary union.

While the Second World War also created financial stress, Liechtenstein would ultimately prosper due to its low tax corporate rate drawing many companies to the country. At the beginning of the 21st century, with its

COMPANY PERSPECTIVES

Versatility and special competence, wherever you need us. Teams from all business areas bundle their knowledge to continually exceed your expectations. Whether you require classical banking services, private banking, asset management, trust services or fund services: we'll provide you with made to measure services and we'll find the optimal solution for you. We all work together to achieve one common goal: your success. Independent companies complement our business activities, enhance our expertise and expand our offer to cover your requirements.

maximum tax rate of 20 percent as well as its easy rules of incorporation, Liechtenstein had more than twice as many registered holding companies as citizens. The country is not a part of the European Union but is a member of the European Free Trade Association.

FOUNDING AND GROWTH OF THE LANDESBANK

The history of LLB is tied to significant milestones in the history of Liechtenstein. In the middle of the 19th century, Governor Karl Haus von Hausen created a new constitution for the Principality of Liechtenstein, greatly improving the nation's living conditions. In another effort to improve his country, on December 5, 1861, von Hausen established what would eventually become the LLB, the Zins- und Credit-Landes-Anstalt (Savings and Loan Bank). The creation of the state-owned financial institution made it easer for farmers and home builders to obtain loans.

As Liechtenstein advanced into the next century, it became a constitutional monarchy, and two years later, on January 12, 1923, a new savings and lending law was established. The law separated Landesbank from the state, making it, according to the company's website, "a new legal form as an independent institute under public law.", The law also provided for "the introduction of a board of directors as the supreme governing body and the provision of endowment capital with a continuing unlimited state guarantee."

Although Liechtenstein and Landesbank struggled through World War II, they both ultimately flourished. With its tax laws, the country attracted companies to incorporate in Liechtenstein, and Landesbank was there to provide financial services. Landesbank succeeded especially in attracting wealthy individuals, with its traditions of strict privacy and secrecy. By the mid-1980s the bank issued for the first time bearer participation certificates valued at 20 million Swiss francs to private investors. The Principality of Liechtenstein issued a stamp on June 9, 1986, honoring LLB's 125th anniversary and its founder, Karl Haus von Hausen.

LLB went through another transformation in the early 1990s. The Liechtenstein Parliament (Landtag) enacted the Law Concerning Liechtensteinische Landesbank on October 21, 1992. Effective beginning January 2, 1993, the law enabled the conversion of Liechtensteinische Landesbank into a public limited company (Aktiengesellschaft, or AG), and LLB was listed on the Swiss Stock Exchange.

As Liechtenstein focused on new business development and expansion in the late 1990s, so did LLB. LLB expanded abroad in 1998 with the founding of the Liechtensteinische Landesbank (Switzerland) Ltd., with its head office in Zurich, a branch office in Lugano, Switzerland, and a representative office in Abu Dhabi in the United Arab Emirates. Additional offices later opened in the United Arab Emirates.

SCANDAL AND THE TWENTY-FIRST CENTURY

In 2004 the tradition-oriented LLB was the target of a blackmail scheme in which a former employee demanded CHF 18 million ($17.3 million at the time) or he would publish secret details about the accounts of German clients. The employee was arrested and sentenced in 2004. However, an accomplice, Michael Freitag, continued the blackmail, and LLB paid out €9 million ($13.5 million) as part of the extortion campaign, according to the German magazine *Der Spiegel.* In September 2007 German prosecutors learned that Freitag had deposited €1.4 million ($1.7 million) in cash at the Rostock Commerzbank, which began a money laundering investigation, but there were no connections to LLB. When one of Freitag's accomplices contacted two LLB clients and told them details of their accounts, those clients then contacted LLB. As part of its own investigation, using former agents of Germany's Federal Office of Criminal Investigation, LLB learned Freitag's identity and informed German authorities.

Freitag and three accomplices were arrested in September 2007. After the story was featured in *Der Spiegel* in 2008, an LLB spokesperson commented, as quoted by Reuters, "The bank clients who have been affected have been informed. ... We cannot comment beyond the statement. This is an ongoing investigation."

KEY DATES

1861: The Zins- und Credit-Landes-Anstalt (Savings and Loan Bank) is founded in the Principality of Liechtenstein.
1921: Liechtenstein becomes a constitutional hereditary monarchy.
1923: A new savings and lending law is established in Liechtenstein, bringing a separation from government administration for Landesbank.
1992: Law Concerning Liechtensteinische Landesbank is passed, providing for the conversion of Liechtensteinische Landesbank into a public limited company.
1998: Liechtensteinische Landesbank (Switzerland) Ltd. Is established, with a head office in Zurich.
2005: Liechtensteinische Landesbank increases its shareholding in swisspartners Investment Network AG from 20 percent to 51 percent.
2007: Liechtensteinische Landesbank takes over a majority shareholding in Bank Linth LLB AG, greatly expanding its business operations in Switzerland.

Hundreds of German clients with secret savings accounts were affected, but LLB's investigators were able to recover two-thirds of the documents concerning customer accounts.

The German investigation of the LLB data theft led to prosecutions for tax fraud and evasion by German citizens. Similarly, in violation of Liechtenstein's bank secrecy and criminal laws (which legally prevent banks from disclosing information from depositors in connection with foreign tax law violations), information was purchased by the German Federal Intelligence Service (Bundesnachrichtendienst) from a former employee at the LGT Bank in Liechtenstein AG. Crown Prince Alois von und zu Liechtenstein criticized German authorities and called its investigation tactics an attack on the Principality of Liechtenstein. The events called negative attention to the banking secrecy custom in Liechtenstein, Luxembourg, and Switzerland, a tradition that has attracted wealthy customers from around the world to bank large quantities of money and potentially avoid paying taxes on that money. In the wake of the scandal, Liechtenstein stood by its laws, while LLB was left with concerns about its unrecovered stolen records concerning more than a thousand customers.

FURTHER EXPANSION

In spite of the years it was being blackmailed, LLB continued to thrive. On April 1, 2005, LLB increased its shareholding in swisspartners Investment Network AG, an asset management firm, from 20 percent to 51 percent. That same year, LLB launched a series of professional seminars called "Financial Perspectives" in conjunction with the Financial Services Institute of the University of Applied Sciences Liechtenstein. Two seminars are conducted each year on current topics from the world of finance.

In December 2006 LLB made a public purchase offer for Bank Linth in Uznach, Switzerland. Seventy-four percent of Bank Linth's shareholders approved of the purchase. On March 8, 2007, LLB took over a majority shareholding in Bank Linth LLB AG, thereby greatly expanding its business operations in Switzerland. In May 2008 Konrad Schnyder, a member of the board of directors of Bank Linth since 1998, was elected to LLB's board of directors at the annual general meeting. Three of LLB's board of directors' members are elected at the general shareholder's meeting, and four members are elected by the Principality of Liechtenstein's Landtag, which also appoints the LLB chairman.

LLB also increased its holdings in Jura Trust to 100 percent, as well as its holdings in swisspartners Investment Network to 61.74 percent. In November 2009 LLB opened a bank in Vienna, Austria. LLB also holds a 17.5 percent share in MBPI AG, a small, independent asset management firm in Triesen, Liechtenstein. In addition, LLB has a 48 percent equity stake in the life insurance company Elips Life AG. By 2009 LLB was one of the leading asset management institutes in Switzerland and Liechtenstein, with client assets under management of CHF 49.4 billion ($45.4 billion).

LOOKING TO THE FUTURE

Maintaining its traditions but sensing the necessity of information technology, LLB, including the LLB Group, Liechtensteinische Landesbank (Switzerland) AG, and Bank Linth LLB AG, paired with SunGard, a leading software and technology services firm. SunGard's Ambit Risk & Performance Management solution, according to a press release, "will help LLB Group's risk management team meet new liquidity risk requirements, employ new risk and profitability metrics in their banking and investment book positions and obtain a single view of all the group's current and future positions. This will help the team to better perform risk, treasury and margin analysis on these positions."

In other efforts to work more efficiently and reduce costs, in March 2010 LLB announced it would partner with Liechtenstein's VP Bank (Verwaltungs- und Privat-Bank AG) in the business sectors of logistics and information technology. "Specifically," according to a press release, "this involves combining print and dispatch infrastructure and shared use of buildings to accommodate computer centers." VP Bank, founded in 1956, is one of the largest banks in Liechtenstein, offering asset management services to wealthy clients.

As LLB closed the first decade of the new century in the midst of a global economic downturn, it seemed more than capable of weathering the storm. Commenting on 2009 business results, Dr. Hans-Werner Gassner, chairman of LLB's board of directors, was quoted on the company's website as saying: "We cannot escape the effects of international crises. Nevertheless we know how to hold our ground in these difficult business conditions, and we are continuing to expand our position in our target markets. In 2009 we intentionally made long-term investments because we are convinced that we can benefit substantially in the long term from a stabilization of the economic and political situation. On the whole, the result we achieved in 2009 was within our expectations and we are satisfied with it. We want our shareholders to participate in this solid business result and in the LLB Group's strong position by providing them with an unchanged dividend." In the first quarter of 2010 the company announced a rise in net profits by 20.2 percent.

Inextricably tied to the history of the Principality of Liechtenstein, LLB maintains close ties to the nation's people and culture. The bank has sponsored the Vaduz Film Fest for 15 years, as well as involved itself in blues, jazz, theater, and opera events. LLB sponsors a program for the Vaduz Light Athletic Club, which promotes physical activity among Liecthenstein's citizens, and has been the major sponsor of FC Vaduz (the nation's football club) for more than a decade.

Louise B. Ketz

PRINCIPAL SUBSIDIARIES

LLB Group; Liechtensteinische Landesbank (Switzerland) Ltd.; Bank Linth LLB AG; Liechtensteinische Landesbank (Österreich) AG; LLB Fondsleitung AG; LLB Fund Services AG; LLB Asset Management AG; Jura Trust AG.

PRINCIPAL OPERATING UNITS

Domestic Clients; International Clients; Institutional Clients; Corporate Center.

PRINCIPAL COMPETITORS

LGT Group; VP Bank; Basellandschaftliche Kantonalbank; Basler Kantonalbank AG; Berner Kantonalbank AG; Luzerner Kantonalbank.

FURTHER READING

"Bank LLB Secret Accounts Hit by Blackmail." Reuters, February 11, 2008.

Beattie, David. *Liechtenstein: A Modern History.* London: I. B. Tauris, 2004.

Donahue, Patrick, and Joshua Gallu. "Liechtenstein under Siege Clings to Bank Secrecy to Outdo Swiss." Bloomberg, February 27, 2008.

Jaeger, Ulrich, and Gunther Latsch. "Chasing Stolen Bank Data: How a Liechtenstein Bank Helped German Investigators." *Der Spiegel*, March 3, 2008.

"LLB Group Selects SunGard's Ambit Risk & Performance Management Solution for Liquidity Risk Management" (press release). SunGard, September 7, 2009. Accessed November 13, 2010. http://www.sungard.com/pressreleases/2009/ambit090709.aspx.

Pancevski, Bojan. "Taxation HMRC May Pay More for Liechtenstein Tax Details." *Daily Telegraph* (London), March 10, 2008.

"VP Bank and LLB Join Forces in Logistics and IT" (press release). VP Bank, March 2, 2010. Accessed November 13, 2010. http://www.vpbank.com/htm/1397/en/Publikationen-Detail.htm?Article=50313&ArticleReturn=589.

Wiesmann, Gerrit. "Data Handover Could Boost German Crusade against Tax Evaders." *Financial Times*, Augusts 4, 2008.

Little Caesar Enterprises, Inc.

2211 Woodward Avenue
Detroit, Michigan 48201
U.S.A.
Telephone: (313) 983-6000
Toll Free: (800) 722-3727
Fax: (313) 983-6197
Web site: http://www.littlecaesars.com

Private Company
Founded: 1959
Incorporated: 1962
Sales: $1.13 billion (2009)
NAICS: 722211 Limited-Service Restaurants

■ ■ ■

Founded by Michael and Marian Ilitch, Little Caesar Enterprises, Inc., is the largest carryout pizza restaurant in the world, with locations on five continents. It is the fourth-largest pizza restaurant chain in the United States, with 2,600 franchise and company-owned restaurants. Little Caesars serves a menu of several types of pizza, breads, and chicken wings made with only natural ingredients and all-natural spices. Its locations offer carryout service only. Little Caesar Enterprises, headquartered in Detroit, Michigan, achieved sales of $1.13 billion in 2009.

IN THE BEGINNING

Michael and Marian Ilitch are the founders of Little Caesar Enterprises, Inc. They opened their first Little Caesars Pizza restaurant in 1959 in Garden City, Michigan. The restaurant offered spaghetti, fried chicken, and french fries, as well as pizza. In their first week, the Ilitches sold 296 pizzas and soon realized they had found a niche by offering quality at low prices. They opened their second restaurant just two years later.

In 1962 the Ilitches sold their first franchise restaurant. By the end of the 1960s, they had built or franchised over 50 restaurants, including one in Canada. During that decade, delivery was a service of most Little Caesars restaurants, but in 1971 the chain moved to carryout only. The restaurant set itself apart from many competitors by using only natural ingredients, including high-gluten flour in the pizza dough, specially grown California tomatoes, and grade A cheese. Little Caesars prided itself on the use of all-natural spices, as opposed to the synthetic flavorings used throughout the pizza industry.

The 1970s were years of innovation and phenomenal growth for Little Caesars. In 1971 the company began its two-for-one "Pizza! Pizza! Two Great Pizzas! One Low Price!" concept and made it a permanent feature of the company's marketing campaigns in 1975. The marketing strategy forced competitors in some heavily saturated areas to mimic the two-for-one offer. In 1977 Little Caesars also introduced drive-through windows at its quick-serve locations, and in 1979 developed a pizza conveyor oven that sped up the production of pizza and other baked items.

COMPANY PERSPECTIVES

Our mission is to provide delicious, high-quality products at an affordable price, with friendly, prompt, and courteous service.

BUILDING AN EMPIRE

In 1980 Little Caesars had 226 restaurants with sales of $63.6 million. By mid-decade annual sales had grown more than fivefold to $340 million. The company emphasized three simple concepts: market saturation, two pizzas for the price of one, and carryout only. Approximately 98 percent of Little Caesars restaurants were 1,200 to 1,800 square feet, offering carryout only. Overhead and maintenance expenses for these locations was considerably lower than that of competitors who offered sit-down or even delivery-only service, because the restaurants did not require servers, busboys, dishwashers, or delivery personnel.

In 1984 the company built its 500th restaurant. The 1,000th Little Caesars opened just two years later. By that time, the company was well established in 38 states and parts of Canada and had one location in Great Britain. Marketing innovations included the first college campus restaurant, at the University of Oklahoma in Norman, Oklahoma, and the first hospital restaurant, at Mt. Carmel Mercy Hospital in Detroit, Michigan.

JOINT VENTURES AND ADVERTISING

In the early 1990s marketing and promotion efforts for Little Caesar focused on value ("Pizza! Pizza! Two Great Pizzas! One Low Price!") and quality ("When you make pizza this good, one just isn't enough"). The company invested a minimum of 5 percent of its sales on advertising, and franchises, which constituted 75 percent of all locations, spent a comparable percentage on local and corporate promotions. The company also initiated its first network television campaign. Seven, 30-second commercials were developed, featuring comical situations that became the hallmark of Little Caesars promotions.

Little Caesar also began experimenting with the basic carryout, two-for-one pizza concept. Variations included restaurants with limited seating, drive-through units, and arena concessions. In a joint venture with Kmart Corporation, Little Caesar built over 400 Pizza Stations in Kmart stores and the resulting self-serve restaurants (featuring pasta and vegetable salads, soups, fresh fruits, and the standard pizza, sandwiches, and hot pasta) constituted almost half of Little Caesars 1992 growth. The company also introduced new items, such as Crazy Bread, Chocolate! Chocolate!, Ravioli! Ravioli!, and Baby Pan! Pan! lunch pizzas

In the early 1990s Little Caesars' sales outpaced the industry's growth by 24 percent; yet the company remained locked in a closely fought battle with its two largest competitors, Pizza Hut and Domino's Pizza and faced growing competition from the rapidly emerging Papa John's pizza chain. In the summer of 1995 Little Caesar introduced a nationwide delivery service that was not as successful as planned. Yet 1995 was still a decent year for Little Caesars. Its new, stuffed-crust pizza was enormously popular, and revenues were more than $1.1 billion.

GROWING PAINS

The late 1990s were challenging for Little Caesars. The company slashed its national advertising budget by nearly 23 percent from 1994 to 1996, and laid off 27 managers at its headquarters in Detroit. The jobs represented 1 percent of its corporate workforce, and rumors linked the purge to Harsha Agadi's appointment as chief operating officer and the company's 8 percent decline in domestic sales in 1996. In addition, Little Caesars market share fell from 14.5 to 13.4 percent for the year, and 184 restaurants closed, leaving 4,004 still in operation. Meanwhile, over at Papa John's, same-store sales grew by 10 percent, and restaurants mushroomed by 32.1 percent to 1,160.

On the positive side, Little Caesars broadened its marketing efforts substantially with three major moves. The first was a joint venture with Holiday Inn in Florida to put pizza kiosks in two of the chain's biggest-draw hotels. The second was the unveiling of a new strategy calling attention to Little Caesars long-held creed of value. In a risky move, it proudly proclaimed "Bigger is Better," with pizzas 80 percent larger (or four inches in diameter per pie) at the same price. Third, the company's venture with Kmart stores expanded into 1,500 of the chain's over 2,000 stores in 1997.

In the late 1990s Little Caesars was still battling its old foes Domino's and Pizza Hut, and Papa John's relentless growth had become a serious threat. Its same-store sales were up 12 percent and profits up 66 percent in 1997, and the chain planned to open dozens of new stores each month during 1998. To counter its slipping market share, Little Caesars began accepting American Express credit cards at its locations in Utah. It also of-

KEY DATES

1959: The first Little Caesars restaurant opens in Garden City, Michigan.
1962: The first franchise opens in Detroit, Michigan.
1971: The chain ends delivery service, switching to carryout only; two-for-one "Pizza! Pizza!" concept is introduced.
1986: The 1,000th Little Caesars opens.
2000: Michael and Marian Ilitch turn over control of the company to their children, Christopher and Denise Ilitch.
2001: The Manage to Own program debuts, establishing incentives for company employees to become franchise owners.

fered pizza at 39 cents a slice on May 7, 1998, to mark its 39th anniversary. For all of 1998, however, the chain shrank from 4,500 locations to 4,100, an 8.9 percent decline.

NEW MARKETING

Little Caesars decided to try a different marketing approach. It hired a new ad agency, Bozell Worldwide, which deemphasized the chain's traditional "zany" advertising in a new campaign that put the focus on quality and value. This was coupled with a direct-mail campaign offering a money-back guarantee. The new approach was intended to play subtly on issues raised by rival Pizza Hut's lawsuit against Papa John's over the latter's claims to have the best-quality pies. The new TV spots also promoted an offer of two 12-inch pizzas with up to three toppings for $10.99, the first time Little Caesars offered three toppings in a national promotion.

The new marketing focus did not get a good response from all franchisees, however, some of whom criticized the company for changing its message too often and introducing innovations, such as fountain service, then not sticking with them. Another complaint was that its two-for-one deals were squeezing profit margins. The bad news continued into 1999, peaking in July, when the chain abruptly closed more than 300 locations across the United States, in some cases without notice to employees or customers. Workers at the restaurants were laid off. A month later Little Caesars auctioned off all the equipment from the restaurants.

A company spokesperson told reporters that the closings were part of a national remodeling program in Colorado, Indiana, Texas, North Carolina, Pennsylvania, and Florida and denied rumors that Little Caesar Enterprises was in financial trouble. The company did not say when the locations would reopen, although some were being modified to accommodate drive-through business. Meanwhile, Little Caesars cancelled a national, network-television advertising buy planned for the fall. The closings punctuated a year that saw further declines in sales for the chain. Sales plunged 11.2 percent in 1999 to $1.47 billion, after having dropped 7 percent the year before.

MAJOR CHANGES

The first Little Caesars in Egypt and in Aruba opened in 1998. A year later the company bought Pan Smak, a chain of eight pizza restaurants in Poland. In March 2000 the Ilitches created a new, wholly owned subsidiary, LC Trademarks Inc., into which Little Caesar Enterprises transferred its trademarks, real estate valued at $4.3 million, and $750,000 in cash. The decision prompted opinions by some attorneys that it was a ploy to protect the company and its assets from litigation.

In June 2000, after more than 40 years running Little Caesars, Mike and Marian Ilitch turned over daily operation of the chain as well as their other holdings to their son, Christopher, and their daughter, Denise. That same month, Little Caesars and Bozell, now known as FCB Worldwide, split, less than two years after the ad agency was hired. Also in 2000 Little Caesars sales dropped for the eighth straight year to an estimated $1.3 billion, 11.3 percent down from the previous year, and Papa John's overtook Little Caesars as the third-largest pizza chain in the United States.

Little Caesars reported in 1999 that the ranks of its franchise and company-owned locations had thinned by 1,086 since 1998, meaning it had lost 41 percent of its traditional carryout and delivery locations over three years. Nonetheless, some observers considered this to be a positive sign that the company was refocusing on its most profitable locations and starting to attend more to the needs of franchisees. That began to emerge more distinctly in June 2001, when a group of ex–Pizza Hut executives agreed to buy 59 company-owned stores in North Carolina, South Carolina, Maryland, Missouri, and Kansas.

In October 2001 the company announced it would sell 500 of its 4,000 company-owned locations to franchisees, leaving it with only 50 to 100 outlets under direct corporate control. The shift accompanied a new program called Manage to Own in which a Little Caesars restaurant manager could become a franchisee over time by moving up a ladder from salary to bonus to a percentage of profits and then 100 percent ownership of a restaurant. The initial investment could be as little as $10,000. Part of the goal was to improve recruitment by offering incentives to high-performing, loyal managers.

MENDING FENCES, MAKING IMPROVEMENTS

Meanwhile, Little Caesars was mending fences with existing franchisees. In November the company settled a class-action lawsuit brought by a group of 250 franchise owners. The owners balked at Little Caesars mandatory fee of 4 percent of gross sales for national advertising and wanted its supply costs brought in line with what other pizza chains charged. The settlement was valued at $350 million but gave the company the opportunity to start fresh with franchisees. The deal included instituting shared governance of marketing and operations, elimination of $14 million of debt owed by the franchisees, a half share of profits to franchisees from Little Caesars supply division, a 10-year extension of franchise agreements, and a $5 million investment by the company for building new restaurants.

Bolstering the new start, the company made improvements in its menu items and promotions. Already in May 2000, Little Caesars introduced Caesar Sticks, 11-inch cinnamon bread sticks brushed with a buttery mixture, rolled in cinnamon and sugar, and baked golden brown. They proved popular. In February 2002 the company rolled out a new deep-dish pizza, its first major new menu item in two years. It also introduced two limited-time promotional pies in some markets: a pepperoni deluxe with two kinds of pepperoni and a buffalo chicken pizza with celery and blue-cheese dressing.

FOCUSING ON GOOD VALUE

Five months later, Little Caesars announced that sales were up 11 percent for the first half of the year and credited the new deep-dish pizza. In summer 2003 the chain introduced a one-topping, large pizza for $5, again focusing on good value and competitiveness and again the company saw traffic at its restaurants jump. Sales dropped again to an estimated $1.16 billion in 2002, but then started to climb. In 2003 they rose slightly to $1.2 billion, as the pizza restaurant business in general began to revive. Same-store sales rose an average 18.2 percent, marking the first of a string of consecutive years of sales growth for Little Caesar.

By 2004 the company reported that it had 1,731 locations, including franchises and corporate-owned restaurants. Denise Ilitch left the company in July 2004, and her brother, Christopher, took over as CEO. Dave Scrivano was named president of Little Caesar Enterprises, Inc., the following January. In another sign that all was not entirely well with franchisees, the company filed a lawsuit in U.S. District Court in Detroit in May 2004 against 39 franchisees for using ingredients that did not meet its specifications, which it said violated their agreements. The 39 owners had set up a collective to purchase ingredients from a distributor not approved by Little Caesars. Little Caesars sought unspecified damages, arguing that different ingredients could alter the look or taste of the pizza.

RENEWED GROWTH

Little Caesars' plans to restore sales growth and mend fences with franchisees were successful. Now the company focused on reversing the shrinkage in its national footprint during the late 1990s. Little Caesars exceeded its 2006 projections, building more than 200 new stores in 32 states and 9 countries, while average sales per store rose as well. It attracted more new franchisees that year than in any previous year.

In 2007 Little Caesars topped all U.S. pizza chains in store growth. While the pizza restaurant business in general was sluggish, the company was maintaining its pace partly due to value offerings, such as carryout pizza by the slice and $5 Hot-N-Ready pies that customers could buy in multiples. The Manage to Own program was also showing results. The company announced in 2009 that more than 50 corporate employees, ranging from field colleagues to executives, had transitioned to franchise owners under the program, while nearly 50 percent had opened three or more stores.

Another element in the company's expansion was an initiative that Michael Ilitch, a former Marine, spearheaded starting on Veterans Day in 2006. Little Caesars offered a discount of up to $5,000 on franchise fees and up to $5,000 off the cost of equipment to military veterans who wanted to start their own franchise; veterans who were disabled while serving in the military were eligible for up to $68,000. In April 2007 the company conducted its first three-day training class for six veterans who had been awarded franchise opportunities. Ilitch was honored for his work by the U.S. Department of Veterans Affairs later that year with the department's highest honor for a private citizen, the Secretary's Award. By 2009 more than 50 veterans had applied for more than $1.5 million in credits and benefits through the program to become franchisees.

When Little Caesars celebrated its 50th birthday in 2009, it was the fastest-growing pizza chain in the world, with a presence in all 50 states and in 20 countries. The previous year, the U.S. Small Business Administration (SBA) had listed Little Caesars as one of its best loan performers among franchises with more than 60 SBA-guaranteed loans. "Our excellent listing with the SBA reflects our solid operating system and strong brand," Bob Mazziotti, senior vice president of franchise development, said in a press statement on August 14, 2008.

NEW PROMOTIONS AND PLANNING FOR THE FUTURE

New promotions were helping bolster the business. For the 2006 holiday season, Little Caesars introduced prepaid gift cards. Two years later it made a special deal with Wal-Mart to offer gift cards at Wal-Mart stores in 29 states. In 2009 Little Caesars took over sponsorship of the Motor City Bowl football classic, renaming it the Little Caesars Pizza Bowl and launching a promotion, offering customers across the country a chance to win tickets to the event as well as other college bowl games. Deepening the tie-in, it dropped the price for its large Hot-N-Ready pies from $5 to $3.99 plus tax for two days in December only, with the coupons available at http://www.littlecaesars.com.

While sales for all pizza restaurants were flat in 2008 and 2009 due to the recession, Little Caesars sales grew to $1.13 billion in 2009. It was, however, still looking for ways to stay competitive and extend its brand. In March 2010 it deepened its association with the military by signing on as a sponsor of Cell Phones for Soldiers for March and April, committing to collect used cell phones to help raise money for calling cards so U.S. service members could call home. Meanwhile, the company signaled its commitment to continued expansion outside the United States by announcing the appointment of James C. Hartenstein as vice president, international. Hartenstein had previously spent more than a decade working with Wendy's international business.

April Dougal Gasbarre
Updated, Taryn Benbow-Pfalzgraf; Eric Laursen

PRINCIPAL COMPETITORS

CiCi's Pizza; Papa John's International, Inc.; Pizza Hut Inc.; Domino's Pizza, Inc.

FURTHER READING

Frank, Robert. "Marketing & Media: Building a Better Pie—Pizza Hut Is Topping Rivals with Cheese." *Wall Street Journal*, January 18, 1996.

Garfield, Bob. "Little Caesars Cheesy Ad Really Pulls in Audience." *Advertising Age*, November 25, 1991.

Gindin, Rona. "A Fight to Stay on Top." *Restaurant Business*, July 1, 1986.

Gosselin, Susan. "Pizza Wars." *Lane Report*, September 1, 2001.

"Ilitches Give Control of Businesses to Son, Daughter." Associated Press, June 19, 2000.

"Little Caesars Pizza Names James C. Hartenstein Vice President, International." PR Newswire, April 26, 2010.

Maki, Dee Ann. "Ilitch-Lites Is Helping Growth Plans Pan Out for Little Caesars Pizza." *Advertising Age*, May 2, 1988.

Poling, Travis E. "Little Caesars Franchises Win Settlement Victory." Knight-Ridder Tribune Business News, November 7, 2001.

Rubenstein, Ed. "Size Matters in New Campaigns Set to Attack the Competition." *Nation's Restaurant News*, September 22, 1997, 18.

Snavely, Brent. "A Bigger Slice: Little Caesars Expansion Helps Add Sales, Increase Market Share." *Crain's Detroit Business*, February 26, 2007.

Strong, Michael. "Caesars $5 Pizza Has Competitors Scrambling." *Crain's Detroit Business*, December 15, 2003.

Lost Arrow, Inc.

259 West Santa Clara Street
Ventura, California 93001
U.S.A.
Telephone: (805) 643-8616
Toll Free: (800) 638-6464
Fax: (800) 543-5522
Web site: http://www.patagonia.com

Private Company
Founded: 1957 as Chouinard Equipment
Incorporated: 1972 as Great Pacific Iron Works
Employees: 1,300
Sales: $330 million (2009)
NAICS: 315239 Women's and Girls' Cut and Sew Other Outerwear Manufacturing; 315299 All Other Cut and Sew Apparel Manufacturing; 448190 Other Clothing Stores; 451110 Sporting Goods Stores; 454111 Electronic Shopping; 454113 Mail-Order Houses

■ ■ ■

Lost Arrow, Inc., is the holding company for Patagonia (a designer and manufacturer of outdoor equipment and clothing), Lotus Designs (a supplier of swim vests, rescue jackets, and accessories for the paddle-sports market), and Water Girl (a women's surf apparel line). The company sells its products through a catalog and out of more than 40 stores in the United States, Europe, and Japan as well as through thousands of dealers worldwide. Its customers include serious and casual outdoors enthusiasts as well as people who only want to dress like outdoor adventurers. Lost Arrow is owned by founder Yvon Chouinard and his wife.

EARLY HISTORY

Yvon Chouinard founded Lost Arrow as Chouinard Equipment in 1957. Born in Maine in 1938, he moved with his family to Burbank, California, when he was eight. In high school Chouinard became fascinated with falconry and learned to rappel down cliffs to reach falcon nests. After a scary rappelling accident, he decided to learn to climb up the cliffs instead.

After high school, Chouinard met a Swiss blacksmith, who was also a dedicated rock climber. The blacksmith had made his own pitons, metal spikes that are wedged into rock to hold a rope during climbing, out of old car axles. The tough, unmalleable steel alloy seemed to make the pitons much safer. They would not bend or come out of the rock if a climber fell. So Chouinard learned blacksmithing from a book and began making his own pitons out of chrome-molybdenum steel. He made them on a portable coal forge and sold them from his car at various favorite rock climbing sites.

In 1957 Chouinard borrowed a little over $800 from his parents and bought a forging die. He set himself up in a shed behind his parents' house in Burbank and manufactured aluminum carabiners, D-ring shaped pieces of a climbing harness. This backyard venture became Chouinard Equipment. The company's first mail-order catalog came out in 1964. It was a one-

COMPANY PERSPECTIVES

Build the best product, cause no unnecessary harm, use business to inspire and implement solutions to the environmental crisis.

page list of equipment and prices that included a note to customers that speedy delivery should not be expected during the climbing season.

As demand for his climbing equipment grew, Chouinard moved his workshop to a shed near the beach in Ventura, California, and took on a partner, Thomas Frost. Also an avid climber, Frost had a degree in aeronautical engineering. His expertise allowed the company to take on more complicated designs and make more pieces by machine. Sales in the first few years were only several thousand dollars, and Chouinard frequently took time off to climb.

SALES INCREASE

The company grew in spite of itself. The quality of Chouinard's products was clearly better than those made in Europe, and while they were more costly, climbers were happy to pay. Sales doubled each year from 1966 to 1972, and the catalog became more impressive, including climbing instructions, discussions of the ethics of removing pitons from the rock versus leaving them in, quotations from diverse sages, and in-depth descriptions of each piece of equipment. It resembled a book more than a commercial catalog. The 1972 edition was reviewed in the *American Alpine Journal* because it was considered among the finest literature available on climbing.

Chouinard Equipment incorporated in 1972, changing its name to Great Pacific Iron Works. There were about a dozen employees, many of them climbers with little business background. Chouinard also enticed some craftsmen to join the company, bringing in artisans from Korea and Mexico. The company printed 10,000 catalogs in 1972, and by 1976 it was distributing over 35,000.

In 1974 sales stood at around $2 million. The company's market share was enviable. In the 1970s Great Pacific Iron Works was an unchallenged leader in the U.S. climbing equipment market with an estimated 80 percent share.

AN INFORMAL COMPANY

Great Pacific Iron Works was run extremely informally. Chouinard's wife and nephew worked for the company, and many employees were attracted to it because of its location near a prime surfing beach. Chouinard himself was notorious for not being at his desk. He ran the company from afar while fly-fishing in Idaho or climbing in Argentina. The ethos was that Great Pacific Iron Works was selling equipment for outdoors enthusiasts, made by outdoors enthusiasts.

Many of Chouinard's ideas for new equipment and designs came from his actual needs. He seemed to have an uncanny ability to rethink items others only made do with. His innovations ranged from comfort items to lifesaving safety devices. The Great Pacific Iron Works catalog listed items from a cool-mesh fishing vest to the Chouinard-Frost ice axe, which had revolutionized ice climbing.

ADDING CLOTHES

The company really began to grow when the catalog expanded its clothing line. Chouinard's focus was on extremely durable clothing, such as shorts made from a heavy-duty corduroy imported from England. In the mid-1970s Great Pacific began selling rugby shirts and shorts, also produced in the United Kingdom. They proved extremely popular, and other new clothing sold well, too.

The catalog also introduced jackets made from pile, a synthetic fleece material. Pile was advertised as an improvement over wool, because it was lighter weight and quicker to dry. This was the first of the technologically advanced materials that became a hallmark of the company.

In 1976 Chouinard consolidated the clothing part of the business into a separate company, named Patagonia after the remote region of Argentina. Clothing made from the new pile material soon accounted for more than half of all Patagonia's sales. The climbing equipment business continued under the original name, Chouinard Equipment. In 1984 Chouinard changed the name of Great Pacific Iron Works to Lost Arrow Corporation, making it a parent holding company for Chouinard Equipment and Patagonia.

PATAGONIACS

In 1986 Galliano Mondin became chief financial officer (CFO). Mondin struggled to bring order to the company's finances, which was a difficult job given the company's noncorporate culture but also because Pat-

KEY DATES

1957: Yvon Chouinard starts Chouinard Equipment in a shed behind his parents' house in Burbank, California.

1964: Chouinard Equipment distributes its first mail-order catalog.

1972: Chouinard Equipment incorporates, changing its name to Great Pacific Iron Works.

1976: Chouinard creates Patagonia, a separate company for the clothing line, and resumes selling climbing equipment under the name Chouinard Equipment.

1984: Chouinard changes the name of Great Pacific Iron Works to Lost Arrow Corporation, making it a parent holding company for Chouinard Equipment and Patagonia.

1989: Chouinard Equipment files for bankruptcy and is sold.

1995: Company-wide sales reach $154 million.

1999: Lost Arrow acquires Lotus Designs and Water Girl; Chouinard retires.

2006: Patagonia's first surf shop opens, in Cardiff-by-the-Sea, California.

2009: Lost Arrow expands its Reno, Nevada, distribution center by 50 percent.

agonia was experiencing rocketing growth. Sales grew from about $3 million in the late 1970s to about $24 million in 1986. By 1988 sales had quadrupled to $96 million. Also in 1988 Chouinard hired a former ski resort president, Pat O'Donnell, as chief executive officer (CEO), and O'Donnell hired a new CFO with experience in apparel as well as a former Marshall Field executive to take over the catalog operation.

The hiring did not stop there. Chouinard hired more designers and let them hire more designers, or hire their friends, and he continued to bring in people he had met surfing or elsewhere. Payroll and other costs burgeoned at the end of the 1980s, despite the advice of the new, more traditional executives. Many of the employees were uncommonly dedicated, calling themselves "Patagoniacs," and the company was becoming a great place for creative, individualistic people to work. Workers were encouraged to take off in the middle of the day to jog, surf, or play volleyball, and their input on the clothes and equipment was of utmost value.

EXPANDING CUSTOMER BASE

The untraditional nature of Patagonia encouraged almost cultish admiration for the company and its products. The catalog, its most visible marketing feature, advertised Patagonia's toll-free numbers for rock climbing or kayaking advice. The number to call to order clothes, however, was not toll free and notoriously hard to find. Almost every aspect of the publication went against the grain of traditional marketing advice. Nonetheless, the Patagonia catalog had become one of the most successful mail-order businesses in the United States.

Patagonia's popularity boomed beyond its earliest customer core of experienced outdoor enthusiasts. Less-experienced and novice enthusiasts were fast becoming customers, too. In 1989 Chouinard Equipment was sued by several customers who claimed that the company failed to properly warn them about the dangers of climbing. To protect the rest of its businesses from liability, Lost Arrow placed Chouinard Equipment in bankruptcy, and a group of former employees purchased it in a leveraged buyout, naming their new company Black Diamond.

By the early 1990s Patagonia was firmly the focus of Lost Arrow's overall business, and many of its fans were people who only wanted to look like outdoor adventurers. The clothing had a high reputation for quality, matched by high prices. Many manufacturers by now had successfully imitated Patagonia style and materials and were selling comparable garments for much less. As leaner economic times affected retail markets by 1991, Patagonia found itself with a huge domestic backlog and a bloated payroll. Although its international business was still growing, the U.S. market was stagnant.

TEMPORARY SETBACKS

In 1991 the company's bank shortened its line of credit and later required an immediate cash payment of $2.5 million on an earlier loan. In July Patagonia was forced to sell inventory below cost and lay off 20 percent of its workforce, which was 150 people. The next catalog featured a new, pared-down stock. It was now not necessary to sell "volleyball shorts," just shorts would do. Instead of five styles of ski pants, only two were offered.

Overall the number of items for sale dropped by 40 percent. Catalog distribution was also curtailed. Chouinard at first announced that he wanted to halt the catalog altogether, but it was eventually cut back from four to two mailings a year. Chouinard also announced in various interviews that he wanted to halt the company's growth altogether. He was more interested in ecology than in business and he did not want his company to get any larger.

NEW STORES AND ACQUISITIONS

Despite the founder's dire talk, Patagonia continued to prosper. After the drastic measures taken in 1991, the company seemed under better control. Hiring was no longer indiscriminate, although workers still received some of the most generous benefits in the United States, with a subsidized child-care center adjoining the company cafeteria, a generous 401(k) match, and, of course, surfing breaks. In 1990 the company began a streak of continuous appearances on *Working Mother*'s list of the 100 best companies that lasted throughout the decade. A long run on *Fortune*'s list of the top 100 places to work began in 1998.

Expansion and sales growth continued as the company branched out beyond its catalog business into direct retail sales and augmented various lines of goods through selective acquisitions. Patagonia opened more retail stores in the United States and abroad. In 1995 a Patagonia store opened in a fashionable district in Manhattan, New York, alongside some of the city's most trendy retailers. Sales in 1995 were the company's best ever, close to $154 million, more than double the 1988 total of $75 million.

By 1999 catalog distribution had reached 725,000 worldwide. That same year Lost Arrow acquired Lotus Designs. Located in Weaverville, North Carolina, Lotus Designs was a supplier of swim vests, rescue jackets, and accessories for the paddle-sports market. In 2000 Lost Arrow moved all of its own similar products under the Lotus Designs label. At about the same time, Lost Arrow added another new business, Water Girl, a women's surf apparel line.

By 2000 sales had climbed to about $220 million. Although other retailers copied Patagonia's products and even the style of its catalog, a cachet still clung to the Patagonia brand, in part because the company continued to innovate. In 1993, for example, it was the first to market clothing made from a fleece fabric derived from recycled soda bottles, which it dubbed synchilla.

ENVIRONMENTALLY ACTIVE

The company continued to give generously to environmental funds and established itself as a standout in the garment industry for monitoring contractors for labor law violations. In November 1998 Patagonia, along with Nike, Reebok, and other leading brands, signed an agreement negotiated by a White House task force under which they pledged not to do business with companies that use forced labor or require employees to work more than 60 hours a week. If anything, Patagonia and Lost Arrow were accelerating their efforts to embed environmentally sound practices into their business model and persuade other companies to go along. In 1994, after commissioning a study that found that oil-based synthetics like polyester and nylon were less harmful to people and the environment than conventionally grown cotton, Patagonia converted its entire cotton line to organic fiber and did so within 18 months. Three years later, as part of its campaign to promote the use of organic cotton, the company helped a group of cotton farmers in California and Texas convince Levi Strauss, Nike, and The Gap to help stabilize the market for the organic fiber by buying it to mix with their larger supplies of nonorganic cotton.

In October 1999 Chouinard retired, although he remained very involved with the company. Michael Crooke, formerly an executive with Pearl Izumi, an activewear apparel maker, became CEO. In October 1999 Crooke told *Outdoor Retailer*, "My goals are to maintain and grow the guiding principles that Yvon and Melinda Chouinard started the company on." Patagonia suffered a rare public-relations embarrassment two years later when Mary Collins, a small-scale maker of clothing for whitewater sports under the Aquafur label, won a lawsuit against the company for using the same brand name. Mostly, however, the first decade of the new century saw steady success and growth for all of Lost Arrow's businesses.

CONTINUED GROWTH IN THE NEW CENTURY

In the first decade of the 21st century, Patagonia opened new stores in Chicago, Illinois (2002); Westport, Connecticut (2005); Cardiff-by-the-Sea, California (2006); Boulder, Colorado (2007); and Austin, Texas (2008), bringing the total number of stores in the United States to 26. The company grew from 10 locations in Japan, where it had an especially avid following, to 16. Growth was slower in Europe, due in part to high costs and strict labor laws. There, Patagonia's strategy centered on an e-commerce website.

The Cardiff-by-the-Sea location, 25 miles outside San Diego, in particular represented an important new focus for the company. This was Patagonia's first surf shop. Among the offerings at the new store were wetsuits and boards from Fletcher Chouinard Designs, headed by Yvon's 31-year-old son. The environmentally friendly boards, selling for $650 to $1,275 each, used polystyrene foam blanks instead of polyurethane, which was considered more toxic. In 1998, two years after the surf line debuted, it accounted for about 10 percent of sales.

Soon Patagonia was splitting its product offerings evenly between mountain and water sports. In September 2006 Chouinard told *Women's Wear Daily*, "With global warming, there's no ice. There will be no skiing. The waves will get bigger." He also said, "I see the writing on the wall. You can look at it and say, 'Hey, it's an opportunity. You've got to change.'"

Patagonia could make such strategic decisions, Chouinard noted, because it remained a privately held company, a status he was not interested in changing despite inquiries from prospective buyers. "Everybody tells me it's an undervalued company, that we could grow this business like crazy and then go public, make a killing," Chouinard said, as reported by Susan Casey in *Fortune* (May 29 2007). "But that would be the end of everything I've wanted to do. It would destroy everything that I believe in."

PLANNING FOR THE FUTURE

In 2005 Lost Arrow signed a deal with Wolverine World Wide's Merrell footwear brand to design, manufacture, and market footwear under the Patagonia, Water Girl, and Lotus Designs brands. That same year, Patagonia commenced an innovative arrangement with Teijin Ltd., a Japanese company that used a proprietary technology to recycle polyester fiber from clothing. Under the deal, Patagonia collected used Capilene sports underwear sold at its stores worldwide and transported them to a Teijin plant in Japan for recycling as new polyester fiber. Teijin then sold the new fabric made from the fiber to Patagonia. Two years later, Patagonia expanded the program, called Common Threads Recycling, to include Polartec-branded garments and Patagonia cotton T-shirts.

The company's environmental efforts continued in the new decade. In 2001 Patagonia made headlines when it rejected a highly touted new fabric made from corn because the corn was genetically altered. In 2005 it pulled polycarbonate plastic water bottles off the shelves of its 40 stores when it became known that the plastic contained a chemical that can disrupt a person's hormonal system. The following year the company launched a new website, Footprint Chronicles, that showed the carbon footprint that resulted from production and distribution of Patagonia products like its synchilla vest.

By 2006 annual sales topped $250 million and were evenly split between wholesale business to other retailers and direct channels, including the catalog and Patagonia stores. As sales grew, so did Patagonia's demand for distribution space. In 2009 the company constructed an addition to its 12-year-old, 342,000-square-foot distribution center in Reno, Nevada, that enlarged the older facility by 50 percent. The "green" distribution center, which was expected to accommodate the company's growth plans at least through 2016, was built using recycled steel, insulation, and window glass; tile and carpet made from recycled materials; lighting that used motion sensors to conserve electricity; and radiant heat using copper tubing and hot water to save on natural gas. Also in 2009 sales increased 12 percent to $330 million, giving the company its best back-to-back years since its incorporation.

A. Woodward
Updated, Eric Laursen

PRINCIPAL SUBSIDIARIES

Patagonia, Inc.; Lotus Designs; Water Girl.

PRINCIPAL COMPETITORS

Columbia Sportswear Company; VF Outdoors, Inc.; adidas AG.

FURTHER READING

Adelson, Andrea. "Casual, Worker-Friendly, and a Moneymaker, Too." *New York Times*, June 30, 1996.

Bernstein, Jeremy. "Ascending." *New Yorker*, January 31, 1977, 36–52.

Brown, Paul B. "The Anti-Marketers." *Inc.*, March 1988, 62–72.

Casey, Susan. "Patagonia: Blueprint for Green Business." *Fortune*, May 29 2007.

Chouinard, Yvon. *Let My People Go Surfing: The Education of a Reluctant Businessman*. New York: Penguin Press, 2005.

Earnest, Leslie. "Patagonia's Founder Seeks to Spread Environmental Gospel." *Los Angeles Times*, November 5, 2005.

Foy, Paul. "What Recession? US Outdoor Gear Makers 'Buoyant.'" Associated Press, August 8, 2010.

Gutner, Toddi. "Travails in Patagonia." *Forbes*, September 2, 1991, 14.

Randall, Glenn. "Riding Herd on the Charity Trail." *Backpacker*, July 1988, 26–27.

Serwer, Andrew E. "Patagonia CEO Reels Company In." *Fortune*, December 14, 1992, 177.

Tran, Khanh T. L. "Patagonia Jumps into Surf." *Women's Wear Daily*, September 27, 2006.

Lucite International, Limited

Queens Gate, Queens Terrace
Southampton, SO 14 3BP
United Kingdom
Telephone: (+44 870) 240-4620
Fax: (+44 870) 240-4626
Web site: http://www.lucite.com

Private Company, Wholly Owned Subsidiary of Mitsubishi Rayon Co., Ltd.
Founded: 1993
Employees: 1,800
Sales: $1.50 billion (2010)
NAICS: 325211 Thermoplastic Resins and Plastics Materials Manufacturing

■ ■ ■

Lucite International, Limited, designs, develops, and manufactures acrylic-based products, which include such well-known brands as Lucite, TufCoat, Perspex, Elvacite, and Colacryl. It is one of the world's largest manufacturers of methyl methacrylate (MMA), supplying approximately 25 percent of the world's MMA. Lucite's products are divided into four major segments: specialty monomers, methyl methacrylates, resins and polymers, and sheets and composites. Lucite's consumer and trade products have applications in a wide range of industries such as textiles; floor polishes; adhesives; lubricants; coatings; automotive; inks; LCD; lighting; signage; optics; dental; and bath, spa, and other solid surfaces. The company has manufacturing, sales, and research and development facilities in the Americas, Asia, and Europe, and an MMA plant in China. Lucite International became a wholly owned subsidiary of Mitsubishi Rayon Company, Ltd., after its acquisition in 2009.

LUCITE'S BEGINNINGS

In the late 1920s the German-American chemical firm Rohm and Haas developed polymethyl methacrylate (PMMA), or clear acrylic, and trademarked it as Plexiglas in 1934. One year later, London-based Imperial Chemical Industries PLC (ICI) invented the first commercial process for methyl methacrylate (MMA), which was used to manufacture PNMA, and began producing acrylic under the name Perspex. The U.S. chemical giant E.I. DuPont de Nemours and Company also developed MMA in the early 1930s, registering it under the name Lucite. DuPont opened its first MMA production plant two years later.

By the 1950s Lucite had become a household name, and the durable translucent material was used to produce a wide range of products, including furniture, china, car hood ornaments, and designer handbags (which would become collector's items decades later). During the 1960s DuPont established MMA operations in Memphis, Tennessee, and Parkersburg, West Virginia.

Meanwhile ICI's expansion included a PMMA plant in Rozenburg, Netherlands. In 1976 ICI expanded further when it entered into a joint venture with the China Petroleum Development Corporation to establish an MMA operation in Taiwan, the Kaohsiung Monomer Company, Ltd. During this same period, DuPont

COMPANY PERSPECTIVES

Our company is single-minded in its determination to achieve excellence in all that we do. We are dedicated to achieving the highest standards in the areas of safety, health and environmental and cost performance, and in our research and development.

installed the world's first continuous cast sheet line at its Memphis facility.

In 1989 ICI entered the North American market when it acquired St. Louis, Missouri–based K-S-H Inc., an acrylic polymers and sheet manufacturer with operations in Ohio, Missouri, and Toronto, Canada. Two years later, ICI doubled its production base in North America when it purchased Continental Polymers in Compton, California, for £20 million and established its North American headquarters in St. Louis. By 1991 ICI was the world's third-largest acrylics producer, with 2,500 employees and annual sales of approximately $500 million.

As part of an effort to cut costs and streamline operations, in 1994 ICI sold its polypropylene business to BASF AG of Germany in return for BASF's acrylics business. In 1993 ICI and DuPont agreed to a swap, whereby DuPont would acquire ICI's European nylon business in exchange for DuPont's U.S. acrylics business and a cash payment. The business merger formed ICI Acrylics, Inc., and the new company embarked on a global expansion in excess of $600 million, acquiring facilities in the United States, United Kingdom, Taiwan, and Thailand. Under the terms of the agreement, the U.S. Federal Trade Commission stipulated that ICI Acrylics divest one of its three U.S. plants as well as the machinery, equipment, inventory, technology, patents, and customer lists to an independent company so as not to lessen competition in the U.S. acrylics market.

ICI ACRYLICS' EXPANSION

ICI Acrylics' European expansion efforts in 1995 included the acquisition of an acrylic and polycarbonate sheet plant in Nischwitz, Germany, from Klöckner Pentaplast, and an increase of its PMMA production to 40,000 tons per year at its Rozenburg site. In January 1997 ICI Acrylics moved to its new 51,000-square-foot headquarters in Cordova, Tennessee. By 2010 ICI Acrylics had announced that it would invest $22 million to expand its MMA plant in Beaumont, Texas, increase production capacity at its Taiwan facility, and construct a new unit in Malaysia, moves that would increase the company's global output to 1.2 billion pounds per year and make it the world's largest supplier of MMA.

In May 1997 ICI unveiled a three-year program of divestments designed to raise $5 billion for an $8 billion takeover of Unilever's specialty chemical assets. ICI planned to sell its industrial chemicals businesses and other traditional areas of activity and focus entirely on specialty chemicals, coatings, and other materials. National Starch and Chemical Company, Unichema International, Quest International, and Crosfield, four of the businesses within the Unilever takeover, were already market leaders in their respective sectors.

Also in May 1997, ICI entered into a joint venture with competitor Mitsubishi Rayon Company, Ltd., to develop an acrylic recycling technology at ICI's main research center in Wilton, England, capable of handling all types of acrylic waste, including materials used in bathtubs and large signage. By February 1998 the partners had announced that an acrylics recycling plant with an annual capacity of up to 5,000 metric tons would be functional in Hoddesdon, England, within the year.

Although ICI's Specialties Division trading profits had increased from £30 million to £205 million by the end of 1997, due in large part to the Unilever acquisition, ICI's 1998 half-year results were disappointing. The strength of the pound, weakening markets in Asia, falling volumes in acrylics, and the still up-for-sale industrial chemicals division contributed to a 14 percent drop in the company's share price, and analysts reduced their full-year projections by 25 percent.

In January 1999 ICI announced a restructuring of its U.S. paints business that included 500 job cuts and several closings of its plants and stores. The restructuring was part of a wider plan to eliminate 1,000 jobs worldwide and reduce ICI's fixed costs by $116 million over two years. While ICI Acrylics worked to raise awareness of its new Lucite, TufCoat resin siding, ICI was forced to cut an additional 600 administrative and support jobs. In October 1999 the Ineos Group, in partnership with Charterhouse Capital Partners, acquired ICI Acrylics from ICI for £505 million and renamed the company Ineos Acrylics, Inc.

INEOS ACRYLICS' EXPANSION AND TRANSFORMATION

Ineos Acrylics maintained the Cordova, Tennessee, headquarters, while Ineos's corporate headquarters were in Southampton, England. Soon after the acquisition, Ineos unveiled plans to significantly expand the acrylics

KEY DATES

1934: Imperial Chemical Industries (ICI) invents the first commercial process for methyl methacrylate (MMA).

1993: ICI's acrylics business merges with DuPont's acrylics business to form ICI Acrylics.

1999: The Ineos Group in partnership with Charterhouse Capital Partners purchases ICI Acrylics and renames the company Ineos Acrylics.

2002: Ineos Acrylics is rebranded as Lucite International.

2009: Mitsubishi Rayon Company acquires Lucite International.

business by building MMA plants that utilized new and improved processing technologies. The expansion plans included a $13 to $15 million investment in its Beaumont, Texas, plant to increase annual MMA capacity by 50 million pounds per year, a $10 million expansion of the Missouri plant, and construction of a pilot plant at its Wilton, England, site for a new ethylene-based MMA process. In February 2001 the company broke ground on an acetone cyanohydrin plant at BASF's Seal Sands site in England.

Ineos's expansion through acquisitions included the July 2000 purchase of Acrylic Products, a leading South African producer of acrylic sheet, and the England-based Bonar Polymers, a manufacturer of specialty acrylic resin for dental applications. In December 2000 Ineos announced that it would buy ICI's Klea chlorofluorocarbon (CFC) replacement and Crosfield businesses for £300 million. In the deal, Ineos and ICI also formed a joint venture called Ineos Chlor made of ICI's chlor-alkali business with Ineos holding an 85 percent share. The following month, Ineos agreed to acquire EVC International, Europe's leading producer of polyvinyl chloride (PVC).

LUCITE INTERNATIONAL

In May 2002 Lucite International was officially unveiled as the new name of Ineos Acrylics. Scott Davidson was named chairman and CEO of the company that boasted16 manufacturing sites across the globe, 2,000 employees, sales offices in 28 countries, and $1 billion in annual sales. Davidson, who had joined ICI as an economist in 1968 at the age of 22, died in 2003. Ian Lambert, an ICI employee since 1985 and Lucite's CFO, was appointed the new CEO.

In 2003 Lucite formed Lucite International (China) Chemical Industry Company Ltd. and began construction on a new MMA plant at Caojing, near Shanghai. Although the costs of raw materials had risen in 2004 while the U.S. dollar weakened, the increase in the demand for acrylics and polymers insured that Lucite remained profitable. Lucite suffered a setback when in August 2005 it was cited by the European Commission, along with ICI, BASF, and a number of other companies, with price fixing between 1995 and 2003. More of a blow to the company's reputation than its pocket, in May 2006 Lucite was ordered to pay $32 million of the total $442.3 million fine.

In October 2005 Lucite announced plans to take over DuPont's acrylonitrile (ACN) facility in Beaumont with the intention of expanding the site's hydrogen cyanide (HCN) capabilities. (HCN was used in MMA production.) The move was designed to reduce costs incurred in shipping HCN from its Memphis site to the Beaumont facility. In July 2006 Lucite began construction in Singapore on its first MMA plant that would use the company's proprietary Alpha technology. The state-of-the-art technology, which eliminated the ammonium bisulfate by-product and the need for HCN, would reduce manufacturing costs by 40 to 50 percent. In 2007 Lucite sold its facilities in Olive Branch, Mississippi, and Monterrey, Mexico, to Plaskolite, Inc. In 2008 Perspex South Africa Limited purchased Lucite's South African plant.

In November 2008, as the new 120,000-ton-per-year Alpha plant on Jurong Island in Singapore began production, one of Lucite's main competitors, Mitsubishi Rayon Company, announced its intention to acquire the company. The deal, worth $1.6 billion, was completed in May 2009. In September 2009 the Beaumont facility ceased ACN production. Lucite International also planned to expand its plant at Caojing in 2010 and complete a second 250,000-ton-per-year Alpha plant by 2011. In a company press release, Mitsubishi announced its medium-term plan to March 2011 was to expand the company's core MMA business through development, acquisitions, and technological advances.

Marie O'Sullivan

PRINCIPAL DIVISIONS

Sheets and Composites; Resins and Polymers; Methyl Methacrylates; Specialty Monomers.

PRINCIPAL COMPETITORS

Arkema Inc.; Asahi Kasei Corporation; Evonik Degussa GmbH.

FURTHER READING

Alperowicz, Natasha. "Ineos Acrylics to Expand MMA Capacity." *Chemical Week*, November 10, 1999, 24.

Arnold, Martin, and Michiyo Nakamoto. "Mitsubishi Rayon Buys Lucite in $1.6bn Deal." *Financial Times*, November 12, 2008, 17.

Baker, John. "Lucite Makes Big." *ICIS Chemical Business (Weekly)*, September 24, 2007.

Cameron, Sue. "ICI Chief Who Rescued Nylon." *Financial Times*, April 2, 2003, 23.

Firn, David. "Lucite Gets Back in the Black." *Financial Times*, April 17, 2005, 5.

Gribben, Roland. "ICI Charged with Operating Acrylics Cartel." *Daily Telegraph* (London), August 23, 2005.

Higgs, Richard. "ICI, Mitsubishi Research Acrylic Recycling." *Plastics News*, May 26, 1997, 58.

Milmo, Sean. "Unilever Purchase Transforms ICI into New Firm." *Chemical Market Reporter*, May 12, 1997.

Wellington, Elizabeth. "Summer's Hot Accessories Come in Lucite." *Philadelphia Inquirer*, June 7, 2010.

Young, Ian. "A New Era Beckons for Lucite: Building Up to Commercialization of Novel MMA Technology." *Chemical Week*, July 28, 2008.

Martin Agency, Inc.

One Shockoe Plaza
Richmond, Virginia 23219-4132
U.S.A.
Telephone: (804) 698-8000
Fax: (804) 698-8001
Web site: http://www.martinagency.com

Wholly Owned Subsidiary of Interpublic Group of Companies, Inc.
Founded: 1965
Employees: 340
Sales: $129 million (2009 est.)
NAICS: 541613 Marketing Consulting Services; 541810 Advertising Agencies; 541820 Public Relations Services; 541910 Marketing Research Services

■ ■ ■

Martin Agency, Inc., is a leading full-service advertising firm, the largest ad agency in the southeastern United States, and one of the fastest growing agencies in the country. Martin's services include print, broadcast, and digital advertising; direct marketing; media planning and buying; Yellow Pages advertising; campaign design; event planning and marketing; data analytics; consumer analysis; and public relations. Based in Richmond, Virginia, the award-winning agency also has offices in New York City and Seattle, Washington. Martin is part of the global advertising corporation Interpublic Group of Companies, Inc., although the firm operates as an independent unit.

COMPANY FORMATION AND INITIAL DEVELOPMENT: 1965–85

With one account from A.H. Robins Company and a three-person staff, the Martin Agency was established in 1965 by the advertising executives David Martin and George Woltz. In 1969 the firm launched its "Virginia is for Lovers" campaign for the Virginia State Travel Service, which brought Martin national attention. By the early 1970s Martin was Virginia's second-largest ad agency.

In 1977 Martin lured the talented adman Harry Jacobs from Cargill, Wilson & Acree to be president of the firm. The following year Jacobs hired another major talent, Mike Hughes, to be the chief creative officer. The Jacobs-Hughes team soon brought recognition to Martin, which was named one of the top-10 creative agencies in 1981 by *Advertising Age*.

During the early 1980s Martin began competing with New York City firms by producing creative ads, hiring excellent talent, earning awards, and gradually developing a national clientele. By 1984 Martin was the largest ad agency in Virginia and one of the biggest in the Southeast. Martin was also at the center of a trend that found ad agencies outside of major markets getting attention from national customers.

Martin landed sizable regional accounts during the mid-1980s, including the Life Insurance Company of Virginia, the Bank of Virginia, Coty Fragrances, ITT Telecommunications, Kings Dominion Theme Park, and Blue Cross and Blue Shield of Virginia. Pushing Martin to the national stage was its print ad in 1984 for General Motors Electro-Motive Division, which was

COMPANY PERSPECTIVES

We are at our core a strategic and creative company that generates ideas for our clients. With all of our resources under one roof, we are structured to put fewer boundaries on ideas than any other agency in the country. We do our best work for game-changing brands—brands that transform categories, consumer perceptions, and the cultural landscape in their pursuit of dramatic growth. Brands that sell everyday products to everyday people in not-so-everyday ways.

named one of the Best Magazine Ads of Year by *Adweek*. By 1985 four-fifths of Martin's billings were from companies outside of Virginia and half of its accounts were national.

SERVICE EXPANSION AND OWNERSHIP CHANGES: 1986–89

Martin gradually expanded its services to include direct marketing, market research, and Yellow Pages marketing. In 1986 the Scali, McCabe, Sloves Group acquired a majority stake in Martin. The firm continued to operate as a standalone unit, and the following year it acquired Husk Jennings Overman, a Florida agency.

By 1987 approximately 80 percent of Martin's accounts were from outside the state. During the late 1980s Martin secured accounts from the Pennsylvania snack food maker Snyders of Hanover, Blue Cross and Blue Shield of Florida, the Florida-based Barnett Banks, the railroad and ocean shipping firm CSX/Sea-Land Intermodal, the telecommunications firm Teli USA, Maserati automobiles, Residence Inn, Wrangler apparel, the fleece-wear maker Bassett-Walker, and Banc One Corporation.

David Martin stepped down as chairman and chief executive officer (CEO) in 1988. Jacobs took over the leadership of Martin. In 1989 Martin opened an office in Columbus, Ohio, to serve its $12 million client Banc One.

GROWTH AND NEW OWNERSHIP: 1990–93

By 1990 Martin's annual billings were $175 million, having grown from just $4 million in 1977. The company was developing a name for itself in New York City, as ads for Signet Banking Corporation, Wrangler, and Residence Inn garnered awards. Martin became known for its innovation, unconventionality, humor, and ability to deliver a simple but interesting message.

New accounts during the early 1990s included the children's clothier Health-tex, the branded apparel provider VF Corporation, the luxury-apparel retailer London Fog, and Mercedes-Benz. The Mercedes-Benz account, the largest at the agency, necessitated a staff increase of 70 employees.

In 1992 Don Just, who as company president helped bring national accounts to the company during the late 1980s, left the firm, and John B. Adams was named president. In November 1993 the Lowe Group, which was owned by the Interpublic Group of Companies, acquired the Scali, McCabe, Sloves Group, which included Martin. In spite of the acquisition, the firm continued to operate independently.

After Martin launched its Health-tex magazine advertisements, sales for the children's clothier rose more than 40 percent, and Martin earned several awards for the campaign. In 1993 Martin landed several new national accounts, including those for Coca-Cola's Mello Yello, Remy Martin cognac, Seiko's Pulsar watches, Sky Radio, and the electronic-messaging provider SkyTel.

GROWTH OF NATIONAL ACCOUNTS: 1994–99

Between 1994 and 1995 Martin landed accounts for the child care provider KinderCare, the auto insurer GEICO, the Coca-Cola brand Mr. Pibb, Fairfield Inns, PING golf products, and Sprint Cellular. The company also formed Martin Interactive to address the electronic needs of its clientele. In 1996 Martin secured accounts with the Columbia/HCA Healthcare Corporation, the National Geographic Society, and *Men's Health* magazine. That same year Martin had $310 million in billings and $48 million in revenues.

The agency expanded its national reputation in 1997 by landing contracts with Saab Cars USA, Finlandia vodka, Turner Classic Movies, and the outdoor clothier Timberland Company. For the year, Martin was named one of the world's top-10 creative firms by the international design publication *Graphis Magazine*. Martin opened offices on the West Coast and in Charlotte, North Carolina, the latter to handle its Remy Martin cognac and Coca-Cola Mello Yello campaigns. Jacobs, the chairman and CEO of Martin, retired in 1997 and passed his titles to Adams. Adams was succeeded as president by Hughes, who retained his post as chief creative officer.

KEY DATES

1965: David Martin and George Woltz found Martin Agency, Inc.
1977: The firm hires Harry Jacobs.
1993: The agency becomes part of the Interpublic Group of Companies.
2007: Martin lands a $570 million account with Wal-Mart.
2009: Martin is named U.S. Agency of the Year by *Adweek*.

During the late 1990s Martin landed several dot-com accounts. The agency also added to its client roster the American Stock Exchange, PageNet, the wireless services provider Alltel, Lender's Bagels by Kellogg's, Kohler bath and kitchen products, Carfax, and the Charlotte Hornets of the National Basketball Association. After abandoning its Mercedes-Benz account in 1998 to make a play for a Saab account, Martin landed a $55 million contract with Saab. The agency also launched the Wrangler branding tag "Real. Comfortable. Jeans." Before the decade closed, Martin parted ways with the American Stock Exchange, Banc One, and Wrangler, but the jeans company continued to use the Martin-coined three-word phrase throughout the next decade.

Martin followed its accounts during the 1990s. Late in the decade the agency added and subtracted regional offices, establishing new satellites as business seemed to dictate. Martin had a successful 1999, which included its first Super Bowl advertisement for Yellow Pages, a new campaign for TV Land channel, and its initial work for Kellogg's, as well as awards for its Saab campaign. The firm also opened its new headquarters in Richmond's Shockoe district, where it combined several company businesses into one building for the first time.

NEW CLIENTS AND SUCCESSFUL CAMPAIGNS: 2000–04

Martin began the new century with a television spot for GEICO that debuted the green gecko, which began a long and successful run for the popular reptile. The firm continued landing dot-com accounts in 2000, as well as contracts with Carfax and Charles Schwab. Martin parted ways with Finlandia and launched a branch office in Reston, Virginia, to serve dot-com companies and opened a San Francisco, California, office to service its new Schwab account.

By 2001 the dot-com bubble had burst and advertising business for Internet-based companies had fizzled. During an 18-month period two-thirds of an estimated $200 million in billings from dot-com companies failed to materialize. Martin also lost its valuable Saab advertising account, which had brought in $180 million in billings over the four previous years. In response, the firm laid off 40 people from its 415-member staff. The company restructured Martin Interactive, which was moved to New York following the folding of its dot-com clients. The agency also lost Timberland and closed its San Francisco office.

In 2001 Martin landed a contract with the investment management firm U.S. Trust, United Parcel Service (UPS), and Advance Auto Parts. In May of that year Martin Public Relations, which was started by the firm during the 1980s, was renamed Slay Public Relations, with Joe Slay taking over as president. The renaming was meant to signal that Slay was a division of Martin but independently run.

The following year Martin launched its initial campaigns for Hanes and for another Coca-Cola brand, Vanilla Coke. The firm also debuted the first in an 18-spot GEICO campaign, which featured a screen test waiting room where the gecko met an apparently washed-up Taco Bell chihuahua. That same year Martin rolled out what would become the well-known "What can Brown do for you?" UPS campaign.

Martin's campaigns for GEICO had discernible results: two years after the gecko debuted, the insurer passed the 5 million policyholder mark. In 2004 Martin launched its GEICO Cavemen ads with the tagline "so easy a caveman could do it," which helped push the number of policyholders to 8 million within three years. The firm was also credited with improving brand awareness for and shipping volume at UPS.

That same year Martin landed Miller Genuine Draft and Time Warner Internet accounts and a contract with the American Ad Council to discourage voter apathy. In December of that year Martin's relationship with UPS and the National Association for Stock Car Auto Racing helped the firm earn a campaign promoting *NASCAR Nation*, a new Speed Channel show that was developed in consultation with Martin, which provided the market research for the program.

MAJOR AWARDS AND WAL-MART ACCOUNT: 2005–08

Martin opened 2005 with a Super Bowl ad for an Olympus digital music player. In 2006 the firm lost the Olympus and Miller Genuine Draft accounts but had twice as many gains as losses. *Advertising Age* named

Martin as one of the top-five ad firms in the United States and ranked two GEICO ads among the top three ads in 2006. Between early 2006 and mid-2007 Martin landed $775 million in new business, including accounts for Barely There bras, BFGoodrich, Burt's Bees, Cruzan Rum, Discover Card, ESPN's X Games, Sirius satellite radio, and The Learning Channel. In 2007, after Wal-Mart fired its advertising agency following allegations of improprieties, Martin was awarded a $570 million account with the uber-retailer.

In late 2007 a massive recession began to overshadow the country. By 2008 the recessionary conditions were beginning to affect the firm's business. In response, Martin cut 5 percent of its workforce.

MORE AWARDS AND NATIONAL CLIENTS: 2009–10

In 2009 the agency initiated a multifaceted advertising and marketing campaign to launch Microsoft's first two Microsoft Stores in the United States. Martin developed the store logo, store bags, employee study guides, and the world's largest high-definition display wall for the campaign. Latter that year *Adweek* named Martin as U.S. Agency of the Year after the firm recorded a double-digit revenue gain that pushed sales to an estimated $129 million.

In 2010 Martin picked up accounts with the financial services firm Morgan Stanley and Johnson & Johnson's Tylenol and Motrin brands. That same year the agency launched ESPN3.com, which was an enhanced version of the sports channel's online broadband network. Martin was also awarded the top Creativity Award by *Ad Age* for the agency's John F. Kennedy Library and Museum ad commemorating the 40th anniversary of the moon landing.

In early 2010 Martin recruited John Norman to become the new chief creative officer. Norman was hired to replace Hughes, who had been the head of the creative department for 28 years and who remained president. Late in the year Norman restructured the creative department by replacing the assembly-line approach in which ad development began with a copywriter and proceeded from department to department with a system in which an entire team from various departments worked on a project from concept to completion. Norman also established DesignMartin, a digital arts unit.

As the end of the decade neared, Martin was considered to be the fastest growing U.S. ad agency by *Ad Age*. With a growing list of high-profile clients, the firm had both talent and a long national résumé to help maintain growth and future success.

Roger Rouland

PRINCIPAL SUBSIDIARIES

Digital Leadership Group; Ingenuity Media, Inc.; Slay Public Relations.

PRINCIPAL COMPETITORS

Crispin Porter & Bogusky, LLC; GSD&M Idea City LLC; Wieden + Kennedy, Inc.

FURTHER READING

DeLouise, Amy. "The Martin Agency." *Back Stage*, July 24, 1987, 8.

Dougherty, Philip H. "The Rising Regional Agencies." *New York Times*, February 21, 1986.

Furchgott, Roy. "Fully Martinized: The Martin Agency Still Strives to Preserve Its Brand of Southern Hospitality." *Adweek Eastern Edition*, January 18, 1993, 35.

Gianatasio, David, and Eleftheria Parpis. "Enfatico, Martin Agency Slash Staff." *Adweek*, February 24, 2009.

Hatfield, Stefano. "Lowe's Manifesto." *Campaign*, November 19, 1993, 32.

Malis, Elizabeth Levy. "The Martin Agency's Unconventional Wisdom." *Back Stage*, May 18, 1990, 48.

Parekh, Rupal. "Martin Agency." *Advertising Age*, January 19, 2009, 30.

Parpis, Eleftheria. "The Martin Agency: Master Storytellers Mix Creative with an Aggressive New Business Strategy." *Mediaweek*, January 25, 2010, 10.

Stevenson, Richard W. "Scali to Get Big Share of Martin." *New York Times*, January 14, 1986.

Tischler, Linda. "Clan of the Caveman." *Fast Company Online*, June 1, 2007. Accessed November 12, 2010. http://www.fastcompany.com/magazine/116/features-clan-of-the-caveman.html.

MSNBC Cable, L.L.C.

30 Rockefeller Plaza
New York, New York 10112
U.S.A.
Telephone: (212) 664-4444
Fax: (212) 664-4085
Web site: http://www.msnbc.com

82 Percent Owned Subsidiary of NBC Universal, Inc.
Incorporated: 1996
Employees: 900
Sales: $368 million (2009)
NAICS: 515210 Cable and Other Subscription Programming

■ ■ ■

MSNBC Cable, L.L.C., is a 24-hour, all-news cable television channel that provides a variety of programming, including live and breaking news, news feature programs, political analysis, documentaries, and news talk shows. Controlled by NBC Universal, Inc., MSNBC derives its content from NBC News, which maintains editorial control over the cable network. MSNBC, based in the United States where it reaches 90 million U.S. households, is also available in the United Kingdom, Canada, and the Middle East. Originally started as a 50-50 joint venture between Microsoft Corporation and NBC (later renamed NBC Universal), MSNBC Cable since 2006 has been 82 percent controlled by NBC Universal. In late 2009 Comcast agreed to acquire a majority stake in NBC Universal in a deal that was approved in January 2010. Microsoft and NBC jointly own the Web site MSNBC.com, which is operated as a separate company.

THE FOUNDATION FOR MSNBC: PRELAUNCH PERIOD

MSNBC Cable, L.L.C., traces its roots to two major media companies, the computer software giant Microsoft Corporation and the television network NBC, a subsidiary of General Electric Company (GE). These two companies agreed in late 1995 to create two 50-50 joint-venture news companies: MSNBC Cable, L.L.C., a cable television network, and MSNBC Interactive News, L.L.C., which would operate a sister Web site, MSNBC.com. In 1996 the two joint ventures were officially incorporated and both the network and Web site were launched, but NBC and Microsoft had laid the groundwork for their new businesses separately in the immediate years preceding.

After being acquired by GE in 1985, NBC in 1989 launched its first cable venture, the business news network CNBC. In 1992 NBC formed the joint venture Desktop Video, with IBM Corporation and NuMedia Corporation, to deliver a fee-based multimedia news service to personal business computers. NBC provided the content, IBM the marketing, and NuMedia the software (IBM later sold its share to Microsoft). In 1994 NBC launched a second cable channel, America's Talking. This all-talk network was established by Roger Ailes, who would later become president of Fox News. By 1995 NBC had gained both cable and computer-based business experience.

COMPANY PERSPECTIVES

Built on the worldwide resources of NBC News, MSNBC defines news for the next generation with world-class reporting and a full schedule of live news coverage, political analysis, and award-winning documentary programming—24 hours a day, seven days a week. MSNBC's home on the Internet is msnbc.com, which boasts the state-of-the-art technology of Microsoft and the first-rate reporting of NBC News. Employing the newsgathering resources of NBC News and its more than 200 affiliate stations, MSNBC offers viewers the highest-quality news coverage.

Microsoft, after becoming a $1 billion company in 1990, set its sights on non-software ventures to help sell its software. Corresponding with Microsoft's release of its Windows 95 operating system, the company in 1995 launched Microsoft Network (MSN), an Internet service provider and online service that, along with its free e-mail service, Hotmail, quickly grew in popularity. Within a few months, MSN had enrolled 500,000 customers, and Microsoft was ready to further expand its online ventures.

FORMATION AND LAUNCH OF MSNBC

In December 1995 Microsoft and NBC agreed to establish two joint ventures under the name MSNBC (short for Microsoft, or MS, and NBC). MSNBC was designed to be an integrated news operation combining the broadcasting expertise of NBC with the technical know-how of Microsoft. The software firm invested $220 million, and the two companies split the cost of a $200 million Web site newsroom for MSNBC.com, located in Redmond, Washington, where Microsoft was headquartered. NBC provided the broadcasting space for the MSNBC channel.

MSNBC's business plan called for the conversion of the America's Talking network, with about 18 million subscribers, into its news channel. The company's cable distribution leaders forcefully marketed the network, and, despite an initial reluctance from cable providers to add the channel, MSNBC lined up 22 million subscribers for its debut.

MSNBC launched from the CNBC studios on July 15, 1996, with Jodi Applegate anchoring the first show with a mix of news, interviews, and opinion. John Gibson and John Seigenthaler also anchored daytime news shows. The channel's prime-time lineup began with a retrospective-styled documentary drawing from NBC News archives, *Time and Again*, hosted by Jane Pauley. It was followed by the newsmakers talk show *Internight*, the all-things-tech show *The Site*, and *The News with Brian Williams*.

MSNBC's first marketing mantra reflected the network's initial relationship to technology: "It's Time to Get Connected." The motto was best reflected in *The Site*, a newsmagazine devoted to the Internet revolution hosted by Soledad O'Brien. *The Site* and its companion Web site won several awards during the show's brief tenure and enjoyed a type of geek-based cult following. Following the death of Diana, Princess of Wales, in August 1997, the program (which had reached as many as 35 million homes) was preempted for two weeks in favor of Diana-related news, and it never returned. Nicknamed "television's first cyberbabe" by Lloyd Grove of the *Washington Post*, O'Brien (who would later cohost a CNN morning show) gained Internet fame through *The Site*, and many of her online fans protested the cancellation. Another eclectic program initially featured on MSNBC was the Saturday night newsmagazine *Edgewise*, which featured a mix of art and news. Hosted by Peabody Award-winner John Hockenberry, *The Edge* was never wholly embraced by network executives and was canceled before the fall of 1997.

COMPETITION IN THE MID-NINETIES

MSNBC faced competition from not only the well-established CNN but also Fox News, which debuted just a few months after MSNBC. Early on, MSNBC made a name for itself by being the first to break news, scooping CNN in 1996 with the announcement of the TWA Flight 800 crash, which at the time was the second-worst aircraft disaster in U.S. history. Without a morning show such as CNN had, MSNBC in September 1996 began simulcasting *Imus in the Morning*, a popular New York-based syndicated radio program.

MSNBC's initial objective was to attract a new generation of tech-savvy news watchers. After one year, however, the network was garnering a nightly audience of only 24,000 households and trailed both CNN and Fox in viewer numbers. In 1997 MSNBC began to cut costs (laying off one-fifth of its staff) and move away from its Internet-based origins. The channel replaced *Internight* with the topic-driven *The Big Show*, hosted by the popular former ESPN sportscaster Keith Olbermann.

KEY DATES

1996: MSNBC Cable, L.L.C., is established as a 50-50 joint venture between NBC and Microsoft Corporation; MSNBC begins broadcasting.

2006: NBC Universal acquires a majority stake in MSNBC, leaving Microsoft owning 18 percent.

2008: For the first time, MSNBC tops CNN in several key ratings areas.

2009: General Electric agrees to sell Comcast Corporation a controlling interest in NBC Universal, the parent company of MSNBC.

MSNBC's ratings grew 10-fold during the Bill Clinton impeachment hearings in late 1998 and early 1999 when the channel adopted an approach to news that provided saturation coverage of major stories. The network, however, suffered fallout: In November 1998 Olbermann resigned in protest over the continuing impeachment-related news focus. He was replaced by Hockenberry, whose new namesake show occasionally beat its Fox counterpart, *The Crier Report* (hosted by Catherine Crier). Hockenberry lasted only six months, however, before MSNBC pulled the plug on his show. He was replaced by Chris Matthews, a former political staffer and presidential speech writer, historian, and Washington bureau chief for the *San Francisco Examiner*. Matthews, a veteran of the America's Talking network, brought a revised version of his first cable show to MSNBC under the name *Hardball with Chris Matthews*. The program generated a nightly audience of 400,000 to 500,000, better than twice that of *Hockenberry*, and Matthews soon became one of the enduring faces associated with MSNBC.

REPACKAGED NEWS SHOWS AND NEW PROGRAMMING IN A NEW CENTURY

Following the Clinton impeachment hearings, MSNBC's ratings slid. In 1999 MSNBC tried a short-lived John McLaughlin program and a version of CNN's popular *Crossfire*, named *Equal Time*, but its ratings were lackluster. To cut costs, MSNBC replaced its own midday news program with a rebroadcast of *NBC News Today*, repackaged as *Today on MSNBC*. The cable network repackaged other NBC News shows, including *Dateline*, which was renamed *MSNBC Investigates*, in a move that irritated NBC affiliates.

MSNBC in 2000 used more repackaged shows, including *Special Edition* and *Crime Files*. For weekend filler, the channel acquired original documentaries commissioned from the Discovery Channel. During the 2000 election cycle, MSNBC borrowed heavily from NBC News. During the presidential election recount in Florida in November 2000, however, the daily coverage of Florida events by the newly hired Lester Holt provided a ratings boost for MSNBC, and the network topped Fox News for the month in certain ratings categories.

To generate a larger female audience, MSNBC tried the three-woman program *Home Page*, hosted by Ashleigh Banfield, Mika Brzezinski, and Gina Gaston in 2000. The channel also began simulcasting two hours of the Detroit-based radio program *The Mitch Albom Show*. Both programs were canceled the same year, *Home Page* because of low ratings and *Albom* because of ongoing show preemptions by his home radio station. MSNBC also canceled *Equal Time* and watched the departure of Gibson (a future Fox News star), who had anchored a show since MSNBC's launch.

SEPTEMBER 11 AND WAR COVERAGE

MSNBC ratings dropped 75 percent in 2001, and the channel turned to still more repackaged programs and documentary-style programs. Then, in a reversal of its programming direction, MSNBC hired opinionated hosts such as Mike Barnicle, whose show flopped and was canceled quickly. What boosted ratings that year was coverage of the September 11, 2001, terrorist attacks and related events that followed. MSNBC was the first of the three major cable news outlets to broadcast the attack on the Twin Towers, and, in a switch in roles, NBC News used MSNBC to provide ongoing coverage of terrorist-related events.

On September 11, 2001, an MSNBC star was born as Banfield literally rose from the ashes to become a popular figure and major force at the network. Banfield covered the terrorist attacks from New York's ground zero and was seen on television covered in ashes. Her reporting that day earned her an Emmy Award, and MSNBC soon sent Banfield overseas, to Afghanistan, to host *A Region in Conflict*, and then to other areas, for *Ashleigh Banfield on Location*, both of which were prime-time programs. The *New York Times*, in a May 5, 2003, article, claimed Banfield "fit nicely with MSNBC's positioning as the news network of choice for younger viewers."

MSNBC latched onto a patriotic theme in 2002 and adopted the slogan "America's Newschannel." Former Republican presidential candidate Alan Keyes briefly hosted an opinionated talk show as did veteran talk-show host Phil Donahue, hired for a prime-time spot. Daytime talk shows replaced news coverage, and *The News with Brian Williams* was moved to CNBC, until Williams assumed the NBC News anchor job in 2004.

In 2003 NBC Universal, Inc., was born through a merger of GE's subsidiary NBC and Vivendi Universal Entertainment, the U.S. unit of the French media group Vivendi Universal S.A. (later renamed simply Vivendi). That same year, Banfield publicly criticized the Iraq War at a time of patriotic fervor and quickly fell out of favor. The network's concern for pro-war public sentiment was reflected in the 2003 hiring of Joe Scarborough, a former Republican congressman who hosted the prime-time *Scarborough Country*. Olbermann also returned to the network to host his own prime-time show, *Countdown*, replacing antiwar advocate Donahue, whose show was the highest rated on the network at the time. Many industry observers later concluded that the pacifistic Donahue was released for the same reason Scarborough was hired: a concern for appearing patriotic.

Olbermann quickly drew liberal viewers and gained a cultlike following for his antiwar, anti-George W. Bush positions, especially those espoused on *Countdown*'s "special comment" segments. As the war in Iraq continued, Olbermann's comments became progressively more caustic and controversial while his viewership rose to one million each evening, which was better than any show in MSNBC history. By mid-decade Olbermann's identity grew to, in many respects, define the network, or at least how it was perceived by its viewers and its critics.

OLYMPICS, KATRINA, AND OWNERSHIP CHANGES

In 2004 the network's election coverage boosted nightly viewership during the national party conventions. In 2005 the ratings of CNN and Fox both fell as MSNBC's ratings remained basically stable. MSNBC fared better in part because of its Hurricane Katrina-related coverage, garnering 1.24 million viewers during the initial week of the hurricane news. The network in 2005 hired CNN *Crossfire*-veteran Tucker Carlson, a libertarian-conservative commentator, to host his own show, which was soon moved from prime time to late afternoon. In September Neal Shapiro resigned as president of NBC News and was replaced with Steve Capus, a former executive producer of *NBC Nightly News*. Capus was charged with overseeing both NBC News and MSNBC.

In 2006 NBC Universal acquired a portion of Microsoft's share in MSNBC, boosting its own stake from 50 to 82 percent. The change in network control eliminated the veto power that Microsoft held on any NBC-proposed investments in MSNBC. MSNBC then promoted to general manager Dan Abrams, an attorney who had hosted his own MSNBC show on legal issues, and named Phil Griffin, an NBC News vice president, to oversee the channel.

In 2007 NBC News and MSNBC both began broadcasting from newly renovated studios at 30 Rockefeller Plaza in New York. That year, Olbermann signed a contract extension with MSNBC, guaranteeing the host $4 million a year through 2013. Jeff Zucker, NBC Universal chief executive, called Olbermann's show "one of the signature brands of the entire company." Nielsen Media Research found that Olbermann's "special comments," during a 12-month span, resulted in a 33 percent ratings increase for his show, enough to pass CNN's counterpart in the same time slot, *Paula Zahn Now*, which was soon canceled. Olbermann's ratings even neared those of *Bill O'Reilly* on Fox News within the 25 to 54 age-group demographic.

In 2007 Abrams moved back to the anchor chair, putting Griffin completely in charge of MSNBC management. Abrams's prime-time show replaced Scarborough's, who, along with Brzezinski, began cohosting the new *Morning Joe* show, designed to compete directly with CNN. *Morning Joe* also provided a replacement for the radio simulcast of Don Imus, whose show had been canceled after he made what were deemed racially charged remarks.

POLITICAL COVERAGE AND RATINGS INCREASES: 2008–09

MSNBC gained publicity and a popular political following during the 2008 election cycle. The February 2008 debate between Barack Obama and Hillary Rodham Clinton, broadcast on MSNBC, was the highest-rated program in MSNBC history, generating 7.8 million viewers. The debate actually introduced many viewers who had never before heard of MSNBC to the network. The network decided a brand awareness campaign was warranted and used the slogans "Where Politics Comes First" and "The Place for Politics." During the election cycle, Carlson's show was canceled and replaced by White House correspondent David Gregory's *Race for the White House*, and another NBC correspondent, Andrea Mitchell, was given a politics-oriented weekdays show. With its increased political coverage, MSNBC in

2008 ranked as the fastest-growing cable news network and the leader among 18- to 34-year-old viewers, the most important group to advertisers.

MSNBC stacked left-leaning hosts in its prime-time spots during the 2008 election season. In September 2008 MSNBC hired popular progressive radio talk-show host Rachel Maddow, who replaced Abrams, for a show to directly follow *Countdown. The Rachel Maddow Show* launched during MSNBC's election-season ratings climb, and within just a few days, Maddow doubled the ratings for her time slot. In less than a month, Maddow's audience share was neck and neck with CNN's *Larry King Live*. In the lead-up to the November election, MSNBC anchored primary election night and party convention coverage with Olbermann and Matthews. In September 2008 the network handed these duties to Gregory, although Olbermann and Matthews remained as analysts. The switch came in response to growing claims of left-leaning political bias and tension between NBC News and MSNBC. Nonetheless, the cable network doubled its political-coverage audience in 2008.

In January 2009 MSNBC hired liberal radio personality Ed Schultz to host an early evening, pre-prime-time talk show. During early 2009 MSNBC for the first time topped CNN in overall weekday prime-time viewer numbers and in the key 25 to 54 age-group demographic. Olbermann's *Countdown* and *The Rachel Maddow Show* topped their CNN competitors in viewer numbers, while *Morning Joe* bested CNN's morning program in certain ratings categories.

In late 2009 Comcast Corporation, the leading U.S. cable television company and a major Internet service provider, entered into merger talks with GE to acquire a majority interest in NBC Universal. The parties reached an agreement for Comcast to acquire a 51 percent stake in NBC Universal, parent of MSNBC and all other NBC Universal cable networks. While NBC was losing money, MSNBC for 2009 earned $149.6 million on revenues of $368 million. Audience numbers rose slightly during the year as the network increasingly came to be identified with a liberal brand.

2010 AND BEYOND: POLITICAL COVERAGE, PROGRESSIVE HOSTS, AND PERHAPS COMCAST

During the first quarter of 2010, the entire MSNBC prime-time lineup beat its CNN counterparts, and *Morning Joe* topped CNN's *American Morning* in total viewership for the first time ever. For the fall of 2010, MSNBC promoted network commentator Lawrence O'Donnell to anchor his own prime-time show on politics and pop culture, and it hired Martin Bashir, former coanchor of ABC's *Nightline*, to host a weekday current-events show.

As it entered the new decade, MSNBC seemed to be defined by being "the place for politics" and its left-leaning prime-time hosts. Despite not having a Republican president to criticize, the network continued to grow its liberal brand through new host hires. The biggest gains for MSNBC, like Fox, came from political-oriented programming with opinionated hosts. MSNBC's *Rachel Maddow Show*, for example, realized a 13 percent viewership increase between 2008 and 2009.

In January 2011, the Comcast-NBC Universal merger received government regulatory approval. The deal involved Comcast buying Vivendi's 20 percent stake in NBC Universal as well as a 31 percent share from GE, which resulted in the cable company owning a majority stake of 51 percent. Comcast would thus control NBC Universal, including MSNBC and NBC.

Roger Rouland

PRINCIPAL COMPETITORS

ABC, Inc.; Cable News Network, Inc.; CBS Corporation; Fox News Network, LLC.

FURTHER READING

Baird, Julia. "When Left Is Right." *Newsweek*, November 22, 2008, 55.

Calderone, Michael. "For First Time, MSNBC Tops CNN in Primetime." Politico.com, March 31, 2009. Accessed November 9, 2010. http://www.politico.com/blogs/michaelcalderone/0309/For_first_time_MSNBC_tops_CNN_in_primetime_.html.

Lesly, Elizabeth, and Kathy Rebello. "Network Meets Net: How Big an Audience Is There for Microsoft and NBC's Cable-Web News Venture?" *BusinessWeek*, July 15, 1996.

Mermigas, Diane. "Multimedia Synergy NBC: Microsoft Co-venture Will Link NBC Units." *Electronic Media*, June 3, 1996, 20.

Rutenberg, Jim. "From Cable Star to Face in the Crowd." *New York Times*, May 5, 2003.

Schatz, Amy, and Sam Schechner. "Comcast Rivals, Partners Seek Conditions on NBC Deal." *Wall Street Journal*, June 23, 2010.

Steinberg, Jacques. "Cable Channel Nods to Ratings and Leans Left." *New York Times*, November 6, 2007.

Stelter, Brian. "MSNBC Takes Incendiary Hosts from Anchor Seat." *New York Times*, September 7, 2008.

———. "MSNBC's Tag for Now: 'The Power of Change.'" *New York Times*, November 9, 2008.

NCC AB

Vallgaten 3
Solna, Stockholm, S-171 80
Sweden
Telephone: (+46 8) 585 510 00
Fax: (+46 8) 85 77 75
Web site: http://www.ncc.se/en

Public Company
Founded: 1988
Employees: 18,000
Sales: SEK 52 billion ($6.65 billion) (2009)
Stock Exchanges: Stockholm
Ticker Symbol: NCC A
NAICS: 237990 Other Heavy and Civil Engineering Construction; 236115 New Single-Family Housing Construction (except Operative Builders); 236116 New Multi-family Housing Construction (except Operative Builders); 236117 New Housing Operative Builders; 236220 Commercial and Institutional Building Construction

■ ■ ■

Based in the Solna municipality of Stockholm, Sweden, NCC AB is the second-largest construction company in Scandinavia. A developer and builder of commercial and residential properties, industrial facilities, public buildings, and civil engineering structures, NCC also builds roads, provides paving and road services, and produces construction materials such as asphalt and aggregate rock products. NCC's operations are combined under NCC Construction, NCC Housing, NCC Property Development, and NCC Roads. In 2009 the Scandinavian construction market generated SEK 883 billion ($114 billion), of which NCC had a market share of 6 percent.

BEGINNINGS AS A SHIPPING COMPANY

NCC's history dates back to 1890, when the Swedish businessman Axel Johnson established what would eventually become one of the top shipping companies in Scandinavia, Nordstjernan (North Star). Almost 100 years later, in 1987, Nordstjernan began acquiring shares in the construction company Armerad Betong Vägförbättring (ABV), even though Nordstjernan already had its own construction company, Johnson Construction Company (JCC), established in 1961.

By May 1988 ABV was officially a Nordstjernan subsidiary, and Torsten Eriksson, the president of JCC, was made president of ABV. By September of that year restructuring of employees and business contacts was complete, and the new company resulting from the merging of JCC and ABV was named Nordic Construction Company AB (NCC). Nordstjernan acquired all the shares in NCC from JCC, and the construction operations of JCC and ABV were transferred to NCC.

ACQUISITIONS AND NOTABLE PROJECTS: 1990–2005

Less than two years after NCC was formed, the company began to expand outside Sweden, starting with the acquisition of the Danish construction company

COMPANY PERSPECTIVES

NCC's vision is to be the leading company in the development of future environments for working. NCC's overriding objective is to have the industry's highest production efficiency and the best employees and thereby be able to develop the most attractive customer offerings.

NCC's competitive edge derives from its production and aftermarket expertise, its size combined with a strong local presence and its financial strength. By thinking globally and acting locally, NCC strengthens its offering, thus creating the conditions for continued profitable growth.

Modulbeton A/S in 1990. It expanded into Norway with the acquisition of EEG-Henriksen Gruppen in 1995. The following year it expanded into Finland with the acquisition of Puolimatka and acquired another Danish company, Rasmussen & Schiøtz.

In 1997 NCC acquired Siab AB, another of Sweden's large construction and property companies. Like NCC, Siab was involved with the construction of residential and nonresidential buildings, highways, and streets, and it also managed real estate property in Sweden, Germany, and Malaysia. Before its acquisition by NCC, Siab had made five major acquisitions of its own: Anders Dios in 1990; Industribau Furstenwalde GMBH in 1991; NPL BYGG in 1992; Byggnad Sao Le Lundbergs in 1994; and Kraftbyggarna in 1995. After the Siab purchase, NCC continued to make acquisitions, specifically in Denmark (Superfos Construction and Bûlow & Nielsen in 1999, and Holmbo-Hijse Orla Christensen in 2004) and Norway (Rjeber & Sønasa in 2000).

One of NCC's first projects was the Stockholm Globe Arena and accompanying office buildings, completed in 1988. The Vasa Museum opened in June 1990. Built by NCC Sweden, it became Scandinavia's most popular museum, housing the 17th-century shipwrecked *Vasa* and the 46,000 objects that were found with it. The 64-gun *Vasa* was a Swedish warship that set sail on the Baltic Sea in 1628 and sank after sailing only 1,300 meters. Pieces of the ship were salvaged in 1961, and the ship was reconstructed with 95 percent of the original wood.

When NCC finished construction of the Kista Science Tower in Stockholm in 2003, the building was Sweden's tallest, at 117 meters. NCC trumped its own height records two years later when it completed the Turning Torso, at 190 meters. A mixture of commercial, office, and residential space in the Swedish seaport of Malmö, opposite Copenhagen, Denmark, the striking structure is constructed of nine five-story cubes and twists 90 degrees from bottom to top. It won the 2005 MIPIM Award in Cannes, France, as the Best Residential Building.

NCC continued to amass more notable projects during the decade. The Öresund Tunnel, completed in 2005, became the world's largest immersed tunnel and enabled direct travel by train or car between Sweden and Denmark. NCC led the Öresund Tunnel Contractors, an international consortium that built the 3.7-kilometer tunnel, which was 40 meters wide and had four traffic lanes and two railway tracks.

MULTIPLE BUSINESS UNITS BY END OF DECADE

After two decades of operation, NCC eventually organized its business operations into several divisions. NCC Construction built residential and office properties, industrial facilities, arenas and other buildings, civil engineering structures, and roads in the Scandinavian region, the Baltic countries, and Germany. NCC Construction Sweden operated only in Sweden, with its operations divided among the four major regions of the country: southern, western, and northern Sweden and the Stockholm/Mälardalen region. NCC Housing was formed in January 2009 to develop and sell housing in the Scandinavian region, the Baltic countries, and Germany. Until the end of 2008 its operations were conducted within NCC Construction.

NCC Roads supplied products and services used for building roads, including the production of aggregates and asphalt products as well as paving work and road service. Its major market was Sweden, but NCC Roads also operated in the St. Petersburg area of Russia, as well as in Denmark, Finland, and Norway. NCC Roads employed environmentally friendly techniques by using energy-saving paving technologies, recycling asphalt, and using alternative fuels. In 2009 NCC Roads was producing 6 million tons of asphalt and 25 million tons of stone materials and aggregates each year. That same year NCC Roads had revenue of SEK 10.3 billion ($1.3 billion) and 4,040 employees and was the largest operation in the asphalt and aggregates industry in the Scandinavian region.

NCC Property Development, another unit within NCC, developed and sold commercial properties in emerging markets in the Scandinavian and Baltic

KEY DATES

1988: The Nordic Construction Company (NCC) is formed.
1990: The Vasa Museum, built by NCC, opens in Malmö, Sweden.
1997: NCC acquires Siab AB, another of Sweden's largest construction and property companies.
2003: Kista Science Tower, then Sweden's tallest building, opens in Stockholm.
2005: The award-winning Turning Torso, Sweden's tallest building at the time, opens.
2006: NCC Property Development becomes a GreenBuilding partner with the European Commission.
2010: NCC is commissioned by the Swedish Road Administration to construct a new Highway 50 and to operate and maintain it for 20 years.

regions. In 2006 NCC Property Development partnered with GreenBuilding, the European Commission's program for energy-efficient buildings. The firm was the first developer in Europe to become a GreenBuilding corporate partner. In 2007 NCC Property Development had SEK 5 billion ($645 million) invested in ongoing projects and 120 employees in Sweden, Denmark, Norway, Finland, and Latvia.

MOVING INTO A THIRD DECADE OF BUSINESS: 2010

At the beginning of its third decade, NCC was fortunate to have many projects on its plate. The company was commissioned in the construction of Sweden's Citytunnel, a transport system designed to connect the railway north of Malmö with lines running to Trelleborg and Ystad, Sweden, and to Copenhagen. NCC's part of the project was building the new segment at Malmö, the "C Nedre," which included the installation of a platform connecting the existing railway to an underground station.

NCC ended 2009 with a commission to build a football (soccer) and other events arena for the Kalmar Football Club, an order worth SEK 230 million ($29.7 million), and a contract to build a school in Oslo, Norway, for SEK 194 million ($25.1 million). It also divested itself in December 2009 of land with a residential construction contract outside Stockholm for SEK 400 million ($51.7 million).

NCC began 2010 with an announcement in January that NCC Construction Sweden was commissioned to build a forensic psychiatric care facility in Gothengen for SEK 500 million ($64.7 million) and NCC Construction Finland was commissioned to construct a new shopping center and apartments in Helsinki for SEK 425 million ($55 million). NCC announced in February it had been commissioned by the Swedish Road Administration to construct a new Highway 50 in Östergötland County, a contract valued at SEK 1.3 billion ($168.2 million). The road contract stipulated that NCC would be responsible for highway operations and maintenance for 20 years.

In March NCC Property Development sold the first two stages of the Zenit Company House office project (a GreenBuilding endeavor) in Aarhus, Denmark, for SEK 256 million ($33.1 million). NCC Construction Sweden was commissioned to build a new arena in Ystad for SEK 240 million ($31 million). That same month NCC Sweden was awarded the commission to expand the country's E45 Highway, a project valued at SEK 340 million ($44 million).

The litany of new projects continued for NCC into the second quarter of 2010. NCC Construction Sweden had already built several of Sweden's hydropower plants, including Kvarnforsen, outside Sveg, and the firm announced in April that it was commissioned to expand the Bålforsen hydropower plant at Umeälven, a project valued at SEK 210 million ($27.2 million).

Facing the reality of the global economic recession that began in late 2007, Olle Ehrlén maintained an outlook of cautious optimism in the company's interim report ending March 31, 2010: "Demand in the Nordic construction market recovered.... Orders received by NCC increased during the first quarter." The report's market outlook assessed the challenges presented by the downturn in housing and construction, confirming that "NCC expects no or only little growth in construction investments in housing, offices and other building during 2010" and that "demand for aggregates was lower during the first quarter." However, the report forecast that growth was expected in the civil engineering sector, resulting in new construction and in demand for asphalt and aggregate materials. In other good news, the housing markets in the region during the first quarter had stabilized, and "NCC's assessment is that demand for housing will be stable or rise modestly during 2010." Nonetheless, "the leasing market for commercial properties deteriorated somewhat during early 2010, with rising vacancy rates and falling rents.... NCC's assessment is that market conditions for commercial properties will be challenging in 2010." Even though NCC was the leading construction company in the region, it still had its work cut out for itself in the years to come.

Louise B. Ketz

PRINCIPAL DIVISIONS

NCC Construction Denmark; NCC Construction Finland; NCC Construction Norway; NCC Construction Sweden; NCC Housing; NCC Property Development; NCC Roads.

PRINCIPAL COMPETITORS

Colas Group; CRH PLC; Destia; JM AB; Mesta Konsern AS; MT Højgaard; Peab AB; Skanska AB; Svevia; Veidekke Group; YIT Corporation.

FURTHER READING

"Financial Report: NCC." *CisionWire*, March 29, 2010.

"Hydropower Plant Construction Contract Awarded to NCC." AZoBuild, April 15, 2010. Accessed November 2, 2010. http://www.azobuild.com/news.asp?newsID=9960.

Interim Report for the Period January 1–March 31, 2010. NCC AB, May 2010. Accessed November 2, 2010. http://www.ncc.se/Global/About_NCC/ir/rapporter/2010/Q1/NCC_Q1_eng.pdf.

"Key Developments: NCC Actiebolag." Reuters, June 9, 2010.

"NCC to Construct Hydropower Plant outside Lycksele for SEK 210 Million." *Business Wire*, April 14, 2010.

"NCC Construction Awarded E45 Highway Expansion Project." AZoBuild, March 30, 2010. Accessed November 2, 2010. http://www.azobuild.com/news.asp?newsID=9770.

The NORDAM Group, Inc.

6911 North Whirlpool Drive
Tulsa, Oklahoma 74117
U.S.A.
Telephone: (918) 878-4000
Fax: (918) 878-4849
Web site: http://www.nordam.com

Private Company
Founded: 1969
Incorporated: 1977
Employees: 2,000
Sales: $600 million (2007 est.)
NAICS: 336412 Aircraft Engine and Engine Parts Manufacturing; 336413 Other Aircraft Parts and Auxiliary Equipment Manufacturing

■ ■ ■

The NORDAM Group, Inc., is a family-owned manufacturer of commercial, military, and general aircraft parts and equipment and a provider of aircraft repair and maintenance services. In addition to its primary operation in Tulsa, Oklahoma, NORDAM operates facilities in Wichita, Kansas; the United Kingdom; and Singapore. NORDAM operates the largest privately owned U.S. Federal Aviation Administration–approved repair station in the world for composite aircraft structures and is a vertically integrated manufacturer, possessing complete product life-cycle design capabilities. The company also manufactures complex structures like thrust reversers and assembles customer-supplied aircraft engines. NORDAM customers include more than 150 commercial air carriers, the U.S. military, the military of other countries, other aircraft maintenance providers, and aircraft equipment manufacturers.

COMPANY FOUNDED: 1969

NORDAM was founded in 1969 by Ray H. Siegfried II, who was born and raised in Tulsa, Oklahoma. After earning a degree in business administration at the University of Norte Dame in 1965, Siegfried joined the U.S. Army, serving his two-year term in South Korea. He returned home in 1967 to complete his military service in the army reserve and went to work as an agent for his family's insurance company, R.H. Siegfried Co. One of its clients was a company on the verge of liquidation called the Northeastern Oklahoma Research Development and Manufacturing Company, or NORDAM, for which the insurance company had issued a performance bond. The Siegfried family bought the business, and Ray Siegfried took over the management of NORDAM in April 1969.

Siegfried found NORDAM with $1.2 million in debt, just eight employees, a handful of products, and no focus. The company's most important asset was a $125,000 contract to manufacture military equipment parts for Texas-based LTV Corp. Siegfried decided to keep the NORDAM name but essentially reinvented the company. Eventually focusing on aircraft component manufacturing and repair, the company started out manufacturing helicopter components, turned to military shelters, then expanded into commercial aircraft interiors and aviation product repair, including the rebuilding of jet engines, the manufacture of noise sup-

COMPANY PERSPECTIVES

Our products must be the benchmark for value to our customers; the services we provide must be the envy of our competitors; our business results must be the standard for everyone else; our safety record must remain exemplary; and, we must be the employer of choice in the communities where we operate.

pression kits for older jet engines, and the manufacture and repair of acrylic aircraft windows and windshields.

In Siegfried's first three months overseeing the company, NORDAM lost $250,000. Then in 1970 the company landed its first aircraft repair job, which involved the repair of a wingtip lens on a 727 aircraft. A year later the company built an autoclave for honeycomb bonding, which led the U.S. military to award it a major contract to repair honeycomb-bonded panels on helicopters damaged in the Vietnam War. As a result, NORDAM turned profitable during the second year under Siegfried's leadership. In 1973 annual sales increased to $3 million, and the company employed 100 people.

MANUFACTURING DIVISION FORMED: 1978

NORDAM enjoyed steady growth during the balance of the 1970s, expanding in a number of directions while establishing a reputation as an innovative firm. The company acquired its first commercial helicopter repair job, servicing Canadian helicopters damaged by hail, in 1974. NORDAM's first major manufacturing contract followed two years later when the U.S. Federal Aviation Administration hired the company to construct 400 lightweight, portable shelters out of pressed honeycomb-bonded panels. This job led to the creation of the Manufacturing Division in 1978.

In the meantime, Siegfried's younger brother, Robin Siegfried, joined NORDAM as a salesman after graduating from the University of Oklahoma in 1972. Three years later he was sent on the road to generate international business by cold calling on potential customers. What was supposed to be a short trip lasted several months as the younger Siegfried enjoyed solid success and laid the foundation for NORDAM's international business. In 1976 NORDAM established its LORI Division, which started out repairing aircraft heat exchangers, and Robin Siegfried headed the unit. In 1996 NORDAM sold the LORI Division.

Sales reached $11 million in 1978 and increased a year later when the Manufacturing Division was contracted by Bell Helicopter to provide honeycomb-bonded engine decks and interiors. To support its growth, NORDAM opened a new 60,000-square-foot facility in Tulsa. Two years later the company opened its first international office, establishing a branch in Singapore. In 1983 NORDAM completed its first acquisition, adding TK International and its 200 employees.

Also in 1983 NORDAM's Manufacturing Division added 120,000 square feet to accommodate two new contracts. One contract was with British Airways for 1,100 windows for 737 and 747 aircraft. The other was a $25 million contract to manufacture aircraft interiors for China. In 1984 NORDAM's Repair Division also expanded, doubling in space to 240,000 square feet.

SALES REACH $100 MILLION: 1985

Sales reached $100 million in 1985 and steady growth continued. NORDAM acquired Texas-based M&N Aerospace in 1986, and two years later launched its Transparency Division. In 1989 the Transparency Division turned out 2,000 new acrylic windows every month, but was unable to keep up with demand. This lead to an expansion of its facility in 1990 to 140,000 square feet.

The late 1980s also brought several notable contracts, such as producing interior parts for Air Force One, the aircraft used by the president of the United States. An agreement was reached in 1987 with Pratt & Whitney to develop, manufacture, and sell a hush kit system for one of its jet engines. In 1988 NORDAM negotiated a long-term contract with American Airlines to overhaul and repair all of the carrier's large reverser components. The following year the LORI Division secured a contract with the airline to repair all of its heat exchangers.

NORDAM continued to expand through the 1990s. It acquired World Aviation Associates, a global sales and marketing company, in 1990. It opened a new LORI plant in Singapore in 1991, and it acquired Rohr's Business Jet Nacelle and Thrust Reverser Division in 1994. Two years later NORDAM Europe began operations in Cardiff, Wales. In 1999 NORDAM acquired the thrust reverser business of the Dee Howard subsidiary of Finmeccanica.

TRYING TIMES

The year 2001 was a difficult one for NORDAM. The terrorist attacks on the United States on September 11,

KEY DATES

1969: Ray H. Siegfried II acquires NORDAM.
1978: NORDAM establishes the Manufacturing Division.
1985: Sales reach $100 million.
2005: Ray Siegfried dies.
2009: Ray Siegfried's children assume top executive posts.

2001, hurt the aviation industry, which was already suffering the adverse effects of a recession. In October NORDAM's president and chief operating officer, Charles Ryan, died in a plane crash. Soon after Ryan's death, Ray Siegfried was diagnosed with amyotrophic lateral sclerosis, a muscular system disorder commonly known as Lou Gehrig's disease.

In the spring of 2002 Ray Siegfried stepped down as chief executive officer (CEO), but remained chairman of the board. He was succeeded by Robin Siegfried and longtime NORDAM executive Ken Lackey, who served as co-CEOs. In February 2003 Robin Siegfried resigned from the company, and in July 2004 he filed a lawsuit, claiming that he was forced to resign. He also claimed that his brother, majority shareholders, and other board members tried to force him to sell his 28 percent interest in the company at a distressed value, that the 2002 promotion to co-CEO was "a hoax," and that a plan was already in place at the time of the promotion to force him out.

In 2007 a judge granted the defendant's motions for summary judgment, maintaining that the charges of Robin Siegfried were not supported by the facts. The matter remained the subject of litigation for another year before a settlement was reached in the summer of 2008. Meanwhile, Ray Siegfried died at the age of 62 in October 2005. Despite his deteriorating condition, he had remained involved in the affairs of NORDAM. In the final months when he could no longer speak and was confined to a wheelchair, he made use of an Eyegaze computer to communicate with the movement of his eyes.

POSITIONED FOR FUTURE SUCCESS

Following the events of 2001, NORDAM experienced a steady dip in sales. When business bottomed out in 2003, the company had lost 40 percent of its business in two years, forcing it to cut 40 percent of its workforce. With the commercial air industry struggling, NORDAM focused more attention on the military market, since it offered much greater promise due to the ongoing wars in Afghanistan and Iraq. NORDAM successfully acquired military work, including the fabrication of flaps, doors, covers, and skins for the F-16 fighter aircraft; engine bay doors for the F-18 fighter aircraft; spoilers and radomes for the C-5 transport and E-3A surveillance aircraft; and windows for the Black Hawk helicopter. As a result of the new military work, the company resumed hiring, adding people with the necessary specialized skills.

Sales began to improve in 2003. By late 2005 NORDAM was experiencing accelerated growth, and sales reached $550 million in 2006. Lackey, who was ready to retire, was asked in 2006 to stay another two years as CEO. This move did not come without a cost, however. His heir apparent, 48-year-old-president John Uczekaj, promptly resigned to pursue other opportunities.

In early 2009 Lackey left NORDAM, and 61-year-old Bill Peacher, who had headed the Repair Group since 2002, assumed the position of CEO. In addition to Peacher's appointment, three of Ray Siegfried's children accepted executive positions. In keeping with their father's wishes, each of them had worked elsewhere at least three years to prove themselves. As a result, NORDAM appeared to be well positioned for long-term success as a family enterprise.

Ed Dinger

PRINCIPAL SUBSIDIARIES

World Aviation Association.

PRINCIPAL COMPETITORS

AAR CORP.; Goodrich Corporation; Triumph Group, Inc.

FURTHER READING

Caliendo, Heather. "Ken Lackey, CEO of Tulsa-Based NORDAM Group: The 'Executive's Executive.'" *Oklahoma City Journal Record*, July 7, 2008.

———. "The Kids Are All Right: The Siegfried Dynasty in Tulsa." *Journal Record*, January 5, 2009.

"Employees Hold Key to Success at Tulsa, Okla.–Based Manufacturer." *Tulsa World*, September 18, 2002.

Maurer, Mitch. "Reinforced Values." *Tulsa World*, August 26, 1996.

Stancavage, John. "Head of Tulsa, Okla.–Based Aviation Firm Passes Torch." *Tulsa World*, May 1, 2002.

———. "Suit Alleges Power Fight at Tulsa, Okla.–Based Aerospace Firm." *Tulsa World*, July 7, 2004.

Stewart, D.R. "NORDAM Executive Named CEO." *Tulsa World*, December 5, 2008.

———. "NORDAM Pulling Out of Aerospace's Slump." *Tulsa World*, June 29, 2006.

"Tulsa Industrialist Ray H. Siegfried II Dies." *Tulsa World*, October 7, 2005.

Nordzucker AG

Küchenstraße 9
Brunswick, D-38100
Germany
Telephone: (+49 531) 2411-0
Fax: (+49 531) 2411-100
Web site: http://www.nordzucker.de

Private Company
Incorporated: 1997
Employees: 4,346
Sales: EUR 1.81 billion ($2.45 billion) (2009)
NAICS: 311313 Beet Sugar Manufacturing; 311312 Cane Sugar Refining

■ ■ ■

Nordzucker AG is Europe's second-largest sugar producer, relying on readily available beets rather than sugarcane. In 2009 the company produced some 2.9 million tons of sugar from 17.5 million tons of sugar beets. Most of the sugar, about 80 percent, is sold in bulk to the food industry, mostly to confectionery manufacturers but also to the makers of dairy products, ice cream, jams, and beverages. The company also serves the retail sector with its SweetFamily and Dansukker brands of household sugar. Sugar beet by-products are put to use as well. The dried pulp is used in animal feed, while beet pellets are blended into feed as well as cereals. Another by-product resulting from the sugar extraction process is molasses, which is sold to feed manufacturers and to firms in the yeast and alcohol industries.

Early in the 21st century, sugar beet molasses has also found an additional use in the production of bioethanol fuel. Another niche product is ambrosia bee feed, used by beekeepers during certain development phases. Other customers of Nordzucker products include chemical and pharmaceutical companies. The company maintains five sugar beet processing plants in Germany as well as operations in Denmark, Finland, Lithuania, Poland, Slovakia, and Sweden. Although a stock company, Nordzucker's shares are not listed on any exchange. Rather, shares are owned by three holding companies, Nordharzer Zucker AG, Union-Zucker Südhannover GmbH, and Nordzucker Holding AG (the largest shareholder with about a 76 percent stake), and a number of direct shareholders, who own about 5 percent of the company.

19TH-CENTURY ROOTS

The production of sugar from beets developed in Europe during the early decades of the 1800s following a continental blockade imposed by Napoléon Bonaparte, the French emperor. Trade between Great Britain and other European countries was disrupted, and imports of cane sugar were prevented, thus forcing Europeans to turn to beet sugar. Although the blockade came to an end after the Napoleonic Empire was crushed in 1814, the advantages of beet sugar prompted the rise of beet processing plants in the 1830s, some of which later became a part of Nordzucker. The number of factories increased dramatically as the century came to a close, as did beet production in Europe. In the 20th century, two world wars brought devastation to both farmers and processors alike. In Germany, which following World

COMPANY PERSPECTIVES

We are one of the leading sugar producers in Europe. Working together with our beet farmers we ensure that the inhabitants of Europe enjoy reliable and sustainable supplies of the important foodstuff sugar as well as other products—especially in the animal feed sector.

War II was split between the East and West, a reconfigured sugar industry began to take shape in the 1950s.

In the northern part of Germany, sugar factories came together in a series of mergers and acquisitions. The key step came in 1958 when several sugar factories in the Brunswick (Braunschweig) area of West Germany joined together. Other factories were added in the 1960s and 1970s. Another important development came in 1968 when the European Economic Community laid the foundation for what would be known as the Sugar Regime. In short, maximum production volumes were set for each sugar-producing country in Europe as well as price guarantees. The high price set by the regime created an incentive to grow beets, resulting in Europe producing more sugar than it consumed. The excess was dumped on the world market below the cost of its production, depressing local prices and adversely affecting poorer countries that grew sugarcane and could produce sugar more efficiently than beet sugar producers were it not for European government support for beets. Greater beet production also required increased irrigation, leading to additional environmental consequences.

NORDZUCKER AG FORMED: 1997

In 1985 another major merger resulted in the creation of Zucker-Aktiengesellschaft Uelzen-Braunschweig (ZAG). Further acquisitions followed, and after German reunification in 1991 the sugar industry in the former East Germany was restructured and ZAG acquired three of the sugar factories. Other additions followed until 1997 when the assets of ZAG were transferred to Zucker Verbund Nord AG, which subsequently took the name Nordzucker, or "north sugar." As such, the Brunswick-based company became Europe's third-largest sugar producer, maintaining factories at 11 locations in Germany and investments in four factories in the Czech Republic that were managed by Nordzucker's international division.

Nordzucker was initially owned by seven sugar companies but soon a holding structure was adopted. The company wasted little time in pursuing a strategy of diversification. To build a pharmaceutical business, it acquired NPE Natur Pharma GmbH in 1998, adding a company that used natural ingredients to develop and market pharma products as well as food and snacks. Also in the final years of the decade, Nordzucker acquired a half-interest in Slovakia's largest sugar company, WORD A.S., which owned a controlling interest in three sugar factories, and Nordzucker entered the promising market of Poland by acquiring a majority stake in Cukrownia Opalenica S.A.

At the start of the new century Nordzucker adhered to a strategy of diversification and organic growth, especially in Eastern Europe, as a way to become more efficient and prepare for the eventual end of trade protections provided by the European Union. In 2000 the company furthered its commitment to Poland by acquiring a majority interest in Cukrownia Wschowa S.A., which controlled four sugar factories. As a result, Nordzucker increased its share of the Polish sugar market to 10 percent. Through other acquisitions, Nordzucker added new natural sweetener products and expanded its range of food supplements and pharmaceutical ingredients. In 2001 the company entered the pet accessories market by introducing an organic cat litter product that was made from beet pulp.

EASTERN EUROPEAN EXPANSION

Nordzucker widened its geographic footprint in 2003. It acquired a 96 percent interest in a Slovakian company, Považský Cukor a.s., to increase its share in the Slovakian market to 40 percent, and acquired three Hungarian sugar factories to gain a 36 percent market share in Hungary. Nordzucker also forged a joint venture with Swedish-Danish dairy group Arla Foods, creating SweetGredients to produce a new sweetener called tagatose. Made from milk (lactose), tagatose contained one-third the calories of real sugar yet retained sugar's look, feel, and taste. Thus, it was ideally suited for a wide variety of functional food products.

Other new products Nordzucker introduced during this time included diet-preserving sugar, organic-preserving sugar, brown tea sugar, organic sugar, and a branded product, Backträume (Baking Dreams), available in vanilla, cinnamon, and rum flavors. Nordzucker also revamped its research and development unit. Renamed InnoCenter GmbH, this unit was charged with developing new alternative sweeteners as well as educating farmers about biomass. Nordzucker also formed InnoSweet GmbH to help commercialize these sweeteners and special sugars and keep pace with changing nutritional trends and markets. Later, in 2005, the

KEY DATES

1968: Europe's Sugar Regime establishes quotas and price supports.
1997: Nordzucker AG is formed.
2006: Sugar Regime quotas expire.
2009: Nordzucker acquires the sugar unit of the Danish firm Danisco A/S and renames it Nordic Sugar A/S.
2010: CEO Hans-Gerd Birlenberg resigns.

operations of InnoCenter would be folded into InnoSweet.

To standardize its continental branding efforts, Nordzucker in 2004 created the SweetFamily master brand, which featured a particular shade of blue and adorned all of the company's household sugar products available in Hungary, Poland, and the Czech Republic. In 2004 the company added a pair of new products: brown sugar cubes and brown sugar in a convenient shaker. A year later minicubes of white and brown sugar were added, along with Sugar Dreams, which, like Baking Dreams, was available in vanilla, cinnamon, and rum flavors.

QUOTAS EXPIRE: 2006

At the end of June 2006, the quotas that had been set by the Sugar Regime expired. Under the new terms, Nordzucker lost 200,000 tons of sugar (although it was able to acquire 72,000 tons of extra quota from the German Ministry of Nutrition, Agriculture, and Consumer Protection), resulting in its area of beet cultivation decreasing by 15 to 20 percent. Subsidies also came to an end. With diversification more important than ever, the company and its joint-venture partners petitioned the European Union to form an international distribution company. Additionally, the company began construction on a bioethanol plant in Klein Wanzleben, Germany, for an entrance into the biofuels industry. Nordzucker's CEO, Ulrich Nohle, also initiated a cost-savings program to deal with the new realities. The InnoSweet operation was shut down during this time. Many of the company's shareholders did not agree with his actions, and in early 2007 Nohle left Nordzucker "under hostile circumstances," according to the *Financial Times*.

Nordzucker was forced to shut down some production facilities in 2007. Along with its partners, however, it received permission to form Eurosugar to market sugar across Europe. Later in the year Eurosugar created a joint venture with an Italian company to market and import sugar in central and southern Italy, and another partner was taken on to market sugar in Ireland. The year also saw the opening of Nordzucker's bioethanol plant, the first in Germany to produce bioethanol exclusively from sugar beets.

Nordzucker closed additional sugar production plants in 2008. In exchange for restructuring grants, the company renounced 13.5 percent of its production quota in Germany, 13.5 percent in Poland, 10.5 percent in Slovakia, and 31.6 percent in Hungary. In the meantime, Nordzucker opened a pilot plant on the site of a former sugar factory to test the feasibility of generating biogas from beet and beet pulp.

NORDIC SUGAR ACQUIRED: 2009

To fortify its position in the European sugar market, Nordzucker engineered a major acquisition in 2008. In a deal finalized in March 2009, it paid $937 million for the sugar unit of the Danish firm Danisco A/S. This unit, which was renamed Nordic Sugar A/S, contributed 40 percent of Nordzucker's revenues that year and elevated Nordzucker to a strong number two position in the European sugar market. The acquisition also led to a reorganization of Nordzucker's operations, which were divided into three regions: central Europe, northern Europe, and eastern Europe.

Although there was general agreement over the direction Nordzucker needed to take in light of Europe's changing sugar market, there remained disagreement in the top ranks of the company over the specific strategy to adopt. As a result, another chief executive resigned. In January 2010 CEO Hans-Gerd Birlenberg, the man responsible for the Nordic Sugar acquisition, tendered his resignation because of differences with the company's supervisory board over Nordzucker's future plans. He was replaced by Hartwig Fuchs, chairman of the managing board of Alfred C. Toepfer International GmbH.

Fuchs took the helm at a time of uncertainty for both Nordzucker and Europe's sugar industry. Although no further quota reductions were expected, the company expected pricing pressure to continue with little hope of being able to pass cost increases on to the market. Hence, it was likely that consolidation in the sugar industry would continue in Europe. Nordzucker had little choice than to continue to grow. Size mattered because it provided the necessary economies of scale to improve the company's cost structure while increasing Nordzucker's market presence. Later in 2010 Nordzucker took a step to craft a new market opportunity by forming a joint venture with PureCircle, a Malaysia-based company, to develop and market products that combined sugar and stevia to create a new reduced-calorie product to market to food and beverage companies. Nordzucker faced clear challenges, but it had wisely prepared for the end of the Sugar Regime and demonstrated that it was as well positioned as any company in the industry to remain competitive in the years ahead.

Ed Dinger

PRINCIPAL SUBSIDIARIES

CENTRAL EUROPE: Nordzucker GmbH & Co. KG; fuel 21 GmbH & Co. KG; Anton Hübner GmbH & Co. KG; Medopharm Arzneimittel GmbH & Co. KG. NORTHERN EUROPE: Nordic Sugar A/S (Denmark); Nordic Sugar AB (Sweden); Suomen Sokeri OY (Finland; 80%); Sucros OY (Finland; 80%); AB Nordic Sugar Kèdainiai (Lithuania; 71%); Maribo Seed Holding A/S (Denmark); Sugarpartners Partnership (Ireland). EASTERN EUROPE: Považský Cukor a.s. (Slovakia; 97%); Nordzucker Polska S.A. (Poland; 99%); Mátra Cukor Zrt. (Hungary; 99%); Sunoko d.o.o. (Serbia; 51%).

PRINCIPAL OPERATING UNITS

Central Europe Region; Northern Europe Region; Eastern Europe Region.

PRINCIPAL COMPETITORS

Südzucker Aktiengesellschaft; Tate & Lyle PLC; Tereos SA.

FURTHER READING

Dengel, Birgit. "Departure of Nordzucker's CEO under Hostile Circumstances." *Europe Intelligence Wire*, February 5, 2007.

"Nordzucker Buys Three Beghin-Say Sugar Refineries in Hungary." *Europe Intelligence Wire*, January 3, 2003.

"Nordzucker CEO Resigns over 'Differences.'" *just-food.com*, January 29, 2010. Accessed November 4, 2010. http://www.just-food.com/news/nordzucker-ceo-resigns-over-differences_id109628.aspx.

"Danish Food Ingredients Producer Danisco A/S Agrees to Complete Sale of Danisco Sugar to Nordzucker." *Nordic Business Report*, February 20, 2009.

"PureCircle and Nordzucker Joint Venture." *Food Product Design*, September 24, 2010. Accessed November 4, 2010. http://www.foodproductdesign.com/news/2010/09/purecircle-and-nordzucker-joint-venture.aspx.

Overwaitea Food Group

19855-92A Avenue
Langley, British Columbia V1M 3B6
Canada
Telephone: (604) 888-1213
Toll Free: (800) 242-9229
Fax: (604) 888-2258
Web site: http://www.overwaitea.com

Subsidiary of The Jim Pattison Group
Founded: 1915
Employees: 14,000
Sales: $2.67 billion (2009)
NAICS: 445110 Supermarkets and Other Grocery (Except Convenience) Stores

■ ■ ■

Based in Langley, British Columbia, Overwaitea Food Group (OFG) is one of western Canada's largest grocers, operating about 120 supermarkets in 80 communities. In addition to Overwaitea Foods, the company uses four other supermarket formats: Cooper's Foods, PriceSmart Foods, Save-On-Foods, and the more upscale Urban Fare. Most OFG stores offer a full range of specialty departments, including bakery, deli, health and beauty, pharmacy, book, video, and floral departments. OFG's Bulkley Valley Wholesale unit supplies OFG stores as well as other supermarkets and convenience stores in western Canada. OFG is a subsidiary of The Jim Pattison Group, Canada's third-largest private company, with interests in the automotive, media, packaging, magazine distribution, entertainment, and financial industries.

ROOTS: 1915

OFG traces its history to 1915 when Robert C. Kidd opened a tea importing, blending, and packing shop. To attract customers, he sold 18-ounce bags of tea for the price of a pound. Customers referred to the shop as the "overweight-tea store." Kidd embrace the name and shortened it to "Overwaitea." The business was later reorganized as Overwaitea Ltd., for which Kidd served as president until his death in 1932. Over the years, Kidd's lone shop evolved into a chain of stores, and in addition to tea, groceries were added.

By the late 1960s there were 50 independently operated Overwaitea stores located in British Columbia, primarily found in the outskirts of Vancouver and Victoria. Combined sales were in the CAD 40 million range, but the chain's prospects were dim. The stores were small, averaging about 8,000 square feet in size, and outdated. Moreover, Overwaitea lacked the financial backing needed to fend off challenges from multinational chains, in particular Canada Safeway. Thus, in 1968 Overwaitea's directors elected to sell a controlling interest to Neon Products Ltd., one of Canada's largest sign companies, which had been acquired by businessman Jim Pattison a year earlier.

Pattison was very much a self-made man. As a youth he helped his father "de-moth" pianos, drumming up business by going door-to-door. He then honed his salesmanship by hawking any number of products, including garden seed and adhesive tape, before becom-

COMPANY PERSPECTIVES

We are BC's very own food people.

ing a car salesman. By the late 1950s he was managing a Vancouver car lot, and in 1961, at the age of 33, he used a $40,000 loan to acquire a General Motors dealership in Vancouver and strike out on his own. He then used proceeds from the dealership to acquire a string of related businesses to achieve some diversity. Because he advertised on the radio, he bought a struggling Vancouver radio station, which would serve as the foundation for a media unit that would also come to include television stations and newspapers. Advertising also led Pattison to acquired Neon Products, which he then used as an acquisition vehicle to pick up Overwaitea.

FIRST WAREHOUSE STORE OPENS

Pattison's holdings were varied and expanding and he provided the necessary resources to grow OFG. In the same year he acquired the chain, OFG opened its first warehouse stores. Although the selection was modest and no perishables were offered, the new store demonstrated that customers were eager to save money, and OFG's management made steady improvements to the format. Later a warehouse format that included perishables was launched under the Mark-It Foods banner.

Money was also invested in the original Overwaitea stores. During the 1970s every store was upgraded. Furthermore, new stores were opened as the chain made a concerted effort to fill in its footprint in British Columbia by adding locations in the Victoria and lower mainland areas of the province. By the mid-1980s OFG was operating 46 Overwaitea supermarkets, the average size of which was now 27,000 square feet.

OFG's efforts in the warehouse store category led to the 1982 launch of the Save-On-Foods format in Delta, British Columbia. About twice the size of an Overwaitea store, and located in more densely populated markets, the new Save-On-Food stores offered a better shopping environment and emphasized fresh products. The produce section was extensive, and meat cutting and preparation was done in the open behind the meat counter to reinforce the idea of fresh preparation. Unlike previous warehouse formats, Save-On-Foods did not cater solely to large-quantity customers. The stores also offered small quantities with the same price per pound as bulk packages. By 1986 OFG was operating eight Save-On-Foods stores in the lower mainland area of the province, where at the time they were the most progressive discount supermarkets the industry had to offer. To keep pace with the growth of both warehouse and conventional stores, OFG expanded its distribution center to 500,000 square feet in 1986.

ASSOCIATED GROCERS ACQUIRED: 1989

Because of changes in the grocery sector, OFG's management sought to become more proactive in the 1980s. For example, it decided to become involved in wholesaling to gain diversity. In 1989 OFG acquired Associated Grocers, a grocery wholesaler based in Calgary, Alberta. It was a well-established operation, formed in 1927 as a voluntary association of independent grocers who joined together to gain leverage with suppliers. The addition of Associated Grocers allowed OFG to extend its reach to communities that were too small to support one of its corporate stores. Through its wholesale arm, OFG could now supply an independent grocer to serve that market.

During most of the 1990s OFG was led by longtime employee Brian Piwek. His tenure with the company predated Pattison's involvement. Piwek's first position in the OFG organization was as a junior clerk for an Overwaitea store in Terrace, British Columbia, in 1965. He would go on to other jobs in many other locations in the province before working his way up through the organization at the home office. He was named president of OFG in 1991. Soon after taking the reins, he began visiting the stores to develop a turn-of-the-21st-century vision for OFG.

Under Piwek's leadership, the company placed more emphasis on the Save-On-Foods brand. Overwaitea was well entrenched in some markets, but its brand value was regional. As a result, OFG elected to use the Save-On-Foods banner in new markets, especially in communities that saw an influx of new population, and where the inherent message of Save-On-Foods was more readily understandable than the more obscure Overwaitea name. The change in focus led OFG to sell four Overwaitea stores in 1992.

Margins in the grocery field grew thinner in the early 1990s when Canada Safeway launched a price war as part of an effort to regain lost market share in the Alberta market. Other chains were forced to follow suit and operating costs were cut to the bone. To save on transportation costs, OFG formed Save-On-Foods Transport in 1993. Based in the United States, the new unit primarily delivered U.S. produce to OFG distribution centers as well as hauling other goods for OFG and

KEY DATES

1915: Robert C. Kidd opens tea store.
1932: Kidd dies.
1968: Jim Pattison acquires Overwaitea chain.
1982: Save-On-Food format is launched.
2001: Bulkley Valley Wholesale is acquired.

serving outside clients. OFG also looked to improve efficiencies and lower costs through technology. A private communications network was installed at the stores, distribution facilities, and head office to provide accurate inventory information.

NEW AUTOMATED PROTOTYPE STORE: 1994

In 1994 OFG invested in a new automated store prototype. Ahead of its time, the store included self-scanning checkout lanes, although customers were still required to pay a cashier. Another innovation was electronic shelf labels that allowed prices to be adjusted electronically. Electronic customer counters also monitored shopper traffic to allow the store manager to make the best use of the employees on hand.

The need to grow larger and more diverse only increased as the 1990s unfolded and the pace of consolidation increased in Canada's supermarket industry. OFG added to its wholesale business in 1995 by acquiring a pair of small British Columbia companies, Buy-Low Foods Ltd. and G&H Marketing Enterprise Inc. In 1999 OFG acquired Cooper's Foods, adding nine stores. A chain of smaller neighborhood stores, Cooper's focused on convenience and service to remain competitive. OFG was hardly alone in its efforts to expand. All across Canada retailers were eager to gain market share, due in some measure to the prospect of competition with Wal-Mart. The U.S. retailing giant had already established a Canadian operation, and Canadian supermarket chains believed Wal-Mart was likely to expand into their sector. Most of the attractive available sites were already occupied, but that would not prevent Wal-Mart from improving its position through acquisitions.

OFG remained one of Canada's largest grocers in the new century by adopting a strategy of using multiple formats to meet the specific needs of each community. On one end of the spectrum were the small footprint Cooper's Foods stores, while on the other was the new Urban Fare format that catered to the more upscale customer in Vancouver. In between were the Overwaitea and Save-On-Food formats. In 2001 OFG added another format, PriceSmart Foods. Building upon the automated store prototype of the 1990s, PriceSmart combined low prices with self-checkout and other self-service options. OFG's parent company took the concept of community-tailored formats even further with separately run Buy-Low Foods, which operated 26 corporate and franchise stores in western Canada under its own slate of brands: Buy-Low Foods, Giant Foods, Shop n' Save, Budget Foods, and Nesters Market.

WHOLESALER ACQUIRED: 2001

Another part of OFG's strategy was to continue to diversify, something its larger rivals had failed to pursue. In 2001 the company acquired Bulkley Valley Wholesale, a wholesaler that started out in 1959 as a confection and tobacco supplier and expanded into groceries. Shortly before its acquisition by OFG, it opened its doors to the public, adding retail sales to its primary wholesale business. In addition to serving independent grocers, Bulkley supplied mining camps, lodges, and restaurants in northwest British Columbia. Also in 2001 Pattison acquired Van-Whole Produce Ltd, a Vancouver distributor of fresh fruits and vegetables.

The threat of Wal-Mart opening superstores carrying groceries in Canada continued to concern supermarket chains in the first decade of the 21st century. Industry leader Loblaw Cos. expanded its discounted superstore format to new markets and lowered prices in 2003 in anticipation of a Wal-Mart invasion that never materialized. Nevertheless, Loblaw emerged as western Canada's largest retailer, passing Safeway, which had a 21.5 percent market share in 2003 compared to Loblaw's 22.5 percent. Safeway maintained prices that were significantly higher than the competition, relying instead on its excellent store locations to retain customers. Although this strategy allowed Safeway to maintain profits, it came at the cost of shrinking market share. OFG, in the meantime, held the third slot in western Canada, with a 10 percent market share.

By staying nimble, OFG remained competitive in the new century, unafraid to serve every market size. In 2008, for instance, it opened its first store, a Save-On-Foods format, in downtown Vancouver. It was also quick to adjust to changing conditions. When sustainable sources of fish became an important issue, OFG created a plan in 2009 and a year later became the first retailer to sell sustainably grown Coho salmon in all of its stores. In 2010 OFG also became the first, and only, Canadian retailer to receive a passing grade for seafood sustainability from Greenpeace's annual "Taking Stock" report. OFG had proven adept at fending off competition in western Canada, and at the very least made itself an attractive acquisition property. Because Pattison, who was now more than 80 years of age, had already arranged to leave his business empire to charities rather than his children, the long-term independence of OFG remained very much an open question.

Ed Dinger

PRINCIPAL DIVISIONS

Bulkley Valley Wholesale; Cooper's Foods; Overwaitea Foods; PriceSmart Foods; Save-On-Foods; Urban Fare.

PRINCIPAL COMPETITORS

Canada Safeway Limited; Loblaw Companies Limited; Sobeys Inc.

FURTHER READING

"Brian Piwek: Leading Overwaitea into the Next Millennium." *Canadian Grocer*, November 1996, 10–12.

Cohn, Cathy. "Overwaitea Produces." *Supermarket News*, January 27, 1986, 1.

Dunn, Brian. "Canadian Price Wars." *Supermarket News*, June 7, 2004, 44.

Kane, Michael. "Convenience, Specialty Products Keep Small Groceries in Food Fight." *Vancouver Sun*, February 24, 2006, H3.

Zwiebach, Elliot. "Consolidation Heats Up in Canada." *Supermarket News*, September 20, 1999, 42.

Pilot Flying J Inc.

5508 Lonas Drive
Knoxville, Tennessee 37909
U.S.A.
Toll Free: (800) 562-6210
Web site: http://www.pilotflyingj.com

Private Company
Incorporated: 1958
Employees: 20,000+
Sales: $17.28 billon (2008 est.)
NAICS: 447110 Gasoline Stations with Convenience Stores; 722110 Full Service Restaurants

■ ■ ■

Pilot Flying J Inc. is the nation's largest retail supplier of diesel fuel for over-the-road trucks. It runs a network of roughly 550 "travel centers," truck stops providing fuel, food, hospitality, convenience stores, truck maintenance, and numerous other roadside amenities. The company is also among the nation's top franchisees of quick-service restaurants, such as Subway and Denny's. Formerly known as Pilot Travel Centers, the company swelled in size in 2010 by acquiring its chief competitor, the travel center network Flying J, when that company filed for bankruptcy protection. The acquisition vaulted Pilot, renamed Pilot Flying J, to the top of the travel center industry and made it one of the ten largest private companies in the United States.

FROM ONE TINY PILOT STATION

The history of Pilot Corporation begins with James A. Haslam II, an athlete who played starting tackle for the University of Tennessee football team. After he graduated in 1952, Haslam joined the U.S. Army and served a tour of duty in the Korean War. Upon his return, he went to work for Fleet Oil Co., an independent enterprise based in LaFollette, Tennessee.

"Dad always wanted his own business," said James A. Haslam III, son of the founder, in an interview with *Nation's Restaurant News* (January 26, 1998). Consequently, he explained, the elder Haslam went into business for himself in 1958, opening the first Pilot gas station in the small town of Gate City, Virginia. That first station was a tiny, four-pump affair, with cigarettes and soft drinks available at the counter.

Slowly the company grew, adding more small gas stations throughout the Southeast. In 1965 Pilot Corporation brought in about $2 million per year. That year Marathon Oil Company purchased 50 percent of Pilot Corporation and loaned its tiny new business interest $4 million, which was earmarked to build new Pilot gas station locations. By 1973 Pilot Corporation was operating more than 50 stores and boasted annual sales of $30 million, mostly in gasoline, motor oil, and cigarettes. In 1976 Pilot opened its first convenience store on the Alcoa Highway in Knoxville, Tennessee. The following year Pilot bought Lonas Oil Company, also headquartered in Knoxville, converting most of that company's locations into convenience stores.

With 100 convenience stores in 1981 and total annual sales of $175 million, Pilot set out to grow by means of an expanded concept, the "travel center": a truck stop with both a convenience store and shower facilities for drivers on long-haul trips. Pilot opened its

COMPANY PERSPECTIVES

We are now one great company, two great brands. Our new organization is a combination of two of the best-known brands in the travel center industry, both with strong family histories and shared values. So, whether you are a professional driver, a trucking company, a business traveler, a family on vacation, or a nearby resident, our new company is ready to serve your interstate fueling, dining, or other consumer needs. We look forward to a bright future as our customers' preferred stop for highway hospitality.

first travel center in 1981 in Corbin, Kentucky. The centers also featured some of the earliest full-length truck platform scales, installed by the CAT Scale company, which would become the largest truck-scale network in the world.

EXPANDING INTO THE RESTAURANT INDUSTRY

Pilot started to branch out into the restaurant industry in 1984 when it opened the first Pilot Kitchen in one of its travel centers. The Pilot Kitchen was a deli counter that offered sandwiches, salads, and soups. Rather than develop the quick-food arm of the business on its own, the company approached fast food chains to create locations within Pilot travel centers. In 1988 the first Pilot travel center–based Dairy Queen opened in Hebron, Ohio. Three years later, the sandwich shop Subway opened its first truck-stop location in a Pilot Travel Center. Restaurant franchising grew to become a major component of Pilot's business.

Also during 1988, some 33 years after Marathon Oil gave Pilot Corporation a much-needed infusion of cash, Pilot bought out its larger partner's interest. It would not be the end of the relationship between the two companies, however. Marathon remained the company's major fuel supplier and later resumed a prominent ownership stake.

James Haslam's sons, James A. "Jimmy" Haslam III and William "Bill" Haslam, joined the family business, taking executive positions and raising the family's profile in Tennessee. In addition to working for Pilot, in the 1990s Jimmy Haslam joined the board of directors of two other companies, the First Tennessee National Corporation and Ruby Tuesday Inc. Pilot CEO and president Bill Haslam served on the Knoxville, Tennessee, Community Development Corporation from 2001 to 2003. Also during 2001, Bill organized a group of investors (including his brother and father) to purchase the Tennessee Smokies, a local Class AA baseball team, for $7.5 million. In 2003 Bill Haslam left Pilot after he was elected mayor of Knoxville. Seven years later he was elected governor of Tennessee.

As the Haslam family gained prominence, it also continued to grow the family business. By 1997 Pilot Corporation ranked 99th on *Forbes* magazine's list of the 500 largest privately held companies in the United States. In 1998 the company overtook its chief competitor in the travel center business, Flying J, to become the nation's largest supplier of diesel fuel for over-the-road trucks. Pilot had also cracked the top 25 U.S. restaurant franchises. That year T. J. Cinnamons baked goods and coffee shops joined the ranks of the company's in-store partners, which by then included Subway, Arby's, KFC, Pizza Hut, Steak 'n Shake, Taco Bell, and Wendy's.

PILOT TRAVEL CENTERS LLC CREATED

Early in 2001 Pilot Corporation teamed up with Speedway SuperAmerica LLC (a wholly owned subsidiary of Marathon Ashland Petroleum LLC that was a joint venture between Marathon Oil and Ashland Petroleum) to create Pilot Travel Centers LLC. The 50-50 joint venture folded Speedway's 96 travel center operations into the Pilot business. CAT Scale Company also was brought into the venture, providing its truck scales to various locations. The initiative expanded Pilot's travel center network to approximately 235 locations in 35 states. That number rose again with Pilot's $170 million acquisition of its competitor Williams Travel Centers in 2003.

In the early 2000s the company also expanded the range of services available at its travel centers. Working with IdleAire Technologies Corporation, Pilot began to offer air conditioning, heating, and electric hookups at its travel centers. Telephone, Internet, and cable television access were also added to some of the locations, creating what essentially amounted to "hotels" for truckers: a place where they could park their trucks, sleep in their cabs, and enjoy the amenities without having to keep their engines on and idling. Pilot began a project in 2004 to introduce 24-hour truck maintenance and repair centers at more than 100 of its travel centers, at a cost of $1.8 million apiece. In 2007 the company announced it would open medical clinics at its travel centers. Joe Neely, CEO of Roadside Medical Labs and Clinics, succinctly explained the rationale for this partnership to *Fleet Owner* (December 20, 2007), asking, "Have you ever tried to park a rig at your doctor's

KEY DATES

1958: James Haslam II opens the first Pilot gas station in Gate City, Virginia.
1965: Marathon Oil Co. buys half of Pilot and loans $4 million to build new locations.
1976: Pilot opens its first convenience store, in Knoxville, Tennessee.
1981: Pilot opens its first travel center, in Corbin, Kentucky.
1985: Pilot adds national restaurant chains to travel centers.
1998: Pilot is the 25th-largest restaurant franchise in the United States.
2003: Pilot acquires Williams Travel Centers, doubling the size of the company.
2008: Marathon Petroleum Company sells its 50 percent stake in Pilot Travel Centers to Pilot Corp.
2010: Flying J and Pilot Travel Centers merge, creating one of the nation's 10 largest private companies.

office?" With these and other additional services, Pilot hoped to motivate more individual truckers and trucking companies, recreational-vehicle enthusiasts, and other motorists to utilize its travel centers as one-stop solution providers.

Pilot's expansion hit a snag in California in 2007, when state attorney general Jerry Brown filed a complaint against the company for violating environmental regulations in its handling of hazardous materials. Pilot officials maintained that the company had done no damage to the environment but negotiated a $7.5 million settlement with the state in September 2007. The amount was lowered to $5 million when the company voluntarily altered its maintenance of underground storage tanks. In April 2008 Jimmy Haslam announced that Pilot would stop opening new travel centers in California, saying that the state's regulatory environment made it too costly to do business there.

NEW PARTNERS: 2008–10

In October 2008 Pilot announced that it would buy out Marathon Oil's 50 percent interest in Pilot Travel Centers. At the same time, it sold a 47.5 percent stake in the business to the private equity firm CVC Capital Partners, which had facilitated the deal.

By 2009 Pilot had reached the top 15 on *Forbes*'s list of largest private companies in the United States, with 2008 revenues of $17.28 billion. Pilot soon seized another opportunity to grow by an order of magnitude. Its close competitor Flying J, overextended and hindered by the financial crisis that began in late 2008, filed for Chapter 11 bankruptcy protection. Using $1.8 billion in credit obtained from Bank of America, Merrill Lynch, and Wells Fargo, Pilot made an offer on Flying J's main asset, its national network of 250 travel centers. The Federal Trade Commission initially held up the deal out of antitrust concerns but gave its approval when Pilot agreed to relinquish 26 of the centers to another company in the business, Love's Travel Stops & Country Stores.

The deal, which went into effect on July 1, 2010, allowed Flying J to make a successful exit from bankruptcy, albeit as a much smaller company. Both parties involved in the deal took on new corporate names. Pilot Travel Centers became Pilot Flying J, styling itself as "one great company, two great brands." Flying J, which would then be called FJ Management, retained an 11.7 percent stake in Pilot Flying J.

The clear industry leader, Pilot controlled more than 550 travel centers in 43 states and 6 provinces in Canada. It planned to turn over dozens of Flying J's Country Market restaurants to national fast food chains, choosing Denny's as its preferred restaurant operator. Pilot was already the largest franchisee of Subway restaurants in the world.

Daryl F. Mallett
Updated, Roger K. Smith

PRINCIPAL COMPETITORS

7-Eleven, Inc.; Love's Travel Stops & Country Stores; Road Ranger, LLC; Stuckey's, Inc.; TravelCenters of America.

FURTHER READING

Beebe, Paul. "Successful Flying J Bankruptcy a Throwback to Different Time." *Salt Lake Tribune*, August 1, 2010.

"Coast-to-Coast Trucker Medical Clinics." *Fleet Owner*, December 20, 2007. Accessed October 20, 2010. http://fleetowner.com/management/trucker_medical_clinics_1220/

Donahue, Bill. "Pilot Gets into a Fix." *Convenience Store Decisions*, June 2004, 60.

Flory, Josh. "California Won't See More Pilot Travel Centers." *Knoxville News-Sentinel*, April 18, 2008.

Gates, Nick, and Stan DeLozier. "Smokies Purchase Nets Pilot a Publicity Vehicle." *Knoxville News-Sentinel*, December 28, 2001.

Gordetsky, Margaret. "Gingrich on Bandwagon for Truck Stop Heating, Cooling, Entertainment Units." *Transport Topics*, December 11, 2000.

"Pilot Buys Marathon Stake in Travel Centers." *Knoxville News-Sentinel*, October 1, 2008.

Pomerleau, Charlie. "Merger Official Today for Two Companies." *Ogden (UT) Standard-Examiner*, July 1, 2010.

Smyth, Whit. "The NRN Fifty: The Franchisees—Pilot Corp.: Launch into the Restaurant Business Has Sales Taking Off." *Nation's Restaurant News*, January 26, 1998.

Pizza Hut Inc.

14841 Dallas Parkway
Dallas, Texas 75254
U.S.A.
Telephone: (972) 338-7700
Toll Free: (800) 948-8488
Fax: (972) 338-6869
Web site: http://www.pizzahut.com

Wholly Owned Subsidiary of Yum! Brands, Inc.
Founded: 1958
Incorporated: 1959
Employees: 300,000
Sales: $10 billion (2008)
NAICS: 722110 Full-Service Restaurants

■ ■ ■

Pizza Hut Inc. is the largest pizza restaurant company in the world, based on both number of outlets and percentage of market share. A subsidiary of Yum! Brands, Inc., the company oversees more than 6,000 pizza restaurants and delivery outlets in the United States and more than 5,700 in 94 other countries and territories. A number of Pizza Hut restaurants also serve as locations for another rapidly growing Yum! Brands subsidiary, the chicken-wing chain WingStreet. Well before Pizza Hut celebrated its 50th birthday in 2008, its size and presence marked it as the leader in the $37 billion pizza category. Characteristic of the company as it entered its sixth decade were a constantly evolving menu aimed at satisfying the latest trends among its customers; regular launches of new promotions and marketing programs; and strong efforts to increase its presence in new technologies, from the Internet to Twitter.

EARLY HISTORY

Pizza Hut was founded in 1958 by brothers Dan and Frank Carney in their hometown of Wichita, Kansas. When a friend suggested opening a pizza parlor, then a rarity, they agreed that the idea could prove successful, and they borrowed $600 from their mother to start a business with partner John Bender. Renting a small building at 503 South Bluff in downtown Wichita and purchasing secondhand equipment to make pizzas, the Carneys and Bender opened the first Pizza Hut restaurant. On opening night, they gave pizza away to encourage community interest. A year later, in 1959, Pizza Hut was incorporated in Kansas, and Dick Hassur opened the first franchise unit in Topeka, Kansas.

In the early 1960s Pizza Hut grew on the strength of aggressive marketing of the pizza restaurant idea. In 1962 the Carney brothers bought out John Bender's interest, and Robert Chisholm joined the company as treasurer. In 1966, when the number of Pizza Hut franchise units had grown to 145, a home office in Wichita was established to coordinate the businesses.

Two years later the first Pizza Hut franchise was opened in Canada. This was followed by the establishment of the International Pizza Hut Franchise Holders Association (IPHFHA). It aimed to acquire 40 percent of the company's franchise operations, or 120 stores, and add them to the six outlets wholly owned by Pizza Hut. The acquisitions, however, brought turmoil to the

COMPANY PERSPECTIVES

Your Favorites. Your Pizza Hut.

chain. Varied accounting systems used by previous franchise owners had to be merged into one operating system, a process that took eight months to complete. In the meantime, sales flattened and profits tumbled.

TURMOIL BRINGS NEW STRUCTURE

In 1970 Frank Carney decided that the company needed to develop a long-term business strategy. The first priority was increasing sales and profits. Second was to continue building a strong financial base to support further growth. The strategy also called for adding new restaurants to the chain in emerging and growing markets. In 1970 Pizza Hut opened units in Munich, Germany, and Sydney, Australia. That same year, the chain's 500th restaurant opened, in Nashville, Tennessee. Further acquisitions that year included an 80 percent stake in Ready Italy, a frozen crust maker, and a joint venture with Sunflower Beef, Inc., called Sunflower Food Processors. Also in 1970 all Pizza Hut restaurants added sandwiches to their menu. In 1971 Pizza Hut became the world's largest pizza chain, according to sales and number of restaurants, then numbering just a little more than 1,000 in all.

At the end of 1972 Pizza Hut made its first, long-anticipated offer of 410,000 shares of common stock to the public on the New York Stock Exchange. The company expanded by purchasing three restaurant divisions: Taco Kid, Next Door, and the Flaming Steer. In addition, Pizza Hut acquired Franchise Services, Inc., a restaurant supply company, and J & G Food Company, Inc., a food and supplies distributor. The company also added a second distribution center in Peoria, Illinois.

In 1973 Pizza Hut expanded further by opening outlets in Japan and Great Britain. Three years later the chain had more than 100 restaurants outside the United States and 2,000 units in its franchise network. The company's 2,000th restaurant was opened in Independence, Missouri. It also established the 35-by-65-meter red-roof Pizza Hut restaurant building as the regulation size and design for all its new establishments. The new construction standard called for free-standing buildings built in a distinctive one-story brick design. The sites seated from 60 to 120 people.

Advertising played an increasingly influential role at Pizza Hut, broadening the chain's public profile. Campaigns were run both nationally and locally in the U.S. market. Spending on local advertising increased from $942,000 in 1972 to $3.17 million in 1974.

PEPSICO BUYS OUT COMPANY IN 1977

In 1977 Pizza Hut merged with PepsiCo, becoming a division of the global soft drink and food conglomerate. Sales that year reached $436 million, and a new headquarters opened in Wichita. The 1980s brought new competitors to Pizza Hut as the pizza restaurant trade climbed to $15 billion in annual sales in the United States alone. The company's main competitors had previously been regional chains such as Dallas-based Pizza Inn, Denver-based Shakey's, and Phoenix-based Village Inn and Straw Hat. Fierce competition in the 1980s brought new entrants into the quick-service pizza category, including Little Caesar's, Domino's Pizza International, and Pizza Express.

To raise its profile, Pizza Hut introduced the Pan Pizza in 1980. The product, with a thicker crust made in deep pans, soon became popular. The success of new additions to Pizza Hut's menu was facilitated by the marketing resources provided by PepsiCo. For example, in 1983 Pizza Hut introduced its Personal Pan Pizza, offering customers a guarantee that their single-serving pizzas would arrive quickly and steaming hot in five minutes. The aim was to make a quick, affordable pizza the ideal lunchtime meal.

STRONG GROWTH

In 1984 Steven Reinemund was appointed president and chief executive officer of Pizza Hut. He oversaw a period of unprecedented growth. In 1986 Pizza Hut opened its 5,000th franchise unit, in Dallas, Texas, and began its successful home delivery service. By the 1990s the delivery and carryout business had grown to account for approximately 25 percent of the company's total sales.

In 1990 Pizza Hut opened its first restaurant in Moscow. Russians' pizza of choice, "Moskva," a pie topped with sardines, tuna, mackerel, salmon, and onion, became a favorite at the Moscow restaurant, which quickly established itself as Pizza Hut's highest-volume unit in the world. Restaurants just behind in total volume served were found in France, Hong Kong, Finland, and Britain.

By 1991 company sales at the pizza chain were up 10 percent worldwide, at $5.3 billion, as growing health awareness and the popularity of vegetarianism had

KEY DATES

1958: Pizza Hut is founded in Wichita, Kansas, by brothers Dan and Frank Carney.
1959: The company is incorporated, and its first franchise unit opens in Topeka.
1971: Pizza Hut becomes the world's largest pizza chain by sales and number of restaurants.
1972: Pizza Hut goes public.
1977: PepsiCo buys out the company.
1997: PepsiCo spins off Pizza Hut, KFC, and Taco Bell into Tricon Global Restaurants, Inc., an independent publicly traded company.
2003: The company creates WingStreet, a chicken-wing chain with locations in Pizza Hut restaurants.
2008: The company creates iPhone and iPad applications that allow customers to place delivery orders.
2009: Pizza Hut begins to remodel its restaurants at locations in Jacksonville, Florida.

prompted many people to view pizza as a nutritious fast-food alternative. Pizza Hut Delivery, the home delivery operation, provided $1.2 billion in sales alone, and overall Pizza Hut sales, added to those of PepsiCo subsidiaries Taco Bell and KFC (formerly Kentucky Fried Chicken), gave the parent company more than $21 billion in sales that year on its restaurant and fast food side.

In the early 1990s Pizza Hut was concerned with making itself more accessible. Drive-through units were added for customers' convenience, and Pizza Hut Express units were being developed. The Express unit originated in shopping malls, providing fast food at affordable prices made possible by lower operating overheads. Pizza Hut then positioned Express units in school cafeterias, sports arenas, office buildings, and major airports. Such nontraditional locations became the fastest-growing sector of operations for Pizza Hut in the early 1990s.

DECLINING PROFITS AND RECOVERY

In 1994 Pizza Hut experienced its first decline in operating profits in 15 years. The pizza market was no longer growing, fast food rivals had cut prices, and investment in new outlets was draining corporate resources. For PepsiCo's restaurant division, sales in restaurants open at least one year fell 6 percent, contributing to a 21 percent drop in profits (to $295 million).

In an effort to change direction, Roger A. Enrico moved from PepsiCo's beverage and snack food divisions to head the restaurant division in 1994. His first move was to heavily promote a new product: stuffed crust pizza, a pie with a ring of mozzarella folded into the outer edge of the crust. The company used a massive advertising campaign to promote the new product, including television commercials that paired celebrities eating their pizzas crust first.

Some indicators were promising: market share rose from 25.6 to 27 percent; 1995 sales increased 16 percent to $5.2 billion; and operating income rose to $414 million, up 40 percent from the prior year. Pizza Hut planned to launch a major new product and two or three line extensions each year. In 1997 it introduced Totally New Pizzas, with 67 percent more toppings and thicker sauce. The company allocated $50 million for the project, in part to install new or improved ovens. In 1996 Pizza Hut accounted for 17 percent of PepsiCo's total sales and 13 percent of its operating profit.

TRICON GLOBAL RESTAURANTS

The parent company's return on assets, however, was significantly greater in its beverage and snack food divisions than in its restaurant division. In the late 1990s PepsiCo drew together its restaurant businesses, including Pizza Hut, Taco Bell, and KFC. All operations were overseen by a single senior manager, and most back-office operations, including payroll, data processing, and accounts payable, were combined. In October 1997 the company spun off the restaurant division, creating an independent, publicly traded company called Tricon Global Restaurants, Inc.

Enrico, now CEO of PepsiCo, explained in a January 23, 1997, press release, "Our goal in taking these steps is to dramatically sharpen PepsiCo's focus. Our restaurant business has tremendous financial strength and a very bright future. However, given the distinctly different dynamics of restaurants and packaged goods, we believe all our businesses can better flourish with two separate and distinct managements and corporate structures." By then Pizza Hut had 7,600 restaurants and delivery units in the United States and more than 3,000 in 86 other countries.

The move to a new corporate banner did not interrupt the steady evolution of Pizza Hut's menu. New offerings included the Edge, a pizza with toppings placed all the way to the edge of the pie, leaving virtually no crust, and the Sicilian Pizza, which combined basil, oregano, and garlic baked directly into a thicker, 8-by-12-inch rectangular crust. By early 1998 executives were already crediting the new products, as well as the previous year's promotional spending, for what appeared to be a turnabout in revenues.

"The Edge doubled our traffic" and boosted revenues 5 percent in fourth quarter 1997, Randy Gier, chief marketing officer, told Candace Talmadge of Reuters News (April 24, 1998). The rollouts continued in 1999 with the Big New Yorker Pizza, a "traditional style" pizza with a bigger, 16-inch crust with larger slices that could be folded and a sweeter sauce.

EMBRACING INTERNATIONAL MARKETS AND NEW TECHNOLOGY

Pizza Hut looked for new ways to appeal to its customers outside the United States. The company announced in September 1999 that it would keep its products in the United Kingdom free of genetically modified grain. Three years later, the company paid to have its new logo placed on a Russian rocket carrying a piece of the International Space Station.

Pizza Hut also worked to control costs and improve revenues, however. In 1999 it began experimenting with charging for delivery from its locations in Texas. Earlier that year, Tricon reported that it earned $151 million in the fourth quarter of 1998, a year after taking a quarterly loss, on strong sales in all three of its restaurant units, including a 4 percent improvement at Pizza Hut. Staying abreast of new technologies, Pizza Hut in 1997 became the first pizza chain to approve use of credit cards for payment on deliveries. The following year, it created a new Web site, www.orderpizzahut.com, allowing customers in northern California to order pizza on the Internet. The company promoted the new site the following January by giving northern California consumers the option to order pies online in advance of the Super Bowl to avoid busy signals.

LAWSUITS

The dawn of a new century was punctuated by a high-profile lawsuit that Pizza Hut brought against competitor Papa John's. In November 1999 a jury in federal court in Dallas ruled that Papa John's claim to have "Better Ingredients, Better Pizza" was "false, misleading and deceives a substantial number of American consumers." The case was significant because it marked the first time a company was held liable for an advertising slogan and forbidden to use it in the future. "This is a victory for consumers as much as it is for Pizza Hut because the jury declared that truth in advertising really does matter," Pizza Hut president Mike Rawlings said in a November 29, 1999, press statement. Less than two months later, the court enjoined Papa John's from using the slogan, a recognizable variation of it, or the word "better" in any future marketing campaign.

Papa John's obtained a stay of enforcement as it appealed to the U.S. Fifth Circuit Court in New Orleans. In September 2000 the court ruled that the Papa John's ads were misleading but that the company could continue to use its slogan and did not have to pay the $468,000 in damages Pizza Hut sought. The court reasoned that the slogan was "puffery": a claim so exaggerated and general that it could not be misleading by itself. Pizza Hut appealed to the U.S. Supreme Court, which in March 2001 let the appeals court ruling stand.

NEW PROMOTIONS

Pizza Hut continued to launch new promotions, often combining its offerings with products from other companies. In July 2000 it teamed up with America Online to offer $30 in online shopping to customers who bought a Big New Yorker pizza. The next year, Pizza Hut and Blockbuster collaborated to offer a certificate good toward one free new-release movie rental to every customer who ordered Pizza Hut's new Twisted Crust pizza.

Promotion rose to new heights in 2001, however, when Pizza Hut became the first company to deliver pizza to outer space. Together with Russian scientists, the company developed a pizza that could be consumed in space, then had it delivered to the International Space Station, where the crew ate it. The pie was six inches in diameter, the size of a Pizza Hut Personal Pan Pizza, to fit into the space station's smaller oven, and used salami instead of pepperoni because it better withstood the process.

The company, meanwhile, launched new menu items tailored to more terrestrial tastes. The P'zine, "the pizza that eats like a sandwich," was introduced in 2002 and revived periodically thereafter. Later that year, Pizza Hut introduced the Chicago Dish Pizza, a deep-dish pie. It also brought back an earlier offering, the Insider, which included a full pound of cheese, prompting Pizza Hut to estimate it would use 100 million pounds of cheese that summer alone.

The menu was widening in other ways too. In 2003 Pizza Hut introduced Fit 'N Delicious pizzas with lower fat. In 2004 it launched a line of salads and promoted a new buffalo chicken wing pizza. The following year saw the premiere of Dippin' Strips Pizza, which was cut into rectangles that could be dipped into sauce.

Pizza Hut was continuing to expand geographically. In 2001 it said it planned to open 50 new outlets in China in the following two years, the same number it had opened in its first decade operating in that country. Domestically, however, the company had slimmed down to less than 7,000 units from its height of 7,600 in the late 1990s. Pizza Hut maintained its leading position in the industry, however. In 2001 it was named the number one national pizza chain in the United States in *Restaurants & Institutions'* annual Choice in Chains survey.

TAPPING THE ELECTRONIC MARKET

Consumer use of new technologies grew and evolved rapidly in the latter half of the 2000s, and with each new device and application, Pizza Hut developed a presence geared to its audience. In 2007 it announced that online ordering was available at nearly all of its U.S. delivery locations. In 2008 Pizza Hut offered Total Mobile Access, which allowed orders from mobile phones via text messaging or mobile web, making Pizza Hut the first restaurant chain to offer both services nationwide.

The same year, Pizza Hut introduced a downloadable widget enabling customers to place pizza orders directly from their computer desktops, and a Facebook application that allowed users to place orders without leaving the site. By 2009 Pizza Hut's own Facebook page had more than one million fans. Meanwhile, the company had created new, free applications for the iPhone and iPad for placing orders directly from those devices. The iPhone application reached $1 million in sales in less than a year.

In July 2006 Pizza Hut settled two class-action lawsuits in which it was alleged to have improperly classified managers as exempt from overtime pay, even though they performed many of the same functions (taking orders, answering the phone, making pizzas, and cleaning up) as workers who received overtime. The principal lawsuit sought damages based on one-and-a-half times the members' pay, plus penalties, potentially costing Pizza Hut more than $300 million. In the two settlements, Pizza Hut agreed to pay a total of $12.5 million.

While the company continued to introduce new menu items (such as Cheesy Bits Pizza and a Lasagna Pizza in 2006, Double Deep Pizza and Hand Tossed-Style Pizza in 2007, Ultimate Grill Pizza in 2008, and Stuffed Crust Pan Pizza in 2009), it also found new ways to appeal to customers and expand its profile. For instance, in 2005 the company became the primary sponsor of Chevrolets driven by Terry Labonte and Brian Vickers in two NASCAR series.

Pizza Hut's biggest success during the second half of the decade, however, was WingStreet, a chicken-wing chain with locations in Pizza Hut restaurants. Introduced in 2003, WingStreet had expanded to 1,000 points of access by 2007 and was aiming to be available at more than 4,000 within three years. WingStreet won the Hot Concepts! Award in 2007 from *Nation's Restaurant News*. Pizza Hut also widened its offerings in March 2008 by introducing Tuscani Pastas, the first line of pasta dishes to be delivered by a national chain. It sold more than 2 million in the product's first month.

YUM! BRANDS

In 2006 Pizza Hut's parent, now known as Yum! Brands, reorganized its businesses, naming Scott Bergren, formerly the company's executive vice president and chief marketing and food innovation officer, as president of Pizza Hut. Yum! Brands by then had more than 34,000 restaurants worldwide and had acquired the A&W and Long John Silver's chains.

By the middle of the decade, however, pizza chains were experiencing a cost squeeze due to rising cheese and flour prices. Sales continued to be dampened by an economic recovery that had not translated into rising wages after the recession of 2000–01. In 2007 Pizza Hut chalked up $10 billion in sales but closed more U.S. restaurants than it opened, attributing this in part to leases ending and restaurants being sold.

Pizza Hut celebrated its 50th birthday in 2008. The following year it launched the first stage of a program to recast itself physically with a more contemporary look. The $5 million project, begun in June 2009, involved remodeling all of the chain's locations in the Jacksonville, Florida, area, including 7 dine-in restaurants and 23 delivery and carry-out-only restaurants. "With the introduction of Tuscani Pastas last year and the expansion of our WingStreet wing concept at hundreds of Pizza Hut locations, there's a lot more than just pizza at Pizza Hut," Pat Murtha, chief operating officer, said in a June 25 press statement. "While as a company we'll always be known as Pizza Hut, the contemporary new look of our restaurant reflects our expanding menu, while keeping our overall restaurant feel fresh and contemporary." Pizza Hut intended to expand the new look to other markets in the future.

RECESSION AND BEYOND

With the recession that began in 2008, Pizza Hut tailored its marketing to its customers' realities. In

February 2009 it held an all-day "pizza for a penny" promotion on Abraham Lincoln's birthday. At the end of the year, it announced a limited-time $10-for-any-pizza deal, and in August 2010 it introduced everyday low prices on its flagship menu items. Some items would experience "almost a 50 percent reduction," Brian Niccol, chief marketing officer, told Stuart Elliott of the *New York Times* (August 18, 2010).

Aiming to build a following on social networks, Pizza Hut in April 2009 announced a search for a new short-term intern, a Pizza Hut "Twintern," to manage its voice on Twitter. The campaign generated sufficient interest that the company hired the intern to manage Pizza Hut's Twitter account full-time.

Etan Vlessing
Updated, Susan Windisch Brown; Eric Laursen

PRINCIPAL COMPETITORS

Domino's Pizza, Inc.; Little Caesar Enterprises, Inc.; Papa Gino's, Inc.; Papa John's International, Inc.

FURTHER READING

Clifford, Stephanie. "Tweeting Becomes a Summer Job Opportunity." *New York Times*, April 19, 2009.

Collins, Glenn. "PepsiCo to Get $4.5 Billion in Spinoff of Restaurant Units." *New York Times*, August 15, 1997.

Elliott, Stuart. "Pizza Hut Cuts Prices Again to Counteract the Slow Recovery." *New York Times*, August 18, 2010.

Forest, Stephanie Anderson. "How Enrico Put the Spice Back in Pizza Hut." *BusinessWeek*, March 11, 1996, 72.

Gumpert, David. *The Pizza Hut Story*. Wichita: Pizza Hut, 1989.

"Pizza Hut Debuts a Brand New Look and Menu in Jacksonville." PR Newswire, June 25, 2009.

Rudnitsky, Howard. "Leaner Cuisine." *Forbes*, March 27, 1995, 43–44.

Schreiner, Bruce. "Pizza Hut Turns 50 in Tough Time for the Industry." Associated Press, May 30, 2008.

Talmadge, Candace. "For Pizza Hut, New Products Are Recipe for Success." Reuters News, April 24, 1998.

Vicini, James. "U.S. Court Denies Pizza Hut Appeal on Ads." Reuters News, March 19, 2001.

Planned Parenthood Federation of America

434 West 33rd Street
New York City, New York 10001
U.S.A.
Telephone: (212) 541-7800
Toll Free: (800) 230-7526
Fax: (212) 245-1845
Web site: http://www.plannedparenthood.org

Nonprofit Company
Founded: 1916
Employees: 210
Sales: $106.36 million (2009)
NAICS: 621410 Family Planning Centers

■ ■ ■

The Planned Parenthood Federation of America is the largest and oldest family planning organization in the United States. Headquartered in New York City, Planned Parenthood provides family planning information and services through a network of 86 affiliate organizations that operate 825 health centers in all fifty states and the District of Columbia. Active internationally, Planned Parenthood has a world regional office in Nairobi, Kenya; Guatemala City, Guatemala; Abuja, Nigeria; and Khartoum, Sudan. It serves Latin America and the Caribbean through an international office in Miami, Florida. Besides family planning education and services, each Planned Parenthood affiliate offers information on human sexuality and provides maternal and infant health care. Along with contraception, including sterilization procedures, each affiliate also offers infertility counseling, assisted reproductive technology services, and medically safe and legal abortions. With over 25,000 volunteers and staff assisting the organization in the United States and abroad, Planned Parenthood provides health care, information, and education to 10 million men, women, and teens worldwide each year.

MARGARET SANGER BEGINS: 1916–23

In 1916 the family planning activist Margaret Sanger joined with her sister and a friend to found a clinic in New York City that provided contraceptive advice to poor and immigrant women. The era's strict laws, specifically the so-called Comstock Laws, which dated back to 1873, defined birth control information and materials as obscene and prohibited their distribution. In the state of New York the law allowed the distribution of birth control information and materials only to prevent or cure disease. That same year local authorities raided the clinic and arrested its founders. Sanger spent 30 days in a women's prison but appealed her conviction on the charges against her.

In 1923 she incorporated the Birth Control Clinical Research Bureau in New York City, a clinic where physicians hoping to bring about a new, more liberalized interpretation of the Comstock Laws prescribed and provided contraceptives and collected statistics on their safety and efficacy. By 1925 the clinic had served over 1,600 women.

COMPANY PERSPECTIVES

The mission of Planned Parenthood is to provide comprehensive reproductive and complementary health care services in settings which preserve and protect the essential privacy and rights of each individual, to advocate public policies which guarantee these rights and ensure access to such services, to provide educational programs which enhance understanding of individual and societal implications of human sexuality, and to promote research and the advancement of technology in reproductive health care and encourage understanding of their inherent bioethical, behavioral, and social implications.

AMERICAN BIRTH CONTROL LEAGUE: 1923–28

In 1923 Sanger also founded the American Birth Control League, which involved itself in issues of disarmament and world famine, as well as in population growth and birth control. During the 1920s the league offered a vocal and increasingly effective rallying point for proponents of birth control. Sanger, along with her family and supporters, played a vital role in the league's work and development. Sanger's husband, the oil company executive James Noah Henry Slee, donated a tenth of his income to the league and served as its treasurer. By 1926 Slee had donated over $56,000 to the league. *Time* noted on March 18, 1929, that when Slee sought to deduct the donations from his taxable income, citing the league's "charitable, scientific and educational purposes," the U.S. Board of Tax Appeals indicated that the American Birth Control League sought "to enlist the support and co-operation of legal advisers, statesmen and legislators in effecting the lawful repeal and amendment of State and Federal statutes which deal with the prevention of conception." Even though the tax appeals board did not find such aims objectionable, it also did not find them strictly charitable, scientific, or educational. As a result, Slee had to pay tax on a portion of the money that he donated to the league. Regardless, *Time* indicated that "the significance of the incident was that one important Governmental agency accepted in passim the League's contraceptive activities as normal and acceptable in present U. S. culture."

When the American Birth Control League met in January 1928, its leaders reported increasing interest in birth control among both medical professionals and women. The league also noted that the Birth Control Clinical Research Bureau had served approximately 4,500 women the previous year. The league announced plans to raise funds for a second clinic in New York City.

Another notable development in the league's history occurred that same year, when James F. Cooper, the league's director of clinical research, published the book *Technique of Contraception: The Principles and Practice of Anti-conceptional Methods*. The book dealt with the significance of birth control, temporary and permanent methods of contraception, physical and mental effects of contraception, and common misunderstandings regarding the subject. Day-Nichols, Inc., of New York published the book, which was the first book on birth control allowed to be published and distributed within the United States. However, it could only be sold to physicians.

CHALLENGES AND GROWTH CONTINUE: 1929–62

In 1929 New York authorities raided the Birth Control Clinical Research Bureau's office because its actions continued to violate the Comstock Laws. Physicians and nurses working at the bureau were arrested and the patients' confidential medical records were seized. In response, Sanger founded the National Committee on Federal Legislation for Birth Control to direct efforts to overturn the Comstock Laws.

By 1931 the American Birth Control League had established state birth control leagues in Connecticut, Illinois, Massachusetts, New Jersey, and Pennsylvania. Furthermore, cities in California, Colorado, Georgia, Michigan, Maryland, North Carolina, and Ohio had local chapters. A total of 58 birth control clinics were open and active throughout the United States.

Five years later, in 1936, a federal court significantly liberalized the Comstock Laws in New York, Connecticut, and Vermont. In its decision, the court held that the phrase "to prevent or cure disease" in New York state Comstock Laws should be interpreted to include prevention of pregnancy. The following year the American Medical Association officially recognized birth control as an important feature in women's health.

By the American Birth Control League's 1938 convention, 374 birth control clinics served communities throughout the United States. The league estimated that approximately 200,000 women visited these clinics. League members expressed concern regarding the relatively small number of women who used clinic services given that, as reported by *Time* on February 7, 1938, approximately "50% to 75% of the married couples in the U. S. want to space or prevent the birth

KEY DATES

1916: Margaret Sanger opens the first birth control clinic in the United States.
1923: Margaret Sanger opens the Birth Control Clinical Research Bureau and incorporates the American Birth Control League.
1939: The Birth Control Research Bureau and the American Birth Control League merge to form the Birth Control Federation of America.
1942: The Birth Control Federation of America is renamed Planned Parenthood Federation of America.
1965: The U.S. Supreme Court rules in *Griswold v. Connecticut* that the U.S. Constitution protects the use of contraceptives by married couples.
1973: The U.S. Supreme Court rules in *Roe v. Wade* that abortion is legal.

of children." At the 1938 convention Richard Norris Pierson, a New York obstetrician and the new league president, stressed the need for continued fund-raising and announced the league's new fund-raising slogan: "Planned Parenthood."

The Birth Control Clinical Research Bureau and the American Birth Control League merged in 1939, creating the Birth Control Federation of America. Three years later, in 1942, the organization changed its name to Planned Parenthood Federation of America.

In 1948 representatives from 20 countries attended the International Conference on Population and World Resources in Relation to the Family and formed the International Planned Parenthood Committee. Twelve years later, in 1960, the U.S. Food and Drug Administration approved the sale and distribution of the first birth control pill. By 1962, 1.2 million women in the United States used the oral contraceptive.

SUPREME COURT RULINGS AND CONGRESSIONAL ACTIONS: 1965–73

Planned Parenthood's history is closely aligned with U.S. Supreme Court rulings and congressional actions that directly affected the services the organization provided. One of the earliest of these, in 1965, was the Court's *Griswold v. Connecticut* decision, which allowed married couples throughout the United States access to contraception and struck down state laws forbidding it, including the long-standing Comstock Laws that had jailed Sanger and her supporters in 1916.

In 1971 Congress officially repealed most of the Comstock Laws that were still in place around the country. That same year Planned Parenthood established its own international program, Family Planning International Assistance. The organization eventually became the largest U.S.-based nongovernmental provider of family planning services to millions of women and men in developing countries around the world.

The U.S. Supreme Court's *Roe v. Wade* ruling in 1973 struck down state laws prohibiting abortion. At the time of the landmark decision only four states, Washington, Hawaii, Alaska, and New York, allowed unrestricted abortions. The other states had restrictions on the procedure, such as requiring the mother's life to be in danger or the pregnancy to have resulted from rape or incest. The Court decision allowed states only minimal restrictions, such as limiting abortions to medically licensed facilities, but otherwise removed significant obstacles to a woman's decision to terminate a pregnancy.

FAYE WATTLETON: 1978–92

Besides Sanger, the most publicly recognizable leader of Planned Parenthood was Faye Wattleton, who became president of the organization in 1978. A former nurse and midwife, Wattleton had previously led the Planned Parenthood affiliate in Dayton, Ohio. Her selection as the national president lent a highly visible face to an organization that had maintained a relatively low profile for many years and had, except for Sanger, been led by men.

As political hostility to abortion rights increased in the United States during the 1980s, Wattleton mobilized Planned Parenthood supporters. A direct result of this mobilization was that the organization became an increasingly public and outspoken advocate for abortion rights. Wattleton also launched a political action fund that allowed Planned Parenthood to endorse political candidates. In a profile of Wattleton, Richard Stengel wrote in *Time* on December 11, 1989, "In an era when nonprofit organizations seek out celebrity spokespeople to get their message across, she is the public relations ideal, a spokeswoman who has become a celebrity." In 1989, 177 Planned Parenthood affiliates operated 850 clinics in 46 states. Wattleton remained president until 1992.

FUTURE PROSPECTS

In 2001 Planned Parenthood announced several major goals for its next 25 years. The organization would continue to work toward ensuring that individuals understood that sexuality is an essential, lifelong aspect of their humanity and that they should celebrate their sexuality in a context of respect, openness, and mutual consent. Planned Parenthood also intended to create a new media company to counteract what the organization saw as potential censorship of reproductive and sexual health information. The organization also wanted to create the largest volunteer citizen-action base of support of any social movement in the United States.

The Planned Parenthood Action Fund, an affiliated but separately incorporated organization, supported Planned Parenthood's political activities with lobbying efforts and voter education programs. The action fund's lobbying efforts focused on funding for domestic and international family planning and support for various political candidates and platforms.

Joyce Helena Brusin

FURTHER READING

"Birth Control (Medicine)." *Time*, March 18, 1929, 38.

"Birth Control (Medicine)." *Time*, January 26, 1931, 56.

Chesler, Ellen. *Woman of Valor: Margaret Sanger and the Birth Control Movement in America.* New York: Simon & Schuster, 1992.

Conlin, Michelle. "Birth Control of a Nation." *Business Week*, September 13, 2004, 18.

"Controller (Medicine)." *Time*, February 7, 1938, 49.

Davis, Tom. *Planned Parenthood and Its Clergy Alliances.* New Brunswick, NJ: Rutgers University Press, 2005.

Stengel, Richard. "Nothing Less Than Perfect: Faye Wattleton," *Time*, December 11, 1989, 82.

Wattleton, Faye. *Life on the Line.* New York: Ballantine, 1996.

Pro-Football, Inc.

21300 Redskin Park Drive
Ashburn, Virginia 20147-6100
U.S.A.
Telephone: (703) 726-7000
Fax: (703) 726-7086
Web site: http://www.redskins.com

Private Company
Founded: 1932
Employees: 250
Sales: $345 million (2009)
NAICS: 711211 Sports Teams and Clubs

■ ■ ■

Pro-Football, Inc., is the parent company of the Washington Redskins franchise of the National Football League (NFL). In its history, the team has won three Super Bowls and prior to that a pair of NFL championships. Although the Redskins claim Washington, D.C., as their home, the team maintains its headquarters and training facilities at Redskins Park in Ashburn, Virginia, and plays its home games at FedExField in Landover, Maryland, the largest stadium in the league, with a seating capacity of nearly 92,000. Since its acquisition by businessman Daniel Snyder in 1999, the Redskins have enjoyed limited success on the field, but the franchise has increased significantly in value. According to *Forbes* in 2010, the Redskins were the second-most-valuable NFL franchise, trailing only the Dallas Cowboys, and the fourth-most-valuable sports franchise in the world, worth an estimated $1.55 billion.

DEPRESSION ERA ROOTS

The person behind the creation of the Washington Redskins was George Preston Marshall, born in Grafton, Virginia, in 1896. He inherited his father's laundry business and grew it into a highly profitable chain, but he also harbored a desire to become involved in a less mundane field. He tried his hand at show business, producing several theatrical shows in Washington, before turning to professional sports. In 1925 he founded a team in the fledgling American Basketball League (ABL), the Washington Palace Five, named after his Palace Laundry. Although the ABL would fold in 1931, Marshall made the acquaintance of one of the league's founders, George Halas, who was also interested in promoting professional football and who became a driving force behind the creation of the NFL. Halas recruited Marshall to buy the league's defunct Duluth Eskimo franchise. Thus, in 1932 Marshall and three partners paid $100 for the Eskimo franchise. They moved it to Boston where the team became known as the Boston Braves, sharing the stadium of the Boston Braves of Major League Baseball.

Neither the baseball nor football Braves fared well in Boston. Marshall bought out his partners before the start of the 1933–34 NFL season and moved the team across town to Fenway Park, where he hoped attendance would improve. No longer affiliated with the Braves, the team was also renamed the Redskins. Attendance continued to struggle, even when Marshall brought

COMPANY PERSPECTIVES

The mission of Player Development is to challenge National Football League players to be lifelong learners while pursuing continuous improvement in family relations, social interactions, personal growth and career development during and beyond their NFL careers.

Boston a championship-caliber team in 1936. The Redskins were slated to play the championship game against the Green Bay Packers at home, but Marshall moved the game to New York City where a larger crowd could be expected. His team lost at the neutral-site game, and the following year Marshall moved the Redskins closer to his home, recasting them as the Washington Redskins.

MARSHALL THE INNOVATOR

The idea of a championship game was one of many contributions Marshall made to the growth of the NFL. Although he did not pretend to know the nuances of the game, he brought a much needed sense of showmanship to the professional game. In addition to splitting the league into two divisions to create a championship game, Marshall also urged the NFL to move the goalposts to the front of the goal line to make kicking field goals easier, suggested that the rules governing the forward pass be liberalized to increase scoring, and proposed that the ball be moved from the sidelines to the hash marks near the center of the field at the end of each play.

Marshall also proved adroit at promoting the Redskins in Washington. In 1937 his team drafted highly touted quarterback Sammy Baugh from Texas Christian University and Marshall made sure to outfit the new player with a cowboy hat to play to the public's impression of Texans. Unlike the proverbial Texan who was all hat and no cattle, Baugh proved to be one of the most productive football players in league history. He was not only one of the greatest passers the game would see but also a prolific punter and skilled defensive back. Over the next nine years, Baugh led the Redskins to five NFL championship games, of which they won two.

Marshall sold his laundry business in 1945 to focus all of his attention on the Redskins. He remained innovative, quick to embrace television and form a lucrative network of southern television stations to carry the Redskins' games. At the same time, he refused to join the movement to bring in African-American players. The NFL had employed African-American players in its early days, and many historian believed that it was Marshall who led the effort following the 1933–34 season to segregate the NFL. Regardless, Marshall refused after World War II to even try out African-American players, preferring instead to draft white southerners while having the team's volunteer marching band play "Dixie." Although such decisions played well to the Redskins' southern television audience, they did not help the team on the field. The other teams in the league began to add African-American talent and the Redskins fell to the bottom of the league standings, posting only three winning seasons in the final 23 years of Marshall's life.

MARSHALL DIES: 1969

Under pressure from the Kennedy administration, the Redskins were finally integrated in 1962. A year later Marshall suffered a stroke. Three court-appointed conservators, headed by attorney Edward Bennett Williams, ran the team until Marshall's death in 1969. Marshall's stake in the team had been reduced to 52 percent by this time. The largest of the minority owners was Jack Kent Cooke, who bought a 25 percent stake in 1960 for $350,000.

Cooke, a naturalized U.S. citizen born in Canada, was a high school dropout who sold encyclopedias door-to-door during the Great Depression of the 1930s before becoming a radio station manager. He became a success in broadcasting as well as publishing, emerging as a millionaire who left Canada for a Beverly Hills, California, mansion in 1960. Along the way he became interested in sports ownership. In 1965 he bought the Los Angeles Lakers of the National Basketball Association, followed by the Los Angeles Kings franchise- of the National Hockey League (NHL).

Following Marshall's death, the Redskins conservators voted to sell Marshall's 52 percent interest back to the club. As a result, Cooke's 25 percent interest grew to slightly more than 50 percent, giving him majority control. Because of cross-ownership rules imposed by the NFL, Cooke was not permitted to actively run the team, which continued to be operated by Williams. It was under Williams that the Redskins enjoyed a resurgence on the field. Legendary Green Bay Packers Coach Vince Lombardi was hired as the Redskins head coach in 1969. Although he would die less than two years later, Lombardi would bring the team its first winning season since 1955. He was soon replaced by George Allen, who would steer the team to its first Super Bowl appearance in 1973.

KEY DATES

1932: George Preston Marshall acquires Duluth Eskimo franchise to form Boston Braves.
1937: Renamed as the Redskins, team moves to Washington, D.C.
1979: Jack Kent Cooke takes control of team.
1997: Team moves into new stadium.
1999: Daniel Snyder buys Redskins.

A GOLDEN ERA: 1982–91

Cooke and his wife divorced after 42 years of marriage in the mid-1970s, leading to an extended property settlement suit. The $42 million he paid his wife was a then-record settlement and resulted in Cooke selling the Lakers and Kings. No longer saddled with cross-ownership rules, Cooke moved to Virginia in 1979 and took direct control of the Redskins. In 1981 he turned over day-to-day control of the Redskins to his son, John Kent Cooke, but not before making one of the most important decisions in club history. In early 1981 Jack Cooke hired the offensive coordinator of the San Diego Chargers, Joe Gibbs, to become the Redskins' new head coach. The following decade would prove to be a golden era for the team, which won the Super Bowl in the 1982–83, 1987–88, and 1991–92 seasons. Gibbs would retire in the spring of 1993 to pursue a new career in stock-car racing, heading a NASCAR team.

Since 1961 the Redskins had been playing in Robert F. Kennedy Memorial Stadium, originally known as District of Columbia Stadium. With a seating capacity of fewer than 57,000, it was the NFL's smallest site by the 1990s. Cooke searched for a new home for the Redskins and in 1995 found it in Maryland's Prince George's County. Cooke paid for the $160 million stadium, while the state of Maryland contributed $77 million to cover infrastructure costs. Cooke would not live to see the opening of the facility, however. He died at the age of 84 in April 1997. In September of that year the Redskins' new home was named Jack Kent Cooke Stadium in his honor.

Cooke's death also necessitated a change in ownership. According to his will, the team and stadium were to be sold to support a scholarship fund. The trustees of his estate then hired Morgan Stanley Dean Witter to conduct the sale. There was no lack of interest, with bids coming from likes of groups headed by Gibbs, John Cooke, and others. A 35-year-old entrepreneur who grew up a devoted Redskins fan, Daniel M. Snyder, was also an eager participant. Snyder had made his fortune in niche marketing and in 1996 took Snyder Communications public, becoming the youngest CEO of a company listed on the New York Stock Exchange. By 1999 he had a personal worth of $500 million.

SNYDER BUYS REDSKINS: 1999

To strengthen his position in acquiring the Redskins and stadium, Snyder joined forces with New York real estate mogul Howard Milstein (who also owned the New York Islanders of the NHL), Milstein's brother Edward, and media heavyweight Mort Zuckerman (who had played a pivotal role in Snyder's business career). After a five-month process, the group in early 1999 submitted a winning bid of $800 million, a record amount of money for a U.S. sports franchise, but it was rejected by the NFL. The league was supposedly unhappy with the way the deal was structured, but there were also reported concerns about Milstein's penchant to engage in litigation. Snyder struck out on his own and was able to secure $800 million in cash and financing to satisfy the NFL. The sale was completed in July 1999.

Snyder wasted little time in making changes to the Redskins, using his marketing expertise to extract a great deal of hidden value in the franchise. The team sold 6,000 previously unsold club seats while doubling the price, along with eight luxury suites. Another 740 feet of rotational and other signs were made available for sale in the stadium. Rights' fees from local television shows were increased, the use of the Redskins trademark was increased, and new sponsorship deals were struck. The team also looked to sell the naming rights of the stadium, exchanging the tribute to the Redskins' former owner for the $250 million Federal Express paid to have their name attached to the stadium for 27 years.

There was no doubt that Snyder had turned the Redskins into a moneymaking machine, but his hands-on approach to developing new revenue streams did not serve him well in putting together a winning team. He showed little patience, hiring and firing a succession of head coaches, which included top college coach Steve Spurrier as well as a return of Gibbs. Snyder also expanded FedExField, increasing the seating capacity from 80,000 to nearly 92,000. Because of the NFL's mandatory cap on players' salaries, Snyder was not able to use that extra cash to make up for several disappointing, expensive free-agent signings. Coaching salaries, however, had no cap. Snyder spent lavishly in this area but again received little return on his investment. The Redskins remained an extremely valuable property despite the team's inability to field a Super Bowl-worthy squad.

Ed Dinger

PRINCIPAL OPERATING UNITS

FedExField; Redskins Park.

PRINCIPAL COMPETITORS

Dallas Cowboys Football Club, Ltd.; New York Football Giants, Inc.; Philadelphia Eagles Limited Partnership.

FURTHER READING

Barnes, Bart. "A Washington Monument: The Master Salesman's Biggest Success Was Himself." *Washington Post*, April 7, 1997, A1.

Epstein, Noel, ed. *Redskins: A History of Washington's Team.* Washington, D.C.: Washington Post, 1997.

"George Preston Marshall Dies." *New York Times*, August 10, 1969.

Lombardo, John. "Snyder Changes Begin to Pay Off for New Redskins." *Washington Business Journal*, October 29, 1999, 42.

———. "Snyder Switches Focus to External Changes." *Washington Business Journal*, August 13, 1999, 13.

Loverro, Thom. *Hail Victory*. Hoboken, NJ: John Wiley & Sons, 2006.

Pulley, Brett. "The $1 Billion Team." *Forbes*, September 20, 2004, 34.

Schaffer, Athena. "Cooke Finds New Site for Redskins." *Amusement Business*, December 11, 1995, 11.

Shapiro, Leonard. "If Only the Gridiron Was a Business." *Washington Post*, September 1, 2005.

Steinberger, Mike. "Money Buys NFL Boss Failure and Insults." *Financial Times*, December 22, 2000, 15.

Promotora de Informaciones S.A.

Gran Via, 32
Madrid, 28013
Spain
Telephone: (+34 91) 330 10 00
Web site: http://www.prisa.com

Public Company
Incorporated: 2000
Employees: 14,987
Sales: EUR 3.21 billion ($4.04 billion) (2009)
Stock Exchanges: Madrid
Ticker Symbol: PRS
NAICS: 511110 Newspaper Publishers; 511130 Book Publishers; 515110 Radio Networks; 515120 Cable and Other Subscription Programming; 611310 Colleges, Universities, and Professional Schools

■ ■ ■

Promotora de Informaciones S.A. (PRISA) is the world's leading Spanish- and Portuguese-language media group. Its business areas include publishing, print journalism, radio and television broadcasting, film, and digital media. PRISA products reach 50 million readers, listeners, and viewers in 22 countries through such brands as Santillana and Alfaguara publishing, *El País*, Unión Radio, and Canal+ television. The company has a presence in Brazil and in the Hispanic community in the United States, with a potential global market of 700 million people.

PRISA was founded by Jesús de Polanco Gutiérrez, an entrepreneur who sold books door-to-door to support himself while earning a law degree. The organization that would become PRISA began in 1958 when Polanco established the textbook publisher Santillana. The company grew throughout the 1960s, expanding into journalism with the sports newspaper *Diario As* in 1967. In 1976 the newspaper *El País* was launched, during a period in which Spain was making the transition to democratic government following 40 years of authoritarian rule by Francisco Franco. Taking strong positions defending civil rights, *El País* grew into Spain's largest and most influential newspaper. The company introduced *Cinco Días*, which became Spain's leading business and finance daily, in 1978. The publisher El País-Aguilar was established in the late 1980s and produced books on such topics as travel, leisure, and gastronomy. Its popular travel series include Guías Visuales ("visual guides") and Guías con Encanto ("guides to charming places").

EXPANDING BEYOND PRINT: 1980–2000

As PRISA's influence grew during the 1980s, the company collaborated with the Autonomous University of Madrid to establish the El País/Universidad Autónoma de Madrid School of Journalism, a training center for journalists. The school, which opened in 1986, offered a master's degree in journalism and supplemented student coursework with internships within the PRISA organization. In 1989 PRISA expanded its media range with the creation of Sogecable, a company that oversaw the development of audiovisual projects including television and film production,

COMPANY PERSPECTIVES

A commitment to society is the essence of PRISA. From the very beginning, the founders and promoters of *El País* have been committed to Spanish society, to defending and expanding democratic liberty, equality, and civil rights for all. Three decades after the first issue of *El País*, this commitment remains as strong and vital as ever, and today, PRISA continuously re-evaluates the concepts of social responsibility in order to better champion a free, socially aware, responsible, tolerant, and sustainable society. This vision is shared by all those who work in our organization and is evident in the work and in the day-to-day operations of all those who work for PRISA.

PRISA is active in promoting and defending the social and cultural values of those areas where we operate, through, for example, initiatives aimed at recognizing, fostering and stimulating literary creativity, the media, film, and music.

distribution, and screening. It launched the cable company Canal+ in 1990.

The Sogecable organization expanded in 1994 when it formed Canal Satélite Digital, a satellite television provider that offered an array of subscription channels. At the same time, Canal+ continued to grow, reaching one million subscribers by the mid-1990s. In the late 1990s Canal Satélite Digital debuted the first Spanish-language subscription package in the European market. PRISA print media also experienced growth during this period, with the introduction of *El País* online and the acquisition in 1996 of a controlling interest in the thriving sports publication *As*.

Augmenting the company's educational services, Santillana Formación was created in 1998 to provide postgraduate training over the Internet, and in 2000 Prisacom was set up to oversee a wide range of digital activities within the PRISA organization. Online learning expanded in 2001 with the establishment of Santillana Formación's Instituto Universitario de Posgrado (IUP), a virtual business school associated with the University of Alicante, the Autonomous University of Barcelona, and the University of Carlos III in Madrid. IUP offered postgraduate study in business and finance through online courses. By 2010 IUP was among the largest business schools in Spain and a leading provider of online executive education.

INTERNATIONAL GROWTH: 2000–09

To fund its international growth, PRISA was taken public with an IPO on the Madrid Stock Exchange in 2000. It then expanded into Brazil with the acquisition of the textbook publisher Moderna and entered an agreement with Televisa to collaborate on broadcasting ventures in Mexico. In April 2002 PRISA established Grupo Latino de Radio (GLR), a joint venture with Valores Bavaria of Colombia, to develop a radio network throughout the Americas. Two years later PRISA bought out Valores to take full control of GLR and added the Argentinean outlets Radio Continental and Radio Estéreo to the network. In April 2005 GLR's U.S. office began Spanish-language radio broadcasts in southern California. PRISA'a print media were also expanding their international operations, with a 75 percent stake in Editora Objetiva, a publisher of biography, fiction, history, and politics based in Rio de Janeiro, Brazil. In addition, the company invested in media businesses in France and Portugal.

During this period PRISA pursued partnerships and acquisitions in print media in France, Portugal, Bolivia, and Mexico. In 2005 it increased its share to just over 15 percent in Groupe Le Monde et Partenaires Associés, which published the French daily *Le Monde*. Also in 2005, PRISA became the largest shareholder in the Portuguese magazine publisher Media Capital Edições (MCE), which produced such periodicals as *Lux* (celebrity news), *Revista de Vinhos* (wine), and *Casas de Portugal* (home decoration).

In 2006 PRISA entered a joint venture with the Barcelona-based media company Grupo Godó to create Unión Radio, the world's largest Spanish-language radio broadcasting system, with more than 1,250 stations in Spain, Argentina, Chile, Colombia, Costa Rica, Mexico, Panama, and the United States. Unión Radio's flagship station in Spain was Cadena SER (Sociedad Española de Radiodifusíon), which began operating in 1926. In October 2006 PRISA acquired Media Capital of Lisbon, Portugal, the parent company of MCE, with business interests in television and radio broadcasting, video and film distribution, magazine publishing, and Internet service. PRISA's extensive radio holdings expanded further in December 2006, when Unión Radio acquired Iberoamerican Radio Chile, a leading broadcaster with more than 100 stations. In 2008 PRISA and Grupo Godó, which owned 20 percent of Unión Radio, brought in another partner, selling a 16.2 percent share to the British venture capital firm 3i.

KEY DATES

1958: Jesús de Polanco establishes Santillana publishing house.
1976: First issue of *El País* is published on May 4.
1997: Canal Satélite Digital launches Europe's first Spanish-language pay-television package.
2000: PRISA goes public on the Madrid Stock Exchange.
2007: Jesús de Polanco dies, and his son Ignacio becomes PRISA's president.

In July 2007 PRISA founder Jesús de Polanco died, and his son Ignacio Polanco assumed the role of president. The following year PRISA solidified its ownership of Sogecable after securing financing to acquire 100 percent of the company stock through a takeover. In order to raise money to help fuel further international growth, the company sold 25 percent of the Santillana Group to DLJ South American Partners, a private equity firm with significant holdings in Latin American markets. Further capital was raised through the sale of 35 percent of Media Capital to Ongoing Strategy Investments, a Portuguese firm headed by the fifth generation of the Rocha dos Santos family and active in such industries as agriculture, chemicals, finance, health care, media, and real estate. Also in 2009 PRISA entered a partnership to merge the Sogecable general-interest television channel Cuatro with Telecinco, another of the leading channels in Spain. The agreement created Gestevisión Telecinco.

OPERATIONS IN 2010

By the end of the first decade of the 21st century, PRISA comprised a business empire that extended through traditional and new media in more than 20 countries. Its publishing holdings as of 2010 included Grupa Santillana, with products and services organized by market, including literary works for all ages, travel, reference, and philosophy publications. Among the leading imprints, Alfaguara published works of fiction. Alfaguara Infantil y Juvenil published fiction for children and teenagers, and Alamah published titles on personal development and spirituality. Santillana Education was the leading publisher of school textbooks in Spain, Portugal, and Latin America and published language books for children and adults through Richmond Publishing, with centers in Buenos Aires, London, Madrid, Mexico City, and Sao Paulo. As part of Santillana Online, Santillana en Red developed technological solutions with Prisacom to support students and teachers in Spanish and Portuguese-speaking countries.

Periodical publishing included *El País*, which was printed at eight plants in Spain and in Argentina, Belgium, and Mexico. The newspaper had an agreement with the *New York Times* to publish a Spanish-language supplement containing articles from the U.S. paper. Similarly, the *International Herald Tribune* included an English-language version of *El País* alongside its edition in Spain. Online, the company published general interest news through Elpaís.com and Cadenaser.com, business and financial news through Cincodias.com, and sports content through As.com.

As of 2010 PRISA was one of the world's leading production and distribution companies for Spanish- and Portuguese-language audiovisual content and the largest operator in Spain and Portugal. Sogecine was Spain's leading film producer, and Sogepaq (a part of Sogecable) acquired and marketed rights for cinemas, film distribution, and television. In Portugal PRISA operated through the production company Plural Entertainment, established in 2001, and through the broadcast and distribution firm Media Capital, owner of TVI. Plural Entertainment also created film and television content for the Hispanic market in the United States and Latin American markets, including television series, films, television news magazines, entertainment programs, documentaries, and game shows. As of 2010 Sogecable television was broadcasting three digital terrestrial channels: CNN+, Cuatro, and the music channel 40 Latino. In addition, under the brand name Canal+, Sogecable produced nine premium content channels that were part of DIGITAL+, Spain's leading pay TV package. Canal+ also produced a number of themed channels, including DCine Español, Golf+, and Canal+ Comedia, available through DIGITAL+ and other cable operators. DIGITAL+ programming included entertainment and news on more than 150 channels, and its movie premieres and live sports events made it the leading nationwide digital TV provider.

PRISA's radio holdings were thriving in 2010. Cadena SER was the most popular station in Spain with more than five million daily listeners for its news, talk, and sports programming. The most popular music radio station in Spain was PRISA's 40 Principales, with 3.3 million daily listeners. Another PRISA station, Cadena Dial, broadcast Spanish music from a base in Seville and counted 1.7 million listeners daily. In the United States GLR operated Spanish-language radio in Los Angeles and Miami. Unión Radio operated in Mexico through Radiópolis, 50 percent of which was owned by Televisa. Radiópolis had 88 stations, including W Radio in the talk radio segment and Bésame and 40 Principales for music radio. Los40.com extended the brand of Spain's leading music channel and showcased content and services from several of PRISA's channels, including 40 Principales, M80 Radio, and Cadena Dial. Radiolé.com was the top-ranked web portal for Spanish music.

As of 2010 PRISA was restructuring its debt to provide capital to take advantage of expansion opportunities. On March 5, 2010, PRISA and Liberty Acquisitions Holding Corporation announced a merger of the two companies that resulted in $900 million cash infusion in PRISA. Ignacio Polanco, PRISA's chairman of the board, stated: "Liberty's investment in PRISA demonstrates the strong belief in the underlying value of Grupa PRISA's market-leading positions in educational publishing, press, audiovisual and digital, and in our strategy for growth." Liberty's chairman, Martin E. Franklin, added: "We are confident in PRISA's potential to increase its digital market penetration to leverage its print and broadcast content and to accelerate its revenue growth in Latin America."

Louise B. Ketz; Laurie DiMauro

PRINCIPAL DIVISIONS

Cinco Días; Diario As; El País; Grupo Santillana; Progresa; Sogecable; Unión Radio.

PRINCIPAL COMPETITORS

El Mundo, Cadena COPE; *Marca*; Telefonica,; Vocento S.A.; Univision.

FURTHER READING

Burnett, Victoria. "Jesús de Polanco, 77, Media Mogul, Helped Revive Free Speech in Spain." *New York Times*, July 23, 2007.

Carvajal, Doreen. "Europe Teems with Web Dailies." *New York Times*, June 29, 2003.

Goodman, Al. "At the Helm of a Media Great as Spain's Political Wind Shifts to Starboard." *New York Times*, April 29, 1996.

"Grupa Prisa and Liberty Acquisition Holdings Announce Deal to Drive Prisa Digital, Latin American Growth." *Wall Street Journal MarketWatch*, March 5, 2010.

"Prisa Holds over 95 Percent of Sogecable after Full Bid." *Forbes*, May 12, 2008.

Riding, Alan. "Press Empire Wields Great Power in Spain." *New York Times*, April 1, 1991.

"Stars of Europe: Jesús de Polanco." *BusinessWeek*, July 7, 2003.

Tagliabue, John. "For Growth, Spanish Media Company Plans to Go West." *New York Times*, December 8, 2003.

———. "With Capital in Hand, Spain Revisits Its Empire." *New York Times*, June 29, 2003.

QIAGEN N.V.

Spoorstraat 50
Venlo, 5911 KJ
Netherlands
Telephone: (+31-77) 320-8400
Fax: (+31-77) 320-8409
Web site: http://www.qiagen.com

Public Company
Founded: 1984
Incorporated: 1996
Employees: 3,500
Sales: $1.01 billion (2009)
Stock Exchanges: NASDAQ Frankfurt
Ticker Symbols: QGEN (NASDAQ); QIA (Frankfurt)
NAICS: 325413 In-Vitro Diagnostic Substance Manufacturing; 334516 Analytical Laboratory Instrument Manufacturing; 551112 Offices of Other Holding Companies

■ ■ ■

Biotechnology pioneer QIAGEN N.V. (Qiagen) is the world leader in sample and assay technologies, tools that allow the extraction of ultrapure DNA, RNA, and protein as well as single nucleotide polymorphism (SNP) screening, enabling the analysis of nucleic acids and the information hidden therein. The company holds the patent for a revolutionary and proprietary resin-based DNA extraction process developed by one of its founders, Metin Colpan, in the early 1980s that has since become a standard throughout the world. Qiagen has successfully leveraged and extended that technology to offer a wide array of products, primarily in the form of consumable testing "kits," to more than 500,000 customers worldwide, including academic research centers, pharmaceutical and biotechnology companies, applied testing centers, and molecular diagnostics laboratories.

Qiagen's panel of molecular diagnostic tests includes the *digene* HPV test, which is regarded as a "gold standard" in testing for high-risk types of human papillomavirus (HPV), the primary cause of cervical cancer, as well as a broad suite of solutions for infectious disease testing and companion diagnostics. Qiagen also sells complete robotics systems that enable automated DNA extraction using its kits, freeing up valuable laboratory time and manpower. The company's technology, which has been used in such infamous circumstances as the O. J. Simpson murder trial and the testing of Monica Lewinsky's dress stains, has helped reduce DNA extraction times from several days to just two hours, allowing for large-scale production of the ultrapure DNA and RNA necessary for the booming genomics industries, the application of genetic research to the health field. Qiagen, with its holding company based in Venlo, Netherlands, and its operational headquarters in Hilden, Germany, maintains facilities in more than 35 locations around the world.

DNA EXTRACTION PIONEER IN THE EIGHTIES

Extracting the pure DNA from bacteria or from cells of human or animal tissues was a tedious and even dangerous process in the early 1980s, requiring the handling of

COMPANY PERSPECTIVES

As the innovative market and technology leader, Qiagen creates sample and assay technologies that enable access to content from any biological sample. Our mission is to enable our customers to achieve outstanding success and breakthroughs in life sciences, applied testing, pharma, and molecular diagnostics. We thereby make improvements in life possible. Our commitment to the markets, customers, and patients we serve drives our innovation and leadership in all areas where our sample and assay technologies are required. The exceptional talent, skill, and passion of our employees are key to Qiagen's excellence, success and value.

toxic and extremely harsh chemicals and involving several days to complete. Nonetheless, the availability of large and reliable quantities of pure DNA and RNA was a requirement for the building of the nascent biotechnology field, then just gathering steam with the launch of the human genome project and other genetic breakthroughs being made at the time. Among those working in genetics technology in the late 1970s was Turkish-born Metin Colpan.

Colpan had come to Germany at the age of six with his parents, who were part of the wave of "guest workers" entering Germany in the 1960s. Colpan was to consider this background as an important part of his later success, giving him the flexibility to meet the ever-changing demands of the biotechnology industry. He went on to complete a PhD in chemical engineering at the University of Darmstadt. Colpan's PhD thesis was to provide the foundation for his later success. By the late 1970s, Colpan had become convinced of the need for new methods and technologies for extracting the pure nucleic acid needed for genetics research. His thesis detailed the development of a silica resin-based anion-exchanger that could separate out nucleic acids from cells more rapidly than the traditionally time-consuming and more dangerous chemical methods.

Completing his thesis in 1983, Colpan applied for a U.S. patent for his technology (which he received in 1987). Colpan then made the rounds of Germany's pharmaceutical industry seeking financial backing to implement his resin-based technology from such firms as Roche and Bayer. Nevertheless, as Colpan told *Forbes* in 1999, these companies thought him "too entrepreneurial." His fortunes changed in 1984, however, after a one-hour meeting at the Frankfurt airport with Moshe Alafi, a prominent California-based investor in the nascent biotechnology sector. Alafi, who had been among the earliest investors in such biotechnology pioneers as Biogen and Amgen, agreed to provide Colpan with a letter of commitment. With Alafi's backing, Colpan was able to raise some $3 million to launch his company.

LAUNCH OF QIAGEN

In 1984 Colpan joined with three other partners to launch Qiagen in Düsseldorf, Germany (the operational headquarters was later moved to nearby Hilden, Germany). The company claimed the distinction of being the first venture capital-backed German company. Colpan's resin-based anionic-extraction technology also was set to revolutionize the biotechnology industry. In 1986 Qiagen introduced its first ready-to-use plasmid kit, which offered customers all the materials and equipment needed for the company's breakthrough nucleic acid cleansing process.

The company, however, which remained the exclusive manufacturer of Colpan's anion-exchange resin, quickly ran into trouble. Part of the company's troubles came from its eagerness to adapt its product to a broad variety of applications, targeting a range of industries from agricultural products to veterinary research laboratories, and thus spreading the company too thin. Another factor in the company's initial growing pains could be found in the hostile climate toward genetic research in Germany during the mid-1980s. Reeling from the forced shutdown of another company's insulin production facility, the country's biotechnology sector took the better part of a decade to regain its footing. Meanwhile, Qiagen found itself shunned by its potential German customers.

Facing the brink of financial failure, Qiagen turned its attention to the booming U.S. market for biotechnology, which was quickly capturing the lead in what many began to see as the gold rush for the 21st century. Rather than compete in the end-products sphere, such as in drug development and gene therapies, which required years of costly research with no guarantee of success, Qiagen remained focused on providing what it liked to call "the picks and shovels" of the new gold rush. As Peer Schatz, who was named the company's CFO in 1993, told the *Financial Times*: "You know in the gold rush it was the Levi Strausses and Wells Fargoes that made the money, not the gold diggers. We think genomics will equal significant growth for Qiagen without having to compete with our customers."

KEY DATES

1984: Metin Colpan and partners found Qiagen in Düsseldorf, Germany.
1986: Qiagen introduces the first ready-to-use plasmid kit.
1996: Holding company Qiagen N.V. is incorporated in the Netherlands; initial public offering of stock is completed on the NASDAQ.
1997: Company stock is listed on the Frankfurt exchange.
1999: Qiagen and Becton, Dickinson and Company launch the joint venture PreAnalytiX.
2001: Qiagen launches PAXgene.
2007: Company merges with Digene to become the market and technology leader in molecular diagnostics.
2009: Sales exceed $1 billion for the first time.

GATHERING STRENGTH IN THE NINETIES

Qiagen was increasingly finding customers for its revolutionary technique. The company also worked closely with its customers (it was later to claim that its customers represented all of the researchers active in the field throughout the world), a strategy that bore fruit especially in enabling the company to spot new trends in biotechnology research. A contract in 1991 for a large-scale order of DNA led the company to become one of the earliest entrants in developing products for gene therapy applications, a biotechnology segment that was to become one of the fastest growing by the end of the decade. By the end of that year, the company was profitable, while still posting less than $10 million in total sales.

The arrival of Schatz as CFO in 1993 helped the company put an end to its shaky financial condition. The Austrian-born and U.S.-educated Schatz helped Colpan redefine the company's strategy, narrowing its sights on the market for genetics research and also thereby more narrowly deploying its resources. The new business plan helped the company focus not only its research and development resources but also its sales and marketing budget. At the same time, the company continued to expand its array of products as it adapted its patented technology to the needs of the various branches of biotechnology research.

In 1995 Qiagen launched a new line of so-called BioRobot workstations. The BioRobot was intended to automate a number of the steps in the DNA purification process, freeing up researchers' time. Although the company's automated equipment remained a sideline to its main consumable products business, Qiagen continued to develop new automated equipment across a wide range of laboratory processes.

By 1996 Qiagen had turned the corner, posting revenues of more than $50 million per year and profits of more than $5 million. The company had successfully positioned itself as the world leader in its product niche, raising its kits (which cost customers between $50 and $2,500 each, while returning margins of up to 70 percent to Qiagen) to an industry standard. As Schatz described the company product to *Business Week* in 2000: "We're the Post-Its of the biotech industry."

GOING PUBLIC: 1996

While keeping its operational headquarters in Germany, the company in 1996 was reorganized under a holding company, Qiagen N.V., based in Venlo, Netherlands. That same year, Qiagen went public and was listed on the NASDAQ, an offering that allowed two of the original four partners to cash out. Qiagen was to see its stock soar, boasting one of the highest price-to-earnings ratios (reaching 295 by the end of the decade) in its market, and valuing the company at some $6 billion. The NASDAQ offering was followed by a secondary offering on the Frankfurt Stock Exchange's Neuer Markt in 1997.

The public offerings gave Qiagen the financing to begin expanding its operations into new biotechnology areas. One of the company's first moves was to expand its automated process capacity with the acquisition of Rosys AG, based in Switzerland, which the company combined into a new subsidiary, Qiagen Instruments AG. That subsidiary produced a new successor to the original BioRobot in 1999 and continued to develop automated instruments for the biomedical research laboratory. In 1998 Qiagen launched a new subsidiary in Japan, Qiagen K.K., held at 60 percent.

Recognizing the growing maturation of its core plasmid market, Qiagen began taking steps to gain expertise in other fast-growing and complementary biotechnology areas. At the end of 1999, the company acquired a new product area when it bought Seattle-based Rapigene, Inc., bringing Qiagen that company's Masscode screening technology for single nucleotide polymorphisms (SNPs). SNPs are the human DNA sequence variations that can affect an individual's propensity for certain diseases and for particular reactions to pathogens, chemicals, drugs, and vaccines. The addition of Rapigene, subsequently renamed Qiagen Genomics, Inc., gave the company a strong entry into the booming genomics market.

Qiagen also was forming a number of strategic partnerships and alliances, joining with other companies such as Evotec, Zeptosens, and Affymetrix. In 1999 the company joined with Becton, Dickinson and Company to create the joint venture partnership PreAnalytiX in order to create standardized systems for nucleic acid collecting, stabilizing, and cleansing.

WORLD LEADER IN THE BIOTECH BOOM OF THE 21ST CENTURY

The biotechnology sector was sure to revolutionize much of medical care and the pharmaceutical industry in the 21st century, and Qiagen was well-positioned to partake in the ongoing biotech boom. In 2001 PreAnalytiX launched PAXgene, a revolutionary technology that consolidated and integrated the key steps of whole-blood collection, nucleic acid stabilization, and RNA purification, enabling a streamlined sequence from blood collection to pure DNA. In 2004 QIAamp became the world's first stand-alone product for sample preparation to receive the coveted CE mark, certifying that the product had met all consumer safety, health, and environmental requirements of the European Union. The year 2005 saw the development of several products to aid disease detection such as the *artus* Influenza Kit for the rapid detection of all known variants of the avian flu virus H5N1, which reduced the time of detection to a mere 75 minutes. A portfolio for the surveillance of the swine flu, including a test for the detection of the influenza A/H1N1 virus, was added in 2009.

In 2006 Qiagen acquired multiplexing assay technology, which enables the testing for several pathogens in one single run. A year later, the firm introduced QIAcube, a platform fully automating the processing of Qiagen consumable products. Pyrosequencing, which refined high-resolution detection and quantification down to a single base-pair level and thus could identify DNA sequences and their pathological mutations, was introduced in 2008. In 2010 Qiagen completed the European certification for its careHPV test, a diagnostic test important in cancer research.

Many of these technological developments were made possible through a series of acquisitions completed during the first decade of the 21st century. This buying spree began in 2000 with the acquisition of California-based Operon Technologies, Inc., a maker of synthetic DNA and other synthetic genetic materials used for pharmaceuticals testing.

SHIFT TOWARD MOLECULAR DIAGNOSTICS

When in 2004 Colpan moved to Qiagen's supervisory board, making room for Schatz to become CEO in his stead, the company's strategy included a shift toward molecular diagnostics, a field with tremendous potential for growth and one promising to enhance the quality of health care while also making it more cost efficient. In 2007 Qiagen merged with the U.S.-based Digene Corporation, thus creating the new market leader in molecular diagnostics. In 2009 Qiagen acquired a molecular diagnostics distribution business in China, adding to its presence on the Asian continent. That same year, Qiagen also acquired Explera s.r.l., SABiosciences Corporation, and DxS Ltd. By the time ESE GmbH was added in early 2010, molecular diagnostics made up almost 50 percent of Qiagen's revenue.

With more than $1 billion in sales, organic growth of 13 percent, and an adjusted net profit of 22 percent, Qiagen enjoyed the most successful year in its history in 2009, a clear testament to the success of the strategic move toward molecular diagnostics. Consequently, that same year Qiagen was included in the NASDAQ 100 Index.

With a comprehensive portfolio of more than 500 consumable products and automated solutions for sample collection, Qiagen continued to offer technologies that could be applied to cancer research, prevention, and eradication; diagnostics; genetic fingerprinting; life science research; and pharmaceutical research. Such applications, in turn, could, for example, help identify suspects, clarify an individual's lineage, or help detect pandemic threats ranging from animal diseases to bioterrorism. In addition, Qiagen, always the biotech pioneer, was actively pursuing the field of personalized medicine, which had the potential to provide pharmaceutical health-care solutions based on a patient's particular genetic makeup.

M. L. Cohen
Updated, Helga Schier

PRINCIPAL SUBSIDIARIES

Qiagen Deutschland Holding GmbH (Germany); Qiagen GmbH (Germany); Qiagen Hamburg GmbH (Germany); Qiagen, Inc. (Canada); Qiagen, Inc. (USA); Qiagen Instruments AG (Switzerland); Qiagen Ltd. (UK); Qiagen North American Holding Inc. (USA); Qiagen S.A. (France); Qiagen Sciences, Inc. (USA); Qiagen Gaithersburg, Inc. (USA); Qiagen SpA (Italy); eGene, Inc. (USA).

PRINCIPAL COMPETITORS

Beckman Coulter; Life Technologies Corporations; Roche Diagnostics Corporation; Sigma-Aldrich Corporation.

FURTHER READING

Bishop, Tricia. "Digene Sold to Dutch Biotech." *Baltimore Sun*, June 4, 2007.

Bowley, Graham. "Qiagen: A Success Worth Replicating." *Financial Times*, September 3, 1998.

Firn, David. "Qiagen in Deal to Buy Operon." *Financial Times*, June 13, 2000.

Frost & Sullivan Healthcare Practice. "Movers and Shakers Interview: Peer Schatz," June 23, 2004. Accessed July 26, 2010. http://www.frost.com/prod/servlet/market-insight-top.pag?docid=20584675.

Karnitschnig, Matt. "The 'Post-Its' of the Biotech Industry." *Business Week International*, July 17, 2000, 26.

Krause, Carey. "Executive Insights: Qiagen." *Chemical Market Reporter*, October 29, 2001, 22.

Moukheiber, Zina. "Gold Digger." *Forbes*, November 1, 1999, 408.

"Qiagen and Abbott Enter into Agreement on Molecular Tests for HIV, HCV and HPV." *Women's Health Weekly*, October 28, 2010, 376.

"Qiagen Buys Rapigene; Allies with Zeptosens." *Chemical Market Reporter*, January 17, 2000, 5.

Red Robin Gourmet Burgers, Inc.

6312 South Fiddler's Green Circle, Suite 200N
Greenwood Village, Colorado 80111
U.S.A.
Telephone: (303) 846-6000
Fax: (303) 846-6048
Web site: http://www.redrobin.com

Public Company
Founded: 1940s as Sam's Tavern
Incorporated: 1969 as Red Robin Enterprises, Inc.
Employees: 24,038
Sales: $841.05 million (2009)
Stock Exchanges: NASDAQ Global Market
Ticker Symbol: RRGB
NAICS: 533110 Franchise Agreements, Leasing, Selling or Licensing, without Providing Other Services; 722110 Full-Service Restaurants

■ ■ ■

Red Robin Gourmet Burgers, Inc., is a casual dining restaurant chain with a menu that features more than two dozen gourmet burgers and chicken sandwiches with toppings such as grilled pineapple, guacamole, barbecue sauce, and sautéed mushrooms. Red Robin's burgers include beef, turkey, chicken, fish, and vegetarian alternatives, all free of preservatives and artificial ingredients. Offerings also include Bottomless Steak Fries (i.e., free refills) and a distinctive line of Bottomless Beverages. Red Robin emphasizes a fun, relaxed, family-friendly environment and encourages diners to customize their meals. Another distinctive feature of the environment at Red Robin is Unbridled Acts: random acts of kindness that employees perform for customers and each other.

The chain evolved from a single restaurant that started as a tavern near the University of Washington during the 1940s. As of January 2010, Red Robin operated 430 restaurants across the United States and Canada, including both corporate-owned locations and restaurants operating under franchise agreements.

ORIGINS

Red Robin originated as Sam's Tavern near the University of Washington during the 1940s. The owner, who sang in a barber shop quartet, loved the song "When the Red, Red Robin Comes Bob, Bob, Bobbin Along," so much so that he changed the name of the tavern to Sam's Red Robin. In 1969 the owner Gerald Kingen converted the tavern into the first Red Robin restaurant that specialized in gourmet hamburgers.

The 1,200-square-foot establishment proved popular, encouraging Kingen to develop a chain of restaurants as Red Robin Enterprises, Inc. From the start, franchising agreements drove the chain's expansion. One franchisee was Mike Snyder, a regular Red Robin customer and a native of Yakima, Washington. Snyder opened his first Red Robin restaurant there in 1979 and thereafter opened others, developing his own chain under the control of his company, the Snyder Group Company.

By 1985 the entire Red Robin chain consisted of 22 restaurants, now known as Red Robin International,

COMPANY PERSPECTIVES

Red Robin Gourmet Burgers, Inc., was founded on four core values: Honor, Integrity, Continually Seeking Knowledge and Having Fun. These core values are the foundation for every Red Robin decision from creating its mouthwatering gourmet burgers to hiring energetic Team Members and even to deciding new restaurant locations. They also are the foundation for how the company treats its Team Members, Guests and communities. Red Robin's core values can be found embroidered on the sleeve of every Team Member's uniform, which serves as a constant reminder of what makes the company unique and special.

Inc., to reflect the company's expansion into Canada. In that year Kingen sold the seven company-owned restaurants to the restaurant operator Skylark Co. Ltd., which also acquired oversight of Red Robin's 15 franchised locations. Skylark initiated a decade of rapid growth that also included the introduction of one of its distinctive menu attractions: Bottomless Steak Fries. Performance slumped, however, generating concerns that the chain was losing its focus. The problems were acute at company-owned restaurants, which by 1995 were generating sales of nearly one-quarter below the total average of the chain's franchised units. The contrast was especially strong with the performance of the 14 profitable restaurants that were controlled by the Snyder Group Company.

Skylark turned to Snyder for help. In April 1996 the company appointed him president and chief operating officer (COO). That same year Red Robin cut its ties with Skylark and moved its headquarters from Irvine, California, to Greenwood Village, Colorado. The following year Red Robin's board of directors made Snyder chief executive officer (CEO) and, shortly thereafter, chairman of the board.

GROWTH UNDER SNYDER: 1996–2002

Already known as an aggressive operator, Snyder instituted a new regime at Red Robin. Paying close attention to costs and efficiency, he improved the profitability of the chain store by store. Snyder rallied the workforce by instituting a new system of financial rewards for performance. For example, store managers were given bonuses for reaching sales objectives. A new upper-level management team was recruited and the restaurants' menu was expanded. As part of the program to streamline the operation of restaurants, 10 units were deemed underperformers and closed. In 1995, the year before Snyder assumed control, Red Robin's company-owned restaurants generated an average of $2.1 million in annual sales, with an average profit margin of 13 percent per store. Five years later company-owned restaurants were generating an average of $3 million in annual sales and a 19.2 percent profit margin per store.

As profitability improved, the company management wanted to return Red Robin to growth mode. Several structural changes facilitated this. In 2000 the company completed a recapitalization and acquired the 14-unit Snyder Group Company, giving the CEO a significant equity interest in Red Robin. Quad-C, a private equity firm, invested $25 million in Red Robin, becoming its largest stockholder. In January 2001 Red Robin Gourmet Burgers, Inc., was formed. The new entity acquired all the operation's outstanding capital stock, although its business was operated primarily through Red Robin International, Inc.

In April 2002 the company made its initial public offering (IPO) of stock. The company management hoped to raise $60 million, which would be used for expansion and debt reduction. By this point Red Robin had nearly 200 restaurants in the chain, and the company management announced long-term plans to boost this to 850. Given the scale of its ambitions (it cost $1.7 million to build a new Red Robin unit), some analysts were concerned whether a chain relying on gourmet burgers could reach this goal while maintaining its ability to increase profits. Executives deemed their goals justified given the projected growth of Red Robin's core demographic: teens and preteens.

In July Red Robin reported that the IPO raised $45 million and that it sold 4 million shares at $12 per share. Even though the IPO failed to raise the projected $60 million, it was still deemed a success. That same month the company management stuck to its plans by entering into a three-year, $40 million revolving credit agreement. Together, proceeds from the IPO and the credit line gave the company the financial fuel to drive its expansion.

EXPANSION RESUMES: 2002–05

As Red Robin entered its first decade as a publicly traded company, it concentrated on expanding in the Southwest and Midwest and on the East Coast. During the year following its IPO Red Robin made major strides in these directions. In July 2002 it opened two

KEY DATES

1940s: Sam's Tavern is established near the University of Washington in Seattle.
1969: Gerald Kingen converts Sam's Tavern to the first Red Robin restaurant.
1979: Mike Snyder, a Red Robin franchisee, opens his first restaurant.
1985: Gerald Kingen sells his stake in the company to Skylark Co. Ltd.
1996: Mike Snyder is appointed company president and chief operating officer; Red Robin cuts ties with Skylark.
2002: Red Robin completes its initial public offering of stock; its long-term expansion plan is initiated.
2005: Mike Snyder resigns and Dennis Mullen is named chief executive officer (CEO).
2006: The annual promotion "Next Gourmet Burger Kids Contest" is inaugurated.
2009: The Clinton Group, Inc., and Spotlight Advisors, LCC, acquire over 7 percent of company stock.
2010: Stephen E. Carley becomes the new CEO.

new restaurants, one in Fenton, Missouri, and another in Toledo, Ohio, increasing its presence in the Midwest to 27 restaurants. In September it bolstered its presence in the Southwest by opening three company-owned restaurants in Arizona, giving it a total of eight corporate and franchise locations in the state. In October Red Robin added a new franchise partner, Centex Red Bird LLC, which signed on to open seven restaurants in San Antonio and Austin, Texas, by 2007. Another new franchisee, PB&J, was added in December, which agreed to open seven restaurants in Kansas by 2007.

Expansion continued in 2003. The company opened two new restaurants in Omaha, its first in Nebraska, and another in Columbia, Maryland, its fifth unit in that state. In March Red Robin signed another franchise partner, Mandes Restaurant Group, LLC, which agreed to open eight new restaurants in the greater Dallas, Texas, area by 2008. Looking for a franchise partner on the East Coast, Red Robin signed a deal the following year with the Connecticut-based Swan Concepts, Inc., which agreed to build five restaurants in five years in the mid-Hudson and Upstate regions of New York state.

Meanwhile, Red Robin was working to make certain that it could handle the increasing scale of operations. In May 2003 it hired a director of food safety and quality assurance. To better meet Wall Street's demand for quarterly forecasts, it implemented a new analytic software package from Cognos to perform forecasting, budgeting, and ad hoc what-if scenarios. In May 2005 Red Robin signed a deal to serve Coca-Cola products at all of its restaurants, replacing a previous deal with PepsiCo Inc. By this time the company had hired its first executive chef and was expanding its burger menu, adding a turkey club burger and a pot roast burger in February 2005.

TURBULENT TIMES: 2005

Expansion appeared to be paying off. Red Robin posted a 59.6 percent return during the third quarter of 2004, prompting Snyder to tell David Milstead in the *Rocky Mountain News* on October 1, 2004, "I feel like we've just started. I can see and touch and feel 1,000 units." He attributed Red Robin's success to "the mutual trust and respect between our restaurants and the communities they serve."

Less than a year later, however, both Snyder and the longtime chief financial officer (CFO) Jim McCloskey had left the company and Red Robin was struggling to restore its luster amid concerns about corporate controls and practices. The first sign of trouble surfaced on November 16, 2004, when David Milstead reported in the *Rocky Mountain News* that the company's board had waived its code of ethics for Snyder and Robert J. Merullo, the senior vice president of operations. Snyder and Merullo together owned more than one-third of Mach Robin LLC, a Red Robin franchisee that operated 32 Red Robin restaurants in Idaho, Illinois, Nevada, New Mexico, and Canada. When Mach Robin signed an area development agreement for Boise, Idaho, the board waived a portion of the code of ethics that stated, "You may not take advantage of a corporate opportunity yourself or give it to another person or firm."

A year later Red Robin had to delay filing a 10-K statement for fiscal year 2005 after the company changed how it accounted for leases. The delay nearly resulted in the company being delisted from the NASDAQ. In June 2005 the company announced that McCloskey was stepping down as CFO. McCloskey had recently made remarks at an investor conference, calling the company's values "Christian" and saying it did not hire employees with an "urban" image. Company officials said the remarks had nothing to do with McCloskey's replacement.

Then Reuters reported on August 11, 2005, that Snyder had retired after an internal investigation "identified various expenses by Mr. Snyder that were inconsistent with the company policies or lacked sufficient documentation." Specifically, the probe targeted "use of chartered aircraft and travel and entertainment expenses." According to Reuters, the company said in a statement that it had notified the U.S. Securities and Exchange Commission (SEC) of the investigation and that it would record an after-tax charge of some $1.8 million "for stock options that were accelerated and exercised in 2002," an event also connected to Snyder's departure.

Red Robin's shares tumbled after this announcement, and the company soon faced a class action shareholder lawsuit alleging it had issued materially false and misleading statements about its business and prospects. Snyder repaid $1.3 million for the questionable travel and entertainment expenses dating back to 2001, but the SEC soon announced it was stepping in with its own investigation. That probe continued until June 2007, when the SEC charged Snyder with misrepresentation of personal travel expenses as business expenses. Snyder settled the case, agreeing to pay a $250,000 civil penalty and to be barred from serving as an officer or director of a public company.

Meanwhile, the Red Robin board quickly filled the leadership gap. It named Dennis Mullen, a restaurant industry veteran who had served on the board since 2002, as chairman and CEO, and promoted Eric Houseman, who had been the vice president of restaurant operations, to president and COO.

ECONOMIC CHALLENGES AND LEADERSHIP CHANGE: 2006–09

The new executive team took charge at a difficult time. In January 2006 Red Robin slashed its profit forecast for 2005 and missed its fourth-quarter earnings estimate by 20 percent due to lower same-store sales and underperformance by its newer restaurants. However, the company continued with its long-range expansion plan and inaugurated a drive to convert more of the chain into company-owned locations. In March 2006 it signed a deal to acquire 13 franchise restaurants in Washington state for $42 million plus $1.4 million in assumed debt. The following January it agreed to purchase 17 more in California, and in 2008 it bought eight in New Jersey and 11 in Wisconsin and Minnesota. That same year the company also completed a $50 million stock repurchase program. By August 2008 the chain included over 400 locations.

The company was also developing new promotions. In 2006 it held the "Next Gourmet Burger Kids Contest," in which children aged 10 years and younger were asked to create their own original burgers. More than 16,000 entries were submitted during the contest. The winning burger was offered in every Red Robin restaurant during the summer while more than 50 other burgers were featured in a cookbook that was sold to benefit the National Center for Missing and Exploited Children. Given the positive response to the contest, the company decided to make it an annual event.

During this period revenues were on a rollercoaster, veering higher in 2006 and then heading lower in 2007 amid broader economic troubles in the restaurant industry. In part, the decrease in revenues was attributed to higher gas prices, which prompted diners to cook more at home. However, Red Robin was also experiencing investor unrest. Analysts questioned the company's investment in purchasing franchise-controlled restaurants. They also criticized both the site location of the units and the stock buyback.

In May 2008 Institutional Shareholder Services Inc. recommended that investors vote against an equity incentive plan that was proposed by the company management. In spite of this recommendation, the proposal was accepted. Regardless, analysts and investors were again concerned in January 2009, when Red Robin reduced the number of new restaurants it planned to open during the year and announced that it was cutting its 2009 marketing budget and canceling plans to advertise on national cable television.

That same month the company beat Wall Street's profit projections, which gave its shares a boost. Red Robin felt it could ride out the economic downturn that began in late 2007 and resist the encroachments of the fast-food chains by playing up its profile as a good value for the money. "We're trying to make sure they know about our value proposition," Susan Lintonsmith, the chief marketing officer, told the *Wall Street Journal*'s Paul Ziobro on February 25, 2009. "People are still looking for the experience and the quality of the food when they go out."

NEW ADVERTISING CAMPAIGN AND MANAGEMENT: 2009–10

In June 2009 Red Robin decided to resume advertising on national cable television after an eight-month hiatus. It also released details of its marketing and development plan for fiscal year 2010, which included more television buys to support a spring 2010 limited-time-only menu promotion. The advertising campaign consisted of integrated television, radio, and online ads and was scheduled to run for four of the eight weeks of the product promotion at a cost of approximately $6.7 million. "The campaign is aimed at keeping current guests engaged in the brand and driving new and prospective guests into the restaurant to experience first-hand our fun atmosphere and craveable gourmet burgers," Jennifer Rivas, the director of national marketing, told Dianna Dilworth in *DMNews* on February 19, 2010. In June 2010 Red Robin announced that the campaign was being extended through the summer.

Investors were pressing for a change of leadership, however. The investment firms Clinton Group, Inc., and Spotlight Advisors, LCC, together had acquired 7.7 percent of Red Robin stock by the end of 2009. In March 2010 the company reshuffled its board and concluded a standstill agreement with the firms under which they agreed not to take certain actions until December 31. Shortly thereafter, pursuant to the agreement, Red Robin formed a committee to replace Mullen as CEO. The company had already split the CEO's and chairman's roles when it installed Pattye Moore, a board member, as chair.

These changes sparked interest from other institutional investors. In March Scopus Asset Management disclosed that it had boosted its Red Robin holdings to 6 percent of stock. In July the restaurant investor Biglari Holdings Inc. also announced that it had acquired a same-sized stake. Red Robin's shares fell in May when the company cut its full-year profit outlook. Regardless, the company declared that its advertising campaign was a success and announced that it would continue to hold prices on its menu steady, as it had for the previous two years.

The search for a new CEO ended in August, when the company selected Stephen E. Carley, a veteran of the restaurant, food-service, and consumer products industries. The following month the company announced that it was again extending its integrated marketing campaign through the fall of 2010.

Jeffrey L. Covell
Updated, Eric Laursen

PRINCIPAL SUBSIDIARIES

Red Robin International, Inc.

PRINCIPAL COMPETITORS

Applebee's Services, Inc.; Brinker International, Inc.; California Pizza Kitchen, Inc.; Carlson Restaurants Worldwide, Inc., TGI Friday's Inc.

FURTHER READING

Berta, Dina. "Bob Merullo: A Weil-Done Menu and Beefed-Up Operations Send Sales Soaring at Red Robin." *Nation's Restaurant News*, January 27, 2003, 138.

Gerst, Virginia. "Burger Boom: The Reinvention of America's National Sandwich Continues Unabated." *Restaurants & Institutions*, September 1, 2004.

Milstead, David. "Red Robin Cuts the Mustard." *Rocky Mountain News*, October 1, 2004, 4B.

"Red Robin Announces Stephen E. Carley Will Be Appointed Chief Executive Officer." *Business Wire*, August 12, 2010.

"Red Robin CEO Ousted on Internal Probe." Associated Press, August 11, 2005.

"Red Robin Getting More Gourmet Investors." *Dow Jones News Service*, March 25, 2010.

"Red Robin Raises $48M in IPO, Bucks Stock Slide." *Nation's Restaurant News*, July 29, 2002, 6.

"SEC Opens Probe of Ex-CEO of Red Robin." *Rocky Mountain News*, February 3, 2006, 2B.

Ziobro, Paul. "Fast-Food Chains Go after Sit-Down Customers." *Wall Street Journal*, February 25, 2009.

Reyes Holdings L.L.C.

9500 West Bryn Mawr Avenue
Rosemont, Illinois 60018
U.S.A.
Telephone: (847) 227-6550
Fax: (847) 227-6550
Web site: http://www.reyesholdings.com

Private Company
Founded: 1976
Employees: 10,300
Sales: $12 billion (2010)
NAICS: 424410 General Line Grocery Merchant Wholesalers; 424810 Beer and Ale Merchant Wholesalers

■ ■ ■

Reyes Holdings L.L.C. is a leading wholesale food and beverage distributor with warehouses in the United States, Canada, Ireland, and Latin America. Through Reyes Beverage Group it distributes beer to more than 26,000 U.S. accounts, making it the largest beer distributor in the United States. Its Martin-Brower Company provides food, beverages, and other products to almost 10,000 McDonald's restaurants. Reyes's Reinhart FoodService supplies more than 40,000 customers in schools, hospitals, military bases, and sporting facilities throughout the United States. According to *Forbes*, it is the 25th-largest privately held company in the United States.

BUSINESS BEGINNINGS

In 1976 Joseph Reyes and his son J. Christopher "Chris" Reyes bought Dixie Systems, a small dirt-floor Schlitz beer distributor in South Carolina, for $740,000. The elder Reyes, trained as an engineer, designed radar programs for the U.S. Navy and coordinated development programs with the National Aeronautics and Space Administration. With Chris, a recent graduate from the state university in Maryland, he purchased what he described in 2005 as "a low-tech, high-profitability cash-and-carry" business, as reported by Steven R. Strahler in *Crain's Chicago Business* on May 23, 2005. Reyes added, "We had the instinctive (nature of) peddlers—not just sit on your ass but maneuver, because things change all the time."

This perspective resulted in the company growing through a long series of strategic acquisitions. In less than a year, Joseph's son Jude transferred to a university in South Carolina and joined his older brother. Shortly thereafter the family purchased Savannah Beverage, a small distribution outlet in Georgia.

By 1979, with Joseph still providing backing and support, the Reyeses moved into the Chicago market after the company persuaded the Miller Brewing Company to allow them to take over Campbell Distributing in Illinois, a floundering Miller distributorship. When the Reyeses formed Chicago Beverage Systems, Inc., Miller had less than 10 percent of the Chicago market. The Reyeses were determined to improve on that position.

COMPANY PERSPECTIVES

What's casual about business?

EARLY ACQUISITIONS

Joseph Reyes (pronounced "Rays" in an early Anglicization of the family's Hispanic name) with his sons Chris and Jude developed the Chicago business through their ability to inspire a team spirit in their organization and a willingness to incorporate the newest technology to improve service to their clients. They also welcomed more Reyes brothers into the company management.

David "Duke" Reyes soon joined Reyes Holdings. The company then acquired Premium Distributors of Virginia while divesting its original distributorships, Dixie Systems and Savannah Beverage. In 1989 Reyes extended its operations to the West Coast with the purchase of Harbor Distributing in Long Beach, California. Joseph became the company's chairman emeritus in 1990.

From 1993 to 1995, with David as the California-based CEO of the beer business, and Chris and Jude as the Chicago-based company cochairmen, the Reyes organization bought five additional southern California distributorships. In 1996 Reyes extended its East Coast operations with the purchase of Premium Distributors of Washington, D.C. James and Tom, two younger Reyes brothers, also joined the company.

DIVERSIFICATION AND DISTINCTION

In 1998 Reyes branched out from beer distribution and purchased the Martin-Brower Company for $200 million. Martin-Brower, which had begun in 1934 as the Brower Paper Company and later merged with the Martin Paper Company, manufactured and supplied paper products to a variety of customers. In 1956 Martin-Brower was selected to supply paper products to the first McDonald's restaurant, in Des Plaines, Illinois.

In 1972, when McDonald's initiated a program using a single distribution network to provide all the dry goods, frozen foods, and paper products for its restaurants, Martin-Brower was selected to supply the Baltimore, Maryland, market. Soon the company also secured McDonald's Canadian market. In 1987 Martin-Brower established MBX Logistics as a dedicated provider of transportation logistics management services supporting Martin-Brower and McDonald's.

With its new division, Reyes used its beverage-distribution savvy to supply a new range of products, from paper napkins to burger buns. It also entered the international market through Martin-Brower's Canadian and Latin American operations. The acquisition of MBX gave Reyes enhanced access to state-of-the-art technology and the ability to deliver time-sensitive and temperature-controlled products.

While expanding the scope of Reyes Holdings from its origins in beer distribution, the Reyeses were quietly rising to the top of Chicago's corporate and philanthropic elite. Despite their increasing prominence, the Reyeses remained reticent and private. As Christopher told *Crain's Chicago Business* (May 23, 2005), "If no one knew me, I'd be just as happy."

INCREASING ACQUISITIONS

Reyes Holdings continued its policy of growth through acquisitions by using private market financing for its new purchases. Its Virginia operations expanded by adding several new companies under Premium Distributors of Virginia and merging Northern Virginia Beverage with Premium in 2004. The company clearly held Reyes Holdings' criteria for acquisitions: a privately held business (preferably family owned) that provided distribution services, was an established and profitable company with a strong management team, and whose owners wanted to sell quickly, confidentially, and fairly.

In 2004 the company identified an organization that clearly fit those criteria when Reyes acquired Reinhart FoodService in 2005. Reinhart had been established in Wisconsin in 1972 originally as Reinhart Institutional Foods and was an expansion of D. B. Reinhart's wholesale grocery company Gateway Foods. By 1988 the company had acquired several additional food service companies in Wisconsin and Minnesota, including Thoreson Food Service, Marshall Fruit and Produce, Walters Foods, and the Dernehl-Taylor Company, and it divested itself of the Gateway Foods grocery business to specialize in institutional food service.

Reinhart, like Reyes, continued growing through a series of acquisitions and added Jeanette Foodservice, Midwest Foodservice Distributors, Sugar Incentives, and Weis Foodservice as well as the food service divisions of several organizations that supplied major chain restaurants. By 2005, when Reyes Holdings acquired the company, Reinhart had more than $2 billion in revenue and 12 distribution centers from Pittsburgh to Omaha. The acquisition increased Reyes employees by 50 percent.

By that time Reyes Beverage division had expanded its Chicago distributorship from the 500,000 cases of

KEY DATES

1976: The Reyes family purchases its first beer distributorship, marking the founding of Reyes Holdings.
1979: Reyes acquires Campbell Distributing, which becomes Chicago Beverage Systems.
1998: Reyes acquires Martin-Brower Company.
2005: Reyes acquires Reinhart FoodService.
2009: Reyes acquires Metroplex Holdings.

Miller beer it sold when purchased in 1979 to annual sales of nine million cases with multiple brands. Reyes Holdings sold 40 million cases of beer nationwide. After its expansion into food service, however, its beer distributorships accounted for just 15 percent of Reyes Holdings' annual revenues.

Reyes Holdings quickly extended its new Reinhart division into territories with established Reyes operations. In January 2006 Reinhart FoodService opened offices and a distribution center in Richmond, Virginia. In April the company purchased Frank J. Catanzaro Sons and Daughters in Ohio and King Provisions in Georgia, in May it bought King Provisions of Florida, in June it added Burlington FoodService in Vermont, and in July the Nebraska distribution center was expanded through the purchase of Food Services of America. The Florida center was set up to serve customers in the southeastern United States as well as international clients in Latin America, Europe, the Middle East, and the Pacific Rim.

MORE ACQUISITIONS AND EXPANSION

The Reyeses' penchant for ongoing acquisitions continued. In 2006 Reyes bought Larkin Wholesale Company, a beer distributor in Maryland. In 2007 the company purchased Gate City beverage Distributors in California as well as Dearing Beverage Company in Virginia. In 2008 Reyes acquired Mesa Distributing, the largest beverage wholesaler in San Diego, with about $200 million in annual revenue and more than 200 employees. Through Reinhart, Reyes extended its food service operations in the southeastern United States by purchasing the IJ Company, a leading regional food supplier with four distribution facilities headquartered in Tennessee.

In 2008, through Martin-Brower Company, Reyes acquired full control of its joint venture in Brazil with Bunge Alimentos. Then in 2009 Reyes purchased Metroplex Holdings. Martin-Brower, already the largest McDonald's distributor, then added more than 600 McDonald's and Chipotle stores in New York and New Jersey, as well as more than 100 McDonald's in Ireland, to its distribution network.

GROWTH

As the organization acquired more businesses, the individual units also grew. The company employed sophisticated technology, including robotics, Global Positioning Systems (GPS), and mobile tracking devices to support efficiency and reliability. MBX Logistics, once a dedicated logistics provider for Martin-Brower and McDonald's, began managing transportation logistics for a variety of companies in the food, beverage and manufacturing industries, including Coca-Cola and Lopez Foods. When Reyes purchased MBX it handled fewer than 8,000 loads annually. By 2010 MBX managed more than 68,000 loads in its clients' supply chain networks.

Reyes Beverage Group, which once controlled a single beer distributorship in South Carolina, by 2010 operated 12 warehouses in 9 different areas, from Los Angeles to Washington, D.C., and delivered more than 80 million cases of beer annually. Although it had begun with a single product, by 2010 it carried Corona, Molson-Coors, Heineken USA, Miller Brewing Company, Boston Beer, Sierra Nevada, New Belgium, Yuengling, and Diageo brands. Reyes Beverage Group managed more than 26,000 accounts each year and had become the largest beer distributor in the United States.

Martin-Brower, already McDonald's largest supplier in the United States when it was acquired by Reyes, continued to expand its service areas. By 2010 it supplied more than 8,000 McDonald's stores worldwide. Reinhart, the third-largest private food distributor in the United States, by 2010 was operating from 24 national locations.

The increasing prominence of the Reyes operations did not, however, increase the visibility of Reyes family members. Although Chris maintained his participation in civic organizations, he gradually withdrew from membership in corporate boards. He reportedly joined other Chicago corporate titans, however, in an unpublicized investment group aimed at supporting Chicago technology start-ups with venture capital.

Reyes Holdings continued to grow even during the economic downturn after 2008 and, by, 2010, was, according to *Forbes*, the 25th-largest privately held company in the United States, with reported annual sales of $12 billion. Its organizational strategy, outlined on its Web site, clearly attributed its success to the more than 60 acquisitions Reyes had made since its founding in 1976. It is also, clearly, the company's formula for its future.

Grace Murphy

PRINCIPAL DIVISIONS

Reyes Beverage Group; Martin-Brower Company; Reinhart FoodService.

PRINCIPAL COMPETITORS

Atlantic Dominion Distributors; SYSCO; Wirtz Beverage Group; Republic National Distributing Company; U.S. FoodserviceGroup; The Anderson-DuBose Company; Golden State Foods.

FURTHER READING

"#236 J. Christopher Reyes & Family—The Forbes 400 Richest Americans 2009." *Forbes*, September 30, 2009.

Allen, Mike. "Mesa Distributing Sold; Businessman Reflects on Stadium." *San Diego Business Journal*, June 2, 2008.

"Beer Here! Reyes Holdings Seeks $200M in Fixed, Floating Notes." *Private Placement Letter*, January 17, 2005.

Daniels, Steve. "Reyes Departing Allstate Board." *Crain's Chicago Business*, July 25, 2008.

Ford, George C. "Chicago Firm Buys Reinhart FoodService." *Cedar Rapids (IA) Gazette*, December 29, 2004.

Pletz, John. "Cash of the Titans: Corporate Giants Join Ferro to Back Startups, Fill City's Funding Gap." *Crain's Chicago Business*, March 15, 2010.

Segal, Robert B. "McDonald's Primary Distributors Are Sold." *AllBusiness.com*, July 1, 1998. Accessed October 25, 2010. http://www.allbusiness.com/services/business-services-mailing-reproduction/4438651-1.html.

Strahler, Steven R. "Chris Reyes Revealed." *Crain's Chicago Business*, May 23, 2005.

Reynolds Group Holdings Ltd.

4 Henderson Place
Onehunga, Auckland 1061
New Zealand
Telephone: (+64 9) 622-3500
Fax: (+64 9) 366-6263
Web site: http://www.reynoldsgroupholdings.com

Wholly Owned Subsidiary of Rank Group Ltd.
Founded: 1919 as United States Foil Company
Incorporated: 1928
Employees: 29,450
Sales: $9.48 billion (2009)
NAICS: 322221 Coated and Laminated Packaging Paper and Plastics Film Manufacturing; 322223 Plastics, Foil, and Coated Paper Bag Manufacturing

■ ■ ■

When Rank Group Ltd., the investment vehicle of New Zealand billionaire Graeme Hart, created Reynolds Group Holdings Ltd. in October 2009, it welded a rapid-fire series of acquisitions into one of the largest makers of consumer food and beverage packaging and closure products in the world. As of June 2010, the company consisted of four principal units: Closure Systems International, Evergreen, Reynolds Packaging Group, and SIG. In August 2010 Reynolds signed a deal to acquire Pactiv, maker of Hefty garbage bags and Slide-Rite zip-lock seals, for $6 billion in cash and debt.

Reynolds has its roots in Reynolds Metals Company, which in turn evolved out of the United States Foil Company and which introduced one of the signature U.S. consumer brands, Reynolds Wrap, in 1947. Reynolds is a leader in production and conversion of flexible packaging, including laminated and multilayered substrates and plastic shrink film along with aluminum foil. Along with its branded products, it produces a range of products used by leading consumer manufacturers, from Coca-Cola Bottlers to packaged food producers.

Reynolds possesses a virtual monopoly of the foil market in the United States and controls 19 percent of the global market for packaging with aseptic closures. Its specialized products include printed and laminated lightweight foils used in food and consumer product packaging, laminated and printed paper stock for health care–related products such as alcohol towelettes, tablets, and transdermal patches, and foil and film coverings for food and pharmaceutical containers.

THE FIRST 25 YEARS

The Reynolds name has always been at least partially synonymous with aluminum foil. The company was founded by R. S. Reynolds, a former law student and nephew of R. J. Reynolds, one of the first U.S. tobacco barons. After several years working for his uncle, R. S. Reynolds borrowed $100,000 and in 1919 purchased a small, one-story building in Louisville, Kentucky, and founded the United States Foil Company (U.S. Foil). The increased demand for foil was the result of the ever-rising public appetite for cigarettes, the demand for which created constant shortages of the foil used for packaging.

KEY DATES

1919: United States Foil Company is founded.
1928: Reynolds Metals Company incorporates.
1938: Founder R. S. Reynolds moves the company headquarters from New York City to Richmond, Virginia.
1947: Reynolds Wrap is introduced.
1986: Gold is discovered at Reynolds's bauxite properties in Australia.
2000: Reynolds merges with Alcoa Inc. in a stock-swap valued at about $4.34 billion.
2005: Alcoa reorganizes its Packaging and Consumer Group, including Reynolds consumer and food packaging products and Closure Systems International.
2008: Alcoa sells the Packaging and Consumer Group to Rank Group Ltd. for $2.7 billion.
2009: Rank reorganizes its global beverage packaging holdings as Reynolds Group Holdings Ltd.
2010: Reynolds Group Holdings Ltd. purchases Pactiv Corporation for $6 billion.

U.S. Foil's entrance into the market generated a price war with other foil manufacturers, who hoped that by cutting prices they could drive the fledgling company out of business. Their plan did not work, as Reynolds created a more efficient production process at the Louisville plant. Lower manufacturing costs allowed the company to undersell its competitors by several cents per pound, ensuring the company's share of the growing market. During the 1920s Reynolds pioneered the use of lighter weight, less-expensive aluminum foil. In 1928, after buying back stock he had sold to R. J. Reynolds to start U.S. Foil, R. S. Reynolds built the company's first aluminum foil plant and rolling mill in Louisville, and the Reynolds Metals Company was formed.

The company thrived during the Great Depression. It recorded annual sales of $13 million in 1930 and moved its corporate headquarters to New York City. In 1935 Reynolds developed a method of printing on aluminum foil employing the rotogravure process. This enabled the company to expand quickly into other aluminum foil packaging markets. The following year, Reynolds ventured outside the United States for the first time, opening a foil production plant in Havana, Cuba.

In 1938 R. S. Reynolds moved the company's headquarters south again. Taking his son Richard S. Reynolds, Jr., with him as assistant to the president, the company settled in Richmond, Virginia. Reynolds, Jr., had previously founded a stock-brokerage firm that would later become Reynolds Securities, which eventually merged with Dean Witter.

Reynolds continued to increase its production capacity. It borrowed $15 million and began construction on its first smelting facility, in Sheffield, Alabama. It also acquired a bauxite mining operation in Arkansas to help feed the smelters. Reynolds's World War II production was extensive. By the end of the war, the company had increased production capacity to more than 450 million pounds.

POSTWAR EXPANSION

The postwar demand for aluminum, chiefly for use in consumer goods and construction, was even greater. Reynolds developed aluminum siding for the booming housing market. In 1946 it leased, then purchased, six government-owned production plants, doubling its production capacity. Reynolds Wrap, the company's now well-known household aluminum foil, was introduced in 1947.

R. S. Reynolds, Jr., was named the company's new president in 1948. His three brothers (David, William G., and J. Louis) also assumed much of the responsibility for running the business, concentrating primarily on a program of rapid overseas expansion. In 1953 the company organized Reynolds International, Inc., in an effort to consolidate and further expand foreign operations. Reynolds closed the 1950s with a move to a new, modern corporate headquarters in suburban Richmond.

During the 1960s the company continued to grow and introduce new all-aluminum products for home and industry. These included the first aluminum drill pipe in 1960 and the first aluminum beverage can in 1963, both successful. An attempt to increase production capacity by 20 percent cost Reynolds an estimated $650 million in the mid-1960s. The project was plagued by cost overruns and delays, and by the time it was completed, aluminum demand had leveled off.

REORGANIZATION AND RECYCLING

Reynolds's leadership came under criticism from financial analysts, particularly for what was perceived as the Reynolds family's tight control over the company. A reorganization commenced during the late 1960s, including the creation of separate operating divisions, each responsible for its own profit performance. Control remained with the Reynolds family, however. In 1976

David P. Reynolds was its chairman, J. Louis and William G. Reynolds were board members, a cousin, A. D. Reynolds, was a vice president, and William G. Reynolds, Jr., was treasurer.

The company continued to offer new products to the marketplace. In 1970 it introduced the first all-aluminum automobile engine block. All-aluminum car bumpers came on line in 1973. The beverage can with the stay-on, pull-top tab was well received in 1975.

In 1973 a Reynolds unit pleaded guilty to charges of importing ores from Rhodesia in violation of U.S. government sanctions against the country. In 1975 the company's assets in Guyana were nationalized, and Reynolds was forced to settle for a $10 million payment for its Guyanese holdings. In 1980, 51 percent of its Jamaican assets and operations and all of its Jamaican land holdings were sold to the Jamaican government.

Reynolds had begun a major recycling effort in 1968, which expanded steadily. As of 1980 the company was recycling almost half the number of cans it produced. In 1981 it enlarged its recycling capacity with two more facilities. In 1990 Reynolds recycled 438 million pounds of consumer-generated aluminum scrap, paying out $123 million to the recycling public. By then the company was recycling more cans than it produced. In addition to environmental advantages, recycled aluminum required only 5 percent of the energy needed to produce aluminum from virgin materials.

MODERNIZATION AND A GOLD STRIKE

Like most U.S. industrial giants, Reynolds lost sales in the recession of the early 1980s. David Reynolds and William Bourke, a former Ford Motor Company vice president and now Reynolds's chairman and CEO, realized that Reynolds's upstream costs (for mining, smelting, and refining) were cutting into downstream profits on finished goods like aluminum foil and cans. Reynolds embarked on a multibillion-dollar capital improvements program that included shutting down some of the company's less profitable operations. By 1988 Reynolds had cut its employee count by one-third and reduced its production costs by almost 25 percent, reversing the drain on profits.

Gold was discovered at one of the company's bauxite properties in Australia in 1986. Reynolds's entrance into the gold market, an unexpected upsurge in aluminum prices in the late 1980s, continuing modernization of the company's production facilities, and the expansion of its consumer products division made Reynolds a solid, profitable enterprise.

Under Bourke's leadership, the company increased its focus on consumer products and gold. Using its well-established marketing, sales, and distribution organizations, it was able to add new products without increasing employment. Reynolds introduced a line of colored plastic wraps and resealable plastic bags. In May 1988 it acquired Presto Products, Inc., a $200-million-a-year producer of plastic bags for indoor and outdoor use, including freezer, sandwich, and food storage bags, along with a line of moist paper tissues and cotton swabs. In line with its commitment to recycling, Reynolds set a long-term goal of recycling more plastics each year than it produced.

Modernization of its plants continued with construction of a new 120-metric-ton-per-year facility at the company's Baie Comeau, Quebec, smelter, along with expansion and modernization of other company plants, in western Australia, Texas, and Louisiana. Reynolds invested more than $400 million in Alabama to ensure its position as a world-class producer of aluminum can stock and can-end stock. In addition, it expanded its research-and-development efforts. Reynolds created new process technologies in aluminum-lithium casting and electromagnetic casting and various techniques in automation. It also developed technology for manufacture of aluminum automobile drive shafts and radiators. In 1989 the company acquired an interest in Italy's Fata European Group, a company with strong ties to and business experience in Eastern Bloc countries. Fata, Reynolds, and a group of post-Soviet organizations began constructing a $200 million aluminum-foil plant in Siberia in the 1990s.

REORGANIZATION

In 1990 the company introduced Reynolds Microwave Wrap, a nonstick cooking paper designed to help dishes cook evenly and not spatter in microwave ovens. The company anticipated $20 million in retail sales in the product's first year. In 1992 Reynolds sold its wire and cable operations as well as its 84 percent interest in Eskimo Pie. The company also announced a 12 percent cut in employment to reduce costs. A 1993 restructuring included reducing alumina and aluminum production by 21 percent, and Reynolds sold its aluminum reclamation plant in Benton Harbor, Michigan.

Reynolds struggled to adjust to a difficult and evolving business environment in the 1990s. In 1994 it purchased the aluminum and stainless steel products distribution business of Prime Metals. The company also sold its 40 percent interest in Australia's Boddington gold mine and exited the gold business altogether the following year. However, a 1994 pact among the chief aluminum-producing nations to scale back production over the following two years helped Reynolds achieve strong sales. A decline in demand for beer beverage cans continued, however, and a can-making plant was closed in Fulton, New York, followed by the shuttering of the company's Houston facility in 1996. Meanwhile, the company modernized its plant in Torrance, California, reducing the number of manufacturing lines there from six to three. Other Reynolds plants were making cans with smaller, lighter ends that reduced the amount of metal needed by 3 percent.

Recycling reached record levels. Reynolds recycled 584 million pounds of aluminum, including more than 11 billion aluminum beverage cans, and nearly 228 million pounds of non-can aluminum scrap in 1996 alone. Furthermore, the company noted that as more aluminum was used in automobiles, appliances, building products, packaging items, foil and foil products, and other household goods, more metals would be entering the recycling stream.

FURTHER RESTRUCTURING AND MERGER

Disappointing sales in 1996, due to low aluminum prices and lower demand for some of its products, led to another restructuring. Effective April 1, 1997, the company was organized into 6 global units, down from 20, focusing on the most profitable aluminum markets around the world. The new units were packaging and consumer products, construction and distribution, transportation, metals and carbon products, bauxite and alumina, and cans. The year also saw a milestone for Reynolds Wrap Aluminum Foil, which celebrated its 50th year. In tribute, Reynolds donated $1 million to Meals on Wheels, with which the company had a five-year alliance.

Non-U.S. expansion was still part of the company's plans. In 1999 Reynolds launched a food-service packaging and consumer products subsidiary in Brazil. Called Reyco, the new company would sell products, including aluminum foil containers and institutional aluminum foil, under the Reynolds brand name.

Reynolds came under criticism in the face of a more competitive aluminum market. The company was considered to perform well in the early stages of aluminum production, transforming mined bauxite into sheets of metal, and dominated the consumer foil market. By 1997 packaging and cans generated about 35 percent of the company's revenue. Yet analysts considered the company weak in the middle stages of production: rolling metal into parts for automobiles and airplanes, for example. Reynolds was criticized in particular for not following its main competitors, Alcoa Inc. and Canada's Alcan Aluminium Ltd., which made major investments in rolling plants in the 1980s. The company, which employed about 30,000, planned more job cuts.

In August 1999, Alcoa, alarmed by an announced three-way merger of Alcan, Pechiney SA of France, and Alusuisse-Lonza Holding AG of Switzerland, launched an unsolicited tender offer for Reynolds. Within weeks Reynolds agreed to a stock-swap merger with Alcoa valued at about $4.34 billion, creating the largest aluminum company in the world, with $21 billion in annual sales and 126,700 employees. When the deal closed the following May, Alcoa anticipated that the vast majority of Reynolds's 19,000 employees would keep their jobs.

THE ALCOA ERA

Alcoa quickly served notice that it intended to expand its new Reynolds Food Packaging unit. Three months after completing the merger, it purchased Baco Consumer Products Ltd., the United Kingdom's leading seller of household wraps, aluminum foil, and plastic bags. Alcoa intended to expand beyond aluminum and become one of the top 10 global packaging companies. In January 2004 Reynolds leased a facility in the Cedar Grove (Kentucky) Business Park for a new 527,000-square-foot distribution center. In August it announced plans to introduce Reynolds Wrap and other products into India, hoping to quickly secure a 25 percent share of the country's total aluminum foil market.

Reynolds continued to introduce new products and improvements on old ones. In 2004 it unveiled the first variation on Reynolds Wrap since 1947, called Reynolds Release. The new product had a nonstick coating on one side so that the frosting on a cake, for example, would not cling when the wrap was removed. Reynolds's concern was in part to defend the market for aluminum foil in the face of the growing popularity of takeout meals.

The following year Alcoa reorganized its Packaging and Consumer Group, creating a new research and development group and splitting its manufacturing operations into two units: Alcoa Packaging (focused on growing market segments such as medical, pharmaceutical, health care, food, electronics and film products) and Reynolds Food Packaging (focused on the needs of food service providers such as distributors, processors, agriculture, bakeries, and restaurants). Also falling under the Packaging and Consumer Group were Alcoa Consumer Products (producing private label and branded offerings such as Reynolds Wrap) and Closure Systems International (Alcoa's large and expanding global unit that produced plastic and aluminum bottle caps, plastic bottles, and packaging services and supplies).

REALIGNMENTS

Fierce competition continued in the aluminum business, however, prompting more realignments among the top players. In 2005 Alcoa began discussions with Alcan about a possible merger. The talks continued sporadically for two years, but in May 2007 Alcan executives rejected a $27.4 billion takeover offer, which they told Bill Bregar of *Plastics News* (May 28, 2007) was "inadequate in multiple respects."

Meanwhile, Alcoa disclosed it was exploring strategic alternatives to disposition of the Packaging and Consumer Group, which in 2006 had generated some $3.2 billion in revenues and $95 million in after-tax operating income, representing 10 percent of the company's total revenues and some 3 percent of after-tax income. The unit employed about 10,000 workers in 22 countries. In December 2007 it found a buyer and announced the sale of the Packaging and Consumer Group to Rank Group Ltd., the investment vehicle of New Zealand billionaire Graeme Hart, for $2.7 billion. The deal closed in the first quarter of 2008.

RANK GROUP ACQUISITIONS

Hart was in the process of rapidly shifting Rank Group's holdings from a mix of food and forestry holdings to packaging. In early 2006 Rank completed the acquisition of Carter Holt Harvey, Ltd. (CHH), Australasia's leading forest products company with market-leading positions in building supplies, pulp, paperboard, and packaging, then sold CHH's forests properties. In December, CHH agreed to buy International Paper's beverage packaging business, Evergreen Packaging, for $413 million. That same month, Rank launched a bid for Swiss milk carton maker SIG, completing the acquisition the following May for $3.2 billion. The following month, Rank purchased another forestry and paper company, North Carolina–based Blue Ridge Holding Corp., for $338 million. In September 2007 Rank put CHH's wood products business up for sale. Meanwhile, Hart was exiting the food business by selling the Bluebird snack line in Australia to PepsiCo and divesting a 20 percent stake in the Australasian food company Goodman Fielder Ltd.

The purchase of Alcoa's Packaging and Consumer Group was one of the largest deals ever by a New Zealand company. In January 2008 Rank launched a $1.6 billion one-year leveraged loan to fund the acquisition. Hart quickly set about remodeling Reynolds. The unit in September closed its aluminum foil operations in Richmond after 70 years there, shutting down 2 plants and a distribution site and eliminating about 490 local jobs. The company said that it would move operations to other U.S. sites.

REYNOLDS LAYOFFS AND FURTHER RANK GROUP ACQUISITIONS

More downsizings and realignments followed. In January 2009 Reynolds Packaging Group, as it was then known, sold the production equipment in its medical thermoformed packaging plant in Downingtown, Pennsylvania, to Brentwood Industries Inc. In March it shut down the Downingtown factory, resulting in 144 jobs lost. The same month, Reynolds licensed to Winpak Ltd. exclusive rights to the formulas it used to produce packaging materials for pharmaceutical and health care manufacturers. Another 158 layoffs were announced for the Richmond facilities in June. In November Multi-Plastics Inc., a supplier of film products to the printing and packaging industries, purchased two plastics extrusion facilities from Reynolds Packaging, in Pennsylvania and New Jersey.

Rank Group, meanwhile, made more acquisitions, molding its packaging properties, now the second-largest beverage packaging producer after Tetra Pak, into a more unified global company. Hart announced a $3.5 billion debt refinancing in March 2009 and said he was positioning himself for expansion. "I'd be better not to comment but you can be very confident I'm always watching the market for acquisitions," he told the *Australian Financial Review*, as reported in the *New Zealand Herald* on March 3, 2009. "Public or private, there's never any merit discussing in a newspaper what you're looking at buying or selling. But there's a lot going on; it's great."

THE CREATION OF REYNOLDS GROUP HOLDINGS

Hart failed in a bid to acquire the packaging assets of Alcan from Rio Tinto, which had purchased Reynolds's old rival in 2007. In October 2009, in a complicated transaction funded by new debt, cash contributed by SIG, and equity from a sister company called Beverage Packaging Holdings (Luxembourg) I, another Rank subsidiary, Beverage Packaging Holdings (Luxembourg) III, bought Reynolds Consumer Products and Closure Systems International from Rank. The deal ultimately led to creation of Reynolds Group Holdings Ltd., a holding company for all of Rank's packaging units. The entire group of properties reported $3.9 billion in revenues for 2009, down 3 percent from the previous year.

The consolidation continued in April 2010, when Rank sold Evergreen Packaging and a New Zealand paper mill owned by CHH to Reynolds, funded by $1.75 billion in new debt. Reynolds Foodservice purchased shortly thereafter. By then rumors were afloat that Hart was preparing to spin off his packaging empire in a public offering, and later, that he was considering a bid for Pactiv Corporation, manufacturer of consumer products including Hefty garbage bags and Slide-Rite zip-lock seals. A deal was struck in August for Reynolds Group Holdings to pay $6 billion for Pactiv, with $4.4 billion in cash and the remainder in debt. Those acquisitions strengthened the company's focus on consumer products.

Eric Laursen

PRINCIPAL SUBSIDIARIES

Closure Systems International; Evergreen; Pactiv; Reynolds Consumer; Reynolds Foodservice; SIG.

PRINCIPAL COMPETITORS

Anchor Packaging Inc.; Dart Container Corporation; Genpak, LLC; Handi-Foil Corp.; Rio Tinto Alcan Inc.; Solo Cup Company; Tetra Pak Group.

FURTHER READING

Bradley, Grant. "Hart Wraps up $3.5 Billion Packaging Deal." *New Zealand Herald*, December 24, 2007.

Bregar, Bill. "Alcan Rejects Bid from Alcoa." *Plastics News*, May 28, 2007.

Cienski, Jan. "Global Competition, Weak Profits Prompts Reynolds Metals to Restructure." Associated Press, June 16, 1997.

DeRosa, Angie. "Alcoa Unveils Reorganization in Packaging." *Plastics News*, November 7, 2005.

"Hart Bundles Packaging Assets, Loads Debt into RGH." *Business Wire*, April 20, 2010.

Labs, Wayne. "Fillers That Fit the Bill: Faced with Changing Consumer Demands, Processors Require Quick Turnarounds, Accurate Fills and Decreasing Energy Costs." *Food Engineering*, October 1, 2009.

Maynard, Micheline. "Wrapping a Familiar Name around a New Product." *New York Times*, May 22, 2004.

"Refinanced Hart on the Lookout for Packaging Buys." *New Zealand Herald*, March 3, 2009.

"Strategies of the Aluminium Giants." *Metal Bulletin*, January 22, 2003.

Witkowski, Wallace. "Graeme Hart: Cornering Packaging, Coming and Going." *MarketWatch*, August 17, 2010.

Roku, Inc.

12980 Saratoga Avenue, Suite D
Saratoga, California 95070
U.S.A.
Toll Free: (888) 600-7058
Fax: (408) 446-1734
Web site: http://www.roku.com

Private Company
Incorporated: 2002
Employees: 10
Sales: $60 million (2010 est.)
NAICS: 334310 Audio and Video Equipment Manufacturing

■ ■ ■

Based in Saratoga, California, Roku, Inc., is a privately held consumer electronics company that is best known for its digital video player. Originally developed for Netflix, Inc., Roku's player is a small set-top box that streams Netflix videos and content from other providers to standard definition and high-definition (HD) televisions. Even though the barebones player has no hard drive and maintains just enough memory to create a two-minute buffer of data, it offers a full range of video outputs, as well as built-in wired and wireless Internet connections. The remote is also basic but functional. The Roku player lineup has grown to three products. Besides the base model, the Roku HD, the company sells the Roku XD, which is capable of playing full HD video and offers extended-range wireless capabilities and a remote with an instant replay button. The top-of-the line Roku XD/S model adds dual-band wireless capabilities, component video and optical audio outputs, and a universal serial bus (USB) port for playing stored videos, music, and photos. In addition, Roku sells SoundBridge, a Wi-Fi tabletop unit that accesses Internet radio stations, and BrightSign, a digital sign controller for standalone or networked messaging displays.

EARLY YEARS

Roku was founded by Anthony Wood. Wood possessed both an interest in technology and an entrepreneurial spirit. As a high school student he formed his first company, which developed software programs for RadioShack Corporation's TRS-80 minicomputer. After enrolling at Texas A&M University, he turned his attention to developing video editing software for the Commodore computer. Wood was posting sales of more than $100,000 a year, but his success came at the expense of missing many classes. On the verge of being dismissed from school, he decided to abandon the business and complete his electrical engineering degree.

Wood's first venture after college was starting a software company called iBand that simplified the creation of Web sites. It also became his first major payday in 1996, when he sold the business to Macromedia, which was subsequently acquired by Adobe Systems Incorporated. His product was renamed DreamWeaver and became the industry's premiere Web design software program. He also spent some time at Macromedia, serving as vice president of Internet authoring.

COMPANY PERSPECTIVES

Roku is a leading supplier of innovative and easy to use digital media products. Our best known consumer products are the Roku digital video player and the stylish SoundBridge Internet radio line.

WOOD SELLS REPLAYTV: 2001

Wood's next big idea was to create a new way to record television shows. Rather than use a video cassette recorder, which he found cumbersome, he wondered if there was a way to record shows on a computer hard drive. In June 1997 he launched ReplayTV but soon found that he faced competition from a company called Teleworld, which eventually changed its name to TiVo Inc. The two companies both debuted their new video recorder at the 1999 Consumer Electronics Show. ReplayTV was better received and actually beat TiVo to the market by two weeks, but other factors intervened to allow TiVo to win out in the marketplace. TiVo was better financed than ReplayTV and it did not alienate the major Hollywood studios as Wood had by incorporating a feature that could completely skip commercials. Thus, Wood was tied up in litigation with the studios at a crucial time when he was vying with TiVo for consumer acceptance. In 2001 he sold ReplayTV for $125 million plus the assumption of debt. The underlying technology eventually found its way to DirecTV.

At age 36 Wood was between endeavors. During the summer of 2002 he took his family to an Oregon resort and once again found inspiration for a new product. He wanted to display pictures of his children and art on his flat-screen television and discovered that there was no way to do it. Assuming there were many other people who would want to do the same thing, he began to sketch out what kind of equipment and software would be needed, as well as a way to make money out of the idea. By the end of the summer he was convinced that a HD digital media player could form the foundation for a profitable company.

ROKU LAUNCHED: 2002

In the fall of 2002 Wood launched his sixth company, Roku, which is Japanese for "six." Because of his experience with ReplayTV, which required him to spend an inordinate amount of time raising money and placating investors, he decided to supply the seed money himself and spent about $3 million of his own money over the next year. Moreover, in the wake of the dot-com bubble bursting, most venture capital firms were not willing to offer generous terms. By eschewing outside money, Wood avoided giving away a major stake in his new business.

Roku's first product, the Roku HD 1000, was a plug-in appliance that allowed an HDTV to access digital photos, music, and movies from a personal computer. The first units began shipping in October 2003. Roku also sold art packs, which were collections of classic art work, nature photos, and other visual displays. In January 2004 Roku introduced its second product, the SoundBridge network music player. Shaped as a cylinder, it allowed music stored on a personal computer to be played through a stereo system, and like the later digital video player it offered both wired and wireless networking capabilities. The SoundBridge also supported Internet radio, making hundreds of free radio stations available to users. The product was initially priced at $449, but by the end of 2004 a lower-cost version, priced at $199, was made available.

BRIGHTSIGN INTRODUCED: 2006

In 2006 Roku ventured beyond the consumer electronics field when it used its expertise to introduce the BrightSign digital sign and kiosk controller, a product that was geared toward small businesses and corporate merchandising departments. Designed as a turn-key system, the controller could be connected to computer monitors and HDTVs to display looping videos or slide shows. Content could be developed by end users with off-the-shelf photo or video editing tools. As was the case with other Roku products, BrightSign offered a full range of connectivity options, including Ethernet and serial ports, USB speakers, and infrared remote control.

Because of his previous experience with ReplayTV and Roku, Wood was hired as a consultant by Netflix. In January 2007 Netflix introduced its Watch Now service that allowed subscribers to watch select television shows and movies on their computers, and the company was eager to make that content available on television sets. Wood was subsequently asked to join Netflix. Allowed to continue running Roku, he accepted and was named vice president of Internet television.

The idea of delivering video over the Internet was not new to Reed Hastings, the cofounder and chief executive officer of Netflix. He said as much when Netflix was launched in 1997 and the name of the company itself implied that long-term goal. Delivering digital video discs (DVDs) by mail rather than by the Internet was a matter of practicality, not design. In 2000 Hastings's engineers developed a rudimentary Internet

KEY DATES

2002: Anthony Wood founds Roku, Inc.
2003: Roku HD 1000, the company's first product, is introduced.
2004: The company introduces SoundBridge.
2007: Anthony Wood is hired by Netflix, Inc.
2008: Roku's digital video player is launched as the Netflix Player.

delivery system, but it required 16 hours to download a two-hour movie. Hastings canceled the program but soon hired a new team of engineers. In 2003 the team constructed a small computer that connected to a television, but it cost $300 and still took two hours to download a film. Not satisfied with the results, Hastings decided to pull the plug a second time.

When he was ready to try again in 2006, the landscape had changed considerably. Consumers were replacing slow dial-up connections with broadband, and the popularity of YouTube made them comfortable with the idea of streaming video rather than downloading and saving a copy. A new team of engineers developed a method of making video streaming more reliable on home networks by creating a way to adjust quality to the user's Internet speed to avoid unnecessary interruptions. Hastings made the service available to Netflix subscribers, but he was well aware that the vast majority were not interested in watching television shows and movies on their computer screens. They wanted content delivered to their television sets.

Wood and his team designed a small streaming video box. Beta testers expressed their pleasure with the device and in mid-December 2007 efforts were well under way to introduce the Netflix Player to the market when Hastings had second thoughts. Rather than have Netflix be a device manufacturer, Hastings decided to spin off the player to Wood and Roku. Netflix would, instead, seek to have its streaming video service incorporated into additional devices, such as game consoles, DVD players, televisions, and smartphones.

NETFLIX PLAYER INTRODUCED: 2008

Netflix invested in Roku, as did the venture capital firm Menlo Ventures, but Wood was on his own once again. In May 2008 Roku launched its digital video player, which for several months would be known as the Netflix Player. Even though Netflix's revised strategy created a host of potential competitors, Roku benefited from a head start, allowing it to build market share. The box was also heavily promoted by Netflix, which was eager to build its streaming video business for obvious reasons. Netflix spent a quarter of its revenues on postage. The more customers streamed videos, no matter the licensing cost, the less Netflix would have to spend on postage.

Roku's success hinged on a number of factors. The video player itself was designed to be inexpensive and small, yet it was robust and easy to use. Initially priced at $99 it was essentially an impulse purchase in consumer electronics. In the long term, however, Wood recognized that content was the key. Netflix's ability to increase the amount and quality of its streaming library was an obvious necessity, but out of Roku's control. To help its own cause, the company sought other content providers, in particular Amazon.com, which offered new content on a pay-per-view basis. The combination of Netflix, with its all-you-can-eat subscription model, and Amazon provided the Roku player with a solid foundation. Roku also upgraded the player, adding the capability of streaming HD content.

The courting of content partners continued in 2009. In August of that year Major League Baseball games became available on the Roku player, which was an important development for several reasons. It demonstrated Roku's ability to carry live content, added sports to the menu, and aligned the company with another high-profile partner. Roku also created a developer's kit and opened a channel store where in 2010 dozens of niche channels became available. In the fall of 2010 a subscription version of the highly successful Hulu online video service was added as well.

NETGEAR ALLIANCE: 2010

Having learned a difficult lesson with ReplayTV, Wood made sure that the Roku player was built below cost to ensure a profit. Sales grew at a steady pace, increasing to $17 million in 2008, $33 million in 2009, and about $60 million in 2010. The company relied solely on Internet sales until the fall of 2010, when the player became available in retail stores for the first time. A media player that was co-branded with Netgear became available at chain stores such as Best Buy and RadioShack. There was no shortage of competition, however. Apple, for one, elected to pay new attention to the set-top box field by reconfiguring its long neglected Apple TV. Roku responded by slashing prices and introducing a new, more powerful media player. There were also other set-top box manufacturers introducing new products, along with Blu-Ray players and television sets incorporating streaming capabilities. In the fall of 2010 Roku began licensing its technology so that it could be incorporated into other devices. Roku had proven to be nimble, but its long-term prospects remained far from certain.

Ed Dinger

PRINCIPAL COMPETITORS

Apple Inc.; Boxee, Inc.; OpenTV Corp.; Syabas Technology; Technicolor; TiVo Inc.

FURTHER READING

Berkman, Johanna. "Hit Replay," *New York Times Magazine*, November 16, 2003, 76.

Edwards, Cliff. "A $99, No-Frills Player from Netflix." *Business Week Online*, May 30, 2008.

Graham, Jefferson. "Roku's $99 Player Aims to be the Hub for Streaming Movies." *USA Today*, September 14, 2009.

Hansell, Saul. "Why the Roku Netflix Player Is the First Shot of the Revolution." *New York Times*, May 20, 2008.

Hiltzik, Michael. "Roku Box Developer Has a Sixth Sense about Video." *Los Angeles Times*, October 13, 2010.

Muller, Tom. "Netflix Inside." *Wired*, October 2009, 120.

"Netflix Hires Anthony Wood to Get Its Internet TV Operation Going." *Online Reporter*, April 21, 2007, 21.

Roush Enterprises, Inc.

12445 Levan Road
Livonia, Michigan 48150
U.S.A.
Telephone: (734) 779-7006
Toll Free: (800) 215-9658
Fax: (734) 779-7950
Web site: http://www.roush.com

Private Company
Founded: 1976 as Jack Roush Performance Engineering
Employees: 2,500
NAICS: 541330 Engineering Services; 711211 Sports Teams and Clubs

■ ■ ■

Although best known for its NASCAR racing teams, Roush Enterprises, Inc., based in Livonia, Michigan, is a multifaceted company. Roush Fenway Racing operates seven race teams in the NASCAR Sprint Cup, Nationwide, and Truck series. The Roush subsidiary offers automotive engineering services, including computer-aided design and engineering, body and chassis engineering, power-train engineering, noise and vibration engineering, electrical systems engineering, thermal systems engineering, and program management. Roush also offers testing and development services, creates prototypes, and manufactures components for niche vehicles and provides similar services for the consumer products and medical device markets.

Roush also serves the aerospace industry with engineering, prototyping, and engineering services and the defense market by providing body and chassis engineering and power-train engineering for military vehicles. Additionally, Roush is involved in the entertainment field by using its capabilities to design and fabricate roller coasters and other amusement park rides, and it serves the renewable energy field by producing wind turbines. Subsidiary Roush Performance Products, Inc., is a specialty vehicle company offering special-edition Ford Mustang automobiles and F150 trucks, alternative-fuel vehicles, parts, and engines. Another unit, Performance Assembly Solutions, is a full-service supplier of niche and specialty power-train modules. Finally, Roush Life Sciences offers such products as storage and centrifuge bottles as well as laboratory filtration systems and provides services including design and engineering, prototyping, reverse engineering, fabrication, tooling, machining, and sound and vibration analysis. Roush Enterprises is a private company whose chairman is its founder, Jack Roush.

FOUNDER'S LIFE AND CAREER

Jack Ernest Roush was born in Manchester, Ohio, in 1942. His father, Charles, was a farmer and businessman with a variety of interests but limited financial success. Charles Roush was also a mechanic, and his son often watched him rebuild truck engines in their driveway. During high school, Jack Roush worked at a Chevrolet dealership parts counter and service center and sanded and painted cars at an automotive body shop. He also developed an interest in aviation. After failing to gain admission to the Air Force Academy, he enrolled at Berea College in Kentucky, graduating in 1964 with a degree in mathematics and a minor in

COMPANY PERSPECTIVES

We are focused on performance, driven by technology, and committed to success ... your success.

physics. He then moved to Detroit to become an assembly process engineer at Ford Motor Company and indulge his interest in street and drag racing. He joined forces with like-minded Ford colleagues, and calling themselves the Fastbacks they pooled their money and talents to build competitive drag cars. On the side, Roush made money building Ford engines for race cars of all sorts as well as racing boats, tractor pullers, and truck pullers.

Roush went to work for Chrysler in 1969 to expand his knowledge of engines. He also furthered his education, earning a master's degree in mathematics from Eastern Michigan University in 1970. In that same year, he struck out on his own to start an engineering business but primarily made his living teaching mathematics, physics, and automotive subjects at nearby community and junior colleges. In this way, Roush freed up his summers for racing. He also formed a partnership with Wayne Gapp in 1970 to pursue motor sports, primarily drag racing, working his way up through the power classes to the NHRA Pro Stock division.

Roush split with Gapp in 1976 and formed Jack Roush Performance Engineering, his success in drag racing serving as a calling card that led to contracts with car manufacturers as well as race teams. In 1978 he put a hold on his own drag racing activities to focus on the business. With the launch of the Ford Special Vehicle Operations in 1980, Roush began developing blocks, heads, manifolds, and engines for the Ford racing program and eventually produced racing Mustangs, Capris, and Merkurs. In 1982 he returned to active participation in motor sports through a partnership with Zakspeed Racing, which had enjoyed success in Europe and was interested in racing in the United States. The partnership focused on running Ford GTX and GTP cars.

ROUSH RACING

Having enjoyed success as a businessman, Roush decided to go it alone on the track in 1984, forming Roush Racing. Initially he pursued road racing, entering cars in events sponsored by the International Motor Sports Association and Sports Car Club of America. He enjoyed a good deal of success, his teams winning several series titles and manufacturers championships over the next few years. By 1988 Roush was ready to try NASCAR and enter a car in its elite Winston Cup series. He had been a fan of the premiere stock car racing circuit for many years, in particular of driver Richard Petty. During his college days Roush's only hobby was listening to radio broadcasts of NASCAR races.

NASCAR success proved elusive for Roush. Although his driver, Mark Martin, won a pole position and earned 10 top 10 finishes during the first year, it was not until October 1989 that Martin won his first NASCAR Winston Cup race for Roush. A year later, Martin was in contention for the championship but lost out to driver Dale Earnhardt by just 26 points. Earlier in the year Martin had been disqualified for an engine specification violation and docked 46 points. Roush insisted he had been singled out by NASCAR, which he claimed had unfairly denied his team the championship. The incident also resulted in a longtime feud with Earnhardt.

LAUNCH OF ROUSH PERFORMANCE

While Roush Racing enjoyed NASCAR success in the 1990s, its drivers winning numerous races, the championship continued to elude Jack Roush. In the meantime, he continued to build his business empire. He acquired Anatrol VNH Services, an established provider of mechanical noise and vibration analysis, naming it Roush Anatrol. Roush Performance was launched in 1995 to produce niche vehicles and vehicle component packages. In 1997 he acquired Detroit Art Services to add technical publication services that included print and video products, technical documentation, as well as web-based materials. The unit also provided graphic services and promotional materials for Roush customers.

Expansion continued as the decade came to a close with the 1999 acquisition of Crucam Inc., which added rapid prototyping, machining, and manufacturing tools to Roush's capabilities. Crucam formed the foundation for the Roush Manufacturing Services division. Also in 1999, Roush forged a joint venture with Uni Boring Company, Inc., a manufacturer of power-train components, creating Performance Assembly Solutions. This unit provided engine development services that spanned the gamut, from concept to assembly.

At the start of the new century, Roush Performance Products began selling customized Ford Mustangs as well as other custom cars and parts. Roush Anatrol invested $3 million to construct a new 300,000-square-

KEY DATES

1976: Jack Roush Performance Engineering is formed.
1984: Roush Racing is formed.
1988: Roush enters NASCAR racing.
1995: Roush Performance is launched.
2008: Roush Life Sciences is formed.

foot engineering center for its lab in Livonia, Michigan, providing noise, vibration, and harshness testing for all of Roush's divisions. Jack Roush also won his first title in NASCAR's three premiere series. In 2000 his driver Greg Biffle won the Truck Series, and two years later he won the Nationwide Series. Meanwhile, Roush drivers were closing in on the ultimate prize, a Sprint Cup (the renamed Winston Cup) Series championship. Roush almost failed to witness his long-anticipated triumph, however.

An experienced pilot, Roush flew his fully restored P-51 Mustang World War II fighter aircraft to a private hangar in Troy, Alabama, where friends were gathered to celebrate his 60th birthday before a scheduled NASCAR race in Talladega. Another aviation enthusiast at the party offered Roush a chance to fly his new Aircam, an experimental, lightweight, low-flying, open-cockpit plane. Roush took the Aircam for a flight over a nearby lake, but was unfamiliar with the terrain, which featured two groups of power lines. After negotiating the first set, Roush failed to anticipate the second, clipped them on a low-altitude bank, and flipped into the lake, trapped upside down underwater.

CHEATING DEATH

Roush enjoyed a stroke of improbable good fortune. Watching the accident from his living room window was a state game warden named Larry Hicks. A former Marine he had been trained in the search and rescue of pilots downed in water. Although he had never been called upon to actually use his training, he responded immediately, using his fishing boat to rush to the scene of the accident. He dove into the water and freed Roush, who suffered from multiple injuries, including a shattered thigh bone, a knee broken in three places, a mangled ankle, broken ribs, a collapsed lung, and other injuries to his tailbone, head, and shoulder. He also was not breathing.

Hicks performed CPR to resuscitate Roush until an emergency medical team arrived. Although in critical condition, Roush survived the accident but spent six weeks in the hospital recovering. Hicks was also injured, suffering aviation fuel burns and a detached finger tendon. Nevertheless, he steadfastly refused to accept any money from Roush, preferring instead the friendship of the man whose life he saved.

The accident was also a moment of testing for Roush Enterprises. President and chief executive officer Evan Lyall flew to Alabama to visit Roush in the hospital over the weekend of the accident and returned to work on Monday morning to report Roush's condition to employees. He then followed up with e-mail updates twice daily during Roush's recovery. Lyall and other executives also reassured customers and vendors that Roush Enterprises was conducting business as usual. Fortunately, Roush had put in place a succession plan that made it possible for the company to function properly despite the absence of its charismatic leader.

FIRST SPRINT CUP SERIES CHAMPIONSHIP WIN

Roush Racing won its first Sprint Cup Series Championship in 2003 with driver Matt Kenseth and defended the title a year later with driver Kurt Busch. There was now no doubt that Roush Racing was one of the top NASCAR teams. To help the organization stay in the top ranks, Roush teamed up with NASCAR legend Robert Yates in 2005 to form Roush Yates Engines to design and produce high-performance racing engines. In 2007 Jack Roush sold a near 50 percent interest in Roush Racing to John Henry and the Fenway Sports Group, owners of Major League Baseball's Boston Red Sox, to create Roush Fenway Racing. Jack Roush continued to manage the race operations, while Fenway Sports Group provided its marketing and sales expertise and looked to improve racing interest in New England. The move was also made in large part to keep the racing team financially competitive with Toyota, which was poised to become involved in NASCAR racing.

While racing remained the face of the company, Roush Enterprises continued to look for new opportunities. In 2008 it acquired Massachusetts-based Nypro, a global supplier of precision plastic parts for a variety of industries, including automotive, consumer, electronics, health care, and packaging. Roush used Nypro's capabilities to form Roush Life Sciences and participate in the fast-growing market for OEM (original equipment manufacturer) health care and laboratory research products. The new unit also allowed Roush to make full use of its design, engineering, prototyping, and manufacturing capabilities. There was every reason to believe that Roush Enterprises would continue to excel in NASCAR racing and find new ways to take commercial advantage of the capabilities racing required.

Ed Dinger

PRINCIPAL SUBSIDIARIES

Roush; Roush Fenway Racing; Roush Life Sciences; Roush Performance Products, Inc.

PRINCIPAL COMPETITORS

Cragar Industries, Inc.; Hendrick Motorsports, Inc.; Wood Brothers Racing Inc.; Specialty Vehicle Acquisition Corp.; Magna International, Inc.

FURTHER READING

Anderson, Lars. "Born Again." *Sports Illustrated*, December 1, 2002.

Bernstein, Viv. "Racecar Owner Happy to Have a New Lease on Life." *New York Times*, July 10, 2003.

Kosdrosky, Terry. "Roush Enterprises Rallies after Crash." *Crain's Detroit Business*, May 6, 2002, 3.

McCraw, Jim. "Smilin' Jack." *Hot Rod*, May 1997.

"Roush Enters Life Sciences Market." *Chemical Business Newsbase*, October 22, 2008.

Spencer, Lee. "Top Cat." *Sporting News*, November 24, 2003, 22.

Ryohin Keikaku Co., Ltd.

4-26-3 Higashi-Ikebukuro, Toshima-ku
Tokyo, 170-8424
Japan
Telephone: (+81 03) 3989-4403
Fax: (+81 03) 5954-7022
Web site: http://ryohin-keikaku.jp/eng

Public Company
Founded: 1989
Incorporated: 1989
Employees: 4,680 (est.)
Sales: ¥14.27 billion ($15.27 million) (2009)
Stock Exchanges: Tokyo
Ticker Symbol: 7453
NAICS: 442110 Furniture Stores; 442299 All Other Home Furnishings Stores; 448140 Family Clothing Stores; 424320 Men's and Boys' Clothing and Furnishings Merchant Wholesalers; 445110 Supermarkets and Other Grocery (Except Convenience) Stores; 454111 Electronic Shopping

■ ■ ■

With a sensible, creative approach to product development and a distinct contrast to Madison Avenue's branding, the Japanese firm Ryohin Keikaku Co., Ltd., has put its stamp on retailing. Since the 1980s its Muji brand products, such as folding bicycles, wall-mounted CD players, and unbleached fabric clothing, have gained a wide following, especially among young adults and aficionados of new ideas in architecture and design. As of 2010 Ryohin operated through five business groups: stores, franchises, and distribution in Japan; marketing and operations in the United States, Europe, and Asia; a florist business, Hana-Ryohin Co.; modular houses, furniture, and household items; campsites; carryout food and cafés; and Idée, which is responsible for product development.

FROM PRIVATE LABEL TO INDEPENDENCE: 1980–89

In 1980 Ikko Tanaka, Kazuko Koike, and Takashi Sugimoto created the concept and initial products known as *mujirushi ryohin*. Later shortened to *muji*, the phrase meant "no brand, good quality." The venture was backed by Seiji Tsutsumi, a principal figure in Japan's distribution industry and head of the Seibu Saison Group. Tanaka, Koike, and Sugimoto were specialists in graphic design, advertising, and interior design. Tanaka became Muji's first art director, and Koike, a copywriter, created the brand's first tagline, "Lower Priced for a Reason." Another forebear, Kaoru Ariga, designed Muji's popular 26-inch bicycle in 1983. Along with Muji's dye-free stationery (an early indication of the company's environmental interests), the bike's simplicity, functionality, and affordability became a talisman for the budding company.

Muji began as a private-label line for The Seiyu Ltd., a chain of supermarkets in Japan that was part of the Seibu Saison Group. Initially the Muji line comprised mainly food products such as soups, seasonings, and noodles. In 1981 unbleached cotton underwear was added to Muji's offerings. Three years after the label's debut, a 103-square-meter store

COMPANY PERSPECTIVES

Since its independence from The Seiyu Ltd. in 1989, Ryohin Keikaku Co., Ltd., has been developing and supplying consumer driven daily necessities including clothing, household goods and food. The company's basic principle is to develop new, simple products at reasonable prices by making the best use of the materials while considering environmental issues. Ryohin Keikaku has been steadily developing its design concept and the popularity of its products sold under the Muji brand is spreading worldwide as a global trend originating in Japan.

dedicated to the Muji brand, Mujirushi Ryohin, opened in Tokyo's Aoyama district. By the mid-1980s Seibu had created a distinct Mujirushi Ryohin division, and Muji outlets were set up within Seiyu stores.

Ryohin's initial success was partly because of its parent company. Established in 1963 by the Seibu Saison Group, Seiyu opened its first store near the main site of the 1964 Tokyo Olympics. In addition to targeting its inventory at young people, the store also offered convenience. Extra-long work weeks and the urban sprawl that had sprung up around many Japanese cities created a demand for one-stop shopping in far-flung residential areas. Tsutsumi also owned railway and transit lines, and Seibu and Seiyu stores were opened in train stations along these routes.

Seibu's venturelike strategy for its subsidiaries by not endowing Seiyu, Muji, and its other companies with the Seibu name but undertaking financial risk on their behalf, occasionally led to selling or spinning them off. Thanks in part to connections via Seiyu and Seibu, Muji was strengthened by production and procurement agreements obtained at facilities in Japan, Hong Kong, and elsewhere from 1986 to 1988. Progress spurred a spinoff. In 1989 Ryohin Keikaku Co. became a separate entity, and developing and selling Muji brand products became its primary business in 1990. From this point on, Ariga, Tanaka, and others held responsibility for the company's next moves.

EXPANSION AND PROGRESS: 1990–2000

The company spent the 1990s undergoing expansion. In 1991 it opened a Muji store in London, the first one outside Japan. Other stores and franchises followed during the early to mid-1990s, in Hong Kong, Singapore, and elsewhere in the United Kingdom and Japan. By 1996 more than 300 employees worked at 221 stores in Japan and 15 stores overseas. Another expansion occurred regarding shipping and distribution: in 1993 Ryohin Keikaku started a trucking subsidiary, RK Truck Co. The next year Ryohin Keikaku Europe became the entity for that continent's operations. Based within one location, administrative procedures, distribution, and inventory were more efficient and communication with headquarters in Tokyo was expedited.

Ryohin's net profit for 1995 was ¥834 million. That year the company held its initial public offering, with the Japan Securities Dealers Association, and also began operating its first campgrounds, the Muji Tsunan Campsite. By entering the outdoor recreation business and inviting the public's involvement, the company combined a commitment to the environment with a welcoming of public participation. From 1995 to 2000 Ryohin added two more campsites, using the 231 total hectares (571 acres) for children's educational events, group holiday activities, and summer vacationing.

As the 1990s ended, Ryohin maintained its approach to designing, selling, and promoting its "no-brand" products, and customers flocked to its 248 stores. As Alexandra Harney observed in her *Financial Times* article on October 1, 1998, "Behind the low prices is one of the most efficient manufacturing and distribution networks in the industry." Harney reported that 80 percent of Ryohin's clothing and 50 percent of its household goods were produced at its facilities in Japan and China. Experiencing lackluster revenues, rival chains, including former parent company Seiyu, were forced to restructure. In 1998, as the company opened its first store in Paris, net revenues for the year's first half were ¥2.1 billion ($15.7 million).

In 1998 Ryohin became Japan's sole retail holder of ISO 9001 certification, verifying its quality control and manufacturing systems. That year the company was listed on the Tokyo Stock Exchange's second section, for mid-size companies. In 2000 Ryohin's listing on the Tokyo Stock Exchange was shifted to the first section, reserved for large firms.

GOOD QUALITY FOR THE 21ST CENTURY

Ryohin's e-commerce for the U.S. market launched fully in 2000. By 2010 www.muji.us had joined www.muji.com as the company's websites for e-commerce in the United States and around the globe. Aficionados of up-and-coming Muji products who had shopped for or heard about the sweaters, dishes, and other items avail-

KEY DATES

1980: The Muji brand debuts.
1989: Seiyu Ltd. spins off Ryohin Keikaku Co.; Ryohin Keikaku Co., Ltd., is established.
1991: The first store outside Japan opens.
2000: The Muji brand celebrates its 20th anniversary; the company launches e-commerce for customers in the United States.
2007: The first store in the United States opens.

able in Japan, Singapore, the United Kingdom, and France could now purchase these products online. The "no-brand" had developed a far-reaching name and a steady success rate.

Muji House, later enfolded into the subsidiary Muji.net Co., was founded in 2000. Its focus on housing was possible because of Ryohin's financial resources and designers' expertise. Japanese architect Kazuhiko Namba was a creative force behind the two-story, box-shaped Muji houses with open floor plans and shoji screens to separate spaces at will. Another prominent influence was graphic designer Kenya Hara, chosen by founding art director Ikko Tanaka as the next head of Ryohin's design team. In his 2008 book *Designing Design*, Hara delineated Japan's cultural influence on Muji: "Japan, looking upon the world from its detached location at the eastern end of Asia, has built an aesthetic that is infinitely attractive to human rationality, not within luxury or extravagance, but simplicity." At Hara's urging, product designer Naoto Fukasawa joined Ryohin's transitional efforts.

From 2000 to 2005 more stores opened as the company continued its expansion. In 2001 the Muji Yurakucho store in Tokyo became Ryohin's flagship site. New stores opened in Ireland, Taiwan, Italy, and South Korea in 2003 and 2004. By 2005 Muji stores had been established in Germany and Shanghai. The design community's acknowledgment of Muji's excellence included five gold awards from International Forum Design in 2005 for Muji's DVD player, shredder, telephone, CD storage system, and CD player with clock radio.

EXPANDED U.S. PRESENCE

In 2006 Ryohin launched its subsidiary Idée Co., a collaboration among in-house staff, consultants, and others designing and packaging small appliances, electronic items, furniture, and products for the home. That autumn Muji U.S.A. Limited was founded in preparation for the opening in 2007 of the first store in the United States, located in Manhattan's SoHo neighborhood. While interest was sufficient that by 2009 Ryohin had opened two more stores in New York City in partnership with the Museum of Modern Art and a site at JFK International Airport, these were just one part of near-term plans. Indonesia got its first Muji store in 2009, a store in Poland was ahead for 2010, and Muji Beauty, a skin-care line for young women, was also scheduled for a 2010 launch.

Known as Muji to Go, the shop at JFK Airport was part of a kiosk business begun in 2008 operating alongside Meal Muji, featuring food for travelers. The division known as Café & Meal Muji hearkened back to the brand's origins, when Muji products were sold in transit stations for busy commuters who still sought good quality. The commitment to excellent designs and to producing items that people want, with cost effectiveness in mind and attention paid to simple packaging and efficient manufacturing, have been threads that Ryohin has maintained throughout its existence. Success placed the brand and the company onto a far-flung path, but as Kenya Hara stated in *Designing Design*, "As long as the corporate seedbed is basically the Japanese market, the product will remain appropriate to the Japanese market."

Mary C. Lewis

PRINCIPAL SUBSIDIARIES

Hana-Ryohin Co. Ltd.; Idée Co. Ltd.; Muji (Beijing) Co. Ltd. (China); Muji Deutschland GmbH; MUJI Europe Holdings Limited (UK, 66%); Muji (Hong Kong) Co. Ltd.; Muji Italia SpA; Muji Korea Co. Ltd. (South Korea, 60%); Muji.net Co. Ltd. (60%); Muji (Shanghai) Co. Ltd. (China); Muji Singapore Pte. Ltd.; RK Trucks Co. Ltd.; Muji Taiwan Co. Ltd. (39%); Muji USA Limited (80%); Ryohin Keikaku Europe Ltd. (UK); Ryohin Keikaku France SAS.

PRINCIPAL DIVISIONS

Café & Meal Muji Business; Muji Business in Japan; Muji Campsite Operation; Muji House; Muji Overseas Marketing Business; Flower Business; Idée.

PRINCIPAL OPERATING UNITS

Muji Global Sourcing Pte. Ltd. (Singapore); MGS (Shanghai) Trading Co. Ltd.

PRINCIPAL COMPETITORS

Carrefour SA; Gap Inc.; Inter IKEA Systems B.V.; Metro AG; Target Corporation; Tesco PLC; Wal-Mart Stores Inc.

FURTHER READING

Bayley, Stephen. "Pure and Simple; R+R." *Times* (London), June 9, 2001, 51.

Furukawa, Tsukasa, and Valerie Seckler. "Muji to Make U.S. Footprint with Two New York Openings." *WWD*, January 25, 2007, 14.

Hara, Kenya. *Designing Design*. Baden, Switzerland: Lars Müller, 2008.

Harney, Alexandra. "Japanese Retailer Blooms in a Recessionary Wilderness: Muji Has Found That Its No-Frills Approach Has Won It a Loyal Consumer Base." *Financial Times*, October 1, 1998, 33.

Hayashibara, Mariko. "Mujirushi Ryohin: Success Made Simple." *Asian Business*, March 1998, 10, 12, 14.

Hoggard, Liz. "Living in a Box." *Independent* (London), November 11, 2006, 78.

"Japanese Retailers Drawn to Mass C&T." *Cosmetics International*, March 26, 2010, 3.

Katayama, Osamu. "Muji Rejuvenated." *Japan Journal*, June 2005, 14–16.

"Muji Online Bows in North America." *WWD*, November 6, 2000, 23.

Ueno, Chizuko. "Seibu Department Stores and Image Marketing: Japanese Consumerism in the Postwar Period." In *Asian Department Stores*. Ed. Kerrie L. MacPherson. Honolulu: University of Hawaii Press, 1998, 177–84.

SanDisk®

SanDisk Corporation

601 McCarthy Boulevard
Milpitas, California 95035
U.S.A.
Telephone: (408) 801-1000
Fax: (408) 801-8657
Web site: http://www.sandisk.com

Public Company
Founded: 1988
Employees: 3,267
Sales: $3.57 billion (2009)
Stock Exchanges: NASDAQ
Ticker Symbol: SNDK
NAICS: 334112 Computer Storage Device Manufacturing

■ ■ ■

SanDisk Corporation, based in Milpitas, California, became a pioneer in flash storage cards during the early 1990s and is still a world-leading manufacturer in this field. Flash storage cards have been adapted into many electronic applications, ranging from mobile phones to digital cameras and portable music players. SanDisk markets its own branded flash cards and consumer electronics in many retail venues. The company has offices or production facilities in China, France, Germany, Hong Kong, Ireland, Israel, Japan, South Korea, Spain, Sweden, and Taiwan.

EARLY YEARS: 1988–94

During the 1960s Eli Harari moved from his native Israel to the United States, where he became a innovative researcher of electronic memory chips. In 1988 Harari joined with Sanjay Mehrotra and Jack Yuan to establish SunDisk Corporation in Santa Clara, California. The founders of the start-up firm believed that a new technology, flash memory chips, provided an ideal data storage medium for portable electronic devices. Flash memory could be deleted and rewritten extremely swiftly, consumed little power, and had no moving parts. Flash memory cards were small and portable and had much larger storage capacity than floppy discs, making them well suited for transferring data among different devices.

The company's founders struggled to raise funds from skeptical potential investors, yet they rejected offers that did not suit their corporate vision. The venture capitalist Irwin Federman contributed some of his own money to SunDisk and arranged for crucial financing from venture funds and corporations. Its first flash memory chips were 4 megabytes (MB) in size and fabricated by Matsushita Electronics. In 1991 SunDisk won its first major contract to supply IBM with 20MB flash drives installed in a new line of personal computers.

SunDisk staked strong hopes that digital cameras would quickly supersede conventional film cameras. The company anticipated additional demand for flash memory due to the boom in mobile phones, the rollout of personal digital assistants, and the launch of personal computers equipped with external memory slots. However, markets for these products were frustratingly slow to develop. Seagate Technology Inc. helped support SunDisk by paying $30 million for a 25 percent stake in the company in 1992. The company also supplemented

COMPANY PERSPECTIVES

SanDisk's reputation and brand name have been built upon and will continue to be built upon the innovation and quality of our products and services. We strive to meet the highest standards for manufacturing quality and performance for our products. We are committed to ensuring that consumers can continue to trust SanDisk products for their reliability, quality, and superior performance. To meet this goal, we must always strive to manufacture products that meet or exceed our performance and quality standards.

its income by designing specialized memory systems for clients such as the National Aeronautics and Space Administration and the Boeing Company.

By the mid-1990s SunDisk had become an industry leader in flash memory, as its revenues rose to $35.4 million in 1994. The company forged ahead into the next generation of 16MB and 32MB chips. SunDisk introduced the CompactFlash card in 1994, which it offered as an open standard to encourage other chip manufacturers to adopt it. CompactFlash won out over the competing MiniCard and SmartMedia standards thanks in part to being promoted by the CompactFlash Association, which included Apple Computers, Hewlett-Packard, Motorola, and Eastman Kodak. Even though CompactFlash was higher in unit price than rival flash cards, its larger storage capacity and installed controllers attracted many equipment manufacturers.

EXPANDING PRODUCT LINE: 1995–2000

In August 1995 SunDisk changed its name to SanDisk Corporation because it had been facing frequent confusion with the industry giant Sun Microsystems. Shortly thereafter the company conducted an initial public offering by issuing stock on the NASDAQ. That same year SanDisk reported for the first time a yearend net profit of $14.5 million on revenues of $62.8 million.

SanDisk's revenues steadily increased and the company remained profitable throughout the late 1990s. In 1996 SanDisk and Matsushita announced a 64MB Double Density flash chip, which stored two bits of data in each cell rather than one. The following year SanDisk and Siemens Microelectronics introduced the MultiMediaCard format. Smaller than CompactFlash, the new format was designed to enable advanced wireless communication and supported by the leading cellular phone manufacturers.

In 1995 SanDisk charged Samsung Electronics Co., Ltd., with using several of its patents without a license. In turn, Samsung filed a countersuit accusing SanDisk of violating its patents. In August 1997, after rulings against Samsung led the U.S. government to exclude its flash products from the United States, the two companies agreed to cross-license each other's patents. SanDisk's fierce defense of its patents yielded benefits through its competitors' licensing fees that in time amounted to hundreds of millions of dollars annually.

Originally, SanDisk was a "fabless" chip designer that contracted with foundries to fabricate its products. Frustrated by unreliable availability of chip supply, the company reversed an industry trend and began boosting its own production capacity. In 1997 SanDisk purchased a share of a chip fabrication plant to be constructed in Taiwan to receive a guaranteed portion of output. Three years later, in 1999, SanDisk established FlashVision, a joint venture with Toshiba Corporation. In 2000 SanDisk acquired a 10 percent stake in Tower Semiconductor Ltd. to help finance construction of a chip foundry in Israel.

By 2000 digital cameras were at last becoming mainstream consumer products. The flash memory market expansion brought opportunities and perils for SanDisk. The steady decline in unit prices of flash chips and cards drove sales of consumer electronics devices, but the same price decline threatened SanDisk's operating margins. SanDisk reported $26.6 million in net income and $247 million in revenues in 1999. These figures soared in 2000 to $298.7 million in net income and $601.8 million in revenues. The company shipped over 13 million units that year, up from barely 500,000 in 1996. SanDisk also collaborated with Toshiba to create the SD Memory Card, which was intended to store copyright-protected content on portable digital music players.

ECONOMIC VOLATILITY AND STRATEGY CHANGE: 2001–07

In 2001 SanDisk's growth suffered a sharp reverse. On the one hand, the collapse of the dot-com bubble and the telecommunications industry depressed demand for flash memory. On the other hand, Samsung poured competing flash products on the market, causing a sudden oversupply and plunging flash card prices by nearly 70 percent. A direct result from this decrease in prices was that SanDisk's revenues dropped to $366.3 million as the company recorded $297.9 million in losses and had to institute a series of layoffs. However, by the

KEY DATES

1988: Eli Harari, Sanjay Mehrotra, and Jack Yuan found SunDisk Corporation.
1994: SunDisk introduces CompactFlash cards.
1995: SunDisk Corporation changes its name to SanDisk Corporation, makes an initial public offering.
1999: SanDisk and Toshiba Corporation begin a joint venture, FlashVision.
2008: Samsung Electronics Co., Ltd., makes takeover offer for SanDisk, then rescinds it.

second quarter of 2002 SanDisk reported profits again, driven by the relentless consumer shift to digital cameras and MP3 players.

This downturn convinced SanDisk that the only way to keep ahead of plunging prices was to eliminate inessential costs and emphasize its retail division. Following Intel's lead in personal computers, SanDisk began marketing branded flash memory cards in camera shops, computer stores, and office-supply stores on the premise that consumers would be willing to pay more for quality accessories. By 2004, 70 percent of the company's revenues came from its retail division. This strategy enabled SanDisk's retail lines to absorb its chip production, and in turn it did not have to purchase chips from outside vendors at higher cost.

The company also marketed its own branded electronic devices. The SanDisk Photo Album, released in 2004, could show digital photographs or video on a television screen and play MP3 files through television speakers. During the fall of 2004 SanDisk introduced a portable music player, the SanDisk Sansa. Although the Apple iPod Shuffle soon dominated the category, the Sansa remained the second-leading brand, which offered extra features such as a video screen and FM radio.

In 2004 USB flash drives were beginning to rival digital cameras as a source of revenue for SanDisk, which with its Israeli partner M-Systems introduced the U3 flash drive at an industry trade show in January 2005. Touting U3 as an open platform, SanDisk sought to establish U3 as an industry standard despite the hostility from the USB Flash Alliance, which was upset that flash drive manufacturers would have to pay licensing fees. That same year SanDisk brought out TrustedFlash technology that enabled transfer of protected digital files among cell phones and other devices. Harari was convinced that mobile phones would eventually feature many portable device functions, so he wanted to position SanDisk as the go-to supplier of memory for these phones.

In April 2007 SanDisk launched the Sansa Connect model. A step up from the SanDisk Sansa, the new model provided Wi-Fi connectivity and Yahoo Music channels. That October SanDisk introduced TakeTV, which played downloaded digital video files on a television set and was coupled with the Fanfare service to provide movies and television shows over the Internet. The success of these products and SanDisk's flash drives continued to drive sales. In 2007 SanDisk reported $218 million in net profits and $3.9 billion in revenues.

TEMPORARY SETBACK AND RENEWED HOPE: 2008–10

A conjunction of economic trends caught up with SanDisk and its rivals in 2008. The aftershocks of the world financial crisis that began in late 2007 dissuaded many consumers from purchasing new electronic devices. Chip manufacturers suffered further due to a combination of continued falling prices and a glut of production. In September Samsung publicized its offer to purchase SanDisk for $5.9 billion. Despite pressure from investors, SanDisk spurned this offer as too low. Toshiba boosted SanDisk through refinancing their joint venture, paying nearly $1 billion to acquire a 20 percent share. Samsung eventually withdrew its takeover offer, citing SanDisk's mounting losses and plunging stock price. Burdened by a heavy debt load, SanDisk reported a loss of $1.9 billion in the fourth quarter of 2008.

The following year SanDisk recovered swiftly, reporting a record net income of $415.3 million and revenues of $3.2 billion. The company's large investments in ramping up production capacity bore fruit. Growth was also based on sales to other manufacturers as retail sales remained sluggish. Furthermore, Samsung renewed its license to use SanDisk's patents for another seven years, which helped maintain another vital income stream.

In July 2010 Harari startled many industry watchers when he declared that he would step down from his company posts at the start of 2011. Mehrotra was slated to become SanDisk's chief executive officer and Michael Marks its chairman. Through the first half of 2010 SanDisk continued to post impressive revenues and profits. Given its position in the flash drive industry, SanDisk was prepared to be at the forefront of new technological advances for the second decade of the 21st century.

Stephen V. Beitel

PRINCIPAL SUBSIDIARIES

M-Systems, Inc.; SanDisk 3D LLC; SanDisk Equipment Ltd. (Japan); SanDisk IL Ltd. (Israel); SanDisk India Device Design Centre, Ltd.; SanDisk International Limited (Ireland); SanDisk Israel (Tefen) Ltd.; SanDisk Limited (Japan); SanDisk Manufacturing (Ireland); SanDisk Secure Content Solutions, Inc.; SanDisk Semiconductor (Shanghai) Co. Ltd. (China); SanDisk Taiwan Limited (Taiwan).

PRINCIPAL DIVISIONS

SanDisk Enterprise.

PRINCIPAL COMPETITORS

Elpida Memory, Inc.; Intel Corporation; Lexar Media, Inc.; Micron Technology, Inc.; Samsung Electronics Co., Ltd.; Silicon Motion Technology Corp.; Sony Corporation; Spansion Inc.; Toshiba Corporation.

FURTHER READING

Arensman, Russ. "Eli's Big Adventure." *Electronic Business*, December 1, 2006, 26.

Clarke, Peter. "SanDisk Stakes $75M on Foundry Partnership." *Electronic Engineering Times*, July 10, 2000, 22.

Cohen, Shlomi. "Three Brilliant Moves by the SanDisk CEO." *Israel Business Arena*, August 17, 2010.

DeTar, James. "Opposing Camps Could Slow Advances in Flash Memory." *Investor's Business Daily*, January 31, 2005, 4.

DeTar, Jim. "SunDisk Eyes Flash Ramp to Meet Rivals." *Electronic News*, January 10, 1994, 1.

"New Deal with Samsung Bolsters Flash Maker SanDisk." *eWeek*, May 27, 2009.

Ojo, Bolaji. "SanDisk, Samsung Settle Legal Battle—Companies Sign New Seven-Year Cross-Licensing Agreement." *Electronic Buyers' News*, August 26, 2002, 13.

"Samsung Drops $5.85 Billion Bid for SanDisk." *Information-Week*, October 22, 2008.

Thomas, Owen. "SanDisk Plays Its Cards Right: Eli Harari Isn't Wary of Ever-Plunging Prices." *Business 2.0*, May 2004, 60.

Yi, Matthew. "Maximum Exposure; SanDisk, the Leading Maker of Memory Cards, Tries to Be the Kodak of the Digital Age." *San Francisco Chronicle*, March 1, 2004, E1.

Sealed Air Corporation

200 Riverfront Boulevard
Elmwood Park, New Jersey 07407
U.S.A.
Telephone: (201) 791-7600
Fax: (201) 703-4205
Web site: http://www.sealedair.com

Public Company
Incorporated: 1960
Employees: 16,200
Sales: $4.24 billion (2009)
Stock Exchanges: New York Stock Exchange
Ticker Symbol: SEE
NAICS: 322221 Coated and Laminated Packaging Paper Manufacturing; 322232 Envelope Manufacturing; 326111 Plastics Bag and Pouch Manufacturing; 326112 Plastics Packaging Film and Sheet (Including Laminated) Manufacturing; 326140 Polystyrene Foam Product Manufacturing; 326150 Urethane and Other Foam Product (except Polystyrene) Manufacturing; 326199 All Other Plastics Product Manufacturing

■ ■ ■

Sealed Air Corporation, a leading global manufacturer of food, protective, and specialty packaging materials, operates over 100 facilities in 52 countries. Reaching nearly 80 percent of the world's population, its products serve a variety of food, industrial, medical, and consumer applications and include AirCap and Bubble Wrap air cellular cushioning materials, Jiffy brand mailers and bags, Cryovac food packaging systems, Fill-Air inflatable packaging, Instapak foam packaging, Shanklin shrink packaging machinery, Ethafoam high recycled content polyethylene foam, and Nelipak trays and blister sealing machines. Sealed Air derives the majority of its revenues from its line of food packaging products that are marketed primarily under the Cryovac trademark. However, it is also focused on growth through leveraging its core technologies in new markets, including energy conservation and design and testing services.

BUBBLE WRAP BEGINNINGS: 1960–77

Sealed Air was founded by Alfred W. Fielding and Marc A. Chavannes, the two men who gave the world Bubble Wrap. First developed in 1957, the product was initially created in response to a client's request for a new type of plastic wallpaper. When that idea fizzled, the pair found some success marketing the product as a greenhouse insulator. They finally stumbled onto the idea of adapting it for the packaging market. After a few years of tinkering with manufacturing methods and searching for seed capital, Fielding and Chavannes launched Sealed Air Corporation in 1960. With $85,000 raised through an initial public stock offering, production of the AirCap material began in earnest the following year. In its earliest form, AirCap packaging material suffered from leaky bubbles. In spite of this problem the product gained popularity throughout the 1960s, and by the middle of the decade research efforts had led to the development of a special coating that prevented the

COMPANY PERSPECTIVES

Sealed Air will be the global supplier of choice for solutions, products and services that improve our customer's bottom-line in the markets we serve.

We will be an exceptional company for our customers, employees and communities.

Our Code of Conduct is fully in effect ... all the time ... everywhere.

Our #1 Priority: Putting our Customer 1st.

bubbles from losing air. By 1969 Sealed Air reported sales of $4 million. This represented nearly the entire market for Bubble Wrap, because the product was still proprietary at the time.

Sealed Air added another product to its line in 1970. By laminating AirCap cushioning material to craft paper, the company developed its Mail Lite shipping envelope. That same year the company became international when it acquired Smith Packaging Ltd., later renamed Sealed Air of Canada Ltd. In 1971 T. J. Dermot Dunphy was named chief executive officer (CEO). Under his leadership the company flourished. By 1972 Sealed Air's sales had passed the $10 million mark. Another new product, PolyMask, was introduced in 1973. Poly-Mask, a pressure sensitive polyethylene film for protecting delicate surfaces against scratches, was the first Sealed Air product not based on its air bubble technology. At yearend 1973 the company's net profits topped $1 million. Of its $13.6 million in sales for that year, about 60 percent came from AirCap and about 20 percent from Mail Lite. The rest came mostly from the manufacture and distribution of a variety of packaging products by its Canadian subsidiary. The company's biggest customer was the electronics industry, which accounted for about 40 percent of sales.

During the mid-1970s Sealed Air developed another innovative use for its air cell technology. The Suncap solar pool blanket was essentially a big sheet of Bubble Wrap that was placed on swimming pools. The solar pool blanket allowed the sun's rays to heat the water and sharply reduced the evaporative loss of water and treatment chemicals. By 1977 the solar pool blanket was generating 6 percent of company sales. As an offshoot of the pool blanket, the company began making a roof-mounted solar water heater that was designed mainly for heating swimming pools.

EXPANSION THROUGH ACQUISITION: 1977–83

The most important development of 1977 was the acquisition of Instapak Corporation, the producer of a revolutionary "foam-in-place" cushioning system. The foam-in-place process involved surrounding a product with liquid urethane that then expanded into a semirigid foam. Instapak was made a division of Sealed Air, and it quickly became one of the company's most important products, generating almost as great a share of total sales as Bubble Wrap by the end of the decade. Foreign sales also increased dramatically during the second half of the 1970s, accounting for nearly a quarter of the company's total in 1977. By 1979 Sealed Air's annual sales had grown to more than $70 million.

By the beginning of the 1980s foam-in-place was clearly a product destined for bigger things, and Sealed Air had virtually no competition in the area. The pool blankets were also doing well, selling as fast as the company could make them. In 1981 Sealed Air added PolyCap to its product line. PolyCap was essentially a lower-cost, less durable version of AirCap, without the barrier coating, providing a less expensive option for products that required only a relatively short period of protection.

Sealed Air broadened its product line further in 1983 by purchasing Cellu-Products Co. for $20 million. The Cellu-Products acquisition added thin-grade polyethylene foam, coated films, and other plastic and paper materials to the company's growing collection of packaging products. That same year Sealed Air gained its first presence in the food packaging business through the acquisition of the Dri-Loc line of absorbent pad products, which were used underneath meat, fish, and poultry sold in supermarkets. Even though the recession of 1982 lowered Sealed Air's revenue and earnings figures, the emergence of personal computers and other related electronics products brought a new wave of business, and by 1983 the company's sales had increased to $124 million.

ACQUISITIONS AND RECAPITALIZATION: 1984–91

In an effort to diversify its product line further, and in part to prepare itself for the impending expiration of its Bubble Wrap patents, Sealed Air acquired several smaller companies during the mid-1980s. In 1984 it acquired Cortec Corporation, a small anticorrosive chemical firm. Cortec was sold only a few years later after it was caught illegally shipping chemicals to Libya. Other acquisitions that yielded happier results included Static Inc. in 1985, a Canadian spa manufacturer in 1987, and a Swedish

KEY DATES

1960: Alfred W. Fielding and Marc A. Chavannes found Sealed Air Corporation.
1970: Sealed Air acquires Smith Packaging Ltd.
1977: Sealed Air acquires Instapak Corporation; the company begins selling the Suncap solar pool blanket.
1983: Sealed Air acquires Cellu-Products Co.; first foray into food packaging comes via the purchase of the Dri-Loc absorbent pad product line.
1987: Sealed Air acquires Jiffy Packaging Corporation.
1995: Sealed Air acquires Trigon Industries Limited, nearly doubling Sealed Air's food packaging operations.
1998: Sealed Air merges with W.R. Grace & Company.
2002: Sealed Air agrees to settle all current and future asbestos-related claims connected with Grace.
2006: Sealed Air acquires Nelipak.

packaging company that same year. More important was the company's 1987 purchase of Jiffy Packaging Corporation, which manufactured padded mailers for items such as floppy disks and books. The addition of Jiffy solidified Sealed Air's dominant position in the protective mailer market. During this period Sealed Air also began incorporating recycled materials into a number of its air bubble and paper packaging products, at a time when few companies in the industry were doing so.

By 1988 Sealed Air had annual sales of $346 million and a net profit of $42 million. Over 36 percent of the company's annual sales came from Instapak, which by this time had more or less replaced Bubble Wrap as the flagship product. One new development for the year was a pair of systems called InstaPacker and VersaPacker, which could produce bags full of protective foam at the touch of a button.

Dunphy pulled off a remarkable financial maneuver in 1989. The company had been so profitable over the previous few years that it found itself with a huge cash surplus. Because Dunphy could not find any more companies that he felt were good acquisition candidates, he had no obvious outlets for this cash buildup. To avoid becoming too attractive a target for a takeover, as well as to create a so-called controlled crisis to shake his managers out of their complacency, Dunphy decided to give the money away. He announced a $40-per-share special dividend, amounting to a $328 million gift to shareholders. The move increased the company's long-term debt from $19 million to over $300 million.

Dunphy hoped that leveraging the company would push it to new heights of efficiency, and he was correct. The new debt situation necessitated changes in the way the company handled inventory and led to other cost-cutting measures. These changes enabled the company to begin repaying its debts ahead of schedule, thereby creating further savings. At the same time, an unexpected reduction in the cost of raw materials resulted in more opportunities to pay down part of the debt with extra cash. By the early 1990s Sealed Air was ready to go shopping once again. In 1991 it acquired Korrvu, which produced transparent suspension packaging that protected fragile items in a trampoline-like membrane, and Sentinel Foam & Envelope Corporation, a packaging firm based in Philadelphia, Pennsylvania.

SIGNIFICANT INTERNATIONAL EXPANSION: 1993–97

Sealed Air's sales figures stalled somewhat during the first part of the 1990s, advancing from $413 million in 1990 to only $452 million in 1993. Nevertheless, the company was able to generate solid profits each year. To boost revenue, Dunphy began concentrating heavily on worldwide expansion. Instapak was introduced in Mexico, and the company opened manufacturing facilities in Germany and Spain. Meanwhile, the company continued to emphasize research and development, and new products were unveiled at a steady pace. One such product was Floral, introduced in 1993. Floral was a foam that served as a base in artificial flower arrangements. Within a year of its first appearance, Floral was generating sales in the neighborhood of $5 million.

In 1993 the company purchased the Shurtuff Division of Shuford Mills Inc. Shurtuff's extremely durable plastic-based mailers meshed well with Sealed Air's existing protective mailer product line. The company reinforced its European food pad business with the 1994 purchase of Hereford Paper and Allied Products Ltd., a food pad manufacturing firm based in England. Packaging companies based in France, Italy, and Norway were also acquired during the year. The French acquisition added two product lines, Sup-Air-Pack and Fill Air, to the company's collection of inflation-based systems, an area that was considered to hold great promise for the future. Toward the end of the year the company reorganized its management structure so that its important product lines were coordinated globally rather than country by country. This move reflected an increasing focus on the international market. The combination of acquisitions and new products helped boost Sealed Air's sales in 1994 to over $500 million for the first time in company history. Its net profits of $31.6 million also reached record levels.

Sealed Air's largest acquisition during this period was in January 1995, when it acquired Trigon Industries Limited, a New Zealand company with operations in Australia, England, Germany, and the United States, for $54.6 million. With annual sales of $72 million, Trigon had an immediate and significant impact on Sealed Air's balance sheet as well as on its geographic reach by providing a base for expansion in the South Pacific. Trigon's lines of packaging films and systems for perishable foods almost doubled Sealed Air's food packaging operations.

The Trigon purchase was followed in June 1996 by the acquisition of Southcorp Holdings Limited, an Australian and New Zealand protective packaging firm. This purchase bolstered Sealed Air's position in the South Pacific, as the company saw its overseas sales grow from 18 percent of overall sales in 1985 to nearly 40 percent in 1997. At yearend 1997 the company reported net sales of $843 million, while its operating profits were a record $138 million.

MERGER WITH CRYOVAC: 1998–2000

In March 1998 Sealed Air completed the largest deal in its history, when it merged with the Cryovac packaging business of W.R. Grace & Company in a complicated stock and cash transaction valued at $4.9 billion. W.R. Grace transferred Cryovac to Sealed Air in return for $1.3 billion, which was given to Grace's other subsidiaries. This group of subsidiaries was spun off to shareholders as a separate publicly owned company that assumed the W.R. Grace name. The merged Cryovac–Sealed Air entity became a subsidiary of the old W.R. Grace, which was renamed Sealed Air Corporation. The deal was undertaken in such a complex way to ensure that it was done on a tax-free basis and to shield Sealed Air from the mounting asbestos liabilities of one of the spun-off Grace units, Grace Construction Products, that had made asbestos-containing products.

The addition of Cryovac was a dream deal for Dunphy, who had held off on discussions with Grace executives about a merger for two decades. The Cryovac operations were in fact much larger than those of the old Sealed Air, and the company saw its sales triple to more than $2.5 billion following the merger. Cryovac specialized in food packaging products, making that segment Sealed Air's largest, accounting for 60 percent of sales. The acquired lines were led by Cryovac itself, a material used to vacuum-seal food packages. The deal also significantly enhanced Sealed Air's worldwide profile by adding operations in nearly 20 more countries. Following the merger, Sealed Air remained headquartered in Saddle Brook, New Jersey, and Dunphy continued to serve as chairman and CEO.

Sealed Air continued its history of innovation in 1999 by introducing VistaFlex inflatable packaging, which was designed as an alternative to corrugated inserts and other premolded shapes and die cuts used in high-volume protective packaging applications. Also debuting that year was Instapak Quick, a simplified version of the Instapak foam-in-bag product that was targeted toward smaller companies selling products over the Internet. The company also completed a number of small acquisitions between 1999 and 2001. These included manufacturers of air cellular cushioning products in Latin America, Asia, and Africa and producers of foam and solid plastic trays used in food packaging in Latin America, Europe, and Australia. During the third quarter of 2000 a larger deal was finalized, with Sealed Air paying approximately $119 million for Dolphin Packaging PLC, a maker of foam food trays based in England. Another significant purchase was that of Shanklin Corporation, a U.S. manufacturer of shrink film packaging equipment. Meanwhile, in early 2000 Dunphy retired from the CEO position while remaining chairman. William V. Hickey, the president and chief operating officer of Sealed Air, was promoted to president and CEO.

ASBESTOS-RELATED TRAVAILS: 2000–02

By the turn of the 21st century some analysts were beginning to question the wisdom of the Cryovac merger. The deal had greatly expanded Sealed Air's operations in Asia and Europe, meaning that the company suffered in a more pronounced way from the economic troubles in Asia that cropped up during the late 1990s and from the decline in meat consumption in Europe that followed the outbreaks of mad cow and foot-and-mouth disease. Even more ominously, the merger had left Sealed Air exposed to potential liabilities related to asbestos claims, despite the structure of the merger, which had explicitly shielded Sealed Air from W.R. Grace's asbestos exposure, and the fact that neither Sealed Air nor Cryovac had ever produced or sold any products containing asbestos.

By 2000 Sealed Air had been named a party in a number of lawsuits alleging that the company was responsible for possible asbestos liabilities. The asbestos claimants were suing both Sealed Air and W.R. Grace, charging that Grace had fraudulently transferred Cryovac's assets to shelter them from Grace's asbestos liabilities. They further contended that Sealed Air was the true successor to the "old" W.R. Grace and that without Cryovac the "new" Grace was insolvent at the time of its spin-off because of the growing number of asbestos lawsuits that it faced. Weighed down by these asbestos claims, W.R. Grace filed for Chapter 11 bankruptcy protection in April 2001.

Asbestos-related events dominated 2002. Sealed Air faced a federal fraudulent-transfer lawsuit that was in its pretrial phase. In late July the company suffered a blow when the federal judge in the case issued a ruling that post-1998 asbestos claims could be considered when determining whether the new W.R. Grace was solvent when it transferred Cryovac to Sealed Air. The defendants had contended that only claims pending at the time of the merger should be considered. This news sent Sealed Air's stock plunging by 62 percent over a two-day period.

With the outcome of the trial, which was scheduled to begin in early December 2002, in serious doubt, Sealed Air reached an agreement in late November to settle all current and future asbestos-related claims. The company agreed to pay $834 million in cash and stock into a trust that would be established as part of the bankruptcy-reorganization plan of W.R. Grace. The trust would make payments to asbestos victims on behalf of Grace and its former subsidiaries. To cover the settlement costs and associated legal fees, Sealed Air recorded an $850.1 million charge, leading to a net loss of $309.1 million in 2002. The agreement put air back into the company's stock, sending it ballooning 56 percent and returning it to where it was before the critical July 2002 pretrial ruling.

SHIFTING FORTUNES: 2003–08

After the agreement Sealed Air was able to place its full attention on finding new products and market them. In 2003 the company received three prestigious DuPont Awards for Innovation in Packaging, including one for its new inflatable Bubble Wrap system. By 2004 Sealed Air was reporting an operating profit of $503 million. Sealed Air was ready to move into new areas, and in January 2006 it purchased Nelipak, a manufacturer of medical packaging with headquarters in the Netherlands. The company also expanded its operations in China and introduced shrink wrap products in Europe.

To increase its product line and develop new markets, Sealed Air decided to adopt an open innovative approach. This collaborative strategy, of looking for external partners to help solve technological problems and find additional markets, was employed in an alliance with NineSigma, a company with a large global network of experts. In 2007 Sealed Air also initiated an Annual Bubble Wrap Competition for Young Inventors that promoted brand recognition and supported educational efforts. That same year the company purchased rights to Ethafoam, a Dow Chemical performance foam business.

Sealed Air was selected in 2008 to provide the protective packaging to transport an irreplaceable cargo: Leonardo, a 77-million-year-old mummified dinosaur discovered in Montana. The unique artifact was wrapped by a special Sealed Air team that had designed, developed, and tested the custom protection for this extraordinary task. When Leonardo finally arrived at the Johnson Space Center in Houston, Texas, for scientific study, the fragile specimen was intact, testifying to the exceptional qualities of the Sealed Air products and the expertise of the Sealed Air team.

Despite Sealed Air's accomplishments, it experienced difficulties in a worsening global economy. An increase in resin prices (Sealed Air's primary raw material) and in transportation costs limited the company's profit margins in 2008. The company also agreed to pay $25 million indemnity to the families of 100 people who died in a rock club fire where Sealed Air packaging material had been used as soundproofing, and was continuing to pay for its 2002 asbestos settlement. Even though its revenues increased for 2008, the company reported a 49 percent decline in profits. To compensate, Sealed Air initiated strong cost-cutting measures by aggressively managing overhead costs, instituting programs to increase productivity, consolidating plants, and eliminating almost 1,000 jobs.

INNOVATION FOR FUTURE GROWTH

By 2009 Sealed Air had realized an estimated $45 million in savings. However, its revitalization strategy was not limited to cost reductions. Sealed Air was also increasing production in developing markets, such as China, India, eastern Europe, and Mexico. By building manufacturing facilities close to expanding markets, the company hoped to serve its global markets more effectively and to utilize its diverse distribution channels more efficiently.

In maintaining focus on its core food and protective packaging products, the company invested more than twice the industry average in research and development and launched over 25 new products in 2009. Its innovative edge was particularly strong in areas poised for global growth, including packaging that could be used in microwaves or conventional ovens, vertical pouch packaging, and automated packaging equipment systems. Sealed Air was also expanding into nonpackaging areas. Leveraging its technological expertise, the company had extended the use of its specialty materials into other applications, such as energy conservation and temperature-controlled supply chains.

Sealed Air was founded with an innovative product that began as a wallpaper and became an iconic packaging material. The company planned its continued growth as it had begun: by finding multiple uses for its varied materials and singular solutions to a variety of problems.

Robert R. Jacobson
Updated, David E. Salamie; Grace Murphy

PRINCIPAL SUBSIDIARIES

Cryovac, Inc.

PRINCIPAL OPERATING UNITS

Food Packaging; Protective Packaging; Medical Products; Shrink Packaging; Specialty Materials.

PRINCIPAL COMPETITORS

AEP Industries Inc.; Bemis Company, Inc.; Interplast Group; Pactiv Corporation; Printpack, Inc.; Reynolds Food Packaging; Sonoco Products Company.

FURTHER READING

Dunphy, T. J. Dermot. *Sealed Air Corporation: "Our Products Protect Your Products"—A Story of Modern Day Protective Packaging.* New York: Newcomen Society in North America, 1982.

Egan, Mary Ellen. "Pop Icon." *Forbes*, January 8, 2001, 140.

Hartman, Lauren R. "Shipping Fragile Fossils: After Spending 77 Million Years Underground, a 'Mummified' Dinosaur Is Unearthed." *Packaging Digest*, December 2008, 38.

Jusko, Jill. "Open Innovation Tools: Ninesigma Helps Manufacturer Sealed Air Grow Its Collaboration with External Partners." *Industry Week*, September 2009, 52.

Kim, Queena Sook. "Sealed Air Aims to Prove Cryovac Wasn't Too Big a Bite." *Wall Street Journal*, May 23, 2001, B4.

McGough, Robert. "Controlled Crisis." *Financial World*, February 6, 1990, pp. 74–75.

O'Brien, Timothy L., and Terzah Ewing. "Sealed Air to Buy Grace Packaging Unit." *Wall Street Journal*, August 15, 1997, A3.

Perone, Joseph R. "Sealed Air Agrees to Asbestos Deal." *Newark (NJ) Star-Ledger*, December 7, 2002, 13.

Vigna, Paul, and John Shipman. "Packaging Suppliers Put a Bow on Earnings." *Wall Street Journal*, July 21, 2010.

Welsh, Jonathan. "Sealed Air Moves beyond Success of Its Bubble Wrap." *Wall Street Journal*, March 14, 1997, B3.

Sigma Pharmaceuticals Ltd.

96 Merrindale Drive
South Croydon, Victoria 3136
Australia
Telephone: (+61 03) 9839-2800
Fax: (+61 03) 9839-2801
Web site: http://www.sigmaco.com.au

Public Company
Founded: 1912 as Sigma Company Limited
Incorporated: 1912
Employees: 1,700
Sales: AUD 3.22 billion ($2.54 billion) (2009)
Stock Exchanges: Australian Stock Exchange
Ticker Symbol: SIP
NAICS: 325411 Medicinal and Botanical Manufacturing; 325412 Pharmaceutical Preparation Manufacturing; 424210 Drugs and Druggists' Sundries Merchant Wholesalers; 541712 Research and Development in the Physical, Engineering, and Life Sciences (except Biotechnology)

■ ■ ■

Sigma Pharmaceuticals Ltd. is a leading Australian manufacturer and marketer of prescription, over-the-counter, and generic pharmaceutical products as well as a major wholesaler and distributor to pharmacy retailers. In addition to its manufacturing and wholesale businesses, Sigma owns three of Australia's leading retail pharmacy brands: Amcal, Amcal Max, and Guardian.

COMPANY ORIGINS

Sigma Pharmaceuticals was founded in 1912 as Sigma Company Limited by two Melbourne pharmacists. In an era when the vast majority of Australian medicines and chemicals were imported, the company began as a cooperative pharmaceutical wholesaler of mostly imported ready-to-use products. Together with other Australian drug wholesalers of the time, Sigma established a practice of providing financial backing to retail pharmacies that purchased and sold its wholesale goods.

With the outbreak of World War I in 1914, disruptions in trade revealed the depth of Australian dependence on drugs, chemicals, and scientific instruments imported from Europe, particularly because Germany had been the source of 90 percent of Australia's chemical supplies. Moreover, shortages and submarine warfare forced the British government to forbid or limit drug exports to its colonies. These developments, together with serious outbreaks of disease in 1913 and 1915, led the Australian government to establish the Commonwealth Serum Laboratories (CSL) in 1916 to ensure domestic supplies of drugs to treat meningitis, smallpox, and other potentially epidemic diseases.

ENTRANCE INTO MANUFACTURING

World War II (1939–45) further stimulated Australian pharmaceutical research and manufacturing. Threatened shortages in antimalarials and other essential drugs prompted the CSL to engage university-based scientists

COMPANY PERSPECTIVES

Our aims: grow the market share and profitability of our leading product and retail pharmacy brands; be the preferred supplier of products and services to pharmacies and medical practitioners; build mutually advantageous strategic long-term relationships with key suppliers; provide efficient, "best in class" customer service; operate the most efficient and reliable pharmaceutical manufacturing service in Australia.

in drug research and development, particularly on drugs derived from Australia's native plants. In 1942, in the midst of this domestic research and development effort, Sigma began its long history of manufacturing activities.

In 1950, in an effort to ensure the availability of a small number of life-saving drugs, the Australian government established its Pharmaceutical Benefits Scheme (PBS). The scheme, or medical benefits plan, would go on to bear an enormous influence on the development of Australia's pharmaceutical manufacturing, wholesale, and retail firms. The 1960 National Health Act (NHA) further enhanced the effect of drug benefit schemes. By 1978, however, about 90 percent of the drugs paid for under the PBS and NHA were manufactured by overseas companies, and by 1985, the PBS and NHA subsidized or paid for three-fourths of the prescriptions at privately owned pharmacies. This large percentage, and the NHA's ability to set the rate of payment it provided, diminished financial returns to retail pharmacists and slowed the development of new medicines.

By 1986 Sigma remained one of only three large Australian-owned pharmaceutical manufacturing companies. Many smaller firms whose manufacturing patents had expired had been acquired by large multinational drug companies.

ACQUISITIONS AND GROWTH: 1997–2003

With a view toward becoming a larger and publicly listed company, Sigma began a concerted effort to grow its manufacturing and distribution capabilities by acquiring smaller companies. In 1997 it made the first of two significant acquisitions of leading Australian pharmacy product lines and retailers when it acquired Guardian, and the following year it made a similar move by acquiring Amcal.

The company's 1998 sales were reported at 1.32 billion Australian dollars (AUD), up 11 percent from the previous year, along with net profits of AUD 8.9 million. Analysts attributed the increase to Sigma's active expansion program and its ongoing transformation from a drug warehouse business to an integrated health care services provider. The company continued on this trajectory in 1999 when it acquired the Australian pharmaceutical manufacturing business of British-based SmithKline Beecham, including its facilities located in Dandenong, a suburb of Melbourne. That same year, Sigma Company obtained a full listing on the Australian Stock Exchange (ASX).

In May 2001 three Australian drug producers, including Sigma, were alleged to have offered illegal cash incentives to local pharmacists in exchange for exclusive sales agreements in which pharmacists would buy 90 percent of their stock from the three companies. These agreements also clashed with pharmacists' codes of conduct, which prohibited the compromising of professional independence, judgment, and integrity for commercial gain.

The next year Sigma faced a regulatory hurdle when it proposed a merger with another of Australia's leading pharmaceutical companies, Australian Pharmaceutical Industries (API). Sigma and API each held approximately 30 percent of Australia's drug wholesalers market, and because the proposed merger would have created an entity with a 60 to 70 percent market share in three Australian states, with sales totaling an estimated AUD 3.7 billion, the Australian Competition and Consumer Commission rejected the proposed merger. This setback did not stop Sigma from pursuing a general strategy of growth, however.

In 2003 Sigma acquired the Brisbane-based drug manufacturer Herron Pharmaceuticals for approximately AUD 123 million (AUD 10 million in Sigma Company shares and the remaining balance in cash). At the time of its acquisition by Sigma, Herron generated approximately AUD 80 million annually in sales.

MERGER WITH ARROW PHARMACEUTICALS

In 2005 Sigma merged with Australia's second-largest producer of generic drugs, Arrow Pharmaceuticals. The AUD 2.2 billion merger between Arrow and Sigma Company created the new Sigma Pharmaceuticals Limited. Since its incorporation in 1999, Arrow had obtained roughly 36 percent of Australia's generic pharmaceutical market. Sigma's chief executive, John

KEY DATES

1912: The company is founded as Sigma Company Limited.
1942: Sigma begins pharmaceutical manufacturing activities.
1999: Sigma Company Limited acquires full listing on Australian Stock Exchange (ASX).
2005: Sigma merges with Arrow Pharmaceuticals Limited to become Sigma Pharmaceuticals Limited.
2008: Sigma's profits on generic drugs are threatened when the government reduces the prices it will pay for these medicines.
2009: Financial troubles cause Sigma to alter its long-standing strategy of acquiring smaller companies.
2010: Sigma sells off its generic and over-the-counter drugs unit as the company attempts to recover from a turbulent fiscal year.

Stocker, told the Australian Associated Press on November 25, 2005, that the Arrow merger would "bring together two very complementary businesses," and that it would also grant Sigma exclusive access in Australia to a pipeline of generic drugs and lift the new Sigma Pharmaceuticals into the list of Australia's top 80 publicly listed companies.

Sigma launched renewed attempts to acquire rival Australian Pharmaceutical Industries in the autumn of 2006. Deepening financial problems at API, however, forced Sigma to withdraw from three informal offers before finally ending its bids completely in December.

In 2007 Sigma announced its expectation that underlying profit would increase by 15 percent during the coming fiscal year 2008. The company cited the acquisition of new retail pharmacies and the expansion of markets for generic drugs as reasons for its enhanced expectations. The announcement followed Sigma's report that its full-year net profits for the previous year had reached AUD 101.8 billion, down 2.9 percent from the previous full year.

In late 2008 Sigma acquired the Melbourne-based specialty company Orphan Holding Proprietary Limited for AUD 130 million. The privately held company focused on licensing, marketing, and distributing drugs from abroad in Australia and New Zealand, especially medications used to treat serious or life-threatening illnesses. Sigma's leaders hoped the acquisition would increase its exposure to non-retail markets, particularly hospitals. Analysts expected Orphan to provide Sigma with approximately AUD 40 million in additional annual sales and AUD 13 million in additional annual gross earnings.

PHARMACIST-CORPORATE CONNECTIONS

As the decade drew to a close, Sigma moved to increase its influence over pharmacies and individual pharmacists by means of training programs and economic incentives. In early 2008 Sigma joined with the Pharmacy Guild of Australia to offer a national learning and professional-development program for retail pharmacists. Developed specifically for Sigma's branded pharmacy chains (Amcal, Amcal Max, and Guardian), the Sigma Retail Training Program offered a total of 140 sessions on topics ranging from retail to health and personal development. Supplemented by online learning modules, the classroom-style program was anticipated to serve 10,000 to 15,000 participants in cities across Australia.

At the same time, Sigma continued to pursue its stated intention of bringing half of Australia's 5,000 pharmacies into its retail pharmacy network. Sigma backed its intentions with an ambitious AUD 6 billion plan to help finance pharmacy purchases by young pharmacists who wanted to acquire businesses from their older colleagues entering retirement. Under the plan, banks continued to finance 90 percent of pharmacy purchases, but Sigma offered 8.5 percent of funding, along with another 1.5 percent originating from equity investors. The arrangement allowed pharmacists to acquire longer-term financing at lower interest rates. It was similar to the kinds of financial assistance that Australian pharmaceutical wholesalers had provided in the early 20th century.

ALTERED STRATEGIES ON GENERIC DRUGS

Australia's government made significant reforms to its health care system in 2008, including drastically reducing the prices that the government would pay for generic medicines. Australian pharmaceutical companies claimed that the reductions in reimbursement, which they had lobbied against, contributed to major financial hardship and unexpected increases in debt.

In the wake of these reforms, Sigma unsuccessfully filed a court action in 2009 against multinational drug manufacturer Wyeth Pharmaceuticals for the right to release a generic version of Wyeth's antidepressant Efexor (known in the United States as Effexor), which had generated global sales of $3.9 billion in 2007–08. Sigma claimed that Wyeth's patents for the drug were invalid on a number of grounds, but the court dismissed the claims in November 2010.

ADDITIONAL GROWTH AND READJUSTMENTS

In October 2009 Sigma acquired a portfolio of pharmaceutical brand drugs and an additional manufacturing facility in Dandenong from the multinational drug company Bristol-Myers-Squibb. The estimated cost of $51.1 million gave Sigma access to 15 prescription brand-name drugs (including leading cholesterol treatments) for manufacture and distribution in Australia and New Zealand.

Sigma's growth strategy was seriously threatened, however, as the company defaulted on debt repayments in late 2009 and was forced to sell assets in order to pay creditors. Although it managed to renegotiate repayment terms with creditors at the end of November 2009, additional crises loomed in 2010. Following allegations of accounting irregularities and of the preferential treatment of large pharmacy retailers over smaller ones, the trading of Sigma shares on the Australian Stock Exchange was suspended on February 25, 2010, at Sigma's request. The halt lasted for five weeks while the company prepared revised earnings statements. On March 31 Sigma announced that it had suffered a loss of nearly AUD 389 million the preceding year. The Australian Associated Press reported that same day that Sigma attributed the loss to "deterioration in competitive conditions and a changing regulatory environment" as it saw its stock value diminished by half.

SALE OF PHARMACEUTICALS DIVISION TO ASPEN

Sigma was in serious financial trouble when Aspen Pharmacare, South Africa's largest drug company, agreed in August 2010 to purchase Sigma's generic and over-the-counter drugs unit for AUD 900 million. The sale enabled Sigma to retain its wholesale and retail businesses.

In its annual report to shareholders in September 2010, Sigma acknowledged the challenges of the preceding year and the significant impact of market conditions and other concerns. The report noted, however, that "Sigma has a unique vertically integrated and diversified business model with leading market positions in generics, over-the-counter, and consumer, medical, manufacturing, wholesale, and retail banners."

At the close of 2010, Sigma remained Australia's largest pharmaceutical manufacturer and Australian-owned supplier, utilizing five manufacturing sites across the continent. The company retained a significant share of the market in generic drugs and sought to maintain its place by aggressively pursuing a first-to-market strategy for generic drugs once their patents had expired. Its portfolio of prescription drugs included pain relievers and respiratory medications as well as the antibiotic Minomycin (minocycline), the cardiovascular medication Lanoxin (digoxin), and the sleep medication Normison (temazepam). Sigma also owns Australia's largest portfolio of over-the-counter medications, including pain relievers and cough-and-cold remedies, as well as hay fever and gastrointestinal medications. The company continued to manufacture medicinal creams, ointments, and dietary supplements such as vitamins and minerals. Sigma benefits from a long-term supply contract to manufacture antibiotics for Japan. Besides Japan, Sigma's largest established markets in the Asia-Pacific region included New Zealand and Hong Kong. Sigma also continued to export its products to markets in the Middle East and Europe, most notably Sweden. Major emerging foreign markets for Sigma-manufactured drugs included Malaysia, Taiwan, the Philippines, and Thailand.

As Australians continued to age along with their counterparts in other developed nations, they could be expected to demand increasing amounts of drugs used to address diseases and conditions more prevalent among an aging population. Moreover, Australia continued to provide a strong base for private and government-supported biotechnology research. Despite the worldwide economic downturn that began in 2008 and the changes brought to Australia's pharmaceutical industry by government benefit reforms, steady or increasing demand for pharmaceuticals and other health care products could be expected to create ongoing opportunities for pharmaceutical and health care companies in Australia.

Joyce Helena Brusin

PRINCIPAL SUBSIDIARIES

Sigma Company, Ltd.; Arrow Pharmaceuticals Proprietary, Ltd.; Sigma Pharmaceuticals (Australia) Proprietary, Ltd., including Herron Pharmaceuticals Proprietary, Ltd.; Chemist Club Proprietary, Ltd.; Amcal Proprietary, Ltd.; Commonwealth Drug Company Proprietary, Ltd.; Fawns & McAllan Proprietary Limited; Guardian Pharmacies Australia Proprietary, Ltd.; Sigma Finance Proprietary, Ltd.; Extend-A-Care Proprietary, Ltd.; Sigma New Zealand, Ltd.; Sigma (Hong Kong) Proprietary, Ltd.; Sigma (Western

Australia) Proprietary, Ltd.; Sigma Services Proprietary, Ltd.; Sigma Research Proprietary, Ltd.

PRINCIPAL COMPETITORS

Australian Pharmaceutical Industries; Halcygen Pharmaceuticals Limited; CSL Limited; Novogen Limited.

FURTHER READING

"Aspen Pharma's A$900-Million Lifeline Resuscitates Sigma." *Information Company*, August 16, 2010.

Greenblat, Eli. "Sigma Seals Painless $2bn Drug Merger." *Australasian Business Intelligence*, August 22, 2005.

———. "Sigma Switches Focus to 'Embrace' Strategy." *Australian Financial Review*, March 13, 2007.

"Sigma, Arrow Get Green Light from Shareholders to Merge." Australian Associated Press, November 25, 2006.

"Sigma Makes $1.085b Joint Bid for Symbion Health." *Gold Coast Bulletin*, June 20, 2007.

"Sigma Pharmaceuticals in $900m Aspen Deal." *Australian*, August 16, 2010.

"Sigma Reports $389m Annual Loss." Australian Associated Press, March 31, 2010.

"Sigma's Big Call." *Gold Coast Bulletin*, March 27, 2007.

"Spotlight on the Australian and New Zealand Pharmaceutical and Biotechnology Industries." In *Wiley Handbook of Current and Emerging Drug Therapies*, vol. 4. Hoboken, NJ: Wiley-Interscience, 2007, 151–74.

SRG Global, Inc.

23751 Amber Avenue
Warren, Michigan 48089-6000
U.S.A.
Telephone: (586) 757-7800
Fax: (586) 757-8329
Web site: http://www.srgglobalinc.com

Wholly Owned Subsidiary of Guardian Industries Corp.
Founded: 2009
Employees: 4,000
Sales: $670 million (2008)
NAICS: 336399 All Other Motor Vehicle Parts Manufacturing

■ ■ ■

If you purchased your car in North America, chances are better than even that its grille was made by SRG Global, Inc. Since its predecessor company was founded in 1946, SRG Global has built itself into a leading global manufacturer of advanced, high-value coatings on plastics, principally for the automotive industry. Just about anything in an automobile, commercial truck, or household appliance that combines chrome and plastic (including not only grilles but also exterior trim, door handles, and other items) comes out of the company's facilities in the United States, Europe, and Asia.

SRG Global's evolution parallels that of the U.S. auto industry in the postwar era. First it was a parts supplier with an innovative streak and close ties to Detroit's automobile companies in the 1950s and 1960s, and then it extended its production facilities into China and Europe. As auto production and consumption spread from its traditional bases in North America and Europe, SRG Global became what its name implies: a global manufacturing company with an increasingly international base of customers. In 2010 *Plastics Week* ranked it as the fifth-largest North American maker of injection molds, with an estimated $550 million in sales.

SIEGEL-ROBERT AUTOMOTIVE

Siegel-Robert Automotive, Inc., was founded in 1946 and quickly established itself as one of the niche parts suppliers to Ford Motor Company, General Motors, Chrysler, and the American Motor Company. In the 1960s the Missouri-based company pioneered chrome-plated plastics and thereafter expanded its client roster to include non-automotive manufacturers such as Whirlpool that shared a demand for this process. Also in the decades that followed, Siegel-Robert continued to expand in the lower Midwest, establishing new operations in Tennessee (its electroplating plant in Ripley, Tennessee, opened in 1964), Kentucky, and Indiana.

Growth of the automotive unit's business quickened in the 1990s, as Detroit's automakers coped with economic challenges in part by outsourcing more of the production process. In 1996, for example, GM shifted production of car and truck grilles from its Delphi Flint West plant to a Siegel-Robert Automotive facility in Tennessee. By then Siegel-Robert Automotive had 3,200 U.S. workers.

Over the years Siegel-Robert Automotive expanded into a more diversified company, Siegel-Robert, Inc.,

COMPANY PERSPECTIVES

Our vision is to become the global leader in high-value coatings on plastics.

based in St. Louis. That company's other holdings included Advantek, Inc., which made products used in the assembly of electronic goods such as computers and medical components; Continental Disc Corporation, a manufacturer of disc devices for chemical and other industries; and Sensidyne, LP, a maker of industrial health and safety instrumentation.

Siegel-Robert's automotive unit maintained a reputation for innovation and continuous process improvement. One area on which it concentrated its attention was streamlining the manufacturing process for each of its products. For instance, its plant in Farmington, Missouri, worked to improve the "assembly assists" at each stage of production of its automotive grilles. Process economies in two areas, clip driving and hot air staking, resulted in creation of a two-station dial assembly machine that could assemble a complete grille in one setup. Such innovations led *Industry Week* to name the Farmington facility one of the best plants of the year in 2006. Innovation also helped Siegel-Robert expand its client group to include Toyota, Honda, Nissan, and motorcycle manufacturer Harley-Davidson.

SIEGEL-ROBERT'S INTERNATIONAL EXPANSION: 2004–06

As U.S. automakers began expanding their overseas manufacturing presence, so did Siegel-Robert. In 2004 it opened a sales and engineering office in Shanghai to support sales to Chinese automakers as well as work with U.S. auto companies and so-called Tier 1 parts suppliers that were expanding their production into China. The following year it opened a new 22,000-square-meter production facility in Suzhou, near Shanghai, producing high-quality decorative trim (essentially the same injection-molding and chrome-plate product line as manufactured in the company's U.S. facilities) and including design capabilities. The new operation cost $30 to $40 million to launch, and plans called for doubling its size by mid-2006.

In a press release dated October 12, 2005, Robert Simpson, president of Siegel-Robert Automotive, stated, "We plan to grow our business in Asia. We selected China because of the growing Chinese market, its proximity to current and potential customers, and its status as a low-cost country for global sourcing opportunities." In 2006 the automotive unit registered $363 million in sales out of $500 million-plus for parent Siegel-Robert, Inc., according to *Automotive News*, and was the largest manufacturer of chrome-plated plastic parts for the automotive industry in North America.

ACQUISITION AND GROWTH

In May 2008 Siegel-Robert, Inc., decided to reshuffle its mix of businesses, and it sold Siegel-Robert Automotive to Guardian Industries Corp., a maker of glass and other materials for the automotive and construction industries. The terms were undisclosed. Guardian Industries, based in Warren, Michigan, had an existing trim operation within its Guardian Automotive unit. At the same time, Siegel-Robert, Inc., also sold Sensidyne and refocused on its remaining two units, Advantek and Continental Disc, reincorporating itself in Nevada as Robert Family Holdings, Inc. In 2008 Siegel-Robert Automotive posted revenues of about $670 million.

In March 2009, at the Geneva International Motor Show, Guardian announced the creation of SRG Global, Inc., a new subsidiary combining Siegel-Robert Automotive, Guardian Automotive's trim operations, and a European trim operation, Lab Radio SA. The latter, located in Valencia, Spain, was a leader in wheel covers. The new company started with about 3,100 employees in the United States and 4,000 globally. Although the announcement came during a slump in auto sales and Chapter 11 filings by two of the Big Three U.S. automakers, Kevin Baird, SRG Global's president and chief executive officer, told the *Detroit News* (March 3, 2009) that "we've got a contrarian view." Guardian aimed to create a global trim maker that developed products in one country and manufactured them in many, making it more competitive in the regional markets it supplied.

Also in March 2009, SRG Global announced that it would build a new $25.3 million factory in Boleslawiec, Poland, creating at least 160 direct jobs in a region that had been attracting a string of new investments in parts and components facilities from European, North American, and Japanese companies. *Crain's Detroit Business* reported on January 12, 2010, that SRG Global was close to choosing a site in Mexico for a new 175,000-square-foot plant, in which it would invest some $30 million. "It's our goal for our business to resemble the global marketplace," director of marketing Thomas Schneider told *Crain's*.

Baird stressed that the company would, however, continue to reduce its workforce in response to the poor

KEY DATES

1946: Siegel-Robert Automotive, Inc., is founded.
2005: Siegel-Robert Automotive opens its first non-U.S. production facility, in Suzhou, China.
2008: Siegel-Robert, Inc., sells Siegel-Robert Automotive to Guardian Industries Corp.
2009: Guardian creates SRG Global, Inc., combining Siegel-Robert Automotive, Guardian Automotive's trim operations, and Lab Radio SA.
2010: Advanced Development Center opens in Taylor, Michigan.

auto market. It followed the announcement of the new Polish plant with news of the indefinite closing of its Bowling Green, Kentucky, location. After Guardian acquired Siegel-Robert Automotive, it reduced the number of facilities run by the three units that would form SRG Global from 15 to 10.

CONTINUED INNOVATION

SRG Global was also making sure it maintained its ability to innovate. In May 2010 it opened a new 46,000-square-foot Advanced Development Center in Taylor, Michigan, aimed at speeding development, testing, and time to market of its next generation of coatings for plastics. One of its first products was a new prototype louvered grille for GM that was said to improve the efficiency of the automaker's full-size pickup trucks and help it meet new U.S. emissions and fuel economy standards. "What we heard is that GM is moving 100 percent of their vehicles to louvered grilles," Jon DeGaynor, SRG Global's vice president of business development and strategy, told WardsAuto.com (May 18, 2010). "We're trying to find a way to do it more efficiently, less expensively, as an integrated part."

In a more difficult economic environment, Baird told *Automotive News* (July 5, 2010), the challenge for SRG Global and other parts suppliers was to find a way to improve its profitability with lower sales volume. "We're definitely experiencing the new normal," he said. "We've all scaled our business to allow us to ensure profitability at a much lower level than before."

A rebound in sales at the end of 2009 enabled SRG Global to post $423 million in sales to North American automakers for the year, and the improvement continued into 2010. In August the Ford Motor Company gave its "Q1" quality award to SRG's Ripley, Tennessee, plant, where it produced parts for Ford, including the grille for the popular Ford Escape SUV.

Eric Laursen

PRINCIPAL COMPETITORS

Automotive Components Holdings LLC; Berry Plastics Corp.; International Automotive Components Group LLC; Magna International Inc.; Neaton Auto Products Manufacturing Inc.; Newell Rubbermaid Inc.; Nypro Inc.

FURTHER READING

"Automotive Grille Assembly Yields Process Efficiencies." *Industrial Equipment News*, March 1, 2004.

Beene, Ryan. "SRG Global Inc. Eyeing Site in Central Mexico for New Plant." *Crain's Detroit Business*, January 12, 2010.

Diem, William. "SRG Targets Global Chrome Market." *Ward's Auto World*, April 1, 2009.

Lampinen, Megan. "Guardian Industries to Acquire Siegel-Robert's Automotive Business." *Automotive World*, April 17, 2008.

Miel, Rhoda. "New SRG Center Marries Molding, Coating." *Plastics News*, June 14, 2010.

Priddle, Alisa. "SRG of Warren to Grow Globally." *Detroit News*, March 3, 2009.

Swietek, Wes. "Auto Woes: 213 Losing Jobs: Parts Manufacturer S-R Closing Indefinitely; Corvette Plant Shutting Down for Six Weeks." *Bowling Green (KY) Daily News*, March 25, 2009.

Taninecz, George. "Best of Times in a Tough Industry: Technical Expertise and Lean Are Key to One Auto Supplier's Success." *Industry Week*, October 1, 2006.

Treece, James B. "The New Normal: Suppliers Who Survived Are Lean Enough to Thrive in an 11-millon Market." *Automotive News*, July 5, 2010.

Webb, Alysha. "Siegel-Robert Follows Top Customer to China." *Automotive News*, November 7, 2005.

Sylvia Woods, Inc.

328 Lenox Avenue
New York City, New York 10027
U.S.A.
Telephone: (212) 996-0660
Toll Free: (800) 263-4825
Fax: (212) 427-6389
Web site: http://www.sylviassoulfood.com

Private Company
Founded: 1962
Employees: 100
Sales: $60.3 million (2009 est.)
NAICS: 311422 Specialty Canning; 722110 Full-Service Restaurants; 722320 Caterers

■ ■ ■

Sylvia Woods, Inc., is a private company based in New York City that operates the iconic Sylvia's Restaurant, which is frequented by countless celebrities, politicians, businesspeople, and tourists from around the world as well as by local residents. The soul food eatery offers a full slate of southern dishes, including barbecued ribs, fried chicken, smothered chicken, smothered pork chops, collard greens, black eyed peas, peach cobbler, and sweet potato pie. Private dining rooms are available and the restaurant's menu is available thorough Sylvia's Catering Corp. The Sylvia's name is also applied to a line of products that are marketed by the subsidiary Sylvia's Food Products and are available in supermarkets around the country. They include sauces, spices, sausages, black eyed pea soup, navy bean soup, and canned vegetables. In addition, the company offers mixes for gravy, cornbread, fish fry, fried chicken, flapjacks and pancakes, peach cobbler, sweet potato pie, and apple crisp. Finally, the real estate firm ATOC, Inc., is controlled by the company, which in turn is owned and managed by the family of Sylvia Woods.

FOUNDER, SOUTH CAROLINA BORN: 1926

Sylvia Woods was born Sylvia Pressley in Hemingway, South Carolina, in 1926. She endured a hardscrabble childhood. When she was just three days old her father died and her mother soon left for New York to earn some much-needed money. During her mother's absences, Woods was raised by her grandmother and a close-knit rural community. Her grandmother gave cooking lessons to Woods, who at the age of eight needed to cook because her mother had returned home and was working in the fields. Woods also worked in the fields when she was older. At the age of 11 she met her future husband who was a year older, Herbert Woods, in a bean field. Although less known than his celebrated wife, Herbert would play a key role in the success of Sylvia Woods, Inc.

Sylvia and Herbert's courtship was hindered by her mother, who limited their dates to Wednesday and Sunday evenings. Then in 1939 Sylvia and her mother moved to New York. In an effort to continue the courtship, Herbert joined the U.S. Navy in hopes of making port in Brooklyn and seeing her on shore leave. He never came closer than Norfolk, Virginia, and soon he found himself in the Pacific Ocean working as a cook

COMPANY PERSPECTIVES

Sylvia Woods, the "Queen of Soulfood," is the founder and owner of the world famous Sylvia's Restaurant, located in the historical village of Harlem, since 1962.

on a battleship during World War II. When he was finally discharged from the service in 1944, he was reunited with Sylvia and they married.

Sylvia Woods had no interest in becoming a restaurateur. In fact, because of her modest upbringing, she had rarely passed through the doors of a restaurant. Instead, she worked at a hat factory while Herbert drove a cab. In 1954 she switched jobs to become a waitress at Johnson's Luncheonette in Harlem. Woods waited tables for eight years, when in 1962 the owner ran into financial difficulties and offered to sell the business to her.

WOODS BUYS LUNCHEONETTE: 1962

Woods's mother provided the funds to purchase the luncheonette by taking out a $20,000 loan. Woods took over a small operation that consisted of just six booths and 15 counter stools and renamed the luncheonette Sylvia's Restaurant. Despite the small size, Sylvia's succeeded. To help make sure the restaurant could pay the bills, Herbert became a long-distance truck driver, a job that he held into the late 1970s. He also put his training as a navy cook to good use by serving an occasional shift as a chef.

Woods explained the nature of the cuisine in an interview with *Restaurant Hospitality* in January 1995: "Chitlins and pigs' tails, those were the things you would get from the white folks' homes. That's soul food. We didn't have much, but we made the best out of what we had." Initially, Sylvia's Restaurant served Harlem's black community. There was enough business that in 1968 Woods relocated to a larger property on Lenox Avenue between 126th and 127th Streets. Over the years Sylvia's also became popular with customers outside of Harlem, who were more than willing to make the trek to Harlem at a time when the neighborhood was not considered especially safe. The *New York Times* writer Bryan Miller noted in his "Diner's Journal" on November 4, 1983, that seeing Cadillacs and Mercedes-Benzes double-parked outside Sylvia's was "not an uncommon sight in Manhattan's tonier neighborhoods. But such a scene outside an unglamorous-looking eating place … surrounded by neon-flashing, fried-chicken carryout shops, is curious indeed."

TOURISTS TARGETED

During the early 1980s Lloyd Williams, a banker and family friend, urged Woods to make an effort to appeal to tourists. While skeptical, she decided to take his advice and soon discovered that tourists from around the world were more than eager to visit, and the business grew to new heights. Herbert bought adjoining properties so that by 1987 the restaurant added three dining rooms and a patio and could seat as many as 315 people.

Besides the food, a major key to the success of Sylvia's Restaurant was the its family atmosphere. Miller described Sylvia's as "a back-slapping, bonhomous kind of place where waitresses call customers 'honey.'" However, there was no doubt that Woods, who was often called the "Queen of Soul Food," was the star attraction. Even though she was busy, she liked to visit freely with her customers, whether they were locals, celebrities, or foreign tourists. She told Jonathan Prober in the *New York Times* on August 5, 1987, "I enjoy laughing, mingling, seeing others enjoying themselves."

Woods was also surrounded by family. Her four children (two sons and two daughters) and seven grandchildren were all working at the restaurant by the late 1980s. The family members were close, but they did not always agree on how to grow the business because some members were more conservative than others. It was a mix that allowed the business to grow at a measured pace. One of the more assertive family members was daughter Bedelia, who was the driving force behind the restaurant expanding into catering. Even though her mother and brother Kenneth insisted that the kitchen was not set up to handle the extra work, Bedelia continued to make her case until the family finally agreed to make the necessary investment. Eventually, Sylvia's was catering major events, such as the Grammy Awards, and feeding as many as 3,000 people.

FOOD PRODUCTS ADDED: 1992

It was another son, Van, who took the lead in forming Sylvia's Food Products. For years customers brought bottles to the restaurant to purchase Sylvia's popular barbecue sauce. Finally, a fireman showed up with a gallon jug asking for the sauce. Van Woods decided the time had come to start bottling the sauce, and in 1992

KEY DATES

1962: Sylvia Woods buys Johnson's Luncheonette and renames it Sylvia's Restaurant.
1968: Sylvia's Restaurant moves to larger location.
1992: Sylvia's Food Products is established.
1997: Sylvia's Restaurant opens in Atlanta, Georgia.
2001: Sylvia's Express opens in John F. Kennedy International Airport.

he established Sylvia's Food Products and launched the Queen of Soul Food line with $200,000 in start-up capital. Initially, the only product was the barbecue sauce, but the line soon added hot sauce. Because the company wanted to gain entry to supermarkets, it decided to develop a more extensive line of products. Another popular restaurant item, collard greens, was added along with other canned vegetables. The initial 17-product soul food line became available in supermarkets throughout New York City and in the Northeast and the South. The line gradually gained national coverage and by 1997 Sylvia's Food Products was booking $6 million in annual sales.

Woods's popularity caught the attention of the book publisher William Morrow and Company, and in 1992 she published the cookbook *Sylvia's Soul Food Cookbook: Recipes from Harlem's World Famous Restaurant.* The book sold well enough that in 1999 Morrow published a second book with her, *Sylvia's Family Soul Food Cookbook: From Hemingway, South Carolina, to Harlem.* The branding possibilities of the Sylvia's name were not lost on others. During the late 1990s a group of investors led by the J.P. Morgan Community Development Corporation attempted to duplicate the success of Sylvia's Restaurant in other parts of the country. In 1997 a 250-seat Sylvia's Restaurant opened in Atlanta, Georgia. There were plans to open other restaurants in Baltimore, Maryland; Chicago, Illinois; Detroit, Michigan; Houston, Texas; and Los Angeles, California. However, they never materialized and after several years the Atlanta restaurant closed as well. Sylvia's also attempted to take advantage of its name recognition by opening an express outlet at New York's John F. Kennedy International Airport in 2001. However, the outlet eventually failed.

HARLEM REVITALIZED

Sylvia's Food Products and Sylvia's Catering Corp. were the only businesses using the Sylvia's name that had staying power. In Harlem, however, the restaurant retained its iconic status, along with the nearby Apollo Theater, and in the new century the restaurant played an important role in revitalizing the community. The former president Bill Clinton established his office in Harlem, and members of the upper-middle class also descended on the neighborhood by purchasing boarded-up brownstones and gentrifying a neighborhood that had suffered through decades of decline. To many New Yorkers and tourists, Sylvia's Restaurant had been one of the few reasons to venture to the area north of Central Park.

The new century was a time of change for the Woods family. In 2001 Herbert passed away at the age of 76. That same year the family established the Sylvia and Herbert Woods Scholarship Endowment Foundation to make scholarships available to children who lived in Harlem and in the surrounding communities. The restaurant remained as popular as ever, although the recipes had to be modified in 2007 to adhere to the city's ban on the use of trans fats. In 2010 Woods was named by *Crain's New York Business* to its Restaurateurs Hall of Fame, joining the founders of Le Circe, TGIF's, and Union Square Café among other notable eateries. The restaurant she founded and nurtured was in good hands with her children and grandchildren and was expected to remain popular for many years to come.

Ed Dinger

PRINCIPAL SUBSIDIARIES

ATOC, Inc.; Sylvia's Catering Corp.; Sylvia's Food Products.

PRINCIPAL COMPETITORS

Del Monte Foods Company; Dinosaur Bar & Char Inc.; Glory Foods, Inc.

FURTHER READING

Hayes, Jack. "NY-based Sylvia's to Launch Chains, Sets Sights First on Atlanta." *Nations Restaurant News*, March 10, 1997, 37.

Marriott, Michel. "Queen of Soul Food Taking 'Down Home' on the Road." *New York Times*, September 3, 1997.

Martin, Douglas. "Herbert Woods, Consort of a Soul Food Queen, Dies at 76." *New York Times*, June 15, 2001, A29.

Miller, Bryan "Diner's Journal." *New York Times*, November 4, 1983.

Probber, Jonathan. "Sylvia's, a Harlem Institution, Celebrates 25th Anniversary." *New York Times*, August 5, 1987.

"Soul Survivor." *Restaurant Hospitality*, January 1995, 24.

Townsel, Lisa Jones. "Mother-Daughter Business Buddies." *Ebony*, June 1997, 90.

Tengelmann Warenhandelsgesellschaft KG

Wissollstrasse 5-43
Mülheim an der Ruhr, 45478
Germany
Telephone: (+49 208) 5806 0
Fax: (+49 208) 208 5806 6401
Web site: http://tengelmann.de

Private Company
Founded: 1867
Employees: 84,516
Sales: €11.34 billion ($15.05 billion) (2009)
NAICS: 445110 Grocery Stores; 444110 Home Centers; 448110 Clothing Stores, Men's and Boys'; 448120 Clothing Stores, Women's and Girls'; 454111 Internet Retail Sales Sites

■ ■ ■

Headquartered in Mülheim an der Ruhr, Germany, Tengelmann Warenhandelsgesellschaft KG is among the world's largest retail supermarket and distribution groups, ranking number four behind Wal-Mart Stores Inc., REWE Group, and METRO AG. Tengelmann employees over 84,000 people in supermarkets, discount markets, do-it-yourself stores, clothing retailers, and Internet distributors and is present in 16 countries in Europe. In the United States, Tengelmann is represented through its 41 percent control of the Great Atlantic and Pacific Tea Company, which includes the A&P, Kohls, Waldbaums, Super Fresh, Food Emporium, and Pathways banners.

Tengelmann remains the property of the founding Scholl and Haub family. Karl-Erivan Haub and Christian Haub, the great-great-grandsons of the company's founder, have led the company since the beginning of the 21st century by taking the company into its newest direction: e-commerce.

FROM COFFEE TO RETAIL: 1867–93

During the early 1800s the Scholl family provided ferry services on the Rhine River from their home in Mulheim. By midcentury the building of a bridge had ended the need for a ferry service, so the family business was transformed into a cargo service for the growing industrial presence in the Ruhr valley region. Among the cargo the family carried were products from the German and other European colonies, including spices, tea, cacao, and coffee, which arrived in the Dutch ports to be transported throughout Europe.

In 1867 Louise Scholl married Wilhelm Schmitz, who operated the wholesale business Schmitz & Lindgens, which focused on colonial products. Schmitz and Scholl joined their business interests to form the trading firm Wilhelm Schmitz-Scholl.

The growing popularity of coffee led Schmitz-Scholl to explore a new market. For most of the century coffee reached the end consumer as unroasted green beans. This meant that customers were required to roast their own coffee. Schmitz-Scholl saw an opportunity to provide an expanded service to its customers, so the company started roasting its own coffee for sale. This process remained small scale until 1882, when the

COMPANY PERSPECTIVES

With its modern structure and international outlook, the Tengelmann Group is a multi-sector retailer represented across Europe.

company purchased an industrial-sized roasting oven and opened a coffee roasting plant across the street from its headquarters. By the mid-1880s the Schmitz-Scholl Kaffeerösterei produced more than 1,000 pounds of coffee per day. After adding a second roaster, the company moved its coffee roasting operations to a new, larger production plant.

When Wilhelm Schmitz died in 1887, his sons Karl and Wilhelm Schmitz-Scholl took over the company's operations and began orienting the company toward further expansion. The brothers began advertising their products, and Schmitz-Scholl's coffee soon reached new popularity under the Plantagen Kaffee and Storch Kaffee brand names.

The company eventually grew dissatisfied with its distribution arrangements, in which it used third-party distributors or sold directly to retailers. Schmitz-Scholl took pride in the quality of its products, in particular its coffee, a pride that was not always reflected in the care with which retailers stored and displayed its products. Therefore, during the 1890s the company became determined to take over the distribution of its products.

The first Schmitz-Scholl retail store opened in 1893 in Düsseldorf and was called Tengelmann, after their longtime employee Emil Tengelmann. Firma Hamburger Kaffee-Import-Geschaft Emil Tengelmann, a retail subsidiary, was set up under the Schmitz-Scholl operation. The Tengelmann store featured the company's coffees, cacao, and teas, as well as other grocery items.

GROWTH AND EXPANSION: LATE 19TH AND EARLY 20TH CENTURIES

The Scholls quickly expanded the Tengelmann concept from a single store to a true retail organization with branches spreading throughout Germany. Driving this growth was the company's coffee, which had become a popular brand name, making the Scholl-Tengelmann operation one of Europe's leading coffee importers. The success of its wholesale and retail distribution activities encouraged the company to increase its production capacity. At the turn of the 20th century the company opened three new grocery branches that featured their own coffee roasting plants. The Tengelmann stores also began providing a wider assortment of goods and eventually became full-fledged grocery stores.

Among the company's imported products were items such as vanilla, anise, cinnamon, cane sugar, and other spices that, coupled with the firm's cacao imports, led the Scholl-Tengelmann concern to expand in a new direction. During the early 1900s the company established a second production line by producing its own sweets and confectionery products. This production line resulted in the formation of Rheinische Zuckerwarenfabrik GmbH, which was established in Düsseldorf in 1906 under the direction of Wilhelm Schmitz-Scholl.

The launch into candies was followed by the construction of the company's own chocolate and cacao factory in Mülheim, which opened in 1912. The company's chocolate and cacao products were sold under the Wissoll brand name, formed by the contraction of the Wilhelm Schmitz-Scholl company name. During the 1920s the company began selling its candy products on the international market.

By the outbreak of World War I the Schmitz-Scholl company encompassed more than 560 Tengelmann stores. With the German defeat in 1918 and the reparations toll, which included the loss of parts of German territory, including the Ruhr valley region, Tengelmann (as the company began to call itself) lost approximately 160 of its grocery stores. The postwar period resulted in rampant inflation, so much so that the German mark became virtually worthless. To continue operations, Tengelmann adapted its product assortment by adding inexpensive items such as ersatz coffee and pudding powders.

During the Weimar Republic in the 1920s Tengelmann began an expansion drive by dividing its operations into regional divisions and modernizing its store design. Beginning in the 1930s, however, an economic depression that exacerbated the volatility of the German political scene enabled the Nazi Party to take power. Tengelmann had also come under new leadership. When Karl Schmitz-Scholl died in 1933, his son, Karl Jr., became the company's chief. Following the eruption of World War II, Tengelmann's operations were placed under the ultimate control of the Nazi government.

NATIONAL EXPANSION: 1945–69

By the end of the war most of Tengelmann's facilities were in ruins. Many of the company's urban-based stores and factories had been damaged during the war,

KEY DATES

1867: Foundation of trading forms Wilhelm Schmitz-Scholl.
1893: Opening of first retail store in Düsseldorf under the name Tengelmann.
1953: Tengelmann introduces self-service grocery stores.
1971: Tengelmann acquires Kaiser's Kaffee Geschäft AG.
1972: Tengelmann opens the first Plus store.
1979: Tengelmann acquires a controlling share of the Great Atlantic and Pacific Tea Company and its A&P chain of supermarkets.
1985: Tengelmann acquires OBI.
1994: Tengelmann launches Kik.
2002: Tengelmann changes its name to Tengelmann Warenhandelsgesellschaft KG.
2009: Plus Warenhandel GmbH merges with Netto Marken-Discount GmbH & Co OHG.
2010: Tengelmann E-Commerce GmbH is launched.

and of the facilities that had not be damaged, most were located in Soviet-controlled East Germany. Moreover, the shortage of goods following the war made it difficult for the company to resume its operations. Complicating matters, Karl Jr. had received a jail sentence because of his membership in the Nazi Party. In spite of these challenges, Tengelmann resumed operations in 1945 under the direction of Schmitz-Scholl's sister, Elisabeth Haub. Product assortment was limited, but the company developed several powdered products that were used as protein supplements.

By 1949 Tengelmann employed over 2,000 people in 222 branches. Perhaps the most significant move that enabled Tengelmann to become one of West Germany's top grocery chains was the institution of an innovative shopping concept that Erivan Haub, Karl Jr.'s nephew, had brought back from the United States. Then 20 years old, Haub had been sent to the United States to spend time working for U.S. supermarkets, where he discovered the relatively new but successful self-service concept. Upon Haub's suggestion, the first self-service Tengelmann opened its doors in 1953. The success of the new concept was immediate. By the end of the 1950s Tengelmann had restructured all of its stores to the self-service format. During the 1960s the company began expanding its retail operations into newly developing segments. The first was a new department store concept called the hypermarket, which combined traditional supermarket operations with an expanded range of products, from hardware to small appliances to books and records. In 1967 Tengelmann inaugurated its first hypermarket under the Grosso-Markt name. The Grosso-Markt led to the launch of another concept store called the Tenga market. This smaller store took an opposite approach by providing a vastly reduced product assortment at discounted prices. The Tenga markets eventually gave way to other Tengelmann names, such as Ledi and Plus.

By 1968 Tengelmann had grown into a nationwide chain of more than 400 branch operations that included over 350 Tengelmann supermarkets, a growing number of Tenga discount stores and Grosso-Markt hypermarkets, and the company's chocolate production operations. That same year the company reported revenues of more than DEM 1 billion for the first time.

When Karl Jr. died in 1969, Erivan Haub took over the company and became the chief architect of Tengelmann's greatest expansion. Under Haub, the company began a string of important acquisitions that would not only strengthen the company's domestic position but also transform it into a major international player.

GROWTH THROUGH ACQUISITIONS: 1971–85

Tengelmann's first acquisition was in 1971, when the company bought its struggling archrival, Kaiser's Kaffee Geschäft AG. Founded in 1880, Kaiser's had grown into a chain of more than 500 supermarkets with revenues of DEM 875 million. During the late 1960s the company had run into difficulties. The acquisition by Tengelmann brought a restructuring of the Kaiser chain, including the conversion of a number of its smaller stores to the Tengelmann Plus format. Those stores, launched in 1972, took over the company's Tenga discount operations by expanding the small-store format to include fresh fruits and vegetables. Throughout the 1970s the company made a number of other domestic acquisitions, including firms such as C.F. Beck, Wedi, Carisch, Hillko, Bronner, Schwörer, and Schade & Füillgrabe.

The first step toward international expansion was the acquisition of Löwa Warenhandelgesellschaft, the Austrian supermarket chain, in 1972. In 1979 Tengelmann acquired a 24 percent controlling share of the Great Atlantic and Pacific Tea Company and its A&P chain of supermarkets. Once the world's largest supermarket chain, with more than 12,000 branches, A&P had fallen into disarray. However, under Tengelmann's control A&P restructured rapidly, revitalized its operations, and returned to profitability during the early 1980s.

Tengelmann expanded into the Netherlands by purchasing that country's number-four supermarket group, the Hermans Groep, in 1986. By the end of the decade Tengelmann had moved into two more European countries: Italy, with the acquisition of the Superal chain, and Hungary, with the acquisition of the Skála-Coop chain of supermarkets.

Tengelmann's international acquisition drive was partly in response to the increasingly limited growth opportunities in West Germany, but the company nevertheless sought means to continue its growth in West Germany. During this period Tengelmann began to diversify its product line. In 1985 the company acquired the holding company OBI and its chain of OBI do-it-yourself (DIY) hardware and building supply stores.

EXPANSION IN EASTERN EUROPE: 1990–2000

The purchase of the DIY chain encouraged Tengelmann to diversify even further. The takeover of the Modea clothing store chain in 1990 marked the company's move into clothing and accessories, and in 1994 Tengelmann launched the textile discount store KiK.

During the 1990s Tengelmann's international expansion continued with the extension of its discount store format into new markets, particularly in eastern Europe, which since the end of the cold war was open to western shopping experiences. In 1992 Plus stores were opened in Prague, Czech Republic, and Tatabánya, Hungary, and in 1995 in Dabrowa Górnicza, Poland.

With profits under increasing pressure because of a global recession, the cost of German reunification, and competition from other national discount stores such as Lidl and ALDI, Tengelmann was forced to decrease costs by refocusing on its core business. The company's short-lived deep discount chain Ledi was closed in 1997. That same year the Rudis Reste Rampe clothing store chain was sold. In 1999 Modea became the independent Takko Holding GmbH after a management buyout and the Grosso-Markt hypermarkets and Magnet super stores were sold to AVA. In 2000 Erivan Haub became chairman of the board of directors, while his sons Karl-Erivan Haub and Christian Haub began overseeing the day-to-day business operations.

CONSOLIDATION IN A NEW CENTURY: 2001–10

In 2001 the company combined the operations of Kaiser's Kaffee Geschäft AG and the Emil Tengelmann GmbH into Kaiser's Tengelmann AG. In 2002 the company became the Tengelmann Warenhandelsgesellschaft KG. Still essentially a family business, Karl-Erivan Haub became the chief executive officer (CEO) of the European division and Christian Haub became the CEO of the A&P North American division. The new leadership promised to promote stability and further growth by focusing on its major companies: Plus, Kaiser's Tengelmann, A&P, OBI, and Kik.

The beginning of the 21st century was marked by international expansion, particularly of OBI and Plus discount stores. OBI opened stores in Shanghai, China, in 2000 and in Sarajevo, Bosnia Herzegovina, and Moscow, Russia, in 2003. By 2005 OBI operated 500 stores throughout Europe. Plus opened stores in Greece, Portugal, Romania, and Spain. By 2006 Tengelmann operated 4,000 Plus stores, with over 1,000 of them located outside of Germany. Another 2,000 Kik stores were located throughout Germany.

In 2007, amid the global recession that was brought about by the collapse of the U.S. subprime mortgage market and the ensuing global banking crisis, Tengelmann reported a growth of 4.9 percent. In an effort to sustain this growth, Tengelmann began shedding its less profitable sectors. In 2008 Plus sold its stores in the Czech Republic, Greece, Poland, Portugal, and Spain. The following year Plus merged with Netto Marken-Discount GmbH & Co. OHG. Tengelmann retained only a 15 percent interest in the new company. Plus online, an Internet distributor of various nonfood items, severed its ties to Plus Warenhandelsgesellschaft and began operating independently under the Tengelmann umbrella. Two years later, in 2010, Tengelmann sold its Kaiser's Tengelmann branches in the Rhein-Main-Neckar area in southern Germany to the REWE Group and Tegut Gutberlet Stiftung & Co., citing difficult logistics in an area too large to blanket with only a few stores.

At the close of the first decade of the 21st century the company entered the e-commerce market by investing in several Internet distributors such as Lando, Brands4Friends, Baby-Markt, and You Tailor. Even though Kaiser's Tengelmann still made up the bulk of the company's revenue in 2010, closely followed by OBI and Kik, the new Tengelmann E-Commerce GmbH promised sustainable future growth. Paired with Tengelmann New Media GmbH, the company's online marketing arm, Tengelmann E-Commerce had the potential to become a potent global force online.

M. L. Cohen
Updated, Helga Schier

PRINCIPAL OPERATING UNITS

Kaiser's Tengelmann GmbH; OBI; Kik; A&P (41%); Tengelmann E-Commerce GmbH; Plus Eastern Europe

PRINCIPAL COMPETITORS

ALDI Group; H&M Hennes & Mauritz AB; Lidl Dienstleistung GmbH & Co. KG; METRO AG; REWE Group; Edeka Zentrale AG & Co. KG.

FURTHER READING

"A&P's Haub Is Calling for Private-Label Growth." *Supermarket News*, November 23, 1998.

Baumeister, Rosemarie, ed. *Ein Jahrhundert Tengelmann.* Mülheim an der Ruhr: Unternehmensgruppe Tengelman, 1993.

"Changes at Tengelmann Boost Store Brands." *Private Label*, November 1998.

"85 Filialen verkauft: Die Handelskette Tengelmann zieht sich komplett aus dem Rhein-Main-Neckar-Raum zurück." Nicos Weinwelten.de, March 17, 2010. Accessed October 27, 2010. http://www.nikos-weinwelten.de/home/beitrag/archive/2010/march/17/tengelmann_zieht_sich_zurueck/index.htm.

Funke, Eva. "Tengelmann knippst das Licht aus." *Stuttgarter Nachrichten*, August 26, 2010.

"Tengelmann CEO Eyes A&P Merger with Larger Peer." Reuters, August 26, 2010.

"Haub Zeichnet Ein Trübes Bild für den Lebensmittelhandel." *Frankfurter Allgemeine Zeitung*, December 18, 1998.

Kaczmarek, Joel. "Ein Spätzünder immt Fahtrt auf – wie Tengelmann den E-Commerce erschliessen möchte." Gruenderszene.de, March 19, 2010. Accessed October 27, 2010. http://www.gruenderszene.de/allgemein/ein-spatzunder-nimmt-fahrt-auf---wie-tengelmann-den-ecommerce-erschliesen-mochte.

"Lebensmittelkette Kaiser's Strafft Filialnetz und Geht Neue Wege." *Die Welt*, December 16, 1998.

Spector, Mike, and Timothy W. Martin. "Boxed in by Debt, A&P Solicits Advice." *Wall Street Journal*, October 13, 2010.

TomoTherapy Incorporated

1240 Deming Way
Madison, Wisconsin 53717-1954
U.S.A.
Telephone: (608) 824-2800
Fax: (608) 824-2996
Web site: http://www.tomotherapy.com

Public Company
Founded: 1997
Incorporated: 1997
Employees: 600
Sales: $270 million (2009)
Stock Exchanges: NASDAQ
Ticker Symbol: TOMO
NAICS: 334519 Other Measuring and Controlling Device Manufacturing

■ ■ ■

TomoTherapy Incorporated develops, manufactures, markets, and sells medical equipment capable of providing image-guided radiation therapy to treat cancer. TomoTherapy Hi-Art systems use external radiation beams to combine the 360-degree imaging capabilities of computed tomography (CT) with the therapeutic power of radiation. This method allows radiation oncologists and other members of the treatment team to more exactly focus radiation treatment and thus reduce unnecessary radiation exposure to surrounding healthy tissue. Doctors, medical physicists, and other specialists can use the narrow "slices" of X-ray obtained by a CT scan to vary therapeutic radiation intensity according to need, and can more accurately adjust to changes in a patient's anatomy as treatment progresses.

Headquartered in Madison, Wisconsin, and with European offices in Brussels, Belgium, TomoTherapy has placed more than 200 of its Hi-Art systems at cancer treatment centers in 16 countries around the world. It offers customer support services in each region, either directly or through third-party distributors.

BEGINNINGS OF A GOOD IDEA

Medical physicist Thomas Rockwell Mackie and mathematician and software engineer Paul Reckwerdt first discussed the ideas behind the TomoTherapy technology while waiting in line together at a University of Wisconsin cafeteria. In 1990 they joined forces to begin exploring how so-called slice therapy might improve radiation cancer treatment. Radiation oncologists, or cancer specialists who treat patients with radiation, had previously relied on CT or X-ray images obtained prior to therapy. Markings drawn on the patient's skin aligned external radiation therapy with the malignant tumors inside the patient. This approach could compromise accuracy and unnecessarily expose healthy surrounding tissue to radiation.

The slice therapy envisioned by Mackie and Reckwerdt promised to provide faster and more accurate treatments that minimized damage to surrounding tissue. Their method combined a radiation therapy unit with a circular CT scanner that could obtain cross-sectional, three-dimensional images of affected areas of the patient's body. After the CT scan determined the exact shape and location of the tumor, a radiation on-

COMPANY PERSPECTIVES

TomoTherapy Incorporated is an innovative company seeking to provide the best radiation treatment for patients worldwide.

cologist could more expertly determine treatment needs and, using a large rotating fiberglass cabinet, administer therapeutic radiation in a helical, or circular, pattern around the patient's body.

As Mackie and Reckwerdt continued to work on integrating imaging and radiation therapy, they launched a related venture in 1992. They established their first company, Geometrics, to produce software that could interpret CT scans more accurately and help oncologists plan cancer treatment.

In the winter of 1993, Mackie published the first medical research paper on tomotherapy in the journal *Medical Physics*. In 1994 Mackie and Reckwerdt established a tomotherapy research group at the University of Wisconsin. In 1996 they sold Geometrics, their first medical technology company, to ADAC Laboratories of California for nearly $4 million. The next year Mackie and Reckwerdt went on to found and incorporate TomoTherapy.

WISCONSIN INVESTORS STEP IN

TomoTherapy attracted its first investors in 1999. At the time Mackie and Reckwerdt were assembling their prototype machine in an underground cement bunker at the University of Wisconsin's Physical Science Laboratory. Each TomoTherapy machine cost $1.5 million to manufacture. The company's manufacturing start-up costs were estimated at approximately $6 million. The General Electric Company, which had previously signed a contract to produce the machines, abruptly withdrew its offer when it closed its radiation therapy division.

According to reports in Madison newspapers, investors were reluctant to back a venture that did not promise the quick, megamillion-dollar turnaround afforded by some Internet start-up companies at the time. The location of TomoTherapy also posed a challenge. Company cofounder Reckwerdt told the *Wisconsin State Journal* in a February 25, 1999, article that "venture capitalists have told us, if we were in [California's] Silicon Valley, they would do it tomorrow, or if this was Internet software, 'we'd back you tomorrow. You're in the Midwest; you can't do manufacturing out there,' they told us."

TomoTherapy did, however, attract Madison investors. The Wisconsin Alumni Research Foundation, the licensing and patenting arm of the University of Wisconsin, invested approximately $1.5 million in more than 100 tomotherapy-related patent applications in 12 countries. The Madison-based venture-capital group Venture Investors Management invested $1 million of the $16 million it had available in TomoTherapy

The medical establishment also greeted the machine's promise with enthusiasm. Even though TomoTherapy had not applied for U.S. Food and Drug Administration (FDA) approval for the device, a Canadian hospital and a University of Wisconsin hospital placed units on order. TomoTherapy also received a $500,000 technology development loan from the Wisconsin State Department of Commerce, along with a $100,000 small business innovation research grant from the federal government.

TREATMENTS BEGIN

In September 2001 the Cross Cancer Institute in Edmonton, Alberta, Canada, became the first cancer treatment center in the world to install and use TomoTherapy's Hi-Art units. The Canadian hospital, outside the jurisdiction of the FDA, had begun fund-raising in 1998 to cover the $3 million cost of the machine.

In February 2002 the FDA granted approval to TomoTherapy to market its new Hi-Art treatment system in the United States. The system was the first fully integrated radiation therapy system to offer patient imaging with treatment delivery. Previous systems had merely adapted existing CT scanners to also provide therapy. TomoTherapy anticipated selling six units in 2002 but hoped to sell as many as eight. According to company marketing director Andrew Jones, hospitals acquiring the units were required to build "radiation bunkers" with thick cement walls before installing the devices. In anticipation of increased demand for their product, TomoTherapy company executives announced plans to hire an additional 50 employees in 2002. In 2003 TomoTherapy delivered the first Hi-Art models to cancer treatment centers in the United States and clinical treatment of cancer patients began.

In June 2002 TomoTherapy won the statewide 2002 Emerging Entrepreneur of the Year Award at the annual awards ceremony for Wisconsin Entrepreneurs of the Year. Sponsored by the accounting firm of Ernst & Young, the award recognized companies in business fewer than five years.

In July 2003 TomoTherapy received a $900,000 Small Business Innovative Research grant from the

KEY DATES

1990: Thomas Mackie and Paul Reckwerdt first explore concept of "slice therapy."
1994: Tomotherapy research group is established at the University of Wisconsin, Madison.
1997: TomoTherapy Incorporated is founded.
2002: Company is granted U.S. Food and Drug Administration approval to market Hi-Art treatment system.
2007: Company is listed on the NASDAQ.

National Cancer Institute. The grant was awarded to support continued research and the development of new oncology imaging methods. Innovations under development at TomoTherapy in 2003 included methods to create images of patients in real-time during radiation therapy treatments. Dr. Guang Feng, a senior physicist at TomoTherapy, told the *Madison (Wisconsin) Capital Times* in a July 4, 2003, article that the new methods under development promised significant breakthroughs. "Since organ motion is a significant obstacle to precise treatment delivery, we are talking about major improvements in cancer treatment," he said.

In late December 2005 TomoTherapy succeeded in raising $14 million in new equity capital. "This could very well be our last round of private financing," said CEO Frederick Robertson in an interview published in the January 13, 2006, issue of *Medical Device Week*. The new capital was expected to accelerate growth, increase manufacturing capacity, and expand operations to meet increasing demand for TomoTherapy treatment systems. Expanding operations also increased the number of TomoTherapy employees from 171 at the end of 2004 to 327 at the close of 2005.

INTERNATIONAL SALES AND LOCAL SUPPORT

At the beginning of 2006, TomoTherapy announced that its 2005 revenues would top $85 million, nearly twice its 2004 revenues. January 2006 orders for Hi-Art units were not anticipated to be filled until the summer. By 2006 over 50 units were installed in treatment facilities around the world, including hospitals in Belgium, Hong Kong, Italy, and Japan, as well as at the prestigious Johns Hopkins Hospital in Baltimore, Maryland. More than 600 patients a day received cancer treatment with TomoTherapy equipment. By 2006 sales offices had opened in Brussels, Belgium, and Bangkok, Thailand.

At least two other Wisconsin communities, Middleton and Fitchburg, attempted to woo TomoTherapy away from its Madison headquarters. In response, the Madison City Council and the Madison Development Corporation lent TomoTherapy nearly $1 million to help pay for new equipment to expand production. According to Madison's director of planning and development, Mark Olinger, this was not an unusual practice. In the January 1, 2006, edition of the *Wisconsin State Journal*, Olinger said "I think anything that we do that helps us continue to have home-grown firms [is important.]" Regarding TomoTherapy, he added, "They're rapidly growing; they continue to hire people; they're really a cutting-edge, high-tech firm."

INITIAL PUBLIC OFFERING AND OTHER MILESTONES

On May 9, 2007, TomoTherapy celebrated 10 years of expansion and growth when it became a publicly traded company on the NASDAQ. TomoTherapy's initial public offering (IPO) raised $223 million on the sale of 11.7 million shares. Shares initially priced at $19 at the beginning of the day rose to $22.67 at the close of trading. The Wisconsin Alumni Research Foundation still retained 3.3 percent of equity in the new public company, based on its early investment in patent applications. Other Wisconsin-based firms also retained interests. Venture Investors LLC of Madison owned as much as 12 percent of the outstanding shares.

In February 2008 TomoTherapy celebrated an important milestone when it produced its 200th Hi-Art unit and shipped it abroad to Italy. In May 2008 TomoTherapy acquired the privately owned Chengdu Twin Peak Accelerator Technology, Inc., of China for an undisclosed sum. Linear accelerators, such as those manufactured by Twin Peak, were key components in radiation therapy systems because they created the high-energy X-rays needed for cancer therapy. TomoTherapy announced it would use the accelerators manufactured by Twin Peak to supplement its existing supply sources. TomoTherapy CEO Robertson commented in the May 1, 2008, issue of the journal *Biomedical Business & Technology* that "the acquisition of Twin Peak represents a substantial advance in our ability to control the quality and features of our products. This is also a piece of our long-term strategy of reducing the cost of the Hi-Art treatment system to improve margins."

RESPONSE TO CHALLENGES AND THE LONG VIEW

In January 2009 TomoTherapy announced a 12 percent reduction in its workforce. Calculated to save approximately $5.4 million annually, the move came in response to what CEO Robertson described to *Biotech Business Week* in the January 5, 2009, issue as slow growth in challenging economic conditions. "It is essential in the current environment to effectively manage costs while continuing to provide outstanding service and support to our global customer base," said Robertson.

In addition to the original Hi-Art units, available TomoTherapy products in 2010 included the TomoMobile, a portable unit that could be transported and relocated to improve patient access to cancer care. Another product, the TomoHD treatment system, combined helical and direct radiation treatment methods in a single device to enable clinics to serve a broader population of cancer patients.

Although the company had begun experiencing slower growth, a number of factors continued to have a positive effect on sales of TomoTherapy products. These included increased patient and physician awareness of product availability and the treatment methods offered, potentially lower health-care costs, and the rising number of cancer treatment procedures performed around the world. Any reluctance on the part of hospitals or clinics to adopt TomoTherapy systems might have been influenced by other factors, including limited reimbursement levels, a scarcity of trained personnel, lengthy training times, time required to plan patient treatment, and the relatively high average selling price of the TomoTherapy units.

Joyce Helena Brusin

PRINCIPAL COMPETITORS

Accuray Incorporated; BrainLAB AG; Elekta AB; Siemens Healthcare; Varian Medical Systems, Inc.

FURTHER READING

"Cancer Killer: Big Idea, Little Money. UW Offshoot Company Working on Machine That Delivers Radiation." *Wisconsin State Journal*, February 25, 1999.

"Financings Roundup." *Medical Device Week*, January 13, 2006.

"International Report: Chengdu Twin Peak Accelerator Technology." *Biomedical Business & Technology*, May 1, 2008.

Mackie, Thomas, et al. "Tomotherapy: A New Concept for the Delivery of Dynamic Conformal Radiotherapy." *Medical Physics*, November–December 1993.

Newman, Judy. "Tomotherapy Riding a Wave: Company That Makes Cancer-Treatment Equipment Is Growing at a Serious Pace." *Wisconsin State Journal*, January 1, 2006.

Richgels, Jeff. "New Grants to Firms Here Will Advance Technologies." *Madison (WI) Capital Times*, July 4, 2003, 7C.

"TomoTherapy Announces Workforce Reduction." *Biotech Business Week*, January 5, 2009.

Williams-Masson, Ellen. "Striking Gold: TomoTherapy a Bold Example of University Spin-Off Success." *Wisconsin State Journal*, July 13, 2008. Accessed November 11, 2010. http://host.madison.com/business/article_5baec918-205f-5704-9daa-de47808fc46a.html.

Transocean Ltd.

Turmstrasse 30
Zug, Ch-6300
Switzerland
Telephone: (+41 41) 749 0500
Web site: http://www.deepwater.com

Public Company
Founded: 1919 as Danciger Oil and Refining Company
Incorporated: 1953 as The Offshore Company
Employees: 19,300
Sales: $11.6 billion (2009)
Stock Exchanges: NYSE Zurich
Ticker Symbol: RIG (NYSE) RIGN (SIX)
NAICS: 213111 Drilling Oil and Gas Wells

■ ■ ■

Transocean Ltd. is the world's largest offshore drilling company. With official headquarters in Switzerland and a major operating center in Houston, Texas, the company fields more than 19,000 employees around the globe. Transocean's drilling rigs and work crews are contracted by petroleum companies at a day rate, over the course of long-term and short-term contracts. Transocean's mobile rigs cover all of the world's major offshore drilling markets off five continents. Although the company offers inland drilling barges and shallow-water drilling rigs, Transocean is especially active in the deepwater and harsh environment drilling segment, offering semisubmersible rigs as well as massive drill ships that have drilled to record depths of more than 35,000 feet. The rig that set this world depth record, *Deepwater Horizon*, exploded on April 20, 2010, in the Gulf of Mexico, setting off the largest environmental disaster in the history of the petroleum industry.

CORPORATE LINEAGE DATING BACK TO 1953

Transocean is composed of a number of drilling operations that were merged, especially during the late 1990s and 2000s when the offshore drilling industry as a whole consolidated. The surviving corporate structure belongs to The Offshore Company, incorporated in Delaware in 1953. It was created when the pipeline company Southern Natural Gas Co. (SNG) purchased DeLong-McDermott, which was a contract drilling joint venture of DeLong Engineering and J. Ray McDermott's marine construction business.

A year later, Offshore established the first jackup drilling rig in the Gulf of Mexico. Oil and gas exploration then began to move farther offshore and to more remote areas of the world. In the 1960s Offshore became one of the earliest companies to operate jackups in the inhospitable environment of the North Sea, which would develop into one of the world's most significant sources of oil.

In 1967 Offshore went public. Ten years later it expanded its range of operations to Southeast Asia, where it drilled its first deepwater well. In 1978 the company became a wholly owned subsidiary of SNG, which had greatly increased its emphasis on offshore drilling and exploration operations. As a result, Offshore developed one of the largest U.S. fleets of drilling rigs. When SNG changed its name to Sonat in 1982, The

COMPANY PERSPECTIVES

Our mission is to be the premier offshore drilling company providing worldwide rig-based, well-construction services to our customers through the integration of motivated people, quality equipment, and innovative technology, with a particular focus on technically demanding environments.

Offshore Company became known as Sonat Offshore Drilling Inc.

RISE AND FALL OF OIL PRICES

During the 1970s new "floaters" were developed to accomplish deepwater drilling. Semisubmersible rigs were partially submerged and usually moored to the ocean floor for stability. Drill ships, able to reach depths of 3,000 feet and particularly useful in exploring remote areas, were also introduced as a cost-effective option during this period. By the late 1970s a large number of companies began to build and operate floaters, leading to a highly fragmented industry. When oil prices reached $32 a barrel in 1981, a drilling boom ensued, with oilfield service companies purchasing a great deal of equipment and saddling themselves with considerable debt.

As the price of oil plunged in the mid-1980s, reaching a level below $10 by 1986, oil companies canceled drilling programs or negotiated much lower day rates for offshore rigs. A 300-foot jackup in the Gulf of Mexico that once commanded $50,000 a day now rented for less than $10,000. Many service companies went bankrupt or were swallowed up by stronger rivals. During this decade-long lean period, the number of offshore drilling rigs in operation declined precipitously, from more than 1,000 in the early 1980s to around 500.

When oil and gas prices appeared to be rising in 1993, Sonat took advantage of investor optimism to spin off Sonat Offshore, making $340 million while retaining a 40 percent interest, which would then be sold off in 1995. In this way the parent company hoped to transform itself from a diversified pipeline company into an exploration and production company.

The newly independent Sonat Offshore, as a result of the offering, had a clean balance sheet and money in the bank, and was well positioned to weather an ensuing decline in gas prices. Moreover, the company's emphasis on deepwater oil drilling also would prove to be a wise strategy. It was recognized that the most desirable energy plays that remained in the world resided under great depths of ocean. Although the technology existed to tap these deposits, only until oil prices reached a certain level would it become economical for a company like Sonat Offshore to invest in a new generation of drill ships. The cost of such rigs was so high that only large companies were able to afford them.

CONSOLIDATION AMONG OFFSHORE DRILLING CONTRACTORS

There were other reasons why consolidation among offshore drilling contractors became desirable in the mid-1990s. It would likely bring pricing discipline to a highly fragmented industry, in which the top three companies served just 27 percent of the market. In 1995 there were about 400 jackup rigs owned by as many as 80 companies, creating a supply/demand imbalance that gave oil producers tremendous leverage over contractors. A small drop in the price of gas or oil could result in a major decrease in day rates.

Clearly, companies could not expect to achieve long-term health by simply building more rigs to expand their business. Growth had to come by acquiring existing rigs, to gain some leverage with producers. With fewer but larger contractors in the industry, the addition of new rigs would hopefully become more of a rational and systematic process. In addition, larger players could operate more efficiently around the world, with rigs strategically positioned to save on moving charges while building a more diversified customer base.

In 1995 Sonat Offshore announced its proposal to acquire Reading & Bates Corp., which began offshore drilling operations in 1955. Although discussions continued over the next several months, in the end Reading & Bates rejected a $501 million cash and stock offer. In May 1996 Sonat Offshore announced a $1.5 billion stock and cash deal to acquire Norway's Transocean ASA, which a few months earlier had announced that it was looking for a partner. Transocean ASA had been created in the mid-1970s when a Norwegian whaling company entered the semisubmersible business, then later consolidated with a number of other companies. Because of its large North Sea operations, Transocean ASA was considered a prize catch, one that would automatically make the buyer into the unquestioned leader in deepwater drilling.

Reading & Bates attempted to outflank Sonat Offshore, venturing an unsolicited bid for Transocean ASA, which because of Norway law did not have any of the U.S. takeover defenses at its disposal, such as

KEY DATES

1942: Forex is founded in France.
1947: Southeastern Drilling Company (Sedco) is founded.
1953: The Offshore Company is incorporated.
1978: The Offshore Company becomes a wholly owned subsidiary of Sonat Inc., formerly Southern Natural Gas Co. (SNG).
1993: Sonat Offshore is spun off.
1996: Sonat Offshore acquires Transocean ASA to become Transocean Offshore.
1999: Transocean Offshore merges with Sedco Forex Drilling to become Transocean Sedco Forex Inc.
2001: Transocean acquires R&B Falcon to become the world's largest offshore drilling company; two rivals, Global Marine and Santa Fe International, combine to form Global Santa Fe, Transocean's closest competitor.
2007: Transocean merges with Global Santa Fe.
2010: Transocean's *Deepwater Horizon* rig, leased by British Petroleum in the Gulf of Mexico, explodes, leading to the largest accidental oil spill in history.

"poison pill" provisions. After a month-long skirmish, Sonat Offshore sweetened its bid and agreed to retain much of Transocean's management team, the fate of which was uncertain under the Reading & Bates offer. The deal became effective in September 1996, and Sonat Offshore changed its name to Transocean Offshore.

TRANSOCEAN OFFSHORE

Rising oil prices, in the meantime, benefited offshore drilling contractors. Day rates by December 1996 had doubled over the previous year, topping $130,000 a day. The chairman of Transocean Offshore, J. Michael Talbert, concluded that the trend could continue for as long as 20 years and made a commitment to expand on the company's fleet.

With long-term contracts with oil companies in hand, Transocean Offshore began the development of a new generation of massive drill ships, featuring the latest in technological advances, and designed to drill to 10,000 feet, as opposed to the 3,000-foot capacity of the drill ships built in the mid-1970s. The first ship, the *Discoverer Enterprise*, would be 834 feet in length with a derrick that stood 226 feet high. It could sleep 200 and carry 125,000 barrels of oil and gas. Because it featured two drilling systems in one derrick, the ship could reduce the time to drill a development well by up to 40 percent and could drill and lay pipeline without the need of a pipelay barge.

With its increased productivity the ship could command much higher day rates, in the neighborhood of $200,000. Moreover, the *Enterprise* would essentially serve as a floating research and development project for two additional high-tech ships. Due to some setbacks partly caused by accident and weather, it would be more than a year late in becoming serviceable and see its price tag grow from $270 million to more than $430 million.

PROPOSED MERGER

In April 1999 Transocean Offshore was approached by Schlumberger Ltd., which proposed spinning off its offshore drilling operations, Sedco Forex Limited, as part of a merger of equals. Paris-based Schlumberger had been involved in offshore drilling for many years. The Forex (*Forages et Exploitations Pétrolières*) company was created in France in 1942 to engage in land drilling in North Africa and the Middle East, as well as France.

Forex teamed with Languedocienne to create a company called Neptune to engage in offshore drilling. Forex had gained complete control of Neptune by 1972, when Schlumberger bought the remaining interest in Forex. The Southeastern Drilling Company, Sedco, was a U.S. firm, founded in 1947 by future Texas governor Bill Clements to drill in shallow marsh water. In the 1960s it began to provide drilling services in deeper water. Schlumberger acquired Sedco in 1984 and a year later combined it with Forex to create Sedco Forex Drilling.

The proposed Transocean Offshore and Sedco Forex merger was announced in July 1999. It called for an exchange of stock valued at approximately $3.2 billion. Both Schlumberger and Transocean would receive five seats on the board, while Schlumberger's vice-chairman would serve as the chairman of the company and Transocean's Talbert would become president and CEO.

TRANSOCEAN SEDCO FOREX

With a market capitalization of more than $9 billion by mid-March 2000, Transocean Sedco Forex was an independent powerhouse among offshore drilling contractors and the fourth-largest oilfield service company. Its fleet included 46 semisubmersibles and seven deepwater drill ships, with others under construction. It was widely expected that the deal would create added pressure on other contractors to merge, as much-needed consolidation in the industry continued to gain momentum.

Transocean Sedco Forex was added to the Standard & Poor's (S&P) 500 Index on the first day of trading on the New York Stock Exchange in 2000. It enjoyed an immediate boost in price, caused in large part by money managers adding the stock to their funds that mirrored the S&P 500. The company soon was involved in another major expansion, acquiring R&B Falcon for more than $9 billion in an all-stock transaction, which included the assumption of $3 billion in debt.

After failing to beat out Sonat Offshore in the Transocean ASA acquisition, Reading & Bates had merged with Falcon Drilling Co. in 1997 and then acquired Cliffs Drilling in 1998. The company's fortunes suffered a downturn in 1998 and although it had made strides in redressing its situation, its debt load remained high, and management decided that the time was ripe to merge with Transocean Sedco Forex. Under terms of the deal R&B Falcon owned approximately 30 percent of the new company and received three new seats on the board of directors.

MOVING FROM FOURTH- TO THIRD-LARGEST OILFIELD SERVICE COMPANY

Transocean Sedco Forex was now a company worth approximately $14 billion and was the third-largest oilfield service company, eclipsed only by Halliburton and Schlumberger. With 165 offshore rigs, inland barges, and supporting assets, the combined company easily outpaced its closest rival, Pride International, with just 59 offshore rigs, of which 45 were shallow-water jackups. Moreover, Transocean provided almost half of the world's ultra-deep drilling ships. In effect, Transocean Sedco Forex was able to expand its global fleet with the most extensive range of offshore rigs and markets, while gaining a presence in the shallow and inland waters of the Gulf of Mexico, where it previously had no fleet.

Because of high gas prices R&B Falcon's 27 jackups in the Gulf and more than 30 inland barges promised to be an attractive addition. Because the company had changed its origin of incorporation to the Cayman Islands in late 1999, it was not allowed by law to operate vessels in U.S. waters. The company complied with the law by becoming a 25 percent joint venture partner in the former R&B Falcon transportation business, which consisted of 102 inland and offshore tugboats, four crew boats, and 58 inland and offshore flat deck cargo barges and inland shale barges.

MERGER WITH GLOBALSANTAFE

Transocean, which deleted the "Sedco Forex" from its name in 2003, had clearly taken the lead in the consolidation of offshore drilling contractors, but it was not done snapping up desirable rivals. Its crowning acquisition came in 2007 when it merged with GlobalSantaFe, the second-largest contractor in the offshore drilling business. This company was the product of the merger of Global Marine Inc. and Santa Fe International Corporation in 2001.

The Global Marine Exploration Company was incorporated in 1958, but its origins date back a decade earlier to a consortium of four oil companies, Continental, Union, Superior, and Shell. Global Marine was among the earliest oil contractors in the North Sea. In 1986, following a steep drop in oil prices, Global Marine entered bankruptcy protection, emerging three years later and managing to retain its administrative structure and much of its fleet. The Santa Fe Drilling Company began in California in 1946, and soon began operations in Venezuela, the Middle East, North Africa, Europe, and the Caribbean.

The 2007 merger of equals between Transocean and GlobalSantaFe yielded a company whose enterprise value was estimated at $53 billion, with a fleet of roughly 140 rigs. Transocean's CEO, Robert L. Long, would become chief executive of the merged company, while GlobalSantaFe chairman Robert E. Rose would head the combined board.

DEEPWATER HORIZON DISASTER OF 2010

Transocean's slogan, "We're never out of our depth," illustrated the company's image as the most aggressive player in the drilling industry, especially in the deepwater segment. Throughout the first decade of the 21st century, the company set numerous world records for drilling depth. In 2003 the *Discoverer Deep Seas* became the first offshore rig to reach a depth below 10,000 feet. A year later the *Deepwater Horizon* set a depth record for its class of semisubmersible rigs. The company's financial performance was equally robust: from 2004 to 2009, Transocean's revenue grew at an average annual rate of 34 percent.

In addition to plumbing the nether regions of the ocean floor, Transocean also became known for pushing the envelope of government regulations and tax policies. In 2008 the company relocated its incorporation from the Cayman Islands to Switzerland, in order to secure a lower corporate tax rate. At the time, the company was tied up in tax disputes with the U.S., Brazilian, and Norwegian governments involving nearly $700 million.

Among the petroleum companies who leased Transocean equipment, BP was the company's most important partner in 2009, furnishing more than $1 billion in revenue, 12 percent of Transocean's earnings for the year. In September the company announced that the *Deepwater Horizon* rig had set another depth record, a well measuring more than 35,000 feet in vertical depth, while drilling for BP in the Gulf of Mexico.

The rig was still in the Gulf, about 40 miles off the Louisiana coast, on April 20, 2010. Shortly before 10:00 that evening, a large volume of high-pressure gas erupted out of the well, igniting in the open air. Eleven workers, nine of them Transocean employees, died in the explosion and ensuing fire on the rig platform.

Hours after the *Deepwater Horizon* sank on April 22, an oil slick indicated a severely gushing leak at the well. Nearly five months passed before authorities were confident that the leak had been permanently sealed. It was the largest accidental spill in the history of petroleum extraction. The estimated 4.9 million barrels of oil released into the Gulf easily surpassed the volume of the 1989 *Exxon Valdez* spill in Alaska's Prince William Sound. Untold damage was done to the Gulf's ecosystem and the livelihoods of those employed in the fishing industry.

LOOKING AHEAD

BP was quickly identified as the main party responsible for the accident, but as the rig's owner, Transocean was also subject to intensive investigation by Congress and federal authorities as well as the press. It emerged that numerous components and pieces of equipment aboard the rig were either known to be faulty or had not been properly inspected for years. This included the "blowout preventer," the failure of which was an instrumental factor behind the accident. Moreover, Transocean officials had voiced safety concerns about several of its Gulf of Mexico rigs in the weeks before the catastrophe.

Despite these revelations, Transocean appeared unlikely to be saddled with a major proportion of the accident's cleanup costs, due to federal legislation as well as the limited liability clauses in its contract with BP. It remained to be seen whether the damage to the company's image and reputation would hinder its growth and profitability in the long run. Nevertheless, with all its other rigs still booked solid for years to come, Transocean seemed to retain the industry's confidence and remained its largest and deepest driller.

Ed Dinger
Updated, Roger K. Smith

PRINCIPAL SUBSIDIARIES

Transocean Inc.; Transocean Management Ltd.; Applied Drilling Technology, Inc.; ADT International; Challenger Minerals Inc.; Transocean Pacific Drilling Inc.; Angola Deepwater Drilling Company Limited; Overseas Drilling Limited; Global Marine Inc.; GSF Leasing Services GmbH; Sedco Forex International Inc.; Transocean Offshore Deepwater Drilling Inc.; Transocean Offshore Holdings Ltd.; Transocean Offshore International Ventures Ltd.; Transocean Worldwide Inc.; Triton Asset Leasing GmbH; Triton Nautilus Asset Leasing GmbH.

PRINCIPAL COMPETITORS

Diamond Offshore Drilling, Inc.; Noble Drilling Services Inc.; Saipem S.p.A.; Seadrill Ltd.; Ensco International, Inc.; Halliburton; Helmerich & Payne, Inc.

FURTHER READING

Antosh, Nelson. "Sonat, Norwegian Firm Strike Deal." *Houston Chronicle*, May 3, 1996.

DeLuca, Marshall, and William Furlow. "Driller Consolidation Begins, but Will It Continue?" *Offshore*, August 1999, 56.

Harrison, Joan. "Transocean Rounds Out Its Service Offerings with R&B Falcon Deal." *Mergers and Acquisitions*, October 2000, 22.

Krauss, Clifford, and Tom Zeller Jr. "A Behind-the-Scenes Firm in the Spotlight." *New York Times*, May 24, 2010.

Mack, Toni. "Learning from Experience." *Forbes*, December 2, 1996, 102–08.

Meier, Barry. "Owner of Exploded Rig Is Known for Testing Rules." *New York Times*, July 8, 2010.

Mouawad, Jad. "Top Oil Drilling Companies to Merge." *New York Times*, July 24, 2007.

Opdyke, Jeff D. "Mergers Could Improve Prospects among Stocks of Offshore Drillers." *Wall Street Journal*, March 15, 1995.

Tejada, Carlos. "Schlumberger's Sedco and Transocean to Merge." *Wall Street Journal*, July 13, 1999.

Urbina, Ian. "Oil Rig's Owner Had Safety Issue at Three Other Wells." *New York Times*, August 5, 2010.

Trinity Biotech plc

One Southern Cross
IDA Business Park
Bray, Wicklow
Ireland
Telephone: (+353 1) 276-9800
Fax: (+353 1) 276-9888
Web site: http://www.trinitybiotech.com

Public Company
Founded: 1992
Incorporated: 1992
Employees: 330
Sales: $125.9 million (2009)
Stock Exchanges: NASDAQ
Ticker Symbol: TRIB
NAICS: 325412 Pharmaceutical Preparation Manufacturing

■ ■ ■

A relatively young company, Trinity Biotech plc is a global leader in the development, manufacture, and marketing of diagnostic test kits for the clinical laboratory and point-of-care (POC) markets. The company also provides raw materials to the life sciences industry. Trinity Biotech has grown to include manufacturing facilities in Lemgo, Germany; Carlsbad, California; Kansas City, Missouri; and Jamestown, New York, and has direct sales forces in France, Germany, the United Kingdom, and the United States. The company's product line, which is used to detect diabetes; autoimmune, infectious, and sexually transmitted diseases; and disorders of the blood, liver, and intestine, includes some of the world's most highly respected brands such as Uni-Gold, Amax, Primus, MarDx, and Destiny. Although the company's principal POC product line is its range of tests for the detection of HIV antibodies, three major product portfolios initially constituted the clinical laboratory product line: coagulation, infectious diseases, and clinical chemistry.

In 2010 Trinity Biotech sold its worldwide coagulation business to the Stago Group, a move that included the transfer of 320 employees and an expected reduction in annual revenues of up to 40 percent. Trinity Biotech planned to concentrate on developing its POC business, focusing on those areas with the greatest growth rates, particularly infectious diseases and diabetes. Ronan O'Caoimh, Trinity Biotech's cofounder, served as the company's CFO before becoming its CEO in 1994, a position he still held, as well as chairman of the board, in 2010.

TECHNOLOGICAL ACHIEVEMENTS

Trinity Biotech was established in Bray, Ireland, in 1992 and listed on the NASDAQ shortly after its establishment. Its rapid expansion over its first two decades, both organically and through acquisitions, made it a global leader in the diagnostics industry. Trinity Biotech expanded into the United States in March 1994 with the acquisition of Acquired Disease Detection International of Irvine, California.

The following year, Trinity Biotech received a favorable evaluation from the World Health Organization for

COMPANY PERSPECTIVES

Since its formation in 1992, Trinity Biotech has actively pursued the aim of becoming a leading player in the international diagnostics industry. A combination of strong organic growth and a progressive acquisition-led strategy has seen the company assemble an impressive portfolio of over 400 products to date.

Specializing in the development, manufacture and marketing of diagnostic test kits, Trinity Biotech's continued success is based on the fact that as a company it consistently achieves standards of excellence in the quality of all it does.

its SeroCard HIV, and was soon awarded a $500,000 tender to supply the product to the Mexican Department of Social Security through its distributor, Biocard S.A. de C.V. One of Trinity Biotech's most important technological advances came in 1996 when the Uni-Gold HIV one-step test was launched. The following year, the product was submitted to the U.S. Food and Drug Administration (FDA) for approval. Trinity Biotech also received a $600,000 assistance package from the Irish Trade Board to market the product within Europe. Other acquisitions in that year included Centocor UK Holdings in Cambridge, England, and Clark Laboratories, a manufacturer of infectious disease and autoimmune diagnostic kits, in Jamestown, New York. By June 1997 the Jamestown facility was producing and shipping five new Trinity products that had received FDA approval: Lyme IgG, Lyme IgG/IgM, Legionella, Chlamydia IgG and Herpes Group Antigen.

In January 1998 Trinity Biotech received FDA clearance to market its test kit for the adenovirus, a leading cause of infectious gastroenteritis. The following month, Trinity Biotech signed an agreement with SmithKline Beecham International to launch Uni-Gold in Africa, and acquired a tender from the government of Malaysian to distribute the product throughout that country. In March of that year, the company expanded its manufacturing capacity in Ireland with the purchase of a 50,000-square-foot facility in Bray, Ireland, and transferred all of the Centocor infectious disease product line from the United Kingdom to the new site.

For the year ending December 31, 1997, the company reported revenues of $16.83 million, a staggering 142 percent increase over the previous year. Acquisitions in 1998 included the Microzyme product line for hormones and drugs of abuse from Diatech, Inc., in Boston, Massachusetts; the Macra lipoprotein assay for the detection and risk assessment of coronary heart disease from Strategic Diagnostics, Inc., in Newark, Delaware; the infectious disease diagnostics business from Cambridge Diagnostics Ireland Ltd.; and the Microtrak product line for the detection of sexually transmitted diseases from Syva Company, a subsidiary of Dade Behring, Inc. Net profits for 1998 were $2.55 million, with revenues increasing by 38 percent over the previous year to $23.17 million.

BROADENING THE SHAREHOLDER BASE

In March 1999, in a vote of confidence, CEO O'Caoimh, President Brendan Farrell, CFO Jonathan O'Connell, and COO Jim Walsh acquired 557,656 ordinary shares in the company. Two months later, Trinity Biotech began trading its common shares on the Dublin Stock Exchange, a move the management hoped would broaden its shareholder base and attract more corporate investors. By April 2000 the company had raised $12.54 million through a placement of four million shares, with a total of 16 long-term institutional shareholders in Ireland, the United Kingdom, and the United States, coming onboard.

Trinity Biotech planned to put the proceeds toward reducing debt, establishing direct sales points within Europe, and acquisitions, including the recently acquired MarDx Diagnostics, Inc., a Carlsbad, California-based manufacturer of test kits for the detection of Lyme disease. The year closed with the acquisition of 33.3 percent of HiberGen Ltd., an Irish genomics company, and 100 percent of Washington State-based Bartels, Inc., a leading manufacturer of diagnostics for the detection of cell-dependent infectious agents.

Because of the absence in the U.S. market of other rapid tests for HIV, in March 2001 the FDA's Center for Biologics Evaluation & Research granted Trinity Biotech an Investigational Device Exemption for the Uni-Gold HIV test. "We are particularly pleased that our test will be used to provide a currently unmet public health need," O'Caoimh said in a March 7, 2001, press release. Six months later, Trinity Biotech launched a Uni-Gold Malaria one-step test. In that same month, the company established Trinity Biotech GmbH, a sales and marketing subsidiary in Frankfurt, Germany. In December 2001 Trinity Biotech acquired the Biopool Hemostasis Division of Xtrana Inc. for $6.25 million.

In January 2002 Trinity Biotech received FDA approval for the Uni-Gold Strep A one-step test for the diagnosis of group A streptococcus. The following

KEY DATES

1992: Trinity Biotech plc is founded and listed on the NASDAQ.
1996: Trinity Biotech launches the Uni-Gold HIV one-step test.
2003: Company receives clearance for Uni-Gold Recombigen HIV test.
2005: Research Diagnostics Inc. of Flanders, New Jersey, and Primus Corporation of Kansas City, Missouri, are acquired.
2010: Trinity Biotech sells its coagulation line to the Stago Group for $90 million.

month the company increased its share in HiberGen to 66 percent. Six months later, Trinity Biotech completed its purchase of Sigma Diagnostics' coagulation business and followed this with the purchase of Sigma's clinical chemistry product line in December. The Trinity Biotech U.K. sales and marketing subsidiary was established that same month.

Trinity Biotech raised $20 million in July 2003 in a private placing of convertible notes with three U.S. institutions, with analysts speculating that the company would use the proceeds to make further acquisitions in the areas of infectious diseases and hemostasis. In December 2003 the FDA granted Trinity Biotech approval to market the Uni-Gold Recombigen HIV test in the United States. Adaltis US, Inc., a distributor of diagnostic instruments and reagents for infectious diseases, was purchased in April 2004 for $3.5 million, giving Trinity Biotech exclusive distribution rights in the United States and nonexclusive rights worldwide with the exception of China.

In that same month, the company acquired the U.S.-based Fitzgerald Industries International, Inc., a provider of immunodiagnostic products. With sales, general, and administration costs increasing by $10.7 million in 2004 over 2003, particularly in the United States, the company reported a 34 percent drop in pretax profits. Revenues, however, were still positive, increasing by 22 percent over the previous year.

DONATIONS AND ACQUISITIONS

In March 2005 Trinity Biotech acquired Research Diagnostics, Inc., in Flanders, New Jersey, for $4.2 million. On National HIV Testing Day in June 2005, the company announced that it would be donating $1 million worth of the Uni-Gold Recombigen HIV tests to community-based organizations and public health facilities throughout the United States. The following month, Trinity Biotech completed the $12 million acquisition of Primus Corporation in Kansas City, Missouri. For 2005 the company reported an increase in revenues of 23.2 percent to $98.6 million.

In 2006 the company once again saw a rise in revenues, to $118.7 million, a 20 percent increase over the previous year. The company's largest acquisition in 2006 was the $51.9 million purchase of the coagulation division bioMérieux, of Lyon, France. In June 2006 Trinity Biotech entered into an agreement with the Planned Parenthood Federation of America (PPFA) to provide the Uni-Gold Recombigen HIV test to all of its affiliates, with the PPFA committed to purchasing 50,000 tests per year.

In May 2007 Trinity Biotech's profile was significantly raised when the company entered into an agreement with UNITAID, a foundation committed to the efficient dissemination of high-quality drugs and diagnostics to countries in need, and the Clinton Foundation's Clinton HIV/AIDS Initiative (CHAI). Under the terms of the agreement, Trinity Biotech would offer its test kits at discounted prices to UNITAID-eligible countries and members of the CHAI Procurement Consortium, a group of more than 60 developing countries throughout the world. In October of that year, the company announced that it had decided to delist from the Irish Stock Exchange. The following month, Trinity Biotech embarked on a group restructuring, the key elements of which included reorganizing the sales and marketing function; streamlining the hemostasis and infectious disease product lines; implementing a more focused research and development program; closing its manufacturing facility in Umea, Sweden; and reducing the workforce, for an estimated annual savings of $5 million.

In January 2008 the company launched a new line of Lyme enzyme immunoassay products designed specifically for the detection of the European forms of the disease. The GeneSys system for testing genetic blood disorders in infants was introduced in April 2008. In that same month, the company announced that it was placing $7.1 million of American Depositary Shares in a registered public offering, the proceeds of which would be used for general administrative expenses, as well as the final payment for the 2006 bioMérieux deal. Other product launches in 2008 included HIV-1 BED, a new HIV incidence assay. The year closed with Trinity Biotech announcing that it planned to implement further cost-cutting measures by reducing overhead and eliminating 70 jobs, with an expected savings of $6 million of profit before tax.

REACHING A MILESTONE

A major achievement for the company in March 2009 was the FDA's approval of the Destiny Max analyzer product for use in the U.S. market. It was "a key strategic milestone for Trinity. This completes the roll out of Destiny Max in all major worldwide markets thus providing Trinity with access to the high throughput haemostasis market, estimated to be US$500 million per annum," O'Caoimh said in a July 7, 2009, press release.

In May 2010 Trinity Biotech sold its worldwide coagulation business to the Stago Group for $90 million, which included the transfer of 320 employees and a $6.8 million reduction of property, plants, and equipment. With coagulation revenues decreasing, the company planned to concentrate on the POC business, with a focus on infectious diseases, the hemoglobin A1c test for diabetes, and coagulation. The company also planned to supplement organic growth through licensing agreements, partnerships, and small acquisitions. The company reported revenues of $22.6 million in its second quarter of 2010, down from $32.3 million for the same period the previous year, a decline that was attributed mainly to the divestiture of the coagulation business.

Marie O'Sullivan

PRINCIPAL SUBSIDIARIES

Trinity Biotech Manufacturing Limited; Trinity Research Limited; Benen Trading Limited; Trinity Biotech Manufacturing Services Limited; Trinity Biotech Financial Services Limited; Trinity Biotech Inc. (USA); Clark Laboratories Inc. (USA); Mardx Diagnostics Inc. (USA); Fitzgerald Industries International, Inc. (USA); Biopool US Inc. (USA); Primus Corporation (USA); Trinity Biotech (UK Sales) Limited; Trinity Biotech GmbH (Germany); Trinity Biotech France SARL.

PRINCIPAL DIVISIONS

Clinical Laboratory; Point of Care.

PRINCIPAL COMPETITORS

Johnson & Johnson; Roche Diagnostics Corporation; Siemens Healthcare Diagnostics Inc.

FURTHER READING

"Biotech Company Acquires Sigma's Clinical Chemistry Business." *Biotech Business Week*, January 27, 2003, 2.

Hunt, Joanne. "Trinity Biotech Posts Revenues of $22.6m." *Irish Times*, July 30, 2010.

Kennedy, Emma. "Profits, Revenues Up at Trinity Biotech." *Irish Independent*, March 7, 2007.

Sheridan, Cormac. "Trinity Biotech Raises US$20M by Placing Convertible Notes." *BioWorld International*, July 16, 2003, 1.

"Trinity Biotech Acquires Coagulation Product Line of bioMérieux." *Internet Wire*, May 25, 2006.

"Trinity Biotech Announces Agreement with the Clinton Foundation HIV/AIDS Initiative (CHAI)." *Internet Wire*, May 23, 2007.

"Trinity Biotech Announces Group Restructuring." *Internet Wire*, December 7, 2007.

"Trinity Biotech Closes Deal to Sell Its Worldwide Coagulation Business Line to Stago." *Internet Wire*, May 5, 2010.

"Trinity Biotech Completes Acquisition of Biopool Hemostasis Business and Strengthens Board of Directors." *PR Newswire*, February 1, 2002.

"Trinity Biotech Receives FDA Approval for Uni-Gold Recombigen HIV Test." *PR Newswire*, December 29, 2003.

United Drug PLC

United Drug House
Magna Drive
Magna Business Park
Citywest Road
Dublin, 24
Ireland
Telephone: (+353 1) 463-2300
Fax: (+353 1) 459-6893
Web site: http://www.united-drug.ie

Public Company
Founded: 1948
Employees: 6,000
Sales: $2.3 billion (2009)
Stock Exchanges: London Dublin
Ticker Symbol: UN6A (Dublin) UDG (London)
NAICS: 424210 Drugs and Druggists' Sundries Merchant Wholesalers US; 423410 Photographic Equipment and Supplies Merchant Wholesalers; 423450 Medical, Dental, and Hospital Equipment and Supplies Merchant Wholesalers

■ ■ ■

United Drug PLC is a leading European health care services provider and the primary pharmaceutical wholesaler and distributor in Ireland. Headquartered in Dublin, Ireland, United Drug operates 35 businesses in Europe and the United States. In addition to pharmaceutical preparations, the company distributes perfumes, cosmetics, and photographic products. It also markets medical equipment.

United Drug operates through four divisions. The Healthcare Supply Chain division oversees the company's offerings in health care logistics. The Packaging and Specialties division offers packaging solutions for pharmaceutical manufacturers through facilities in the United States, the United Kingdom, Belgium, and The Netherlands. The Contract Sales and Marketing division provides contract sales and related marketing services to health care product manufacturers in the United Kingdom, the Republic of Ireland, and the United States. The Medical and Scientific division operates business units in Ireland and the United Kingdom. It provides contract distribution, sales, and marketing services, supported by clinical and technical support expertise, to manufacturers of medical and scientific equipment and products.

COOPERATIVE ROOTS

Founded as a cooperative on January 1, 1948, in Ballina, County Mayo, Ireland, United Drug set out to provide enhanced services to western Ireland's pharmacists. Its founders were a group of pharmacists who had grown tired of the inadequate service provided to them by the national distributors based in the capital city of Dublin.

United Drug's first real expansion occurred four years later, in 1952, when an additional distribution center was established in Limerick. In 1971 the company relocated to Dublin, and with the introduction of Ireland's General Medical Scheme, or health plan, it began offering free medicine to 40 percent of the Irish population. In 1972 United Drug gained

> **COMPANY PERSPECTIVES**
>
> Our vision is to be a dynamic, leading international healthcare services company, fostering enhanced patient outcomes through partnerships with healthcare manufacturers, government agencies, providers and payors.

national recognition when it acquired the British pharmaceutical company Ayrton Saunders. That year it also moved into new expanded facilities in Dublin.

EARLY GROWTH

During the 1970s and 1980s, United Drug expanded steadily throughout Ireland. The company entered the medical and scientific sector for the first time in 1990, when it acquired Trinity Instruments. In 1992 United Drug became a public limited company, or PLC, and listed on the Dublin and London Stock Exchanges. Later that year the company achieved a foothold in Northern Ireland with the acquisition of the wholesale firms Smiths and Sangers. In 1995 United Drug further added to its capacity in medicine and science by acquiring Novapath Supplies.

United Drug became more widely recognized in June 1996 when it entered into a joint venture with the British company Unichem Group to provide distribution services to pharmaceutical manufacturers and health care companies in the British market. Unichem and United Drug each owned half of the new joint venture they named UniDrug. UniDrug provided order processing, warehousing, and information services to its clients. By 1996 established United Drug clients included the pharmaceutical companies Eli Lilly, Bristol Myers Squibb, Zeneca, and Astra Pharmaceuticals.

By 1997 United Drug's subsidiary Sangers Wholesale was servicing 500 community pharmacies and 27 hospitals in Northern Ireland through distribution depots in Belfast and Omagh. United Drug itself operated depots in Dublin, Limerick, and United Drug's hometown of Ballina. These three depots served 1,000 community pharmacies and 200 hospitals in the Republic of Ireland. United Drug's founding goal, to provide enhanced services to western Ireland's pharmacists, had succeeded far beyond its original borders.

The 1997 acquisition of Dublin Drug, a leading Irish wholesaler and distributor, set in motion another period of substantial growth for United Drug. By 1999 the company's pretax profits had increased 33 percent over the previous year to £8.7 million. Pharmaceutical industry analysts attributed much of the increase to the Dublin Drug acquisition. In 2000 United Drug's longtime chief executive officer, Jerry Liston, who had held the post for 27 years, retired. The youngest person ever to lead an Irish public company would succeed him. Liam FitzGerald was just 34 when he became CEO of United Drug.

In 2000 United Drug bought the United Kingdom's second-largest pharmaceutical contract sales company, Ashfield Healthcare, for an undisclosed sum. In 2001 the company opened a new headquarters at Magna Park in Dublin, where the increased space available reflected the company's substantial growth. The move also heralded several acquisitions that in rapid succession expanded on the company's already significant presence among contract distributors and pharmaceutical sales companies in Ireland and the United Kingdom.

MORE ACQUISITIONS AND A NEW FOCUS ON INDEPENDENT PHARMACIES

In April 2002 United Drug began a year of important acquisitions with the purchase of the privately owned British medical-device supplier New Splint. The specialist wholesaler, headquartered in Hampshire, supplied orthopedic devices and implants. The purchase price of £7 million was slated to increase by £1 million with the attainment of specific agreed-upon profit margins. In September 2002 United Drug acquired all shares in Oremelt Company, a specialized distributor of medical, surgical, pharmaceutical, and critical-care products. The acquisition cost of €13.3 million included cash, interest-bearing loans, and shares of United Drug stock.

In October 2002 Ventiv Health, Inc., based in the United States, sold its contract services organization, based in the United Kingdom, to United Drug for a cash purchase price of €7.7 million. Ventiv provided companies in the pharmaceutical and life sciences industries with various services, including consulting, analytics, market research, and strategic and tactical planning. In 2002 United Drug also acquired the Irish medical devices company IntraVeno Healthcare for €19.5 million. In February 2003 United Drug executives announced a 20 percent increase in the company's profits over the previous 18 months. Analysts attributed much of the increase to a decision by a major United Drug competitor, the German distributor Gehe AG, to enter Ireland's retail pharmaceutical market. Gehe's move to retail left United Drug the principal

KEY DATES

1948: United Drug is founded as a cooperative in Ballina, County Mayo, Ireland.

1952: A United Drug distribution center is established in Limerick.

1972: United Drug gains national recognition with the acquisition of Ayrton Saunders and a move to Dublin.

1992: United Drug becomes a public limited company (PLC) and acquires listings on the London and Dublin Stock Exchanges.

2007: With its acquisition of the pharmaceutical and health care division of the Belgian company Budelpack International, United Drug expands operations to continental Europe.

wholesale supplier to 800 of Ireland's 1,200 independent pharmacists.

A year later, in February 2004, board chairman Martin Rafferty told United Drug investors at the company's annual meeting that they could expect another strong year. Rafferty also, however, warned Ireland's remaining independent pharmacists that major United Drug competitors Gehe and Uniphar now owned a significant number of retail pharmacies throughout Ireland. "Unless you are a customer of United Drug," Rafferty told pharmacists, "your wholesaler is now your competitor as well and is in danger of undermining you in the future." According to published reports, many independent pharmacies during the previous three years had already switched to United Drug as their wholesaler, and the company expected many more to follow.

United Drug actively sought to increase the number of independent pharmacists in Ireland by offering a financial support plan known as the Catalyst scheme. The debt-based plan, offered at a fixed rate, assisted noncorporate pharmacists in acquiring adequate financing to buy pharmacies that came on the market. The plan did not impose ownership rights or loyalty contracts on the pharmacists it assisted.

ACQUISITIONS LEAD TO DIVERSIFICATION

Two acquisitions in June 2005 promised to strengthen United Drug's position among outsourcing businesses serving UK manufacturers. In early June the company acquired In2Focus Sales Development Services, a leading contract sales services provider, for a purchase price of £15 million. Later that month United Drug acquired TD Packaging, one of Europe's largest independent contract packaging companies, for £11 million.

In July 2006 United Drug announced it had acquired Medical Advisory Service for Travellers Abroad (MASTA), a British distributor of branded vaccines. The acquisition cost of £14.5 million would be supplemented by an additional £4.5 million upon the completion of agreed-upon profit targets achieved over the following two years. In February 2007 United Drug acquired Pyramed Ltd, a British distributor of medical devices, for £8.5 million in cash and stock. Based in Surrey, Pyramed specialized in selling and distributing products used in interventional cardiology and the treatment of vascular diseases. It enjoyed a reputation for best-in-class clinical and technical knowledge.

United Drug made its first foray into continental Europe in April 2007, when it acquired the pharmaceutical and health care division of Budelpack International, a Belgian provider of specialty contract packaging services. Pharmaceutical packaging, such as that produced by Budelpack, included prefilled syringes, prefillable inhalers, plastic bottles for liquid medication, and pouches to hold medicinal powder mixes. Financial terms of the Budelpack business acquisition were not announced. Later that same year, United Drug acquired another contract packaging provider, European Packaging Centre, based in The Netherlands.

In July 2007 United Drug merged its subsidiaries Ashfield Healthcare and In2Focus Sales Development Services into a new subsidiary, Ashfield In2Focus Ltd, through which United Drug conducted its contract sales services in the United Kingdom and Europe. In November 2007 United Drug announced the purchase of Procon Conferences Ltd, a British pharmaceutical conference services company based in Yorkshire. Procon provided corporate event management services to the pharmaceutical and health care sector. The company secured event venues, handled association memberships, coordinated delegate registration, and provided overall management of events.

UNITED DRUG'S BOLT-ON STRATEGY

In an interview with London's *Sunday Times* (April 22, 2007), United Drug CEO Liam FitzGerald addressed how United Drug's smaller-scale acquisitions, sometimes called "bolt-ons," fit into the company's larger plans. "The history of United Drug has been to gain 80% of growth through organic growth and 20% through bolt-ons. As the company gets bigger, either the magnitude of the deals has to increase, or the number of deals has to get bigger." FitzGerald also addressed United Drug's tendency to avoid large so-called transformational deals that make headlines but can change the character of a company in unexpected ways. "We're not tempted into doing a transformational deal just because it's big," he said. "If something big comes along in the markets we are chasing, we'll certainly take a look at it. But we're not going to get into mad auctions against private equity players and overpay. That's bad business."

In August 2009 United Drug entered into a joint venture with Medco Health Solutions, Inc., to provide home-based pharmacy care services to patients in the United Kingdom's National Health Service (NHS) who live with chronic or complex conditions. Services would include drug dispensing and delivery, on-site nursing, and case management. United Drug and Medco estimated that more than 96 percent of all pharmacy costs and 70 percent of overall health costs in the United Kingdom were related to the care of patients with chronic and complex conditions. According to analysts, appropriate transfer of care and services from hospital to home-based settings would lower costs while also increasing patient access to care.

In a move intended to broaden its sales and marketing services, in August 2010 United Drug announced the purchase of the health care communications and consultancy firm InforMed Group. InforMed Group provided medical writing, publication planning, market research, and business analysis services, as well as marketing and sales training. The initial purchase price of £11.4 million was expected to increase by as much as £5.9 million with the completion of agreed-upon targets over the next three years.

DEMOGRAPHICS AND DIVERSIFICATION HOLD FUTURE PROMISE

United Drug PLC, along with other wholesalers active in the medical and pharmaceutical sectors, could expect to profit from its ability to address the needs of a rapidly aging Irish population. Experts predicted that the number of Irish residents who were 65 or older, numbering fewer than half a million in 2006, would increase 1.4 million by the year 2041. In 2010 United Drug continued to hold a strong position along Ireland's pharmaceutical supply chain. Its forays into the medical supply pipeline in Northern Ireland, Britain, and elsewhere in Europe would continue to benefit earnings, as would its ability to respond to Ireland's shifting demographics. While the wholesale drug business remained potentially susceptible to government reforms, fiscal analysts expected United Drug to continue to manage regulatory change through diversification and continued gains in productivity.

Joyce Helena Brusin

PRINCIPAL SUBSIDIARIES

Sangers (Northern Ireland) Ltd; Dublin Drug Company Ltd; Procon Conferences Ltd; Pyramed Ltd; MASTA Ltd; TD Packaging Ltd; New Splint Ltd; IntraVeno Healthcare Ltd; Ashfield In2Focus Ltd.

PRINCIPAL DIVISIONS

Healthcare Supply Chain; Packaging and Specialty; Contract Sales and Marketing Services; Medical and Scientific.

PRINCIPAL COMPETITORS

Cahill May Roberts Ltd, a subsidiary of Celesio AG (formerly Gehe AG); Uniphar Group PLC; Alliance Boots GmbH; McSweeney Pharmacy Group.

FURTHER READING

Carroll, Steve. "United Drug Buys Consultancy Firm." *Irish Times*, August 11, 2010.

Creaton, Siobhán. "United Drug Sounds Alarm for Pharmacies." *Irish Times*, February 12, 2004.

Labanyi, David. "United Drug Agrees [to] New UK Homecare Joint Venture Deal." *Irish Times*, August 14, 2009.

"New United Drug Venture." *Irish Times*, June 25, 1996.

Pan, Kwan Yuk. "UK and Ireland: United Aims to Wrap Up Packaging." *Financial Times*, May 10, 2007.

Paul, Mark. "United Drug Boss Takes Life at a Run." *Sunday Times*, April 22, 2007.

"Pharmacy Group Is Ageing Well." *Sunday Times*, May 11, 2008.

"United Drug Acquires Oremelt Company for €13.3m." *M2 Europharma*, September 10, 2002.

"United Drug Beefs Up UK Position with TD Deal." *Printing World*, June 23, 2005.

Vaupell Inc.

1144 Northwest 53rd Street
Seattle, Washington 98107-3735
U.S.A.
Telephone: (206) 784-9050
Fax: (206) 784-9708
Web site: http://www.vaupell.com

Wholly Owned Subsidiary of H.I.G. Capital, L.L.C.
Founded: 1947 as Vaupell Industrial Plastics
Employees: 500
Sales: $76 million (2007 est.)
NAICS: 326199 All Other Plastics Product Manufacturing; 332997 Industrial Pattern Manufacturing; 326122 Plastics Pipe and Pipe Fitting Manufacturing

■ ■ ■

Vaupell Inc. is a big name in plastics. Its history parallels the rise and evolution of large-scale, sophisticated manufacturing in the United States, with its increasing reliance on synthetic materials. Established in Seattle, Washington, soon after the end of World War II, the company was the first plastics supplier to the Boeing Company and for many years specialized in serving the aerospace industry. Beginning in the 1990s, it expanded into the medical market. Since then the company has added clients in defense, additional transportation sectors, and electronics.

Vaupell also owns AntiWave Pool Products, in Sanger, Texas, which manufactures products for competitive-level swimming pools using injection-molding technology, and Golston Product Solutions, also in Sanger, which designs and manufactures carriers for pneumatic-tube delivery systems. In 1998 Vaupell was acquired by H.I.G. Capital, L.L.C., a Miami-based private investment firm. Vaupell's operations have since expanded to include Vaupell China Molding & Tooling, a joint venture based in Shenzhen, China.

Throughout its history, Vaupell has focused on supplying sophisticated groups of clients with components and applications requiring high-level engineering skills and state-of-the-art facilities. As the second decade of the 21st century begins, it has become one of the largest plastic molders in the United States, operating more than 110 injection-molding presses of various sizes and the third-largest molder of high-heat advanced polymers used for critical medical and aerospace applications.

AEROSPACE SPECIALIST

Vaupell Industrial Plastics was founded by Leonard J. Vaupell in Seattle in 1947. The company soon made its name by supplying the first plastic parts to Boeing. For most of its first five decades, it remained a family-owned business making components and applications for the aerospace industry. Another longtime major client was the General Electric Company's GE Plastics division, for which Vaupell developed flame-retardant resins used in aircraft. Along the way, Vaupell was a party to numerous innovations and technological advances for the industry. One such advance was the use of corrosion-resistant PEEK (polyetheretherketone)-based compounds for the engine frame on the Boeing 757, to protect the engine during fuel leaks, and for the starter air discharge duct

COMPANY PERSPECTIVES

Vaupell Holdings, Inc., is a global contract manufacturer of custom injection molded components and assemblies focused on the aerospace, medical, and defense marketplaces. We provide advanced, integrated solutions to select customers in these niche markets and can assist in all phases of a company's product life cycle.

in the Boeing 737. In 1996 Vaupell received the President's Award for Excellence from Boeing Commercial Airplane Group.

Along the way, Vaupell spread its reach into smaller niche markets, notably by the purchase of AntiWave Pool Products in 1982. AntiWave had been founded six years earlier by Anton Kajlich, a former All-American water polo player and member of the Czechoslovakian national team. AntiWave's products included water polo balls, floating goals, and a turnbuckle tensioning device used to move lane lines in and out of pools for competitive swimming and water polo.

DIVERSIFICATION INTO PROTOTYPE TESTING

Diversification stepped up to a new level in the mid-1990s. Increasingly, Vaupell's clients were relying on it to create prototypes to assess the form and function of new products. The company became especially adept at stereolithography, a sophisticated process that uses resins to build parts a layer at a time. A laser beam first traces a cross-section pattern on the surface of the liquid resin, then solidifies it and binds it to the layer below. Vaupell's mastery of this process was especially attractive to medical product designers and makers, and, beginning in the late 1990s, over the course of 10 years, the company participated in the design review phase for more than 1,000 new medical devices.

Vaupell was also investing to keep its facilities up to date, streamline and cut production costs, and maintain a top-flight staff of engineers and production workers. In 1991 it joined the wave of manufacturers adopting computer-aided design systems. "[Before,] it was paper- and drawing-based. Now we very rarely receive a drawing except by downloading it directly into our computer," Syd Darlington, marketing vice president, told Bill Virgin of the *Seattle Post-Intelligencer* for an article in the May 2, 1994, edition. In 1996 Vaupell participated in the initial survey of jobs that began the process of establishing a National Employee Certification Program for Plastics Molding. Two years later, faced with 35 to 45 percent increases in resin prices, it helped form Outsourced Purchasing Management LLC, a new plastic processors purchasing alliance.

That same year, Vaupell Industrial Plastics attracted the attention of H.I.G. Capital, a Miami-based investment group. After purchasing Vaupell in October 1998, H.I.G. named Joseph Jahn, a veteran plastics industry executive, as president and CEO. A new period of expansion and acquisition was about to begin for Vaupell.

GROWTH AND DIVERSIFICATION

The recession of 2000–01 cut deeply into Vaupell's balance sheet as Boeing and other aerospace clients retrenched. Rather than downsize, however, Vaupell decided to bet on an industry recovery. It kept its entire staff of 25 engineers, despite not having sufficient workload for all of them at the time, and accepted a drop in the profit margin. Financial help from H.I.G. helped Vaupell to weather the period. "It would have been irreparable," Jahn told Steve Wilhelm of the *Puget Sound Business Journal* in the April 9, 2007, issue, "to come out of the business downturn and try to pick up the pace again, as well as expand our capacity, as well as participate at the tier-one level, had we made a short term business decision, to shed the cost of these critical sources we had."

By 2007 Vaupell had been designated a tier-one supplier on the new Boeing 787 jet, supplying three components: attendant modules, magazine racks, and literature pockets. As such, Vaupell positioned itself to benefit from an evolution in the aircraft manufacturing business. Although in the past Boeing had designed every part of its aircraft, with the 787 it had decided to shift the actual design of major parts and assemblies to its suppliers, instead assuming the role of a "large-scale integrator," putting the sections together and monitoring the overall process.

Vaupell by this time had 190 employees, up from 135 during the economic slump. One reason for this growth was that in 2004 H.I.G. acquired SciTech Plastics Group, another leading, fully integrated injection-molding manufacturer, which had 400 employees. SciTech, which had been founded in 1998 and had grown through acquisitions, had been forced to declare bankruptcy because of overleveraging and the economic downturn. H.I.G. combined Vaupell Industrial Plastics and the SciTech properties into a new company, Vaupell Inc., with Jahn continuing as

KEY DATES

1947: Leonard Vaupell founds Vaupell Industrial Plastics.
1998: Vaupell is acquired by H.I.G. Capital.
2004: Vaupell Industrial Plastics merges with SciTech Plastics Group to form Vaupell Inc.
2006: Joint venture, Vaupell China Molding & Tooling, is established in Shenzhen, China.
2010: Vaupell works with SABIC Innovative Plastics to introduce a stronger, lighter-weight compound for aircraft interior features.

president and CEO while Mark Evans, SciTech's chief operating officer, assumed that role at the new company.

The merger especially strengthened Vaupell's position in the medical products field. "This acquisition is the culmination of several years of pursuing a strategic integration with a technical supplier to medical markets," Jahn said in a May 3, 2004, press statement. "We believe the resulting position in medical and aerospace, in addition to the other unique segments we serve, will differentiate us from the vast majority of custom injection molders in the United States."

PLANT CONSOLIDATION

Following the merger, Vaupell consolidated SciTech's four plants in Massachusetts and Connecticut, closing existing factories and moving the operations into a 187,000-square-foot plant in Agawam, Massachusetts, near Springfield. The move was aimed at improving efficiency (the new site had more clean-room molding capacity and additional injection presses, and was located near several of Vaupell's medical developer customers) as well as cutting rental costs, which were more reasonable in the western part of the state.

The consolidation cost Vaupell more than $4 million to carry out. Although Vaupell had no problem getting engineers (who tended to be a highly mobile workforce) to make the move, the company was concerned about finding highly skilled tradespeople such as machinists and toolmakers. In the January 9, 2007, issue of the *Christian Science Monitor*, Evans told reporter Ben Arnoldy, "There's a generation gap. People are not going to school for the trades. I'm looking for 18-year-olds who want to get into a career, and who want to learn the business from people that we have." The state was helpful, however, providing Vaupell with $191,320 in Workforce Training Fund grants in 2005, followed by further grants in succeeding years.

Vaupell secured its first foothold outside the United States in September 2006 when it set up Vaupell China Molding & Tooling, a joint venture with Shenzhen RongChangSheng Plastic Mould Co. Ltd. The new facility, located in Shenzhen, was another cost saver, helping Vaupell to more economically supply steel molds to existing customers, including for the Boeing 787. Going forward, however, Jahn told Wilhelm in the *Puget Sound Business Journal* article that Vaupell also anticipated staking out new business prospects in China. "China has a real design to become an aerospace manufacturer," he said. "We are participating in the [Chinese] advanced regional jet, which will be made outside Shanghai."

The company's revenues by this point were divided roughly equally between aerospace, medical equipment, and other applications. Operations were split between Seattle, site of corporate headquarters and the facilities for Vaupell Northwest Molding & Tooling (which had become the world's leading manufacturer of aircraft interior components), and five other facilities: Vaupell Rapid Solutions in Hudson, New Hampshire, a rapid prototyping facility; Vaupell Northeast Molding & Tooling in Agawam, specializing in injection molding and mainly serving the medical market; Vaupell Midwest Molding & Tooling in Constantine, Michigan, an injection-molding operation serving orthopedic and surgical instruments makers; the Shenzhen joint venture; and, in Sanger, Texas, AntiWave Pool Products and another proprietary company, Golston Product Solutions, which designed and manufactured carriers for pneumatic-tube delivery systems.

TECHNOLOGY IMPROVEMENT

Vaupell was also improving its capacities at each location. In 2006 the Hudson operation added a direct metal laser-sintering system that could produce tooling inserts, prototype parts, and metal end products in about half the time needed with traditional tools. A year later, responding to customer demand, the company switched from two-dimensional to three-dimensional computer modeling at its Constantine prototyping facility. The change enabled it to work better with medical device makers who were producing ever more miniaturized designs. In 2009 the Agawam plant obtained a used 440-ton Milacron injection-molding press so that it could take orders for much larger parts.

The company was not ignoring its core aerospace business, however. In 2010 Netherlands-based SABIC Innovative Plastics introduced a new high-performance compound that could replace heavier airline-grade die-cast and machined aluminum, cutting the weight of some interior aircraft components by up to 50 percent and improving strength by 40 percent. Vaupell worked with SABIC to create the first practical application of the new compound: a new tray table arm, which was exhibited at the Aircraft Interiors Expo in May. According to the Web site IDES—The Plastics Web, in an item dated May 27, 2010, Mike Hamm, vice president of sales at Vaupell, stated that carbon-fiber-filled Ultem resin, the basic element, "is a true industry game changing material that not only slashes part weight for greater fuel savings, but also offers a balance of other high-performance properties to meet aircraft industry demand for the best materials on the market for next-generation planes."

Eric Laursen

PRINCIPAL SUBSIDIARIES

Vaupell Northwest Molding & Tooling; Vaupell Rapid Solutions; Vaupell Northeast Molding & Tooling; Vaupell Midwest Molding & Tooling; Vaupell China Molding & Tooling; Golston Product Solutions; AntiWave Pool Products.

PRINCIPAL COMPETITORS

AptarGroup, Inc.; Berry Plastics Group Inc.; BWAY Corporation; Cascade Engineering Inc.; Illinois Tool Works Inc.; Letica Corporation; Magna International Inc.; Newell Rubbermaid Inc.; Nypro, Inc.; SRG Global Inc.

FURTHER READING

Arnoldy, Ben. "Too Prosperous, Massachusetts Is Losing Its Labor Force." *Christian Science Monitor*, January 9, 2007.

"H.I.G. Capital Acquires SciTech and Vaupell." Press release, May 3, 2004. Accessed November 10, 2010. http://www.higprivateequity.com/NewsRelease.php?id=368.

"SABIC Innovative Plastics' Revolutionary New Carbon-Fiber-Filled Ultem Resin Is 50% Lighter, 40% Stronger vs. Aluminum for Aircraft Interior Parts." IDES—The Plastics Web, May 27, 2010. Accessed November 10, 2010. http://ides.typepad.com/plastics_news/2010/05/.

Virgin, Bill. "Diversification Key to Survival, Companies Find." *Seattle Post-Intelligencer*, May 3, 1994.

———. "New Wave of New Ways Brings Resurgence in Manufacturing." *Seattle Post-Intelligencer*, May 2, 1994.

Wilhelm, Steve. "Ballard-Based Supplier for Boeing Has a World-Class Reputation." *Puget Sound Business Journal*, April 9, 2007.

Vocus, Inc.

4296 Forbes Boulevard
Lanham, Maryland 20706-4329
U.S.A.
Telephone: (301) 459-2590
Toll Free: (800) 345-5572
Fax: (301) 549-2827
Web site: http://www.vocus.com

Public Company
Incorporated: 1988 as First Data Software Publishing, Inc.
Employees: 518
Sales: $84.6 million (2009)
Stock Exchanges: NASDAQ
Ticker Symbol: VOCS
NAICS: 511210 Software Publishers

■ ■ ■

Vocus, Inc., is a provider of on-demand public relations and government relations management software to organizations of all sizes. A key function of the company's web-based software is news monitoring, allowing customers to keep track of its coverage by the media, whether broadcast, print, or online from blogs and social media sites such as Twitter and Facebook. Vocus also offers press release distribution over the web to more than 30,000 journalists and bloggers. In addition, more than 15 million visits are paid each year to the Vocus news center at PRWeb.com, and 250,000 subscribers tap into its news feeds.

Another service is providing access to the company's daily updated proprietary media database that provides subscribers with information about one million journalists, analysts, media outlets, and publicity possibilities. Not only can subscribers use the data to determine the ideal media people to cover their companies or organizations and create subject-specific distribution lists, they can also learn background information about contacts before talking to them. Vocus on-demand software is offered mostly on an annual subscription basis, while press release distribution is primarily a per-transaction service. Rates, which range from $3,000 to $50,000 per year, are determined by the size of a company. All told, Vocus has nearly 4,500 customers in such sectors as finance, insurance, health care, pharmaceuticals, retail, and consumer products, as well as educational institutions and nonprofit corporations. Vocus is a public company listed on the NASDAQ Global Market. In addition to its Lanham, Maryland, headquarters, Vocus maintains offices in Herndon, Virginia; London; and Düsseldorf, Germany.

COMPANY FOUNDED: 1988

Vocus was cofounded in 1988 as First Data Software Publishing, Inc., by its longtime president and chief executive officer, Richard Rudman, and Chief Technology Officer Robert Lentz. Rudman was born and raised in the Washington, D.C., area. After graduating from high school in 1979, he enlisted in the U.S. Air Force, where he became familiar with electronics and computers. After a four-year stint in the service, he earned a degree in accounting from the University of Maryland and went to work as an accountant at Barlow

COMPANY PERSPECTIVES

Vocus has changed the way communications professionals do their jobs. Vocus provides the ability to leverage the ubiquity of the Internet to interact with the media, publish their news online where it can be found by millions, monitor news and social media conversations from virtually any source and track their results to compare them with key competitors.

Corporation, a real estate development and management company. To automate some of his accounting work, Rudman learned dBase, the first widely used database management system developed for personal computers (PCs). He became enamored with the technology, which shifted the direction of his career.

In 1986 Rudman joined with Lentz (the two had been friends in junior high school) to design and implement mission-critical PC-based software and networks. After high school, Lentz had gone to work as a bank teller but soon left because he had always wanted to start his own business. He eventually launched a computer consulting company, Dataway Corporation, and soon Rudman joined him. They would serve such clients as the U.S. Navy, Booz Allen, and KPMG.

LOBBYIST PRODUCT LAUNCHED: 1992

In order to grow Dataway, Rudman and Lentz decided to start a software company, First Data Software Publishing, which planted the seeds for Vocus. First Data developed a product that was well suited to the company's home market of the nation's capital. In 1992 it introduced Capitol Hill Lobbyist, which streamlined the collection and dissemination of legislative information, making it ideal for grassroots lobbying. The program was also combined with *Congressional Quarterly*, which provided coverage of Congress, to create a congressional and regulatory online tracking service called Washington Alert LinkService.

Because the lobbying product introduced First Data to the vertical software market (that is, catering to a specific industry or market), Rudman and Lentz consider 1992 as the beginning of Vocus. In addition to *Congressional Quarterly*, Capitol Hill Lobbyist was sold to companies as well as associations to allow their employees and associates to more effectively lobby Congress. This product remained the focus of the company for about five years, generating revenues of about $2 million a year.

In 1997 Rudman and Lentz were approached by a party interested in buying the business. "They wanted us to handle the grassroots management software," Rudman told Sramana Mitra in a 2010 interview, "and have us integrate with another portfolio company's media relations software." The resulting combination would be a corporation communications software company. A deal was reached to sell First Data for $6 million, closing documents were signed, and all that was needed was a wire transfer of the funds. Instead, Rudman and Lentz received a telephone call canceling the deal without explanation.

The aborted sale proved to be a blessing in disguise. Rudman and Lentz quickly realized that the idea of extending its government relations technology to the public relations field was a good one. With an eye toward the Public Relations Society of America annual conference just three months away, they launched a crash program to develop and launch a public relations software package. They met their deadline and were able to unveil their software at the conference, making an entry into the public relations market.

In the first year, First Data generated $400,000 in sales from its public relations product, which at the time was a desktop application. Total sales were in the $4 million range by 1999. Rudman and Lentz began receiving feedback from customers who expressed a desire to access the program over the Internet. In meeting this request, Rudman and Lentz realized they could transform the software into a flagship offering by adopting a software-as-a-service (SaaS; also called software on demand) model that generated revenues through web-based subscriptions rather than selling a desktop application under a perpetual license model.

SAAS MODEL ADOPTED: 1999

Late in 1999 the partners decided that it would not be practical to continue to sell the desktop application while pursuing a web-based product, and they elected to focus all of their efforts on the SaaS service. It was not an easy choice at the time, given that the concept was so new that there were no on-demand companies in the market. Rudman and Lentz had to make a presentation to their 50 employees to explain the concept. The advantages of reengineering the application to the Internet became evident. The number of potential customers increased significantly while at the same time there was no need to pay on-site visits to make sales presentations. Moreover, there was no need for users to purchase expensive hardware, making the service affordable to a wider range of customers.

KEY DATES

1988: First Data Software Publishing, Inc., is formed.
1992: Capitol Hill Lobbyist product is introduced.
1999: Company name is changed to Vocus, Inc.
2000: First and second rounds of venture capital are raised.
2005: Vocus is taken public.

In 1999 First Data was reincorporated in Delaware as Vocus, Inc. In that same year, it became the first company to offer on-demand software for public relations, initially sold under the name PRality. It was also the first to offer on-demand software for government relations and political action committees, marketed under the GRality label. Vocus began to actively sell SaaS software in 2000, but in order to build the necessary sales and marketing operation, the company needed venture-capital money. Thus, in January 2000 the company raised $2 million from Edison Venture Fund. Rudman and Lentz could have likely raised more money, but not pleased with the company's valuation, elected to take a smaller amount of money. Nonetheless, they were not sure how to best use the money. "We experimented a lot with that money," Rudman admitted to Mitra. "We blew the whole $2 million on sales and marketing. We made a lot of mistakes." As a result, Rudman was glad the company did not raise any more money during its initial round of funding.

Over the course of 2000 the valuation of Vocus increased. Just eight months after its first round of funding, Vocus raised a second round led by Lazard Technology Partners. The company netted $8.4 million, but having learned its lessons from the first round, the company would make more judicious use of its cash. When Vocus went public in 2005 it still retained $4 million of those proceeds.

EUROPEAN OFFICES OPEN: 2002

Vocus enjoyed steady growth in the first decade of the 21st century, supported by acquisitions and internal growth. In the summer of 2001 the company acquired Astrum Digital Information, a television monitoring and clipping service. To generate international sales, the company opened an office in London as well as offices in France and Hong Kong in 2002. The company increased sales from $4.72 million in 2000 to $7.95 million in 2001.

Sales continued to grow, reaching $11.5 million in 2002 and $15.4 million in 2003. Also in 2003, Vocus added customers through the acquisition of Public Affair Technologies (PAT). Additionally, Vocus received new technology to bolster its public relations product, in particular PAT's mile-radius search capabilities that allowed users to search for reporters on a local basis.

To support its expanding business in Western Europe, Vocus opened an office in Madrid, Spain, in 2004 as well as an office in Prague, Czech Republic, to support growth in Central and Eastern Europe, followed by an office in Stockholm, Sweden, to serve customers in the Scandinavian countries. Another important step was an alliance with Durrants, a U.K.-based media-monitoring company that would provide Vocus customers with global news and monitoring services. Also of note in 2004, Vocus expanded its government relations business through the acquisition of Gnossos Software, Inc., adding hundreds of new customers. These moves helped Vocus to increase sales to $20.3 million in 2004.

TAKEN PUBLIC: 2005

Vocus became cash-flow positive in 2005, posting revenues of more than $28 million. In December of that year the company went public, netting $40 million in its initial stock offering. Shares of Vocus then began trading on the NASDAQ, providing Vocus with an initial market capitalization of $120 million. The company took advantage of its public status to complete a significant acquisition in August 2006. It paid $28 million in cash and stock for PRWeb, a press release distribution company that in 1999 had been the first to deliver press releases online.

Revenues increased to $40.3 million in 2006 and Vocus posted its first profitable year, netting $442,000. Not only did sales improve to $58.1 million and net income to $1 million in 2007, the price of Vocus stock increased to more than $25, or almost triple its opening $9 price. To keep pace with changes in the marketplace, Vocus continually updated its software. In 2007, for example, it added a service that allowed customers to incorporate videos from YouTube and other websites into news releases. In August 2007 Vocus launched Issues Wire, an online distribution service for news releases related to political and public issues.

Vocus hired more salespeople in 2008, allowing the company to increase the number of customers from 2,427 at the end of 2007 to 3,370 one year later. As a result, revenues improved 33 percent to $77.5 million in 2008 and net income approached $7 million. A year later the number of active subscribers grew to 4,438, leading to an increase in sales to $84.6 million in 2009.

Vocus looked to expand its international business in 2010 by acquiring a French public relations software company, Datapresse. It also purchased a privately held Chinese company, BDL Media Ltd., the addition of which brought more than 100 Chinese companies as customers, providing Vocus with a promising platform for the future in a fast-growing market.

Ed Dinger

PRINCIPAL SUBSIDIARIES

PAT LLC; Vocus International Holdings LLC; Vocus Europe Limited.

PRINCIPAL COMPETITORS

PR Newswire Association LLC; Reuters Group PLC; United Business Media Limited.

FURTHER READING

"Congressional Quarterly Initiates Washington Alert LinkService." *Online*, September 1991, 11.

Gonsalves, Antone. "Vocus Expands Relationship Management Software." *TechWeb*, September 8, 2000.

Huslin, Anita. "Vocus Puts Playtime on the Agenda." *Washington Post*, August 27, 2007.

Jarboe, Kathleen Johnston. "With Md. Stocks Rising, Lanham Firm Files $40M IPO." *Baltimore (MD) Daily Record*, June 20, 2005.

Mazzucca, Timothy. "Rick Rudman." *Washington Business Journal*, December 1, 2000, 29.

Mitra, Sramana. "On the Way to $100 Million in SaaS Revenue: Vocus CEO Rick Rudman." March 18, 2010. Accessed October 19, 2010. http://www.sramanamitra.com/2010/03/19/on-the-way-to-100-million-in-saas-revenue-vocus-ceo-rick-rudman-part-3.

"Vocus Projecting Major Growth with Acquisition of PAT." *PR Week*, February 3, 2003, 7.

Winpak Ltd.

100 Saulteaux Crescent
Winnipeg, Manitoba R3J 3T3
Canada
Telephone: (204) 889-1015
Fax: (204) 888-7806
Web site: http://www.winpak.com

Public Company
Founded: 1977
Employees: 1,750
Sales: US$506 million (2009)
Stock Exchanges: Toronto
Ticker Symbol: WPK
NAICS: 326111 Plastics Bag and Pouch Manufacturing; 326112 Plastics Packaging Film and Sheet (including Laminated) Manufacturing; 326199 All Other Plastics Product Manufacturing; 33399 All Other General Purpose Machinery Manufacturing

■ ■ ■

Based in Winnipeg, Canada, Winpak Ltd. is a leading North American manufacturer and distributor of high-quality packaging materials and packaging machines. The company was founded in 1977 and has been publicly traded since 1986, although it continues to be majority owned by Wihuri Oy, a conglomerate headquartered in Finland whose holdings extend from packaging to private air charter to food wholesaling.

Winpak's main lines of products include rigid packaging materials and lidding for perishable foods and beverages and flexible packaging materials for health care applications. The company distributes packaging materials throughout Canada, the United States, Mexico, the Caribbean, and other parts of Latin America. It also has customers for its rigid packaging and flexible lidding products in the United Kingdom.

ORIGINS AND EARLY EXPANSION: 1977–86

Winpak's origins extend back to 1974, when Wihuri executives made an exploratory visit to Winnipeg. Looking to expand its plastic packaging business to North America, Wihuri commissioned John Robert Lavery, a 32-year-old partner with Ernst & Whinney, to conduct a feasibility study. Lavery recommended that Wihuri build a plant in Winnipeg. He also introduced company officials to the Investors Group, which was based in the city and became a partner in the new operation. After securing further funding from the Federal Business Development Bank, the project went forward with Lavery as president and chief executive officer. Winpak's newly constructed plant was operational by late 1977, and its first item was plastic packaging for bacon.

Winpak's first year produced nearly CAD 4 million in sales but no profits. Its second year ended no better. After losing a combined CAD 5.5 million during its first two years, Winpak's management made a case to Wihuri to continue rather than rethink the venture. Certain of the company's future success, Lavery and 11 other managers decided to chip in their own capital to become part owners. In 1980 Winpak turned a small profit. Within a few years the company was comfortably profitable and searching for opportunities to expand.

COMPANY PERSPECTIVES

Winpak manufactures and distributes high-quality packaging materials and related innovative packaging machines. The Company's products are used primarily for the protection of perishable foods, beverages, and in health care applications.

Winpak, part of a global packaging group, operates nine production facilities in Canada and the United States. The Company offers customers global coverage and expertise. The North American business units assist customers throughout the United States, Canada, Latin America, the Pacific Rim countries and, for certain products, Europe. Winpak's strategic alliance with Winpak, one of Europe's leading manufacturers of packaging materials, allows global customers to reduce costs, simplify product development and consolidate packaging solutions.

From the start, Winpak's policy was to grow both internally and externally. During its first year of operations it hired sales staff throughout Canada and the United States. Ten years later it acquired operations in Philadelphia, Pennsylvania, Los Angeles, California, Chicago, Illinois, and Boston, Massachusetts. By 1986 it had annual sales of CAD 42.2 million and was the third-largest supplier of multilayered vacuum packaging in North America. In August of that year Winpak completed its initial public offering (IPO) on the Toronto Stock Exchange, selling 1.6 million common shares for CAD 8.25 a share. The transaction reduced Wihuri's stake in the company from 77 percent to 51 percent.

Wihuri and Winpak continued to maintain a close and supportive relationship by sharing information on market trends, research and development costs, and information technology. Under a mutual agreement, Wihuri confined its packaging unit to Europe while Winpak concentrated on the Americas. Winpak's aim was to diversify by expanding the types of plastic packaging it could supply.

EXPANSION THROUGHOUT NORTH AMERICA: 1987–94

In 1987 Winpak acquired 80 percent of the shares of Flex-On Inc., a packaging company based in Senoia, Georgia, that operated two plants that used the extrusion method to produce blown films for flexible packaging applications. Winpak acquired the remainder of the shares in 1989. Three years later, in 1992, the company acquired PNG Flexible Packaging, a Toronto-based operation that specialized in printing plastic packages for items such as candy bars and cookies and renamed it Winpak Technologies. The following year Winpak bought the Consumers' Portion Packaging division of Consumers Packaging Inc. The transaction gave Winpak control of the largest North American manufacturer of individual thermoformed plastic packaging systems for creamers, margarine and other blends, and condiments. In 1995 the company followed up with the acquisition of W. A. Lane, Inc., a maker of packaging machines that was based in San Bernardino, California.

At the end of its first decade as a public company, Winpak was already a market leader in Canada and had established a strong position in the United States. Seventy percent of its sales took place in the United States, 25 percent in Canada, and the remainder in Mexico and other Latin American countries. At the May 1996 annual meeting in Toronto, Lavery told investors that Winpak was still looking for acquisition opportunities in plastic packaging, especially in food packaging. According to *Plastics News* on May 13, 1996, Lavery explained that the global packaging industry "is ripe for consolidation, despite the hundreds of mergers and acquisitions in the past five years." He believed the world market, which was estimated at CAD 500 million a year, was "still highly fragmented."

Rapidly rising demand for plastic packaging was boosting Winpak's revenues and profits. Sales doubled between 1992 and 1993, and in spite of rising raw materials prices the company posted a 20.3 percent increase in net earnings for the first six months of 1995. In an interview with Martin Cash in the *Winnipeg Free Press* on July 30, 1993, Lavery attributed these results in part to continual technological upgrades and efforts to improve internal efficiency. In 1992 the company spent CAD 5 million upgrading its plants in Winnipeg and Georgia. It also made a CAD 400,000 investment in a quality management program. In 1994 Winpak announced that it would spend CAD 30 million over the next two years to build a new manufacturing plant for Winpak Technologies.

STAYING STATE-OF-THE-ART: 1997–2001

In 1997 Winpak installed its first dedicated polypropylene sheet and thermoforming line at its factory in South Chicago Heights, Illinois, which broadened the range of food packaging types it could offer. Later that year the company announced that it would spend CAD 33.8 million over the next five years to further expand and upgrade its Winnipeg plant. Meanwhile, Winpak

KEY DATES

1977: Winpak Ltd. is established in Winnipeg with Wihuri Oy as a majority shareholder.
1986: Winpak launches an initial public offering on the Toronto Stock Exchange.
1998: Winpak establishes American Biaxis with Nichimen Corporation.
2005: Winpak signs a licensing agreement with Asahi Kasei Life and Living Corporation.
2009: Winpak signs a licensing agreement with Reynolds Packaging LLC.

acquired the Quebec-based producer Heat Seal Packaging Inc., an industry leader in developing and manufacturing plastic membranes and lids for dairy, food, beverage, and pharmaceutical makers.

Winpak concluded in 1998 a joint venture agreement with Nichimen Corporation, a leading Japanese trading concern, to manufacture and sell biaxially oriented nylon film used to make sanitary food containers. Winpak had a 51 percent stake in the new Winnipeg operation, American Biaxis, which paralleled a similar joint venture that Wihuri had already set up with Nichimen in Europe. "The product we produce there will be partially sold to Nichimen and partially sold to ourselves for our own consumption," Lavery told John Schreiner in the *Financial Post* on June 15, 1999. "So we're going to end up with a new product that is going to reduce the purchases that we have and it will be at a lower price than what we're paying and a better quality. That's always our goal, to be the low-cost producer. We do it through investing in high technology."

Winpak continued to enjoy rising sales and earnings, but it was also feeling pressures from increased competition, customer consolidations, and rising prices for raw materials. In 1999 it closed the Bristol, Pennsylvania, manufacturing facility and transferred production to its Chicago and Toronto plants. Nevertheless, expansion and upgrading continued. In 2000 Winpak began a CAD 46 million capital project to expand the Winnipeg and Chicago facilities. Early in 2001, after announcing another year of record earnings with its net income increasing from CAD 16.6 million to CAD 23.3 million, the company indicated that it would spend nearly CAD 20 million on new equipment for the Winnipeg plant over two years.

DECREASING COSTS AND WASTE: 2002–03

Winpak added more packaging technology to its arsenal in 2002 when it acquired Webkote, a leading manufacturer of die-cut lids for dairy, food, beverage, and pharmaceutical companies. The following year Winpak began a CAD 13 million expansion project that would double American Biaxis's production capacity and size. The move was also seen as a vote of confidence by Winpak of keeping Winnipeg the center for its operations. "The workforce is very reliable in Winnipeg," Murray Johnston, the vice president and chief financial officer of Winpak, told Murray McNeill in the *Winnipeg Free Press* on April 19, 2003, adding that Winpak's heavy use of hydroelectricity made Manitoba's low electricity rates an advantage. The decision to expand American Biaxis's presence there "does demonstrate that the company is very content with its business presence in Winnipeg."

Over the previous five years the company had invested nearly CAD 200 million in property, plant, and new advanced manufacturing equipment, which generated incremental net earnings of CAD 23.4 million in sales. Even though the economy had been sluggish following the dot-com crash, Winpak had managed to produce record profits in some quarters by lowering costs and by reducing waste at its plants. It also continued to produce new package types that were geared to lower costs and improve efficiency for users. Sales in 2002 alone were CAD 454 million, up from CAD 47.5 million in 1987, Winpak's first full year as a public company.

"We have almost $70 million of high-tech capacity available to increase sales," Lavery told Geoff Kirbyson in the *Winnipeg Free Press* on May 31, 2002. "With respect to capacity, this is our best position in many years. We can respond quickly to new opportunities and we have the technology and cost structure to be successful when opportunities are presented." At the end of 2003 Lavery retired, and Bruce Berry was named president and chief executive officer.

STAYING PROFITABLE IN TOUGH TIMES: 2004–06

Winpak announced in early 2004 that it would begin reporting its financial results in U.S. dollars, acknowledging that the United States was the company's major market. Even though a strong Canadian dollar threatened to depress profits, the company was committed to investing approximately CAD 120 million over the next three years to further expand and upgrade production throughout its facilities. This included expanding its operations and opening a new plant in Senoia, adding new technologies to the Montreal and Winnipeg plants, and building a new plant in Pekin, Illinois.

Winpak was also on the lookout for new acquisitions, particularly packaging companies that made items such as meat trays and packaging for medical devices. However, its targets would not necessarily be in its home markets. According to McNeill in the *Winnipeg Free Press* on April 20, 2004, Berry told shareholders, "Expanding our geography outside North America is also a priority. We believe South America and China are regions providing opportunities for Winpak."

That same year Winpak acquired the MAP FRESH division of Clear Lam Packaging, Inc., which made it a significant player in the market for barrier trays for fresh meat using modified atmosphere packaging. In 2005 the company signed a licensing agreement with Asahi Kasei Life and Living Corporation of Japan to buy Asahi Kasei's technology for shrink wrapping red meat and poultry products. The agreement made Winpak one of only four companies in North America able to use the technique. The new process was installed at the Senoia plant with the goal of securing 5 percent of the CAD 850 million annual market for meat and poultry packaging within five years. Later that year it sold the assets of a Toronto operation that made printed paper bags to Color Ad Packaging Ltd. and consolidated other production lines. In 2006 it sold some property and buildings in Toronto.

MAJOR ACQUISITIONS: 2008–10

In 2008 Winpak purchased Walsroder Packaging LLC, a film packaging company based in Willowbrook, Illinois. The following year the company signed a licensing deal for exclusive rights to use Reynolds Packaging LLC's formulations and specifications to produce packaging materials used in the pharmaceutical and health care industries. Reynolds had announced a year earlier that it would no longer be producing these materials. "It's a big deal for us," Berry told McNeill in the *Winnipeg Free Press* on March 31, 2009. Winpak beat several other packaging firms for the deal, which would help the company to expand its pharmaceutical and health care product offerings. Berry explained that obtaining government approval for new packaging materials for these industries was expensive and time consuming, whereas Reynolds already had the proper approvals. "So with this deal we can bypass all of that," Berry noted.

Winpak recorded one of its best financial performances of the decade in 2008 and followed up with record first-quarter results in 2009, despite a severe economic downturn that began in late 2007. According to McNeill in the *Winnipeg Free Press* on April 23, 2009, Winpak's success could be attributed to the fact "that 90 per cent of the plastic packaging materials it produces are used to package perishable foods and beverages and health-care products—things that consumers need even during tough economic times." Berry told McNeill, "Winpak may not be recession proof, but it is the next best thing to it."

That being the case, Winpak showed no signs of diverging from its long-term strategy of investing for the future. At the company's April 2010 shareholders' meeting, Berry announced a CAD 30 million round of capital spending to be completed that year. The project would include adding an additional coextrusion line and a new 10-color printing press at one of its two Winnipeg production plants to keep up with demand from U.S. food producers.

Eric Laursen

PRINCIPAL SUBSIDIARIES

Winpak Portion Packaging Ltd.; Winpak Heat Seal Packaging Inc.; Winpak Portion Packaging Inc.; Winpak Heat Seal Corporation; Winpak Films Inc.; Winpak Lane, Inc.; Winpak Inc.; American Biaxis Inc.

PRINCIPAL DIVISIONS

Flexible Lidding; Flexible Packaging; Health Care Packaging; Packaging Machinery and Parts; Rigid Packaging.

PRINCIPAL COMPETITORS

Bemis Company, Inc.; Sealed Air Corporation; Sonoco Products Company.

FURTHER READING

Cash, Martin. "Packaging Team Delivers Goods." *Winnipeg Free Press*, July 30, 1993.

"Finnish Wihuri's Winpak Significant Player in North America." *Kauppalehti*, March 15, 1996, 12.

Gordon, Sheldon. "How to Succeed in the U.S. Market by Really Really Trying." *National Post*, June 3, 1999, 76.

McNeill, Murray. "Winpak on Hunt for Acquisitions." *Winnipeg Free Press*, April 23, 2009, B7.

———. "Winpak Ramps up Package Production." *Winnipeg Free Press*, April 21, 2010, B5.

———. "Winpak Stays Local for Expansion." *Winnipeg Free Press*, April 19, 2003, B5.

———. "Winpak's a Winner Built on Risk." *Winnipeg Free Press*, February 2, 2004, D5.

Schreiner, John. "Winpak Offers Solid Performance Package." *Financial Post*, June 15, 1999, D3.

Taylor, Fabrice. "Winpak Seems a Good Package." *Globe and Mail* (Toronto), August 14, 2002, B8.

"Winpak Sees Its Opportunity in Vacuum Pack." *Globe and Mail* (Toronto), March 9, 1987, B10.

Wüstenrot & Württembergische AG

Gutenbergstrasse 30
Stuttgart, D-70176
Germany
Telephone: (+49 711) 662-0
Fax: (+49 711) 662-722520
Web site: http://www.ww-ag.com

Public Company
Founded: 1828 as Württembergische Privat-Feuer-Versicherung-Gesellschaft
Incorporated: 1923 as Württembergische Feuerversicherung AG
Employees: 8,267
Sales: €5.48 billion ($7.89 billion) (2009)
Stock Exchanges: Berlin
Ticker Symbol: WUW
NAICS: 236116 New Multifamily Housing Construction (except Operative Builders); 236117 New Housing Operative Builders; 522110 Commercial Banking; 522120 Savings Institutions; 522292 Real Estate Credit; 524113 Direct Life Insurance Carriers; 524114 Direct Health and Medical Insurance Carriers; 524126 Direct Property and Casualty Insurance Carriers; 531210 Offices of Real Estate Agents and Brokers

■ ■ ■

Wüstenrot & Württembergische AG (W&W) is among Germany's top 10 mortgage banking and insurance companies. Its mortgages are overseen by two major subsidiaries: Wüstenrot Bausparkasse AG, which is one of the country's largest providers of home loan savings plans, and Wüstenrot Bank AG Pfandbriefbank, which is a mortgage bank for private customers that also issues mortgage bonds in the capital markets. W&W's second field of activity, insurance, is carried out by five main subsidiaries: Württembergische Versicherung AG, which offers a broad variety of property and casualty insurance plans to individuals and corporate clients; the life insurers Württembergische Lebensversicherung AG and Karlsruher Lebensversicherung AG; Württembergische Krankenversicherung AG, which provides health and medical insurance; and ARA Pensionskasse AG, which offers corporate pension plans.

In addition, W&W is also active in real estate brokering, in the construction of residential dwellings, and, through two subsidiaries in Ireland, in financial asset management. Its core market is in Germany, where the company serves approximately 6 million customers, but it also has subsidiaries in the Czech Republic and other east European countries as well as in Ireland and Luxembourg.

WÜRTTEMBERGISCHE'S EARLY YEARS: 1828–99

W&W's roots go back to 1825, when Georg Wessler, a young entrepreneur and tobacco factory owner in Ulm, published an advertisement in the *Schwäbischer Merkur* daily newspaper to find other businesspeople who were interested in jointly establishing insurance for movable property such as machinery, inventories, and merchandise against losses due to fire and other casualties. Even though building owners were required

COMPANY PERSPECTIVES

W&W—We've got it covered. Having united the forces of Wüstenrot and Württembergische, we've become a one-stop shop for comprehensive financial planning. We leverage the combined power of our two equally strong pillars, a home loan savings bank and an insurance provider, to respond to our clients' needs like no other financial services provider in Germany.

to buy fire insurance from a state-owned agency, insurance coverage for movable property could only be obtained from a handful of private insurers, none of which were based in the southwestern German kingdom of Württemberg.

Three years later, in 1828, Württembergische Privat-Feuer-Versicherung-Gesellschaft, the first privately held movable property insurer in southern Germany, was founded in Stuttgart. Unlike its competitors, Württembergische granted fire insurance coverage to poor people through much lower premiums. During its first year Württembergische issued nearly 5,000 insurance certificates to private individuals and businesses. By the end of the 1830s Württembergische covered roughly two-thirds of Württemberg.

With industrialization in full swing during the second half of the 19th century, Württembergische grew leaps and bounds. The rise of steam-powered factories attracted a growing number of workers from other parts of the country, with the number of inhabitants in Stuttgart alone reaching 120,000 by the late 19th century. Because both businesses and individuals were potential insurance customers, Württembergische's business thrived, enabling the mutual insurer to pay its members a 30 percent dividend for the first time during the late 1850s. Massive growth continued throughout the 19th century, with dividends reaching 40 percent by the late 1860s and 60 percent a decade later. By the end of the 19th century Württembergische reported 170,000 insurance certificates with a total amount insured of DEM 1 billion.

REORGANIZATION, EXPANSION, AND INFLATION: 1900–35

At the turn of the 20th century Württembergische focused on internal reorganization and external expansion. Reinsurance arrangements were completely restructured, which decreased related costs during the first decade of the new century. Typewriters were introduced to speed up the creation and processing of documents, which previously had been written out by hand, and women began working as telephone operators at the much larger headquarters in Stuttgart. To extend its reach beyond Württemberg, the mutual insurer changed its name to Württembergische Feuerversicherung auf Gegenseitigkeit and started cooperating with Allgemeiner Deutscher Versicherungsverein, a Stuttgart-based liability and accident insurer that had a national sales organization. In addition, Württembergische's own sales network was strengthened and the company's commissions for its sales agents were raised to increase their motivation to close deals.

The beginning of World War I in 1914 drastically slowed Württembergische's growth. Left with less than half of its workforce, the insurer had to extend work hours to manage its day-to-day operations. During the war years Württembergische acquired the German fire insurer Lübecker Feuerversicherungsgesellschaft and the Dutch fire and burglary insurer Niederländische Lloyd. As the company's insurance portfolio increased, its workforce doubled, reaching 400 by the early 1920s.

Between 1918 and the early 1920s the company struggled to maintain its financial reserves as postwar inflation enveloped the country. Eventually, most of its reserves were exhausted, except for its real estate in which Württembergische had invested part of its capital. To raise new capital, the insurer was transformed into Württembergische Feuerversicherung AG, a joint stock corporation, in 1923. One of its main shareholders was Allgemeine Rentenanstalt zu Stuttgart (ARA), a private pension insurer in which Württembergische also acquired a major stake. The mutual shareholdings marked the beginning of a successful business partnership of the two insurers.

During the mid-1920s Württembergische expanded its line of insurance plans to include liability, accident, auto, glass, and water pipeline coverage. Even though the company's sales agents were able to offer a broad variety of products to customers, the growing number of claims and decreasing price levels due to fierce competition posed a serious challenge. The number of fire insurers alone had more than doubled during the 1920s. To make matters worse, the Great Depression, which reached Germany by the early 1930s, caused a sudden contraction of the insurance market.

WORLD WAR II LOSSES AND POSTWAR BOOM: 1935–74

The German economy did not show signs of recovery until the mid-1930s. However, by that point the

KEY DATES

1828: Württembergische Privat-Feuer-Versicherung-Gesellschaft is founded in Stuttgart.
1921: Verein Gemeinschaft der Freunde is established in Wüstenrot.
1999: Wüstenrot and Württembergische merge to form Wüstenrot & Württembergische AG (W&W).
2005: W&W acquires Karlsruher Versicherung.
2010: W&W acquires Allianz Dresdner Bauspar AG.

National Socialist party had taken over the German government. During this period Württembergische had a workforce of roughly 700 employees and was, according to *175 Jahre Württembergische*, heavily influenced by Nazi ideology. During World War II the remaining employees had to shoulder a heavier workload and work at different branch offices. To escape the Allied bombings, important business operations were moved outside of Stuttgart. By 1945 over two-thirds of its facilities had been destroyed or heavily damaged.

Although Württembergische lost several offices in the Soviet-occupied Eastern German zone, it was determined to make a fresh start in the newly founded Federal Republic of Germany. During the postwar economic boom the insurance business flourished again. By 1953 Württembergische reported revenues from insurance premiums that were three times higher than prewar revenues. To tap into the rapidly growing market for private financial security, the company established in 1954 a life insurance department and intensified its cooperation with ARA.

As the company's revenues continued to climb during the 1960s and 1970s, Württembergische made an effort to use new electronic data processing technologies. It first system was based on punch cards, which were replaced by mainframe computers during the early 1970s. By that time its annual premiums had grown fivefold, reaching DEM 500,000 in 1973.

Württembergische also continued to add new products. In 1971 Württembergische Rechtsschutzversicherung, a new subsidiary for legal expense insurance, was established. Three years later, in 1974, the company started a close cooperation with Leonberger Bausparkasse, a mutual mortgage savings bank, by selling its mortgage savings plans to the bank's customers.

COMPUTERIZATION AND EXPANSION: 1983–99

The introduction of personal computers at Württembergische in 1983 was the first step toward the computerization of all aspects of the insurance business. During the 1980s the company also established an information system for its sales personnel and a central department for its accounts receivable collection. In 1990, one year after the fall of the Berlin Wall, Württembergische sent a convoy of recreational vehicles to eastern Germany to sell auto insurance to as many East Germans as possible, whose policies were set to expire at the end of the year. As a result, the company reported 127,000 new insurance contracts in only eight weeks. That same year Württembergische opened 10 new branch offices in eastern Germany.

During the 1990s Württembergische was confronted with an increasingly fierce competitive climate in the German insurance market. The company reacted by investing more in television advertising and in customer loyalty programs. It also teamed up with strategic partners to further expand its product range and to maintain its independence within the rapidly consolidating industry. In 1991 Württembergische merged with its longtime partner ARA to form WürttAG, which served as a holding company for the insurance group. The company's fire insurance business was transferred to the newly established Württembergische Versicherung AG while ARA, which was renamed Württembergische Lebensversicherung, operated the life insurance and private pension business.

By the mid-1990s Württembergische's premium income passed the DEM 1 billion mark for the first time. However, the claims that were filed following a major fire at Düsseldorf International Airport in 1996 drastically affected its revenues for the year. Two years later the company founded the health and medical insurance subsidiary Württembergische Krankenversicherung to tap into an additional revenue source. Nonetheless, by the late 1990s nearly half of the insurer's shareholders signaled that they were ready to sell their stake in the company. In 1999 Württembergische announced that it was merging with Wüstenrot, one of Germany's largest home building savings and mortgage banks.

WÜSTENROT'S EARLY YEARS: 1921–52

Wüstenrot was founded on the initiative of Georg Kropp, a pharmacist and social activist. Kropp had a vision of enabling families with few financial resources to save money for building their own homes, which was a revolutionary idea at a time of extreme housing shortages in post–World War I Germany. Despite the resistance of the established savings banks and other opponents, Kropp was relentless in propagating his idea of a self-help organization in which every member who regularly paid a certain amount into a joint account could receive a loan to build a home. By 1921 Kropp had assembled a small group of investors, and together they founded the mutual home loan savings association Verein Gemeinschaft der Freunde (GdF) in Wüstenrot.

However, shortly thereafter the country was beginning to feel the crippling effects of rising postwar inflation. Just before all the association's funds were used up, Kropp and his partners paid out every member and stopped their activities until 1924, when they launched a revised model of a home loan savings plan and began to acquire members again. In 1926 GdF's home loan savings business was transferred to a nonprofit limited liability company. Four years later GdF's headquarters were moved to Ludwigsburg and the company was renamed Bausparkasse Gemeinschaft der Freunde Wüstenrot. Its home loan savings model not only increased the number of new customers but also of competitors. However, after the German government passed a law in 1931 that regulated the market and established a new agency to oversee private mortgage savings banks, their number was reduced from over 400 before 1931 to less than 60.

GdF's first subsidiary abroad was established in Salzburg, Austria, in 1930, but after 1945 the Austrian government controlled it. Beginning with the postwar economic boom in West Germany, Wüstenrot enjoyed an extended period of massive growth that was driven by constantly rising standards of living and by a 1952 law that guaranteed an extra financial bonus from the state to people with mortgage savings plans. The company established Hausbau Wüstenrot, a new nonprofit subsidiary for the construction of condominiums, and launched a savings plan that was geared toward individuals who wanted to buy an apartment instead of a house.

DIVERSIFICATION AND FURTHER EXPANSION: 1960–98

During the 1960s Wüstenrot began modernizing its offices, training its staff, and establishing a network of 20 branch offices in major cities. By the mid-1960s the company's building society savings program reached almost DEM 4.5 billion. A major strategic step followed in 1968 with the foundation of Wüstenrot-Bank AG für Wohnungswirtschaft, in which the company's own bank offered its customers supplemental financing for residential construction projects. The following year Wüstenrot and the German insurer Allianz established Wüstenrot Lebensversicherung AG, which provided life insurance policies for mortgage savings plan holders. Additional subsidiaries for services in connection with the development of residential construction projects and for market research were developed during the early 1970s.

Geographic expansion began in 1978 with the establishment of a mortgage savings subsidiary in Luxembourg. During the 1980s the company greatly expanded its network of branch offices. In 1990 Wüstenrot established 11 sales offices in eastern Germany. The following year Wüstenrot and its Austrian counterpart founded mortgage banking subsidiaries in the Czech Republic and Slovakia. The company eventually became active in Croatia, Hungary, and Poland.

Diversification continued in 1991, when Wüstenrot created Wüstenrot Immobilien, a real estate brokerage that in the following years established a national network of brokers who advised their clients in mortgage financing and financial risk management. Wüstenrot Hypothekenbank, a mortgage bank that also issued mortgage bonds, was founded in 1995. Three years later, in 1998, Wüstenrot restructured its group of companies. GdF's mortgage savings business was spun off to the newly founded Wüstenrot Bausparkasse AG, while GdF itself was transformed into the Wüstenrot Beteiligungs AG, a holding company for most of GdF's remaining subsidiaries.

RESTRUCTURING AFTER MERGER: 1999–2006

In 1999 Wüstenrot and Württembergische merged to form Wüstenrot & Württembergische AG. Both companies were active in the same geographic region and served a similar customer base, but their product portfolios supplemented each other perfectly. The companies continued to operate as two separate organizations during the first few years after the merger. At the turn of the 21st century W&W was hit hard by an estimated €100 million in losses following the terrorist attacks on the World Trade Center on September 11, 2001. The following the year a major flood catastrophe along the Oder River in Germany cost the company another €100 million.

The value of Württembergische's stock declined, but the liaison with Wüstenrot prevented the worst. Württembergische divested itself of its reinsurance activities, but extended its mortgage banking activities to the Czech Republic. Meanwhile, Wüstenrot acquired Leonberger Bausparkasse, the home loan savings association that Württembergische had cooperated with for many years, in 2001. However, it continued to lose market share to competitors. Consequently, W&W slipped deeply into the red. After the company worked on cutting costs and strengthening its sales network and customer relationships, W&W returned to profits.

In 2005 W&W acquired Karlsruher Versicherung, a major German life insurer that had annual revenues of €1.2 billion and a workforce of 7,400. The acquisition catapulted W&W into the top 10 of Germany's direct insurance groups. However, the turnaround for the company was in 2006, when Alexander Erdland, the head of Schwäbisch Hall, became the company's new chairman.

TURNAROUND UNDER NEW LEADERSHIP: 2006–10

Erdland initiated a three-year restructuring program that focused on streamlining the company's organization, setting up joint operational structures, strengthening its sales force, and building a group identity between the mortgage banking and insurance branches. In February 2007 the company sold its Dutch life and property insurance subsidiary Erasmus, and the following month it signed a cooperation agreement with the Spanish bank Santander to use cross-selling opportunities. As a result of these measures, W&W's revenues continued to rise significantly, and its market share in German home mortgage savings increased.

The company acquired the home mortgage savings bank Vereinsbank Victoria Bauspar AG in 2009 and merged it with Wüstenrot Bausparkasse. The following year W&W acquired Allianz Dresdner Bauspar AG from Commerzbank. These acquisitions not only boosted the company's market share in home loan and savings to over 11 percent but also gave W&W access to the sales networks of major German financial institutions, including Commerzbank, HypoVereinsbank AG, and ERGO Versicherungsgruppe AG, for its home mortgage savings business.

In 2009 W&W reported profits of €220 million. In September 2010 it became Commerzbank's exclusive provider of home loan and savings plans. With its the new positioning as a major financial security specialist, W&W saw itself as a key player in the German market for tailor-made individual financial services and had a strategic goal of achieving annual profits of €250 million by 2012.

Evelyn Hauser

PRINCIPAL SUBSIDIARIES

Wüstenrot Bausparkasse AG; Wüstenrot Bank AG Pfandbriefbank; Württembergische Versicherung AG; Karlsruher Lebensversicherung AG (82%); Württembergische Krankenversicherung AG; Württembergische Lebensversicherung AG (72%); Allgemeine Rentenanstalt Pensionskasse AG; Wüstenrot Haus- und Städtebau GmbH; 3B Boden-Bauten-Beteiligungs GmbH; W&W Gesellschaft für Finanzbeteiligungen mbH; Württembergische Immobilien AG; Wohnimmobilien GmbH & Co. KG der Württembergischen; W&W Advisory Dublin Ltd. (Ireland); W&W Asset Management Dublin Ltd. (Ireland); W&W Asset Management GmbH; W&W Asset Management AG (Luxembourg); W&W Europe Life Limited (Ireland).

PRINCIPAL COMPETITORS

Allianz SE; AWD Holding AG; Bausparkasse Schwäbisch Hall AG; ERGO Versicherungsgruppe AG; HUK-COBURG-Versicherungsgruppe; HypoVereinsbank AG; LBS Landesbausparkasse Baden-Württemberg; MLP AG; MPC Münchmeyer Petersen Capital AG; R+V Versicherung AG.

FURTHER READING

"Commerzbank Closes Sale of Allianz Dresdner Bauspar." *ENP Newswire*, July 12, 2010.

"Further Job Cuts at W&W (Neuer Chef krempelt Wustenrot um)." *Europe Intelligence Wire*, June 23, 2006.

Langer, Eberhard. *Werke, nicht Worte. 75 Jahre Wüstenrot.* Frankfurt am Main, Germany: Verlag Fritz Knapp GmbH, 1996.

"Munich Re Sells Karlsruher to W&W (Munchener Ruck verkauft Karlsruher)." *Europe Intelligence Wire*, October 11, 2005.

175 Jahre Württembergische. Vom "Provisorischen Verein" zum Fels in der Brandung. Stuttgart, Germany: Wüstenrot & Württembergische AG, 2003.

"Wustenrot Building Society Receives Mortgage License." *Czech Business News*, November 12, 2002.

"Wustenrot Improves Share of Building Society Market." *Europe Intelligence Wire*, August 18, 2008.

"Wüstenrot & Württembergische to Sell Erasmus Groep (W&W stosst Tochter Erasmus ab)." *Europe Intelligence Wire*, February 9, 2007.

"W&W Restructures to Get Back in Profit." *Europe Intelligence Wire*, December 19, 2002.

"W&W to Cooperate with Santander." *Europe Intelligence Wire*, March 1, 2007.

Yankees Entertainment & Sports Network, LLC

Chrysler Building, 405 Lexington Avenue, 36th Floor
New York, New York 10174
U.S.A.
Telephone: (646) 487-3600
Fax: (646) 487-3612
Web site: http://www.yesnetwork.com

Private Company
Founded: 2001
Employees: 140
Sales: $417.1 million (2009 est.)
NAICS: 515210 Cable and Other Subscription Programming

■ ■ ■

The Yankees Entertainment & Sports Network, LLC, operates the Yankees Entertainment and Sports (YES) Network, the largest regional sports network in the country. The network broadcasts New York Yankees baseball games and New Jersey Nets basketball games, as well as pregame and postgame shows, regional college games, and Emmy Award–winning original programming, including sports talk and interview shows, sports news, and other sports-related entertainment productions. Distributed locally in New York, New Jersey, Connecticut, and Pennsylvania, the YES Network is controlled by the Steinbrenner family. Others with interests in the YES Network include an investment group led by Ray Chambers, the former Nets owner, and the global investment banker Goldman Sachs.

FOUNDATION FOR THE NETWORK

In 1973 George M. Steinbrenner III acquired the Yankees from the CBS television network. During the 1970s the franchise won three pennants and two World Series. After those titles, the team did not return to winning form until the late 1990s, when the Yankees won the World Series in 1998 and 1999. That same year the franchise was merged with the New Jersey Nets to create the holding company YankeesNets LLC. It was hoped that the merger would provide greater leverage for both teams in selling their broadcast rights.

During the 1990s those broadcasting rights belonged to the New York cable powerhouse Cablevision Systems Corporation, which had acquired smaller cable operators and came to hold broadcasting rights for all seven New York–area major league franchises in baseball, basketball, and hockey. Cablevision controlled Yankees broadcasting through the Madison Square Garden (MSG) Network and Nets broadcasting through SportsChannel New York (which later became Fox Sports Net New York and then MSG Plus).

Following the merger, YankeesNets attempted to put its two-team leverage to use in subsequent talks with Fox Sports Net New York, Cablevision, and Time Warner. Discussions with the latter two involved not only broadcasting rights but also the possibility of the joint establishment of a sports network. In 2000 the Yankees and International Management Group (IMG) tried to form such a network, but MSG Network filed suit to protect its Yankees broadcasting rights through the 2001 season, and the New York Supreme Court

COMPANY PERSPECTIVES

YES Network is a 24-hour-a-day, 7-day-a-week premier sports and entertainment television network featuring the 27-time World Champion New York Yankees Major League Baseball team and the New Jersey Nets NBA team. The YES Network is available to viewers in New York, Connecticut, and parts of New Jersey and Pennsylvania. In addition to 130 Yankees games, YES broadcasts other professional and collegiate sports teams as well as classic sports footage. We are the No. 1 Regional Sports Network in the country.

ultimately blocked the IMG-Yankees deal in April 2001. Under the court-sanctioned settlement terms, MSG Network was also given the right to broadcast 85 Yankees games in 2002, but YankeesNets controlled an option to repurchase those rights for $30 million, which it did in June 2001. The payoff freed the Yankees from Cablevision's clutches and placed the team in a position to start its own network.

With the Cablevision-Yankees broadcasting deal set to expire after the 2001 season and the Nets contract set to expire after its 2001–02 season, YankeesNets decided to start its own network, which would effectively end Cablevision's monopoly over New York sports. Playing a role in the decision was the growing value of the Yankees: the team had become a major brand because of successes on the field during the late 1990s.

FORMATION OF THE NETWORK

At the turn of the 21st century the Yankees kept winning. After notching their third consecutive World Series victory in 2000, the franchise went back to the October finale in 2001 and was defeated by the San Diego Padres. Nonetheless, the Yankees appeared on the upswing, especially with Steinbrenner annually pitching millions of dollars at free-agent players to improve the team.

To launch the YES Network, YankeesNets secured as financial partners Goldman Sachs, the global investment banker group, and the Quadrangle Group, a small investment partnership. Goldman Sachs in turn brought on board Leo J. Hindery Jr., the former AT&T Broadband president, and Quadrangle encouraged the billionaire cable and communications businessman Amos Barr Hostetter Jr. to join the new partnership. The investors agreed to contribute a total of $340 million for a collective stake of 40 percent. Goldman Sachs and Quadrangle agreed to be 50-50 partners, each contributing $150 million, and Hindery and Hostetter each agreed to contribute $20 million, with the total sum dedicated to paying off the debt of YankeesNets. Steinbrenner tapped Hindery to be the network's president and chief executive officer (CEO).

In September 2001 Quadrangle and Hostetter backed out of their YES Network investment, so Goldman Sachs moved to cover their share. The YES Network also struggled in securing carriage deals with Cablevision and Time Warner, which demanded that the network be part of their premium service rather than their basic cable service. This was something that ran counter to the network's business plan because basic service would deliver greater advertising revenues.

In spite of these troubles, by October the formation of Yankees Entertainment & Sports Network, LLC, had been solidified. The network's initial broadcasting team included Fred Hickman, the former coanchor of CNN's *Sports Tonight* who would host studio coverage of Yankees broadcasts, and Suzyn Waldman, a former Broadway actress and sports reporter who was hired to do play-by-play for 35 games and host pre- and postgame shows. Michael Kay, a sports-radio veteran, was named the television commentator, and the ESPN anchor Charlie Steiner was hired to call the games. In late 2001 the YES Network signed WCBS-AM to air radio broadcasts of the Yankees in the New York area and WCBS-TV purchased the rights to broadcast 20 regular season games.

PREPARATION FOR THE NETWORK'S LAUNCH

The YES Network was launched in February 2002. Hindery tapped John Filippelli, a former ABC Sports executive producer, as vice president of programming and production for the network. Hindery also hired a number of executives from two of his former companies, AT&T and GlobalCenter Inc.

Once the YES Network was established and its top-tier management was in place, it had to secure carriage deals with cable companies in the New York metro area and the territory surrounding it, which included parts of Connecticut, New Jersey, New York, and Pennsylvania. During the first three months of 2002 the network had signed carriage deals with DIRECTV, Comcast, Time Warner Cable, RCN Cable, and AT&T Broadband, leaving Cablevision as the one significant holdout. The companies were charged a fee of $2 per month per subscriber for the right to distribute the YES Network,

KEY DATES

2001: Yankees Entertainment & Sports Network, LLC, is launched.
2002: Yankees Entertainment and Sports (YES) Network is launched.
2004: Cablevision Systems Corporation becomes a YES Network carrier.
2007: Hal Steinbrenner becomes chairman of Yankee Global Enterprises LLC.
2008: Hal Steinbrenner becomes managing general partner and cochairman of the Yankees and Hank Steinbrenner becomes general partner and cochairman.
2010: George M. Steinbrenner III dies.

which made it the most expensive cable network in the New York metro area. In March 2002 the YES Network began running ads in major newspapers that encouraged Cablevision subscribers to switch to DIRECTV. The network's ads complemented a print and radio marketing program by DIRECTV. Before the first game, the network had signed season agreements with six charter advertisers: American Honda Motor Company, Continental Airlines, Coors Brewing Company, Corona Beer, Tri-State Dodge Dealers, and Sears.

NETWORK'S DEBUT

On March 19, 2002, the YES Network broadcast its first game: a Yankees home exhibition game against the Cincinnati Reds. Hickman and Waldman anchored the Yankees coverage and were joined by the former Yankees player Bobby Murcer and Paul O'Neill. By then, the network had filled out its initial program schedule, which included *Minor League Mondays*; *Yankeeography*, a John Sterling–hosted program that featured biographies of famous Yankees players; *Yankee Magazine*, hosted by Hickman; and *Stepping Up to the Plate*, which introduced the Yankees lineup and the network's principal personalities. Between 1 p.m. and 6 p.m. each weekday the network aired a simulcast of the popular *Mike and the Mad Dog*, a leading New York sports-radio call-in show that starred Mike Francesca and Chris Russo. The simulcast became a YES Network staple for the remainder of the decade.

Cablevision became the only major regional cable company to refuse to be a YES Network carrier. Instead, Cablevision offered its subscribers a rebate for the Yankees games not shown on its network. One month into the 2002 Major League Baseball (MLB) season the YES Network brought suit against Cablevision, claiming the cable company refused to carry the network only for anticompetitive reasons. In December Cablevision came under federal investigation for alleged antitrust violations involving its refusal to carry the YES Network.

With the new MLB season approaching, Michael Bloomberg, the mayor of New York City, stepped in to help broker a deal. When he failed, Eliot Spitzer, the attorney general of New York, helped the two parties reach agreement on a one-year pact. The brokered deal put the federal antitrust suit against Cablevision on a stay, while the YES Network lawsuit against Cablevision continued but at a slower pace. The one-year agreement called for the two sides to continue discussions for a long-term contract and, if a new deal was not reached by February 1, 2004, the matter would go to a binding arbitration.

In late 2003 the Yankees and the Nets agreed to end their relationship, and the Nets were sold to the real estate developer Bruce Ratner. After the separation, the company was renamed Yankee Global Enterprises LLC. Controlled by the Steinbrenner family, the company was the owner of the Yankees and held a 34 percent stake in the YES Network, although the team and the network each operated as a separate entity.

CABLEVISION IN, HINDERY OUT

In 2003 Bloomberg called on Robert M. Gutkowski, a former MSG president, and Tom Rogers, a former NBC Cable president, to help facilitate a durable deal between the YES Network and Cablevision. However, the former executives accomplished nothing concrete, so Cablevision and the network were forced into a binding arbitration. In March 2004 Cablevision announced that it was required to carry the YES Network as part of its expanded basic cable package and that a six-year agreement with the network had been established.

In April 2004 Hindery resigned from his posts as president and CEO of the network. In September the network named Tracy Dolgin, a former president of FOX Sports Net, as its new president and CEO. Dolgin promoted Filippelli from executive vice president to president of production and programming. Filippelli was responsible for popular shows such as the one-hour interview program *Center Stage*, hosted by Michael Kay, and *Yankeeography*. Filippelli was also credited with helping to drive up ratings of Yankees games by more than 30 percent in 2004.

The YES Network upgraded its broadcast offerings in 2005, when it launched a high-definition (HD) version of its network that was made available through most of its major carriage operators. The network, serving 10.4 million viewers after three years in business, also sought to widen the type of programs shown. That year it debuted *Poker Challenge* and the reality series *Ultimate Road Trip*, which followed several Yankees fans chosen to attend all 162 games in a season. The network also added several major advertisers, including Bank of America, Kia, and Suzuki.

By the end of the Yankees 2005 season, the YES Network had the highest ratings and sales of any sports network. For 2005, advertising for Yankees games, including extra innings, was sold out, and the network generated between $44 million and $62 million in ad sales and about $190 million in subscriber revenues.

NEW TECHNOLOGY AND ADVERTISING SOURCES

After a successful first-season run in 2005, *Ultimate Road Trip* was given a second go-round in 2006. The new season featured four Yankees fans attending all 162 games using a variety of network sponsors such as Continental Airlines and Dodge pickups to make their way to the games. Other advertisers featured were Blimpie, Dunkin' Donuts, Fujifilm, and area restaurants. For the YES Network, *Ultimate Road Trip* drove in revenues.

In February 2006 the network laid the groundwork for additional advertising opportunities through new interactive Yankees broadcasts. Partnering with MLB.com and its carrier DIRECTV, the YES Network added interactive features to its Yankees broadcasts, allowing subscribers with DIRECTV set-top boxes to access box scores, statistics, and special views from a second camera via remote control. The network found that its interactive viewers watched games more than 50 percent longer than those who did not have or use the interactive features and that the interactivity helped propel ratings growth of nearly 10 percent in one year.

In 2006 the network received permission from the MLB to show video highlights of New York Mets games on the network's website. The deal involved the newly founded SportsNet New York (SNY), which was launched in 2006 and became the television broadcaster of the New York Mets, Jets, and Big East Conference games. The YES Network's site also received approval to show SNY original content, including local college and professional team web pages, 90-second wrap-ups on area sports, and blogs from SNY writers. Between July and October the website saw an increase in traffic and a spike in unique visitors of more than 75 percent, resulting in an expanded collection of advertisers. Between its launch and 2006 the number of YES Network clients grew more than fourfold to more than 400, with several major firms also advertising through the growing digital-media portfolio of the network's offerings. In 2006 the YES Network's advertising generated between $300 million and $340 million, its cash flow was about $185 million, and it had nearly 12 million subscribers through satellite and cable networks.

MANAGEMENT CHANGES AND NEW REVENUE STREAMS

Between 2006 and 2007 the YES Network became a trendsetter through its aggressive moves in the digital video field by extending the Yankees brand and bringing in fans from around the world. The network signed deals with Amazon.com, Joost (an Internet television service), ROO (an online video network), and Yahoo. These deals expanded how the YES Network could reach viewers and bring advertisers into its fold, while increasing brand awareness. The network's agreement with Joost called for the network to receive a dedicated channel that regularly ran updated long-form programs, sports highlights, and interviews. Amazon.com agreed to sell DVDs of original YES Network programming, including its popular series *Center Stage*.

In 2007 the YES Network made several upgrades to its content and brand marketing. It became the first 24/7 HD regional sports network when it launched a full-time HD simulcast of its regular channel. In addition, the network tapped into the growing wireless broadcast market by teaming up with the mobile-phone search service 4INFO to provide real-time sports updates on mobile phones. That same year YES Interactive on DIRECTV opened its second season with new features, including "Rivals Alerts" and real-time statistics of pitchers.

Goldman Sachs announced in August 2007 that it was reevaluating its investment in the YES Network. At the time of the announcement, 35 percent of the network was owned by the Steinbrenner family and a small group of other investors. Even though the Steinbrenner group did not control the network, it did oversee Yankees interests, which in turn included the major asset held by the network: rights to carry Yankees games for 15 more years. Goldman Sachs said it was getting a current read on the marketplace and on the network's value and that any new YES Network partner would need to be approved by both the Steinbrenner group and the Yankees.

That same year, with Steinbrenner reportedly in declining health, his son, Hal Steinbrenner, was named chairman of Yankee Global Enterprises. Hal had already been appointed a general partner of the Yankees club and was serving as a board member of Yankee Global Enterprises when he assumed the position of its chairman. In 2008 Hal also assumed the roles of managing general partner and cochairman of the Yankees team, and his younger brother, Hank, was named general partner and cochairman.

RENEWAL OF REVENUE GROWTH

In 2008 the former Marlins coach Joe Girardi was named manager of the Yankees. For the 2008 season, the YES Network opted to end *Ultimate Road Trip* and launch three new series: *The Joe Girardi Show*, a 30-minute Sunday program; *Sportslife: NYC*, a series focusing on New York's culture of sports; and *YESterdays*, a program that featured former Yankees players.

The network announced in June 2009 a landmark agreement involving the MLB and Cablevision that allowed Cablevision subscribers with the YES Network tier to view live games streamed online within the New York metro area. The arrangement was a trial test by the MLB that made the YES Network the first sports network to provide broadband streaming of live professional games within its own market.

By April 2010 the network had four carriers for its live in-market streamed games: Blue Ridge Communications, Cablevision, Verizon Communications's FiOS TV, and Time Warner Cable. Broadband viewers could watch Yankees broadcasts on home computers, laptops, or other portable devices. In another YES Network first, in July 2010 the network utilized Cablevision's iO TV 1300 to broadcast its first Yankees game against the Seattle Mariners in three-dimensional (3D) television. A second 3D game was aired the following day.

Following a decline in revenues over the past few years, the network reported that sales were beginning to increase in 2010. The rally actually began in late 2009, when the Yankees battled the Philadelphia Phillies in the World Series. By mid-2010 the YES Network was collecting 50 percent more advertising dollars than a year prior.

END OF AN ERA

On July 13, 2010, George Steinbrenner died from a heart attack at the age of 80. Steinbrenner had owned the Yankees for 37 years. When he bought the club in 1973, it was worth $8.7 million. By 2010 the club's value was estimated to be more than $3 billion. During his tenure as owner, Steinbrenner proved that astutely spending millions of dollars on free agents could translate into championships.

Following his passing, the Steinbrenner family announced that the Yankees and the YES Network were not for sale and that a succession plan was in place. Hal and Hank became cochairmen of the Yankees organization in 2008, when Hal was named managing general partner. Hal had also been serving as chairman of Yankees Global Enterprises, the parent company of the Yankees and the YES Network, since 2007. Thus, the team and the regional sports network that George built remained connected to the Steinbrenner family.

Roger Rouland

PRINCIPAL COMPETITORS

CBS Broadcasting Inc.; Comcast SportsNet; ESPN, Inc.; FOX Sports Net, Inc.; Madison Square Garden, Inc.; NBC Television Network; New England Sports Network, Ltd.; VERSUS, L.P.

FURTHER READING

Birger, Jon, and Tim Arango. "The Dismantling of the Yankee Empire." *Fortune*, August 2, 2007.

Dempsey, John. "Yankees B'casts Stack up Stats." *Daily Variety*, July 26, 2006, 1.

"End of an Era: Yankees Likely Staying in Steinbrenner Family." *Street & Smith's SportsBusiness Daily*, July 14, 2010.

Fatsis, Stefan. "Yankees Holding Company Set to Form a Sports Network Valued at $850 Million." *Wall Street Journal Western Edition*, September 11, 2001, B4.

Kerschbaumer, Ken. "Yes, Yes, Yes, Yes, No: Most NYC Systems Carry New Yankees Network, but Cablevision Still Balks." *Broadcasting & Cable*, March 25, 2002, 14.

Klayman, Ben. "Yankees Pinstripes, Operations to Remain Unchanged." *Reuters*, July 13, 2010.

McConville, Jim. "YES Network on Deck to Air Yankees," *Hollywood Reporter*, September 11, 2001, 4.

Reynolds, Mike. "ITV in YES's Year-5 Plan." *Multichannel News*, March 19, 2007, 24.

Sandomir, Richard. "Steinbrenner Faces Suit over Idea for YES." *New York Times*, August 28, 2009.

"Steinbrenner May Get New Partners in YES." *Multichannel News*, August 21, 2006, 12.

Cumulative Index to Companies

Listings in this index are arranged in alphabetical order under the company name. Company names beginning with a letter or proper name such as Eli Lilly & Co. will be found under the first letter of the company name. Definite articles (The, Le, La) are ignored for alphabetical purposes as are forms of incorporation that precede the company name (AB, NV). Company names printed in **bold** *type have full, historical essays on the page numbers appearing in bold. Updates to entries that appeared in earlier volumes are signified by the notation* **(upd.)**. *This index is cumulative with volume numbers printed in bold type.*

1–999

A

B

Banco do Brasil S.A., **II** 199–200; **113** 33–36 (upd.)
Banco Espírito Santo e Comercial de Lisboa S.A., **15** 38–40 *see also* Espírito Santo Financial Group S.A.
Banco Itaú S.A., **19** 33–35
Banco Popular *see* Popular, Inc.
Banco Santander, S.A., **36** 61–64 (upd.); **111** 12–17 (upd.)
Banco Serfin *see* Grupo Financiero Serfin, S.A.
Bancomer S.A. *see* Grupo Financiero BBVA Bancomer S.A.
BancorpSouth, Inc., **116** 70–73
Bandag, Inc., **19** 36–38
Bandai Co., Ltd., **55** 44–48 *see also* Namco Bandai Holdings Inc.
Banfi Products Corp., **36** 65–67; **114** 73–76 (upd.)
Banfield, The Pet Hospital *see* Medical Management International, Inc.
Bang & Olufsen Holding A/S, **37** 25–28; **86** 24–29 (upd.)
Bank Austria AG, **23** 37–39; **100** 57–60 (upd.)
Bank Brussels Lambert, **II** 201–03
Bank Hapoalim B.M., **II** 204–06; **54** 33–37 (upd.)
Bank Leumi le-Israel B.M., **60** 48–51
Bank of America Corporation, **46** 47–54 (upd.); **101** 51–64 (upd.)
Bank of Boston Corporation, **II** 207–09 *see also* FleetBoston Financial Corp.
Bank of China, **63** 55–57
Bank of Cyprus Group, **91** 40–43
Bank of East Asia Ltd., **63** 58–60
Bank of Granite Corporation, **89** 87–91
Bank of Hawaii Corporation, **73** 53–56
Bank of Ireland, **50** 73–76
Bank of Mississippi, Inc., **14** 40–41
Bank of Montreal, **II** 210–12; **46** 55–58 (upd.)
Bank of New England Corporation, **II** 213–15
Bank of New York Company, Inc., **II** 216–19; **46** 59–63 (upd.)
The Bank of Nova Scotia, **II** 220–23; **59** 70–76 (upd.)
The Bank of Scotland *see* The Governor and Company of the Bank of Scotland.
Bank of the Ozarks, Inc., **91** 44–47
Bank of the Philippine Islands, **58** 18–20
Bank of Tokyo-Mitsubishi Ltd., **II** 224–25; **15** 41–43 (upd.) *see also* Mitsubishi UFJ Financial Group, Inc.
Bank of Valletta PLC, **111** 18–22
Bank One Corporation, **36** 68–75 (upd.) *see also* JPMorgan Chase & Co.
BankAmerica Corporation, **II** 226–28 *see also* Bank of America.
Bankers Trust New York Corporation, **II** 229–31
Banknorth Group, Inc., **55** 49–53
Bankrate, Inc., **83** 38–41
Banner Aerospace, Inc., **14** 42–44; **37** 29–32 (upd.)
Banner Corporation, **106** 54–57
Banner Health, **119** 84–87
Banorte *see* Grupo Financiero Banorte, S.A. de C.V.
Banque Nationale de Paris S.A., **II** 232–34 *see also* BNP Paribas Group.
Banta Corporation, **12** 24–26; **32** 73–77 (upd.); **79** 50–56 (upd.)
Banyan Systems Inc., **25** 50–52
Baptist Health Care Corporation, **82** 37–40
Bar-S Foods Company, **76** 39–41
Barbara's Bakery Inc., **88** 21–24
Barça *see*Futbol Club Barcelona.
Barclay Furniture Co. *see* LADD Furniture, Inc.
Barclays PLC, **II** 235–37; **20** 57–60 (upd.); **64** 46–50 (upd.)
BarclaysAmerican Mortgage Corporation, **11** 29–30
Barco NV, **44** 42–45
Barden Companies, Inc., **76** 42–45
Bardwil Industries Inc., **98** 15–18
Bare Escentuals, Inc., **91** 48–52
Barilla G. e R. Fratelli S.p.A., **17** 35–37; **50** 77–80 (upd.)
Barings PLC, **14** 45–47
Barloworld Ltd., **I** 422–24; **109** 57–62 (upd.)
Barmag AG, **39** 39–42
Barnes & Noble, Inc., **10** 135–37; **30** 67–71 (upd.); **75** 50–55 (upd.)
Barnes & Noble College Booksellers, Inc., **115** 44–46
Barnes Group, Inc., **13** 72–74; **69** 58–62 (upd.)
Barnett Banks, Inc., **9** 58–60 *see also* Bank of America Corp.
Barnett Inc., **28** 50–52
Barneys New York Inc., **28** 53–55; **104** 26–30 (upd.)
Baron de Ley S.A., **74** 27–29
Baron Philippe de Rothschild S.A., **39** 43–46
Barr *see* AG Barr plc.
Barr Pharmaceuticals, Inc., **26** 29–31; **68** 46–49 (upd.)
Barratt Developments plc, **I** 556–57; **56** 31–33 (upd.)
Barrett Business Services, Inc., **16** 48–50
Barrett-Jackson Auction Company L.L.C., **88** 25–28
Barrick Gold Corporation, **34** 62–65; **112** 38–44 (upd.)
Barrière *see* Groupe Lucien Barrière S.A.S.
Barry Callebaut AG, **29** 46–48; **71** 46–49 (upd.)
Barry-Wehmiller Companies, Inc., **90** 40–43
The Bartell Drug Company, **94** 62–65
Barton Malow Company, **51** 40–43
Barton Protective Services Inc., **53** 56–58
The Baseball Club of Seattle, LP, **50** 81–85
BASF SE, **I** 305–08; **18** 47–51 (upd.); **50** 86–92 (upd.); **108** 85–94 (upd.)
Bashas' Inc., **33** 62–64; **80** 17–21 (upd.)
Basic Earth Science Systems, Inc., **101** 65–68
Basin Electric Power Cooperative, **103** 43–46
The Basketball Club of Seattle, LLC, **50** 93–97
Basketville, Inc., **117** 31–34
Bass PLC, **I** 222–24; **15** 44–47 (upd.); **38** 74–78 (upd.)
Bass Pro Shops, Inc., **42** 27–30; **118** 55–59 (upd.)
Bassett Furniture Industries, Inc., **18** 52–55; **95** 44–50 (upd.)
BAT Industries plc, **I** 425–27 *see also* British American Tobacco PLC.
Bata Ltd., **62** 27–30
Bates Worldwide, Inc., **14** 48–51; **33** 65–69 (upd.)
Bath Iron Works Corporation, **12** 27–29; **36** 76–79 (upd.)
Battelle Memorial Institute, Inc., **10** 138–40
Batten Barton Durstine & Osborn *see* Omnicom Group Inc.
Battle Mountain Gold Company, **23** 40–42 *see also* Newmont Mining Corp.
Bauer Hockey, Inc., **104** 31–34
Bauer Publishing Group, **7** 42–43
Bauerly Companies, **61** 31–33
Baugur Group hf, **81** 45–49
Baumax AG, **75** 56–58
Bausch & Lomb Inc., **7** 44–47; **25** 53–57 (upd.); **96** 20–26 (upd.)
Bavaria N.V., **121** 59–62
Bavaria S.A., **90** 44–47
Baxi Group Ltd., **96** 27–30
Baxter International Inc., **I** 627–29; **10** 141–43 (upd.); **116** 74–78 (upd.)
Baxters Food Group Ltd., **99** 47–50
The Bay *see* The Hudson's Bay Co.
Bay State Gas Company, **38** 79–82
Bayard SA, **49** 46–49
BayBanks, Inc., **12** 30–32
Bayer AG, **I** 309–11; **13** 75–77 (upd.); **41** 44–48 (upd.); **118** 60–66 (upd.)
Bayer Hispania S.L., **120** 37–40
Bayerische Hypotheken- und Wechsel-Bank AG, **II** 238–40 *see also* HVB Group.
Bayerische Landesbank, **116** 79–82
Bayerische Motoren Werke AG, **I** 138–40; **11** 31–33 (upd.); **38** 83–87 (upd.); **108** 95–101 (upd.)
Bayerische Vereinsbank A.G., **II** 241–43 *see also* HVB Group.
Bayernwerk AG, **V** 555–58; **23** 43–47 (upd.) *see also* E.On AG.
Bayou Steel Corporation, **31** 47–49
BayWa AG, **112** 45–49
BB&T Corporation, **79** 57–61
BB Holdings Limited, **77** 50–53
BBA *see* Bush Boake Allen Inc.
BBA Aviation plc, **90** 48–52
BBAG Osterreichische Brau-Beteiligungs-AG, **38** 88–90
BBC *see* British Broadcasting Corp.
BBDO Worldwide *see* Omnicom Group Inc.

C

CIBC *see* Canadian Imperial Bank of Commerce.
Ciber, Inc., **18** 110–12
CiCi Enterprises, L.P., **99** 94–99
CIENA Corporation, **54** 68–71
Cifra, S.A. de C.V., **12** 63–65 *see also* Wal-Mart de Mexico, S.A. de C.V.
CIGNA Corporation, **III** 223–27; **22** 139–44 (upd.); **45** 104–10 (upd.); **109** 121–31 (upd.)
Cimarex Energy Co., **81** 73–76
Cimentos de Portugal SGPS S.A. (Cimpor), **76** 92–94
Ciments Français, **40** 107–10
Cimpor *see* Cimentos de Portugal SGPS S.A.
Cinar Corporation, **40** 111–14
Cincinnati Bell Inc., **6** 316–18; **105** 112–18 (upd.)
Cincinnati Financial Corporation, **16** 102–04; **44** 89–92 (upd.)
Cincinnati Gas & Electric Company, **6** 465–68 *see also* Duke Energy Corp.
Cincinnati Lamb Inc., **72** 69–71
Cincinnati Milacron Inc., **12** 66–69 *see also* Milacron, Inc.
Cincom Systems Inc., **15** 106–08
Cinemark Holdings, Inc., **95** 95–99
Cinemas de la República, S.A. de C.V., **83** 84–86
Cinemeccanica S.p.A., **78** 70–73
Cineplex Odeon Corporation, **6** 161–63; **23** 123–26 (upd.)
Cinnabon, Inc., **23** 127–29; **90** 132–36 (upd.)
Cinram International, Inc., **43** 107–10
Cintas Corporation, **21** 114–16; **51** 74–77 (upd.)
CIPSA *see* Compañia Industrial de Parras, S.A. de C.V. (CIPSA).
CIPSCO Inc., **6** 469–72 *see also* Ameren Corp.
The Circle K Company, **II** 619–20; **20** 138–40 (upd.)
Circon Corporation, **21** 117–20
CIRCOR International, Inc., **115** 122–25
Circuit City Stores, Inc., **9** 120–22; **29** 120–24 (upd.); **65** 109–14 (upd.)
Circus Circus Enterprises, Inc., **6** 203–05
Cirque du Soleil Inc., **29** 125–28; **98** 46–51 (upd.)
Cirrus Design Corporation, **44** 93–95
Cirrus Logic, Inc., **11** 56–57; **48** 90–93 (upd.)
Cisco-Linksys LLC, **86** 88–91
Cisco Systems, Inc., **11** 58–60; **34** 111–15 (upd.); **77** 97–103 (upd.)
Cisneros Group of Companies, **54** 72–75
CIT Group Inc., **76** 95–98
Citadel Communications Corporation, **35** 102–05
CitFed Bancorp, Inc., **16** 105–07 *see also* Fifth Third Bancorp.
CITGO Petroleum Corporation, **IV** 391–93; **31** 113–17 (upd.)
Citi Trends, Inc., **80** 72–75
Citibank *see* Citigroup Inc
CITIC Pacific Ltd., **18** 113–15; **116** 110–15 (upd.)
Citicorp, **II** 253–55; **9** 123–26 (upd.) *see also* Citigroup Inc.
Citicorp Diners Club, Inc., **90** 137–40
Citigroup Inc., **30** 124–28 (upd.); **59** 121–27 (upd.)
Citizen Watch Co., Ltd., **III** 454–56; **21** 121–24 (upd.); **81** 77–82 (upd.)
Citizens Communications Company, **79** 105–08 (upd.)
Citizens Financial Group, Inc., **42** 76–80; **87** 104–112 (upd.)
Citizens Utilities Company, **7** 87–89 *see also* Citizens Communications Company
Citrix Systems, Inc., **44** 96–99
Citroën *see* PSA Peugeot Citroen S.A.
City Brewing Company LLC, **73** 84–87
City Developments Limited, **89** 153–56
City Lodge Hotels Limited, **114** 134–37
City National Bank, **116** 116–20
City Public Service, **6** 473–75
CJ Banks *see* Christopher & Banks Corp.
CJ Corporation, **62** 68–70
CJSC Transmash Holding, **93** 446–49
CJSC Transmash Holding, **93** 446–49
CKE Restaurants, Inc., **19** 89–93; **46** 94–99 (upd.)
CKX, Inc., **102** 84–87
Claire's Stores, Inc., **17** 101–03; **94** 125–29 (upd.)
CLARCOR Inc., **17** 104–07; **61** 63–67 (upd.)
Clare Rose Inc., **68** 83–85
Clarins S.A., **119** 106–09
Clarion Company Ltd., **64** 77–79
The Clark Construction Group, Inc., **8** 112–13
Clark Equipment Company, **8** 114–16
Classic Vacation Group, Inc., **46** 100–03
Clayton Homes Incorporated, **13** 154–55; **54** 76–79 (upd.)
Clayton Williams Energy, Inc., **87** 113–16
Clean Harbors, Inc., **73** 88–91
Clean Venture, Inc., **104** 79–82
Clear Channel Communications, Inc., **23** 130–32; **116** 121–25 (upd.)
Clearly Canadian Beverage Corporation, **48** 94–97
Clearwire, Inc., **69** 95–97
Cleary, Gottlieb, Steen & Hamilton, **35** 106–09
Cleco Corporation, **37** 88–91
The Clemens Family Corporation, **93** 156–59
Clement Pappas & Company, Inc., **92** 52–55
Cleveland-Cliffs Inc., **13** 156–58; **62** 71–75 (upd.)
The Cleveland Clinic Foundation, **112** 91–95
Cleveland Indians Baseball Company, Inc., **37** 92–94; **115** 126–31 (upd.)
Click Wine Group, **68** 86–88
Clif Bar Inc., **50** 141–43
Clifford Chance LLP, **38** 136–39
Clinton Cards plc, **39** 86–88
Cloetta Fazer AB, **70** 58–60
Clondalkin Group PLC, **120** 62–65
Clopay Corporation, **100** 106–10
The Clorox Company, **III** 20–22; **22** 145–48 (upd.); **81** 83–90 (upd.)
Close Brothers Group plc, **39** 89–92
The Clothestime, Inc., **20** 141–44
Cloud Peak Energy Inc., **116** 126–29
Clougherty Packing Company, **72** 72–74
Cloverdale Paint Inc., **115** 132–34
Club de hockey Canadien, Inc., **121** 89–92
Club Méditerranée S.A., **6** 206–08; **21** 125–28 (upd.); **91** 121–27 (upd.)
ClubCorp, Inc., **33** 101–04
CMC *see* Commercial Metals Co.
CME *see* Campbell-Mithun-Esty, Inc.; Central European Media Enterprises Ltd.; Chicago Mercantile Exchange Inc.
CMG Worldwide, Inc., **89** 157–60
CMGI, Inc., **76** 99–101
CMIH *see* China Merchants International Holdings Co., Ltd.
CML Group, Inc., **10** 215–18
CMO *see* Chi Mei Optoelectronics Corp.
CMP Media Inc., **26** 76–80
CMS Energy Corporation, **V** 577–79; **14** 114–16 (upd.); **100** 111–16 (upd.)
CN *see* Canadian National Railway Co.
CNA Financial Corporation, **III** 228–32; **38** 140–46 (upd.)
CNET Networks, Inc., **47** 77–80
CNG *see* Consolidated Natural Gas Co.
CNH Global N.V., **38** 147–56 (upd.); **99** 100–112 (upd.)
CNN Worldwide, **121** 93–96
CNP *see* Compagnie Nationale à Portefeuille.
CNP Assurances, **116** 130–33
CNPC *see* China National Petroleum Corp.
CNS, Inc., **20** 145–47 *see also* GlaxoSmithKline plc.
Co-operative Group (CWS) Ltd., **51** 86–89
Coach, Inc., **10** 219–21; **45** 111–15 (upd.); **99** 113–120 (upd.)
Coach USA, Inc., **24** 117–19; **55** 103–06 (upd.)
Coachmen Industries, Inc., **77** 104–07
Coal India Limited, **IV** 48–50; **44** 100–03 (upd.)**115** 135–40 (upd.)
Coalition America Inc., **113** 87–90
Coastal Corporation, **IV** 394–95; **31** 118–21 (upd.)
Coats plc, **V** 356–58; **44** 104–07 (upd.)
COBE Cardiovascular, Inc., **61** 68–72
COBE Laboratories, Inc., **13** 159–61
Coberco *see* Friesland Coberco Dairy Foods Holding N.V.
Cobham plc, **30** 129–32
Coborn's, Inc., **30** 133–35
Cobra Electronics Corporation, **14** 117–19

Companhia Vale do Rio Doce, IV 54–57; 43 111–14 (upd.) *see also* Vale S.A.
Compania Cervecerias Unidas S.A., 70 61–63
Compañia de Minas BuenaventuraS.A.A., 92160–63
Compañia Española de Petróleos S.A. (Cepsa), IV 396–98; 56 63–66 (upd.)
Compañia Industrial de Parras, S.A. de C.V. (CIPSA), 84 59–62
Compañia Sud Americana de Vapores S.A., 100 121–24
Compaq Computer Corporation, III 124–25; 6 221–23 (upd.); 26 90–93 (upd.) *see also* Hewlett-Packard Co.
Compass Bancshares, Inc., 73 92–94
Compass Diversified Holdings, 108 182–85
Compass Group plc, 34 121–24; 110 97–102 (upd.)
Compass Minerals International, Inc., 79 109–12
CompDent Corporation, 22 149–51
Compellent Technologies, Inc., 119 114–18
CompHealth Inc., 25 109–12
Complete Business Solutions, Inc., 31 130–33
Complete Production Services, Inc., 118 103–06
Comprehensive Care Corporation, 15 121–23
Comptoirs Modernes S.A., 19 97–99 *see also* Carrefour SA.
Compton Petroleum Corporation, 103 120–23
CompuAdd Computer Corporation, 11 61–63
CompuCom Systems, Inc., 10 232–34
CompuDyne Corporation, 51 78–81
CompUSA, Inc., 10 235–36; 35 116–18 (upd.)
CompuServe Interactive Services, Inc., 10 237–39; 27 106–08 (upd.) *see also* AOL Time Warner Inc.
Computer Associates International, Inc., 6 224–26; 49 94–97 (upd.)
Computer Data Systems, Inc., 14 127–29
Computer Learning Centers, Inc., 26 94–96
Computer Sciences Corporation, 6 227–29; 116 144–49 (upd.)
ComputerLand Corp., 13 174–76
Computervision Corporation, 10 240–42
Compuware Corporation, 10 243–45; 30 140–43 (upd.); 66 60–64 (upd.)
Comsat Corporation, 23 133–36 *see also* Lockheed Martin Corp.
comScore, Inc., 119 119–23
Comshare Inc., 23 137–39
Comstock Resources, Inc., 47 85–87
Comtech Telecommunications Corp., 75 103–05
Comverse Technology, Inc., 15 124–26; 43 115–18 (upd.)
Con Ed *see* Consolidated Edison, Inc.
Con-way Inc., 101 130–34
ConAgra Foods, Inc., II 493–95; 12 80–82 (upd.); 42 90–94 (upd.); 85 61–68 (upd.)
Conair Corporation, 17 108–10; 69 104–08 (upd.)
Conaprole *see* Cooperativa Nacional de Productores de Leche S.A. (Conaprole).
Concentra Inc., 71 117–19
Concepts Direct, Inc., 39 93–96
Concha y Toro *see* Viña Concha y Toro S.A.
Concord Camera Corporation, 41 104–07
Concord EFS, Inc., 52 86–88
Concord Fabrics, Inc., 16 124–26
Concord Music Group, Inc., 118 107–10
Concur Technologies, Inc., 106 118–22
Concurrent Computer Corporation, 75 106–08
Condé Nast Publications Inc., 13 177–81; 59 131–34 (upd.); 109 143–49 (upd.)
Cone Mills LLC, 8 120–22; 67 123–27 (upd.)
Conexant Systems Inc., 36 121–25; 106 123–28 (upd.)
Confluence Holdings Corporation, 76 118–20
Congoleum Corporation, 18 116–19; 98 52–57 (upd.)
CONMED Corporation, 87 117–120
Conn-Selmer, Inc., 55 111–14
Connecticut Light and Power Co., 13 182–84
Connecticut Mutual Life Insurance Company, III 236–38
The Connell Company, 29 129–31; 104 83–87 (upd.)
Conner Peripherals, Inc., 6 230–32
Connetics Corporation, 70 64–66
Connors Bros. Income Fund *see* George Weston Ltd.
Conn's, Inc., 67 128–30
ConocoPhillips, IV 399–402; 16 127–32 (upd.); 63 104–15 (upd.)
Conrad Industries, Inc., 58 68–70
Conseco, Inc., 10 246–48; 33 108–12 (upd.); 112 102–08 (upd.)
Conso International Corporation, 29 132–34
CONSOL Energy Inc., 59 135–37
Consolidated Contractors Company, 115 141–45
Consolidated Delivery & Logistics, Inc., 24 125–28 *see also* Velocity Express Corp.
Consolidated Edison, Inc., V 586–89; 45 116–20 (upd.) 112 109–15 (upd.)
Consolidated Freightways Corporation, V 432–34; 21 136–39 (upd.); 48 109–13 (upd.)
Consolidated Graphics, Inc., 70 67–69
Consolidated Natural Gas Company, V 590–91; 19 100–02 (upd.) *see also* Dominion Resources, Inc.
Consolidated Papers, Inc., 8 123–25; 36 126–30 (upd.)
Consolidated Products, Inc., 14 130–32
Consolidated Rail Corporation, V 435–37
Consorcio ARA, S.A. de C.V., 79 113–16
Consorcio Aviacsa, S.A. de C.V., 85 69–72
Consorcio G Grupo Dina, S.A. de C.V., 36 131–33
Constar International Inc., 64 85–88
Constellation Brands, Inc., 68 95–100 (upd.)
Constellation Energy Group, Inc., 116 150–55 (upd.)
Consumers' Association, 118 111–14
The Consumers Gas Company Ltd., 6 476–79; 43 154 *see also* Enbridge Inc.
Consumers Power Co., 14 133–36
Consumers Union, 26 97–99; 118 115–19 (upd.)
Consumers Water Company, 14 137–39
The Container Store, 36 134–36
ContiGroup Companies, Inc., 43 119–22 (upd.)
Continental AG, V 240–43; 56 67–72 (upd.)
Continental Airlines, Inc., I 96–98; 21 140–43 (upd.); 52 89–94 (upd.); 110 103–10 (upd.)
Continental Bank Corporation, II 261–63 *see also* Bank of America.
Continental Cablevision, Inc., 7 98–100
Continental Can Co., Inc., 15 127–30
Continental Corporation, III 239–44
Continental General Tire Corp., 23 140–42
Continental Grain Company, 10 249–51; 13 185–87 (upd.) *see also* ContiGroup Companies, Inc.
Continental Graphics Corporation, 110 111–14
Continental Group Co., I 599–600
Continental Medical Systems, Inc., 10 252–54
Continental Resources, Inc., 89 161–65
Continucare Corporation, 101 135–38
Continuum Health Partners, Inc., 60 97–99
Control Data Corporation, III 126–28 *see also* Seagate Technology, Inc.
Control Data Systems, Inc., 10 255–57
Controladora Comercial Mexicana, S.A. de C.V., 36 137–39
Controladora Mabe, S.A. de C.V., 82 74–77
Convergys Corporation, 119 124–29
Converse Inc., 9 133–36; 31 134–38 (upd.)
Conzzeta Holding, 80 76–79
Cook Group Inc., 102 93–96
Cooker Restaurant Corporation, 20 159–61; 51 82–85 (upd.)
Cookson Group plc, III 679–82; 44 115–20 (upd.)
CoolBrands International Inc., 35 119–22

D

E

F

Fyffes PLC, **38 196–99**; **106 196–201 (upd.)**

G

G&K Holding S.A., **95 159–62**
G&K Services, Inc., **16 228–30**
G-III Apparel Group, Ltd., **22 222–24**; **117 107–11 (upd.)**
G A Pindar & Son Ltd., **88 101–04**
G.D. Searle & Co., **I 686–89**; **12 186–89 (upd.)**; **34 177–82 (upd.)**
G. Heileman Brewing Co., **I 253–55** *see also* Stroh Brewery Co.
G.I.E. Airbus Industrie, **I 41–43**; **12 190–92 (upd.)**
G.I. Joe's, Inc., **30 221–23** *see also* Joe's Sports & Outdoor.
G. Leblanc Corporation, **55 149–52**
G.S. Blodgett Corporation, **15 183–85** *see also* Blodgett Holdings, Inc.
Gabelli Asset Management Inc., **30 211–14** *see also* Lynch Corp.
Gables Residential Trust, **49 147–49**
Gadzooks, Inc., **18 188–90**
GAF, **I 337–40**; **22 225–29 (upd.)**
Gage Marketing Group, **26 147–49**
Gaiam, Inc., **41 174–77**
Gainsco, Inc., **22 230–32**
Galardi Group, Inc., **72 145–47**
Galaxy Investors, Inc., **97 178–81**
Galaxy Nutritional Foods, Inc., **58 135–37**
Gale International LLC, **93 221–24**
Galenica AG, **84 139–142**
Galeries Lafayette S.A., **V 57–59**; **23 220–23 (upd.)**
Galey & Lord, Inc., **20 242–45**; **66 131–34 (upd.)**
Galiform PLC, **103 179–83**
Gallaher Group Plc, **49 150–54 (upd.)**
Gallaher Limited, **V 398–400**; **19 168–71 (upd.)**
Gallo Winery *see* E. & J. Gallo Winery.
Gallup, Inc., **37 153–56**; **104 156–61 (upd.)**
Galoob Toys *see* Lewis Galoob Toys Inc.
Galp Energia SGPS S.A., **98 135–40**
Galtronics Ltd., **100 174–77**
Galyan's Trading Company, Inc., **47 142–44**
The Gambrinus Company, **40 188–90**
Gambro AB, **49 155–57**
The GAME Group plc, **80 126–29**
Games Workshop Group plc, **121 203–10**
GameStop Corp., **69 185–89 (upd.)**
GAMI *see* Great American Management and Investment, Inc.
Gaming Partners InternationalCorporation, **92225–28**
Gander Mountain Company, **20 246–48**; **90 203–08 (upd.)**
Gannett Company, Inc., **IV 612–13**; **7 190–92 (upd.)**; **30 215–17 (upd.)**; **66 135–38 (upd.)**
Gano Excel Enterprise Sdn. Bhd., **89 228–31**
Gantos, Inc., **17 199–201**
Ganz, **98 141–44**
GAP *see* Grupo Aeroportuario del Pacífico, S.A. de C.V.
The Gap, Inc., **V 60–62**; **18 191–94 (upd.)**; **55 153–57 (upd.)**; **117 112–17 (upd.)**
Garan, Inc., **16 231–33**; **64 140–43 (upd.)**
The Garden Company Ltd., **82 125–28**
Garden Fresh Restaurant Corporation, **31 213–15**
Garden Ridge Corporation, **27 163–65**
Gardenburger, Inc., **33 169–71**; **76 160–63 (upd.)**
Gardner Denver, Inc., **49 158–60**
Garmin Ltd., **60 135–37**
Garst Seed Company, Inc., **86 156–59**
Gart Sports Company, **24 173–75** *see also* Sports Authority, Inc.
Gartner, Inc., **21 235–37**; **94 209–13 (upd.)**
Garuda Indonesia, **6 90–91**; **58 138–41 (upd.)**
Gas Natural SDG S.A., **69 190–93**
GASS *see* Grupo Ángeles Servicios de Salud, S.A. de C.V.
Gasunie *see* N.V. Nederlandse Gasunie.
Gate Gourmet International AG, **70 97–100**
GateHouse Media, Inc., **91 196–99**
The Gates Corporation, **9 241–43**
Gateway Corporation Ltd., **II 628–30** *see also* Somerfield plc.
Gateway Group One, **118 158–61**
Gateway, Inc., **10 307–09**; **27 166–69 (upd.)**; **63 153–58 (upd.)**
The Gatorade Company, **82 129–32**
Gatti's Pizza, Inc. *see* Mr. Gatti's, LP.
GATX, **6 394–96**; **25 168–71 (upd.)**
Gaumont S.A., **25 172–75**; **91 200–05 (upd.)**
Gaylord Bros., Inc., **100 178–81**
Gaylord Container Corporation, **8 203–05**
Gaylord Entertainment Company, **11 152–54**; **36 226–29 (upd.)**
Gaz de France, **V 626–28**; **40 191–95 (upd.)** *see also* GDF SUEZ.
Gazprom *see* OAO Gazprom.
GBC *see* General Binding Corp.
GC Companies, Inc., **25 176–78** *see also* AMC Entertainment Inc.
GDF SUEZ, **109 256–63 (upd.)**
GE *see* General Electric Co.
GE Aircraft Engines, **9 244–46**
GE Capital Aviation Services, **36 230–33**
GEA AG, **27 170–74**
GEAC Computer Corporation Ltd., **43 181–85**
Geberit AG, **49 161–64**
Gecina SA, **42 151–53**
Gedney *see* M.A. Gedney Co.
Geek Squad Inc., **102 138–41**
Geerlings & Wade, Inc., **45 166–68**
Geest Plc, **38 200–02** *see also* Bakkavör Group hf.
Gefco SA, **54 126–28**
Geffen Records Inc., **26 150–52**
GEHE AG, **27 175–78**
Gehl Company, **19 172–74**
GEICO Corporation, **10 310–12**; **40 196–99 (upd.)**
Geiger Bros., **60 138–41**
Gelita AG, **74 114–18**
GEMA (Gesellschaft für musikalische Aufführungs- und mechanische Vervielfältigungsrechte), **70 101–05**
Gemini Sound Products Corporation, **58 142–44**
Gemplus International S.A., **64 144–47**
Gen-Probe Incorporated, **79 185–88**
Gencor Ltd., **IV 90–93**; **22 233–37 (upd.)** *see also* Gold Fields Ltd.
GenCorp Inc., **9 247–49**
Genentech, Inc., **I 637–38**; **8 209–11 (upd.)**; **32 211–15 (upd.)**; **75 154–58 (upd.)**
General Accident plc, **III 256–57** *see also* Aviva PLC.
General Atomics, **57 151–54**; **112 194–98 (upd.)**
General Bearing Corporation, **45 169–71**
General Binding Corporation, **10 313–14**; **73 159–62 (upd.)**
General Cable Corporation, **40 200–03**; **111 154–59 (upd.)**
The General Chemical Group Inc., **37 157–60**
General Cigar Holdings, Inc., **66 139–42 (upd.)**
General Cinema Corporation, **I 245–46** *see also* GC Companies, Inc.
General DataComm Industries, Inc., **14 200–02**
General Dynamics Corporation, **I 57–60**; **10 315–18 (upd.)**; **40 204–10 (upd.)**; **88 105–13 (upd.)**
General Electric Company, **II 27–31**; **12 193–97 (upd.)**; **34 183–90 (upd.)**; **63 159–68 (upd.)**
General Electric Company, PLC, **II 24–26** *see also* Marconi plc.
General Employment Enterprises, Inc., **87 172–175**
General Growth Properties, Inc., **57 155–57**
General Host Corporation, **12 198–200**
General Housewares Corporation, **16 234–36**
General Instrument Corporation, **10 319–21** *see also* Motorola, Inc.
General Maritime Corporation, **59 197–99**
General Mills, Inc., **II 501–03**; **10 322–24 (upd.)**; **36 234–39 (upd.)**; **85 141–49 (upd.)**
General Motors Corporation, **I 171–73**; **10 325–27 (upd.)**; **36 240–44 (upd.)**; **64 148–53 (upd.)**
General Nutrition Companies, Inc., **11 155–57**; **29 210–14 (upd.)** *see also* GNC Corp.
General Public Utilities Corporation, **V 629–31** *see also* GPU, Inc.

General Re Corporation, III 258–59; 24 176–78 (upd.)
General Sekiyu K.K., IV 431–33 *see also* TonenGeneral Sekiyu K.K.
General Signal Corporation, 9 250–52 *see also* SPX Corp.
General Tire, Inc., 8 212–14
Generale Bank, II 294–95 *see also* Fortis, Inc.
Générale des Eaux Group, V 632–34 *see also* Vivendi.
Generali *see* Assicurazioni Generali.
Genesco Inc., 17 202–06; 84 143–149 (upd.)
Genesee & Wyoming Inc., 27 179–81
Genesis Health Ventures, Inc., 18 195–97 *see also* NeighborCare,Inc.
Genesis HealthCare Corporation, 119 185–89
Genesis Microchip Inc., 82 133–37
Genesys Telecommunications Laboratories Inc., 103 184–87
Genetics Institute, Inc., 8 215–18
Geneva Steel, 7 193–95
Genmar Holdings, Inc., 45 172–75
Genovese Drug Stores, Inc., 18 198–200
Genoyer *see* Groupe Genoyer.
GenRad, Inc., 24 179–83
Gentex Corporation, 26 153–57
Genting Bhd., 65 152–55
Gentiva Health Services, Inc., 79 189–92
Genuardi's Family Markets, Inc., 35 190–92
Genuine Parts Co., 9 253–55; 45 176–79 (upd.); 113 150–55 (upd.)
Genworth Financial Inc., 116 250–53
Genzyme Corporation, 13 239–42; 38 203–07 (upd.); 77 164–70 (upd.)
geobra Brandstätter GmbH & Co. KG, 48 183–86
Geodis S.A., 67 187–90
The Geon Company, 11 158–61
GeoResources, Inc., 101 196–99
Georg Fischer AG Schaffhausen, 61 106–09
Georg Jensen A/S, 110 173–77
George A. Hormel and Company, II 504–06 *see also* Hormel Foods Corp.
The George F. Cram Company, Inc., 55 158–60
George P. Johnson Company, 60 142–44
George S. May International Company, 55 161–63
George W. Park Seed Company, Inc., 98 145–48
George Weston Ltd., II 631–32; 36 245–48 (upd.); 88 114–19 (upd.)
George Wimpey plc, 12 201–03; 51 135–38 (upd.) *see also* Taylor Wimpey PLC.
Georgia Gulf Corporation, 9 256–58; 61 110–13 (upd.)
Georgia-Pacific LLC, IV 281–83; 9 259–62 (upd.); 47 145–51 (upd.); 101 200–09 (upd.)
Geotek Communications Inc., 21 238–40
Geox S.p.A., 118 162–65
Gerald Stevens, Inc., 37 161–63
Gerber Products Company, 7 196–98; 21 241–44 (upd)
Gerber Scientific, Inc., 12 204–06; 84 150–154 (upd.)
Gerdau S.A., 59 200–03
Gerhard D. Wempe KG, 88 120–25
Gericom AG, 47 152–54
Gerling-Konzern Versicherungs-Beteiligungs-Aktiengesellschaft, 51 139–43
German American Bancorp, 41 178–80
Gerresheimer Glas AG, 43 186–89
Gerry Weber International AG, 63 169–72
Gertrude Hawk Chocolates Inc., 104 162–65
Gesellschaft für musikalische Aufführungs- und mechanische Vervielfältigungsrechte *see* GEMA.
Getrag Corporate Group, 92 137–42
Getronics NV, 39 176–78
Getty Images, Inc., 31 216–18; 121 211–17 (upd.>
Gevaert *see* Agfa Gevaert Group N.V.
Gévelot S.A., 96 132–35
Gevity HR, Inc., 63 173–77
GF Health Products, Inc., 82 138–41
GFI Informatique SA, 49 165–68
GfK Aktiengesellschaft, 49 169–72
GFS *see* Gordon Food Service Inc.
Ghirardelli Chocolate Company, 30 218–20; 121 218–22 (upd.>
Gianni Versace S.p.A., 22 238–40; 106 202–07 (upd.)
Giant Cement Holding, Inc., 23 224–26
Giant Eagle, Inc., 86 160–64
Giant Food LLC, II 633–35; 22 241–44 (upd.); 83 155–161 (upd.)
Giant Industries, Inc., 19 175–77; 61 114–18 (upd.)
Giant Manufacturing Company, Ltd., 85 150–54
GIB Group, V 63–66; 26 158–62 (upd.)
Gibbs and Dandy plc, 74 119–21
Gibraltar Steel Corporation, 37 164–67
Gibson Greetings, Inc., 12 207–10 *see also* American Greetings Corp.
Gibson Guitar Corporation, 16 237–40; 100 182–87 (upd.)
Gibson, Dunn & Crutcher LLP, 36 249–52
Giddings & Lewis, Inc., 10 328–30
Giesecke & Devrient GmbH, 83 162–166
GiFi S.A., 74 122–24
Gifts In Kind International, 101 210–13
GigaMedia Limited, 109 264–68
Gilbane, Inc., 34 191–93
Gildan Activewear, Inc., 81 165–68
Gildemeister AG, 79 193–97
Gilead Sciences, Inc., 54 129–31
Gillett Holdings, Inc., 7 199–201
The Gillette Company, III 27–30; 20 249–53 (upd.); 68 171–76 (upd.)
Gilman & Ciocia, Inc., 72 148–50
Gilmore Entertainment Group L.L.C., 100 188–91
Gilster-Mary Lee Corporation, 120 139–42
Ginnie Mae *see* Government National Mortgage Association.
Giorgio Armani S.p.A., 45 180–83
Girl Scouts of the USA, 35 193–96
The Gitano Group, Inc., 8 219–21
GIV *see* Granite Industries of Vermont, Inc.; Gruppo Italiano Vini
Givaudan SA, 43 190–93
Given Imaging Ltd., 83 167–170
Givenchy *see* Parfums Givenchy S.A.
GKN plc, III 493–96; 38 208–13 (upd.); 89 232–41 (upd.)
GL Events S.A., 107 150–53
Glaces Thiriet S.A., 76 164–66
Glacier Bancorp, Inc., 35 197–200
Glacier Water Services, Inc., 47 155–58
Glamis Gold, Ltd., 54 132–35
Glanbia plc, 59 204–07, 364
Glatfelter Wood Pulp Company *see* P.H. Glatfelter Company
Glaverbel Group, 80 130–33
Glaxo Holdings plc, I 639–41; 9 263–65 (upd.)
GlaxoSmithKline PLC, 119 190–202 (upd.); 46 201–08 (upd.)
Glazer's Wholesale Drug Company, Inc., 82 142–45
Gleason Corporation, 24 184–87
Glen Dimplex, 78 123–27
Glico *see* Ezaki Glico Company Ltd.
The Glidden Company, 8 222–24
Global Berry Farms LLC, 62 154–56
Global Cash Access Holdings, Inc., 111 160–63
Global Crossing Ltd., 32 216–19
Global Hyatt Corporation, 75 159–63 (upd.)
Global Imaging Systems, Inc., 73 163–65
Global Industries, Ltd., 37 168–72
Global Marine Inc., 9 266–67
Global Outdoors, Inc., 49 173–76
Global Partners L.P., 116 254–57
Global Payments Inc., 91 206–10
Global Power Equipment Group Inc., 52 137–39
GlobalSantaFe Corporation, 48 187–92 (upd.)
Globe Newspaper Company Inc., 106 208–12
Globex Utilidades S.A., 103 188–91
Globo Comunicação e Participações S.A., 80 134–38
Globus SB-Warenhaus Holding GmbH & Co. KG, 120 143–47
Glock Ges.m.b.H., 42 154–56
Glon *see* Groupe Glon.
Glotel plc, 53 149–51
Glu Mobile Inc., 95 163–66
Gluek Brewing Company, 75 164–66
GM *see* General Motors Corp.

Great-West Lifeco Inc., III 260–61 *see also* Power Corporation of Canada.
Great Western Financial Corporation, 10 339–41 *see also* Washington Mutual, Inc.
Great White Shark Enterprises, Inc., 89 242–45
Great Wolf Resorts, Inc., 91 222–26
Greatbatch Inc., 72 154–56
Greater Washington Educational Telecommunication Association, 103 197–200
Grede Foundries, Inc., 38 214–17
Greek Organization of Football Prognostics S.A. (OPAP), 97 182–85
The Green Bay Packers, Inc., 32 223–26
Green Dot Public Schools, 99 186–189
Green Mountain Coffee Roasters, Inc., 31 227–30; 107 158–62 (upd.)
Green Tree Financial Corporation, 11 162–63 *see also* Conseco, Inc.
Green Tree Servicing LLC, 109 282–84
The Greenalls Group PLC, 21 245–47
Greenberg Traurig, LLP, 65 161–63
The Greenbrier Companies, 19 185–87
Greencore Group plc, 98 168–71
Greene King plc, 31 223–26
Greene, Tweed & Company, 55 170–72
Greenhill & Co., Inc., 119 208–12
GreenMan Technologies Inc., 99 190–193
Greenpeace International, 74 128–30
GreenPoint Financial Corp., 28 166–68
Greenwood Mills, Inc., 14 219–21
Greg Manning Auctions, Inc., 60 145–46
Greggs PLC, 65 164–66
Greif Inc., 15 186–88; 66 154–56 (upd.)
Grendene S.A., 102 154–57
Grévin & Compagnie SA, 56 143–45
Grey Global Group Inc., 6 26–28; 66 157–61 (upd.)
Grey Wolf, Inc., 43 201–03
Greyhound Lines, Inc., I 448–50; 32 227–31 (upd.)
Greylock Partners, 116 258–61
Greyston Bakery, Inc., 101 220–23
Griffin Industries, Inc., 70 106–09
Griffin Land & Nurseries, Inc., 43 204–06
Griffith Laboratories Inc., 100 196–99
Griffon Corporation, 34 194–96
Grill Concepts, Inc., 74 131–33
Grinnell Corp., 13 245–47
Grist Mill Company, 15 189–91
Gristede's Foods Inc., 68 31 231–33; 180–83 (upd.)
The Grocers Supply Co., Inc., 103 201–04
Grohe *see* Friedrich Grohe AG & Co. KG.
Grolier Inc., 16 251–54; 43 207–11 (upd.)
Grolsch *see* Royal Grolsch NV.
Grontmij N.V., 110 190–94
Grossman's Inc., 13 248–50
Grote Industries, Inc., 121 226–29
Ground Round, Inc., 21 248–51
Group 1 Automotive, Inc., 52 144–46
Group 4 Falck A/S, 42 165–68
Group Health Cooperative, 41 181–84
Groupama S.A., 76 167–70
Groupe Air France, 6 92–94 *see also* Societe Air France.
Groupe Alain Manoukian, 55 173–75
Groupe André, 17 210–12 *see also* Vivarte SA.
ARES *see* Groupe Ares S.A.
Groupe Bigard S.A., 96 151–54
Groupe Bolloré, 67 196–99
Groupe Bourbon S.A., 60 147–49
Groupe Bull *see* Compagnie des Machines Bull.
Groupe Caisse d'Epargne, 100 200–04
Groupe Casino *see* Casino Guichard-Perrachon S.A.
Groupe Castorama-Dubois Investissements, 23 230–32 *see also* Castorama-Dubois Investissements SCA
Groupe CECAB S.C.A., 88 131–34
Groupe Crit S.A., 74 134–36
Groupe Danone, 32 232–36 (upd.); 93 233–40 (upd.)
Groupe Dassault Aviation SA, 26 179–82 (upd.) *see also* Dassault Aviation S.A.
Groupe de la Cité, IV 614–16
Groupe DMC (Dollfus Mieg & Cie), 27 186–88
Groupe Dubreuil S.A., 102 162–65
Groupe Euralis, 86 169–72
Groupe Flo S.A., 98 172–75
Groupe Fournier SA, 44 187–89
Groupe Genoyer, 96 155–58
Groupe Glon, 84 155–158
Groupe Go Sport S.A., 39 183–85
Groupe Guillin SA, 40 214–16
Groupe Henri Heuliez S.A., 100 205–09
Groupe Herstal S.A., 58 145–48
Groupe Jean-Claude Darmon, 44 190–92
Groupe Lactalis, 78 128–32 (upd.)
Groupe Lapeyre S.A., 33 175–77
Groupe LDC *see* L.D.C. S.A.
Groupe Le Duff S.A., 84 159–162
Groupe Léa Nature, 88 135–38
Groupe Legris Industries, 23 233–35
Groupe Les Echos, 25 283–85
Groupe Limagrain, 74 137–40
Groupe Louis Dreyfus S.A., 60 150–53
Groupe Lucien Barrière S.A.S., 110 195–99
Groupe Monnoyeur, 72 157–59
Groupe Open, 74 141–43
Groupe Partouche SA, 48 196–99
Groupe Pinault-Printemps-Redoute *see* Pinault-Printemps-Redoute S.A.
Groupe Promodès S.A., 19 326–28
Groupe Rougier SA, 21 438–40
Groupe SEB, 35 201–03
Groupe Sidel S.A., 21 252–55
Groupe Soufflet SA, 55 176–78
Groupe Stalaven S.A., 117 126–29
Groupe Vidéotron Ltée., 20 271–73
Groupe Yves Saint Laurent, 23 236–39 *see also* Gucci Group N.V.
Groupe Zannier S.A., 35 204–07
Grow Biz International, Inc., 18 207–10 *see also* Winmark Corp.
Grow Group Inc., 12 217–19
GROWMARK, Inc., 88 139–42
Groz-Beckert Group, 68 184–86
Grubb & Ellis Company, 21 256–58; 98 176–80 (upd.)
Gruma, S.A.B. de C.V., 31 234–36; 103 205–10 (upd.)
Grumman Corp., I 61–63; 11 164–67 (upd.) *see aslo* Northrop Grumman Corp.
Grunau Company Inc., 90 209–12
Grundfos Group, 83 171–174
Grundig AG, 27 189–92
Gruntal & Co., L.L.C., 20 274–76
Grupo Aeroportuario del Centro Norte, S.A.B. de C.V., 97 186–89
Grupo Aeroportuario del Pacífico, S.A. de C.V., 85 160–63
Grupo Aeropuerto del Sureste, S.A. de C.V., 48 200–02
Grupo Algar *see* Algar S/A Emprendimentos e Participações
Grupo Ángeles Servicios de Salud, S.A. de C.V., 84 163–166
Grupo Brescia, 99 194–197
Grupo Bufete *see* Bufete Industrial, S.A. de C.V.
Grupo Carso, S.A. de C.V., 21 259–61; 107 163–67 (upd.)
Grupo Casa Saba, S.A. de C.V., 39 186–89
Grupo Clarín S.A., 67 200–03
Grupo Comercial Chedraui S.A. de C.V., 86 173–76
Grupo Comex, 115 224–26
Grupo Corvi S.A. de C.V., 86 177–80
Grupo Cydsa, S.A. de C.V., 39 190–93
Grupo Dina *see* Consorcio G Grupo Dina, S.A. de C.V.
Grupo Dragados SA, 55 179–82
Grupo Elektra, S.A. de C.V., 39 194–97
Grupo Eroski, 64 167–70
Grupo Ferrovial S.A., 40 217–19; 118 166–70 (upd.)
Grupo Ficosa International, 90 213–16
Grupo Financiero Banamex S.A., 54 143–46
Grupo Financiero Banorte, S.A. de C.V., 51 149–51
Grupo Financiero BBVA Bancomer S.A., 54 147–50
Grupo Financiero Galicia S.A., 63 178–81
Grupo Financiero Serfin, S.A., 19 188–90
Grupo Gigante, S.A. de C.V., 34 197–99
Grupo Herdez, S.A. de C.V., 35 208–10
Grupo IMSA, S.A. de C.V., 44 193–96
Grupo Industrial Bimbo, 19 191–93
Grupo Industrial Durango, S.A. de C.V., 37 176–78
Grupo Industrial Herradura, S.A. de C.V., 83 175–178
Grupo Industrial Lala, S.A. de C.V., 82 154–57

H

Hamilton Beach/Proctor-Silex Inc., 17 213–15
Hammacher Schlemmer & Company Inc., 21 268–70; 72 160–62 (upd.)
Hammerson plc, IV 696–98; 40 233–35 (upd.)
Hammond Manufacturing Company Limited, 83 179–182
Hamon & Cie (International) S.A., 97 190–94
Hamot Health Foundation, 91 227–32
Hampshire Group Ltd., 82 170–73
Hampton Affiliates, Inc., 77 175–79
Hampton Industries, Inc., 20 280–82
Hancock Fabrics, Inc., 18 222–24
Hancock Holding Company, 15 207–09
Handleman Company, 15 210–12; 86 185–89 (upd.)
Handspring Inc., 49 183–86
Handy & Harman, 23 249–52
Hanesbrands Inc., 98 185–88
Hang Lung Group Ltd., 104 184–87
Hang Seng Bank Ltd., 60 161–63
Hanger Orthopedic Group, Inc., 41 192–95
Hangzhou Wahaha Group Co., Ltd., 119 227–30
Haniel *see* Franz Haniel & Cie. GmbH.
Hanjin Shipping Co., Ltd., 50 217–21
Hankook Tire Company Ltd., 105 200–03
Hankyu Corporation, V 454–56; 23 253–56 (upd.)
Hankyu Department Stores, Inc., V 70–71; 62 168–71 (upd.)
Hanmi Financial Corporation, 66 169–71
Hanna Andersson Corp., 49 187–90
Hanna-Barbera Cartoons Inc., 23 257–59, 387
Hannaford Bros. Co., 12 220–22; 103 211–17 (upd.)
Hanover Compressor Company, 59 215–17
Hanover Direct, Inc., 36 262–65
Hanover Foods Corporation, 35 211–14
Hansen Natural Corporation, 31 242–45; 76 171–74 (upd.)
Hansgrohe AG, 56 149–52
Hanson Building Materials America Inc., 60 164–66
Hanson PLC, III 501–03; 7 207–10 (upd.); 30 228–32 (upd.)
Hanwha Group, 62 172–75
Hapag-Lloyd AG, 6 397–99; 97 195–203 (upd.)
Happy Kids Inc., 30 233–35
Harbert Corporation, 14 222–23
Harbison-Walker Refractories Company, 24 207–09
Harbour Group Industries, Inc., 90 226–29
Harcourt Brace and Co., 12 223–26
Harcourt Brace Jovanovich, Inc., IV 622–24
Harcourt General, Inc., 20 283–87 (upd.)
Hard Rock Café International, Inc., 12 227–29; 32 241–45 (upd.); 105 204–09 (upd.)
Harding Lawson Associates Group, Inc., 16 258–60
Hardinge Inc., 25 193–95
HARIBO GmbH & Co. KG, 44 216–19
Harkins Amusement Enterprises, Inc., 94 227–31
Harland and Wolff Holdings plc, 19 197–200
Harland Clarke Holdings Corporation, 94 232–35 (upd.)
Harlem Children's Zone, Inc., 121 234–37
Harlem Globetrotters International, Inc., 61 122–24
Harlequin Enterprises Limited, 52 153–56
Harley-Davidson, Inc., 7 211–14; 25 196–200 (upd.); 106 223–28 (upd.)
Harley Ellis Devereaux Corporation, 101 229–32
Harleysville Group Inc., 37 183–86
Harman International Industries, Incorporated, 15 213–15; 101 233–39 (upd.)
Harmon Industries, Inc., 25 201–04 *see also* General Electric Co.
Harmonic Inc., 43 221–23; 109 285–88 (upd.)
Harmonix Music Systems, Inc., 121 238–40
Harmony Gold Mining Company Limited, 63 182–85
Harnischfeger Industries, Inc., 8 241–44; 38 224–28 (upd.) *see also* Joy Global Inc.
Harold's Stores, Inc., 22 248–50
Harper Group Inc., 17 216–19
HarperCollins Publishers, 15 216–18
Harpo Inc., 28 173–75; 66 172–75 (upd.)
Harps Food Stores, Inc., 99 206–209
Harrah's Entertainment, Inc., 16 261–63; 43 224–28 (upd.); 113 160–65 (upd.)
Harris Corporation, II 37–39; 20 288–92 (upd.); 78 142–48 (upd.)
Harris Interactive Inc., 41 196–99; 92 148–53 (upd.)
Harris Publishing *see* Bernard C. Harris Publishing Company, Inc.
The Harris Soup Company (Harry's Fresh Foods),92 154–157
Harris Teeter Inc., 23 260–62; 72 163–66 (upd.)
Harrisons & Crosfield plc, III 696–700 *see also* Elementis plc.
Harrods Holdings, 47 171–74
Harry & David Holdings, Inc., 118 175–80 (upd.)
Harry London Candies, Inc., 70 110–12
Harry N. Abrams, Inc., 58 152–55
Harry Winston Inc., 45 184–87; 104 188–93 (upd.)
Harry's Farmers Market Inc., 23 263–66 *see also* Whole Foods Market, Inc.
Harry's Fresh Foods *see* The Harris Soup Company (Harry's Fresh Foods)
Harsco Corporation, 8 245–47; 105 210–15 (upd.)
Harte-Hanks Communications, Inc., 17 220–22; 63 186–89 (upd.)
Hartford Financial Services Group, Inc., 116 267–70
Hartmann Inc., 96 172–76
Hartmarx Corporation, 8 248–50; 32 246–50 (upd.)
The Hartstone Group plc, 14 224–26
The Hartz Mountain Corporation, 12 230–32; 46 220–23 (upd.)
Harvey Norman Holdings Ltd., 56 153–55
Harveys Casino Resorts, 27 199–201 *see also* Harrah's Entertainment, Inc.
Harza Engineering Company, 14 227–28
Hasbro, Inc., III 504–06; 16 264–68 (upd.); 43 229–34 (upd.); 112 199–206 (upd.)
Haskel International, Inc., 59 218–20
Hästens Sängar AB, 121 241–44
Hastings Entertainment, Inc., 29 229–31; 104 194–99 (upd.)
Hastings Manufacturing Company, 56 156–58
Hauser, Inc., 46 224–27
Havas, SA, 10 345–48; 33 178–82 (upd.) *see also* Vivendi.
Haverty Furniture Companies, Inc., 31 246–49
Hawaiian Airlines Inc., 22 251–53 (upd.) *see also* HAL Inc.
Hawaiian Electric Industries, Inc., 9 274–77; 120 157–62 (upd.)
Hawaiian Holdings, Inc., 96 177–81 (upd.)
Hawk Corporation, 59 221–23
Hawker Siddeley Group Public Limited Company, III 507–10
Hawkeye Holdings LLC, 86 246–49
Hawkins Chemical, Inc., 16 269–72
Haworth, Inc., 8 251–52; 39 205–08 (upd.); 118 181–87 (upd.)
Hay Group Holdings, Inc., 100 210–14
Hay House, Inc., 93 241–45
Hayel Saeed Anam Group of Cos., 92 158–61
Hayes Corporation, 24 210–14
Hayes Lemmerz International, Inc., 27 202–04
Hayneedle Incorporated, 116 271–74
Haynes International, Inc., 88 163–66
Haynes Publishing Group P.L.C., 71 169–71
Hays plc, 27 205–07; 78 149–53 (upd.)
Hazelden Foundation, 28 176–79
Hazlewood Foods plc, 32 251–53
HBO *see* Home Box Office Inc.
HCA, Inc., 35 215–18 (upd.); 111 181–88 (upd.)

I

Julius Baer Holding AG, **52** 203–05
Julius Blüthner Pianofortefabric GmbH, **78** 185–88
Julius Meinl International AG, **53** 177–80
Jumbo S.A., **96** 221–24
Jumeirah Group, **83** 227–230
Jungheinrich AG, **96** 225–30
Juniper Networks, Inc., **43** 251–55
Juno Lighting, Inc., **30** 266–68
Juno Online Services, Inc., **38** 269–72 *see also* United Online, Inc.
Jupitermedia Corporation, **75** 222–24
Jurys Doyle Hotel Group plc, **64** 215–17
JUSCO Co., Ltd., **V** 96–99 *see also* AEON Co., Ltd.
Just Bagels Manufacturing, Inc., **94** 268–71
Just Born, Inc., **32** 305–07
Just For Feet, Inc., **19** 228–30
Justin Industries, Inc., **19** 231–33 *see also* Berkshire Hathaway Inc.
Juventus F.C. S.p.A, **53** 181–83
JVC *see* Victor Company of Japan, Ltd.
JWP Inc., **9** 300–02 *see also* EMCOR Group Inc.
JWT Group Inc., **I** 19–21 *see also* WPP Group plc.
Jysk Holding A/S, **100** 241–44

K

K-Paul's Louisiana Enterprises Inc., **109** 326–30
K+S Aktiengesellschaft, **112** 242–47
K-Swiss Inc., **33** 243–45; **89** 277–81 (upd.)
K-tel International, Inc., **21** 325–28
K-Tron International Inc., **115** 259–62
K-VA-T Food Stores, Inc., **117** 189–92
K&B Inc., **12** 286–88
K & G Men's Center, Inc., **21** 310–12
K.A. Rasmussen AS, **99** 241–244
K2 Inc., **16** 295–98; **84** 206–211 (upd.)
Kable Media Services, Inc., **115** 263–66
Kadant Inc., **96** 231–34 (upd.)
Kagome Company Ltd., **120** 193–96
Kaiser Aluminum Corporation, **IV** 121–23; **84** 212–217 (upd.)
Kaiser Foundation Health Plan, Inc., **53** 184–86; **119** 272–76 (upd.)
Kajima Corporation, **I** 577–78; **51** 177–79 (upd.); **117** 193–97 (upd.)
Kal Kan Foods, Inc., **22** 298–300
Kaman Corporation, **12** 289–92; **42** 204–08 (upd.); **118** 224–33 (upd.)
Kaman Music Corporation, **68** 205–07
Kampgrounds of America, Inc., **33** 230–33
Kamps AG, **44** 251–54
Kana Software, Inc., **51** 180–83
Kanebo, Ltd., **53** 187–91
Kanematsu Corporation, **IV** 442–44; **24** 259–62 (upd.); **102** 192–95 (upd.)
The Kansai Electric Power Company, Inc., **V** 645–48; **62** 196–200 (upd.)
Kansai Paint Company Ltd., **80** 175–78
Kansallis-Osake-Pankki, **II** 302–03
Kansas City Power & Light Company, **6** 510–12 *see also* Great Plains Energy Inc.
Kansas City Southern Industries, Inc., **6** 400–02; **26** 233–36 (upd.)
The Kansas City Southern Railway Company, **92** 198–202
Kantar Group, **119** 277–81
Kao Corporation, **III** 38–39; **20** 315–17 (upd.); **79** 225–30 (upd.)
Kaplan, Inc., **42** 209–12; **90** 270–75 (upd.)
KappAhl Holding AB, **107** 225–28
KAR Auction Services, Inc., **117** 198–201
Kar Nut Products Company, **86** 233–36
Karan Co. *see* Donna Karan Co.
Karl Kani Infinity, Inc., **49** 242–45
Karlsberg Brauerei GmbH & Co KG, **41** 220–23
Karmann *see* Wilhelm Karmann GmbH.
Karstadt Aktiengesellschaft, **V** 100–02; **19** 234–37 (upd.)
Karstadt Quelle AG, **57** 195–201 (upd.)
Karsten Manufacturing Corporation, **51** 184–86
Kash n' Karry Food Stores, Inc., **20** 318–20 *see also* Sweetbay Supermarket
Kashi Company, **89** 282–85
Kasper A.S.L., Ltd., **40** 276–79
kate spade LLC, **68** 208–11
Katokichi Company Ltd., **82** 187–90
Katy Industries Inc., **I** 472–74; **51** 187–90 (upd.)
Katz Communications, Inc., **6** 32–34 *see also* Clear Channel Communications, Inc.
Katz Media Group, Inc., **35** 245–48
Kaufhof Warenhaus AG, **V** 103–05; **23** 311–14 (upd.)
Kaufman and Broad Home Corporation, **8** 284–86 *see also* KB Home.
Kaufring AG, **35** 249–52
Kawai Musical Instruments Manufacturing Co.,Ltd., **78** 189–92
Kawasaki Heavy Industries, Ltd., **III** 538–40; **63** 220–23 (upd.)
Kawasaki Kisen Kaisha, Ltd., **V** 457–60; **56** 177–81 (upd.)
Kawasaki Steel Corporation, **IV** 124–25
Kay-Bee Toy Stores, **15** 252–53 *see also* KB Toys.
Kayak.com, **108** 286–89
Kaydon Corporation, **18** 274–76; **117** 202–06 (upd.)
Kayem Foods Incorporated, **118** 234–37
KB Home, **45** 218–22 (upd.)
KB Toys, Inc., **35** 253–55 (upd.); **86** 237–42 (upd.)
KBC Group N.V., **116** 313–16
KBR Inc., **106** 264–70 (upd.)
KC *see* Kenneth Cole Productions, Inc.
KCPL *see* Kansas City Power & Light Co.
KCSI *see* Kansas City Southern Industries, Inc.
KCSR *see* The Kansas City Southern Railway.
KDDI Corporation, **109** 331–35
Keane, Inc., **56** 182–86
Keds, LLC, **118** 238–41
Keebler Foods Company, **36** 311–13
Keio Corporation, **V** 461–62; **96** 235–39 (upd.)
The Keith Companies Inc., **54** 181–84
Keithley Instruments Inc., **16** 299–301
Kelda Group plc, **45** 223–26
Keller Group PLC, **95** 221–24
Kelley Blue Book Company, Inc., **84** 218–221
Kelley Drye & Warren LLP, **40** 280–83
Kellogg Brown & Root, Inc., **62** 201–05 (upd.) *see also* KBR Inc.
Kellogg Company, **II** 523–26; **13** 291–94 (upd.); **50** 291–96 (upd.); **110** 265–73 (upd.)
Kellwood Company, **8** 287–89; **85** 203–08 (upd.)
Kelly-Moore Paint Company, Inc., **56** 187–89; **112** 232–36 (upd.)
Kelly Services, Inc., **6** 35–37; **26** 237–40 (upd.); **109** 336–43 (upd.)
The Kelly-Springfield Tire Company, **8** 290–92
Kelsey-Hayes Group of Companies, **7** 258–60; **27** 249–52 (upd.)
Kemet Corp., **14** 281–83
Kemira Oyj, **70** 143–46
Kemper Corporation, **III** 269–71; **15** 254–58 (upd.)
Kemps LLC, **103** 235–38
Kendall International, Inc., **11** 219–21 *see also* Tyco International Ltd.
Kendall-Jackson Winery, Ltd., **28** 221–23
Kendle International Inc., **87** 276–279
Kenetech Corporation, **11** 222–24
Kenexa Corporation, **87** 280–284
Kenmore Air Harbor Inc., **65** 191–93
Kennametal, Inc., **13** 295–97; **68** 212–16 (upd.)
Kennecott Corporation, **7** 261–64; **27** 253–57 (upd.) *see also* Rio Tinto PLC.
Kennedy-Wilson, Inc., **60** 183–85
Kenneth Cole Productions, Inc., **25** 256–58
Ken's Foods, Inc., **88** 223–26
Kensey Nash Corporation, **71** 185–87
Kensington Publishing Corporation, **84** 222–225
Kent Electronics Corporation, **17** 273–76
Kentucky Electric Steel, Inc., **31** 286–88
Kentucky Fried Chicken *see* KFC Corp.
Kentucky Utilities Company, **6** 513–15
Kenwood Corporation, **31** 289–91
Kenya Airways Limited, **89** 286–89
Keolis SA, **51** 191–93
Kepco *see* Korea Electric Power Corporation; Kyushu Electric Power Company Inc.
Keppel Corporation Ltd., **73** 201–03
Keramik Holding AG Laufen, **51** 194–96
Kerasotes ShowPlace Theaters LLC, **80** 179–83

Cumulative Index to Companies

L

M

Mazzio's Corporation, 76 259–61
MBB *see* Messerschmitt-Bölkow-Blohm.
MBC Holding Company, 40 306–09
MBE *see* Mail Boxes Etc.
MBI Inc., 120 230–33
MBIA Inc., 73 223–26
MBK Industrie S.A., 94 303–06
MBNA Corporation, 12 328–30; 33 291–94 (upd.)
MC Sporting Goods *see* Michigan Sporting Goods Distributors Inc.
MCA Inc., II 143–45 *see also* Universal Studios.
McAfee Inc., 94 307–10
McAlister's Corporation, 66 217–19
McBride plc, 82 226–30
MCC *see* Morris Communications Corp.
McCain Foods Limited, 77 253–56
McCarthy Building Companies, Inc., 48 280–82; 120 234–38 (upd.)
McCaw Cellular Communications, Inc., 6 322–24 *see also* AT&T Wireless Services, Inc.
McClain Industries, Inc., 51 236–38
The McClatchy Company, 23 342–44; 92 231–35 (upd.)
McCormick & Company, Incorporated, 7 314–16; 27 297–300 (upd.)
McCormick & Schmick's Seafood Restaurants, Inc., 71 219–21
McCoy Corporation, 58 223–25
McDATA Corporation, 75 254–56
McDermott International, Inc., III 558–60; 37 242–46 (upd.)
McDonald's Corporation, II 646–48; 7 317–19 (upd.); 26 281–85 (upd.); 63 280–86 (upd.)
McDonnell Douglas Corporation, I 70–72; 11 277–80 (upd.) *see also* Boeing Co.
McGrath RentCorp, 91 326–29
The McGraw-Hill Companies, Inc., IV 634–37; 18 325–30 (upd.); 51 239–44 (upd.); 115 304–14 (upd.)
MCI *see* Melamine Chemicals, Inc.
MCI WorldCom, Inc., V 302–04; 27 301–08 (upd.) *see also* Verizon Communications Inc.
McIlhenny Company, 20 364–67
McJunkin Corporation, 63 287–89
McKechnie plc, 34 270–72
McKee Foods Corporation, 7 320–21; 27 309–11 (upd.); 117 255–58 (upd.)
McKesson Corporation, I 496–98; 12 331–33 (upd.); 47 233–37 (upd.); 108 334–41 (upd.)
McKinsey & Company, Inc., 9 343–45
McLanahan Corporation, 104 302–05
McLane Company, Inc., 13 332–34
McLeodUSA Incorporated, 32 327–30
McMenamins Pubs and Breweries, 65 224–26
McMoRan *see* Freeport-McMoRan Copper & Gold, Inc.
McMurry, Inc., 105 296–99
MCN Corporation, 6 519–22
McNaughton Apparel Group, Inc., 92 236–41 (upd.)
McPherson's Ltd., 66 220–22
McQuay International *see* AAF-McQuay Inc.
MCSi, Inc., 41 258–60
McWane Corporation, 55 264–66
MDC Partners Inc., 63 290–92
MDU Resources Group, Inc., 7 322–25; 42 249–53 (upd.); 114 294–301 (upd.)
MDVIP, Inc., 118 281–85
Mead & Hunt Inc., 113 252–56
The Mead Corporation, IV 310–13; 19 265–69 (upd.) *see also* MeadWestvaco Corp.
Mead Data Central, Inc., 10 406–08 *see also* LEXIS-NEXIS Group.
Mead Johnson & Company, 84 257–262
Meade Instruments Corporation, 41 261–64
Meadowcraft, Inc., 29 313–15; 100 283–87 (upd.)
MeadWestvaco Corporation, 76 262–71 (upd.)
Measurement Specialties, Inc., 71 222–25
MEC *see* Mitsubishi Estate Company, Ltd.
Mecalux S.A., 74 183–85
Mechel OAO, 99 278–281
Mecklermedia Corporation, 24 328–30 *see also* Jupitermedia Corp.
Medarex, Inc., 85 256–59
Medco Containment Services Inc., 9 346–48 *see also* Merck & Co., Inc.
Medco Health Solutions, Inc., 116 335–39
Médecins sans Frontières, 85 260–63
MEDecision, Inc., 95 263–67
Media Arts Group, Inc., 42 254–57
Media General, Inc., 7 326–28; 38 306–09 (upd.)
Media Sciences International, Inc., 104 306–09
Mediacom Communications Corporation, 69 250–52
MediaNews Group, Inc., 70 177–80
Mediaset SpA, 50 332–34
Medical Action Industries Inc., 101 338–41
Medical Information Technology Inc., 64 266–69
Medical Management International, Inc., 65 227–29
Medical Staffing Network Holdings, Inc., 89 320–23
Medicine Shoppe International, Inc., 102 253–57
Medicis Pharmaceutical Corporation, 59 284–86
Medifast, Inc., 97 281–85
MedImmune, Inc., 35 286–89
Mediolanum S.p.A., 65 230–32
Medipal Holdings Corporation, 120 239–43
Medis Technologies Ltd., 77 257–60
Meditrust, 11 281–83
Medline Industries, Inc., 61 204–06
Medtronic, Inc., 8 351–54; 30 313–17 (upd.); 67 250–55 (upd.)
Medusa Corporation, 24 331–33
Mega Bloks, Inc., 61 207–09
MegaChips Corporation, 117 259–62
Megafoods Stores Inc., 13 335–37
Meggitt PLC, 34 273–76
Meguiar's, Inc., 99 282–285
Meidensha Corporation, 92 242–46
Meier & Frank Co., 23 345–47 *see also* Macy's, Inc.
Meijer, Inc., 7 329–31; 27 312–15 (upd.); 101 342–46 (upd.)
Meiji Dairies Corporation, II 538–39; 82 231–34 (upd.)
Meiji Mutual Life Insurance Company, III 288–89
Meiji Seika Kaisha Ltd., II 540–41; 64 270–72 (upd.)
Mel Farr Automotive Group, 20 368–70
Melaleuca Inc., 31 326–28
Melamine Chemicals, Inc., 27 316–18 *see also* Mississippi Chemical Corp.
Melco Crown Entertainment Limited, 103 262–65
Melitta Unternehmensgruppe Bentz KG, 53 218–21
Mello Smello *see* The Miner Group International.
Mellon Financial Corporation, II 315–17; 44 278–82 (upd.)
Mellon-Stuart Co., I 584–85 *see also* Michael Baker Corp.
The Melting Pot Restaurants, Inc., 74 186–88
Melville Corporation, V 136–38 *see also* CVS Corp.
Melvin Simon and Associates, Inc., 8 355–57 *see also* Simon Property Group, Inc.
MEMC Electronic Materials, Inc., 81 249–52
Memorial Sloan-Kettering Cancer Center, 57 239–41
Memry Corporation, 72 225–27
Menard, Inc., 104 310–14 (upd.)
Menasha Corporation, 8 358–61; 59 287–92 (upd.); 118 286–93 (upd.)
Mendocino Brewing Company, Inc., 60 205–07
The Men's Wearhouse, Inc., 17 312–15; 48 283–87 (upd.)
The Mentholatum Company Inc., 32 331–33
Mentor Corporation, 26 286–88
Mentor Graphics Corporation, 11 284–86
MEPC plc, IV 710–12
Mercantile Bankshares Corp., 11 287–88
Mercantile Stores Company, Inc., V 139; 19 270–73 (upd.) *see also* Dillard's Inc.
Mercer International Inc., 64 273–75
The Merchants Company, 102 258–61
Mercian Corporation, 77 261–64

Millennium & Copthorne Hotels plc, 71 231–33
Millennium Pharmaceuticals, Inc., 47 249–52
Miller Brewing Company, I 269–70; 12 337–39 (upd.) *see also* SABMiller plc.
The Miller Group Ltd., 119 316–21
Miller Industries, Inc., 26 293–95
Miller Publishing Group, LLC, 57 242–44
Millicom International Cellular S.A., 115 340–43
Milliken & Co., V 366–68; 17 327–30 (upd.); 82 235–39 (upd.)
Milliman USA, 66 223–26
Millipore Corporation, 25 339–43; 84 271–276 (upd.)
The Mills Corporation, 77 280–83
Milnot Company, 46 289–91
Milton Bradley Company, 21 372–75
Milton CAT, Inc., 86 268–71
Milwaukee Brewers Baseball Club, 37 247–49
Mine Safety Appliances Company, 31 333–35
Minebea Co., Ltd., 90 298–302
The Miner Group International, 22 356–58
Minera Alumbrera Ltd., 118 300–02
Minera Escondida Ltda., 100 293–96
Minerals & Metals Trading Corporation of India Ltd., IV 143–44
Minerals Technologies Inc., 11 310–12; 52 248–51 (upd.)
Minnesota Mining & Manufacturing Company, I 499–501; 8 369–71 (upd.); 26 296–99 (upd.) *see also* 3M Co.
Minnesota Power, Inc., 11 313–16; 34 286–91 (upd.)
Minnesota Twins, 112 276–80
Minntech Corporation, 22 359–61
Minolta Co., Ltd., III 574–76; 18 339–42 (upd.); 43 281–85 (upd.)
The Minute Maid Company, 28 271–74
Minuteman International Inc., 46 292–95
Minyard Food Stores, Inc., 33 304–07; 86 272–77 (upd.)
Miquel y Costas Miquel S.A., 68 256–58
Mirage Resorts, Incorporated, 6 209–12; 28 275–79 (upd.) *see also* MGM MIRAGE.
Miramax Film Corporation, 64 282–85
Mirant Corporation, 98 243–47
Miroglio SpA, 86 278–81
Mirror Group Newspapers plc, 7 341–43; 23 348–51 (upd.)
Misonix, Inc., 80 248–51
Mississippi Chemical Corporation, 39 280–83
Mississippi Power Company, 110 315–19
Misys PLC, 45 279–81; 46 296–99
Mitchell Energy and Development Corporation, 7 344–46 *see also* Devon Energy Corp.
Mitchells & Butlers PLC, 59 296–99
Mitel Corporation, 18 343–46
MITRE Corporation, 26 300–02; 107 269–72 (upd.)
MITROPA AG, 37 250–53
Mitsubishi Bank, Ltd., II 321–22 *see also* Bank of Tokyo-Mitsubishi Ltd.
Mitsubishi Chemical Corporation, I 363–64; 56 236–38 (upd.)
Mitsubishi Corporation, I 502–04; 12 340–43 (upd.); 116 346–52 (upd.)
Mitsubishi Electric Corporation, II 57–59; 44 283–87 (upd.); 117 263–69 (upd.)
Mitsubishi Estate Company, Limited, IV 713–14; 61 215–18 (upd.)
Mitsubishi Heavy Industries, Ltd., III 577–79; 7 347–50 (upd.); 40 324–28 (upd.); 120 252–58 (upd.)
Mitsubishi Materials Corporation, III 712–13
Mitsubishi Motors Corporation, 9 349–51; 23 352–55 (upd.); 57 245–49 (upd.)
Mitsubishi Oil Co., Ltd., IV 460–62 *see also* Nippon Mitsubishi Oil Corp.
Mitsubishi Rayon Co. Ltd., V 369–71
Mitsubishi Trust & Banking Corporation, II 323–24
Mitsubishi UFJ Financial Group, Inc., 99 291–296 (upd.)
Mitsui & Co., Ltd., I 505–08; 28 280–85 (upd.); 110 320–27 (upd.)
Mitsui Bank, Ltd., II 325–27 *see also* Sumitomo Mitsui Banking Corp.
Mitsui Marine and Fire Insurance Company, Limited, III 295–96
Mitsui Mining & Smelting Co., Ltd., IV 145–46; 102 274–78 (upd.)
Mitsui Mining Company, Limited, IV 147–49
Mitsui Mutual Life Insurance Company, III 297–98; 39 284–86 (upd.)
Mitsui O.S.K. Lines Ltd., V 473–76; 96 282–87 (upd.)
Mitsui Petrochemical Industries, Ltd., 9 352–54
Mitsui Real Estate Development Co., Ltd., IV 715–16
Mitsui Trust & Banking Company, Ltd., II 328
Mitsukoshi Ltd., V 142–44; 56 239–42 (upd.)
Mity Enterprises, Inc., 38 310–12
MIVA, Inc., 83 271–275
Mizuho Financial Group Inc., 25 344–46; 58 229–36 (upd.)
MN Airlines LLC, 104 321–27
MNS, Ltd., 65 236–38
Mo och Domsjö AB, IV 317–19 *see also* Holmen AB
Mobil Corporation, IV 463–65; 7 351–54 (upd.); 21 376–80 (upd.) *see also* Exxon Mobil Corp.
Mobile Mini, Inc., 58 237–39
Mobile Telecommunications Technologies Corp., 18 347–49
Mobile TeleSystems OJSC, 59 300–03
Mocon, Inc., 76 275–77
Modell's Sporting Goods *see* Henry Modell & Company Inc.
Modern Times Group AB, 36 335–38
Modern Woodmen of America, 66 227–29
Modine Manufacturing Company, 8 372–75; 56 243–47 (upd.)
MoDo *see* Mo och Domsjö AB.
Modtech Holdings, Inc., 77 284–87
Moelven Industrier ASA, 110 328–32
Moen Incorporated, 12 344–45; 106 295–98 (upd.)
Moe's Southwest Grill *see* MSWG, LLC.
Moët-Hennessy, I 271–72 *see also* LVMH Moët Hennessy Louis Vuitton SA.
Mohawk Fine Papers, Inc., 108 353–57
Mohawk Industries, Inc., 19 274–76; 63 298–301 (upd.)
Mohegan Tribal Gaming Authority, 37 254–57
Moksel *see* A. Moksel AG.
MOL *see* Mitsui O.S.K. Lines, Ltd.
MOL Rt, 70 192–95
Moldflow Corporation, 73 227–30
Molex Incorporated, 11 317–19; 14 27; 54 236–41 (upd.)
Moliflor Loisirs, 80 252–55
Molina Healthcare, Inc., 116 353–56
Molinos Río de la Plata S.A., 61 219–21
Molins plc, 51 249–51
The Molson Companies Limited, I 273–75; 26 303–07 (upd.)
Molson Coors Brewing Company, 77 288–300 (upd.)
Monaco Coach Corporation, 31 336–38
Monadnock Paper Mills, Inc., 21 381–84
Monarch Casino & Resort, Inc., 65 239–41
The Monarch Cement Company, 72 231–33
Mondadori *see* Arnoldo Mondadori Editore S.p.A.
Mondragón Corporación Cooperativa, 101 347–51
MoneyGram International, Inc., 94 315–18
Monfort, Inc., 13 350–52
Monnaie de Paris, 62 246–48
Monnoyeur Group *see* Groupe Monnoyeur.
Monoprix S.A., 86 282–85
Monro Muffler Brake, Inc., 24 337–40
Monrovia Nursery Company, 70 196–98
Monsanto Company, I 365–67; 9 355–57 (upd.); 29 327–31 (upd.); 77 301–07 (upd.)
Monsoon plc, 39 287–89
Monster Cable Products, Inc., 69 256–58
Monster Worldwide Inc., 74 194–97 (upd.)
Montana Coffee Traders, Inc., 60 208–10

New York Restaurant Group, Inc., 32 361–63
New York Shakespeare Festival Management, 92328–32
New York State Electric and Gas Corporation, 6 534–36
New York Stock Exchange, Inc., 9 369–72; 39 296–300 (upd.)
The New York Times Company, IV 647–49; 19 283–85 (upd.); 61 239–43 (upd.)
New York Yacht Club, Inc., 103 290–93
The Newark Group, Inc., 102 302–05
Neways, Inc., 78 251–54
Newcom Group, 104 345–48
Newcor, Inc., 40 332–35
Newegg Inc., 107 291–94
Newell Rubbermaid Inc., 9 373–76; 52 261–71 (upd.); 120 267–76 (upd.)
Newfield Exploration Company, 65 260–62
Newhall Land and Farming Company, 14 348–50
Newly Weds Foods, Inc., 74 201–03
Newman's Own, Inc., 37 272–75
NewMarket Corporation, 116 371–74
Newmont Mining Corporation, 7 385–88; 94 331–37 (upd.)
NewPage Corporation, 119 333–38
Newpark Resources, Inc., 63 305–07
Newport Corporation, 71 247–49
Newport News Shipbuilding Inc., 13 372–75; 38 323–27 (upd.)
News America Publishing Inc., 12 358–60
News Communications, Inc., 103 294–98
News Corporation, IV 650–53; 7 389–93 (upd.); 46 308–13 (upd.); 109 408–15 (upd.)
Newsday Media Group, 103 299–303
Newsquest plc, 32 354–56
NewYork-Presbyterian Hospital, 59 309–12
Nexans SA, 54 262–64
NEXCOM *see* Navy Exchange Service Command.
Nexen Inc., 79 282–85
Nexity S.A., 66 243–45
Nexstar Broadcasting Group, Inc., 73 238–41
Next Media Ltd., 61 244–47
Next plc, 29 355–57
Nextel Communications, Inc., 10 431–33; 27 341–45 (upd.) *see also* Sprint Nextel Corp.
NextWave Wireless Inc., 112 291–94
Neyveli Lignite Corporation Ltd., 65 263–65
NFC plc, 6 412–14 *see also* Exel plc.
NFL *see* National Football League Inc.
NFL Films, 75 275–78
NFO Worldwide, Inc., 24 352–55
NG2 S.A., 120 277–80
NGC Corporation, 18 365–67 *see also* Dynegy Inc.
NGK Insulators Ltd., 67 264–66
NH Hoteles S.A., 79 286–89
NHK, III 580–82; 115 361–65 (upd.)
Niagara Corporation, 28 314–16
Niagara Mohawk Holdings Inc., V 665–67; 45 296–99 (upd.)
NICE Systems Ltd., 83 280–283
Nichii Co., Ltd., V 154–55
Nichimen Corporation, IV 150–52; 24 356–59 (upd.) *see also* Sojitz Corp.
Nichirei Corporation, 70 203–05
Nichiro Corporation, 86 299–302
Nichols plc, 44 315–18
Nichols Research Corporation, 18 368–70
Nicklaus Companies, 45 300–03
Nicole Miller, 98 257–60
Nicor Inc., 6 529–31; 86 303–07 (upd.)
Nidec Corporation, 59 313–16
Nielsen Business Media, Inc., 98 261–65
Nigerian National Petroleum Corporation, IV 472–74; 72 240–43 (upd.)
Nihon Keizai Shimbun, Inc., IV 654–56
NII *see* National Intergroup, Inc.
NIKE, Inc., V 372–74; 8 391–94 (upd.); 36 343–48 (upd.); 75 279–85 (upd.)
Nikken Global Inc., 32 364–67
The Nikko Securities Company Limited, II 433–35; 9 377–79 (upd.)
Nikon Corporation, III 583–85; 48 292–95 (upd.)
Nilson Group AB, 113 273–76
Niman Ranch, Inc., 67 267–69
Nimbus CD International, Inc., 20 386–90
Nine West Group Inc., 11 348–49; 39 301–03 (upd.)
Nintendo Co., Ltd., III 586–88; 7 394–96 (upd.); 28 317–21 (upd.); 67 270–76 (upd.)
NIOC *see* National Iranian Oil Co.
Nippon Credit Bank, II 338–39
Nippon Electric Glass Co. Ltd., 95 301–05
Nippon Express Company, Ltd., V 477–80; 64 286–90 (upd.)
Nippon Life Insurance Company, III 318–20; 60 218–21 (upd.)
Nippon Light Metal Company, Ltd., IV 153–55
Nippon Meat Packers, Inc., II 550–51; 78 255–57 (upd.)
Nippon Mining Holdings Inc., IV 475–77; 102 306–10 (upd.)
Nippon Oil Corporation, IV 478–79; 63 308–13 (upd.); 120 281–87 (upd.)
Nippon Paint Company Ltd., 115 366–68
Nippon Seiko K.K., III 589–90
Nippon Sheet Glass Company, Limited, III 714–16
Nippon Shinpan Co., Ltd., II 436–37; 61 248–50 (upd.)
Nippon Soda Co., Ltd., 85 303–06
Nippon Steel Corporation, IV 156–58; 17 348–51 (upd.); 96 317–23 (upd.)
Nippon Suisan Kaisha, Limited, II 552–53; 92 269–72 (upd.)
Nippon Telegraph and Telephone Corporation, V 305–07; 51 271–75 (upd.); 117 279–85 (upd.)
Nippon Yusen Kabushiki Kaisha (NYK), V 481–83; 72 244–48 (upd.)
Nippondenso Co., Ltd., III 591–94 *see also* DENSO Corp.
NIPSCO Industries, Inc., 6 532–33
NiSource Inc., 109 416–20 (upd.)
Nissan Motor Company Ltd., I 183–84; 11 350–52 (upd.); 34 303–07 (upd.); 92 273–79 (upd.)
Nisshin Seifun Group Inc., II 554; 66 246–48 (upd.)
Nisshin Steel Co., Ltd., IV 159–60
Nissho Iwai K.K., I 509–11
Nissin Food Products Company Ltd., 75 286–88
Nitches, Inc., 53 245–47
Nixdorf Computer AG, III 154–55 *see also* Wincor Nixdorf Holding GmbH.
NKK Corporation, IV 161–63; 28 322–26 (upd.)
NL Industries, Inc., 10 434–36
Noah Education Holdings Ltd., 97 303–06
Noah's New York Bagels *see* Einstein/Noah Bagel Corp.
Nobel Biocare Holding AG, 119 339–42
Nobel Industries AB, 9 380–82 *see also* Akzo Nobel N.V.
Nobel Learning Communities, Inc., 37 276–79; 76 281–85 (upd.)
Nobia AB, 103 304–07
Noble Affiliates, Inc., 11 353–55
Noble Group Ltd., 111 338–42
Noble Roman's Inc., 14 351–53; 99 297–302 (upd.)
Nobleza Piccardo SAICF, 64 291–93
Noboa *see also* Exportadora Bananera Noboa, S.A.
Nocibé SA, 54 265–68
NOF Corporation, 72 249–51
Nokia Corporation, II 69–71; 17 352–54 (upd.); 38 328–31 (upd.); 77 308–13 (upd.)
NOL Group *see* Neptune Orient Lines Ltd.
Noland Company, 35 311–14; 107 295–99 (upd.)
Nolo.com, Inc., 49 288–91
Nomura Securities Company, Limited, II 438–41; 9 383–86 (upd.)
Noodle Kidoodle, 16 388–91
Noodles & Company, Inc., 55 277–79
Nooter Corporation, 61 251–53
Noranda Inc., IV 164–66; 7 397–99 (upd.); 64 294–98 (upd.)
Norcal Waste Systems, Inc., 60 222–24
The NORDAM Group, Inc., 121 317–20
Norddeutsche Affinerie AG, 62 249–53
Nordea Bank AB, 40 336–39; 117 286–90 (upd.)
Nordex AG, 101 362–65
NordicTrack, 22 382–84 *see also* Icon Health & Fitness, Inc.
Nordisk Film A/S, 80 269–73

O

Occidental Petroleum Corporation, IV 480–82; 25 360–63 (upd.); 71 257–61 (upd.)
Océ N.V., 24 360–63; 91 359–65 (upd.)
Ocean Beauty Seafoods, Inc., 74 209–11
Ocean Bio-Chem, Inc., 103 308–11
Ocean Group plc, 6 415–17 *see also* Exel plc.
Ocean Spray Cranberries, Inc., 7 403–05; 25 364–67 (upd.); 83 284–290
Oceaneering International, Inc., 63 317–19
Ocesa *see* Corporación Interamericana de Entretenimiento, S.A. de C.V.
O'Charley's Inc., 19 286–88; 60 229–32 (upd.)
OCI *see* Orascom Construction Industries S.A.E.
OCLC Online Computer Library Center, Inc., 96 324–28
The O'Connell Companies Inc., 100 306–09
Octel Messaging, 14 354–56; 41 287–90 (upd.)
Ocular Sciences, Inc., 65 273–75
Odakyu Electric Railway Co., Ltd., V 487–89; 68 278–81 (upd.)
Odebrecht S.A., 73 242–44
Odetics Inc., 14 357–59
Odfjell SE, 101 383–87
ODL, Inc., 55 290–92
Odlo Sports Group AG, 120 297–300
Odwalla Inc., 31 349–51; 104 349–53 (upd.)
Odyssey Marine Exploration, Inc., 91 366–70
OEC Medical Systems, Inc., 27 354–56
OENEO S.A., 74 212–15 (upd.)
Office Depot, Inc., 8 404–05; 23 363–65 (upd.); 65 276–80 (upd.)
OfficeMax Incorporated, 15 329–31; 43 291–95 (upd.); 101 388–94 (upd.)
OfficeTiger, LLC, 75 294–96
Officine Alfieri Maserati S.p.A., 13 376–78
Offshore Logistics, Inc., 37 287–89
Ogden Corporation, I 512–14; 6 151–53 *see also* Covanta Energy Corp.
OGF S.A., 113 282–86
Ogilvy Group Inc., I 25–27 *see also* WPP Group.
Oglebay Norton Company, 17 355–58
Oglethorpe Power Corporation, 6 537–38
Ohbayashi Corporation, I 586–87
The Ohio Art Company, 14 360–62; 59 317–20 (upd.)
Ohio Bell Telephone Company, 14 363–65; *see also* Ameritech Corp.
Ohio Casualty Corp., 11 369–70
Ohio Edison Company, V 676–78
Ohio National Financial Services, Inc., 118 327–30
Oil and Natural Gas Commission, IV 483–84; 90 313–17 (upd.)
Oil-Dri Corporation of America, 20 396–99; 89 331–36 (upd.)
Oil States International, Inc., 77 314–17
Oil Transporting Joint Stock Company Transneft, 92450–54
The Oilgear Company, 74 216–18
Oji Paper Co., Ltd., IV 320–22; 57 272–75 (upd.)
OJSC Novolipetsk Steel, 99 311–315
OJSC Wimm-Bill-Dann Foods, 48 436–39
Oki Electric Industry Company, Limited, II 72–74; 15 125; **21** 390
Oklahoma Gas and Electric Company, 6 539–40
Okuma Holdings Inc., 74 219–21
Okura & Co., Ltd., IV 167–68
Olan Mills, Inc., 62 254–56
Old America Stores, Inc., 17 359–61
Old Dominion Freight Line, Inc., 57 276–79
Old Dutch Foods, Inc., 118 331–34
Old Kent Financial Corp., 11 371–72 *see also* Fifth Third Bancorp.
Old Mutual PLC, IV 535; **61 270–72**
Old National Bancorp, 15 332–34; 98 266–70 (upd.)
Old Navy, Inc., 70 210–12
Old Orchard Brands, LLC, 73 245–47
Old Republic International Corporation, 11 373–75; 58 258–61 (upd.)
Old Spaghetti Factory International Inc., 24 364–66
Old Town Canoe Company, 74 222–24
Old Vic Productions plc, 108 371–74
Oldcastle, Inc., 113 287–90
Oldenburg Group Inc., 113 291–95
Olga's Kitchen, Inc., 80 274–76
Olin Corporation, I 379–81; 13 379–81 (upd.); 78 270–74 (upd.)
Olivetti S.p.A., 34 316–20 (upd.)
Olsten Corporation, 6 41–43; 29 362–65 (upd.) *see also* Adecco S.A.
Olympia & York Developments Ltd., IV 720–21; 9 390–92 (upd.)
Olympic Entertainment Group A.S., 117 291–94
Olympus Corporation, 106 332–36
OM Group, Inc., 17 362–64; 78 275–78 (upd.)
OMA *see* Grupo Aeroportuario del Centro Norte, S.A.B. de C.V.
Omaha Steaks International Inc., 62 257–59
Omega Protein Corporation, 99 316–318
O'Melveny & Myers, 37 290–93
Omni Hotels Corp., 12 367–69
Omnicare, Inc., 13 49 307–10; 111 366–70 (upd.)
Omnicell, Inc., 89 337–40
Omnicom Group Inc., I 28–32; 22 394–99 (upd.); 77 318–25 (upd.)
Omnilife *see* Grupo Omnilife S.A. de C.V.
OmniSource Corporation, 14 366–67
OMNOVA Solutions Inc., 59 324–26
Omrix Biopharmaceuticals, Inc., 95 314–17
OMRON Corporation, 28 331–35 (upd.); 115 369–74 (upd.)
Omron Tateisi Electronics Company, II 75–77
OMV AG, IV 485–87; 98 271–74 (upd.)
On Assignment, Inc., 20 400–02
One Price Clothing Stores, Inc., 20 403–05
O'Neal Steel, Inc., 95 306–09
Oneida Ltd., 7 406–08; 31 352–55 (upd.); 88 280–85 (upd.)
ONEOK Inc., 7 409–12; 116 375–81 (upd.)
Onet S.A., 92 292–95
Onex Corporation, 16 395–97; 65 281–85 (upd.)
Onion, Inc., 69 282–84
Onoda Cement Co., Ltd., III 717–19 *see also* Taiheiyo Cement Corp.
Onoken Company Ltd., 110 346–49
Ontario Hydro Services Company, 6 541–42; 32 368–71 (upd.)
Ontario Teachers' Pension Plan, 61 273–75
Onvest Oy, 117 295–99
Onyx Acceptance Corporation, 59 327–29
Onyx Pharmaceuticals, Inc., 110 350–53
Onyx Software Corporation, 53 252–55
OOC Inc., 97 316–19
OPAP S.A. *see* Greek Organization of Football Prognostics S.A. (OPAP)
Opel AG *see* Adam Opel AG.
Open *see* Groupe Open.
Open Text Corporation, 79 301–05
Openwave Systems Inc., 95 318–22
Operadora Mexicana de Aeropuertos *see* Grupo Aeroportuario del Centro Norte, S.A.B. de C.V.
Operation Smile, Inc., 75 297–99
Opinion Research Corporation, 46 318–22
Oplink Communications, Inc., 106 337–41
The Oppenheimer Group, 76 295–98
Oppenheimer Wolff & Donnelly LLP, 71 262–64
Opsware Inc., 49 311–14
OPTEK Technology Inc., 98 275–78
Option Care Inc., 48 307–10
Optische Werke G. Rodenstock, 44 319–23
Opus Corporation, 34 321–23; 101 395–99 (upd.)
Oracle Corporation, 6 272–74; 24 367–71 (upd.); 67 282–87 (upd.)
Orange 21 Inc., 103 312–15
Orange Glo International, 53 256–59
Orange S.A., 84 286–289
Orascom Construction Industries S.A.E., 87 349–352
OraSure Technologies, Inc., 75 300–03
Orbit International Corp., 105 336–39
Orbital Sciences Corporation, 22 400–03; 107 324–30 (upd.)
Orbitz, Inc., 61 276–78

P

The PNC Financial Services Group Inc., **II 342–43**; **13 410–12 (upd.)**; **46 350–53 (upd.)**; **117 321–26 (upd.)**
PNM Resources Inc., **51 296–300 (upd.)**
Pochet SA, **55 307–09**
PODS Enterprises Inc., **103 327–29**
Pogo Producing Company, **39 330–32**
Pohang Iron and Steel Company Ltd., **IV 183–85** *see also* POSCO.
Polar Air Cargo Inc., **60 237–39**
Polaris Industries Inc., **12 399–402**; **35 348–53 (upd.)**; **77 330–37 (upd.)**
Polaroid Corporation, **III 607–09**; **7 436–39 (upd.)**; **28 362–66 (upd.)**; **93 345–53 (upd.)**
Polartec LLC, **98 319–23 (upd.)**
Policy Management Systems Corporation, **11 394–95**
Policy Studies, Inc., **62 277–80**
Poliet S.A., **33 338–40**
Polish & Slavic Federal Credit Union, **113 300–03**
Polk Audio, Inc., **34 352–54**
Polo/Ralph Lauren Corporation, **12 403–05**; **62 281–85 (upd.)**
Polski Koncern Naftowy ORLEN S.A., **77 338–41**
PolyGram N.V., **23 389–92**
PolyMedica Corporation, **77 342–45**
PolyOne Corporation, **87 384–395 (upd.)**
Pomare Ltd., **88 304–07**
Pomeroy Computer Resources, Inc., **33 341–44**
Ponderosa Steakhouse, **15 361–64**
Poof-Slinky, Inc., **61 298–300**
Poore Brothers, Inc., **44 348–50** *see also* The Inventure Group, Inc.
Pop Warner Little Scholars, Inc., **86 335–38**
Pope & Talbot, Inc., **12 406–08**; **61 301–05 (upd.)**
Pope Cable and Wire B.V. *see* Belden CDT Inc.
Pope Resources LP, **74 240–43**
Popular, Inc., **41 311–13**; **108 396–401 (upd.)**
The Porcelain and Fine China Companies Ltd., **69 301–03**
Porr *see* Allgemeine Baugesellschaft – A. Porr AG.
Porsche AG, **13 413–15**; **31 363–66 (upd.)**
The Port Authority of New York and New Jersey, **48 317–20**
Port Imperial Ferry Corporation, **70 226–29**
Portal Software, Inc., **47 300–03**
Portillo's Restaurant Group, Inc., **71 284–86**
Portland General Corporation, **6 548–51**
Portland Trail Blazers, **50 356–60**
Portmeirion Group plc, **88 308–11**
Ports Design Ltd., **117 327–31**
Portucel *see* Grupo Portucel Soporcel.
Portugal Telecom SGPS S.A., **69 304–07**
Posadas *see* Grupo Posadas, S.A. de C.V.
POSCO, **57 287–91 (upd.)**
Positivo Informatica S.A. *see* Grupo Positivo.
Post Office Group, **V 498–501**
Post Properties, Inc., **26 377–79**
La Poste, **V 470–72**
Poste Italiane S.p.A., **108 402–06**
Posterscope Worldwide, **70 230–32**
Posti- Ja Telelaitos, **6 329–31**
Potash Corporation of Saskatchewan Inc., **18 431–33**; **101 409–15 (upd.)**
Potbelly Sandwich Works, Inc., **83 307–310**
Potlatch Corporation, **8 428–30**; **34 355–59 (upd.)**; **87 396–403 (upd.)**
Potomac Electric Power Company, **6 552–54**
Potter & Brumfield Inc., **11 396–98**
Pou Chen Corporation, **81 309–12**
Pou Sheng International Ltd., **110 376–80**
Powell Duffryn plc, **31 367–70**
Powell's Books, Inc., **40 360–63**
Power Corporation of Canada, **36 370–74 (upd.)**; **85 332–39 (upd.)**
Power-One, Inc., **79 334–37**
PowerBar Inc., **44 351–53**
Powergen PLC, **11 399–401**; **50 361–64 (upd.)**
Powerhouse Technologies, Inc., **27 379–81**
POZEN Inc., **81 313–16**
PP&L *see* Pennsylvania Power & Light Co.
PPB Group Berhad, **57 292–95**
PPG Industries, Inc., **III 731–33**; **22 434–37 (upd.)**; **81 317–23 (upd.)**
PPL Corporation, **41 314–17 (upd.)**
PPR S.A., **74 244–48 (upd.)**
PR Newswire, **35 354–56**
Prada Holding B.V., **45 342–45**
Prairie Farms Dairy, Inc., **47 304–07**
Praktiker Bau- und Heimwerkermärkte AG, **103 330–34**
Pranda Jewelry plc, **70 233–35**
Pratt & Whitney, **9 416–18**
Praxair, Inc., **11 402–04**; **48 321–24 (upd.)**; **113 304–09 (upd.)**
Praxis Bookstore Group LLC, **90 339–42**
Pre-Paid Legal Services, Inc., **20 434–37**; **120 321–25 (upd.)**
Precision Castparts Corp., **15 365–67**; **111 397–402 (upd.)**
Precision Foods, Inc., **120 326–29**
Preferred Hotel Group, **103 335–38**
Prelle & Cie *see* Manufacture Prelle & Cie
Premark International, Inc., **III 610–12** *see also* Illinois Tool Works Inc.
Premcor Inc., **37 309–11**
Premier Industrial Corporation, **9 419–21**
Premier Parks, Inc., **27 382–84** *see also* Six Flags, Inc.
Premiere Radio Networks, Inc., **102 335–38**
Premium Brands Holdings Corporation, **114 333–36**
Premium Standard Farms, Inc., **30 353–55**
PremiumWear, Inc., **30 356–59**
Preserver Group, Inc., **44 354–56**
President Casinos, Inc., **22 438–40**
Pressman Toy Corporation, **56 280–82**
Presstek, Inc., **33 345–48**
Preston Corporation, **6 421–23**
Preussag AG, **17 378–82**; **42 279–83 (upd.)**
PreussenElektra Aktiengesellschaft, **V 698–700** *see also* E.On AG.
PRG-Schultz International, Inc., **73 264–67**
Price Communications Corporation, **42 284–86**
The Price Company, **V 162–64** *see also* Costco Wholesale Corp.
Price Pfister, Inc., **70 236–39**
Price Waterhouse LLP, **9 422–24** *see also* PricewaterhouseCoopers
PriceCostco, Inc., **14 393–95** *see also* Costco Wholesale Corp.
Priceline.com Incorporated, **57 296–99**
PriceSmart, Inc., **71 287–90**
PricewaterhouseCoopers, **29 389–94 (upd.)**; **111 403–10 (upd.)**
PRIDE Enterprises *see* Prison Rehabilitative Industries and Diversified Enterprises, Inc.
Pride International, Inc., **78 319–23**
Primark Corp., **13 416–18** *see also* Thomson Corp.
Prime Hospitality Corporation, **52 280–83**
Primedex Health Systems, Inc., **25 382–85**
Primedia Inc., **22 441–43**
Primerica Corporation, **I 612–14**
Prince Sports Group, Inc., **15 368–70**
Princes Ltd., **76 312–14**
Princess Cruise Lines, **22 444–46**
The Princeton Review, Inc., **42 287–90**
Principal Financial Group Inc., **116 395–99**
Principal Mutual Life Insurance Company, **III 328–30**
Printpack, Inc., **68 293–96**
Printrak, A Motorola Company, **44 357–59**
Printronix, Inc., **18 434–36**
PRISA *see*Promotora de Informaciones S.A.
Prison Rehabilitative Industries and Diversified Enterprises, Inc. (PRIDE), **53 277–79**
Pro-Build Holdings Inc., **95 344–48 (upd.)**
Pro-Football, Inc., **121 343–46**
The Procter & Gamble Company, **III 50–53**; **8 431–35 (upd.)**; **26 380–85 (upd.)**; **67 304–11 (upd.)**
Prodigy Communications Corporation, **34 360–62**
Prodware S.A., **102 339–42**
Proeza S.A. de C.V., **82 288–91**

Professional Bull Riders Inc., 55 310–12
The Professional Golfers' Association of America, 41 318–21
Proffitt's, Inc., 19 323–25 *see also* Belk, Inc.
Programmer's Paradise, Inc., 81 324–27
Progress Energy, Inc., 74 249–52
Progress Software Corporation, 15 371–74; 120 330–35 (upd.)
The Progressive Corporation, 11 405–07; 29 395–98 (upd.); 109 451–56 (upd.)
Progressive Enterprises Ltd., 96 339–42
The Progressive Inc., 110 381–84
ProLogis, 57 300–02
Promotora de Informaciones S.A., 121 347–50
Promus Companies, Inc., 9 425–27 *see also* Hilton Hotels Corp.
ProSiebenSat.1 Media AG, 54 295–98
Proskauer Rose LLP, 47 308–10
Prosper De Mulder Limited, 111 411–14
Protection One, Inc., 32 372–75
Provell Inc., 58 276–79 (upd.)
Providence Health System, 90 343–47
The Providence Journal Company, 28 367–69; 30 15
The Providence Service Corporation, 64 309–12
Provident Bankshares Corporation, 85 340–43
Provident Life and Accident Insurance Company of America, III 331–33 *see also* UnumProvident Corp.
Providian Financial Corporation, 52 284–90 (upd.)
Provigo Inc., II 651–53; 51 301–04 (upd.)
Provimi S.A., 80 292–95
PRS *see* Paul Reed Smith Guitar Co.
Prudential Financial Inc., III 337–41; 30 360–64 (upd.); 82 292–98 (upd.)
Prudential plc, III 334–36; 48 325–29 (upd.)
PSA Peugeot Citroen S.A., 28 370–74 (upd.); 54 126
PSF *see* Premium Standard Farms, Inc.
PSI Resources, 6 555–57
Psion PLC, 45 346–49
PSS World Medical, Inc., 115 397–402 (upd.)
Psychemedics Corporation, 89 358–61
Psychiatric Solutions, Inc., 68 297–300
PT Astra International Tbk, 56 283–86
PT Bank Buana Indonesia Tbk, 60 240–42
PT Gudang Garam Tbk, 103 339–42
PT Indosat Tbk, 93 354–57
PT Semen Gresik Tbk, 103 343–46
PTT Public Company Ltd., 56 287–90
Pubco Corporation, 17 383–85
Public Service Company of Colorado, 6 558–60
Public Service Company of New Hampshire, 21 408–12; 55 313–18 (upd.)
Public Service Company of New Mexico, 6 561–64 *see also* PNM Resources Inc.
Public Service Enterprise Group Inc., V 701–03; 44 360–63 (upd.)
Public Storage, Inc., 21 52 291–93
Publicis Groupe, 19 329–32; 77 346–50 (upd.)
Publishers Clearing House, 23 393–95; 64 313–16 (upd.)
Publishers Group, Inc., 35 357–59
Publishing and Broadcasting Limited, 54 299–302
Publix Super Markets, Inc., 7 440–42; 31 371–74 (upd.); 105 345–51 (upd.)
Puck Lazaroff Inc. *see* The Wolfgang Puck Food Company, Inc.
Pueblo Xtra International, Inc., 47 311–13
Puerto Rico Electric Power Authority, 47 314–16
Puget Sound Energy Inc., 6 565–67; 50 365–68 (upd.)
Puig Beauty and Fashion Group S.L., 60 243–46
Pulaski Furniture Corporation, 33 349–52; 80 296–99 (upd.)
Pulitzer Inc., 15 375–77; 58 280–83 (upd.)
Pulsar Internacional S.A., 21 413–15
Pulte Homes, Inc., 8 436–38; 42 291–94 (upd.); 113 310–15 (upd.)
PUMA AG Rudolf Dassler Sport, 35 360–63; 120 336–41 (upd.)
Pumpkin Masters, Inc., 48 330–32
Punch International N.V., 66 258–60
Punch Taverns plc, 70 240–42
Puratos S.A./NV, 92 315–18
Pure World, Inc., 72 285–87
Purina Mills, Inc., 32 376–79
Puritan-Bennett Corporation, 13 419–21
Purolator Products Company, 21 416–18; 74 253–56 (upd.)
Putt-Putt Golf Courses of America, Inc., 23 396–98
PVC Container Corporation, 67 312–14
PW Eagle, Inc., 48 333–36
PWA Group, IV 323–25 *see also* Svenska Cellulosa.
Pyramid Breweries Inc., 33 353–55; 102 343–47 (upd.)
Pyramid Companies, 54 303–05
PZ Cussons plc, 72 288–90

Q

Q.E.P. Co., Inc., 65 292–94
Qantas Airways Ltd., 6 109–13; 24 396–401 (upd.); 68 301–07 (upd.)
Qatar Airways Company Q.C.S.C., 87 404–407
Qatar National Bank SAQ, 87 408–411
Qatar Petroleum, IV 524–26; 98 324–28 (upd.)
Qatar Telecom QSA, 87 412–415
Qdoba Restaurant Corporation, 93 358–62
QIAGEN N.V., 39 333–35; 121 351–55 (upd.>
QLT Inc., 71 291–94
QRS Music Technologies, Inc., 95 349–53
QSC Audio Products, Inc., 56 291–93
QSS Group, Inc., 100 358–61
Quad/Graphics, Inc., 19 333–36
Quaker Chemical Corp., 91 388–91
Quaker Fabric Corp., 19 337–39
Quaker Foods North America, II 558–60; 12 409–12 (upd.); 34 363–67 (upd.); 73 268–73 (upd.)
Quaker State Corporation, 7 443–45; 21 419–22 (upd.) *see also* Pennzoil-Quaker State Co.
QUALCOMM Incorporated, 20 438–41; 47 317–21 (upd.); 114 337–43 (upd.)
Quality Chekd Dairies, Inc., 48 337–39
Quality Dining, Inc., 18 437–40
Quality Food Centers, Inc., 17 386–88 *see also* Kroger Co.
Quality King Distributors, Inc., 114 344–47
Quality Systems, Inc., 81 328–31
Quanex Corporation, 13 422–24; 62 286–89 (upd.)
Quanta Computer Inc., 47 322–24; 110 385–89 (upd.)
Quanta Services, Inc., 79 338–41
Quantum Chemical Corporation, 8 439–41
Quantum Corporation, 10 458–59; 62 290–93 (upd.)
Quark, Inc., 36 375–79
Quebéc Hydro-Electric Commission *see* Hydro-Quebéc.
Quebecor Inc., 12 412–14; 47 325–28 (upd.)
Quelle Group, V 165–67 *see also* Karstadt Quelle AG.
Quest Diagnostics Inc., 26 390–92; 106 383–87 (upd.)
Questar Corporation, 6 568–70; 26 386–89 (upd.)
The Quick & Reilly Group, Inc., 20 442–44
Quick Restaurants S.A., 94 357–60
Quicken Loans, Inc., 93 363–67
Quidel Corporation, 80 300–03
The Quigley Corporation, 62 294–97
Quiksilver, Inc., 18 441–43; 79 342–47 (upd.)
QuikTrip Corporation, 36 380–83
Quill Corporation, 28 375–77; 115 403–06 (upd.)
Quilmes Industrial (QUINSA) S.A., 67 315–17
Quinn Emanuel Urquhart Oliver & Hedges, LLP, 99 350–353
Quintiles Transnational Corporation, 21 423–25; 68 308–12 (upd.)
Quixote Corporation, 15 378–80
Quiznos Corporation, 42 295–98; 117 332–37 (upd.)
Quovadx Inc., 70 243–46
QVC Inc., 9 428–29; 58 284–87 (upd.)

Qwest Communications International, Inc., 37 312–17; 116 400–05 (upd.)

R

R&B, Inc., 51 305–07
R&R Partners Inc., 108 407–10
R.B. Pamplin Corp., 45 350–52
R.C. Bigelow, Inc., 49 334–36
R.C. Willey Home Furnishings, 72 291–93
R.G. Barry Corp., 17 389–91; 44 364–67 (upd.)
R. Griggs Group Limited, 23 399–402; 31 413–14
R.H. Kuhn Company, Inc., 117 338–41
R.H. Macy & Co., Inc., V 168–70; 8 442–45 (upd.); 30 379–83 (upd.) *see also* Macy's, Inc.
R.J. Reynolds Tobacco Holdings, Inc., 30 384–87 (upd.)
R. M. Palmer Co., 89 362–64
R.P. Scherer Corporation, I 678–80 *see also* Cardinal Health, Inc.
R.R. Bowker LLC, 100 362–66
R.R. Donnelley & Sons Company, IV 660–62; 38 368–71 (upd.); 113 316–21 (upd.)
R.T. Vanderbilt Company, Inc., 117 342–45
Rabobank Group, 26 419; **33 356–58; 116 406–09 (upd.)**
RAC *see* Roy Anderson Corp.
Racal-Datacom Inc., 11 408–10
Racal Electronics PLC, II 83–84 *see also* Thales S.A.
RaceTrac Petroleum, Inc., 111 415–18
Racing Champions Corporation, 37 318–20
Rack Room Shoes, Inc., 84 314–317
Radeberger Gruppe AG, 75 332–35
Radian Group Inc., 42 299–301 *see also* Onex Corp.
Radiant Systems Inc., 104 383–87
Radiation Therapy Services, Inc., 85 344–47
@radical.media, 103 347–50
Radio Flyer Inc., 34 368–70; 118 366–69 (upd.)
Radio One, Inc., 67 318–21
RadioShack Corporation, 36 384–88 (upd.); 101 416–23 (upd.)
Radius Inc., 16 417–19
RAE Systems Inc., 83 311–314
RAG AG, 35 364–67; 60 247–51 (upd.)
Rag Shops, Inc., 30 365–67
Ragdoll Productions Ltd., 51 308–11
Raha-automaattiyhdistys (RAY), 110 390–94
Raiffeisen Zentralbank Österreich AG, 85 348–52
RailAmerica, Inc., 116 410–14
RailTex, Inc., 20 445–47
Railtrack Group PLC, 50 369–72
Rain Bird Corporation, 84 318–321
Rainbow Media Holdings LLC, 109 457–60
Rainforest Café, Inc., 25 386–88; 88 312–16 (upd.)
Rainier Brewing Company, 23 403–05
Raisio PLC, 99 354–357
Rakuten Inc., 118 370–73
Raleigh UK Ltd., 65 295–97
Raley's Inc., 14 396–98; 58 288–91 (upd.)
Rallye SA, 54 306–09
Rally's, 25 389–91; 68 313–16 (upd.)
Ralph Lauren *see* Polo/Ralph Lauren Corportion.
Ralphs Grocery Company, 35 368–70
Ralston Purina Company, II 561–63; 13 425–27 (upd.) *see also* Ralcorp Holdings, Inc.; Nestlé S.A.
Ramsay Youth Services, Inc., 41 322–24
Ramtron International Corporation, 89 365–68
Ranbaxy Laboratories Ltd., 70 247–49
RAND Corporation, 112 307–10
Rand McNally and Co., 28 378–81; 120 342–47 (upd.)
Randall's Food Markets, Inc., 40 364–67 *see also* Safeway Inc.
Random House Inc., 13 428–30; 31 375–80 (upd.); 106 388–98 (upd.)
Randon S.A. Implementos e Participações, 79 348–52
Randstad Holding nv, 16 420–22; 43 307–10 (upd.); 113 322–26 (upd.)
Range Resources Corporation, 45 353–55
The Rank Group plc, II 157–59; 14 399–402 (upd.); 64 317–21 (upd.)
Ranks Hovis McDougall Limited, II 564–65; 28 382–85 (upd.)
RAO Unified Energy System of Russia, 45 356–60
Rapala-Normark Group, Ltd., 30 368–71
Rare Hospitality International Inc., 19 340–42
RAS *see* Riunione Adriatica di Sicurtà SpA.
Rascal House *see* Jerry's Famous Deli Inc.
Rasmussen Group *see* K.A. Rasmussen AS.
Rathbone Brothers plc, 70 250–53
RathGibson Inc., 90 348–51
ratiopharm Group, 84 322–326
Ratner Companies, 72 294–96
Rautakirja Oy, 104 388–92
Rautaruukki Oyj, 115 407–10
Raven Industries, Inc., 33 359–61; 120 348–52 (upd.)
Ravensburger AG, 64 322–26
Raving Brands, Inc., 64 327–29
Rawlings Sporting Goods Company, 24 402–04; 107 368–72 (upd.)
Raychem Corporation, 8 446–47
Raycom Media, Inc., 106 399–402
Raymarine plc, 104 393–96
Raymond James Financial Inc., 69 308–10
Raymond Ltd., 77 351–54
Rayonier Inc., 24 405–07
Rayovac Corporation, 13 431–34; 39 336–40 (upd.) *see also* Spectrum Brands.
Raytech Corporation, 61 306–09
Raytheon Aircraft Holdings Inc., 46 354–57
Raytheon Company, II 85–87; 11 411–14 (upd.); 38 372–77 (upd.); 105 352–59 (upd.)
Razorfish, Inc., 37 321–24
RCA Corporation, II 88–90
RCM Technologies, Inc., 34 371–74
RCN Corporation, 70 254–57
RCS MediaGroup S.p.A., 96 343–46
RDO Equipment Company, 33 362–65
RE/MAX International, Inc., 59 344–46
Read-Rite Corp., 10 463–64
The Reader's Digest Association, Inc., IV 663–64; 17 392–95 (upd.); 71 295–99 (upd.)
Reading International Inc., 70 258–60
The Real Good Food Company plc, 99 358–361
Real Madrid C.F., 73 274–76
Real Times, Inc., 66 261–65
Real Turismo, S.A. de C.V., 50 373–75
The Really Useful Group, 26 393–95
RealNetworks, Inc., 53 280–82; 109 461–68 (upd.)
Realogy Corporation, 112 311–14
Reckitt Benckiser plc, II 566–67; 42 302–06 (upd.); 91 392–99 (upd.)
Reckson Associates Realty Corp., 47 329–31
Recordati Industria Chimica e Farmaceutica S.p.A., 105 360–64
Recording for the Blind & Dyslexic, 51 312–14
Recoton Corp., 15 381–83
Recovery Engineering, Inc., 25 392–94
Recreational Equipment, Inc., 18 444–47; 71 300–03 (upd.)
Recycled Paper Greetings, Inc., 21 426–28
Red Apple Group, Inc., 23 406–08
Red Bull GmbH, 60 252–54
Red Hat, Inc., 45 361–64
Red McCombs Automotive Group, 91 400–03
Red Robin Gourmet Burgers, Inc., 56 294–96; 121 356–60 (upd.>
Red Roof Inns, Inc., 18 448–49 *see also* Accor S.A.
Red Spot Paint & Varnish Company, Inc., 55 319–22; 112 315–19 (upd.)
Red Wing Pottery Sales, Inc., 52 294–96
Red Wing Shoe Company, Inc., 9 433–35; 30 372–75 (upd.); 83 315–321 (upd.)
Redback Networks, Inc., 92 319–22
Redcats S.A., 102 348–52
Reddy Ice Holdings, Inc., 80 304–07
Redflex Holdings Limited, 116 415–18
Redhook Ale Brewery, Inc., 31 381–84; 88 317–21 (upd.)
Redken Laboratories Inc., 84 327–330
Redland plc, III 734–36 *see also* Lafarge Cement UK.
Redlon & Johnson, Inc., 97 331–34
Redner's Markets Inc., 111 419–22
RedPeg Marketing, 73 277–79

S

Softbank Corporation, 13 481–83; 38 439–44 (upd.); 77 387–95 (upd.)
Sohu.com Inc., 119 419–22
Sojitz Corporation, 96 395–403 (upd.)
Sol Meliá S.A., 71 337–39
Sola International Inc., 71 340–42
Solar Turbines Inc., 100 402–06
Solarfun Power Holdings Co., Ltd., 105 429–33
SolarWinds, Inc., 116 447–50
Sole Technology Inc., 93 405–09
Solectron Corporation, 12 450–52; 48 366–70 (upd.)
Solo Cup Company, 104 424–27
Solo Serve Corporation, 28 429–31
Solutia Inc., 52 312–15
Solvay & Cie S.A., I 394–96; 21 464–67 (upd.)
Solvay S.A., 61 329–34 (upd.)
Somerfield plc, 47 365–69 (upd.)
Sommer-Allibert S.A., 19 406–09 *see also* Tarkett Sommer AG.
Sompo Japan Insurance, Inc., 98 359–63 (upd.)
Sonae SGPS, S.A., 97 378–81
Sonat, Inc., 6 577–78 *see also* El Paso Corp.
Sonatrach, 65 313–17 (upd.)
Sonera Corporation, 50 441–44 *see also* TeliaSonera AB.
Sonesta International Hotels Corporation, 44 389–91
Sonic Automotive, Inc., 77 396–99
Sonic Corp., 14 451–53; 37 360–63 (upd.); 103 386–91 (upd.)
Sonic Innovations Inc., 56 336–38
Sonic Solutions, Inc., 81 375–79
SonicWALL, Inc., 87 421–424
Sonnenschein Nath and Rosenthal LLP, 102 384–87
Sonoco Products Company, 8 475–77; 89 415–22 (upd.)
SonoSite, Inc., 56 339–41
Sony Corporation, II 101–03; 12 453–56 (upd.); 40 404–10 (upd.); 108 460–69 (upd.)
Sophus Berendsen A/S, 49 374–77
Sorbee International Ltd., 74 309–11
Soriana *see* Organización Soriana S.A.B. de C.V.
Soros Fund Management LLC, 28 432–34
Sorrento, Inc., 19 51; **24 444–46**
SOS Staffing Services, 25 432–35
Sotheby's Holdings, Inc., 11 452–54; 29 445–48 (upd.); 84 360–365 (upd.)
Soufflet SA *see* Groupe Soufflet SA.
Sound Advice, Inc., 41 379–82
Souper Salad, Inc., 98 364–67
The Source Enterprises, Inc., 65 318–21
Source Interlink Companies, Inc., 75 350–53
The South African Breweries Limited, I 287–89; 24 447–51 (upd.) *see also* SABMiller plc.
South Beach Beverage Company, Inc., 73 316–19
South Dakota Wheat Growers Association, 94 397–401
South Jersey Industries, Inc., 42 352–55
Southam Inc., 7 486–89 *see also* CanWest Global Communications Corp.
Southcorp Limited, 54 341–44
Southdown, Inc., 14 454–56 *see also* CEMEX S.A. de C.V.
Southeast Frozen Foods Company, L.P., 99 423–426
The Southern Company, V 721–23; 38 445–49 (upd.)
Southern Connecticut Gas Company, 84 366–370
Southern Electric PLC, 13 484–86 *see also* Scottish and Southern Energy plc.
Southern Financial Bancorp, Inc., 56 342–44
Southern Indiana Gas and Electric Company, 13 487–89 *see also* Vectren Corp.
Southern New England Telecommunications Corporation, 6 338–40
Southern Pacific Transportation Company, V 516–18 *see also* Union Pacific Corp.
Southern Peru Copper Corporation, 40 411–13
Southern Poverty Law Center, Inc., 74 312–15
Southern Progress Corporation, 102 388–92
Southern States Cooperative Incorporated, 36 440–42
Southern Sun Hotel Interest (Pty) Ltd., 106 435–39
Southern Union Company, 27 424–26
Southern Wine and Spirits of America, Inc., 84 371–375
The Southland Corporation, II 660–61; 7 490–92 (upd.) *see also* 7–Eleven, Inc.
Southtrust Corporation, 11 455–57 *see also* Wachovia Corp.
Southwest Airlines Co., 6 119–21; 24 452–55 (upd.); 71 343–47 (upd.)
Southwest Gas Corporation, 19 410–12
Southwest Water Company, 47 370–73
Southwestern Bell Corporation, V 328–30 *see also* SBC Communications Inc.
Southwestern Electric Power Co., 21 468–70
Southwestern Public Service Company, 6 579–81
Southwire Company, Inc., 8 478–80; 23 444–47 (upd.)
Souza Cruz S.A., 65 322–24
Sovereign Bancorp, Inc., 103 392–95
Sovran Self Storage, Inc., 66 299–301
SP Alpargatas *see* Sao Paulo Alpargatas S.A.
Spacehab, Inc., 37 364–66
Spacelabs Medical, Inc., 71 348–50
Spadel S.A./NV, 113 363–67
Spaghetti Warehouse, Inc., 25 436–38
Spago *see* The Wolfgang Puck Food Company, Inc.
Spangler Candy Company, 44 392–95
Spanish Broadcasting System, Inc., 41 383–86
Spansion Inc., 80 352–55
Spanx, Inc., 89 423–27
Spar Aerospace Limited, 32 435–37
Spar Handelsgesellschaft mbH, 35 398–401; 103 396–400 (upd.)
Spark Networks, Inc., 91 437–40
Spartan Motors Inc., 14 457–59
Spartan Stores Inc., 8 481–82; 66 302–05 (upd.)
Spartech Corporation, 19 413–15; 76 329–32 (upd.)
Sparton Corporation, 18 492–95
Spear & Jackson, Inc., 73 320–23
Spear, Leeds & Kellogg, 66 306–09
Special Broadcasting Service Corporation, 115 433–36
Special Olympics, Inc., 93 410–14
Specialist Computer Holdings Ltd., 80 356–59
Specialized Bicycle Components Inc., 50 445–48
Specialty Coatings Inc., 8 483–84
Specialty Equipment Companies, Inc., 25 439–42
Specialty Products & Insulation Co., 59 381–83
Spec's Music, Inc., 19 416–18 *see also* Camelot Music, Inc.
Specsavers Optical Group Ltd., 104 428–31
Spector Photo Group N.V., 82 344–47
Spectra Energy Corporation, 116 451–54
Spectrum Brands, Inc., 109 514–20 (upd.)
Spectrum Control, Inc., 67 355–57
Spectrum Organic Products, Inc., 68 346–49
Spee-Dee Delivery Service, Inc., 93 415–18
SpeeDee Oil Change and Tune-Up, 25 443–47
Speedway Motorsports, Inc., 32 438–41; 112 396–400 (upd.)
Speedy Hire plc, 84 376–379
Speidel Inc., 96 404–07
Speizman Industries, Inc., 44 396–98
Spelling Entertainment, 14 460–62; 35 402–04 (upd.)
Spencer Stuart and Associates, Inc., 14 463–65 *see also* SSI (U.S.), Inc.
Sperian Protection S.A., 104 432–36
Spherion Corporation, 52 316–18
Spicy Pickle Franchising, Inc., 105 434–37
Spie *see* Amec Spie S.A.
Spiegel, Inc., 10 489–91; 27 427–31 (upd.)
SPIEGEL-Verlag Rudolf Augstein GmbH & Co. KG, 44 399–402
Spin Master, Ltd., 61 335–38
Spinnaker Exploration Company, 72 334–36

Sunshine Village Corporation, **103** 415–18
Sunsweet Growers *see* Diamond of California.
Suntech Power Holdings Company Ltd., **89** 432–35
Sunterra Corporation, **75** 354–56
Suntory Ltd., **65** 328–31
Suntron Corporation, **107** 421–24
SunTrust Banks Inc., **23** 455–58; **101** 458–64 (upd.)
SunWize Technologies, Inc., **114** 398–402
Super 8 Motels, Inc., **83** 381–385
Super Food Services, Inc., **15** 479–81
Supercuts Inc., **26** 475–78
Superdrug Stores PLC, **95** 390–93
Superior Energy Services, Inc., **65** 332–34
Superior Essex Inc., **80** 364–68
Superior Industries International, Inc., **8** 505–07
Superior Uniform Group, Inc., **30** 455–57
Supermarkets General Holdings Corporation, **II** 672–74 *see also* Pathmark Stores, Inc.
SUPERVALU INC., **II** 668–71; **18** 503–08 (upd.); **50** 453–59 (upd.); **114** 403–12 (upd.)
Suprema Specialties, Inc., **27** 440–42
Supreme International Corporation, **27** 443–46 *see also* Perry Ellis International Inc.
Suramericana de Inversiones S.A., **88** 389–92
Surrey Satellite Technology Limited, **83** 386–390
The Susan G. Komen Breast CancerFoundation, **78** 373–76
Susquehanna Pfaltzgraff Company, **8** 508–10
Susser Holdings Corporation, **114** 413–16
Sutherland Lumber Company, L.P., **99** 431–434
Sutter Home Winery Inc., **16** 476–78 *see also* Trinchero Family Estates.
Suzano *see* Companhia Suzano de Papel e Celulose S.A.
Suzuki Motor Corporation, **9** 487–89; **23** 459–62 (upd.); **59** 393–98 (upd.)
SVB Financial Group, **109** 521–25
Sveaskog AB, **93** 430–33
Svenska Cellulosa Aktiebolaget SCA, **IV** 338–40; **28** 443–46 (upd.); **85** 413–20 (upd.)
Svenska Handelsbanken AB, **II** 365–67; **50** 460–63 (upd.)
Svenska Spel AB, **107** 425–28
Sverdrup Corporation, **14** 475–78 *see also* Jacobs Engineering Group Inc.
Sveriges Riksbank, **96** 418–22
SVP Worldwide LLC, **113** 384–89
SWA *see* Southwest Airlines.
Swagelok Company, **120** 425–29
SWALEC *see* Scottish and Southern Energy plc.
Swales & Associates, Inc., **69** 336–38
Swank, Inc., **17** 464–66; **84** 380–384 (upd.)
Swarovski International Holding AG, **40** 422–25 *see also* D. Swarovski & Co.
The Swatch Group Ltd., **26** 479–81; **107** 429–33 (upd.)
Swedish Match AB, **12** 462–64; **39** 387–90 (upd.); **92** 349–55 (upd.)
Swedish Telecom, **V** 331–33
SwedishAmerican Health System, **51** 363–66
Sweet Candy Company, **60** 295–97
Sweetbay Supermarket, **103** 419–24 (upd.)
Sweetheart Cup Company, Inc., **36** 460–64
The Swett & Crawford Group Inc., **84** 385–389
SWH Corporation, **70** 307–09
Swift & Company, **55** 364–67
Swift Energy Company, **63** 364–66
Swift Transportation Co., Inc., **42** 363–66
Swinerton Inc., **43** 397–400
Swire Pacific Ltd., **I** 521–22; **16** 479–81 (upd.); **57** 348–53 (upd.)
Swisher International Group Inc., **23** 463–65
Swiss Air Transport Company Ltd., **I** 121–22
Swiss Army Brands, Inc. *see* Victorinox AG.
Swiss Bank Corporation, **II** 368–70 *see also* UBS AG.
The Swiss Colony, Inc., **97** 395–98
Swiss Federal Railways (Schweizerische Bundesbahnen), **V** 519–22
Swiss International Air Lines Ltd., **48** 379–81
Swiss Reinsurance Company (Schweizerische Rückversicherungs-Gesellschaft), **III** 375–78; **46** 380–84 (upd.)
Swiss Valley Farms Company, **90** 400–03
Swisscom AG, **58** 336–39
Swissport International Ltd., **70** 310–12
Sybase, Inc., **10** 504–06; **27** 447–50 (upd.)
Sybron International Corp., **14** 479–81
Sycamore Networks, Inc., **45** 388–91
Syco Entertainment, Ltd., **118** 421–26
Sykes Enterprises, Inc., **45** 392–95
Sylvan, Inc., **22** 496–99
Sylvan Learning Systems, Inc., **35** 408–11 *see also* Educate Inc.
Sylvia Woods, Inc., **121** 401–03
Symantec Corporation, **10** 507–09; **82** 372–77 (upd.)
Symbol Technologies, Inc., **15** 482–84 *see also* Motorola, Inc.
Symrise GmbH and Company KG, **89** 436–40
Syms Corporation, **29** 456–58; **74** 327–30 (upd.)
Symyx Technologies, Inc., **77** 420–23
Synaptics Incorporated, **95** 394–98
Synchronoss Technologies, Inc., **95** 399–402
Syneron Medical Ltd., **91** 471–74
Syngenta International AG, **83** 391–394
Syniverse Holdings Inc., **97** 399–402
SYNNEX Corporation, **73** 328–30
Synopsys, Inc., **11** 489–92; **69** 339–43 (upd.)
SynOptics Communications, Inc., **10** 510–12
Synovus Financial Corp., **12** 465–67; **52** 336–40 (upd.)
Syntax-Brillian Corporation, **102** 405–09
Syntel, Inc., **92** 356–60
Syntex Corporation, **I** 701–03
Synthes, Inc., **93** 434–37
Sypris Solutions, Inc., **85** 421–25
SyQuest Technology, Inc., **18** 509–12
Syral S.A.S., **113** 390–93
Syratech Corp., **14** 482–84
SYSCO Corporation, **II** 675–76; **24** 470–72 (upd.); **75** 357–60 (upd.)
System Software Associates, Inc., **10** 513–14
Systemax, Inc., **52** 341–44
Systembolaget AB, **113** 394–98
Systems & Computer Technology Corp., **19** 437–39
Sytner Group plc, **45** 396–98
Szerencsejáték Zrt., **113** 399–402

T

T&D Holdings Inc., **114** 417–21
T-Netix, Inc., **46** 385–88
T-Online International AG, **61** 349–51
T.J. Maxx *see* The TJX Companies, Inc.
T. Marzetti Company, **57** 354–56
T. Rowe Price Associates, Inc., **11** 493–96; **34** 423–27 (upd.)
T-3 Energy Services, Inc., **119** 441–44
TA Triumph-Adler AG, **48** 382–85
TAB Products Co., **17** 467–69
Tabacalera, S.A., **V** 414–16; **17** 470–73 (upd.) *see also* Altadis S.A.
TABCORP Holdings Limited, **44** 407–10
Tabio Corporation, **120** 430–34
TACA *see* Grupo TACA.
Taco Bell Corporation, **7** 505–07; **21** 485–88 (upd.); **74** 331–34 (upd.)
Taco Cabana, Inc., **23** 466–68; **72** 344–47 (upd.)
Taco John's International Inc., **15** 485–87; **63** 367–70 (upd.)
Tacony Corporation, **70** 313–15
TADANO Ltd., **119** 445–49
TAG Heuer S.A., **25** 459–61; **77** 424–28 (upd.)
Tag-It Pacific, Inc., **85** 426–29
Taiheiyo Cement Corporation, **60** 298–301 (upd.)
Taittinger S.A., **43** 401–05
Taiwan Semiconductor Manufacturing Company Ltd., **47** 383–87
Taiwan Tobacco & Liquor Corporation, **75** 361–63

Vestey Group Ltd., **95** 433–37
Vêt'Affaires S.A., **120** 472–75
Veuve Clicquot Ponsardin SCS, **98** 447–51
VEW AG, **39** 412–15
VF Corporation, **V** 390–92; **17** 511–14 (upd.); **54** 398–404 (upd.); **119** 506–14 (upd.)
VHA Inc., **53** 345–47
Viacom Inc., **7** 560–62; **23** 500–03 (upd.); **67** 367–71 (upd.) *see also* Paramount Pictures Corp.
Viad Corp., **73** 376–78
Viag AG, **IV** 229–32 *see also* E.On AG.
ViaSat, Inc., **54** 405–08
Viasoft Inc., **27** 490–93; **59** 27
VIASYS Healthcare, Inc., **52** 389–91
Viasystems Group, Inc., **67** 372–74
Viatech Continental Can Company, Inc., **25** 512–15 (upd.)
Vicarious Visions, Inc., **108** 529–32
Vicat S.A., **70** 341–43
Vickers plc, **27** 494–97
Vicon Industries, Inc., **44** 440–42
VICORP Restaurants, Inc., **12** 510–12; **48** 412–15 (upd.)
Victor Company of Japan, Limited, **II** 118–19; **26** 511–13 (upd.); **83** 444–449 (upd.)
Victoria Coach Station Ltd.*see* London Regional Transport.
Victoria Group, **III** 399–401; **44** 443–46 (upd.)
Victorinox AG, **21** 515–17; **74** 375–78 (upd.)
Victory Refrigeration, Inc., **82** 403–06
Vicunha Têxtil S.A., **78** 441–44
Videojet Technologies, Inc., **90** 424–27
Vidrala S.A., **67** 375–77
Viel & Cie, **76** 372–74
Vienna Sausage Manufacturing Co., **14** 536–37
Viessmann Werke GmbH & Co., **37** 411–14
Viewpoint International, Inc., **66** 354–56
ViewSonic Corporation, **72** 365–67
Viking Office Products, Inc., **10** 544–46 *see also* Office Depot, Inc.
Viking Range Corporation, **66** 357–59
Viking Yacht Company, **96** 446–49
Village Roadshow Ltd., **58** 356–59
Village Super Market, Inc., **7** 563–64
Village Voice Media, Inc., **38** 476–79
Villeroy & Boch AG, **37** 415–18
Vilmorin Clause et Cie, **70** 344–46
Vilter Manufacturing, LLC, **105** 475–79
Vin & Spirit AB, **31** 458–61 *see also* V&S Vin & Sprit AB.
Viña Concha y Toro S.A., **45** 432–34
Viña San Pedro Tarapacá S.A., **119** 515–19
Vinci S.A., **27** 54; **43** 450–52; **113** 455–59 (upd.)
Vincor International Inc., **50** 518–21
Vinmonopolet A/S, **100** 434–37
Vinson & Elkins L.L.P., **30** 481–83
Vintage Petroleum, Inc., **42** 421–23
Vinton Studios, **63** 420–22
Vion Food Group NV, **85** 438–41
Virbac Corporation, **74** 379–81
Virco Manufacturing Corporation, **17** 515–17
Virgin Group Ltd., **12** 513–15; **32** 491–96 (upd.); **89** 479–86 (upd.)
Virginia Dare Extract Company, Inc., **94** 447–50
Viridian Group plc, **64** 402–04
Visa Inc., **9** 536–38; **26** 514–17 (upd.); **104** 464–69 (upd.)
Viscofan S.A., **70** 347–49
Vishay Intertechnology, Inc., **21** 518–21; **80** 401–06 (upd.)
Vision Service Plan Inc., **77** 473–76
Viskase Companies, Inc., **55** 379–81
Vista Bakery, Inc., **56** 365–68
Vista Chemical Company, **I** 402–03
Vistana, Inc., **22** 537–39
VistaPrint Limited, **87** 451–454
Visteon Corporation, **109** 572–76
VISX, Incorporated, **30** 484–86
Vita Food Products Inc., **99** 478–481
Vita Plus Corporation, **60** 315–17
Vitacost.com Inc., **116** 455–58
Vital Images, Inc., **85** 442–45
Vitalink Pharmacy Services, Inc., **15** 522–24
Vitamin Shoppe Industries, Inc., **60** 318–20
Vitasoy International Holdings Ltd., **94** 451–54
Viterra Inc., **105** 480–83
Vitesse Semiconductor Corporation, **32** 497–500
Vitro Corp., **10** 547–48
Vitro Corporativo S.A. de C.V., **34** 490–92
Vivarte SA, **54** 409–12 (upd.)
Vivartia S.A., **82** 407–10
Vivendi, **46** 438–41 (upd.); **112** 462–68 (upd.)
Vivra, Inc., **18** 545–47 *see also* Gambro AB.
Vizio, Inc., **100** 438–41
Vlasic Foods International Inc., **25** 516–19
VLSI Technology, Inc., **16** 518–20
VMware, Inc., **90** 428–31
VNU N.V., **27** 498–501
VNUS Medical Technologies, Inc., **103** 485–88
Vocento, **94** 455–58
Vocus, Inc., **121** 430–33
Vodacom Group Pty. Ltd., **106** 481–85
Vodafone Group Plc, **11** 547–48; **36** 503–06 (upd.); **75** 395–99 (upd.)
voestalpine AG, **IV** 233–35; **57** 399–403 (upd.); **115** 473–78 (upd.)
Voith Sulzer Papiermaschinen GmbH *see* J.M. Voith AG.
Volcan Compañia Minera S.A.A., **92** 403–06
Volcom, Inc., **77** 477–80
Volga-Dnepr Group, **82** 411–14
Volkert and Associates, Inc., **98** 452–55
Volkswagen Aktiengesellschaft, **I** 206–08; **11** 549–51 (upd.); **32** 501–05 (upd.); **111** 519–25 (upd.)
Volt Information Sciences Inc., **26** 518–21
Volunteers of America, Inc., **66** 360–62
Von Maur Inc., **64** 405–08
Vonage Holdings Corp., **81** 415–18
The Vons Companies, Inc., **7** 569–71; **28** 510–13 (upd.); **103** 489–95 (upd.)
Vontobel Holding AG, **96** 450–53
Voortman Cookies Limited, **103** 496–99
Vornado Realty Trust, **20** 508–10; **112** 469–74 (upd.)
Vorwerk & Co. KG, **27** 502–04; **112** 475–79 (upd.)
Vosper Thornycroft Holding plc, **41** 410–12
Vossloh AG, **53** 348–52
Votorantim Participaçoes S.A., **76** 375–78
Vought Aircraft Industries, Inc., **49** 442–45
Vranken Pommery Monopole S.A., **114** 501–05
VSE Corporation, **108** 533–36
VSM *see* Village Super Market, Inc.
VTech Holdings Ltd., **77** 481–84
Vueling Airlines S.A., **97** 445–48
Vulcabras S.A., **103** 500–04
Vulcan Materials Company, **7** 572–75; **52** 392–96 (upd.)

W

W + K *see* Wieden + Kennedy.
W.A. Whitney Company, **53** 353–56
W. Atlee Burpee & Co., **27** 505–08
W.B Doner & Co., **56** 369–72
W.B. Mason Company, **98** 456–59
W.C. Bradley Co., **69** 363–65
W.H. Brady Co., **16** 518–21 *see also* Brady Corp.
W. H. Braum, Inc., **80** 407–10
W H Smith Group PLC, **V** 211–13
W Jordan (Cereals) Ltd., **74** 382–84
W.L. Gore & Associates, Inc., **14** 538–40; **60** 321–24 (upd.)
W.P. Carey & Co. LLC, **49** 446–48
W.R. Berkley Corporation, **15** 525–27; **74** 385–88 (upd.)
W.R. Grace & Company, **I** 547–50; **50** 522–29 (upd.)
W.S. Badcock Corporation, **107** 461–64
W.W. Grainger, Inc., **V** 214–15; **26** 537–39 (upd.); **68** 392–95 (upd.)
W.W. Norton & Company, Inc., **28** 518–20
Waban Inc., **13** 547–49 *see also* HomeBase, Inc.
Wabash National Corp., **13** 550–52
Wabtec Corporation, **40** 451–54
Wachovia Bank of Georgia, N.A., **16** 521–23
Wachovia Bank of South Carolina, N.A., **16** 524–26
Wachovia Corporation, **12** 516–20; **46** 442–49 (upd.)

Index to Industries

Accounting

American Institute of Certified Public Accountants (AICPA), 44
Andersen, 29 (upd.); 68 (upd.)
Automatic Data Processing, Inc., III; 9 (upd.); 47 (upd.)
BDO Seidman LLP, 96
BKD LLP, 96
CPP International, LLC, 103
CROSSMARK, 79
Deloitte Touche Tohmatsu International, 9; 29 (upd.)
Ernst & Young Global Limited, 9; 29 (upd.); 108 (upd.)
FTI Consulting, Inc., 77
Grant Thornton International, 57
Huron Consulting Group Inc., 87
JKH Holding Co. LLC, 105
KPMG International, 33 (upd.); 108 (upd.)
L.S. Starrett Co., 13
LarsonAllen, LLP, 118
McLane Company, Inc., 13
NCO Group, Inc., 42
Paychex Inc., 15; 46 (upd.); 120 (upd.)
PKF International, 78
Plante & Moran, LLP, 71
PRG-Schultz International, Inc., 73
PricewaterhouseCoopers International Limited, 9; 29 (upd.); 111 (upd.)
Resources Connection, Inc., 81
Robert Wood Johnson Foundation, 35
RSM McGladrey Business Services Inc., 98
Saffery Champness, 80
Sanders\Wingo, 99
Schenck Business Solutions, 88
StarTek, Inc., 79
Travelzoo Inc., 79
Univision Communications Inc., 24; 83 (upd.)

Advertising & Business Services

1-800-FLOWERS.COM, Inc., 26; 102 (upd.)
4imprint Group PLC, 105
24/7 Real Media, Inc., 49
ABM Industries Incorporated, 25 (upd.)
Abt Associates Inc., 95
Accenture Ltd., 108 (upd.)
AchieveGlobal Inc., 90
Ackerley Communications, Inc., 9
ACNielsen Corporation, 13; 38 (upd.)
Acosta Sales and Marketing Company, Inc., 77
Acsys, Inc., 44
Adecco S.A., 36 (upd.); 116 (upd.)
Adelman Travel Group, 105
Adia S.A., 6
Administaff, Inc., 52
The Advertising Council, Inc., 76
The Advisory Board Company, 80
Advo, Inc., 6; 53 (upd.)
Aegis Group plc, 6
Affiliated Computer Services, Inc., 61
Affinion Group, Inc., 121
AHL Services, Inc., 27
Alibaba.com, Ltd., 119
Allegis Group, Inc., 95
Alloy, Inc., 55
Amdocs Ltd., 47
American Building Maintenance Industries, Inc., 6
Amey Plc, 47
Analysts International Corporation, 36
aQuantive, Inc., 81
The Arbitron Company, 38
Ariba, Inc., 57
Armor Holdings, Inc., 27
Asatsu-DK Inc., 82
Ashtead Group plc, 34
Avalon Correctional Services, Inc., 75
Bain & Company, 55
Barrett Business Services, Inc., 16
Barton Protective Services Inc., 53
Bates Worldwide, Inc., 14; 33 (upd.)
Bearings, Inc., 13
Berlitz International, Inc., 13; 39 (upd.)
Bernard Hodes Group Inc., 86
Bernstein-Rein, 92
Big Flower Press Holdings, Inc., 21
Billing Concepts, Inc., 26; 72 (upd.)
Billing Services Group Ltd., 102
The BISYS Group, Inc., 73
Booz Allen Hamilton Inc., 10; 101 (upd.)
Boron, LePore & Associates, Inc., 45
The Boston Consulting Group, 58
Bozell Worldwide Inc., 25
BrandPartners Group, Inc., 58
Bright Horizons Family Solutions, Inc., 31
Broadcast Music Inc., 23; 90 (upd.)
Bronner Display & Sign Advertising, Inc., 82
Buck Consultants, Inc., 55
Bureau Veritas SA, 55
Burke, Inc., 88
Burns International Services Corporation, 13; 41 (upd.)
Cambridge Technology Partners, Inc., 36
Campbell-Ewald Advertising, 86
Campbell-Mithun-Esty, Inc., 16
Cannon Design, 63
Capario, 104
Capita Group PLC, 69

Aerospace

Agribusiness & Farming

Airlines

Automotive

Beverages

Bio-Technology

ArQule, Inc., 68
Becton, Dickinson and Company, I; 11 (upd.); 36 (upd.); 101 (upd.)
Biogen Idec Inc., 14; 36 (upd.); 71 (upd.)
bioMérieux S.A., 75
Bio-Rad Laboratories, Inc., 93
BTG Plc, 87
Caliper Life Sciences, Inc., 70
Cambrex Corporation, 44 (upd.)
Cardiac Science Corporation, 121
Celera Genomics, 74
Centocor Inc., 14
Charles River Laboratories International, Inc., 42
Chiron Corporation, 10; 36 (upd.)
Covance Inc., 30; 98 (upd.)
CryoLife, Inc., 46
Cytyc Corporation, 69
Delta and Pine Land Company, 33
Dionex Corporation, 46
Dyax Corp., 89
Ebro Foods S.A., 118
Embrex, Inc., 72
Enzo Biochem, Inc., 41
eResearch Technology, Inc., 115
Eurofins Scientific S.A., 70
Genentech, Inc., 32 (upd.)
Gen-Probe Incorporated, 79
Genzyme Corporation, 38 (upd.)
Gilead Sciences, Inc., 54
Hindustan Lever Limited, 79
Howard Hughes Medical Institute, 39
Huntingdon Life Sciences Group plc, 42
IDEXX Laboratories, Inc., 23; 107 (upd.)
ImClone Systems Inc., 58
Immunex Corporation, 14; 50 (upd.)
IMPATH Inc., 45
Incyte Genomics, Inc., 52
Inverness Medical Innovations, Inc., 63
Invitrogen Corporation, 52
Judge Group, Inc., The, 51
Kendle International Inc., 87
Landec Corporation, 95
Life Technologies, Inc., 17
LifeCell Corporation, 77
Lonza Group Ltd., 73
Martek Biosciences Corporation, 65
Medarex, Inc., 85
Medtronic, Inc., 8; 30 (upd.); 67 (upd.)
Meridian Bioscience, Inc., 115
Millipore Corporation, 25; 84 (upd.)
Minntech Corporation, 22
Mycogen Corporation, 21
Nektar Therapeutics, 91
New Brunswick Scientific Co., Inc., 45
Novozymes A/S, 118
Omrix Biopharmaceuticals, Inc., 95
Pacific Ethanol, Inc., 81
Pharmion Corporation, 91
QIAGEN N.V., 39; 121 (upd.)
Quintiles Transnational Corporation, 21
RTI Biologics, Inc., 96
Seminis, Inc., 29
Senomyx, Inc., 83
Serologicals Corporation, 63
Sigma-Aldrich Corporation, I; 36 (upd.); 93 (upd.)
Starkey Laboratories, Inc., 52
STERIS Corporation, 29
Stratagene Corporation, 70
Talecris Biotherapeutics Holdings Corp., 114
Tanox, Inc., 77
TECHNE Corporation, 52
Trinity Biotech plc, 121
TriPath Imaging, Inc., 77
Viterra Inc., 105
Waters Corporation, 43
Whatman plc, 46
Wilmar International Ltd., 108
Wisconsin Alumni Research Foundation, 65
Wyeth, Inc., 50 (upd.); 118 (upd.)

Chemicals

A. Schulman, Inc., 8; 49 (upd.)
Aceto Corp., 38
Air Products and Chemicals, Inc., I; 10 (upd.); 74 (upd.)
Airgas, Inc., 54
Akzo Nobel N.V., 13; 41 (upd.); 112 (upd.)
Albaugh, Inc., 105
Albemarle Corporation, 59
AlliedSignal Inc., 9; 22 (upd.)
ALTANA AG, 87
American Cyanamid, I; 8 (upd.)
American Vanguard Corporation, 47
Arab Potash Company, 85
Arch Chemicals Inc., 78
ARCO Chemical Company, 10
Arkema S.A., 100
Asahi Denka Kogyo KK, 64
Atanor S.A., 62
Atochem S.A., I
Avantium Technologies BV, 79
Avecia Group PLC, 63
Azelis Group, 100
Baker Hughes Incorporated, III; 22 (upd.); 57 (upd.); 118 (upd.)
Balchem Corporation, 42
BASF SE, I; 18 (upd.); 50 (upd.); 108 (upd.)
Bayer AG, I; 13 (upd.); 41 (upd.); 118 (upd.)
Betz Laboratories, Inc., I; 10 (upd.)
BFGoodrich Company, The, 19 (upd.)
BOC Group plc, I; 25 (upd.); 78 (upd.)
BorsodChem Zrt., 113
Braskem S.A., 108
Brenntag Holding GmbH & Co. KG, 8; 23 (upd.); 101 (upd.)
Burmah Castrol PLC, 30 (upd.)
Cabot Corporation, 8; 29 (upd.); 91 (upd.)
Calgon Carbon Corporation, 73
Caliper Life Sciences, Inc., 70
Calumet Specialty Products Partners, L.P., 106
Cambrex Corporation, 16
Campbell Brothers Limited, 115
Catalytica Energy Systems, Inc., 44
Celanese Corporation, I; 109 (upd.)
Celanese Mexicana, S.A. de C.V., 54
CF Industries Holdings, Inc., 99
Chemcentral Corporation, 8
Chemi-Trol Chemical Co., 16
Chemtura Corporation, 91 (upd.)
China Petroleum & Chemical Corporation (Sinopec Corp.), 109
Church & Dwight Co., Inc., 29
Ciba-Geigy Ltd., I; 8 (upd.)
Clorox Company, The, III; 22 (upd.); 81 (upd.)
Croda International Plc, 45
Crompton Corporation, 9; 36 (upd.)
CVR Energy Corporation, 116
Cytec Industries Inc., 27
Degussa-Hüls AG, 32 (upd.)
DeKalb Genetics Corporation, 17
Dexter Corporation, The, I; 12 (upd.)
Dionex Corporation, 46
Dow Chemical Company, The, I; 8 (upd.); 50 (upd.); 114 (upd.)
DSM N.V., I; 56 (upd.)
Dynaction S.A., 67
E.I. du Pont de Nemours & Company, I; 8 (upd.); 26 (upd.); 73 (upd.)
Eastman Chemical Company, 14; 38 (upd.); 116 (upd.)
Ecolab Inc., I; 13 (upd.); 34 (upd.); 85 (upd.)
Eka Chemicals AB, 92
Elementis plc, 40 (upd.)
Engelhard Corporation, 72 (upd.)
English China Clays Ltd., 15 (upd.); 40 (upd.)
Enterprise Rent-A-Car Company, 69 (upd.)
Equistar Chemicals, LP, 71
Ercros S.A., 80
ERLY Industries Inc., 17
Ethyl Corporation, I; 10 (upd.)
Evonik Industries AG, 111 (upd.)
Ferro Corporation, 8; 56 (upd.)
Firmenich International S.A., 60
First Mississippi Corporation, 8
FMC Corporation, 89 (upd.)
Formosa Plastics Corporation, 14; 58 (upd.)
Fort James Corporation, 22 (upd.)
Fuchs Petrolub AG, 102
G.A.F., I
General Chemical Group Inc., The, 37
Georgia Gulf Corporation, 9; 61 (upd.)
Givaudan SA, 43
Great Lakes Chemical Corporation, I; 14 (upd.)
GROWMARK, Inc., 88
Grupo Comex, 115
Guerbet Group, 46
H.B. Fuller Company, 8; 32 (upd.); 75 (upd.)
Hauser, Inc., 46
Hawkins Chemical, Inc., 16
Henkel KGaA, III; 34 (upd.); 95 (upd.)
Hercules Inc., I; 22 (upd.); 66 (upd.)
Hexion Specialty Chemicals, Inc., 116
Hillyard, Inc., 114
Hoechst A.G., I; 18 (upd.)
Hoechst Celanese Corporation, 13
Huls A.G., I
Huntsman Corporation, 8; 98 (upd.)
Ikonics Corporation, 99

Conglomerates

Procter & Gamble Company, The, III; 8 (upd.); 26 (upd.); 67 (upd.)
Proeza S.A. de C.V., 82
PT Astra International Tbk, 56
Pubco Corporation, 17
Pulsar Internacional S.A., 21
R.B. Pamplin Corp., 45
Rank Organisation Plc, The, 14 (upd.)
Raymond Ltd., 77
Red Apple Group, Inc., 23
Roll International Corporation, 37
Rubbermaid Incorporated, 20 (upd.)
S.C. Johnson & Son, Inc., III; 28 (upd.); 89 (upd.)
Samsung Group, I
Sara Lee Corporation, II; 15 (upd.); 54 (upd.); 99 (upd.)
Schindler Holding AG, 29
Scott Fetzer Company, 12; 80 (upd.)
Sea Containers Ltd., 29
Seaboard Corporation, 36; 85 (upd.)
Sealaska Corporation, 60
Sequa Corporation, 13; 54 (upd.)
Sequana Capital, 78 (upd.)
SHV Holdings N.V., 55
Sideco Americana S.A., 67
Sime Darby Berhad, 14; 36 (upd.)
Sistema JSFC, 73
SK Group, 88
Société du Louvre, 27
Sojitz Corporation, 96 (upd.)
Sonae SGPS, S.A., 97
Spectrum Brands, Inc., 109 (upd.)
Standex International Corporation, 17; 44 (upd.)
Steamships Trading Company Ltd., 82
Stinnes AG, 23 (upd.)
Sudbury Inc., 16
Sumitomo Corporation, I; 11 (upd.); 102 (upd.)
Swire Pacific Limited, I; 16 (upd.); 57 (upd.)
Talley Industries, Inc., 16
Tandycrafts, Inc., 31
TaurusHolding GmbH & Co. KG, 46
Teijin Limited, 61 (upd.)
Teledyne, Inc., I; 10 (upd.)
Tengelmann Warenhandelsgesellschaft KG, 27; 121 (upd.)
Tenneco Inc., I; 10 (upd.)
Textron Inc., I; 34 (upd.); 88 (upd.)
Thomas H. Lee Co., 24
Thorn Emi PLC, I
Thorn plc, 24
TI Group plc, 17
Tokyu Corporation, 47 (upd.)
Tomen Corporation, 24 (upd.)
Tomkins plc, 11; 44 (upd.)
Toshiba Corporation, I; 12 (upd.); 40 (upd.); 99 (upd.)
Tractebel S.A., 20
Transamerica–An AEGON Company, I; 13 (upd.); 41 (upd.)
Tranzonic Cos., The, 15
Triarc Companies, Inc., 8
Triple Five Group Ltd., 49
TRW Inc., I; 11 (upd.)
Tyco International Ltd., III; 28 (upd.); 63 (upd.)
UAB Koncernas MG Baltic, 117
Unilever, II; 7 (upd.); 32 (upd.); 89 (upd.)
Unión Fenosa, S.A., 51
United Technologies Corporation, I; 10 (upd.); 34 (upd.); 105 (upd.)
Universal Studios, Inc., 33; 100 (upd.)
Valhi, Inc., 19
Valorem S.A., 88
Valores Industriales S.A., 19
Veba A.G., I; 15 (upd.)
Vendôme Luxury Group plc, 27
Viacom Inc., 23 (upd.); 67 (upd.)
Virgin Group Ltd., 12; 32 (upd.); 89 (upd.)
Vivartia S.A., 82
Vivendi, 112 (upd.)
Votorantim Participaçoes S.A., 76
W.R. Grace & Company, I; 50
Walter Industries, Inc., III; 22 (upd.); 72 (upd.)
Washington Companies, The, 33
Washington H. Soul Pattinson and Company Limited, 112
Watsco Inc., 52
Wesfarmers Limited, 109
Wheaton Industries, 8
Whitbread PLC, I; 20 (upd.); 52 (upd.); 97 (upd.)
Whitman Corporation, 10 (upd.)
Whittaker Corporation, I
Wilh. Werhahn KG, 101
Wirtz Corporation, 72
WorldCorp, Inc., 10
Worms et Cie, 27
Yamaha Corporation, III; 16 (upd.); 40 (upd.); 99 (upd.)
Yildiz Holding A.S., 117
Zorlu Holding A.S., 117

Construction

A.G. Spanos Companies, 115
A. Johnson & Company H.B., I
ABC Supply Co., Inc., 22
Abertis Infraestructuras, S.A., 65
Abrams Industries Inc., 23
Acciona S.A., 81
Acergy SA, 97
Aecon Group Inc., 121
Aegek S.A., 64
Alberici Corporation, 76
Allgemeine Baugesellschaft – A. Porr AG, 120
Amec Spie S.A., 57
AMREP Corporation, 21
Anthony & Sylvan Pools Corporation, 56
Asplundh Tree Expert Co., 59 (upd.)
Astec Industries, Inc., 79
ASV, Inc., 34; 66 (upd.)
Auchter Company, The,, 78
Austin Company, The, 8
Autoroutes du Sud de la France SA, 55
Autostrada Torino-Milano S.p.A., 101
Balfour Beatty plc, 36 (upd.)
Bamburi Cement Limited, 116
Baratt Developments PLC, I
Barton Malow Company, 51
Bauerly Companies, 61
BE&K, Inc., 73
Beazer Homes USA, Inc., 17
Bechtel Corporation, I; 24 (upd.); 99 (upd.)
Bellway Plc, 45
BFC Construction Corporation, 25
BICC PLC, III
Bilfinger & Berger AG, I; 55 (upd.)
Bird Corporation, 19
Birse Group PLC, 77
Black & Veatch LLP, 22
Boral Limited, III; 43 (upd.); 103 (upd.)
Bouygues S.A., I; 24 (upd.); 97 (upd.)
Bowen Engineering Corporation, 105
Branch Group, Inc., The, 72
Brasfield & Gorrie LLC, 87
Bread Loaf Corporation, 107
BRISA Auto-estradas de Portugal S.A., 64
Brock Group of Companies, The, 114
Brown & Root, Inc., 13
Bufete Industrial, S.A. de C.V., 34
Building Materials Holding Corporation, 52
Bulley & Andrews, LLC, 55
C.R. Meyer and Sons Company, 74
CalMat Co., 19
Cavco Industries, Inc., 65
Centex Corporation, 8; 29 (upd.); 106 (upd.)
Chicago Bridge & Iron Company N.V., 82 (upd.)
Chugach Alaska Corporation, 60
Cianbro Corporation, 14
Clark Construction Group, Inc., The, 8
Coachmen Industries, Inc., 77
Colas S.A., 31
Comfort Systems USA, Inc., 101
Consolidated Contractors Company, 115
Consorcio ARA, S.A. de C.V., 79
Corporación Geo, S.A. de C.V., 81
Costain Group PLC, 115
D.R. Horton, Inc., 58
Day & Zimmermann, Inc., 31 (upd.)
Desarrolladora Homex, S.A. de C.V., 87
Dick Corporation, 64
Dillingham Construction Corporation, I; 44 (upd.)
Dominion Homes, Inc., 19
Doosan Heavy Industries and Construction Company Ltd., 108
Doprastav A.S., 113
Downer EDI Limited, 119
Drees Company, Inc., The, 41
Dycom Industries, Inc., 57
E.W. Howell Co., Inc., 72
Edw. C. Levy Co., 42
Eiffage S.A., 27; 117 (upd.)
Ellerbe Becket, 41
EMCOR Group Inc., 60
Empresas ICA Sociedad Controladora, S.A. de C.V., 41
Encompass Services Corporation, 33
Engelberth Construction, Inc., 117
Engle Homes, Inc., 46
Environmental Industries, Inc., 31
Eurotunnel PLC, 13

Containers

Drugs & Pharmaceuticals

Education & Training

Electrical & Electronics

Ingram Micro Inc., 52
Innovative Solutions & Support, Inc., 85
Integrated Defense Technologies, Inc., 54
Intel Corporation, II; 10 (upd.); 75 (upd.)
Intermec Technologies Corporation, 72
International Business Machines Corporation, III; 6 (upd.); 30 (upd.); 63 (upd.)
International Electric Supply Corp., 113
International Rectifier Corporation, 31; 71 (upd.)
Intersil Corporation, 93
Ionatron, Inc., 85
Itel Corporation, 9
Jabil Circuit, Inc., 36; 88 (upd.)
Jaco Electronics, Inc., 30
JDS Uniphase Corporation, 34
Johnson Controls, Inc., III; 26 (upd.); 59 (upd.); 110 (upd.)
Juno Lighting, Inc., 30
Katy Industries, Inc., I; 51 (upd.)
Keithley Instruments Inc., 16
Kemet Corp., 14
Kent Electronics Corporation, 17
Kenwood Corporation, 31
Kesa Electricals plc, 91
Kimball International, Inc., 12; 48 (upd.)
Kingston Technology Company, Inc., 20; 112 (upd.)
KitchenAid, 8
KLA-Tencor Corporation, 45 (upd.)
KnowledgeWare Inc., 9
Kollmorgen Corporation, 18
Konami Corporation, 96
Konica Corporation, III; 30 (upd.)
Koninklijke Philips Electronics N.V., 50 (upd.); 119 (upd.)
Koor Industries Ltd., II
Kopin Corporation, 80
Koss Corporation, 38
Kudelski Group SA, 44
Kulicke and Soffa Industries, Inc., 33; 76 (upd.)
Kyocera Corporation, II; 21 (upd.); 79 (upd.)
L-3 Communications Holdings, Inc., 111 (upd.)
LaBarge Inc., 41
Lamson & Sessions Co., The, 13; 61 (upd.)
Lattice Semiconductor Corp., 16
LDK Solar Co., Ltd., 101
LeCroy Corporation, 41
Legrand SA, 21
Lenovo Group Ltd., 80
Leoni AG, 98
Lexmark International, Inc., 18; 79 (upd.)
Linear Technology Corporation, 16; 99 (upd.)
Littelfuse, Inc., 26
Loewe AG, 90
Loral Corporation, 9
LOUD Technologies, Inc., 95 (upd.)
Lowrance Electronics, Inc., 18
LSI Logic Corporation, 13; 64
Lucent Technologies Inc., 34
Lucky-Goldstar, II
Lunar Corporation, 29
Lynch Corporation, 43
Mackie Designs Inc., 33
MagneTek, Inc., 15; 41 (upd.)
Magneti Marelli Holding SpA, 90
Marconi plc, 33 (upd.)
Marquette Electronics, Inc., 13
Marshall Amplification plc, 62
Marvell Technology Group Ltd., 112
Matsushita Electric Industrial Co., Ltd., II; 64 (upd.)
Maxim Integrated Products, Inc., 16
McDATA Corporation, 75
Measurement Specialties, Inc., 71
Medis Technologies Ltd., 77
MEMC Electronic Materials, Inc., 81
Merix Corporation, 36; 75 (upd.)
Methode Electronics, Inc., 13
Micrel, Incorporated, 77
Midway Games, Inc., 25; 102 (upd.)
Mitel Corporation, 18
MITRE Corporation, 26
Mitsubishi Electric Corporation, II; 44 (upd.); 117 (upd.)
Molex Incorporated, 11; 54 (upd.)
Monster Cable Products, Inc., 69
Motorola, Inc., II; 11 (upd.); 34 (upd.); 93 (upd.)
N.F. Smith & Associates LP, 70
Nam Tai Electronics, Inc., 61
National Instruments Corporation, 22
National Presto Industries, Inc., 16; 43 (upd.)
National Semiconductor Corporation, II; 26 (upd.); 69 (upd.)
NEC Corporation, II; 21 (upd.); 57 (upd.)
Network Equipment Technologies Inc., 92
Nexans SA, 54
Nintendo Company, Ltd., III; 7 (upd.); 28 (upd.); 67 (upd.)
Nokia Corporation, II; 17 (upd.); 38 (upd.); 77 (upd.)
Nortel Networks Corporation, 36 (upd.)
Northrop Grumman Corporation, 45 (upd.); 111 (upd.)
Oak Technology, Inc., 22
Océ N.V., 24; 91 (upd.)
Oki Electric Industry Company, Limited, II
Omnicell, Inc., 89
OMRON Corporation, II; 28 (upd.); 115 (upd.)
Onvest Oy, 117
Oplink Communications, Inc., 106
OPTEK Technology Inc., 98
Orbit International Corp., 105
Orbotech Ltd., 75
Otari Inc., 89
Otter Tail Power Company, 18
Pacific Aerospace & Electronics, Inc., 120
Palm, Inc., 36; 75 (upd.)
Palomar Medical Technologies, Inc., 22
Parlex Corporation, 61
Peak Technologies Group, Inc., The, 14
Peavey Electronics Corporation, 16
Philips Electronics N.V., II; 13 (upd.)
Philips Electronics North America Corp., 13
Pioneer Electronic Corporation, III; 28 (upd.)
Pioneer-Standard Electronics Inc., 19
Pitney Bowes Inc., III; 19 (upd.); 47 (upd.)
Pittway Corporation, 9; 33 (upd.)
Pixelworks, Inc., 69
Planar Systems, Inc., 61
Plantronics, Inc., 106
Plessey Company, PLC, The, II
Plexus Corporation, 35; 80 (upd.)
Polaroid Corporation, III; 7 (upd.); 28 (upd.); 93 (upd.)
Polk Audio, Inc., 34
Potter & Brumfield Inc., 11
Premier Industrial Corporation, 9
Protection One, Inc., 32
QUALCOMM Incorporated, 114 (upd.)
Quanta Computer Inc., 47; 79 (upd.); 110 (upd.)
Racal Electronics PLC, II
RadioShack Corporation, 36 (upd.); 101 (upd.)
Radius Inc., 16
RAE Systems Inc., 83
Ramtron International Corporation, 89
Raychem Corporation, 8
Raymarine plc, 104
Rayovac Corporation, 13; 39 (upd.)
Raytheon Company, II; 11 (upd.); 38 (upd.); 105 (upd.)
RCA Corporation, II
Read-Rite Corp., 10
Redback Networks, Inc., 92
Reliance Electric Company, 9
Research in Motion Ltd., 54
Rexel, Inc., 15
Richardson Electronics, Ltd., 17
Ricoh Company, Ltd., III; 36 (upd.); 108 (upd.)
Rimage Corp., 89
Rival Company, The, 19
Rockford Corporation, 43
Rogers Corporation, 61; 80 (upd.)
Roku, Inc., 121
S&C Electric Company, 15
SAGEM S.A., 37
St. Louis Music, Inc., 48
Sam Ash Music Corporation, 30
Samsung Electronics Co., Ltd., 14; 41 (upd.); 108 (upd.)
SanDisk Corporation, 121
Sanmina-SCI Corporation, 109 (upd.)
SANYO Electric Co., Ltd., II; 36 (upd.); 95 (upd.)
Sarnoff Corporation, 57
ScanSource, Inc., 29; 74 (upd.)
Schneider Electric SA, II; 18 (upd.); 108 (upd.)
SCI Systems, Inc., 9
Scientific-Atlanta, Inc., 45 (upd.)
Scitex Corporation Ltd., 24
Seagate Technology, 8; 34 (upd.); 105 (upd.)
SEGA Corporation, 73
Semitool, Inc., 79 (upd.)
Semtech Corporation, 32

Engineering & Management Services

Entertainment & Leisure

Financial Services: Banks

Financial Services: Excluding Banks

Food Products

Food Services, Retailers, & Restaurants

Health, Personal & Medical Care Products

Andis Company, Inc., 85
AngioDynamics, Inc., 81
Ansell Ltd., 60 (upd.)
ArthroCare Corporation, 73
Artsana SpA, 92
Ascendia Brands, Inc., 97
Atkins Nutritionals, Inc., 58
Aveda Corporation, 24
Avon Products, Inc., III; 19 (upd.); 46 (upd.); 109 (upd.)
Ballard Medical Products, 21
Bally Total Fitness Holding Corp., 25
Bare Escentuals, Inc., 91
Bausch & Lomb Inc., 7; 25 (upd.); 96 (upd.)
Baxter International Inc., I; 10 (upd.); 116 (upd.)
BeautiControl Cosmetics, Inc., 21
Becton, Dickinson and Company, I; 11 (upd.); 36 (upd.); 101 (upd.)
Beiersdorf AG, 29
Big B, Inc., 17
Bindley Western Industries, Inc., 9
Biolase Technology, Inc., 87
Biomet, Inc., 10; 93 (upd.)
BioScrip Inc., 98
Biosite Incorporated, 73
Block Drug Company, Inc., 8; 27 (upd.)
Body Shop International plc, The, 11; 53 (upd.)
Boiron S.A., 73
Bolton Group B.V., 86
Borghese Inc., 107
Bristol-Myers Squibb Company, III; 9 (upd.)
Bronner Brothers Inc., 92
Burt's Bees, Inc., 58
C.O. Bigelow Chemists, Inc., 114
C.R. Bard Inc., 9; 65 (upd.)
Candela Corporation, 48
Cantel Medical Corporation, 80
Cardinal Health, Inc., 18; 50 (upd.); 115 (upd.)
Carl Zeiss AG, III; 34 (upd.); 91 (upd.)
Carma Laboratories, Inc., 60
Carson, Inc., 31
Carter-Wallace, Inc., 8
Caswell-Massey Co. Ltd., 51
CCA Industries, Inc., 53
Chanel SA, 12; 49 (upd.)
Chattem, Inc., 17; 88 (upd.)
Chesebrough-Pond's USA, Inc., 8
Chindex International, Inc., 101
Chronimed Inc., 26
Church & Dwight Co., Inc., 68 (upd.)
Cintas Corporation, 51 (upd.)
Clarins S.A., 119
Clorox Company, The, III; 22 (upd.); 81 (upd.)
CNS, Inc., 20
COBE Cardiovascular, Inc., 61
Cochlear Ltd., 77
Colgate-Palmolive Company, III; 14 (upd.); 35 (upd.)
Combe Inc., 72
Conair Corporation, 17; 69 (upd.)
CONMED Corporation, 87
Connetics Corporation, 70
Cook Group Inc., 102
Cooper Companies, Inc., The, 39
Cordis Corporation, 19; 46 (upd.); 112 (upd.)
Cosmair, Inc., 8
Cosmolab Inc., 96
Coty Inc., 36; 115 (upd.)
Covidien Ltd., 91
Cyberonics, Inc., 79
Cybex International, Inc., 49
Cytyc Corporation, 69
Dade Behring Holdings Inc., 71
Dalli-Werke GmbH & Co. KG, 86
Datascope Corporation, 39
Del Laboratories, Inc., 28
Deltec, Inc., 56
Dentsply International Inc., 10; 109 (upd.)
DEP Corporation, 20
DePuy Inc., 30; 37 (upd.)
DHB Industries Inc., 85
Diagnostic Products Corporation, 73
Dial Corp., The, 23 (upd.)
Direct Focus, Inc., 47
Drackett Professional Products, 12
Drägerwerk AG, 83
drugstore.com, inc., 109
Drypers Corporation, 18
Duane Reade Holdings Inc., 109 (upd.)
Dynatronics Corporation, 99
DynaVox, Inc., 116
Edwards Lifesciences LLC, 112
Elizabeth Arden, Inc., 8; 40 (upd.)
Elscint Ltd., 20
Emerging Vision, Inc., 115
Empi, Inc., 26
Enrich International, Inc., 33
Essie Cosmetics, Ltd., 102
Essilor International, 21
Estée Lauder Companies Inc., The, 9; 30 (upd.); 93 (upd.)
Ethicon, Inc., 23
Exactech, Inc., 101
E-Z-EM Inc., 89
Farnam Companies, Inc., 107
Farouk Systems Inc., 78
Forest Laboratories, Inc., 11
Forever Living Products International Inc., 17
FoxHollow Technologies, Inc., 85
Franz Haniel & Cie. GmbH, 109
French Fragrances, Inc., 22
G&K Holding S.A., 95
Gambro AB, 49
General Nutrition Companies, Inc., 11; 29 (upd.)
Genzyme Corporation, 13; 77 (upd.)
GF Health Products, Inc., 82
Gillette Company, The, III; 20 (upd.); 68 (upd.)
Given Imaging Ltd., 83
GN ReSound A/S, 103
GNC Corporation, 98 (upd.)
Golden Neo-Life Diamite International, Inc., 100
Goody Products, Inc., 12
Groupe Yves Saint Laurent, 23
Grupo Omnilife S.A. de C.V., 88
Guerlain, 23
Guest Supply, Inc., 18
Guidant Corporation, 58
Guinot Paris S.A., 82
Hanger Orthopedic Group, Inc., 41
Health O Meter Products Inc., 14
Helen of Troy Corporation, 18
Helene Curtis Industries, Inc., 8; 28 (upd.)
Henkel KGaA, III; 34 (upd.); 95 (upd.)
Henry Schein, Inc., 31; 70 (upd.)
Herbalife Ltd., 17; 41 (upd.); 92 (upd.)
Huntleigh Technology PLC, 77
ICON Health & Fitness, Inc., 38; 102 (upd.)
Immucor, Inc., 81
Inamed Corporation, 79
Integra LifeSciences Holdings Corporation, 87
Integrated BioPharma, Inc., 83
Inter Parfums Inc., 35; 86 (upd.)
Intuitive Surgical, Inc., 79
Invacare Corporation, 11; 47 (upd.)
Invivo Corporation, 52
IRIS International, Inc., 101
IVAX Corporation, 11
IVC Industries, Inc., 45
Jean Coutu Group (PJC) Inc., The, 46
John Frieda Professional Hair Care Inc., 70
John Paul Mitchell Systems, 24; 112 (upd.)
Johnson & Johnson, III; 8 (upd.); 36 (upd.); 75 (upd.)
Kanebo, Ltd., 53
Kao Corporation, III; 79 (upd.)
Kendall International, Inc., 11
Kensey Nash Corporation, 71
Keys Fitness Products, LP, 83
Kimberly-Clark Corporation, III; 16 (upd.); 43 (upd.); 105 (upd.)
Kiss My Face Corporation, 108
Kolmar Laboratories Group, 96
Kyowa Hakko Kogyo Co., Ltd., III
Kyphon Inc., 87
Laboratoires de Biologie Végétale Yves Rocher, 35
Lamaur Corporation, The, 41
Laserscope, 67
Lever Brothers Company, 9
Lion Corporation, III; 51 (upd.)
L'Oréal SA, III; 8 (upd.); 46 (upd.); 109 (upd.)
Lush Ltd., 93
Luxottica SpA, 17; 52 (upd.)
Mandom Corporation, 82
Mannatech Inc., 33
Mary Kay Inc., 9; 30 (upd.); 84 (upd.)
Matrix Essentials Inc., 90
Maxxim Medical Inc., 12
Medco Containment Services Inc., 9
MEDecision, Inc., 95
Medical Action Industries Inc., 101
Medicine Shoppe International, Inc., 102
Medifast, Inc., 97
Medline Industries, Inc., 61
Medtronic, Inc., 8; 30 (upd.); 67 (upd.)
Melaleuca Inc., 31

Health Care Services

Haemonetics Corporation, 20
Hamot Health Foundation, 91
Hazelden Foundation, 28
HCA, Inc., 35 (upd.); 111 (upd.)
Health Care & Retirement Corporation, 22
Health Management Associates, Inc., 56
Health Net, Inc., 109 (upd.)
Health Risk Management, Inc., 24
Health Systems International, Inc., 11
HealthSouth Corporation, 14; 33 (upd.)
Henry Ford Health System, 84
Highmark Inc., 27
Hillhaven Corporation, The, 14
Holiday Retirement Corp., 87
Hologic, Inc., 106
Hooper Holmes, Inc., 22
Hospital Central Services, Inc., 56
Hospital Corporation of America, III
Hospital for Special Surgery, 115
Howard Hughes Medical Institute, 39
Humana Inc., III; 24 (upd.); 101 (upd.)
IASIS Healthcare Corporation, 112
Intermountain Health Care, Inc., 27
Jenny Craig, Inc., 10; 29 (upd.); 92 (upd.)
Kaiser Foundation Health Plan, Inc., 53; 119 (upd.)
Kinetic Concepts, Inc. (KCI), 20
LabOne, Inc., 48
Laboratory Corporation of America Holdings, 42 (upd.); 119 (upd.)
LCA-Vision, Inc., 85
Legacy Health System, 114
Life Care Centers of America Inc., 76
Lifeline Systems, Inc., 53
LifePoint Hospitals, Inc., 69
Lincare Holdings Inc., 43
Manor Care, Inc., 6; 25 (upd.)
Marshfield Clinic Inc., 82
Matria Healthcare, Inc., 17
Maxicare Health Plans, Inc., III; 25 (upd.)
Mayo Foundation for Medical Education and Research, 9; 34 (upd.); 115 (upd.)
McBride plc, 82
McKesson Corporation, 108 (upd.)
MDVIP, Inc., 118
Medical Management International, Inc., 65
Medical Staffing Network Holdings, Inc., 89
Memorial Sloan-Kettering Cancer Center, 57
Merge Healthcare, 85
Merit Medical Systems, Inc., 29
MeritCare Health System, 88
Molina Healthcare, Inc., 116
Mount Sinai Medical Center, 112
Myriad Genetics, Inc., 95
National Health Laboratories Incorporated, 11
National Jewish Health, 101
National Medical Enterprises, Inc., III
National Research Corporation, 87
Natus Medical Incorporated, 119
Navarro Discount Pharmacies, 119
New York City Health and Hospitals Corporation, 60
New York Health Care, Inc., 72
NewYork-Presbyterian Hospital, 59
NovaCare, Inc., 11
NSF International, 72
Omnicare, Inc., 111 (upd.)
Option Care Inc., 48
OrthoSynetics Inc., 35; 107 (upd.)
Oxford Health Plans, Inc., 16
PacifiCare Health Systems, Inc., 11
Palomar Medical Technologies, Inc., 22
Pediatric Services of America, Inc., 31
Pediatrix Medical Group, Inc., 61
PHP Healthcare Corporation, 22
PhyCor, Inc., 36
Planned Parenthood Federation of America, 121
PolyMedica Corporation, 77
Primedex Health Systems, Inc., 25
Providence Health System, 90
Providence Service Corporation, The, 64
Psychemedics Corporation, 89
Psychiatric Solutions, Inc., 68
Quest Diagnostics Inc., 26; 106 (upd.)
Radiation Therapy Services, Inc., 85
Ramsay Youth Services, Inc., 41
RehabCare Group, Inc., 114
Renal Care Group, Inc., 72
Res-Care, Inc., 29
Response Oncology, Inc., 27
Rural/Metro Corporation, 28
Sabratek Corporation, 29
St. Jude Children's Research Hospital, Inc., 114
St. Jude Medical, Inc., 11; 43 (upd.); 97 (upd.)
Salick Health Care, Inc., 53
Scripps Research Institute, The, 76
Select Medical Corporation, 65
Shriners Hospitals for Children, 69
Sierra Health Services, Inc., 15
Sisters of Charity of Leavenworth Health System, 105
Smith & Nephew plc, 41 (upd.)
Sports Club Company, The, 25
SSL International plc, 49
Stericycle Inc., 33
Sun Healthcare Group Inc., 25
Sunrise Senior Living, Inc., 81
SwedishAmerican Health System, 51
Tenet Healthcare Corporation, 55 (upd.); 112 (upd.)
The Cleveland Clinic Foundation, 112
Twinlab Corporation, 34
U.S. Healthcare, Inc., 6
U.S. Physical Therapy, Inc., 65
Unison HealthCare Corporation, 25
United HealthCare Corporation, 9
United Surgical Partners International Inc., 120
UnitedHealth Group Incorporated, 9; 103 (upd.)
Universal Health Services, Inc., 6
Vanderbilt University Medical Center, 99
Vanguard Health Systems Inc., 70
VCA Antech, Inc., 58
Vencor, Inc., 16
VISX, Incorporated, 30
Vivra, Inc., 18
WellPoint, Inc., 25; 103 (upd.)

Hotels

Accor S.A., 69 (upd.)
Amerihost Properties, Inc., 30
Ameristar Casinos, Inc., 69 (upd.)
Archon Corporation, 74 (upd.)
Arena Leisure Plc, 99
Aztar Corporation, 13; 71 (upd.)
Bass PLC, 38 (upd.)
The Biltmore Company, 118
Boca Resorts, Inc., 37
Boyd Gaming Corporation, 43
Boyne USA Resorts, 71
Bristol Hotel Company, 23
Broadmoor Hotel, The, 30
Caesars World, Inc., 6
Candlewood Hotel Company, Inc., 41
Carlson Companies, Inc., 6; 22 (upd.); 87 (upd.)
Castle & Cooke, Inc., 20 (upd.)
Cedar Fair Entertainment Company, 22; 98 (upd.)
Cendant Corporation, 44 (upd.)
Choice Hotels International, Inc., 14; 83 (upd.)
Circus Circus Enterprises, Inc., 6
City Developments Limited, 89
City Lodge Hotels Limited, 114
Club Mediterranée S.A., 6; 21 (upd.); 91 (upd.)
Compagnia Italiana dei Jolly Hotels S.p.A., 71
Daniel Thwaites Plc, 95
Doubletree Corporation, 21
EIH Ltd., 103
Extended Stay America, Inc., 41
Fairmont Hotels & Resorts Inc., 69
Fibreboard Corporation, 16
Four Seasons Hotels Limited, 9; 29 (upd.); 106 (upd.)
Fuller Smith & Turner P.L.C., 38
Gables Residential Trust, 49
Gaylord Entertainment Company, 11; 36 (upd.)
Gianni Versace S.p.A., 22; 106 (upd.)
Global Hyatt Corporation, 75 (upd.)
Granada Group PLC, 24 (upd.)
Grand Casinos, Inc., 20
Grand Hotel Krasnapolsky N.V., 23
Great Wolf Resorts, Inc., 91
Grupo Posadas, S.A. de C.V., 57
Helmsley Enterprises, Inc., 9
Hilton Hotels Corporation, III; 19 (upd.); 49 (upd.); 62 (upd.)
Holiday Inns, Inc., III
Home Inns & Hotels Management Inc., 95
Hospitality Franchise Systems, Inc., 11
Host Hotels & Resorts, Inc., 112
Hotel Properties Ltd., 71
Hotel Shilla Company Ltd., 110
Howard Johnson International, Inc., 17; 72 (upd.)
Hyatt Corporation, III; 16 (upd.)
ILX Resorts Incorporated, 65
InterContinental Hotels Group, PLC, 109 (upd.)

Information Technology

Insurance

White Mountains Insurance Group, Ltd., 48
Willis Group Holdings Ltd., 25; 100 (upd.)
Winterthur Group, III; 68 (upd.)
Wüstenrot & Württembergische AG, 121
Yasuda Fire and Marine Insurance Company, Limited, The, III
Yasuda Mutual Life Insurance Company, The, III; 39 (upd.)
Zurich Financial Services, 42 (upd.); 93 (upd.)
Zürich Versicherungs-Gesellschaft, III

Legal Services

Akin, Gump, Strauss, Hauer & Feld, L.L.P., 33
American Bar Association, 35
American Lawyer Media Holdings, Inc., 32
Amnesty International, 50
Andrews Kurth, LLP, 71
Arnold & Porter, 35
Baker & Daniels LLP, 88
Baker & Hostetler LLP, 40
Baker & McKenzie, 10; 42 (upd.)
Baker and Botts, L.L.P., 28
Bingham Dana LLP, 43
Brobeck, Phleger & Harrison, LLP, 31
Cadwalader, Wickersham & Taft, 32
Chadbourne & Parke, 36
Cleary, Gottlieb, Steen & Hamilton, 35
Clifford Chance LLP, 38
Coudert Brothers, 30
Covington & Burling, 40
CRA International, Inc., 93
Cravath, Swaine & Moore, 43
Davis Polk & Wardwell, 36
Debevoise & Plimpton, 39
Dechert, 43
Dewey Ballantine LLP, 48
DLA Piper, 106
Dorsey & Whitney LLP, 47
Drinker, Biddle and Reath L.L.P., 92
Faegre & Benson LLP, 97
Fenwick & West LLP, 34
Fish & Neave, 54
Foley & Lardner, 28
Fried, Frank, Harris, Shriver & Jacobson, 35
Fulbright & Jaworski L.L.P., 47
Gibson, Dunn & Crutcher LLP, 36
Greenberg Traurig, LLP, 65
Heller, Ehrman, White & McAuliffe, 41
Hildebrandt International, 29
Hogan & Hartson L.L.P., 44
Holland & Knight LLP, 60
Holme Roberts & Owen LLP, 28
Hughes Hubbard & Reed LLP, 44
Hunton & Williams, 35
Jenkens & Gilchrist, P.C., 65
Jones, Day, Reavis & Pogue, 33
Kelley Drye & Warren LLP, 40
King & Spalding, 23; 115 (upd.)
Kirkland & Ellis LLP, 65
Lambda Legal Defense and Education Fund, Inc., 106
Latham & Watkins L.L.P., 33; 117 (upd.)
LeBoeuf, Lamb, Greene & MacRae, L.L.P., 29
LECG Corporation, 93
Legal Aid Society, The, 48
Mayer, Brown, Rowe & Maw, 47
Milbank, Tweed, Hadley & McCloy, 27
Morgan, Lewis & Bockius LLP, 29
Morrison & Foerster LLP, 78
O'Melveny & Myers, 37
Oppenheimer Wolff & Donnelly LLP, 71
Orrick, Herrington and Sutcliffe LLP, 76
Patton Boggs LLP, 71
Paul, Hastings, Janofsky & Walker LLP, 27
Paul, Weiss, Rifkind, Wharton & Garrison, 47
Pepper Hamilton LLP, 43
Perkins Coie LLP, 56
Phillips Lytle LLP, 102
Pillsbury Madison & Sutro LLP, 29
Pre-Paid Legal Services, Inc., 20; 120 (upd.)
Proskauer Rose LLP, 47
Quinn Emanuel Urquhart Oliver & Hedges, LLP, 99
Robins, Kaplan, Miller & Ciresi L.L.P., 89
Ropes & Gray, 40
Saul Ewing LLP, 74
Seyfarth Shaw LLP, 93
Shearman & Sterling, 32
Sidley Austin Brown & Wood, 40
Simpson Thacher & Bartlett, 39
Skadden, Arps, Slate, Meagher & Flom LLP, 18; 120 (upd.)
Slaughter and May, 112
Snell & Wilmer L.L.P., 28
Sonnenschein Nath and Rosenthal LLP, 102
Southern Poverty Law Center, Inc., 74
Stroock & Stroock & Lavan LLP, 40
Sullivan & Cromwell, 26
Troutman Sanders L.L.P., 79
Vinson & Elkins L.L.P., 30
Wachtell, Lipton, Rosen & Katz, 47
Weil, Gotshal & Manges LLP, 55
White & Case LLP, 35
Williams & Connolly LLP, 47
Willkie Farr & Gallagher LLP, 95
Wilmer Cutler Pickering Hale and Dorr L.L.P., 109
Wilson Sonsini Goodrich & Rosati, 34
Winston & Strawn, 35
Womble Carlyle Sandridge & Rice, PLLC, 52

Manufacturing

A.O. Smith Corporation, 11; 40 (upd.); 93 (upd.)
A.T. Cross Company, 17; 49 (upd.)
A.W. Faber-Castell Unternehmensverwaltung GmbH & Co., 51
AAF-McQuay Incorporated, 26
Aalborg Industries A/S, 90
ACCO World Corporation, 7; 51 (upd.)
Acme United Corporation, 70
Acme-Cleveland Corp., 13
Acuity Brands, Inc., 90
Adolf Würth GmbH & Co. KG, 49
AEP Industries, Inc., 36
Aga Foodservice Group PLC, 73
Agfa Gevaert Group N.V., 59
Ahlstrom Corporation, 53
Airsprung Group PLC, 121
Aktiebolaget Electrolux, 22 (upd.)
Albert Trostel and Sons Company, 113
Alfa Laval AB, III; 64 (upd.)
Alliance Laundry Holdings LLC, 102
Allied Defense Group, Inc., The, 65
Allied Products Corporation, 21
Alltrista Corporation, 30
ALSTOM, 108
Alvis Plc, 47
American Cast Iron Pipe Company, 50
American Equipment Company, Inc., 104
American Homestar Corporation, 18; 41 (upd.)
American Locker Group Incorporated, 34
American Seating Company, 78
American Tourister, Inc., 16
American Woodmark Corporation, 31
Amerock Corporation, 53
Ameron International Corporation, 67
AMETEK, Inc., 9; 114 (upd.)
Ampacet Corporation, 67
Anchor Hocking Glassware, 13
Andreas Stihl AG & Co. KG, 16; 59 (upd.)
Andritz AG, 51
Applica Incorporated, 43 (upd.)
Applied Films Corporation, 48
Applied Materials, Inc., 10; 46 (upd.)
AptarGroup, Inc., 69
Aquatic Company, 121
Arc International, 76
Arçelik A.S., 100
Arctic Cat Inc., 16; 40 (upd.); 96 (upd.)
AREVA NP, 90 (upd.)
Ariens Company, 48
Aristotle Corporation, The, 62
Armor All Products Corp., 16
Armstrong Holdings, Inc., III; 22 (upd.); 81 (upd.)
Art's Way Manufacturing Co., Inc., 101
Ashley Furniture Industries, Inc., 35
Assa Abloy AB, 112
Atlantis Plastics, Inc., 85
Atlas Copco AB, III; 28 (upd.); 85 (upd.)
Atrium Companies, Inc., 121
Atwood Mobil Products, 53
Austin Powder Company, 76
AZZ Incorporated, 93
B.J. Alan Co., Inc., 67
Babcock & Wilcox Company, The, 82
Badger Meter, Inc., 22
Baldor Electric Company, 21; 97 (upd.)
Baldwin Technology Company, Inc., 25; 107 (upd.)
Ballantyne of Omaha, Inc., 27
Bally Manufacturing Corporation, III
Baltimore Aircoil Company, Inc., 66
Bandai Co., Ltd., 55
Barmag AG, 39
Barnes Group Inc., 13; 69 (upd.)
Barry-Wehmiller Companies, Inc., 90

Materials

Mining & Metals

Nonprofit & Philanthropic Organizations

Paper & Forestry

Universal Forest Products, Inc., 10; 59 (upd.)
UPM-Kymmene Corporation, 19; 50 (upd.)
Wausau-Mosinee Paper Corporation, 60 (upd.)
West Fraser Timber Co. Ltd., 17; 91 (upd.)
West Linn Paper Company, 91
Westvaco Corporation, IV; 19 (upd.)
Weyerhaeuser Company, IV; 9 (upd.); 28 (upd.); 83 (upd.)
Wickes Inc., 25 (upd.)
Willamette Industries, Inc., IV; 31 (upd.)
WTD Industries, Inc., 20

Personal Services

24 Hour Fitness Worldwide, Inc., 71
Adelman Travel Group, 105
ADT Security Services, Inc., 12; 44 (upd.)
Akal Security Incorporated, 119
Alderwoods Group, Inc., 68 (upd.)
Ambassadors International, Inc., 68 (upd.)
American Retirement Corporation, 42
Ameriwood Industries International Corp., 17
Aquent, 96
Aurora Casket Company, Inc., 56
Bidvest Group Ltd., 106
Blackwater USA, 76
Bonhams 1793 Ltd., 72
Brickman Group, Ltd., The, 87
CareerBuilder, Inc., 93
Carriage Services, Inc., 37
CDI Corporation, 6; 54 (upd.)
Central Parking System, 18; 104 (upd.)
CeWe Color Holding AG, 76
Chemed Corporation, 13; 118 (upd.)
Chubb, PLC, 50
Correctional Services Corporation, 30
CUC International Inc., 16
Curves International, Inc., 54
eHarmony.com Inc., 71
Franklin Quest Co., 11
Gateway Group One, 118
Gold's Gym International, Inc., 71
Granite Industries of Vermont, Inc., 73
Greg Manning Auctions, Inc., 60
Gunnebo AB, 53
Hair Club For Men Ltd., 90
Herbalife Ltd., 17; 41 (upd.); 92 (upd.)
I Grandi Viaggi S.p.A., 105
Imperial Parking Corporation, 58
Initial Security, 64
Jazzercise, Inc., 45
Jostens, Inc., 7; 25 (upd.); 73 (upd.)
Kayak.com, 108
Kiva, 95
Lifetouch Inc., 86
Loewen Group Inc., The, 16; 40 (upd.)
Mace Security International, Inc., 57
Manpower, Inc., 9
Martin Franchises, Inc., 80
Match.com, LP, 87
Michael Anthony Jewelers, Inc., 24
Michael Page International plc, 45
OGF S.A., 113
Orkin, Inc., 104
PODS Enterprises Inc., 103
Prison Rehabilitative Industries and Diversified Enterprises, Inc. (PRIDE), 53
Randstad Holding nv, 113 (upd.)
Regis Corporation, 18; 70 (upd.)
Rollins, Inc., 11; 104 (upd.)
Rose Hills Company, 117
Rosenbluth International Inc., 14
Screen Actors Guild, 72
Segway LLC, 48
Service Corporation International, 6; 51 (upd.)
Shutterfly, Inc., 98
Snapfish, 83
SOS Staffing Services, 25
Spark Networks, Inc., 91
Stewart Enterprises, Inc., 20
Supercuts Inc., 26
Town & Country Corporation, 19
UAW (International Union, United Automobile, Aerospace and Agricultural Implement Workers of America), 72
Weight Watchers International Inc., 12; 33 (upd.); 73 (upd.)
Yak Pak, 108
York Group, Inc., The, 50
YTB International, Inc., 108

Petroleum

Abraxas Petroleum Corporation, 89
Abu Dhabi National Oil Company, IV; 45 (upd.); 114 (upd.)
Adani Enterprises Ltd., 97
Aegean Marine Petroleum Network Inc., 89
Agland, Inc., 110
Agway, Inc., 21 (upd.)
Alberta Energy Company Ltd., 16; 43 (upd.)
Alon Israel Oil Company Ltd., 104
Amerada Hess Corporation, IV; 21 (upd.); 55 (upd.)
Amoco Corporation, IV; 14 (upd.)
Anadarko Petroleum Corporation, 10; 52 (upd.); 106 (upd.)
ANR Pipeline Co., 17
Anschutz Corp., 12
Apache Corporation, 10; 32 (upd.); 89 (upd.)
Aral AG, 62
Arctic Slope Regional Corporation, 38
Arena Resources, Inc., 97
Ashland Inc., 19; 50 (upd.); 115 (upd.)
Ashland Oil, Inc., IV
Atlantic Richfield Company, IV; 31 (upd.)
Atwood Oceanics, Inc., 100
Aventine Renewable Energy Holdings, Inc., 89
Badger State Ethanol, LLC, 83
Baker Hughes Incorporated, 22 (upd.); 57 (upd.); 118 (upd.)
Basic Earth Science Systems, Inc., 101
Belco Oil & Gas Corp., 40
Benton Oil and Gas Company, 47
Berry Petroleum Company, 47
BG Products Inc., 96
Bharat Petroleum Corporation Limited, 109
BHP Billiton, 67 (upd.)
Bill Barrett Corporation, 71
BJ Services Company, 25
Blue Rhino Corporation, 56
Blue Sun Energy, Inc., 108
Boardwalk Pipeline Partners, LP, 87
Bolt Technology Corporation, 99
Boots & Coots International Well Control, Inc., 79
BP p.l.c., 45 (upd.); 103 (upd.)
Brigham Exploration Company, 75
British Petroleum Company plc, The, IV; 7 (upd.); 21 (upd.)
British-Borneo Oil & Gas PLC, 34
Broken Hill Proprietary Company Ltd., 22 (upd.)
Bronco Drilling Company, Inc., 89
Burlington Resources Inc., 10
Burmah Castrol PLC, IV; 30 (upd.)
Callon Petroleum Company, 47
Caltex Petroleum Corporation, 19
Calumet Specialty Products Partners, L.P., 106
CAMAC International Corporation, 106
Cano Petroleum Inc., 97
Carrizo Oil & Gas, Inc., 97
Chevron Corporation, IV; 19 (upd.); 47 (upd.); 103 (upd.)
Chiles Offshore Corporation, 9
The China National Offshore Oil Corp., 118
China National Petroleum Corporation, 46; 108 (upd.)
China Petroleum & Chemical Corporation (Sinopec Corp.), 109
Chinese Petroleum Corporation, IV; 31 (upd.)
Cimarex Energy Co., 81
CITGO Petroleum Corporation, IV; 31 (upd.)
Clayton Williams Energy, Inc., 87
Coastal Corporation, The, IV; 31 (upd.)
Compañia Española de Petróleos S.A. (Cepsa), IV; 56 (upd.)
Complete Production Services, Inc., 118
Compton Petroleum Corporation, 103
Comstock Resources, Inc., 47
Conoco Inc., IV; 16 (upd.)
ConocoPhillips, 63 (upd.)
CONSOL Energy Inc., 59
Continental Resources, Inc., 89
Cooper Cameron Corporation, 20 (upd.); 58 (upd.)
Cosmo Oil Co., Ltd., IV; 53 (upd.)
CPC Corporation, Taiwan, 116
Crimson Exploration Inc., 116
Crown Central Petroleum Corporation, 7
Daniel Measurement and Control, Inc., 16; 74 (upd.)
Dead River Company, 117
DeepTech International Inc., 21
Den Norse Stats Oljeselskap AS, IV
Denbury Resources, Inc., 67
Deutsche BP Aktiengesellschaft, 7
Devon Energy Corporation, 61
Diamond Shamrock, Inc., IV

Publishing & Printing

Real Estate

Retail & Wholesale

Rubber & Tires

Telecommunications

Textiles & Apparel

Tobacco

Transport Services

Santa Fe Pacific Corporation, V
Schenker-Rhenus AG, 6
Schneider National, Inc., 36; 77 (upd.)
Sea Ray Boats Inc., 96
Seaboard Corporation, 36; 85 (upd.)
SEACOR Holdings Inc., 83
Securicor Plc, 45
Seibu Railway Company Ltd., V; 74 (upd.)
Seino Transportation Company, Ltd., 6
Simon Transportation Services Inc., 27
Skeeter Products Inc., 96
Smithway Motor Xpress Corporation, 39
Société Nationale des Chemins de Fer Français, V; 57 (upd.)
Société Norbert Dentressangle S.A., 67
Southern Pacific Transportation Company, V
Spee-Dee Delivery Service, Inc., 93
Stagecoach Group plc, 30; 104 (upd.)
Stelmar Shipping Ltd., 52
Stevedoring Services of America Inc., 28
Stinnes AG, 8; 59 (upd.)
Stolt-Nielsen S.A., 42
Sunoco, Inc., 28 (upd.); 83 (upd.)
Swift Transportation Co., Inc., 42
Swiss Federal Railways (Schweizerische Bundesbahnen), The, V
Swissport International Ltd., 70
Teekay Shipping Corporation, 25; 82 (upd.)
Tibbett & Britten Group plc, 32
Tidewater Inc., 11; 37 (upd.)
TNT Freightways Corporation, 14
TNT Post Group N.V., V; 27 (upd.); 30 (upd.)
Tobu Railway Company Ltd., 6; 98 (upd.)
Todd Shipyards Corporation, 14
Tokyu Corporation, V
Totem Resources Corporation, 9
TPG N.V., 64 (upd.)
Trailer Bridge, Inc., 41
Transnet Ltd., 6
Transport Corporation of America, Inc., 49
Trico Marine Services, Inc., 89
Tsakos Energy Navigation Ltd., 91
TTX Company, 6; 66 (upd.)
U.S. Delivery Systems, Inc., 22
Union Pacific Corporation, V; 28 (upd.); 79 (upd.)
United Parcel Service, Inc., 63
United Parcel Service of America Inc., V; 17 (upd.)
United Road Services, Inc., 69
United States Postal Service, 14; 34 (upd.); 108 (upd.)
Universal Truckload Services, Inc., 111
US 1 Industries, Inc., 89
USA Truck, Inc., 42
Velocity Express Corporation, 49
Werner Enterprises, Inc., 26
Westinghouse Air Brake Technologies Corporation, 116
Wheels Inc., 96
Wincanton plc, 52
Wisconsin Central Transportation Corporation, 24
Wright Express Corporation, 80
Yamato Transport Co. Ltd., V; 49 (upd.)
Yellow Corporation, 14; 45 (upd.)
Yellow Freight System, Inc. of Delaware, V
YRC Worldwide Inc., 90 (upd.)

Utilities

ACEA S.p.A., 115
AES Corporation, 10; 13 (upd.); 53 (upd.)
Aggreko Plc, 45
AGL Resources Inc., 116
Air & Water Technologies Corporation, 6
Akeena Solar, Inc., 103
Alberta Energy Company Ltd., 16; 43 (upd.)
Allegheny Energy, Inc., V; 38 (upd.)
Alliant Energy Corporation, 106
Ameren Corporation, 60 (upd.)
American Electric Power Company, Inc., V; 45 (upd.)
American States Water Company, 46
American Water Works Company, Inc., 6; 38 (upd.)
Aquarion Company, 84
Aquila, Inc., 50 (upd.)
Arkla, Inc., V
Associated Natural Gas Corporation, 11
Atlanta Gas Light Company, 6; 23 (upd.)
Atlantic Energy, Inc., 6
Atmos Energy Corporation, 43; 118 (upd.)
Avista Corporation, 69 (upd.)
Baltimore Gas and Electric Company, V; 25 (upd.)
Basin Electric Power Cooperative, 103
Bay State Gas Company, 38
Bayernwerk AG, V; 23 (upd.)
Berlinwasser Holding AG, 90
Bewag AG, 39
Big Rivers Electric Corporation, 11
Black Hills Corporation, 20
Bonneville Power Administration, 50
Boston Edison Company, 12
Bouygues S.A., I; 24 (upd.); 97 (upd.)
British Energy Plc, 49
British Gas plc, V
British Nuclear Fuels plc, 6
Brooklyn Union Gas, 6
BW Group Ltd., 107
California Water Service Group, 79
Calpine Corporation, 36
Canadian Utilities Limited, 13; 56 (upd.)
Cap Rock Energy Corporation, 46
Carolina Power & Light Company, V; 23 (upd.)
Cascade Natural Gas Corporation, 9
Cascal N.V., 103
Centerior Energy Corporation, V
CenterPoint Energy, Inc., 116
Central and South West Corporation, V
Central Hudson Gas and Electricity Corporation, 6
Central Maine Power, 6
Central Vermont Public Service Corporation, 54
Centrica plc, 29 (upd.); 107 (upd.)
ČEZ a. s., 97
Chesapeake Utilities Corporation, 56
China Shenhua Energy Company Limited, 83
China Southern Power Grid Company Ltd., 116
Chubu Electric Power Company, Inc., V; 46 (upd.); 118 (upd.)
Chugoku Electric Power Company Inc., V; 53 (upd.)
Cincinnati Gas & Electric Company, 6
CIPSCO Inc., 6
Citizens Utilities Company, 7
City Public Service, 6
Cleco Corporation, 37
CMS Energy Corporation, V, 14 (upd.); 100 (upd.)
Coastal Corporation, The, 31 (upd.)
Cogentrix Energy, Inc., 10
Columbia Gas System, Inc., The, V; 16 (upd.)
Comisión Federal de Electricidad, 108
Commonwealth Edison Company, V
Commonwealth Energy System, 14
Companhia Energética de Minas Gerais S.A. CEMIG, 65
Compañia de Minas Buenaventura S.A.A., 93
Connecticut Light and Power Co., 13
Consolidated Edison, Inc., V; 45 (upd.); 112 (upd.)
Consolidated Natural Gas Company, V; 19 (upd.)
Constellation Energy Group, Inc., 116 (upd.)
Consumers' Gas Company Ltd., 6
Consumers Power Co., 14
Consumers Water Company, 14
Copperbelt Energy Corporation PLC, 116
Covanta Energy Corporation, 64 (upd.)
Crosstex Energy Inc., 107
Dalkia Holding, 66
Delmarva Power & Light Company, 118
Destec Energy, Inc., 12
Detroit Edison Company, The, V
Dominion Resources, Inc., V; 54 (upd.)
DPL Inc., 6; 96 (upd.)
DQE, Inc., 6
Drax Group PLC, 119
DTE Energy Company, 20 (upd.)
Duke Energy Corporation, V; 27 (upd.); 110 (upd.)
E.On AG, 50 (upd.)
Eastern Enterprises, 6
Edison International, 56 (upd.)
EDP - Energias de Portugal, S.A., 111 (upd.)
El Paso Electric Company, 21
El Paso Natural Gas Company, 12
Electrabel N.V., 67
Electricidade de Portugal, S.A., 47
Electricité de France S.A., V; 41 (upd.); 114 (upd.)
Electricity Generating Authority of Thailand (EGAT), 56

Waste Services

Geographic Index

Albania

Algeria

Argentina

Australia

Brunei

Canada

Cayman Islands

Chile

China

Colombia

Croatia

Cyprus

Czech Republic

Denmark

Ecuador

Egypt

El Salvador

Estonia

Ethiopia

Ethiopian Airlines, 81

Fiji

Air Pacific Ltd., 70

Finland

Ahlstrom Corporation, 53
Alma Media Corporation, 98
Amer Group plc, 41
Dynea, 68
Enso-Gutzeit Oy, IV
Finnair Oyj, 6; 25 (upd.); 61 (upd.)
Fiskars Corporation, 33; 105 (upd.)
Fortum Corporation, 30 (upd.)
Hackman Oyj Adp, 44
Huhtamäki Oyj, 64
Imatra Steel Oy Ab, 55
Kansallis-Osake-Pankki, II
Kemira Oyj, 70
Kesko Corporation, 8; 27 (upd.); 114 (upd.)
KONE Corporation, 27; 76 (upd.)
Kymmene Corporation, IV
Metsa-Serla Oy, IV
Metso Corporation, 30 (upd.); 85 (upd.)
M-real Oyj, 56 (upd.)
Myllykoski Oyj, 117
Neste Oil Corporation, IV; 85 (upd.)
Nokia Corporation, II; 17 (upd.); 38 (upd.); 77 (upd.)
Onvest Oy, 117
Orion Oyj, 72
Outokumpu Oyj, 38; 108 (upd.)
Posti- ja Telelaitos, 6
Raha-automaattiyhdistys (RAY), 110
Raisio PLC, 99
Rautakirja Oy, 104
Rautaruukki Oyj, 115
Saarioinen Oy, 117
Sanitec Corporation, 51
SanomaWSOY Corporation, 51
Seppälä Oy, 113
Sonera Corporation, 50
Stora Enso Oyj, 36 (upd.); 85 (upd.)
Tamfelt Oyj Abp, 62
Tieto Oyj, 117
Tulikivi Corporation, 114
United Paper Mills Ltd. (Yhtyneet Paperitehtaat Oy), IV
UPM-Kymmene Corporation, 19; 50 (upd.)
Vaisala Oyj, 104
Valio Oy, 117
Valmet Corporation (Valmet Oy), III
Wärtsilä Corporation, 100

France

Accor S.A., 10; 27 (upd.); 69 (upd.)
Actes Sud S.A., 120
Actia Group S.A., 107
Aéroports de Paris, 33
Aerospatiale Group, The, 7; 21 (upd.)
Agence France-Presse, 34
Air France–KLM, 108 (upd.)
Akerys S.A., 90
Alain Afflelou SA, 53
Alcatel S.A., 9; 36 (upd.)
Alcatel-Lucent, 109 (upd.)
Alès Groupe, 81
ALSTOM, 108
Altran Technologies, 51
Amec Spie S.A., 57
Arc International, 76
AREVA NP, 90 (upd.)
Arianespace S.A., 89
Arkema S.A., 100
Association des Centres Distributeurs E. Leclerc, 37
Assurances Générales de France, 63
Atochem S.A., I
Atos Origin S.A., 69
Au Printemps S.A., V
Aubert & Duval S.A.S., 107
Auchan Group, 37; 116 (upd.)
Automobiles Citroen, 7
Autoroutes du Sud de la France SA, 55
Avions Marcel Dassault-Breguet Aviation, I
AXA Group, III; 114 (upd.)
Babolat VS, S.A., 97
Baccarat, 24
Banque Nationale de Paris S.A., II
Baron Philippe de Rothschild S.A., 39
Bayard SA, 49
Belvedere S.A., 93
Bénéteau SA, 55
Besnier SA, 19
BigBen Interactive S.A., 72
bioMérieux S.A., 75
BNP Paribas Group, 36 (upd.); 111 (upd.)
Boiron S.A., 73
Boizel Chanoine Champagne S.A., 94
Bonduelle SA, 51
Bongrain S.A., 25; 102 (upd.)
Boulanger S.A., 102
Bouygues S.A., I; 24 (upd.); 97 (upd.)
Bricorama S.A., 68
Brioche Pasquier S.A., 58
Brossard S.A., 102
BSN Groupe S.A., II
Buffalo Grill S.A., 94
Bugatti Automobiles S.A.S., 94
Bull S.A., 43 (upd.)
Bureau Veritas SA, 55
Burelle S.A., 23
Business Objects S.A., 25
Caisse des Dépôts et Consignations, 90
Camaïeu S.A., 72
Canal Plus, 10; 34 (upd.)
Cap Gemini Ernst & Young, 37
Carbone Lorraine S.A., 33
Carrefour SA, 10; 27 (upd.); 64 (upd.)
Carrere Group S.A., 104
Casino Guichard-Perrachon S.A., 59 (upd.)
Castorama-Dubois Investissements SCA, 104 (upd.)
Cegedim S.A., 104
Celio France S.A.S., 113
Cemoi S.A., 86
Cetelem S.A., 21
Champagne Bollinger S.A., 114
Chanel SA, 12; 49 (upd.)
Chantiers Jeanneau S.A., 96
Charal S.A., 90
Chargeurs International, 6; 21 (upd.)
Christian Dalloz SA, 40
Christian Dior S.A., 19; 49 (upd.); 110 (upd.)
Christofle SA, 40
Ciments Français, 40
Clarins S.A., 119
Club Mediterranée S.A., 6; 21 (upd.); 91 (upd.)
CNP Assurances, 116
Coflexip S.A., 25
Colas S.A., 31
Compagnie de Saint-Gobain, III; 16 (upd.); 64 (upd.)
Compagnie des Alpes, 48
Compagnie des Machines Bull S.A., III
Compagnie Financiere de Paribas, II
Compagnie Financière Sucres et Denrées S.A., 60
Compagnie Générale d'Électricité, II
Compagnie Générale des Établissements Michelin, V; 42 (upd.); 117 (upd.)
Compagnie Générale Maritime et Financière, 6
Comptoirs Modernes S.A., 19
Coopagri Bretagne, 88
Crédit Agricole Group, II; 84 (upd.)
Crédit Industriel et Commercial S.A., 116
Crédit Lyonnais, 9; 33 (upd.)
Crédit National S.A., 9
Dalkia Holding, 66
Damartex S.A., 98
Darty S.A., 27
Dassault Aviation S.A., 114 (upd.)
Dassault Systèmes S.A., 25
DCN S.A., 75
De Dietrich & Cie., 31
Delachaux S.A., 76
Délifrance S.A., 113
Deveaux S.A., 41
Devoteam S.A., 94
Dexia Group, 42
Doux S.A., 80
Du Pareil au Même, 43
Dynaction S.A., 67
Dyneff S.A., 98
EADS SOCATA, 54
ECS S.A, 12
Ed S.A.S., 88
Éditions Gallimard, 72
Editis S.A., 78
Eiffage S.A., 27; 117 (upd.)
Electricité de France S.A., V; 41 (upd.); 114 (upd.)
Elf Aquitaine SA, 21 (upd.)
Elior SA, 49
Eram SA, 51
Eramet, 73
Eridania Béghin-Say S.A., 36
Essilor International, 21
Etablissements Economiques du Casino Guichard, Perrachon et Cie, S.C.A., 12
Établissements Jacquot and Cie S.A.S., 92
Etablissements Maurel & Prom S.A., 115
Etam Developpement SA, 44
Eurazeo, 80

Germany

Ghana

Greece

Guatemala

Hong Kong

Hungary

Iceland

India

Bharat Electronics Limited, 113
Bharat Heavy Electricals Limited, 119
Bharat Petroleum Corporation Limited, 109
Bharti Tele-Ventures Limited, 75
Britannia Industries Ltd., 117
Coal India Limited, IV; 44 (upd.); 115 (upd.)
Dr. Reddy's Laboratories Ltd., 59
EIH Ltd., 103
Essar Group Ltd. 79
Essel Propack Limited, 115
Hindustan Lever Limited 79
Hindustan Petroleum Corporation Ltd., 116
Indian Airlines Ltd., 46
Indian Oil Corporation Ltd., IV; 48 (upd.); 113 (upd.)
Infosys Technologies Limited, 38; 119 (upd.)
Jaiprakash Associates Limited, 101
Jet Airways (India) Private Limited, 65
Larsen and Toubro Ltd., 117
Mahindra & Mahindra Ltd., 120
Minerals and Metals Trading Corporation of India Ltd., IV
MTR Foods Ltd., 55
Neyveli Lignite Corporation Ltd., 65
Oil and Natural Gas Corporation Ltd., IV; 90 (upd.)
Ranbaxy Laboratories Ltd., 70
Raymond Ltd., 77
Reliance Industries Ltd., 81
Rolta India Ltd., 90
Satyam Computer Services Ltd., 85
State Bank of India, 63
Steel Authority of India Ltd., IV; 66 (upd.)
Sun Pharmaceutical Industries Ltd., 57
Tata Consultancy Services Limited, 119
Tata Iron & Steel Co. Ltd., IV; 44 (upd.)
Tata Motors, Ltd., 109
Tata Steel Ltd., 109 (upd.)
Tata Tea Ltd., 76
Wipro Limited, 43; 106 (upd.)

Indonesia
Djarum PT, 62
Garuda Indonesia, 6; 58 (upd.)
Pertamina, 56 (upd.)
PERTAMINA, IV
PT Astra International Tbk, 56
PT Bank Buana Indonesia Tbk, 60
PT Gudang Garam Tbk, 103
PT Indosat Tbk, 93
PT Semen Gresik Tbk, 103

Iran
IranAir, 81
National Iranian Oil Company, IV; 61 (upd.)

Ireland
Aer Lingus Group plc, 34; 89 (upd.)
Allied Irish Banks, plc, 16; 43 (upd.); 94 (upd.)
Baltimore Technologies Plc, 42
Bank of Ireland, 50
Cahill May Roberts Group Ltd., 112
Clondalkin Group PLC, 120
CRH plc, 64
CryptoLogic Limited, 106
DCC plc, 115
DEPFA BANK PLC, 69
Dunnes Stores Ltd., 58
eircom plc, 31 (upd.)
Elan Corporation PLC, 63
Fyffes PLC, 38; 106 (upd.)
Glanbia plc, 59
Glen Dimplex, 78
Grafton Group plc, 104
Greencore Group plc, 98
Harland and Wolff Holdings plc, 19
IAWS Group plc, 49
Independent News & Media PLC, 61
Ingersoll-Rand PLC, 115 (upd.)
IONA Technologies plc, 43
Irish Distillers Group, 96
Irish Food Processors Ltd., 111
Irish Life & Permanent Plc, 59
Jefferson Smurfit Group plc, IV; 19 (upd.); 49 (upd.)
Jurys Doyle Hotel Group plc, 64
Kerry Group plc, 27; 87 (upd.)
Musgrave Group Plc, 57
Paddy Power plc, 98
Ryanair Holdings plc, 35
Shannon Aerospace Ltd., 36
Shire PLC, 109
SkillSoft Public Limited Company, 81
Smurfit Kappa Group plc, 112 (upd.)
Stafford Group, 110
Telecom Eireann, 7
Thomas Crosbie Holdings Limited, 81
Trinity Biotech plc, 121
United Drug PLC, 121
Waterford Wedgwood plc, 34 (upd.)
WPP Group plc, 112 (upd.)

Israel
Aladdin Knowledge Systems Ltd., 101
Alon Israel Oil Company Ltd., 104
Amdocs Ltd., 47
Bank Hapoalim B.M., II; 54 (upd.)
Bank Leumi le-Israel B.M., 60
Blue Square Israel Ltd., 41
BVR Systems (1998) Ltd., 93
Castro Model Ltd., 86
Check Point Software Technologies Ltd., 119
ECI Telecom Ltd., 18
EL AL Israel Airlines Ltd., 23; 107 (upd.)
Elscint Ltd., 20
Emblaze Ltd., 117
EZchip Semiconductor Ltd., 106
Galtronics Ltd., 100
Given Imaging Ltd., 83
IDB Holding Corporation Ltd., 97
Israel Aircraft Industries Ltd., 69
Israel Chemicals Ltd., 55
Israel Corporation Ltd., 108
Koor Industries Ltd., II; 25 (upd.); 68 (upd.)
Lipman Electronic Engineering Ltd., 81
Makhteshim-Agan Industries Ltd., 85
NICE Systems Ltd., 83
Orbotech Ltd., 75
Scitex Corporation Ltd., 24
Strauss-Elite Group, 68
Syneron Medical Ltd., 91
Taro Pharmaceutical Industries Ltd., 65
Teva Pharmaceutical Industries Ltd., 22; 54 (upd.); 112 (upd.)
Tnuva Food Industries Ltd., 111

Italy
ACEA S.p.A., 115
Aeffe S.p.A., 119
AgustaWestland N.V., 75
Alfa Romeo, 13; 36 (upd.)
Alitalia—Linee Aeree Italiana, S.p.A., 6; 29 (upd.); 97 (upd.)
Alleanza Assicurazioni S.p.A., 65
Angelini SpA, 100
Aprilia SpA, 17
Arnoldo Mondadori Editore S.p.A., IV; 19 (upd.); 54 (upd.)
Artsana SpA, 92
Assicurazioni Generali S.p.A., III; 15 (upd.); 103 (upd.)
Autogrill SpA, 49
Automobili Lamborghini Holding S.p.A., 13; 34 (upd.); 91 (upd.)
Autostrada Torino-Milano S.p.A., 101
Azelis Group, 100
Banca Commerciale Italiana SpA, II
Banca Fideuram SpA, 63
Banca Intesa SpA, 65
Banca Monte dei Paschi di Siena SpA, 65
Banca Nazionale del Lavoro SpA, 72
Barilla G. e R. Fratelli S.p.A., 17; 50 (upd.)
Benetton Group S.p.A., 10; 67 (upd.)
Brioni Roman Style S.p.A., 67
Bulgari S.p.A., 20; 106 (upd.)
Cantine Giorgio Lungarotti S.R.L., 67
Capitalia S.p.A., 65
Cinemeccanica SpA
Compagnia Italiana dei Jolly Hotels S.p.A., 71
Credito Italiano, II
Cremonini S.p.A., 57
Davide Campari-Milano S.p.A., 57
De Agostini Editore S.p.A., 103
De Rigo S.p.A., 104
De'Longhi S.p.A., 66
Diadora SpA, 86
Diesel SpA, 40
Dolce & Gabbana SpA, 62
Ducati Motor Holding SpA, 30; 86 (upd.)
Enel S.p.A., 108 (upd.)
ENI S.p.A., 69 (upd.)
Ente Nazionale Idrocarburi, IV
Ente Nazionale per L'Energia Elettrica, V
Ermenegildo Zegna SpA, 63
Fabbrica D' Armi Pietro Beretta S.p.A., 39
FASTWEB S.p.A., 83
Ferrari S.p.A., 13; 36 (upd.)
Ferrero SpA, 54
Ferretti Group SpA, 90
Ferrovie Dello Stato Societa Di Trasporti e Servizi S.p.A., 105
Fiat S.p.A., I; 11 (upd.); 50 (upd.); 120 (upd.)

Jamaica

Japan

Jordan

Kenya

Kuwait

Latvia

Lebanon

Libya

Liechtenstein

Lithuania

Luxembourg

Macedonia

Malaysia

Malta

Mauritius

Mexico

Mongolia

Nepal

The Netherlands

Netherlands Antilles

New Zealand

Nigeria

Norway

Oman

Pakistan

Panama

Papua New Guinea

Paraguay

Peru

Philippines

Poland

Portugal

Puerto Rico

Qatar

Romania

Russia

Saudi Arabia

Scotland

Singapore

Slovakia

South Africa

South Korea (Republic of Korea)

Spain

Sri Lanka

Sweden

Switzerland

Taiwan

Thailand

Trinidad and Tobago

Tunisia

Turkey

Ukraine

United Arab Emirates

United Kingdom

United States

Gap, Inc., The, V; 18 (upd.); 55 (upd.); 117 (upd.)
Garan, Inc., 16; 64 (upd.)
Garden Fresh Restaurant Corporation, 31
Garden Ridge Corporation, 27
Gardenburger, Inc., 33; 76 (upd.)
Gardner Denver, Inc., 49
Garst Seed Company, Inc., 86
Gart Sports Company, 24
Gartner, Inc., 21; 94 (upd.)
GateHouse Media, Inc., 91
Gates Corporation, The, 9
Gateway Group One, 118
Gateway, Inc., 10; 27 (upd.); 63 (upd.)
Gatorade Company, The, 82
GATX Corporation, 6; 25 (upd.)
Gaylord Bros., Inc., 100
Gaylord Container Corporation, 8
Gaylord Entertainment Company, 11; 36 (upd.)
GC Companies, Inc., 25
GE Aircraft Engines, 9
GE Capital Aviation Services, 36
Geek Squad Inc., 102
Geerlings & Wade, Inc., 45
Geffen Records Inc., 26
Gehl Company, 19
GEICO Corporation, 10; 40 (upd.)
Geiger Bros., 60
Gemini Sound Products Corporation, 58
GenCorp Inc., 8; 9
Genentech, Inc., I; 8 (upd.); 32 (upd.); 75 (upd.)
General Atomics, 57; 112 (upd.)
General Bearing Corporation, 45
General Binding Corporation, 10; 73 (upd.)
General Cable Corporation, 40; 111 (upd.)
General Chemical Group Inc., The, 37
General Cigar Holdings, Inc., 66 (upd.)
General Cinema Corporation, I
General DataComm Industries, Inc., 14
General Dynamics Corporation, I; 10 (upd.); 40 (upd.); 88 (upd.)
General Electric Company, II; 12 (upd.); 34 (upd.); 63 (upd.)
General Employment Enterprises, Inc., 87
General Growth Properties, Inc., 57
General Host Corporation, 12
General Housewares Corporation, 16
General Instrument Corporation, 10
General Maritime Corporation, 59
General Mills, Inc., II; 10 (upd.); 36 (upd.); 85 (upd.)
General Motors Corporation, I; 10 (upd.); 36 (upd.); 64 (upd.)
General Nutrition Companies, Inc., 11; 29 (upd.)
General Public Utilities Corporation, V
General Re Corporation, III; 24 (upd.)
General Signal Corporation, 9
General Tire, Inc., 8
Genesco Inc., 17; 84 (upd.)
Genesee & Wyoming Inc., 27
Genesis Health Ventures, Inc., 18
Genesis HealthCare Corporation, 119
Genesis Microchip Inc., 82
Genesys Telecommunications Laboratories Inc., 103
Genetics Institute, Inc., 8
Geneva Steel, 7
Genmar Holdings, Inc., 45
Genovese Drug Stores, Inc., 18
Gen-Probe Incorporated 79
GenRad, Inc., 24
Gentex Corporation, 26
Gentiva Health Services, Inc. 79
Genuardi's Family Markets, Inc., 35
Genuine Parts Co., 9; 45 (upd.); 113 (upd.)
Genworth Financial Inc., 116
Genzyme Corporation, 13; 38 (upd.); 77 (upd.)
Geon Company, The, 11
GeoResources, Inc., 101
George A. Hormel and Company, II
George F. Cram Company, Inc., The, 55
George P. Johnson Company, 60
George S. May International Company, 55
George W. Park Seed Company, Inc., 98
Georgia Gulf Corporation, 9; 61 (upd.)
Georgia-Pacific LLC, IV; 9 (upd.); 47 (upd.); 101 (upd.)
Geotek Communications Inc., 21
Gerald Stevens, Inc., 37
Gerber Products Company, 7; 21 (upd.)
Gerber Scientific, Inc., 12; 84 (upd.)
German American Bancorp, 41
Gertrude Hawk Chocolates Inc., 104
Getty Images, Inc., 31; 121 (upd.)
Gevity HR, Inc., 63
GF Health Products, Inc., 82
Ghirardelli Chocolate Company, 30; 121 (upd.)
Giant Cement Holding, Inc., 23
Giant Eagle, Inc., 86
Giant Food LLC, II; 22 (upd.); 83 (upd.)
Giant Industries, Inc., 19; 61 (upd.)
Gibraltar Steel Corporation, 37
Gibson Greetings, Inc., 12
Gibson Guitar Corporation, 16; 100 (upd.)
Gibson, Dunn & Crutcher LLP, 36
Giddings & Lewis, Inc., 10
Gifts In Kind International, 101
G-III Apparel Group, Ltd., 22; 117 (upd.)
Gilbane, Inc., 34
Gilead Sciences, Inc., 54
Gillett Holdings, Inc., 7
Gillette Company, The, III; 20 (upd.); 68 (upd.)
Gilman & Ciocia, Inc., 72
Gilmore Entertainment Group L.L.C., 100
Gilster-Mary Lee Corporation, 120
Girl Scouts of the USA, 35
Gitano Group, Inc., The, 8
Glacier Bancorp, Inc., 35
Glacier Water Services, Inc., 47
Glamis Gold, Ltd., 54
Glazer's Wholesale Drug Company, Inc., 82
Gleason Corporation, 24
Glidden Company, The, 8
Global Berry Farms LLC, 62
Global Cash Access Holdings, Inc., 111
Global Crossing Ltd., 32
Global Hyatt Corporation, 75 (upd.)
Global Imaging Systems, Inc., 73
Global Industries, Ltd., 37
Global Marine Inc., 9
Global Outdoors, Inc., 49
Global Partners L.P., 116
Global Payments Inc., 91
Global Power Equipment Group Inc., 52
GlobalSantaFe Corporation, 48 (upd.)
Globe Newspaper Company Inc., 106
Glu Mobile Inc., 95
Gluek Brewing Company, 75
GM Hughes Electronics Corporation, II
GMAC, LLC, 109
GMH Communities Trust, 87
GNC Corporation, 98 (upd.)
Go Daddy Group Inc., The, 102
Godfather's Pizza Incorporated, 25
Godiva Chocolatier, Inc., 64
Goetze's Candy Company, Inc., 87
Gold Kist Inc., 17; 26 (upd.)
Golden Belt Manufacturing Co., 16
Golden Books Family Entertainment, Inc., 28
Golden Corral Corporation, 10; 66 (upd.)
Golden Enterprises, Inc., 26
Golden Krust Caribbean Bakery, Inc., 68
Golden Neo-Life Diamite International, Inc., 100
Golden Star Resources Ltd., 117
Golden State Foods Corporation, 32
Golden State Vintners, Inc., 33
Golden Valley Electric Association, 110
Golden West Financial Corporation, 47
Goldman Sachs Group, Inc., The, II; 20 (upd.); 51 (upd.); 110 (upd.)
Gold'n Plump Poultry, 54
Gold's Gym International, Inc., 71
GoldToeMoretz, LLC, 102
Golfsmith International Holdings, Inc., 120
Golin/Harris International, Inc., 88
Golub Corporation, 26; 96 (upd.)
Gomez Inc., 104
Gonnella Baking Company, 40; 102 (upd.)
Good Guys, Inc., The, 10; 30 (upd.)
Good Humor-Breyers Ice Cream Company, 14
Goodby Silverstein & Partners, Inc., 75
Goodman Holding Company, 42
GoodMark Foods, Inc., 26
Goodrich Corporation, 46 (upd.); 109 (upd.)
GoodTimes Entertainment Ltd., 48
Goodwill Industries International, Inc., 16; 66 (upd.)
Goody Products, Inc., 12
Goodyear Tire & Rubber Company, The, V; 20 (upd.); 75 (upd.)
Goody's Family Clothing, Inc., 20; 64 (upd.)
Google, Inc., 50; 101 (upd.)
Gordmans, Inc., 74

Siskin Steel & Supply Company, 70
Sisters of Charity of Leavenworth Health System, 105
Six Flags, Inc., 17; 54 (upd.)
SJW Corporation, 70
Skadden, Arps, Slate, Meagher & Flom, 18; 120 (upd.)
Skechers U.S.A. Inc., 31; 88 (upd.)
Skeeter Products Inc., 96
S-K-I Limited, 15
Skidmore, Owings & Merrill LLP, 13; 69 (upd.)
skinnyCorp, LLC, 97
Skyline Chili, Inc., 62
Skyline Corporation, 30
SkyMall, Inc., 26
SkyWest, Inc., 25
Skyy Spirits LLC, 78
SL Green Realty Corporation, 44
SL Industries, Inc., 77
Sleepy's Inc., 32
SLI, Inc., 48
Slim-Fast Foods Company, 18; 66 (upd.)
Sling Media, Inc., 112
SLM Corp., 25 (upd.); 116 (upd.)
Small Planet Foods, Inc., 89
Small World Toys, 115
Smart & Final LLC, 16; 94 (upd.)
Smart Balance, Inc., 100
SMART Modular Technologies, Inc., 86
SmartForce PLC, 43
Smead Manufacturing Co., 17
Smith & Hawken, Ltd., 68
Smith & Wesson Corp., 30; 73 (upd.)
Smith & Wollensky Restaurant Group, Inc., The, 105
Smith Barney Inc., 15
Smith Corona Corp., 13
Smith International, Inc., 15; 59 (upd.); 118 (upd.)
Smith Micro Software, Inc., 112
Smithfield Foods, Inc., 7; 43 (upd.); 114 (upd.)
SmithKline Beckman Corporation, I
Smith-Midland Corporation, 56
Smith's Food & Drug Centers, Inc., 8; 57 (upd.)
Smithsonian Institution, 27
Smithway Motor Xpress Corporation, 39
Smurfit-Stone Container Corporation, 26 (upd.); 83 (upd.)
Snapfish, 83
Snap-on Incorporated, 7; 27 (upd.); 105 (upd.)
Snapple Beverage Corporation, 11
Snell & Wilmer L.L.P., 28
Society Corporation, 9
Soft Pretzel Franchise Systems, Inc., 108
Soft Sheen Products, Inc., 31
Softbank Corporation, 77 (upd.)
Sola International Inc., 71
Solar Turbines Inc., 100
SolarWinds, Inc., 116
Sole Technology Inc., 93
Solectron Corporation, 12; 48 (upd.)
Solo Cup Company, 104
Solo Serve Corporation, 28
Solutia Inc., 52
Sonat, Inc., 6
Sonesta International Hotels Corporation, 44
Sonic Automotive, Inc., 77
Sonic Corp., 14; 37 (upd.); 103 (upd.)
Sonic Innovations Inc., 56
Sonic Solutions, Inc., 81
SonicWALL, Inc., 87
Sonnenschein Nath and Rosenthal LLP, 102
Sonoco Products Company, 8; 89 (upd.)
SonoSite, Inc., 56
Sorbee International Ltd., 74
Soros Fund Management LLC, 28
Sorrento, Inc., 24
SOS Staffing Services, 25
Sotheby's Holdings, Inc., 11; 29 (upd.); 84 (upd.)
Sound Advice, Inc., 41
Souper Salad, Inc., 98
Source Enterprises, Inc., The, 65
Source Interlink Companies, Inc., 75
South Beach Beverage Company, Inc., 73
South Dakota Wheat Growers Association, 94
South Jersey Industries, Inc., 42
Southdown, Inc., 14
Southeast Frozen Foods Company, L.P., 99
Southern Company, The, V; 38 (upd.)
Southern Connecticut Gas Company, 84
Southern Financial Bancorp, Inc., 56
Southern Indiana Gas and Electric Company, 13
Southern New England Telecommunications Corporation, 6
Southern Pacific Transportation Company, V
Southern Poverty Law Center, Inc., 74
Southern Progress Corporation, 102
Southern States Cooperative Incorporated, 36
Southern Union Company, 27
Southern Wine and Spirits of America, Inc., 84
Southland Corporation, The, II; 7 (upd.)
Southtrust Corporation, 11
Southwest Airlines Co., 6; 24 (upd.); 71 (upd.)
Southwest Gas Corporation, 19
Southwest Water Company, 47
Southwestern Bell Corporation, V
Southwestern Electric Power Co., 21
Southwestern Public Service Company, 6
Southwire Company, Inc., 8; 23 (upd.)
Sovereign Bancorp, Inc., 103
Sovran Self Storage, Inc., 66
Spacehab, Inc., 37
Spacelabs Medical, Inc., 71
Spaghetti Warehouse, Inc., 25
Spangler Candy Company, 44
Spanish Broadcasting System, Inc., 41
Spansion Inc., 80
Spanx, Inc., 89
Spark Networks, Inc., 91
Spartan Motors Inc., 14
Spartan Stores Inc., 8; 66 (upd.)
Spartech Corporation, 19; 76 (upd.)
Sparton Corporation, 18
Spear & Jackson, Inc., 73
Spear, Leeds & Kellogg, 66
Special Olympics, Inc., 93
Specialized Bicycle Components Inc., 50
Specialty Coatings Inc., 8
Specialty Equipment Companies, Inc., 25
Specialty Products & Insulation Co., 59
Spec's Music, Inc., 19
Spectra Energy Corporation, 116
Spectrum Brands, Inc., 109 (upd.)
Spectrum Control, Inc., 67
Spectrum Organic Products, Inc., 68
Spee-Dee Delivery Service, Inc., 93
SpeeDee Oil Change and Tune-Up, 25
Speedway Motorsports, Inc., 32; 112 (upd.)
Speidel Inc., 96
Speizman Industries, Inc., 44
Spelling Entertainment, 14; 35 (upd.)
Spencer Stuart and Associates, Inc., 14
Spherion Corporation, 52
Spicy Pickle Franchising, Inc., 105
Spiegel, Inc., 10; 27 (upd.)
Spinnaker Exploration Company, 72
Spirit Airlines, Inc., 31
Sport Chalet, Inc., 16; 94 (upd.)
Sport Supply Group, Inc., 23; 106 (upd.)
Sportif USA, Inc., 118
Sportmart, Inc., 15
Sports & Recreation, Inc., 17
The Sports Authority, Inc., 16; 43 (upd.); 120 (upd.)
Sports Club Company, The, 25
Sportsman's Guide, Inc., The, 36
Springs Global US, Inc., V; 19 (upd.); 90 (upd.)
Sprint Nextel Corporation, 9; 46 (upd.); 110 (upd.)
SPS Technologies, Inc., 30
SPSS Inc., 64
SPX Corporation, 10; 47 (upd.); 103 (upd.)
Spyglass Entertainment Group, LLC, 91
Square D, 90
Squibb Corporation, I
SRA International, Inc., 77
SRAM Corporation, 65
SRC Holdings Corporation, 67
SRG Global, Inc., 121
SRI International, Inc., 57
SSI (U.S.), Inc., 103 (upd.)
SSOE Inc., 76
STAAR Surgical Company, 57
Stabler Companies Inc., 78
Stage Stores, Inc., 24; 82 (upd.)
Stanadyne Automotive Corporation, 37
StanCorp Financial Group, Inc., 56
Standard Candy Company Inc., 86
Standard Commercial Corporation, 13; 62 (upd.)
Standard Federal Bank, 9
Standard Microsystems Corporation, 11
Standard Motor Products, Inc., 40
Standard Pacific Corporation, 52
Standard Register Company, The, 15, 93 (upd.)

Titan Machinery Inc., 103
Titanium Metals Corporation, 21
TiVo Inc., 75
TJ International, Inc., 19
The TJX Companies, Inc., V; 19 (upd.); 57 (upd.); 120 (upd.)
TLC Beatrice International Holdings, Inc., 22
TMP Worldwide Inc., 30
T-Netix, Inc., 46
TNT Freightways Corporation, 14
Today's Man, Inc., 20
TODCO, 87
Todd Shipyards Corporation, 14
Todd-AO Corporation, The, 33
Todhunter International, Inc., 27
Tofutti Brands, Inc., 64
Tokheim Corporation, 21
TOKYOPOP Inc. 79
Toll Brothers Inc., 15; 70 (upd.)
Tollgrade Communications, Inc., 44
Tom Brown, Inc., 37
Tom Doherty Associates Inc., 25
Tombstone Pizza Corporation, 13
Tommy Bahama Group, Inc., 108
TomoTherapy Incorporated, 121
Tom's Foods Inc., 66
Tom's of Maine, Inc., 45
Tone Brothers, Inc., 21; 74 (upd.)
Tonka Corporation, 25
Too, Inc., 61
Tootsie Roll Industries, Inc., 12; 82 (upd.)
Topco Associates LLC, 60
Topps Company, Inc., The, 13; 34 (upd.); 83 (upd.)
Tops Appliance City, Inc., 17
Tops Markets LLC, 60
Torchmark Corporation, 9; 33 (upd.); 115 (upd.)
Toresco Enterprises, Inc., 84
Toro Company, The, 7; 26 (upd.); 77 (upd.)
Torrington Company, The, 13
Tosco Corporation, 7
Total Entertainment Restaurant Corporation, 46
Total System Services, Inc., 18
Totem Resources Corporation, 9
TouchTunes Music Corporation, 97
Tower Air, Inc., 28
Tower Automotive, Inc., 24
Towers Perrin, 32
Town & Country Corporation, 19
Town Pump Inc., 113
Town Sports International, Inc., 46
Townsends, Inc., 64
Toy Biz, Inc., 18
Toymax International, Inc., 29
Toys "R" Us, Inc., V; 18 (upd.); 57 (upd.); 110 (upd.)
TPI Composites, Inc., 112
Tracor Inc., 17
Tractor Supply Company, 57
Trader Joe's Company, 13; 50 (upd.); 117 (upd.)
TradeStation Group, Inc., 83
Traffix, Inc., 61
Trailer Bridge, Inc., 41
Trammell Crow Company, 8; 57 (upd.)
Trane, 78
Trans World Airlines, Inc., I; 12 (upd.); 35 (upd.)
Trans World Entertainment Corporation, 24; 68 (upd.)
Transaction Systems Architects, Inc., 29; 82 (upd.)
Transamerica–An AEGON Company, I; 13 (upd.); 41 (upd.)
Transammonia Group, 95
Transatlantic Holdings, Inc., 11
Transco Energy Company, V
TransDigm Group Incorporated, 119
Transitions Optical, Inc., 83
Trans-Lux Corporation, 51
Transmedia Network Inc., 20
TransMontaigne Inc., 28
Transport Corporation of America, Inc., 49
TransPro, Inc., 71
Tranzonic Companies, The, 37
Travel Ports of America, Inc., 17
TravelCenters of America LLC, 108
Travelers Corporation, The, III
Travelocity.com LP, 46; 113 (upd.)
Travelzoo Inc. 79
Travis Boats & Motors, Inc., 37
TRC Companies, Inc., 32
Treadco, Inc., 19
Treasure Chest Advertising Company, Inc., 32
Tredegar Corporation, 52
Tree of Life, Inc., 29; 107 (upd.)
Tree Top, Inc., 76
TreeHouse Foods, Inc. 79
Trek Bicycle Corporation, 16; 78 (upd.)
Trend-Lines, Inc., 22
Trendwest Resorts, Inc., 33
Trex Company, Inc., 71
Tri Valley Growers, 32
Triarc Companies, Inc., 8; 34 (upd.)
Tribune Company, IV; 22 (upd.); 63 (upd.)
Trico Marine Services, Inc., 89
Trico Products Corporation, 15
Trident Seafoods Corporation, 56
Trigen Energy Corporation, 42
TriMas Corp., 11
Trimble Navigation Limited, 40
Trinchero Family Estates, 107 (upd.)
Trinity Industries, Incorporated, 7
TRINOVA Corporation, III
TriPath Imaging, Inc., 77
Triple Five Group Ltd., 49
Tripwire, Inc., 97
TriQuint Semiconductor, Inc., 63
Trisko Jewelry Sculptures, Ltd., 57
Tri-State Generation and Transmission Association, Inc., 103
Triton Energy Corporation, 11
Triumph Group, Inc., 31
TriZetto Group, Inc., The, 83
TRM Copy Centers Corporation, 18
Tropicana Products, Inc., 28; 73 (upd.)
Troutman Sanders L.L.P. 79
True North Communications Inc., 23
True Religion Apparel, Inc. 79
True Temper Sports, Inc., 95
True Value Company, 74 (upd.)
TruFoods LLC, 114
Truman Arnold Companies, Inc., 114
Trump Organization, The, 23; 64 (upd.)
TruServ Corporation, 24
Trustmark Corporation, 106
TRW Automotive Holdings Corp., 75 (upd.)
TRW Inc., I; 11 (upd.); 14 (upd.)
T-3 Energy Services, Inc., 119
TTX Company, 6; 66 (upd.)
Tubby's, Inc., 53
Tucson Electric Power Company, 6
Tuesday Morning Corporation, 18; 70 (upd.)
Tully Construction Co. Inc., 114
Tully's Coffee Corporation, 51
Tultex Corporation, 13
Tumaro's Gourmet Tortillas, 85
Tumbleweed, Inc., 33; 80 (upd.)
Tumi, Inc., 112
Tupperware Corporation, 28; 78 (upd.)
TurboChef Technologies, Inc., 83
Turner Broadcasting System, Inc., II; 6 (upd.); 66 (upd.)
Turner Construction Company, 66
Turner Corporation, The, 8; 23 (upd.)
Turtle Wax, Inc., 15; 93 (upd.)
Tuscarora Inc., 29
Tutogen Medical, Inc., 68
Tuttle Publishing, 86
TV Guide, Inc., 43 (upd.)
TVI Corporation, 99
TVI, Inc., 15
TW Services, Inc., II
Tweeter Home Entertainment Group, Inc., 30
Twentieth Century Fox Film Corporation, II; 25 (upd.)
Twin Disc, Inc., 21
Twinlab Corporation, 34
Twitter, Inc., 118
II-VI Incorporated, 69
Ty Inc., 33; 86 (upd.)
Tyco Toys, Inc., 12
Tyler Corporation, 23
Tyler Perry Company, Inc., The, 111
Tyndale House Publishers, Inc., 57
Tyson Foods, Inc., II; 14 (upd.); 50 (upd.); 114 (upd.)
U.S. Aggregates, Inc., 42
U.S. Army Corps of Engineers, 91
U.S. Bancorp, 14; 36 (upd.); 103 (upd.)
U.S. Borax, Inc., 42
U.S. Can Corporation, 30
U.S. Cellular Corporation, 31 (upd.); 88 (upd.)
U.S. Delivery Systems, Inc., 22
U.S. Foodservice, Inc., 26; 120 (upd.)
U.S. Healthcare, Inc., 6
U.S. Home Corporation, 8; 78 (upd.)
U.S. Music Corporation, 108
U.S. News & World Report Inc., 30; 89 (upd.)
U.S. Office Products Company, 25
U.S. Physical Therapy, Inc., 65
U.S. Premium Beef LLC, 91